ABSTRACT

OF

NORTH CAROLINA WILLS

COMPILED FROM

ORIGINAL AND RECORDED WILLS IN THE
OFFICE OF THE SECRETARY OF STATE

BY

J. BRYAN GRIMES

SECRETARY OF STATE

Baltimore
GENEALOGICAL PUBLISHING CO., INC.
1980

Originally published: Raleigh, North Carolina, 1910
Reprinted: Genealogical Publishing Co., Inc.
Baltimore, 1967, 1975, 1980
Library of Congress Catalogue Card Number 67-28615
International Standard Book Number 0-8063-0163-5
Made in the United States of America

INTRODUCTION.

The increasing interest of the public in the old wills filed in the office of the Secretary of State has caused the Trustees of the Public Libraries to authorize the Secretary of State to prepare the within publication. An abstract of every will found in the office of the Secretary of State is published herein. These abstracts show the name of the testator, place of residence, names of wife, children, legatees, witnesses, probate officer, etc.; also, names of plantations mentioned and remarkable items or noteworthy passages in wills.

The first record I have been able to find providing for the keeping of wills in the office of the Secretary of State is the following order:

> Order'd that a Commission be Deliver'd to ye Honble Majr Samuel Swann Esqr Secretary of State for this province Impowering him to keep an office for ye proving of Wills Granting administrats & probetts and all other Matters for ye Ordering & Securing of Dead Mens Estates according to ye foll Rules.
> 1. The Honble Secretary of State for ye time being shall atend ye Secretaries Office att ye Genrll Court House ye first thursday in every mo who shall have full power to prove Wills grant probetts & administrations & take care of Dead Mens Estates.
> 2. No will shall be proved or administration ordered either in ye Genrll Court or in ye precinct Court of Chowan Pequimans or Pascotant after ye first day of August next but only before ye sd Officer appoynted as afs'd and ye Clarks of each Respective precinct aforesd are hereby required to Return all papers and wrightings Relateing to wills & administrations and all other Concerns relating to Dead Mens Estates which shall Ly in their Respective offices into ye Secretaryes office within two mo.
> 3. Iff no person with in 2 months after ye Date of any person Dying Intestate appeare to sue for administration it shall be in ye power of ye sd officer to assigne an administrator.
> 4. Iff an Executor shall neglect to make proof of the will wthin 6 mo ye time Limitted by Law it shall be in ye power of ye sd Officer to Grant administration to the nearest of kinn if any sue for ye same if not to such pesons as he shall think fitt.
> 5. And ye sd Officer shall not grant administran or probatt of Will till Certificate be produced of ye Register ye Death of ye pson decd in ye Respective Registers as ye Law Directs.
> 6. And every prson suing for Admintrat Shall give in Sufficient Security before ye sd Officer & before whom all Evidence shall be brought to prove wills.

iv   INTRODUCTION.

7. And every prson who shall obtain admintrati or Probett shall within one year after such adminstrat. or probatt obtaind bring in a true Inventory with acct of ye Estate in their hands until they shall obtaine further time which ye sd Officer hath power & liberty to grant.

The original of this paper was found by the late J. R. B. Hathaway in the courthouse at Edenton.[1] This order is without date, but was issued about 1700, as Samuel Swann was Secretary of State in that year and the first of his records are dated at that time.

The next legislation I find in reference to wills is an act of the General Assembly of 1715, chapter 48, the caption and first three sections of which are as follows:

AN ACT CONCERNING PROVEING WILLS AND GRANTING LETTERS OF ADMINISTRATION AND TO PREVENT FRAUDES IN THE MANAGEMENT OF INTESTATES ESTATES.

I. Be It Enacted by his Excellency the Pallatine & and the rest of the True & Absolute Lords Proprietors of the Province of Carolina by & with the advice & consent of the rest of the Members of the General Assembly now met at Little River for the No. East part of the province & by the Authority of the same.

II. It is Hereby Enacted & declared that all Wills & Administrations heretofore proved & granted by the Council, General Court, Precinct Court or by powers or Commission heretofore granted by any Governor, Deputy Governor, President & Council to any particular person or persons shall be deemed adjudged & taken to be good & effectual to all Intents & Purposes whatsoever as if proved before Or granted by any Ordinary or other Ecclesiastical Judge or person.

III. And Be It Further Enacted by the Authority afors'd that it shall & may be lawfull for the Governor or Commander in Chief for the time being the General Court or Precinct Court to have Wills proved before them and Grant Orders for Administration. Provided the same be not repugnant to the Rules & Methods prescribed in this Act And Provided that the Granting Letters Testamentary or Letters of Administration allways Excepted which shall be allways from & after the Ratification of this Act signed by the Governor or Commander in Chief for the time being and sealed with the Colony seale & only Issuing out of the Secretary's Office & Counter signed by the Secretary or Deputy. * * * * * * * *

This act validates probates up to that time, confirms letters of administration previously granted and provides for the better regulation of these matters.

---

[1]Published in *The North Carolina Historical and Genealogical Register*, Vol. III, p. 57.

In 1723 a law was enacted more rigidly enforcing the making and filing of inventories. Both the acts of 1715 and of 1723 were brought forward and confirmed in 1749.

During Governor Dobbs' administration, in 1760, acts were passed[2] "to establish Inferior Courts of Pleas and Quarter Sessions in the several counties in this Province," and[3] "for establishing Superior Courts of Pleas and Grand Sessions and regulating the proceedings therein." These acts provided for the filing and recording of wills in the clerk's office, which is still the law.

In an act of the General Assembly of 1754, ch. 6, sec. 8,[4] it was recited that "many original wills, patents and deeds have been lost for want of convenient offices to keep the same." The various migrations of our capital since that date have undoubtedly added to these losses.

Many of the wills here are in bad order, decayed, foxed and faded, and some of them are illegible. Where there is doubt as to correct recording of a will it is so stated or queried. The earliest will found is that of Mary Fortsen, which was made in 1663, but there are not many before 1690. There are a few wills filed here since 1760 which have been included in the abstract list. Occasionally it is found that a testator who was known to be an educated person signed his will by making his mark, so it is not always an evidence of illiteracy when the will is signed by a mark, nor is the signature to the will generally a satisfactory signature of the testator, as often he was sick, weak or infirm in body at the time of signing the will. The original spelling has been preserved in making abstracts of wills and the same name is often found spelled in several different ways. It will be observed that the terms "father-in-law" or "mother-in-law" often mean stepfather or stepmother; sometimes they

---

[2]Col. Rec., Vol. XXV, p. 405.
[3]Col. Rec., Vol. XXV, p. 433.
[4]Col. Rec., Vol. XXV, p. 306.

are referred to as "father" or "mother." The term "cousin" will be frequently found to mean nephew or niece.

It is interesting to note that in wills prior to 1752, two years are generally named for dates in the months of January, February and March; for instance, January 20, 1718-9; but this was not always the case, and occasionally only one year is given. As examples, see wills of

CATHERINE BUSBEY, made January 22, 1738-9. Proved February Court, 1738.

THOMAS BARCLIFT, made November 14, 1750. Proved at January Court, 1750.

NICHOLAS BLACKMAN, made August 26, 1730. Probated March 11, 1730.

On the continent and in Scotland the Gregorian Calendar was in use, but it was not adopted in England until 1751, when Parliament passed "An Act for Regulating the Commencement of the Year, and for Correcting the Calendar now in use." This act provided that the year begin on the first day of January, 1752, and not on the twenty-fifth of March, as was then the usage. The same act provided that eleven days be omitted in September, 1752,[5] "and that the natural Day next immediately following the said second Day of September, shall be called, reckoned and accounted to be the fourteenth Day of September, omitting for that Time only the eleven intermediate nominal Days of the common Calendar, and that the several natural Days which shall follow and succeed next after the said fourteenth Day of September shall be respectively called, reckoned and numbered forwards in numerical Order from the said fourteenth Day of September, according to the Order and Succession of Days now used in the Present Calendar." If this is kept in mind, it will reconcile many apparently contradictory dates.

The abstracts were prepared by Messrs. WM. H. SAWYER

---

[5]Statutes at Large, Vol. VII, 1747-1756; 24 Geo. II., C. 23, A. D. 1751, and as amended by 25 Geo. II., C. 30 A. D. 1752.

and JOSEPH E. SAWYER, the proof read by Messrs. W. P. BATCHELOR and JOSEPH E. SAWYER, and the index made by Mr. W. P. BATCHELOR. To these gentlemen I desire to make acknowledgment for their faithful service.

It is expected that this work will be interesting and helpful in genealogical research and especially valuable as illustrative of the domestic history of our people. It will also be found useful in tracing titles to properties.

J. BRYAN GRIMES.

ABSTRACT OF WILLS.

ABERCROMBIE, HANNAH.   Pasquotank County.

August 12, 1754. January Court, 1755. *Daughter:* CATHRINE CHAMBERLIN. *Grandchildren:* LUCY and JEREMIAH CHAMBERLIN, DANIEL EVERTON, WILLIAM, HANNAH and JAMES EVERTON, COURTNEY and ABY CHAMBERLIN. *Executrix:* CATHERINE CHAMBERLIN. *Witnesses:* THOMAS TAYLOR, WILLIAM COALE. *Clerk of the Court:* THOMAS TAYLOR. Executrix qualified before ROBERT MURDEN.

ABINGTON, JOSEPH.   Currituck County.

January 2, 1734–1735. July Court, 1735. *Son:* WILLIAM (land on the Banks). *Daughter:* MARY ABINGTON. *Executor:* HENRY WOODAS. *Witnesses:* MATHIAS and MARY TOLER, FRANCIS HODGES, OTHO HOLLAND. *Clerk of the Court:* JAMES CRAVEN.

ABINGTON, THOMAS.   Pasquotank Precinct.

November 13, 1707. December 28, 1707. *Legatees:* MARY TULLY, GEORGE ELLIS, CHARLES GRIFFIN, ELIZABETH HECKLEFIELD. *Executors:* TOBIAS KNIGHT, JOHN and THOMAS PALIN. *Witnesses:* JOHN HECKLEFIELD, FRANCIS GILBERT, MARY COOKOO. Proven before W. GLOVER.

ADAMS, ABRAHAM.

(No date). *Sons:* ABRAM ADAMS (land lying on Pamlico River), RICHARD ADAMS (land on Pamlico River), WILLIAM ADAMS and WILLOBY ADAMS. *Daughter:* OBIA. *Wife:* BATHIA, who is appointed executrix. Part of this will is missing and no dates are given.

ADAMS, ABRAHAM.

October 3, 1733. *Witnesses:* PHILIP and MARY SHUTE, JOHN COLLISON. Only last page of will is found.

ADAMS, ABRAHAM.   Bath County.

December 18, 1734. Probate not dated. *Sons:* JAMES and JOSEPH (lands on Kengens Mill Creek and Old Town Swamp). Negroes bequeathed to sons. *Daughters:* SARAH ADAMS, ELIZABETH ADAMS. *Wife and Executrix:* ANNE. *Guardian and Trustee:* JOHN HODGSON. *Witnesses:* JOHN COLLISON, JAMES ADAMS, PETER CAILAG (or Cailaugh). Proven before GAB. JOHNSON.

ADAMS, CHARLES.   Craven County.

March 21, 1757. April 20, 1757. *Wife:* MARGARET. *Executor:* JOHN STARKEY. *Witnesses:* JER. VAIL, NATHL. RICHARDSON, VINYD. BOND. Proven before ARTHUR DOBBS.

ADAMS, JOHN.   Bath County.

February 17, 1733-1734. No probate. *Sons:* ABRAHAM, JAMES, EMANUEL, JOHN, THOMAS. *Daughters:* MARTHA, RACHEL and MARY ADAMS. *Executors:* ABRAHAM and JAMES ADAMS (sons). *Witnesses:* OLIVER BLACKBURN, ROBERT SHARPLES, JOHN ALDERSHIRE.

ADAMS, JOHN.   Craven County.

September 19, 1750. *Friends:* JOSEPH BALCH and JOHN GOWEL, FRANCIS MERRINGER and WM. HERRITAGE. *Wife:* MARY ADAMS, to whom is devised a sloop called "Adventure." *Executors:* JOSEPH BALCH and MARY ADAMS. *Witnesses:* GEARSHAM SPEAR, RD. LOVETT. Will proven by J. VAIL. *Clerk of Court:* PHIL SMITH.

ADAMS, MARGARET.   Craven County.

July 8, 1765. September 1, 1773. *Executor and sole legatee:* BERNARD PARKINGTON. *Witnesses:* MARY HAWKS, AMBCOX BAYLEY, PERRIGAN COX. Proven before Jo. MARTIN.

ADAMS (spelled ADDOMES), MATTHEW.   Chowan Precinct.

August 9, 1703. November 25, 1708. *Wife and Executrix:* SARAH. *Son:* MATTHEW. *Daughter:* ELIZABETH. *Witnesses:* THOMAS BLOUNT, THOMAS BLOUNT, JR., JAMES BONNER. Proven before THOMAS CARY. Seal of the Colony affixed on probate.

ADAMS, PETER.   Chowan County.

December 13, 1745. March 31, 1746. *Sister:* MARY MOUNCE of Crediton in Devonshire. *Son:* JOHN. Wife not named. *Executors:* WILLIAM HOSKINS, HENRY BONNER, and JOHN LEWIS. *Witnesses:* JOHN HULL, WILLIAM LUTEN and WILLIAM LEWIS. Proven before E. HALL, C. J.

ADAMS, ROGER.   Bladen County.

August 2, 1739. August 6, 1739. *Wife and Executrix:* FRANCES. *Other legatees:* LUCY and JOHN GREEN, GABRIEL JOHNSTON, SAMUEL WOODWARD, JAMES INNES, JAMES MURRAY. *Witnesses:* THOMAS HART, ROBERT KNOWLS, JAMES MENZIES. Proven before GABRIEL JOHNSTON.

ADDISON, RICHARD.   Chowan County.

August 12, 1720. January Court, 1724. *Wife and Executrix:* SARAH. *Witnesses:* SAMUEL SPRUILL, ROBERT FEWOX, CHARLES CRADOCK. *Clerk of the Court:* ROBERT FOSTER.

ABSTRACT OF WILLS, 1690—1760.

AHIER, JOHN.   Onslow County.

January 11, 1744-1745. October Court, 1746. *Son:* WILLIAM. *Daughter:* ELIZABETH AHIER. *Wife and Executrix:* ELIZABETH. *Witnesses:* STEPHEN HOWARD, STEPHEN HOWARD, JR. *Clerk of the Court:* WILL HEDGES.

ALBERTSON, ALBERT, SR.   Perquimans Precinct.

February 10, 1701. April 14, 1702. *Sons:* PETER, NATHANIEL, ALBERT and EASAW. Wife not named. *Executors:* PETER and NATHANIEL ALBERTSON (sons). *Witnesses:* JOHN FALCONER, NATHANIEL NICKOLSON, JOSEPH SUTON. *Clerk of the Court:* JOHN STEPNEY.

ALBERTSON, ISAAC.   Pasquotank County.

February 12, 1759. March Court, 1759. *Wife and Executrix:* JEMIMA· *Daughter:* RUTH ALBERTSON. *Witnesses:* THOMAS CRAGHILL, ISAAC SITTEN (or Litten), SARAH MARTIN. *Clerk of the Court:* THOS. TAYLOR.

ALBERTSON, JOSHUA.   Perquimans County.

August 5, 1753. October Court, 1753. *Son:* FRANCIS (plantation). *Daughters:* ELIZABETH, MARY and PENELOPY ALBERTSON. *Wife and Executrix:* MARY. *Executors:* AARON and WILLIAM ALBERTSON (brothers). *Witnesses:* PHINEUS NIXON, NATHANIEL ALBERTSON, JOHN ANDERSON. *Clerk of the Court:* EDMUND HATCH.

ALBERTSON, MARY.   Perquimans County.

Will not dated. Probated January 10, 1720-1721. *Son:* ALBERT. *Grandchildren:* MARY, JOHN and ELISABETH ALBERTSON. *Executor:* ALBERT ALBERTSON (son). *Witnesses:* THOMAS STAFFORD, ALBERT ALBERTSON, JR. *Clerk of the Court:* RICHARD LEARY.

ALBERTSON, NATHANIEL.   Perquimans County.

December 4, 1751. January Court, 1752. *Sons:* JOSHUA (land on Long Branch and Creek Swamp), WILLIAM ("my manner plantation"), AARON. *Grandsons:* BENJAMIN and CHALKLEY ALBERTSON. *Daughters:* HANNAH ALBERTSON, ELIZABETH NEWBY, LYDDA TRUEBLOOD. Negroes bequeathed to sons. Three sons appointed executors. *Witnesses:* JOSHUA PERISHO, JAMES HENBE, MARY MORRIS. *Clerk of the Court:* EDMUND HATCH.

ALDERSON, SIMON.   Beaufort County.

Will not dated. Probated at December Court, 1740. *Sons:* LEVIN and JOHN. *Daughters:* ELIZABETH and SARAH ALDERSON. *Other legatee:* JOHN ODEON. No executor appointed. *Witnesses:* ROBERT HOWARD, WILLIAM MARTIN. *Clerk of the Court:* ROGER JONES.

ABSTRACT OF WILLS, 1690—1760.

ALDRIDGE, JOHN. County not given.

December 28, 1705. April 2, 1706. *Wife and Executrix:* DOROTY. *Witnesses:* SAMUL SLOCUMB, RICHARD SMITH, JOHN WILSON. *Clerk of the Court:* LEVI TRUEWHITT.

ALEXANDER, ANTHONY. Tyrrell County.

July 29, 1741. November 3, 1741. *Sons:* ANTHONY, JOSEPH, LAMUEL, BENJAMIN, ISAAC, JOHN (plantation known by name of Mockason), JOSIAS (plantation known as Tuttellfields), GIDDEON, JOSHUA. *Daughters:* ANNE, RACHEL, PRISCILLA, SARAH, JANE, NAOMI, CASIAH, SETH. *Son-in-law and Executor:* THOMAS BATEMAN. *Witnesses:* BENJAMIN GIDGOOD, THOMAS BEST, CHRISTIAN ALEXANDER. Proven before J. MONTGOMERY.

ALFORD, JABEZ. Chowan Precinct.

July 9, 1705. July Court, 1706. *Legatees:* GEORGE TAYLER, ESAYAH HENLY, LUKE HAMAN, JAMES DAMEVALL, MARY DAMEVALL, THOMAS DANIELL, SARAH JONES. *Executor:* THOMAS POLLOCK. *Witnesses:* THOMAS JONES, HENRY BROOKS, JAMES FITZGERALD. *Clerk of the Court:* N. CHEVIN.

ALFORD, JOHN. Albemarle County.

April 16, 1691. May 4, 1691. *Daughters:* TABITHA and SARAH. *Executor:* CHARLES JONES (father-in-law). *Witnesses:* JOHN HUNT, WILLIAM PINDOR, HANNAH WOOD. *Clerk of the Court:* RICHARD PLATER.

ALLDAY, THOMAS. Bertie County.

March 16, 1754. May Court, 1754. *Sons-in-law:* WILLIAM and BENJAMIN COWARD (land on Cotahney). *Other legatees:* THOMAS HIGHMAN, ISAAC, (a molato boy), WILLIAM HIGHMAN, DIANA SANDERLIN. *Executors:* HENRY HUNTER and JOHN SMITH. *Witnesses:* JOHN BROGDEN, THOMAS HYMAN, MOSES HUNTER, PETER BROGDEN. *Clerk of the Court:* SAMUEL ORMES.

ALFORD, JOSEPH. Albemarle County.

December 8, 1689. No probate. *Wife and Executrix:* ANN. *Witnesses:* CHARLES JONES, JOHN BARBER, LUDFORD IVY.

ALLEN, ANDREW. Dobbs County.

October 29, 1762. November 18, 1762. *Wife:* PRISCILLA. *Devisees:* THOMAS WALTON, HANNAH WALTON, GRACE MEERS, GILBERT KER, JOHN VANSSELT, JOSEPH PARKER. *Executors:* JACOB VANSSELT, PRISCILLA ALLEN, JOSEPH KERR. *Witnesses:* ANTHONY VANSSELT, FREDERICK GIBBLE, ANNA GIBBLE. Name of Clerk of Court is torn off.

ABSTRACT OF WILLS, 1690—1760.   5

ALLEN, ELEAZAR.   New Hanover County.

January 1, 1742. *Wife and Executrix:* SARAH. *Nephews and Niece:* WILLIAM, DANIEL and CATHERINE WILLARD, children "of JOSIAH WILLARD, of Boston, by my sister, CATHERINE WILLARD." *Executors:* JAMES HASSELL and NATHANIEL RICE. *Witnesses:* SUSANN HASELL, JAS. HASELL, *Clerk of the Court:* ISAAC FARIES. Impression of rope and anchor on seal.

ALLEN, HUGH.   Chowan County.

July 5, 1752. No probate. *Sons:* JOSIA, JOHN and GEORGE. *Daughters:* EALCE, MARY and SARAH. *Wife and Executrix:* ELIZABETH. *Witnesses:* RICHARD BOND, RICHARD STALLINGS, JAMES BOND.

ALLEN, JAMES.   Edgecombe County.

December 4, 1733. February Court, 1733. *Legatees:* JAMES KELLEY, JOHN NAIRNE (executor). *Witnesses:* WILLIAM BELL, ANNE and JOHN STONE. *Clerk of the Court:* ROBERT FORSTER. Impression of head on seal.

ALLEN, JOHN.   Bertie County.

January 8, 1735-1736. August Court, 1736. *Sons:* WILLIAM and RICHARD. *Daughters:* CATHRINE and MARGARET ALLIN. *Wife and Executrix:* ELIZABETH. *Witnesses:* THOMAS MANDEN, ISAAC RICKS and HENRY TUDOR. *Clerk of the Court:* JNO. WYNNS.

ALLEN, SARAH, wid. of ELEAZAR ALLEN. New Hanover Co.

January 28, 1761. April 1, 1761. "My body I commit to the earth, to be buried as near the remains of my late husband as not to hurt the foundations of his tomb, which was bestowed on him by my beloved niece, MRS. SARAH FRANKLAND.

"It is my will that all my just debts and funeral charges be paid * * * hoping that THOMAS FRANKLAND, my said niece's husband (whose mortgage on the said ELEAZAR ALLEN's estate may perhaps go near to swallow the whole), will not avail himself of that mortgage so as to cut off the just demands of my other creditors.

"To my beloved niece, MRS SARAH FRANKLAND, my wedding ring (plain gold) as a particular mark of my affection and a memento of my conjugal happiness, not doubting hers is equal, and may it be as lasting. Item: To my beloved niece, MRS. MARY JANE DRY, I give and bequeath my gold watch (not of modern taste, but an excellent piece of mechanism), the gold chain and all the trinkets belonging thereto * * *. Item: To my beloved nieces, the daughters of my sister MOORE, MRS. SARAH SMITH of Charlestown, MRS. MARY HARLSTON of the same place, and MRS. ANN SWANN of Cape Fear, I give a mourning ring to each of them * * *. Item:

To my beloved grandniece, MISS MARY FRANKLAND, I give and bequeath my silver-chased teakettle and cream pot and lamp, also my walnut tree fineered tea chest containing three pieces of plate chased as the teakettle, in the form of urns for tea and sugar * * *. Item: I give to my grandniece, MISS HARIAT FRANKLAND, my largest silver waiter * * *. Item: To my grandniece, MISS REBECCA DRY, * * * a dozen teaspoons and strainer in a black shagreen case, designated to accompany an eight-sided silver coffee pot, put into her possession when I went to England in the year 1756, together with a shagreen writing stand, quite new, to encourage her in that part of her education in which she seems to be making great progress * * * To my beloved niece, MRS. MARY JANE DRY, one silver saucepan. I give to my grandniece, SUSANNAH HASELL, a mahogany dressing-table and a little gilt smelling bottle. I give to my grandniece, MARY HASELL, a little mahogany tea chest. I give all the books of modern taste to my grandnieces, REBECCA DRY and SUSANNAH HASELL. I give to my generous and constant friend, WILLIAM DRY, a mourning ring. I give to my friend, MRS. DEROSSETT, SR., my silver etice in a black shagreen case. As to all my other letters to and from my several correspondents abroad and in America, etc., etc.

"It is my will that one acre of ground around the tomb of my said husband be reserved sacred for the use of our cemetery when the rest of the plantation of "Lilliput" shall be sold † † †.

Executors: JAMES MURRAY, WILLIAM DRY, HENRY HYRNES, FREDERICK JONES of the OAK & WILLIAM BAMPFIELD of South Carolina. *Witnesses*: GEORGE MOORE, ELIZABETH CATHERINE DEROSSET, JAMES COLSON. Proven before ARTHUR DOBBS. Coat of arms on seal at top of first page of will.

ALLIGOOD, RICHARD.   Beaufort County.

January 22, 1751. September 19, 1752. *Sons:* HILLERY, WILLIAM. *Daughter:* MATHEW BAUER. Sons appointed executors. *Witnesses:* GEORGE JENKINS, JOHN ALLEGOOD and MARTHA JENKINS. *Clerk of the Court:* WILL ORMOND.

ALSTON, JOHN.   Chowan County.

February 20, 1755. December 2, 1758. *Sons:* JOSEPH JOHN ALSTON (land on White Oak River), SOLOMON ALSTON (one negro), WILLIAM and PHILLIP ALSTON, JAMES ALSTON. *Daughters:* MARY SEWARD, ELIZABETH WILLIAMS, SARAH KEARNY, CHARITY DAWSON. *Grandchildren:* JOHN, ELIZABETH, PATTY and WILLIAM ALSTON. *Executor:* JAMES ALSTON (son). *Witnesses:* SCASBROOK WILSON, THOMAS BYARD, JOSEPH PARKER. Proven before ARTHUR DOBBS.

AMBLER, WILLIAM.   Perquimans County.

April 27, 1745. July Court, 1745. *Friends:* JOHN STEVENSON, WILLIAM STEVENSON (land on Perquimans River), ZACHARIAH NIXON, ELIZA-

BETH PHELPS, HENRY PHELPS, JONATHAN PHELPS, JOHN BARCLIFT of Wearneck, ELIZABETH WILLIAMS, BENJAMIN BAPTIST, JOHN READ, ELIZABETH REED, JOSEPH SUTTON. *Executor:* JOHN STEVENSON. *Witnesses:* SAM SCOLLAY, WILLIAM HAROLD, FRANCIS LAYDEN. *Clerk of the Court:* EDMUND HATCH.

AMBROS, DAVID.   Chowan County.

July 14, 1745. August 1, 1745. *Sons:* DAVID, WILLIAM, JESSE and ISRAEL. *Daughters:* MARY, SUSANNAH and MORNING AMBROS. *Wife and Executrix:* SUSANNAH. *Witnesses:* JACOB PRIVETT, DAVID BUSH, JAMES CRAVEN. Proven before ENOCH HALL, C. J. Coat of arms on seal.

ANDERSON, CAROLUS.   Northampton County.

February 10, 1752. February Court, 1753. *Daughters:* RACHEL WARREN and MARY ANDERSON (land and negroes), SARAH ANDERSON (land on Kubys Creek). Wife and Executrix not named. *Witnesses:* NICHOLAS and WILLIAM BOONE. *Clerk of the Court:* I. EDWARDS.

ANDERSON, ELIZABETH.   Bertie Precinct.

November 5, 1732. August Court, 1733. *Sons:* JAMES, CARROLUS. *Daughter:* ELIZABETH PITMAN. *Granddaughters:* ELIZABETH and SARAH ANDERSON (executrix) *Witnesses:* ELIAS FORTT, EALCER FORTT, HENRY CROMPTON. *Clerk of the Court:* ROBERT FORSTER.

ANDERSON, ELISABETH.   Perquimans County.

May 25, 1757. January Court, 1760. *Sons:* JOHN and SAMUEL, *Daughter:* ABIGAIL CHARLES. *Granddaughters:* ELIZABETH and SARAH HENBE. *Grandsons:* WILLIAM ARNOLD and JOSHUA ALBERTSON. *Executors:* WILLIAM ARNOLD, JOHN ANDERSON and WILLIAM ALBERTSON. *Witnesses:* JOHN BOSWELL, JOSEPH BOSWELL, SARAH ANDERSON. *Clerk of the Court:* MILES HARVEY.

ANDERSON, GEORGE.   Granville County.

July 6, 1757. March 7, 1758. *Wife and Executrix:* MARY. *Daughter:* EAVE ANDERSON. *Brother:* WILLIAM ANDERSON. *Nephew:* GEORGE ANDERSON (son of William). *Other legatees:* ELIZABETH and JOHN UNDERWOOD. *Executor:* OSBORNE JEFFREYS. *Witnesses:* JAMES BRAEZAR, WILLIAM ANDERSON, THOMAS SMITH. *Clerk of the Court:* DANIEL WELDON.

ANDERSON, JAMES.   Perquimans County.

February 6, 1741-1742. December 14, 1742. *Sons:* JAMES and JOHN. *Executor:* RICHARD SKINNER. *Witnesses:* THOMAS JESSOP and THOMAS BATEMAN. Proven before W. SMITH.

8   ABSTRACT OF WILLS, 1690—1760.

ANDERSON, JOHN.   Perquimans County.
January 27, 1744-1745. March 5, 1745. *Executors:* CHRISTOPHER
SUTTON and ABRAHAM MULLEN. *Other legatee:* JANE MULLEN. *Witnesses:*
GEORGE WOOD, ELENDER MULLEN. Proven before GAB JOHNSTON.

ANDERSON, JOSEPH.   Chowan County.
1750. January Court, 1750. *Daughter:* MARY ANDERSON. *Guardians
of daughter:* THOMAS BARKER, DR. SAMUEL SABINE PLOMER and WILLIAM
MEARNS. *Brother:* JAMES ANDERSON, near Lundy. *Sister:* MARGARET
ANDERSON, in Bonnetown, near Leish. *Daughters-in-law:* LUCY and
AGNES MARTIN. *Executors:* THOMAS BARKER and JOSEPH BLOUNT.
Wife: ANN. *Witnesses:* JOHN HALSEY, WILLIAM LUTEN and JAMES
CRAVEN. Codicil bearing date December 24, 1750, makes further provision for daughter and confirms appointment of THOMAS BARKER as
executor. *Witnesses to Codicil:* PETER PAYNE and JOHN MCKILDO.
Clerk of the Court: WILL MEARNS.

ANDERSON, JOSEPH.   Perquimans County.
September 23, 1751. October Court, 1751. *Daughter:* ELIZABETH
(land on Moses Creek, and two negroes). *Executor:* ZACHARIAH NIXON.
Witnesses: JAMES and SILVANUS HENBE, SAMUEL ANDERSON. *Clerk of the
Court:* EDMUND HATCH.

ANDREWS, JOHN.   Rowan County.
October 3, 1756. No probate. *Sons:* JAMES and JOHN. *Daughter:*
JANET. *Wife:* AGNES. *Executors:* THOMAS DOUGLAS and JAMES ANDREWS. *Witnesses:* JOHN MARTIN, WILLIAM NIBLACK, ELISABETH LAWRENCE. Codicil dated October 3, 1756, makes provision for minor children.
Witnesses: ELISABETH LAWRENCE, WILLIAM NIBLACK, JOHN MARTEN.

ANDREWS, THOMAS.   Bertie Precinct.
January 12, 1736-1737. March 31, 1737. *Legatees:* ROBERT BELL,
THOMAS ANDREWS (executor). *Witnesses:* THOMAS DAVY, ANN and PENELOPE BELL. Proven before W. SMITH, C. J.

ANDREWS, WARREN.   Tyrrell County.
May 4, 1772. February 28, 1774. *Sons:* LEVI, EDMUND and ETHELDRED ANDREWS. *Daughters:* MILLEE BLUNT, MARTHA PEARSE, ELISABETH ANDREWS. *Wife:* SARAH. Three sons appointed executors. *Witnesses:* WILLIAM ELLIS, ROBEN SHERROD. Proven before JO MARTIN.

ANELYN, PETER.
March 14, 1710. No probate. *Sons:* HENRY, PETER and JOHN.
Daughter: ANN. *Executor:* THOMAS POLLOCKE. *Witnesses:* LAURANCE
SARSON, ROBERT WEST, JOHN JONES, THOMAS ASHLY.

ANSELL, JOHN. Currituck County.

September 12, 1738. April Court, 1740. *Son and Executor:* JOHN. *Daughter:* SARAH ROBERTS. *Grandson:* JAMES ROBERTS. *Witnesses:* HENRY WHITE, HILARY WHITE, LEADY WHITE. *Clerk of the Court:* WILLIAM SHERGOLD.

ANSELL, JOHN, "of Netsiland." Currituck County.

April 6, 1753. March Court, 1755. *Sons:* JOHN, WILLIAM, JAMES, CALEB. *Daughters:* MARY and LETESSHA. Wife not named. *Executor:* JOHN ANSELL (son). *Witnesses:* CALEB WHITE, JOSHUA WHITE, PAUL ELISON. *Clerk of the Court:* WILLIAM SHERGOLD.

ANSLEY, SOLOMON. Tyrrell County.

August 27, 1750. March Court, 1750. *Daughters:* MARY, SARAH, ELIZABETH, ANN, RACHEL and EASTER ANSLEY. *Sons:* JOHN and JOSEPH. *Wife and Executrix:* SARAH. *Witnesses:* SAMUEL SPRUILL, MATTHEW CARSWELL, SAMUEL SPRUILL, JR. *Clerk of the Court:* EVAN JONES.

ARDERNE, JOHN.

October 22, 1707. May 17, 1712. *Kinsman:* WILLIAM DUCKENFIELD (tract of land known by name of Salmon Creek, "all negro, indian, molato slaves, all horses, mares, cobbs, cattle, hoggs, young and old, and everything else in America, England, or any other part of the world.") *Executor:* WILLIAM DUCKENFIELD, Esq. *Witnesses:* HENRY LYSLE, THO. ARNOLD, GEO. BLAINYE, CHARLES BARBOUR, JOHN TALOR.

ARENTON, CHRISTOPHER. Chowan County.

April 22, 1753. July Court, 1753. *Son:* WILLIAM. *Daughter:* ABEGELL HUBARD. *Wife and Executrix:* SARAH. *Witnesses:* THOMAS PEIRCE, MARY CREECY, JOHN FENNELL. *Clerk of the Court:* WILL HALSEY.

ARENTON, WILLIAM. Craven County.

January 23, 1761. *Daughters:* REBECKAH, MARY and LEAH. *Wife:* MARY. *Executor:* HENRY SHIPPARD. *Witnesses:* EDMUND HATCH, MARTIN SHIPPARD. No probate.

ARMSTRONG, JEAMS.

June 22, 1684. November 2, 1685. *Executor and sole legatee:* RICHARD CRAGE (1). *Witnesses:* HENRY WHITE and WILLIAM JACKSON. No probate officer.

ARLOW, JAMES.

December 27, 1757. February Court, 1758. *Nephew:* JOHN ARLOW. *Wife and Executrix:* BRIDGET (house and lot in Wilmington). *Executor:*

BENJAMIN MORISON. *Witnesses:* BEN WHEATLEY, ARTHUR MABSON, JOHN JONES. *Clerk of the Court:* JA. MORAN.

ARMOUR, JOHN.   Pasquotank County.

March 21, 1728. March Court, 1729. *Son:* JOHN. *Daughters:* MARY, ANN. *Other legatees:* JOHN DAVIS and WILLIAM DAVIS (brothers of former wife). Wife and Executrix not named. *Executor:* DAVID BARLY (father-in-law). *Witnesses:* (Signatures of witnesses, probate and portion of will missing.)

ARMOR, WILLIAM.   Pasquotank Precinct.

December 13, 1719. January 25, 1719. *Legatees:* THOMAS and THEOPHILUS ARMOR (sons), ROBERT and JOHN ARMOR and ANN MEADS, WILLIAM BROTHERS. *Executor:* JOHN ARMOR. *Witnesses:* WILLIAM JAMES, THOMAS CRANK. Proven before JNO. PALIN.

ARMSTRONG, JOHN.   Currituck County.

March 28, 1753. March Court, 1755. *Wife and Executrix:* ASIAH. *Witnesses:* THOS. WILLIAMS, JOSHUA BRENT, LUCY PUTT. *Clerk of the Court:* WILLIAM SHERGOLD.

ARNOLD, EDWARD.   Chowan County.

February 23, 1748. April Court, 1752. *Son and Executor:* EDWARD. *Daughter:* HANNAH STALLINGS. *Wife:* PLEASANT (plantation and negroes). *Witnesses:* JOHN SUMNER, RICHARD BROTHERS, APSILLA WEBB. *Clerk of the Court:* JAMES CRAVEN. Impression of lion rampant on seal.

ARNOLD, JOHN.   Perquimans Precinct.

March 21, 1723. July 14, 1724. *Sons:* JOHN, LAWRENCE, WILLIAM and JOSEPH. *Daughter:* ELIZABETH ARNOLD. *Wife and Executrix:* MARY. *Witnesses:* WILLIAM HAN, JAMES JONES, ABRAHAM REIGS, JOHN REIGS. *Clerk of the Court:* RICHD LEARY.

ARNOLD, JOHN.   Perquimans County.

April 11, 1735. July 21, 1735. *Son:* JOHN. *Wife and Executrix:* ELIZABETH (land at Deep Creek). *Executor:* SAMUEL PARSONS. *Witnesses:* JAMES GIBSON, WILLIAM ARNELL. *Clerk of the Court:* JAMES CRAVEN. Crest on seal.

ARNOLD, JOSEPH.   Perquimans County.

November 30, 1751. April Court, 1752. *Daughter:* MARY. *Executors:* WILLIAM and LAWRENCE ARNOLD (brothers). *Witnesses:* JAMES GIBSON and WILLIAM BATEMAN. *Clerk of the Court:* EDMUND HATCH.

ABSTRACT OF WILLS, 1690—1760.   11

ARNOLD, LAWRENCE.   Albemarle County.
December 14, 1691. February 2, 1691. *Son and Executor:* JOHN. *Other legatee:* LAWRENCE GODFREY. *Witnesses:* ELIZABETH JENKINS, ISAAC ROWDEN. *Clerk of the Court:* RICHARD PLATER.

ARRINGTON, WILLIAM.   Northampton County.
January 11, 1750. February Court, 1752. *Sons:* BRIGGS and WILLIAM (plantation to each). *Other legatees:* JAMES ROSS, NATHANIEL WILLIAMS. *Executors:* JOHN DAWSON and NATHAN WILLIAMS. *Witnesses:* HENRY DAWSON, JOHN PITMAN, JOHN BROCK. *Clerk of the Court:* I. EDWARDS.

ARTHUR, JOHN.   Chowan County.
May 29, 1735. October Court, 1735. *Legatees:* WILLIAM FALAW, JACOB PRIVIT, JOHN HANAH. *Executors:* THOMAS LUTEN and CONSTANT LUTEN. *Witnesses:* WILLIAM GOOLDSBERRY, HUMPHREY WEBB, EDWARD HOWCOTT. *Clerk of the Court:* JAMES CRAVEN.

ARTHUR, JOHN.   Craven County.
January 7, 1751. March 2, 1751. *Sons:* JOHN, JAMES, MATTHEW and WILLIAM. *Daughters:* ANN and MARY. *Wife and Executrix:* BRIDGET. *Witnesses:* CHARLES EVITT, ROBERT MOORE, AMMEY MOORE. Proven before GABRIEL JOHNSTON.

ASHE, JOHN BAPTISTA.   Bath County.
November 2, 1731. November 15, 1734. *Sons:* JOHN and SAMUEL. *Daughter:* MARY. *Brothers:* JOHN and SAMUEL SWANN. *Other legatees:* JOHN RUSSELL, DANIEL HENDRICK of South Carolina. The following lands devised: "lands up the northwest branch of Cape Fear River, called Ashwood, situated between the lands of JOHN PORTER of Virginia, merchant, and the plantation whereon DANIEL DONAHO now lives." "My other lands on the north side of the river directly opposite to those aforementioned"; * * * land on Stumpy Sound called Turkey Point; 100 acres called Stumpy Island or New River Banks; 400 acres "above WILLIAM LEWIS's plantation on the Main Branche of Old Towne Creek"; 2,560 acres near Rockfish Creek on the northwest branch of Cape Fear River; 640 acres of land on the northeast branch of Cape Fear River." The following item may be of interest: "I will that my slaves be kept to work on my lands and that my estate be managed to the best advantage so as my sons may have as liberal an education as the profits thereof will afford; and in their education I pray my executors to observe this method: Let them be taught to read and write and be introduced into the practical part of Arithmetick, not too hastily hurrying them to Latin or Grammar; but after they are pretty well versed in these, let them be taught Latin and Greek. I propose

this may be done in Virginia; after which let them learn French; perhaps some Frenchman at Santee will undertake this. When they are arrived to years of discretion let them study the Mathematicks. To my sons when they arrive at age I recommend the pursuit and study of some profession or business (I could wish the one to ye Law, the other to Merchandize), in which let them follow their own inclinations. I will that my daughter be taught to write and read and some feminine accomplishments which may render her agreeable; and that she be not kept ignorant of what appertains to a good housewife in the management of household affairs. Item: I give to each of my executors a gold ring as a token of the respect, etc. I will that a brick Vault may be built at Groveley and my Dear Wife's body taken up out of the Earth and brought and laid there; if it should be my fortune to die in Carolina so as my corpse may be conveyed thither, I desire that one large Coffin may be made and both our bodys laid together therein and lodged in the said Vault." *Executors:* EDWARD MOSELEY, ROGER MOORE, NATHANIEL RICE, SAMUEL and JOHN SWANN, WILLIAM DOWNING and EDWARD SMITH. *Witnesses:* MEHITTOBEL RUTTER, JOHN HAWKINS, CORNELIUS DARGAN, MICH RUTTER. Codicil dated October 16, 1734, appoints JOB HOWS and THOMAS JONES *Executors* and directs interest in sawmill owned by testator and MATT ROWAN to be sold. *Witnesses:* JAMES INNES, JOSEPH WALTERS, EDWARD SMITH. Proven before GAB JOHNSTON. *Executors* qualified before W. SMITH, C. J. Impression of dragon's head on seal.

ASHLEY, JOHN.   Anson County.

February 1, 1759. No probate. *Sons:* JOHN, FRANCIS and WILLIAM (land on Bare Creek), JURDEN. *Daughters:* MARY ANN FRANKS, ELINOR SUTTON, ROSE TOUCHSTONE, SARAH ASHLEY. *Wife and Executrix:* MARY. *Witnesses:* RICHARD YARBOROUGH, CHRISTOPHER TOUCHSTONE, FREDERICK ———.

ASKUE, JOHN.   Isle of Wight County.

Not dated. No probate. *Son:* WILLIAM. *Brother and Executor:* NICHOLAS ASKUE. *Witnesses:* JOHN BROWNE, WILL WILLIAMS, ELIZABETH BROWNE. Original missing. Abstract made from recorded copy, Book 1712-1722, page 31.

AVENT, THOMAS.   Northampton County.

April 15, 1751. February Court, 1752. *Brother and Executor:* WILLIAM AVENT. *Wife:* USLEA. Children not named. *Executor:* JOHN MOORE. *Witnesses:* RICHARD MOORE and JOHN DAVIS. *Clerk of the Court:* I. EDWARDS.

AVERITT, NATHANIEL.   Onslow County.

December 4, 1755. Probate not dated. *Sons:* JOHN, ARTHUR, BENJAMIN NATHANIEL, EPHALY AVERITT. *Son-in-law:* JONATHAN ENNETT. *Daughter:* NANCY AVERITT. *Executors:* STEPHEN LEE, JOHN MILTON and Captain JOHN ASHE. *Witnesses:* NATHANIEL KNOTT, ELIZABETH CAREY, JOHN HUNT. *Clerk of the Court:* WILL CRAY. Crest on seal.

AVERY, JOHN.   Hyde County.

October 27, 1740. Probate not dated. *Wife:* JANE. *Other legatees:* MARTHA SMITH, AGNES SLADE, THOMAS, WILLIAM and SAMUEL SMITH (sons of John), LYDIA (wife of Benjamin Russell), ELIZABETH and DORCAS SMITH, JOHN SMITH, DARCAS WORLDLY, JAMES AVERY, GILBERT MACKNARY, KEZIA HADLEY, ELIZABETH (daughter of Uriah Collins), FOSTER JERVIS, LYDIA CATHRIGHT, JAMES AVERY. *Executors:* JOHN SMITH and FOSTER JERVIS. *Witnesses:* URIAH COLLINS, WILLIAM SILVESTER, WILLIAM GIDDENS. *Clerk of the Court:* WILLIAM BARROW.

BADHAM, WILLIAM.   Chowan Precinct.

October 28, 1736. November 3, 1736. *Devisees and legatees:* ELLEN and MARY DUNSTON (daughters of Martha and John Dunston), BARNABY STELY DUNSTON (son of John), RICHARD WILLIAM DUNSTON (son of John), JOHN LAPORTE. The following lands devised: Plantation on Machecomock Creek; lots Nos. 1, 2 and 3 in town of Edenton; land on Rockahock Creek, in Chowan; plantation on Chinkapin Swamp, in Bertie; 640 acres in Bertie precinct; plantation near Edenton, "whereon I now live"; back plantation called "Heldersham"; 305 acres in Chowan. About ten negroes bequeathed. *Wife and Executrix:* MARTHA. *Executors:* THOMAS JONES and JOSEPH ANDERSON. *Witnesses:* THOMAS JONES, BENJAMIN HILL and THOMAS JACKSON. Proven before W. SMITH. Original of this will is missing. Abstract made from recorded copy, No. 136, in Land Grant Records, Book 4.

BAGGETT, NICHOLAS.   Bertie County.

January 9, 1753. April Court, 1755. *Sons:* BENJAMIN, NICHOLAS, ABRAHAM, JOSEPH, BARNABEY, THOMAS ("the plantation whereon I now live"), HARDY, JOHN. *Daughters:* MARY WEST, MARTHA BAGGETT, ELIZABETH WARD, SARAH BAGGETT. *Wife:* MARY. *Executors:* JOSEPH and THOMAS BAGGETT (sons). *Witnesses:* CHARLES HORNE, JOHN HOOKS. *Clerk of the Court:* BENJAMIN WYNNS.

BAGLEY, THOMAS.

July 19, 1727. *Sons:* THOMAS ("plantation whereon I now live"), WILLIAM (land on Great Branch). *Daughter:* HANNA BAGLEY. *Wife:* SU-

SANA. *Executors:* SUSANA BAGLEY (wife) and JOSEPH JESSOP. *Witnesses:* RICHARD WOOD, JOSIAS BAGNE, WILLIAM SHARBO. *Clerk of the Court:* CHARLES DENMAN.

BAILEY, DAVID.   Pasquotank County.

October 6, 1745. March 29, 1746. *Sons:* JOSEPH (one plantation, three negroes, one whipsaw, one steel trap, one corn mill), BENJAMIN (land bought of Ebenezer Hall, and one negro), ROBERT (land and plantation, "The Folly," two negroes, half of new schooner), SIMON (plantation called "Piney Point" lying at Core Sound, one negro). *Daughters:* ELIZABETH BRYANT, SARAH SNOWDON and TAMAR BAILEY. Stock mark of testator, swallow fork in right ear, the left ear off; also poplar leaf in "ye left ear and a crop and a slit in ye right." To daughter TAMAR is bequeathed one woolen wheel made at Core Sound. *Other legatees.* MIRIAM OVERMAN and DAVID WALLIS (children of second wife). *Wife:* THAMAR. *Executors:* JOSEPH BAILEY (son) and SIMON BRYANT (son-in-law). *Witnesses:* THOS. WEEKS, PATRICK BAILEY, JOHN BAILEY. Proven before ENOCH HALL, C. J.

BAILY, JOHN.   Hyde County.

July 23, 1749. March Court, 1758. *Daughter and Executrix:* MARGARET BAILY. *Friend:* THOMAS BARLOW (son of Elizabeth Kelly). *Witnesses:* THOS. LOACH, JOHN SMITH, WM. CARDING. *Clerk of the Court:* STEPHEN DENNING.

BAILEY, JOSEPH.   Pasquotank County.

June 17, 1749. August 4, 1749. *Daughter:* ANNE BAILEY ("plantation whereon I now live"). *Brothers:* SIMON and ROBERT BAILEY. *Sisters:* THAMAR BAILEY, SARAH SNOWDON. *Executors:* ROBERT BAILEY (brother), PATRICK POOL. *Witnesses:* PATRICK BAILEY, DAVID BAILEY, HENRY DE SON. Will proven before GAB. JOHNSTON at Eden House. Coat of arms on testator's seal.

BAIRD, RICHARD.

Sons-in-law: WILLIAM BOGE and ———— BOGE. *Wife:* JEANE. *Cousin:* CATHERN CLARKE. *Other legatees:* JAMES LOADINAR, MARGREETT BOGE. *Executors:* JAMES and CHRISTOPHER ————. *Witnesses:* PETER OREY, PATRICK ————. On the back of this will appears another will of RICHARD BIARD, in which appear the names of JAMES LADMAN, CATRING CLARKE, HANNAH BARD, JANNE BIARD (wife), WILLIAM MOORE, JOHN LILEY (executor), WILLIAM BOGE, WILLIAM LARNESS, CHARLES MCDANIEL, RICHARD HICKNEY, HANNAH HILLE.

BAKER, HENRY.   Chowan County.

January 9, 1737. May 1, 1739. *Sons:* HENRY ("All the land whereon I now live * * * these negroes vizt: Guy, Clouse, Bob, Caesar, Ned, Jacob, Young Diner and Hagar * * * my watch, seal, desk, 6 Russia chares, ye great glass, my sword. one deal table"); JOHN ("All my land at a place called Little Town and my land joining on Banks Wynn & Askue, and the land bought of WILLIAM GARRET in Bertie precinct * * * these negroes, vizt, Arthur, Juno, Finney, Little Bobb and Dick * * *"); BLAKE ("land bought of John and Thomas Wilkins in Chowan * * * land on Ahoskie Marsh in Bertie and the stock thereto belonging * * * these negroes, vizt, Cipio, Joe, Patt and Argalus"); DAVID ("130 acres of land at Meherring Landing adjoining to the ferry"). *Daughters:* MARY and SARAH (two negroes to each), RUTH. *Son:* ZADOCK, (twenty shillings). *Wife:* RUTH (six negroes). *Brothers* and *Executors:* WILLIAM, JAMES and LAWRENCE BAKER. *Witnesses:* EDWARD VANN, JOHN BRADY, EDWARD WARREN. Proven before W. SMITH, C. J.

Original of this will is missing. Abstract made from recorded copy No. 81 in Land Grants, Book 4.

BAKER, MOSES.   Chowan County.

January 26, 1723. January Court, 1724. *Sons:* BENETT, WILLIAM. Wife and three daughters mentioned but not named. *Executors:* Wife and RICHARD MINSHON. *Witnesses:* AARON BLANCHARD, WM. HILL, WILLIAM WESSON. *Clerk of Court:* ROBERT FORSTER.

BALCH, JOSEPH.   Craven County.

December 18, 1750. February 13, 1752. *Friend:* JOHN MARKS. *Wife:* SUSANNAH BALCH. *Her daughters:* PHOEBE and MARY. *Nephew:* JOSEPH BALCH (son of Benjamin Balch). *Executor:* JOHN STARKEY. *Witnesses:* ROBERT MOORE, JNO. SNEAD, CHRISTOPHER NEAL. *Deputy Clerk of Court:* SOL. REW.

BALEY, JOHN.   Chowan County.

July Court, 1716. *Wife:* MAREY. *Friends:* HENREY CLARK, JEFERY LYLES. *Executrix:* MARY BALEY (wife). *Witnesses:* HENREY CLARK, JEFERY LYLES, WILL MITCHELL. *Clerk of the Court:* R. HICKS.

BALL, JOHN.   Carteret County.

November 10, 1749. December Court, 1749. *Sons:* NATHAN ("houses and plantation whereon I now live"), STEPHEN (150 acres land on "west side of Brice's plantation"), JAMES (150 acres land "adjoining plantation whereon I now live"). *Daughters:* SARAH BALL, RACHEL BALL. *Wife:* MAGDALENE BALL. *Executors:* MAGDALENE BALL (wife) and SAMUEL NOBLE. *Witnesses:* DAVID TURNER, FRANCIS EGLETON, REBECCA TURNER. *Clerk of the Court:* GEO. READ.

BALL, THOMAS.   Chowan Precinct.

March 28, 1722. April 17, 1722. *Son:* WILLIAM (200 acres land on Corsaks Swamp; 200 acres land; 400 acres of land). *Daughter:* ANN BALL. *Wife and Executrix:* ELIZEBETH. *Executor:* THOMAS YETTS. *Witnesses:* JOSEPH HUDSON, JOHN BUCKLER, THOS. OLDNEE. *Deputy Clerk of the Court:* W. BADHAM.

BALLARD, ABRAHAM.   Perquimans County.

November 9, 1753. April Court, 1754. *Sons:* JETHRO ("plantation whereon I now live"), KEADAH. *Daughters:* APSILLA BALLARD, BATHSHEBA BALLARD. *Wife:* ELIZABETH. *Executors:* ELIZABETH (wife) and JOHN SUMNER. *Witnesses:* SARAH NORFLEET, PHILLISIA NORFLEET, JOHN SUMNER. *Clerk of the Court:* WILLIAM SKINNER.

BALLARD, JOHN.   Chowan Precinct.

July 12, 1736. November 26, 1736. *Wife:* MARY. *Daughter:* ANN BALLARD. *Daughter-in-law:* SARAH. *Executors:* JOHN LEWISS, JOHN JONES, JR. *Witnesses:* BENJAMIN TALBOT, WILLIAM FALLOW. Proven before W. SMITH.

BALLARD, JOSEPH.   Chowan County.

July 21, 1729. October 14, 1729. *Sons:* JOHN, JOSEPH ("my plantation"), ELISHER, ELIAS. *Daughters:* MARTHA, SUSANNE, ESTHER. *Wife:* ANNE. *Executor:* JOSEPH BALLARD (son). *Witnesses:* JAMES MANY, JOHN HOOKS, JOHN PURVIS. Will proven before RICHARD EVERARD, at Edenton.

BALLENTINE, GEORGE.

January 14, 1723. *Wife, Executrix and sole legatee:* DINAH. *Witnesses:* AARON OLIVER, ALEXANDER BALLENTINE, ELINER WENTFORD.

BANGS, ABIAH, widow of JONATHAN.   Craven County.

June 3, 1755. *Cousin:* ELIZABETH HOBBS ("my lot in Newbern Town"). *Daughter:* BETTY BANGS. *Sisters:* ELIZABETH and MARY CARRUTHERS. *Brothers:* JOHN CARRUTHERS, WILLIAM CARRUTHERS. *Executors:* WILLIAM CARRUTHERS (brother), ROBERT JONES, "oturney at law." *Witnesses:* WILLIAM CREEKMORE, RUBIN HAMMONTREE, WILLIAM CARRUTHERS, SR. No probate.

BANGS, JONATHAN.   Craven County.

October 7, 1743. June 15, 1744. *Wife:* ABIAH. *Daughter:* BETTY BANGS. *Sister:* THANKFULL COVELL. *Executors:* JOHN CARRUTHERS (uncle), ABIAH BANGS (wife). *Witnesses:* FRANCIS BRINLEY, JNO. CARRUTHERS, JO. RD. HICKSON. *Clerk of the Court:* W. ROUTLEDGE. Coat of arms on seal.

BANKS, WILLIAM.   Craven County.
April 7, 1772. May 27, 1772. *Wife:* ANNE. *Daughters-in-law:* SU-
SANNAH and FILLDER MOORE. *Sons-in-law:* JOHN MOORE, WILLIAM
MOORE. *Brother:* JONATHAN BANKS. *Executors:* JONATHAN BANKS
(brother) and CHRISTOPHER NEALE. *Witnesses:* JAMES COOR, BENJA-
MIN FORDHAM, JOHN MOORE. Will proven before Jo. MARTIN.

BAPTIST, BENJAMIN.   Chowan County.
March 24, 1752. April Court, 1752. June 15, 1752. *Son:* EDMUND.
Wife: MARY CLARK BAPTIST. *Executors:* MARY C. BAPTIST (wife),
EDMUND BAPTIST (son) and EDMUND HATCH. *Witnesses:* J. PALMER (?),
EDMUND HATCH, SARAH ARNOLD. *Clerk of the Court:* JAMES CRAVEN.
Executrix qualified before———BLOUNT.

BARBER, JOHN.   Albemarle County.
June 10, 1692. April Court, 1693. *Servant:* ROBERT HARPER, 10
pounds, and servant to be set free at date of death. Remainder of estate
to ANN BOYCE, wife of William Boyce, debarring said William Boyce from
any claim or possession of any of said estate. *Witnesses:* THOMAS PALIN,
EM. NISCON, EDWARD MAYO. *Clerk of the Court:* EDWARD MAYO.

BARCLIFT, JOHN.   Perquimans County.
April 23, 1759. July Court, 1759. *Wife:* ELIZABETH BARCLIFT.
Sons: ASA BARCLIFT, DEMSON BARCLIFT, BENJAMIN BARCLIFT, JOHN
BARCLIFT, NOAH BARCLIFT. *Daughters:* MARY BARCLIFT, ELIZA SAN-
DERSON. *Executors:* SAMUEL SUTTON and THOMAS STEVENSON. *Wit-
nesses:* JAMES GIBSON, SAMUEL BARCLIFT, MATHIAS JOHNSON. *Clerk of
Court:* MILES HARVEY.

BARCLIFT, JOSHUA.   Perquimans County.
November 29, 1755. January Court, 1756. *Sons:* WILLIAM ("planta-
tion whereon I now live"), JAMES, BLAKE. *Daughters:* MIRIAM BARCLIFT,
ANN BARCLIFT. *Wife:* MARY. *Executors:* JOHN BARCLIFT (cousin),
JOSEPH ROBINSON, WILLIAM TRUMBALL (nephew). *Witnesses:* JAMES
GIBSON, TULLE WILLIAMS, GEORGE LEE. *Clerk of the Court:* MILES
HARVEY.

BARCLIFT, THOMAS.   Perquimans County.
November 14, 1750. January Court, 1750. *Sons:* WILLIAM, THOMAS
and JOSEPH. *Daughters:* SARAH BIDGOOD, ELIZABETH WRIGHT, MARY
JACKSON, ANNE GORDEN. *Wife and Executrix:* ELIZABETH. *Witnesses:*
JAMES GIBSON, JOHN BARCLIFT. *Clerk of the Court:* EDMUND HATCH.

BARCLIFT, WILLIAM.   Perquimans Precinct.
   July 25, 1733. December 19, 1733. *Son:* WILLIAM. *Wife:* SARAH.
Executors: SARAH BARCLIFT (wife) and JOSHUA WHITE. *Witnesses:*
JOHN ARNELL, NEHEMIAH WHITE. *Clerk of the Court:* ISAAC PALMER.

BARCLIFT, WILLIAM.   Perquimans County.
   March 22, 1747-1748. January Court, 1748. *Sons:* JOSHUA ("use
and occupation of my mannor plantation for two years"), SAMUEL, JOSEPH,
THOMAS, JOHN. *Daughter:* MARY GIBSON. *Grandson:* WILLIAM BAR-
CLIFT (son of Joshua). *Executors:* JOHN BARCLIFT (cousin), EDMUND
HATCH. *Witnesses:* JOHN NICKOLS, JOHN BARCLIFT, EDMUND HATCH.
Clerk of the Court: EDMUND HATCH. Courthouse at Phelps Point.

BARCOCK, WILLIAM.   Pasquotank Precinct.
   March 5, 1730. July 10, 1731. *Sons:* THOMAS (100 acres land upper
end of my Island"), WILLIAM, DANIELL (100 acres adjoining Thomas),
PETER (100 acres adjoining Daniell), JOHN (100 acres "on bee tree neck"),
JOSEPH ("plantation I now live on," containing 140 acres), LUKE.
Daughters: JANE and ANN. *Wife and Executrix:* JANE. *Witnesses:* JAMES
FORBUS, REBECCA FORBUS, JOHN BELL. *Clerk of the Court:* WILLIAM
WYOTT.

BARECOCK, THOMAS.   Pasquotank County.
   January 1, 1721. January 17, 1721-1722. *Sons:* WILLIAM and THOM-
AS BARECOCK. *Daughters:* ELIZABETH UPTON, SARAH SANDERLIN, PRIS-
CILLA GREGORY, MARGARET GREGORY, REBEKAH FORBUS and MARTHA
FORBUS. *Granddaughter:* MARGARET DAVIS. *Grandson:* CALEB GREG-
ORY. *Executors:* WILLIAM BARECOCK and MARGARET GREGORY. *Wit-
nesses:* BALEY FORBUS, JOHN BELL, GEORGE LUMLEY. *Clerk of the
Court:* EDWARD GALE.

BAREFIELD, RICHARD.   Bertie County.
   November 22, 1728. February Court, 1728. *Sons:* RICHARD, ISHAM,
SOLOMON, JAMES, HENRY, WILLIAM, THOMAS. *Grandson:* RICHARD
BAREFIELD. *Wife:* MARY BAREFIELD. *Executors:* RICHARD BAREFIELD
(son) and WILLIAM MORE. *Witnesses:* WILLIAM JONES, THOMAS WHIPPLE,
ALEXANDER COTTON. Letters were issued August 8, 1729.

BAREFIELD, JOHN, on New River.   Onslow County.
   November 24, 1742. *Son:* LUKE. *Daughters:* MARY EDWARDS, SARAH
JONES, ROSE, JUDITH. *Wife and Executrix:* ELIZABETH. *Witnesses:*
JAMES BARFIELD, RICHARD JOHNSTOUN, JOHN QUARLAY. No probate.

BARFIELD, RICHARD.   Duplin County.

May 1, 1754. *Sons:* HENRY ("plantation I now live on"), JESSE, SOLOMON. *Daughters:* MARY BARFIELD, BETH BARFIELD, AN GRADY, CATTREN TATER. *Granddaughter:* BETH TATER. *Executors:* SOLOMON and JESSE BARFIELD (sons). *Witnesses:* JAMES BARFIELD, JOHN MORRIS, SOLOMON BARFIELD. *Register:* JOHN DUCKSON (or Dickson).

BARLOW, ROBERT.   Hyde County.

November 24, 1751. March. 1752. *Legatees:* FOSTER JERVIS, DINAH SMITH, MARTHA SMITH, HANNAH McNALLIN, WILLIAM SILVESTER. *Executor:* WILLIAM SILVESTER. *Witnesses:* BENJA. RUSSELL, JOEL BARTON. *Clerk of the Court:* FRAN. EGLETON. Courthouse at Woodstock town.

BARNETT, EDWARD.

November 13, 1687. *Wife:* SARAH. *Daughter:* ELENER CONET. *Witnesses:* THOMAS MONEY, THOMAS BUTLER. No probate.

BARNES, JOSEPH.   Northampton County.

April 7, 1751. August Court, 1751. *Sons:* JACOB, MYCAH, DEMSEY, JETHRO, JAMES. *Wife:* ELIZABETH. No executor named. *Witnesses:* JOSEPH CARISSUR, HENRY GAY, CHARLES SKINNER, JULION WHITLEY. *Clerk of the Court:* I. EDWARDS.

BARNES, JOSEPH.   Onslow County.

July 4, 1755. *Son:* HEZEKIAH (land and plantation). *Wife:* ANN. *Executors:* ANN BARNS (wife) and JONATHAN METTON. *Witnesses:* JOHN CHAPMAN, MARGRET MORTON. *Clerk of the Court:* WILL. CRAY.

BARNSFELD, ANNE.   Pasquotank County.

April 23, 1721. July 8, 1721. *Daughters:* ANN COWLES, ELIZABETH ROYAL. *Granddaughter:* ELIZABETH ROYAL. *Executor:* CORNILUS ROYAL. *Witnesses:* ROBERT PALMER and EVAN JONES. Will proven before JOHN PALIN, J. P.

BAROS, MOSES.

March 14, 1733. *Devisee:* MARY LESON. *Executor:* ROBERT PEYTON. *Witnesses:* WILLIAM LANE, TOBE LANE, ROBERT PEYTON, HENRY CRAFTON and EDWARD HADLEY, Justices of Bath Court. JOHN COLLISON, Clerk of Bath Court.

BARROW, EDMUND.   Northampton County.

March 22, 1758. July Court, 1758. *Sons:* BENJAMIN, JOHN, JAMES. *Daughters:* ELIZABETH BARROW, MARY BARROW. *Wife:* MARY. *Execu-

tors: MARY BARROW (wife), Major NICHOLAS MASSENBURG. *Witnesses:*
JOHN TURNER, JAMES CARY, JR. *Clerk of the Court:* I. EDWARDS.

BARROW, JAMES.   Chowan County.

June 17, 1718. *Sister:* JOHANAH. *Brother:* JOSEPH. *Wife:* SARAH.
Daughter: SARAH BARROW. *Cousin:* SARAH BARROW. *Executrix:* SARAH BARROW (wife). *Witnesses:* FRANCIS SMITH, THOMAS PEIRCE, JOHN ANDERSO. Will proven in Perquimans County. *Clerk of the Court:* RICHARD LEARY.

BARROW, JOHN, SR.   Perquimans County.

March 1, 1718. August, 1718. *Sons:* JOHN and JOSEPH ("my manner plantation"), JAMES (300 acres land). *Friend:* JOHN MIDDLETON. *Executors:* JAMES and JOSEPH BARROW. *Witness:* FRANCIS SMITH. Will proven before CHARLES EDEN, Governor and Ordinary.

BARROW, JOHN.   Perquimans Precinct.

June 11, 1718. August 12, 1719. *Son:* JOHN ("all my lands"). *Daughters:* SARAH, REBECCA, ELISABETH, MARGARET. *Wife:* RACHELL. *Executors:* JOSEPH BARROW (brother) and RACHELL BARROW (wife). *Witnesses:* FRANCES SMITH, JAMES BARROW, JOHN WILLIAMS, JOHN LENDION. *Clerk of the Court:* RICHARD LEARY.

BARROW, JOHN.   Perquimans County.

February 17, 1742. March 5, 1742. *Sisters:* SARAH ASHLEY, MARGARET BARROW. *Cousins:* JOHN ASHLEY, JOSEPH ASHLEY. *Executors:* ZACHARIAH NIXON, FRANCIS ETOMS (_). *Witnesses:* JAMES SKINNER and JOSEPH BARROW, JR. (Quakers), WILLIAM JONES. Proven before W. SMITH.

BARROW, JOHN.   Hyde County.

August 23, 1748. September Court, 1748. *Brothers:* ZACHARIAH BARROW ("my house and plantation"), MOSES, THOMAS, GEORGE, FREDERICK. *Sisters:* ANN DOWNING, REBACA BARROW. *Executor:* JOHN BARROW (uncle). *Witnesses:* NATHANIEL EBORNE, JOHN HARVEY, THOMAS SIMONS. *Clerk of the Court:* THOMAS LOACK.

BARROW, JOSEPH.   Perquimans County.

March 17, 1754. January Court, 1755. *Sons:* JOHN ("lower part of my manner plantation"), WILLIAM (300 acres land). *Daughters:* ELIZABETH BUNDAY, ANN and ORPAH BARROW. *Grandson:* WILLIAM BARROW. *Wife:* SARRAH. *Witnesses:* THOMAS PEIRCE, JOHN SWAIN, JOSHUA LANG. *Executors:* JOSIAH BUNDAY, JOHN BARROW, WILLIAM BARROW (sons), ANN BARROW and ORPAH BARROW (daughters). *Clerk of the Court:* RICHARD CLAYTON.

BARROW, JOSEPH.   Beaufort County.

June 19, 1752. *Sons:* JEAMS (plantation bought of John Vernon), JOHN (plantation bought of Thomas Little), JOSEPH and daughter MARY ("place where Davis lives"). *Executors:* Brother JOHN BARROW and wife JEAN BARROW. *Witnesses:* JOHN BERGERON, ROBERT FLAKE, WILLIAM MITCHELL. *Clerk of the Court:* WILL ORMOND.

BARROW, JOSEPH, JR.   Perquimans County.

February 14, 1753. April Court, 1753. *Wife:* SARAH BARROW. *Son:* WILLIAM BARROW. *Executrix:* SARAH BARROW. *Witnesses:* JOSEPH WHITE, MARY SHERWOOD. *Clerk of the Court:* EDMUND HATCH.

BARROW, REBEKAH.   Perquimans Precinct.

January 13, 1721. October 23, 1722. *Sister, Executrix and sole devisee and legatee:* SARAH BARROW. *Witnesses:* WILLIAM DAVIS, JACOB BUTLER and CHRISTOPHER BUTLER. Will proven before C. GALE, Chief Justice.

BARROW, WILLIAM.   Hyde County.

January 8, 1715. October 23, 1716. *Sons:* WILLIAM, JOHN, RICHARD (manor plantation, 1400 acres), SAMUEL, JOSEPH, JAMES (1000 acres land on Broad Creek). *Daughters:* ANN and SARAH BARROW. *Wife:* ELIZA. *Executors:* ELIZA (wife) and WILLIAM (son). *Witnesses:* THOS. BONNER, THOS. MARTIN, JOHN COSTER. Will proven before C. GALE, Chief Justice.

BARROW, WILLIAM.   Hyde County.

April 25, 1746. *Sons:* JOHN, THOMAS ("my manner plantation"), GEORGE, MOSES, ZACHARIAH and HEDRICK (to the two latter sons "land lying on Jacks Creek"). *Daughters:* REBEKAH BARROW and ANNE DOWNING (wife of WILLIAM DOWNING). *Executors:* JOHN BARROW (brother), JAMES COLES (son-in-law), JOHN SMITH. *Witnesses:* NATHANIEL EBORNE, HENRY EBORNE, REBEKAH EBORNE, MARTHA EBORNE, JOHN BARROW. *Clerk of the Court:* THOMAS LOACK.

BARROW, WILLIAM.   Edgecombe County.

October 20, 1758. December Court, 1758. *Son:* WILLIAM BARROW (plantation lying on Kehukey Swamp). *Daughter:* ANNA FORT. *Granddaughter:* ELIZABETH FORT. *Executor:* WILLIAM BARROW. *Witnesses:* JAMES BARNES, DREW SMITH, WILLIAM BARNES. *Clerk of the Court:* JOS. MONTFORT.

BARRY, WILLIAM.   Bath County.

December 14, 1721. *Brothers:* DAVID BARRY, MARION BARRY. *Executor:* THOMAS MORRIS. *Witnesses:* RICHARD HARVEY, ANN GREEN. *Clerk of the Court:* RT. FORSTER.

BARTLETT, WILLIAM.   Albemarle County.

March 14, 1694-1695. July Court, 1698. *Eldest son:* WILLIAM (plantation adjoining William Arnold). *Son:* THOMAS (land from branch adjoining home plantation to Thomas Godfrey's line). *Executors:* ELIZABETH and WILLIAM BARTLETT. *Witnesses:* THOS: TWEDY, JOHN NORTHCOAT, GILBERT GOODALL. *Clerk of the Court:* WILLIAM GLOVER.

BARTON, VALLENTIN.   Albemarle County.

March 6, 1685. March 24, 1686. *Wife:* HANNAH. *Brothers-in-law:* WILLIAM FYAM, JOSEPH WILLIAMS. *Friends:* HANNA FORD, LEDY HARRISON. *Executors:* HANNA BARTON (wife) and GEORGE FORDISE (brother-in-law). *Witnesses:* ANN SYMONS, RICHARD FOUNTAIN, WILLIAM WILKJON. Will proven before WILLIAM WILKJON.

BARTRAM, ELIZABETH, relict of WM. BARTRAM. Bladen Co.

December 27, 1771. August Court, 1772. *Daughters:* SARAH BROWN (husband, Thomas Brown), MARY ROBESON (husband, Thomas Robeson). *Executors:* THOMAS BROWN (son-in-law) and SARAH BROWN (his wife). *Witnesses:* JNO. JONES, HENRIETTA JONES, MARY SYON (LYON). *Clerk of the Court:* MATURIN COLVELL. Will also proven before the Governor and Council, February 2, 1773, as attested by J. BIGGLESTON. Executor qualified before Jo. MARTIN, at New Bern, February 3, 1773. Sealed with signet ring.

BASS, EDWARD.   Northampton County.

July 25, 1748. August Court, 1750. *Sons:* BENJAMIN (plantation on Quarter Swamp), JOSEPH (50 acres of land and orchard), SAMPSON (50 acres land on Quarter Swamp), EDWARD (50 acres of land), JAMES (50 acres land), REUBEN ("my mannor plantation"). *Grandson:* ELIJAH BASS. *Daughters:* KATHERINE ANDERSON, DINAH BASS, KIZIAH BASS, MARY BASS. *Wife:* LOVEWELL BASS. *Executor:* BENJAMIN BASS (son). *Witnesses:* WILLIAM BASS, DINAH BASS, JOHN SUTTON. *Clerk of the Court:* I. EDWARDS.

BASS, JOHN.   Bertie Precinct.

January 18, 1732. February Court, 1732. *Sons:* MOSES (all land on north side of "Baire Swamp"), JOHN, EDWARD ("my maner plantation"), WILLIAM ("my land at ye Beaver dam"), ARON ("plantation on south side of Baire Swamp"). *Grandson:* ARON JOHNSTUN (100 acres of land). *Daughters:* JEUDATH CANADY (100 acres of land), SARAH ANDERSON (100 acres of land), LOVEY BASS (100 acres land), MARY (100 acres land), PACEunce Bass ("plantation on south side of Baire Swamp"). *Wife:* MARY. *Executors:* JOHN and EDWARD BASS (sons). *Witnesses:* THOMAS BRYANT, JAMES GUIE, EDWARD BASS. *Clerk of Court:* RT. FORSTER.

BASTABLE, WILLIAM. Perquimans Precinct.

March 9, 1727-1728. *Wife:* HANNAH. *Daughter:* HANNAH BASTABLE. *Other legatees:* MARY and ANN SCETTISON (daughters of JAMES SCETTISON), RACKES WHITE. *Executors:* SAMUEL PHELPS and ROBERT WILLSON. *Witnesses:* JONATHAN SHEARWOOD, JOHN HARRES, BENJAMIN SANDERS. *Clerk of the Court:* CHARLES DENMAN.

BATCHELOR, EDWARD.

September 21, 1706. *Wife:* (Mentioned, but not named). *Friend:* ROBERT FEWOX. *Executor:* JOHN FEWOX. *Witnesses:* SAMUEL BREUITT, JOHN GATE. No probate.

BATCHELOR, EDWARD. Newbern, Craven County.

1777. *Sons:* JOHN BATCHELOR (tract of land on Susquehanna, in "Pensilvania"), EDWARD BATCHELOR. *Daughters:* FRANCIS BATCHELOR and ELIZABETH BATCHELOR. *Wife:* FRANCIS BATCHELOR. *Friend and partner in business:* THOMAS ASHETON. *Executors:* THOMAS ASHETON, of Philadelphia; DR. THOMAS HASTINE, Newbern; FRANCIS BATCHELOR (wife). This will was not signed, which fact is explained by affidavits of RICHARD COGDELL (taken by JOSEPH LEECH, J. P.), MICH'L. GORMAN (taken by JOSEPH LEECH), THOMAS FLYNN (taken by JOSEPH LEECH, J. P.). Executors qualify before RICHARD CASWELL, Governor.

BATE, HENRY LAWRENCE. County not given.

May 12, 1740. July 9, 1740. *Son:* AUGUSTINE BATE (land bought of Jonathan Taylor). *Wife and Executrix:* MARTHA. *Sister:* ANN BATE (one gold ring). *Mother:* SARAH SANDERS. *Executors:* HUMPHREY BATE (brother), THOMAS WHITMELL (brother-in-law). *Witnesses:* WILL CATHCART, HENRY HUNTER, SARAH HUNTER. Proven before GAB. JOHNSTON. Coat of arms, a shield bearing a lion rampant on seal.

BATEMAN, JOHN. Perquimans County.

February 4, 1747-1748. July Court, 1750. *Nephew:* THOMAS BATEMAN ("plantation whereon I now live," also plantation called "Broad Neck"). *Brother:* THOMAS BATEMAN (father of nephew THOMAS), MARY HAWKINS (daughter of nephew JOHN HAWKINS), ELIZABETH PHELPS (daughter of brother JONATHAN BATEMAN), MARY PHELPS (daughter of brother THOMAS), WILLIAM BATEMAN (son of brother THOMAS), SARAH BUTTERRE (daughter of brother JONATHAN). *Executors:* THOMAS BATEMAN (brother), WILLIAM BATEMAN (nephew). *Witnesses:* SAMUEL

SWANN, FRANCIS LAYDEN, CATHERINE DAVIS.
BENJ. SCARBOROUGH, for EDMUND HATCH, Clerk

BATEMAN, JONATHAN.

January, 1694-1695. February 25, 1695. W
MARGARET. *Sons:* JONATHAN, JOHN, THOMAS
ecutor: JONATHAN (son). *Witnesses:* THOMAS
DIANA WHITE. *Clerk of the Court:* W. GLOVE

BATEMAN, WILLIAM.

March 30, 1703. April 25, 1704. *Daughters*
BELL (300 acres of land "back in the woods").
("dwelling plantation"), WILLIAM, SAMUELL.
named). *Witnesses:* ROBERT SMITH, DANNIEL
DREW MAKEFASHION. *Clerk of the Court:* EDV

BATTERS, THOMAS.

November 29, 1733. June 11, 1734. *Daug*
BATTERS ("my manor plantation"). *Wife a*
Witnesses: ELIZABETH COUPPER, PHILO. WILL
Will proven at Bath town. *Justices:* ROBT. I
ROGER KENYON, EDWD. HADLEY. *Clerk of the*

BATTLE, JOHN.

April 22, 1740. May Court, 1740. *Sons:* WII
PRISSILLA BATTLE, SARAH BATTLE. *Wife:* SA
BATTLE (wife), WILLIAM BATTLE (brother). *Wit*
JAMES GRIFFEN, MARTHA KNIGHT. *Clerk of the*

BAYER, DAVID.

August 8, 1696. October, 1696. *Clerk of t.*
Witnesses: THOS. LUTEN, CASTEN ROBISON. T

BAYES, EDWARD.

August 8, 1696. October Court, 1696. *Son:*
ELIZ., MARY and ANN BAYES. *Executrix:* M
THOS. LUTON and COTTON ROBISON. *Clerk of th*

BEASLEY, FRANCES.

April 17, 1719. May 20, 1719. *Son:* JEAME
south side of Perquimans River), ROBERT (a t1
side of Morattock River). *Wife:* MARY BEA

ABSTRACT OF WILLS, 1690—1760.   25

BEASLEY (brother) and friend JOHN SMITHWICK. *Witnesses:* JOHN LESSHONS, WILLIAM MIZELL, JOHN BENTLEY. Proven before CHAS. EDEN, Governor and Ordinary.

BEASLEY, JAMES.   Bertie County.

January 2, 1758. January Court, 1758. WILLIAM BENTLEY (son of JOHN BENTLEY). *Godson:* LUKE SMETHWICK. *Executors:* JOHN SMETHWICK, JNO. WARD. *Witnesses:* JON. SMETHWICK, EDMUND SMETHWICK. *Clerk of the Court:* BENJ'N WYNNS.

BEASLEY, SAMUEL.   County not given.

November 13, 1735. *Brothers:* FRANCIS and THOMAS. *Other legatees:* JOHN BEASLEY, MARY BEASLEY (grandmother), THOMAS HUTSSOON, JAMES BEASLEY, JUNR. No executor. *Witnesses:* WILLIAM CROPLY, THOMAS BENTLEY, ELIZABETH WELLS. No probate.

BECTON, JOHN.   Craven County.

January 13, 1753. May Court, 1753. *Sons:* FREDERICK, GEORGE (340 acres land at "ye little creek"), EDMOND (land "known by ye name of Jacobbs Wells"), MICHAEL (lands "called the Snow Hills"). *Daughters:* MARY and SARAH. *Wife:* ANN. *Executors:* FREDRICK ESLER, FREDRICK BECTON (son). *Witnesses:* WALTER JONES, THOMAS BRANTON, CLEMENT DYSON. *Clerk of the Court:* SOL. REW.

BEELS, JACOB.   Pasquotank County.

May 15, 1746. July Court, 1746. *Daughters:* TABITHA and MARY (manor plantation), BARBRAY, ELIZABETH. *Brother:* JOHN BEELS. *Executor:* JOHN BEELS (brother). *Witnesses:* CHARLES WRIGHT, WILLIAM ANDREWS, MARY WRIGHT. *Clerk of the Court:* THOS. TAYLOR.

BEELS, JAMES.   Pasquotank County.

November 3, 1721. April 17, 1722. *Wife and Executrix:* ANN. *Son:* JOHN BEEL (plantation). *Witnesses:* JOHN PERKENS, HENRY CREECH, GEORGE LUMLEY. *Clerk of the Court:* EDW'D GALE.

BEEZLEY, THOMAS.   No county given.

April 15, 1733. July 3, 1733. *Sons:* JOHN and THOMAS. *Wife:* ELIZA. *Friend:* THOMAS OWIN. *Executors:* ELIZABETH BEEZLEY (wife), JOHN BEEZLEY (son). *Witnesses:* JNO. FREDERICK, JOHN KING. *Clerk of the Court:* WM. CRAWFORD (or CRANFORD).

BEFRET, BENJAMIN, Mulberry Neck, New Hanover County.

October 25, 1749. August 24, 1753. August 30, 1753. *Son:* BENJAMIN (plantation and lands). *Executors:* HENNERY CASTER and THOMAS

KENNAN. *Witnesses:* WILLIAM SAVAGE, HOUGH MCCANNE, JOHN DICKSON, Register of Duplin County; JOSEPH WILLIAMS, Justice of the Peace; JA. MURRAY, Sec. *Remarks:* This will mentions wife and four children, but does not name the wife, and names only one of the children.

BELL, CORNELIUS.   Beaufort and Hyde Precincts.

August 26, 1729. December Court, 1729. *Sons:* CORNELIUS ("third part of my land"), GEORGE ("one third part of my land"). *Daughter:* MARY. *Grandson:* JAMES NEVEL. *Friend:* JOHN LATHY BELL. *Executor:* CORNELIUS BELL (son). *Witnesses:* EDWD. HADLEY, THOMAS TULLE. *Clerk of the Court:* JOHN MATTOCKE.

BELL, ELIZABETH.   Tyrrell County.

June 16, 1750. November 30, 1750. "Sister Margarett's daughter in London" (wedding ring and necklace). CAPT. WILLIAM MACKEY, deceased husband's nephew (all residue of estate). *Executors:* CULLEN POLLOCK and WM. MACKEY. *Witnesses:* THOS. LEE, JOHN GORMAN, BEDFORD FAGON   Proven before GAB. JOHNSTON, at Eden House.

BELL, GEORGE.   Edgecombe County.

December 21, 1751. February Court, 1752. *Sons:* ARTHUR, GEORGE, WILLIAM. *Daughter:* ELIZABETH FLOYD. *Granddaughter:* MARY BELL. *Executors:* FRANCIS FLOYD and ARTHUR BELL. *Witnesses:* WILLIAM PARTIS, THOS. BELL, THOS. FLOYD. *Clerk of the Court:* BENJAMIN WYNNS.

BELL, GEORGE.   Edgecombe County.

February 18, 1755. May, 1755. *Sons:* JOHN ("plantation whereon I now live"), DAVID, GEORGE. *Wife:* SARAH BELL. *Executors:* SARAH BELL (wife) and JOHN BELL (son). *Witnesses:* ARTHUR BELL, GEORGE BELL, RAFE CHANNEL. *Clerk of Court:* JOS. MONTFORT.

BELL, JOHN.   Pasquotank County.

March 1, 1720. March 29, 1721. *Sons:* JAMES ("all my land att Alegator"), JOHN, WILLIAM, GEORGE, NATHANIEL (to these four "all my land on the north side of Pasquotank River"), HENRY, JOSEPH, BENJAMIN. *Daughter:* MARY BELL. *Wife and Executrix:* MARY. *Witnesses:* WILLIAM WILLSON, SAMUEL COCK, DARBEY SIVILENANT. Will proven before R. HICKS, Clerk, at Court held at Queen Anne's Creek, in Chowan Precinct.

BELL, JOSEPH.   Carteret County.

March 12, 1744. June Court, 1745. *Wife:* MARGRIT. *Son:* THOMAS ("my plantation"). *Friend:* JOHN NELSON. *Executors:* JOHN NELSON and THOMAS BELL. *Witnesses:* THOMAS HARRISS, RACHEL BOOTH, MARTHA BOOTH. *Clerk of the Court:* GEO. READ.

ABSTRACT OF WILLS, 1690—1760.   27

BELL, ROSS.   Carteret County.

January 24, 1726. *Sons:* GEORGE, ROSS, JOSEPH. *Daughter:* MARY BELL. *Executor:* JOSEPH BELL. *Witnesses:* GEO. WHITAKER, JAMES HINES, MARGRETT BELL. *Clerk of the Court:* JOHN GALLAND.

BELL, THOMAS.   Chowan County.

December 11, 1733. January Court, 1733. *Cousins:* WILLIAM BELL (land in Perquimans called "Matthew's Point"), THOMAS BELL (land on Kendricks Creek), ANNE and JANE BELL (daughters of brother JOHN BELL), WILLIAM MACKAY. *Wife and Executrix:* ELIZABETH. "It is my will that no sale be made of any slaves, but that my estate be kept intire except my Sloop————". *Witnesses:* SAML DURRANCE, W. DOWNING, HANAH GIRKIN. *Clerk of the Court:* MOSELEY VAIL.

BELL, THOMAS.   Chowan County.

August 28, 1751. October Court, 1751. *Cousins:* (the surviving children of ROBT. MCCLEE and JAMES OAR. *Friend:* CAPT. WILLIAM MACKEY. *Executors:* ALEXANDER STEWART (brother-in-law), JAMES WADDAL. *Witnesses:* JAMES TROTTER, JEMIMA ALLEN, JAMES CAMPBELL. *Clerk of the Court:* JAS. CRAVEN.

BELL, WILLIAM.   Currituck County.

August 27, 1721. August 31, 1721. *Son:* WILLIAM. Wife and children mentioned, but not named. *Witnesses:* THOMASIN ONEAL, MARY ONEAL, DEBORAH PELL, SARAH WALKER. Proven before THOS. TAYLOR, JOHN WOODHOUSE. This is a nuncupative will proven by witnesses after testator's death.

BELL, WILLIAM.   Edgecombe County.

December 1, 1752. May and August Courts, 1754. *Sons:* ARTHUR BELL (390 acres land in the River Island), JOSHUA BELL (plantation where he now lives). *Daughters:* MARY PYRENT, ANNE BELL. *Executors:* ARTHUR and JOSHUA BELL. *Witnesses:* JAMES ATKISON, WILLIAM CAIN, REBECAH CAIN. *Clerk of Court:* BEN'J. WYNNS.

BELLMAN, JOHN.   Perquimans County.

July 10, 1740. October, 1740. *Wife:* MARY. *Daughter:* SARAH BELLMAN. *Executors:* MARY BELLMAN (wife), ROBERT WILLSON, JAMES SITTERSUN, ZACK ELSON. *Clerk of the Court:* JAMES CRAVEN.

BELMAN, JOHN.   Pasquotank Precinct.

November 5, 1706. January Court, 1706-1707. *Sons:* JOHN and ROBERT. *Wife and Executrix:* SARAH. *Witnesses:* THO. BOYD, BENJ'N WEST. *Clerk of the Court:* THO. ABINGTON.

BENBOW, GERSHON.   Bladen County.

January 12, 1750. *Sons:* POWEL, RICHARD and EVANS. *Daughter:* SUSANNAH. *Executors:* POWELL BENBOW (son) and CHARLES BENBOW (brother). *Witnesses:* ABRAM SANDERS, RICHARD MAY, JOHN JONES. No probate.

BENBURY, WILLIAM.   Chowan County.

April, 1755. *Wife:* BRIGETT. *Sons:* WILLIAM, JOHN, JOSEPH, JAMES, MILES, EDMOND. *Brother:* JOHN BENBURY. *Daughter:* SARAH. *Executors:* JOHN BENBURY, WM. BENBURY and wife of testator. *Witnesses:* JOHN BEASLEY, SAMUEL BENBURY, J. BENBURY. *Clerk of the Court:* WILL HALSEY.

BENDER, MARTIN.   Craven County.

October 19, 1750. December Court, 1750. *Sons:* DANIEL (plantation), JOHN (150 acres land in Carteret County on the north side of White Oak River). *Daughters:* SALOME and MARY BENDER (250 acres land on north side of White Oak River). *Executors:* JOHN SIMMONS and JOHN GRANADE. *Witnesses:* BENJAMIN SIMMONS and ELIZABETH MORREY. *Clerk of the Court:* PHIL. SMITH.

BENNET, JOHN.   Currituck Precinct.

December 10, 1710. *Sons:* JOSEPH ("my plantation"), BENJAMIN (land bought of JOSEPH NICKER). *Wife and Executrix:* MARY. *Brother:* JOSEPH BENNET. Portion of lands devised to use of poor "old men and women who have been honest, etc.," and portion left for education of poor children. *Witnesses:* GEORGE and ANN THOMPSON, EDWARD COB and EDWARD STAFFORD. Recorded in Book 1712-1722, page 49. Original missing.

BENNET, JOSEPH.   Currituck Precinct.

March 9, 1751-1752. April 9, 1723. *Sons:* JOSEPH ("plantation now dwell on") WILLIAM, SAMUEL (84 acres land), JOHN. *Daughters:* MARY SAYRS, ALICE BENNET. *Wife:* ANNE. *Executors:* ANNE BENNET (wife) and JOSEPH BENNET (son). *Witnesses:* JOHN WILSON, EDWARD COX. *Clerk of the Court:* JAMES WICKER.

BENNET, NEHEMIAH.   Currituck County.

March 11, 1753. April Court, 1753. *Sons:* JOHN ("plantation I now dwell on"), JOSIAH ("lands on west side of the road"). *Daughter:* SUSAN BENNET. *Wife and Executrix:* ELIZABETH. *Witnesses:* JAMES BURNHAM, GEORGE DAVIS, SOLOMON BENNET. *Clerk of the Court:* WILLIAM SHERGOLD.

BENNET, SOLOMON. Currituck County.

March 23, 1753. March Court, 1755. *Sons:* MOSES (plantation), BENJAMIN (150 acres of land on Mozark Creek). *Daughters:* REBECKER BENNET, MARY BENNET, BETSSE BENNET. *Wife and Executrix:* DARKES BENNET. *Witnesses:* PHILIP NORTHERN, MARY ETHERIGS, TIMOTHY ETHRIGS. *Clerk of the Court:* WILLIAM SHERGOLD.

BENTLEY, JOHN, OF MORATOCK RIVER.

December 15, 1728. July 15, 1741. *Sons:* WILLIAM ("plantation he now lives on"), JOHN and JOSEPH ("my manner plantation to be equally divided between them"), JEREMIAH ("plantation at Tuttsnia"), JAMES, ("plantation at fork of Rockner's"). *Daughters:* MARY BENTLEY, LIDIA. *Grandson:* JOHN BENTLEY. *Granddaughter:* HANAH BENTLEY. *Wife:* SARAH. *Executors:* SARAH BENTLEY (wife), WILLIAM BENTLEY (son). *Witnesses:* WILL LATTIMER, MOSES GROOME, ELIZABETH LATTIMER. Will proven before GAB. JOHNSTON, at Eden House.

BENTLEY, JOHN. Perquimans Precinct.

October 15, 1695. November, 1695. *Brother:* RICHARD BENTLEY. *Cousin:* ELIZABETH LEARY. *Wife:* ANN. JOHN and ROGER WILLIAMS (sons of brother-in-law, JENKINS WILLIAMS). *Brother-in-law:* WILLIAM BARROW. *Friend:* JONATHAN ASHFORD. *Executors:* ANN BENTLEY (wife) and WILLIAM BARROW (brother-in-law). *Witnesses:* JOHN BARROW, ELIZABETH GARDINER, GEORGE BARROW. *Clerk of Court:* W. GLOVER.

BENTLEY, JOHN. Bertie County.

March 12, 1754. May Court, 1754. *Sons:* WILLIAM ("plantation whereon I now live"), JOHN (lands known as "Island lands"). *Sister-in-law:* ANN BENTLEY. *Executor:* RICHARD TOMLINSON. *Witnesses:* JOHN HYMAN, JOHN WARD, REBEKAH WARD. *Clerk of the Court:* SAMUEL ORMES.

BENTLEY, JOHN. Albemarle County.

October 15, 1695. November Court, 1695. *Brother:* RICHARD BENTLEY. *Cousin:* ELIZABETH LERRY. JOHN WILLIAMS and ROGER WILLIAMS, WILLIAM BARROW. *Executor:* WILLIAM BARROW. *Witnesses:* JOHN BARROW, ELIZABETH GARDNER, GEORGE BARROW. *Clerk of the Court:* W. GLOVER.

BENTLEY, JOHN. Tyrrell County.

March 25, 1754. June Court, 1754. *Wife:* SARAH. *Son:* ISAAC. *Brothers:* WILLIAM BENTLEY and JAMES BENTLEY. *Executors:* WILLIAM GARDNER, JAMES and ISAAC GARDNER. *Witnesses:* LUKE MIZELL, MARY GARDNER, SARAH MIZELL. *Clerk of the Court:* EVAN JONES.

BENTLEY, RICHARD.   County not given.

April 6, 1697. May 27, 1697. *Executrix and sole legatee:* DIANA WHITE. *Witnesses:* JAMES BASET (?), ALEXANDER LILLINGTON. *Clerk of the General Court:* W. GLOVER. Coat of arms on seal.

BENTON, JOHN.   Chowan County.

February 28, 1748–1749. October Court, 1750. *Sons:* EPOPHRODITUS, ELIJAH, JETHRO ("manner plantation"), JOHN, MOSES. *Daughter:* JUDITH RABEY, MARY PARKER, CHARITY PARKER. *Grandsons:* WILLIAM PARKER (son of MARY), JAMES PARKER (son of CHARITY). *Executors:* JOHN and JETHRO BENTON (sons). *Witnesses:* HENRY MORGIN, JOHN WEAVER, WILLIAM PARKER. *Clerk of the Court:* JAMES CRAVEN.

BERGERON, JUDITH.   Beaufort County.

November 14, 1742. December Court, 1742. *Sons:* ELIAS, JOHN. *Daughters:* JUDETH WILKINS, JEAN BARROW, MARGRET GIDDINS. *Executor:* ELIAS BERGERON (son). *Witnesses:* MIKEL WARD, JACOB MERCER, THOMAS MERCER. *Clerk of the Court:* JOHN FORBES.

BERRY, CORNEALUS.   Currituck County.

April 17, 1751. April 7, 1752. *Wife:* COMFORT. *Other legatees:* LITTLETON BERRY, CORNEALUS BERRY and JOHN BERRY (presumably sons). *Executrix:* COMFORT BERRY (wife). *Witnesses:* WILL WHITE, THOMAS MILLER. *Clerk of the Court:* WILLIAM SHERGOLD.

BEVANS, RICHARD.   Hyde County.

1744. *Wife:* MARY. All the land of the testator is bequeathed "to the Baptism ministers that Coms heare to the County of hide to preach the gospel." *Executor:* ROBERT SPRING. *Witnesses:* TIMOTHY ALLEN, PASHE BARTLETT, NAITHANE DAVIS. Will proven before ENOCH HALL, C. J.

BEVERLEY, JOHN, SR.   Bertie County.

December 22, 1737. February Court, 1737. *Sons:* JOHN and ROBERT (to whom is bequeathed "the manner plantation"). *Daughters:* SARAH COX, MARY PEEK. *Granddaughters:* RACHEL BEVERLEY, SARAH BEVERLEY. *Grandsons:* WILLIAM COX, WILLIAM and HENRY BEVERLEY. *Wife:* MARGARETT BEVERLY. *Executors:* JOHN JONES and JOSEPH JONES. *Witnesses:* JAMES DOUGLASS, ELIZA DOUGLASS and JOHN SUTTON. *Clerk of the Court:* JOHN WYNNS.

BEVINS, MARY.   Hyde County.

July 27, 1753. December Court, 1754. *Sons:* JOHN and ROBERT. *Daughters:* ELIZABETH, MARY, ANN. *Granddaughters:* MARY ARTRY, ANN

DICKS. *Friend:* JAMES CHAPMAN. *Executors:* ROBERT and JOHN BEVINS (sons). *Witnesses:* ABRAHAM COX, THOMAS MACKWILLIAMS, SARAH MATHERS. *Clerk of the Court:* STEPN. DENNING.

BEXLEY, WILLIAM.
March 13, 1745. *Daughter:* REBECKAH BEXLEY. *Witnesses:* WM. LANE, NICHS. ROUTLEDGE, PHILIP KESSLER, KATHN. COLESTON, CHARLES STEWART, PETER HENDRIKSON, ELIZTH. HENDRICKSON. Will proven before WM. LANE. This is a nuncupative will.

BIDDLE, JACOB. Onslow County.
February 24, 1755-1756. April Court, 1758. *Sons:* JACOB ("a pease of land lying on the North side of the Branch that runs by plantation and binding on John Simson's Branch"), ISAAC. *Wife:* ANNE. *Grandsons:* WILLIAM BIDDLE (son of ISAAC), ISAAC BIDDLE (son of ISAAC). *Other legatees:* ABRAM SIMSON, ANTHONY and JACOB CHARLESCRAFT. *Executors:* ANNE BIDDLE (wife) and ISAAC BIDDLE (son). *Witnesses:* SAMUEL PEIRSON, WILLIAM GIBSON, JAMES ATKINS. *Clerk of the Court:* WILLIAM CRAY, Court House on New River. JNO. STARKEY and others, *Justices*.

BILLET, JOHN. Pasquotank Precinct.
February 29, 1719–1720. April 19, 1720. *Son:* DANIEL (plantation adjoining BENJAMIN PRITCHARD). *Daughter:* SARAH. *Son-in-law:* JAMES BELL. *Wife and Executrix:* ALLICE. *Witnesses:* W. NORRIS, THOS. SAWYER, JONTH. JONES, JAMES BELL. Recorded in book 1712–1722, page 223. Original missing.

BIRNIE, WILLIAM. New Hanover County.
September 28, 1752. December 14, 1752. *Wife:* ILLIN. *Executors:* ILLIN BIRNIE (wife) and MOSES JNO. DEROSSET. *Witnesses:* JOHN CAMPBELL, MARY MASON, JOHN MAULTSBY. *Clerk of the Court:* ISAAC FARIES.

BIROTE, PETER. Edenton in Chowan County.
January 15, 1742. April 21, 1743. *Son:* BENJAMIN BIROTE ("all my estate"). *Executor:* PETER PAYNE. *Witnesses:* BENJAMIN TALBOT, HUMPHRY ROBINSON, WM. ARKILL. *Codicil:* January 22, 1742. MARY GASTON "one bed." *Witness:* BENJA. TALBOT. *Clerk of the Court:* RICHARD MCCLURE.

BISHOP, GEORGE. Onslow County.
December 20, 1743. September Court, 1743. *Brothers:* STOAKLEY (325 acres land in Onslow Co.), JAMES SIDBURY ("one Indian man"), WOODMAN STOAKLEY SIDBURY. *Sister:* BETTIE DUDLEY. *Cousins:* BISHOP DUDLEY,

ESTER DUDLEY, COMFORT SIDBURY, MOSES SIDBURY. *Mother:* ELIZABETH BISHOP. *Father and Executor:* GEORGE BISHOP. *Other legatees:* JANE MORGAN, MORGAN MORGAN, JR. *Witnesses:* RICE RICE, MORGAN MORGAN, JAMES SMALLWOOD. Will proven in New Hanover Court. JAMES SMALLWOOD, *Deputy Clerk.*

BLACK, ISAAC. New Hanover County.

June 22, 1754. August Court, 1754. *Brother:* JOHN BLACK. *Sisters:* ELIZABETH WOODS, JANE BLACK. *Executor:* JOSHUA TOOMER. *Witnesses:* WILLM. GREGORY, JAS. CAMPBELL, MARK GIBBINS. *Clerk of the Court:* ISAAC FARIES.

BLACK, MICHAEL. Craven County.

January 16, 1760. May 3, 1760. *Friend: Executor and sole legatee:* JOSEPH WILLIS. *Witnesses:* JACOB MILLER, GEORGE FISHER, JAMES WILLIS. Will proven before ARTHUR DOBBS, at Newbern.

BLACKALL, ABRAHAM. Edenton, Chowan County.

February 1, 1739–1740. February 23, 1749. January Court, 1749. *Wife:* SARAH. *Daughters:* PENELOPE and SHARLOT. *Executrix:* SARAH BLACKALL (wife). *Witnesses:* RD. FORSTER, JAMES PATTER, JAMES TROTTER. Executrix qualified before JOS. ANDERSON, Justice of the Peace. Will proven before WILL MEARNS, *Clerk of the Court.*

BLACKALL, SARAH. Edenton, Chowan County.

January 29, 1754. April Court, 1754. *Daughters:* SARAH ROWDEN, PENELOPE, CHARLOT. *Deceased husband:* DR. BLACKALL. *Executor:* DR. SAMUEL LABAN PLOMMER. *Witnesses:* FRANCIS OLIVER, ABIGAIL SLAUGHTER. *Clerk of the Court:* WILL HALSEY. Coat of arms on seal.

BLACKLEDGE, RICHARD, SENR. Craven County.

February 20, 1776. October 15, 1777. *Wife:* ANN. *Sons:* RICHARD ("manor plantation and ½ of 275 acres land on Pecoson Point"), WILLIAM, BENJAMIN ("200 acres Moseleys Creek," this to three sons above named), THOMAS ("land bought of Wm. Farmer and wife and 100 a. on Bever Dam"). *Sons-in-law:* SPYERS SINGLETON, CAP. JOHN JONES. *Daughters:* ELLENER (wife of CAPT. JOHN JONES), ANN BLACKLEDGE. *Friends:* MRS. MARY NEALE and MRS. BETSEY BAKER (ten pounds for mourning ring and gold buttons). *Father:* BENJAMIN BLACKLEDGE, SR. *Executors:* JACOB BLOUNT, CHRISTOPHER NEALE, RICHARD BLACKLEDGE, JR. (son) and SPYERS SINGLETON (son-in-law). *Witnesses:* J. BLOUNT, HENRY CANNON, READING BLOUNT. Will proven before RD. CASWELL.

BLACKMAN, JOHN.   Bertie County.

November 19, 1736. November Court, 1736. *Wife:* SARAH. *Sons:* JOHN, BENNET, ARTHUR, JOSEPH, STEAVEN. *Daughter:* ELIZABETH. *Executors:* BENNET BLACKMAN (son) and THEOPHILUS WILLIAMS. *Witnesses:* WILLIAM TAYLOR, ARTHUR MAIKDSUNACE, PHEBE JERNIGAN. *Clerk of the Court:* JNO. WYNNS.

BLACKMAN, NICHOLAS.   Bertie Precinct.

August 26, 1730. March 11, 1730. *Wife:* ALLISON. *Sons-in-law:* GEORGE SMITH and WILLIAM SMITH. *Executrix:* ALLISON BLACKMAN (wife). *Witnesses:* EDWD. COLLINS, RICHARD MOORE, JAMES BAKER. Will proven before GEO. BURRINGTON, Governor.

BLAKE, DAVID.   Currituck Precinct.

October 9, 1714. January 13, 1714–1715. *Sons:* THOMAS, DAVID. *Daughters:* SARAH, ELIZABETH, MATHEW. *Friends:* MATHIAS TOWLER, JOHN MASON. *Executors:* RALPH MATHAM, JNO. MASON. *Witnesses:* THOMAS EVANS, JOHN EVANS, RICH'D SMITH. *Clerk of the Court:* JO. WICKER.

BLANCHARD, BENJAMIN.   Upper part of Nansimond County.

June 5, 1719. *Sons:* ROBERT ("land on Beverdam Swamp in Chowan Precinct in North Carolina"), ABSALOM, BENJAMIN ("land on Beverdam"). *Son-in-law:* WILLIAM WESTON (wife CATHERINE). *Wife:* CATHERINE. *Executors:* CATHERINE (wife) and ROBERT (son). *Witnesses:* WILL. HILL, JAMES GRISING, THOMAS ROUNTREE. No probate.

BLANCHARD, EPHRAIM.   Chowan County.

July 22, 1745. April, 1749. *Son:* AARON ("plantation on west side of Beaverdam Swamp." "Land on Walroy Swamp;" "100 acres in Pasquotank known by the name of the Sound Neck;" "place in Pasquotank called Nobbs Crook"). *Son:* EPHRAIM ("100 acres in Chowan Co.;" "100 acres on Walroy Swamp;" "200 acres in Pasquotank County on Sound Neck;" "50 acres at the head of Nobbs Crook in Pasquotank"). *Son:* MICAJAH ("manor plantation on east side of Beaverdam Swamp-450 acres;" "50 acres at Nobbs Crook"). *Granddaughter:* MARY GRIFFIN. *Wife:* ISABEL BLANCHARD. *Executors:* ISABEL BLANCHARD (wife) and EPHRAIM BLANCHARD (son). *Witnesses:* THOS. ROUNTREE, SR., CHAS. ROUNTREE, THOMAS ROUNTREE. *Clerk of the Court:* WILL MEARNS.

BLANING, HUGH.   Bladen County.

May 10, 1751. March Court, 1752. *Wife:* ELIZABETH. *Wife's children:* WILLIAM and ELIZABETH HALL. *Sister:* SARAH STAR. *Executors:* ELIZA-

BETH BLANING (wife), MATTHEW ROWAN. *Witnesses:* ROBERT DOWIE, THOS. HALL and ———. *Clerk of the Court:* THOS. ROBESON. Coat of arms on seal.

BLICHENDEN, THOMAS. Perquimans County.

April 12, 1744. July Court, 1745. *Sons:* JOHN (plantation on Sound Side), WILLIAM ("plantation whereon I now live"), ABRAHAM. *Daughter:* SARAH. *Wife:* MARY. *Executors:* MARY BLICHENDEN (wife), ABRAHAM and WILLIAM BLICHENDEN (sons). *Witnesses:* MAC. SCARBOROUGH, NATH'L CARRUTHERS, ZACH. CHANCEY. *Clerk of Court:* EDMUND HATCH. Courthouse on Phelps Point. Coat of arms on seal.

BLIN, DANIEL. Bath Town, Beaufort County.

September 23, 1742. March 13, 1753. *Wife, Executrix and sole devisee:* MORNING BLIN. *Witnesses:* MARY SMITH, JOHN RIEUSSETT, PATRICK BRAHAM. *Clerk of the Court:* WILL ORMOND.

BLISH, JOHN. Pasquotank County.

November 17, 1718. *Devisees:* MARTHA FOSTER (daughter of THOMAS FOSTER), ELIZABETH FLEMEN, EDWARD JAMES, STEPHEN SALL, WILLIAM WILLSON (mairener). *Executor:* WILLIAM WILLSON. *Witnesses:* JOSEPH CAPE, MARY MILLER, JOHN BETT Senor. No probate.

BLOUNT, BENJAMIN. Tyrrell County.

February 1, 1739. June Court, 1740. *Sons:* JAMES, JACOB, EDMUND, ISAAC and BENJAMIN (to the latter is given "my manner plantation"). *Daughters:* ESTHER, MARY, SARAH. *Wife:* ELIZABETH. *Executors:* BENJAMIN (son) and ELIZABETH (wife). *Witnesses:* ANN HALLIS, ZACHARIAH GURKIN. *Justice of the Peace:* JAMES TURNBULL. *Deputy Clerk of the Court:* THOS. LEARY.

BLOUNT, EDMUND. Tyrrell County.

February 12, 1754. June Court, 1754. *Son:* EDMUND ("manner plantation") *Wife:* ELIZABETH. *Executors:* ELIZABETH BLOUNT (wife), BENJAMIN BLOUNT. *Witnesses:* BENJAMIN BLOUNT, JACOB BLOUNT. *Clerk of Court:* EVAN JONES. Other children are mentioned, but not named.

BLOUNT, ELIZABETH. Chowan County.

February 8, 1732. March 12, 1732. *Sons:* JOHN, THOMAS, JAMES, JOSEPH, CHARLES (to the two latter is bequeathed land at Bare Swamp and Haughton land). *Daughters:* ANNE WARLEY, RACHELE. *Executors:* JOHN LOVICK, SAMLL. PAGETT and JONATHAN JACOCKS. *Witnesses:* R.

ABSTRACT OF WILLS, 1690—1760. 35

HICKS and MARY COLESON. Will proven before GEORGE BURRINGTON, at Edenton. A tract of land at Barrow's Hole is ordered sold and proceeds applied to payment of doctor.

BLOUNT, JOHN. Chowan County.

January 27, 1725–1726. May 18, 1726. *Sons:* JOHN, THOMAS (manor, fronting on Albemarle Sound, John to have eastern and Thomas western portion), JAMES and CHARLES (land on Welches Creek), JOSEPH (land at Mattehapungo, known by the name of Goshen). *Wife:* ELIZABETH (land at Bear Swamp and at Barrow Hole). *Daughters:* MARY JACOCKS, ELIZA PAGET, SARAH LOVICK, MARTHA WARSLEY and HESTER WORLEY. *Executrix:* ELIZABETH BLOUNT (wife), to be assisted by friends JOHN LOVICK and THOS. POLLOCK. *Witnesses:* SAMLL. WARNER, WM. BENBURY, MAGNES PLOWMAN. Will proven before RICHARD EVERARD, Governor, etc.

Codicil to will of JOHN BLOUNT. Dated January 27, 1725–1726. *Daughters:* ANN and RACHEL (a gold ring each). CHRISTOPHER GALE appointed assistant together with JNO. LOVICK and THOS. POLLOCK. Coat of arms on seal of both will and codicil. The testator mentions in the will having broken the entail.

BLOUNT, ————. County not given.

Dates missing. *Wife:* ELIZABETH. *Sons:* JOHN and THOMAS ("Beech Island land and land on Welches' Creek up Moratock;" JOSEPH (land at Matchapungo known by name of "Goshan"); JAMES (land at Bear Swamp). *Daughters:* MARY JACOCS, ELIZABETH PAGET and MARTHA WEST. Remainder of will missing.

BLOUNT, JAMES. Albemarle County.

March 10, 1685. July, 1686. *Sons:* THOS. BLOUNT and JOHN BLOUNT. *Son:* JAS. BLOUNT. *Daughters:* ANN SLOCUM and ELIZ. HAWKINS. *Grandchildren:* JAMES and SARAH BLOUNT and ANN SLOCUM, and JOHN HAWKINS. *Wife:* ANN BLOUNT. *Executrix:* ANN BLOUNT. *Witnesses:* JNO. HALL, JANE MILLER and WM. DOBSON. Proven before SETH SOTHELL.

BLOUNT, JAMES. Chowan County.

February 12, 1716. March 27, 1717. *Wife:* ELIZABETH. *Daughters:* ANNE BLOUNT ("my plantation with 240 acres of land"), ELIZABETH YELVERTON, MARY. *Sons:* JOHN BLOUNT, JAMES BLOUNT and JOHN YELVERTON. *Grandsons:* JAMES YELVERTON and JOHN YELVERTON. *Granddaughter:* SARA PHILLIPS. *Executrixes:* ELIZABETH BLOUNT (wife) and ANNE BLOUNT (daughter). *Witnesses:* J. TURNER, ANNE DUGLES, JOHN YELVERTON. *Clerk of Court:* R. HICKS.

BLOUNT, JOHN.   Chowan County.

December 8, 1753. April Court, 1754. *Sons:* JAMES (plantation and three negroes), FREDERIC (four negroes), WILSON (three negroes). *Sister-in-law:* Mrs. MARY MOOR. *Daughters:* ELIZABETH, MARTHA, MARY. *Wife:* SARAH (three negroes). Chaise, boat, blacksmith tools and watch ordered sold. *Brothers:* CHARLES BLOUNT and JOSEPH BLOUNT (*executors*). *Witnesses:* J. HALSEY, JNO. SMITH, JOHN BEASLEY, RICHARD DUNBAR. *Clerk of the Court:* WILL HALSEY. The following item may be of interest: "My Will and desire is * * * * That no Stranger shall be admitted to live on any part of the back land to destroy the timber and that no Person shall on any Consideration whatsoever be admitted to live on any part of my land excepting an overseer."

BLOUNT, THOMAS.   Kendricks Creek, Albemarle County.

September 3, 1701. March 28, 1706. *Sons:* JOHN and JAMES. Following lands devised: "Midle plantation; land at the mouth of Kendricks Creek, whereon I now live; land called Cabbin Necke." *Daughters:* BILLAH (wife of KELLEM TYLER), SARAH PEIRCE, CHRISTIAN LUDFORD and ANN WILSON. *Wife:* MARY. *Executor:* JAMES BLOUNT (son). *Witnesses:* WM. WILLSON, JOHN BLOUNT, THOMAS GREEN. Proven before THOMAS CARY.

BLYE, WILLIAM.   Bertie County.

November 29, 1748. May Court, 1749. *Sons:* WILLIAM ("manner plantation"), THOMAS. *Daughters:* SARAH BLYE, ELIZABETH BLYE. *Wife:* ELIZABETH. *Executors:* WILLIAM BLYE (son), ELIZABETH BLYE (wife). *Witnesses:* JOHN THOMAS, NATHANIEL WILLIAMS, TIMOTHY WILLIAMS. *Clerk of the Court:* JOHN LOVICK.

BOBBIT, JOHN.   Bertie County.

May 7, 1736. November 6, 1736. *Son:* WILLIAM (100 acres land in the "Orraneechey Neck"). *Son:* THOMAS (100 acres land in the "Orraneechey Neck"). *Daughters:* FRANCIS, MARY and AMEY. *Executors:* WILLIAM BOBBIT, ROBERT GREEN, JOHN MASSY and JAMES BROGDEN. *Witnesses:* FRANCIS BETTES, RICHARD MASSY, FRANCIS MASSY, and C. EVANS. *Clerk of the Court:* JOHN WYNNS.

BOGE (or BOGUE), JOSIAH.   Perquimans County.

March 1, 1752. July Court, 1752. *Sons:* JESSE, JOSEPH, JOBE ("all my lands"). *Daughters:* MARY BOGE, MIRIAM BOGE, LIDY BOGE. *Wife:* DEBORAH. *Executors:* DEBORAH BOGE (wife), JOHN MOOR, TRUMAN MOOR. *Witnesses:* JOSHUA PARISHE, JOSHUA HASKET, THOMAS HOLLOWELL. *Clerk of the Court:* EDMUND HATCH.

BOGE, WILLIAM.   Perquimans Precinct.

December 20, 1720. April 11, 1721. *Sons:* WILLIAM and JOSIAH ("my manner plantation"). *Daughters:* ELIZABETH HILL, JEAN BOGE, MYRIAM BOGE, RACHEL BOGE. *Wife:* ELLENDER. *Grandson:* WILLIAM HILL. *Executors:* WILLIAM BOGE (son), JACOB HILL (son-in-law). *Witnesses:* BENJAMIN MUNDY, JOHN MOOR. *Clerk of the Court:* RICH'D LEARY.

BOGUE, WILLIAM.   Perquimans County.

June 29, 1744. October Court, 1745. ("On the North East side of Perquimans River"). *Wife and Executrix:* SARAH. *Sons:* WILLIAM BOGUE (100 acres land on the East side Sutens Creek"), JAK BOGUE. *Witnesses:* JOHN MORE, THOMAS BAGLEY. *Clerk of Court:* EDMUND HATCH. Courthouse on Phelps Point.

BOND, JOHN.   Beaufort County.

July 8, 1749. September Court, 1749. *Sons:* WILLIAM (land on the West side of Middle Swamp), JOHN, JAMES (land on South side Pamplico River), ROBERT ("plantation I now live on"), RICHARD (land called Piners). *Daughters:* MARY and ANNA, and SARAH. *Wife:* (mentioned, but no name given). *Executors:* WILLIAM, JOHN and JAMES BOND (sons). *Cousin:* MARTHA SPRING. *Witnesses:* ABRAM PRITCHETT, JOHN TURNER, PHILLIP PRITCHETT, JOSHUA PRITCHETT. *Clerk of Court:* JOSIAH PRATHER.

BOND, LEWIS.   Chowan County.

February 22, 1753. April Court, 1753. *Sons:* RICHARD ("my mannar plantation"), WILLIAM, JOHN, *Daughters:* ELISABETH and SARAH BOND. *Wife:* REBECKER. *Executor:* RICHARD BOND (brother-in-law). *Witnesses:* JAMES BOND, DEMSEY CASTEN, ROBERT STEWART. *Clerk of the Court:* JAS. CRAVEN.

BOND, RICHARD.   No county.

January 15, 1725. *Sons:* RICHARD and HENRY (land on Maidenhare Creek), HANCE, WILLIAM, LEWIS ("maner plantation"). *Daughter:* MARY BOND. *Executrix:* Wife (mentioned, but not named). This is a copy of Bond's will and no signature, witness or probate appears.

BOND, ROBERT.   Craven Precinct.

January 6, 1737. June, 1738. *Son:* FRANCIS ("plantation whereon I now live"). *Daughters:* SARAH BOND (100 acres land at Broad Creek), ELISEBETH (50 acres of land), MARTHA BOND. *Wife and Executrix:* SARAH. *Witnesses:* F. DAWSON, JOHN GOOD. *Clerk of the Court:* JAMES COOR.

ABSTRACT OF WILLS, 1690—1760.

BOND, SAMUEL. Perquimans County.

October 12, 1721. March 26, 1723. *Sons:* SAMUELL (land on Perquimans River), LUKE (land on Perquimans River). *Daughters:* MARY, SUSANA, ELIZEBETH BOND, JANE BOND. *Friends:* JOSEPH SMITH, TIMOTHY CLEARE, JOS. JESSOP. *Executor:* SAMUELL BOND (son). *Witnesses:* JAMES SMITH, SUSANA SMITH, JOSEPH JESSOP. Will proven before C. GALE, Chief Justice.

BOND, VINYARD. Beaufort County.

March 25, 1762. November 8, 1762. *Wife:* SARAH. *Son:* SWEETING. *Daughter:* SARAH. (Plantations on Care Point, Trent River and Town Creek to wife and children for support of children). *Sisters:* SUSANNAH KERSHAW, SARAH, MARY and MARGARET. *Executors:* SARAH BOND (wife) and JOHN CARRUTHERS (brother of wife). *Witnesses:* WILL'M PEYTON, WILL'M TRIPPE, HENRY LOCKEY, THOMAS LEE. Will proven before ARTHUR DOBBS at Newbern.

BOND, WILLIAM. Beaufort County.

November 6, 1757. December Court, 1757. *Sons:* JOHN ("plantation wheareon I doe live" and one-half of the "Old Box Neak," together with one negro). WILLIAM (land "where Samuell Daves lives and land where Jarves Smith did live, one par of Silver Shue buckles, one par of Nea buckles and one Stock Buckall"). *Daughter:* REBECCA (one negro). *Other legatees:* KNIGA (?) and MARY ERKMAN. *Executors:* JAMES and RICHARD BOND and SAMUELL DAVES. *Witnesses:* FRS. GILBERT, FRANCES WARNER, ANN MAYO. *Clerk of the Court:* WALLEY CHAUNCEY.

BONNER, HENRY. Chowan County.

September 1, 1738. October 7, 1738. *Sons:* HENRY (plantation lying in Greenhall), THOMAS (three plantations called "Brins," "Hales's" and "Jones's"). *Grandson:* RICHARD LEWIS ("Bayes plantation"). *Daughters:* ELIZABETH, DEBORAH and MARY. *Granddaughters:* SARAH LEWIS and DEBORAH LEWIS. *Executor:* HENRY BONNER (son). *Witnesses:* JOS. ANDERSON, ABRA'M BLACKALL, JAMES POTTER. *Clerk of the Court:* W. SMITH.

BONNER, JOHN. Chowan County.

November 11, 1753. January Court, 1754. *Cousins:* WILLIAM, ELIZABETH, MARY and EDWARD HOWCOTT (negroes). *Godson:* THOMAS ECLESTON (one negro). *Brother:* THOMAS BONNER (plantation). *Executors:* JOHN BENBURY and HENRY BONNER. *Witnesses:* JEREH MICHENER, JOHN SMITH, GEORGE LILES. *Clerk of the Court:* WILL HALSEY.

BONNER, MARY.   Chowan County.

January 30, 1749–1750. July Court, 1750. *Friend:* DEBROH THOMPSON. Two brothers and a sister mentioned, but not named. *Executor:* JAMES TOMPSON. *Witnesses:* JOHN LEWIS, JOHN LEWIS, JUNIOR. *Clerk of the Court:* WILL MEARNS.

BONNER, THOMAS.   County not given.

March 6, 1685. November 24, 1685. *Son:* THOMAS. *Wife and Executrix:* MARY. *Witnesses:* HENRY BONNER, SAMUEL WARREN, WILLIAM BONNER. Proven before WM. WILKISON.

BONNER, THOMAS.   Bertie County.

November 11, 1755. April Court, 1756. *Sons:* THOMAS, HENRY, MOSES. *Daughters:* ESTER MORE, ELISEBATH WHELER, ANNA BYRDE, SARAH WHARTON, PACHENCE BYRDE. *Wife:* ELISEBATH BONNER. *Executrix:* ELISEBATH BONNER (wife). *Witnesses:* MOSES BONNER, EDMON BYRDE, ARTHUR MOOR, ABRAHAM BLITCHENDEN. *Clerk of the Court:* BENJN WYNNS. WM. WYNNS, P. J.

BOON, JOSEPH.   No county given.

February 19, 1728. *Sons:* JAMES, JOSEPH, THOMAS, RATLIF. *Sister:* MARTHA BAYLEY. *Daughters:* MARY and ELIZABETH. *Executrix:* ——— BOON. *Wife:* Not named. *Witnesses:* THOMAS BOON, NATHANIEL COOPER. No probate.

BOONE, JAMES.   Bertie Precinct.

June 8, 1733. March 31, 1735. *Sons-in-law:* JOHN EARLY (one negro woman and fifty apple trees); JOHN WYNNS (my negro man called Charles and 1000 foot of plank); CULLINEUR SESSUMS (one negro). *Daughters:* MARY WYNNS, ELIZA EARLY. *Grandsons:* GEORGE AUGUSTUS WYNNS, JAMES EARLY. *Other legatees:* WILLIAM BURKE, JOHN ASSKEW, MARTHA DAVIS. *Wife and Executrix:* ELIZABETH. *Witnesses:* JOHN WILLSON, THOMAS LEE, JAMES MARTIN. Proven before GAB. JOHNSTON.

BOON, NICHOLAS.   No date and no county given.

Sons: NICHOLAS (dwelling plantation), WILLIAM, JOSEPH. *Daughters:* MARY, MARTHA and ANN. *Wife:* MARY. *Executors:* MARY BOONE (wife), WILLIAM BOON (brother) and THOMAS BOON, JUNR. *Witnesses:* JOHN STRICKLAND, JOHN FORD, NATHANIEL COOPER. No probate.

BOOTH, GEORGE.   Knott's Island, Currituck County.

February 12, 1729. July 7, 1730. *Sons:* JOHN and GEORGE (land lying in "Viriana"). *Daughter:* HANNAH SIMMONS. *Wife:* MARY BOOTH. *Executrix:* MARY BOOTH. *Clerk of the Court:* J. MARTYN.

BOOTH, JAMES.   Newton in Cape Fear.

February 12, 1737–1738. February 18, 1737–1738. *Devisees:* ROGER ROLFE, JONATHAN OGDEN, SEN'R, and JONATHAN OGDEN. *Executors:* JONATHAN OGDEN and ROGER ROLFE. *Witnesses:* RICHARD OGDEN, ANN SHIRLEY, ANN ROLFE. (Seal with coat of arms.) Proven before GAB. JOHNSTON, *Governor*, etc.

BOOTH, JOHN.   Carteret County.

December 14, 1751. March Court, 1752. Nuncupative will spoken to JOHN SIMPSON and GEORGE BELL, who made oath to same before RICHARD WARD Estate left to *Wife*, RACHEL, and *Children* (not named). *Clerk of the Court:* GEO. READ.

BOOZMAN, RALPH.   Perquimans County.

January 1, 1744–1745. January Court, 1750. *Sister:* MARY BULLOCK. *Executors:* JOSEPH BULLOCK and THOMAS BULLOCK. *Niece:* SARAH BULLOCK (daughter of MARY BULLOCK). *Witnesses:* JOSHUA HOBART, JAMES LITTLETON, JR., HANNAH LITTLETON. *Clerk of the Court*: EDMUND HATCH.

BORDEN, WILLIAM.   Carteret County.

February 10, 1748–1749. August 1, 1749. *Son:* WILLIAM ("my manner plantation" and also 800 acres of land on Harlor's Creek and Core Creek). *Daughters:* ALICE STANTON, KATHERINE BORDEN, HANNAH BORDEN, SARAH PRATT. *Nephew:* WILLIAM BORDEN. *Brothers:* THOMAS BORDEN, BENJAMIN BORDEN. *Sister :* AMY CHASE. *Executors :* BENJAMIN BORDEN (brother). HENRY STANTON (son-in-law), SUSANNAH BORDEN (wife). *Witnesses:* SAMUEL NEWBY, JOSEPH NEWBY, JOSEPH ROBINSON. Will proven before GAB. JOHNSTON, *Governor*, at Edenhouse.

BOSWELL, GEORGE.   Perquimans County.

December 30, 1741. January 7, 1741. *Sons:* GEORGE ("my dwelling plantation"), ISAC. *Daughter:* EZIBELL. *Sister-in-law:* HANNAH MORGIN. *Executors:* THOMAS HALLOWELL, CHARLES OVERMAN, HANNAH MORGIN. *Witnesses:* THOMAS NICHOLSON, JOHN BOSWELL, JOSIAH BUNDY. Will proven before J. MONTGOMERY, C. J.

BOSWELL, WILLIAM.   Perquimans Precinct.

February 1, 1734–1735. February 17, 1734. *Sons:* THOMAS (land at the head of Little River), JOHN (one-half of plantation "that I now dwell on"), ICHABOD ("remainder part of said tract"). *Daughter:* MARY BOSWELL. *Executors:* THOMAS OVERMAN and THOMAS NICHOLSON. *Witnesses:* JOHN BOSWELL, GEORGE BOSWELL, WM. BUNDY. *Codicil:* Places children in hands of executors to be brought up. Will and codicil proven before GAB. JOHNSTON, *Governor*, at Edenton.

BOSWORTH, JOSEPH.   Carteret Precinct.
    June 18, 1734. June 3, 1735. *Sons:* JOSEPH, EPHRAIM and ROBERT. *Wife:* MARY. *Executors:* MARY BOSWORTH (wife), JOSEPH WEEKS, DR. SOLOMON BACON. *Witnesses:* JAMES BALL, EPHRAIM CHADWICK, WILLIAM WALDRON. *Clerk of the Court:* JAS. WINRIGHT. All estate of testator is ordered sold and proceeds deposited with some person at Boston for use and benefit of wife and children.

BOTNETT, JOHN.   Albemarle County.
    October 30, 1703. April 17, 1704. *Friend and Executor:* DAVID PRICHARD. *Witnesses:* WM WARREN, WM JOY, MARGARE JOY. Will proven before WM ROLFE.

BOUDE, JOHN.   Bertie County.
    May 18, 1738. August 25, 1738. *Wife:* KATHERINE. *Reputed son* (son of Catherine Deed), 603 acres land. *Brother:* THOMAS BOUDE, of Philadelphia. *Friends:* JAMES WILKINGS, THOMAS BOXLY. *Cousin:* JOHN BOUDE. *Executors:* KATHERINE BOUDE, GODFREY LEA, EDWARD BARNS, JOHN DAYTON. *Witnesses:* ROBERT MACRAE, JAMES WILKINS, MARY HARBERTT, SARAH LEE. Proven before W. SMITH, C. J.

BOULD, GEORGE.   Craven County.
    July 12, 1745. September Court, 1745. *Brother:* JOSEPH BOULD. *Friends:* FRANCIS STRINGER, JOHN SNEAD (ten acres of marsh "opposite to Newbern Town"), GEORGE POWELL, son of JOHN POWELL. *Wife:* MARY BOULD. *Executrix:* MARY BOULD. *Witnesses:* FEILDER POWELL, JAMES COAR, THOS. FOX, MARY COAR. *Clerk of the Court:* JNO. RICE.

BOUND, RICHARD.   Perquimans Precinct.
    November 22, 1720. July 11, 1721. *Sons:* EDWARD (200 acres of land), SAMUELL (200 acres of land). *Daughters:* ELIZABETH, HORNER, ABIGALL. *Wife:* ABIGALL. *Executors:* ABIGALL BOUND (wife) and JAMES MINGE. *Witnesses:* HANAH BURROES, ELIZABETH PHETTS. *Clerk of the Court:* RICH'D LEARY.

BOUREN, EDMUND.   Currituck Precinct.
    July 29, 1711. No probate. *Son:* JOSEPH (land on Youpim Ridge). *Daughters:* SARAH, JANE and SUSANNAH BOUREN. *Wife and Executrix:* SARAH. *Witnesses:* WILLIAM WILLIAMS, JO WICKER, THOMAS POYNER. Original missing. Recorded in Book 1712-22, page 42.

BOYCE, ISAAC.   Perquimans County.
    January 15, 1750. July Court, 1751. *Uncles:* NICHOLAS and ELIAS STALLINGS. *Sons:* JOB, JOSEPH and BENJAMIN. *Wife:* JUDE. *Executors:* JOS. NICHOLAS and ELIAS STALLINGS. *Witnesses:* ABRAHAM SANDERS, WHITE, ELIZABETH SANDERS. *Clerk of Court:* EDMUND HATCH.

BOYCE, JOHN.   Perquimans County.

February 12, 1748. July Court, 1749. *Sons:* ISAAC, JOHN, MOSES. *Daughters:* JEAN, ELIZABETH, RACHEL. *Grandson:* JOB BOYCE. *Wife:* SUSANNAH BOYCE. *Executors:* SUSANNAH BOYCE (wife) and ISAAC BOYCE (son). *Witnesses:* NICHOLAS STALLINGS, WILLIAM EASON, HENRY STALLINGS. *Clerk of the Court:* EDMUND HATCH.

BOYCE, WILLIAM.   Albemarle County.

August 30, 1688. April Court, 1693. All estate, real and personal, to *wife*, ANN BOYCE. *Executrix:* ANN BOYCE. *Witnesses:* PAUL LATHAM, JOHN BARBER, JACOB FIELDS. *Clerk of the Court:* EDWARD MAYO.

BOYCE, WILLIAM.   Perquimans County.

June 11, 1703. October 12, 1703. *Mother:* MARY (of Yarmouth, England). *Friends:* MR. JULIAN LAKERS, MR. ROBERT BRADLEY (Prince George Co., Maryland). Gold rings to following parties: COLL. WM. WILKINSON, his wife, MRS. JULIANA LAKERS, JAMES STODDART (Prince George Co., Maryland), his wife, JNO. COBB, PETER GODFREY. *Executrix:* JOANNA KESLER. *Witnesses:* DAVID HARRIS, ELIZ. STUART, P. GODFREY. *Clerk of the Court:* THOS. SNODEN.   Coat of arms on seal.

BOYD, JOHN.   Chowan County.

October 9, 1737. July Court, 1738. *Son:* WILLIAM. *Daughters:* ANNE, MARION and LYDIAR BOYD. *Wife:* LYDIA. *Executors:* LYDIA BOYD (wife), PHILIP AYDLETT (of Virginia), ANDREW IRVING. *Witnesses:* JOHN ROWSOM, JAS. WILLIAMS, EDWARD SILK. *Clerk of the Court:* JAMES CRAVEN.

BOYD, JOHN.   Pasquotank County.

January 29, 1741. July Court, 1742. *Sons:* WILLIAM ("Westeard parte of my land"), THOMAS ("Eastard part of my land"). *Daughter:* WINEFRUIT BOYD. *Wife and Executrix:* ANN BOYD. *Witnesses:* JOHN MCKEEL, WM. WALLIS, ANTHONY MARKHAM. *Clerk of the Court:* THOS. TAYLOR.

BOYD, THOMAS.   Bath County.

December 17, 1725. April Court, 1726. *Son:* JOHN. *Wife:* KATHERINE (use of plantation on Broad Creek, "where I now dwell"). *Friends:* COL. EDWARD MOSELEY, ROBERT TURNER (five pounds for ring), CAPT. SIMON ALDERSON. *Executors:* EDWARD MOSELEY, SIMON ALDERSON. This is a holograph will and a caveat was entered thereto by one John Bond. Several affidavits, together with portions of briefs and argument of counsel are filed with the original.

BOYD, WINEFRED.   Pasquotank County.

June 15, 1720. July 19, 1720. *Sons:* JOHN and THOMAS BOYD (negroes). BENJAMIN and CHARLES WEST (executors). *Witnesses:* LEWIS KNIGHT, RICHARD STAMP. Recorded in Book 1712–22, page 242. Original missing.

BOYINTONE, JOSEPH.   Chowan Precinct.

September 25, 1738. January, 1738. *Brother and Executor:* BENJAMIN BOYINTONE of Gloster, New England. *Friend:* JOHN RICHARDS of Edenton. *Witnesses:* ABNER BLACKALL, THOS. MORTIMORE, JAMES MITCHELL. *Clerk of the Court:* JAMES CRAVEN.

BOYKIN, THOMAS.   Northampton County.

April 13, 1748. February Court, 1750. *Wife:* MELDRED. *Son:* THOMAS (land and plantation). ANN CRAFORD, MARTHA THORNTON, ELIZABETH STRICKLAND and PATTIENCE STRICKLAND (one shilling each). *Executors:* MELDRED BOYKIN (wife) and THOMAS BOYKIN (son). *Witnesses:* JNO. SIMPSON, JOSEPH ROGERS, JOHN REYNOLDS. *Clerk of the Court:* I. EDWARDS.

BOYKIN, EDWARD.   Northampton County.

June 8, 1743. *Sons:* THOMAS (lands lying between Richard Walls and Meadow Branch), SOLOMON (lands above Meadow Branch), HARDY (land on Cypress Swamp), EDWARD, BENJAMIN. *Daughter:* RACHEL HERON. *Grandson:* HENRY BOYKIN. *Wife:* JUDITH. *Executors:* JUDITH (wife) and SOLOMON BOYKIN (son). *Witnesses:* CHAS. CAMPBELL, RICHARD WALL. *Clerk of the Court:* I. EDWARDS.

BRACK, GEORGE.   Onslow County.

September 25, 1750. April 2, 1751. *Sons:* GEORGE (160 acres land on "head of the Rich Neck"), ELIAZAR, RICHARD, WILLIAM (160 acres of land "whereon I now live"). *Grandson:* JOHN LEWIS. *Daughter:* ELIZABETH BRACK. *Son-in-law:* MATHEW LEWIS. *Wife:* GEAN. *Executors:* MATHEW LEWIS, GEORGE BRACK (son). *Witnesses:* LIONEL BOUTWELL, MOURNING LEWIS, SUSANER MORRIS. *Clerk of the Court:* THO. BLACK.

BRADDY, JAMES.   Chowan County.

August 17, 1750. January Court, 1750. *Sons:* JOHN and JOSEPH, JAMES ("plantation whereon I now live"). *Grandson:* JAMES CONNER. *Wife:* GRACE. *Executors:* GRACE BRADDY (wife) and JAMES BRADDY (son). *Witnesses:* ED. WARREN, MARY POWELL, HENRY GOODMAN. *Clerk of the Court:* WILL MEARNS.

BRADEY, JOHN.   Craven County.

October 11, 1753. November Court, 1753. *Wife:* ABIGAIL. *Executor:* JEREMIAH RHEAM. *Witnesses:* DANIEL PERKINS, JEREMIAH RHEAM. *Clerk of the Court:* SOL REW.

BRADFORD, NATHANIEL.   Edgecombe County.

October 2, 1756. February Court, 1757. *Sons:* JOHN ("plantation whereon I now live"), NATHANIEL ("remainder of my lands"). *Daughters:* MARY BRADFORD and PATIENCE BRADFORD. *Wife:* SARAH: *Executors:* JOHN BRADFORD and JOSEPH LANE. *Witnesses:* SAM'L HARVY, JAMIMA SIMMONS. *Clerk of the Court:* JOSEPH MONTFORT.

BRADLEY, RICHARD.   Currituck County.

April 13, 1756. June Court, 1756. *Sons:* HANER, WILLIAM, ABEL, JOHN, RICHARD. *Daughters:* ANN ETHERIDGE, ALIDEA CORBILL, MARY BRADLEY, ELIZABETH BRADLEY. *Wife:* DORITY BRADLEY. *Executors:* DORITY BRADLEY (wife) and WILLIAM BRADLEY (son). *Witnesses:* KEDAR MARCHANT, JOSIAH DOUGH, ELIZABETH DENBY. *Clerk of the Court:* WILLIAM SHERGOLD.

BRADY, JOSEPH.   Chowan County.

November 19, 1752. July Court, 1753. *Daughters:* ELIZABETH HARTLOCK, BARSHEBA JONES, MARY JONES. *Son:* JOHN BRADY. *Grandson:* JOHN DICKINS (*mother*, SUFFRAH DICKINS). *Granddaughters:* TAMER BRADY and EADY DICKINS. *Witnesses:* JACOB ROGERS, JOSEPH BRADY, TAMER BRADY. *Clerk of the Court:* WILL HALSEY.

BRANCH, FRANCIS.   County not given.

November 14, 1739. December 4, 1739. *Daughter:* SARAH DONNAVAN. *Wife:* ANNE. PHILLIP MAGNIER, PHILLIP MAGNIER, JR., SAMUEL MAGNIER. WILLIAM BRANCH (son of ISAAC BRANCH). *Executors:* JAMES DONNAVON, ANNE BRANCH (wife). *Friends:* WM. ARKILL, WM. LUTEN. *Witnesses:* CONST. LUTEN, WM. LUTEN, WM. LEWIS. Will proven before W. SMITH, C. J.

BRANCH, WILLIAM.   Chowan County.

November 24, 1720. January Court, 1721. *Wife:* MARGRET ("lott of land in Edenton on Queen Anne Creek"). *Sons:* WILLIAM (plantation near Edenton), ISSACHAR (plantation on the southwest side of Mattchacomak Creek), SOLOMON. *Daughter:* ELIZABETH. *Executors:* MARGRET BRANCH (wife), FRANCIS BRANCH (brother). *Witnesses:* JNO. NEW, ANNE BRANCH, THOMAS BRANCH. *Clerk of the Court:* (name torn from will).

BRAND, ISABELLA CAMERON, relict of ANDREW BRAND,
                                  Basterin Cannongate, Scotland.

This is an assignment to ALEX CUNNYNGHAM of Cannongate, Scotland, in case of the death of testatrix who is about to set forth for Carolina and names as legatees, *Nephew:* JOHN MURRAY (son of ROBERT MURRAY of Glencarnock) and ROBINA CAMERON, his wife, and as *Executor*, JOHN RUTH-

ERFORD (Merchant in Cape Fear). This will (or assignment) is written on stamped paper. *Witnessed by* THOMAS AINSLEE and DUN MCDONALD, and proven at August Court, 1748, before JAS. MORAN, *Clerk of the Court*, by ALEXR DUNCAN by "Parity of Hands."

BRASKE, LAURENCE.   Pasquotank County.

June 1, 1687. July 2, 1687. *Devisees:* MARGARET BROWNE and ELIZABETH CRADUCK. *Executrix:* MARGARET BROWNE and ELIZABETH CRADUCK. *Witnesses:* JOHN BROWNE, WM. WOOD, JOHN WILLSON. Will proven before SETH SOTHELL.

BRASWELL, ROBERT.   Bertie Precinct.

September 14, 1734. November Court, 1736. *Sons:* ROBERT, JOHN, RICHARD ("plantation whereon I now live"), VALENTINE (100 acres land). *Daughters:* SARAH DOUGHTRY, JEAN BRASWELL, MARY BRASWELL. *Godson:* DIOMEE SUMNER (100 acres land). *Wife:* SARAH. *Executors:* JAMES BRYANT, JOSHAWAY DAUGHTREY. *Witnesses:* THOS. BRYANT, NICHOLAS BAGET, PACCENCE BRYANT. *Clerk of the Court:* JNO. WYNNS.

BRAY, HENRY.   Pasquotank County.

September 20, 1745. *Sons:* WILLIAM, CHRISTOPHER, JOHN, GEORGE, DANIEL (one shilling each), JEREMIAH ("my plantation containing 100 acres land"), JACOB. *Daughters:* MARY SHAWDAILY, SARAH SQUIERS, ELIZABETH FORBES (one shilling each). *Wife and Executrix:* DINAH. *Witnesses:* JAS. FORBES, JNO. CARTRIET, WILLIAM WRIGHT. Probate illegible.

BRAY, WILLIAM.   Pasquotank Precinct.

August 23, 1725. January 18, 1725. *Sons:* HENERE (the tract of land "that he now liveth on"), GEORGE (plantation "where I now live"). *Executors:* WILLIAM BURGES and GEORGE BRAY. *Witnesses:* STEPHEN BURGES, THOMAS BURGES, ELIZABETH BURGES. *Clerk of the Court:* THO. WEEKES. Executor qualified before JO. PALIN.

BRENT, JAMES.   Currituck County.

February 7, 1753. April Court, 1753. *Sons:* RICHARD ("plantation whereon I now live"), JAMES ("plantation called "Tuckers Ridg"). *Daughter:* ANN BRENT. *Wife and Executrix:* KIZIAH. *Witnesses:* ABSALOM LEGETT, JOHN SIMMONS, HENRY SIMMONS, JR. *Clerk of the Court:* WILLIAM SHERGOLD.

BRENT, THOMAS.   Currituck County.

January 1, 1726. April 11, 1727. *Son:* JAMES (150 acres land known as "Wolfpoint Ridge"). *Wife:* ANN. *Executrix:* ANN BRENT (wife). *Witnesses:* THOS. WILLIAMS, HOLLAND HEATH, CHARLES BRENT. *Clerk of the Court:* J. MARTYN.

BREWER, JANE.   New Hanover County.

August 18, 1739. September 25, 1739. *Daughters:* CATHERINE and HANNAH. *Son-in-law:* RICHARD HOTT. *Executors:* DANIEL DUNBIBIN and RICHARD HOTT. *Witnesses:* RUFUS MARSDEN, ROGER ROLFE, JAMES BROWN. Will proven before GABRIEL JOHNSON, *Governor, etc.,* at Newton.

BREWER, GEORGE.   Northampton County.

January 25, 1757. August Court, 1757. *Sons:* RAWLE, GEORGE, MATTHEW, JOHN. *Wife and Executrix:* MARY. *Witnesses:* JOSEPH SCOULS, ELIZABETH WHITINGTON, WILLIAM CHAPMAN. *Clerk of the Court:* I. EDWARDS.

BRIANT, SAMUEL.   Chowan County.

June 6, 1717. July Court, 1717. *Executor and sole legatee:* JOHN FISHER. *Witnesses:* FRANCIS JOHNSON, EDWARD PHELPS. *Clerk of the Court:* R. HICKS.

BRICE, WILLIAM.   County not given.

November 16, 1718. May 1, 1719. *Sons:* FRANCIS and WILLIAM. *Daughter:* ELIZA BRICE. *Wife and Executrix:* ANN. *Executor:* THOMAS HARVEY. *Witnesses:* THOMAS HARVEY, ELIZ. HARVEY, MARTIN FRANK. *Clerk of the Court:* CALEB METCALFE. Recorded in Book 1712–22, page 226. Original missing.

BRICKELL, JAMES.   Beaufort County.

April 22, 1746. June Court, 1746. *Son:* JAMES (land joining Mr. Ormond's lands). *Daughters:* ANN BRICKELL (land joining Mr. Barrow's lands). *Son of* ELIZABETH GRAY (one cow). *Executors:* WYRIATT ORMOND, *Atty.-at-Law;* ABRAHAM DUNCAN, *Gent.,* and JAMES BRICKELL (son). *Witnesses:* MARY DUNCAN, MARY BRICKELL, WILLIAM GRAY. *Clerk of the Court:* JOHN FORBES.

BRIDGEN, SAMUEL. Ludlow Castle, New Hanover County.

November 30, 1757. February Court, 1758. *Trustees:* JOB HOWES, SEN'R, and JOB HOWES, JR., to whom is conveyed in trust for *daughter,* JANE BENNETT, a tract of land on Old Town Creek. In trust for *son,* EDWARD BRIDGEN, of London, a plantation called "Bridgen's Hall," "Ludlow Castle" and "Bridgen's Pastime." *Daughter:* ELIZABETH CATHARINA, wife of ARMOND DeROSSETT. *Wife:* SARAH. *Brother:* REV. JOHN BRIDGEN (Professor of Gresham College, London). *Nephew:* WILLIAM BRIDGEN (Alderman of London). *Witnesses:* JOHN MOTT, HANNAH MOTT, ARTHUR HOWES. *Clerk of the Court:* JA. MORAN.

ABSTRACT OF WILLS, 1690—1760. 47

BRIDGERS, WILLIAM. Bertie Precinct.

March 11, 1728–1729. November Court, 1729. *Sons:* WILLIAM ("plantation whereon I now live"), JOSEF ("plantation on Fishing Creek"), JOHN (100 acres land). *Daughter:* SARAH BRIDGERS. *Brothers:* BENJAMIN BRIDGERS, WILLIAM BRYANT. *Father:* JOHN DEW. *Wife:* SARAH. *Executors:* WILLIAM BRYANT and JOHN DEW, SENOR. *Witnesses:* JOHN DAWSON, WILLIAM BRYANT, MARY HUISE, RICHARD HUISE. *Clerk of the Court:* RT. FORSTER.

BRIDGERS, WILLIAM. Bertie County.

November 2, 1729. May Court, 1730. *Sons:* JOSEPH, BENJAMIN ("my plantation"), Samuel. *Daughters:* MARY, ELIZABETH. *Executor:* SAMUEL BRIDGERS (son). *Witnesses:* JOHN WEVVRILL, JOHN BARDIN, EDWARD CHITTY. *Clerk of the Court:* RT. FORSTER.

BRIDGERS, WILLIAM. Johnston County.

September 30, 1751. December Court, 1751. JOEL MARTIN and LUCRECE, *legatees.* *Executor:* PHILIP JONES. *Witnesses:* JAS. BRYANT, JAMES ACOCK, JOS. GOODING. *Clerk of the Court:* CHAS. YOUNG.

BRIDGESS, SAMUEL. Northampton County.

December 13, 1748. February Court, 1756. *Daughters:* MARY BRIDGESS, PATIENCE BRIDGESS (to both are bequeathed 200-acre tracts of land on the Tarkill Branch). *Executor:* WILLIAM BOON. *Witnesses:* JOHN CORE, JESSE CARDIN, JOSEPH BRIDGESS. *Clerk of the Court:* I. EDWARDS.

BRIGGS, RICHARD. Chowan County.

March 2, 1754. July Court, 1754. *Sons:* JOHN, SOLOMON, JAMES, MOSES, RICHARD and CHRISTIAN. *Daughters:* TILPAH and RACHEL. *Wife:* ELIZABETH BRIGGS. *Executors:* JOHN DAVIS and JOB HARRISS. *Witnesses:* JOHN DAVIS, JOBE HARRISS, JESSE EASON. *Clerk of the Court:* WILL HALSEY.

BRIGHT, HENERY. Pasquotank County.

July 8, 1734. October Court, 1739. *Son:* ADAM. *Daughter:* LEVINAH UPTON. *Wife and Executrix:* ELIZABETH. *Witnesses:* WILLIAM OVERENTON, JOSEPH MAKEFARSON. *Clerk of the Court:* JAMES CRAVEN.

BRIGHT, HENRY. Currituck County.

May 23, 1749. July Court, 1749. *Sons:* CALEB, SILAS, JOHN, HENRY. *Daughters:* BRIDGES, MARY ANN, SUSY, CORTNEY. *Executor:* HENRY BRIGHT (son). *Witnesses:* JAMES BURNHAM, SAMUEL BRIGHT, ANN BRIGHT. *Clerk of the Court:* RICH'D MCCLURE.

BRIGHT, JAMES.   Hyde County.

March 29, 1735. *Wife, Executrix and sole devisee:* ANN. *Witnesses:* GILES WILLIAMS, HANAH ADAMS, RICH'D WM. SILVESTER. *Clerk of the Court:* JNO. COLLISON.

BRIGHT, RICHARD.   Currituck County.

December 12, 1734. *Sons:* EPHRAM, WILLIAM. *Daughters:* CASIAH, ELIZABETH. *Wife:* ELIZABETH (who is appointed executrix). *Witnesses:* SAMLL. BALLANCE, JOHN WEST, MOSES LINTON. *Clerk of the Court:* THOMAS LOWTHER.

BRIGHT, RICHARD.   Currituck County.

February 20, 1733. July 1, 1740. *Sons:* RICHARD, HANSON, SOLLOMON, ("ye maner plantation"), WILLIAM, JAMES, SAMLL. *Daughters:* ANN COX, ELENER ETHERIDGE, EDEE BRIGHT. *Executor:* JOHN ETHERIDGE (son-in-law). *Witnesses:* RICH. ETHERIDGE, HENRY FORSHAW, SAMLL. LEE. *Clerk of Court:* WM. SHERGOLD.

BRIGHT, SIMON.   Dobbs County.

November 23, 1775. January 18, 1777. *Sons:* SIMON ("the plantation wheron I now live," together with 200 acres of land on the Briery Branch), GRAVES (lands known by name of Haskins land), JAMES (500-acre and 160-acre tracts of land). *Daughters:* MARY BRIGHT, NANCY BRIGHT, SALLY BRIGHT, ELIZABETH BRIGHT. *Wife:* MARY. *Executors:* RICHARD CASWELL and JOHN COOKE (friends) and JAMES BRIGHT (brother). *Witnesses:* E. COOKE, RD. CASWELL and J. GLASGOW. Will proven before RD. CASWELL, at New Bern.

BRIGHT, SOLOMON.   Currituck County.

February 4 (no year). June, 1755. *Sons:* HANCE and SOLOMON (plantation). *Wife and Executrix:* MARY BRIGHT. *Witnesses:* THOS. WILLIAMS, WILLIAM WILLIAMS, THOMAS DAVIS. *Clerk of the Court:* WILLIAM SHERGOLD.

BRIGHT, WILLIAM.   Craven County.

January 12, 1754. November 6, 1754. *Son:* STOCWELL ("all my land down the Riever * * * * one plantation on Orched Creek and one Do. on Loer Broad Creek"). *Daughters*: SUSANAH BRIGHT, ELENAR BRIGHT, MARY BRIGHT, SARAH BRIGHT, ANN NELSON. *Grandson:* HARMON GASKINS. *Granddaughters:* MARY and SARAH BRIGHT. *Wife and Executrix:* ANN. *Witnesses:* JAMES ARTHER, SARAH ARTHER, W. CARRUTHERS, JUNR. *Clerk of the Court:* SOL. REW.

BRILL, WILLIAM.   County not given.

November 27, 1752. April 2, 1753. *Sons:* WILLIAM ("my Richland plantation"), RIGDON ("plantation I now dwell on"), ACTON, FRANCIS. *Executors:* FRANCIS BRIN, SAMELL HATCH and NATHAN SMITH. *Witnesses:* MARY MOORE, BENETA SMITH, MATTHEW SAMIN (?), JOSEPH BATCHER. Will proven before MATT ROWAN.

BRITT, WILLIAM.   County not given.

June 25, 1711. No probate. *Daughter:* MARY. *Wife:* ELIZABETH. *Executors:* SAMUEL EDMUNDS, ROBERT and THOMAS WEST. *Witnesses:* JOHN JORDAN, MATT ADAMS, MARY ADAMS. Will recorded in book 1712–22, page 34. Original missing.

BROCHETT, BENJAMIN.   Craven County.

July 9, 1750. August Court, 1758. *Wife and Executrix:* SARAH. *Witnesses:* MARY GARDNER, MARY PRINGELL, JOHN GRANADE. *Clerk of the Court:* PETER CONWAY.

BRODERICK, THOMAS, late of the Island of Granada,
                                          but now of Wilmington.

May 6, 1770. May 16, 1770. *Friends:* "MR. PARNERA, *Priest of the Roman Catholick Religion* in Philadelphia" (30 pounds "Pensilvania Currency"), MR. HARDIN, *of the same Profession*"), CHRISTIAN CAIN, Wilmington (40 gallons of rum). *Nephew:* ANDREW BRODRICK (son of brother DAN'L BRODRICK, of Philadelphia). *Executor:* CORNELIUS HARNETT. *Witnesses:* JAMES MCCAN, THO. LOYD, ARCHY WARD. Will proven before WM. TRYON, at Wilmington. *Executor* qualified before FRED'K GREGG.

BROMLEY, GEORGE.   Bertie Precinct.

March 21, 1726. September 20, 1728. *Friend and sole legatee and devisee:* THOMAS BETTERLEY. *Witnesses:* GO. ALLEN, WILL'M WILLIAMS, JNO. MATHEWS, W. BIGGS. Will proven before RICH'D EVERARD.

BROOKS, JOHN.   Currituck County.

July 9, 1707. April 27, 1708. *Son:* JOHN ("plantation whereon I now live"). *Daughters:* ELIZABETH BROOKS, FRANCES BROOKS, MARY BROOKS. *Son-in-law:* WILLIAM SCOTT. *Wife:* MARY. *Executrix:* MARY BROOKS (wife). *Witnesses:* WM. SWANN, JAMES BETTS. *Clerk of the Court:* EDWARD TAYLOR.

4

ABSTRACT OF WILLS, 1690—1760.

BROTHERS, JOHN.   Pasquotank Precinct.

November 28, 1733. April 8, 1735. *Sons:* JOSEPH (200 acres of land known as Kirks plantation), WILLIAM (150 acres of land), JOHN (100 acres of land on North side of Gum Pole Swamp), SAMUELL (129 acres of land), THOMAS, RICHARD, SAMUEL. *Daughter:* ELIZABETH BROTHERS. *Wife:* MARY. *Executors:* MARY BROTHERS (wife), JOSEPH BROTHERS (son), WILLIAM BROTHERS (brother). *Witnesses:* THOMAS WOODLEY, MARY WOODLEY, JAMES CRAVEN. *Clerk of Court:* JOS. SMITH. Courthouse in Broomfield.

BROTHERS, WILLIAM.   Pasquotank Precinct.

January 3, 1711. *Sons:* WILLIAM (126 acres of land), THOMAS (126 acres of land), RICHARD (126 acres of land), JOHN (126 acres of land), BENJAMIN. *Daughters:* ELINOR CARP, ELIZABETH, MARY, HANAH, SARAH, REBEKAH, DOROTY. *Wife and Executrix:* SARAH BROTHERS. *Witnesses:* HOWELL BROWNE. No probate.

BROWN, FRANCIS.   Bertie County.

November 7, 1748. May Court, 1750. *Sons:* FRANCIS (plantation purchased from Dan'l Brown), WILLIAM (150 acres of land), JOHN (land in Cypress Swamp), BENJAMIN. *Daughters:* ANNE, MARY, SARAH, JANE and ELIZABETH. *Executor:* JOHN WYNNS. *Witnesses:* ISAAC HILL, DAN'L VANPELT, GEORGE RIVET. *Clerk of the Court:* SAM'L ORMES.

BROWN, JAMES.   Currituck County.

April 5, 1721. *Wife and Executrix:* MARY. *Son:* WILLIAM (plantation). *Witnesses:* JAMES ADAMS, JOSEPH SANDERSON, ELIZABETH SANDERSON, *Clerk of the Court:* ———.

BROWN, JAMES.   Bath Town, Beaufort County.

November 13, 1746. *Daughters:* MARY BROWN and ANN BROWN. *Wife:* DOROTHY. *Executors:* MITCHELL COURTANCH (?), ABRAHAM DUNCAN. *Witnesses:* DAN'L BLIZ, RICHARD BASSETT, JAMES RIGNEY. No probate.

BROWN, JAMES.   Edgecombe County.

March 26, 1773. March 25, 1774. *Son:* JAMES ("my plantation"). *Daughters:* MOLLY BROWN, RACHEL BROWN, CATHARINE BROWN, SALLY BROWN, ANNY BROWN. *Executor:* BENJAMIN AMASON. *Witnesses:* JAMES AMASON, JESSE AMASON, WILLIAM AMASON. Will proven before Jo. MARTIN.

ABSTRACT OF WILLS, 1690—1760.   51

BROWN, JOHN.   Pasquotank Precinct.

February 15, 1698–1699. October 17, 1699. *Sons:* DANIEL and PEETER ("my plantation"). *Daughters:* MARGARET and JEAN. *Executrix:* WIFE (not named). *Witnesses:* DANIEL AKEHURST, WILLIAM REED. *Clerk of the Court:* THO. ABINGTON.

BROWN, JOHN.   Edgecombe County.

March 13, 1758. June Court, 1759. *Sons:* NATHAN ("land, still and cyder hogsheads"), HARDY. *Daughters:* PATIENCE POPE, ELISABETH EDWARDS, PRISCILLA BROWN, HANRENITTIA BROWN, SARAH BROWN, OLIVE BROWN. *Grandson:* BURAL SHELTON. *Wife:* PATIENCE. *Executors:* NATHAN BROWN, SAMUEL EDWARDS and SOLOMON. *Witnesses:* JOHN POPE, GEORGE CRUDUP, NICHOLAS DIXON. Will proven in Halifax Court. JOS. MONTFORT, *Clerk.*

BROWN, JONAS.   Northampton County.

January 26, 1741. August Court, 1743. *Brother:* WM. BROWN. *Nephew:* JONAS BROWN (son of William). *Wife and Executrix:* EDITH BROWN. *Witnesses:* WM. BODDIE, MARY BODDIE. *Clerk of Court:* I. EDWARDS.

BROWN, PHILIP.   Bertie County.

December 10, 1725. *Wife:* TEMSIN. *Friend:* JOHN MCHARLIN. *Executors:* TEMSIN BROWN (wife) and JOHN MCHARLIN. *Witnesses:* WILL ADAMS, JOHN WHITE, BENJAMIN SANDERS. No probate.

BROWN, RICHARD.   Bertie County.

April 8, 1734. May Court, 1736. *Sons:* DANIEL, RICHARD, WILLIAM, JAMES, STEPHEN. *Daughters:* ELIZABETH, AGNIS, MARGARETT. *Wife:* MARGARETT. *Executrix:* MARGARETT BROWN (wife). *Witnesses:* NICHS TAINLESS, EDWARD TIDMAN, AGNIS BROWN. *Clerk of the Court:* JNO. WYNNS.

BROWN, THOMAS.   Chowan County.

April 1, 1718. October 21, 1718. *Sons:* THOMAS, JOHN, HOWELL, JAMES. *Daughter:* SARAH MACDONEL. *Wife:* CHRISTIAN. *Witnesses:* JUDETH PERRY and THOMAS PERRY. *Clerk of the Court:* R. HICKS.

BROWN, THOMAS.   New Hanover County.

July 16, 1748. May 10, 1749. *Wife:* FORTUNE (400 acres land on the Sound). *Daughters:* ISABELLA (plantation "up the North West"), ELIZABETH ("plantation I purchased of WILLIAM SALTER"). *Executors:* JOHN BROWN (brother), RICHARD QUINCE. *Witnesses:* GEO. MERRICK, HENRY WRIGHT, ANN WRIGHT. Will proven before E. MOSELEY, *Associate Justice,* at Wilmington.

BROWN, WILLIAM.   Chowan Precinct.

December 15, 1718. July 21, 1719. *Sons:* JOHN ("ye manner plantation"), THOMAS (150 acres of land), JACOB (150 acres of land). *Daughters:* ANN, MARTHA, MARY, SARAH (each 150 acres of land). *Executors:* THOMAS MONDERS. *Witnesses:* THOMAS MONDERS, THOMAS SMITH, MARTHA BROWN. *Clerk of the Court:* R. HICKS. *Wife* of testator mentioned, but not named.

BROWN, WILLIAM.   Beaufort County.

September 9, 1751. December 10, 1751. *Wife:* ELIZABETH. *Son:* JOHN BROWN. *Daughters:* MARY BROWN and SARAH BROWN. *Executrix:* ELIZABETH BROWN (wife). *Witnesses:* JOHN LINTON, JOHN CHESTER, SAMUEL COAKSON. *Clerk of the Court:* WILLIAM ORMOND.

BROWNE, JOHN.   Chowan County.

November 28, 1718. October 21, 1718. *Wife:* ANNE. *Stepson:* JACOB PRITCHARD. *Witnesses:* JAMES ROBERTSON, ELIZA SWANN, EDW'D MOSELEY. *Clerk of the Court:* R. HICKS. *Remarks:* The date of probate of this will is prior to date of signing.

BROWNE, WALTER.   Bertie County.

October 17, 1735. February Court, 1735. *Son:* JOSIAH BROWNE ("dwelling plantation"). *Cousin:* JESSE DRAKE. *Wife:* MARY BROWNE ("plantation on the South side of Cattawaske marsh"). *Executrix:* MARY BROWNE. *Witnesses:* JESSE BROWNE, JOHN BATTLE, JOHN BROWNE. *Clerk of the Court:* JOHN WYNN. *Remarks:* The date of probate is evidently incorrect, as the will is dated eight months later. Probably this date was 1736, as the will was recorded March 2, 1736.

BROWNING, JOHN.   Albemarle County.

April 29, 1723. September 4, 1733. *Wife:* MARGETT. *Son:* JOHN (plantation 250 acres). *Daughters:* ELIZABETH BROWNING, DARKESS. *Executors:* WIFE, son JOHN BROWNING, MR. COLLIN POLLOCK. *Witnesses:* THOS. HOBBS, JOHN COOTHEN. Will proven before W. LITTLE, C. J.

BRYAN, ANNE.   Craven County.

October 25, 1767. March 9, 1773. *Sons:* WILLIAM, JOHN and JESSE. *Daughters:* MARY COOK and ELIZABETH DAWSON. *Grandsons:* JOSEPH STOCKLEY and JOHN DAWSON. *Executors:* WILLIAM, JOHN and JESSE BRYAN (sons). *Witnesses:* JAMES CARRAWAY, ANN CARRAWAY, ELIES JUSTES, GIDEON CARRAWAY. Proven before JO. MARTIN.

ABSTRACT OF WILLS, 1690—1760.

BRYAN, EDWARD.   Craven County.

January 28, 1745. May 9, 1746. *Sons:* JOHN BRYAN (220 acres land bought of Martin and Edward Frank, called "New Germany"), WILLIAM BRYAN (300 acres land, called "New Germany"), EDWARD BRYAN (lot in Newbern). *Daughter:* PENELIPY BRYAN (lot in Newbern). *Wife:* ANN BRYAN ("one plantation, called paradice"). *Executors:* ANN BRYAN (wife), HARDY BRYAN (brother), LEWIS BRYAN (brother). *Witnesses:* WM. WHITFORD, JANE HAND, RICHARD HART. Will proven before E. HALL, Chief Justice of North Carolina.

BRYAN, HARDY.   Craven County.

February 28, 1760. May 6, 1760. *Sons:* THOMAS, WILLIAM, HARDY (one-half of manor, including houses), NATHAN, LEWIS (lots in Newbern), ISAAC. *Daughter:* MARY (front lot in Newbern). *Wife:* SARAH. *Executors:* THOMAS and WILLIAM BRYAN (sons). *Witnesses:* JAMES REED, SHADRACH ALLEN, MATTHEW ARTER. Will proven before ARTHUR DOBBS.

BRYAN, SIMON.   Bertie County.

November 26, 1751. May Court, 1753. *Son:* DAVID. *Wife:* ANN. *Brother:* EDWARD BRYAN. *Executors:* ANN BRYAN (wife), EDWARD BRYAN (brother) and DAVID BRYAN (son). *Witnesses:* MARTHA BRYAN, ISABEL DEAL, JAS. LOCKHART, LILLINGTON LOCKHART. *Clerk of the Court:* BENJ. WYNNS. The will mentions three children, but names only one.

BRYAN, THOMAS.   County not given.

December 1, 1760. *Wife:* RACHEL BRYAN. *Daughters:* SARAH and ANN BRYAN. *Executors:* RACHEL BRYAN, WM. BRYAN (brother of testator) and JOHN LAVENDER. *Witnesses:* SARAH BRYAN, HARDY BRYAN, WM. WHITE. No probate appears.

BRYAN, WILLIAM.   Craven County.

December 12, 1746. June Court, 1747. *Wife:* ANNE. *Sons:* WILLIAM, LEWIS, JOHN, JESS. *Daughters:* ELIZABETH and ANNE. *Executors:* ANNE BRYAN (wife), JOSEPH BRYAN (brother) and WILLIAM BRYAN (son). *Witnesses:* LAZARUS PEARSE, JAMES CARRAWAY, WILLIAM CARRAWAY, JR. *Clerk of the Court:* WILL HEDGES.

BRYANT, JAMES.   Bertie Precinct.

March 11, 1731. *Son:* WILLIAM BRYANT. JOHN DEW, RICHARD BRASWELL, JAMES BRYANT, THOMAS BRYANT and MATTHEW TELAR are named as *children*. *Executors:* JOHN DEW and JAMES BRYANT. *Witnesses:* ARON DRAKE and JOHN DANIEL. No probate.

BRYANT, JOHN.   Edgecombe County.

September 14, 1734. May Court, 1735. *Wife:* ELIZABETH. *Sons:* WILLIAM BRYANT (tract of land known by the name of Ballards), ARTHUR BRYANT and DAVID HOPPER. *Friend:* JAMES TURNER. *Executors:* WM. BRYANT and DAVID HOPPER (sons). *Witnesses:* ROBT. REDFORD, ARCHBALD THOMPSON and ANN FRAZIER. *Clerk of the Court:* ———(?).

BRYANT, WILLIAM.   Edgecombe County.

September 21, 1749. February Court, 1749. *Sons:* JOSEPH, WILLIAM. *Daughter:* PATIENCE ("my house, land and plantation"), SARAH MYHAND. *Grandson:* JAMES MCDANIEL. *Friends:* THOMAS HUYANDINE. *Executors:* ABRAM DEW and EDWARD BROWN. *Witnesses:* THOS. POPE, WM. ANDREWS, JAMES MYHAND. *Clerk of the Court:* BENJ'N WYNNS.

BUCKLY, ELENDER.   Pasquotank County.

February 26, 1704. April 17, 1705. *Sons:* HENRY, JORGE. *Daughter:* ELIZABETH BUCKLY. *Executor:* SON (not named). *Witnesses:* WM. SIMSON, MARY SIMSON, JOANA PRITCHARD. *Clerk of the Court:* THOS. ABINGTON.

BUCK, JOHN.   County not given.

June 27, 1710. *Sons-in-law:* LEM'LL. BARBER and JACOB BARBER (all lands after wife's decease). JOSHUA BARBER (son to CHARLEY BARBER), BENJAMIN TULLE. *Executrix:* ANNE BUCK. *Witnesses:* RICHD. THEARSSE, ELIZA BEAY and JNO. WICKER. *Clerk of the Court:* ROBERT BUCKNER.

BUGNION, RALPH.   New Hanover County.

December, 1751. February 25, 1754. *Wife and Executrix:* ELIZABETH. *Sister:* MARGARET BUGNION. *Witnesses:* CALEB GRAINGER, JOHN DAVIS, JUNR. *Clerk of the Court:* ISAAC FARIES.

BUMPAS, JOB.   Onslow County.

September 5, 1746. October, 1746. *Sons:* DAVID (200 acres of land on the North East of New River adjoining the Desert), CORNELIUS (300 acres of land on the North side of the North East of New River with a grist mill on the same), JOHN (320 acres of land on the South side of the North East of New River). *Daughter:* ABIGGAIL LEWIS. *Executors:* DAVID and CORNELIUS BUMPAS (sons). *Witnesses:* ELMAR ANDERSON, TABAS BUMPAS, ANN HALL. *Clerk of the Court:* WILL HEDGES.

BUN, JOHN.   Bertie County.

January 27, 1727. *Sons:* JOHN (300 acres land on South side Orreroy Swamp), DAVID ("plantation lying in Verjenea"), BENJAMIN ("plantation

ABSTRACT OF WILLS, 1690—1760. 55

where I now live"). *Daughter:* ANN. *Wife and Executrix:* ELEANER BUN. *Witnesses:* WM. RICH, RICHARD HAREN, WILLIAM BUN. (Two wills, one original and one copy.) No probate.

BUNDY, ANNE.   Pasquotank County.

November 16, 1743. December, 1744. *Sons:* GIDEÒN (wife MIRIAM), ABRAHAM. *Granddaughter:* LYDIA BUNDY. *Executors:* GIDEON and ABRAHAM BUNDY (sons). *Witnesses:* JACOB OVERMAN, ABRAHAM HENDRICK, THOS. WILKES. *Clerk of the Court:* THOS. TAYLOR.

BUNDY, BENJAMIN.   Pasquotank County.

October 5, 1728. October 26, 1728. *Wife:* HANNAH BUNDY (plantation of 1,200 acres). *Brother:* SAMUEL BUNDY. *Executors:* HANNAH BUNDY and SAMUEL BUNDY. *Witnesses:* ZACHARIAH FEILD, THOMAS WOODLEY, JOHN PHITT. Will proven before C. GALE, C. J.

BUNDY, CALEB.   Pasquotank Precinct.

Brothers: WILLIAM and JOHN BUNDY. *Executor:* WILLIAM BUNDY (brother). *Witness:* RUTH RECTON. *Clerk pro tem. of the Court:* J. PALIN.

BUNDY, CALEB.   Pasquotank Precinct.

April 27, 1721. *Sons:* JOHN ("land I bought of THOMAS STANTON"), BENJAMIN ("tract of land whereon I now dwell"), SAMUEL ("all my land up Little River"). *Daughter:* MARY BUNDY ("tract of land I bought of my brother SAMUEL BUNDY"). *Granddaughter:* LIDAY BUNDY (daughter of son WILLIAM BUNDY). *Executors:* JOHN and BENJAMIN BUNDY (sons). *Witnesses:* THOMAS WOODLEY, RUTH RETTON, JOHN SYMONS. *Clerk of the Court*: EDW'D GALE.

BUNDY, DAVID.   Perquimans County.

January 22, 1749. April Court, 1750. *Brothers:* JEREMIAH, MOSES and CALEB BUNDY. *Uncle:* JOSIAH BUNDY. *Executor:* JOSIAH BUNDY. *Witnesses:* RICHARD SKINNER and GRAHAM SANDERS. *Clerk of the Court:* EDMUND HATCH.

BUNDY, SAMUEL.   Pasquotank County.

January 6, 1737. July Court, 1740. *Friend:* THOMAS NICHOLSON. *Sons:* WILLIAM, ABRAHAM, GIDEON, JOSIAH. *Daughter:* JANE PIKE, wife of BENJAMIN PIKE. *Wife:* ANNE. *Cousin:* SAMUEL BUNDY. *Executors:* ANNE BUNDY (wife) and THOMAS NICHOLSON. *Witnesses:* JOHN NIXON, PHINEAS NIXON, JOSEPH ROBINSON. *Clerk of the Court:* JAMES CRAVEN.

BUNDY, WILLIAM.   Perquimans County.

December 12, 1749. January Court, 1749. *Daughter*: SARAH BARROW ("plantation whereon I now live"). *Wife:* MARY BUNDY. *Executor:*

JOSEPH BARROW (son-in-law). *Witnesses:* THOMAS OVERMAN, CHARLES OVERMAN, PETER MUNDEN. *Clerk of the Court:* EDMUND HATCH. Codicil to this will.

BURGESS, STEPHEN. County not given.

December 19, 1729. January 13, 1729–1730. *Sons:* STEPHEN (plantation called "Beach Reag"), THOMAS (100 acres of land "commonly called Bridg Nack"), ("all the rest of my children one shilling starling money apeas"). *Wife and Executrix:* ELIZABETH. *Witnesses:* GEORGE BRAY, HENRY BRAY, WILLIAM BRAY. *Clerk of the Court:* W. MINSON.

BURGESS, STEPHEN. Pasquotank County.

January 21, 1734–1735. April 13, 1736. *Sons:* THOMAS ("plantation I now live on"), STEPHEN (plantation called Beach Ridge), DAVID (plantation called Bridg Nack). *Wife:* ELIZABETH. *Executors:* ELIZABETH BURGES (wife) and WILLIAM BURGES (brother). *Witnesses:* PETER BROWN, MATTHEW HARENDEEN, SARAH BROWN. *Clerk of the Court:* JAS. SMITH.

BURKETT, JOHN. Perquimans County.

February 4, 1728–1729. March 7, 1728. *Sons:* JOHN, JOSEPH. *Executor:* JOSEPH BURKETT (son). *Witnesses:* CHARLES DENMAN, JOSIAH GILBERT, JANE ALMES. Will proven before RICH'D EVERARD.

BURLEIGH, ROBERT. Wilmington, New Hanover County.

September 12, 1757. *Wife:* SARAH. *Sons:* ROBERT and JAMES. *Executors:* DANIEL DUNBIBIN, CORNELIUS HARNETT. *Witnesses:* SAM'LL GREEN, THOS. JAMES, THOMAS NEWTON. *Clerk of the Court:* JAMES MORAN. Will orders that houses and lots in Wilmington be sold.

BURNASS, JOHN. Onslow County.

March 11, 1741–1742. January Court, 1744. Children mentioned, but not named. *Executor:* JOHN STARKEY. *Witnesses to Will:* JOHN MCGRAH, JACOB BIDDLE, ISAAC EVANS. *Witnesses to Codicil:* STEPHEN LEE, RICH'D ———— and JACOB BIDDLE. *His Majesty's Justices:* JOHN STARKEY, ABM. MITCHELL, JOHN HOWARD. *Clerk of the Court:* ANDR. MURRAY.

BURNBY, JOHN. Pasquotank Precinct.

April 8, 1705. August 19, 1707. *Son:* JOHN. *Grandson:* JOHN MASON. *Granddaughters:* MARGUERITT BURNBY, ELIZABETH BURNBY, ELIZABETH COBB, SARAH MASON, MARY MASON. *Wife and Executrix:* ELIZABETH. *Witnesses:* SAMUEL PIKE, GORG ELLES, JOHN CORP. *Clerk of the Court:* THO. ABINGTON.

ABSTRACT OF WILLS, 1690—1760.   57

BURNBY, THOMAS.   Pasquotank County.

May 12, 1687. October 6, 1687. *Wife*: HANNAH. *Brothers:* EDWARD and WILLIAM STANLY, JOHN and WILLIAM BURNBY. *Father:* JOHN BURNBY. *Executrix:* HANNAH BURNBY. *Witnesses:* QUITH CRADDOCK, ELIZABETH MABRY, DORITHY SHILO, JOHN BULL. Proven before SETH SOTHELL.

BURNET, GEORGE.   Bertie County.

September 11, 1752. August Court, 1753. *Wife:* SUSANNA (*Executrix and sole devisee*). *Witnesses*: JOSEPH MINTON, WILLIAM CARTER. *Clerk of the Court:* SAM'L ORMES.

BURNHAM, ELIZABETH.   Currituck County.

April Court, 1755. *Witnesses:* GEORGE BURGES, WILLIS MILLER, PHILIP NORTHERN. *Clerk of the Court:* RICH'D MCCLURE. This will is illegible, except the names above given.

BURNHAM, ESEBEL.   Currituck County.

January 1, 1749–1750. *Sons:* SOLOMON BENNET, JOHN BENNET, NEHEMIAH BENNET. *Daughter:* SUSIAS ABIAR. *Granddaughter:* ISABEL ARMSTRONG. The probate and signatures of testatrix and witnesses are missing.

BURT, MARY, Widow of WM. BURT.   Bertie County.

September 10, 1724. February Court, 1724; January 2, 1724. *Sons:* JAMES and EGO GLYON. *Daughter:* MARY GLYON. *Witnesses:* JOSEPH HUTSON, JAMES KEETER, JOYCE HOKINS. Proven before E. MOSELBY. *Clerk of the Court:* R. W. MILLERTON.

BURTENSHALL, RICHARD.   Tyrrell County.

September 15, 1740. September Court, 1743. *Wife:* MARGARET BURTENSHALL. *Daughters:* SUSANNA COFFT, DOREAS WATTS, ELIZABETH WEST, PRISCILLA SMITH. *Grandson:* RICHARD BURTENSHALL. *Executrix:* MARGARET BURTENSHALL. *Witnesses:* MARY ROGERS, MARY TURNER, JOSHUA TURNER. *Clerk of the Court:* J. J. BARRETT.

BUSBEY, CATHERINE.   Bertie Precinct.

January 22, 1738–1739. February Court, 1738. THEOPHILUS WILLIAMS ("my plantation liing on the North side of Roneoake River"). HESTER WILLIAMS (daughter of THEOPHILUS), JESSE PAGE (1 cow and calf). *Executor:* THEOPHILUS WILLIAMS. *Witnesses:* NEEDHAM BRYAN, H. BATE, SUSAN BRYAN. *Clerk of the Court:* JNO. WYNNS.

BUSH, WILLIAM, SR.   Chowan Precinct.

April 5, 1716. October Court, 1716. *Sons:* WILLIAM ("that plantation whereon he now lives"), JOHN ("plantation whereon I now live"). *Daughters:* MARY EARLY, MARTHA WILLIAMS, ROSE WINNS, ELINORE MACLENDAN (one shilling each), ELIZABETH BUSH. *Wife and Executrix:* MARTHA BUSH. *Witnesses:* WILLIAM CRANFORD, JOHN SMITH. *Clerk of the Court:* R. HICKS.

BUTLER, JACOB.   Chowan County.

May 24, 1745. *Wife:* MARY. *Son:* CHRISTOPHER BUTLER (dwelling and plantation). *Daughter:* SARAH BUTLER. *Grandson:* JACOB SIMONS. *Executors:* CHRISTOPHER BUTLER (son) and MARY BUTLER (wife). *Witness:* CHRIS'R BUTLER. *Clerk of the Court:* JOS. CRAVEN. This will is proven by affidavits of JOSEPH MING and DAVID BUTLER.

BUTLER, DAVID.   Chowan County.

August 13, 1742. October Court, 1749. *Wife and Executrix:* MARY (all land and estate of testator in trust for children). *Witnesses:* NATHANIEL MING, MARTHA MING. *Clerk of the Court:* WILL MEARNS.

BULTER, JOHN.   Tyrrell County.

December 24, 1772. October 14, 1773. *Wife:* ELIZABETH. *Sons:* WILLIAM, JOHN, JAMES (plantation on Turkey Swamp). *Daughters:* PHEREBY MCHENRY (wife of GEORGE AUGUSTUS MCHENRY, "manner plantation"), ELIZABETH JOHNSON, SARAH GARNER, MARTHA CHERRY, MARY LEGGITT. *Granddaughters:* SARAH ANN MCHENRY, SUSANNA MCHENRY, WINEFORD MCHENRY, ELIZABETH CHERRY (daughter of ARTHUR GARNER and SARAH) *Grandsons:* JAMES CHERRY (son of MARTHA), JAMES GARNER (son of ARTHUR and SARAH GARNER), SIMON BUTLER (son of JOHN), JOHN BUTLER (son of JAMES). *Executors:* ELIZABETH BUTLER (wife), JOHN and JAMES BUTLER (sons). *Witnesses:* EDMUND ANDREWS, JOHN WHITEHURST, SOLO. WILSON. Will proven before Jo. MARTIN.

Codicil to Will of JOHN BUTLER: Dated November 5, 1773. *Grandson:* ANDREW BUTLER. *Granddaughter:* ELIZABETH CHERRY. *Daughter:* PHEREBY MCHENRY. *Witnesses:* JACOB HARRIS, SOLO. WILSON.

BUXTON, SAMUEL.   Northampton County.

February 11, 1743–1744. February Court, 1743. *Sons:* SAMUEL, WILLIAM, GEORGE, JACOB. *Daughters:* ANN BUXTON, PETRONELIA BUXTON (to each of the above-named children is bequeathed five pounds Virginia currency). *Son:* LEWIS ("my plantation and land"). *Wife and Executrix:* ANN. *Witnesses:* ELIZABETH EDWARDS, ISAAC EDWARDS, J. EDWARDS. *Clerk of the Court:* I. EDWARDS.

BYRD, JOHN.   Chowan County.

September 13, 1716. October Court, 1716. *Son:* JOHN ("tract of land, 640 acres lying at New Market). *Son:* EDWARD (365 acres land), WILLIAM (365 acres land). *Son:* RICHARD ("plantation I now live upon"). *Wife:* REBECCA. *Daughter:* ANNE. *Executors:* REBECCA BYRD and JOHN HARDY. *Witnesses:* JNO. CRAMBIE, SUSANNAH WILLIAMS, MARY DAMRELL. *Clerk of the Court:* R. HICKS.

BYRD, THOMAS.   Bertie County.

December 14, 1742. February Court, 1742. *Sons:* THOMAS (water mill), EDMAN (still). *Daughters:* HONER BAKER, ELIZABETH JONES, MARGERRIT HOLLOMAN, SARAH BIRD, ANN BIRD. *Wife:* ELIZABETH (*Executrix*). *Witnesses:* CHRISFOR HALLOMON, THOMAS BAKER, ANTHO. WEBB. *Clerk of the Court:* HENRY DESON. Court held at the house of John Collins.

BYROM, THOS.   Pasquotank County.

March 13, 1709–1710. *Friend:* BENJAMIN WEST. *Executors:* JOHN PALIN, BENJAMIN WEST. *Witnesses:* ARTHUR HATCH, BARTHOLEMEW HEWITT. Coat of arms seal. No probate.

CAIN, HARDY.   Edgecombe County.

December 21, 1754. May Court, 1755. *Daughters:* ISABELL CAIN ("plantation whereon I now live"), PLURITY. *Wife and Executrix:* RACHEL. *Brother and Executor:* JAMES CAIN. *Witnesses:* WALLIS JONES, JAMES CORRELL. *Clerk of the Court:* JOS. MONTFORT.

CAIN, JOHN.   Edgecombe County.

February 9, 1755. February Court, 1757. *Sons:* JONATHAN, ABIJAH (dwelling plantation). *Daughter:* ZIPPORAH. *Executor:* JONOTHAN CAIN (son). *Witnesses:* JAS. DEHORTY, JOHN TANNER, REBEKAH DEHORTY. *Clerk of the Court:* JOS. MONTFORT.

CAIN, WILLIAM.   Bertie Precinct.

March 3, 1732. *Sons:* HARDY ("my plantation"), WILLIAM (290 acres of land), JAMES (upper part of dwelling plantation). *Daughters:* PATIENCE CAIN, UNIS CAIN, SARY CAIN, RACHELL CAIN. *Wife and Executrix:* ELIZABETH. *Witnesses:* RICHARD PACE, JUNR., WILLIAM CANE. No probate.

CALDWELL, ROBERT.   Bladen County.

March 24, 1749. June 20, 1750. *Brother:* JOSHUA CALDWELL. Wife and two sons mentioned, but not named. *Friend:* WILLIAM NEALE. *Executors:* JOSHUA CALDWELL (brother), JOSEPH CLARK. *Witnesses:* GERSHAN BENBOW, JOHN LEARY, SAMUEL NEALE. *Clerk of the Court:* THOS. ROBESON.

CALLAWAY, CALEB.   County not given.

June 10, 1706. June 13, 1706. *Son and Executor:* JOSUA (plantation on Yawpim). *Daughter:* RACHEL, wife of JOHN WIATT. *Granddaughter:* ELIZABETH WIATT, daughter of JOHN WIATT (one negro). *Wife:* ELIZABETH. *Witnesses:* THOMAS LONG, JOHN BARROW, ANTHONY WHERRY. *Clerk of the Court:* THOS. SNODEN.

CALLAWAY, JOSHUA.   Perquimans County.

February 23, 1741. July Court, 1742. *Sons:* THOMAS ("plantation whereon he now lives"), JOHN, CALEB. *Daughter:* ELIZABETH HARMAN. *Granddaughter:* ELIZABETH CALLAWAY (daughter of CALEB). *Wife and Executrix:* ELIZABETH. *Executor:* JOHN CALLAWAY (son). *Witnesses:* WILLIAM WYATT, THOMAS LONG, JOHN STEPNEY.

CALLIO, JOSEPH.   County not given.

April 29, 1719. July 22, 1719. *Wife and daughter:* JANE and ELIZABETH CALLIO (*Executors*). *Witnesses:* THOMAS HARRYS, ADAM MOORE, LOUIS THOMAS. Recorded in Book 1712–1722, page 217. Original missing.

CAMBRELL, ALEXANDER.   Chowan Precinct.

February 4, 1726. February 21, 1726. *Wife and Executrix:* ANNE. *Daughter:* SARAH CAMBRELL. *Executor:* WILLIAM COTRELL. *Witnesses:* ROBERT JEFFRYS, PAUL BUNCH, THOMAS MUNS. Will proven before RICH'D EVERARD.

CAMBRIDGE, FRANCIS.   Upper Parish of Nansemond County.

February 2, 1710. *Wife and Executrix:* ELIZABETH. *Witnesses:* ANDREW ROSS, JAMES HAWARD, JNO. SUMNER. Recorded in Book 1712–1722, page 36. Original missing.

CAMBRILL, ANNE.   Chowan Precinct.

February 16, 1726. February 21, 1726. *Sole devisee and legatee:* DAUGHTER (not named). *Witnesses:* ROBERT JEFFREYS, THOMAS SMITH. Will proven before RICH'D EVERARD.

CAMERLEN, DANIEL.   Northampton County.

January 7, 1747. May Court, 1752. *Son:* PHILIP ALEXANDER CAMERLEN. *Daughters:* RACHEL CAMERLEN, ANN WHITLEY, BRIDGET GODWIN, ELEZIN TEWE, MARY BEST, ELISABETH WHITLEY. *Grandson:* JOSEPH GODWIN. *Granddaughter:* BELASON. *Wife and Executrix:* ANN. *Witnesses:* WILLIAM WHITLEY, JOSHUA WILLIAMS. *Clerk of the Court:* I. EDWARDS.

CAMPBELL, HUGH. County not given.

January 28, 1737. February 20, 1737. *Executors:* ROGER MOORE, ELEAZAR ALLEN. *Wife and Executrix:* MAGDALEN CAMPBELL. *Witnesses:* CORNELIUS HARNETT, RICHARD SHAW. Will proven before GAB. JOHNSTON. No devisees or legatees in this will.

CAMPBELL, JAMES. New Hanover County.

July 30, 1759. October 10, 1759. Wilmington. *Brothers:* WILLIAM CAMPBELL (½ of land on North West Brown Marsh, one lot in Wilmington on Market Street, also 3 other lots in Wilmington), ROBERT CAMPBELL (other half of lands on Brown Marsh, three lots in Wilmington), SAMUEL (tract of land on Hammond Creek in Bladen Co.), lots in Wilmington. *Executors:* MOTHER (not named) and WILLIAM CAMPBELL (brother). *Witnesses:* MARMADUKE JONES, CALEB GRAINGER, MOSES JNO. DEROSSET. Will proven before ARTHUR DOBBS at Brunswick.

CAMPBELL, JOHN. New Hanover County.

February 4, 1770. May 16, 1770. *Wife and Executrix:* MARY. *Daughters:* MARY CAMPBELL, RACHEL CAMPBELL, ANN CAMPBELL. *Executor:* HENRY TOOMER. *Witnesses:* THOS. HENDERSON, ROBERT WEIR, DAVID ROSS. Will proven before WM. TRYON at Wilmington. Executrix qualified before CORNELIUS HARNETT, *Justice of the Peace.*

CAMPBELL, WILLIAM. Beaufort County.

October 8, 1743. March Court, 1743. *Wife and Executrix:* ANN. *Son:* WILLIAM ("all my lands"). *Son-in-law:* JOHN LEWINTON. *Brother-in-law:* JOHN BARROW. *Witnesses:* MARY HOWARD, JOHN EVERTON, ROBERT HOWARD. *Clerk of the Court:* M. GOOLD. (?)

CANADY, RICHARD. Tyrrell County.

April 20, 1744. October 23, 1749. *Son:* JOHN ("plantation whereon I now live"). *Daughter:* KEZIA. *Wife:* KATHERINE. *Executors:* JOHN CANADAY (son) and STEVENS LEE. *Witnesses:* RICHARD DRAPER, EVAN JONES. *Clerk of the Court:* JOSIAH HART. Executors qualified before STEVENS LEE.

CANADY, SAMUEL. County not given.

January 2, 1727-1728. *Sons:* WILLIAM, SAMUEL ("my manor plantation"). *Daughter:* ELIZABETH. *Executors:* WILL BENETT and JOHN BARFIELD. *Witnesses:* JOHN PUFFIELDS, MARGRET WASTANDS, JOHN SMITH. No probate.

CANLEPI, MICHAEL. Craven County.

October 31, 1743. December 22, 1743. *Godson and Executor:* JOHN FONVILLE. *Witnesses:* JOSEPH HANNIS, JOSEPH HANNIS, SR., JNO. MARTIN. *Clerk of the Court:* N. ROUTLEDGE.

CANNINGS, JOSEPH. Albemarle County.

October 12, 1728. September 22, 1729. *Wife and Executrix:* REBEKA. *Friends:* JOSHUA TURNER and MARY TURNER (gold ring to each). *Witnesses:* JONATHAN BATEMAN, THOMAS BATEMAN, ELIZABETH BATEMAN. Will proven before RICH'D EVERARD.

CANNON, EDWARD. Beaufort and Hyde Precinct.

June 10, 1729. *Sons:* EDWARD, DENNIS, WILLIAM, HENRY, DAVID, JOHN ("my plantation"). *Daughters:* MARGARET, SARAH WOODARD, JANE, MARY, OLIF, RUTH. *Wife and Executrix:* SARAH. *Witnesses:* JOHN KNOWIS, JOHN LAWHON, RICHARD ABEL. *Clerk of the Court:* JNO. MATLOCK.

CAPPS, DENNIS. Currituck County.

April Court, 1749. *Sons:* EDWARD ("land he now lives on"), MOSES ("eastern part of my land"), WILLIAM ("western part of my land"), HENRY (one shilling), DENNIS (one shilling), PHILLIP ("all ye rest of my estate"). *Grandson:* ENOCH CAPPS. *Daughters:* SARAH BARRY, MILLBOROUGH BRYAN, MARY STRIPES, ELIZABETH CAPPS. *Executors:* WIFE (not named), MOSES CAPPS (son). *Witnesses:* ROBERT SIMMONS, WILLIS SIMMONS, ELIAS CORNISH, DOYLEY LATTER. *Clerk of the Court:* RICHARD MCCLURE.

CAR, PATRICK. Bertie County.

November 7, 1742. February Court, 1742. *Sons:* JONATHAN ("plantation whereon I now live"), THOMAS. *Daughter:* MARGARET CAR. *Wife and Executrix:* TAMAR. *Executor:* RICHARD WILLIAMS. *Witnesses:* MICAJAH HINTON, ELIZABETH BENTON, ROSANNAH WOOD. *Clerk of the Court:* HENRY DESON.

CARLETON, ARTHUR. Chowan Precinct.

January 9, 1718–1719. April 22, 1719. *Wife:* (mentioned, but not named). *Witnesses:* JAMES WARD, WM. HOUGHTON, WM. GROSSVENOR. *Clerk of the Court:* R. HICKS.

CARMAN, WILLIAM. County not given.

August 12, 1725. November 1, 1727. *Wife and Executrix:* ELIZABETH. *Granddaughters:* ANN CARMAN and SARAH SIMMONS. *Witnesses:* TIMOTHY WINSLOE, WILLIAM TATE, GILBERT ———. Will proven before RICH'D EVERARD.

Abstract of Wills, 1690—1760. 63

CARR, WILLIAM.   Duplin County.

December 5, 1753. October Court, 1754. *Son:* ARCHBALD (plantation and houses). *Daughter:* JANE CARR. *Wife and Executrix:* HANNAH. *Witnesses:* JOHN DICKSON, WILLIAM MCREE, SUSANNAH MCALEXANDER. *Clerk of the Court:* JOHN DICKSON.

CARRAWAY, JAMES.   Craven County.

March 9, 1773. *Sons:* ENOCH (100 acres of land on Bay River), FRANCIS (150 acres of land on Bay River), JOSEPH, GIDEON. *Daughters:* NANCY, FANNY. *Wife:* ANN. *Executors:* JOSEPH and GIDEON CARRAWAY (sons). *Witnesses:* THOS. NELSON, THOMAS CARRAWAY, JESSE BRYAN. Will proven before JO. MARTIN.

CARRUTHERS, JOHN.   Perquimans County.

February 2, 1751–1752. April Court, 1752. *Wife and Executrix:* ELIZABETH ("plantation whereon I now dwell lying on Yopim"). *Brothers:* JAMES and JACOB (tract of land on Deadman's Swamp), NATHANIEL and ROBERT (land up Roanoke). *Executor:* JOHN WILKINS. *Witnesses:* J. HALSEY, DEBROH WILKINS, JAMES BRINKLEY. *Clerk of the Court:* EDMUND HATCH.

CARRUTHERS, JOHN.   Craven County.

September 20, 1751. February Court, 1752. *Daughters:* SARAH RICE (gold buttons), ROCKSOLANAH WITHERINTON (1 lot in Newbern joining Pollock Street and Eding Street, known as No. 98), FRANCES HODGES (cattle and one slave). *Sons:* JOHN ("riding sadal & bridle, one pr. large money seals and silver shu-buckels and Knee Buckels"), JOSEPH (6 large silver tea spoons, silver tea tongs and strainer and four large silver spoons), WILLIAM. *Sons-in-law:* FRANCES HODGES and JOHN WITHERINTON. *Wife:* CONTENT. All lands and lots in Newbern (including the two where "the long house stands"), together with slaves, ordered to be sold and proceeds divided among three sons. *Executors:* JOHN and JOSEPH (sons). *Witnesses:* SARAH BETSWORTH, ABIAH BANGS, SOL. REW. *Clerk of the Court:* PHIL. SMITH.

CARRUTHERS, NATHANIEL.   Perquimans County.

June 22, 1745. January Court, 1750. *Sons:* JAMES, JACOB and JOHN. *Executors:* JAMES and JOHN CARRUTHERS (sons). *Witnesses:* JOHN STEPNEY, JOHN RONSHAM, JACOB CARRUTHERS. *Clerk of the Court:* EDMUND HATCH. *Justice of the Peace:* PETER PAYNE.

CARRUTHERS, ROBERT.   Newbern, Craven County.

March 14, 1758. March 27, 1758. *Wife and Executrix:* UNICE. *Daughter:* LYDIA RALIER. (To these two is devised "all my lotts in New Bern and all my land in this Province.") *Witnesses:* MICH SMITH, THOS. HASLEN, RD. COGDELL. Will proven before ARTHUR DOBBS at New Bern.

CARTER, ANN.   Onslow County.

July 21, 1770. July 25, 1770. *Legatees and Devisees:* MARY CLEAREY (of Philadelphia), ABRAHAM DAWS, WILLIAM JAMESON, STEPHEN LEE. *Executors:* WILLIAM JAMESON and STEPHEN LEE. *Witnesses:* EDWARD MOREY, LYDIA GILLESPYE, JOSEPH LITTLEBRIDGE. *Clerk of the Court:* WM. CRAY. Will proven before Gov. WM. TRYON.

CARTER, HENRY.   Bath, Beaufort and Hyde.

February 3, 1735–1736. March 9, 1735. *Sons:* JOHN ("plantation I now live on"), HENRY, SOLOMON, WALTER. *Wife and Executrix:* MARGRET. *Executor:* JOHN CARTER (son). *Witnesses:* EDW'D HADLEY, GILBERT MCNEARY, GILD SILVERTHORN. *Justices:* ROBT. TURNER, SIMON ALDERSON, SETH PILKINTON. *Clerk of the Court:* JOHN COLLISON.

CARTWRIGHT, GRACE.   Pasquotank Precinct.

December 30, 1728. June 3, 1729. *Daughter:* ELIZABETH TRUEBLOOD. *Son:* JOSEPH. *Other legatees:* JOSIAH TRUEBLOOD, JOSHUA TRUEBLOOD, JOHN TRUEBLOOD, ELIZABETH TRUEBLOOD, MIRIAM TRUEBLOOD, ELIZABETH MURDEN, JEREMIAH MURDEN, MARY MURDEN, JOHN MURDEN, JOB CARTWRIGHT, SENR, BENJAMIN CARTWRIGHT (son of Joseph), ELIZABETH CARTWRIGHT (daughter of Joseph), THOMAS CARTWRIGHT (son of THOMAS). *Executor:* JOSEPH CARTWRIGHT (son). *Witnesses:* BENJAMIN MILLER, WILLIAM LEWIS, MARTHA LEWIS. Will proven before RICHARD EVERARD.

CARTWRIGHT, JOHN.   Pasquotank Precinct.

April 23, 1714. *Brothers:* JOB CARTWRIGHT, THOS. CARTWRIGHT, JOS. CARTWRIGHT. *Sisters:* ELIZA CARTWRIGHT, CATHERINE CARTWRIGHT. *Friend:* JOHN MURDEN (son of JERROM MURDEN). *Executors:* THOMAS and JOB CARTWRIGHT (brothers). *Witnesses:* GRAN CARTWRIGHT, WILL NORRIS. No probate.

CARTWRIGHT, ROBERT.   Pasquotank County.

April 15, 1746. July Court, 1746. *Sons:* HEZEKIAH ("plantation whereon I now live"), JOSIAH, EZEKIEL. *Daughter:* MARTHA CARTWRIGHT. *Grandson:* CLAUDIUS CARTWRIGHT. *Wife and Executrix:* MARTHA. *Executor:* HEZEKIAH CARTWRIGHT (son). *Witnesses:* JAMES PIKE, EDWARD TADLOCK, JOS. MARTIN. *Clerk of the Court:* THOS. TAYLOR.

CARTWRIGHT, THOMAS.   Pasquotank Precinct.

March 4, 1706. April 15, 1707. *Sons:* THOMAS, ROBERT, JOB, JOHN, WILLIAM. *Daughters:* CATREN, MARY, ELISABETH. *Wife and Executrix:*

GRACE CARTWRIGHT. *Executor:* JOHN CARTWRIGHT (son). *Witnesses:* THOMAS TWIDDY, GEORGE HARRIS and WILLIAM WARREN. *Clerk of the Court:* THO. ABINGTON.

CARTWRIGHT, WILLIAM. Chowan or Pasquotank County.

February 2, 1731. February 16, 1730. *Brothers:* ROBERT and THOMAS. *Other legatees:* OWEN REES, HANNAH STAFFARD, JOSEPH STOCKLEY, MARY REES (sister), ELIZABETH CLARK. *Executors:* JEREMIAH MURDEN and STEPHEN DELEMARE. *Witnesses:* ELISABETH CLARK, JONATHAN HIBBS, MARY MURDEN. Proven before RICHARD EVERARD.

CARTRIGHT, WILLIAM. Pasquotank County.

January 15, 1733. April Court, 1734. *Sons:* THOMAS, ROBERT, JOSEPH ("plantation whereon I now dwell"), CALEB and DAVID (land called the Sandy Run), JOHN. *Daughters:* HANNAH CARTRIGHT ("land above the pigpens"), TAMER CARTRIGHT (tract of land called the Little For). *Other legatees:* OEN RESE, ELIZABETH CARTRIGHT, daughter of son JOHN, deceased (forty acres of land on the South side of the Creek swamp known by the name of Maverts). *Wife and Executrix:* SARAH. *Witnesses:* EDWARD WHORTEN, JOHN RICHARDSON, JAMES GREAVES. *Clerk of the Court:* JOSEPH ANDERSON.

CARVER, JAMES. Bladen Precinct.

May 7, 1738. June 7, 1739. *Sons and Executors:* JAMES (land on North side of the North West River), Samuel. *Daughters:* MARY BENBOW, ANN CARVER. *Wife and Executrix:* ELIZABETH. *Witnesses:* RICHARD HELLIER, ANN HELLIER. Will proven before GAB. JOHNSTON.

CARVER, JAMES. Bladen County.

February 27, 1753. June Court, 1753. *Son:* JOB (house and land "where I now live"). *Daughter:* ELIZABETH CARVER. *Brother:* SAMUEL CARVER. *Executors:* SAMUEL CARVER (brother) and ELIZABETH CARVER (wife). *Witnesses:* RICHARD MALLINGTON, PATRICK MCCONKEY, GEORGE WILLISS. *Clerk of the Court:* THOS. ROBESON. The testator devises two acres of land "where the meeting house now stands," "to our society of People called Quakers."

CARVER, SAMUEL. Bladen County.

April 23, 1758. July Court, 1758. *Wife and Executrix:* ARCADIA. *Sons:* SAMUEL ("plantation whereon I now live"), JAMES (lot in Wilmington). *Daughters:* SARAH and MARY CARVER. *Brother:* WILLIAM MAULTSBY. *Witnesses:* SAML. MILHOUS, CHARLES BENBOW, RICHARD MARLINGTON. *Clerk of the Court:* C. BURGWIN.

CASTELLAW, WILLIAM.   Bertie County.

June 18, 1749. August Court, 1749. *Mother and Executrix:* SARAH CASTELLAW. *Brothers:* JOHN, JAMES and THOMAS CASTELLAW. *Sisters:* BATHIAH, SARAH and KATHERINE CASTELLAW. *Executor:* THOS. WHITMELL. *Witnesses:* SARAH SANDERSON, HARDY MOORE. *Clerk of the Court:* JOHN LOVICK.

CASWELL, RICHARD.   Dobbs County.

July 2, 1789. January Court, 1790. Revokes will made at death of son, WILLIAM CASWELL. One-half acre of ground reserved as burying ground at place called "The Hill," where mother and father are buried; one-half acre near "Red House," where wife and son WILLIAM are buried. Disclaims any interest in land of MARTIN CASWELL. SAMUEL CASWELL and NATHANIEL BIRD mentioned. Land near MRS. SHINES' dwelling to ELEANOR CASWELL, wife of SAMUEL CASWELL, dec'd, until her son SHINE CASWELL becomes of age. *Grandsons:* RICHARD WILLIAM CASWELL and RICHARD FRANCIS MACKILEWEAN. Land bought of RICH'D CASWELL, JR'S., estate to be sold to JONATHAN MORRIS, if he desires it. *Daughter-in-law:* MRS. RICHARD CASWELL, 1½ lots in Kinston. *Granddaughter:* MARY CASWELL, mentioned. *Daughter:* ANNA FONVILLE, land called "Walnut Hill." *Sons:* WINSTON, DALLAM and JOHN. *Daughter:* SUSANNAH. *Executors:* WINSTON, DALLAM and JOHN. *Friend:* JAMES GLASGOW, to advise them. *Friends:* SPYERS SINGLETON, ROBERT WHITE, JOHN HERRITAGE, JESSE COBB, FRANCIS CHILD, SIMON BRIGHT, JOSHUA CROOM, BENJAMIN CASWELL, JOHN COART, to divide all other property into five equal shares, after inventory, one share for wife, SARAH CASWELL, and one share each for WINSTON, DALLAM, JOHN and SUSANNAH CASWELL.

* A codicil includes further disposition of property to sons WINSTON, DALLAM and JOHN, and daughters ANNA and SUSANNAH. *Witnesses:* SIMON BRIGHT, JAMES BRIGHT. *Clerk of Court:* N. CASWELL.

Attested as a true copy of will on file in office of Clerk of the Court of Lenoir County, July 20, 1799.   S. BRIGHT, *Clerk.*

CASWELL, MATTHEW.   Tyrrell County.

March 24, 1754. June Court, 1754. *Sons:* MATTHEW (plantation "formerly belonging to Edward Phelps"), SAMUEL ("my Log house plantation"), ELISHA ("my manner plantation"). *Daughters:* JOANNA (land called the Red Banks), ELIZABETH CASWELL (plantation known by the name of Briffit's Island and also land on Scuppernong River), TABITHA CASWELL (land known by the name of the Loghouse land adjoining brother Samuel). *Other legatee:* CASWELL HASSELL. *Wife and Executrix:* ELIZABETH. *Executors:* SAMUEL SPRUILL (father-in-law) and MATTHEW CASWELL (son). *Witnesses:* JOSHUA TURNER, ROBERT ELTON, EDWD. PHELPS. *Clerk of the Court:* EVAN JONES.

CAVENA, CHARLES.   Edgecombe County.

April 8, 1756. February Court, 1757. *Sons:* DAVID (one shilling), NEEDHAM (50 acres of land on Beech run), AQUILLA (60 acres land on west side of Beech Run), NICOLAS (one shilling), ARTHER (60 acres of land "joining to Needham land on the River"), CHARLES and HENRY ("the remainder of my land"). *Daughter:* MARY CAVENA (300 acres land "on the south side of Northuntee Mach"). *Witnesses:* JOHN FOUNTAINE, JOHN MURPHREE, ABIGAL PITTMAN. *Clerk of the Court:* JAS. MONTFORT.

CAWDREY, THOMAS.   Craven County.

August 1, 1748. December, 1748. *Executor and sole devisee and legatee:* JOHN BROWN. *Witnesses:* PETER GLAIR, PATTERSON GILLETT and JOHN HARPER. *Clerk of the Court:* ———SMITH.

CHADWICK, SAMUEL.   Carteret County.

October 4, 1749. December 5, 1749. *Sons:* THOMAS, JOSIAH, GAYER ("my manner plantation"). *Daughters:* TAMAR CHADWICK, SARAH CHADWICK, MARY CHADWICK. *Wife:* MARY. *Executors:* SAMUEL WHITHURST, THOMAS CHADWICK, ISAIAH CHADWICK. *Witnesses:* JOSEPH BRAY, REBECKAH CHADWICK, RACHEL YOUNG. *Clerk of the Court:* GEO. READ.

CHALKHILL, JOHN.   New Hanover County.

November 14, 1757. February Court, 1758. *Wife:* DORCAS. *Daughters:* MARY (my ring), LYDIA. *Wife's daughter:* RACHEL HOWISON. *Executors:* GEORGE MOORE and WM. DRY. *Witnesses:* RD. HARDY, DAVID BROWN, MARGARET MCCORKHILL. *Clerk of the Court:* JA. MORAN.

CHAMBERLAIN, JOHN.   Pasquotank County.

January 10, 1743-1744. April Court, 1753. *Sons:* JOHN ("plantation whereon I now live"), WILLIAM (land on Brights Branch), JEREMIAH ("plantation joining upon his grandfather's, Jeremiah Everton"). *Daughters:* MARY BRIGHT (wife of ISACK BRIGHT), ANN CHAMBERLIN, BETTIE CHAMBERLIN, LUCY, AMY and MARTHA CHAMBERLIN. *Executors:* JOHN CHAMBERLIN (son) and ISACK BRIGHT. *Witnesses:* SAM'L ETHERIDGE, GABR. BURNHAM, ROBERT CHAMBERLIN, BENJAMIN BURNHAM. *Clerk of the Court:* THOMAS TAYLOR.

CHAMBERS, EDMOND.   County not given.

December 3, 1693. January 2, 1693. *Friend:* FRANCIS HENRY. *Witnesses:* HENRY PALIN, ANN MADREN. *Clerk of the Court:* EDWARD MAYO.

CHAMPION, EDWARD.   Chowan Precinct.

January 6, 1717-1718. April Court, 1718. *Sons:* JOSEPH (land on the West side of Miery Branch), THOMAS (land on the East side of Miery

Branch), EDWARD. *Daughters:* ELIZABETH CHAMPION, MARY CHAMPION *Wife and Executrix:* MARY. *Witnesses:* WILLIAM SADLER, HENRY LISLER. *Clerk of the Court:* R. HICKS.

CHAMPEN, JOHN.   Chowan County.

October 10, 1749. April Court, 1751. *Grandsons:* CHAMPEN SPIVEY, son of NATHANIELL and MARTHA SPIVEY (250 acres land on South side of Stoping Creek), JAMES BLY, son of WILLIAM and ELIZABETH BLY (250 acres land "whereon I now dwell"), PETER COPELAND, son of WILLIAM and SARAH COPELAND (250 acres of land). *Daughter:* MARGRET WARD (250 acres of land). *Wife:* SARRAH. *Executors:* SARAH CHAMPEN (wife), NATHANIEL SPIVEY (son-in-law). *Witnesses:* JOHN ARLIN, MARY ARLIN, ROBT. ELLIOTT. *Clerk of the Court:* JAS. CRAVEN.

CHAMPION, ORLANDO.   Chowan County.

December 13, 1744. January 9, 1744. *Daughter and Executrix:* ELIZABETH NEAL ("plantation I now live on"). *Other legatees and devisees:* MARY, wife of WILLIAM RICHARDS; ANN, the wife of JOSEPH ANDERSON; EDWARD CHAMPION (brother), WILLIAM RICHARDS. *Executors:* JOSEPH ANDERSON and JOSEPH BLOUNT. *Witnesses:* NATHANIEL MATTHEWS, JOHN VERLIN, JAMES FENNISON. *Justice:* J. HALSEY. Will proven before GAB. JOHNSTON, *Governor.*

CHANCEY, EDMUND.   Pasquotank County.

March 15, 1753. July Court, 1754. *Grandsons:* EDMUND CHANCEY, son of STEPHEN ("easternmost part of my plantation"), EDMUND CHANCEY, son of JACOB ("middlemost part of my plantation"), EDMUND CHANCEY, son of ZACHARIAH ("my Sand Hills land"). *Sons:* DANIEL (a riding horse, saddle and bridle, dozen spoons, pair of brass scales, large Bible and three young horses); ZACHARIAH (one shilling "sterling money to cutt him off from my rail and personal Estate because of the Wickedness that he committed in my House in the time of my Absence"). *Daughter-in-law:* RACHEL CHANCEY (16 barrels of corn, 450 lbs dried meat, 3 gallons fatt, "my wheat patch, all my black pepper and all my flax and wool and one half of my sweetening"). *Granddaughters:* MARY and HANNAH CHANCEY. To JAMES FURBUSH is bequeathed book "No Cross, No Crown." Children of *Daughter* RUTH: JOHN BAKER, MARY DEGRAFINRED, BLAKE BAKER, SARAH, RUTH and ZADOCK BAKER. *Executor:* JOHN BAKER. *Witnesses:* ROBT. HALL, WM. SWANN. *Clerk of the Court:* THOS. TAYLOR.

CHANCEY, WILLIAM.   Pasquotank County.

April 18, 1736. May 13, 1736. *Father:* WILLIAM CHANCEY. *Brother:* JEREMIAH CHANCEY. *Sisters:* ANN BOID, ELESABETH SUTTON, MARY CHANCEY, DEBORAH CHANCEY. *Cousins:* JOSEPH SUTTON, DEBORAH SUTTON,

JOHN SYMONS. *Executors:* JEREMIAH CHANCEY, JOHN BOIDE (brothers). *Witnesses:* JOE SYMONS, MARY LOWRY. Will proven before W. SMITH, C. J.

CHANCEY, WILLIAM. Pasquotank County.

July 17, 1746. August 4, 1749. *Daughters:* ANN WHEEDBEY, MARY COMMANDER, DEBORAH BALEY. *Grandsons:* WILLIAM CHANCEY ("plantation whereon I do now live"), WILLIAM BOYD, WILLIAM CHANCEY COMMANDER, JOSEPH SATTEN, THOMAS BOYD. *Granddaughters:* DEBORAH SATTEN, ELIZABETH BOYD, WINEFRED BOYD, ANN BALEY, MARY BALEY. *Executors:* JOSEPH BALEY and JOSEPH COMMANDER (sons-in-law). *Witnesses:* WILLIAM BROTHERS, DARCUS BROTHERS, ROBERT LOWRY. Will proven before *Gov.* GAB. JOHNSTON at Eden House.

CHAPMAN, CHAS. Northampton County.

May 19, 1753. November Court, 1753. *Sons:* CHARLES (100 acres land), HENRY (100 acres), WILLIAM ("my plantation"), DANIEL HAWKINS (100 acres on East side of cedy branch). *Wife and Executrix:* FRANCIS. *Witnesses:* DANIEL HAWKINS, CHARLES CHAPMAN, HENRY CHAPMAN. *Clerk of Court:* I. EDWARDS.

CHAPMAN, JOHN. Carteret County.

November 2, 1770. December 10, 1770. *Sister and Executrix:* SARAH CHAPMAN ("all my lands"). *Brother and Executor:* SAMUEL CHAPMAN. *Witnesses:* MICAJAH FRAZIER, JOB CALLOWAY. Will proven before *Gov.* WM. TRYON.

CHAPMAN, MARY. Pasquotank County.

September 2, 1728. December 9, 1729. *Daughters:* ELIZABETH LANDWELL, SARAH DAVIS (wife of ROBERT DAVIS). *Granddaughter:* MARY DAVIS. *Executor:* ROBERT DAVIS. *Witnesses:* ABRAHAM WHITE, JER. SYMONS. Will proven before RICHD. EVERARD.

CHAPPEL, RICHARD. Chowan County.

March 5, 1734–1735. October Court, 1735. *Sons:* MOSES, MICHAIAH, RICHARD. *Daughters:* JUDAH and SARAH CHAPPEL. *Wife and Executrix:* ELIZA. *Executor:* MOSES BAKER. *Witnesses:* MICHAEL BRINKLEY, WM. TREVETHAN. *Clerk of the Court:* JAMES CRAVEN.

CHARLES, DANIELL.

April 17, 1687. *Brothers:* JOHN CHARLES, SAMUELL CHARLES. *Sister:* JEANE CHARLES. *Executors:* FRANCIS TOMAS, CHRISTOPHER———. *Witnesses:* DAVID BLAKE, DAVID SHERROD, PETER GREY. No probate.

CHARLES, JOHN.   County not given.

Sisters: JANE and ELIZABETH CHARLES. *Brother*: SAMUEL CHARLES. *Friends*: MARY TONIE and WILLIAM BOGE. No probate. *Endorsement*: "David Sharpe owes me fourteen shillings, John Steyne twenty shillings, Edward Mayo owes me 3 L D."

CHARLES, HANNAH.   Perquimans County.

October 1, 1750. July Court, 1752. *Son*: EDWARD MOUDLIN. *Daughters*: ELISABETH WHITE, SARAH PERRY, ANN COX. *Grandsons*: JOHN MOUDLIN and JOHN COX. *Granddaughters*: MARY MOUDLIN (daughter of JOHN MOUDLIN). *Son-in-law*: ROBERT COX. *Executors*: JOHN MOUDLIN (grandson), ROBERT COX (son-in-law). *Witnesses*: JACOB MARGIN, HANNAH MOUDLIN, DAVENPORT GOODING. *Clerk of the Court*: EDMUND HATCH.

CHARLES, JEANE.   Perquimans Precinct.

July 11, 1688. *Aunt*: MARIE STEPNEY. *Other legatees*: JOHN STEPNEY, *brother and sister* (not named), *father* (not named). *Executors*: CRISTIFER NISBRALE, FRANCES TOMES. *Witnesses*: THOMAS STEELL, JOHN STEELL, JOHN HARLEE. No probate. Coat of arms on seal.

CHARLES, SAMUEL.   Perquimans County.

March 12, 1727–1728. *Sons*: SAMUEL ("plantation whereon I now live), JOHN (tract of land on gum swamp and Bull Branch), JOSUAY (tract of land on gum Swamp). *Daughters*: LIDEY CHARLES, SARAH CHARLES, HANNAUGH. *Granddaughter*: ELIZABETH OAVERMAN. *Executors*: SAMUELL and JOHN CHARLES (sons). *Witnesses*: JOHN KEATTEN, NATHANIEL ALBURT, EDWARD MOUDLIN. *Clerk of the Court*: CHARLES DENMAN.

CHARLES, WILLIAM.   County not given.

April 7, 1687. *Brother*: JOHN CHARLES (120 acres of land). *Daughter*: JANN CHARLES ("plantation I now live on"). *Wife*: ELIZABETH. *Friend*: JAMES HOGG. *Executors*: FRANCIS TOMES (father), JONATHAN PHILIPS. *Witnesses*: JAMES HOGG, DANIELL PINBROW. No probate.

CHARLTON, JOHN.   Chowan Precinct.

May 13, 1735. April 15, 1736. *Sons*: JOB ("plantation whereon I now live"), JOHN (land called "Stacyes"), WILLIAM (fifty pounds). *Wife and Executrix*: SARAH. *Executor*: WILLIAM HASKINS. *Witnesses*: SARAH WARDNAR, RICHARD FITCHJARREL. *Clerk of the Court*: JAMES CRAVEN.

CHEASTEN, RICHARD.   Perquimans County.

October 22, 1715. November 22, 1715. *Wife*: ANNE. *Son*: RICHARD ("all my real estate"). *Grandson*: DANIELL LAYTON. *Executors*: JOSEPH JESSOP, RICHARD CHEASTEN (son). *Witnesses*: ANTHONY HASKIT, TABITHA HASKIT, ANNE HASKIT. *Secretary to the Governor*: J. KNIGHT.

CHEEK, RICHARD.   Beaufort County.

September 29, 1743. April 30, 1745. *Sons:* RANDOLPH ("plantation I now live on"), WILLIAM (150 acres land), JAMES (140 acres of land), JOHN (150 acres land), ROBERT (150 acres of land). *Daughters:* ELIZBETH BURNEY, JANE CHEEK, ANN CHEEK. *Wife:* JANE. *Executors:* WM. CHEEK, RICHARD CHEEK, JR., and JOHN BURNEY. *Witnesses:* WM. HIX, JOHN THIGPEN, ROBT. CHEEK. Will proven before E. MOSELEY, *Chief Justice.* *Clerk of the Court:* JOHN FORBES.

CHERRY, SAMUEL.   Beaufort County.

July 14, 1754. September Court, 1754. *Sons:* JOHN ("manner plantation"), WILLIAM (400 acres land on the Beaverdam), CADO (400 acres of land on Briery Swamp), CHARLES (land on Meadow Branch), SAMUEL, SOLOMON, SAMUEL, GEORGE, WILLIS. *Daughters:* ELIZABETH, ABIGAIL, PATIENCE, MARY and COURTNEY CHERRY, REBECKAH HODGES. *Executors:* JOHN CHERRY (son) amd WM. WILLIS. *Witnesses:* WM. WILLIS, GRIFFIN FLOYD, PETER FLOYD. *Clerk of the Court:* WALLEY CHAUNCY.

CHESTER, JOHN.   Bertie Precinct.

January 22, 1728. February Court, 1728. *Daughters:* ELIZABETH CHESTER (land lying on Apple tree, Meratuck, and a place called frog Hall), MARY CHESHER ("all my tract of land I now live on"), SARAH CHESHER (land "betwixt the land of John Bowds and the land I now live on"). *Son-in-law:* JAMES FALK (land on Buck Horn). *Wife and Executrix:* ELIZABETH. *Executors:* ARTHUR WILLIAMS, JOHN DEW. *Witnesses:* JOSEPH DARDEN, WILLIAM SMITH. *Clerk of the Court:* RT. FORSTER.

CHESSON, ANNE.   Perquimans County.

January 3, 1727. January 17, 1727. *Sons*: JOHN, JAMES and JOSHUA. *Sister:* ESBELL GARRET. *Executors:* DANIEL and WILLIAM GARRETT (brothers). *Witnesses:* JOSEPH OATES, JEAN AMES. Will proven before RICH'D EVERARD.

CHESSON, JAMES.   Perquimans County.

May 19, 1729. *Sons*: JOHN ("all my right of land lying in the crik fork in jowan), JAMES (land "where I now dwell"). *Wife and Executrix:* ANN. *Executor:* WILLIAM EGERTON. *Witnesses:* JEREMIAH PRATT, WILLIAM EGARTON, JOB. PRATT. Will proven before RICH'D EVERARD, *Governor.*

CHESTER, JOHN.   County not given.

December 18, 1733. *Son:* JOHN. *Daughters:* LEATH ADAMS, RACHELL HOCKINGS, MARY CHESTER, SARY CHESTER, ELIZABETH CHESTER. *Son-in-law:* BENJAMIN HOCKINGS. *Executors:* SIMON ALDERSON, WILLIAM ADAMS. *Witnesses:* ANNE JACKSON, PHILO. WILLIAMS. *Clerk of the Court:* JNO. COLLISON.

CHESTER, SAMUEL.　　　　Wilmington, New Hanover County.

October 10, 1758. November Court, 1758. *Wife and Executrix:* MARTHA. *Children:* mentioned, but not named. *Witnesses:* WILLIAM VAUGHAN, WM. WILKINSON, ROBERT FREEMAN. *Clerk of the Court:* JA. MORAN.

CHEVIN, NATHANIEL.　　　　　　　　　Pasquotank Precinct.

March 3, 1719–1720. *Son of wife:* NATHANIEL CALEY. *Other legatees:* DANIEL RICHARDSON, JOHN FARRY, EDW'D BAPER, LEVI MARCUM, CHARLES MARCUM, ROBERT KEELS. *Executors:* DANIEL RICHARDSON and JOHN FARRY. Proven before JOHN PALIN and RICHARD SANDERSON. Recorded in Book 1712–1722, page 219. Original missing.

CHEW, HENRY, SR.　　　　　　　　　　　Carteret County.

May, 1753. March 9, 1758. *Sons:* HENRY, JOSEPH ("plantation whereon I now dwell" and 640 acres of land on Newport River). *Daughters:* SARAH DEAL, JANE PARKER, ELISABETH HUNT. *Friend:* CALEB MARYLAND. *Executors:* JOSEPH CHEW (son) and ELISABETH HUNT (daughter). *Witnesses:* ANN READ, MARY LUDFORD and GEORGE READ. WM. ROBERTSON, *Clerk of the Court.*

CHURCH, JOSEPH.　　　　　　　　　　　Currituck Precinct.

February 28, 1722–1723. April 9, 1723. *Son:* RICHARD. *Daughters:* LEDY WHITE, ANN CHURCH, *Wife and Executrix:* JULIAN. *Executor:* RICHARD CHURCH (son). *Witnesses:* HESTER JARVES, SENR., AZRIAM PARKER, THOMAS PARKER. *Clerk of the Court:* JOS. WICKER.

CLAPHAM, JOSEPH.　　　　　　　　　　Bertie Precinct.

March 25, 1733. May 8, 1733. *Sons:* SAMUELL ("my farm and stock in the parish Dewsbery in Yorkshire in old England"), JOSIAS (plantation lying on Long Marsh at the head of Tuckahoo creek in Queen Anne Co., Maryland, also plantation in Bertie precinct on the Runaray Marshes). *Executor:* JOSIAS CLAPHAM (son). *Witnesses:* JUDETH WALKER, HENRY WALKER, JOHN NAIRNS. *Clerk of the Court:* RT. FORSTER.

CLARE, HANNAH.　　　　　　　　　　　Perquimans Precinct.

August 26, 1726. *Daughters:* HESTER WINSLOW, HANNAH BUNDY (husband BENJAMIN). *Granddaughter:* MARY JONES. *Grandson:* WILLIAM JONES. *Son-in-law and Executor:* BENJAMIN BUNDY. *Witnesses:* JOHN BUNDY, ELIZA BUNDY, JOHN SIMONS. *Clerk of the Court:* THOS. WEEKES.

CLARK, GEORGE. Bertie Precinct.

February 25, 1723-1724. July 31, 1724. *Friends:* THOMAS TAYLOR, JOHN SWAN, JONATHAN TAYLOR. *Wife:* ELISABETH. *Executor:* JONATHAN TAYLOR. *Witnesses:* JNO. SMITHWICK, GEORGE SMITH, PATRICK SMITH. Will proven before C. GALE, *Chief Justice. Clerk of the Court:* JOHN CARNICK.

CLARK, JAMES, SENR. Bladen County.

April 26, 1757. On Cow Branch upon Drowning Creek. This is more a deed of assignment than a will and assigns all right, title and interest of JAMES CLARK of "the plantation I now live upon" to JOHN STACK. *Witnesses:* WILLIAM BARTRAM, JOHN MITCHELL.

CLARKE, JOHN. County not given.

May 30, 1689. *Wife and Executrix:* MARY. *Guardians of children:* DANIEL AKHURST, JOHN WEST and EDWARD SMITH. *Friend:* WILLIAM CURRY. *Witnesses:* HENRY PALIN, SENR., JOHN HAWKINS, JOHN CABEY. Will proven before SETH SOTHELL.

CLARK, JOHN. Perquimans County.

September 3, 1716. November 14, 1717. *Sons:* JOHN and THOMAS (estate divided between them). *Wife:* ANN. *Other legatees:* SIMON and THOMAS TROMBELL, SARAH TROMBELL, ELIZABETH TROMBELL. No Executor named. *Witnesses:* RICHARD SANDERSON, JOHN GRAY, SIMON TRUMBELL. Will proven before CHARLES EDEN.

CLARK, ROBERT. Edgecombe County.

December 12, 1752. August Court, 1753. *Sons:* WILLIAM, MOSES, AARON, ROBERT, LEVI. *Daughters:* ANN TATUM, JEAN CLYBUN, MARY DUGLIS, RACHEL ETHEREDG, AGNESS ETHEREDG, HANNAH UNDERWOOD. *Wife:* JEAN. *Executor:* THOMAS TATUM. *Witnesses:* WM. WIGGONS, MARY WIGGONS. *Clerk of the Court:* BENJ'N WYNNS.

CLARKE, THOMAS. Bertie Precinct.

April 25, 1728. *Sons:* THOMAS, LEWIS, WILLIAM, JOHN, MATTHEW. *Daughters:* ELIZABETH, MARY, GRACE and BRIDGET. *Executors:* WIFE (not named) and THOMAS CLARKE (son). *Witnesses:* NEHEMIAH JOYNER, ELLIS BRADEY, EDWARD HOOD. No probate.

CLAYTON, ELIZABETH. Perquimans County.

January 13, 1737-1738. February 2, 1737. *Daughter:* MARY CLAYTON. *Executors:* JOHN STEVENSON, JOHN BARCLIFT. *Witnesses:* CHRISTIAN REED, BENJAMIN BAPTISTE, MARY DURANT. Will proven before W. SMITH, C. J.

CLAYTON, HENRY.   Chowan Precinct.

January 20, 1725. July 26, 1725. *Wife:* ELIZABETH. *Daughter:* SARAH CLAYTON. *Trustees for daughter:* CHRISTOPHER GALE, JOHN LOVICK and WILLIAM LITTLE (to whom is conveyed tract of land on Perquimans River called the "Vinyard," in trust for daughter SARAH). *Brother:* RICHARD CLAYTON (of London). *Executors:* CHRISTOPHER GALE (father-in-law), JOHN LOVICK and WILLIAM LITTLE. *Witnesses:* WILLIAM WILLIAMS, BARTHALM SCOTT, JOHN―――. Will proven before RICH'D EVERARD, *Governor.* Coat of arms on seal.

CLEARE, TIMOTHY.   Perquimans County.

November 10, 1724. November 17, 1724. *Daughters:* MARY MAYO, ELIZABETH WINSLOWE, JANE JESSOP, SARAH WHITE, HANNAH CLEARE, HEPZIBAH BERRY. *Sons-in-law:* THOS. WINSLOW (his sons, TIMOTHY and JESSE), THOMAS JESSOP. *Grandson:* JOHN ROBINSON. *Wife:* HANNAH. *Executors:* THOS. WINSLOW and THOS. JESSOP (sons-in-law). *Witnesses:* THOMAS BAGLEY, SMITH COLLA, J. JESSOP. *Clerk of the Court:* E. MOSELEY.

CLEMENT, JOHN.   Bertie Precinct.

January 2, 1734. January 29, 1734. *Friends:* JOHN BELL (*Executor*), ARCHIBALD BELL, GEORGE BELL, ROBERT BELL, PENELOPE BELL. *Witnesses:* ROBT. SHARMAN, MIKEL KING, LUCY SHARMAN. Will proven before GAB. JOHNSTON, *Governor*, at Edenton.

CLEMENTS, GEORGE.   Bertie County.

February 22, 1729. May Court, 1730. *Sons:* BENJAMIN and GEORGE. *Daughter:* ELIZABETH CLEMENTS. *Wife and Executrix:* SUSANNA. *Witnesses:* THOMAS BUSBY, GEORGE FRENCH, WILLIAM SMITH. *Clerk of the Court:* RT. FORSTER.

CLIFFORD, THOMAS.

October 9, 1735. "Late of Charlestown in South Carolina, but at present residing in New Hanover Precinct in North Carolina." *Wife and Executrix:* MARY. *Witnesses:* M. MOORE, ELIZA SWANN, E. MOSELEY. Proven before GAB. JOHNSTON.

CLOASE, GEORGE.   New Hanover County.

August 8, 1750. April 28, 1760. *Father-in-law:* NEWORK INGRIM. *Mother:* JEAN INGRIM. *Executor:* ALEXANDER DUNCAN. *Witnesses:* A. MCKEITHEN, JAS. CAMPBELL, JR. Will proven before ARTHUR DOBBS.

COEN, BENJAMIN. Pasquotank Precinct.
November 29, 1734. January 4, 1734. *Son-in-law:* JAMES MACK-
BRIDE. *Daughter*: BELEY COEN. *Wife:* BRIDGET. *Executors:* CHARLES
SAWYER, BENNETT MORGAN. *Witnesses:* CALEB KOEN and BENNETT
MORGAN. *Clerk of the Court:* JOS. SMITH.

COFFINE, MARY. Perquimans County.
June 17, 1707. July 8, 1707. *Deceased husband:* JOHN THURSTON.
Daughter: HANNAH THURSTON. *Granddaughter:* SARAH ROSE. *Executor:*
EDMOND MODLIN. *Witnesses:* GILBERT SMITH, DERBY BRAYEN. *Clerk of
the Court:* THOS. SNODEN.

COGWELL, HENRY. Perquimans Precinct.
February 26, 1716. October 3, 1719. *Daughters:* BETTIE COGWELL
("land whereon I now live"), SARAH COGWELL (75 acres of land in Chowan
precinct). *Wife and Executrix:* MARY. *Executor:* PETER JAMES. *Witnesses:* JOHN JONSON, WM. EGERTON, JAMES WILSON. *Clerk of the Court:*
RICH'D LEARY.

COKER, CALEB. Edgecombe County.
June 11, 1748. November Court, 1748. *Wife:* MARY. *Sons:* RICHARD,
JAMES and THOMAS. *Daughters:* MARY NARRON, ANN BRUN, FRANCIS
WALL, ELIZABETH SPEIR, SARAH COKER, AGNES COKER. *Executors:* MARY
COKER (wife) and JAMES SPEIR. *Witnesses:* MARGRET COKER and JAMES
COKER. *Clerk of the Court:* BENJ'N WYNNS.

COKER, RICHARD. Beaufort County.
March 26, 1756. June Court, 1756. *Wife and Executrix:* MARGREAT.
Executor: WM. SPEIR. *Witnesses:* JOHN SPEIR, WM. SPEIR, ELIZABETH
SPEIR. *Clerk of the Court:* WALLEY CHAUNCEY.

COLEMAN, WILLIAM. Edgecombe County.
December 29, 1749. February Court, 1752. *Son:* SAMUEL ("plantation whereon I now live"). *Daughters:* SARAH, SUSANNAH. *Wife and Executrix:* JANE. *Executor:* ROBERT COLEMAN (brother). *Witnesses:* MOSES
COLEMAN, CORNELIUS JORDAN, ELIN JORDAN. *Clerk of the Court:* BENJ'N
WYNNS.

COLEMAN, ROBERT. Bath County.
July 9, 1721. September 25, 1721. March 29, 1722. *Wife and Executrix:* MARY. *Daughters:* ELIZABETH ISLER, MARY WHITE. *Granddaughter:* MARY ISLER. *Grandson:* DAVID DUPUISE. *Wife's son:* DENNIS ODIER.

Son-in-law and Executor: CHRISTOPHER RUNNILLS. *Witnesses:* RICHARD CARY, JOHN BUTLER, PETER GREEN. *Clerk of the Court of Isle of Wight Co., Virginia:* W. BRIDGERS. C. GALE, C. J.

COLEMAN, WILLIAM.   Anson County.

May 1, 1750. June Court, 1750. *Sons:* WILLIAM, THOMAS, JOHN, JAMES and SAMUEL (To the 1st three is given "the plantation whereon I now live" and to the other two is given "plantation lying upon mountain creek"). *Wife and Executrix:* ELISABETH. *Executor:* JOSEPH WHITE. *Witnesses:* JOHN HAMER, MARY COLEMAN, ANTHONY HUTCHINGS. *His Majesty's Justices:* JAMES MCCWEAN, JOSEPH WHITE, CHARLES ROBINSON, EDM'D CARTLIDGE, SAM DAVIS, ALEX'R OSBORN. *Clerk of the Court:* THOMAS JONES.

COLES, JAMES.   Perquimans Precinct.

February 20, 1711. *Daughter:* ELIZABETH COLES (tract of land in Nansemond County, Va., "whereon my father James Coles lived"; tracts of land at Somertowne and Buckland). *Wife and Executrix:* MARY. *Witnesses:* RICH FRENCH, ELIZ. FRENCH, SARAH EVENS. *Clerk of the Court:* HENRY CLAYTON. Coat of arms on seal.

COLESON, WILLIAM.   Bertie Precinct.

February 9, 1736. *Brothers:* ABRAHAM and JOSEPH COLESON. *Sister:* SARAH LUNDY. *Executors:* THOMAS WHITMELL and EDWARD COLLINS. *Witnesses:* EDW'D COLLINS, JAMES WARD, THOMAS FALCONER. Will proven before W. SMITH, C. J.

COLLEY, MAGDALEN.   Albemarle County.

December 10, 1699. Ratifies and confirms will of MATTHEW COLLEY, except one feather bed and appurtenances which she wills to *daughter* REBECCA. *Witnesses:* HENRY WHITE, JACOB OVERMAN.

COLLEY, MATTHEW.   Albemarle County.

April 16, 1699. *Children:* ELIZABETH, JOHN and REBECCA, one plantation each. JOHN NUBY. No Executor. No probate. *Witnesses:* FENN. WHITE, JAMES DAVIS.

COLLEY, ROBERT.   Craven County.

April 15, 1744. June 26, 1744. *Son:* JAMES. *Wife:* KATHERINE. *Executor:* DR. FRANCIS STRINGER. *Witnesses:* WM. BUIE, ED. WARNSLEY, ANDREW BASS. *Clerk of the Court:* N. ROUTLEDGE.

COLLIER, CORNELIUS.   Beaufort County.

September 6, 1741. December 8, 1741. *Friends:* ABRAHAM GRAY, REBECKAH GRAY, CORNELIUS GRAY, ELIZABETH GRAY. *Executor:* RICHARD NEWMAN. *Witnesses:* WM. BARROW, JONAS SQUIRES. *Clerk of the Court:* JOHN FORBES.

COLLINS, CHARLES.   Newberne, Craven County.

March 3, 1738. March 7, 1738. *Wife, Executrix and sole legatee and devisee:* ANN. *Witnesses:* JOHN REED, MARG'TT REED, JNO. WILLIAMS. Will proven before GAB. JOHNSTON.

COLLINS, JAMES.   Perquimans County.

April 15, 1730. May 19, 1730. *Sons:* WILLIAM, THOMAS. *Daughter:* ALIE COLLINS. *Wife and Executrix:* LUIEE. *Executor:* WILLIAM COLLINS (son). *Friend:* JOSEPH JESSOP. *Witnesses:* THOS. LILLEY, SARAH LILLEY. Will proven before RICH'D EVERARD, *Governor*.

COLLINS, JOHN.   Craven County.

February 20, 1748–1749. March Court, 1750. *Sons:* SAMUEL, JOSEPH. *Granddaughters:* ELISEBETH JONES, MARY JONES, VINI JONES. *Wife and Executrix:* MARY. *Executor:* SAMUEL COLLINS (son). *Witnesses:* WILLIAM SMITH, GEORGE BARBER, JACOB TAYLER. *Clerk of the Court:* PHIL SMITH.

COLLINS, JOHN.   Bertie County.

December 27, 1749. March 18, 1752. *Sons:* WILLIAM (land on Casshi River purchased of Jonathan Standley), JOHN and DAVID (bible to each), JOSEPH (plantation on Guy hall swamp purchased of Hardy Keele), MIKELL (survey on Redbud), DEMSEY (plantation on Gie hall Swamp "where Henry Ballentine formerly lived"), JESSE ("my plantation"), ABSOLUM (247 acres of land on the Deep Branch). *Grandsons:* JOHN KEEN and JOHN COLLINS. *Wife and Executrix:* MARY. *Witnesses:* MOSES HILL, JETHRO ROUNTREE. Proven before GAB. JOHNSTON.

COLLINS, LUIEE.

April 18, 1730. May 19, 1730. *Son-in-law:* WILLIAM COLLINS. *Son:* THOMAS. *Daughter-in-law:* ALLIE COLLINS. *Executor:* JOSEPH JESSOP. *Witnesses:* SUSANAH SMITH, MARTIN ASPILL, ELIZABETH FERRILL. Will proven before RICHARD EVERARD.

COLLINS, RICHARD.   Bath County.

September 23, 1707. October, 1707. *Legatees and devisees:* EDMON PARSE, ANN NOLSON, JOHN BUNTING. *Executor:* ROGER MOUNTERY. *Witnesses:* EDWARD PITT, JOSEPH HALEBROOK, JAMES PEIRCE. *Clerk of the Court:* LEVI EMEWHITT.

COLLINS, URIAH.   Hyde County.

January 3, 1751–1752. March Court, 1752. *Son:* HENRY ("house and plantation"). *Daughters:* ELIZABETH COLLINS and HANNAH COLLINS. *Executor and Guardian of Children:* TIMOTHY GRADLESS. *Witnesses:* JOEL BARTRE, RICHARD WOOD. *Clerk of the Court:* FRANCIS EGLETON. Courthouse in Woodstock town.

COLLINGS, WILLIAM.   Pasquotank Precinct.

April 8, 1706. July 19, 1709. *Wife and Executrix:* ELISIBETH. *Cousin:* THOMAS WODLEY. *Witnesses:* (CAPT.) JOHN HUNT, SAMUELL DAVIS, ELISIBETH DAVIS. *Clerk of the Court:* JOHN BISHOP.

COLLIS, THOMAS.   Pasquotank Precinct.

September 3, 1719. *Legatees:* GEORGE LUMLEY, SAMUEL BARNET (*executor*). *Witnesses:* GRIFFITH JONES, EDWARD COOPER, EDWARD FAIRCLOTH. Recorded in Book 1712–22, page 217. Original missing.

COLLSON, JOHN.   Bertie Precinct.

May 3, 1730. February Court, 1736. *Sons:* JOHN, THOMAS, JACOB, SANDOWS and JOSEPH (land on Rognes Swamp to be equally divided between them). *Daughters:* MARY and MARTHA COLLSON. *Wife:* SUSANNAH. *Executors:* SUSANNAH COLLSON (wife), JOHN COLLSON (son), THOS. BLOUNT, THOS. WHITMELL. *Witnesses:* AGNESS LEAGETT, JOHN LEAGETT, CHARLES HAVENTON. *Clerk of the Court:* JOHN WYNNS.

COLSTON, MARY (Widow of Jacob).

July 20, 1732. *Son:* WILLIAM COLSTON. *Daughter:* SARAH LUNDY. *Executors:* JOHN GRAY, THOMAS WHITTMEAL. *Witnesses:* JOHN LEGGET, THOS. KEARNY. No probate.

COLTEN, JAMES.   Bertie County.

January 14, 1758. April Court, 1758. *Sons:* JAMES ("plantation where I now live"), HENRY, SOLOMON, THEOPHILUS. *Daughter:* CHRISTIAN COLTEN. *Wife and Executrix:* SARAH. *Executors:* ARTHUR and JOHN COLTEN (brothers). *Witnesses:* SAMUELL COLTEN, THOMAS ROCHE, MARY ROCHE. *Clerk of the Court:* BENJ. WYNNS.

COMBS, WINNIFITT.   Tyrrell County.

October 31, 1749. March Court, 1750. *Sons:* ROBERT and SAMUELL. *Daughters:* MARY COMBS, ELISEBETH BRADY, ANN WREN. *Grandson:* JAMES COMBS. *Executor:* ROBT. COMBS (son). *Witnesses:* DAVID DUNCAN, JOHN WARD, JOHN COMBS. *Clerk of the Court:* EVAN JONES.

COMMANDER, JOSEPH MATTHEW.

April 23, 1698. *Sons:* THOMAS and JOSEPH. *Executors:* JAMES TUKE, JOHN TUKE. *Witnesses:* DANIEL AKEHURST, THOMAS BLOUNT, JEREMIAH SYMONS, WILLIAM NICHOLSON. *Clerk of the Court:* W. GLOVER.

COMMANDER, THOMAS. Pasquotank County.

August 25, 1739. October Court, 1739. *Sons:* JOHN ("the west side of my land"), SAMUEL ("land east of the flat branch"), BENJAMIN ("great iron pott"). THOMAS and JOSEPH. *Daughters:* MARY and SARAH. *Executors:* THOMAS and JOSEPH COMMANDER (sons). *Witnesses:* SIMON BRYAN, T. SWEENY, THOMAS SYMONS. *Clerk of the Court:* JAMES CRAVEN. Executors qualified before W. SMITH, C. J.

COMMANDER, THOMAS. Pasquotank County.

February 16, 1741-1742. April Court, 1742. *Son:* JOSEPH ("all my land"). *Wife and Executrix:* ELISABETH. *Brother and Executor:* JOSEPH COMMANDER. *Sisters:* SARAH COMMANDER and MARY COMMANDER. *Witnesses:* ROBERT LOWRY, ANN OVERMAN, SIMON BRYAN. *Clerk of the Court:* THOMAS TAYLOR.

COMMINFORT, HENDRICK. Currituck Precinct.

July 7, 1712. *Sons:* WILLIAM, ANDREW (*executor*). *Daughter:* MARGARET. *Witnesses:* RICHARD BALLANCE, JANE VANDERMULER, EVAN MILLER and THOMAS VANDERMULER. Recorded in Book 1712-22, page 44. Original missing.

COMINFORT, RICHARD. County not given.

December 7, 1704-1705. *Legatees:* THOMAS VINCE, RICHARD CANNADY, THOMAS VANDERMULEN, JANE VANDERMULEN, MARY VINCE (sister), MARGARET and SARAH VINCE. *Mother and Executrix:* HENDRICK COMINFORT. *Witnesses:* WILL SWANN, JOHN BROWN, THOMAS PLATT. *Clerk of the Court:* JOSEPH WICKER. Recorded in Book 1712-22, page 244. Original missing.

CONGLETON, WILLIAM. Beaufort County.

July 21, 1755. December Court, 1755. *Sons:* JAMES, WILLIAM ("my plantation on the Briery Branch"), JOHN ("plantation that George Hill now lives on"), HENRY and DAVID ("plantation whereon I now live"). ABRAHAM (my still). *Daughter:* ELIZABETH CONGLETON. *Wife:* SARAH. *Executors:* JAMES and WILLIAM CONGLETON (sons) and SARAH CONGLETON (wife). *Witnesses:* JAS. BONNER, THOS. BONNER, JUNR., WILLM. PHELPS. *Clerk of the Court:* WALLEY CHAUNCEY.

CONNER, ANDREW.   Bath Town.
   January 14, 1754. March Court, 1754. *Friends:* ROGER and HENRY
ORMOND, sons of WYRIOTT ORMOND (972 acres of land on North side of
Pamplico River). *Daughter:* SARAH CONNER. *Executor:* WYRIOTT OR-
MOND. *Witnesses:* WILLM. MORE, WILL ORMOND, JAS. ELLISON, THOMAS
WILLIAMS. *Clerk of Craven County Court:* JNO. SNEAD.

CONNER, DEMSEY.   Pasquotank County.
   December 5, 1753. January Court, 1754. *Daughter:* ANNLATITIA
CONNER. *Wife and Executrix:* MARY. *Witnesses:* MATTHIAS JORDAN,
JOSEPH JORDAN, ELIZABETH JORDAN. *Clerk of the Court:* THOS. TAYLOR.

CONNER, JOHN.   Pasquotank County.
   October 5, 1753. October Court, 1753. *Sons:* JOHN, CADOR. *Daughters:* MARY CONNER and RUTH CONNER. *Wife and Executrix:* ELISEBETH.
Executor: JOS. SCOTT. *Witnesses:* JOS. JORDAN, PENELOPE JORDAN. *Clerk
of the Court:* THOS. TAYLOR.

CONNERLY, JOHN.   Johnston County.
   October 17, 1751. March Court, 1751. *Sons:* WILLIAM and CULLEN
(300 acres of land in Duplin Co.). *Wife:* KESIAH. *Daughter:* PATIENCE.
Brothers: RICHARD JONES, STEPHEN HERRING. *Executor:* ANTHONY HER-
RING. *Witnesses:* ELIZABETH JONES, GRIFFIN JONES. *Clerk of the Court:*
CHAS. YOUNG.

CONWAY, MARY.   New Bern, Craven County.
   August 17, 1774. August 26, 1774. *Son:* WILLIAM CONWAY ("lands
and lotts in the town of New Bern, together with all negroe slaves, two
pair of gold Buttons and the residue of My Gold Rings * * * * And I
do earnestly intreat my Executors to pay strict regard to the education
of my said son in such manner as shall be necessary to qualify him for
such Business or profession as his Genius shall most incline to"). *Other
legatees:* MARY GORDON, SUSANNAH (wife of EDMUND WRENFORD) and
ELIZABETH ELMSLEY (silk and linen wearing apparel). *Executors:* JOHN
HAWKS and EDMUND WRENFORD. *Witnesses:* JOHN BONNER, JOSEPH
DOWSE and HENRY VIPON. Proven before Jo. MARTIN.

COOK, JOHN.   Bertie County.
   November 24, 1744. January 30, 1745. *Sons:* SAMUEL (plantation on
Black Walnut Swamp), ISAAC (100 acres land), DAVID (100 acres of land
on Salmon Creek). *Daughters:* SARAH, ELIZABETH and ANNA COOK.
Wife and Executrix: ANNA. *Executor:* ISAAC COOK (son). *Witnesses:*
THOS. RYAN, WM. BALL, ISAAC RATLIFF. Will proven before GAB.
JOHNSTON at Eden House.

COOK, SAMUEL.   Bertie County.

October 2, 1756. January Court, 1757. *Sons:* JOHN ("my plantation, containing 162 acres), JESSE (100 acres of land at the head of Black Walnut), BENJAMIN, WILLIAM. *Daughters:* FRANCES, MARY and ELIZABETH COOK. *Wife and Executrix:* MARY. *Executors:* EDWARD BRYAN, JOHN COOK (son), ROBERT WEST. *Witnesses:* JOHN BURN, JOHN PERRY, ROBERT WEST. *Clerk of the Court:* BENJ. WYNNS.

COOK, JOHN.   County not given.

August 19, 1696. *Son:* THOMAS. *Wife and Executrix:* ELIZABETH. *Witnesses:* HENDERSON WALKER, ANN WALKER, ARGELL SIMONS. *Clerk of the Court:* W. GLOVER.

COOK, THOMAS.   Chowan County.

November 20, 1734. January 20, 1734. *Legatees:* GRIZELL BULL ("houses and lots in Edenton and negroes), JOHN COOK (uncle). *Executors:* JOHN PAYLEN and EDMUND GALE. *Witnesses:* CHARLES WESTBEERE, SAMUEL SNOWDEN, PETER YOUNG. Proven before GABRIEL JOHNSTON. Recorded in Book 1722-35, page 344. Original missing.

COOK, WILLIAM.   Northampton County.

April 3, 1758. October Court, 1758. *Sons:* WILLIAM, JAMES, ELIMELEACH, JOHN, LAZARUS, DANIEL, HENERY, EPHRAIM, MERCURIUS (to each is bequeathed one shilling). *Daughters:* ELIZABETH COOK, MARY COOK (one shilling each). *Wife and Executrix:* NEOMY (balance of estate). *Witnesses:* EMELIUS DERING, RICHARD WORRELL, THOMAS PAIRE. *Clerk of the Court:* I. EDWARDS.

COOPER, JOSEPH.   Pasquotank County.

April 3, 1753. April Court, 1754. *Sons:* JOSEPH, JAMES. *Daughters:* SARAH and MARY COOPER. *Wife and Executrix:* SARAH ANN COOPER. *Witnesses:* JARVIS JONES, ANTONY FOREHAND, BRIDGITT JONES. *Clerk of the Court:* THOS. TAYLOR.

COPELAND, JAMES.   Chowan County.

March 13, 1752. *Son:* JAMES (tract of land on Chowan River). *Daughter:* MARY COPELAND. *Wife and Executrix:* DIANA. *Witnesses:* JAMES FALLAW, ISAC WILLIAMS, JOHN THACH. No probate.

COPELAND, WILLIAM.

October 23, 1720. *Sons:* WILLIAM ("plantation whereon I now live"), JOHN, JAMES and CHARLES ("land betwixt Sandy Run and Bear Swamp"). *Daughters:* CHRISTIAN and SARAH COPELAND. *Wife and Executrix:*

CHRISTIAN. *Witnesses:* JOHN EARDAN, GEORGE TURNEDGE, ELIZABETH TURNEDGE. Will proven before CHRISTOPHER GALE. *Clerk of the Court:* JOHN CARNICK.

COPELAND, WILLIAM.   Chowan Precinct.

January 26, 1753. April Court, 1753. *Sons:* WILLIAM ("plantation whereon I now live"), JESSE. *Daughters:* ANNE COPELAND, JUDATH COPELAND. *Wife and Executrix:* SARAH. *Witnesses:* EVERARD GARRETT, THOMAS SMALL, CHARLES COPELAND. *Clerk of the Court:* JAS. CRAVEN.

CORBETT, THOMAS.   Albemarle County.

January 10, 1692. April 3, 1693. *Legatees and Devisees:* SARAH LILY (daughter of JOHN LILY), REBEKAH, ANN, JONATHAN and RICHARD VINS (children of RICHARD VINS, SR.) *Executor:* RICHARD VINS, SR. *Witnesses:* BENJAMIN GIDON, JOHANNAH GIDON, ANTHONY DAWSON. *Clerk of the Court:* JOHN STEPNEY.

CORBIN, JEAN (widow of FRANCIS CORBIN), Chowan County.

February 10, 1775. April 3, 1775. *Legatees:* JOHN RUTHERFORD, JR., WILLIAM GORDON RUTHERFORD and FRANCIS RUTHERFORD, "children of my good friend JOHN RUTHERFORD of New Hanover County" (1,260 acres of land on the East Branch of Long Creek; plantation on the North east side of the North West branch of Cape Fear adjoining Henry Simmons; plantation in Bladen County adjoining Macknights on the West side of the Northwest branch of Cape Fear River, together with all negroes, household furniture and personal estate of testatrix). *Executors:* LEWIS HENRY DEROSSET, JOHN RUTHERFORD and THOMAS HOLLOWAY. *Witnesses:* SAM ASHE, DANIEL and DAVID MORGAN. Proven before JO. MARTIN. Executor qualified before RICHARD CASWELL.

CORE, THOMAS.   Northampton County.

October 26, 1751. May Court, 1752. *Sons:* THOMAS, ARTHUR. *Daughters:* MARGET COOPER, MARY HOLLAND, ELIZABETH CORE, GRACE CORE. *Wife and Executrix:* MARGITT. *Executor:* ARTHUR CORE (son). *Witnesses:* JAMES BOYTE, JOHN RIGHT, WM. MURFREE. *Clerk of the Court:* I. EDWARDS.

COREY, JOHN.   Pasquotank County.

February 18, 1757. March 25, 1757. *Sons:* JOHN, THOMAS and JOSEPH. *Wife and Executrix:* LUCA. *Executor:* THOMAS COREY (son). *Witnesses:* ANN COAK, JOHN MCKEEL. *Clerk of the Court:* THOS. TAYLOR.

CORP, JOHN.

December 20, 1718. February 10, 1718–1719. *Son and Executor:* WILLIAM. *Daughter:* ELNER CORP. *Wife and Executrix:* ELINOR. *Brother:*

ABSTRACT OF WILLS, 1690—1760. 83

RICHARD CORP. *Brother-in-law:* RICHARD BROTHERS. *Witnesses:* J. PALIN, CHAS. BULL, SARAH BULL. Will proven before JOHN ROBISON, *Justice of the Peace.*

CORP, JOHN.   Pasquotank County.

March 10, 1753. April Court, 1753. *Brother and Executor:* WILLIAM KNIGHTS. *Wife and Executrix:* ELIZABETH. *Witnesses:* THOMAS MC-KEELS, EDWARD KNIGHTS. *Clerk of the Court:* THOS. TAYLOR.

CORPREW, THOMAS.   Chowan County.

August 18, 1748. January Court, 1748. *Sons:* JOHN (400 acres land in Perquimans and 200 in Chowan Co.), GEORGE DURANT CORPREW ("plantation whereon I now live; plantation of 700 acres in Princess Ann County, Va."). *Wife:* SARAH. *Daughter-in-law:* MARY BUNCOMB. Poor of the PARISH of ST. PAUL in CHOWAN CO. (one negro man). *Executors:* SARAH CORPREW (wife), JOSHUA CORPREW (brother), BENJAMIN PAYTON, MILES GALE, WILLIAM HASKINS. *Witnesses:* CLEMENT HALL, JOHN REMBOUGH, JOHN ROSS. *Clerk of the Court:* WILL MEARNS. Executors qualified before JOS. ANDERSON, J. P.

CORREE, JAMES.   Bertie County.

October 22, 1750. May Court, 1754. *Sons:* JAMES ("manner plantation"), DAVID, JOHN and JACOB. *Daughters:* MARGRET CORREE, JANIT CORREE. *Wife and Executrix:* MARY. *Executors:* THOMAS WHITMILL, ARTHUR WILLIAMS. *Witnesses:* ABRAHAM JORDAN, HESTER BROADWELL, ARTHUR WILLIAMS. *Clerk of the Court:* SAML. ORMES.

COSTE, EPHRAIM.   County not given.

November 14, 1719. *God-daughter:* ELIZABETH MARKHAM. *Executor:* ANTHONY MARKHAM. *Witnesses:* LEVI MARKHAM LENERTON. No probate.

COTTEN, JOHN.   Northampton County.

Date of death, February 2, 1741. *Sons:* JOHN ("plantation whereon I dwell"), BENJAMIN ("plantation whereon Philip Edens lives"). *Daughters:* MARY BRUCLE (or Breecle) (land at Blue water), ANNE COTTEN, SARAH COTTEN (one negro). *Wife and Executrix:* ANNE. *Executor:* WILLIAM COTTEN (brother). *Witnesses:* RICHD. BARFIELD, THOMAS COWMAN, JOHN DAWSON. *Clerk of the Court:* I. EDWARDS. This is a nuncupative will proven before ISAAC HUNTER by the witnesses above named.

COTTEN, SAMUELL.   Northampton County.

January 16, 1774. May 18, 1774. *Sons:* SAMUELL ("my manor plantation"), JOHN. *Wife and Executrix:* LIDIA. *Wife's children:* ELISABETH COTTEN EWELL, SALLY COTTEN EWELL, RODERICK COTTEN EWELL. *Other legatees:* THOMAS THOMAS, EURIDICE GARDINAR (bound boy), JOHN FRANKLIN. *Executor:* ROBERT HILLIARD. *Witnesses:* C. E. TAYLOR, JNO. BARNES, SARAH JOSSEY. Will proven before Jo. MARTIN at Halifax.

COTTEN, SARAH.   Northampton County.

December 7, 1753. February Court, 1754. *Sons:* WILLIAM BRIDGERS, JOSEPH BRIDGERS, JOHN BRIDGERS, CHARLES COTTEN, WILLIAM COTTEN, ROBERT COTTEN. *Daughters:* SARAH COTTEN, PATIENCE COTTEN, PRISCILLA WILLS, MARY COTTEN, MARTHA SCOTT. *Executor:* WILLIAM BRIDGERS (son). *Witnesses:* JOHN DAWSON, RICHD. WILLS, JOHN SCOTT. *Clerk of the Court:* I. EDWARDS.

Codicil: Dated December 13, 1753. Mentions *sons*: JOSEPH BRIDGERS, CHARLES, WILLIAM. *Witnesses:* JOHN DAWSON, JOHN SCOTT.

COTTON, JOHN.   Bertie County.

May Court, 1728. *Sons:* JOHN, WILLIAM, SAMUEL, THOMAS, ARTHUR, JAMES, JOSEPH, ALEXANDER. *Wife:* MARTHA COTTON. *Sons-in-law:* JOHN THOMAS, CAPT. JOHN SPEARS. *Daughters:* SUSANNAH and PRISCILLA COTTON, MARTHA BENTON, widow of FRANCIS BENTON. *Executors:* THOMAS BRYAN and WILLIAM BENNET. *Witnesses:* THOMAS BRYANT, THOS. STRANGE, MARY PARKER. *Clerk of the Court:* RT. FORSTER. The following lands devised: 320 acres on Ahoskey Marsh; 150 acres in the Oserow Meadow; land bought of Charles Stevenson; land called the Green Pond Neck; lower survey on Fishing Creek; 400 acres of land in upper survey on Fishing Creek. Several negro slaves bequeathed, together with a great quantity of personal property in the shape of wearing apparel, household furniture, etc.

COTTON, JOHN.   Pasquotank County.

March 1, 1791. July 4, 1792. *Son:* HUMFRE. *Executors:* THOMAS SYONS, JARAMIAH SYMONS, JOSEPH COMMANDER. *Witnesses:* CALEB BUNDY, JANE BUNDY. *Clerk of the Court:* PAUL LATHAM.

COULSON, WILLIAM.   County not given.

November 18, 1712. *Wife:* ELIZABETH. *Executors:* DAVID HENDERSON and JOHN BOYD. *Witness:* WM. DOWNING. Original missing. Recorded in Book 1712–1722, page 53.

COURTNEY, ROBERT.   Onslow County.

January 17, 1750. April 2, 1751. *Sons:* JOHN (1 shilling), ROBERT (land on the Half Moon Creek on the East side of the Northwest branch of New River called Wallins), JONATHAN (plantation whereon "I now live"), ROWLAN (100 acres land on lower end of plantation). *Son-in-law:* RICHARD CURTIS. *Friend:* BENJAMIN EASON. *Wife:* HANNAH. *Daughter:*

PHEBE CURTIS. *Executors:* ROBERT and JONATHAN COURTNEY (sons). *Witnesses:* MATTHEW LEWIS, JOS. STURGES, BENJAMIN EASON. *Clerk of Court:* THOS. BLACK.

COWARD, JOHN.   Bertie Precinct.

March 8, 1737. August Court, 1737. *Sons:* WILLIAM and JOHN (plantation whereon I now live), BEVARD. *Wife:* ELISABETH. *Executor:* JOSEPH WIMBERLEY. *Witnesses:* EDWARD VANN, HENRY VANN, JOHNATHAN TALER. *Clerk of the Court:* JNO. WYNNS.

COWEN, GARRETT.   Albemarle County.

July 6, 1720. April Court, 1721. *Son:* DANIEL. *Wife:* not named. *Witnesses:*—— and ELIZABETH KOWEN. *Clerk of the Court (pro tem.):* J. PALIN.

COWELL, BENJAMIN.   Currituck County.

October 5, 1752. March Court, 1756. *Sons:* BENJAMIN, SOLOMON, WILLIAM, BUTLAR, EDMOND, JOHN, THOMAS. *Daughters:* REBECCA COWELL, ELIZABETH COWELL, DORCAS. *Wife and Executrix:* ELIZABETH. *Executor:* SOLOMON COWELL (son). *Witnesses:* JOS. CAMPBELL, JOHN WOODHOUSE, JORDAN ROGERS. *Clerk of the Court:* WILLIAM SHERGOLD.

COX, EDWARD.   Currituck County.

September 26, 1748. July Court, 1751. *Sons:* THOMAS ("plantation whereon I now live"), ABSALOM (plantation of 75 acres), ELIJA ("remainder of my land"). *Daughter:* JEMIMA PARKER. *Executors:* THOMAS, ABSALOM, ELIJAH COX (sons). *Witnesses:* WM. SHERGOLD, NATHL. WILSON, MALACHI WILSON. *Clerk of the Court:* RICH'D MCCLURE.

COX, CHARLES.   Duplin County.

November 24, 1752. April 10, 1759. *Daughter:* ANNE COX (500 acres of land in the province of "pencelvany" (Pennsylvania) in the County of Newcastle). *Wife and Executrix:* FRANCESINA ("plantation whereon I now live"). *Executor:* JOSEPH WILLSON. *Witnesses:* AMBROSE DUDLEY, AARON HODESEN. *Clerk of the Court:* JOHN DICKSON.

COX, JOHN.   Onslow County.

April 18, 1743. *Wife:* CHRISTIAN ("one-half my plantation"). *Daughter:* MARTHA COX (other half plantation). *Executor:* JOHN STARKEY. *Witnesses:* JAMES HOYLE, DANIEL SHORLY, MARY PELWOOD. *Clerk of the Court:* WM. CRANFORD.

COXE, ROBERT.   Little River Precinct.

February 21, 1725. November 25, 1730. *Son:* ROBERT. *Daughters:* SARAH COXE, ANNE WEEKS. *Wife and Executrix:* ELIZABETH. *Witnesses:* MARY COLLINGS, JOHN BOSWEL. Will proven before RICHD. EVERARD.

Cox, Thomas. Currituck County.

April 30, 1743. July 5, 1743. *Sons:* EDWARD (land called the "Wolfpit Ridge"), SOLOMON ("maner plantation"), MARMEDUKE (41 acres of land)· *Daughters:* MARY COX, DINAH COX, ANN COX. *Wife and Executrix:* ANN. *Witnesses:* JOHN SHURLEY, LUCY PLATTS. *Clerk of the Court:* JOHN LANG.

CRADDOCK, RICHARD. Pasquotank County.

January 9, 1685. *Wife, Executrix and sole legatee and devisee:* ELIZABETH. *Witnesses:* ANTHONY HATCH, STEVEN STELL, JOHN BOWND, MARGRET BOWND. No probate.

CRAIG, RICHARD.

February 9, 1695–1696. April Court, 1696. *Friends:* PATRICK BEALLY (*Executor*), JOHN and DAVID BEALLY (sons of PATRICK). *Witnesses:* SAMUELL DAVIS, JOHN DAVIS. *Clerk of the Court:* EDWARD MAYO.

CRANFORD, WILLIAM. Onslow County.

October 4, 1743. April Court, 1745. *Sons:* JAMES ("plantation whereon he now lives"), JOHN ("plantation whereon I now live"). *Son-in-law and Executor:* PHILLIP FINSINGER. *Wife and Executrix:* KATHERINE. *Witnesses:* THOS. ROBERTS, RICHD. MELTEN, ROBERT MELTEN. *Clerk of the Court:* ANDR. MURRAY.

CRAVEN, JAMES.

September 28, 1755. October 11, 1755, "late of Droughton near Skipton in Craven in the County of York in Great Britain, now of Edenton in North Carolina." "I give to my *wife* PENELOPE CRAVEN (formerly HODGSON) all the Black cattle, sheep and hogs at the "Brick House" and the "Ould plantation called Pagetts Plantation" and in the Range commonly called the Great Marsh," together with ten negroes and all "the Craven Silver Plate" and furniture; fifty books and horse and side saddle. *Other legatees:* "DOCKTER ABRAHAM BOULTON (brother), THOMAS CRAVEN HODGSON ("my large gold seal"), WILLIAM BADHAM (six silver spoons), DOCTOR JOHN CRAVEN, MARY LEEMING (sister), PETER LEEMING. *Executors:* FRANCIS CORBIN, WYRIOT ORMOND, WILLIAM HERITAGE of North Carolina and JOHN WATSON of Suffolk, Virginia. *Witnesses:* SARAH BLOUNT, JOSEPH HARRON, JOHN WILLIAMS, JOHN PINDOR. Proven before ARTHUR DOBBS.

CRAWFORD, WILLIAM. Chowan County.

May 12, 1732. January 13, 1735. *Daughters:* ELIZABETH, wife of ALEXANDER OLIVER; HONNER, wife of EDWARD DILLDAY. *Granddaughter:* MARY OLIVER. *Wife and Executrix:* MARY. *Grandsons:* WM. CRAWFORD (*appointed Executor*), THOMAS JENKINS. *Witnesses:* JOSEPH VAUN, ANNE VAUN, RICHARD TAYLOR. Will proven before W. SMITH, C. J.

ABSTRACT OF WILLS, 1690—1760.   87

CREECH, HENRY.   Albemarle County.

August 16, 1709. No probate. *Son-in-law:* JOHN DAILIE (land at ye beetree neck). *Sons:* THOMAS and WILLIAM (land "called ye bald ridge"), RICHARD, HENRY. *Wife and Executrix:* JOYCE. *Witnesses:* ELENOR JAMES, TAMER CREECH, JOHN BELT. Original missing. Recorded in Book 1712–1722, page 28.

CRESSY, LEVI.   Perquimans County.

October 21, 1734. October 28, 1734. *Sons:* JOHN, JOSEPH. *Daughter:* ELIZABETH CRESSY. *Executors:* JOHN CRESSY (son) and ZACHARIAH CHANEY. *Witnesses:* NANN JONES, JOHN MOORE, ZACHARIAH CHANEY. Will proven before GEO. BURRINGTON.

CRICKET, JOHN.   Bertie County.

October, 1753. April Court, 1755. *Sons:* JOHN (300 acres of land on the Middle Swamp), THOMAS ("plantation whereon I now live" and land on South side of the Branch), CHARLES (land on the North side of the Branch). *Wife and Executrix:* MARY. *Executor:* JOHN CRICKET (son). *Witnesses:* ROT. LENOX, ALEXR. FORD, EDWARD RASON. *Clerk of the Court:* BENJAMIN WYNNS.

CRISP, NICHOLAS.   Chowan Precinct.

March 22, 1727. May 23, 1727. *Grandsons:* RICHARD CRISP (lands and plantations in Chowan precinct; plantation known by the name of Windlys; lot and warehouse in Edenton; land in Perquimans precinct known by the name of Fendals; the Island called Batts Grove), GEORGE DURANT. *Granddaughters:* MARY DURANT (plantation and lands in Perquimans precinct lying on Albemarle Sound between Norcombs and Col Harneys), SARAH DURANT ("all my lands lying on Moratoke River in Bertie Precinct at and near Shauwaukee and Hennunteh containing 1120 acres); ANN DURANT, ELIZABETH DURANT. *Daughter-in-law:* ELIZABETH CRISP (widow of son, JOHN CRISP). *Daughter:* HAGAR DURANT. *Executors:* EDWARD MOSELEY and JEREMIAH VAIL. *Witnesses:* WILLM. WILLIAMS, HUMPHRY ROBINSON, JAMES BUSH. Will proven before C. GALE, C. J.

CROCKER, PETER.   Edgecombe County.

October 24, 1752. August Court, 1753. *Wife:* SARAH. *Children:* mentioned, but not named. *Witnesses:* JAMES WILLIAMSON, THOMAS BARRAN, JOSEPH BRIDGERS. *Executors:* FRANCIS WILLIAMSON and SARAH CROCKER (wife). *Clerk of the Court:* BENJN. WYNNS.

CROFTON, HENRY.   Beaufort County.

October 6, 1756. March Court, 1757. *Sons:* THOMAS ("plantation whereon I now live"), THEOPHILUS, WILLIAM and AMBROS (plantation lying in Crofton's Cut). *Daughters:* ELIZABETH CROFTON, MARY and MARTHA. *Executors:* JOHN BOYD (brother), EDWARD SALTER and JOHN SLADE. *Witnesses:* SAM'LL DUNBAR, ROBT. PHILIPS, ELIZABETH CROFTON. *Clerk of the Court:* WALLEY CHAUNCEY.

CROKER, ANTONY.   Granville County.

July 28, 1754. September 3, 1754. *Sons:* THOMAS ("plantation whereon I now live" on Sandy Creek), ARTER ("plantation he now lives on"), JACOB. *Executors:* ARTER and JACOB CROKER (sons). *Witnesses:* JAMES WHITE, EDWARD THOMAS, JOHN BRANTLY. *Clerk of the Court:* DAN'L WELDON.

CROMEN, MARTIN.   Bertie Precinct.

May 1, 1733. August Court, 1733. *Brother:* THOMAS CROMEN (of Bolart in the County of Limerick, Kingdom of Ireland, "all my lands within this province"). *Legatees:* WM. KENEDY, JR., FRANCIS KENEDY, JOHN GRAY, JR., ELIZABETH FROST (daughter-in-law), THOMAS COPLAND (son-in-law), JONATHAN RIDING, MICHAL ELLIS, WILLIAM KENEDY. *Executors:* WM. KENEDY, JAMES CONER, JOHN GRAY. *Witnesses:* MICHAEL ELLIS, GRACE KENEDY. *Clerk of the Court:* RT. FORSTER.

CRONEY, DINNIS.   Pasquotank Precinct.

March 24, 1735. April 8, 1735. *Son:* WILLIAM. *Daughters:* ELENDER CRONEY, MARY CRONEY, SARAH WALLARD. *Wife:* ANNE. *Executor:* WM. CRONEY (son). *Witnesses:* JOHN SCARBOROUGH, JEAN BILLITT. *Clerk of the Court:* JOSA. SMITH.

CROSLAND, ELIZABETH.   Albemarle County.

October 18, 1693. April Court, 1694. *Father:* RICHARD STIBETT (STIVER). *Witnesses:* CHRISTOPHER BUTLER, WILLIAM SPRICK, ANHORETTA BUTLER. No probate.

CROSLEN, JOHN.   Albemarle County.

May 6, 1693. Chowan Court, April, 1694. *God-daughter:* CONSTANT STIVER. ANN STIVER, HANER STIVER, RICH STIVER, JOHANER STIVER. *Executor:* RICH STIVER. *Witnesses:* JONES BREFOT, ARTHUR CARLETON, COTTON COLLES. *Clerk of the Court:* NATHANIEL CHEVIN.

CROPLEY, JOHN.   Albemarle County.

January 25, 1685. March 29, 1686. *Son:* VINS ("land where I now live"). *Wife:* ANN. *Wife's father:* JOHN VINS. No executor named. *Witnesses:* WILLIAM WILKJON, GEORGE FORDYSE, EDWARD HARRISON. Will proven before WM. WILKJON.

CROPLEY, VINES.   Chowan Precinct.

April 10, 1719. July 31, 1719. *Son:* WILLIAM ("all my estate"). *Executor:* JAMES BEASLEY. *Witnesses:* JAMES BEASLEY, JACOB PRIVET, MARY BEASLEY. *Clerk of the Court:* R. HICKS. Coat of arms on seal.

CROSSOT, JOSEPH.   Carteret Precinct.

October 28, 1728. December 3, 1728. *Legatees:* DAVID SHEPHERD, JOSEPH FULFORD. This is a nuncupative will proven by the oaths of THOMAS DUDLEY and ELIZABETH, his wife, before JOHN GALLAND, *Clerk of the Court.*

CRUISE, LAWRENCE.   Albemarle County.

January 13, 1690. *Daughter:* MARY CRUISE. *Friends:* ROBERT JENKISSON and wife, ELIZABETH. *Executor:* THOMAS CLARCK (of "yawe pime River"). *Witnesses:* WILLIAM PRIVIT, DAVID PERKINS. No probate.

CRUMP, JOSEPH.   Northampton County.

May 5, 1758. October Court, 1759. *Wife:* CASSANDRA. *Sons:* JOSIAS, RICHARD (in Virginia), CHARLES, JOSEPH. *Daughters:* PATTY CRUMP, KATY CRUMP. *Executrix:* CASSANDRA CRUMP (wife) and CHAS. CRUMP (son). *Witnesses:* WM. HALL, CLEMT. LANIER. *Clerk of the Court:* I. EDWARDS.

CRUMPTON, HENERY.   Bertie Precinct.

January 11, 1735. February Court, 1735. *Sons:* HENERY, WILLIAM. *Daughters:* SUSANNAH, ELIZABETH, JANE and ANNE (to each of the above named is given five shillings). *Friend and Executor:* SAMUELL PEACOCK ("all my land" on pattecasi Creek on the beaverdam). *Witnesses:* ABRAHAM BURTON, ARTHUR SELLERS, ARTHUR WILLIAMS. *Clerk of the Court:* JNO. WYNNS.

CUNNINGHAM, MORRIS.   Albemarle County.

July 19, 1696. *Executor and sole devisee and legatee:* MATHEW KELLEY. *Witnesses:* THOMAS SYMONS, ARNOLD WHITE. *Clerk of the Court:* EDWARD MAYO.

CURRIR, JOHN.

May 1, 1681. February 5, 1683. *Daughter:* SARAH. *Witnesses:* THOMAS LUTON, MARTHA CULLEN. Will proven before SETH SOTHELL.

DALRYMPLE, JOHN.   New Hanover County.

(Second son to Sir John Dalrymple of Cowsland, Baronet of the Kingdom of Scotland.) February 25, 1742-1743. January 26, 1767. *Wife and Executrix:* MARTHA. *Friend:* ROGER MOORE. *Brothers:* WM. WALTERS,

JOSEPH WALTERS, JOHN WALTERS, SAMUEL WALTERS. *Sisters:* SARAH
LILLINGTON, ELIZABETH HAWES. *Executors:* ROGER MOORE, WM. and
JOSEPH WALTERS. *Witnesses:* JNO. SWANN, GEO. LOCKHART, GEORGE
MOORE. Assistant Judge of New Hanover County, THOS. LLOYD.

DAMERELL, JAMES. Chowan Precinct.

June 22, 1692. October 3, 1704. *Daughters:* RACHELL DAMERELL.
Wife: LUCY. *Witnesses:* DANIELL HALLSEY, WILLM. JONES. *Clerk of the Court:* NA. CHEVIN.

DANIEL, ELISABETH. Tyrrell County.

March 1, 1752. June 9, 1752. *Sons:* ROBERT, THOMAS, JOHN ("my manner plantation"), WILLIAM, AARON, JOSIAH. *Daughters:* SARAH WILLSON, ELISABETH DANIEL, MARY WARD, RUTH DANIEL, PRICILAH DANIEL. *Executors:* THOMAS and JOHN DANIEL (sons). *Witnesses:* WM. WILLIS, JOHN BROWN, SENIOR, MARY WILLIS. *Clerk of the Court of Beaufort County:* WILL ORMOND.

DANIEL, JOHN. Northampton County.

November 13, 1754. February Court, 1755. *Sons:* EZEKIEL ("my plantation"), EPHRAIM, JOSEPH, JOHN, ABRAHAM, ISAAC. *Daughters:* SARAH DANIEL, ELIZABETH DANIEL. *Wife and Executrix:* SARAH. *Executor:* JOHN DANIEL (son). *Witnesses:* SAMUEL PARKER, JOSEPH DANIEL. *Clerk of the Court:* I. EDWARDS.

DANIELL, OWEN. Chowan Precinct.

March 7, 1700. *Executor:* THOMAS JONES (to take care of two of the testator's children until they arrive at age). *Son:* THOMAS (in care of THOMAS POLLOCK). *Daughter:* MARY (in care of JAMES HIRES (?)). *Witnesses:* CORNELIUS BENNINGTON, JOHN JONES. *Clerk of the Court:* N. CHEVIN.

DANIEL, THOMAS. Tyrrell County.

July 11, 1749. September Court, 1749. *Sons:* ROBERT LANIER DANIEL, THOMAS, JOHN, WILLIAM, ARON, JOSIAH. *Daughters:* SARAH WILLSON, ELISABETH DANIEL, MARY DANIEL, RUTH DANIEL, PRISILIA DANIEL. (To all of the above named is bequeathed one shilling.) *Wife and Executrix:* ELISABETH ("all my estate"). *Witnesses:* WM. WILLISS, JOHN WILLSON, JOHN BROWN. *Clerk of the Court:* EVAN JONES.

DANIELL, WILLIAM. Bath Town, Beaufort County.

December 31, 1740. March Court, 1740. *Wife and Executrix:* FRANCES. *Wife's Grandson:* WILLIAM DANIELL PENKET. *Witnesses:* JAS. CALEPS, THOMAS OWEN, WM. FOREMAN, ROGER JONES. *Clerk of the Court:* ROGER JONES.

DANN, JOHN, SENR.   Albemarle County.
    January 7, 1696–1697. May Court, 1697. *Sons:* JOHN, LUIA. *Daughter:* ELIZABETH DANN. *Wife and Executrix:* JEANE. *Witnesses:* ARCHIBALD BURNETT, HUGH―――, JONATHAN BURDET. *Clerk of the Court:* W. GLOVER.

DANSBE, DANIEL.   Edgecombe County.
    January 21, 1749–1750. August Court, 1750. *Son:* ISOME ("my plantation"). *Daughters:* MARY, ELIZABETH and CLEAREMON DANSBE. *Wife and Executrix:* ELIZABETH. *Executor:* DAVID ROZIER. *Witnesses:* ROBERT TAYLOR, DAVID COLLINS, REUBEN ROZIER. *Clerk of the Court:* BENJ'N WYNNS.

DARDEN, JOSEPH.   Bertie Precinct.
    February 18, 1732–1733. August Court, 1733. *Sons:* WEST (119 acres of land), JOSEPH (110 acres of land), HENAREY (320 acres of land on the horse pasture swamp). *Daughters:* AMERICA DARDEN, REBEC DARDEN. *Wife and Executrix:* ALSE. *Executor:* ARTHUR WILLIAMS. *Witnesses:* ELIZABETH JONES, MARY POWERS, JOHN EGERTON. *Clerk of the Court:* RT. FORSTER.

DARLING, RICHARD.   Chowan Precinct.
    April 8, 1702. *Son:* THOMAS. *Wife and Executrix:* ELIZABETH. *Witnesses:* COLLUMB. FLYN, DANIEL DEENS, JAMES LONG. No probate.

DARNALL, ANN.   Currituck Precinct.
    June 17, 1720. July 20, 1720–1721. *Son:* WILLIAM DARNALL. *Executor:* RICHARD DAUGE. *Witnesses:* PETER DAUGE, SUSANNAH DAUGE. *Clerk of the Court:* JOS. WICKER.

DAUGHTREY, THOMAS.   Northampton County.
    November 15, 1757. November Court, 1757. *Sons:* SAMUEL ("plantation whereon I now live"), JOHN, THOMAS, JESSE. *Daughters:* MARY ROOKS, ELIZABETH WILLIAMS, SARAH RICE, MARTHA RUTLAND, PATIENCE MONSON, PLEASANTS DAUGHTREY. *Wife:* MARY. *Grandson:* JOHN DAUGHTREY. *Executors:* BRYAN DAUGHTREY (cousin), ROBERT PEELLE. *Witnesses:* SAMUELL PIRKINS, JOSHUA DAUGHTREY, ALEXANDRIA DAUGHTREY. *Clerk of the Court:* I. EDWARDS.

DAVENPORT, JACOB.   Tyrrell County.
    July 29, 1746. *Wife:* RACHEL. *Daughter:* ANN. *Brothers:* JAMES and JOHN DAVENPORT (*Executors*), WILLIAM DAVENPORT. *Witnesses:* EDWARD PHELPS, JOHN BROWN, JOHN DAVENPORT, SENIOR.

DAVEY, WALTER.   Beaufort County.

June 22, 1743. October 24, 1743, "late of the City of Dublin, now resident in Beaufort County." *Sons:* SAMUELL, JOSEPH. *Daughters:* JANE, MARGARETT and RACHELL. *Executor:* ABRAHAM DUNCAN. *Witnesses:* EDWARD HOWCOTT, JAMES BROWN, SAML. BUNDY. Will proven before J. MONTGOMERY, C. J.

DAVID, PHILIP.   Wilmington, New Hanover County.

August 5, 1747. December Court, 1747. *Son and Executor:* DAVID (land lying on North East River). *Daughter:* MARY MCKEITHEN. *Executor:* JAMES SMALLWOOD. *Witnesses:* WM. HARRISON, CHARLOTTE SMALLWOOD, JOSEPH JONES. *Clerk of the Court:* JAMES SMALLWOOD.

DAVIES, FRANCIS.   County not given.

February 10, 1749. April 30, 1753. Cape Faire. *Wife and sole legatee and devisee:* JUDITH. *Witnesses:* BENJ'N MORISON, ROBERT HALTON. Will proven before MATT. ROWAN.

DAVIS, ARTHUR.   County not given.

February 2, 1733–1734. April 1, 1735. *Sons:* ARTHUR (land on "ye rainbow banks"), LEWIS (200 acres of land on Banbow Creek). *Son-in-law:* WILLIAM FORK (100 acres of land adjoining Lewis' plantation). *Wife:* ELIZABETH. *Executors:* ARTHUR and LEWIS DAVIS (sons). *Witnesses:* SAMUEL WHEATLEY, STEPHEN ANDREWS. Will proven before *Governor* GAB. JOHNSTON at Edenton.

DAVIS, DAVID.   Bladen County.

December 9, 1740. September Court, 1741. *Sister:* RACHEL DAVIS (plantation purchased of GABRIEL WAYNE). *Executor:* WILLIAM BARTRAM. *Witnesses:* JONATHAN EVANS, THOS. WALKER, THOMAS JONES. *Clerk of the Court:* JOHN CLAYTON. *Chief Justice:* J. MONTGOMERY.

DAVIS, HUGH.   County not given.

December 7, 1729. *Legatees and devisees:* JOHN HARMAN (plantation on the Sound Side), ROBERT HARMAN, MARY HARMAN, ANN LONGLAD. *Executrix:* JULIANA LAKER. *Witnesses:* THOMAS CALLOWAY, WILLIAM———. *Clerk of the Court:* EDWARD MOSELEY.

DAVIS, ISAAC.   Currituck County.

March 21, 1742. July 13, 1743. *Son:* CORNELIUS ("all my land and plantation"). *Wife and Executrix:* RACHEL. *Executor:* CORNELIUS JONES (father-in-law). *Witnesses:* DANIELL PHILLIPS, FRANCES HODGES, FRANCIS STAFFORD. *Clerk of the Court:* JOHN LURRY.

ABSTRACT OF WILLS, 1690—1760.

DAVIS, JAMES.   County not given.

April 22, 1715. *Sons:* WILLIAM, JAMES, JOHN, ROBERT, HENRY. *Wife and Executrix:* ELIZABETH. *Executors:* ROBERT WHITE, JOHN WHITE and JOHN SYMONS. *Witnesses:* HENRY WHITE, ARNOLD WHITE, JR., DAMARIS WHITE, ARNOLD WHITE, SENR. No probate.

DAVIS, JOHN.   County not given.

April 26, 1688. May 12, 1688. *Daughter:* ELIZABETH. *Friend and Executor:* WILLIAM WILKISON. *Witnesses:* MATHEW LYAL, WILLIAM ELFISK, JANE MILLER. Will proven before SETH SOTHELL.

DAVIS, JOHN.   Hyde County.

December 17, 1751. March Court, 1752. *Sons:* SAMUEL (plantation on the river side), JOHN. *Daughters:* TEMPERANCE DAVIS, JEMIMA BALLARD. *Wife:* SARAH DAVIS. *Executors:* NATHANIEL DAVIS and THOS. SMITH. *Witnesses:* THOS. SMITH, JER. SLADE, RICHARD WOOD. *Clerk of the Court:* FRAN. EGLETON.

DAVIS, JOHN.   Pasquotank County.

March 28, 1753. April Court, 1753. *Sons:* JOSEPH ("my plantation"), WILLIAM, JOHN, SAMUEL. *Daughter:* SARAH GORDEN. *Executors:* JOSEPH DAVIS (son), WILLIAM GORDEN (son-in-law). *Witnesses:* WILLIAM SYMONS, THOMAS LOWRY, MARY TART. *Clerk of the Court:* THOS. TAYLOR.

DAVIS, JOHN.   Pasquotank County.

January 10, 1754. April Court, 1754. *Brothers:* SAMUEL and WILLIAM DAVIS. *Cousins:* JOHN DAVIS, JR., MARY DAVIS. *Friends:* JAMES TURNER, WILLIAM GORDEN, JOHN GORDEN. *Executor:* JOSEPH DAVIS (brother). *Witnesses:* JOHN TURNER, JOSEPH LOWRY, THEOPHILUS LEONARD. *Clerk of the Court:* THOS. TAYLOR.

DAVIS, PETER.   Bertie Precinct.

April 29, 1719. May Court, 1723. *Daughter:* SARY DAVIS. *Brother:* DAVIS. *Cousins:* ARTHUR and HENERY CRAWFORD. *Executrix:* WIFE (mentioned, but not named). *Witnesses:* ARTHUR CRAFFORD (Crawford), WILLIAM CROFORD (Crawford). *Clerk of the Conrt:* RT. FORSTER.

DAVIS, RICHARD.   Pasquotank County.

June 9, 1737. June 14, 1737. *Sons:* JOSHUA ("plantation whereon I now live"). *Daughters:* ALEE and ABIGILL (DAVIS). *Guardians:* ELIZABETH HALL and JAMES COPLAND. *Executor:* ZACH NIXON. *Witnesses:* RICHARD CHEASTEN, RALPH FLETCHER, SAMUELL MOORE. Will proven before W. SMITH, *Chief Justice.*

DAVIS, ROBERT.   Pasquotank County.

December 30, 1749. January Court, 1750. *Sons:* JAMES ("maner plantation"), THOMAS ("my other plantation which lies next to JAMES LOWRY"). *Daughters:* ELIZABETH, RUTH. *Wife:* SARAH. *Executors:* JAMES and THOMAS (sons). *Witnesses:* JOSHUA WHITE, JAMES NEWBY. *Clerk of the Court:* THOS. TAYLOR.

DAVIS, SAMUELL.   Albemarle County.

January 11, 1687–1688. *Wife:* ELIZABETH. *Witnesses:* ROBERT WALLIS, JOHN BILLITT. No probate. Device on seal is three arrows and tomahawk.

DAVIS, SOLOMON.   Pasquotank County.

January 12, 1737. January Court, 1739. *Daughters:* DOROTHY DAVIS, MARGARET FORSTER, ELIZABETH DAVIS. *Son-in-law:* CALEB COEN. *Grandson:* DANIEL KOEN. *Friend:* JOHN SAWYER. *Wife and Executrix:* SARAH. *Witnesses:* B. MORGAN, JOHN GRAY. *Clerk of the Court:* JAMES CRAVEN.

DAVIS, THOMAS.   Bath County.

February 15, 1711–1712. January 4, 1714. *Son:* PHILLIP ("my manner plantation on Oyster Creek, West side of Pamlico River), THOMAS (land on Matchepungo River). *Daughters:* SARAH, RACHELL, CHARITY and MARY DAVIS. *Wife and Executrix:* THOMESON. *Witnesses:* none given. No signature. Will proven by GYLES SHUTE and THOMASIN DAVIS. *Clerk of the Court:* JOHN DRINKWATER.

DAVIS, THOMAS.   Perquimans County.

December 14, 1745. April Court, 1746. *Son and Executor:* MOSES ("plantation whereon I now live"). *Daughters:* ELIZABETH DAVIS, SARAH BOND. *Wife and Executrix:* ELIZABETH. *Witnesses:* WILLIAM EASON, THOMAS EASON, ISAAC SPEIGHT. *Clerk of the Court:* EDMUND HATCH.

DAVIS, THOMAS.   Granville County.

August 20, 1754. March 7, 1758. *Sons:* JOHN, THOMAS, RUBIN and RICHARD. *Daughter:* MARY DAVIS. *Wife and Executrix:* ELISABETH. *Executors:* DANIEL UNDERWOOD, RICHARD PINNIL. *Witnesses:* JOHN GIBBS, THOS. COOK, THOMAS ZACEE. *Clerk of the Court:* DANIEL WELDON.

DAVIS, THOMAS.   Bladen County.

October 2, 1761. May Court, 1769. *Daughter-in-law:* KATHERINE GREADY. *Daughter:* MARY GREADY (500 acres of land adjoining "Secretary Rice's backland"). *Brother:* WILLIAM DAVIS. *Executors:* WILLIAM DAVIS and JOHN LUCAS. *Witnesses:* JNO. TURNER, RALPH MILLER,

THOS. NEWTON. Codicil to will appoints ANN DAVIS (wife) and THOMAS OWEN *Executors* in place of WILLIAM DAVIS and JOHN LUCAS. *Witnesses to codicil:* THOS. HALL, JOHN ROOT, RALPH MILLER. *Clerk of the Court:* ARTHUR HOWE.

DAVIS, WILLIAM.   Carteret County.

June Court, 1756. *Sons:* NATHAN, JOSEPH, WICKER, CALLIP, BENIEMEN, WILLIAM, SOLOMON. *Daughter:* ABIGARL. *Wife and Executrix:* MARY. *Executors:* NATHAN and JOSEPH (sons). *Witnesses:* GEORGE BELL, RILIND BELL and JAMES SHAFORD (Shackleford). *Clerk of the Court:* JOHN SMITH.

DAVISON, JOHN.   Bertie County.

August 6, 1752. October Court, 1756. *Son and Executor:* JOHN ("plantation whereon I now live"). *Grandson:* JOHN DAVISON (land on Chinkopin Creek). *Granddaughter:* MARY DAVISON. *Wife and Executrix:* MARY. *Witnesses:* JOHN FREEMAN, ABRAM HARRILL, JACOB LASITER, THOMAS HARRILL. *Clerk of the Court:* BENJN. WYNNS.

DAVISON, JOHN.   Edenton, Chowan County.

November 1, 1773. December 9, 1773. *Wife:* ELESHEA CHRISTIANA DAVISON. *Brother and Executor:* ROBERT DAVISON. *Friends and Executors:* JOHN SMITH, ANDREW LITTLE. *Witnesses:* JOHN ROM COUGH, CHAS. BONDFIELD, GEO. GRAY. Will proven before JO. MARTIN.

DAWE, WILLIAM.   Beaufort County.

January 20, 1745. March Court, 1745. *Son:* WILLIAM (100 acres of land on Durham's Creek), JOHN ("the plantation whereon I now live"). NICHOLAS and WILLIAM. *Daughters:* DIANA DAWE, SARAH DIXON, LYDIA COE. *Wife and Executrix:* DINAH. *Witnesses:* EDWARD CAMPEN, JOHN CORREE. *Clerk of the Court:* JOHN FORBES.

DAWS, WILLIAM.   Chowan Precinct.

July 21, 1719. October Court, 1719. *Sons:* WILLIAM and ELYJAH (268 acres of land). *Executors:* WILLIAM BAKER and JOHN BROWN. *Witnesses:* JOHN BROWN, JOHN MANEAR, ELIZABETH BAKER. *Clerk of the Court:* R. HICKS.

DAWSON, JOHN.   Edgecombe County.

November 22, 1748. May Court, 1749. *Sons:* JOHN, DEMEY, SOLLOMON. *Daughters:* MARTHA, PATIENCE. *Wife and Executrix:* MARY. *Witnesses:* BENJ. CHAMPION, FRANCES BYTHELL HAYNES. *Clerk of the Court:* BENJN. WYNNS.

DEANE, GEORGE, SENR.   Albemarle County.
April 10, 1700. GEO. DEANE (150 acres of land). *Daughter:* CHRISTIAN. HUMPHREY LEGG and JOHN BATCHELOR (150 acres each). *Executrix:* ELIZABETH DEANE. *Witnesses:* JOHN PROCTOR, MARY SECHEWRAA, HUMPHREY LEGG. (No probate.)

DEIPTT, JOHN.   Bath County.
January 17, 1723-1724. June 17, 1724. *Sons:* PETTER DEIPTT (plantation in Machapongo containing two hundred acres), JOHN (200 acres of land). *Wife and Executrix:* PENON. *Daughter and Executrix:* ANN DEIPTT. *Witnesses:* PETER HAND, JOHN FONVIELLE. *Clerk of the Court:* JOHN CORNICK. *Clerk of the Court at Newbern:* C. METCALFE.

DELAMAR, FRANCIS.   Beaufort County.
May 15, 1739. March, 1741. *Son:* THOMAS ("plantation on the South side of Broad Creek"). *Wife and Executrix:* SUSANNAH. *Son:* FRANCIS ("plantation whereon I now live"). *Witnesses:* ROBERT WENHAM, BENJA. RICE, MARY RICE. *Clerk of the Court:* JOHN FORBES.

DELAMARE, STEPHEN.   Pasquotank Precinct.
October 2, 1732. October Court, 1732. *Nephew:* JOSEPH STOCKLEY ("plantation whereon I now live"), ISAAC STOCKLEY. *Cousin:* EDWARD MAYO. *Sister and Executrix:* ANN STOCKLEY. *Brother:* FRANCIS DELAMARE. *Witnesses:* HARRAL BLY, SAMUEL REDING, JO. PALIN. *Clerk of the Court:* H. MINSON.

DELOHOIDE, WILLIAM.   New Hanover County.
October 3, 1738. This is a nuncupative will proven by MRS. ELIZABETH ROWAN, and provides for the lading of his sloop (WILLIAM O'BRYAN, Master), and of his brig by CAPT. ROWAN and cargo delivered to THOMAS FARREN and JOHN ———. Proven before ROBT. HALTON, J. P.

DENEHAM, ELIZABETH.   Bath County.
July 9, 1716. *Legatees:* ANN CLEWES, ELIZABETH LEIGH, JOSEPH TREWETT, ELEZABETH DENEHAM, JOHN LEIGH, JOHN DENEHAM. *Witnesses:* ELIZABETH LEE and JAMES LEE, JUNR. *Clerk of the Court:* JNO. DRINKWATER.

DENSON, JAMES.   Onslow County.
May 3, 1756. *Legatees:* JAMES HOWARD, JOHN HOWARD, LUKE BAREFIELD, SARAH ASHBURN. *Wife and Executrix:* ELIZABETH. *Witnesses:* WM. ROYAL, MOSES ANDERSON, JOSEPH STURGES. *Clerk of the Court:* WILLM. CRAY.

DEPT, PENELOPE.

March 25, 1732. August 27, 1735. *Sons:* PETER, JOHN *(Executor).* *Daughters:* ANN, JANE and ELIZABETH. *Witnesses:* MARY LANE, ELIZABETH NORWOOD, EDWARD BROUGHTON. Will proven before W. SMITH, C. J. Executor qualified before C. POWELL and N. ROUTLEDGE.

DERBY, WILLIAM.

March 10, 1687. March 13, 1688. *Daughter:* JUDITH ("plantation whereon I now live"). *Witnesses:* JOHN PRIVETT, ROBERT LINDSAY, JOHN DAWLEY. Will proven before SETH SOTHELL.

DERHAM, ELIZABETH. Bath County.

July 17, 1716. *Legatees:* ANNE CLOWS, KATHERINE DERHAM, ELIZABETH LEIGH, JOSEPH TRUWITT, ELIZABETH DERHAM, JOSEPH DERHAM, JOHN LEIGH, JAMES LEIGH. *Brother:* JOHN DERHAM. *Father-in-law and Executor:* JAMES LEIGH. *Witnesses:* names not given. *Clerk of the Court:* JOHN DRINKWATER. Original missing. Recorded in Book 1712-22, page 125.

DEROSSET, MOSES JOHN. New Hanover County.

November 30, 1767. March 1, 1768. ("Practitioner in physic and surgery"). *Wife and Executrix:* MARY. *Daughter:* MAGDALENE MARY DEROSSET. *Son:* ARMOND JOHN DEROSSET. *Executors:* LEWIS HENRY DEROSSET (brother), JOHN DUBOIS, JAMES MOORE and MARMADUKE JONES. *Witnesses:* ANN MOORE, A. MACLAINE, E. JUSTUCE (?). Will proven before Gov. WM. TRYON at Wilmington.

DEXTER, HOPE. New River, in Onslow County.

March 10, 1745. April 1, 1746. *Brother:* PHILLIP DEXTER (all the land that lies between the main road and Mitiams Creek). *Friend:* JAMES THOMSON (land "between my land and the land above named"). *Nephew:* HOPE DEXTER (one watch). *Witnesses:* DANIEL MCFETERS, JOHN HOLMES, CHARLES STOUT, JOSHUA, JAMES. *Clerk of the Court:* GEO. CLOPTON.

DEVIS, JOHN. Newberne, in Craven County.

March 11, 1754. March 25, 1754. *Legatees and Devisees:* JOHN FREEMAN, ANN NELSON, JOHN STARKEY *(Executor),* MARY WIGMORE, RICHARD LYON. *Witnesses:* EUPHEMIA WHITE, RICHARD LYON, CHARLES FARQUHARSON. Will proven before MATT. ROWAN.

DEW, JOHN. Bertie County.

September 5, 1740. November Court, 1744. *Sons:* JOHN ("all my horses and mairs that run on the South side of the Meharin River"), JOSEPH (land lying on the East side of the "Rode from Cornell hills ferry and also land on Buckhorse swamp"), SPENSER ("plantation whereon I now live"), WILLIAM, MORVEN. *Daughter:* PATIENCE. *Wife and Executrix:* SUSANNAH. *Executor:* JOSEPH DEW (son). *Witnesses:* EDWARD MOSELEY, ALES MOSELEY, CONSTANT DEW. *Clerk of the Court:* RT. FORSTER. (Northampton County.)

DIAS, HENRY. Beaufort Precinct (Bath County).

December 8, 1737. March Court, 1737. *Sons:* RICHARD (plantation on Blounts Creek), JOHN (land called Forke neck), THOMAS (land on WALLASES Creek), HENRY ("plantation whereon I now live"). *Daughter:* ANN DIAS. *Wife and Executrix:* REBECCA. *Executor:* JOHN PURSELL. *Witnesses:* RICHARD EVANS, JAMES PERDUE, MARY PERKINS. *Clerk of the Court:* ROGER JONES.

DICKENSON, JOHN. Northampton County.

February 4, 1742. August Court, 1749. *Sons:* DANIEL, JOHN, DAVID, ISAAC. *Daughters:* SARAH DANIEL, ELIZABETH FUTREL, REBECKAH NEWSOM, CHARITY DICKENSON, MARY DICKENSON. *Wife:* REBECCA. *Executors:* DANIEL and JOHN DICKENSON (sons). *Witnesses:* JOSEPH JORDAN, ROBERT PEELLE, ISAAC PARKER. *Clerk of the Court:* I. EDWARDS.

DICKINSON, MARY. Northampton County.

October 6, 1753. November Court, 1753. *Brothers:* DAVID, ISAAC (*Executors*), DANIEL and JOHN DICKINSON. *Sisters:* CHARITY PEELLE, SARAH DANIEL, ELIZABETH FUTRELL. *Kinsman:* WILLIAM ROWSUM. *Witnesses:* JOHN BROWN, SUSANAH PARKER, SUSANAH HORTON. *Clerk of the Court:* I. EDWARDS.

DICKINSON, REBECKAH. Northampton County.

July 1, 1750. February Court, 1753. *Sons:* JOHN and ISAAC DICKINSON (*Executors*), DAVID. *Daughters:* SARAH DANIEL, ELIZABETH FUTURELL, REBECCAH NEWSOM, CHARITY DICKINSON, MARY DICKINSON. *Witnesses:* ISAAC PARKER, JOHN HORTON. *Clerk of the Court:* I. EDWARDS.

DICKS, JOHN. Chowan Precinct.

February 10, 1705. October 2, 1706. *Son-in-law:* RICHT LEWIS. *Wife and Executrix:* PHELIS. *Witnesses:* THOS. LUTEN, JON JONES, JON WHEATLY. *Clerk of the Court:* N. CHEVIN.

DICKSON, JOHN. Dobbs County.

April 16, 1769. *Father:* JAMES DICKSON. *Mother:* JENNET. *Uncle:* ROBERT GRACEY. *Friends:* JAMES CUMMIN, JAMES GIBSON (*Executor*), JAMES LINDSAY (*Executor*). *Witnesses:* ANTHONY HERRING, CHRISTOPHER BLANSHARD, CHARLES HINES. No probate.

ABSTRACT OF WILLS, 1690—1760.   99

DISCORAH, THOMAS.   Perquimans County.

January 11, 1726–1727. February 2, 1726–1727. *Legatees:* SAMUEL PHELPS, SARAH SHEARWOOD, MARY SHEARWOOD, JAMES SITERSON (*Executor*). *Witnesses:* RALPH BOOSMAN, R. WILSON. Will proven before RICH'D EVERARD.

DIXON, JOHN.   Beaufort County.

March 23, 1772. December 11, 1773. *Son and Executor:* CHOOSEWELL ("my land"). *Daughter:* BIATHA. *Witnesses:* NICHOLAS DAW, LEVIN STANFORD, THOMAS DIXON. Will proven before JO. MARTIN.

DIXON, ROBERT.   Bertie Precinct.

April 4, 1727. August Court, 1727. *Sons:* TOBIAS, JAMES, ROBERT. *Daughter:* FRANCES. *Wife and Executrix:* CHRISTIANA. *Executor:* JOHN LOWE. *Witnesses:* ABRAHAM BURTON, BEREBE MELTON, WILLIAM LOWE. *Clerk of the Court:* RT. FORSTER.   Coat of arms on seal.

DOBBS, ARTHUR.   Brunswick, in New Hanover County.

"Governor and Captain General of the Province of North Carolina." August 31, 1763. April 24, 1765. *Sons:* CONWAY RICHARD DOBBS, EDWARD BRICE DOBBS. *Wife:* JUSTINA. *Brother:* REVEREND DOCTOR RICHARD DOBBS. *Witnesses:* JAMES HASELL, LEWIS DEROSSET, JOHN SAMPSON. Proven before WM. TRYON. The following items are of interest: "instead of immoderate funeral expenses I desire that one hundred pounds Sterling money may be paid and distributed proportionately among the housekeepers of the Parrishes of Ballynure and Kilroot in the County of Antrim and Kingdom of Ireland, and one other hundred pounds of like money among the poor freemen House-keepers who reside within the county of the town of Carrick-fergus to be paid — — — — out of my Demesnes at Castle Dobbs or out of the arrears of rents I reserved out of a Moiety of lands in that Kingdom during my life." All slaves, plate, etc., is bequeathed to wife, together with "the money and interest due to me by the General Assembly for the lands called Tower hill in Johnston County, purchased from me by the publick." "Whereas, I have a right to the Moiety of two hundred thousand acres of land granted to me by the Crown in Sixteen patents of twelve thousand five hundred acres each in Mecklinburgh (late Anson) County as one of the associates of HUEY and CRYMBLE ————etc." To each of children is bequeathed fifty pounds and to brother twenty pounds. "Item. Whereas I am entitled to a Moiety of Twelve Thousand acres of land by a purchase from MR. PATRICK SMITH of Waterford, merchant, for which a patent was granted to him as an associate of HUEY and CRYMBLE, subdivided from the great tract No. 4, the heirs and assigns of MR. JAMES BENNING of Lisburn, Ireland, being entitled to the other moiety." "I give and bequeath to my son CONWAY RICHARD DOBBS

—————— all my plate goods, Household furniture, arrears, Rents and other chattels whatsoever which are now belonging to me at my decease, which are now or hereafter may be at Castle Dobbs in the County of Antrim and Kingdom of Ireland." Sons and wife appointed executors and executrix. Impression of head on seal.

DOBSON, WILLIAM. Chowan Precinct.

August 23, 1690. October 13, 1690. *Wife and Executrix:* KATEREN. *Witnesses:* JOHN LEWIS, THOMAS MUNS, JOHN WINGATE. *Clerk of the Court:* JOHN WINGATE.

DOLEER, GYLES. Albemarle County.

February 26, 1687–1688. January 6, 1689. *Legatees and Devisees:* JOHN VALLENTINE ROE, DAVID PRITCHETT, ROWLAND BUCKLY, MARY GARNETT ("my plantation"). *Executor:* RALPH GARNETT. *Witnesses:* PAUL LATHUM, FRANCIS HENRY, ROWLAND BUSSLY. Will proven before THO. ROLFE, ROBERT WALLIS, PAUL LATHUM———, THOMAS SYMONS.

DONOHO, JOHN. New Hanover County.

June 6, 1743. June 24, 1743. *Friend, Executor and sole legatee and devisee:* WILLIAM WHITE of Wilmington. *Witnesses:* JAMES SMALLWOOD, GEO. OWEN, ANN HIGGINES. *Clerk of the Court:* JAMES SMALLWOOD.

DOOLES, THOMAS. Edgecombe County.

November 28, 1756. May Court, 1757. *Sons:* JOSEPH ("plantation whereon I now live"), JOHN. *Daughters:* SARAH, CATTEREN, BITHA. *Wife:* PATIENCE. *Executors:* JOSEPH DOOLES (son), ROBERT PURRER. *Witnesses:* JAMES MYHAN, MOSES HORNE, ROBERT PURYEAR, JOSEPH DOOLES. *Clerk of the Court:* JOS. MONTFORT.

DOUGE, TULL. Currituck County.

May 18, 1746. July 1, 1746. *Brother and Executor:* JAMES DOUGE. *Brother:* JOHN DOUGE. *Sisters:* SARAH SOREY, SUSANNAH CLASCO (or GLASCO), MARY DOUGE. *Other legatees:* PETER SOREY, CALEB GLASCO. *Witnesses:* JOSA CAMPBELL, HENRY SIMMONS, JOAB DOUGE. *Clerk of the Court:* RICHARD MCCLURE.

DOUGHTY, JOHN. Wilmington, New Hanover County.

June 9, 1742. August 31, 1749. *Wife:* MARIAN. *Witnesses:* THOMAS CHINAGAM, JOSA GRAINGER. *Clerk of the Court:* ISAAC FARIES.

DOUGLASS, DAVID. Northampton County.

March 29, 1753. November Court, 1753. *Sons:* WILLIAM ("land whereon he now lives"), JOHN ("manner land and plantation"). *Daughters:* MOLLEY CARRILL, ELIZABETH HARWELL, SUSANAH DOUGLASS. *Grand-*

daughter: ELIZABETH CARRIL. *Wife and Executrix:* ELIZABETH. *Executor:* WILLIAM DOUGLASS (son). *Witnesses:* CHRISMASS RAY, JOHN DOUGLASS. *Clerk of the Court:* I. EDWARDS.

DOUGLAS, JAMES.   Bertie County.

October 6, 1750. July 11, 1752. *Sons:* KESIA (plantation), JAMES. *Daughter:* ANN. *Granddaughter:* ELIZABETH DOUGLAS. *Wife and Executrix:* ELIZABETH. *Witnesses:* JOHN BROWN, ELIZABETH ROBERTSON, JOSEPH MADLIN. *Secretary to the Governor:* SAML. ORMES. Lands on Hoskie Swamp devised to children.

DOWAY, ROBERT.   Bladen County.

January 30, 1756. January Court, 1758. *Sons:* JAMES and ROBERT. *Daughter:* ELIZABETH. *Wife:* CATHERINE. *No executors. Witnesses:* JOHN STACK, HENRY LEWIS, JAMES WHITE. *Clerk of the Court:* J. BURGWIN.

DOWNER, WILLIAM.   Brunswick, New Hanover County.

December 10, 1745. March Court, 1745. *Executors:* CAPT. HUGH BLANING and CAPT. RICHARD QUINCE. The will directs the executors to sell so much of the estate as may be necessary to pay the debts of the testator and to pay to themselves 80 pounds each in addition to their legal fees of seven and one-half per cent, and to ship the remainder to WILLIAM WYNN and wife RUTH at ALDGATE in the City of London, and BENJAMIN and MARY SANDWELL in Wapping, London. *Witnesses:* HUGH MACKAY, RALPH SUGNION, THOMAS CAMPBELL. *Clerk of the Court:* JAMES SMALLWOOD.

DOWNING, WILLIAM.   Tyrrell County.

April 1, 1739. April 6, 1739. *Sons:* WILLIAM ("my plantation, except sawmill, which is bequeathed to CULLEN POLLOCK and STEPHEN LEE, proceeds to be applied to debt due SAMUEL HERRING of London, woolen draper). *Brothers-in-law:* EBENEZER SLADE (450 acres of land on Moratock River), HENRY SLADE. *Son-in-law:* THOMAS LEE. *Executors:* CULLEN POLLOCK, JOHN MONTGOMERY, STEPHEN LEE, PETER PAYNE. *Witnesses:* WM. MAXWELL, SAM SCOLLAY, DAVID COLTRANE. Codicil bearing same date as will provides for working slaves in mill. Will proven before W. SMITH, C. J.

DOWNING, WILLIAM.   Tyrrell County.

February 24, 1748. March 7, 1748. *Son:* HENRY ("plantation whereon I now dwell"). *Wife:* ANN. *Daughters:* MARY, ELIZABETH. *Friend:* JOHN HUGHES. *Executors:* STEVENS LEE, JOHN BARROW. *Witnesses:* JACOB BLOUNT, JAMES JONES, MARY JONES. *Clerk of the Court:* EVAN JONES.

DRAKE, JOHN.   Bertie Precinct.

January 5, 1728. May Court, 1729. *Son:* JAMES ("my manner plantation"). *Wife:* SARAH. *Executor:* JAMES BRYANT (father-in-law). *Witnesses:* JOHN SUTTON, JOHN DICKINSON, RICHARD SUMNER. *Clerk of the Court:* RT. FORSTER.

DREDING, JOHN.   Craven County.

December 22, 1757. February Court, 1758. *Executor:* JOSEPH PRINGLE ("plantation whereon I now live"). *Wife and Executrix:* CHARITY. *Witnesses:* SAMUEL SLADE, JOHN SLADE, SAMUEL SLADE, JUNR. *Clerk of the Court:* PETER CONWAY.

DRINKWATER, JOHN.   Bath County.

August 7, 1717. May 30, 1718. *Devisees:* PHILLIP SHUTE, son of GYLES and CHARITY SHUTE (plantation containing 820 acres, lying between Mallard Creek and Goose Creek; 320 acres on South Dividing Creek; house and lot in Bath Town; money and plate on hand), GYLES SHUTE (wearing apparel), CHARITY SHUTE (all lands in event of death of PHILLIP. *Executors:* GYLES and CHARITY SHUTE. *Witnesses:* PATRICK CAVAN, ELIZABETH ELLEBAR. Will proven before CHAS. EDEN, at Bath Town.

DUBOIS, JOHN.   Wilmington, New Hanover County.

September 13, 1767. March 1, 1768. *Sons:* PETER, WALTER, JOHN (house in Dock Street, also plantation on Smith Creek containing 300 acres; also a large diamond ring), ISAAC (two houses in Dock Street), JAMES (two lots in front street and houses thereon). *Daughters:* ANNE JEAN DUBOIS, MAGDALENE MARGARET DUBOIS (two brick houses on Dock Street and two diamond rings), MARGARET DUBOIS (lot on the north side of Market Street.) *Wife and Executrix:* JEAN. *Friends:* CALEB and CORNELIUS GRAINGER (sons of COLONEL CALEB GRAINGER). *Executors and Guardians of children:* JEAN DUBOIS (wife), PETER, WALTER and JOHN DUBOIS (sons), LEWIS HENRY and MOSES JOHN DEROSSET. *Witnesses:* J. EUSTACE, EDWARD CHIVERS, ARCHIBALD MACLAINE. *Secretary:* BENJ'N HERON. Will proven before WM. TRYON at Wilmington.

DUCKENFIELD, NATHANIEL. Utkinton, in the County of Chester, England.

July 4, 1746. January Court, 1756. *Wife and Executrix:* MARGRET (lands in County of Chester during widowhood, leasehold estate in Ludgate Street, London). *Friend and Executor:* JOSEPH COLLET, merchant of London (lands in North Carolina to be sold and proceeds applied according to directions). *Brother and Executor:* JOHN CHORLEY. *Nephew:* JOHN CHORLEY (son of sister, JANE CHORLEY). *Nephew and Executor:* SAMUEL

DUCKENFIELD (son of JOHN DUCKENFIELD of Bristol). *Witnesses:* WILLIAM PRIOR, JOSEPH COLLET, DOROTHY POTTS. Will proven before ROBERT CHAPMAN, Doctor of Laws, Surrogate to JOHN BETTESWORTH, certified by THOMAS, Archbishop of Canterbury, over the seal of the town of London. *Deputy Registers:* WM. LEGARD, PETER ST. ELY, HEN. STEPHENS. JOSEPH COLLET refused the trust imposed by this will in a writing witnessed by SAMUEL DUKINFIELD and BENJAMIN ROSEWELL. Letters of administration granted to MARGARET DUCKINFIELD by Bertie County Court, January, 1756. *Clerk of the Court:* BENJ. WYNNS. This will is illegible, but is recorded in Bk. Wills, 1755–58, at page 144.

DUCKENFIELD, WILLIAM. Chowan Precinct (formerly of Cheshire, in Great Britain).

May 17, 1720. February 27, 1721. *Brother:* JOHN DUCKENFIELD. *Cousins:* CHARLES BARBER, NATHANIEL DUCKENFIELD (son "of my brother, SIR ROBERT DUCKENFIELD, BARONET"), MARY, ANN, SUSANNA, JANE, SARAH, KATHERINE and JUDITH DUCKENFIELD (sisters of NATHANIEL). *Executor:* NATHANIEL DUCKENFIELD. *Witnesses:* THOMAS ASHLY, JOHN POWELL, BENJA. SOAMES, JOHN CHERYHOLME, JOHN DUCKENFIELD, E. MOSELEY. Will proven before CHAS. EDEN, *Governor.* Coat of arms on seal.

DUDLEY, CHRISTOPHER. Onslow County.

March 19, 1744–1745. February 26, 1746. *Sons:* EDWARD, WILLIAM, THOMAS and CHRISTOPHER DUDLEY (land on "the River"). *Grandsons:* GEORGE (son of EDWARD) and CHRISTOPHER (son of THOMAS) DUDLEY. *Daughter:* ANN HOUSTON (one negro). Other negroes bequeathed to wife and sons. *Wife and Executrix:* MARY. *Executor:* JOHN STARKEY. *Witnesses:* JANE SIMPSON, JOHN SIMPSON, MARY TROTT. Proven before GAB. JOHNSTON.

DUDLEY, EDWARD. County not given.

January 22, 1744–1745. April 3, 1745. *Son:* GEORGE. *Daughters:* HANNAH, ANNE, MARY. *Executors:* JOHN STARKEY and JOHN DUDLEY. *Witnesses:* JOHN HENAGAN ("nicknamed SWENNY"), WILLIAM SIMPSON, HANNAH PITTS. Will proven before GAB. JOHNSTON. *Chief Justice:* E. MOSELEY.

DUDLEY, JOHN. Onslow County.

September 12, 1748. April 2, 1751. *Sons:* JOHN and DAVID ("my cow pen land to be equally divided between them"), WILLIAM ("my manor plantation"). *Daughter:* SARAH. *Wife:* ELIZABETH. *Executors:* JOHN STARKEY and THOMAS DUDLEY. *Witnesses:* JOHN WELLS, NATHNELL BURNAP, RICHARD STEVENS. *Clerk of the Court:* THOS. BLACK. Courthouse at Johnston, on New River.

DUDLEY, THOMAS.   Carteret County.

  May 13, 1753. June Court, 1753. *Sons:* CHRISTOPHER (250 acres of land on East side of White Oak River), ELIJAH, JACOB, STEPHEN, ABRAHAM and THOMAS (to the last two is bequeathed "plantation where I now live"). *Daughters:* ELISABETH DUDLEY, SARAH GILLITT. *Granddaughters:* ELIZABETH and SARAH GILLITT. *Son-in-law:* JOHN GILLITT. *Wife:* ELIZABETH. *Executors:* JOHN STARKEY and MOSES HOUSTON. *Witnesses:* CHARLES COGDELL, EZEKILL HUNTER, WILLIAM HOUSTON. *Clerk of the Court:* GEO. READ.

DUDLEY, THOMAS.   Currituck County.

  December 15, 1755. March, 1757. *Sons and Executors:* WILLIAM, THOMAS ("one-half of the plantation whereon I now live"). *Grandson:* MALAKIE DUDLEY ("one-half of the plantation whereon I now live "). *Daughter:* MARY WILLIAMS. *Wife:* MARY. *Witnesses:* CHARLES WILLIAMS, THOMAS WILLIAMS, SOLOMON ASHLEE, OEN SLATTER. *Clerk of the Court:* WILL MEARNS.

DUGGAN, THOMAS.   Tyrrell County.

  May 9, 1754. June Court, 1754. *Sons:* THOMAS, JESSE. *Apprentice:* JOHN SEALS. *Wife and Executrix:* MARY. *Executor:* CAPT. JOHN HARDISON. *Witnesses:* JNO. BENNET, HIGASON KING, WILLIAM KING. *Clerk of the Court:* EVAN JONES.

DUNBAR, DUN.   Beaufort County.

  May 18, 1747. December Court, 1747. *Son:* SAMUELL (300 acres of land on the West side of Goos Creek). *Daughters:* ELISABETH DUNBAR (300 acres of land on Rush Marsh and Goose Creek), SARAH DUNBAR (tract of land and also "plantation I now live on"), MARY DUNBAR ("small neck of land" on "the River and South Dividing Creek") HANNAH DUNBAR (tract of land on the South side of a creek formerly called Hendersons), ESTER (stock of hogs and cattle). *Wife and Executrix:* SARAH BARR. *Executors:* JOSIAH JONES, JOHN TRIPPE, JUNR. *Witnesses:* JOSHUA PRITCHET, EDMOND CAMPEN, ROBERT CAMPEN. *Clerk of the Court:* JOHN FORBES.

DUNCAN, ABRAHAM.   Beaufort County.

  February 3, 1749. June Court, 1751. *Wife and Executrix:* MARY (land on Kenyon's Savannah; house and storehouse in Bath Town; lot No. 65 in Bath Town). *Nephews:* GEORGE and ABRAHAM DUNCAN, sons of JOHN DUNCAN of Londonderry, New England (my plantation on the South Side of Pamplico River, land on Southside of Tar River, land on Swifts Creek). *Brothers:* JAMES, WILLIAM, JOHN and ROBERT. *Sister:* HESTER

CASON. *Witnesses:* THOMAS PEARSON, JOHN SIMPSON, JUNR., JAMES ADAMS, W. ORMOND, *Clerk of the Court:* WILLIAM ORMOND. Coat of arms on seal.

DUNCAN, ALEXANDER.   Wilmington, New Hanover County.

May 11, 1767. May 18, 1768. *Brother:* ROBERT DUNCAN. *Other legatees:* ALEXANDER PURVES of Edinburgh, JOHN CLARK GOLDSMITH, THOMAS SMITH, JOHN RUTHERFORD (1000 pounds sterling), JAMES MOORE (eight young negroes), THOMAS CUNNINGHAM, JR., FRANCES RUTHERFORD, daughter of JOHN RUTHERFORD (8 young negroes), JOHN WALKER, CORNELIUS HARNETT, MARY, wife of CALEB GRAINGER, MAURICE MOORE and WIFE, CAPT. JOHN FORSTER and WIFE, ALEXANDER CHAPMEN (20 pounds to each), ARTHUR BENNET, ROBERT SCHAW, JOHN ANCRUM (two last named appointed executors). Proven by THOMAS COBHAM and WILLIAM LORD before WM. TRYON.

DUPEE, ELIAS.   Craven County.

August 14, 1750. February Court, 1754. *Father and Executor:* DANIEL DUPEE ("my share of all prize money to me belonging while on board his Majesty's Ship 'Bedford,' CAPT. JAMES CORNWELL, Commander"). *Witnesses:* JOHN MILL, FRAN. FONTAINE, JNO. FOSTER. *Clerk of the Court:* SOL. REW.

DURANT, ANN, widow of GEORGE.   Albemarle River.

January 23, 1694. June 22, 1695. *Son and Executor:* THOMAS DURANT. This is a nuncupative will proven by JOHN NORTHCOATE, JOHN CLAPPAR, ELENOR MOLINES, before WILLIAM DUCKENFIELD. *Clerk of the Court:* W. GLOVER. *Executor* qualified in Palatine Court—JOHN ARCHDALE, *Governor*, DANIEL AKEHURST, FRANCIS ———, BENJAMIN LATEN. Seal of the Palatine on probate.

DURANT, GEORGE.   Albemarle County.

October 9, 1688. April 26, 1693–1694. *Sons:* JOHN ("½ of my plantation"), THOMAS ("ye other half"). *Nephews:* GEORGE DURANT, HENRY DURANT (son of brother JOHN). *Daughters:* SARAH, MATYTYA, PERTYENIA, and ANN DURANT. *Wife and Executrix:* ANN. *Witnesses:* JOHN PHILPOTT, FRANCES HOSSTEN, JOHN CULLY. *Clerk of the Court:* EDWARD MAYO.

DURANT, GEORGE.   Albemarle County.

May 25, 1730. September 29, 1730. *Son:* GEORGE. *Daughters:* ANNE DURANT, MARY DURANT, SARAH DURANT, ELIZABETH DURANT. *Friend:* ANNE LONGLARTHER. *Executors:* ZEBULON CLAYTON, RICHARD WHIDBEE (brothers). *Witnesses:* THOMAS SNOWDEN, ELIZABETH GIBSON, JOHN STEVENS. Will proven before RICHARD EVERARD.

DURANT, THOMAS.   Perquimans Precinct.
   May 8, 1728. April 15, 1734. *Sons:* ABRAHAM JETNETT and AARON
MOSES DURANT. *Friend:* JOSHUA DICKS. *Witnesses:* ZEB CLAYTON,
JOHN MITCHELL, PELEG ROGERS. *Justice of the Peace:* SAMUEL SWANN.
Clerk of the Court: CHARLES DENMAN.

DURRANCE, SAMUEL.   Tyrrell County.
   November 21, 1756. December Court, 1756. *Sons:* WELLCOM, WIL-
LIAM, FRANCIS ("all my land to be equally divided between them").
"Ungratefull wife, Late": ELIZABETH DURANT. *Executors:* WILLIAM
SWINSON, FRANCIS WARD. *Witnesses:* ALEXANDER MACCLELEAN, MARY
COMBS, FR. WARD. *Clerk of the Court:* FR. WARD.

DWIGHT, MATHEW.   Chowan County.
   February 27, 1737–1738. *Executrix, Wife and sole legatee and devisee:*
ELIZABETH. *Witnesses:* CHARLTON MIZELL, SUSANNAH MIZELL. Probate
illegible.

EADEY, HENRY.   Pasquotank County.
   April 11, 1750. July Court, 1750. *Brother:* JOHN EADEY (land in Curri-
tuck County). *Daughter-in-law:* MARY WALSON. *Wife and Executrix:*
ELIZABETH. *Witnesses:* SARAH WILLSON, PETER WREN, SAMUEL LOW-
MAN. *Clerk of the Court:* THOS. TAYLOR.

EAGAN, JAMES.   "Cape Fare, in Bladen Precinct."
   October 30, 1737. March Court, 1738. *Executor:* WILLIAM CARY.
Wife and daughter: mentioned, but not named. *Witnesses:* THOMAS LOCK,
WILLIAM BARTRAM, ARTHUR DANIEL. *Clerk of the Court:* RICHARD HET-
EIER.

EAGLE, RICHARD.   Brunswick County.
   March 23, 1769. March 31, 1769. *Son:* JOSEPH ("House, plantation,
saw and grist mills"). *Daughter:* SUSANNAH EAGLE. *Wife:* MARGARET
HENRIETTA EAGLE (formerly BUGNION). *Cousins:* JEAN and ELIZABETH
DAVIS. *Sister:* ELIZABETH DAVIS. *Other legatees:* JEANET MCFARLING,
JOHN EAGLESON. *Executors:* JOHN GIBBS, ROBERT SHAW, JOHN ANCRUM
and THOMAS OWEN. *Witnesses:* JOHN WALKER, JOHN FERGUS, MARY
WALKER. Will proven before WM. TRYON. Codicil to this will, of even
date. Confirms title to MR. WM. DRY in and to a tract of land "bought of
my father, RICH'D EAGLES."

EARLY, ELIONOR.   Albemarle County.
   September 2, 1732. *Grandsons:* THOS. SUTTON, JAMES CURLEE. *Granddaughters:* SARAH SUTTON, MARY DALE (my plantation called by the name
of "Blew Water"). *Executrix:* MARY DALE. *Witnesses:* ROBT. EVANS,
NICHOLAS FAIRLESS, NATHANIEL KEELE. No probate.

EARLY, JOHN.   Bertie County.
August 6, 1740. October 20, 1740. *Son:* JOHN (plantation on horse swamp). *Daughters:* MARGARET MACHENRY, MARTHA THOMSON, MARY BLAKE, SARAH REEF, ELISABETH WILLSON, BETHSHABA MORRIS, REBEKAH MORRIS. *Wife:* ANN. *Executors:* JOHN EARLY (son), WILLIAM WILLSON (son-in-law). *Witnesses:* JOHN WILLIAMS, EDWARD WILLIAMS, WILLIAM WILLSON. Will proven before GAB. JOHNSTON at Eden House.

EASON, WILLIAM.   Perquimans County.
January 20, 1718–1719. July 14, 1719. *Sons:* WILLIAM (land on South side of Cypress Swamp), THOMAS, GEORGE ("plantation whereon I now live"). *Daughters:* MARY, SUSANNA, RACHEL and JANE EASON. *Wife and Executrix:* MARY. *Witnesses:* THOMAS DAVIS, ELISEBETH DAVIS, THO. SPEIGHT. *Clerk of the Court:* RICHD. LEARY.

EASON, WILLIAM.   Bertie Precinct.
January 27, 1734. May Court, 1736. *Sons:* WILLIAM and GEORGE. *Wife:* ANNE. *Executors:* THOMAS and GEORGE EASON (brothers). *Witnesses:* HENRY BAKER, JUNR., SAMUELL SMITH, JOHN HENNARD. *Clerk of the Court:* JNO. WYNNS.

EASTER, ABRAHAM.   Hyde County.
November 18, 1751. December Court, 1751. *Son:* JAMES ("choice of two plantations my father left me"). *Daughter:* MARY EASTER (fifty-three acres of land on Swan Quarter"). *Wife:* ELIZABETH. *Brothers and Executors:* JOHN and THOMAS EASTER. *Witnesses:* WILLIAM CARON, SABBASTIN SILVERTHORN, URIAH COLLINS. *Clerk of the Court:* THOS. LOACK.

EASTER, JOHN.   Hyde Precinct.
October 27, 1732. March Court, 1733. *Sons:* ABRAHAM ("my plantation"), THOMAS. *Daughters:* SARAH and DINAH. *Wife and Executrix:* Mentioned, but not named. *Witnesses:* EDWD. HADLEY, THOMAS GOODING, THOMAS RICHARDS. *Clerk of Beaufort Court:* JNO. COLLISON.

EASTER, JOHN.   Hyde County.
January 17, 1751–1752. March Court, 1752. *Sister:* LIDA EASTER. *Friend:* ELIZABETH LOACK. *Brothers and Executors:* THOMAS and WILLIAM EASTER. *Witnesses:* JOHN HOUREN, JOHN WINLY, SARAH WINDLY. *Clerk of the Court:* FRANS. EGLETON.

EASTER, MOVY.   Hyde County.
November 4, 1751. December Court, 1751. *Sons:* ABRAHAM, JOHN, WILLIAM and THOMAS. *Daughters:* LYDIA EASTER, MARY EASTER, ANN

and SARAH EASTER. *Executors:* JOHN and THOMAS EASTER (sons). *Witnesses:* JOHN MASON, JACOB TULE, ANN JASPER. *Clerk of the Court:* THOS. LOACK.

EATON, JAMES. Chowan Precinct.

December 11, 1729. January 6, 1729. *Wife:* MARY. *Executor:* WILLIAM WILLIAMS of Edenton. *Witnesses:* JOHN MATTHEWS, WM. BAELEY, DAVID DAVIS. Will proven before RICHARD EVERARD.

EATON, WILLIAM. Granville County.

February 19, 1759. March 20, 1759. Saint Johns Parish in the County of Granville. *Sons:* WILLIAM (lands in Dinwiddie and Brunswick counties in Virginia, except land received of William Scoggan), THOMAS, CHARLES RUST. *Daughters:* JANE, wife of COLO. NATHANIEL EDWARDS; ANNE HAYNES, relict of ANDREW HAYNES; MARY, wife of ROBERT JONES; SARAH, wife of CHARLES JOHNSON; ELIZABETH, wife of DANIEL WELDON; MARTHA EATON. *Grandson:* EATON HAYNES. *Wife and Executrix:* MARY. The following lands devised: plantation in Granville "whereon I now live"; land in Granville called Bowsers; land where LEWIS BALLARD and CORMELIAL EARLS live; land in Northampton called Cumboes; lots in the town of Halifax; land "where Granville Court house is built"; land on Tabbs Creek; lot in the town of Petersburg; land in Granville called Gould's; land on Little Fishing Creek called Youngs; land on Andersons Swamp; two tracts on Smiths Creek called Hughes and Rayborn's; lot in Halifax adjoining the Market place and Main street. A large number of negroes bequeathed, some being on plantations at Tabbs Creek and others on Mush Island. *Witnesses:* WM. PERSON, JAS. PAINE, RICHD. COLEMAN. *Clerk of the Court:* DANIEL WELDON.

EBURN (or EBORNE), ELIZABETH. Hyde County.

May 23, 1745. June Court, 1751. *Sons:* LITTLETON, HENRY, NATHANIEL. *Daughters:* ELIZABETH MACKNICOL, REBECCA JONES, ANN JONES. *Granddaughter:* MARY STEPHENS. *Executor:* HENRY and LITTLETON EBURN (sons). *Witnesses:* EDWARD DAVIS, ELISABETH BELL, WM. HARRIS. *Clerk of the Court:* THOS. LOACK.

EBORN, HENRY. Hyde County.

October 20, 1732. March Court, 1732. Matchepungo in Hyde County. *Sons:* HENRY ("my plantation"), LITTLETON (land on Broad Creek and plantation Pantego; one negro). *Daughters:* MARY EBORN, RHODA LAYSON, ELIZABETH EBORN, ANNE JONES and REBECKER DEEDAN. *Other legatees:* NATHANIEL EBORN, son of HENRY and ELIZABETH EBORN (land between George Mixon and William Cambal on Matchepungo Creek); SALATHYEL LAYSON, son of EVENS RHODA LAYSON. *Wife and Executrix:*

ELIZABETH. *Executors:* WILLIAM BARROW, NATHANIEL EBORN and THOMAS SMITH. *Witnesses:* GEORGE MIXON, ELIZABETH WILLIAMSON, CHARLES JOHNSON. *Clerk of the Court:* JNO. COLLISON.

EBORN, LITTLETON. Hyde County.

April 13, 1758. June Court, 1758. *Brothers:* AARON EBORN ("my dwelling plantation"), JAMES EBORN, WILLIAM EBORN. *Executors:* WILLIAM BOYD (brother-in-law), WILLIAM EBORN. *Witnesses:* WM. HARRIS, MARTHA EBORN, WILLIAM MACNORAL. *Clerk of the Court:* STEPHN DENNING.

EBORN, NATHANIEL. Hyde County.

October 1, 1753. March Court, 1754. *Sons:* JAMES ("My plantation and one negro"), LITTLETON (plantation on Matchapungo Creek); WILLIAM (land on Matchapungo Creek adjoining HENRY EBORN, "holden by a bond in the hands of THOMAS, GEORGE and ZACERIA BARRAH," and 1 negro), AARON (land on Matchapungo adjoining THOMAS BARRAH, and one negro). *Daughter:* ELIZABETH EBORN (one negro). *Wife:* REBECCA. *Executors:* JAMES and LITTLETON EBORN (sons). *Witnesses:* ISRAEL WINDLY, ELIZABETH WINDLY, JOHN HOUREN. *Deputy Clerk:* STEPHEN DENNING.

EBORNE, REBEKAH. Hyde County.

October 30, 1754. June Court, 1758. *Sons:* LITTLETON (*Executor*), WILLIAM and AARON. *Daughter:* ELIZABETH EBORNE. *Witnesses:* GEORGE BARROW, ZACHARIAH BARROW. *Clerk of the Court:* STEPN. DENNING.

EDEN, CHARLES. County not given.

Governor of North Carolina, December 26, 1721. April 2, 1722. *Niece:* MARGARET PEUGH, daughter of ROBERT PEUGH. *Other legatees:* JOHN HOLLOWAY, DANIEL RICHARDSON, JAMES HENDERSON (land on Derhams Creek), JOHN LOVICK (executor). *Witnesses:* MARY BADHAM, H. CLAYTON, W. BADHAM. *Clerk of the Court:* W. BADHAM. Original missing. Recorded in Book 1712-1722, page 299.

EDMONDS (spelled EDDMONDS), RICHARD. Northampton Co.

September 26, 1750. November Court, 1750. *Sons:* THOMAS and DAVID. *Daughters:* MAREY, REBEKAH, ELIZABETH and SUSANNAH EDMONDS. *Wife:* ELIZABETH. *Executor:* BERABE MELTON. *Witnesses:* SAMUEL HACKNEY, SAMUEL JORDAN, JENINGS HACKNEY. *Clerk of the Court:* I. EDWARDS.

EDMONDS, SAMUEL. Chowan County.

November 3, 1720. April Court, 1721. *Son:* HENRY ("my plantation") *Daughters:* SARAH EDMONDS, ANN SMITH, ELISABETH MEDLETON. *Wife:*

MARY. *Executor:* JOHN EDWARDS, SENR. *Witnesses:* JOHN WILLIAMS, GEO. EUBANK, THEOPHILUS WILLIAMS, EDWARD MORE. *Clerk of the Court:* THOS. HENMAN.

EDMONDSON, JOSEPH.   Craven County.

August 4, 1743. *Sons:* JOHN (*Executor*), THOMAS. *Daughter:* PRISELOW EDMONDSON. *Wife and Executrix:* PRISELOW. *Witnesses:* RICHD. BATH, ELIAS MARTIN, JOSEPH GAD. No probate.

EDNYE (EDNEY), ROBERT.   Pasquotank County.

April 4, 1752. December Court, 1758. *Sons:* SAMUEL, NUTON RENSHER EDNYE. *Daughters:* ANN EDNYE (land on "the long ridge"), AHINOAM EDNYE (land on "ash branch"), ELIZABETH CARTWRIGHT (land on "broad neck branch"). *Wife and Executrix:* ANN. *Witnesses:* SAMUEL SMITH, JOSEPH SPENCE, THOS. LOADS (RHODES). *Clerk of the Court:* THOS. TAYLOR.

EDWARDS, CATHERINE.   Bladen County.

May 2, 1755. October Court, 1755. *Son:* ROBERT ("ye plantation I formerly lived on"). *Daughter:* ANN SUTTON. *Grandsons:* JOHN, SAMUEL and ISAAC HOLLINGSWORTH. *Executors:* ROBERT EDWARDS (son) and VALENTINE HOLLINGSWORTH. *Witnesses:* JAMES PROTHRO, JEREMIAH PROTHRO, ANN D. LAURENCY. *Clerk of the Court:* EDWARD NUGENT.

EDWARDS, EDWARD.   Northampton County.

February 27, 1758. July Court, 1758. *Wife and Executrix:* ANNE. *Witnesses:* JAMES LEAY, WILLIAM WINBORNE. *Clerk of the Court:* J. EDWARDS.

EDWARDS, HENRY.   Edgecombe County.

January 14, 1758. June Court, 1758. *Sons:* NATHAN, BRITAIN and JESSE ("my plantation"), SAMUEL and HENRY (*executors*). *Witnesses:* ARTHUR BOWIN, JOHN NORWOOD. *Clerk of the Court:* JOS. MONTFORT.

EDWARDS, ISAAC.   Northampton County.

December 18, 1758. January Court, 1759. *Sons:* JOSIAH ("plantation whereon I now live, including all the lands lying between Roanoque River and Uraha Swamp"), JOHN (land on North side Uraha Swamp), THOMAS ("100 acres of land, including Davise's plantation"), WILLIAM. *Daughter:* ELIZABETH FERGUSON. *Son-in-law:* SAMUEL PHILIPS. *Grandchildren:* ELIZABETH PHILIPS, JOHN EDWARDS. *Daughter-in-law:* ANN EDWARDS. *Wife and Executrix:* ELIZABETH. *Witnesses:* JOHN SAWKILL, ROBERT DUKES, JOHN EDWARDS. *Clerk of the Court:* J. EDWARDS.

ABSTRACT OF WILLS, 1690—1760.   111

EDWARDS, JOHN.   New Hanover County.
June 19, 1743. May 15, 1744. *Sons:* JOHN, THOMAS. *Daughter:* CHARITY EDWARDS. *Wife and Executrix:* MARY. *Executor:* HENRY BARON. *Witnesses:* THOMAS HOBBY, WILLM. STEPHENS, HENRY BARON. Will proven before E. MOSELEY, *Chief Justice.*

EDY, JOHN.   County not given.
November 7, 1726. December 2, 1726. *Daughter:* DIANA EDY. *Brother:* HENRY EDY. This is a nuncupative will proven before THOS. TAYLOR by THOMAS SPENCER, HENRY EDEN and ESTHER DUDLY.

EGERTON (spelled EGGERTON), JAMES. Perquimans County.
September 11, 1749. January Court, 1750. *Sons:* JAMES (plantation in Chowan County), WILLIAM (plantation on Mill Swamp). *Daughters:* ANN and MARY EGERTON. *Wife and Executrix:* SARAH. *Executors:* JOHN HALCEY, JOHN WILKINS. *Witnesses:* THOMAS CALLOWAY, WILLIAM HALL, RICHARD CLEMENS. *Clerk of the Court:* EDMUND HATCH.

ELDRIDGE, WILLIAM.   Northampton County.
May Court, 1751. *"Supposed son":* MATTHEW MOOR. *Wife:* MARY. *Other legatees:* MELA MOOR, CHARITY MOOR, PATTY PEACOCK (daughter of ELIZABETH PEACOCK). *Brother:* SAMUEL. *Sisters:* MARTHA, THOMAS NIXON, MARTHA MOOR. *Executors:* WILLIAM KECHEN, JAS. WASHINGTON, BENJN. DEBERRY. *Witnesses:* JNO. DEBERRY, WILLIAM RICHARDSON. RABACKAH DAWSON. *Clerk of the Court:* I. EDWARDS.

ELKS, JOHN.   County not given.
January 23, 1707–1708. *Sons:* JOHN ("my dwelling plantation"), THOMAS, AMANUEL (land called "rich neck"), MARMADUKE. *Wife and Executrix:* MARY. *Witnesses:* EDWARD OLD, JUNIOR, GEORGE WARRENTON, SENIOR, GEORGE WARRENTON, JUNIOR, REBEKAH OLD. *Clerk of the Court:* JOS. WAKER (or WALKER).

ELKS, RICHARD.   Albemarle County.
September 21, 1687. October 6, 1687. *Executor and sole legatee and devisee:* WILLIAM DARBY ("plantation upon Yawpin River"). *Witnesses:* THOMAS POLLOCK, HANNA HAILE, JOHN WOLFENDEN, JOHN LEWIN. Will proven before SETH SOTHELL, *Governor.*

ELLEGOOD, MATTHIAS.   Pasquotank County.
September 10, 1773. March 7, 1774. *Friends and Executors:* COLO. JOHN SAWYER, JONATHAN HEARRING. *Wife and Executrix:* MARGREAT. *Witnesses:* SAMUEL SPENCE, THOS. ETHERIDGE, THOMAS GRANDY. Will proven before JO. MARTIN.

ELIOTT, CHARLES. Enfield.

October 15, 1753. May Term, 1757. *Executor and sole legatee:* HON. JOHN RUTHERFORD. *Witnesses:* THOS. LOWE, JOHN LAWSON. *Clerk of the Court:* I. EDWARDS.

ELLIOTT, GEORGE. Pasquotank Precinct.

February 7, 1727–1728. April Court, 1728. *Daughter:* MARY WALLIS. *Other legatees:* JOHN CLARKE, ANN ASKINS, ANN GRAY. *Executor:* RICHARD GRAY. *Witnesses:* THOMAS BEDFORD, WILLIAM WALLIS, JAMES COLLINS. *Clerk of the Court:* WM. MINSON.

ELIOT, MICHEL. Orange County.

October 25, 1756. December Court, 1756. *Executor and sole legatee and devisee:* WILLIAM PHILLIPS. *Witnesses:* WILLIAM OFFILL, JAMES HOPKINS, WILLIAM HOPKINS. *Clerk of the Court:* JAMES WATSON.

ELLIOTT, MOSES. Perquimans County.

February 22, 1756. January Court, 1756. *Sons:* JOSEPH, MOSES, BENJAMIN. *Daughter:* MARGRET ELLIOT. *Wife and Executrix:* JUDAH. *Witnesses:* ABRAHAM HASKIT, SAMUEL BAGLEY. *Clerk of the Court:* MILES HARVY.

ELLIOT, THOMAS. Perquimans County.

April 2, 1720. December 16, 1729. *Sons:* CALEB ("plantation on which I now dwell"), JOSHUA (200 acres of land), ISAAC ("remaining part of ye tract"), WILLIAM (1 shilling), THOMAS, ABRAHAM, SOLOMON, MOSES, JOSEPH and BENJAMIN. *Daughters:* MARY BROWN, URSELY. *Wife and Executrix:* MARGARET. *Witnesses:* SARAH WARNER, WILLIAM———, R. WILSON. Will proven before RICH'D EVERARD.

ELLIS, GEORGE. Pasquotank Precinct.

January 30, 1720. July Court, 1720. *Brother and Executor:* THOMAS PALIN. *Daughter:* ANN ELLIS. *Wife and Executrix:* HANNAH. *Witnesses:* SARAH BULL, KATH. TOWER, JANE DANN. *Clerk of the Court pro tem.:* J. PALIN.

ELLIS, MARY. County not given.

Executor and Guardian of son: THOMAS CLARKE. *Witnesses:* ELIZABETH WILLIS, ELLIS WILSON, JOHN WILSON. No probate.

ELLIS, ROBERT. Northampton County.

January 28, 1740. February Court, 1743. *Son:* JNO. ELLIS (one shilling). *Grandsons:* ROBERT and JOHN ELLIS (160 acres of land to each).

Neighbor and Executor: PHIL SMITH ("plantation whereon I now dwell").
Witnesses: PHIL SMITH, MOSES BECK, ELIZABETH SMITH. *Clerk of the Court:* I. EDWARDS.

ELLISON, WILLIAM.   New Hanover County.

June 23, 1737. July 2, 1737. *Brother and sole devisee and legatee:* ANDREW ELLISON. *Executor:* JAMES MURRAY. *Witnesses:* JA. PATERSON, THOMAS CLARKE, JA. MURRAY. Will proven before ROBT. HALTON and GAB. JOHNSTON.

ELTON, ZACHARIAH.   Perquimans County.

October 5, 1752. October Court, 1752. *Devisees and Legatees:* JONATHAN PHELPS, SEN., JOSEPH WHITE, MARY BARKER, WILLIAM LAMB. *Executors:* JONATHAN PHELPS, JOSEPH WHITE. *Witnesses:* WILLIAM TOWNSEN, THOMAS MARTIN. *Clerk of the Court:* EDMUND HATCH.

ENGEL, PETER.   Craven Precinct.

September 20, 1722. December Court, 1722. *Godson:* WILLIAM MORE. *Other legatees:* ANN CARTUS, SUSAN MOORE, SURITY MOORE, MARY LOTS, ADAM MOORE, GEORGE MALS. *Witnesses:* MATTHEW REASON, PETER HAND. *Clerk of the Court:* C. METCALFE.

ENGLISH, JOSEPH.   Beaufort County.

November 20, 1744. December Court, 1744. *Friends:* MARY PALLEE, DOCR. PETTER COLAXE. *Executor:* PETTER SOLE. *Witnesses:* JOHN BROCK, JOHN FULKER, NATHAN ARCHBELL. *Clerk of the Court:* FR. GOOLD, JNO. TURNER.

ENNET, EDMUND.   New River.

February 24, 1734. April 11, 1735. *Sons:* JOHN (land on Kisable Creek), EDMOND and JOSEPH ("my dwelling plantation"). *Daughter:* ELLINOR ENNET. *Executors:* NATHANIEL EVERET and JOHN WARREN. *Witnesses:* MARTHA HOLT, WILLIAM MARCHMENT, JONATHAN PIKE, MARY PATTER. Will proven before GOVERNOR GAB. JOHNSTON at New River.

ESPY, JAMES.   Brunswick, in New Hanover County.

October 3, 1739. October 9, 1739. *Son:* USHER. *Daughter:* SARAH ESPY. *Wife:* MARGARET. *Executors:* JOHN MONTGOMERY and WILLIAM DRY. *Witnesses:* RICHARD HELLIER, WM. GRAY, JAMES LYON. Will proven before GAB. JOHNSTON at Newton.

ETHERIDGE, HENRY.   Currituck County.

March 14, 1742-1743. July Court, 1743. *Sons:* SAMUEL, WILLIAM, RICHARD, JOHN, HENRY. *Daughters:* ANN ETHERIDGE, TEDY ETHERIDGE,

MARY ETHERIDGE. *Wife and Executrix:* SUSEY. *Witnesses:* JOHN BALLANCE, WILLIAM MAKEFASHION, MOSES LINTON. *Clerk of the Court:* JOHN LURRY.

ETHERIDGE, JOHN.   Currituck County.

April 3, 1744. July Court, 1744. *Sons:* AMOS (land known as the "Bull yard"), WILLIS (411 acres of land), CALLIB (land known as "Northerns"), JAMES ("plantation where Henry Blount now liveth"), JOHN ("plantation whereon I now live"), JOSIAS ("plantation where Samuel Jones now liveth"). *Daughters:* SARAH BIGGS, DOROTHY ETHERIDGE. *Wife and Executrix:* ELINER. *Witnesses:* THOS. WILLIAMS, SOLOMON ETHERIDGE, JOHN PIRKENS, ABSALOM LEGETT. *Clerk of the Court:* RICHD. MCCLURE.

ETHERIDGE, LUKE.   Currituck County.

February 25, 1732. *Daughters:* SARAH ETHERIDGE ("land I now live on"), ELIZABETH ETHERIDGE ("land in ye great swamp"), ANN ETHERIDGE. *Wife and Executrix:* CHRISTON. *Witnesses:* ELISABETH DANIEL, OTHO HOLLAND. *Clerk of the Court:* THOS. LOWTHER.

ETHERIDGE, MARMADUKE.   Currituck County.

February 3, 1734. *Devisees and legatees:* CALEB, MARMADUKE and MARY BELL (children of Sarah Bell). *Executrix:* SARAH BELL. *Witnesses:* JOHN HOUREN, JOSEPH BOURN, PETER DOUGE. *Clerk of the Court:* THOS. LOWTHER.

ETHERIDGE, RICHARD.   "Currituck Banks and Bay of Kitty Hawk."

February 12, 1739–1740. April Court, 1750. *Sons:* ADAM ("plantation whereon I now live, commonly known by the name of the Whale House"), SAMPSON. *Daughters:* DIANAH DOWE, HELLENA DOWDY, ELIZABETH DOWDY. *Grandson:* ROBERT TUCKER. *Granddaughters:* PRISSELLA ETHERIDGE, DEBORAH FEILDS. *Wife:* SARAH. *Executors:* ADAM, SAMPSON ETHERIDGE (sons). *Witnesses:* THOMAS MAYO, CHARITY SIVELLS, LENINE MAYO. *Clerk of the Court:* RICH'D MCCLURE.

ETHERIDGE, SOLOMON.   Currituck County.

November 7, 1749. January Court, 1749. *Sons:* ABNER ("plantation I now live on"), SOLOMON, ABSALOM. *Daughters:* SARAH ETHERIDGE, LETTISHA ETHERIDGE, BARBY ETHERIDGE, REDAH ETHERIDGE. *Witnesses:* WILLIAM ETHERIDGE, CALEB ETHERIDGE. *Clerk of the Court:* RICHD. MCCLURE.

EUBANK, GEORGE.   Bertie Precinct Society Parish.

March 2, 1732–1733. March 12, 1732. *Brother:* JAMES EUBANK. *Sisters:* ELIZABETH and ISABELL EUBANK. To brothers and sisters is devised all estate in Great Britain. *Other legatees:* THOMAS, ELIZABETH and MARTHA WHITMELL, WILLIAM GRAY. *Executors:* JAMES CASTELLAW, THOMAS WHITMELL and JOHN GRAY. *Witnesses:* JAMES BULOCK, JOHN BARTON. Proven before GEORGE BURRINGTON.

EVANS, BARWELL. Beaufort County.

April 1, 1756. June Court, 1756. *Daughters:* SARAH EVANS ("plantation whereon I now live and forty acres of land on the creek I live on"), SUSANNAH EVANS ("plantation whereon William Brantly lives and three hundred acres of land on the mill creek"). *Nephews:* JACOB and BARWELL EVANS. *Friend:* WILLIAM STOKES. *Wife and Executrix:* SUSANNAH. *Executors:* JACOB, BENJAMIN and CHARLES EVANS (brothers). *Witnesses:* GEORGE SUGG, PETER HULL and RICHARD HURLEY. *Clerk of the Court:* WALLEY CHAUNCEY.

EVANS, CHARLES. Tarr River, in Edgecombe County.

June 1, 1759. June Court, 1759. *Sons:* JACOB (land in Beaufort County), BENJAMIN, CHARLES (land on Tar river and town Creek). *Grandchildren:* CHARLES EVANS (son of BENJAMIN), JOHN EVANS (son of CHARLES and ELIZABETH), ANN EVANS (daughter of CHARLES and ELIZABETH). *Witnesses:* JOHN TISON, CHARLES EVANS, JR. *Clerk of the Court:* JOS. MONTFORT.

EVANS, HUNT. Pasquotank Precinct.

December 15, 1729. January 13, 1729. *Brothers:* BARTHOLOMEW EVANS, THOMAS ARMORE. *Father-in-law and Executor:* LOUIS MARKHAM. *Witnesses:* ROBERT KEEL, ANN CRANK, ISAAC FINNEY. *Clerk of the Court:* H. MINSON.

EVANS, JOHN. Chowan County.

August 24, 1739. January 15, 1739. *Sons:* JOHN ("plantation whereon I now live"), THOMAS, BENJAMIN. *Daughters:* JANE EVANS, MARY EVANS, RACHEL EVANS. *Wife and Executrix:* JANE. *Witnesses:* JOHN EVANS, CHARLES JORDAN. Will proven before W. SMITH, *Chief Justice.*

EVANS, MARY. Perquimans County.

April 8, 1720. March 7, 1723. *Son:* WILLIAM. *Executors:* FRANCIS PENRINE, DARBY BRYAN. *Witnesses:* JOHN DICK, HARRIS WILLOUGHBY, FRANCIS LAYDAIN. Will proven before GEO. BURRINGTON, *Governor.*

EVANS (spelled "EIVENS"), RICHARD. Albemarle County.

September 7, 1692. October 2, 1693. *Sons:* JONATHAN, RICHARD. *Daughters:* RABAKAH EIVENS, ANN EIVENS. *Executors:* ELIZABETH EIVENS (wife), ALEXANDER LILLINGTON. *Witnesses:* DAVID SHEARWOOD, JANE ARNOLD, BENJAMIN CIDDEN. *Clerk of the Court:* JOHN STEPNEY.

EVANS, RICHARD. Beaufort County.

December 26, 1752. June Court, 1753. *Sons:* RICHARD and GEORGE (lands in Onslow on the mouth of New River). *Daughter:* MARY EVANS. About thirteen negroes bequeathed. *Executor:* MICHAEL CAUTANCHE. *Witnesses:* EDMUND PEARCE, JOSHUA PEARCE, READING BLOUNT. *Clerk of the Court:* WALLEY CHAUNCEY.

EVANS, ROBERT. Perquimans County.

March 20, 1754. January Court, 1758. *Sons:* JOHN, ROBERT (*Executor*). *Daughters:* SARAH GRIFFIN, ELISABETH EVANS, MARY EVANS. *Grandchildren:* DEMSEY, ARON, ROBERT and HULDAH BLANSHARD. *Witnesses:* WILLIAM KELLY, NATHAN CULLENS, DAVENPORT GOODING. *Clerk of the Court:* MILES HARVEY.

EVANS, THOMAS. Chowan Precinct.

February 29, 1731–1732. November 2, 1732. *Son and Executor:* THOMAS ("my maner plantation"). *Daughters:* ALLIS WILLIAMSON, SARAH BROWNEY, ELIZEBETH WALKER. *Wife and Executrix:* ELLENER. *Witnesses:* THO. HOBBS, CORNELIUS COLLEHAN. Will proven before WM. LITTLE, *Chief Justice.*

EVANS, THOMAS. Tyrrell County.

March 14, 1744–1745. June Court, 1745. *Mother:* ELENER EVANS. *Daughters:* ELIZABETH, MARY, CATHERINE, ALCE and SARAH EVANS. *Wife and Executrix:* MARY. *Executors:* SAMUEL DURRANCE, MATHIAS ADAMS. *Witnesses:* JOHN NICHALLS, JOHN GARRETT, JOHN WALKER. *Clerk of the Court:* JAS. CONNER.

EVATT, WILLIAM. Northampton County.

April 10, 1758. July Court, 1758. *Daughter:* MARY EVATT. *Wife and Executrix:* SARAH. *Executor:* DANIEL DUNKIN. *Witnesses:* GERARD YOUNG, THOMAS WILBORN. *Clerk of the Court:* I. EDWARDS.

EVERETT, JOHN. Tyrrell County.

March 16, 1754. June Court, 1754. *Brother:* JOSHUA (145 acres of land known as "the Stamping place"), THOMAS (*Executor*). *Father and Executor:* NATHANIEL EVERETT. *Cousins:* JOHN and ELISABETH EVERETT. *Witnesses:* SAMUEL DURRANCE, DANIEL YARRETT, NATHANIEL EVERITT. *Clerk of the Court:* EVAN JONES.

EVERITT, NATHANIEL. Tyrrell County.

November 2, 1749. December 5, 1749. *Legatees and devisees:* NATHANIELL EVERITT of New River, NATHANIEL EVERITT of Mereland, NATHANIEL EVERITT of the parish of St. Andrews ("my plantation"), MARY EVERITT,

ELISABETH RAY, SARY FUGGIN. *Executor:* NATHANIEL EVERITT of St. Andrews. *Witnesses:* THOMAS EVERITT, JAMES RHOUDES, ANN BEESLEY. *Clerk of the Court:* EVAN JONES. Courthouse on Kindrecks Creek.

EVERTON, JEREMIAH. Pasquotank County.

January 3, 1736. October Court, 1740. *Sons:* SOLOMON (1 shilling), JAMES ("my dwelling plantation"). *Daughters:* SARAH FOREHAND, RACHEL EVERTON, KATHERINE CHAMBERLAIN. *Wife and Executrix:* HANNAH. *Witnesses:* JOHN SCARF, JAMES SCARF, THOMAS CROMWELL. *Clerk of the Court:* JAMES CRAVEN.

EYRES, RICHARD. County not given.

October 2, 1685. November 11, 1685. *Executor and sole legatee:* CHARLES PROWS. *Witnesses:* RICHARD ROOKE, MARY ROOKE. *Clerk of the Court:* HENDERSON WALKER.

FAGAN, ENOCH. Tyrrell County.

January 16, 1777. April 29, 1777. *Daughter:* MARY FAGAN. *Wife and Executrix:* RUINA. *Executor:* BENJAMIN BLOUNT. *Witnesses:* SAMUEL BLACK, ISHAM WEBB, FR. WARD. Will proven before RD. CASWELL, *Governor.*

FALCONER, JOHN. Chowan County.

July 28, 1739. August 5, 1741. *Sons:* THOMAS, GEORGE. *Daughters:* ANN FALCONER, MARY FRAZIER, HESTER GRAVENOR. *Wife and Executrix:* SARAH. *Witnesses:* JOHN RONSHAM, EDWD. AURENDELL, PATINES EVERAY. Will proven before J. MONTGOMERY, C. J.

FALCONER, THOMAS. Chowan County.

February 1, 1756. April Court, 1756. *Nephew:* JAMES BEASLEY. *Wife:* SARAH (plantation and all personal property). *Other legatees:* SARAH FREEMAN, daughter of THOMAS FREEMAN; RICHARD LEARY of Tyrrell County; JOHN, son of JAMES BEASLEY; JAMES, son of JOHN BEASLEY and THOMAS son of JAMES BEASLEY; MARY PAIN, daughter of JAMES BEASLEY. *Executors:* JOHN HALSEY and CORNELIUS LEARY. *Witnesses:* ROBERT BEASLEY, JAMES FRANCIS, EDWARD ROBINS, ELIZABETH ROWSUM, THOMAS PEIRCE, JOHN CREECY. *Clerk of the Court:* THOMAS JONES.

FALK, RICHARD. Chowan Precinct.

March 15, ———. No probate. *Sons:* JONATHAN, WILLIAM, JOHN and RICHARD (lands on Maheron River). *Wife and Executrix:* ELIZABETH. *Witnesses:* RICHARD FALK, WILLIAM MAULE, THOMAS BUSBE. Original missing. Recorded in Book 1712–1722, page 27.

FARLEE, JAMES.   Chowan Precinct.

May 1, 1727. May 15, 1727. *Wife:* mentioned, but not named. Testator's lands left to JAMES BENTLEY, son of SARAH BENTLEY. *Guardians:* HENRY BONNER, SAMUELL PAGETT. *Executor:* EDWARD MOSELEY. *Witnesses:* ROBERT JEFFREYS, WM. HALLSEY, JOHN HALLSEY. Will proven before RICHARD EVERARD, *Governor.*

FARLEE, JAMES.   Chowan County.

January 12, 1750. January Court, 1750. *Sons:* SAMUEL ("all my land"), JAMES. *Daughters:* MARY PARKER, SARAH FARLEE, CHRISTIANA FARLEE. *Wife:* RACHEL. *Executor:* JOHN CAMPBELL. *Witnesses:* WILLIAM BOYD, AMOS PARKER, JOHN BACKCUS. *Clerk of the Court:* WILL. MEARNS. Executor qualified before JAMES CRAVEN.

FARR, RICHARD.   Onslow County.

November 8, 1757. July Court, 1758. *Sons:* RICHARD, TITUS GREEN FARR, WILLIAM, JAMES. *Executors:* HANNAH FARR (*wife*), STEPHEN LEE, JOHN MILTON. *Witnesses:* THOS. HILL, ROBERT MILTON, DNL. AUSTIN. *Clerk of the Court:* WILLIAM CRAY.

FARROW, FRANCIS.   Currituck County.

October 7, 1721. February 9, 1722–1723. *Wife and Executrix:* BARBARY. *Children:* mentioned, but not named. *Friend:* WILLIAM ROLLISON. *Witnesses:* DANIEL GUTHRIE, JOHN MACQUIN, RICHARD JOHNSON. Will proven before WM. REED, "presedent of North Carolina."

FEARE, OBADIAH.   Pasquotank Precinct.

June 5, 1719, "of Alligater in the presinck of Pascotank." *Legatees and Devisees:* WILLIAM LUDFORD (*Executor*), SARAH LUDFORD, ANNE LUDFORD, CHRISTIAN LUDFORD, MARY LUDFORD, MARTHA LUDFORD, TOMSON LUDFORD, THOMAS LUDFORD, ANN FEARE (wife). *Witnesses:* EDWD. LININGTON, JOSEPH WINSHAPP, ANDREW OLIVER. No probate.

FEILDS, JAMES.   Perquimans County.

February 15, 1750–1751. April Court, 1751. *Sons and Executors:* RUBIN, MOSES. *Daughters:* ANN FEILDS, ZEBIAH FEILDS. *Son-in-law:* JAMES PRICE (*Executor*). *Witnesses:* NICHOLAS STALLINGS, ELIAS STALLINGS, MOSES ROUNTREE. *Clerk of the Court:* EDMUND HATCH.

FEILD, RICHARD.   Onslow County.

June 24, 1742. January Court, 1744. *Wife and Executrix:* ANN. *Sons:* JOHN and SAMUEL (550 acres of land up White Oak river), RICHARD and SMITH (my plantation), JAMES (300 acres land). *Executor:* JOHN STARKEY. *Witnesses:* ABRA. MITCHELL, ABRAHAM MITCHELL, JAMES ATKINS. *Clerk of the Court:* ANDREW MURRAY.

FELTHEN, JAMES.   Bertie County.

March 16, 1726. July, 1726. *Wife and Executrix:* ANN. *Witnesses:* FRED. RASOR, CHRISTOPHER VANLUVAN, MARTHA HOOPER. Will proven before RICHD. EVERARD.

FELTS, HUMPHREY.   Perquimans County.

1726. July, 1726. *Son:* JOHN. *Daughter:* ELISABETH. *Executor:* WILLIAM LONG. *Witnesses:* EDWD. STANDIN, JOSHUA LONG, SAMUEL WIATT. *Clerk of the Court:* RICH'D LEARY. Court held at the house of ROBERT MOORE.

FENDALL, JOHN.   Chowan County.

December 17, 1695. April Court, 1696. *Wife:* ELIZABETH. *Brother:* ROBERT FENDALL. *Father-in-law and Executor:* ALEXANDER LILLINGTON. *Witnesses:* JOHN DIX, ANN WALKER, HENDERSON WALKER. *Clerk of the Court:* NA. CHEVIN.

FENDALL, ROBERT.   Perquimans County.

November 30, 1711. January, 1711–1712. *Daughter:* ELIZABETH LILLINGTON. *Other devisees and legatees:* ISAAC WILLSON (land on Kendricks Creek known as Hawkinses Neck), RICHARD LOWRY. *Executor:* THOMAS LONG. *Witnesses:* JOHN WIAT, JOHN LONG, THOMAS WYATT. Will proven in Council: N. CHEVIN, *Clerk.*

FEPS, WILLIAM.   Beaufort County.

January 11, 1753. June, 1754. *Sons:* WILLIAM ("my maner plantation"), NATHANIEL, JOSIAH. *Daughters:* LU. RAINER, MOLLE, SARAH *Wife and Executrix:* MARY. *Witnesses:* ROBERT SPRING, CHARLES HOWARD, WILLIAM MORRIS. *Clerk of the Court:* WALLEY CHAUNCY.

FERGUSON, ADAM.   Craven Precinct.

October 13, 1715. February 15, 1715. *Son:* MARK ("my plantation"). *Daughters:* SARAH FERGUSON, JANE FERGUSON. *Wife:* ELIZABETH FERGUSON. *Executor:* DANIELL MCFARLAN. *Witnesses:* ROBT. RAMSEY, PETER CROPELY, FRANCIS HUTSON. *Clerk of the Court:* DANIELL MCFARLAN.

FERGUSON, MARK.   Craven County.

April 16, 1751. September Court, 1751. *Sons:* ADAM (350 acres of land on the East side of Slocumb's Creek), SLOCUMB (800 acres of land on

Mill Creek). *Cousin:* BENJAMIN CUMMINGS (land on East side of Adams Creek). *Wife and Executrix:* ELIZABETH. *Witnesses:* ADAM WALLIS, ROBERT WALLIS, JOHN CUMMINGS. *Clerk of the Court:* PHIL. SMITH.

FERIEL, RICHARD. Pasquotank County.

January 31, 1738–1739. July Court, 1740. *Sons:* ERASMUS and JOHN (*Executor*). *Witnesses:* JOHN HOUREN, THOMAS and WILLIS JAMES. *Clerk of the Court:* JAMES CRAVEN.

FERRIL, WILLIAM. Currituck County.

November 7, 1742. January Court, 1742–1743. *Sons:* JOSEPH, CALEB, SAMUEL. *Daughters:* TAMER, MARY and ANN FERRIL. *Sister:* ESBEL BURKET. *Wife and Executrix:* SARAH. *Witnesses:* GEORGE FEREBEE, JOSEPH FEREBEE, WILLIAM FEREBEE. *Clerk of the Court:* JOHN LURRY.

FEWOX, JAMES. County not given.

March 2, 1710. January 9, 1711–1712. *Son:* ROBERT. *Wife:* ANN. *Other legatees and devisees:* JNO. LAWSON, MARY LAWSON, SAMUEL HARDY, son of WM. HARDY. *Executrix:* MARY LAWSON, widow of NATHANIEL LAWSON. *Witness:* GEO. GLADSTAIN. Codicil, dated May 5, 1711, provides for use of gristmill. *Witnesses:* GEO. GLADSTAIN, JOSEPH FANINGS, JOHN SNELL. Will proven in Council: ROBERT BUCKNER, *Clerk*.

FIGURES, BARTHOLOMEW. Northampton County.

March 16, 1758. July Court, 1758. *Sons:* JOHN (700 acres of land), RICHARD (275 acres of land), BARTHOLOMEW ("my plantation"), JOSEPH ("land whereon he now lives"), WILLIAM (700 acres of land). *Daughters:* REBEKAH DERRING, ELIZABETH LEWIS. *Witnesses:* JOSEPH DEW, CHARLES DEW, WILLIAM SHERARD, JOHN DEW. Codicil to this will of even date makes more bequests to JOHN and BARTHOLOMEW. *Executors:* JOHN and BARTHOLOMEW FIGURES. *Clerk of the Court:* I. EDWARDS.

FILLIAW, JOHN. Craven County.

August 31, 1747. March 15, 1748. *Sons:* JOHN, JOSEPH, JAMES. *Daughters:* ANN FILLIAW, PRISILLAR FILLIAW, MARY FILLIAW. *Wife and Executrix:* JANE. *Witnesses:* ALEXANDER BLACKSHIRE, N. WOLF, WM. GRAY. *Clerk of the Court:* JOHN RICE.

FILLINGHAM, JOHN. Pitt County.

November 11, 1771. December 22, 1773. *Sons:* JOHN, ROBERT, SAMUEL, JARVIS, BENJAMIN. *Daughters:* MATHEW WHITE, MARY HAYS. *Wife:* MARGARET. *Executors:* JOHN and ROBERT (sons). *Witnesses:* JOSIAH LITTLE, ALEXR. STEWART. Will proven before JO. MARTIN.

FISH, WILLIAM.   Bertie County.

August 10, 1750. May Court, 1751. *Sons:* JOHN, WILLIAM ("plantation whereon I now live"). *Daughters:* ANN FERRILL, MARY FISH ("100 acres of land in Johnston County on Marsh Branch"). *Grandsons:* JOHN and WM. FISH. *Wife:* MARY. *Executor:* SAMUELL WILLIAMS. *Witnesses:* SARAH LEE, SAMUEL WILLIAMS, MARY CALVART. *Clerk of the Court:* BENJ. WYNNS.

FISHER, JAMES.   County not given.

August 13, 1702. No probate. "This being my last desire from all wills that all my whole estate both real and personal I give to my *wife and to my children* and my deare friend MR. WILLIAM WILKESON. I would have you if you please to assist them, that they may not be wronged." *Witnesses:* WILLIAM LONG, PETER JONES.

FISHER, RANDOLPH.   Craven County.

March 31, 1747. June Court, 1751. *Sons:* THOMAS and GEORGE (*Executor*). *Witnesses:* GEORGE GRAHMS, THOS. MATCHETT, RICHD. BATH. No signature to probate.

FITZGARRALD, JOHN.   Johnston County.

August 14, 1749. September Court, 1751. *Sons:* JOHN and THOMAS. *Son-in-law:* ARTHUR PEIRCE (*Executor*). *Wife:* ANN. *Executor:* RICHARD PEIRCE. *Witnesses:* ROBT. BUTLER, ANTHONY FULGHAM, ANNE PEIRCE. *Deputy Clerk of the Court:* JAMES OATES.

FITZPATRICK, BRYAN.   Allegator Creek, in Chowan County.

March 26, 1709. *Sons:* CORNELIUS, VINNEY, DINIS ("my dwelling plantation called Hunts"). *Son:* CONRELIUS, appointed *Executor*. Negroes bequeathed to sons. *Witnesses:* SAMUEL BROOKE, DAVID ELDER, JOHN MACKER. Original missing. Recorded in Book 1712–22, page 64.

FITZPATRICK, CORNELIUS.   Allegator, in Albemarle County.

August 21, 1716. *Wife and Executrix:* ELIZABETH. *Sons:* JOHN, CORNELIUS and BRYANT. *Daughters:* ELENDER, MARY, SARAH, ELIZABETH. *Other legatees:* GEO. WHIDBEE, JOHN WOODLAND, ELIZABETH WHIDBEE, RICHARD WHIDBEE, JOHN MARKE. *Witnesses:* JOHN WOODLAND, GEORGE WHIDBEE, RICHARD WHIDBEE. Will proven before THOS. POLLOCK, May 4, 1722.

FLANAKIN, RICHARD.   South Dividing Creek, in Bath Co.

September 5, 1739. June Court, 1741. *Sons:* JAMES ("the mannour plantation"), THOMAS, RICHARD, WILLIAM. *Daughter:* LEAH FLANAKIN.

Wife: KATHERINE. *Executors:* ABRM. PRITCHETT (brother), JAMES FLANAKIN (son). *Witnesses:* PORTER FINCH, DOROTHY FINCH, SAMUEL GOODIN. *Clerk of Beaufort Court:* ROG. JONES.

FLEMING, GEORGE. Pasquotank Precinct.

May 27, 1694. July 16, 1694. *Daughter:* ELIZABETH FLEMING. *Friends:* THOMAS ELLIOTT, JAMES ROBINSON. *Executor:* SIMON RICE. *Witnesses:* WILLIAM BRAY, ISAAC GILFORD, ELIZEBETH JONES, JOHN PHILPOTT. *Clerk of the Court:* EDWARD MAYO.

FLEMING, ROSANNA. Perquimans County.

May 20, 1758. October Court, 1758. *Son:* JAMES (*Executor*). *Daughters:* SARAH SCRIMSHER, MARTHA FLEMING, ELIZABETH FLEMING, MARY FLEMING. *Witnesses:* ZACHARIAH WEBB, SENR., JAMES GIBSON, ZACHARIAH WEBB, JUNR. *Clerk of the Court:* M. HARVEY.

FLETCHER, CURTIS. County not given.

March 28, 1671. April 15, 1671. *Legatees:* WILLIAM BRAY, THOMAS TULLEY, BENJAMIN TULLEY. *Witnesses:* WILLIAM BAYS, DAVID PRISHET. Proven before RICHARD FOSTER and PATRICK WHITE.

FLETCHER, FRANCIS. Pasquotank County.

January Court, 1743. *Wife and Executrix:* MARGARET. *Witnesses:* BENJAMIN BAPTISTE, JONATHAN LANGATHEN, WILLIAM DELENY. *Clerk of the Court:* THOS. TAYLOR.

FLETCHER, RALPH. Perquimans County.

February 20, 1726–1727. January 21, 1728. *Sons:* RALPH ("my manner house & plantation"), GEORGE ("my lower house and plantation"), JAMES, JOSUA. *Daughters:* JANE and ELIZABETH FLETCHER. *Executors:* RICHARD SKINNER and RICHARD CHEASTEN. *Witnesses:* ELIZABETH FRENCH, SARAH SKINNER, THOMAS RATTLIFF. *Clerk of the Court:* THOMAS CREW.

FLETCHER, RALPH. Perquimans County.

April 5, 1752. July Court, 1752. *Sons:* RALPH ("the manner plantation"), JOSHUA. *Daughters:* JANE, MIRIAM and RUTH FLETCHER, MARY RATTLIFF. *Wife:* MARY. *Executors:* JOSEPH RATLIFF (son-in-law). *Witnesses:* FRANCIS TOMS, FRANCIS NEWBY, WILLIAM LASEY. *Clerk of the Court:* EDMUND HATCH.

FLETCHER, THOMAS. Chowan County.

May 10, 1727. April Court, 1734. *Wife:* DOROTHA. *Son:* THOMAS. *Witnesses:* ROBERT LACITER, GEORGE LACITER. *Clerk of the Court:* MOSELY VAIL.

FLOOD, JAMES.   "Cape Fare."
1731. June 10, 1736. *Wife and Executrix:* ELIZABETH. *Witnesses:*
TUNIS VAN GOLDER, ELIZABETH HARNETT, MARY PARKER. *Clerk of the
Court:* HUGH CAMPBELL.

FLOOD, JAMES.   Chowan County.
November 15, 1750. November 30, 1750. *Wife and Executrix:* ELIZABETH. *Children:* WILLIAM and ANN BRASWELL. *Executors:* JAMES CRAVEN and THOMAS BARKER. *Witnesses:* EDMUND HATCH, JOHN MC-KILDO, RICHARD MCCLURE. Will proven before *Gov.* GAB. JOHNSTON.

FLOVELL, WILLIAM.   Newton, county not given.
December 18, 1737. March 1, 1737. Two hundred pounds South Carolina currency to be paid towards the erection of an English Church. *Niece:* ELIZABETH CALLETON, wife of GEORGE CALLETON of South Carolina. *Uncle:* WILLIAM HALE ("late of Nassau in New Providence"). *Executors:* WILLIAM ROPER, ELIZABETH CALLETON, RUFUS MARSDEN, JOHN DAVIS and JOSEPH WRAGG. *Witnesses:* ROGER ROLFE, ARMAND DEROSSET, M. D., MICH. HIGGINES. Will proven before GAB. JOHNSTON. Coat of arms on seal.

FLOYD, JOHN.   Northampton County.
August 3, 1756. November Court, 1756. *Sons:* MORRISE (80 acres of land in King William County, Va.), THOMAS ("plantation whereon I now live"), STEPHEN, JESSEE, JOHN and WILLIAM. *Daughter:* ELIZABETH COOKER. *Executors:* THOMAS and WILLIAM (sons). *Witnesses:* CHAS. CAMPBELL, JAMES STANTON. *Clerk of the Court:* I. EDWARDS.

FLYN, COLLUMB.   Bath County.
August 22, 1721. September 9, 1737. *Son and Executor:* COLLUMB ("all my real estate"). *Daughters:* MARY SMITH, MARGARET PRITCHARD. *Witnesses:* MARTIN FRANCK, ANDREW BALLEAU, THOS. BOYD. Will proven before GAB. JOHNSTON at Newton.

FOGG, MOSES.   Craven County.
December 3, 1751. March 20, 1751. *Legatees and devisees:* GRACE FOGG (daughter of JOHNWATS FOGG, 300 acres of land on Nuse River), MATHIAS BENSTON. *Executor:* JOHN LANE. *Witnesses:* JOHN DUNCAN, NICHOLAS ROUTLEDGE and NATHAN ALEXANDER. *Clerk of the Court:* JNO. SNEAD.

FONVIELLE, JOHN.   Craven County.
January 24, 1773. January 27, 1773. *Sons:* JOHN ("240 acres of land where he now lives; 120 acres of land between ISAAC FONVIELLE and

ARTHOR BLACKMAN; lot No. 6 in Newbern"), WILLIAM BRICE FONVIELLE (640 acres of land where he now dwells; Lot No. 5 in Newbern), FRANCIS (510 acres of land where he now lives; lot No. 7 in Newbern), FREDERICK ("land where he now lives and lot in Newbern"), STEPHEN ("500 acres of land where he now lives on New River; my lower tract on Stone Bay"), JEREMIAH ("770 acres of land in the mouth of Stone Creek; upper part of the lower tract on Stone Bay; half lot in Newbern"). *Daughters:* MARY HATCH (two half lots in Newbern and two hundred acres of land on the North side of Nuce River), ELIZABETH HATCH (lot in Newbern by the West gate; 360 acres of land in New Hanover County), EASTER FONVIELLE (one lot in Newbern). *Granddaughter:* ELIZABETH FONVIELLE. *Wife:* MARY. *Executors:* JOHN, WILLIAM BRICE and FRANCIS FONVIELLE (sons). *Witnesses:* JOHN TURNER, WILLIAM BALLARD, ISAAC ESLECK. Will proven before JO. MARTIN.

FORASTER, JAMES. Orange County.

September 5, 1755. December Court, 1755. *Sons:* WILLIAM, JAMES (to both is given land on Eno River), BENJAMIN and THOMAS ("my plantation"). *Son-in-law:* JOHN MANNING (200 acres of land on Eno River). *Wife and Executrix:* ANN. *Witnesses:* PATT MCCULLOCH, HUGH WOOD. *Clerk of the Court:* JAS. WATSON.

FORBES, JOHN. Pasquotank County.

November 24, 1747. July Court, 1750. *Son:* JAMES. *Wife and Executrix:* MARTHA. *Witnesses:* PETER BROWN, SARAH BROWN. *Clerk of the Court:* THOS. TAYLOR.

FOREHAND, CORNELIUS. Pasquotank County.

February 24, 1727. July 26, 1728. *Sons:* JOHN, CORNELIUS, JAMES, RICHARD, THOMAS. *Daughters:* ELIZEBETH and MARY FOREHAND. *Wife and Executrix:* ELIZABETH. *Witnesses:* ISAAC JONES, WILLIAM PHILLIPS and JOHN KIGHT. *Clerk of the Court:* R. EVERARDE. Executrix qualified before JOHN SOLLEY.

FOREMAN, JOHN. Hyde County.

September 25, 1744. December Court, 1744. *Sons:* CALEB, JOHN FYDINGS FOREMAN, ALEXANDER, WILLIAM, JOSHUA, JOSEPH, LAZARUS (plantation on North side of Pongo Creek). *Daughters:* CHARITY LUCAS, DOROTHY KIPPS. *Wife and Executrix:* MARGARET. *Witnesses:* THOS. LOACK, ELIS LOACK, JOSHUA FOREMAN. *Clerk of the Court:* THOS. LOACK.

FOREMAN, JOHN TIDINGS. Hyde County.

April 1, 1758. September Court, 1758. *Wife and Executrix:* MARGARETT. *Brother and Executor:* SANDERS FOREMAN. *Nephew and Executor:* JOHN FOREMAN (son of SANDERS). *Witnesses:* WM. DUNBARR, SAMUEL DUNBARR. *Clerk of the Court:* STEPHEN DENNING.

FORT, GEORGE.   Chowan Precinct.

May 15, 1719. October 2, 1719. *Sons:* ELIAS, GEORGE, BENJAMIN, JOHN, SAMUELL. *Daughters:* PHELIS FIBATH, ELIZEBETH FORT, CATHERINE FORT, ALICE FORT. *Wife:* ELISABETH FORT. *Executor:* ELIAS FORT. *Witnesses:* WILLIAM BOON, NICCOLIS BOON. *Clerk of the Court:* R. HICKS.

FORT, JOHN.   Craven County.

August 6, 1745. March Court, 1745–1746. *Sons:* ARTHUR, JOHN (plantation and mill at Conohoe) DUNLY (550 acres of land on lower side of falling Creek), MOSES (400 acres land on Cohary Swamp). *Daughters:* JERUSHAH FORT. *Wife and Executrix:* MARY. *Executors:* ARTHUR and JOHN FORT. *Witnesses:* JOHN PIPKIN, JOHN FORT, JUNIER. *Clerk of the Court:* JOHN RICE.

FORT, JOHN.   Johnston County.

May 16, 1748. June Court, 1748. *Brothers:* MOSES and ARTHUR and DRULY. *Sister:* JERUSHA. *Executors:* WILLIAM HOLMES (father-in-law). DRULY FORT (brother). *Witnesses:* ROBERT BUTLER, JOHN PIPKIN, JETHRO PIPKIN. *Deputy Clerk of the Court:* RICHARD CASWELL.

FORT, RICHARD.   Craven County.

March 6, 1745. December Court, 1746. *Brothers:* THOMAS, ELIAS and WILLIAM FORT. *Sisters:* SARAH WALL, MARY BYNUM, HANNAH PHILLIPS. *Nephew:* AUTHOR FORT. *Executors:* THOMAS and ELIAS FORT. *Witnesses:* JOHN PHILLIPS, ROBERT HOOD, AMBRUS PITTMAN, BENJAMIN BLACKBURN. *Deputy Clerk of Johnston County Court:* WM. CASWELL.

FORTSEN, MARY.   County not given.

January 28, 1663. November 15, 1665. *Son:* THEOPHILUS. *Witnesses:* JU. LAWRENCE, WM. EMLY, ELIZABETH ROSY, ELLINER WARDELL. *Clerk of the Court:* THOMAS HARRIS.

FOSCUE, JOHN.   Hyde County.

November 18, 1751. March Court, 1752. *Sons:* MOSES ("my mannor plantation"); JOHN, WILLIAM. *Daughters:* MARY and LYDIA FOSCUE. *Executors:* WILLIAM SLADE and ABIGAIL FOSCUE (wife). *Witnesses:* SIMON FOSCUE, MARY HAMILTON, URIAH COLLINS. *Clerk of the Court:* FRAN. EGLETON.

FOSCUE, SIMON.   Hyde County.

November 11, 1751. December Court, 1751. *Sons:* RICHARD, BELL (my mannour plantation), SIMON, WILLIAM, LUKE, JOHN. *Daughters:*

MARY SILVERTHORN, SARA SANDERSON, BARBARIE BAILEY. *Executors:* LUKE, JOHN and BELL (sons). *Witnesses:* URIAH COLLINS, ABRAHAM EASTER, COMFORT RUE. *Clerk of the Court:* R. LOACK.

FOSTER, HANNAH.   Perquimans County.

June 27, 1727. July Court, 1728. *Grandson:* SAMUEL RIT. *Granddaughter:* COMFORT RIT. *Daughter-in-law:* JEMINAH RIT. *Executors:* THOMAS AWEEDY, GEORGE GORDIN. *Witnesses:* THOS. and JEMINAH WRIT. *Clerk of the Court:* R. EVERARD.

FOSTER, JAMES.   County not given.

October 23, 1726. March 29, 1727. *Friend:* SAMUEL WITE (son of "old SAMUEL WITE"). *Wife:* HANNAH. No Executor. *Witnesses:* ELIJAH STANTON, ELEZBETH STANTON. Will proven before *Governor* RICHARD EVERARD.

FOSTER, JOHN.   Craven County.

October 9, 1754. November Court, 1754. *Son:* THOMAS. *Daughter:* LYDIE FOSTER. *Wife:* ELIZABETH. *Executors:* JEREMIAH VAILE, ZECHARIAH SAWTELL (uncle). *Witnesses:* WM. WRIGHT, CHARLES COGDELL, jun., WILL. MONAT. Codicil of even date makes bequests to *son*, PARKER, *wife*, ELIZABETH, and *uncle*, ZACHARIAH SAWTELL. Same witnesses. *Clerk of the Court:* SOL. REW. Coat of arms on seal.

FOSTER, ROBERT.   Bertie County.

February 12, 1739–1740. May Court, 1740. *Grandchildren:* JOHN BROWN, ANN BROWN, JEMIMA COTTEN and SUSANNA COTTEN (land on Meherin Creek), MARY BROWN. *Son-in-law:* ALEXANDER COTTEN. *Daughter:* ANN COTTEN. *Wife's grandson:* WILLIAM NIGHT. *Executrix:* WIFE (not named). *Witnesses:* WM. WHITFIELD, CHRISTIAN DENTON, MARGREAT LACEY. *Clerk of the Court:* JNO. WYNNS.

FOSTER, WILLIAM.   County not given.

October 9, 1687. *Son:* FRANCIS. *Daughter:* ELIZABETH FOSTER. *Wife:* DIANA. *Witnesses:* JONATHAN HOLEMAN, WILLIAM HUGHES, SAMUEL PRICKLOVELL. No Executors. No probate.

FOURRE, JOHN.   Pasquotank County.

March 13, 1730. April Court, 1732. *Sons:* ISAAC ("ye mannor plantation"), NATHANIELL (plantation on Lettel River). *Daughters:* ELIZABETH FOURRE, MAHER FOURRE. *Sister:* MARY CORRY. *Wife and Executrix:* mentioned, but not named. *Witnesses:* JNO. MILLS, JO. CORRY, THOMAS CORRY. *Clerk of the Court:* W. MINSON.

FOURREE, PETER.   Albemarle County.

August 6, 1697. November 3, 1697. *Son:* JOHN. *Daughters:* NICOLE, MARGUERITT, MARY. *Wife and Executrix:* CATHERINE. *Witnesses:* ANTHONY MARCKHUM, FRANCIS DELAMARE. *Clerk of the Council:* W. GLOVER.

FOX, JAMES.   Tyrrell County.

August, 1754. June Court, 1755. *Son and Executor:* THOMAS. *Daughters:* ANN FOX (*Executrix*), SUSANNA ALEXANDER, MARY WISE. *Witnesses:* JOSHUA ALEXANDER, ABRAHAM JENNET, BENJAMIN CHAPMAN. *Clerk of the Court:* FR. WARD.

FRANCK, JOHN MARTIN.   Craven County.

November 3, 1744. *Sons:* JOHN and EDWARD. *Wife:* SEVIL. *Daughters:* SUSANNAH, SEVIL, BARBARA and CATHERINE FRANCK, MARY WORSLEY, ELIZABETH HARROLD. *Executor:* FREDERICK ISLER. *Witnesses:* CHRISTIAN ISLER, MELCHER REMM, FREDERICK ISLER. The following lands devised: plantation called "Chinpin"; 500 acres on Trent River adjoining Chinpin; 640 acres commonly called "James Marchels plantation." About 20 negroes bequeathed. To each of children is bequeathed cattle and riding horses, and to each of sons is bequeathed a watch. No probate.

FRASER, DUNCAN.   Craven County.

September 8, 1773. September 23, 1773. *Legatees:* PEGGY and JOHN ("two mulatto children, the offspring of Phillis, a free negro woman now in my possession"). *Executor:* JOHN MCKAY of Newbern. *Witnesses:* THOS. SITGREAVES, JOHN SITGREAVES. Will proven before Jo. MARTIN.

FRAZIER, DAVID.   County not given.

September 20, 1729. October Court, 1729. *Executor and sole legatee:* ROBERT BELL. *Witnesses:* JOHN CLEMET, GEORGE BELL. Will proven before RICHD. EVERARD.

FRAZIER, SAMUEL.   Craven County.

May 3, 1772. May 20, 1772. *Wife:* MARY. *Daughter:* MARY. *Sisters:* JANE FRUME and ELIZABETH HEADLY. *Father:* SAMUEL. *Mother:* ELIZABETH. *Executors:* JOHN HAWKS and JAMES COOR. *Will proven before:* JO. MARTIN. *Witnesses:* CORNELIUS GROENENDEYK, JNO. TURNER, JUN., JOSEPH RAWLINGS.

FREEMAN, JOHN.   Chowan Precinct.

February 19, 1729–1730. *Sons:* JOHN, JAMES, MATHEW. *Wife:* MARY. *Executors:* WILLIAM FREEMAN (brother), JOHN FREEMAN (son) and MICHEALL WARD. *Witnesses:* EDWARD WOOD, GEORGE WHITE, THOMAS ROWNTREE. No probate.

FREEMAN, JOHN. Beaufort County.

December 19, 1752. March 13, 1753. *Son:* JOHN. *Wife:* MARY (lots in Bath Nos. 16, 17 and 18). *Executors:* WIFE and SON, who are authorized and directed to sell 1300 acres of land on Tarr River and 1900 acres on Core Creek for the payment of debts. *Witnesses:* JAMES CALEF, JAMES PILKINGTON, WY. ORMOND. *Clerk of the Court:* WILL. ORMOND.

FREEMAN, WILLIAM. Chowan County.

February 7, 1736. August 13, 1737. *Sons:* JOHN ("plantation whereon he now lives"); WILLIAM, THOMAS, RICHARD, ARON, SAMUEL (plantations to each). *Wife and Executrix:* MARY. *Witnesses:* WALTER DROUGHAN, JOHN FREEMAN, JUNER, THOMAS ROWNTREE. Will proven before W. SMITH, C. J.

FRENCH, RICHARD. Perquimans County.

December 17, 1712. April 13, 1716. *Wife and Executrix:* ELIZABETH. *Witnesses:* THOMAS BLICHENDEN, RICHARD SKINNER, JUNR., SARAH EVENS. *Clerk of the Court:* RICH'D LEARY.

FRESHWATER, JOHN. Pasquotank County.

April 9, 1753. July Court, 1753. *Sons:* WILLIAM ARMSTED FRESHWATER, JOHN FRESHWATER. *Daughters:* FRANCES ARMSTEAD FRESHWATER and PHADDUS FRESHWATER. *Wife and Executrix:* ELIZABETH. *Witnesses:* JOSEPH PENDLETON, ABRAHAM HOSEA, ANN PENDLETON. *Clerk of the Court:* THOS. TAYLOR.

FROST, WILLIAM. Albemarle County.

May 30, 1717. April Court, 1718. "Kisey River in Albemarle County." *Sons:* JAMES, WILLIAM. *Daughters:* ELENOR FROST, MARY JOHNSON. *Wife:* JOAN. No Executor named. *Witnesses:* WILL LATTIMER, JOHN STANCELL. *Clerk of Chowan Court:* R. HICKS.

FRY, THOMAS. Bath County.

March 18, 1724–1725. January Court, 1726. "Late of London in Great Britain, now of Bath County in N. C." *Mother:* ELIZABETH FRY of Milton in Southton. *Wife and Executrix:* ELIZABETH. *Witnesses:* PATRICK MAULE, THOMAS HARDING, SARAH SWANN, JNO. BAPTA. ASHE. *Clerk of the Court:* THOMAS JONES.

FRYLY, WILLIAM. Tyrrell Precinct.

August 28, 1737. March 7, 1737. *Daughter and Executrix:* MARY JONES. *Grandsons:* EVEN and FRYLY JONES. *Wife and Executrix:* GRACE. *Witnesses:* STEVENS LEE, ROBERT MCBRIE, THOMAS LEE. *Clerk of the Court:* ANDERSON LEGGET. Executor qualified before JAMES CRAVEN, *Clerk of Court.*

ABSTRACT OF WILLS, 1690—1760. 129

FULLERTON, ROBERT. Chowan County.

December 30, 1749. January Court, 1750. *Daughters:* MARY TOMSON, SUSANNA. *Wife:* MARY. *Executors:* JOHN THOMPSON and MATTHIAS FULLERTON. *Witnesses:* JOHN LEWIS, DAVID BUSH, LEWIS JONES. *Clerk of Court:* WILL. MEARNS.

FURBISH, THOMAS. Pasquotank County.

April 26, 1732. July Court, 1732. *Sons:* WILLIAM, THOMAS, ISAAC. *Wife:* ABIGAIL. *Executor:* THOMAS BURGES. *Witnesses:* ALICE FURBISH, MARY JONES, JUDA HANBURY. *Clerk of the Court:* H. MINSON.

FUSSEL, THOMAS. Parish of Cartee.

June 4, 1735. *Son:* AARON (*Executor*). *Daughters:* ELIZABETH WEAVER (husband GILBERT), MARY RAINWATER (wife of JOHN), MARTHA ARNAL (wife of JOHN), SARAH, ANN. *Witnesses:* WILLIAM WEAVER, RICHARD HEAD, JOHN COOK. No probate.

GAD, JAMES. Pasquotank County.

March 1, 1699. July 15, 1701. *Wife and Executrix:* SARAH. *Sister:* ELIZABETH RIGGENS. *Brother-in-law:* WM. TRANES. *Sister-in-law:* MARJORY LOMBROSER. *Witnesses:* SAMUEL AKEHURST, STEPHEN SCOTT, KATHERN TONER. *Clerk of the Court:* THO. ABINGTON.

GAINER, MARY. Edgecombe County.

October, 1751. November Court, 1751. *Legatees:* HESTER GAINER, MARTHA GAINER (sister), LIDDAY LASATER (sister), WILLIAM GAINER (brother). *Executor:* WILLIAM GAINER. *Witnesses:* ARTHUR BELL, MARTHA GAINER, ESTER BELL. *Clerk of the Court:* BENJAMIN WYNNS.

GAINER, SAMUEL. Tyrrell County.

October 1, 1751. June Court, 1752. *Sons:* JAMES, SAMUEL, WILLIAM, THOMAS, ARTHER, ˙JOSEPH, BENJAMIN. *Daughters:* MARY WHITTEY, ELIZABETH GRIFFEN, SARY GAINER. *Executors:* WIFE (not named), SAMUEL (son). *Witnesses:* WILLIAM GAINER, THOMAS GAINER, JOSEPH GAINER. *Clerk of the Court:* EVAN JONES.

GAINER, WILLIAM. Edgecombe County.

March 11, 1746. November Court, 1750. *Wife and Executrix:* HESTER. *Sons:* WILLIAM and JOSEPH. *Daughters:* MARTHA, MARY, LYDDA, ELIZA. *Executors:* WILLIAM and JOSEPH (sons). *Witnesses:* JOHN COLLINS, WILLIAM BELL, MATTHEW LOWRY. *Clerk of the Court:* BENJAMIN WYNNS.

GALE, CHRISTOPHER. County not given.

February 17, 1734. March 12, 1734. "Born at York in the kingdom of Great Britain, but now Collector of his Majestys Customs at the port of Roanoak." *Executors:* SARAH CATHERINE GALE (wife), EDMOND GALE (brother) and MILES GALE (son). *Daughter:* PENELOPE LITTLE. *Granddaughter:* SARAH CLAYTON. *Nephews:* EDMOND GALE, ROGER GALE. *Friends:* DAVID O'SHEAL, of Nancimond in Va. and WILLIAM BADHAM. *Witnesses:* E. MOSELEY, LOUIS ALLAIRE, MARGARET ALLAIRE. Will proven before GAB. JOHNSTON at Edenton. Coat of arms on seal.

GALE, EDMOND.   Chowan County.

December 6, 1738. January 27, 1738. *Sons:* ROGER and EDMOND. *Wife and Executrix:* MARY. *Witnesses:* THOS. BLOUNT, HENRY BONNER, JOS. ANDERSON. Will proven before W. SMITH, C. J.

GALLEY, JOHN.   Pasquotank County.

October 6, 1729. October 15, 1729. *Sole legatee:* PATRICK LAUGHLIN. *Witnesses:* THOS. GREORGY, RICHARD GREORGRY, JOHN BELL. *Clerk of the Court:* WM. MINSON.

GALLUAY, THOMAS.   Chowan County.

July 27, 1753. October Court, 1753. *Executors and sole devisees:* JACOB ODOM, MARY GALLUAY (mother). *Witnesses:* WILLIAM FRYER, THOMAS FRYER, JEAMES FRYER. *Clerk of the Court:* WILL. HALSEY.

GAMBELL, ADAM.   County not given.

November 14, 1694. November, 1694. "Glaskow in the Kingdom of Scotland." *Legatees:* JOHN GAMBELL, JOHN LOVE (both of London), ADAM HILL (of Glasgow), JOHN ARGY (of Arranthrew), ROBERT, THOMAS and JOHN WEST (sons-in-law of THOMAS POLLOCK), CAPT. JOHN HUNT, JAMES GAMBELL (brother, of Glasgow). *Executors:* COL. THOS. POLLOCK, CAPT. JOHN HUNT. *Witnesses:* HENE MCGREGORE, ELIZABETH HUNT, MICH. LYNCEY (or LYNCH). Will proven before W. GLOVER.

GAMMIDGE, FRANCIS.   Currituck County.

October 19, 1719. January 6, 1738. *Cousin, Executor and sole legatee:* HUMPHREY VINCE. *Witnesses:* MOSES PRISCOD, ISABELL PRISCOD, AND. PEACOCK. *Clerk of the Court:* JOSN. SMITH.

GARDNER, JOHN.   Tyrrell County.

April 13, 1749. June 6, 1749. *Son:* JAMES SMEATHWICK GARDNER. *Daughters:* DUNSILA and ANN GARDNER, JEMIMAH WALLBUTON, ELISABETH MOY, ASHE MOY, REBECCAH WARD. *Wife:* ELISABETH. *Executors:* JOHN WALLBUTTON, JOHN WARD. *Witnesses:* WILLIAM GARDNER, WILLIAM GARDNER, JUN., EDWARD GRIFFEN. *Clerk of the Court:* EVAN JONES.

GARDNER, MARTIN.   Bertie County.

October 6, 1755. January Court, 1760. *Sons:* JOHN, WILLIAM, JAMES, MARTAIN. *Daughters:* ANN, ANNAH and JANE. *Wife and Executrix:* ANNAH. *Executor:* NEEDHAM BRYAN. *Witnesses:* BENJAMIN CARTER, JOSEPH HOLLAND. *Clerk of the Court:* BENJAMIN WYNNS.

GARDNER, WILLIAM.   Tyrrell County.

February 11, 1754. June Court, 1754. *Sons:* WILLIAM, THOMAS, SAMUEL, ISAAC ("ye manner plantation"). *Friend:* MARY COOPER. *Executors:* WILLIAM and SAMUEL GARDNER. *Witnesses:* THOMAS and ISAAC GARDNER, CLOANAH SMITHWICK. *Clerk of the Court:* EVAN JONES.

GARFORT, GREGORY.   Albemarle County.

October 1, 1703. July Court, 1704. "To my mate WILLIAM PARGITER all my whole estate reall & personall * * * *." *Executor:* WM. PARGITER. *Witnesses:* FRANCIS TOMES, JR., MARGARETT TOMES, THO. HOUGHTON. *Clerk of the Court:* THO. SNODEN.

GARNER, JOHN.   Northampton County.

March 23, 1746. February Court, 1755. *Son and Executor:* JOHN. *Grandsons:* JOHN GARNER and THOMAS MACKOONE. *Daughters:* MOURNING HARE, HANNER. *Wife and Executrix:* MARY. *Witnesses:* BENET SMITH, JOHN MACKCONE, SAMUEL WARREN. *Clerk of the Court:* I. EDWARDS.

GARNER, RALFE.   Albemarle County.

May 31, 1695. August Court, 1695. *Daughters:* MARY, ELIZABETH and ESTOR. *Executrix:* JOAN GARDNER. *Witnesses:* THOMAS BARKOCK, GARRETT KEEN. EDWARD MAYO, *Clerk of the Court.*

GARRET, JOHN.   Currituck Precinct.

January 27, 1734–1735. July 1, 1735. *Wife and Executrix:* SARAH. *Sons:* JOHN and JONATHAN. *Witnesses:* JOHN HAWREN, SAMUEL STEVENS, SAMUEL JARVIS. *Clerk of the Court:* JAMES CRAVEN.

GARRETT, THOMAS.   Chowan Precinct.

January 30, 1733. January 31, 1734. *Sons:* HUMPHREY (*Executor*), THOMAS. *Daughters:* CATREN WHITE, SARAH GARRETT, ANN LASITTOR, JANE GARRETT, MARY GARRETT, LETTES GARRETT, PRUDENCE GARRETT. *Executor:* HUMPHREY GARRETT (son). *Wife:* mentioned, but not named. *Witnesses:* ORLANDO CHAMPION, WILLIAM HASE. Will proven before GAB. JOHNSTON, Jan. 31, 1734, at Edenton.

GARRET, WILLIAM.   Albemarle County.

March 23, 1734. March 27, 1735. *Wife and Executrix:* MARY. *Other legatees:* JAMES CHASON, THOMAS HARDISON, RICHARD HARDISON, JOSEPH HARDISON. *Witnesses:* JOHN HARDISON, JASPER HARDISON. Will proven before GAB. JOHNSTON at Edenton.

GASKILL, WILLIAM.   Pasquotank County.

May 4, 1703. July 20, 1703. *Sons:* WILLIAM, THOMAS. *Daughters:* JEAN and FANE GASKILL, ELIZABETH DURANT. *Wife and Executrix:* JANE. *Witnesses:* THO. ABINGTON, RICHARD NETT, WM. HARLOW. *Clerk of the Court:* THO. ABINGTON.

GASKINS, CATRIN.   Pasquotank County.

August 25, 1755. September Court, 1755. *Son and Executor:* THOMAS. *Daughter:* ANN CARTRIGHT. *Witnesses:* SAMUEL DAVIS, JOSEPH PINDLETON. *Clerk of the Court:* THOS. TAYLOR.

GASKINS, FISHER.   Craven County.

November 15, 1757. August Court, 1758. *Son:* JOSEPH. *Daughter:* ANN GASKINS. *Wife and Executrix:* ANN. *Executor:* THOMAS GASKINS (brother). *Witnesses:* ANN BRIGHT, SARAH ARTHER. *Clerk of the Court:* PETER CONWAY.

GASKINS, WILLIAM.   Pasquotank County.

November 4, 1711. *Sons:* WILLIAM (plantation at mouth of Great Flatty Creek), BENJAMIN (plantation in "letel flate creek"). *Executrix:* WIFE (not named). *Witnesses:* EVAN JONES, JOSEPH PEGS. No probate.

GATHIN, EDWARD.   Craven Precinct.

January 3, 1725–1726. March 5, 1725–1726. *Sons:* JOHN. *Wife:* ELIZABETH. *Executors:* JOHN and ELIZABETH (son and wife). *Witnesses:* ROBERT PITTS, MARY PITTS, CALEB METCALFE. *Clerk of the Court:* C. METCALFE.

GEORGE, DAVID.   Pasquotank County.

February 29, 1747–1748. July Court, 1748. *Sons:* JAMES, DAVID ("plantation whereon I now live"). *Daughter:* MARGARET GEORGE. *Wife and Executrix:* ELIZABETH. *Trustees:* JOHN BARCLIFT (brother) and JOHN EVERIGIN. *Witnesses:* WILL GREGORY, STEPHEN SCOTT, SAMUEL SCOTT. *Clerk of the Court:* THOS. TAYLOR.

GEORGE, HENRY.   County not given.

December 3, 1711. *Legatees:* SUSANNAH and ELIZABETH MITCHELL, WILLIAM MITCHELL, JOHN BROWNING, SARAH and JANE BROWNING. *Ex-*

ecutor: JOHN BROWNING. *Witnesses:* JOHN BROWNING, FECEY TICEHORE, JOHN JORDAN. Original missing. Recorded in Book 1712–1722, page 34.

GERFORT, GREGORY.   Perquimans County.

October 1, 1703. July 11, 1704. *Friend, Executor and Sole Legatee:* WILLIAM PERGIFER. *Witnesses:* FRANCIS TOMES, MARGARET TOMES, THO. HAGHTON (or RAGHTON). *Clerk of the Court:* THOS. SNODEN.

GEWIN, CHRISTOPHER.   Edgecombe County.

April 2, 1748. February Court, 1749. *Son and Executor:* CHRISTOPHER. *Daughter and Executrix:* MARY HARRELL. *Grandsons:* LOT, ABELL and CHRISTOPHER HARRELL. *Witnesses:* JAMES BRASWELL, BENJAMIN BRASWELL, ABRAHAM DEW. *Clerk of the Court:* BENJN. WYNNS.

GIBLE, DEDERICK.   Pasquotank County.

June 25, 1720. July 19, 1720. *Sons:* DEDERIK and FREDERICK. *Daughter:* MARY GIBLE. *Wife and Executrix:* MARY. *Witnesses:* JOHANN BARNHART SCHONNEWOLF, ANN———. *Clerk of the Court:* W. NORRIS.

GIBBLE, DEDERICK.   Carteret County.

August 25, 1754. September Court, 1754. *Sons:* DEDERICK, FREDERICK. *Daughter:* SUSANNAH GIBBLE. *Wife and Administratrix:* HANNAH. *Witnesses:* JOHN KILBE, DANIEL REESE, PRUDENCE LEWIS. *Clerk of the Court:* GEO. READ.

GIBSON, THOMAS.   Cumberland County.

February Court, 1762. This is a nuncupative will proven by JOHN CAMPBELL, NEILL MCNEILL and CATHERINE MCNEILL. *Wife:* MARY. *Brother:* WALTER GIBSON. *Executors:* MARY and WALTER GIBSON and ROBERT SMITH. *Justices:* HUTON MCNEILL, ALEZR MCALISTER, FERGD CAMPBELL. *Clerk of the Court:* RICH'D GROVE.

GIDDINGS, THOMAS.   Johnston County.

July 13, 1747. September 5, 1747. *Sons:* JACOB, WILLIAM, ISAAC, BENJAMIN, ABRAHAM. *Granddaughter:* ELIZABETH. *Executor:* JACOB GIDDINGS. *Witnesses:* GEORGE DYCKES, THOS. GRISARD, TH. LAMBERTHSON. Will proven before E. HALL, C. J.

GIDDINGS, WILLIAM.   Hyde County.

November 10, 1757. March Court, 1758. *Sons:* THOMAS, JACOB, JOHN. *Daughters:* AGNIS, LIDEA and DARKIS GIDDINGS. *Wife and Executrix:* FRANCES. *Executor:* JOHN SLADE. *Witnesses:* TIMOTHY GREEN, BENJAMIN SLADE, KEATREN LEATH. *Clerk of the Court:* STEPHN DENNING.

GILBERD, THOMAS.   Chowan Precinct.

October 14, 1719. October 20, 1720. *Sons:* THOMAS ("plantation whereon I now live"), WILLIAM, JOHN. *Executor:* JOHN BRYAN. *Witnesses:* JOHN BRYAN, PHILIP BROWN, TOMSIN BROWNE. *Clerk of the Court:* THOMAS HENMAN.

GILBERT, FRANCIS.   Bath County.

December 30, 1725. July Court, 1726. *Sons:* FRANCIS and HENRY GILBERT. *Wife and Executrix:* ELIZABETH. *Witnesses:* WM. SPARRY, SAMUEL PEEK, WILLIAM MOOR. *Clerk of the Court:* THO. JONES (Clerk of Beaufort and Hyde prect. court).

GILBIRT, JOSIAH.   Perquimans County.

March 14, 1758. April Court, 1760. *Wife and Executrix:* SARAH. *Sons:* JOSEPH (*Executor*); JEREMIAH, THOMAS, JOEL. *Daughter:* JEMIMA COX. *Witnesses:* JOSEPH WHITE, MARY STEWART, DINAH GILBIRT. *Clerk of the Court:* MILES HARVEY.

GILFORD, JOHN.   Pasquotank County.

January 15, 1741. July Court, 1743. *Brother and Executor:* JOSEPH GILFORD (100 acres of land on the Northeast side of Pasquotank River known as "Cabbing Ridge"). *Witnesses:* BENNETT MORGAN, PETER SAWYER. *Clerk of the Court:* THOS. TAYLOR.

GILLETT, JOHN.   Craven County.

May 17, 1749. October 18, 1749. *Sons:* JOHN, PATTERSON, ANDERSON, MOSES. *Executors:* JOHN HARPER, PRISCILLA HALL. *Witnesses:* JOHN SIMMONS, EMMANUEL SIMMONS, MARY DUDLEY. Will proven before GAB. JOHNSTON.

GILLETT, JOHN.   Carteret County.

September 29, 1753. *Daughters:* BETTY and SARAH GILLET. *Brothers:* PATERSON and ANDERSON and MOSES GILLETT. *Executors:* MOSES GILLETT and MOSES HOUSTON. *Witnesses:* EML JONES, JOHN PEGGOTT, EZEKIL HUNTER. No probate.

GILLYAM, THOMAS.   County not given.

October 10, 1702. *Wife and Executrix:* SARAH. *Witnesses:* WM. WILKJON, JOHN TYLER, MARGRETT HOLBROOK. No probate.

GLADSTAINE, GEORGE.   Scuppernong, county not given.

November 6, 1712. *Legatees:* EDWARD PHELPS and MARY LAWSON. *Witnesses:* ROBERT HICKSON, JOHN HASTEL, SAMLL BRIFFET. Original missing. Recorded in Book 1712–1722, page 44.

GLAISTER, MARY.   Pasquotank County.

June 9, 1740. October Court, 1740. *Cousins:* HENRY PALIN (son of Thomas), THOMAS PALIN (son of THOMAS), ANN READING and MARY GLAISTER PALIN (daughters of THOMAS PALIN), MARY CLARK PALIN (daughter of JOHN PALIN), JOHN PALIN (son of JOHN), SARAH PALIN, SUSANNAH PRITCHARD. *Other legatees:* ELISABETH SCOTT (daughter of STEPHEN SCOTT), MARY JONES, MARY MORRIS, SAMIVEL NEWBY, SARAH MARTIN (wife of NATHANIEL). Other bequests made to negro slaves. *Executrix:* SARAH and MARY CLARK PALIN. *Witnesses:* DAVID GEORGE, JOHN HENLEY, JOSHUA SCOTT. *Clerk of the Court:* JAMES CRAVEN.

GLASCO, ROBERT.   Chowan Precinct.

March 26, 1690. October 6, 1690. *Wife and Executrix:* JAN. *Witnesses:* RICHARD SKEBELL, JOHN CROSSLLAN, RICHARD WOLLARD. *Clerk of the Court:* JOHN WINGATE.

GLASGOW, WILLIAM.   Currituck County.

September 30, 1746. April 7, 1747. *Son:* CALEB GLASGOW. *Daughters:* SARAH, ABIAH, ELIZABETH, LOWDENNER. *Wife and Executrix:* SUSANNAH. *Witnesses:* WILLIAM SHERGOLD, PETER DAUGE, WILLIAM BRAY. *Clerk of the Court:* RICHD. MCCLURE.

GLAUSTER, JOSEPH.   Pasquotank County.

January 27, 1718-1719. February 11, 1718-1719. *Wife and Executrix:* MARY. *Daughters:* RUTH and SARAH GLASTER (or GLAUSTER). *Friend:* NATHANIEL MARTIN. *Cousin:* THOMAS PALIN. *Witnesses:* JNO. PALIN, CHAS. BULL, SARAH BULL. Will proven before JOHN ROBISON, *Justice of the Peace.*

GLIN, RICHARD.   Chowan Precinct.

October 5, 1728. November 4, 1728. *Cousins (nephews):* WILLIAM POWELL, son of sister ELIZABETH GLYN; JOHN THORNTON. *Executor:* JOHN AVERETT. *Witnesses:* JOHN POWELL, JAMES STONE, JOHN ROBERTSON. Will proven before RICHD. EVERARD.

GLISHAN, JOHN.   Runeroy Marshes, Bertie Precinct.

September 20, 1734. *Wife and Executrix:* JEAN. *Witnesses:* THEOPHILUS WILLIAMS, LAZARUS BENTON, THOMAS JONES. No probate.

GLOVER (spelled "GLOVEYER"), WILLIAM. Northampton Co.

July 30, 1754. August Court, 1754. *Sons:* JOHN, WILLIAM, GEORGE, JOSEPH, BENJAMIN. *Daughters:* LIDDY HARRIS, SARAH PARRISH. *Grand-*

daughter: MORNING HARRIS. *Wife:* MARY. *Executors:* JOHN and WILLIAM GLOVER (sons). *Witnesses:* JOHN DAY, SILVESTER EASTIS, SAMMUEL HARRIS. *Clerk of the Court:* I. EDWARDS.

GODBY, CARY.   Onslow County.

September 17, 1758. February 28, 1759. *Son:* WILLIAM. *Daughters:* SARAH, ELIZABETH, RACHEL and MARY. *Wife:* ANN. *Executor:* JOHN STARKEY. *Witnesses:* HENRY GODBE, W. MOLSEED, JAMES FOYLE. Will proven before *Governor* ARTHUR DOBBS. *Secretary to the Governor:* RICHD. SPAIGHT.

GODFREY, FRANCIS.   Albemarle County.

October 20, 1675. November 5, 1675. *Sons:* WILLIAM, JOHN. *Wife and Executrix:* JOANE. *Witnesses:* PAUL LATHUM, WM. WESTERMAN, JOHN CULPEPER. *Reg. Pub.:* THOMAS HARRIS. *Clerk of the Court:* RALPH COATES.

GODFREY, MATTEW.   Craven County.

December 8, 1744. *Sons:* MATHEW, JAMES. *Daughters:* SARAH GODFREY, ANN GODFREY, FILLAMER GODFREY. *Executors:* JOSIAH MASTRES, ELISABETH SIMENS. *Witnesses:* THOS. MASTRES, DAVID RAMSEY, THOS. ABETT. No probate.

GODFREY, THOMAS.   Perquimans County.

November 26, 1748. April Court, 1749. *Sons:* WILLIAM, THOMAS, FRANCIS ("my plantation"), JOSEPH. *Daughters:* SARAH GODFREY, ELLINOR GODFREY. *Wife and Executrix:* ELLINOR. *Witnesses:* JAMES GIBSON, BENJAMIN BIDGOOD, AMEY STAFFORD. *Clerk of the Court:* EDMUND HATCH.

GODLY, JOHN.   Bertie County.

January 22, 1731–1732. May Court, 1732. *Sons:* NATHAN ("plantation on Tarr River known by ye name of Tubbago's folly"), JOHN (300 acres of land on South side of Swifts Creek), THOMAS ("plantation on Lookinglass Swamp whereon I now live"). *Daughters:* MARY and AMY GODLY. *Wife and Executrix:* KATHERINE. *Executor:* JOHN EDWARDS "of Roneoke." *Witnesses:* ANN WILLIAMS, SAMUELL HENLEY, WILLIAM PORGEN. *Clerk of the Court:* RT. FORSTER.

GODWIN, NATHAN.   Beaufort County.

February 27, 1751–1752. June 9, 1752. *Executors:* JOSEPH BARROW, GEORGE SUGG, MARY GODWIN (wife). *Daughter:* MARY GODWIN. *Witnesses:* RICHD LATTEN, MARY WILLIAMS, ELISEBETH CHURCH. *Clerk of the Court:* WILL. ORMOND.

GODWIN, WILLIAM.   Bertie County.

May 4, 1752. May Court, 1753. *Sons:* BARNSBY, WILLIS, KEARNEY, JOSIAS. *Wife:* MARTHA. *Daughters:* JULIAN, SILVIA GODWIN, COURTNEY GODWIN, MARTHA GODWIN. *Executor:* JOHN BRICKELL. *Witnesses:* JOHN BROWN, RICHARD ROBERTS, GILSTRAP WILLIAMS. *Clerk of the Court:* BENJN. WYNNS.

GOFFE, ARTHUR.   Craven County.

November 29, 1725. June Court, 1737. *Friend, Executor and sole legatee:* JAMES WINRIGHT. *Witnesses:* TH. BELL, TH. WILSON, PATR. OGILBY. *Clerk of the Court:* JAMES COOR.

GOMM, JOHN.   Tyrrell County.

March 25, 1754. June Court, 1754. *Godson:* GODFREY GRAY, son of HENRY GRAY (tract of land known as Stults Hall). *Wife and Executrix:* MARY. *Witnesses:* JOHN PAGETT, SAMUEL NORMAN, JOSEPH NORMAN. *Clerk of the Court:* EVAN JONES.

GONSOLVO, LAURENCE.   County not given.

December 25, 1687. *Wife and child:* mentioned, but not named. *Witnesses:* WILLIAM PRIVIT, WILLIAM STEWART, RICHARD WILLIAMS. No probate.

GONSOLVO, LAWRENCE.   Albemarle County.

July 2, 1698. July Court, 1698. All worldly goods bequeathed to *father-in-law and mother.* *Witnesses:* THOS. NORSEM, ALICE CHEW, MARY NORCOMB, SARAH BLANK. *Clerk of the Court:* JOHN STEPNEY.

GONSOLVO, THOMAS.   County not given.

1698. Bequeathed all estate to *Mother and Father-in-law,* who are not named. *Witnesses:* THOMAS NORCAM, ALISE OHONE, MARY NORCAM, SARA BLANCK. *Clerk:* JOHN STEPNEY.

GOODALL, GILBERT.   Albemarle County.

September 3, 1712. *Legatees:* ELIZABETH HOSEA, THOMAS ARNOLD, JR., JOHN WINBERY, WILLIAM COLLSON, GEORGE TAYLOR, SARAH WHIDBE, CHARLES BARCLIF, GEORGE DURANT, JOHN STIVERS, RICHARD WHIDBE (*executor*). *Witnesses:* WILLIAM STEVENS, MARGARETT SLATER, MARY DURANT. Original missing. Recorded in Book 1712–1722, page 47.

GOREHAM, JOHN.   Chowan Precinct.

September 30, 1717. October Court, 1717. *Wife and Executrix:* ELINOR ("plantation on Queen Anne Creek I now dwell on"). *Nephew:* JOHN

GOREHAM (land on Darby Creek "called in Indian Renocooset," and also lands on Kesiah River). *Witnesses:* R. HICKS, JOSEPH YOUNG, JOHN CASS.

GORDEN, GEORGE.   Perquimans County.

August 14, 1748. January Court, 1748. *Sons and Executors:* NATHANIEL and WILLIAM ("land I now live on"). *Daughter:* HANNER. *Granddaughter:* TAMER. *Witnesses:* ELIJAH STANTON, WM. TOMBLIN, JEREMIAH HENDRECK. *Clerk of the Court:* EDMUND HATCH.

GORDON, JOHN.   Perquimans County.

April 25, 1754. April Court, 1758. *Sons:* JOHN ("plantation whereon I now live"), GEORGE. *Grandchildren:* MARY and JACOB GORDON, MARMADUKE NORFLEET. *Executors:* JOHN and GEORGE GORDON (sons). *Witnesses:* JESSE EASON, MOSES EASON, JOSHUA SMALL. *Clerk of the Court:* MILES HARVEY.

GORDEN, NATHANIEL.   Perquimans County.

July 14, 1755. January Court, 1756. *Sons:* NATHANELL ("plantation and house whereon I now live"), GEORGE. *Daughters:* ELIZABETH and TAMER. *Wife and Executrix:* ANN. *Witnesses:* ELIJAH STANTON, THOMAS, BARTLET, SAMUILL DAVIS. *Clerk of the Court:* MILES HARVEY.

GORDON, PATRICK.   County not given.

(Attorney-at-law.) November 5, 1773. November 12, 1773. *Wife and Executrix:* MARY. *Witnesses:* JOHN BURNSIDE, ARCHD NELSON. Will proven before JO. MARTIN.

GORMACK, PATRICK.   Pasquotank County.

April 9, 1708. July 21, 1708. *Wife and Executrix:* ELIZABETH. *Other legatees:* JOHN and ALEXANDER CRUIKSHANK, sons of PATRICK CRUIKSHANK and JOANE GORMACK; CAPT. JOHN ROBISON. *Witnesses:* RICHARD MADREN, GEORGE HARRIS, SR., ANN MADREN, GEORGE HARRIS, JR. *Clerk of the Court:* J. PALIN.

GOSBE, JOHN.   County not given.

August 17, 1693. October 2, 1693. *Son:* JOHN. *Executors:* SAMUELL and JOSEPH NICHOLSON (cousins). *Wife:* mentioned, but not named. *Witnesses:* RICHARD DORMON, FRANCES TOMES, JOSEPH SUTTEN. *Clerk:* JOHN STEPNEY.

GOUGH, THOMAS.   County not given.

December 18, 1694. April 8, 1695. *Sons:* ROBERT GOUGH. *Daughter:* SARAH GOUGH. *Wife and Executrix:* SARAH. *Witnesses:* ANTHONY DAWSON, JOHN WILLIAMS, JULIAN TAYLOR. *Clerk of the Court:* JOHN STEPNEY. *Clerk (probably of the Council):* W. GLOVER.

GOURLEY, JOHN. Onslow County.

January 2, 1746. January 7, 1747. *Mother:* ELIZABETH GOURLEY. *Brother:* GEORGE GOURLEY. *Sisters:* GRISLE, MARY. *Executor:* SAMUEL JOHNSTON. *Witnesses:* JAMES GLAUSTER, GEORGE COHERNAN, JOHN DAVIS. Proven before GAB. JOHNSTON at Eden House. Testator left in hands of his executor "forty pounds currency or four pounds sterling to be laid out in Bibles and New Testaments to be distributed among poor children on New River."

GRAINGER, CALEB. New Hanover County.

1763. October 31, 1765. *Sons:* CALEB (houses and lands on Smiths Creek and No. Et. River, north side of the Main or King's Road); CORNELIUS HARNETT GRAINGER (houses and lands on Smiths Creek on South side of the Main Road); WILLIAM (land on the Sound). *Daughter:* MARY GRAINGER. *Wife and Executrix:* MARY. *Executors:* MAURICE MOORE, CORNELIUS HARNETT, ALEXANDER DUNCAN. *Witnesses:* SAMUELL GREEN, ANTHONY WARD, JOSEPH STOCKLEY. Testator was a Mason and desired to be buried with Masonic honors. Codicil to will dated October 5, 1765, provides for child *in ventre sa mere*, and also for erection of sawmill. *Witnesses to codicil:* MARY GRAINGER, MARGARITT DOUGLASS, EDMOND FOGER. Will proven before the Lieutenant Governor, as evidenced by letter from FOUNTAIN ELWIN.

GRAINGER, JOSHUA. New Hanover County.

Sons: CALEB and JOSHUA. *Wife and Executrix:* ELIZABETH. *Daughter:* ANN, ―― DEROSSET, JNO. SITE (?), ―― BRADDISH. No probate. Will almost illegible.

GRANBARY, SAMUEL. Craven County.

January 15, 1760. *Sons:* JOHN ("plantation whereon I live"), WILLIAM. *Wife and Executrix:* FRANCES. *Executor:* WILLIAM SPEIGHT. *Witnesses:* DAVID LEWIS, WM. WEST, JOELL KING. No probate.

GRANGE, JOHN. New Hanover County.

January 20, 1739–1740. June 4, 1740. *Sons:* JOHN and JAMES ("estate whereon I now live consisting of 1000 acres of land up the No. West River"), HUGH (640 acres in New Hanover County commomly called "Old Town"). *Executors:* JAMES GRANGE (brother), JOHN and JEHN DAVIS (brothers-in-law). *Witnesses:* WM. FORBES, CHA. CODGAN, PAUL GUERAR, ELIZ. GARRAD. Will proven before GAB. JOHNSTON.

GRANT, ALEXANDER. Onslow County.

June 9, 1738. January 2, 1738. *Sons:* SOLOMON, ALEXANDER, JOHN. *Daughter:* MARY. *Neighbor and Executor:* JOHN STARKEY. *Wife:* mentioned, but not named. *Executors:* JOHN and ALEXANDER (sons). *Witnesses:* SAMLL. NOBLE, JOSEPH SMITH, RACLL. (RACHEL) NOBLE. *Clerk of the Court:* WM. CRANFORD.

GRANT, WILLIAM.   Dobbs County.

September 23, 1773. November 11, 1773. *Sole legatee and devisee:* JANE BRODIE. *Executors:* JANE BRODIE, THOMAS SCOTT. *Witnesses:* WILLIAM HOOKS, JOHN TILTEN. Will proven before Jo. MARTIN.

GRAVES, RICHARD.   Craven Precinct.

April 11, 1730. September Court, 1730. *Sons:* THOMAS GRAVES. *Daughter:* MARY GRAVES. *Cousins (nephews):* RICHARD and FRANCIS GRAVES (sons of brother, THOMAS GRAVES). *Son-in-law:* FERNIFOLD GREEN. *Wife and Executrix:* HANNAH. *Witnesses:* JAMES GREEN, ——— JONES, JNO. RICHARDS. *Clerk of the Court:* C. METCALFE.

GRAVES, RICHARD.   Craven County.

May 3, 1774. June 4, 1774. *Nephews:* GRAVES BRIGHT ("my land & mills known as Jumping Run"), RICHARD FONVIELLE (son of WILLIAM BRICE FONVIELLE). *Wife:* ANN. *Mother:* SARAH FONVIELLE. *Executors:* SIMON BRIGHT, CHRISTOPHER NEALE. *Witnesses:* CHRIS'R DAWSON, THOMAS DRINY, SARAH BENSON. Will proven before Jo. MARTIN. R. G. monogram on seal.

GRAY, ALEN (ALLEN).   Onslow County.

January 17, 1755. July Court, 1755. *Sons:* WILLIAM, JOHN, HUGH, THOMAS and JAMES. *Daughters:* JENOT, MARY, ELINOR and SARAH. *Wife and Executrix:* MARY. *Executor:* HUGH GIDDINGS. *Witnesses:* THOS. JENKIN, CASSON MOORE, SAMUEL ALEXANDER. *Clerk of the Court:* WILLM. CRAY.

GRAY, ANN.   Pasquotank Precinct.

March 4, 1731. April Court, 1732. *Sons:* WILLIAM and VALLENTINE WALLIS. *Daughters:* JANE, MARY and SARAH WALLIS, ANN KENNEKUM. *Executor:* WILLIAM WALLIS. *Witnesses:* JOHN MCKEEL, JOHN BOYD, RICHARD GRAY. *Clerk of the Court:* H. MINSON.

GRAY, GRIFEN.   County not given.

October 24, 1684. February 4, 1684. *Son and Executor:* GRIFEN. *Wife:* HANNAH. *Witnesses:* SAMUELL DAVIS, THOMAS FRINCH. Will proven before SETH SOTHELL.

GRAY, JAMES.   Onslow County.

October 21, 1757. January Court, 1758. *Son:* JAMES ("my manner plantation"). *Daughter:* ELIZABETH. *Wife and Executrix:* HANNAR.

Executors: THOMAS JENKINS and HENRY RHODES. *Witnesses:* MARY GRAY, MARGET JENKINS, MARTHA KEEN. *Clerk of the Court:* WM. CRAY. Seal of testator bears impression IG.

GRAY, JOHN (SURVEYOR). Bertie County.

September 20, 1745. November 16, 1750. *Sons:* JOHN ("my lands in Northampton and Edgecombe"), WILLIAM ("my plantation"). *Daughters:* JANET MCKINZIE, BARBARA, ANN, LUCRETIA, AMELIA, LOUISA. *Wife:* ANN. *Executors:* EDWARD BRYAN (brother), THOMAS WHITMELL (nephew). *Witnesses:* JAS. WATSON, DUGALD MCKITHAN. No probate.

GRAY, RICHARD. Pasquotank County.

October 6, 1729. October 15, 1729. *Wife and Executrix:* ANN. *Son:* RICHARD (land on the Sound Side and Flatty Creek). *Daughter:* ANN. *Overseer of son's estate:* LEWY MARCKHAM. *Witnesses:* CHARLES WEST, ALEXR. CRUICKSHANK, ANN CRUICKSHANK. *Clerk of the Court:* H. MINSON.

GREEN, JACOB. Chowan County.

January 9, 1751. April Court, 1752. *Cousins (nephews):* RICHARD and WILLIAM GREEN (sons of brother, THOMAS GREEN). *Executors:* THOMAS GREEN (brother), THOS. HARRELL. *Witnesses:* JAMES WIAT, ANN EVANS, THOS. HARRELL. *Clerk of the Court:* JAS. CRAVEN.

GREEN, JOHN. Bladen County.

April 28, 1749. June Court, 1749. *Sons:* JAMES, ROBERT, JOHN. *Daughter:* SARAH. *Wife:* mentioned, but not named. *Executors:* JAMES GRANGE and JAMES CARR. *Witnesses:* JOHN ELISS, JOHN STUBBS, JAMES JONES, DAVID MONLEY. *Clerk of the Court:* THOS. ROBESON.

GREEN, RICHARD. Chowan County.

September 13, 1742. October Court, 1742. *Sons:* JOHN, THOMAS, LEONARD, JACOB, WILLIAM. *Daughters:* ELSE, CATHERINE and MARY GREEN. *Wife and Executrix:* ELEE (or ELSE). *Witnesses:* WILLIAM WHITFIELD, JOHN SPARKMAN, HENRY GOODMAN. *Clerk of the Court:* RICH'D MCCLURE.

GREEN, SUSANNAH. "Bath County, in Craven Precinct."

June 29, 1732. September 17, 1735. *Son:* JOHN BIGGS. *Granddaughter:* MARY BIGGS. *Executors:* JOHN BIGGS and ROBERT BOND. *Witnesses:* WILLIAM BRIGHT, ROBERT BOND. *Clerk of the Court:* CALEB METCALFE.

GREGORY, JUDATH. Pasquotank County.

October 21, 1753. January Court, 1754. *Sons:* ISAAC, DEMSEY. *Daughters:* MARY, LOUCY. *Friend:* MARY LOYED. *Brother and Executor:* JOSEPH MORGAN. *Witnesses:* WM. BURGES, JOSEPH EVERIGIN, SAMUEL SCOTT. *Clerk of the Court:* THOS. TAYLOR.

GREGORY, MARGARET.   Pasquotank County.

February 3, 1746–1747. July Court, 1753. *Sons:* RICHARD, JAMES, JOHN, CALEB. *Daughters:* MARY UMPHERIS, MARGARET BARBER, SARAH GRANDY. *Granddaughter:* SARAH UMPHERIS. *Executor:* JAMES GREGORY (son). *Witnesses:* JAMES FORBES, ELIZABETH FORBES, REBECCA HARDING. *Clerk of the Court:* THOS. TAYLOR.

GREGORY, RICHARD.   Currituck County.

October 7, 1758. December Court, 1758. *Sons:* GRIFFITH, CORNELIUS, ROBERT ("Easter end of my plantation"), WILLIAM ("dwelling plantation"), JOSEPH ("remainder of my land"). *Daughters:* JUDAH SAWYER, EASTER SAWYER and BRIDGET SAWYER; RUTH GLASGOE, ANNE GREGORY, CHARITY GREGORY. *"Dividers":* JAMES GREGORY (brother), ISAAC and WILLIAM BRIGHT (brothers-in-law). *Executors:* JAMES GREGORY (brother), ROBERT GREGORY (son). *Witnesses:* RICHD. STANLEY, THOMAS HUTCHINGS, AMEA HUTCHINGS. *Clerk of the Court:* WM. MEARNS.

GREGORY, SAMUEL.   Chowan County.

February 5, 1744. August 4, 1747. *Sons:* SAMUELL and LUKE (107 acres of land in Perquimans County), THOMAS ("Hous & lot in Edenton that I now dwell in"). *Daughter:* ELIZEBETH GREGORY. *Wife and Executrix:* ELIZEBETH. *Witnesses:* DAVID BUTLER, JOSEPH MING. Will proven before ENOCH HALL.

GREGORY, THOMAS.   Pasquotank County.

April 10, 1736. June 23, 1740. *Sons:* NATHAN ("my manner plantation"), SAMPSON, JACOB, JOB, RICHARD, WILLIAM. *Daughters:* ELISABETH GODFREE, PRISILLA GRAY. *Grandson:* FREDERICK GREGORY. *Executors:* JACOB and JOB (sons). *Witnesses:* JOHN BELL, JOHN ROBERTS, JOHN BEARCOCK. Will proven before W. SMITH, C. J.

GREGORY, WILLIAM.   Pasquotank County.

June 4, 1748. July Court, 1753. *Son:* JOHN (600 acres of land on Cashie River, and 500 acres called "Goram's neck"). *Daughters:* MARY and BARBRA GREGORY. *Wife:* SARAH. *Executors:* JOSEPH ANDERSON, DR. WILLIAM CALHEART, JOHN GRAY, SR., THOMAS WHITEMELL, JOHN EVREGAN. *Witnesses:* ANN ANDERSON, ELISE SCOLLAY, THOMAS POLLOCK, Will proven in Chowan County before MATT. ROWAN. *Clerk of Pasquotank County:* THOS. TAYLOR.

GREGORY, WILLIAM.   Pasquotank County.

November 24, 1751. April Court, 1752. *Sons:* MARK (100 acres of land on North River Swamp), DEMPSEY, ISAAC. *Daughters:* AFFIAH,

MARY, LOVEY. *Granddaughter:* ANN GREGORY. *Wife and Executrix:* JUDITH. *Witnesses:* JOHN RIDING, JOSEPH JONES, THOMAS RIDING. *Clerk of the Court:* THOS. TAYLOR.

GRICE, FRANCIS. Johnston County.

April 28, 1750. December Court, 1750. *Sons:* THOMAS, ROBERT, JAMES, WILLIAM, JACOB, JOHN. *Daughters:* MARY LITTMAN, FAITH GRICE, ELIZABETH GRICE. *Wife and Executrix:* ELIZABETH. *Executor:* ROBERT (son). *Witnesses:* WILLIAM HALL, SAMUELL LITTMAN, JNO. SUTTON. *Clerk of the Court:* JAMES OATES.

GRIFFIN, EDWARD. Tyrrell County.

April 27, 1753. March Court, 1754. *Sons:* EDWARD and WILLIAM (land in Bertie County on Crofoot Branch adjoining Mikell Hill's land). *Daughters:* MARY and SARAH GRIFFIN, ANN GRIFFIN, ELIZABETH COOPER. *Wife:* GRACE. *Executors:* JOHN GRIFFIN (brother), EDWARD COOPER. *Witnesses:* WILLIAM GARDNER, JOHN GRIFFIN, EDWARD COOPER. *Clerk of the Court:* EVAN JONES.

GRIFFEN, EPENETUS. Tyrrell County.

July 30, 1755. December Court, 1756. *Sons:* ANDREW, EPENETUS, MATTHEW, JOHN (*Executor*). *Daughters:* SARAH COCKBERN, ELISABETH GRIFFEN, ANN GRIFFEN. *Wife and Executrix:* ANN. *Witnesses:* NATHL. COOPER, JOSEPH HILSON WORRIN. *Clerk of the Court:* FR. WARD.

GRIFFIN, JAMES. On Kathrine Creek, Chowan County.

June 13, 1748. April Court, 1749. *Sons:* JAMES, JOSEPH and WILLIAM. *Wife and Executrix:* SARAH. *Witnesses:* WILLIAM HILL, WILLIAM COLTHRED, SUSANNAH OVERMAN. *Clerk of the Court:* WILL. MEARNS.

GRIFEN, MARTIN. Chowan County.

June 3, 1718. July Court, 1718. *Sons:* EDWARD ("my plantation on the North side Cissai River), JOHN and WILLIAM (plantation on South side of Rokquis Creek), MARTIN (plantation on Rokquis Creek). *Daughters:* SARAH GRIFEN, ELIZABETH GRIFEN. *Wife and Executrix:* ELIZABETH. *Other legatees:* MARY STANSILL (daughter of MARY), WILLIAM STANSILL (son of JOHN and CATHERINE), JOHN RODGERS (son of THOMAS and FRANCES). *Witnesses:* THOMAS RODGERS, RICHARD PICKEREN, JOHN SMETHWICK. *Clerk of the Court:* R. HICKS.

GRIFEN, RICHARD. Chowan County.

April 8, 1701. February 7, 1702–1703. *Executrix:* WIFE (not named). *Witnesses:* THOMAS JONES, WILLM. JONES, MARY SKITTLESHARP. *Son-in-law:* JOSEPH SKITTLESHARP. *Clerk of the Court:* N. CHEVIN.

GRIFFIN (spelled "GRIFFON"), WILLIAM.   Carteret Precinct.
June 20, 1681. March 29. *Wife and Executrix:* LIDDIA. *Son:* WILLIAM. *Witnesses:* WM. BATEMAN, ROGER MARTIN. Will proven before THOMAS MILLER.

GRIFFIN, WILLIAM.   Bertie Precinct.
December 10, 1735. February Court, 1735. *Wife and Executrix:* MARY. *Witnesses:* THO. WHITMILL, ALEX. THOMPSON, EDWARD MOORE. *Clerk of the Court:* JNO. WYNNS.

GRIFFETH, JOHN.   Bertie County.
July 1, 1727. February Court, 1727. *Sons:* ARTHER (land on Meherrin Cypress Swamp), EDMOND (550 acres of land), JOHN (*Executor*). *Wife and Executrix:* JEMIMA. *Daughter:* MARY. *Other legatees:* JOHN CLARKE, DANIEL RIGING. *Overseer:* WILLIAM BOLDIN. *Clerk of the Court:* RT. FORSTER.

GRIGGS, SAMUEL.   Kings County, New York.
September 3, 1749. *Wife and Executrix:* ELIZABETH. *Witnesses:* W. BETTS, JANE BROWN, MARY COGAN. *Clerk of Craven County Court:* PHIL SMITH. Will proven June 19, 1750.

GRILLS, RICHARD.
February 1, 1719–1720. April 4, 1720. *Wife and Executrix:* SARAH. *Witnesses:* JNO. NEW, HANNAH DOWERS, PATRICK OGILBY. Original missing. Recorded in Book 1712–1722, page 221.

GRIMES, ABSOLOM.   Pasquotank County.
January 7, 1757. March Court, 1757. *Wife, Executrix and sole legatee:* LIDEA. *Witnesses:* JOHN COX, J. BURGES. *Clerk of the Court:* THOS. TAYLOR.

GRIST, RICHARD.   Beaufort County.
June 6, 1752. March 13, 1753. *Sons:* JOHN, WILLIAM, RICHARD ("my manner plantation"). *Daughters:* FRANCES NOUELL, MARY GRIST, ELIZABETH WALL. *Wife and Executrix:* FRANCES. *Witnesses:* WILLIAM WILLIS, WILLIAM LANIER, ELISABETH HILL. *Clerk of the Court:* WILL ORMOND.

GROSVENOR, WILLIAM.   Perquimans Precinct.
November 5, 1702. *Daughters:* SUSANNAH, ELIZEBETH and ESTER GROSVENOR. *Wife and Executrix:* SARAH. *Witnesses:* JONATHAN TAYLOR, J. WMSON. (WILLIAMSON). No probate.

ABSTRACT OF WILLS, 1690—1760.

GUILLIAMS, GEORGE.   Chowan County.

September 22, 1746. April Court, 1747. *Sons:* ISAAC ("my manner plantation"), SAMUELL, GEORGE. *Executor:* SAMUELL GUILLIAMS (son). *Witnesses:* WILLIAM HUGHES, JUNR., GEORGE GUILLIAMS, SAMUEL GUILLIAMS. *Clerk of the Court:* HENRY DELON.

GUMBS, MATTHEW.   Chowan County.

February 9, 1754. April Court, 1754. *Sons:* ELISHA and ABRAHAM ("my manner plantation"). *Daughters:* SARAH, RACHEL, LEAH and RUTH GUMBS, MARY PATCHET. *Executors:* ELISHA and ABRAHAM GUMBS (sons). *Witnesses:* CHARLES ROBERTS, MARTHA JONES, MARY PREVIT. *Clerk of the Court:* WILL. HALSEY.

GUNTER, JOHN.   Beaufort and Hyde Counties.

March 28, 1722. July Court, 1725. *Executor and sole legatee:* JOHN ODEN. *Witnesses:* THOS. OLDNER, THOMAS WARSLEY, CHAS. ODEN. *Clerk of the Court:* JNO. SWANN.

GUTAN, JOSEPH.

January 30, 1770. *Wife's son:* JOHN SATCHWELL. *Wife's grandson:* JACOB DARDON. *Wife and Executrix:* REBECCA. *Witnesses:* ROBERT DIXSON, WALTER DIXSON, WY. ORMOND, ROGER ORMOND. No probate.

GUTHRIE, JOHN.   Pasquotank County.

October 12, 1748. April Court, 1750. *Uncles and Executors:* CHARLES KEEL and JOHN MCKEEL. *Cousin:* MARY MCKEEL. *Father-in-law:* HENRY PENDLETON. *Witnesses:* HENRY PENDLETON, MARY PENDLETON. *Clerk of the Court:* THOS. TAYLOR.

GUY, WILLIAM.   Perquimans County.

March 17, 1754. April Court, 1754. *Cousins:* JOHN and JAMES GUY (sons of JAMES GUY), BRIGGIT GUY. *Wife and Executrix:* MARY. *Executors:* THOMAS and CHRISTOPHER NICHOLSON. *Witnesses:* THOMAS CRAGHILL, SARAH BARROW, MARY KELLEY. *Clerk of the Court:* RICHD. CLAYTON.

HACKLEFIELD, JOHN.   Chowan County.

August 13, 1739. October 29, 1741. *Legatees:* THOMAS, WILLIAM and SARAH HOSKINS. *Executors:* WILLIAM HOSKINS and JOHN BENBURY. *Clerk of the Court:* J. MONTGOMERY.

HADLEY, EDWARD.   Hyde County.

January 22, 1740. June Court, 1743. *Wife and Executrix:* KEZIAH. *Witnesses:* GILBERT MCNARY, NATHANIEL TULE, JONATHAN BELL. *Clerk of the Court:* WM. BARROW.

HAIG, MARY, widow of WILLIAM. Pasquotank County.

February 9, 1718. January 20, 1718–1719. *Son:* WILLIAM. *Other children:* mentioned, but not named. *Other legatees:* MARY WHITE, JOSEPH GLAISTER, MARY GLAISTER. *Executors:* GABRIEL NEWBY and JOSEPH GLAISTER. *Witnesses:* JNO. FOURRE, THOMAS PENDLETON, JOHN CARP. *Clerk of the Court:* W. NORRIS.

HAIG, WILLIAM. Newbegin Creek, in Pasquotank County.

November 4, 1718. January 9, 1718–1719. *Wife and Executrix:* MARY. *Son:* WILLIAM ("my plantation"). *Daughters:* MARY, SARAH and ANN HAIG. *Witnesses:* JOHN MAN, JOHN CARP, RICHARD BROSSIERS. *Clerk of the Court:* W. NORRIS.

HAIG, WILLIAM. Pasquotank County.

February 20, 1734–1735. July Court, 1735. *Son:* WILLIAM. *Wife:* SARAH. *Executors:* SARAH HAIG, WILLIAM HAIG, JOHN EVERIGIN. *Witnesses:* WILLIAM KELLY, JR., JOSEPH JORDAN, MARY JORDAN. *Clerk of the Court:* JOS. SMITH.

HAKONY, JOHN. Albemarle County.

February 25, 1672. October 1, 1673. *Son:* JOHN. *Wife and other children:* mentioned, but not named. *Witnesses:* AZELL ROBETSON (?), FRANCIS MALLARD. Proven before JOHN JENKINS. *Clerk of the Court:* THOMAS HARRIS.

HALL, AN. Perquimans County.

October 9, 1741. January Court, 1741. *Son and Executor:* SAMUEL. *Daughters:* SARAH WARRIN, MARY JENNET. *Granddaughter:* AN JENNET. *Witnesses:* THOS. CALLAWAY, JOSHUA HOBARD, SARAH CURLING. *Clerk of the Court:* EDMOND HATCH.

HALL, HEZEKIAH. Carteret County.

January 9, 1733–1734. March Court, 1733–1734. *Daughter:* SARAH HALL. *Wife and Executrix:* ANN. *Executor:* DAVID SHIPURD. *Witnesses:* JOHN JERRETT, JNO. NELSON, J. HARRIS. *Clerk of the Court:* JAS. WINRIGHT.

HALL, JOHN. Bertie Precinct.

August 9, 1736. February Court, 1736. *Wife:* MARY. *Executor:* JONATHAN STANDLEY. *Witnesses:* THOMAS WATSON, MARGRETT STANDLY, ELIZABETH KELLY. *Clerk of the Court:* JOHN WYNNS.

HALL, JOSEPH.   Onslow County.

December 16, 1747. July 5, 1748. *Daughters:* MARY BURNS, JANE PARROTT. *Wife:* JANE. *Son:* EDWARD ("my plantation"). *Executors:* JOHN STARKEY, EDWARD HALL (son). *Witnesses:* CHARLES SHARP, MARY EVES, RALPH EVES. *Clerk of the Court:* THOS. BLACK.

HALL, NATHANIEL.   Pasquotank County.

January 31, 1734. February 17, 1734. *Sons:* JOSEPH ("my plantation"), BENJAMIN ("plantation up the river" and also land at Banks called Chickconacomock). *Wife and Executrix:* ELINOR. *Executor:* THOMAS WEEKES. *Witnesses:* DAVID BALEY, ROBERT LOWRY, JR., PATRICK BALEY. Proven before GAB. JOHNSTON at Edenton.

HALL, WILLIAM.   Bladen County.

February 6, 1764. April 21, 1765. *Wife and Executrix:* ELIZABETH. *Witnesses:* A. GREEN, JAMES HENDERSON, MARY GREEN. Proven before WM. TRYON at Wilmington.

HALSEY, DANIEL.   Albemarle County.

March 13, 1719. *Wife and Executrix:* MARY. *Witness:* THOMAS EVANS. Original missing. Recorded in Book 1712–1722, page 222.

HALTON, ROBERT.   New Hanover County.

March 22, 1748. April Court, 1749. *Wife:* MARY (in England). *Sisters:* SUSANNAH WILKINS, MARY, ELIZABETH. *Other legatees:* ELIZABETH WILKINS (niece), MARY WILKINS (niece), GABRIEL JOHNSTON, DR. WM. CATHCART, GEORGE GOULD, THOMAS BARKER, BENJAMIN HILL, JOHN ASHTON (1000 acres of land on So. side Nuse River on Greens past.), SARAH GRAVES, ROBERT HALTON, JR., son of SARAH GRAVES ("my seat called Halton's Lodge"; two tracts in New Hanover Co. known as "Laban" and "Brown Marsh," Laban lying on Mill Creek and Brown Marsh "on the North East River of Cape Fear"). *Executors:* GABRIEL JOHNSTON, WM. CATHCART, THOS. BARKER. *Witnesses:* SAML. ORMES, WM. CHURTON, DAN. WELDON. *Clerk of the Court of Chowan County:* WILL MEARNS.

HAMAN, THOMAS.   Pasquotank County.

March 9, 1720–1721. March 30, 1721. *Son:* JOSEPH. *Wife and Executrix:* SARAH. *Daughters:* SARAH and JANE HAMAN. *Witnesses:* WM. WILLSON, WM. BELL, JOS. BROWN. *Clerk of Chowan Precinct Court:* R. HICKS.

HAMBLETON, JOSEPH.

April 1, 1737. April 11, 1737 ("late of Pensilvania but now of the Province of Carolina"). *Wife and Executrix:* RACHELL (plantation in Buck's

Co., Pa.). *Friends:* DAVID LOYD, CHARLES O'NEIL, EVEN EVENS. *Executors:* DAVID LOYD and THOMAS RUSS. *Witnesses:* WILLIAM SALTAR, MARY RUSS, CHARLES O'NEILL. Proven before GAB. JOHNSTON.

HAMBLETON, JANE. Tyrrell Precinct.

March 20, 173—. April 22, 1734. *Son and daughter:* JOHN GARRETT and MARY his wife (who are also appointed executors). *Witnesses:* SAMEL DURRANCE, MARY SKILES. Will proven before NATHANIEL RICE, *President.*

HAMBLIN, THOMAS. Pasquotank County.

December 31, 1757. March Court, 1758. *Son:* JOHN. *Daughters:* ELIZABETH and MARTHA HAMBLIN. *Wife:* MARTHA. *Executor:* CHARLES MARKHAM. *Witnesses:* LYMAN SPENCE, THOMAS MARKHAM, DAVID SINCLAR. *Clerk of the Court:* THO. TAYLOR.

HAMILTON, JOHN.

Will torn and illegible.

HAMILTON, JOHN. Nansemond County.

February 25, 1706–1707. April 25, 1711. *Sons:* JAMES, WILLIAM and STEWART (land at Salem), JOHN and ANDREW. *Daughter:* MARY HAMILTON. *Daughter-in-law:* MARY HOBGOOD. *Wife and Executrix:* CATHERINE. *Witnesses:* RICHD. WYNNE, HENRY PULLEN, DANIEL ELLETT. *Deputy Clerk:* W. RAGSDALE. *Clerk of Court:* MICHL. ARCHIR. This is a copy of will.

HAMILTON, JOHN. Bladen County.

October 22, 1764. February Court, 1765. *Son:* JAMES. *Wife and Executrix:* ESTHER. *Other legatee:* ESABEL HAMILTON (probably daughter). *Executor:* WM. CREE. *Witnesses:* JOHN KENNEY, LEVI MOORE. *Justices:* GEORGE BROWN, JOHN SMITH, JOHN TURNER, GEORGE GIBBS, JOSEPH CLARK. *Clerk of Court:* MALUNN COLVELL.

HANBY, JOHN. Perquimans County.

May 5, 1752. July Court, 1752. *Son:* SALVANIAS ("the manner and plantation whereon I now live"). *Grandsons:* JOHN and DEMSIE HANBY. *Daughters:* MARY HANBY, HANNAH BISHOP, ELIZABETH GRIFFIN. *Friend:* ZACHARIAH NIXON. *Executors:* SELVANUS HANBY (son) and FRANCIS NEWBY. *Wife:* HANNAH. *Witnesses:* NATHAN NEWBY, SAMUEL ANDERSON, FRANCIS TOMES. *Clerk of the Court:* EDMUND HATCH.

Abstract of Wills, 1690—1760. 149

HAND, PETER. Craven Precinct.
February 1, 1730–1731. March 16, 1730–1731. *Wife and Executrix:* ANN. *Daughters:* ELIZABETH, MARY and JEAN HAND. *Other legatee:* RICHARD HART. *Executor:* JOHN DEPT. *Witnesses:* THOS. FOX, JAMES GREEN, JOHN DEEP. *Clerk of the Court:* CALEB METCALFE.

HANCOCK, HECTOR. Carteret County.
October 27, 1751. December Court, 1751. *Sons:* NATHANIEL, BENJAMIN, HENRY, JOSEPH, JOHN and WILLIAM. *Daughter:* MARY HANCOCK. *Wife:* ANN. *Executors:* NATHANIEL and BENJAMIN HANCOCK (sons). *Witnesses:* ANANIAS CAVENAGH, BENJAMIN HANCOCK, NATHANIEL HANCOCK. *Clerk of Court:* GEO. READ.

HANDCOCK, ELISEBETH. Craven County.
January 20, 1743–1744. June 20, 1744. *Sons and Executors:* SIMON and WM. BRIGHT. *Daughter:* LEDLAY HANDCOCK. *Witnesses:* WALTER JONES, FRANCIS HODGES, HOWEL JONES. *Clerk of Court:* N. ROUTLEDGE.

HANDCOCK, WILLIAM. Craven Precinct.
October 9, 1722. March 16, 1730–1731. *Son:* WILLIAM. *Grandsons:* JOHN HANDCOCK ("my plantation"), WILLIAM HANDCOCK. *Granddaughters:* ELIZABETH and MARY HANDCOCK. *Wife and Executrix:* ELENOR. *Executors:* WILLIAM HANDCOCK (son), RICHARD GRAVES, JOHN SLOCUMB (cousin). *Witnesses:* JAMES KEITH, MOSES THOMAS, THOMAS KNIGHT. *Clerk of the Court:* CALEB METCALFE.

HANDWORKER, DANIEL. Perquimans County.
March 7, 1729–1730. April 4, 1730. *Wife, Executrix and sole legatee:* KATHERINE. *Witnesses:* CHARLES DENMAN, SARAH DENMAN. Will proven before RICHARD EVERARD.

HANNIS, JOSEPH. Craven County.
June 30, 1745. September 7, 1745. "Christ Church Parish & County of Craven." *Son and Executor:* JOSEPH. *Wife and Executrix:* CATHERINE. *Witnesses:* FRANCIS STRINGER, WM. THOMPSON, JOSEPH CARRUTHERS, GEORGE WIGGINS. *Clerk of the Court:* JNO. RICE.

HARBERT, EDWARD. Craven County.
January 20, 1754. May Court, 1754. *Sons:* EDWARD ("200 acres of land on the south side of Contentny"), JOHN. *Four other children:* mentioned, but not named. *Executor:* EDWARD HARBERT (son). *Witnesses:* JAMES COMBS, HENRY GIBBINS, WILLIAM RIGGSBY. *Clerk of the Court:* SOL. REW.

HARDESTY, THOMAS.   Carteret County.
July 16, 1758. September Court, 1758. *Sons:* THOMAS (land at Michael's Bridge), ROBERT HARDESTY, JOSEPH HARDESTY, SAMUEL HARDESTY. *Daughters:* MARY, LUCY and ANNA HARDESTY. *Wife and Executrix:* DOROTHA. *Witnesses:* LEWIS WELCH, HENRY CHEW, ROBERT WELCH. *Clerk of Court:* WILLIAM ROBERTSON.

HARDIN, WILLIAM.   Currituck County.
July 30, 1746. October 5, 1748. *Granddaughters:* JANE and ELIZABETH DUDLEY ("my land on Knott's Island whereon I live"). *Daughter:* ELISABETH DUDLEY. *Executors:* JANE HARDEN (wife) and HENRY WHITE. *Witnesses:* WILLIAM WHITE, THOMAS DUDLEY, JR., THOMAS WILLIAMSON. *Clerk of Court:* RICH'D McCLURE.

HARDING, JOSIAH.   Northampton County.
July 1, 1752. November Court, 1756. *Sons:* JOSIAH, THOMAS, JAMES. *Wife and Executrix:* ANN. *Witnesses:* J. EDWARDS, WM. WINBORNE. *Clerk of the Court:* I. EDWARDS.

HARDING, MARY.   Perquimans County.
October 22, 1743. November 8, 1744. *Legatees:* SARAH SKINNER, RICHARD SKINNER, SR., ZACHARIAH and SARAH SKINNER (children of JAMES). *Executor:* RICHARD SKINNER, SR. *Witnesses:* RICHARD SKINNER, JR., SAM'LL MOORE, SARAH CREECEY. Will proven before E. MOSELEY, *Chief Justice.*

HARDING, RICHARD.   Perquimans County.
December 6, 1741. January Court, 1741. *Wife and Executrix:* MARY. *Executor:* THOMAS PEIRCE. *Other legatees:* THOMAS GILBORD and JAMES SKINER. *Witnesses:* JOSEPH ASHLEY, PETER JONES, THOMAS PEIRCE, JR. *Clerk of the Court:* EDMUND HATCH.

HARDISON, JASPER.   Albemarle County.
May 8, 1733. November 5, 1733. *Sons:* JOHN ("land on South side of Deep run"), JASPAR (200 acres of land on Cheat Neck), CHARLES ("piece of land called Cheat Neck Island"), JOSUAH and THOMAS (land on Cheat Neck branch), RICHARD and JOSEPH ("rest of plantation known by the name of Roses Plantation"). *Other legatees:* MARY CARKEET, JUDAH SUTTON. *Executors:* MARY HARDISON (wife), JOHN HARDISON (son). *Witnesses:* JOSEPH HUDSON, SAMUEL DURRANCE. Will proven before GEO. BURRINGTON.

HARDY, JOHN.   Chowan County.
January 19, 1719. March 16, 1719. *Brothers:* WILLIAM, THOMAS and JACOB HARDY. *Daughters:* ELIZABETH and MARY. *Wife and Executrix:*

REBECCAH. *Other legatees:* KATHERINE STANCELL, RICHARD PICKERING, JOHN BUTLER. *Executors:* WILLIAM HARDY, THOMAS POLLOCK and ROBERT WEST. *Witnesses:* JOHN HOLBROOK, LAURENCE SARTON, JOHN LUERTON. Proven before C. EDEN.

HARDY, RICHARD. Wilmington, New Hanover County.

May 20, 1758. August 6, 1758. *Executors:* DANIEL DUNBIBIN, FRANCIS BEITELLE (uncle). *Wife:* SARAH. *Witnesses:* JAMES GREGORY, AO. ROUTLEDGE, ZACK WEEKS. No signature of probate officer.

HARE, EDWARD. Chowan County.

August 27, 1756. October Court, 1757. *Sons:* EDWARD (lands in Chowan), JOHN (lands in Bertie), THOMAS, BRYAN. *Daughters:* CHRISTIAN WEST, MARY BURGES, ANN SCOT. *Wife:* MARY. *Executors:* JOHN and EDWARD HARE (sons). *Witnesses:* WILLIAM SKINNER, JOSEPH ROOKS, JOSEPH SPEIGHT. *Clerk of the Court:* THOMAS JONES.

HARE, EDWARD. Hertford County.

May 16, 1772. April 22, 1777. *Legatees:* THOMAS HARE (brother), MARY HARE (niece), WYNNE WEST (daughter of PETER WEST), MARY BURGES (sister), ANN SCOT (sister), LUKE LEWIS (son of JOHN LEWIS), LUCRETIA HARE (daughter of BRYAN HARE), EDWARD BRYAN HARE (son of BRYAN HARE), JOHN PIPKEN (son of ISAAC PIPKIN), BRAY WARREN (son of JOSEPH WARREN), EFF LEWIS (son of JOHN LEWIS), JOHN MILLER, EDWARD WARREN, JOHN HARE (brother), MILLS LEWIS (son of JOHN LEWIS), WILLIAM WARREN (son of EDWARD WARREN), PHILLIP LEWIS (son of JOHN LEWIS), JOHN GATTELLEN, ISAAC PIPKEN, JESSE BARNES, FRANCIS SPEIGHT, HENRY SPEIGHT, JOHN GOODMAN, BENJ. WYNNS, JUNR., SOLOMON KING, WILLIAM WEST. *Executor:* THOMAS HARE. *Witnesses:* SOLOMON KING, JOHN LEWIS, ISAAC PIPKIN, EDWARD WARREN. Will proven before *Gov.* RD. CASWELL at New Bern.

HARISON, JOHN. Albemarle County.

February 18, 1693. April Court, Chowan, 1694. *Son:* WILLIAM HARISON. *Son:* JOHN HARISON. *Daughter:* ELIZABETH HARISON. *Son:* THOMAS HARISON. *Executrix:* MARY HARISON. *Witnesses:* GEO. HARDIE and JOHN WATKINS. *Clerk of the Court:* HENDERSON WALKER.

HARKEL, GEORGE. Craven County.

May 2, 1746. March 17, 1746. *Sons:* GEORGE ("plantation whereon I now dwell"), JOSEPH. *Daughters:* MIRIAM, MARGARET and MARY HARKEL. *Wife and Executrix:* ELISABETH. *Executor:* JAMES CONAWAY. *Witnesses:* NICHOLAS HARPER, AMOS CUTHRIS, ISAAC BRAWLER. *Clerk of Court:* JNO. RICE.

HARKER, ELIZABETH. Carteret County.
April 12, 1777. June 9, 1777. *Sons:* EBENEZER, JAMES, ZACHARIAH. *Daughter:* SARAH FRESHWATER. *Other legatee:* JOHN BROOKS. *Executors:* JAMES and ZACHARIAH HARKER (sons). *Witnesses:* JOSEPH YEOMAN, SARAH HARKER, ELIAS REES. Will proven before RD. CASWELL.

HARMAN, CALEB. Perquimans County.
October 2, 1773. March 9, 1774. *Sons:* ROBERT and JAMES ("my plantation to be equally divided between them"), CALEB and JOSHUA. *Daughter:* ORPAH HARMAN. *Wife and Executrix:* ELIZABETH. *Executor:* THOMAS HARMAN (brother). *Witnesses:* J. CARRUTHERS, ZEBULON CALLOWAY, MARY HARMAN. Proven before Jo. MARTIN.

HARMAN, ROBERT. Perquimans County.
January 7, 1758. July Court, 1758. *Sons:* CALEB ("my plantation"), JOHN (land in Beaver Cove), STEPHEN, THOMAS. *Daughter:* MARY HARMAN. *Trustees and Guardians:* FRANCIS JONES, DANIEL SAINT and JOHN WHITE, son of JOSEPH. *Wife and Executrix:* ELIZABETH. *Executors:* CALEB HARMAN, JOHN WHITE. *Witnesses:* THOMAS LONG, ELISABETH LONG, JOSEPH WHITE. *Clerk of the Court:* MILES HARVEY.

HARRELL, ABRAHAM. Bertie County.
May 5, 1755. July Court, 1755. *Sons:* ABBE (or ABLE), JOHN ("my manner plantation"), LOTT, ZACHARIAH, CHRISTOPHER. *Daughters:* ABBAGILL, GRACE, SUSANNAH. *Executors:* ABLE and JOHN HARRELL. *Witnesses:* GEORGE HOUSE, EDWARD TOOLE, ISRAEL HARDY HARRELL. *Clerk of the Court:* BENJAMIN WYNNS.

HARRELL, EDWARD. Bertie County.
August 17, 1752. May Court, 1754. *Sons:* HENRY, JOSHEWA, THOMAS. *Grandson:* JESSE HARRELL. *Daughters:* MARY and REBECCA ANDREWS. *Wife:* ANN. *Executors:* HENRY HARRELL (son) and HENRY ANDREWS (son-in-law). *Witnesses:* JOHN HARRELL, ROBERT HOUSE, GEORGE HOUSE. *Clerk of the Court:* SAML. ORMES.

HARRELL, JOHN. Bertie County.
November 8, 1755. January Court, 1756. *Sons:* GEORGE (land between THOS. WILLIAMS and JNO. RHODES), JESSE, ELISHA and BENJAMIN. To these four sons is bequeathed several tracts bounded and described in the will. *Daughter:* MARY. *Wife:* MARY. *Executors:* GEO. HARRELL (son), JESSE and ISRAEL HARDY HARRELL (brothers), RICHARD WILLIAMS, THOMAS WILLIAMS, WM. ANDREWS, JOHN RHODES. *Witnesses:* THOMAS WILLIAMS, WM. ANDREWS, JOHN SKINNER. *Clerk of Court:* BENJAMIN WYNNS.

HARRELL, JOHN.   Bertie County.
  November 1, 1756. April Court, 1759. *Sons:* JESSE and DAVID (plantation to each, and three negroes), JOSIAH (land bought of THOMAS BARKER), EZEKIEL (160 acres of land). Negroes bequeathed to each of sons. *Grandsons:* ESIAS HARRELL (plantation "whereon JONATHAN SPIVEY now lives who married the widow of Esias Harrell deceased"). *Granddaughter:* SARAH HARRELL (one negro). Copper still bequeathed to four sons. *Executors:* JESSE, DAVID and JOSIAH. *Witnesses:* WM. WILLIAMS, EDWARD TOOLE, JONATHAN TOOLE. *Clerk of the Court:* BENJAMIN WYNNS. Codicil makes bequests to THOMAS WILLIAMS, husband of daughter, SARAH. Same witnesses to codicil.

HARRELL, JOSIAH.   Bertie County.
  March 30, 1773. November 12, 1773. *Sons:* SOLOMON (land in Renneroy Marshes), JOSIAH ("my plantation"), WILLIAM. *Wife:* ANN. *Executors:* EDWARD TOOL, NOAH HINTON. *Witnesses:* JAMES CHURCHWELL, JONATHAN TOOL, MARY TOOL. Will proven before JO. MARTIN.

HARRINGTON, HUMPHREY.   Perquimans Precinct.
  November 2, 1713. *Daughter:* ANN. *Daughter-in-law:* ANN MAJOR. *Wife and Executrix:* ELIZABETH. *Witnesses:* RICHARD MORRIS and FRANCIS THOMAS. Original missing. Recorded in Book 1712–1722, page 18

HARRIS, JAMES.   Edgecombe County.
  January 10, 1749–1750. February Court, 1749. *Sons:* JAMES ("my plantation"), ELI. *Wife and Executrix:* CHEARY. *Executor:* MATHEW JOYNER. *Witnesses:* WM. SKINNER, JOHN BLOUNT, JOHN CRUMPTON. *Clerk of the Court:* BENJAMIN WYNNS.

HARRIS, JOHN.   Craven County.
  January 22, 1749. March Court, 1749. *Legatees:* BRICE and JOHN FONVIELLE, WM. BARRAN, JR. (land on Batchelor's Creek). *Executors:* JOHN FONVIELLE, THOMAS GRAVES. *Witnesses:* JOHN McGIBBINS, AMBROSE FIELD, DOROTHY ROLTON. *Clerk of the Court:* PHIL SMITH.

HARRIS, THOMAS.   Currituck County.
  November 7, 1749. January Court, 1749. *Wife:* ELENDER. *Son and Executor:* THOMAS. *Witnesses:* STEPHEN WILLIAMS, JOHN LURRY, LEVI STEWART. *Clerk of the Court:* RICH'D MCCLURE.

HARRISON, DANIEL.   Chowan County.
  January 14, 1726–1727. *Son:* JOSEPH (100 acres of land). *Wife and Executrix:* ELIZABETH. *Friend:* HILL SAVAGE. *Executor:* EDWARD PADGGETT. *Witnesses:* WILLIAM WILLIAMS, JNO. FALCONAR, MARTHA HAMMOND. No probate.

HARRISON, JOHN.
November 19, 1710. *Brother and Executor:* THOMAS HARRISON. *Witnesses:* ANN MITCHELL and WILLIAM MITCHELL. Original missing. Recorded in Book 1712–1722, page 32.

HARRISON, ROBERT.
March 9, 1713–1714. *Sons:* ROBERT (land bought of GARRETT PURSELL), JOSEPH. *Daughters:* SARAH and ELIZABETH HARRISON. *Wife and Executrix:* SARAH. *Executor:* ROBERT HARRISON. Executors to sell land upon River adjoining CORNELIUS JONES. *Witnesses:* DAN'L GUTHRIE, ELIZABETH JONES, WILL VAUGHAN. No probate. Anchor on seal.

HARRISON, VINES.   Chowan County.
February 25, 1738. March 24, 1738. *Brothers:* WILLIAM and JOSHUAY HARRISON. *Executors:* EDMOND HARRISON. *Sister:* SARAH FELTE. *Witnesses:* THOMAS PEIRCE, THOMAS EVERENDEN, EDWARD LISTER. Proven before W. SMITH, C. J.

HART, MARY.   Northampton County.
July 12, 1750. November Court, 1751. *Sons:* BENJAMIN, JOSEE, JOHN, DAVID. *Daughters:* SARAH HART, LUSEE HART. *Executors:* JOHN LAMAN and GREEN HILL. *Witnesses:* JAMES WRIGHT, JOHN GOODEN, JESSE HART, GEORGE BRACE. *Clerk of the Court:* I. EDWARDS.

HART, JOHN.   Bertie Precinct.
November 13, 1741. May Court, 1746. *Sons:* BENJAMIN (plantation "at Pattycasey"), JESSE (plantation on South side of Tarr River), JOHN (land on Town Creek), DAVID ("plantation whereon I now live"). *Daughters:* SARAH and LUCE. *Other legatee:* THOMAS FOXHALL. *Executors:* ETHELDRED RUFFIN and ROBERT RUFFIN. *Witnesses:* JOHN LAMON, HOWILL BROWNE, JOHN DAVISON. *Clerk of Northampton Court:* RT. FORSTER.

HART, THOMAS.   Northampton County.
March 6, 1748. August Court, 1751. *Son and Executor :* HENRY (plantation in "The Meadowes"). *Grandchildren:* JOHN SANDERS, SARAH SANDERS, EURIDICE, THOMAS, MARY and ROSE SANDERS. *Wife:* MARY. *Witnesses:* JNO. SIMPSON, HOWILL BROWNE. *Clerk of the Court:* I. EDWARDS.

HARTLEY, FRANCIS.   Albemarle County.
February 4, 1691–1692. May 2, 1692. *Wife and Executrix:* SUSANNAH. *Other legatees:* ELIZABETH GLASCOINE, ELIZABETH GRAY, JABUS ALFORD, WILLIAM MORRIS, GEORGE MASCHAMP. *Executor:* THOMAS HARVEY.

Witnesses: G. MASCHAMP, RICHARD SLATER, FRANCIS PARROTT, ANN DURANT, THOMAS DURANT. *Clerk of the Court:* HENDERSON WALKER.

HARVEY, DOROTY. Pasquotank County.

November 14, 1682. January 20, 1682. *Brother and Executor:* THOMAS TOOKE of Isle of Wight County in Virginia. *Children of Brother:* JAMES, THOMAS, DOROTEY, JOHN, ABRAHAM, JOANE and WILLIAM TOOKE. *Cousin:* THOS. HARVEY. *Niece:* MARY CREW. *Other legatees:* DORCAS, wife of THOMAS JARVIS, MARGARET, wife of CAPT. WM. CRAFORD; ABIAH, wife of CHRISTOPHER MERCHANT. *Witnesses:* WILLIAM MICHALLE, JOHN HAWKINS, CHRISTOPHER MERCHANT, JOHN COLPEPER. Proven before SETH SOTHELL. This is a copy of will and not the original.

HARVEY, JOHN. Hyde County.

February 26, 1759. June Court, 1759. *Sons:* JOSHUA, RICHARD, JOHN MARK HARVEY, ARTHUR. *Daughters:* MARY MARTIN, REBECCA HARVEY. *Wife:* FRANCIS. *Grandson:* JOHN HARVEY (house and lot in Woodstock). *Brother:* RICHARD HARVEY. *Executors:* RICHARD and JOHN MARK HARVEY (sons). *Witnesses:* STEPHEN DENNING, WILLIAM WEBSTER, JOHN WRIGHT. *Clerk of the Court:* STEPN. DENNING.

HARVEY, RICHARD.

February 22, 1732–1733. *Sons:* JOHN, RICHARD, PETER, SAMUEL, JAMES, JOSIAS. *Daughter:* BRIDGET HARVEY. *Wife and Executrix:* MARY. *Witnesses:* SAMLL HARVEY, JOHN MILLS, ANDREW CONNER. *Clerk of the Court:* JNO. COLLISON.

HARVEY, THOMAS. Albemarle County.

March 31, 1696. November 2, 1699. *Wife and Executrix:* SARAH. *Son:* THOMAS (plantation called "ye Quarter"). *Daughter:* MARY HARVEY (land called Faulks Point and land on Perquimans River). *Nephew:* THOMAS HARVEY. *Brother:* ROBERT HARVEY. *Witnesses:* HENRY NORMAN, ROBERT FENDALL, JOHN PEIRT, W. GLOVER. Codicil to will dated March 23, 1698–1699. Appoints COL. WM. WILKINSON executor of estate of JOHN HARVEY, dec'd, of which estate the testator was executor at the time of his death. *Witnesses to Codicil:* RICHARD FRENCH, RUTH LUKER. Codicil proven before HENDERSON WALKER.

HARVEY, THOMAS. Perquimans County.

April 10, 1729. November 10, 1729. *Sons:* THOMAS ("Plantation whereon I now live"), JOHN (plantation called the Quarter), BENJAMIN (plantation called Foulks (or Foleks) Point), MILES (land on Chowan River in Rockahock Neck bought of SAMUEL WOODARD). *Brother:* MILES GALE of Boston. *Brother-in-law:* COL. ROBERT WEST. *Nieces:* MARTHA, SAREY and MARY WEST (daughters of ROBT.). *Sisters:* ELIZABETH CLAY-

TEN and PENELOPE LITTLE, wife of WILLIAM LITTLE. *Other legatees:* JAMES SITTERSON, WILLIAM TETTERTON; JOHN son of JOHN COLE of Nansemond, Virginia; JOSHUA WHERRY son of ANTHONY WHERRY; ELIZABETH WHERRY daughter of ANTHONY; EDWARD MOSELEY and THOMAS POLLOCK. *Wife and Executrix:* ELIZABETH. *Executors:* MILES GALE, WILLIAM LITTLE, EDWARD MOSELEY and THOS. POLLOCK, JOHN LOVICK. *Witnesses:* THOMAS NORCOMB, RICHARD SUTTON, JOHN WIAT, CHARLES DENMAN, JOHN MITCHELL. Proven before RICHARD EVERARD.

HARVEY, THOMAS.   Perquimans County.

November 21, 1748. January Court, 1748. *Brothers and Executors:* JOHN, BENJAMIN and MILES HARVEY. *Nephews:* THOMAS and JOHN HARVEY. *Sister-in-law:* HANNAH SALTER. *Cousin:* SARAH ALDERSON. *Aunt:* HANNAH SITTERSON. *Witnesses:* JOHN NICKOLS, STEPHIN MARTIN, JOSEPH ARNOLD. *Clerk of the Court:* EDMUND HATCH.

HARWOOD, EDWARD.   Onslow County.

October 21, 1735. October Court, 1737. *Executor:* JOHN STARKEY. *Witnesses:* EDMD. HUGGER, JOHN MIXON, ELIZA JONES, JOHN STARKEY. *Clerk of the Court:* WM. CRANFORD. The testator provides for the sale of all his effects, proceeds to go to his wife and child, who are not named.

HASKINS, HANNIBAL.

February 11, 1698–1699. *Friend and Executor:* JOHN PORTER. *Witnesses:* HUMPHREY LEGGETT, ARCHIBALD HOLMES, WILLIAM BARROW. No probate.

HASSELL, JOHN.   Tyrrell County.

March 25, 1754. June Court, 1754. *Sons:* JOHN (plantation on West side of Scuppernong river known by the name of Plains), JOSEPH (lands on East side of Scuppernong river), ISAAC (plantation on East side of Scuppernong River), BENJAMIN ("my manner plantation"). *Daughters:* MARY WYNNE, SARAH FOX, ESTHER HASSELL. *Wife and Executrix:* RACHELL. Negroes bequeathed to sons. *Witnesses:* THOS. WYNNE, JEREMIAH WYNNE, PETER WYNNE. *Clerk of the Court:* EVAN JONES.

HATCH, ANTHONY.   Perquimans Precinct.

August 1, 1726. November 18, 1726. *Sons:* EDMUND and LAMB (lands lying in Neuse in the County of Bath), ANTHONY ("my plantation). Lands in Alligator held in common with GEORGE DURANT (brother-in-law) ordered sold. *Wife and Executrix:* ELISABETH. *Daughter:* ELISABETH HATCH. *Executors:* RICHD. WHIDBY and GEORGE DURANT (brothers-in-law). *Witnesses:* J. SWEENY, THOMAS PENRICE, JOHN STEVENS, PARTHENIA STEVENS. Proven before RICHARD EVERARD.

ABSTRACT OF WILLS, 1690—1760. 157

HATCH, ANTHONY.   Perquimans County.

September 30, 1744. October Court, 1744. *Sons:* ANTONY ("my manor plantation"), JOHN (plantation joining SOLOMON SNOWDEN). *Wife and Executrix:* ELIZABETH. *Executors:* COL. MCARORA SCARBOROUGH, EDMUND HATCH ("Brother GERMAN"). *Witnesses:* TULLE WILLIAMS, GEORGE DUVANT, SAM SCOLLAY. *Clerk of the Court:* EDMUND HATCH.

HATCH, LEMUEL.   Craven County.

April 2, 1774. February 3, 1777. *Sons:* LEMUEL (two-thirds of dwelling plantation lying between Sted's and Reasonover's Runs and also land on Trent River), JOHN and EDMUND, DURANT, JOY, ANTHONY (to each is given land which is described in will). *Daughters:* ELIZABETH and MARY HATCH. *Wife:* MARY. *Executors:* LEMUEL and JOHN HATCH (sons). *Witnesses:* EDMD. HATCH, JAMES WATSON, CHAS. MARKLAND. *Executor with sons:* FRANCIS FONVILLE. Witnesses to codicil appointing *Executor:* STOKES NORMENT, ELIZABETH NORMENT, ELIZABETH ANDRESS, EDMD. HATCH, JAMES WATSON. Will proven before RD. CASWELL.

HATTON, JOHN.   Pasquotank County.

March 15, 1697-1698. August 16, 1698. *Executor:* BARTHOLEMEW HEWIT. *Friends:* JOHN CIRBY (or COBY), ELIZABETH FOX. *Witnesses:* DANIEL AKEHURST, HENRY PALIN, JUNR., HUMPHRY BOLTON. *Clerk of the Court:* EDWARD MAYO.

HAUGHTON, CHARLES.   Chowan County.

October 4, 1754. *Sons:* JEREMIAH ("my plantation"), JOHN, CHARLES. *Daughter:* ELIZABETH. *Executors:* JEREMIAH and CHARLES (sons). *Witnesses:* WILLIAM HASKINS, WILLIAM WILKINS, JOHN TALER. No probate.

HAUGHTON, GEORGE.   Chowan Precinct.

December 16, 1718. *Daughter:* ELIZABETH. *Wife and Executrix:* JUDITH. *Executor:* THOMAS HAUGHTON (brother). *Witnesses:* JOSHUA PORTER and CHARLES HAUGHTON. Original missing. Recorded in Will Book 1712-1722, page 171.

HAUGHTON, JAMES.   Perquimans County.

March 8, 1758. April Court, 1758. *Nephews:* JOSHUA HAUGHTON (son of sister, EASTER GARRETT), HENRY and EDWARD HALL (sons of sister, RACHEL HALL). *Niece:* MARY HALL. *Executors:* EDWARD HALL, JOHN HALSEY, ANDREW KNOX. *Witnesses:* JAMES EGGERTON, THOS. MING, SARAH ARRANTON. *Clerk of the Court:* MILES HARVEY.

HAUGHTON, RICHARD. Chowan County.

October 19, 1748. November 25, 1748. *Son:* RICHARD. *Wife and Executrix:* MARY. *Executors:* THOMAS WHITE and JOB CHARLTON. *Witnesses:* THOS. WHITE, CHRIS. BUTLER, LEEY HAMPTON. Will proven before J. HALL, J. P.

HAUGHTON, WILLIAM. Chowan County.

November 17, 1749. January Court, 1752. *Sons:* JOSHUA, JAMES, JOB, DAVID (*Executor*). *Daughters:* RACHEL and EASTER HAUGHTON. *Granddaughters:* MARY and SARAH PENRICE, SARAH and MARY HAUGHTON. *Grandsons:* WILLIAM and JONATHAN HAUGHTON. *Wife:* MARY. *Witnesses:* J. BENBURY, RICHARD BRINN, THOMAS BURKIT. *Clerk of the Court:* JAS. CRAVEN.

HAUSINGTON, BENEDICTUS. Bath County.

November 16, 1729. December 16, 1730. *Daughters:* CATTERN, ELISEBETH, DINAH, MARY, SARAH. *Wife and Executrix:* DINAH. *Witnesses:* ROBERT BOND, ANNE NORWOOD.

HAWKINS, JOHN. Albemarle County.

March 1, 1687-1688. May 13, 1688. *Daughter:* MARY HAWKINS. *Executor:* WILLIAM WEST. *Witnesses:* WILL BENBOW, FRANCIS WELLS, WILL HANCKOCK. Proven before SETH SOTHELL.

HAWKINS, JOHN. Chowan County.

February 8, 1716-1717. August 16, 1719. *Sons:* JOSHUA, JAMES. *Daughter:* ANNE. *Other devisees and legatees:* THOMAS HARTSHORN (plantation on Cushake Creek), ELIZABETH HARTSHORN (son and daughter of JOYCE HARTSHORN, who is appointed *Executor*). *Witnesses:* THOS. ROGERS, FRANCIS ROGERS, JOHN HARDY. Will proven before CHAS. EDEN.

HAWKINS, JOHN. Perquimans County.

October 14, 1744. January Court, 1744. *Daughter-in-law:* MARY TRUMBULL. *Daughter:* MARY HAWKINS. *Wife and Executrix:* MARY. *Executors:* ROBERT HODGES and JAMES PEIRCE. *Witnesses:* FOSTER TOMS, JOHN BARCLIFT. *Clerk of the Court:* EDMUND HATCH.

HAWKINS, SARAH. Pasquotank County.

October 19, 1719. November 2, 1722. *Legatees:* THOS. MERRIDAY, heirs of ELIZABETH STUBBLE, wife of JOHN STUBBLE of Wickham, England; MARY STUBBLE, GEORGE GRIFFING, JOHN CARTWRIGHT, JOHN KING, SUSANNAH TALKSEY, JOHN EVERIGIN, WM. EVERIGIN, JR., EMANUEL LOW, JOHN SYMONS, WM. EVERIGIN, SR. (last-named two appointed *Executors*). *Witnesses:* GARRETT PURSEY, ROBERT HARRISON, SARAH HARRISON. Proven before WM. REED.

ABSTRACT OF WILLS, 1690—1760.

HAWKINS, THOMAS.   Tyrrell County.

October 8, 1730. July 21, 1732. *Son:* THOMAS. *Daughters:* MARY, ELIZABETH and SARAH. *Wife's daughter:* ELIZABETH. *Wife and Executrix:* ELIZABETH. *Witnesses:* RICHD. LEARY, JOHN BROWN, JOHN LONG. Will proven before GEO. BURRINGTON.

HAWLEY, MIKELL.   Northampton County.

March 1, 1752. August Court, 1752. *Sons:* JOSEPH, WILLIAM, CHRISTOPHER, BENJAMIN. *Grandson:* WILLIAM MITCHELL. *Daughters:* ANN, ELIZABETH and MARY. *Executor:* BENJAMIN HAWLEY (son). *Witnesses:* ROBERT HARREN, JOHN JOHNSON, ROBERT SHARP. *Clerk of the Court:* I. EDWARDS.

HAYMAN, HENRY.   Albemarle County.

August 29, 1709. *Sons:* HENRY and THOMAS ("land bought of EDWARD MAIO"), CHARLES and JAMES (two Islands on North River next to Indian Island). *Daughters:* MARY and ELINOR HAYMAN. *Wife and Executrix:* MARTHA. *Witnesses:* JAMES FORBUS, ALICE FORBUS, METHUSALEM VAUGHAN. No probate.

HAYMAN, HENRY.   Pasquotank County.

May 23, 1727. July 18, 1727. *Son:* WILLIAM. *Daughter:* ANN HAYMAN. *Wife and Executrix:* MARY. *Witnesses:* MAC. SCARBOROUGH, SARAH FARECLOF, SARAH JONES. *Clerk of the Court:* THOS. WEEKES.

HAYWOOD, JOHN.   Edgecombe County.

July 23, 1756. December Court, 1758. *Sons:* WILLIAM, JOHN, EGBERT and HARWOOD. *Daughters:* DEBORAH and MARY HAYWOOD (213 acres of land devised to daughters). All six children appointed *Executors*. *Witnesses:* EDWARD CROWELL, WM. CAMPBELL, THOMAS MERRIT. *Clerk of the Court:* JOS. MONTFORT.

HAYWOOD, JOHN.   Edgecombe County.

February 18, 1758. June Court, 1758. *Brothers:* EGBERT, WILLIAM and SHERWOOD HAYWOOD. *Sisters:* DEBORAH and MARY HAYWOOD. *Father:* not named. *Executor:* EGBERT HAYWOOD. *Witnesses:* ROBERT WARREN, JOSEPH POPE, SAMUEL PITMAN. *Clerk of the Court:* JOS. MONTFORT.

HEARESON, JOHN.   Chowan Precinct.

February 18, 1693-1694. April Court, 1694. *Sons:* WILLIAM, THOMAS, JOHN. *Daughter:* ELISABETH. *Executrix:* WIFE (not named). *Witnesses:* GEORGE FORDYES, JOHN WATKENES, WILLIAM HEARESON. *Clerk of the Court:* HENDERSON WALKER.

HEATH (spelled also "HATH"), NEHEMIAH.   Currituck Co.
January 2, 1749-1750. April Court, 1750. *Wife and Executrix:* ELIZABETH. *Other legatee:* ROBERT HATH (or HEATH). *Witnesses:* WILLIS ETHERIDGE, WILLIAM BLUNT, LAZERUS FLOWREY. *Clerk of the Court:* RICH'D McCLURE.

HECKLEFIELD, JOHN.   Chowan County.
May 30, 1721. August 8, 1721. *Son:* JOHN. *Other legatees:* Gov. CHARLES EDEN (mourning ring with a deaths head and christal), EDMUND GALE (1 diamond ring), GEORGE DURANT. *Sister-in-law:* MARY COX. *Executors:* EDMUND GALE and GEORGE DURANT. *Witnesses:* WILLIAM BARCLIFT, DARBEY BRYAN, ENOCH CAWEN. Will proven before CHAS. EDEN. There is filed with this will a memorandum or will made by testator in 1718.

HEDGES, THOMAS.   New Hanover County.
March 23, 1745. November 27, 1746. *Son:* WILLIAM. *Daughter:* ANN HEDGES. *Executors:* WILLIAM HEDGES (son), JAMES SMALLWOOD. *Witnesses:* PHILLIP DAVID, DAVID DAVES, THOS. JAMES. Will proven before GAB. JOHNSTON.

HENBY, JOSEPH.   Perquimans County.
April 8, 1752. July Court, 1752. *Daughter:* CLARKEY HENBY. *Father:* JOHN HENBY. *Sisters:* MARY HENBY, ELISABETH GRIFFIN. *Brothers:* JAMES and SILVANUS HENBY. *Executors:* FRANCIS TOMES, JOSEPH RATLIFF. *Witnesses:* JO. SUTTON, SAMUEL ANDERSON, JOHN HENBY. *Clerk of the Court:* EDMUND HATCH.

HENDERSON, DAVID.   Bertie County.
February 13, 1735-1736. March 9, 1735. *Nephew:* GEORGE HENDERSON. *Sister:* JENNETT. *Executors:* COLO. ROBT. WEST, CULLEN POLLOCK, GEORGE HENDERSON and CAPN. JOHN CALDEN. *Witnesses:* THOS. DAVIS, SIMON DART, JAMES KEETER and ELIZABETH DART. Proven before W. SMITH, C. J.

HENDERSON, GEORGE.   Bertie Precinct.
October 15, 1736. November 27, 1736. *Legatees and devisees:* THOMAS MOOR, JOHN RAY, RACHEL NELSON, MARY GREGORY, ANDREW MOOR, HUGH SCOTT (land on Cashai River); ANDREW SCOTT, GEORGE SCOTT (sons of ANDREW SCOTT, merchant in Glasgow). *Executors:* HUGH SCOTT (merchant in Boston), ANDREW MOORE. *Witnesses:* JOHN RAY, GEORGE STRACHAN, SAMUEL COOK. Will proven before W. SMITH, C. J.

HENDERSON, HENMAN.

February 19, 1728. February 21, 1728. Boston in Massachusetts Bay. *Wife, Executrix and sole devisee:* MARY. *Witnesses:* EB. YOUNGMAN, BEN SOPER, GEORGE WILLIAMS. Proven before R. EVERARD.

HENDRICK, FRANCIS.   Pasquotank County.

May 5, 1714. *Son and Executor:* THOMAS. *Wife and Executrix:* MARY. *Witnesses:* W. NORRIS, LEVI CRESSEY, W. ROLFE.

HENDRICK, FRANCIS.   Craven County.

September 11, 1734. December 17, 1734. *Wife:* ELISHE. *Sons-in-law:* JOHN HILL (*Executor*), MOSES ARNECH. *Witnesses:* JOHN JEAMES, THOS. FISHER, GEORGE FISHER. *Clerk of the Court:* CALEB METCALFE.

HENDRICK, JEREMIAH.   Perquimans County.

June 1, 1756. January Court, 1756. *Son:* GEORGE. *Wife and Executrix:* SARAH. *Executor:* ROBERT COCKS (father-in-law). *Witnesses:* THO. WEEKES, THOS. CRAGHILL, THOS. WEEKES, JR. *Clerk of the Court:* MILES HARVEY.

HENDRICKS, SOLOMON.   Perquimans County.

April 18, 1744. October Court, 1744. *Daughters:* MARY ("plantation whereon I now dwell"), SARAH and FRANCES HENDRICKS. *Executors:* JEREMIAH HENDRICKS (brother), MARY HENDRICKS (wife) and SARAH HENDRICKS (daughter). *Witnesses:* MICHAEL MURPHY, THOMAS OVERMAN, JAMES OVERMAN. *Clerk of the Court:* EDMUND HATCH.

HENLEY, JOHN.   Pasquotank County.

March 21, 1726–1727. July Court, 1728. *Sons:* JOHN ("my plantation"), JESSE. *Daughters:* MARY, MIRIAM and ELIZABETH. *Wife and Executrix:* ISABELL. *Executor:* JOHN HENLEY (son). *Witnesses:* DANIEL GUTHRIE and ISAAIAH CULBERTSON. *Clerk of the Court:* R. EVERARD.

HENLY, JOHN.   Onslow County.

January 14, 1747. April Court, 1747. *Sons:* JOHN, WILLIAM, EDWARD (to each is devised land), BENJAMIN. *Daughter:* ELIZABETH HENLY. *Wife and Executrix:* ELIZABETH. *Executor:* GEORGE CUPER (COOPER). *Witnesses:* RICHD. WHITHURST, HENRY BROWN, ANN EUERE.

HENLEY, JOHN.   Pasquotank County.

June 3, 1753. April Court, 1754. *Sons:* JOHN and JOSEPH ("my plantation to be divided between them"). *Wife and Executrix:* MARY.

Executors: JOHN HENLEY (son) and JOSEPH JORDAN (brother-in-law). *Witnesses:* LEML. COOK, ELIZABETH BROTHERS. *Clerk of the Court:* THOMAS TAYLOR.

HENLEY, PETER, "Chief Justice of the Province of North Carolina."

November 23, 1757. July Court, 1758. *Son:* JOHN. *Executor:* JOHN CAMPBELL. This will provides for the payment of a debt of £400 due one AGNES TUCKER of Coryton, near Honiton, in the County of Devon, for advancement made by her in order to provide for the marriage of herself and testator, which marriage, "to the great disappointment of us both," says the testator, "was postponed to be compleated at a future day." Other creditors mentioned are: MR. SIMON BUNKER, of Axminster, in the County of Devon, attorney-at-law; MR. BENJAMIN MAYBERRY, Taylor of Craven Buildings, near Drury Lane, London. *Witnesses:* SARAH MCCULLOCH, JOSEPH MONTFORT, RICHD. BROWNRIGG. *Clerk of the Court of Chowan County:* THOS. JONES. Endorsement on the will reads: "The last will and testament of PETER HENLEY, ESQR., who departed this life on Tuesday, the 25th day of April, 1738, about nine o'clock in the morning, and was interred in the Church in Edenton on the Evening the 27th of same month at six o'clock in the evening in a decent manner and much lamented by his acquaintance."

HERN, JAMES.   Beaufort County.

February 22, 1751–1752. June 9, 1752. *Sons:* JAMES, WILLIAM, JOHN ("my plantation"), MASON. *Daughters:* MARY, ELLINDER, ELIZEBETH, SARAH and RACHEL HERN. *Wife and Executrix:* MASON. *Executor:* GEORGE SUGG. *Witnesses:* MARY MAYO, NATHAN GODWIN, MARY TYSON. *Clerk of the Court:* WILL ORMOND.

HERRENDEN, HEZEKIAH.

November 5, 1746. May Court, 1754, "of Duxborough in the County of Plymouth in New England." *Wife and Executrix:* HANNAH. *Witnesses:* SILVANUS CURTIS, SAMUEL WESTON, SAMUEL WESTON, JUNR. *Clerk of Bertie Court:* SAML. ORMES.

HERRING, SAMUELL.   Johnston County.

October 22, 1750. December Court, 1750. *Sons:* ANTONY, STEPHEN, MICHAEL ("plantation whereon I now live"). *Daughter:* BARTHENA HERRING. *Son-in-law:* JNO. CONNERLEY. *Executor:* ANTONY HERRING (son). *Wife:* not named. *Witnesses:* ANTONY HERRING and JOSEPH HERRING. *Clerk of the Court:* RICHD. CASWELL.

HERRITAGE, WILLIAM. Craven County.

March 8, 1769. *Sons:* HENEAGE ("plantation whereon I dwell, called Springfield"), JOHN ("plantation called Harrow"), WILLIAM MARTIN HERRITAGE. *Son-in-law:* RICHARD CASWELL. *Daughters:* ELIZABETH HERRITAGE, ANNA LOVICK (wife of GEO. LOVICK), SARAH (wife of RICHARD CASWELL), SUSANNAH. *Executors:* RICHARD CASWELL and JOHN and HENEAGE HERRITAGE. *Witnesses:* DANIEL BARRY, ——— and ———. Several tracts of land, besides the ones above mentioned, are conveyed to sons and son-in-law, for description of which said lands see will. Codicil dated April 10, 1769, devises other lands to son HENEAGE, etc. *Witnesses to Codicil:* DAVID GORDON, MARGRET WIGGINS, ELIZABETH BLOUNT, RD. CASWELL. No probate.

HEWITT, BARTHOLOMEW. Pasquotank County.

July 16, 1719. *Legatees:* ROBERT LOWRY, SAMUEL DAVIS, THOMAS CARTRIGHT, SAMUEL NORRIS. *Executor:* WILLIAM NORRIS. *Witnesses:* WILLIAM JONES, JOHN MACKY. Original missing. Recorded in Book 1712–1722, page 243.

HIBBS, JONATHAN. Pasquotank County.

April 5, 1745. July 15, 1745. *Sons:* JOHN (420 acres of land), JONATHAN. *Executors:* DAVID BOLES and CALEB SAWYER. *Witnesses:* JOHN NORRIS, EDWARD SCOTT, WM. COALE. *Clerk of the Court:* THOS. TAYLOR.

HICKS, AFRICA. Pasquotank Precinct.

November 7, 1711. No probate date. *Two sons:* PATRICK MACKGREGORY and GREGORY MACKGREGORY. *Husband:* ROBT. HICKS. *Sister:* ANN PALIN (widow). *Executors:* PATRICK MACKGREGORY and GREGORY MACKGREGORY, to be in care of MR. JOHN PALIN and NATH. CHEVIN until they are 21 years of age. *Witnesses:* GEORGE ELLIS, ELIZA HARLOW. *Clerk of Court:* ROBERT BUCKNER.

HICKS, DAVID. Chowan County.

September 9, 1732. December 23, 1732. *Son-in-law:* THOMAS ASHLY, JR. *Daughter:* LUCRETIA. *Wife and Executrix:* ELIZABETH. *Other children:* mentioned, but not named. All land to be divided among children. *Witnesses:* MART. FRED RASOR, THOMAS ASHLY, LAMB HARDY. Will proven before GEORGE BURRINGTON.

HICKS, JOHN. Carteret County.

May 15, 1749. September Court, 1749. *Wife and Executrix:* HANNAH. *Brothers:* DAVID HICKS, THOMAS HICKS. *Executor:* DAVID HICKS. *Witnesses:* GEORGE MCKEAN, EVE LEWIS, MARTHA LEWIS. *Clerk of Court:* GEO. READ.

HICKS, THOMAS.
October 26, 1722. August 24, 1724. *Sisters:* HANNAH and ABIGAIL HICKS. *Executor:* JOSEPH SUTTON, JUNR. *Witnesses:* BENJAMIN JACKSON, NATHANIEL SUTTON, SENR., NATHANIEL SUTTON, JUNR. Will proven before C. GALE, C. J. This document is in the form of a power of attorney to JOSEPH SUTTON, JUNR., constituting him trustee for sisters above named, who reside in "ould England."

HIGGINS, MICHALL. Craven County.
April 28, 1753. May Court, 1753. *Sons:* MICHAEL and WILLIAM. *Daughters:* MARY, SARAH, ANN and HANNAH HIGGINS. *Wife and Executrix:* ANN. *Executors:* MICHAEL HIGGINS, JEREMIAH VAIL. *Witnesses:* WM. WICKLIFFE, JOHN MURPHY, THOMAS EVENES. *Clerk of the Court:* SOL. REW.

HILL, BENJAMIN. Bertie County.
June 20, 1752. August Court, 1753. *Son and Executor:* HENRY ("all my lands"). *Daughters:* MARY CAMPBELL, SARAH MCCULLOCH (400 acres of land on Roanoak River), PRISCILLA HILL. *Other legatee:* MARGARET COCKRAN. *Executor:* THOMAS JONES of Petty Shore. *Witnesses:* JESSE BROWNE, ROBERT HARDY, JOHN PITT. Codicil dated June 6, 1753, gives land in Cashia Neck to *grandson*, BENJAMIN MCCULLOCH. Same witnesses to codicil. *Clerk of the Court:* SAMUEL ORMES.

HILL, GEORGE. Bath County.
April 17, 1722. March 30, 1723. *Sons:* JOHN, GEORGE, HARMAN, *Wife and Executrix:* MARY. *Daughter:* RACHEL. *Executors:* JOHN and GEORGE HILL. *Witnesses:* THOMAS GOODIN, JOHN LEATH, JOHN PROCTER. *Clerk:* JOHN CORNICK.

HILL, HARMAN. Beaufort County.
December 4, 1752. March Court, 1755. *Sons:* HARMAN (land on Callums Creek), JAMES and WILLIAM. *Daughters:* ELIZ. HANCOCK, SARAH RICE, ANN SLADE (land on Pamplico River), MARY SMITH, RACHEL HILL. *Executors:* SARAH HILL (wife), JOSEPH SLADE, JOHN BARROW. *Witnesses:* EDMUND PEARCE, JOSHUA PEARCE, GRIFFETH HOWELL. *Clerk of Court:* WALLEY CHAUNCEY.

HILL, ISAAC. Chowan Precinct.
March 3, 1710. *Sons:* MICHAEL, JOHN and ISACK, NATHANIEL. *Daughter:* MARTHA. *Executor:* ROBERT WEST. *Witnesses:* WILLIAM MAULE, EDWARD BRYAN, JOHN HALE. Original missing. Recorded in Book 1712–1722, page 34.

ABSTRACT OF WILLS, 1690—1760.

HILL, MOSES. Chowan County.
Will is illegible.

HILL, JOHN. Bath County.
March 27, 1731. September Court, 1731. *Sons:* JOSHUA, JOHN. *Friend:* THOMAS TISON. *Executors:* WIFE (not named) and EDMUND PEARS. *Witnesses:* THOMAS TISON, HARMAN HILL, WILLIAM NICHOLS. *Clerk of the Court:* FRE. GOOLDE.

HILL, JOHN. Northampton County.
June 15, 1747. August Court, 1747. *Sons:* NATHANIEL ("plantation he now lives on"), DANIEL ("plantation I now live on"), LEWIS ("remainder part of my land"), PETER. *Executors:* DANIEL and NATHANIEL HILL (sons). *Witnesses:* WILLIAM ADDISON, WILLIAM FLOARYDAY, HOSEA TAP-LEY. *Clerk of the Court:* RT. FORSTER.

HILL, RICHARD. Craven County.
February 17, 1728-1729. March 18, 1729. *Granddaughter:* ELISABETH HILL. *Executor:* FRANCIS HILL (brother). *Daughter:* ANN JONES. *Son-in-law:* EVAN JONES. *Witnesses:* JAMES TAYLOR, THOMAS JONES, JOHN LEWEIS, JOHN CUMING. *Clerk of the Court:* CALEB METCALFE.

HILL, ROBERT. Tyrrell County.
January 16, 1735-1736. February 4, 1735-1736. *Son:* ROBERT ("my plantation"). *Wife:* ANN. *Daughter:* SARAH HILL. *Executors:* CULLEN POLLOCK and ROBERT WEST. *Witnesses:* SAMUELL DURRANCE, NATH'L CARRUTHERS, PAUL THORP. Proven before W. SMITH, C. J.

HILL, WILLIAM. Northampton County.
September 3, 1748. November Court, 1748. *Son:* WILLIAM ("my plantation"). *Daughters:* ANN HILL, CELIA PHILLIPS. *Wife and Executrix:* ANN. *Witnesses:* JNO. SIMPSON, JACOB LITTLE, FRANCIS DELOATCH. *Clerk of the Court:* I. EDWARDS.

HILL, WILLIAM. Chowan County.
March 10, 1750-1751. April Court, 1751. *Grandsons:* AARON and ROBERT HILL. *Sons:* WILLIAM and AARON *(Executor)*. *Son-in-law and Executor:* THOMAS NICHOLSON. *Daughters:* RACHEL HILL, SARAH BARROW, wife of JOSEPH BARROW. *Witnesses:* JAMES GRIFFIN, JETHRO RABEY, ANN PETERS. *Clerk of the Court:* JAS. CRAVEN.

HILLIARD, JOHN. Northampton County.
November 6, 1748. November Court, 1748. *Sons:* ROBERT ("my plantation"), JOHN. *Daughter:* SARAH HILLIARD. *Wife and Executrix:* MARY. *Witnesses:* JOHN MOREAN, WILLIAM LIVINGSTONE, JOHN MOLTAN. *Clerk of the Court:* I. EDWARDS.

HILLIARD, ROBERT.   Edgecombe County.

April 13, 1743. May Court, 1751. *Devisees and legatees:* JACOB HILLIARD, ROBERT HILLIARD, JEREMIAH HILLIARD ("plantation on the falls of Teare River"); SAMSONE HILLIARD, MARY HILLIARD (all children of JEREMIAH HILLIARD); WILLIAM HILLIARD, JEAMES HILLIARD (sons of WILLIAM HILLIARD). *Wife:* CHARETY. *Executors:* WILLIAM HILLIARD and OSBORNE JEFFREYS. *Witnesses:* SAM'L HALLIMAN, WILLIAM SIRGENER, BENJ. BOYKIN. *Clerk of Court:* BENJ'N WYNNS.

HILLIARD, WILLIAM.   Northampton County.

July 4, 1754. May Court, 1756. *Sons:* WILLIAM (land known by name of "Hogpen Neck"), JAMES ("plantation whereon I dwell"), ISAAC (land in Edgecombe County on Swift Creek), ELIAS (plantations in Northampton and Edgecombe). *Daughter:* ANN HILLIARD. *Wife and Executrix:* ANN. *Executor:* JAMES HILLIARD (son). *Witnesses:* HENRY HART, JOSEPH BRIDGERS, NATHANIEL HOWEL, CHARLES COTTEN. *Clerk of the Court:* I. EDWARDS.

HILORY, SAMEL.   Bath County.

March 20, 1712–1713. *Executor and sole legatee:* SAMUEL WOODARD. *Witnesses:* ELLICKSANDER OLIVER, HENERREY TURNER. No probate.

HINTON, JOHN.   Chowan Precinct.

June 21, 1730. October Court, 1732. *Sons:* HARDY, JOHN, WILLIAM, MALLACIE. *Executors:* MARY HINTON (wife), HARDIE HINTON (son), WILLIAM HINTON (brother). *Witnesses:* JAMES HINTON, JOSEPH ASHLEY, THOS. ROUNTREE. *Clerk of the Court:* RT. FORSTER.

HINTON, MICAJAH.   Bertie County.

October 5, 1756. January Court, 1757. *Son:* WILLIAM. *Daughter:* ELIZEBETH HINTON. This is a nuncupative will proven before JOHN HARRELL, J. P., by JOHN and JONAS HINTON and HEZEKIAH TOMSON. *Clerk of the Court:* BENJAMIN WYNNS.

HOBBY, JACOB.   Edgecombe County.

January 22, 1758. September Court, 1758. *Son:* MATHEW (all "my land"). *Daughters:* RHODA, SARAH and FRANCES HOBBY. *Wife and Executrix:* JEMIME. *Executor:* JOHN BAKER. *Witnesses:* ANDREW IRWING, BRACEWELL BRIDGES, JOSEPH KELLEY. *Clerk of the Court:* JOS. MONTFORT.

HOBS, JOHN.   Pasquotank County

October 29, 1728. October 14, 1729. *Wife and Executrix:* FRANCES. *Witnesses:* JNO. GALLEY, JAMES SMITH, FRANCES SMITH, PATIENCE PRICK-

ETT. *Clerk of the Court:* H. MINSON. *Justices:* JON. PALIN, ROBT. MORGAN, JNO. ROLF, MCKRONA SCARBOROUGH, GABRELL BURNHAM, NATT HALL.

HOCKINGS (HAWKINS), JOHN. Duplin County.

March 29, 1756. July Court, 1756. *Daughters and Executrices:* MARY, ANN and LATTESS HOCKINGS. *Witnesses:* BENJAMIN FUSSELL, JACOB FUSSELL, THOMAS DAVIS, RICHARD PENNEY, EDWARD SPEARMAN. *Clerk of Court:* JOHN DICKSON.

HOCUT, EDWARD. Beaufort County.

January 19, 1749–1750. March Court, 1750. *Sons:* WILLIAM, NATHANIEL, EDWARD. *Wife and Executrix:* MARTHA. *Executor:* NATHAN ARCHEBALD. *Witnesses:* WALLEY CHAUNCEY, STEPHEN BUCKINGHAM, JOHN BOWIN. *Clerk of the Court:* JOHN ALDERSON.

HODGES, JAMES. Chowan County.

September 23, 1722. October 10, 1722. *Cousin:* ELIZABETH HARRISON. *Wife and Executrix:* SARAH CATHERINE HODGES. *Witnesses:* C. GALE, ROGER HAZARD, SARAH HAZARD. Will proven before WM. REED, *President.* Coat of arms on seal.

HODGES, JAMES. Pasquotank County.

February 2, 1758. March Court, 1758. *Sons:* JOSIAH (plantation and islands on the Northeast side of Pasquotank River bridge), WILLIS (one negro), JAMES (land and Marsh on West side of road going to "ye Great Bridge"), LAMB, PORTLOCK. *Daughters:* KESIAH CURLIN, MOLLY, FRANCES HODGES, MIRIAM HODGES. *Brother:* JOSEPH HODGES. Several negroes and a large quantity of personal property bequeathed to wife and children. Estate to pay for brick chimney to house. *Wife:* MARIAM. *Executor:* COLO. ROBERT MURDON. *Witnesses:* JOHN HARRIS, DANIEL KOEN, JOHN MURDEN. *Clerk of the Court:* THOMAS TAYLOR.

HODGES, RICHARD. Beaufort County.

September 3, 1747. April 16, 1752. *Sons:* JOHN (400 acres of land on "Cochavinity Bay"), HENRY ("the manner plantation"). *Daughter:* SARAH HODGES. *Wife:* SARAH. *Executor:* JOHN HODGES (son). *Witnesses:* JAMES COUPPER, JAMES SINGLETON, THOMAS WILLIAMS. *Clerk of Anson County Court:* ANTHONY HUTCHINS.

HODGES, RICHARD. Currituck County.

March 2, 1748. April Court, 1749. *Daughters:* SARAH BURNHAM, FRANCES BOWRIN, MARY, ELISEBETH and UPHAN HODGES. *Wife and Executrix:* FRANCES. *Witnesses:* CALEB WILSON, GEORGE POWERS, WILLIS ETHERIDGE. *Clerk of the Court:* RICHARD MCCLURE.

HODGSON, JOHN. New Hanover County.

July 6, 1738. December Court, 1738. *Daughters:* MARY and MARGARET HODGSON. *Executor:* ROGER MOORE. *Witnesses:* CORN'S HARNETT, CHAS. HEPBURN, JOHN MARTINDALE. *Clerk of the Court:* JNO. RICE.

HOGBIN, WILLIAM. Albemarle County.

May 4, 1692. July 4, 1692. *Wife:* MARGETT. *Daughters:* SARAH and ELIZABETH HOGBIN. *Executors:* THOMAS and JEREMIAH SIMONS. *Witnesses:* PATRICK BAYLEY, JOHN RAPER. *Clerk of the Court:* PAUL LATHUM.

HOG, RICHARD. Bladen County.

June 18, 1768. September 21, 1769. *Sister:* ELIZABETH HOG of Tisheraw, in the parish of Inveresk in North Brittain. *Executors:* ROBERT JOHNSTON, ROBERT and JOHN HOGG. *Witnesses:* WILLIAM BARTRAM, THOMAS BAYLY, LILLAH JOHNSTON. Proven before WM. TRYON.

HOGGES, ROBERT. Bertie County.

March 30, 1740. August Court, 1742. *Sons:* JOHN and RICHARD and ELIAS. *Daughters:* ANN MOORE, OLIVE WIGONS and MATHEW WILLIAMS. *Wife:* not named. *Executors:* ELIAS and RICHARD HOGGES (sons) and ISAAC WILLIAMS (son-in-law). *Witnesses:* NEEDHAM BRYAN, ADAM RABEY, WILLIAM BRYAN. *Clerk of Court:* HENRY DELON.

HOLBROOK, FARMANESS.

March 8, 1683–1684. This will is so torn and rotten as to be illegible.

HOLBROOK (or HOLEBROUGH), JOSEPH. Bath County and "Pamlicoth Precinct."

October 18, 1711. *Legatees:* ALEXANDER and ELIZABETH AVERA, SWAN SWANSON. *Brother and Executor:* JOHN HOLEBROUGH. *Witnesses:* DANIEL HALLSEY, JAMES LEIG. Original missing. Recorded in Book 1712–1722, page 16.

HOLLADAY, THOMAS. Chowan County.

August 30, 1744. September 8, 1744. *Legatees and devisees:* HARDY HOLLADAY HUTSON, THOMAS HOLLADAY HUTSON, JOHN HOLLADAY HUTSON (land in Virginia to be sold and proceeds divided among above named), WILLIAM HOLLADAY, HANNAH BEDARRIN, ELIZABETH BURTON (daughter). *Executrix:* MARY HUTSON. *Witnesses:* JOHN THACH, JOHN NICHOLLS, PRUDANCE GARRETT. Will proven before GAB. JOHNSTON at Eden House.

HOLLADAY, WILLIAM. Tyrrell County.

April 23, 1754. June Court, 1754. *Sons:* THOMAS, SAMMUELL (appointed Executors). *Wife:* ELIZABETH. *Daughters:* mentioned, but not named. *Witnesses:* WILLIAM JONES and JOHN BENNET. *Clerk of the Court:* EVAN JONES.

HOLLAND, DANIEL.   Craven County.
March 16, 1771. April 20, 1771. *Wife and Executrix:* ANNIE. *Witnesses:* JAMES REED, HANNAH REED, JOHN HOLLAND. Will proven before WM. TRYON.

HOLLBROOK, JOHN.   Bertie County.
April 29, 1740. May Court, 1740. *Son and Executor:* JOHN. *Wife:* DOROTHY. *Executors:* COLL. ROBERT WEST, THOMAS RYAN. *Witnesses:* ROGER SNELL, THOS. ASHLY, JUNR., THOMAS ASHBURN. *Clerk of the Court:* JNO. WYNNS.

HOLLERY, SAMUEL, and SAMUELL WOODARD.
April 13, 1713. This is a contract by the terms of which the survivor of the above-named parties shall take all estate of the other, at his decease, and is proven by HENRY TURNER and ALLIS GIVEN before WM. BRICE.

HOLLIS, JAMES.   Tyrrell County.
May 20, 1735. March Court, 1735. *Son:* ARMIT. *Wife and Executrix:* ANN. *Executor:* THOS. HUBBS. *Witnesses:* MARY FEWAX, WILLIAM TYSAR, MARY HUBBS. *Clerk of Court:* JAMES CRAVEN.

HOLLOWAY, THOMAS.   Perquimans County.
November 3, 1750. January Court, 1750. *Son and Executor:* JOHN (two plantations). *Daughters:* ELIZABETH BARCLIFT, RACHEL TURNBULL, ANN SNODEN, MARY BATEMAN, SARAH COUPLAND, UPHERASHA HOLLOWAY. *Witnesses:* JAMES GIBSON, THOS. BARCLIFT, ELIZABETH BARCLIFT. *Clerk of the Court:* EDMUND HATCH.

HOLLOWELL, EDMUND.   Bertie County.
June 17, 1729. October 20, 1729. *Brothers:* THOMAS HOLLOWELL (*Executor*), JOHN HOLLOWELL. All land is bequeathed to JOHN BACON. *Witnesses:* JOHN HOLLOWELL, RICHD. BACON, THOMAS HOLLOWELL, SENR. *Clerk of the Court:* THOS. CREW.

HOLLOWELL, LUKE.   Perquimans County.
March 22, 1734–1735. April 21, 1736. *Sons:* JOEL ("my dwelling plantation"), WILLIAM, JOHN. *Wife and Executrix:* ELIZABETH. Land in Virginia devised to son JOHN. *Witnesses:* JAMES FEILD, THOMAS ROUNTREE, GILBERT SCOT. Will proven before W. SMITH, C. J.

HOLLOWELL, RUBIN.   Perquimans County.
January 23, 1753. April Court, 1753. *Brothers:* LEVY, JOHN and ABNER HOLLOWELL. *Sister:* ANN BRINKLEY. *Executors:* JOHN and LEVY HOLLOWELL. *Witnesses:* NICHOLAS STALLINGS, THOMAS REDDICK, JOSIAH ROGERSON. *Clerk of the Court:* EDMUND HATCH.

HOLLY, JOHN.   Bertie Precinct.

December 23, 1728. February Court, 1728. *Wife and Executrix:* SARAH. *Son:* RICHARD. *Witness:* JOHN SWENNY (or SWENEY). *Clerk of the Court:* RT. FORSTER.

HOLMES, EBENEZER.   Onslow County.

February 4, 1745–1746. April 1, 1746. *Sons:* JOHN, EBENEZER, SETH, BARNABAS (*Executor*). *Daughters:* REBECCA WRIGHT (wife of JOSEPH), HANNAH WILLIAMS, LYDEL HOLMES, ABIGIL HOLMES. *Wife:* HANNAH. *Witnesses:* ANDREW MURRAY, JAMES THOMSON, ANN HURLEY. *Clerk of the Court:* GEO. CLOPTON.

HOLMES, JOHN.   Edgecombe County.

February 28, 1735–1736. May Court, 1736. *Sons:* JOHN, HARDY, EDWARD, GABRIEL. *Daughters:* ANN SANDERS, CHARITY BROWN, DOROTHY SPIER, ROSE. *Wife:* TAMAR. *Executor:* HARDY HOLMES. *Witnesses:* EDWD. BUXTON, WILLIAM DAVIES, ELIZABETH WELSH. *Deputy Clerk of Court:* THOS. KEARNY.

HOMES, EDWARD.   Perquimans County.

April 14, 1702. *Sons:* THOMAS and JOHN. *Wife and Executrix:* ELIZABETH. *Witnesses:* names illegible. *Clerk of Court:* JOHN STEPNEY.

HOMES, EDWARD.   Bertie County.

August 9, 1750. November Court, 1750. *Cousin and Executor:* WM. BIRD. *Wife and Executrix:* LIDDEA. *Witnesses:* HENRY BONNER, WM. MITCHELL and JOHN PADGE. *Clerk of the Court:* SAM'L ORMES.

HOOK, JOHN.

March 27, 1732. *Sons:* WILLIAM (*Executor*), ROBERT, THOMAS and JOHN. *Daughters:* ELISEBATH, MARY and SARAH. *Wife:* RUTH. *Witnesses:* JOHN MACKCONE, NATHAN BARNES. No probate.

HOOKER, GODPHREY.   Bertie County.

April 2, 1729. *Son:* BENJAMIN ("the manner plantation"). *Daughter:* ELISABETH. *Wife and Executrix:* ELISABETH. *Executor:* ROBERT EVANS. *Witnesses:* ROBERT EVANS, JOHN MORRIS and ———. No probate.

HOOKER, WILLIAM.   Chowan County.

June 8, 1716. October Court, 1717. *Sons:* WILLIAM ("plantation whereon I now live, on Barren Branch and Wickacorn Creek"), GODFREE two hundred and fifty acres of land adjoining COL. POLLOCK). *Daughters:* ANN EVANS, BRIDGETT MANN, MARGARETT LEWIS, JANE BROWN and ELIZABETH SISEMORE. *Son-in-law:* SAMUEL SISEMORE (land on the main road). *Grandson:* WILLIAM LEWIS. *Executor:* WILLIAM HOOKER (son). *Witnesses:* WILLIAM CRANFORD, FRANCIS BROWN. *Clerk of the Court:* R. HICKS.

HOOKER, WILLIAM. Bertie County.

October 20, 1756. January Court, 1757. *Sons:* WILLIAM, JOHN, JAMES, STEPHEN, NATHAN. *Daughters:* ANN LASITER, SARAH HOOKER (*Executrix*). *Witnesses:* WM. WYNNS, JAMES WYNNES, BENJAMIN BAKER, BENJAMIN BAKER, JUNR. *Clerk of the Court:* BENJAMIN WYNNS.

HOOKS, WILLIAM. Chowan County.

February 18, 1746–1747. April Court, 1751. *Son:* WILLIAM. *Grandsons:* WILLIAM, CHARLES, THOMAS and JOHN HOOKS. *Executor:* JOHN HOOKS. *Witnesses:* MARTHA SUMNER, ANN SUMNER, CHAS. KING. *Clerk of Court:* JAS. CRAVEN.

HOPKINS, JAMES. Parish of Saint Matthews, Orange Co.

February 8, 1759. September Court, 1759. *Executors:* WILLIAM HOPKINS, WILLIAM PHILLIPS and JOHN HOPKINS. *Children:* mentioned, but not named. *Witnesses:* ALICKANDER FERGUSON, JOHN DOBBINS, DAVID SMITH. *Clerk of Court:* JAS. WATSON.

HOPKINS, JOHN. Albemarle County.

October 14, 1721. November 8, 1721. *Sons:* mentioned, but not named. *Other legatees:* SARAH HOPKINS (granddaughter), CHARLES CRADOCK. No executor named. *Witnesses:* ANDREW OLOVER, CHARLES CRADOCK, ELESEBETH BATEMAN. *Clerk of the Court:* R. HICKS.

HOPKINS, JOHN. Chowan County.

January Court, 1754. *Wife and Executrix:* MARY. *Executor:* JOHN HALSEY. *Witnesses:* THOMAS SUMNER, JNO. MCKILDO, WM. HORNSBY. *Clerk of the Court:* WILL HALSEY. No date of execution.

HORN, WILLIAM.

September 10, 1753. *Sons:* WILLIAM, HENRY, CHARLES, THOMAS, MOSES, MICHAELL (*Executor*). *Daughter:* MARGARET. *Witnesses:* WM. REYNOLDS, JOYCE REYNOLDS, ANN HILL. No probate.

HORTH, THOMAS. Chowan Precinct.

October 29, 1735. January Court, 1735. *Grandchildren:* SARAH, MARY and THOMAS MING (land, cattle, hogs, horses, etc.). *Daughter:* MARTHA Ming. No executor. *Witnesses:* LUKE GREGORY, WILLIAM POWEL. *Clerk of the Court:* JAMES CRAVEN. The original of this will missing. Abstract made from recorded copy in Grant Book No. 4, Will No. 28.

HOSEA, ABRAM.   Pasquotank County.
   May 31, 1771. December 22, 1773. *Wife:* MARY. *Daughter:* LOVEY, wife of JOHN SMITH ("my manner plantation"). *Nephew:* ABRAM HOSEA (land on Little Alligator, in Tyrrell County). *Brother:* ROBERT HOSEA. *Trustee:* THOMAS NICHOLSON. *Executors:* JOHN POOL and JOHN SMITH. *Witnesses:* MATTHEW PRITCHARD, LEMUEL STONE, PETER ROSHALL. Will proven before Jo. MARTIN.

HOSEA, JOSEPH.   Perquimans County.
   May 10, 1753. July Court, 1753. *Sons:* JOSEPH and WILLIAM HOSEA. *Wife and Executrix:* MARY. *Executor:* JOHN HOSEA (brother). *Witnesses:* JAMES GIBSON, WILLIAM TRUMBALL. *Clerk of the Court:* EDMUND HATCH.

HOSEA, ROBERT.   Perquimans County.
   December 17, 1742. January Court, 1742. *Sons:* ABRAHAM, JOSEPH, WILLIAM (*Executor*), THOMAS (*Executor*). *Wife:* ANN. *Witnesses:* JACOB MULLEN and WM. TOMBLIN. *Clerk of the Court:* EDMUND HATCH.

HOSKINS, THOMAS.   Chowan County.
   October 24, 1733. April Court, 1734. *Son and Executor:* WILLIAM. *Daughters:* SARAH CHASTLON, MATHEW MARY. *Son-in-law:* WM. LUTON. *Executor:* JOHN BENBURY. *Witnesses:* JOHN MITCHENER, JAMES SMITH. *Clerk of the Court:* MOSELEY VAIL.

HOSKINS, WILLIAM. "Matacomack Creek in Albemarle Co."
   January 20, 1692–1693. *Brother:* THOMAS HOSKINS. *Cousin:* DANIEL COX, JR. *Executor:* DANIEL COX. *Witnesses:* THOMAS MORIS, NICHOLAS DAW. No probate.

HOSMER, HANNAH.   Onslow County.
   March 26, 1773. May 18, 1773. *Sons:* JOHN and STANTON SPOONER. *Executor:* STANTON SPOONER. *Other children:* mentioned, but not named. *Witnesses:* REUBEN GRANT, EXPERIENCE GRANT. Will proven before Jo. MARTIN.

HOUGHTON, THOMAS.   Bladen County.
   January Court, 1743. *Daughter:* MARY HOUGHTON. *Executors:* ELIZABETH (wife), JOSHUA and WILLIAM HOUGHTON (brothers). *Witnesses:* DAVID BUTLER, MARY BUTLER. *Clerk of Court:* RICH'D MCCLURE.

HOUGHTON, WILLIAM.   Chowan County.
   February 28, 1744–1745. July Court, 1745. *Son:* JONATHAN. *Daughters:* MARY and SARAH HOUGHTON. *Wife and Executrix:* MARY. *Ex-*

ecutors: WILLIAM HOUGHTON (father), DAVID and JAMES HOUGHTON (brothers). *Witnesses:* DAVID BUTLER, MARY HOUGHTON. *Clerk of the Court:* EDMUND HATCH.

HOUSE, GEORGE.   Bertie County.

September 28, 1770. January 3, 1771. *Son and Executor:* THOMAS. *Grandsons:* GEORGE, BALIS, JAMES and JOHN HOUSE. *Granddaughters:* SARAH HOUSE, EDITH HOUSE, ANN, MARY and ELIZABETH SMITH. *Daughters:* ANN AVERET, ELIZABETH MOORE. *Executor:* JAMES MOORE (son-in-law). *Witnesses:* BENJAMIN PARKER, LEWIS HAYLES, WILLIAM HOUSE. Proven before WM. TRYON. Lands on Flagg Run, Little Roquis and other waters devised to son and grandsons.

HOUSE, THOMAS.   Albemarle County.

July 4, 1733. *Sons:* GEORGE, BAYLIS (*Executor*). *Daughters:* ANN and EDITH HOUSE. *Witnesses:* ROBERT POWELL, MARMADUKE NORFLEET. No probate.

HOUSTON, MOSES.   Carteret County.

January, 1774. January 27, 1774. *Wife:* MARGRETT. *Daughter:* MERIAM WEST (plantation on Whittock River). *Grandson:* HOUSTON ROBERTS. *Granddaughters:* JAMIMA DUDLEY, BONETA WILLIAMS, FANNIE DUDLEY, SARAH MADDUX. *Other legatee:* CAPT. GEORGE MITCHEL. *Executors:* BAZELL SMITH, BRICE WILLIAMS and MICAJAH FRAZIAR. *Witnesses:* JAMES MEAD, WILLIAM RAMSEY, PASLEY JACOBS. Proven before JO. MARTIN.

HOUSTON, THOMAS.   Onslow County.

March 29, 1733. July 3, 1733. *Sons:* WILLIAM, MOSES, JAMES, THOMAS. *Daughter:* ELIZIBETH HOUSTON. *Wife and Executrix:* MARY. *Witnesses:* NICHOLAS HUNTOR, SAM'LL JONES, JR., REBECKAH HUNTER. *Clerk of the Court:* WM. CRANFORD.

HOUSTON, WILLIAM.   Carteret County.

May 6, 1760. January 2, 1761. *Son:* WILLIAM. *Wife and Executrix:* RACHEL. *Executors:* SAMUEL and JAMES NOBLE (brothers of wife). *Witnesses:* JOSEPH NOBLE, MARK NOBLE and BETTY NOBLE. Will proven before ARTHUR DOBBS.

HOVER, JOHN JACOB.   Craven County.

February 15, 1744. November 28, 1744. *Sons:* JACOB, JOHN (plantation on Beards Creek), HENRY, SAMUEL. *Daughters:* MARY SLABBACH, ELIZABETH SLABBACH, MARGARETH. *Wife and Executrix:* MARY MAGDA-

LENA. *Executor:* NICHOLAS PUREFOY. *Witnesses:* JOHN GRANADE, GEORGE GRAHAM, JAMES WILLCOCKS. Will proven before E. MOSELEY, *Chief Justice.*

HOWARD, CHARLES. Craven County.

1754. *Son:* CHARLES. *Daughters:* SARAH BROOKS and COURTNEY IVES. *Son-in-law:* JACOB HANBOX (or HANCOX). To each of these is bequeathed 'one shilling apease as the Law directs." *Granddaughter:* SIBBE BROOKS ("land in the fork of Crounes creek, if not sold before I die, quietly to be possessed during her pleasure.") *Wife, Residuary Legatee, and Executrix:* MARY. *Witnesses:* FRAN. FONTAINE, WILLIAM ARTHER, ANN SPINKS. No probate.

HOWARD, JAMES. Bertie Precinct.

October 6, 1729. *Sons:* SOLOMON ("my plantation"), JAMES, EDWARD, SAMUELL, JOHN. To these sons is conveyed lands in Virginia, and lands on Aharskey Swamp, Cooneriskratt Swamp, Horse Swamp, etc. *Daughter:* SARAH HOWARD. *Wife and Executrix:* SARAH. *Other legatees:* FRANCIS SPEIGHT of Chuckatuck parish in Nancemond County, Va., THOMAS DAVIS (land lying on Rattlesnake Branch). *Executor:* JAMES HOWARD (son). *Witnesses:* JOHN RAWLEY (?), MARY BARKETT, WM. CRAFFORD, GEO. OTWAY. Codicil dated October 9, 1729. *Witnesses to Codicil:* JAS. SPEIR, MARY BURKETT, ANN STONE, GEO. OTWAY. No probate.

HOWCOTT, JOHN. Bertie Precinct.

July 28, 1732. September 12, 1733. *Sons:* EDWARD (land called by the name of Stancells); JOHN (dwelling plantation); RICHARD, NATHANIEL. *Daughters:* ELIZABETH BRANCH, MARY HOWCOTT. *Wife:* MARY. *Executors:* EDWARD HOWCOTT (brother) and EDWARD HOWCOTT (son). *Witnesses:* JOHN FRYARD, EDWARD HOWCOTT, ELIZABETH BRANCH. Will proven before GEO. BURRINGTON.

HOWELL, JOSEPH. Edgecombe County.

January 10, 1749. May Court, 1750. *Sons:* JOSEPH, THOMAS (land on Herricks Creek). *Daughters:* MARY, MURPHREY and MARTHA. *Wife and Executrix:* MARGETT. *Executors:* JOSEPH HOWELL (son), COLL. J. DAWSON, SAMUEL RUFFIN, THOMAS HOWELL and JOSEPH HENDERSON. *Witnesses:* JOS. WILLIAMSON, JAS. BARRAN, THOS. BARRAN. *Clerk of Court:* BENJAMIN WYNNS.

HOWSON, WILLIAM. Beaufort County.

November 13, 1713. April 5, 1715. Testator bequeathes all property to his mother, who is not named. *Witnesses:* HENRY SLADE, WILLIAM CORDING, JOHN STAFFORD. *Clerk of the Court:* JNO. DRINKWATER.

ABSTRACT OF WILLS, 1690—1760.   175

HUBBARD, RANE.
March 30, 1714. *Executors and legatees:* WILLIAM EVERIGIN, JOSEPH GLAISTER. *Witnesses:* WILLIAM SIMSON, MARY MURDEN, MARY MASON. No probate.

HUCKINS, DANIEL.   Bath County.
March 26, 1733. June Court, 1733. *Sons and Executors:* SOLOMON and VALLINTY. *Wife and Executrix:* ANN. *Witnesses:* JOHN JACOB HONOR, RICHARD SCOTT. *Clerk of the Court of Craven County:* CALEB METCALFE.

HUDDE, CHRISTOPHER.   Beaufort County.
July 27, 1714. January 5, 1714. *Daughters:* PRUSILY, ELIZABETH GREEN (*Executrix*). *Witnesses:* THO. HENDERSON, JOHN SNEAD. *Clerk of the Court:* JNO. DRINKWATER.

HUDSON, JOSEPH.
Letters issued May 30, 1745. *Sons:* JOSEPH (*Executor*), LEWIS. *Daughters:* SARAH NEKELLES, SUSANAH, ELESEBETH. *Wife and Executrix:* MARY. *Witnesses:* BENJAMIN CARTREET, JOHN DUGEN, JONATHAN BATEMAN. No probate or county given.

HUGGENS, ANN.   Onslow County.
February 30, 1745–1746. May 22, 1746. *Sons:* CHARLES and BENJAMIN (land in Maryland), MATTHEW and JACOB (*Executors*). *Grandson:* JACOB HURLEY (son of ANN HURLEY). *Granddaughter:* LUCREASEA HUGGENS (daughter of MATTHEW HUGGENS). *Witnesses:* R. CHEASTEN, JOHN NORMAN, CATRINE PAULL. Will proven before E. HALL, C. J.

HUGGINS, EDMOND.   Onslow County.
April 12, 1737. July 6, 1737. *Son:* PHILIP. *Other legatees:* ABRAHAM HUGGINS, MARY HUGGINS (daughter of NEHEMIAH), JOHN HUGGINS, THOMAS HILLIARD, THOMAS OWIN, EDWARD EDWARDS. *Executor:* JOHN STARKEY. *Witnesses:* ABRA. MITCHELL, THOS. OWIN. *Clerk of the Court:* WM. CRANFORD.

HUGGINS, JAMES.   Onslow County.
January 24, 1745–1746. May 22, 1746. *Sons:* CHARLES and BENJAMIN (lands in Maryland); JACOB and MATHEW (*Executors*). *Grandson:* JACOB (son of ANN HURLEY). *Granddaughter:* LUCRESEA (daughter of MATTHEW HUGGINS). *Witnesses:* R. CHEASTEN, JOHN NORMAN, CATRINE PAULL. Will proven before E. HALL, C. J.

HUGGINS, JOHN.   Onslow County.
July 15, 1745. February Court, ———. *Son:* JOHN ("plantation whereon I now dwell on Bear Creek"). *Brother:* NEHEMIAH HUGGENS.

Wife: MARY. *Executors:* JOHN and PETER STARKEY. *Witnesses:* SARAH STARKEY, DANIEL SHERLOW, JOSEPH WATTS. *Clerk of Court:* WILL HEDGES.

HULL, JOHN.   Edenton, Chowan County.

January 14, 1747. March 23, 1752. *Wife:* not named. *Sisters:* CATHERINE and MARY HULL (in Rhode Island). *Other legatee:* ANNAH MARTIN. *Executors:* MILES GALE and JAMES CRAVEN. *Witnesses:* HUMPHREY ROBINSON, SAMUEL ROBINSON, ALEXR. FORBES. Will proven before GAB. JOHNSTON and recorded by SAM'L ORMES, *Deputy Secretary.* The testator makes some interesting provisions as to his burial.

HUMES, JAMES.   Beaufort County.

February 6, 1745. March Court, 1745. *Wife:* ELISABETH. *Daughters:* ABIGAIL ("the plantation whereon I now live called by the name of Cappell Point"), ELISABETH HUCHLEROY, MARY (land on Thomases Creek on South Side of Bear River), RENNIS. *Executor:* JOSIAS JONES. *Witnesses:* WM. BETSWORTH, MARY CRICKMAN, URIAH LAMBERT. *Clerk of the Court:* JOHN FORBES.

HUMPHRIES, JOHN.   Pasquotank Precinct.

December 2, 1708. *Sons:* JOHN, WILLIAM, CHRISTOPHER and JOHN (two JOHNS named). *Daughters:* MARY GRAY, SARAH BRAY. *Son-in-law:* GRIFFITH GRAY. *Executor:* WILLIAM HUMPHRIES (son). *Witnesses:* JOHN ULAN, FR. MCBRIDE, SOL. HARAERY (?). No probate.

HUMPHRIES, RICHARD.   Albemarle County.

October 7, 1688. July 25, 1689. *Mother:* mentioned, but not named. *Other legatees:* WILLIAM NICKOLE, JOHN HUNT. *Executor:* THOMAS POLLOCK. *Witnesses:* ELIZEBETH BARCLIFF, JOHN ROPER, WILLIAM BARCLIFT. Will proven before SETH. SOTHELL.

HUMPHREY, JOSEPH.   Bladen County.

October 14, 1752. December Court, 1752. *Cousin:* SARAH ROBERTS. *Nephew:* JOSEPH HUMPHREY. *Friend:* EVAN ELLIS. To Carvers Creek Meeting is given three pounds. *Executors:* JONATHAN EVANS and ISAAC JONES. *Witnesses:* ALEXANDER MCCONKEY, THOMAS SPEIRS. *Clerk of the Court:* THOS. ROBESON.

HUNT, JOHN.   Little River (county not given).

April 7, 1710. August 26, 1710. *Grandsons:* JOHN HUNT EVANS, BARTHOLOMEW EVANS. *Granddaughter:* ELIZABETH EVANS. *Wife:* ELIZABETH. *Executor:* JAMES TOOKE (TOOLE). *Witnesses:* W. EVERIGIN, JOSEPH PARISE, THO. COMMANDER. Will proven before THOMAS CARY, *President.*

HUNT, THOMAS. Pasquotank County.

May 7, 1688. October 2, 1696. *Brother and Executor:* ANDREW HUNT of Bucks County, England. *Other legatees:* JOHN and THOMAS HAWKINS (sons of JOHN HAWKINS). *Witnesses:* EDWARD SMITH, WILLIAM COLLINGS, JOHN CABAGE. *Clerk:* W. GLOVER.

HUNTER, ANN. Chowan County.

May 24, 1749. October Court, 1751. *Sons and Executors:* WM. HUNTER and EDWARD ARNAL. *Daughters:* JUDITH BLAND, ANN WINBORN, HESTER KNIGHT, ALICE ARNAL. *Witnesses:* SARY OSBORN, WM. HUNTER, JOHN PARKER, JOSEPH PARKER. *Clerk of the Court:* JAMES CRAVEN.

HUNTER, ISAAC. Chowan County.

April 17, 1752. April Court, 1753. *Sons:* ELISHA ("my plantation whereon I now live and plantation whereon he now lives, together with one negro), JESSE (land purchased of THOMAS MORRIS and one negro), ISAAC (land in Bertie, together with one negro), DANIEL (70 pounds "current money"). *Daughters:* HANNAH RIDDICK, ELIZABETH PERRY, ALCE HUNTER, RACHELL WALTON and SARAH HUNTER (one negro to each). *Grandchildren:* JESSE, PHILIP and MARY PERRIES and SARAH FIELD. *Other legatee:* ZILPHEA PARKER. Water-mill bequeathed to son JACOB. *Executor:* ELISHA HUNTER (son). *Witnesses:* MOSES SUMNER, SAMUEL SUMNER, JOHN SUMNER. *Clerk of the Court:* JAMES CRAVEN. Impression of dragon on seal.

HUNTER, JOHN.

June 13, 1753. October 25, 1756, "township of Little Brittan, County of Lancaster and province of Pencalvania." *Wife and Executrix:* AGNESS. *Daughters:* MARY and CATRIN. *Witnesses:* JOHN MCBURNEY, ADAM LECKY. *Deputy Register:* EDWARD SHIPPEN. This is a certified copy from the records of Lancaster County, Pa.

HUNTER, NICHOLAS. Carteret County.

January 3, 1749–1750. March Court, 1749. *Sons:* STEPHEN ("all land on the West side of Gailes Branch"), EZEKELL, LEBBEUS, WILLIAM, JOAB. *Grandson:* GEORGE MILLCHELL. *Daughters:* E———, ZILLAH, REACHELL, KISIAH MILLCHELL, ELIZEBATH, SARAH, RUTH. *Wife and Executrix:* REBECCA. *Executor:* EZEKELL HUNTER (son). *Witnesses:* JOHN WILLCOCKS, MOSES HOUSTON, JOHN GILLETT. *Clerk of the Court:* GEO. READ.

HUNTER, ROBERT. Bertie County.

June 3, 1753. August Court, 1753. *Sons:* HENRY, MOSES (*Executor*). *Daughters:* SARAH DOCTON, MARY GORDON, JUDITH PERRY, SUSANNAH

BENTON, ELIZABETH WILLIAMS. *Executor:* THOS. WHITMELL. *Witnesses:*
JNO. HILL, JOHN SLATTER, OEN SLATTER, LITTLETON SLATTER, KEZIAH
SLATTER, WILLIAM APPERSON. *Clerk of the Court:* SAM'L ORMES.

HUNTER, WILLIAM.   Chowan County.

January 4, 1732–1733. January 18, 1732. *Sons and Executors:* WILLIAM and EPHRAIM. *Daughters:* JUDITH, ALLISE and MARY HUNTER, ANN, EASTER. *Wife:* ANN. *Witnesses:* SPENCER COLE, ISAAC HUNTER, ROBERT HUNTER. *Clerk of the Court:* RT. FORSTER.

HUNTER, WILLIAM.   Chowan County.

March 21, 1749. April Court, 1750. *Sons:* JOHN, NICHOLAS, HARDY, WILLIAM, JOB, JAMES, TIMOTHY. *Wife and Executrix:* SARAH. *Executor:* JOHN HUNTER (son). *Witnesses:* ELISHA HUNTER, JOHN GOURDON, JOHN NORFLEET. *Clerk of the Court:* WILL MEARNS.

HURDLE, BENJAMIN.   Perquimans County.

February 14, 1734. July Court, 1735. *Legatees:* WILLIAM HURDLE, MORING HURDLE and ELIZABETH HURDLE (mother). No executor. *Witnesses:* NATHANIEL WILLIAMS, DANIEL RAGESON, JOSEPH RIDDICK. *Clerk of Court:* JAMES CRAVEN.

HUSBANDS, RICHARD.

August 16, 1732. September 15, 1732, "late of Barbadoes but now of ye Country of North Carolina in ye Cape Fear." *Sons:* RICHARD and JOHN ("now in Barbadoes"). *Executrix and Wife:* JANE. *Witnesses:* ELIZABETH HALL, ELIZABETH BRYAN, THOS. HALL. Will proven before GEO. BURRINGTON.

HUTSON, WILLIAM.   Craven County.

January 29, 1739–1740. March 3, 1739. *Wife:* FRANCES. *Executor:* JOSEPH MARR. *Witnesses:* JOSIAH HART, ELISHA JAQUES. Will proven before GAB. JOHNSTON.

HYRNE, HENRY.   New Hanover County.

September 9, 1772. October 26, 1773. *Nephews:* HENRY WALTERS (plantation called "New Hyrnham"; also 1,747 acres of land in New Hanover), JOSEPH and GEORGE WALTERS, MOSES, FRANCIS and HENERY BRITTON. *Niece:* MARY BRITTON. *Goddaughter:* ELIZABETH JONES (daughter of FREDERICK JONES). *Executor:* FREDERICK JONES (two volumes of Chambers' Dictionary). *Witnesses:* SAM'LL SWANN, JOHN BUFORD, BENJAMIN WILLIAMS, WILLIAM BUFORD. Codicil of even date disposes of wearing apparel. *Witnesses to Codicil:* JOHN BUFORD, WILLIAM BUFORD, BENJAMIN WILLIAMS. Proven before JO. MARTIN.

INGRAM, ABSALOM (or ABRAHAM). Onslow County.

October 20, 1744. November 24, 1744. *Sons:* DAVID (land known as "Weakes Iland"), ISAAC, ABRAHAM and JAMES (20 shillings each). *Executor:* DAVID INGRAM (son). *Witnesses:* JOHN WHITE, LAZARUS KENNY. *Justice of the Peace:* JOHN STARKEY. Will proven before GAB. JOHNSTON.

INNES, JAMES.

July 5, 1754. October 9, 1759. "Of Cape Fear in North Carolina. Col. of the Regement of sd Province raised for His Majesty's imediate Service and Commander in Chief of the Expedition to the Ohio against the French and there Indians who have most unjustly Invaided & Fortified themselves on His Majestys Lands." "Being now reddey to Enter upon action & of sound minde, Memory and understanding etc." "I direct a remittance may be made to Edinburgh Sufficient to pay for a Church Bell for the Parish Church of Cannesby in Caithness agreeable to my letter to MR. JAMES BROADEE Minister there." "I also give and bequeath att the death of my loving wife JEAN INNES my plantation called Point Pleasant & the opposite Mash land over the River for which there is a separate patent, two negro young women, one Negroe young man and there increase, all the Stock of Cattle and Hogs halfe the stock of horses belonging att the time to that plantation with all my Books and one hundred Pounds Sterling or the Equivalent there unto in the Currency of the Country For the Use of a Free School for the Benefite of the Youth of North Carolina." The colonel of the New Hanover Regiment, the Parson and Vestry of the Wilmington Church appointed trustees to carry out the foregoing provision. *Executrix:* JEAN INNES (wife). *Witnesses:* JOHN CARLYLE, W. COCKS, CALEB GRAINGER. Will made and executed at Winchester in Virginia. Proven before ARTHUR DOBBS.

IRBY, HENRY. Brunswick County.

January 30, 1733. February 12, 1733–1734. *Sons:* WILLIAM, HENRY ("plantation up North West and House and Lott in Cape Fair to hold in common with ELIZABETH, his sister, and FORTUNE HOLEDERLEY their mother"). *Daughters:* ANN and ELIZABETH IRBY. *Executrix:* FORTUNE HOLEDERLEY. *Witnesses:* JAMES ESPY, ROBT. EATON, WILLIAM POWER. Will proven before GEO. BURRINGTON.

IRVING, ROBERT. Currituck County.

February 16, 1735–1736. "According to the Computation of the Church of England, April 5, 1737." *Executor and sole legatee and devisee:* GEORGE POWERS. *Witnesses:* W. WHITE, CHARLES WALPOLE, HUMPHRY VINCE, RICHARD SPAN. *Clerk of the Court:* WM. SHERGOLD.

ISHAM, JAMES.   Duplin County.

November 2, 1752. July Court, 1753. *Sons:* JAMES, CHARLES. *Daughter:* MARGARET. *Wife and Executrix:* JANE. *Executors:* EVAN ELLIS and EDWARD HARRISON, JUNIOR (brothers-in-law). *Witnesses:* WM. HOUSTON, WM. MCKEE, JOHN DUNN. *Clerk of the Court:* JOHN DICKSON.

ISLANDS (spelled also "ILANDS"), RICHARD.
                                              Currituck Precinct.

March 7, 1733. October Court, 1735. *Sons:* ROBERT (150 acres of land in Princess Ann County), GEORGE (land in Currituck), RICHARD. *Daughters:* SARAH ILANDS (100 acres of land in Princess Ann County), JANE WAYE, ELIZABETH ROULINGS. *Wife and Executrix:* ELIZABETH. *Witnesses:* FRANCIS MORSE, JOHN ROSE, MOSES FICHER. *Clerk:* JAMES CRAVEN.

ISLER, CHRISTIAN.   Craven County.

October 4, 1747. November 7, 1747. *Sons:* JOHN ("one negro, and horse, saddle & bridle"), WILLIAM (plantation and two negroes). *Daughters:* ELIZABETH and SUSANNAH ISLER. *Wife:* ELIZABETH. *Executors:* FREDERICK ISLER (brother), JOHN and WILLIAM ISLER (sons). *Witnesses:* MELCHER REMM, JAMES MARSHEL, SARAH LICKBLAT. Proven before E. HALL, C. J.

ISMAY, JOHN.   Edenton, Chowan County.

January 12, 1729. August 5, 1732. *Daughter:* NANCY (lots 11 and 12 in Edenton). *Wife and Executrix:* SARAH. *Trustees:* JOHN LOVICK and EDW'D MOSELEY. *Witnesses:* SARAH ROWDEN, JNO. MATTHEWS, WILL'M WILLIAMS. Will proven before GEO. BURRINGTON.

IVES, JOHN.   Craven County.

February 21, 1750. August Court, 1752. *Sons:* JOB ("½ of my land at the head of Broad Creek"), JONAS (" loer half of my land on Broad Creek"). *Daughters:* ESTHER (land on south side of Broad Creek called Giddinses Point). *Executor:* JOB IVES (son). *Witnesses:* JAMES WHITING, JACOB JONES, FRANCES NASH. *Clerk of the Court:* PHIL. SMITH.

IVES, THOMAS.   Currituck County.

October 26, 1750. April Court, 1751. *Daughter:* ELISABETH IVES. *Wife and Executrix:* MARY. *Witnesses:* JOHN WOODHOUSE, JAMES PARKER, RODE ALLEN. *Clerk of the Court:* RICH'D MCCLURE.

JACKSON, DANIEL.   Pasquotank County.

February 14, 1734–1735. January 10, 1737. *Sons:* DANIEL, SAMUEL, DAVID ("my plantation"), WILLIAM, JOAB ("long glade tract of land").

Daughters: RUTH, ANN and ELISABETH JACKSON. *Wife and Executrix:* ANN. *Executors:* ZACHARIAS and SAMUEL JACKSON (sons). *Witnesses:* WM. SIMSON, JR., JOHN SIMSON, JUNR. *Clerk of the Court:* JOS. SMITH. *Justice of the Peace:* JAMES CRAVEN.

JACKSON, DAVID. Little River.

September 12, 1715. January 9, 1715–1716. *Son:* THOMAS. *Daughter:* ELIZABETH. *Wife and Executrix:* MARY. *Brothers:* WILLIAM and AARON DAVIS, SAMUELL JACKSON. *Cousin:* LUCY JACKSON. *Witnesses:* JOS. HORNY, SAMUELL DAVIS, DANIEL JACKSON. No signature of probate officer.

JACKSON, ISAAC. Bath County.

September 7, 1716. April 2, 1718. *Son:* THOMAS ("my plantation"). *Daughters:* ELIZABETH CHESTER, RACHELL ADAMS, MARGRIT. *Friend:* JOHN JORDAN. *Wife and Executrix:* ELIZABETH. *Witnesses:* JOHN JORDAN, THO. MORRIS, ELIZABETH MORRIS. *Clerk of the Court:* JNO. DRINKWATER.

JACKSON, JOHN. Bath County.

July 30, 1728. March Court, 1728. *Legatees:* JOHN CHESTER (*Executor*), EDWARD POYNER (*Executor*), NICHOLASS SMITH, ELIZABETH CHESTER, WILLIAM WHITFORD. *Witnesses:* NICHOLAS SMITH, WILLIAM WHITFORD, JEAN SMITH. *Clerk of the Court:* JOHN MATTOCKE.

JACKSON, ROBERT. Chowan County.

January 21, 1757. October Court, 1757. *Wife and Executrix:* ANN. *Witnesses:* JASPER CHARLTON, ABIGAIL CHARLTON. *Clerk of the Court:* THO. JONES.

JACKSON, SAMUEL. Pasquotank County.

December 3, 1748. January 19, 1748. *Sons:* JOHN ("upper part of plantation"), JOSHUA ("remainder of my land"). *Daughters:* ELISABETH BENTON, MIRIAM POOL, MARY CARTWRIGHT, MARY ANN LOVEL. *Wife:* ELISABETH. *Executors:* JOHN and JOSHUA JACKSON (sons). *Witnesses:* ABRAHAM RANKHORN, SAMUEL BENTON, JOSEPH ROBINSON. Will proven before GAB. JOHNSTON.

JACKSON, SAMUEL. Pasquotank County.

March 20, 1750. April Court, 1750. *Sons:* ABSALOM ("plantashion whereon I now live"), MATHIAS (land described in will). *Daughters:* MARY and HANAH JACKSON. *Wife and Executrix:* MARY. *Executor:* DANIEL JACKSON (brother). *Witnesses:* JACOB MADREN, ANN JACKSON, ELIZABETH BENTON. *Clerk of the Court:* THOMAS TAYLOR.

JACKSON, THOMAS.   Bertie County.
    March 15, 1746. May Court, 1753. *Sons:* THOMAS ("plantation known as Mount Garriot, together with my ferry"), WILLIAM (plantation bought of RICHARD MARTIN), JOHN (plantation in Northampton County), JAMES (plantation in Bertie County). *Wife's daughter:* ELIZABETH HAMMOND GRIFFIN. *Wife:* HESTER. *Executors:* JOHN BROWN, son of DR. JAS. BROWN, dec'd, BENJAMIN WYNNS and HESTER JACKSON. *Brother:* JEREMIAH JACKSON of Boston. Codicil dated April 9, 1749, changes division of land among sons, and appoints as *Executors:* BENJAMIN WYNNS, WILLIAM WYNNS and HESTER JACKSON. No witnesses or signature to codicil. *Witnesses to will:* WM. POWER, JAMES GRIFFIN, BETTY GRIFFIN, CATHERN CONNER. *Clerk of the Court:* BENJAMIN WYNNS.

JACKSON, WILLIAM.   Albemarle County.
    March 3, 1694. *Sons:* ZACHARIAS and DANIELL. *Wife:* ELIZABETH. Will proven before W. GLOVER. Part of this will is torn away.

JACKSON, WILLIAM, SENR.   Albemarle County.
    February 21, 1695–1696. March Court, 1697. *Sons:* WILL JACKSON, JR., ZACHARIAH, DAVID, SAMUEL, DANIEL (plantation on the easternmost branch of Herrin Creek). *Daughter:* RUTH DAVIS. *Wife:* ELIZABETH JACKSON. *Executors:* ZACHARIAH and DANIEL JACKSON. *Witnesses:* HUGH CAMPBELL, RICH'D PLATER, WM. SIMSON. *Clerk of the Court:* WILLIAM GLOVER.

JACKSON, WILLIAM, JR.   Perquimans County.
    February 1, 1734. April 20, 1735. *Sons:* MOSES and AARON ("plantation whereon I now dwell"). *Daughters:* PARTHENIA and MARGARET JACKSON. *Wife and Executrix:* MARGARET. *Witnesses:* GEORGE GORDING, WM. JACKSON, SR., EDWARD JACKSON, THOMAS WEEKES. *Clerk of the Court:* JAMES CRAVEN.

JACKSON, ZACHARIAS.   Pasquotank County.
    October 18, 1748. August 4, 1749. *Sons:* SIMON ("the plantation"), DEMCE (land bought of JOHN ALLBIRD), ACE (plantation bought of THOMAS HARRIS), LAMUEL. *Daughter:* DARKES JACKSON. *Wife:* ELIZABETH. *Executors:* WILLIAM and JOAB JACKSON (brothers). *Witnesses:* DAN'L JACKSON, SR., SAMUEL JACKSON, DAVID JACKSON. Will proven before GAB. JOHNSTON at Eden House.

JACOB, ISAAC.   Currituck County.
    March 19, 1713–1714. July 14, 1714. *Daughters:* SUSANAH JACOB ("my manor plantation at New Corotuck"), JANE JACOB ("a tract of land in New Corotuck on ye head of Deep Creek"). *Overseers:* JOHN PROCKTER, BEN-

JAMIN SANDERSON. *Wife and Executrix:* SARAH. *Witnesses:* JOSEPH SANDERSON, DINAH, NELL, WILLIAM ASHLEY. *Clerk of the Court:* JOS. WICKER.

JACOCKS, THOMAS.   County not given.

May 2, 1692. August Court, 1692. *Executrix and sole legatee: Wife,* not named. *Witnesses:* PATRICK BEALLY (or BAYLEY), RICHARD ROOKE. *Clerk, Sect. Office:* W. GLOVER.

JAMES, EDWARD.   Pasquotank County.

February 8, 1720. April Court, 1721. *Sons:* EDWARD ("my manner plantation"), GILBERT. *Sons-in-law:* DOSER BETS, HEZEKIAH. *Cousins:* JOSEPH and MARY MURFEY. *Witnesses:* STEPHEN SAUL, MARY HUTCHENSON, JOHN MARTYN. *Clerk pro tem.:* JOHN PALIN.

JAMES, WILLIAM.   Pasquotank County.

May 31, 1733. May 9, 1733. *Sons:* THOMAS ("plantation whereon I now live"), WILLIAM ("plantation I bought of THOMAS PALMER"), SAMUEL. *Daughters:* REBECCA JAMES and FRANCIS MACKEELE. *Wife and Executrix:* JANE. *Executor:* THOMAS JAMES (son). *Witnesses:* SAMUEL BUNDAY, JEAN BUNDAY, J. SWEENY. Will proven before GEO. BURRINGTON.

JAMES, WILLIAM.   Pasquotank County.

September 18, 1757. September Court, 1757. *Son:* WILLIAM ("my plantation"). *Daughter:* MILLY. *Wife and Executrix:* ANN. *Executor:* JOSEPH POOL. *Witnesses:* MATTHEW DUAN, ELIZABETH JAMES. *Clerk of the Court:* THOS. TAYLOR.

JARMAN, THOMAS.   Onslow County.

April 5, 1759. January Court, 1760. *Sons:* THOMAS, JOHN, MOSES, LARRANCE, WILLIAM. *Daughter:* MARY JARMAN. *Grandchildren:* WILLIAM and MARY JARMAN (children of WILLIAM). *Wife:* not named. *Executors:* JOHN JARMAN and MIKEL KOONE. *Witnesses:* JOHN JARMAN, JACOB MANER. *Clerk of the Court:* WILL'M CRAY.

JARRATT, JOHN.   Carteret County.

April 13, 1745. June Court, 1745. *Sons:* JOHN, JACOB, ABRAHAM, ISAAC. *Daughters:* SARAH, SUSANNAH and ESTHER JARRATT, SARAH SHEPARD, ELISABETH DUDLEY, ANN GASKILL, MARGARET WORD. *Wife and Executrix:* CATHERINE. *Witnesses:* GEORGE BELL, THOMAS LEWIS. *Clerk of the Court:* GEORGE READ.

JARVIS, FOSTER.   Currituck County.

December 3, 1750. January Court, 1750. *Sons:* SAMUELL (100 acres of land adjoining JOHN WOODHOUSE), JONATHAN (200 acres adjoining tract above devised), MARTAIN (361 acres of land), WILLIAM (360 acres of land), FOSTER. *Daughters:* ELIZABETH and FRANCIS JARVIS. *Grandson:* SAMUEL JARVIS. *Executor:* MARTAIN JARVIS (son). *Witnesses:* SAMUEL SALYER, HILLARY WHITE, MICHAEL O'NEEL, HENRY KINZEY. *Clerk of the Court:* RICH'D MCCLURE.

JASPER, RICHARD.   County not given.

October 30, 1722. *Son and Executor:* SAMUELL ("my plantation'). *Daughters:* ELIZABETH, ANN. *Wife and Executrix:* not named. *Witnesses:* CHARLES SMITH, CHARLES SMITH, JR., MARY SMITH.

JASPER, SAMUEL.   Hyde County.

March 29, 1752. March Court, 1753. *Sons:* SAMUEL ("all my land"), WILLIAM, JONATHAN and ISRAEL. *Daughters:* HANNAH LEATH (her children KEZIA and JOHN), ANN JASPER, MARY JASPER, LYDDELA JASPER. *Wife:* ANN. *Executors:* WILLIAM and JONATHAN JASPER (sons). *Witnesses:* ROGER MASON, JR., JOHN SLADE, JR., DORCAS LEATH. *Clerk of Court:* THOS. JORDAN.

JEFFREYS, CHRISTOPHER.   Perquimans County.

January 23, 1735. April Court, 1736. *Legatees:* ELIZABETH and JOSEPH POTTLE, of Pasquotank. *Executor:* JOSEPH POTTLE. *Witnesses:* SAMUEL SWANN, JOHN WILLCOCKS, PATRICK QUIDLE. *Clerk of Court:* JAMES CRAVEN.

JEFFREYS, ELIZABETH.   Northampton County.

June 20, 1742. February Court, 1742. *Sons:* JOHN HILLIARD, OSBORNE JEFFREYS, ROBERT HILLIARD, WILLIAM HILLIARD. *Daughter:* ELIZABETH (wife of JOHN BODDIE). *Grandsons:* WILLIAM, JAMES, ISAAC and ELIAS HILLIARD (sons of WILLIAM), JEREMIAH, JACOB and JOHN HILLIARD. *Granddaughter:* SARAH HILLIARD. *Executors:* JOHN HILLIARD and OSBORNE JEFFREYS (sons). *Witnesses:* I. EDWARDS, DAVID DICSON, MARY DUKE. *Clerk of the Court:* I. EDWARDS.

JEFFREYS, ELIZABETH.   Northampton County.

January 28, 1742. February 1, 1742. May Court, 1743. This is a nuncupative will proven before JOHN DAWSON by OSBORN JEFFREYS and RACHEL BOLLEN, and bequeathes all property to daughter, ELIZABETH BODDIE. Property consists of land, stock and negroes. *Executor:* OSBORN JEFFREYS. *Clerk of the Court:* I. EDWARDS.

The original of this will missing; abstract made from recorded copy No. 142, in Grant Book 4.

JENKINS, CHARLES.   Hertford County.

September 26, 1772. November 25, 1773. *Sons:* WILLIAM, HENRY ("plantation he now dwells on"), CHARLES ("plantation I now dwell on").

ABSTRACT OF WILLS, 1690—1760.   185

Daughter: ELIZABETH. *Executors:* HENRY JENKINS, WINBOURNE, WILLIAM and CHARLES JENKINS (sons) and WILLIAM MURFREE. *Grandsons:* CHARLES and SHURARD JENKINS (sons of WILLIAM). *Witnesses:* THOMAS WINBORNE, SARAH WINBORN. Will proven before JO. MARTIN.

JENNETT, ABRAHAM.   Perquimans County.

October Court, 1742. *Sons:* ISAKIAH, ABRAHAM, JEREMIAH. *Daughters:* ANN and ELISABETH JENNETT. *Wife and Executrix:* MARY. *Executors:* JOHN MOOR, SAMUEL HALL, RALPH DOE. *Clerk of the Court:* EDMUND HATCH.

JENNETT, JOHN.   Tyrrell County.

August 3, 1738. March Court, 1749. *Sons:* WILLIAM ("all my land"), JOHN and JABEZ. *Daughters:* ELIZABETH ALEXANDER, DOROTHY POPTEWELL, JEAN. *Wife:* DOROTHY. *Executor:* WILLIAM JENNETT (son). *Witnesses:* HENRY NORMAN, JOS. SPRUILL, SAM'L SPRUILL. *Clerk of the Court:* EVAN JONES.

JENNETT, JOHN.   Tyrrell County.

April 9, 1748. June Court, 1749. *Sons:* ABRAHAM, JOHN. *Daughters:* ANN and ELIZABETH JENNETT. *Grandson:* ABRAHAM JENNETT. *Wife and Executrix:* ANN. *Witnesses:* GEORGE CARON, ANN JENNETT ("JABEZ'S Daughter"), DANLL. GRANDIN. *Clerk of Court:* EVAN JONES.

JENNINGS, JOHN.   Pasquotank County.

April 15, 1751. July Court, 1751. *Son:* ISAAC. *Other children:* mentioned, but not named. *Wife and Executrix:* LUSE. *Witnesses:* ZACHARIAH KEETON, JOSEPH LAMBROSHER, NATHAN OVERMAN. Clerk's signature missing.

JENNINGS, MARY.   Currituck County.

December 7, 1725. October 7, 1729. *Son:* JOHN RELF. *Son-in-law and Executor:* JOHN NORTON. *Witnesses:* DAVID LINSEY, HENRY SMITH, JOHN MARTYN. *Clerk of the Court:* J. MARTYN.

JENNINGS, THOMAS.   New Hanover County.

December 23, 1744. *Son:* THOMAS ("my plantation"). *Wife and Executrix:* ELLINER. *Executor:* MICHAEL HIGGINS. *Witnesses:* JAS. MACKILWEAN, DANIEL DUPEE, ―― SHERLOCK. No probate.

JENNINGS, WILLIAM.   County not given.

January 24, 1686–1687. April Court, 1687. *Son and Executor:* JOHN. *Daughter:* ANN LATHUM. *Son-in-law:* RALPH GARRET. *Granddaughter:*

MARY GARRET. *Godson:* WILLIAM BARKCAKE. *Witnesses:* THOS. ROLFE, EDWARD CHAMBARS, WM. ROLFE. Officer before whom probated not named.

JENNINGS, WILLIAM.   Currituck County.

July 11, 1713. October Court, 1729. *Wife, Executrix and sole legatee:* MARY. *Witnesses:* JOHN BLISH, JOHN NORTON, MARGARET NORTON. *Clerk of the Court:* J. MARTYN.

JENOURE, JOSEPH, Surveyor General of North Carolina.

September 30, 1732. January 13, 1732. *Wife and Executrix:* ANN. *Son:* mentioned, but not named. *Witnesses:* WM. LITTLE, R. FOSTER. Proven before GEO. BURRINGTON.

JERNAGAN, JOHN.   Bertie Precinct.

January 10, 1733. February Court, 1733. *Sons:* THOMAS and GEORGE ("200 acres of land"), DAVID, JAMES (100 acres of land). *Executors:* TEMPERANCE JERNAGAN (wife), BENJAMIN HILL. *Witnesses:* JOHN CARROL, BARZILLA HEWITT, BENJAMIN HILL. *Clerk of Court:* RT. FORSTER.

JERNIGIN, HENRY.   Bertie Precinct.

May 9, 1736. August Court, 1736. *Sons:* HENRY (80 acres of land), JACOB ("my plantation"), JESSE (80 acres of land), DEMPSIE ("plantation I bought of THOMAS WATSON"). *Daughter:* ANN JONES. *Wife:* PHEBE. *Executors:* HENRY and JACOB JERNIGIN. To Henry is also given land in Va. in north side of Summersetts Creek. *Witnesses:* THEOPHILUS WILLIAMS, JOHN JERNIGAN, BENNETT BLACKMAN. *Clerk of the Court:* JOHN WYNNS.

JESSOP, JOSEPH.   Perquimans County.

March 12, 1735-1736. August 29, 1735. *Nephews:* THOMAS JESSOP ("plantation whereon I now live"), TIMOTHY and JONATHAN JESSOP. *Granddaughter:* MARY MAYO ("my plantation at the meeting house"). *Kinsman:* THOMAS PRITCHARD. *Brother:* THOMAS JESSOP. *Nieces:* MARY and ELIZABETH (daughters of THOMAS). *Wife and Executrix:* MARGARET. *Executors:* THOMAS JESSOP (brother), WILLIAM WHITE. *Witnesses:* THOMAS WINSLOWE, LEAH WINSLOWE, JOHN WILLSON. Will proven before W. SMITH, C. J.

JEVINS, ELIZABETH.   Pasquotank County.

February 5, 1734-1735. July 8, 1735. *Son:* ISAM SWINNEY. *Husband's nephew:* NATHANIEL CHEVIN. *Executor:* STEPHEN SCOTT. *Witnesses:* JOHN SCOTT, JOSEPH PINDLETON, J. JESSOP. *Clerk of the Court:* JOS. SMITH.

ABSTRACT OF WILLS, 1690—1760.   187

JEVINS, JOHN.   Pasquotank County.
May 14, 1734. April Court, 1735. *Wife and Executrix:* ELIZABETH. *Friend:* EDWARD MAYO. *Witnesses:* EDWARD MAYO, MARY MAYO, ANN BRYAN. *Clerk of the Court:* JOS. SMITH.

JEWELL, JOHN.   Beaufort County.
December 10, 1744. March Court, 1744. *Daughter:* ANNE JEWELL ("plantation whereon I now live on the Eastern Branch of Old Town Creek"). *Wife and Executrix:* MARTHA. *Executor:* JAMES ADAMS. *Witnesses:* JAMES ADAMS, MARY ADAMS, JOHN FORBES. *Clerk of the Court "pro hac vice":* JNO. TURNER.

JEWEL, THOMAS.   Beaufort County.
December 24, 1735. March 9, 1735. *Sons:* JOHN, BENJAMIN, SAMUEL and JAMES ("all my land to be equally divided between them"). *Wife and Executrix:* FRANCES. *Executor:* JOHN JEWEL (son). *Witnesses:* DANIEL BLIN, ELIZ. BEAHAN, JNO. COLLISON. *Justices:* ROBT. TURNER, SIMON ALDERSON, SETH PILKINTON. *Clerk of the Court:* JOHN COLLISON.

JOHNSTON, GABRIEL, Governor of North Carolina.
                                                 Granville County.
May 16, 1751. April 4, 1753. *Wife:* FRANCES (plantation called Possum Quarter in Granville County; plantation called Conahoe in Tyrrell and plantation in Bertie County on Salmon Creek). *Daughter:* PENELOPE JOHNSTON. *Nephews:* SAMUEL and JOHN JOHNSTON, HENRY JOHNSTON ("now at school at Newhaven in the Collony of Connecticut"). *Sister:* ELIZABETH SMEAR, of the County of Fife in North Britain. *Executors:* JOHNSTON and WILLIAM CATHCART. *Witnesses:* ANDREW LEAKE, SAMUEL ORMES, THOMAS WHITMELL. Proven before MATT. ROWAN. The following real estate devised: lands lying in Bertie, Northampton and Granville; 1,000 acres on Cypress Creek on the south side of Trent River; 980 acres on Trent River; 400 acres on the head of Trent and New Rivers; 7,000 acres on Deep River in Bladen County; all the small islands in Roanoke River in the neighbourhood of Mount Gallard. The following are items of interest: "And in case my wife shall choose to remain in North Carolina and reside upon the lands of and live with my daughter * * * my will is that she, my said wife, shall have the use of all my said daughter's plantations and for her encouragement to cultivate and improve these plantations, especially in raising silk, etc. * * * And I earnestly request my dearest wife to be a kind, tender mother to my dear little girl and to bring her up in the Fear of God and under a deep sense of her being always in his presence and in Sobriety and moderation confining her desires to things plain, neat and elegant, and especially to take care to keep within the bounds of her income and by no means to

run in debt." "My books I leave to WILLIAM CATHCART after my wife and brother have choose out of them any number not exceeding forty each. To my sister ELIZABETH SMEAR my large gold watch * * * ." Original missing. Recorded in Book 1755–1758, page 153.

JOHNSON, JAMES.   Albemarle County.

August 21, 1694. October Court, 1694. *Children:* WM. JOHNSON, JAMES JOHNSON and ELIZABETH JOHNSON. *Executor:* RICHARD ATKINSON. *Witnesses:* PATRICK KENADY, ANDREW DAVIE. *Clerk of the Court:* JOHN STEPNEY.

JOHNSON, JOHN.   County not given.

September 10, 1693. *Son-in-law:* LAWRENCE GONSOLVO. *Wife and Executrix:* SARAH. *Overseers:* CALEB CALLOWAY, JAMES HOGG, THO. LEPPER, THO. HAUGHTON, JOHN PORTER. No probate.

JOHNSON, JOHN.   Northampton County.

January 27, 1745–1746. August Court, 1753. *Granddaughter:* MARY JOHNSON BRIDGER. *Wife and Executrix:* MARY. *Witnesses:* JAMES JOHNSON, NICHOLAS BOON. *Clerk of the Court:* I. EDWARDS.

JOHNSON, JOHN.   Brunswick County.

March 1, 1750. February Court, 1752. St. Andrews Parish in Brunswick County. *Son and Executor:* WILLIAM ("my land and plantation"). *Daughters:* AMEY MITCHELL and ANN JELKS. *Granddaughters:* MARTHA and ANNE (daughters of WILLIAM). *Witnesses:* JOHN CARRELL, WILLIAM HOLLOWAY and WILLIAM MOSELEY. *Clerk of Edgecombe Court:* BENJ'N WYNNS.

JOHNSON, JOHN.   Hyde County.

September 1, 1756. March Court, 1757. *Son:* WILLIAM. *Daughter:* CATHERINE. *Wife and Executrix:* SARAH. *Witnesses:* JOHN JENNETT, THOMAS JONES, ABSALOM JONES. *Clerk of the Court:* STEPHEN DENNING.

JOHNSON, LEWIS.   Bath County.

October 9, 1711. *Sons:* RICHARD and WILLIAM. *Executor:* FARNIFOLD GREEN. *Witnesses:* CHRISTOPHER DAUSON, GEORGE GRAVE, ELIZABETH HOG. Original missing. Recorded in Book 1712–1722, page 53.

JOHNSTON, SAMUEL.   Onslow County.

November 13, 1756. January Court, 1736. *Sons:* SAMUEL and JOHN (6,500 acres of land on Cape Fear River). *Daughters:* JOAN, PENELOPE, ISOBELL, ANN, HANNAH (lands on Tuckahoe, together with negro slaves

belonging to testator). *Executor:* JOHN STARKEY. *Witnesses:* CARY
GODBE, WILLIAM WILLIAMS, JOHN MILTON. *Clerk of the Court:* WILLIAM
CRAY. Original missing. Recorded in Book 1753–1763, page 134.

JOHNSON, SUSANAH.   Chowan County.

August 13, 1717. July 29, 1718. *Son:* WILLIAM. *Grandson:* JACOB
PARROT. *Daughter and Executrix:* FRANCES RASOR. *Granddaughters:*
SUSANAH and ELIZABETH PARROT. *Godson:* EDWARD FREDERICK RASOR.
Friend: JOHN HARDY. *Witnesses:* LAURENCE SARTON, E———Z———,
WILLIAM WALTERS, PATRICK CANADA. *Clerk of the Court:* R. HICKS.

JOHNSTON, THOMAS.   Onslow County.

August 13, 1751. April Court, 1752. *Sons:* THOMAS, BENJAMIN, JOHN
("plantation I now live on"). *Daughters:* SARAH POWELL, ANN WHIT-
FIELD. *Granddaughters:* MARY, ANN and PRISCILLA KEEL. *Other legatee:*
MARGARET HOENS. *Wife:* ANN. *Executor:* THOMAS JOHNSTON (son).
Witnesses: ANTHONY LEWIS, JOHN BRABHAM, JOS. STURGES. *Clerk of
Court:* THO. BLACK.

JOHNSON, WILLIAM.   Albemarle County.

January 10, 1689. October 7, 1689. *Sons:* BENJAMIN and THOMAS.
Guardians: JOHN HAWKINS, THOMAS REFFER (?). *Wife and Executrix:*
MARY. *Witnesses:* THOMAS PRISE (PRICE), THOMAS COPER (COOPER),
THOMAS MILLER. *Clerk of the Court:* JOHN PHILPOTT. Will proven also
before THOS. ROLFE.

JOHNSON, WILLIAM.   Carteret County.

November 5, 1726. March 5, 1727–1728. *Sons:* THOMAS, JOHN STE-
PHEN and EZEKEL ("my land"). *Son-in-law:* THEO. NORWOOD. *Wife and
Executrix:* SARAH. *Witnesses:* ENOCH WARD, RICH'D CANADY, JOHN SIMP-
SON. *Clerk of the Court:* JOHN GALLAND.

JONES, ARTHUR.   Bladen County.

October 21, 1750. December Court, 1750. *Sons:* LEWIS, SIPHRES.
Daughter: ANN JONES. *Executors:* GERSHON BENBOW, GRIFFITH JONES.
Witnesses: CYPRIAN SHIPHERD, SAMUEL PIKE. *Clerk of the Court:* THOS.
ROBESON.

JONES, CHARLES.

April 25, 1693. July 15, 1695. *Legatees:* SARAH and TABYTHA ALFORD.
Executors: THOMAS SYMONS, JOHN MEEDS. *Witnesses:* ELLINER MELINE.
JACOB DENILLARD, JAMES DAMERELL. *Clerk Secretary's Office:* W. GLOVER.

JONES, CHARLES.   Bertie County.

February 5, 1739. February Court, 1748. *Sons:* CHARLES, JOHN, LANCELOT. *Daughter:* SARAH OUGHTREE. *Wife's daughter:* MARY JONES (land and plantation). *Wife and Executrix:* KATHIRAN. *Overseers:* CHRISTEFER HOLLOMAN, WILLIAM RASBARNY. *Witnesses:* NATHANIEL NICKLESS, JAMES OVERTON. *Clerk of the Court:* HENRY DELON.

JONES, CORNELIUS.   Albemarle County.

May 18, 1714. January 17, 1715. *Son:* CORNELIUS (land commonly called James Robinsons). *Daughters:* ELIZABETH and ANN. *Wife and Executrix:* ELIZABETH. *Witnesses:* WM. VAUGHAN, JOHN BLISH, FRANCES HARRISON. Will proven before JOHN BLISH and JOHN BETS.

JONES, CORNELIUS.   Currituck County.

August 14, 1749. January Court, 1750. *Sons:* WILLIAM, CORNELIUS ("my plantation"), TAYLOR. *Daughters:* RACHEL WHALE (?), ESTHER WHITE, RHODA CASLE, SARAH MOLBRON, BRIDGET JONES. *Wife and Executrix:* ELISABETH JONES. *Executor:* CORNELIUS JONES (son). *Witnesses:* WILLIAM WHITE, JOHN ANSELL, WILLIAM DUDLEY. *Clerk of Court:* RICH'D MCCLURE.

JONES, DANIELL.   Perquimans County.

October 10, 1713. February 21, 1714–1715. *Wife and Executrix:* SARAH. *Executors:* ARTHUR JONES (brother), TIMOTHY CLARE. *Witnesses:* JAMES MINGE, MATHIAS GILES. Executors qualified before C. EDEN.

JONES, DAVID.   Hyde County.

January 9, 1753. March Court, 1753. *Sons:* MORIS, THOMAS, CHRISTOPHER and ABRAHAM (to these four is devised land in Currituck County), RICHARD ("plantation I now live on"), CORNELIUS, SOLOMON (125 acres of land on Strohorn's Neck). *Daughters:* ELISEBETH MASON, ANN. *Executors:* ELIZABETH JONES (wife), THOMAS and MORRIS JONES (sons). *Witnesses:* SAMUEL SELBY, WILLIAM SELBY, SARAH JONES. *Clerk of the Court:* THOMAS JORDAN.

JONES, DAVID, SR.   Hyde County.

September 25, 1756. March Court, 1757. *Sons:* MORRIS ("my dwelling place"), DAVID, ABSALUM. *Daughter:* ELEZEBETH JONES. *Executors:* MORRIS and THOMAS JONES (brothers). *Wife:* ELEZEBETH. *Witnesses:* BENJA. MASON, EDWARD SPENSER, ABRAHAM JONES. *Clerk of the Court:* STEP'N DENNING.

JONES, EDWARD.   Pasquotank Precinct.

March 30, 1718. July 15, 1720. *Wife and Executrix:* ANN. *Brother:* JAMES JONES. *Daughters:* PRISCILLA JONES, ABIGALL JONES (land called the Ferny Ridge). To wife is given land called Basteba. *Brother-in-law:* WILLIAM ROOS. *Witnesses:* WILLIAM PHILLIPS, SAMUEL RANSHER. Original missing. Recorded in Book 1712–1722, page 246.

JONES, EDWARD.   Bladen County.

October 8, 1751. September Court, 1752. *Son and Executor:* ISAAC. *Daughters:* HANNAH LOCK, JANE ENECKS. *Grandsons:* ISAAC and WILLIAM ENECKS. *Granddaughter:* ANN ENECKS. *Wife:* SUSANNA. To Carver's Creek meeting is given ten pounds. *Witnesses:* JOHN SMITH, WM. SIBBLY, JOHN GRAY. *Justices:* BENJAMIN FITZRANDOLPH, HENRY SIMMOND, JONATHAN EVENS. *Clerk of the Court:* THOS. ROBESON.

JONES, EVAN.   Craven County.

June 10, 1750. November Court, 1751. *Sons:* EVAN (plantation on East side of Clubford's Creek), JAMES (plantation on the East side of Buck Creek), ROGER ("manner plantation on West side of Clubford Creek"), CHARLES (plantation on West side of Cohookey Creek). *Wife:* ANN. *Executors:* EVAN, JAMES and ROGER JONES (sons). *Witnesses:* CATHARINE JONES, BRIGETT CANADY, WILLIAM FLOOD. *Clerk of the Court:* PHIL. SMITH.

JONES, EVAN.   Craven County.

December 23, 1752. March 19, 1753. *Son:* LOVICK ("my plantation & lands on the East side of Clubfords Creek"). *Daughter:* SARAH JONES. *Executors:* THOMAS LOVICK and ROGER JONES. *Witnesses:* JAS. JONES, JOHN TANEYHILL, CHARLES JONES. Will proven before JAS. HASELL. *Clerk General Court:* JNO. SNEAD.

JONES, FRANCIS.   Edgecombe County.

January 14, 1750. August Court, 1755. *Sons:* NATHANIEL and TINGNALL (land on Crabtree Creek in Johnston County), JOHN (land on Crabtree Creek), MATTHEW (land on Swift Creek in Johnston County), FRANCIS (land on Jackit Swamp, Edgecombe County), ALBRIDGTON, RIDLEY. *Son-in-law:* JOHN CULLERS (land on Crabtree Creek). *Daughters:* JUDITH WILSON, MARY CULLERS, LUCY JONES, BETTE DAY JONES, LYDIA JONES, JEMIMA JONES. *Executors:* MARY JONES (wife) and NATHANIEL JONES (son). *Witnesses:* THOS. WIGGINS, FRANCIS DRAKE. *Clerk of the Court:* JOS. MONTFORT.

JONES, FREDERICK.   Chowan Precinct.

April 9, 1722. March 26, 1723. *Sons:* WILLIAM HARDING JONES (lands on the south side of Moratoke River), FREDERICK ("all my lands in Craven Precinct"), THOMAS (land at Maherrin and lands on north side of Moratoke River). To each of sons is bequeathed one diamond ring. Plate divided between sons. To brother THOMAS JONES of Virginia is devised lands in King William County, Virginia, called Horns Quarter. *Daughters:* JANE ("Indian girle, four negroes, diamond ring and diamond earrings, Gold watch with chain, seal, etc."), MARTHA (four young negroes, one diamond ring, diamond earrings, gold shoe-buckles, thimble, etc., and one dozen finest damask napkins, one dozen diaper napkins, Holland sheets, etc.), REBECKAH (one diamond ring, about three dozen damask and diaper napkins, table-cloths, sheets, etc.) *Executors:* THOMAS JONES, of Virginia (brother), WM. HARDING and FREDERICK JONES (sons). *Witnesses:* SARAH STEWART, ROGER HAZARD, JOHN ANSLEY, EDW'D MOSELEY. Codicil bequeathes gold rings to REBECAH JONES and silver-mounted pistols to EDWARD MOSELEY. Proven before C. GALE. Coat of arms on seal.

JONES, FREDERICK.   Craven County.

November 21, 1758. February Court, 1759. *Mother:* MARY MOORE. *Brother:* HARDING JONES. *Niece:* MARY JONES. *Executors:* HARDING JONES (brother) and JOSEPH LEECH. *Witnesses:* ELIZABETH SPAIGHT, MARY VAIL, JANE SWANN. *Clerk of the Court:* PETER CONWAY. Coat of arms on seal.

JONES, HENRY.   Northampton County.

November 14, 1733. November Court, 1757. *Sons:* HENRY (*Executor*), WILLIAM, JOHN (plantation on south side of Roanoke River), PHILIP, JAMES ("plantation whereon I now live"). *Daughter:* ELEZEBETH JONES. *Wife:* CATHERINE. Four oldest sons appointed trustees. *Witnesses:* NEEDHAM BRYAN, GEORGE SMITH, JOHN ELESS. *Clerk of the Court:* I. EDWARDS.

JONES, HENRY.   Northampton County.

November 26, 1751. February Court, 1752. Northwest parish in Northampton County. *Son:* HENRY RESTORE JONES ("my manor plantation"). *Daughters:* PRIOR, GRAY, MARY and KATY JONES. *Wife and Executrix:* SARAH. *Witnesses:* JOHN MANDAR, JOHN CORLEW, JUNR., JOEL MOSELEY. *Clerk of the Court:* I. EDWARDS.

JONES, HENRY.   Chowan County.

February 11, 1754. April Court, 1754. *Son:* WILLIAM. *Daughters:* MARY LOVEL, JANE CHAMPION, SARAH PARKER. *Wife and Executrix:* ELIZABETH. *Executor:* BENJAMIN PARKER. *Witnesses:* HENRY BONNER, JOHN LUTEN, SAMUEL LUTEN. *Clerk of Court:* WILL HALSEY.

ABSTRACT OF WILLS, 1690—1760.

JONES, ISAAC. Pasquotank Precinct.

January 7, 1734. January 31, 1734. *Sons:* JOHN ("my manner plantation"), ISAAC ("my little plantation"), NEHEMIAH (land beginning at "ye Fork Bridge, running, &c."), EVIN (100 acres of land). *Daughters:* DOROTHY and MARY JONES. *Executors:* JOHN JONES (son) and JARNAS JONES (brother). *Witnesses:* ABEL ROSS, JOSHUA GAMBLING, JOHN WALLIS. Will proven before GAB. JOHNSTON, at Edenton.

JONES, ISAM. Edgecombe County.

April 24, 1753. November Court, 1753. *Wife:* MARY. *Daughter:* CREACY. *Executor:* WALLIS JONES. *Witnesses:* RICHARD BURD, MATTHEW JONES. *Clerk of the Court:* BENJ'N WYNNS.

JONES, JAMES. Tyrrell County.

August 3, 1750. No probate. *Sons:* JAMES (150 acres of land), TRALEY, EVAN, BENJAMIN (150 acres of land). *Daughters:* MARY DRAPIR, ANN and ELIZABETH JONES. To JOHN RAY is given "the liberty of dwelling on my land called the Folley." *Wife and Executrix:* MARY. *Witnesses:* JOHN RAY, WILLIAM HOWARD, ELIZABETH HOWARD.

JONES, JOHN. Pasquotank County.

November 23, 1707. January 20, 1707–1708. *Son:* JOHN ("all my land"). *Wife and Executrix:* ELIZABETH. *Witnesses:* ROBERT WALLIS, RICHARD MADREN, HENRY SAWYER. *Clerk of Court:* JOHN PALIN.

JONES, JOHN. Pasquotank County.

March 23, 1719–1720. December 23, 1723. *Father-in-law (meaning, probably, stepfather):* JOHN ROLFE. *Mother and Executrix:* ELIZABETH ROLFE. *Aunt:* MARY BARD. *Witnesses:* JOHN SOLLEY, JNO. ROLFE. Will proven before WILLIAM REED, *President.*

JONES, JOHN. Pasquotank Precinct.

December 12, 1723. *Legatees:* DORITY and ELE MACKDANIEL. *Witnesses:* THOMAS HEARENDEEN, JOHN JENNINGS, BENJAMIN SAWYER. *Clerk of the Court:* JOHN PARKER.

JONES, JOHN. Chowan Precinct.

May 12, 1727. May 15, 1727. *Sons:* WILLIAM, JOHN, THOMAS, DAVID. *Daughter:* ELISABETH. *Granddaughter:* ELISABETH JONES (daughter of DAVID). *Friend:* HENRY BONER. *Executor:* SAMUEL PADETH. *Witnesses:* THOS. JONES, DAVID JONES, WM. YATES. Will proven before RICHARD EVERARD.

JONES, JOHN.   Chowan County.

August 6, 1734. October 18, 1744. *Sons:* JOHN ("my plantation").
LEWES, SAMUEL. *Wife and Executrix:* FLORANCE. *Witnesses:* CONST.
LUTEN, JOHN LEWIS, JACOB PRIVETT. *Clerk of the Court:* EDMUND HATCH.

JONES, JOHN.   Chowan County.

February 2, 1735–1736. October Court, 1736. *Sons:* JAMES and DEMSEY ("all my land at the Loosing Swamp"). *Wife and Executrix:* ANN. *Executor:* JAMES JONES (son). *Witnesses:* JOHN SUMNER, JAMES HUBARD. *Clerk of Court:* JAMES CRAVEN.

JONES, JOHN.   Bertie County.

September 25, 1750. May Court, 1751. *Sons:* SOLOMON and JOSEPH (plantation on Poplar Swamp), WILLIAM, JOHN and JAMES. *Daughter:* MARY JONES. *Wife:* not named. *Executors:* JOHN BROWN, THOMAS EASON. *Witnesses:* THOMAS EASON, JOHN ROBERSON, JOHN HARE, SOLOMON HOWARD. *Clerk of Court:* SAM'L ORMES.

JONES, JOHN.   Chowan County.

June 23, 1754. July Court, 1755. *Sons:* JAMES (plantation on Lousin Swamp), JOHN ("plantation I bought of WM. ASHLEY"), JOSIAS ("my manner plantation which I purchased of JOHN PERRY"). *Daughter:* JUDITH JONES. *Wife and Executrix:* JUDITH. *Executor:* JAMES JONES (son). *Clerk of the Court:* THOMAS JONES.

JONES, JOHN.   Edgecombe County.

October 24, 1757. June Court, 1758. *Sons:* WALLIS, ETHELDRED, JOHN. *Sons-in-law:* THOMAS SPELL, CHARLES JERKINS, PETER MITCHELL. *Other legatees:* ANN and BENJAMIN RICHARDSON, JOHN JONES. *Daughter:* SARAH JERKINS. *Executor:* WALLIS JONES (son). *Witnesses:* HENRY HORN, SIKON HORN, JOSIAH HORN. Codicil dated December 17, 1757, mentions son FREDERICK JONES and makes bequests to other sons. Same witnesses. *Clerk of the Court:* JOS. MONTFORT.

JONES, JOHN.   Duplin County.

March 15, 1759. January 12, 1759. *Sons:* WILLIAM ("plantation whereon I now live"), THOMAS (100 acres of land), JOHN (*Executor*). *Daughters:* PATTE, CATHERINE, ELIZABETH, MARY ANN and SARAH JONES. *Wife and Executrix:* ANN. *Witnesses:* WILLIAM WHITFIELD, ANN JONES, ANN WILLIAMS. *Clerk of Court:* JOHN DICKSON.

JONES, JOHN.   Northampton County.

June 24, 1759. October Court, 1759. *Daughter:* ELIZABETH. *Wife and Executrix:* PRISCILLA. *Brother:* EDMOND JONES. *Friend:* SAMUEL

WELDON (lot No. 90 in town of Halifax). *Executor:* JOHN EDMUNDS. Land in Southampton County, Va., and lot No. 15 in Halifax given to executors to be sold for payment of debts. *Witnesses:* WILL CATHCART, WM. FANNING, JAMES DANCY. *Clerk of the Court:* I. EDWARDS.

JONES, JOHN, SR.   Bertie Precinct.

March 17, 1735. May Court, 1736. *Sons:* JAMES, FREDERICK ("my plantation"), JOHN, JOSEPH. *Grandson:* ABRAHAM JONES. *Daughters:* ANN COTTEN, MARY BONNER. *Wife:* MARTHA. *Trustees:* JOHN BROWN, JOHN BATTLE, WILLIAM MEARS. *Executor:* JOHN JONES (son). *Witnesses:* P. HANFORD, JAMES DOUGLASS, ELIZABETH OQUIN. *Clerk of the Court:* JOHN WYNNS.

JONES, JONATHAN.   Pasquotank County.

April Court, 1740. *Sons:* JONATHAN ("plantation at ye head of Sawyer's Creek"), CORNELIUS ("land below Sawyer's Creek"). *Daughters:* MARY, ELESEBETH, RUTH and DINAH JONES. *Wife:* SUSAN. *Executor:* JOSEPH HUMPHRIES. *Witnesses:* WILLIAM MACKDANIEL, CHRISTOPHER HUMPHRIES, DINAH HUMPHRIES. *Clerk of the Court:* JAMES CRAVEN.

JONES, JOSEPH.

September 10, 1756. *Sons:* JAMES and JOSEPH (land divided between them). *Daughters:* MARY, HANNAH, ELIZABETH and ANN. *Wife and Executrix:* MARTHA. *Executor:* WILLIAM VAUGHAN. *Witnesses:* JOHN WHITE, RICHARD NANSON. *Clerk of the Court:* ISAAC FARIES.

JONES, MARY.   Bertie County.

December 22, 1745. January 9, 1748. *Legatees:* ELISABETH SPRUELL (cousin), SARAH HAWKINS (daughter of THOMAS HAWKINS), THOMAS HACKMAN, THOS. SUTTON (nephew), ELIZABETH SUTTON (sister), JOHN SUTTON (nephew, to whom is bequeathed 100 acres of land "in Cishooke at the head of the Line"), GEORGE SUTTON (nephew). *Executors:* CHARLES JACOCKS, THOMAS and JOHN SUTTON. *Witnesses:* THOMAS HACKMAN, JOHN BURN. Will proven before GAB. JOHNSTON, at Eden House.

JONES, MORRIS.   Hyde County.

September 25, 1756. December Court, 1756. *Son:* HENRY ("my dwelling plantation"). *Daughters:* ELESEBETH, MARY, ANN, NEOMY and SARAH JONES. *Wife:* MARY. *Executors:* THOS. JONES (brother), HENRY GIBBS, JNR. *Witnesses:* BENJN. MASON, EDWARD SPENSER, SOLOMON JONES. *Clerk of Court:* STEPHEN DENNING.

JONES, PETER.   County not given.

April 2, 1731. *Sons:* PETER ("plantation whereon I now live"), ROBERT (374 acres of land on Mash Swamp). *Daughters:* SARAH and MARTHA JONES. *Wife and Executrix:* SARAH. *Witnesses:* WM. WILLIAMS, WILLIAM PAUL. No probate.

JONES, PETER.   Perquimans County.

February 17, 1753. April Court, 1753. *Sons:* THOMAS ("plantation whereon I now live"), ZEPHANIAH (land at head of land given to THOMAS), ZECHARIAH (land purchased of WM. WYATT), MALACHY (land on the Mile Branch). All of the sons to be given "Education to Reade & write a Ledgable hand and work Arithmitick through the single rule of three." *Daughter:* MARY JONES. *Grandson:* JOSEPH JONES. *Wife:* MARY. *Arbitrators to divide estate:* JOHN HARVEY, JOSEPH BARROW, JR., FRANCIS JONES, NATHAN and ROBERT NEWBY. *Executors:* JOSEPH WHITE, JOSEPH RATLIF, THOMAS JONES. *Witnesses:* EVAN SKINNER, WILLM. SKINNER, SARAH SKINNER. *Clerk of the Court:* EDMUND HATCH.

JONES, PETER, SENR.   Perquimans County.

May 15, 1751. April Court, 1752. *Sons:* JOHN ("plantation I now live on," plantation at the Mile Branch), WILLIAM (170 acres of land), PETER ("plantation whereon he now lives"). *Daughters:* MARY and HANNAH JONES, SARAH SUTTON, REBECCA DENMAN, MARGRET. *Grandson:* THOMAS SHERWOOD. *Executors:* JOHN JONES (son), MARY JONES (daughter), THOMAS NICHOLSON. *Witnesses:* MAC SCARBOROUGH, ELIZAB. SCARBROUGH, WILLIAM REED. *Clerk of the Court:* EDMUND HATCH.

JONES, ROGER.   Beaufort County.

July 25, 1741. September Court, 1741. *Sons:* ROGER, GEORGE. *Daughters:* JANE, MARGARET, MARY, HOLLAND and ELIZABETH (to the two last named is given plantation called Holland House, also a plantation on Massapungo Swamp. *Wife and Executrix:* REBECCA. *Witnesses:* JOHN BARROW, LITTLETON EBORN, ELIZABETH JONES. *Clerk of the Court:* JNO. TURNER.

JONES, SAMUELL.   Currituck County.

September 30, 1723. *Sons:* THOMAS (one shilling), SAMUEL and WILLIAM (land called Thurrefare Ridge), IZAYAH and ZACKARYATH ("my dwelling plantation"). *Executors:* WILLIAM WILLIAMS, THOMAS DAYES. *Witnesses:* MARGRET CROSSMAN, DANLL. PHILLIPS. *Clerk of the Court:* THOS. LOWTHER.

JONES, SARAH.   Bath County.

May, 1722. *Daughters:* MONING MITEM, CHARITY SHUTE, ELIZABETH CARNEY, MARY SMITH (*Executrix*). *Grandson:* JAMES SMITH. *Witnesses:* FRANCIS DELAMARE, JOHN MARTIN, THOMAS DAVIS. No probate.

JONES, THOMAS.   Bertie County.

1754. Petty Shore in Bertie County. *Legatees:* MARGRET WEBB (widow of SAMUEL WEBB), SAMUEL WEBB (son of MARGRET), HENRY HILL,

JOHN CAMPBELL (of Lazy Hill). *Executor:* JOHN CAMPBELL. No signature. No witnesses. Will proven before ARTHUR DOBBS by BENJAMIN WYNNS, ALEXANDER FORD and JOSEPH HERON, who made oath as to the handwriting of the testator.

JONES, WILLIAM HARDING.   Chowan County.

January 22, 1730. July 27, 1732. Eastern parish in Chowan County. *Wife:* ANN (4,000 acres of land on Roanoke River, together with "house and plantation whereon I now live with third part of the negroes * * * * except ye family pictures and Court of arms which I give to my well beloved brother FREDDICK JONES and likewise all ye books in ye said house which I give to my brothers FREDDICK and THOMAS JONES"). No executor appointed. *Witnesses:* GEORGE ALLEIGN, SAM'LL SNOWDEN, MATTHEW YOUNG. Proven before JNO. PALIN, C. J. Coat of arms on seal.

JONES, WILLIAM.   Chowan Precinct.

January 9, 1722. *Sons:* JOHN ("land whereon he now lives"), HENRY ("the plantation whereon I now live"), CHARLES (land on Deep run). *Grandson:* WILLIAM JONES. *Daughter:* JANE LISLES. *Granddaughter:* DOROTHY LISLES. *Grandsons:* WILLIAM LISLES (son of JANE), WILLIAM LEWSE (son of ELISABETH SPIER), WILLIAM JONES (son of HENRY JONES), WILLIAM WALSTON (son of DOROTHY WALSTON), WILLIAM JONES (son of JOHN JONES). *Other legatees:* HENRY LISLES, JR., and HENRY LISLES, SR. No executor appointed. *Witnesses:* FRANCES HOWCOTT, HANAH LUTEN, THOMAS LUTEN. No probate.

JONES, WILLIAM.   Chowan Precinct.

May 4, 1722. *Sons:* JOHN (land at "ye Rich Thick'tt in Virginia," after his decease to his sons, JOHN and JAMES), also one hundred acres of land on Deep Run Swamp to go to his sons, DAVID and WILLIAM, after his decease), HENRY ("the plantation whereon I now live," after his death to his son, WILLIAM), CHARLES (100 acres of land). *Daughters:* JEANE LYSLE, ELIZABETH SPIERS, DOROTHY WALSTON. *Other devisee:* WM. LYLES. *Executor:* THOMAS LUTEN. *Witnesses:* ROBERT FULLERTON, MARY FULLERTON, MARY DREACE. No probate.

JONES, WILLIAM.   Bertie Precinct.

March 15, 1736. May 20, 1736. *Son:* EPHRAME ("plantation whereon I now live"). *Wife:* ANN. *Executors:* FRANCIS HOPSON, HENRY JERNIGAN. *Witnesses:* BENNET BLACKMAN, HENRY BAKER, JR. Will proven before W. SMITH, C. J.

JONES, WILLIAM.   Beaufort County.

April 28, 1740. September 1, 1742. *Daughters:* ELISABETH, RUTH, ANN PRISKET, wife of JOHN PRISKET; HANER, wife of SOLOMON ROBSON; JANE, wife of ROBT. DUNBAR. *Grandchildren:* WM. QUINN and WM. ROBSON. *Executors:* MARGET JONES (wife), SOLOMON ROBSON. *Witnesses:* RICHARD CHEEK, WM. MITCHELL, JOHN BRYLY, JOHN HENINTON. Will proven before J. MONTGOMERY, C. J.

JONES, WILLIAM.   Edgecombe County.

November 27, 1749. August Court, 1750. *Sons:* DREURY, PETER ("plantation whereon I now live"), ISAM (grist mill). *Arbitrators to divide land:* THOMAS HILL, GEORGE NICHOLSON, JOHN CLARK, WALLIS JONES. *Executors:* SARAH JONES (wife) and WALLIS JONES. *Witnesses:* THOMAS THROWER, WILLIAM ATKISON, WINNIFRED ATKISON. *Clerk of the Court:* BENJAMIN WYNNS.

JONES, WILLIAM.   Perquimans County.

December 9, 1750. April Court, 1752. *Son:* WILLIAM. *Daughters:* ELISABETH BARBER, REBECKAH JONES. *Arbitrators to divide estate:* JOHN HARVEY, JOSEPH WHITE, JOSEPH RIBINSON, JOSEPH BARROW. *Executors:* PETER JONES (brother), MOSES BARBER (son-in-law), WILLIAM JONES (son). *Witnesses:* JOSEPH BARROW, JUNR., JOHN WILLIAMS, JOHN BARROW. *Clerk of the Court:* EDMUND HATCH.

JONES, WILLIAM.   Halifax County.

January 3, 1758. June Court, 1759. *Sons:* WILLIAM (land he now has possession of), HENRY (300 acres land), BRITTON (300 acres of land "adjoining my mill"), SIMON (500 acres of land with mill). *Daughters:* SARAH, WINNIFRED, AMEY, ELIZABETH, SILVA. *Wife and Executrix:* SARAH. *Executor:* WILLIAM JONES. *Witnesses:* AUGUSTINE BATE, NICHOLAS KILLINGSWORTH, SOLOMON HAWKINS, SARAH JONES. *Clerk of the Court:* JOS. MONTFORT.

JONES, WILLIAM.   Chowan County.

July 15, 1773. March 16, 1774. *Daughters:* CHARITY WALKER, RACHEL LUTEN, ESTER JOHNSTON, SARAH, AN and EDAH JONES. *Son:* JAMES ("my plantation"). *Executors:* THOMAS BONNER, JOHN LEWIS and JAMES JONES. *Witnesses:* JOHN MUSHROW, DANCY TROTMAN. Will proven before JO. MARTIN.

JORDAN, ARTHUR.   Northampton County.

November 13, 1751. May Court, 1752. *Sons:* GEORGE ("land where he now lives"), ARTHUR, JOHN and THOMAS ("land JOHN now lives on"), HENRY (150 acres of land), BENJAMIN ("plantation where I now live"). *Daughters:* ELIZABETH, FORTUNE. *Wife and Executrix:* SARAH. *Executor:* BENJAMIN JORDAN (son). *Witnesses:* CHARLES GREGORY, JAMES JORDAN, WILLIAM BARCROFT. *Clerk of the Court:* I. EDWARDS.

JORDAN, ARTHUR.   Northampton County.
  September 14, 1754. August Court, 1755. *Sons:* SAMUEL and ARTHUR.
Daughters: REBECCA, MARY and SARAH. *Wife and Executrix:* SARAH.
Witnesses: ARTHUR YOUNG, REUDEN ROGERS. *Clerk of the Court:* I.
EDWARDS.

JORDAN, DEBORAH.   Bladen County.
  September 4, 1769. February 14, 1770. *Brothers:* ITHAMAR and JOHN
SINGLETARY. *Daughter:* MARGARET GIBSON. *Niece:* DEBORAH SINGLE-
TARY (daughter of ITHAMAR). *Executors:* JOHN SINGLETARY (brother) and
WALTER GIBSON (son-in-law). *Witnesses:* JOHN RUSS, EPH'M MULFORD,
JOSEPH POWERS. Will proven before WM. TRYON.

JORDAN, JOHN.   Hyde Precinct.
  December 31, 1719. *Son and Executor:* JOHN. *Daughters:* MARGARET,
wife of JOHN FOREMAN; MARY JORDAN. *Witnesses:* PETER MCDULE,
THOMAS TYLER, ISAAC CHABANAS. Original missing. Recorded in Book
1712–1722, page 219.

JORDAN, JOSEPH.   Pasquotank County.
  January Court, 1752. *Witnesses:* SAMUEL HUGHE, DEMSEY CONNOR and
JOSEPH ROBINSON. Will illegible.

JORDAN, SOLOMON.   Tyrrell County.
  March 3, 1721–1722. April 11, 1722. *Sons:* ABRAHAM (200 acres of
land on north side of Cashia River and other tracts described in will).
Daughters: LUARRESIA, REBECCA. *Wife:* not named. *Executor:* MAJ.
ROBERT WEST. *Witnesses:* REBECCA CORRY, RACHEL BUTTLOR, MARTIN
CREMEN. Will proven before THOS. POLLOCK.

JORDAN, WILLIAM.   Tyrrell County.
  July 4, 1732. November 2, 1732. *Sons:* JOHN ("my manner planta-
tion"). *Daughter:* ESTER. *Wife and Executrix:* SARAH. *Executor:*
NATHANIEL EVERETT. *Witnesses:* THOS. HOBBS, WILLIAM GARRETT.
SAM'LL DURRANCE. Will proven before WM. LITTLE, *Chief Justice.*

JOY, WILLIAM.   Pasquotank County.
  December 17, 1725. January 18, 1725. *Wife and Executrix:* MARGERY.
Other devisees: SOLOMON and SARAH EVERTON. *Witnesses:* JEREMIAH
EVERTON, FRANCES EVERTON. *Clerk of the Court:* THO. WEEKES. *Execu-
trix* qualified before GABRIEL BARNHAM.

KALBIN, JOHN.   Perquimans Precinct.
  December 20, 1685. *Executor and sole legatee:* ROBERT INBASON. *Witnesses:* WILLIAM DANSE, ANDREW ROSS. No probate.

KASEWELL, FRANCIS.   Pasquotank Precinct.

January 1, 1712–1713. Allegator in Albemarle County. No probate. *Daughters:* MARTHA and MARY KASEWELL. *Wife and Executrix:* SARAH. *Witnesses:* ANN WHITE, HANNAH MANSFIELD, EBENR. WAITE. Original missing. Recorded in Book 1712–1722, page 42.

KEARSEY (spelled also CEARSEY), THOMAS.   Bertie County.

October 28, 1730. August Court, 1731. *Sons:* JOHN (land on Cashie Swamp), THOMAS and WILLIAM (lands), JAMES and PETER. *Daughter:* MARY POHAGON. *Wife and Executrix:* SUSANNA. *Grandson:* WILLIAM KEARSEY. *Executor:* THOMAS KEARSEY (son). *Witnesses:* THOMAS KEARSEY, JR., MARY POHEAGIN, JOSEPH DARDEN, ARTHUR WILLIAMS. *Clerk of Court:* RT. FORSTER.

KEEFE, FREDERICK.   Bertie County.

November 10, 1723. February Court, 1723. *Wife and Executrix:* ELLINOR. *Sons:* FREDERICK and JOHN. *Witnesses:* JAMES BATES, ELIZABETH KEEFE, MARGRETT KEEFE. *Clerk of Court:* RT. FORSTER.

KEEL, JOHN.   Bath County.

November 18, 1736. *Legatees:* JOHN MAINNER, WILLIAM MAINNER (sons of WM. and SARAH MAINNER). *Brother and Executor:* NATHANIEL KEEL. *Witnesses:* JOB BROOKS, WILLIAM MAINNER. No probate.

KEEL, LEMUEL.   Pasquotank County.

February 11, 1747–1748. April Court, 1748. *Brother:* CHARLES KEEL. *Wife and Executrix:* TAMER. *Witnesses:* HEN. PENDLETON, ROBERT HOSEA. *Clerk of Court:* THOS. TAYLOR.

KEEL, TAMAR.   Pasquotank County.

December 14, 1748. January 19, 1748. *Legatees:* SUSANNAH, wife of THOMAS MEADS; ELIZABETH, daughter of THOS. MEADS, and WILLIAM DAVIS (*Executor*). *Witnesses:* JAS. GREGORY, WILLIAM WALLIS. Proven before GAB. JOHNSTON.

KEELAND, JOHN.   Edgecombe County.

January 21, 1752. March 24, 1752. *Executor and sole legatee:* JAMES CARTER. This is a nuncupative will proven by WILLIAM HORNSBY, WILLIAM TAYLOR and CATTREN CARTER. *Clerk of Court:* BENJ'N WYNNS. Proven before GAB. JOHNSTON.

KEETON, HENRY.   Pasquotank Precinct.

September 20, 1710. *Son:* JOSEPH (plantation at New Begun Creek). *Daughters:* ELIZABETH and MERRIAM. *Overseers of will:* EDWARD MAYO,

BENJAMIN PRICHARD and JOSEPH GLAISTER. *Wife and Executrix:* ELISA-
BETH. *Witnesses:* JOHN JENNINGS, W. NORRIS, JOHN SIMSON. No probate.

KEETON, ZACHARIAH, SR.   Pasquotank County.

April 28, 1743. January Court, 1743. *Sons:* ZACHARIAH and PATRICK. *Daughters:* MARY CORY, ELIZABETH WILLCOCKS. *Granddaughter:* ELINER WINBERG. *Wife:* SARAH. *Executors:* ZACHARIAH and PATRICK (sons). *Witnesses:* STEPHEN SCOTT, JOSEPH LOMBROSKER. *Clerk of Court:* THOS. TAYLOR.

KEILE, THOMAS.   Albemarle County.

September 19, 1682. March 6, 1682–1683. *Sons:* THOMAS, ROBERT. *Daughter:* SARAH. *Wife and Executrix:* MARY. *Guardian:* THO. ROLFE. *Witnesses:* THO. ROLFE, FRANCIS WARDE, WILLIAM BENTLEY. Proven before WILL. CRAFORD.

KELLEY, JOHN.   Pasquotank County.

October 22, 1758. December Court, 1758. *Son:* ASA. *Daughters:* MARY, ELIZABETH, MARTHA and NANNA KELLY. *Wife and Executrix:* ELISABETH. *Executor:* PATRICK KELLY (cousin). *Witnesses:* JOHN MACBRIDE, SAMUEL EDNY, SARAH MACBRIDE. *Clerk of the Court:* THOS. TAYLOR. Coat of arms on seal.

KELLEY, SARAH.   Pasquotank Precinct.

January 1, 1699. April 16, 1700. *Daughter:* SARAH KELLEY. *Executor:* JOHN MACKEELL. *Witnesses:* THO. BOYD, DANIEL MACKEEL, ELIZABETH ———. *Clerk of the Court:* THOS. ABINGTON.

KELLY, MATHEW.   Pasquotank County.

April 16, 1697. January 16, 1699. *Sons:* JAMES and JOHN. *Daughters:* ELIZABETH and REBECCA. *Executrix:* WIFE, not named. *Witnesses:* HENRY WHITE, JAMES DAVIS. MAGDALEN KELLY, probably wife of testator, adopts will as her own by writing dated December 10, 1699. *Witnesses:* HENRY WHITE, JACOB OVERMAN. *Clerk of the Court:* THO. ABINGTON.

KELLY, SMITH.   Perquimans Precinct.

February 2, 1734. April 15, 1734. *Son:* NICHOLAS. *Wife and Executrix:* MARY. No signature. No witnesses. *Clerk of the Court:* CHAS. DENMAN.

KEMP, GEORGE.   Pasquotank County.

January 20, 1723–1724. April Court, 1724. *Sons:* GEORGE and ALLEN (all my lands). *Daughter:* SARAH KEMP. *Wife and Executrix:* MARY. *Witnesses:* MAC. SCARBOROUGH, JOHN TOXEY, THO. HILLARD. *Clerk of the Court:* W. NORRIS.

KEMP, WILLIAM. Anson County.

April 20, 1750. April Court, 1753. *Sons:* JOHN, WILLIAM, THOMAS, JOSEPH and STEVEN. *Daughter:* SARAH KEMP. To the sons is bequeathed land described in will. *Wife and Executrix:* ELIZABETH. *Executors:* JOHN and WILLIAM (sons). *Witnesses:* ANDREW MAREMAN, ANTHONY HUTCHINS. *Clerk of the Court:* JNO. DUNN.

KENEDY, WALTER. Johnston County.

March 25, 1751. June Court, 1751. *Son:* JOHN. *Daughter:* MARY KENNEDY. *Wife and Executrix:* SARAH. *Witnesses:* JOHN KENNEDY, ROBT. FELLOW. *Deputy Clerk of the Court:* JAMES OATES.

KENT, JOHN. Bath County.

September 28, 1719. *Wife and Executrix:* MARY. *Executor:* RICHARD HARVEY. *Witnesses:* ANTHONY MARKHAM, JOHN MCKEEL and JOHN HARVEY. Original missing. Recorded in Book 1712–1722, page 219.

KENYON, JOHN. Perquimans County.

May 19, 1751   July Court, 1752. *Son:* JOAB ("my plantation"). *Wife and Executrix:* MARY. *Executors:* ABRAHAM HENDRIXON (brother-in-law) and JOHN WEAKES. *Witnesses:* JOHN MODLING, SAM'LL MOORE, HANNAH MODLING. *Clerk of the Court:* EDMUND HATCH.

KETON, JOHN, SR. Perquimans County.

February 28, 1734–1735. October 1, 1735. *Sons:* JOHN, LEWIS, JOSEPH. *Daughters:* SARAH HUBBARD, ELIZABETH WIGGINS. *Wife and Executrix:* ELIZABETH. *Executor:* ZACHARIAH NICKSON. *Witnesses:* EDWARD MOORE, JOHN WILLCOCKS, ROBERT COCKS. *Clerk of the Court:* JAMES CRAVEN.

KIBBLE, ABRAHAM. Onslow County.

December 6, 1750. April 2, 1757. *Son:* JAMES. *Daughter:* LUSE. *Stepsons:* THOMAS and DANIEL HIX. *Son-in-law and Executor:* JOSEPH WILLIAMS. *Wife and Executrix:* EDITH. *Witnesses:* THOS. JENKINS, JOSEPH LOYD, WILLIAM LOYD. Codicil provides for education of son "as far as the rule of three." *Witnesses:* THOS. JENKIN, JOSEPH LOYD, WILLIAM LOYD.

KILBEE, CHRISTOPHER. Northampton County.

February 9, 1741–1742. May Court, 1752. *Sons:* EPAPHRODITUS, XPHER (to each is devised land). *Daughters:* SARAH, ELIZABETH, FRANCES. *Wife:* KATHERINE. *Executors:* MAJ. JOSEPH GRAY, THOMAS JARRELL. *Friends:* JOSHUA LEWIS and JOHN FORT. *Witnesses:* JOHN BRASSELL, THOMAS WESBROOK. *Clerk of the Court:* I. EDWARDS.

KILLINGSWORTH, FRANCIS. Johnston County.

March 3, 1751. March Court, 1752. *Son:* NOLS. *Wife:* REBECKAH. *Executors:* ARTHUR FORT, SOLOMON HOMES. *Witnesses:* RACHEL STEPHENS, ELIZABETH PACE. *Deputy Clerk of the Court:* CHAS. YOUNG.

KILLINGSWORTH, RICHARD. Edgecombe County.

December 3, 1733. *Wife and Executrix:* MARY. *Cousin:* RICHARD KILLINGSWORTH. *Witnesses:* BENJAMIN WOOD, FRANCIS WOOD, JNO. SPEIR. No probate.

KINCE, CHRISTIAN. Brunswick County.

December 24, 1761. January 19, 1762. *Sons:* JOHN, EDWARD, WILLIAM. *Daughter:* ELIZABETH. *Executors:* JOHN and JOSEPH KINCE and EDWARD WILLIAMS. *Wife:* mentioned, but not named. *Witnesses:* JOHN FILLYAW, SAMUEL KINCE, JOHN HOWARD. Proven before ARTHUR DOBBS.

KINCHEN, WILLIAM. Edgecombe County.

November 6, 1758. December Court, 1758. *Sons:* JOHN (land on the river adjoining Craghill), WILLIAM ("remainder of my land"). *Daughters:* MARTHA, ELIZABETH, MARY and TEMPERANCE. *Executors:* BLAKE BAKER, HENRY DAWSON (brothers), JOHN KINCHEN (son). *Witnesses:* HENRY CAMPBELL, PETER JONES, WILLIAM MOORE. *Clerk of Court:* JOS. MONTFORT.

KING, HENRY. Chowan County.

February 24, 1714. April 16, 1716. *Sons:* MICHAEL, CHARLES and HENRY (lands in Chowan and in Virginia). *Daughters:* ELISABETH, CATREN and MARY KING. Signatures of witnesses torn off. *Clerk of the Court:* R. HICKS. *Names of witnesses appearing in probate:* CHRISTOPHER VANLUON, JOHN HAYES, JUDITH FOX.

KING, HENRY. Bertie County.

July 1, 1750. May Court, 1751. *Daughters:* CATTREN, ANN and PRUDENCE KING. *Wife and Executrix:* ANN. *Executors:* ROBT. WEST, JOS. HARDY. *Witnesses:* AGNEE MARVELL KNOTT, HANNAH MALTIMER. *Clerk of the Court:* SAM'L ORMES.

KING, JOHN. Onslow County.

January 5, 1743–1744. July 4, 1749. *Sons:* JOHN, CHARLES, WILLIAM, NICHOLAS, HENRY and JACOB, MICHAEL. *Wife:* PRISCILLA. *Executors:* LEWIS JENKINS and GEORGE BISHOP. *Witnesses:* ISABELLA JENKINS, ELIZABETH WINGATE, SARAH HIGMAN. *Clerk of the Court:* THOS. ———. Portion of this will missing.

ABSTRACT OF WILLS, 1690—1760.

KING, MICHAEL.   Bertie County.

May 20, 1741. October 29, 1741. *Sons:* MICHAEL, HENRY and JOHN. *Daughters:* CATHERINE, ISBEL, PENELOPE and MARY KING. *Wife and Executrix:* ISBEL. *Executors:* COLL. ROBERT WEST and his son ROBERT. *Witnesses:* ROGER SNELL, JNO. HILL, J. HOLBROOK. Proven before J. MONTGOMERY, C. J.

KINGSTAN, JAMES.

July 12, 1748. *Legatees and devisees:* JACOB BONI, JR., and WM. THOMAS, JUNR. *Executors:* JACOB BONI, SR., and WILLIAM THOMAS, SR. *Witnesses:* WM. MCCANNE and NAT MCCANNE. No probate.

KINSE, JOHN.   Perquimans County.

October 8, 1718. April 14, 1719. *Daughter:* ELIZABETH KINSEY. *Daughter-in-law:* MARY NICKOLSON. *Son-in-law:* SAMUEL NICKOLSON. *Wife and Executrix:* PRESILLAH. *Executor:* RICHARD RATLIFF. *Witnesses:* EDWARD MAUDLIN, EZEKIEL MAUDLIN. *Clerk of the Court:* RICHARD LEARY.

KINSEY, JOHN.   Craven County.

April 9, 1752. May Court, 1752. *Sons:* JOHN, JOSEPH, ABSALOM, CHRISTIAN and SAMUEL. *Daughter:* EASTER. *Wife and Executrix:* MARY. *Executor:* JOHN GRANADE. *Witnesses:* JNO. SNEAD, HARDING JONES, JOHN DUNN. *Clerk of the Court:* PHIL SMITH.

KIRBY, THOMAS.   Chowan County.

May 7, 1718. July 16, 1719. *Sons:* THOMAS, CHARLES and EDWARD. *Daughters:* MABEL and EASTER. *Wife and Executrix:* EASTER. *Witnesses:* JOHN COLSON, RICHARD HORN, ROBERT SHARAR. Proven before CHAS. EDEN.

KISABLE, MICHAEL.   Craven County.

March 8, 1727-1728. September 24, 1728. *Daughter:* MARY FROWING. *Wife:* mentioned, but not named. *Daughter-in-law:* MARGET TEACHY. *Son-in-law:* DANIEL TEACHY. *Executors:* MATHEW RISNOVER and FLETCHER MILLER. *Witnesses:* ROBT. SMITH, ALEXANDER STEEL, JOHN WAXFIELD. *Clerk of the Court:* C. METCALFE

KITCHING, WILLIAM.   Perquimans Precinct.

May 4, 1736. May 20, 1736. *Devisees and legatees:* DANIEL ROGERSON ("plantation I now live on, called Mount Messeary"), JOSIAH ROGERSON, CHRISTOPHER JACKSON, CHARLES DENMAN, CHRISTOPHER DENMAN, SARAH DENMAN, THOMAS LILLY, JR., WILLIAM LILLEY, SARAH ROBERTS, GILBERT SCOT, JOHN LILLEY, CASIAH ROGERSON, MARGRET ROGERSON, ANN

MOORE, JEAN ASPELL. *Executor:* DAN'LL ROGERSON. *Witnesses:* WALTER ANDREW, WILLIAM ROBERTS, MARY ANDREW. Proven before W. SMITH, C. J.

KNIGHT, LEWIS ALLEXANDER. Pasquotank Precinct.

March 17, 1731. April Court, 1732. *Sons:* EMMANUEL and LEWIS (land "on ye River"). *Wife and Executrix:* ANN. *Witnesses:* JER. SWEENY, TIMOTHY MEADES, MARY SWEENY. *Clerk of the Court:* W. MINSON.

KNIGHT, TOBIAS. Bath County.

June 11, 1719. July Court, 1719. *Wife and Executrix:* CATHERINE. All lands, etc., conveyed to wife and *daughter-in-law:* ELIZABETH GLOVER. *Witnesses:* JNO. HALTON, EDWD. CHAMBERLAYNE, PETER HAND. *Clerk of the Court:* JNO. HALTON.

KNIGHT, WILLIAM. Bertie County.

December 3, 1751. February Court, 1752. *Sons:* JOHN, WILLIAM, NEMIAH. *Wife:* MARTHA. *Friends:* ISAAC CARTER, JOSEPH BENTHALL. *Executors:* ISAAC CARTER, JOHN KNIGHT (son). *Witnesses:* WILLIAM KNIGHT, SUSANNAH SKINER, JOSEPH BENTHALL. *Clerk of the Court:* SAMUEL ORMES.

KNOX, JOHN. Chowan County.

February 11, 1729–1730. November 17, 1730. *Son:* THOMAS. *Wife and Executrix:* MARGRET. *Daughter:* MARY KNOX. *Guardian of daughter:* JOHN PORTER, SR. *Executor:* JOHN PORTER, JR. No witnesses. Proven before RICHARD EVERARD.

KORNEGEY, GEORGE. Craven County.

November 2, 1773. November 29, 1773. *Sons:* DANIEL, ELIJAH (land in Dobbs County on Falling Creek), JOHN JACOB, GEORGE (250 acres of land in the fork of the Beaverdam in Duplin County), WILLIAM, DAVID, JOSEPH (500 acres of land on the northeast of Cape Fear), ABRAHAM. *Daughter:* MARY DEBRUHL. *Executors:* JOHN, JACOB and GEORGE KORNEGEY (sons). *Witnesses:* JOHN GRANADE, MORGAN SMITH SANDERS, RUBEN ANDREWS. Proven before JO. MARTIN.

LACYE, WILLIAM, SENIOR. Albemarle County.

August 3, 1701. July Court, 1704. *Daughter:* BARBARY LACYE. *Granddaughter:* MARY LACYE. *Daughter-in-law:* MARY LACYE. *Son:* WILLIAM LACYE. BARBARY and MARY LACYE, daughters of WILLIAM LACYE, JR. *Executor:* WM. LACYE, JR. *Witnesses:* PETER GREY, SENIOR, PETER GRAY, JR., THOMAS HOLMES. *Clerk of the Court:* THO. SNODEN.

LACY, WILLIAM. Perquimans County.

January 17, 1734–1735. January 29, 1734. *Sons:* WILLIAM and THOMAS ("land and plantation whereon I now live"), JOSEPH. *Executors:* WIFE (not named) and RICHARD CHEASTEN. *Witnesses:* JOHN POWELL, ARTHUR CRAXTON and ISAAC MACKEY. Proven before GABRIEL JOHNSTON at Edenton.

LAFFITTE, TIMOTHY. Edenton Precinct.

November 4, 1742. March 24, 1742. *Wife and Executrix:* SARAH. *Witnesses:* BENJN. TALBOT, JESSE BRENN, THOS. BLOUNT. Proven before W. SMITH, C. J.

LAKARO (or LAKERS), BENJAMIN. Perquimans Precinct.

April 7, 1701. July 8, 1701. *Wife and Executrix:* JULIANA (land on Parishes Creek). *Daughter:* SARAH HARVEY (book, "Grantham's Church Principles"). *Friend:* GEORGE BLEIGHTON ("one book, being an Exposition upon the five books of Moses"). *Witnesses:* RICHARD FRENCH, ELIZABETH STEWARD, DEBORAH THURSTON. *Clerk of the Court:* JOHN STEPNEY.

LAKER, JULIANA. Perquimans County.

September 24, 1735. January Court, 1738. *Great-grandson:* BENJAMIN SCARBOROUGH, son of MACKEORA SCARBOROUGH (plantation called the Chenifen Ridge). *Sister:* NEPTUANIA HUTSON. *Daughter:* JOANNA PALMER. *Other legatees:* HUTSON and JULIANA WORTHAM, MARTHA PALMER, SAMUELL PALMER. *Executor:* MACKEORA SCARBOROUGH. *Witnesses:* JOHN BANCKEY, PACIANA CREACY. *Clerk of the Court:* JAMES CRAVEN.

LAMB, WILLIAM. Perquimans County.

December 4, 1757. April Court, 1758. *Wife and Executrix:* MIRIAM. *Daughters:* ELIZABETH, MIRIAM and MARY. *Brother and Executor:* WILLIAM NEWBY. *Witnesses:* SAMUEL LITTESON (or SITTESON), DAVID POWELL, JACOB WILSON. *Clerk of the Court:* MILES HARVEY.

LAMBERSON, HENRY. Beaufort County.

February 17, 1743–1744. June Court, 1744. *Wife:* MARY. *Son:* JOHN. *Executors:* JAMES HUMES, JESSE JONES and JOHN PHYSIOC and NATHANIEL DRAPER. *Witnesses:* JOHN PHYSIOC, JAMES MACKELWAY, NATH'LL DRAPER. *Clerk of the Court:* THE. GOOLD.

LANE, CHRISTIAN.   Edgecombe County.

October 5, 1747. May Court, 1748. *Daughters:* SARAH and MARY
LANE. *Son:* ABRAHAM. *Other legatees:* CHRISTIAN HILL. *Executor:*
ABRAHAM HILL. *Witnesses:* STEPHEN JACKSON, SARAH HILL. *Clerk of
the Court:* BENJ'N WYNNS.

LANE, EPHRAIM.   Craven County.

July 21, 1773. June 8, 1774. *Wife:* SARAH. *Other devisee and legatee:*
FREDERICK TODVINE. *Brothers:* SAMUEL and GEORGE LANE. *Executors:*
RICHARD CASWELL and FURNIFOLD GREEN. *Witnesses:* EDWARD HALLE,
WM. MIX, RICHARD TEER. Proven before Jo. MARTIN.

LANE, JOSEPH.   Edgecombe County.

December 6, 1757. November Court, 1758. *Brother:* WILLIAM LANE.
Sisters: FAITH BYNUM, DREWSILLER BRYANT. *Other legatee:* WINIFRED
POPE. *Executors:* JOHN BRADFORD and HENRY POPE. *Witnesses:* BENJAMIN MERRYMAN, BARNABAS LANE, DAVID DICKSON. *Clerk of the Court:*
JOS. MONTFORT.

LANE, THOMAS.   Bertie County.

March 30, 1754. November Court, 1754. *Daughters:* ANN ROBESON,
ELIZABETH LANE, SARAH BERRY. *Son:* WILLIAM. *Executors:* JOHN
ROBINSON, ANN ROBINSON and ELIZABETH LANE. *Witnesses:* JOSEPH
BUTTERTON, WILLIAM PERSEY, SAM'LL O'STEEN. *Clerk of the Court:*
SAMUEL ORMES.

LANE, WALTER.   Newbern, in Craven County.

September 13, 1742. August Court, 1757. *Brothers:* WILLIAM, JOHN
and GEORGE LANE. *Sisters:* ELIZABETH MATTO, SARAH GODARD, ELENOR
HIXON, RACHEL. *Son:* GEORGE ("my lot in Newbern, No. 10"). *Grandsons:* WALTER LANE and WALTER HIXON. *Wife and Executrix:* MARY.
Executor: SAMUEL SWANN. *Witnesses:* JOHN LAPIERRE, JOHN BRYAN,
MARTIN FRANCK, DAN'LL GRANDIN. *Clerk of the Court:* PETER CONWAY.

LANIER, ROBERT.   Tyrrell County.

September 20, 1744. March Court, 1744. *Daughters:* JEAN, ELIZABETH, SARAH, ANNANAZAH CRISTANAH, GRASE, SAMARIAH. *Sons:* WILLIAM and JOHN (1 bible each). *Grandsons:* ROBERT DANIELL, JOHN
BRYAN. *Granddaughters:* SARAH and MARY GILBERT. *Wife and Executrix:* SARAH. *Executors:* JOHN and WILLIAM LANIER (sons). *Witnesses:*
WILLIAM WILLIS, ROBERT LANIER DANIEL, JOHN LANIER. *Clerk of the
Court:* THOS. LEE.

LANKTON, THOMAS.

September 11, 1696. WM. STEVENS, JEBAZ. ALFORD, RACHEL and MARY DAMORELL, MR. FRANCIS PARROTT, "NEGRO BETTY" (one son about three years old), ANDREW JAMES. *Executor:* MR. WM. DUNKENFIELD. *Witnesses:* WM. JONES, JAMES DAMORELL. Proven by oath of JAMES DAMORELL before HONBLE. THOS. POLLOCK, *Lords' Deputy,* and by WM. JONES before CAPT. ANTHONY DAWSON, *Justice,* September 14, 1696.

LARKINS, JOHN. New Hanover County.

May 15, 1737. September Court, 1738. *Sons:* WILLIAM and JOHN ("my plantation"), JAMES. *Wife and Executrix:* TABITHA. *Friend:* JAMES INNES. *Witnesses:* JOHN SMITHES, JAMES CARTER, JOHN INNES. *Clerk of the Court:* JNO. RICE.

LASEY, FRANCIS. Perquimans County.

April 16, 1739. July Court, 1739. *Daughter:* JEMIMA LASEY ("plantation whereon I now dwell"). *Wife and Executrix:* MARY ANN LASEY. *Brother:* JOHN LASEY. *Executor:* WILLIAM BOGUE. *Witnesses:* FRANCIS JAMES, MOSES ELLIOTT. *Clerk of the Court:* JAMES CRAVEN.

LASHLY, PATRICK. Granville County.

November 28, 1758. March Court, 1759. *Wife:* LIDDA. *Executor:* PHILIP PRYOR. *Witnesses:* MOSES SPAN, CHRISTIAN LANGSTON. *Clerk of the Court:* DANIEL WELDON.

LATHUM, PAUL. Albemarle County.

October 7, 1692. July 31, 1693. *Son:* GEORGE ("my plantation"). *Daughter:* ELIZABETH LATHUM. *Wife and Executrix:* ELIZABETH. *Witnesses:* GEORGE FLEMMING, MARIA FLEMMING, JOHN PHILPOTT. *Clerk of the Court:* EDWARD MOOR.

LATTIMER, WILLIAM. Bertie County.

August 21, 1750. February Court, 1750. *Wife and Executrix:* ELIZABETH. *Executor:* JAMES LEAGWIT. *Friend:* JAMES SMITH. *Witnesses:* RICHARD TOMLINSON, RICH'D BRADLEY, ROBERT ROGERS. *Clerk of the Court:* SAM'LL ORMES.

LATTIMORE, ELIZABETH. Bertie County.

March 3, 1753. May Court, 1753. *Legatees:* MARY SMITH, JAMES SMITH, ABENEZAR TOMLINSON, RICHARD TOMLINSON ("all my lands and houses"). *Executor:* RICHARD TOMLINSON. *Witnesses:* LUKE MIZELL, JOHN OLIVER, ELIZABETH SMITH. *Clerk of the Court:* BENJ'N WYNNS.

LAWLER, PATRICK.   Chowan County.

November 29, 1728. January 22, 1728. *Sons:* DANBY ("my plantation"), DAVID (appointed *Executor*). *Daughter:* ANN LAWTER. *Wife:* PASHENT. *Witnesses:* THOS. ROUNTREE, JAMES HINTON, JOHN MARTAIN. Proven before C. GALE and also before RICH'D EVERARD.

LAWRENCE, GEORGE.   Bertie County.

March 26, 1752. January Court, 1756. *Daughters:* ANN and SARAH LAWRENCE. *Sons:* JOSHUA and GEORGE ("my lands"). *Wife and Executrix:* SARAH. *Executors:* THOMAS and JOHN LAWRENCE (brothers). *Witnesses:* GEORGE LAWRENCE, JOHN YEATS, ROBERT LAWRENCE, THOMAS LAWRENCE. *Clerk of the Court:* BENJAMIN WYNNS.

LAWRENCE, WILLIAM.   Albemarle County.

July 5, 1694. August Court, 1694. *Daughters:* JANE and RACHELL LAWRENCE. *Wife:* MARGARET LAWRENCE. *Cousin:* RACHEL SNELLING. *Cousin:* WM. LAWRENCE. *Executors:* ISRAEL SNELLING and JOHN LAWRENCE. *Witnesses:* FRANCIS JONES, JR., CHRISTOPHER LACY, LAWRENCE HUNT. *Clerk of the Court:* JOHN STEPNEY.

LAWSON, JOHN, Gent.   Bath County.

August 12, 1708. "To my dearly beloved HANNAH SMITH the house I now live in * * * *." "Remainder of my estate real and personal to my *daughter*, ISABELLA, of Bath County, * * * *." Property to be divided among daughter, ISABELLA, and any other child or children of her mother, HANNAH SMITH, "by me." *Executrix:* HANNAH SMITH. *Witnesses:* RICHARD SMITH and JAMES LEIGH. Original missing. Recorded in Will Book 1712–1722, page 39.

LAWSON, SAMUEL.   Craven County.

April 24, 1758. May 31, 1758. *Son:* DURRAM. *Daughter:* MARY PALLIS LAWSON. *Wife and Executrix:* MARGARET. *Executors:* JOHN HILL and WILLIAM MANSFIELD LIPSCOMB. *Witnesses:* JOHN HARDEE, WM. SPEIR and BENJ'N PANE. Proven before ARTHUR DOBBS. To each of the children is devised a house and lot in Newbern.

LAWTER, DAVID.   Chowan County.

Will is not dated, nor is there any probate. *Wife and Executrix:* MARY ("my plantation" and also tract of land called the Cow Island). *Other legatees and devisees:* WALTERS PHELPS (*Executor*), ELIZABETH HOMES, EDWARD PILAND, DARBY LAWTER (brother), CHRISTIANA LOVEWELL, BENJAMIN LOVEWELL. *Witnesses:* THOMAS PILAND, JOHN PHELPS and THOMAS HOMES.

LAYDEN, FRANCIS.   Albemarle County.

February 23, 1727–1728. Probate not dated. *Wife and Executrix:* ELIZABETH. *Sons:* WILLIAM ("the manor plantation"), FRANCIS (land adjoining JOHN STEVENS), GEORGE and ISAAC. *Daughter:* MARY. *Cousin:* WILLIAM MIDDLETON. *Witnesses:* JOHN STEVENS, WILLIAM MIDDLETON, WILLIAM EVENS. *Clerk of the Court:* CHAS. DENMAN.

LAZY (or LACY), JOHN.   Perquimans Precinct.

December 1, 1682. No probate. *Wife:* ABIGAIL. *Daughter:* SARAH LAZY (or LACY). *Witnesses:* JOHN STEPNEY, WILLIAM CHARLES, WILLIAM LAURENCE. No executrix or executor appointed.

LEAR, JOHN.   Nansemond County.

November 21, 1695. December 12, 1695. *Daughters:* MARTHA BURWELL, ELIZABETH LEAR. *Grandson:* JOHN LEAR. *Other legatees:* CHARLES GOREMGE, JOHN GEORGE. *Executors:* LEWIS BURWELL, CAPT. THOMAS GODWIN. *Witnesses:* WILLIAM COFFIELD, JOHN LOWE, ELIZABETH BRIDGER, ANN COFFIELD. *Deputy Clerk of the Court:* ANDREW ROSS. This is a copy of the original made by the deputy clerk of the Court.

LEARGE, JACOB.   Craven County.

1731. March Court, 1731–1732, "of the Switz Country being in Obar Savenchal." *Sons:* JACOB and CHRISTIAN. *Daughter:* MARY LEARGE. *Executor:* JACOB MILLER. *Witnesses:* PETER CORTNEY, GEORGE SLIDER, VENDAL PHILER. *Clerk of the Court:* CALEB METCALFE.

LEARY, CORNELIUS.   Tyrrell County.

March 30, 1742. September Court, 1742. *Brothers:* JOHN and JAMES LEARY. *Sisters:* SARAH, MARY and REBECCA LEARY. *Mother:* SARY LEARY. *Executor:* JOHN LEARY (brother). *Witnesses:* RICH'D LEARY, JAMES SUTTEN. *Clerk of the Court:* W. DOWNING.

LEARY, RICHARD.   Tyrrell County.

April 20, 1738. September 5, 1738. *Sons:* CORNELIUS and JAMES ("plantation whereon I now live to be equally divided between them"), JOHN (three hundred acres of land commonly known as the Chincquapine ridge), THOMAS, RICHARD. *Daughters:* SARAH, MARY and REBECKAH LEARY. *Wife and Executrix:* SARAH. *Executor:* CORNELIUS LEARY. *Witnesses:* JOHN LONG, ELIZABETH LONG. *Deputy Clerk of the Court:* ANDERSON SAGG.

LEATH, JOHN, SR.   Hyde County.

April 9, 1750. June Court, 1751. *Sons:* THOMAS and SAMUEL (100 acres land), CHARLES and PETER (plantation bought of RICHARD LAMBIRTson), JOHN. *Daughters:* SARAH, FRANCES, DORCAS, CASIA, MARY and CATHERINE LEATH, HANNAH HODGES SLADE, ELIZABETH SLADE. *Executors:* JOHN and CHARLES LEATH (sons), AARON TISON. *Witnesses:* AARON TISON, ROGER MASON, JUNR., WILLIAM RICHARD JASPER. *Clerk of the Court:* THOS. LOACK.

LEATH, JOHN.   Hyde County.

November 10, 1751. March Court, 1752. *Sons:* SAMSON ("my manner plantation"), JOHN. *Daughters:* LYDIA and KEZIAH LEATH. *Wife and Executrix:* HANNAH. *Executors:* AARON TISON and JONATHAN JASPER. *Witnesses:* GEORGE BELL, JONATHAN JASPER, ANN JASPER. *Clerk of the Court:* FRANCIS EGLETON.

LEATH, RICHARD.   Hyde County.

May 10, 1749. *Daughters:* AGNES and RACHEL LEATH. *Wife and Executrix:* MARY. *Witnesses:* HEZEKIAH SLADE, BENJAMIN JEWELL, MARY JEWELL. *Clerk of Court:* THOS. LOACK. Testator describes his stock mark as being "crop and under bit and a hole Left Eare, the right under bit and over bit."

LEE, GEORGE.   Pasquotank Precinct.

May 3, 1729. October 12, 1729. *Sons:* JOHN ("ye plantation whereon I now dwell"), EDWARD (land adjoining the plantation aforesaid), GEORGE and WILLIAM. *Daughters:* ELIZABETH, MARY and SARAH LEE. *Wife and Executrix:* ELIZABETH. *Witnesses:* THOS. WEEKES, ANNE WEEKES, ANNE BUNDY. *Clerk of the Court:* H. MINSON. "*Item:* I give and bequeath * * * * * all ye neat cattle that are to be found of ye following mark (viz.) a crop in ye right ear and two slits in ye left wch mark is recorded * * *."

LEE, JAMES.   Bertie Precinct.

January 17, 1731. November Court, 1732. *Sons:* JAMES ("the plantation whereon I now live"), ROBERT and WILLIAM ("a plantation at a place called Kinyard's"). *Wife and Executrix:* SARAH. *Witnesses:* JOHN MORE, RICHARD MORE, JR. *Clerk of the Court of Edgecombe Precinct:* RT. FORSTER.

LEE, MARY (wife of Capt. Thomas Lee),   Chowan County.

September 26, 1716. October 31, 1716. *Sons:* THOMAS BLOUNT (one-half of the "manner plantation with the manner house"), BENJAMIN and JACOB BLOUNT ("the Middle plantation"). *Daughter:* ZILPLIA BLOUNT ("the other halfe of the said manner plantation"). *Executor:* THOMAS BLOUNT (son). *Witnesses:* JERVIS COLEMAN, JOHN EDWARDS, GILBERT HOLLIDAY and WILLIAM SWINSON. *Clerk of the Court:* R. HICKS. Testatrix states that she is also "widdow of CAPTT. THOMAS BLOUNT of Chowan."

LEE, RICHARD.   Edgecombe County.

April 4, 1756. May Court, 1756. *Sons:* TIMOTHY (100 acres of land on "Contenteny Creek"), ARTHUR, RICHARD, SOLOMON (the plantation "which I now live on"). *Daughters:* ELISABETH LEE, RACHEL BRADLEY, SARRAH HORN, MARTHA LEE. *Witnesses:* ABSALOM HOLLIMAN, WILLIAM FOKES, JAMES PERMENTER. *Clerk of the Court:* JOS. MONTFORT. Stock mark of the testator is described as being "swallow fork in the right ear and a crop and half Crop in ye Left Ear."

LEE, STEVENS.   Tyrrell County.

February 2, 1746–1747. June Court, 1746–1747. *Son:* STEVENS (land on Kendricks Creek, ⅔ of grist mill; plantation on White Oak called Cedar Point). *Daughter:* FRANCES LEE ("plantation where I now live called Cabbin Neck"). *Wife:* ELIZABETH. *Executors:* ROBERT WEST, CULLEN POLLOCK, THOMAS LEE and ROBERT WEST, JR. *Witnesses:* WM. MACKEY, JOHN GOMM, JOHN HUGHES. *Clerk of Court:* EVAN JONES.

LEE, STEPHEN.   Onslow County.

January 25, 1772. December 8, 1773. *Son:* STEPHEN ("my plantation bought of WM. HOUSTON"). *Daughters:* MARY, SARAH and FERREBY LEE. *Wife:* FERREBEE. *Executors:* ROBERT ORME, EDWARD STARKEY, PETER STARKEY. *Witnesses:* STEPHEN GRANT, RICHARD OLDFIELD, SARAH WILLIAMS. Proven before JO. MARTIN. Provision is made for education of son at Boston or Philadelphia.

LEE, THOMAS.   Chowan Precinct.

March 14, 1716–1717. July 6, 1719. *Brother:* WILLIAM LEE ("my plantation called Cabbin Neck lying on the East side of Kendricks Creek"). *Children of brother William:* WILLIAM, ELIZABETH and EDWARD. *Friend:* ZILPHA BLOUNT. *Son:* STEPHENS ("all my lands and my mill"). *Wife:* MARY. *Executors:* FREDERICK JONES, EDWARD MOSELEY, WILLIAM DOWNING. *Witnesses:* C. GALE, JERVIS COLMAN, JOHN EDWARDS. Proven before CHARLES EDEN. To wife is given plantation at Conaby "on the east side of the Creek." "*Item:* It is my will that the ship or pink by me now intended to be built at Kendricks Creek shall be compleatly built, finished and launched, &c &c &c."

LEE, THOMAS.

July 23, 1722. July 28, 1722. *Brother:* WILLIAM LEE ("my third part of the Sloop Sea Flower"). *Daughters:* JANE and RACHEL LEE. *Executor:* COLL. MAURICE MOORE. *Witnesses:* GYLES SHUTE, ANTHONY GREEN, THOMAS PESKET (PRESCOTT). Proven before THOMAS POLLOCK, *President of the Council.*

ABSTRACT OF WILLS, 1690—1760.   213

LEE, THOMAS.   Tyrrell County.
November 1, 1750. April Court, 1753. *Son:* THOMAS (lands between Combee Creek and Morrattock River). *Executors:* FRANCIS BRICE, WILLIAM MACKEY, STEVENS LEE. *Witnesses:* JOHN NICHOLLS, WILLIAM BARRET, JAMES RHOADS. *Clerk of the Court:* EVAN JONES.

LEE, THOMAS.   Bertie County.
March 31, 1751. February Court, 1752. *Sons:* WILLIAM ("my plantation"), STEVEN. *Wife and Executrix:* MARY. *Daughter:* PRISSILLA LEE. *Executor:* BENJAMIN WYNNS. *Witnesses:* JNO. HARRELL, THOS. HUDSON, JACOB LEWESS, JNO. LEWESS. *Clerk of the Court:* SAMUEL ORMES.

LEETH, JOHN.   Anson County.
July 21, 1757. *Legatees:* JOSEPH LEETH (son of GEORGE LEETH), MARY WHITE (daughter of JOSEPH WHITE). *Executor:* ANTHONY HUTCHINS. *Witnesses:* JOHN THORMAIN, SAMUEL SMART, ANTHO. HUTCHINS, MARY THURMAN. No probate.

LEGITT, THOMAS.   Currituck County.
April 10, 1749. July Court, 1749. *Wife and Executrix:* ELISABETH. *Daughter:* ELISABETH LEGITT. *Cousin:* JAMES LEGITT (son of ALEXANDER LEGITT). *Witnesses:* ROBERT SIMMONS, ELIASH CORNISH, MOSES CAPS. *Clerk of the Court:* RICH'D MCCLURE.

LEIGH, ANN.   Beaufort Precinct.
August 9, 1732. March Court, 1732–1733. *Sons:* SAMUEL DARDEN (plantation and three negroes), JOSEPH DARDEN. *Daughters:* ANN ADAMS, JANE WATKINS. *Grandsons:* JACOB DARDEN and JAMES ADAMS. *Granddaughters:* SARAH ADAMS and MARY WATKINS. *Executor:* SAMUEL DARDEN. *Witnesses:* ROBERT CAMPEN, JOHN MAYO, THOS. MALLDEN. *Clerk of the Court:* JNO. COLLISON.

LEIGH, JAMES.   Bath County.
September 23, 1728. October Court, 1728. *Sons:* JAMES ("part of the tract of land I now live on"), JOHN (land called the Accomack Entry), Lyonall (land adjoining the Accomack Entry). *Daughters:* SARAH LEIGH, PATIENCE PURSER, ELIZABETH UNDERWOOD and MILLY DURHAM. *Wife:* ANN. *Grandson:* PETER LEIGH. *Executors:* JAMES and JOHN LEIGH (sons). *Trustee:* ROBERT RURNER. *Witnesses:* ROBERT PEYTON, ROBERT PEYTON, BENJA. PEYTON. *Clerk of the Court:* JOHN MATTOCKE.

LEIRMONT, RICHARD.   Hyde County.
February 24, 1752. March Court, 1752. *Daughters:* AMELIA WEBSTER (plantation on Jordan's Creek commonly known by the name of LODOWICK

MARTIN's plantation), WILLIELMA LEIRMONT (one plantation on Jordan's Creek called Margaret Jordan's Fork), MARGARET LEIRMONT (land known as Hunt's Point). *Executors:* WILLIAM WEBSTER, THOMAS JORDAN and THOMAS SMITH. *Witnesses:* ROGER MASON, DINAH SMITH, THOMAS REW. *Clerk of the Court:* FRAN. EGLETON.

LENNON, JOHN.   Bladen County.

October 13, 1757. October Court, 1757. Parish of St. Martin's. *Sons:* JOHN ("this land I now live on"), DENIS (land on Waccamaw Swamp), EPHRAIM. *Daughter:* PHILLIS ELLICE. *Wife and Executrix:* ANN. *Executor:* EVEN ELLICE (son-in-law). *Witnesses:* SAMU'L BAKER, WM. MCREE (or MCKEE), MARY MACKKEY. *Clerk of the Court:* JNO. BURGWIN.

LEPPER, THOMAS.   Bath County, in Craven Precinct.

October 23, 1715. July 22, 1719. *Legatees:* ANNE and KATHERINE NUSS. *Wife and Executrix:* ANNE. *Executors:* DANIEL McFARLANE and RICHARD GRAVES. *Witnesses:* JOHN NELSON, ELIZABETH FERGUSON, MARY JONES and MARY RIDING. *Clerk of the Court:* C. METCALFE.

LEWERTON, EPHRAIM.   Chowan Precinct.

October 10, 1713. *Cousins:* JOHN LEWERTON, son of JOHN LEWERTON (land on Salmon Creek); WILLIAM, son of WILLIAM JONES (land on Black Walnut Swamp); ELIZABETH LEWERTON, ANN and MARY JONES. *Sister:* MARY JONES. *Friend:* REBECCA HARDY. *Executor:* JOHN HARDY. *Witnesses:* WILLIAM JONES, JOHN HOLBROOK. Original missing. Recorded in Book 1712–1722, page 30.

LEWERTON, WILLIAM.   Chowan Precinct.

January 3, 1698–1699. April Court, 1699. *Sons:* WILLIAM and JOHN. *Daughters:* MARY and ELIZABETH. *Wife and Executrix:* ELIZABETH. *Witnesses:* NICHOLAS FILLBERT, JNO. DAVIS and NATH. CHEVIN. *Clerk of the Court:* NATH. CHEVIN.

LEWIS, DAVID.   Carteret County.

October 6, 1773. November 11, 1773. *Devisees and legatees:* JOHN SHEPARD ("plantation whereon I now dwell known by the name of Indian Town"), WILLIAM SHEPARD (plantation known as Glover's Hammock), DAVID SHEPARD, JOHN SIMMONS, DANIEL, JAMES and BENJAMIN SIMMONS, RICHARD SHEPARD. One hundred pounds is bequeathed toward building a church in Beaufort. *Wife and Executrix:* MARY. *Executors:* JOHN SHEPARD, SOLOMON SHEPARD and JOHN SIMMONS. *Witnesses:* WILLIAM BEVIN, JAMES FRAZIER, SARAH FRAZIER. Proven before JO. MARTIN.

ABSTRACT OF WILLS, 1690—1760.   215

LEWIS, EVAN.   Beaufort County.
June 26, 1713–1714.   January 3, 1714.   *Wife and Executrix:* ELIZABETH LEWIS.   *Other legatee:* MARY MAYO.   *Witnesses:* SAM'LL MELTUM, SWAN SWANSON.   *Clerk of the Court:* JNO. DRINKWATER.

LEWIS, WILLIAM.   Bath County.
December 11, 1731.   August 5, 1732.   *Daughters:* ELIZABETH SINCLARE, MARY DUDLEY, MAGDALEN BIGFORD, EDY BENSON.   *Sons:* WILLIAM and SOLOMON.   *Wife and Executrix:* MARY.   *Executor:* WILLIAM LEWIS (son).   *Witnesses:* ED. SMITH, JOHN HERBERT.   Proven before GEORGE BURRINGTON.

LILE, GEORGE.   Chowan County.
October 29, 1752.   January Court, 1753.   *Sons:* GEORGE ("plantation whereon I now live"), JOHN.   *Executors:* WILLIAM' HOSKINS and HENRY BONNER.   *Witnesses:* JOHN CARLTON, JEREMIAH HAUGHTON, JOHN HOSKINS.   *Clerk of the Court:* JAMES CRAVEN.   Six other children are mentioned, but not named.

LILLINGTON, ALEXANDER.   Perquimans Precinct.
September 9, 1697.   October 8, 1697.   *Sons:* JOHN ("plantation whereon I now live and plantation that was formerly STEPHEN HANCOCKS and my silver hilted sword"), GEORGE ("my plantation at Yawpim River and plantation at Little River whereon FRANCIS PENRIE now lives").   *Daughters:* ANN WALKER, ELIZABETH FENDALL, MARY LILLINGTON, SARAH LILLINGTON.   *Sons-in-law:* HENDERSON WALKER and JOHN FENDALL.   *Wife:* ANN.   *Executors:* COL. WILLIAM WILKISON and HENDERSON WALKER.   *Witnesses:* CALEB CALLAWAY, JOHN BARROW, ROBERT HARMAN.   *Clerk of the Court:* W. GLOVER.   Coat of arms on seal.

LILLINGTON, ANN.   Chowan Precinct.
January 26, 1724.   April 1, 1725.   *Daughter:* ELIZABETH LILLINGTON.   *Grandson and Executor:* JOHN SIMONS.   *Witnesses:* JAMES BEASLEY, ANNA STEWART, MARY STEWART.   Proven before GEORGE BURRINGTON.

LILLINGTON, ELIEZER.   Bath County.
April 28, 1729.   December Court, 1729.   *Wife:* ELIZABETH (also appointed *Executrix*).   *Witnesses:* JOHN BROCK, JOHN CLIFFORD, GILBERT HALIDAY.   *Clerk of the Court:* JOHN MATTOCK.   The testator bequeathed the following books: To NATHAN ARCHBALD, "one come and welcome to Jesus Christ by John Bunyan, Mr. Baxters directions of Geting and attaining peace of Conscience, Measons Hymne Book an old sermon book by several divines called the farewell sermons." To JOHN CLIFFORD: "Allens

call to the unconverted and Lees Triumphs of Mercy with a New England Psalm Book." To GILBERT HALIDAY: "Mathers remarkable Providences and an English Dictionary."

LILLINGTON, ELIZABETH.   Bath County.

July 8, 1734. *Sons:* RICHARD BARROW, JOSEPH BARROW, JAMES BARROW, WILLIAM, JOHN and SAMUEL BARROW (1 shilling each). *Daughters:* MARY BARROW and SARAH HARRIS. *Executors:* RICHARD and JOSEPH BARROW (sons). *Witnesses:* DELIVERANCE LATHAN, ELEANOR HOWARD, ROBERT HOWARD. *Clerk of Hyde County Court:* WM. BARROW. Five negro slaves are bequeathed.

LILLINGTON, JOHN.   Beaufort Precinct.

March 19, 1721–1722. July 2, 1723. *Son:* ALEXANDER (1,000 acres of land, two negro slaves, a family bible, etc.). *Daughters:* ELIZABETH, MARY, ANN. *Wife:* SARAH LILLINGTON. *Executors:* MAURICE MOORE, JOHN PORTER and JOHN BAPTISTE ASHE. *Witnesses:* PAT. MAULE, SAMUEL COOPER, JOHN TRANTER. *Clerk of the Court:* JOHN BAPTISTE ASHE. Five negroes, about sixty cattle bequeathed to children.

LILLY, JOHN.   Perquimans County.

January 26, 1753. April Court, 1753. *Wife and Executrix:* KAZEIAH ("plantation where I now dwell"). *Father-in-law:* DANIEL ROGERSON (163 acres of land in Chowan County called the "beverdams"). *Brother:* JOSHUA LILLY, "and my father-in-law, DANIEL ROGERSON" ("three hundred acres of land lying up the Ridges"). *Executor:* JOSIAH ROGERSON. *Witnesses:* NICHOLAS STALLINGS, JOSEPH LILLY, ISAAC LILLY. *Clerk of the Court:* EDMUND HATCH.

LILLEY, THOMAS.   Perquimans County.

October 12, 1735. January Court, 1735. *Sons:* JOHN ("plantation he now lives on"), THOMAS ("plantation whereon I now live"), WILLIAM (100 acres of land), TIMOTHY and JOSEPH (tract of land to be equally divided between them). *Daughters:* MARGARET REDDICK (wife of JOHN REDDICK), HANNA ROGERSON. *Wife and Executrix:* SARAH. *Executor:* THOMAS LILLEY (son). *Witnesses:* GEORGE SPIVE, DANIEL ROGERSON, GILBERT SCOTT. *Clerk of the Court:* JAMES CRAVEN.

LINDSAY, JAMES.   Dobbs County.

June 15, 1768. May 11, 1770. *Brothers:* PETER, WILLIAM and ROBERT LINDSAY. *Executors:* RICHARD CASWELL, JOHN DICKSON and ROBERT LINDSAY. *Witnesses:* FRAS. MACKILWEAN, RIGDON BRICE. *Clerk Superior Court:* AMBLOX BAGLEY.

LININGTON, EDWARD.   Craven County.

July 9, 1736. September Court, 1736. *Sons:* GEORGE and EDWARD LININGTON. *Daughter:* MARY SHERLOCK. *Grandson:* FRANCIS SHERLOCK ("all my lands in Alligator"). *Executors:* DENNIS SHERLOCK and CAPT. JOSEPH HANNIS. *Witnesses:* KATHERINE HANNIS, ANN DUPARTALL, GASPAR VIALON. *Deputy Clerk of the Court:* WM. LANE. Provision in will that "all the pitch and Tarr my negroes makes shall goe to pay my debts &c."

LININGTON, GEORGE.   Craven County.

January 24, 1741–1742. June 16, 1742. *Daughters:* ANN HUTCHISON LININGTON, ELIZABETH LININGTON, CHRISTIAN LININGTON. *Nephew:* FRANCIS SHEARLOCK (640 acres of land on Neuse River). *Wife:* HANNAH. *Executors:* WM. BRICE and RICHARD NIXSON. *Witnesses:* THOS. SMITH and NATHAN SMITH. *Clerk of Court:* N. ROUTLEDGE.

LINSEY, DANIEL.   Currituck Precinct.

November 6, 1720. January 10, 1721. *Son:* DAVID (1 shilling). *Wife and Executrix:* MARY. *Witnesses:* JOHN NORTON, WILLIAM JOHNSON, JOHN MARTYN. *Clerk of the Court:* JO. WICKER.

LINSEY, DAVID.   Currituck County.

August 17, 1749. October Court, 1750. *Wife and Executrix:* ANN. *Mother:* SARAH LINSEY. *Brother:* BENJAMIN LINSEY. To wife is bequeathed "my house and plantation." *Witnesses:* HENRY WOODHOUSE, SOLOMON SMITH, MENES SMITH. *Clerk of the Court:* RICH'D MCCLURE.

LINSEY, ROBERT.   Albemarle County.

May 16, 1689. July 25, 1689. *Executors:* JOHN WILSON and GEORGE HARDIE. *Legatees and devisees:* ANN MATHEWS, COLLETON STURGON ("my plantation at Yawpim"), MARY STURGON, (son and daughter of JOHN STURGON). *Witnesses:* FRANCIS HARTLEY, THOMAS SLATER, MARGARET SLATER. Proven before SETH SOTHELL.

LINTON, WILLIAM.   Bath County.

January 12, 1725–1726. June 20, 1727. *Wife and Executrix:* MARGARET. *Sons and Daughters:* mentioned, but not named. *Witnesses:* ROBERT WATSON, FRANCIS HILL. *Executor:* THOMAS MISTRES. *Clerk of the Court:* CALEB METCALFE.

LITTLE, GEORGE.   Hertford County.

August 1, 1787. *Son:* WILLIAM. *Daughter:* PENELOPE. *Wife and Executrix:* MARY LITTLE. *Witnesses:* GEORGE SWOPE, JOHN JENKINS, ELIZABETH HURST, JAMES BROWN. No probate. All estate of the testator, both real and personal, is divided between son and daughter.

LITTLE, JOHN.   Anson County.
   December 8, 1755. No probate. *Sons:* THOMAS (of Rowan County), WILLIAM, JOHN, ARCHIBALD, JAMES and ALEXANDER. *Daughters:* MARGARET LITTLE and MARTHA REED, wife of JOHN REED. *Grandson:* THOMAS LITTLE. *Executors:* JOHN LITTLE (son) and JOHN CATHEY. *Witnesses:* CHARLES MOORE, HENRY JOHNSON and MARY RENICK. No probate.

LITTLE, WILLIAM.
   June 25, 1734. September 5, 1734. *Sons:* GEORGE (lands in Meherrin Neck), WILLIAM (lands at Okaneechy). *Daughter:* PENELOPE LITTLE (mill at Hoskins). *Wife and Executrix:* PENELOPE. *Executors:* CRISTOPHER GALE, EDMUND GALE and EDWARD SALTER. *Brothers:* JOHN ARBUTHNOT (also *Executor*), ISAAC LITTLE. *Friend:* PENELOPE LOVICK (widow of JOHN LOVICK). *Witnesses:* JOHN BOND, JOHN CROWELL, JOHN PARKER. Proven before GEO. BURRINGTON. About ten negroes bequeathed.

LITTLE, WILLIAM.   Beaufort County.
   March 1, 1756. March Court, 1756. *Sons:* ABRAHAM (land on Cheek's Mill Creek), JACOB (100 acres of "the tract of Land whereon I now dwell"), WILLIAM, JAMES, ISAAC, JOHN, JOSEPH. *Daughter:* JANE MORING. *Wife:* MORNING. *Executors:* ISAAC and JACOB LITTLE (sons). *Witnesses:* AMOS ATKINSON, MARY JUDKINS, JANE ATKINSON. *Clerk of the Court:* WALLEY CHAUNCEY.

LOADMAN, JAMES.   Albemarle County.
   November 14, 1694. April Court, 1695. JANE BARFIELD, RICHARD BARFIELD, WILLIAM BUTLER, SARAH BEASLEY, TIMOTHY CLEAR, ELIZABETH PHELPS, JAMES KENIDAY. *Executor:* WILLIAM BOGUE. *Witnesses:* JOHANNA BEASLEY, JANE BYARD, PATRICK CENADY. *Clerk of the Court:* JOHN STEPNY.

LOCK, BENJAMIN.   Bladen County.
   April 25, 1756. January Court, 1757. *Son:* JOHN ("my land"). *Wife:* MIRIAM. *Executors:* NEIL BEARD (father) and JOHN LOCK (brother). *Witnesses:* THOMAS THEMS, DANIEL BEARD, ELIZABETH LOCK. *Clerk of the Court:* THOS. ROBESON.

LOCK, THOMAS.   Bladen County.
   August 29, 1739. December 19, 1739. *Wife and Executrix:* SUSANNAH. *Sons:* BENJAMIN, DAVID and LEONARD. JOSEPH (land on Northwest River). *Daughters:* ELIZABETH BARTRAM, MARY LOCK. *Witnesses:* THOMAS WIER, PETER WALLSON, WILLIS HUGHES. Proven before GAB. JOHNSTON at Brompton. Original missing. Recorded in Book 1738–1753, page 123.

ABSTRACT OF WILLS, 1690—1760.

LOCKEY, JOSEPH.   Beaufort County.

January 30, 1746. March Court, 1746. *Sons:* JOSEPH ("plantation whereon I now live"), HENRY (land on Barrows Creek), JAMES. *Daughters:* SARAH and FRAZER LOCKEY. *Wife and Executrix:* SARAH. *Executors:* LEVI ALDERSON, JOHN ODEN, JOHN SLADE. "*Item:* My will and desire is that my executors do finish the Brick House now A Building this Ensueing Summer, and that they putt Ten Large Sash Glass Windows therein." *Witnesses:* WM. DUNBARR, AARON SPRING, JOHN HILL. *Clerk of the Court:* JOHN FORBES.

LOCKHART, JAMES.   Bertie County.

December 7, 1753. May Court, 1754. *Wife and Executrix:* ELIZABETH. *Sons:* LILLINGTON ("plantation whereon I now live"), GEORGE ("my two plantations at Cashoak"), JAMES ("all the rest of my lands"). *Executors:* LILLINGTON LOCKHART, MICHAEL CONTANCH. *Witnesses:* EDWARD BRYAN, JOHN BURN, THOS. JACOCKS, ANDR. BURN. *Clerk of the Court:* SAML. ORMES.

LODMAN, JAMES.

November 14, 1694. April 8, 1695. *Legatees:* WM. BARFIELD, SARAH BASLY, TIMOTHY CLEAR, ELIZABETH PHELPS, JAMES KENEDY, WILLIAM BOOGE (*Executor*). *Witnesses:* JOHANA PASLY, JEANE BYRD, PATRICK KENEDY. *Clerk of the Court:* JOHN STEPNEY.

LOFTIN, LEONARD.   Craven Precinct, Bath County.

April 11, 1720. June 21, 1721. *Sons:* CORNELIUS (220 acres of land where "he now lives"), LEONARD ("plantation I now live on"), BENONIEA. *Daughters:* PERCELLY, JANE and JOYCE. *Executors:* CORNELIUS and LEONARD LOFTIN (sons). *Witnesses:* WM. HANDCOCK, ANN METCALFE, CALEB METCALFE. *Clerk of the Court:* CALEB METCALFE.

LOGAN, ALEXANDER.

October 9, 1739. November 6, 1739. *Executors:* THOMAS BLOUNT of Cape Fear, THOMAS BLOUNT and JESSE BLOUNT of Chowan County. Executors are directed to sell the real and personal estate of the testator, and forward proceeds of sale to MESSRS. JOHNSTON & ROBINSON at Charlestown, to be by them forwarded to THOMAS KENNEDY of Bristol, to be applied by him as before directed. *Witnesses:* J. MONTGOMERY, JOHN DUNCAN, DENNIS SHERLOCK. Proven before W. SMITH, C. J.

LONG, DANIEL.   Perquimans County.

July 28, 1714. January 11, 1715–1716. *Wife:* ELIZABETH. *Friend and legatee:* ANN LONGLATHER, of King and Queen County in Virginia. *Executor:* JOSEPH JESSOP. *Witnesses:* RICHARD FRENCH, ROBERT MOORE. *Clerk of the Court:* RICH'D LEARY.

LONG, GILES.

February 12, 1691–1692. This is a nuncupative will, proven by the oaths of EDWARD SMITHWICKE and THOMAS ———, and gives all estate of the testator to his wife and child, who are not named. No probate.

LONG, JAMES.   Albemarle County.

November 24, 1678. October 7, 1680. *Sons:* JAMES, THOMAS and GILLES. *Wife and Executrix:* mentioned, but not named. *Witnesses:* JOHN WILSON, WILLIAM STANARD. No probate officer.

LONG, JAMES.   Chowan County.

November 15, 1711. July 29, 1712. *Sons:* JAMES, THOMAS ("the brick house plantation"), JOHN ("my plantation at Moratock"). *Daughters:* MARY and ELIZABETH. *Wife and Executrix:* ELIZABETH. *Witnesses:* JAMES HAWKINS, THOMAS HOOPPER, LEONARD LEFTIN. Court held at the house of CAPT. THOMAS LEES in Chowan County. *Clerk of the Court:* J. PALIN.

LONG, JAMES.   Chowan County.

September 1, 1731. April Court, 1734. *Sons:* JAMES, GILES, JOSHUA, JOHN, ANDREW (to each of these sons is devised land). *Daughter:* ELIZABETH LONG. *Executor:* GILES LONG (son). *Witnesses:* RICHARD LEARY, THOMAS LEARY, CORNELIUS LEARY. *Clerk of the Court:* MOSELEY VAIL.

LONG, JOSHUA.   Perquimans County.

May 20, 1741. July Court, 1741. *Sons:* THOMAS ("the manner plantation"), JOSHUA ("the land I purchased of JOHN BANKS, and one hundred acres of land on Yopim River"). *Wife:* ELIZABETH. *Executors:* THOMAS LONG (brother), WILLIAM HOSKINS and JOSEPH SUTTON. *Witnesses:* NATHANIEL CARRUTHERS, JOHN BANCKES, ROBERT HARMAN. *Clerk of the Court:* EDMUND HATCH. To two sons is bequeathed one "peryoger" (periagua).

LONG, JOSHUA.   Tyrrell County.

January 7, 1750. June Court, 1754. *Daughters:* PRISCILLA, KEZIAH and ESTER LONG. *Nephew:* STEPHEN LONG ("my plantation"). *Wife and Executrix:* JEMIMA. *Executor:* JOSHUA SWAIN. *Witnesses:* ANDREW LONG, PRISCILLA LONG, GILES LONG. *Clerk of the Court:* EVAN JONES.

LONG, SARAH.   Perquimans Precinct.

September 10, 1712. July 8, 1718. *Legatees:* THOMAS LONG (brother-in-law), MARY PERCE (sister), THOS. PERCE (brother-in-law), CORNELIUS LEARY (son of RICHARD LEARY), JOHN WIATT (cousin), JONATHAN and WILLIAM TAYLOR, JOSHUWAY LONG (plantation at creek's mouth), WIL-

LIAM LONG ("plantation whereon I now dwell"), JAMES CHESSON. *Executors:* THOS. PERCE and THOS. LONG. *Witnesses:* JAMES CHESSON, WILL'M TETHERTON, RICH'D LEARY. *Clerk of Court:* RICHARD LEARY.

LONG, THOMAS.   Perquimans Precinct.

September 21, 1721. October 10, 1721. *Sons:* WILLIAM ("all my land up ye mill swamp"), JOSHUA ("ye land lying on MAJOR HARVES Quarter"), THOMAS ("my plantation whereon I now live, containing four hundred and seventy acres"). *Daughter:* SARAH LEARY. *Wife and Executrix:* REBECKAH. *Executor:* JOSHUA LONG (son). *Witnesses:* THOMAS PEIRCE, JOHN WIAT, JOSHUA CALLOWAY. *Clerk of the Court:* RICH'D LEARY. Court held at the house of MRS. ELIZABETH FRENCH.

LONG, THOMAS.   Perquimans County.

March 7, 1754. April Court, 1754. *Sons:* JOSHUA, THOMAS (plantation commonly known as DANIEL HALL'S plantation). *Wife and Executrix:* SARAH. *Executors:* JOSEPH CREECY, JOSHUA LONG (brother). *Witnesses:* THOMAS WILLIAMS, ROBERT TURNER, ANDR. KNOX. *Clerk of the Court:* WILL. SKINNER.

LONG, WILLIAM.   Perquimans Precinct.

June 2, 1701. July Court, 1712. *Nephews:* JAMES and WILLIAM LONG ("plantation whereon I now live"). *Brothers:* JOHN LONG and THOMAS LONG. *Wife and Executrix:* SARAH. *Witnesses:* THOMAS LONG, JOHN FOSTER, JOHN STEPNEY. *Clerk of the General Court:* J. PALIN.

LONG, WILLIAM.   Perquimans County.

July 4, 1758. April Court, 1759. *Sons:* SIMEON (part "of my manor plantation"), THOMAS ("part of my manor plantation"), REUBEN (land on Franks Creek), WILLIAM, JAMES (100 acres of land on the west side of Minses Creek). *Grandsons:* LEMUEL and ICHABOD LONG, JOSHUA WYATT. *Granddaughter:* MARY WYATT. *Wife and Executrix:* ANN. *Executors:* JAMES, THOMAS, REUBEN and SIMEON LONG (sons). *Witnesses:* THOMAS JONES, ZEPHANIAH JONES, WILL. SKINNER. *Clerk of the Court:* MILES HARVEY.

LONGLEATHER, DANIEL.   Perquimans Precinct.

July 28, 1714. *Legatees:* ANNE LONGLEATHER, of King and Queen County, Va., WILLIAM and JOSEPH STEWARD (sons of wife). *Wife and Executrix:* ELIZABETH. *Witnesses:* RICHARD FRENCH and ROBERT MOORE. Original missing. Recorded in Book 1712-1722, page 105.

LORD, WILLIAM.   Brunswick, in New Hanover County.
July 5, 1748. August Court, 1749. *Sons:* PETER, WILLIAM, THOMAS. *Daughters:* MARY, MARGARET, AMELIA. *Wife and Executrix:* MARGARET. *Witnesses:* RICH'D QUINCE, WILLIAM ROSS, GEO. NICHOLAS. *Clerk of Court:* ISAAC FARIES.

LOVE, AMOS.
August 15, 1770. October 30, 1773. *Sons:* AMOS, THOMAS, CHARLES. *Daughters:* WINNEFRED, MARY, MARGARET, ELISHE and ELIZABETH LOVE. *Wife and Executrix:* MARY. *Executor:* AMOS (son). *Witnesses:* JOSEPH CHATWIN, JOHN WILKINS, CHARLES HARDISON. Proven before JO. MARTIN.

LOVE, DANIEL.   Duplin County.
November 6, 1752. July Court, 1755. *Son:* JAMES. *Daughter:* SARAH LOVE. *Wife and Executrix:* CATHERINE. *Executors:* WILLIAM MCKEE and JOHN SMITH. *Witnesses:* GEORGE PRICE, RICH'D COCKBURN, JAMES PARTON. *Clerk of the Court:* JOHN DICKSON.

LOVICK, JOHN.
August 27, 1727. November 10, 1733. *Nephew:* JOHN LOVICK, son of brother THOMAS LOVICK (plantation called the Horse Meadow or Pasture). *Wife and Executrix:* PENELOPE. *Friends:* RICHARD EVERARD, CHRISTOPHER GALE, EDMOND GALE, ROBERT FORSTER, WILLIAM LITTLE (to each is bequeathed a mourning ring). To WILLIAM LITTLE is bequeathed: "my best Hat, Wigg & Sword my Gold Buttons, all my Law Books & Lord Clarendons History." Testator was executor of the wills of JOHN PLOWMAN and CHARLES EDEN, and his will recites the following in regard to the will of EDEN: "forasmuch as the said CHARLES EDEN on his death bed did charge me if I met with any Trouble about his will from RODERICK LOYD or any of his family that I should not pay the legacy of five hundred pounds sterling in the sd CHAS. EDENS will given to Mrs. MARGARET PUGH, I do therefore forbid my said Executrix to pay the same I having met with great trouble, Vexation and Charge about the said Will from ye RODERICK LOYD and several of his Family and the sd Mrs. PUGH having once refused the said Legacy too and endeavoured to defeat and overthrow the said CHARLES EDENS Will." The depositions of CHRISTOPHER GALE, WILLIAM LITTLE and DR. ABRAHAM BLACKALL will be found filed with the copy of MR. LOVICK'S will from which this abstract is made.

LOVICK, THOMAS.   Carteret County.
April 4, 1759. June Court, 1759. *Wife and Executrix:* SARAH. *Son:* GEORGE PHENNEY LOVICK. *Sons-in-law:* JOHN BENNERS, JAMES PARKIN-

SON. *Grandson:* THOMAS LOVICK. *Granddaughter:* SARAH JONES. *Witnesses:* WILLIAM ROBERTSON, STEPHEN SMITH, ELIZABETH YARBROUGH. *Clerk of Court:* WILLIAM ROBERTSON.

Low, EMANUEL.   Pasquotank Precinct.

March 2, 1726–1727. August 2, 1727. *Daughter:* ANN LETITIA LOW ("plantation whereon I now live; land called Town Point on the Mouth of the Northwest side of Newbegun Creek; one negro"). *Grandson:* GEORGE LOW ("plantation where my cousin ROBINSON now lives and the plantation called New Abbey;" one negro boy and "my seal Scutcheon of arms"). *Wife and Executrix:* ANN. *Witnesses:* W. NORRIS, EDMD. GALE and CHAS. BULL. Codicil appoints daughter *Executrix* and bequeathes to one JOHANNA PEARCE ten pounds. *Witnesses to Codicil:* W. NORRIS, JOSEPH JORDAN, JOHN CONNER, JOSHUA SCOTT, JOHANA PEARCE. *Clerk of the Court:* THOS. WEEKES. *Executors* qualified before RICHARD EVERARD. Coat of arms on seal.

Low, JOHN.   Pasquotank County.

May 11, 1755. March Court, 1759. *Sons:* THOMAS, JOHN LOW, BARNABE. *Daughter:* LIDIE LOW. *Wife and Executrix:* HANNAH. *Executor:* THOMAS LOWE (son). *Witnesses:* GEORGE LOW, EDWARD EDWARDS, JOHN COCKS. *Clerk of the Court:* THOS. TAYLOR.

LOWDEN, JOHN.   Pasquotank Precinct.

May 5, 1719. July 21, 1719. *Son:* ROBERT. *Daughters:* SARAH and ANN LOWDEN. *Witnesses:* SAMUEL COCK, JUN., HENRY HAYMAN. *Clerk of the Court:* W. NORRIS.

LOWE, ANNE.   Pasquotank County.

November 2, 1729. October Court, 1731. *Grandson:* GEORGE LOWE ("now in old England"). *Daughter and Executrix:* ANNA LATITIA LOWE. *Witnesses:* JNO. PALIN, STEPHEN SCOTT, JOHN SCOTT. *Clerk of the Court:* H. MINSON.

LOWE, WILLIAM.   Chowan County.

July 31, 1720. April 17, 1722. *Sons:* JOHN (land in Prince George County, Virginia), WILLIAM (land in Prince George County, Virginia). *Son-in-law:* ROBERT DIXON. *Daughter:* ELIZABETH PACE. *Wife:* ANN. *Executor:* ROBERT DIXON. *Witnesses:* THOMAS WHITMELL, THOMAS ARINGTON. *Clerk of Court:* N. BADHAM.

LOWELL, EDMUND.   Onslow County.

April 21, 1744. July Court, 1744. *Grandson:* EDMUND THORLA. *Daughter:* REBECCA THORLA. *Wife:* ABIGAILL. *Executor:* JOHN STARKEY. *Witnesses:* JOB HUNTER, WILLIAM WEBB, SARAH MIDDLETON. *Clerk of Court:* ANDREW MURRAY.

LOWRY, GEORGE.   Pasquotank County.

September 19, 1753. October Court, 1753. *Friends:* JOHN LOWRY (*Executor*), WILLIAM, MARY and ELISABETH LOWRY. *Witnesses:* JOSEPH LOWRY, WILLIAM LOWRY. *Clerk of the Court:* THOS. TAYLOR.

LOWRY, JOSEPH.   Pasquotank County.

March 23, 1754. April Court, 1754. *Sons:* BENJAMIN and NOAH LOWRY ("all my lands"). *Daughters:* SARAH, LIDEA and HANNAH LOWRY. *Executors:* SOLOMON POOL and JOSEPH DAVES. *Witnesses:* JOHN LOWRY, THOMAS LOWRY, JAMES NEWBY. *Clerk of the Court:* THOS. TAYLOR.

LOWRY, ROBERT.   Pasquotank County.

October 19, 1750. July Court, 1752. *Sons:* WILLIAM, ROBERT and JOHN LOWRY. *Daughters:* BETEY and MARY LOWRY ("my two Lots att Nixson toune"). *Wife and Executrix:* ELIZEBETH. *Executor:* THOMAS RELF. *Witnesses:* WILLIAM SYMONS, JOHN DAVIS, ANNE DAVIS. *Clerk of the Court:* THO. TAYLOR.

LOWTHER, TRISTRIM.   Northampton County.

June 10, 1754. January Court, 1759. *Mother:* MARGERET. *Brothers:* GEORGE, JOHN and WILLIAM LOWTHER. *Sisters:* NELLY and NANCY LOWTHER. *Executor:* WILLIAM LOWTHER (brother). *Witnesses:* BARTHOLOMEW FIGURES, WILLIAM FIGURES, JOHN FIGURES. *Clerk of the Court:* I. EDWARDS.

LOYDE (spelled also LIDE), JOHN.   Bertie County.

July 31, 1741. May Court, 1742. *Sons:* JOHN (200 acres of land in James Citty County, Virginia), ROBERT ("my manner plantation"), THOMAS (125 acres of land adjoining the "manner plantation"). *Daughter:* ELIZABETH LOYDE. *Wife and Executrix:* SARAH. *Witnesses:* WILLIAM PACE, BARRABEE MILTON, ANTONY TYE. *Clerk of Northampton Court:* I. EDWARDS.

LOYD, ROBERT.

December 10, 1726. October 8, 1728. Edenton. *Wife, Executrix and sole legatee:* SARAH CATHERINE LOYD. *Witnesses:* WILL ROWDEN, SARAH ROWDEN, JNO. SELLWOOD. Proven before RICHARD EVERARD.

LUARTON, JOHN.

August 28, 1722. July Court, 1723. Bath Town Creek. *Wife and Executrix:* ANNE. *Witnesses:* JOHN BUCK, THOS. COOKE, ELIEZR. LILLINGTON. *Clerk of the Court:* JNO. BAPT. ASHE.

LUCAS, MARY.   Beaufort County.

March 24, 1761. April Court, 1761. *Daughters:* ANN ALDERSON (also appointed *Executrix*. *Grandsons:* JAMES ALDERSON, JOEL MARTIN, CHARLES ARDISON MARTIN. *Granddaughters:* FRANCES, SARAH, ANN, MARY and SUSANAH MARTIN. *Executor:* JAMES ELLISON. *Witnesses:* JOHN SMAW, SARAH HOWARD. *Clerk of Court:* JNO. SMITH.

LUDFORD, JOHN.   Tyrrell Precinct.

February 26, 1736. *Sisters:* SARAH and HANAH LUDFORD. *Brother:* THOMAS LUDFORD. *Other legatees:* ISACK FITZPATRICK. *Witnesses:* WILLIAM RAPHELL, WM. WILSON and SAMUEL HOPKINS. *Deputy Clerk of the Court:* ANDERSON SAGG.

LUDFORD, WILLIAM.

May 1, 1702. *Son:* WILLIAM. *Grandson:* WILLIAM LUDFORD. To both son and grandson is given a plantation. *Granddaughter:* SARAH LUDFORD. *Wife:* ANN. *Friend:* SAMUEL COOPER. *Executor:* WILLIAM LUDFORD (son). *Witnesses:* GODFREY SPRUILL, CANON SIMPSON and JOHN ANGELY. *Clerk of the Court:* N. CHEVIN.

LUDFORD, WILLIAM.   Of Allegator in the Precinct of Pasquotank.

October 2, 1732. April 2, 1733. *Sons:* WILLIAM, THOMAS and JOHN. *Daughters:* CHRISTIAN, ANN, MARTHA, MARY, TOMSON, RACHEL, SARAH, JOHANA. *Wife:* CHRISTIAN. *Executors:* EDWARD LININGTON, CAPT. SAMUEL SPRUILL, THOS. and JNO. LUDFORD (sons). *Witnesses:* G. LININGTON, BENJAMIN ALEXANDER, WILLIAM MAN. No signature of probate officer.

LUERTON, JOHN.   Bertie County.

August 23, 1740. February 23, 1742. *Nephew:* JOHN GREGORY. *Sister:* MARY JONES (*Executrix*). *Executors:* JAMES CASTELLAW, THOMAS OSBURN. *Witnesses:* JAMES LOCKHART, JOHN RAY, JOHN HILTON. Proven before GABRIEL JOHNSTON.

LUFMAN, WILLIAM.   Currituck Precinct.

April 1, 1728. July 10, 1728. *Sons:* WILLIAM and DANIEL. *Daughter:* MARY WHEATLEY. *Executors:* WILLIAM LUFMAN (son) and THOMAS DAVIS. *Witnesses:* ANDREW ETHERIDGE, WILLIAM TANT. *Clerk of the Court:* J. MARTYN.

LUFMAN, WILLIAM.   Currituck Precinct.

May 9, 1728. July 10, 1728. *Son:* WILLIAM ("all my lands"). *Executor:* THOMAS DAVIS. *Witnesses:* ANDREW ETHERIDGE, JR., DANIEL LUFMAN. *Clerk of the Court:* J. MARTYN.

LUFTY (or LUTTY), WILLIAM.

August 3, 1701. July 11, 1704. *Son:* WILLIAM. *Granddaughter:* MARY LUFTY (or LUTTY). *"Daughter in Lawe":* MARY LUFTY (or LUTTY). *Executor:* WILLIAM LUFTY (son). *Witnesses:* PETER GREY, SR., PETER GREY, JR., THOMAS HOMES. *Clerk of the Court:* THOS. SNODEN. This will is so torn and faded as to be almost illegible.

LUIS, RICHARD. Chowan Precinct.

Not dated. *Sons:* JOHN, BENJAMIN, WILLIAM. *Daughter:* HUDSON. *Wife and Executrix:* ELIZABETH. *Witnesses:* HENRY, WILLIAM and JANE LISLE. Original missing. Recorded in Book 1712–1722, page 177.

LUMBROSIER, JOHN. Pasquotank County.

August 25, 1740. April Court, 1744. *Son and Executor:* JOSEPH. *Grandson:* JOHN DAWES. *Granddaughter:* ELIZABETH BROSYER. *Witnesses:* WILLIAM POWERS, JOSEPH COTTON, ROBT. KEELL. *Clerk of the Court:* THOS. TAYLOR.

LURRY, WILLIAM. Currituck County.

April 21, 1746. July Court, 1746. *Son:* THOMAS ("plantation whereon I now live"). *Wife:* MIRIAM. *Executor:* WILLIAM MACKIE. *Witnesses:* EDWARD COX, GEORGE GAINWELL, SUSANAH MACKIE. *Clerk of the Court:* RICHARD MCCLURE.

LUTON, ADAM. Onslow County.

February 17, 1740. April 2, 1746. *Wife:* ELIZABETH. *Daughter:* MARY LUTON. *Executor:* THOMAS JENKINS. *Witnesses:* THOMAS GANEY, CHARLES BRUTON, ZACHARIA BLACKMOOR. *Clerk of the Court:* GEO. CLOPTON.

LYNCH, JOHN. Granville County.

August 31, 1753. March 7, 1758. *Daughters:* ELIZABETH and NELLY ("plantation whereon I now live"). *Wife:* ELIZABETH. *Executors:* JAMES JENKINS (son-in-law) and ROBERT BAKER. *Witnesses:* THOMAS PARKER, JOHN BLAKENEY and WILLIAM FROHOCK. *Clerk of the Court:* DANIEL WELDON.

LYON, JAMES. Bladen County.

April 27, 1752. June Court, 1752. *Wife:* ZILLAH. *Son:* GEORGE ("my watch"). *Daughters:* ANN (land on White Marsh), ELIZABETH LYON (land on White Marsh), MARY LYON. *Executors:* ZILLAH LYON, MATT. ROWAN, JOHN LYON. *Witnesses:* THOS. ROBESON, RICH'D MULLINGTON, ROBERT WILSON. *Clerk of the Court:* THOS. ROBESON.

MABSON, ARTHUR.   Carteret County.
June 13, 1748. March Court, 1748. *Daughters:* ELIZABETH (wife of NATHANIEL SMITH), SUSANNA. *Son:* ARTHUR. *Nephew:* WILLIAM COLE. *Grandson:* WALTER SMITH. *Wife and Executrix:* MARY. *Executor:* JOHN STARKEY. *Witness:* THOS. LOACK. *Clerk of the Court:* GEO. READ. Six negroes are bequeathed and others mentioned.

MCADAM, JAMES.   Pasquotank County.
April 27, 1742. February 23, 1742. *Wife and Executrix:* SARAH. *Executor:* JOSHUA WHITE. *Witness:* JAMES FENESON. Proven before W. SMITH, C. J.

MCADAMS, SARAH.   Pasquotank County.
October 10, 1744. January Court, 1744. *Brothers and Executors:* JOSHUA and NEHEMIAH WHITE. *Friend:* THOMAS NICHOLSON. *Son:* JOSEPH MCADAM (all estate, both real and personal). *Witnesses:* CHARLES TAILER, THOMAS NICHOLSON, JONATHAN LANGWORTHY. *Clerk of the Court:* THO. TAYLOR.

MCALPIN, WILLIAM.   Craven County.
October 28, 1747. November 7, 1747. Formerly of Sterlingshire in Scotland. *Wife:* HANNAH (in London). *Daughter:* HANNAH MCALPIN (in London). *Mother:* JANE MACKEY (Earthtown in Sterlingshire, Scotland). *Executor:* THOMAS RICHEY, of Jamaica. *Witnesses:* FRANCIS STRINGER, HONNORA DUNCAN, CATHERINE LIDDLE. Proven before E. HALL, *Chief Justice.*

MCCARTY, BAILEY.   Hyde County.
March 1, 1751. June Court, 1751. *Devisees and legatees:* LEAH ANDERSON, BENJAMIN CLEAVES, BAILY COLLINS. *Brother:* DENNIS MCCARTY (land on Great Neck in Currituck). *Wife and Executrix:* ELINOR. *Executor:* THOMAS SMITH. *Witnesses:* THOS. SMITH, WILLIAM SMITH, JEREMIAH SLADE. *Clerk of the Court:* THOS. LOACK.

MCCARTY, DENNIS.   Hyde County.
April 26, 1758. June Court, 1759. *Wife and Executrix:* MARY. *Other devisee:* ABELL HUDSON (one hundred acres of land on Oyster Shell Creek). *Witnesses:* LUKE FORTESCUE, RACHEL MASON, MARTHA BEETY. *Clerk of the Court:* STEPHN. DENNING.

MCCLALLAND, ANDREW.   Bladen County.
March 21, 1752. *Grandchildren:* THOMAS, JANE, ANDREW and JAMES MCCLALLAND. *Executor:* ANDREW MCCLALLAND (son-in-law). *Witnesses:* GEORGE BROWN, BENJA. MOOR, BENJ. FITZRANDOLPH. *Clerk of the Court:* THOS. ROBESON.

McCLAMMY, THOMAS.   New Hanover County.

May 2, 1772. September 27, 1773. *Sons:* PETER ("my plantation"), LUKE (plantation called The Hammock), WONEY, MARK. *Daughters:* ELLENDER NIXON, CATHERINE HYDLEBYRD. *Executors:* PETER, WONEY and LUKE McCLAMMY. *Witnesses:* EDWARD PILCHER, ANNE SUTTAIN, DAVID FALLE. Proven before Jo. MARTIN.

McCLENDEN, DEBORAH.   Perquimans County.

February 8, 1728–1729. October 15, 1732. *Grandson:* JOSEPH SUTTON. *Son and Executor:* RICHARD WHEEDBEE. *Witnesses:* CHARLES DENMAN, JAMES ANDERSON, SENR., JAMES ANDERSON, JUNR. *Clerk of the Court:* CHARLES DENMAN.

MACCLENDON, DENNIS.   Bertie County.

January 19, 1725–1726. *Sons:* DENNIS, JOHN (to each is devised a plantation). *Daughters:* MARY and ELIZABETH MACCLENDON. *Wife:* MARGARETT. *Executors:* JOHN EARLEY (father), FRANCIS and THOMAS MACCLENDON (brothers). *Witnesses:* JAMES PAGE, NICHOLAS FAIRLESS. No probate. "I desire my two negroes * * * in ye winter to make pitch and tarr, and freight it away to New England for such goods as shall best for my wife, etc."

McCORKEL, ROBERT.   Anson County.

No date given. *Sons:* ARCHIBALD and ROBERT (dwelling plantation and plantation on "Catàbee River"). *Wife and Executrix:* MARGARET. *Executors:* JAMES McCORKEL and JAMES LINN. *Witnesses:* JOHN CROCKETT, ROBT. McCLENACKEN. No probate.

McCOY, DANIELL.   Currituck County.

December 2, 1731. October Court, 1735. *Sons:* JOHN and WILLIAM (plantation). *Daughter:* LIDEA McCOY. *Wife and Executrix:* CHRISTIAN. *Witnesses:* MOSES LINTON, JAMES WILKINS, ELEZABATH WILKINS. *Clerk of the Court:* JAMES CRAVEN.

MACCRARY, ROBERT.   Bertie County.

May 30, 1740. July 30, 1740. *Legatees and devisees:* ELIZABETH BARFIELD, MARY BROWN, SARAH BROWN, PRISCILLA BROWN, ELIZABETH BROWN. *Executor:* THOMAS BARFIELD. *Witnesses:* P. ROCHE, THOMAS BARFIELD, MARY BARFIELD. Proven before W. SMITH, C. J.

McCULLOCH, HENRY.

October 25, 1755. November 15, 1755. "Secretary of the Province of North Carolina." *Wife:* MARY. *Daughters:* HENRIETTA MARY, DOROTHY BERISFORD, ELIZABETH MARGARET and PENELOPE MARTHA.

ABSTRACT OF WILLS, 1690—1760.   229

Executor: JOHN CAMPBELL, of Bertie. *Witnesses:* WM. POWELL, GO. ARTHAUD, WM. ROBERTSON. Proven before ARTHUR DOBBS. Coat of arms on seal.

McDANIELL, DANIEL.   Bertie Precinct

April 16, 1733. May 2, 1734. *Sons:* NICHOLAS, DANIEL, JAMES (negroes to each). *Daughters:* ANN and SARAH McDANIEL. *Wife and Executrix:* SARAH. *Witnesses:* JOHN ANDERSON, ALEX. WIGHT, JOHN BRYAN. Original missing. Recorded in Book 1722–1735, page 295.

MACDANIEL, JAMES.   Craven County.

November 29, 1759. *Sons:* JAMES and JOHN (plantation to each), RISDON. *Daughter:* LEVINAH. *Wife and Executrix:* MARGERET. *Executor:* JOHN OLIVER. *Witnesses:* BASSETT SIMMONS, E. BRYAN, DAVID B———. No probate.

MACDANIELL, OWEN.   Bertie County.

February 7, 1742–1743. May Court, 1743. *Wife:* ELLENER. *Son-in-law and Executor:* JETHRO BUTLER ("my manner plantation and six negroes"). *Witnesses:* HENRY HORNE, JOHN CAMPBELL, RICHARD MEDLIN. *Clerk of the Court:* HENRY DESON.

McDOWELL, JAMES.   Bertie County.

February 10, 1752. March 3, 1752. *Brother-in-law:* JOHN SMITH of Wigtown in Galloway in North Britain. *Sister:* CHRISTIAN McDOWELL. *Nephew and Executor:* JOHN SMITH. *Witnesses:* JAMES TROTTER, DANIEL GOLDSMITH, ANNE ORINDELL. Will proven before GAB. JOHNSTON at Edenhouse.

McDOWELL, JOHN.   Brunswick County.

March 27, 1735. April 19, 1735. "Master of the scooner called the Jolly Batchelor, now riding at anchor in Cape Fear River, But of Brunswick * * *." Ten pounds is bequeathed to the Presbyterian church at Dover, Delaware, and five pounds to the Episcopal Church at the same place. *Brother:* JAMES McDOWELL. *Sister:* ELEANOR NISBETT. *Friend:* LYDIA JONES. *Executors:* HUGH CAMPBELL and JAMES ESPY, of Brunswick. *Witnesses:* STEPHEN MOTT, A. DELABASTIE, ANDW. BLYTH, MAGDALEN CAMPBELL. Proven before GAB. JOHNSTON. Provision in will that "a small brick wall be put around my grave wt two marble stones sett up, one att the head and the other att the foot, as is commonly us'd in such cases att Philadelphia."

MACE, FRANCIS.   Pasquotank County.

February 7, 1748–1749. August 1, 1749. *Wife and Executrix:* ANN. *Sons:* JOHN and FRANCIS. *Daughters:* MARY SYMONS, ELIZABETH, SARAH,

HANNA. *Executor:* PETER SYMONS (son-in-law). *Witnesses:* SAMUEL NEWBY, JAMES NEWBY and WILLIAM NEWBY. Proven before GAB. JOHNSTON at Eden House.

MACE, WILLIAM.

May 10, 1757. *Son:* WILLIAM. *Brothers:* BENJAMIN MACE (30 pounds in Irish Money), JONAS MACE (40 pounds Proclamation Money). *Nephews:* WILLIAM MACE and WILLIAM MORRISON. *Wife and Executrix:* ANNE. *Witnesses:* ARTHUR WILLIAMS, BENJAMIN ELLIS, WILLIAM TEEL, WILLIAM PRESCOTT. The foregoing is made from a copy of the original will, and no probate appears. Provision is made for shipping a cargo of indigo.

McGEE, JOHN.   Guilford County.

November 22, 1773. January 28, 1774. *Sons:* SAMUEL, JOHN, ANDREW (plantation on the waters of the Alamance, known by the name of Graham's Place), WILLIAM ("plantation whereon I now live"). *Daughters:* JEAN (plantation on Shockley Creek), SUSANAH (plantation on Shockley Creek, known by the name of Jarrot Hays Place). *Wife and Executrix:* MARTHA. *Executor:* ROBERT LINDSAY (son-in-law). *Witnesses:* ANN LEWIS, JAMES MORGAN, THOMAS WELBORN, MARTHA McGEE. Codicil makes provision for burying-ground, and devises house and one acre of land to one GEORGE ALEXANDER, SENR., to be used as a meeting house. *Witnesses to codicil:* JAMES MORGAN, THOMAS WELBORN. Will and codicil proven before Jo. MARTIN.

McGREGOR, HUGH.   Pasquotank Precinct.

January 12, 1703–1704. February Court, 1704. *Sons:* PATRICK and GREGOR. *Brother-in-law:* JOHN McGREGOR. *Wife and Executrix:* AFRICA. *Witnesses:* WILLIAM BARNSFELD, THOS. PENDLETON, THO. ABINGTON. *Clerk of the Court:* THO. ABINGTON.

MACKANE, GEORGE.   Carteret County.

October 14, 1753. June 6, 1758. *Son:* JOHN. *Daughters:* SOPHIA, MARY and MARGERET. *Wife and Executrix:* MARY. *Witnesses:* ELIZABETH WALLACE, JOHN FINNY. *Clerk of the Court:* WM. ROBERTSON.

MACKARTY, TIMOTHY.   Chowan Precinct.

February 28, 1717–1718. July 15, 1718. *Godson:* WM. GULLIVER. *Wife:* MARY. *Executors:* MAJ. ROBERT WEST and HENRY SPELLER. *Witnesses:* ARTHUR DUGALL, WM. GADD, PATIENCE SPELLER. *Clerk of the Court:* R. HICKS.

MACKDANIELL, DANIEL.   Bertie Precinct.

April 16, 1733. *Sons:* DANIEL, ARCHBELL, ELEXANDER, JAMES. *Daughters:* MARY, ANN and SARAH MACKDANIELL. *Wife and Executrix:* SARAH. *Witnesses:* JNO. ANDERSON, ALEXR. WEIGHT, JOHN BRYAN. No probate.

MACKEELL, ANTHONY.   Bath County.

November 28, 1723. January Court, 1723–1724. Parish of St. Thomas. *Sons:* ANTHONY (1 shilling), THOMAS (plantation), JOHN (plantation), JOSEPH (plantation). *Daughters:* ANN and SARAH MACKEELL. *Wife and Executrix:* RABACKEY. *Witnesses:* WILLIAM PRICE, JOHN SOUTH, PHILIP BAYNARD. *Clerk of the Court:* JNO. BAPT. ASHE.

MCKEEL, BENJAMIN.   Pasquotank County.

April 11, 1754. July Court, 1754. *Daughter:* SARAH MCKEEL ("my plantation"). *Wife and Executrix:* THAMAR. *Executor:* JOHN MCKEEL (brother). *Witnesses:* JOHN CLARK, JOHN LISTER. *Clerk of the Court:* THO. TAYLOR.

MCKEEL, JOHN.   Pasquotank Precinct.

December 24, 1706. April 15, 1707. *Sons:* NATHANIEL and JOHN ("all my lands"). *Wife:* MARY. *Brothers:* THOMAS and DANIEL MCKEEL. *Executors:* THOMAS MCKEEL, JAMES TOOKES. *Witnesses:* JOHN HUNTT, THOMAS ABINGTON, WALTER TURNER. *Clerk of the Court:* THO. ABINGTON.

MCKEELL, JOHN.   Pasquotank County.

October 27, 1750. January Court, 1750. *Sons:* THOMAS and JOHN. *Daughter:* SOPHIA. *Wife:* MARGRETT. *Executors:* THOMAS JAMES and THOMAS MCKEELL, JUNR. *Witnesses:* THOS. MCKEEL and EMANUEL KNIGHT. *Clerk of the Court:* THOS. TAYLOR.

MCKEEL, REBECCA.   Bath County.

May 7, 1729. December Court, 1729. *Sons:* ANTHONY, THOMAS, JOSEPH and JOHN. *Executor:* JOHN BARROW. *Witnesses:* RICH'D HARVEY, LAM'LL HARVEY, PETER MCDOULE (MCDOWELL). *Clerk of the Court:* JOHN MATTOCKE.

MCKEEL, THOMAS.   Pasquotank County.

December 13, 1729. January 13, 1729. *Sons:* BENJAMIN (plantation called the Old Field), THOMAS and JOHN ("the manner plantation"). *Daughters:* ELIZABETH and MARY MCKEEL. *Executors:* BENJAMIN and THOMAS MCKEEL (sons). *Witnesses:* JNO. MCKEEL, LEVI MARKHAM, JOHN POINTER. *Clerk of the Court:* WM. MINSON.

MCKEEL, THOMAS.   Pasquotank County.

May 3, 1753. October Court, 1753. *Daughter and sole devisee:* MARGARET MCKEEL. *Executors:* ANTHONY and CHARLES MARKHAM. *Witnesses:* JONATHAN HOWELL, THOMAS COREY. *Clerk of the Court:* THOS. TAYLOR.

McKEEL, THOMAS. Pasquotank County.

March 31, 1754. July Court, 1754. *Daughters:* GRACE, WIHNEYFRUIT (WINNIFRED), MILLA and ELIZABETH McKEEL. *Wife:* MIRIAM. *Executors:* JOHN McKEEL (brother) and GRACE McKEEL. *Witnesses:* ANTONY MARKHAM, WINEYFRUIT (WINNIFRED) WOODLY. *Clerk of the Court:* THOS. TAYLOR.

McKEITHAN, DUGALD. Bladen County.

January 1, 1750–1751. March Court, 1750. *Father:* DONALD McKEITHAN. *Brother:* JAMES McKEITHAN. *Wife:* MARY. *Cousins:* JOHN McKEITHAN, JAMES McKEITHAN. *Sisters:* NANCY McLAUCHLIN, SARAH McKEITHAN. *Son-in-law:* ROBERT HILLYARD. *Niece:* MARY McKEITHAN. No executor appointed. *Witnesses:* HECT. McNEILL, ALEXR. McALESTER, ANGUS SHAW. *Clerk of the Court:* THOS. ROBESON.

MACKELROY, JAMES. Beaufort County.

April 23, 1773. October 20, 1773. *Sons:* DAVID ("my plantation"), ADAM (land on south prong of Trents Creek), JAMES (land in the fork of Trent Creek). *Daughters:* SARAH and ELIZABETH (land on Neales Creek), MARY CIRTIS (land on Raccoon Creek). *Grandsons:* JAMES and JOHN MACKELROY (land called Whites Old Field). *Wife and Executrix:* ELISABETH. *Executor:* FRANCIS DELAMAR. *Witnesses:* AMOS SQUIERS, THOMAS MACKELROY, ZEKILL HUDSON. Proven before Jo. MARTIN.

MACKFARRELL, JOHN.

November 27,———. December 1,———. This is a nuncupative will proven before JAMES HOYLE, J. P., by the oaths of WILLIAM HUNTER, BENJAMIN TURNER and JOSEPH BENIMAN, in which the testator desired all of his property sold and the proceeds invested for his son, JACOB MACKFARRELL, which son was to remain with his grandfather, JACOB LEWIS.

MACKGUE, LAWRENCE. Bertie County.

April 26, 1740. May Court, 1740. All of estate, both real and personal, is left to grandchildren, children of daughter, ELICE BRYAN. *Executors:* ELICE BRYAN, JOHN BRYAN, EDWARD BRYAN. *Witnesses:* CHARLES, WILLIAM and JOHN RICKETS. *Clerk of the Court:* JNO. WYNNS.

MACKILWEAN, FRANCIS. Dobbs County.

February 8, 1774. March 10, 1774. *Sons:* FRANCIS MACKILWEAN ("my New plantation" also plantation called Old Ford on Contentnea Creek), JOHN STRINGER (five negroes and three horses). *Daughters:* HANAH, ELIZABETH, GATSEY, MARY, ELINOR, NANCY, PENELOPY MACKILWEAN. *Wife and Executrix:* MARY. *Executors:* FURNIFOLD GREEN and RICHARD NIXON of Craven County. *Witnesses:* RD. CASWELL, JNO. SHINE, MARTIN

Abstract of Wills, 1690—1760. 233

Caswell, Simon Bright. Proven before Jo. Martin. Will provides for division of negro slaves into nine parts, one part to each of children and one to wife. *Codicil of even date makes bequest to brother:* John Mackilwean. Same witnesses to codicil.

MacKinne, Barnabee, Jr.   Edgecombe Precinct.

October 13, 1736. November Court, 1736. *Daughters:* Patience and Mary MacKinne. *Other legatees:* Barnaby, son of Joseph Lane; Barnaby, son of William MacKinne; Joseph Lane, William MacKinne (brother), John Pope, James Nowell, Robert and John MacKinne (brothers), Nathaniel Cooper, John Lane. *Wife and Executrix:* Mary (five negroes). Land devised to daughters. Live stock and land devised to other legatees mentioned. *Witnesses:* Nathaniel Cooper, John Crowell, Jno. Watford. *Clerk of the Court:* Thomas Kerney. Original of this will missing. Abstract made from recorded copy No. 58 in Grant Book, No. 4.

Mackinne, John.   Edgecombe County.

February 28, 1753. May Court, 1753. *Son:* Barnaby. *Daughters:* Mary, Martha and Patience Mackinne, Angelina Parish. *Wife and Executrix:* Mary. *Friend:* Cannon Cumbo. *Executor:* Montfort Elbeck. *Witnesses:* Montfort Elbeck, William Gaddy, Mary Elbeck. *Clerk of the Court:* Benj'n Wynns. "I give and bequeath my loving wife * * * the use of my grist mill on Great Quonkee two years next ensuing for pay for the giveing each of my children before mentioned two years schooling."

Mackinne, Richard.   Edgecombe County.

August 10, 1751. August Court, 1755. *Brother:* Robert Mackinne. *Nephew:* Barnaby McKinnie. *Wife and Executrix:* Mary. *Executors:* William Kinchen and William Kinchen, Junr. *Witnesses:* W. Kinchen, Wm. Baker, Lemuel Kinchen. *Clerk of the Court:* Jos. Montfort.

McKinney, Mary.   Edgecombe County.

October 13, 1754. November Court, 1754. "Imprimis. I most humbly bequeath my Soul to God my Maker beseeching His most Gracious reception of it through the all sufficient merits and Meditations of my Most Compassionate Redeemer Jesus Christ, Who gave himself to be an atonement for my sins, and is able to save to the uttermost all that come unto God by him, Seeing he ever liveth to make intercession for them, and who, I trust will not reject me a returning penitent sinner, when I come to him for mercy; in this Hope & confidence I render up my soul with comfort humbly beseeching the most Blessed and Glorious Trinity, one God most holy, most merciful and gracious to prepare me for the time of my dissolution, and then to take me to himself unto that Place of Rest and incomparable Felicity which he has prepared for all that Love and fear his holy name Amen Blessed be God." (The foregoing is given as a specimen of the preambles to the wills of this period.) *Sons:* JOHN, BARNABY. *Daughters:* ANNJELEANY POPE, MARY, PATIENCE and MARTHA MCKINNE. *Executor:* BARNABY POPE. *Witnesses:* DAVID CRAWLEY, WM. GADDY, ROBERT BELCHER. *Clerk of the Court:* BENJ'N WYNNS.

McKINZIE, JOHN.　　　　　　　　　Nansemond County, Va.

March 2, 1754. April Court, 1754. *Sons:* JOHN (795 acres of land at Skeehawkee in Tyrrell County and 305 acres in the Island of Carolina in Bertie County), KENNETH (1000 acres of land at Skeehawkee), WILLIAM (300 acres of land on Ronoke River in Bartie County). *Daughters:* JANET and ANN. *Executors:* WM. GRAY (brother-in-law), CAPT. JOHN HILL of Bertie County and JAMES PUGH and PASCO TURNER of Nansemond County. *Witnesses:* JAMES PUGH, JAMES WRIGHT, CHRISTIAN GOOD. *Clerk of the Court:* SAMUEL RIDDICK. This is taken from a copy of the will of the above named McKINZIE certified to North Carolina by the Court of Nansemond County. Provision in will directs executors to provide for the removal of family to North Carolina.

MACLEARAN, ARCHIBALD.　　　　　　　　Bladen County.

October 26, 1751. December Court, 1751. *Sons:* JOHN and ARCHIBALD (358 acres of land to be divided between them). *Wife and Executrix:* FLORANCE. *Executor:* DUNCAN MACLEARAN. *Witnesses:* DUSHEE SHAW, ARCHIBALD MACDONALD, DUNCAN MACFEE. *Clerk of the Court:* THOMAS ROBESON.

MACKLEMORE, ABRAHAM.　　　　　　　　Bertie Precinct.

January 4, 1735. November Court, 1736. *Sons:* ATKIN, YOUNG ("manner plantation"), WILLIAM. *Wife and Executrix:* MARY. *Witnesses:* WILLIAM GILLIM, WILLIAM CLANTON, JOSEPH BRADY. *Clerk of the Court:* JNO. WYNNS.

MACKLEMORE, JAMES.

February 13, 1733. *Sons:* WILLIAM, JAMES, CHARLES, EPHRAIM (to each of the above named is given a plantation and cattle), JOHN. *Daughter:* MARGORY. *Wife and Executrix:* FORTAIN. *Witnesses:* JOHN DOYLE, ABRAHAM MACKLEMORE, THOMAS ROBERSON. No probate.

MACKLY, HENRY.　　　　　　　　　　Pasquotank Precinct.

February 11, 1720. April Court, 1721. *Daughters:* MAREY MACKLEY (50 acres of land on the north side of Nuce River), ANNE MACKLEY (50 acres of land on the north side of Nuce River). *Son-in-law:* MARTIN MILLER (50

acres of land on the north side of Nuce River). *Wife and Executrix:* BAR-
BERY. *Witnesses:* JANE RUSEL, ELIZABETH PALMER, EVAN JONES. *Clerk
of the Court pro tem.:* JNO. PALIN.

MACMIEL, JOHN.   Bertie Precinct.

February 26, 1729. February 22, 1730. *Devisees:* JOHN MYHAND (300
acres of land on Tar River), MARY MYHAND ("my plantation"), JOHN GRAY
(*Executor*). *Witnesses:* JOHN HARRISS, ANN MIHAND, HENRY WALKER.
Proven before RICH'D EVERARD.

MCNARY, GILBERT.   Hyde County.

March 11, 1746–1747. June 2, 1747. *Son:* WILLIAM. *Daughters:*
MARY and JANE. *Wife:* ELISABETH. *Executors:* JOHN SMITH, SR., and
JOHN SMITH, JR. *Witnesses:* WM. SPEIR, THOMAS ALLEN, AARON TISON.
Clerk of the Court: THOS. LOACK.

MACNAUGHTEN, RANALD.   Bladen County.

October 5, 1752. December 19, 1752. *Sons:* NEILL and CHARLES.
Wife: ISBELL. *Daughter:* MARY. *Executors:* DUNCAN and NEILL MAC-
COULASKIE. *Witnesses:* ANGUISH SHAW, JOHN OPTAN, JOHN CAMPBELL.
Justices of Bladen County Court: GRIFFITH JONES and BENJAMIN FITZRAN-
DOLPH. *Clerk of the Court:* THOS. ROBESON.

MCREE, WILLIAM.   Duplin County.

March 30, 1751. April 2, 1751. Goshen Settlement. *Sons:* JOHN,
JAMES, WILLIAM, ROBERT, SAMUEL. *Daughters:* SARAH SMITH, ALICE
WILLIAMS, SUSANNAH MCREE. *Executors:* JOHN SMITH and WILLIAM
MCREE. *Witnesses:* WILLIAM KENNAN, SARAH MCALEXANDER, ELIZA-
BETH CHAMBERS. *Clerk of the Court:* JOHN DICKSON.

MACKY, WILLIAM.   Bertie County.

1730. *Son:* DANIEL. *Daughter:* MARGRET. All of estate, both real and
personal, is devised and bequeathed to MARY JONES, daughter of HENRY
JONES, of Greenhall, in Chowan County. No signature, witnesses or probate.

MADDOX, JOHN.   Carteret County.

January 1, 1767. March 22, 1774. *Wife and sole legatee:* MIRIAM.
Executors: MOSES HOUSTON, JAMES BARRY. *Witnesses:* WILLIAM HOUS-
TON, DAVID WILLIAMS. Will proven before JO. MARTIN.

MADREN, RICHARD.

March 10, 1755. June Court, 1755. *Sons:* THOMAS ("my plantation"),
REUBEN. *Daughters:* ELIZABETH, RUTH and ANN MADREN. *Wife and*

Executrix: SARAH. *Executors:* JACOB and JOSEPH MADREN (brothers). *Witnesses:* THOMAS PRITCHARD, JNO. SMITHSON. *Clerk of the Court:* THOS. TAYLOR.

MAKEE, DANIELL.   County not given.

July 15, 1694. July 15, 1695. *Sons:* DANIELL, JOHN. *Daughters:* CATHERINE, ELINOR. *Wife and Executrix:* ELINOR. *Witnesses:* G. MUSCHAMP, PIERRE LOURRE, ROBERT MELLYNE, WILLIAM BROWNE. *Clerk of the Court:* EDWARD MAYO.

MAN, JOHN.   Tyrrell County.

February 19, 1742–1743. March Court, 1744. *Sons:* JOHN, WILLIAM, THEOPHALOS ("land on ye South side of Mesus Creek known by ye name of Volls Island"), EDWARD ("ye southermost part of my plantation"), THOMAS ("land joining my son EDWARD'S"), JOSEPH ("ye other part of my maner plantation"). *Daughters:* DORRITY——— and ELIZABETH MAN. *Wife:* MARGIT. *Executors:* THEOPHALUS, JOSEPH and EDWARD MAN. *Witnesses:* BENJAMIN BIDGOOD, JAMES NAHALE. *Clerk of the Court:* THOS. LEE.

MAN, JOHN.   Northampton County.

April 19, 1757. November Court, 1757. *Sons:* FREDERICK, ABSOLOM, JESSE. *Daughter:* LIZEBETH. *Wife and Executrix:* LIZEBETH. *Witnesses:* JOSEPH SIKES, THOMAS TADLOCK. *Clerk of the Court:* I. EDWARDS.

MAN, THOMAS.   Bertie County.

September 30, 1735. November Court, 1735. *Sons:* JOHN ("my plantation and six hundred and forty acres of land"), THOMAS (plantation on Wickacone Creek). *Cousin:* WILLIAM CRAWMAN (land on Killam Swamp). *Daughter:* MARY. *Grandson:* GEORGE WILLIAMS. *Wife:* BRIDGETT. *Executors:* GEORGE WILLIAMS, SR., and THOMAS BUSBEY. *Witnesses:* CHARLES HORNE, GEORGE WILLIAMS, JUNR. *Clerk of the Court:* JOHN WYNNS.

MANDOVEL, JOHN.   Hyde County.

September 31, 1751. March Court, 1752. *Sons:* SAMUEL and JOHN (a plantation to each). *Daughters:* ELIZABETH, REBECKAH, DINEY. *Wife and Executrix:* ELIZABETH. *Executor:* LITTLE JARMAN. *Witnesses:* STEPHEN MANDOVEL, LITTLE JARMAN, JOSEPH GURGANUS. *Clerk of the Court:* FRAN. EGLETON.

MANDUE, THOMAS.   Bertie Precinct.

April 17, 1736. August Court, 1736. *Grandson:* MANDUE DOTHRY ("my plantation and orchards, and all my books except the ould Bible and the Whole Duty of Man"). *Granddaughter:* PERCILA DOTHERY.

Son: WILLIAM BUNN. *Daughter:* MARY. *Executor:* ARTHUR WILLIAMS. *Witnesses:* H. TUDER, WILLIAM BUN, ISAAC RICKS. *Clerk of the Court:* JOHN WYNNS.

MANER, JOHN.   Bertie County.

February 21, 1728-1729. May Court, 1729. *Sons:* WILLIAM, HENRY, JACOB. *Friend:* SOLOMON ALSTON. *Executor:* HENRY MANER (son). *Witnesses:* ELIZABETH SMITH, MARY ALSTON, JOHN ALSTON. *Clerk of the Court:* ROBT. FORSTER.

MANEY, JAMES.   Northampton County.

November 30, 1751. August Court, 1752. *Son and Executor:* JAMES. *Daughters:* JANE MAGETT (plantation bought of WM. TURNER), SUSANE SKINER (plantations bought of JOHN HOBBS, JOHN ROBENS and NATHAN BARNES, and a new survey on river). *Executors:* NICLAS MAGETT and CHARLES SKINER. *Witnesses:* JOHN MINSEY, DAVID JARNAGAND, THOS. JARNAGAND. *Clerk of the Court:* I. EDWARDS.

MARCKHAM, ANTHONY.   Albemarle County.

September 24, 1710. *Sons:* LEVY, JOSHUA, CHARLES, ANTHONY (to each is given a plantation). *Daughters:* MARY and TAMAR. *Wife:* JOY. *Executor:* LEVY MARCKHAM (son). *Witnesses:* FRANCIS DeLaMARE, EDWARD CHAPMAN. No probate.

MARKHAM, JOSHUA.   Pasquotank County.

August 6, 1746. April Court, 1747. *Devisees and legatees:* TIMER EVINS, BARTHOLOMEW EVINS, JOSHUA EVINS, ANTONY MARKHAM, JOSUA, CHARLES, ELIZABETH and MARY MARKHAM (to these are given negroes). *Executor:* ANTHONY MARKHAM. *Witnesses:* SAMUEL SCOLLAY, THOS. HAMLIN. *Clerk of the Court:* THOS. TAYLOR.

MARKHAM, LEVI.   Pasquotank County.

April 1, 1743. April Court, 1744. *Legatees:* WILLIAM MARKHAM CRANK,, MARY, ANN and ELIZABETH CRANK. *Executrix:* ELIZABETH CRANK. *Executors:* ANTHO. MARKHAM and WILLIAM WALLIS. *Witnesses:* TERENCE SWEENY, WILLIAM JAMES, ANNE BOYD. *Clerk of the Court:* THOS. TAYLOR.

MARR, JOSEPH.   Craven County.

March, 1745. *Wife and Executrix:* ALIF. Three children mentioned, but not named. Dates and names of witnesses illegible.

MARSDEN, ALICE.   New Hanover County.

March 24, 1755. March 1, 1759. Wilmington. *Daughters:* ALICE and PEGGY MARSDEN. *Granddaughter:* ALICE MOBSON. *Executor:* ARTHUR MOBSON (son-in-law). *Witnesses:* ISAAC FARIES, JOHN DAVIS, JUNR., ANTHONY WARD. Proven before ARTHUR DOBBS.

MARSDEN, THOMAS.   New Hanover County.

September 23, 1739. *Father:* RICHARD MARSDEN. *Mother:* ELIZABETH MARSDEN, "of Halifax, in ye County of York in England. *Brother:* WILLIAM MARSDEN. *Executors:* JOHN SWANN and THOMAS JONES. *Witnesses:* WILLIAM DUTTEN, WILL CARR, JNO. MARSHALL. No probate. Coat of arms on seal.

MARSHALL, JOHN.   Edgecombe County.

October 24, 1757. February Court, 1758. *Sons:* JOHN ("plantation I now live on"), HUMPHREY (plantation over Tar River at the head of Middle Creek), ABSOLEM. *Daughters:* ELIZABETH MARSHALL, PRISCILLA MARSHALL, GOODWIN TUCKER (to these are given negroes). *Wife and Executrix:* AMY. *Executor:* JOHN MARSHALL (son). *Witnesses:* BENJA. HAILE, BENJ'N NEVILLE, THOS. MARSHALL. *Clerk of the Court:* JOS. MONTFORT.

MARSHALL, WILLIAM.   Bertie County.

September 4, 1738. May Court, 1739. *Wife:* MARGARET. *Other legatees:* MARGARET ROBERTS, JOHN ROBERTS, SARAH PUKE, JAMES PARROT PUKE, MARY KEEFE, WM. PEEKE, JOHN KEEP. *Executrix:* MARGARET MARSHALL (wife). *Witnesses:* JOHN WYNNS, WILLIAM LEE, WILLIAM LINN. *Clerk of the Court:* JNO. WYNNS.

MARSTON, ELIZABETH.   Bath County.

January 2, 1732. September 11, 1733. *Daughters:* MARY, ANN and MOURNING MARSTON. *Executors:* ANN and MOURNING MARSTON. *Witnesses:* JNO. COLLISON, JAMES ADAMS, ROGER JONES. *Clerk of the Court:* JNO. COLLISON. *Justices of Beaufort and Hyde Precincts:* ROBERT TURNER, BENJ. PEYTON, HENERY CROPTON.

MARTIN, ELIZABETH.   Craven County.

March 30, 1767. South River. *Daughters:* SARAH LOFTIN, ELIZABETH MILL. *Grandsons:* ROBERT and ADAM WALLIS, SLOCUMB FERGUSON, THOMAS PITTMAN. *Granddaughters:* SARAH MAHAINS, ANN STEVENS, COMFT. ROLLINS, ELIZABETH HAMBLETON, PRUDENCE FULFORD, JEAN WALLIS. *Brother:* JOHN CUMINGS. *Executor:* JAMES JONES. *Witnesses:* THOMAS MCLIN, SAM'LL MASTERS, ROBERT OLIVER. No probate.

ABSTRACT OF WILLS, 1690—1760.   239

MARTIN, GEORGE.

October 6, 1734. March 8, 1734. *Wife and Executrix:* mentioned, but not named. *Witnesses:* W. SMITH, NATH. RICE, JOHN MONTGOMERY. A codicil to the will devises to EPHRAIM VERNON, brother-in-law of the testator, all lands taken up by patent. Date of codicil same as will, and same witnesses. Proven before GABRIEL JOHNSTON.

MARTIN, JOEL.   Bath County.

October 24, 1715. July 3, 1716. *Sons:* JOHN (land on Matchapungo Creek), WILLIAM (land in Newport Sound). *Daughters:* ANN MARTIN (320 acres of land), ELIZABETH PENNY, MARY WOODARD, FRANCES JARVIS. *Son-in-law:* JOHN PENNY. *Executors:* ELIZABETH PENNY, JOHN PORTER. *Witnesses:* JOHN DEON, HENRY SMITH, JNO. DRINKWATER. *Clerk of the Court:* JNO. DRINKWATER.

MARTIN, JOHN.   Pasquotank County.

December 25, 1741. January Court, 1741–1742. *Sons:* NATHANIEL, JOSEPH, JOHN, JOSHUA. *Daughters:* ELENER BRYANT, MARYANN JESSOP, ANN MARTIN, ELIZABETH MARTIN, JANE MORGIN. *Executors:* JOHN MORGIN (son-in-law), THOMAS JESSOP. *Witnesses:* WILLIAM DAVIS, JOSEPH PRITCHARD, BENJA. PRITCHARD. *Clerk of the Court:* THO. TAYLOR.

MARTIN, NATHANIEL.   Pasquotank County.

November 28, 1743. January Court, 1743. *Son and Executor:* JOSHUA (my land and plantation). *Daughter:* MIRIAM MARTIN. *Wife:* SARAH MARTIN. *Witnesses:* WILLIAM DAVIS, GEORGE DAWSON, WILLIAM BELLMAN. *Clerk of the Court:* THOS. TAYLOR.

MARTIN, THOMAS.   Craven County.

January 15, 1758. March 23, 1758. South River. *Wife and Executrix:* ELIZABETH. *Nephew:* ROBERT MARTIN, son of brother RICHARD MARTIN. *Other legatees:* SARAH LOFTIN, wife of LEONARD LOFTIN of Handcocks Creek; JOAN MARTIN FERGUSON, daughter of MARK FERGUSON. *Executor:* JOHN THOMLINSON, of Clubfoots Creek. *Witnesses:* JOHN CUMMINGS, ELISHA BELKNAP, STEPHEN WALLIS. Proven before ARTHUR DOBBS at Newbern.

MARTIN, WILLIAM.   Bertie County.

April 8, 1735. August Court, 1736. *Sons:* RICHARD ("plantation whereon I now live"), THOMAS, MOSES, JOHN. *Daughters:* MARY and ELSE MARTEN. *Wife and Executrix:* ELSE MARTIN. *Witnesses:* ALEXR. COTTEN, JOHN CARELL. *Clerk of the Court:* JNO. WYNNS.

MARTIN, WILLIAM.   Hyde County.

  November 12, 1744. December 4, 1744. *Daughter:* ELIZABETH MAR-
TIN. *Wife and Executrix:* MARY. *Executors:* DANIEL BLIN (merchant
in Bath) and ALEXANDER FOREMAN. *Other legatees:* EDNE and RICHARD
MARTIN. *Witnesses:* JOS. TART, JOS. HOLLOWELL, THOMAS PARTREE.
Clerk of the Court: THOS. LOACK.

MARTIN, WILLIAM.   Beaufort County.

  August 23, 1745. February 18, 1745. St. Thomas Parish. *Sons:* JOHN
(land on the Beaver Dams), JOEL, WILLIAM, JOSEPH (to each of the sons
is given a plantation). *Daughters:* ANN, ELIZABETH MARTIN. *Cousin:*
JOHN MARTIN. *Executors:* MARY MARTIN (wife), HENRY SNEAD, JOHN,
JOEL and WILLIAM MARTIN. *Witnesses:* JOHN ALDERSON, MARY ALDER-
SON, HENRY WOODARD. Proven before GAB. JOHNSTON at Eden House.

MARTIN, WILLIAM.   Beaufort County.

  December 21, 1769. *Sons:* WILLIAM, THOMAS, JAMES, HENRY. *Daughters:* LURANE, MARY, ANNES, ANNE. These are named as "MARTIN,
alias SCOTT." *Executors:* MOSES HARE, HENRY BONNER, THOMAS JONES.
Witnesses: ALEX. GASTON, JOHN SMAW, JAMES LANE. No probate.

MASHBORNE, JETHRO.   Onslow County.

  December 17, 1752. January Court, 1753. *Son:* EDWARD ("my plantation" and two negroes). *Daughters:* MARY and SARAH MASHBORNE.
Wife and Executrix: SUSANNA. *Executors:* CHARLES COX and DANIEL
MASHBORNE. *Witnesses:* JOHN JARMAN, WM. WHALEY, ELISABETH
PARKER. *Clerk of the Court:* WM. CRAY. Coat of arms on seal. Court
held for Onslow County at the house of JONATHAN MELTON on the Northeast.

MASKIL, WILLIAM.   Craven County.

  February 21, 1753. November Court, 1753. *Brother:* DANIEL. *Wife
and Executrix:* DOROTHY. *Witnesses:* JAMES WHITING, CHARLES HOWARD.
ELIZABETH WHITING. *Clerk of the Court:* SOL. REW.

MASON, JOHN.   Currituck Precinct.

  August 15, 1720. January 10, 1721. *Sons-in-law:* JAMES and MATTHIAS
TOLER. *Friend:* JOHN EVANS. *Wife and Executrix:* ANN. *Witnesses:*
RICHARD WILLIAMSON, DENNIS CALLIHERN, JOHN MARTYN. *Clerk of the
Court:* JO. WICKER.

MASON, JOHN.   Hyde Precinct.

  February 15, 1737–1738. September Court, 1741. "In New Currituck." *Sons:* ROGER, THOMAS ("my dwelling plantation"). *Daugh-*

ters: MARY and MARGRET MASON. Grandsons: MASON TISON, JOHN MASON. Other legatees: THOMAS TISON and CHARLES HARRINGTON. Wife and Executrix: MARY. Witnesses: SAMUEL JASPER, JOHN TULE, THOM. SRETON CROMWELL. Clerk of the Court: H. BARROW.

MASON, JOHN.   Craven County.

February 27, 1747. September Court, 1748. Sons: THOMAS, JOHN, JOSEPH (to each is given about 100 acres of land). Wife and Executrix: ELIZEBETH. Executor: JEREMIAH PARSONS. Witnesses: SOUTHY REW, BENJAMIN MASON, JAMES BUSH. Deputy Clerk: PHIL. SMITH.

MASON, JNO., SR.   Hyde County.

January 9, 1751–1752. March 1, 1752. Sons: MOSES ("my dwelling plantation"), JOSHUA ("land on Roes Bay"), JOHN, JR. (land at Swanquarter Bay). Daughters: CHARITY, ANN and AGNES MASON. Father: ROGER MASON. Brother: ROGER MASON, JR. Wife and Executrix: CATHARINA. Executors: ROGER MASON, JR., and THOMAS MASON, JR. Clerk of the Court: FRAN. EGLETON.

MASON, MARY.   New Hanover County.

November 20, 1771. February 19, 1772. Wilmington. Devisees and legatees: ANN ROBESON (dwelling house on south side of Dock Street and west side of Second Street), JOHN ROBESON, RICHARD LOWRY (house at corner of Front and Princess Streets occupied by JOHN FORSTER), ROBERT BAIRD (tenements on Front Street "at present occupied by the reverend JAMES TATE and NEIL SCHAW"). Executors: JOHN ROBESON, ROBERT BAIRD and CORNELIUS HARNETT. Witnesses: A. MACLAINE, JA. MORAN, JOHN NUTT. Proven before JO. MARTIN.

MASON, ROGER.   Hyde County.

April 14, 1752. September Court, 1752. Son: ROGER (100 acres of land and one-half estate). Daughter: DORCAS. Wife and Executrix: SARAH (200 acres of land on Contentney). Executors: BENJAMIN and THOMAS MASON. Witnesses: THOMAS EASTER, HANNAH LEATH, SOLOMON CARTER. Clerk of the Court: FRANCIS EGLETON. Coat of arms on seal.

MASON, ROGER.   Hyde County.

December 23, 1754. June Court, 1756. Sons: BENJAMIN ("Gailars Hammocks and the upper old field"), THOMAS ("land up Roes down to the Great Bridges"), JOHN and ROGER MASON. Grandsons: CHRISTOPHER MASON, ROGER MASON, JR., DAVID MASON (land called the paupoy ridge), MOSES MASON. Granddaughter: SUSANNAH MASON. Wife: MARY. Executors: BENJAMIN and THOMAS MASON (sons). Witnesses: JOHN TULE, JEAN TULE, JACOB TULE. Clerk of the Court: STEPHEN DENNING.

MASSEY, HEZEKIAH.   Bertie Precinct.

April 15, 1727. August Court, 1727. *Sons:* HEZEKIAH, RICHARD and WILLIAM (100 acres of land to each), JOHN. *Daughters:* SARAH and LUCEY MASSEY. *Friend:* MATHEW SHEERING. *Wife and Executrix:* ELIZABETH. *Executor:* JOHN MASSEY (son). *Witnesses:* ABRAHAM BURTON, JOHN GREEN, SENIOR, THOMAS HICKS. *Clerk of the Court:* RT. FORSTER.

MASTERS, JOHN.   Craven County.

March 22, 1773. July 27, 1773. *Brothers and Executors:* THOMAS and JOSEPH MASTERS. *Wife:* JULYANN. *Witnesses:* THOS. COOKE, BENJ'N CUMMINGS, SARAH WHITEARD. Proven before JO. MARTIN.

MASTERS, JOSEPH.   Craven County.

November 22, 1759. May 3, 1760. *Sons:* JOHN (plantation on the west side of Little Creek), THOMAS (land on Adams Creek), JOSEPH ("plantation whereon I now live"). *Wife and Executrix:* ARCALA. *Executors:* SAMUEL MASTERS (brother), THOMAS COOK. *Witnesses:* THOS. COOK, ELIZA WEST, WILLIAM NORTHAN, SOLOMON NORTHAN. Proven before ARTHUR DOBBS.

MASTERS, THOMAS.   Craven County.

October 27, 1746. *Sons:* JOSEPH, SAMUEL. *Wife and Executrix:* SARAH. *Witnesses:* THOS. COOK, PETER DUKE, DAVID RAMSEY. No probate. Testator mentions Indian slave.

MATHAM, RALPH.   Currituck County.

January 2, 1749. April 26, 1750. *Devisees:* BENJAMIN SIKES, NICHOLAS LUNR (*Executor*). *Witnesses:* ROBERT STILL, WILLIAM STEVENSON, WILLIAM NORTON. Proven before GAB. JOHNSTON.

MATHERS, EDWARD.   Craven County.

July 17, 1753. *Daughters:* ANN GRAY, MARY MATHERS, ELEZEBETH WINFIELD, SARAH MATHERS, PRISCELLA MATHERS, MATHERS LURENIA MATHERS (*Executrix*). *Executor:* LAWRENCE HYLAND. *Grandson:* WILLIAM NEVILE. *Witnesses:* MARTEN HAGIN, THOS. MATCHETT, ELIZBETH RIGBE. No probate.

MATHEWS, CHARITY (wife of JAMES MATHEWS).
                                                  Tyrrell County.

January 20, 1771. May 16, 1772. *Daughters:* PENELOPE SPEIR (plantation on Conetoe), ELIZABETH HARDY, MARY ANDREWS, SUSSANAH SHERRARD. *Other legatees:* JAMES CONNER WILLIAMS, son of JOSEPH JOHN WILLIAMS, WILLIAM WILLIAMS, THOMAS CARNAL, ELIZABETH BLANCHET. *Executors:* JAMES SHERRARD, JOHN EVERET, PENELOPY SPEIR. Proven before JO. MARTIN.

MATHEWS, THOMAS.   Chowan County.

October 6, 1732. October Court, 1732. *Legatees:* THOMAS WATERS, RICHARD HARECK. *Son-in-law:* SAMUEL BYFIELD. *Wife and Executrix:* PRECILLA. *Witnesses:* SARAH HARECK, WILLIAM HARE, JNO. MCWILLIAMS. *Clerk of the Court:* RT. FORSTER.

MATTHIAS, JOHN.   Perquimans County.

March 3, 1746–1747. April Court, 1748. *Son and Executor:* WILLIAM ("my plantation"). *Wife and Executrix:* ELIZABETH. *Witnesses:* DAVID and MARY BUTLER. *Clerk of the Court:* EDMUND HATCH.

MATTOCKE, JOHN.   Bath County.

October 12, 1732. September 4, 1733. *Daughters:* ANN and ELIZABETH MATTOCKE. *Wife:* MARY. No executor named. *Witnesses:* BEN WHEATLEY, WM. OWEN. *Clerk of the Court:* JNO. COLLISON.

MAUDLIN, EZEKIEL.   Perquimans Precinct.

March 25, 1732. April 17, 1732. *Sons:* JEREMIAH, JOSHUA and JAMES. *Wife and Executrix:* HANNAH. *Executor:* THOMAS WEEKES. *Witnesses:* ZEB. CLAYTON, JOHN STEVENS, TULLE WILLIAMS. *Clerk of the Court:* CHARLES DENMAN. Coat of arms on seal. Will recites that testator had sent to Boston for a negro and some goods.

MAUDLIN, THOMAS.   Perquimans County.

September 16, 1758. January Court, 1759. *Son:* JEREMIAH. *Wife:* SARAH. *Brother:* EDMUND CHANCEY. *Executors:* JOHN CLAYTON (father-in-law), RICHARD CLAYTON (brother-in-law) and WILLIAM TRUMBULL. *Witnesses:* WILLIAM TENNETT, EDMUND CHANCEY, JOSEPH BARCLIFT. *Clerk of the Court:* MILES HARVEY.

MAULE, JOHN.   Beaufort County.

December 11, 1773. February 16, 1774. *Son:* MOSES ("my manor plantation"; six negroes and mill on Blounts Creek with land adjoining). *Daughters:* ELIZABETH MAULE ("my Quarter Plantation" and six negroes), ANNE (400 acres of land and five negroes), PENELOPE (900 acres of land and five negroes), JEMIMA (land on Blounts and Nevils Creeks and in Pitt County and six negroes). *Wife:* ELIZABETH (seven negroes). *Executors:* MOSES HARE (brother-in-law), JOHN PATTEN, READING BLOUNT, JOSEPH BLOUNT. *Witnesses:* WILLIAM GERRARD, FORBIS GERRARD, JOHN NEVIL. Proven before Jo. MARTIN.

MAULE, PATRICK.   Bath County.

April 19, 1736. Beaufort Precinct. *Wife:* ELIZABETH (five negroes "to be delivered after the tar kilns are off and the crop finished"); also plantation at Rumney Marsh with a dwelling house to be built "twenty foot long and sixteen foot wide"). *Son:* JOHN (five negroes, lands at Smiths Point and Blunts Creek and lot in Bath town). *Daughters:* SARAH (five negroes and land at Tranters Creek), BARBARA (four negroes and the land on Matchapungo Swamp), MARY (four negroes and lands on north dividing and Jacks Creeks). *Guardians for children:* JOHN and WILLIAM GRAY. *Executors:* JOHN and WILLIAM GRAY, JOHN CALDOM and ROBERT BOYD. *Witnesses:* BART. FLEMING, ELIZABETH MONTGOMERY, NEHEMIAH MONK. *Clerk of the Court:* JNO. COLLISON. Letters issued June, 1736. Probate not dated.

MAULE, WILLIAM.   Bertie Precinct.

February 25, 1726. March 30, 1726. *Wife:* PENELOPE (plantations called Scotts Hall and Mount Galland). *Daughter:* PENELOPE MAULE ("all the rest and residue of my Estate"). *Brother and Executor:* PATRICK MAULE. *Witnesses:* ROBERT FORSTER, JOHN NAIRN, JAMS EAGLES (?). Impression of head and Latin inscription on seal. Proven before RICHARD EVERARD.

MAULTSBY, JOHN.   Bladen County.

October 5, 1749. July 29, 1757. *Sons:* JOHN and WILLIAM. *Daughters:* HANNAH ROOTS, MARY and SARAH. *Wife and Executrix:* MARY. *Witnesses:* ROBT. FORSHA, JOHN JONES, WILLIAM HARRISON. *Clerk of the Court:* THOS. ROBESON. *Justices of the Peace:* CALEB HOWEL, E. CARTLIDGE. Coat of arms on seal.

MAULTSBY, JOHN.   New Hanover County.

May 17, 1757. November 6, 1757. Wilmington. *Mother:* MARY MAULTSBY. *Sisters:* HANNAH ROOTS and MARY MAULTSBY, SARAH SHEPHERD. *Nephews:* WILLIAM and JOHN MAULTSBY, ROGER ROOTS. *Executors:* THOMAS JONES and DANIEL DUNBIBIN. *Witnesses:* BENJ'N MORISON, JAMES ARLORD, FRAN. BETEITHELLY (or BATHELLY). *Clerk of the Court:* JA. MORAN.

MAYFIELD, PETER.   Albemarle County.

June 13, 1687. October 6, 1687. *Goddaughter:* ANN LOVE. *Wife and Executrix:* ANN. *Witnesses:* JOHN LARANCE, ROBERT WALLIS, THO. ROLFE. Proven before SETH SOTHELL.

MAYO, EDWARD.   Pasquotank County.

October 12, 1724. October 20, 1724. *Sons:* EDWARD ("my plantation"), JOSEPH. *Daughters:* MARY, ANN, ELIZABETH and SARAH MAYO. *Wife and Executrix:* MARY. *Executor:* THOMAS JESSOP (brother). *Witnesses:* CALEB SAWYER, WILLIAM JENNINGS, STEPHEN DELEMARE. *Clerk of the Court:* W. NORRIS.

ABSTRACT OF WILLS, 1690—1760.   245

MAYO, EDWARD.   Pasquotank County.

January 27, 1734–1735. February 14, 1734. *Wife and Executrix:*
MARY. *Daughter:* MARY. *Executor:* JOSEPH JESSOP (wife's father). *Witnesses:* JOHN SCOTT, JEAN BUNDAY, JNO. PALIN. Proven before GAB.
JOHNSTON.

MEADS, TIMOTHY.   Albemarle County.

March 2, 1685. July 15, 1686. *Son:* JOHN. *Brother:* THOMAS MEADES,
of Littleworth, in Warwickshire, England. *Wife:* ANN. *Executors:* MR.
DANELL AKEHURST, ARNALL WHITE and HARDY WHITE. *Witnesses:* JOHN
HUNTT, WILLIAM BENTLEY, WILLIAM HOGBEN. Proven before SETH
SOTHELL.

MEAVIS (or MEVOIS), MARK.   Craven County.

January 11, 1762. February 4, 1762. *Sons:* JOHN ("my plantation"),
NATHAN (land on Trent River), BENJAMIN (land on Indian Grave Branch).
Daughters: LEAH and PIGO. *Executors:* EDMUND HATCH, JAMES FRAZIER
and EMANUELL SIMMONS. *Witnesses:* JAMES MCDONALD, JACOB BALL,
EMMANUEL SIMMONS. Proven before ARTHUR DOBBS.

MEDFORD, HENRY.   Halifax County.

December 19, 1773. February 17, 1774. *Sons:* JOHN, JAMES, HENRY
and DANIEL (to each is given a plantation). *Daughters:* MARY, FERREBEE
and ELIZABETH. *Wife:* ELIZABETH. *Executors:* JONATHAN CAIN and
JOHN MEDFORD. *Witnesses:* DANIEL HULL, THOMAS WEATHERSBEE.
Proven before Jo. MARTIN.

MEEDS, SUSANNAH.   Pasquotank County.

March 26, 1755. June Court, 1755. *Sons:* TIMOTHY MEEDS, WILLIAM
DAVIS. *Daughters:* WINNIFRED DAVIS, ELIZABETH HIGHE, SARAH BARCLIFT. *Executors:* TIMOTHY MEEDS, ROBERT HOSEA. *Witnesses:* ABRAHAM HOSEA, JOHN HOSEA, MARY CROCKER. *Clerk of the Court:* THOS.
TAYLOR.

MEEDS, THOMAS.   Pasquotank County.

March 8, 1750–1751. April Court, 1751. *Son and Executor:* TIMOTHY
("my plantation"). *Daughters:* ANN NIGHTS (two negroes), ELIZABETH
MEEDS (two negroes). *Wife and Executrix:* SUSSANAH. *Executor:* ISAAC
SWENY. *Witnesses:* JOSEPH SCOTT, JOHN BROTHERS, JOB WINSLOW.
Clerk of the Court: (signature missing).

MEED, TIMOTHY.   Pasquotank County.

July 6, 1751. January Court, 1751. *Sons:* JOHN and THOMAS ("my
land"). *Daughter:* MILLOSON MEED. *Wife and Executrix:* MARY. *Executor:* JOSEPH PENDLETON. *Witnesses:* THOS. MCKEELL, MARY ANN SMITH.
Clerk of the Court: THO. TAYLOR.

MEGLOHON, JAMES. Bertie County.

July 4, 1750. September 4, 1750. *Son and Executor:* JAMES ("my plantation"). *Wife:* MARGERIT. *Sons-in-law:* CHRISTOPHER HOLLYMAN, WILLIAM ROADS, SAMUEL HOLLYMAN. *Daughter:* ALCE MEGLOHON. *Witnesses:* WM. WILLIFORD, WM. RASBUERY, J. PARLY. Proven before GAB. JOHNSTON at Eden house.

MELTON, ROBERT. Orange County.

April 24, 1759. November Court, 1759. *Sons:* JAMES, NATHANIEL, NATHAN, ISESUM, ANCEL. *Executor:* NATHAN MELTON (son). *Witnesses:* JAMES SELLARS, MARY STRATTON. *Clerk of the Court:* JAMES WATSON.

MERRIDAY, THOMAS. Pasquotank County.

March 1, 1740. *Daughters:* ELIZABETH ("my plantation in Pasquotank known as Lawsons"), SARAH and MARY ("the plantation whereon I now live"). *Wife and Executrix:* ELIZABETH. *Witnesses:* JULIUS CAESAR CLARKE, JOHN JONES. *Clerk of the Court:* THOS. TAYLOR. Coat of arms on seal.

MERRITT, CHARLES. Chowan County.

April 6, 1718. October 21, 1718. *Sons:* CHARLES, NATHANIEL, WILLIAM, JOHN. *Daughters:* ANN, SARAH, HARDY. *Wife and Executrix:* mentioned, but not named. *Witnesses:* JAMES BRYANT, PETER EVANS. *Clerk of the Court:* R. HICKS.

MERRITT, JOHN. Edgecombe County.

January 13, 1757. *Sons:* THOMAS, JOHN. *Daughter:* PEGEE (wife of JOHN STONE), AMEE (wife of WILLIAM HANBY), and BETTY MERRITT. *Wife and Executrix:* MARY. *Witnesses:* JNO. HAYWOOD, THOS. MERRITT. No probate.

MERRIT, NATHANIEL. Edgecombe County.

April 10, 1735. February Court, 1735. *Wife and Executrix:* MARY. *Sons:* NATHANIEL, EFRUM, BENJAMIN. *Daughters:* SARAH and MARY MERRIT. *Witnesses:* FRANCES WELDON, HENRY JONES. *Deputy Clerk of the Court:* THOS. KEARNY.

MESLER, CEARSMEAR. Albemarle County.

May 2, 1696. October Court, 1696. *Son-in-law:* RICHARD LOWIE. *Executrix:* PHILLIS MESLER. *Witnesses:* THOMAS LUTEN, JOHN FENER, RUTH RANER. *Clerk of the Court:* NATH. CHEVIN.

MESSEX, JOSEPH.   Onslow County.

February 27, 1754. July Court, 1754. *Sons:* LEVEN, JOSHUA, ARON and JOSEPH. *Daughters:* DOROTHY, SARAH, GRACE, ESTER. *Wife and Executrix:* GRACE. *Witnesses:* CHARLES WILLIAMSON, RICHARD WILLIAMSON, LEWIS JENKINS. *Clerk of the Court:* WILL. CRAY.

METCALF, CALEB.   Craven County.

December 31, 1736. This is a nuncupative will made in the presence of JOSHUA PLATT, WILLIAM HERRITAGE, ADAM MOORE and AARON WOOD, and bequeathes all estate to daughter, expressing desire that wife have no part of estate. WILLIAM HERRITAGE appointed *Executor*. Proven before GAB. JOHNSTON at Newton, March 15, 1736.

METS, GEORGE.   Bath County, Craven Precinct.

September 15, 1727. September 19, 1727. *Son:* GEORGE. *Daughter:* ANNE CURTISSE METS. *Wife:* SUSANNAH. *Executors:* ADAM MOORE and MATHIAS RISSONOVER. *Witnesses:* JOSHUA PLATT, PETER BALLARD. *Clerk of the Court:* C. METCALFE.

MEWBOORN, THOMAS.   Bertie County.

February 3, 1749. November Court, 1749. *Sons:* THOMAS, JOSHUA, NICHOLAS (a plantation to each), MOSES, GEORGE, JOHN, NICHOLESS. *Daughter:* MARY. *Wife and Executrix:* ELEANNAR. *Witnesses:* EDWARD RICE, THOMAS MEWBOORN. *Clerk of the Court:* JOHN LOVICK.

MIDDLETON, HENRY.   Tyrrell County.

March 6, 1738–1739. June Court, 1739. *Sons:* JAMES ("my manner plantation"), JOHN and HENRY. *Daughter:* MARY. *Wife and Executrix:* MARTHA. *Executors:* DANIEL GARRET and SAM'LL DURRANCE. *Witnesses:* THOS. LEE, BENJ. WALKER, ABIGAL WALKER. *Clerk of the Court:* JAMES CRAVEN.

MIDDLETON, JOHN.

June 26, 1718. July 8, 1718. *Wife and Executrix:* ELIZABETH. *Daughter:* MARY MIDDLETON. *Witnesses:* CHARLES DENMAN, WILL and ANN HALL. *Clerk of the Court:* RICH'D LEARY.

MIDDLETON, JOHN.   Onslow County.

December 25, 1741. April Court, 1744. *Sons:* JOHN and JAMES (plantation to be divided between them), SAMUEL, ISAAC. *Daughters:* ANN, SARAH, SABRA, SUSSANNA. *Wife:* SARAH. *Executor:* JOHN STARKEY. *Witnesses:* ABRAHAM MITCHELL, ALEXR. MITCHELL, SARAH MITCHELL. *Clerk of the Court:* ANDR. MURRAY.

MIDDLETON, JOHN.   Edgecombe County.

July 20, 1750. November Court, 1750. *Sons:* JAMES and EDWARD. *Daughters:* ELIZABETH PERREY, JANE, SARAH and MILDRED MIDDLETON. *Wife and Executrix:* MARY. *Witnesses:* AMBROSE JOSHUA SMITH, JUDITH SMITH. *Clerk of the Court:* BENJ'N WYNNS.

MIDYETT, MATTHEW.   Currituck County.

December 21, 1734. July Court, 1735. Body Island. *Sons:* SAMUEL (land on Albemarle Sound), JOHN ("one great periauger and sails"), JOSEPH, MATTHEW and THOMAS. *Daughters:* ANN, CATERAN, DINA. *Executors:* JOHN and JOSEPH MIDYETT. *Witnesses:* TULLE WILLIAMS, JOSEPH OLOVER, MARY HUNTER. *Clerk of the Court:* JAMES CRAVEN.

MILLARD, CHARLES.

November 7, 1735. Cape Fear. *Legatees:* CORNELIUS HARNETT and HUGH CAMPBELL (*Executor*). *Witnesses:* SOLOMON DAVIS, JOHN DAVENPORT, MAGDALEN CAMPBELL. No probate.

MILLER, THOMAS.

February 20, 1693–1694. July 16, 1694. *Sons:* WILLIAM, RICHARD, NATHANIEL and THOMAS. *Executor:* EDWARD MAYO. *Witnesses:* JOHN HAWKINS, WILLIAM TEMPLE, JOHN CABEGE. *Clerk of the Court:* EDWARD MAYO.

MILLER, THOMAS.   Pasquotank County.

March 30, 1722. July 27, 1722. *Executor and sole legatee:* WM. WILLSON. *Witnesses:* SAMUEL COCK, ANTHONY COCK, JOHN SCARBOROUGH. Proven before RICH'D EVERARD.

MILLER, WILLIAM.   New Hanover County.

September 9, 1777. October 27, 1777. Wilmington. *Brothers:* DANIEL and JAMES MILLER (of Luss in Dumbartonshire, North Brittain). *Father:* JOHN MILLER, *sister:* ELEANOR MILLER, *brother:* JOHN MILLER (to these three is given testator's interest in a brigantine, which he recites was "built at this place"). *Brother-in-law:* JOHN COWAN ("an Island on the Sound known by the name of Bermuda, and also a piece of land on Smith's Creek"). *Wife and Executrix:* ANNA. *Executor:* ALEXR. HOSTLER. *Witnesses:* JAMES GEEKIE, THOMAS BROWN, DAVID ROSS. Proven before RICHARD CASWELL. *Justice of the Peace:* JONAS DUNBIBIN.

MILNER, JAMES.

September 18, 1771. January 13, 1773. Halifax Town. *Brother:* ARTHUR MILNER ("my land estate in North Britain"). *Other legatees:* MARGARET CATHCART, DOLLY HALL, JACOBINA WYNE, MARY and ELIZA-

BETH MONTFORT, JOSEPH MONTFORT, ANDREW MILLER, WILLIAM CATHCART, REV. WILLIAM WILLIE ("all my Hebrew and Greek books"), HENRY SKIPWITH. *Executors:* JOSEPH MONTFORT, ANDREW MILLER, ABNER NASH, HENRY SKIPWITH, DOUGLAS HAMILTON. *Witnesses:* MONTFORT EELBECH, REBECA BAGLEY. Proven before JO. MARTIN. Codicil provides for sale of negro servant, and devises lands purchased from one JACOB ODANIEL. Coat of arms with motto: "Societas Scientia Virtus."

MILTON, JONATHAN.　　　　　　　　　　Onslow County.

January 18, 1758. April Court, 1758. *Son:* JONATHAN. *Daughter:* ANN. *Wife and Executrix:* PURIFY. *Witnesses:* THOMAS HILL, JOSEPH THOMAS, FRANCES COOPER. *Clerk of the Court:* WILL CRAY. *Item:* "all my *woods*, horses and mares be sold, etc."

MING, JOSEPH.　　　　　　　　　　　　Chowan County.

December 1, 1750. April Court, 1751. *Sons:* THOMAS (2 plantations), JOSEPH. *Daughters:* SARAH WILKINS, ANNARITO COLLINS, MARY MING. *Grandsons:* JOSEPH WILKINS and JOSEPH COLLINS. *Wife and Executrix:* RACHEL. *Executors:* THOMAS WARD, JOSEPH MING (son). *Witnesses:* RACHEL CAMBEL, THOMAS WARD, THO. CALLAWAY. No probate officer. Provision is made for three years' schooling to be given to son THOMAS, "in addition to the one he now has."

MITCHELL, ABRAHAM.　　　　　　　　　Carteret County.

December 30, 1746. March Court, 1746. *Brothers:* ANTHONY, JOHN and GEORGE. *Sister:* REBECKAH. *Wife:* not named. *Executors:* JOHN MITCHELL and ESEKEL HUNTER. *Witnesses:* WILLIAM COOK, WILLIAM WALLIS, PETER ARNOLD. *Clerk of the Court:* GEORGE READ.

MITCHELL, ABRAM.　　　　　　　　　　Onslow County.

December 8, 1747. January Court, 1747. *Sons:* GEORGE (1 plantation), ANTONY (land on Queens Creek). *Wife:* ANN. *Daughter:* REBECCA. *Executor:* JOHN STARKEY. *Witnesses:* SARAH MIDDLETON, EDWARD BURKE, EDMOND THORLA. *Clerk of the Court:* THOS. BLACK

MITCHELL, JAMES.　　　　　　Edenton, Chowan County.

April 22, 1745. July Court, 1745. *Son:* JAMES. *Wife and Executrix:* CATHRINE. *Executors:* PETER PAYNE and SAMUEL STILLWELL. *Witnesses:* JAMES WALLACE, ANDRE RICHARD, ELIZ'TH WALLACE. *Clerk of the Court:* EDMUND HATCH.

MITCHELL, RANDALL.　　　　　　　　Edgecombe County.

September 24, 1756. June Court, 1758. *Brother:* WILLIAM MITCHELL. *Daughter-in-law:* ELIZABETH LEAVET. *Wife and Executrix:* MARY. *Executor:* AQUILA SUGG. *Witnesses:* BAURLEAY BELCHER, JOSEPH HOWELLS, BENJAMIN MITCHELL. *Clerk of the Court:* JOS. MONTFORT.

MOBLEY, JOHN.   Edgecombe County.

August 5, 1752. May Court, 1753. *Sons:* JOHN, MORDECA and EDWARD (one negro each). *Brother:* EDWARD MOBLEY. *Nephew:* SAMUEL MOBLEY (one negro). *Wife and Executrix:* RACHELL (two negroes). *Executor:* EDWARD MOBLEY (son). *Witnesses:* JOHN WILLIAMS, JOHN WARD, LEWIS, ATKINS. *Clerk of the Court:* BENJ'N WYNNS.

MOHOON, JOSIAH.   Halifax County.

January 1, 1772. February 2, 1774. *Sons:* JOSIAH and JAMES (one plantation to each), JOHN, JESSE. *Daughters:* ANN and EDEE MOHOON. Testator bequeaths "remainder part of my estate * * * to give all my children an equal learning * * *." *Executors:* NEEDAM BRYANT, ELIAS BRYANT, THOMAS HYMAN. *Witnesses:* JOHN BRYAN, JAMES BURNET, WILLIAM BLAND. Proven before JO. MARTIN.

MONEREIF, JOHN.   Currituck County.

June 22, 1712. April Court, 1713. *Sons:* THOMAS (160 acres of land), WILLIAM (160 acres adjoining THOMAS), JOHN (160 adjoining WILLIAM), GEORGE (gun and sword). A great number of spoons, "poringers," pewter dishes and plates, etc., bequeathed to wife and children. *Daughter:* MARY MONEREIF. *Wife and Executrix:* MARY. *Witnesses:* ADAM PEARRY, THOMAS DAVIS, DANIEL GLASCOE. *Clerk of the Court:* JOS. WICKER.

MONS, THOMAS.   County not given.

January 5, 1693. *Wife and Executrix:* ANN. *Witnesses:* MATHEW SAYES, WILLIAM WATERS, THOMAS GILBERT. *Clerk of the Court:* HENDERSON WALKER.

MONTGOMERY, ANN.   Chowan County.

August 28, 1741. October 29, 1744. *Legatees:* THOMAS JONS, REBECCA JONS, JANE SWAN, daughter of SAMUEL SWAN, at Cape Fear (one small diamond ring and "my staned taffety gound"); MARY TURNBULL, MARY BUCHAR, ANN ALLIN, SAMUEL SWAN ("the rest of the law books and a mourning ring"), JAMES TURNBULL. *Executors:* JAMES TURNBULL and SAMUEL SWAN. *Mother:* SARAH LASTER in England. *Witnesses:* CULLEN POLLOCK, FRANCES POLLOCK, E. BELL. Proven before E. MOSELEY, C. J. On seal is impression of a dog or lion and the word "canis."

MONTGOMERY, GEORGE.   Bath County.

January 19, 1722–1723. July 2, 1723. *Daughter:* ELIZABETH. *Other legatees:* JAMES, JOSIAS and GEORGE MONTGOMERY. *Executor:* ROBT. TURNER. *Witnesses:* JOSEPH ENGLISH, EDWD. DODD, JNO. BROOK. *Clerk of the Court:* JNO. BAPTISTE ASHE.

ABSTRACT OF WILLS, 1690—1760. 251

MONTGOMERY, JOHN. Chowan County.

August 3, 1741. May 22, 1744. Testator devises all his estate to his *wife*, ANNE, who is also appointed *Executrix*. *Witnesses:* JOS. ANDERSON, JAMES CRAVEN, THE. GOOLD. Proven before GAB. JOHNSTON.

MONTICUE, THOMAS. Perquimans County.

June 5, 1750. *Wife:* ELIZABETH. *Other legatees:* FRANCIS NIXON, ZACHARIAH NIXON, HENRY PHELPS, SAMUEL NEWBY, JOHN NIXON, JOSEPH RATLIFF. *Executor:* ZACHARIAH NIXON. *Witnesses:* JOSIAH BUNDY, ABARAHAM HENDRIXON, JOSEPH RATLIFF. Provision is made in will for bricking up the grave of the testator.

MOORE, DAVID.

March 25, 1670. All estate is bequeathed to one DAVID―――― (name illegible). *Witnesses:* JAMES BLOUNT, ROBERT BONEO. *Clerk of the Court:* THOMAS HARRIS.

MOORE, EPAPHRODITUS. Bertie County.

June 11, 1757. October Court, 1757. *Son:* JOHN (all the lands of testator). *Grandsons:* ELISHA WILSON, THOMAS MOORE (one plantation each, both plantations lying on Fort Branch). *Daughters:* JUDATH HURST, REBECKAH CAIN, CHARITY WALSTON, RACHEL WALSTON, MARY MOORE, ANN MOORE, RACHEL STANDLY, GRACE MOORE, PENELOPE HARE, CHRISTIAN MOORE. *Son-in-law:* JAMES HOWARD. *Wife:* not named. *Executors:* MARY and ANN MOORE. *Witnesses:* CHARLES HORN, DEMCY HOLLAND, LEWIS PERRY. *Clerk of the Court:* BENJAMIN WYNNS.

MOORE, JAMES. Bertie Precinct.

November 28, 1735. December 11, 1735. *Wife:* SUSANAH (one negro). *Son:* MORICE ("my plantation and also a plantation on Fishing Creek"). *Daughter:* SARAH. *Executor:* JOHN DAWSON. *Witnesses:* JAMES BARNS, ROBERT TENELL, JOHN BROWN. Codicil dated November 30, 1735, bequeaths live stock to wife. *Witnesses to codicil:* ROBT. RUFFIN, JAMES TART, SAM'LL COTTEN. Proven before GAB. JOHNSTON.

MOORE, JOHN. Perquimans County.

March 19, 1746. May 18, 1746. *Son:* CHARLES ("my plantation"). *Daughter:* MARY. *Wife:* RACHEL. *Executors:* JOHN HARVEY, CHRISTOPHER DENMAN, JOSHUA SKINNER. *Witnesses:* JONATHAN SKINNER, PETER JONES, JOHN BEMBRIDGE. Proven before GAB. JOHNSTON.

MOOR, JOHN. Perquimans County.

March 11, 1750. October 21, 1755. *Sons:* CORNELIUS, JOSEPH ("plantation lying in baley hack"), GIDEON ("the maner plantation"), JOSEPH.

Daughters: MIRIAM, SARAH and BETEY MOORE. *Wife and Executrix:* MARY. *Executor:* JOSEPH RATLIFF (brother-in-law). *Witnesses:* ZACH. NIXON, WILLIAM MORE, SAMUELL MORE. Proven before JNO. CLAYTON and JOSEPH SUTTON, *Justices.*

MOORE, JOHN.   Northampton County.

September 1, 1753. November Court, 1753. *Sons:* MARK, JOHN, ISHAM, WILLIAM, NATHANIEL, RICHARD. *Daughter:* SARAH MOORE. *Wife and Executrix:* TABITHA MOORE. *Executors:* RICHARD MOORE and THOMAS PACE. *Witnesses:* GEORGE HARPER, JOHN MACDESLEY. *Clerk of the Court:* I. EDWARDS.

MOORE, JOHN.   Bertie County.

February 19, 1754. May Court, 1754. *Son:* BENJAMIN. *Daughter:* ANN. *Executors:* ELIZABETH MOORE (wife) and JOHN MOORE (uncle). *Witnesses:* JOHN PEETERICK, ANNE GAINS, HEZEKIAH HERRENDEN. *Clerk of the Court:* SAM'L ORMES.

MOOR, JOHN.   Bertie County.

March 11, 1754. May Court, 1754. *Sons:* SAMUELL and JOHN MOORE ("my lands"). *Daughter:* MARY BELL. *Wife and Executrix:* ANN. *Executor:* EPHRAIM WESTON. *Witnesses:* STEPHEN EVANS, ANN EVANS, JOS. HARDY. *Clerk of the Court:* SAM'L ORMES.

MOORE, JOSEPH.   Edgecombe County.

February 15, 1753. February Court, 1757. *Sons:* JOSEPH (plantation in Edgecombe County on Little Swamp and plantation in Bertie County on Rockquies Swamp), JAMES (land on Conehoe pocoson), HODGES (land on Conehoe), JESSEE and EZIEKEL ("my water mill"). *Daughters:* ANN MCGEE, MARTHA HINTON, CELIA MOORE (one negro girl each), MELIA MOORE. *Executors:* ANN MOORE (wife) and four sons. *Witnesses:* ELIZABETH WILLIAMS, MARY WHITMILL, WM. WILLIAMS. *Clerk of the Court:* JOS. MONTFORT.

MOORE, JOSHUA.   Perquimans County.

February 12, 1734–1735. February 24, 1734. *Brothers:* SAMUEL, JOHN, TRUEMAN. *Nephew:* CORNELIUS (son of JOHN). *Niece:* ELIZABETH NIXON. *Wife and Executrix:* ELIZABETH. *Witnesses:* ZACHARIAH NIXON, THOMAS WINSLOW, ZACHARIAH NIXON, JR. Proven before GAB. JOHNSTON.

MOORE, MARY.   Perquimans County.

March 24, 1753. April Court, 1756. *Sons:* THOMAS and NATHAN NEWBY (*Executors*). *Daughter:* MARY ROBINSON. *Other legatees:* JEM-

MIME, MARY, SARAH and JOHN ROBINSON, ELIZABETH NEWBY, ELIZABETH HILL, ELIZABETH ELIOT. *Witnesses:* FRANCES JONES, RALPH FLETCHER, ELIZABETH HILL. *Clerk of the Court:* MILES HARVEY.

MOORE, RICHARD.   Bertie County.

November 1, 1748. February Court, 1748. *Son and Executor:* JOHN ("all my lands"). *Brother and Executor:* JOHN MOORE. *Witnesses:* WILLIAM RICE, THOMAS DAVIS, LUCREACY LEE. *Clerk of the Court:* JOHN LOVICK.

MOORE, ROBERT.   Perquimans County.

February 22, 1749. January Court, 1750. *Sons:* SAMUELL ("my plantation"), JOHN. *Daughters:* SARAH and RACHEL MOORE. *Grandchildren:* MARY MOORE, MARTHA and MIRIAM MOORE, ELIAZOR CREESSIE. *Executors:* SAMUELL MOORE, RICHARD SKINNER, ABRAHAM SANDERS and JOSEPH WHITE. *Witnesses:* JOSHUA JONES, JONATHAN PHELPS, ELIZABETH ELLIS. *Clerk of the Court:* EDMUND HATCH.

MOORE, ROGER.   New Hanover County.

March 7, 1747–1748. May Court, 1758. Parish of St. Philips. *Sons:* GEORGE, WILLIAM. *Daughters:* SARAH SMITH, MARY and ANNE MOORE. *Wife:* MARY. The following lands are devised: Plantation called Kendall; land on "Mr. Allens Creek"; lands between Therofaire and Black River in the Neck known by the name of Maultsby's Point and lands on the Island opposite; land in fork of River known by name of Mount Misery; 500 acres on So. West River; land between JOB HOWE and MR. DALLISON; 3,025 acres near Saxpahaw Old Fields, bought of JOHN PORTER; lot in Brunswick where "Mr. Ross at present dwells"; plantation called Orton where "I now dwell"; 640 acres at Rocky Point; land on Smith Creek; 5,000 acres at Eno Old Fields. To *daughters*, ANN and MARY MOORE, is bequeathed 3,600 pounds, 1,800 to each. To *son-in-law*, THOMAS SMITH, is devised lot in Brunswick "where WILLIAM LORD at present dwells." *Grandmother of daughters:* MRS. SARAH TROTT. *Aunt of daughters:* MRS. SARAH ALLEN. About 250 negroes bequeathed. Will mentions mill at Brices Creek. *Executors:* GEORGE and WILLIAM MOORE (sons). *Witnesses:* WM. FORBES, RICH'D QUINCE, GEO. LOGAN, WM. ROSS, REBECCA COKE. *Clerk of the Court:* ISAAC FARIES. Coat of arms on seal.

MOORE, SAMUEL.   Albemarle County.

January 9, 1693–1694. August 20, 1694. *Son:* SAMUELL. *Wife and Executrix:* ABIGAIL. *Witnesses:* JNO. HAWKINS, JOHN CABBIDGE, SARAH HAWKINS. *Clerk of the Court:* EDWARD MAYO.

MOORE, SAMUEL.   Onslow County.

October 11, 1750. April 2, 1751. *Sons:* SAMUEL (plantation on a branch of Stones Creek), THOMAS (250 acres of land). *Daughters:* SARAH, MARY and ALLETHEA. *Executors:* OBADIAH MOORE (brother) and THEOPHILUS WILLIAMS. *Witnesses:* HORATIUS WOODHOUSE, ROBERT NIXON, JOSHUA PAULL. *Clerk of the Court:* THOS. BLACK.

MOORE, SAMUELL.   Perquimans County.

October 25, 1751. January Court, 1752. *Wife and Executrix:* MARY. *Nieces:* MARY, HANNA and MARTHA MOORE (daughters of brother, JOHN MOORE). *Other legatees:* ELIZABETH ELLIOT, FRANCIS and NATHAN NEWBY, JOHN PERISHE, EDWARD DEWISE. *Friends:* RICH'D SKINNER, JOSEPH WHITE and ZACHARIAH NIXON. *Executor:* FRANCIS NEWBY. *Witnesses:* ZACH. NIXON, DANIEL SAINT. *Clerk of the Court:* EDMUND HATCH.

MOORE, SAMUEL.   Perquimans County.

May 26, 1754. January Court, 1756. *Sons:* JOSHUA, AARON, JONATHAN, JOHN (to each is given a plantation). *Daughters:* MARY and SARAH MOORE. *Wife and Executrix:* SARAH. *Witnesses:* JOHN ROBINSON, CORNELIUS MOORE, JOSEPH WHITE, JUNR. *Clerk of the Court:* MILES HARVEY.

MOOR, THOMAS.   New Hanover County.

February 3, 1755. February 4, 1755. "Late of New York now in Wilmington." This will appoints COSMAS FARQUHARSON, *Executor*, and he is directed to transmit all estate to New York "to be disposed of as my former Will in the Hands of MR. ALSOP and CARROLL Directs." *Witnesses:* CALEB MASON, SIMON PAYNE, RD. HARTLEY. *Clerk of the Court:* ISAAC FARIES.

MOORE, TITUS.   Bertie County.

April 26, 1753. January Court, 1757. *Son and Executor:* JAMES. *Wife and Executrix:* ELIZABETH. *Daughter:* MARY ODOM. *Witnesses:* NEEDHAM BRYAN, WILLIAM TURNER, PATIENCE TURNER. *Clerk of the Court:* BENJN. WYNNS.

MOORE, TRUEMAN.   Perquimans County.

December 12, 1752. April Court, 1753. *Sons:* WILLIAM, SAMUEL, THOMAS (to each is given a plantation), JESSE (land in Ballyhack). *Daughters:* JANE and MARY MOORE. *Friends:* JOHN WILSON, WILLIAM WHITE, JOHN MOORE and DANIEL SAINT. *Wife and Executrix:* LEAH. *Executors:* THOS. NICHOLSON and SAMUEL MOORE. *Witnesses:* WILLIAM WHITE, DANIEL SAINT, JOSEPH WINSLOW. *Clerk of the Court:* EDMUND HATCH.

MOORE, WILLIAM. Perquimans County.

February 6, 1726–1727. October 31, 1732. *Sons:* WILLIAM, JOHN, JOSHUA, SAMUELL, TRUMAN (to each of the above is given a plantation). *Daughters:* ELIZABETH and JANE. *Cousin:* ROBERT BOGUE. *Wife and Executrix:* ELIZABETH. *Executors:* JOHN and JOSHUA MOORE. *Witnesses:* JOSEPH WINSLOW, JACOB HILL, J. JESSOP. Proven before GEO. BURRINGTON.

MORE, WILLIAM. Perquimans County.

June 4, 1749. April Court, 1752. *Devisees:* TRUMAN MOORE and WILLIAM WILSON (land obtained from EDW. MOSLEY). *Wife and Executrix:* MARTHA. *Witnesses:* ROBT. NEWBY, JOSHUA HASKET, MARY SAVIG. *Clerk of the Court:* EDMUND HATCH.

MOORHEAD. JAMES. Bladen County.

April 4, 1759. July Court, 1759. *Sons:* WILLIAM and JAMES. *Daughters:* JANE and SARAH. *Wife and Executrix:* SARAH. *Executor:* ALEXANDER MCCONKEY. *Witnesses:* PETER CATES, LAWRENCE BYRNE, MARY ARINTON. *Clerk of the Court:* J. BURGWIN.

MORGAN, JAMES (Son of WILLIAM MORGAN).
Perquimans County.

January 26, 1740–1741. October Court, 1741. *Sons:* JACOB and CHARLES (land on Morgan's Swamp). *Daughters:* ELIZABETH and REBECKAH MORGAN. *Wife and Executrix:* HANNAH. *Executor:* THOMAS OVERMAN (brother-in-law). *Witnesses:* ZACHARIAH NIXON, CHARLES OVERMAN, JOS. ROBINSON. *Clerk of the Court:* EDMUND HATCH.

MORGAN, JANE. Perquimans County.

February 4, 1742. March 22, 1742. *Sons:* JOHN ANDERSON, JAMES MORGAN. *Daughter:* SARAH PARSONS. *Daughter-in-law:* ANN MORGAN. *Granddaughters:* MARY and MIRIAM MORGAN, ELIZABETH COSAN, JANE ANDERSON. *Executors:* JOHN ANDERSON and JAMES MORGAN. *Witnesses:* ABRAHAM ELLIOTT, MARY ELLIOTT, JOSEPH RATLIFF. Proven before GAB. JOHNSTON.

MORGAN, JOHN. Pasquotank County.

October 20, 1754. January Court, 1755. *Sons:* JOHN and JOSEPH (1 shilling). *Daughters:* RACHEL OVERMAN, ELIZABETH ELLIOT, MARY ELLIOT, HANNAH BOSWELL ("my manner plantation"). *Grandson:* JOSEPH BOSWELL. *Executors:* HANNAH and JOSEPH BOSWELL. *Witnesses:* GEORGE LOW, EDWARD WARDSWORTH. *Clerk of the Court:* THO. TAYLOR.

MORGAN, NATHAN.   Onslow County.

February 16, 1749. October 2, 1750. *Sons:* WILLIAM ("mannor house and one-half of mannor plantation"), GOER ("the other half of the land I now live on"). *Daughter:* SUKEE MORGAN. *Brothers:* WILLIAM MORGAN (*Executor*) and JOSEPH MORGAN. *Witnesses:* WILLIAM AMBROSE, FRANCIS SUMNER, JOSEPH STURGES. No probate.

MORGAN, ROBERT.   Pasquotank Precinct.

October 22, 1727. November 26, 1730. *Sons:* BENNET, JOSEPH, ROBERT and MOSES (a plantation to each), AARON. *Daughters:* ALLIS, ELIZABETH, ANN and JUDA. *Wife:* ELIZABETH. *Executors:* BENNET and JOSEPH MORGAN (sons). *Witnesses:* ABEL ROSS, TAMAR ROSS, JERUAS JONES, JAMES ADAMS. Proven before RICHARD EVERARD.

MORRELL, HUMPHREY.

March 10, 1732. *Grandsons:* JOSEPH and JOHN PEARS. *Daughter and Executrix:* ELIZABETH WATS. *Mother:* ELIZABETH MORREL. *Witnesses:* WILLIAM SIMES, ANN BURK, HENRY TUDOR. No probate.

MORIS, JOHN.   Craven County.

August 23, 1742. September 24, 1742. *Wife and Executrix:* MATHEW MORRIS. *Son:* JOHN. *Daughter:* MARY MORRIS. *Executors:* ABRAHAM BUSETT, JOHN HUDLER. *Witnesses:* WM. WICKLIFFE, THOMAS MORE, RICHARD MORGAN. *Clerk of the Court:* N. ROUTLEDGE.

MORRIS, JOHN.   Pasquotank County.

November 18, 1739. January Court, 1739. *Sons:* JOSEPH and JOHN ("my manner plantation"), ZACHARIAH, ISAC, AARON, JOSEPH. *Daughters:* HANNAH and SARAH MORRIS. *Wife and Executrix:* MARY. *Witnesses:* JOHN BELMAN, MARY ALBERTSON, JOSEPH ROBINSON. *Clerk of the Court:* JAMES CRAVEN.

MORRISS, JOHN.   Bertie County.

May 21, 1759. July Court, 1759. *Sons:* JOHN and WILLIAM ("plantation whereon I now live," lying on the main road to Bertie Courthouse), BENJAMIN, NATHAN, JACOB, JAMES EARLY, RICHARD. *Daughters:* MARY STALLINGS, ANN HOLMS, SARAH FARMER, ELIZABETH and JANE MORRIS. *Wife and Executrix:* REBEKAH. *Executors:* JOHN and WILLIAM MORRIS. *Witnesses:* WILLIAM WILLEFORD, JACOB STALLINGS, J. EARLY. *Clerk of the Court:* BENJ'N WYNNS.

MORRIS, THOMAS.   New Hanover County.

August 2, 1744. January 9, 1744. *Sons:* THOMAS, WILLIAM, SOLOMON, JAMES (land on Holly Shelter Creek). *Grandsons:* THOMAS and CHARLES

MORRIS. *Brother:* WILLIAM MORRIS. *Executors:* WILLIAM, SOLOMON and JAMES MORRIS (sons). *Witnesses:* CHAS. HARRISON, THOMAS STEERS, SUSANAH NICHOLS. *Deputy Clerk of the Court:* JAMES SMALLWOOD.

MORRISON, BENJAMIN.   New Hanover County.
April 14, 1760. June 10, 1760. Wilmington. *Executor:* ALEXANDER DUNCAN. *Witnesses:* THOMAS TURNBULL, JAMES RUTHERFURD, HENRY TOOMER. Proven before ARTHUR DOBBS at Brunswick. No legatee named in will.

MORTIMER, JOHN.   New Hanover County.
June 14, 1765. September 26, 1766. Wilmington. *Daughter:* HANNAH MORTIMER (lot in Wilmington on north side of Market Street). *Nephew:* JOHN CONAWAY. *Sister:* MARY MORTIMER. *Wife and Executrix:* REBECCA. *Executors:* DOCTR. SAMUELL GREEN and CORNELIUS HARNETT. *Witnesses:* MOSES JOHN DEROSSETT, WM. PURVIANCE, W. GREGORY. Proven before WM. TRYON. *Executors* qualified before MOSES JNO. DEROSSETT.

MOSELEY, EDWARD.   New Hanover County.
March 20, 1745. August Court, 1749. *Sons:* JOHN (plantation at Rockey Point, on the west side of the northeast branch of Cape Fear River, about 3,500 acres; lot and houses in Brunswick "where my Habitation usually is at Present"; plantation below Brunswick commonly called Macknights), EDWARD (plantation in Chowan County containing 2,000 acres in fee tail; lot and house in Wilmington; 600 acres of land opposite Cabbage Inlet; 500 acres in Tyrrell called Coopers; 450 acres in Tyrrell called Whitemarsh), SAMPSON (land on the east side of the northeast branch of Cape Fear River, lying between Holly Shelter Creek and the bald white sandhills, containing 3,500 acres), JAMES (lands on the east side of the northeast branch of Cape Fear River opposite Rocky Point plantation, containing 1,650 acres), THOMAS (1,880 acres of land on northwest branch of Cape Fear River). To SAMPSON, JAMES and THOMAS is devised "all my lands on the East side of Cape Fear River, on part whereof MR. BUGNION dwelleth." To five sons is devised "my large tract of Land in Edgecomb County called Clur, containing 10,000 acres," and fifty-six slaves. *Wife:* ANN (plantation on the Sound "whereon is a large Vineyard planted"; also 3,200 acres of land in Edgecomb called Alden of the Hill, lying on a branch of Fishing Creek, by "some called Irwins, by Other Butterwood"; also 1,650 acres on the west side of Neuse River, about twenty-four miles above Newbern; also twenty-one slaves, new chaise harness and pair of bay horses, ten cows and calves, ten steers and twenty sheep. *Daughter:* ANER (eleven slaves). *Friends:* SAMUEL SWANN, JOHN SWANN, JEREMIAH VAIL, ALEXANDER LILLINGTON, JAMES HASELL. *Mother-in-law:* MRS. SUSANNAH HASELL. *Brother-in-*

17

law: JAMES HASELL, JR. *Sisters-in-law:* MRS. MARY VAIL, MRS. JOHN PORTER and ELIZABETH, late wife of COL. MAURICE MOORE. *Executors:* JOHN and EDWARD MOSELEY (sons) and ANN MOSELEY (wife). *Witnesses:* ELEAZR ALLEN, ROGR. MOORE, WM. FORBES, MATT. ROWAN. Some interesting provisions in will: "I Recommend it to my Dear and loving wife that one of my sons as shall be thought best qualified for it be bred to the law, it being highly necessary in so large a family, and to him I give all my law books, being upwards of 200 volumes, which are now or shall be in my closet," etc. "*Item:* I give to my dear wife Blome's History of the Bible in folio, 3 volumes in folio of Arch Bishop Tillotson's Works, four volumes in Octavo of Dr. Stanhope's, on the Epistles & Gospels, and all the Books of Physick. *Item:* I give to my daughter, ANN HUMPHRIES, 3 Volumes in folio on the Old & New Testament, and I will that my executors buy for her the work of the Auther of the whole Duty of Man. I give to the oldest of my sons that shall not Study the Law, Chambers Dictionary, 2 Volms in folio, and LeBlond of Gardening in Quarto; and the rest of my books, about 150 Volumes, to be divided among my other three Sons. *Item:* I give and bequeath unto my Eldest Son, JOHN, my large Silver Tea Kettle, Lamp & Server for it to stand on, weighing in all about 170 ounces; To my Son EDWARD, my large silver Coffee Pot Pott; to my son SAMPSON, my large Silver Tea Pot; to my Son JAMES, my Large Silver Tankard, & To my Son THOMAS, a pair of Large Square Silver Servers, my cases of Knifes, Forks, Spoons, Salts, Casters & Other my plate to be divided between my Wife & Daughter * * *." "*Item:* it is my will that the profits arising from the labour of my Two Sons' Slaves & their part of the profits arising by the stocks be laid out in purchasing Young Female slaves * * *." "*Item:* When it shall be necessary to give all or any of my sons Other Education that is to be had from the Common Masters in this Province, for I would have my children well educated, it is then my will that such expence be defrayed out of the profits of such Child's estate, etc."

Codicil to will dated June 9, 1748, gives to son WILLIAM, "born since my said last Will was made," the tract of land in Edgecomb called Alden of the Hill and 300 acres contiguous thereto, and also emancipates three slaves, with the provision, however, that "if it shall not be allowed them, then it is my will that my executrix shall place them jointly or severally, as they shall choose, on any of my lands, to make what they shall judge most for their advantage, rendering one-tenth part of the profits to my executrix." *Witnesses to codicil:* JOHN COCHRAN, JOHN HANCOCK, JOHN COOKE. *Clerk of the Court:* ISAAC FARIES. Coat of arms on seal is illegible, and coat of arms on seal to codicil is said by testator to be "MR. SAMPSON'S (my Wife's Father), mine being lately lost." All land devised to sons is devised in fee tail, showing that entails existed at the time of the will.

MOSLER, CEARSMER.   Chowan Precinct.
May 2, 1696. *Wife and Executrix:* PHILIS. *Witnesses:* THOMAS LATEN, JOHN JONES, RICHARD RANER. No probate. Will almost illegible.

MOSS, GRACE.   Craven County.
June 7, 1771. August 6, 1771. *Daughter:* ANN CONWAY. *Niece:* SIDNEY PITMAN. *Son:* JOSEPH MOSS. *Executors:* THOMAS and JOHN NELSON. *Witnesses:* JAMES SEAVERN, JR., DENEL MOZOR, ELEANOR CLASH. Proven before JAS. HASELL. Provision is made for education of son.

MOUND, NOAH.   Edgecombe County.
February 1, 1752. February Court, 1752. This is a nuncupative will proven before SAM'LL WILLIAMS by ELIZA WEBB and JOSEPH ISENMANGER, in which all estate of testator is left to AQUILA SUGG, who is also appointed *Executor*. *Clerk of the Court:* BENJ'N WYNNS.

MOUNTEAGUE, ELIZABETH.   Perquimans County.
September 20, 1756. July Court, 1757. *Legatees:* JOSIAH RAPER, MIRIAM OVERMAN, NAOMY NEWBY, HANNAH NEWBY, JOSEPH ROBINSON, SAMUEL NEWBY, THOMAS NICHOLSON, WILLIAM HASKIT, CHRISTOPHER and JOSEPH NICHOLSON. *Witnesses:* THOMAS, CHRISTOPHER and JOSEPH NICHOLSON. *Witnesses:* JOHN OVERMAN, SARAH BARROW, JOHN TAYLOR. *Clerk of the Court:* MILES HARVEY.

MOUNTICUE, THOMAS.   Perquimans County.
June 5, 1750. October Court, 1750. *Devisees and legatees:* FRANCIS NIXON (all lands and houses), ZACHARIAH NIXON, HENRY PHELPS (one negro man), SAMUEL NEWBY and JOHN NIXON (ten pounds in good "merchantable barrel pork"), JOSEPH RATLIFF, ZACHARIAH NIXON, JR., and MEHETABLE NIXON. *Wife and Executrix:* ELIZABETH. *Executor:* ZACHARIAH NIXON. *Witnesses:* JOSAH BUNDY, ABRAHAM HENDRIXON, JOSEPH RATLIFF. *Clerk of the Court:* EDMUND HATCH.

MOY, JOHN.   Currituck County.
January 3, 1735. July 1, 1735. *Son:* JOHN ("my maner plantation"). *Daughter:* JANE MOY. *Wife and Executrix:* ANNIE. *Witnesses:* JOHN WARDEN, RICHARD BRADLEY. *Clerk of the Court:* JAMES CRAVEN.

MOYE, THOMAS.   Bertie Precinct.
March 26, 1721-1722. May Court, 1723. *Wife and Executrix:* ELIZABETH. *Wife's sons:* THOMAS and JOHN PHILLIPS. *Witnesses:* JNO. SIMPSON, THOMAS BOYKIN, ISABELL JOYNER. *Clerk of the Court:* RT. FORSTER.

MULKEY, PHILIP.   Edgecombe Precinct.

December 17, 1736. May Court, 1737. *Sons:* DAVID (land on Beaver Ponds), PHILIP ("my plantation"). *Daughters:* JANE, EVE, SCARBROUGH, JUDITH. *Son-in-law:* GEORGE LAWS. *Friends:* BACKLEY KIMBROUGH and JOHN HARDY (land at plumtree). *Wife and Executrix:* SARAH. *Executor:* JAMES SMITH. *Witnesses:* RICHARD HERRING, JOHN CALIHAN, JONATHAN MULKEY. *Clerk of the Court:* THOS. KEARNY.

MULLEN, ISAAC.   Perquimans County.

August 24, 1743. October Court, 1743. *Son:* JOSEPH ("my plantation"). *Wife and Executrix:* ELIZABETH. *Daughter:* REBECCA. *Executors:* ABRAHAM and JACOB MULLEN (brothers). *Witnesses:* SAMUEL BARCLIFT, JOSEPH PERSHER, JOHN ANDERSON. *Clerk of the Court:* EDMUND HATCH.

MULLEN, JACOB.   Perquimans County.

November 5, 1757. January Court, 1758. *Sons:* ISAAC and ABRAHAM ("my plantation containing 229 acres"), JACOB (76 acres of land), THOMAS (land on Suttons Creek). *Daughter:* HANNAH MULLEN. *Executors:* WILLIAM TOMBLIN and WILLIAM HASKET. *Witnesses:* JAMES GIBSON, JAMES PEIRCE, FRANCIS LAYDEN. *Clerk of the Court:* MILES HARVEY.

MUMFORD, JOSEPH.   Onslow County.

October 3, 1732. *Sons:* JOSEPH ("all my lands"), EDWARD. *Daughter:* ELIZABETH MUMFORD. *Executors:* EDWARD HOWARD, THOMAS FULLARD. *Witnesses:* JAMES MURRAY, EDWARD HOWARD, ELIZABETH MURRAY. *Clerk of the Court:* WM. CRANFORD.

MUNDAY, WILLIAM.   Albemarle County.

December 3, 1688. January 28, 1688. *Son:* WILLIAM. *Daughter:* ELIZABETH MUNDAY. *Wife and Executrix:* EMMAY. *Executor:* JOHN STOCKUM. *Witnesses:* JOHN JONES, WILLIAM HANCOCK, ELIZA STOCKUM, JOHN WINGATE. Proven before SETH SOTHELL.

MUNS, THOMAS.   Albemarle County.

January 5, 1693. *Wife:* ANNE MUNS, sole heir and Executrix. *Witnesses:* MATHEW SAYES, WM. WALTERS, THOS. GILBERT. Proved at Chowan. *Clerk of Court:* HENDERSON WALKER.

MURDEN, JEREMIAH.   Pasquotank County.

August 3, 1745. November 20, 1750. *Son and Executor:* ROBERT ("the manner plantation"). *Daughter:* MARY. *Granddaughter:* MARY SPENCE. *Witnesses:* JOHN JONES, ISAAC JONES, JOHN CAMMILL. Proven before GAB. JOHNSTON.

ABSTRACT OF WILLS, 1690—1760.

MURPHY, EDMOND. Craven County.

March 4, 1745. *Sons:* BENJAMIN and JOSUA ("all my lands"), EDMUND. *Wife and Executrix:* ELIZABETH. *Witnesses:* JAMES TUCKER, WM. FLOOD, PAUL PHILLIPS. No probate.

MURPHY, JEREMIAH. Craven County.

November 26, 1750. May Court, 1752. *Son:* THOMAS. *Executors:* GEORGE LANE, THOMAS MURPHY and JOHN LANE. *Witnesses:* JOHN MURPHY, JANE CARRUTHERS, JNO. CARRUTHERS, JR. *Clerk of the Court:* PHIL. SMITH.

MURPHY, THOMAS. Craven County.

October 7, 1746. February 27, 1746. *Sons:* THOMAS (plantation on Trent River), JEREMIAH, JOHN. *Daughter:* BRIDGETT MURPHY. *Wife and Executrix:* SARAH. *Witnesses:* JOHN JOHNS, JOHN ABBOTT, JOHN PETER REMM. Proven before GABRIEL JOHNSTON.

MURPHEY, WILLIAM. Edgecombe County.

January 23, 1736. May Court, 1737. *Daughters:* MARY and MARTHA MURPHEY (one plantation each), ESTHER MURPHY (negroes). *Other legatees:* WILLIAM HURST, JOSEPH BRADSHAW. *Wife and Executrix:* ANN. *Executors:* JOHN EDWARDS and ISAAC RICKS. *Witnesses:* JOHN POPE, WM. GOODWIN, JOHN STRICKLAND. *Deputy Clerk of the Court:* THOS. HARVEY.

MURRAY, ANDREW. Onslow County.

February 9, 1745–1746. April 2, 1746. *Devisee:* JAMES HURLEY. *Executor:* STEPHEN LEE. *Witnesses:* FOYE DEXTER, E. CHADWICK, DANIEL SHESLOW, JAMES HOYLE, ELIZABETH HOYLE. *Clerk of the Court:* GEO. CLOPTON.

NAYLER, WILLIAM. Albemarle County.

April 13, 1696. September 30, 1696. Little River. *Daughters:* MARGARET and MARY "living in Virginia." *Executor:* JOHN KING. *Witness:* MARTHA PLATER. *Clerk of the Court:* W. GLOVER.

NEALE, ABNER. Craven County.

January 5, 1770. October 14, 1772. *Sons:* ABNER (land on Adams Creek), RICHARD (land bought of WILLIAM CARRUTHERS and MATHEW GODFREY), CHRISTOPHER and PHILIP (to each is given land bounded and described in will), MATHEW (lands on Browns Creek), BARRE (land on Goose Creek). *Daughters:* WINIFRED THOMAS, MARY PITTMAN, wife of JOSEPH PITTMAN, HANNAH NEALE, ELIZABETH NEALE, PATIENCE NEALE. *Grandchildren:* JOHN, ABNER, SARAH and WINIFRED THOMAS. Eight negroes bequeathed. *Wife:* ELIZABETH. *Friends:* JAMES JONES, JOHN

BRYAN, THOMAS COOK, SAMUEL MASTERS, PARMENAS HORTON and JOHN THOMLINSON. *Executors:* CHRISTOPHER and RICHARD NEALE (sons) and ROGER JONES. *Witnesses:* ELIJAH JARMAN, ROBERT TURNER, BENJAMIN CUMMINGS. Proven before JO. MARTIN.

NEALE, CHARLES.   Albemarle County.

January 7, 1698–1699. *Daughters:* DORCAS, MARY. *Guardian to daughter:* JOHN MACKEELL. *Son:* CHARLES (negroes). *Wife and Executrix:* MARY. *Witnesses:* JOHN MACKEELL, FRANCIS DELAMARE, JOHN WOODHOUSE, THOMAS BOYD, JOY MARKHAM. *Clerk of the Court:* N. CHEVIN.

NEALE, HENRY.

July 13, 1734. April 30, 1735. *Wife's son:* JOHN, SIMPSON. *Sons:* SAMUEL and HENRY ("my negroes"), THOMAS. *Daughters:* JANE and ELIZABETH NEALE (one negro each). *Wife:* SUSANAH. *Executors:* JANE HUSBANDS (sister), SAMUEL HAZELL (cousin), JOSEPH CLARK. *Witnesses:* THOS. HALL, HANNAH HALL, ELIZ. BRIAN. Proven before GAB. JOHNSTON, at Cape Fear.

NEEDHAM, THOMAS.   Pasquotank County.

October 6, 1740. July Court, 1743. *Sons:* JOHN, GEDEON, THOMAS (a plantation to each), CHRISTOFER (one shilling). *Daughter:* ANN. *Executor:* JOHN NEEDHAM (son). *Witnesses:* DENNIS SAWYER, ROBERT TORKSEY. *Clerk of the Court:* THOS. TAYLOR.

NESSFEILD, JOHN.   Bladen County.

March 27, 1764. April 20, 1764. *Wife and Executrix:* ANN. *Other legatees:* THOMAS WHITE and wife, ANN. *Executor:* JOHN ROBESON of Wilmington. *Witnesses:* HU. WADDELL, JAMES BAILEY, EDW. BRYAN. Proven before ARTHUR DOBBS. Testator provides for sale of all his estate; proceeds to be invested in young female slaves for use of wife and children. Impression of dove with olive branch on seal.

NEVIL, BENJAMIN.   Halifax County.

November 15, 1758. September Court, 1759. *Sons:* BENJAMIN ("plantation whereon I now live"), JESSE (plantations in Edgecombe and Granville Counties). *Daughter:* ELIZABETH NEVIL (one negro). *Wife and Executrix:* ELIZABETH. *Witnesses:* JOHN MARSHALL, AMY MARSHALL, ROBART SANDERS. *Clerk of the Court:* JOS. MONTFORT.

NEVILL, FRANCIS.

April 16, 1735. April 20, 1735. Little River. *Legatees:* JAMES COLLINS and wife, LUCE; JOHN ARMOR ("my bote"), "Old Madum Britt my ring the pose in thy brest my heart dothe rest." *Executor:* JAMES COLLINGS. *Witnesses:* THOMAS BEDFORD, WILLIAM ALLIN. *Clerk of the Court:* JOHN PARKER. *Justice of the Peace:* JNO. PALIN.

NEWBY, BENJAMIN. Pasquotank County.

November 13, 1739. January Court, 1739. *Sons:* JOSEPH (tract of land), BENJAMIN ("the manner plantation"). *Daughter:* SARAH NEWBY. *Wife and Executrix:* SUSANAH. *Executor:* JOHN OVERMAN. *Witnesses:* JAMES NEWBY, JOHN ROBINSON, JOHN LOW. *Clerk of the Court:* JAMES CRAVEN.

NEWBY, EDWARD.

August 6, 1717. *Brother:* WILLIAM. *Father and Executor:* GABRIEL NEWBY. *Witnesses:* BENJAMIN SANDERS, NATHAN and WILLIAM NEWBY. Original missing. Recorded in Book 1712–1722, page 270.

NEWBY, FRANCIS. Perquimans County.

March 18, 1743–1744. April Court, 1744. *Sons:* ROBERT and JESSE ("my plantation"), MARK and FRANCIS. *Daughters:* MARGARET and SARAH (one negro each). *Executors:* ROBERT, MARK, FRANCIS and JESSEE NEWBY. *Witnesses:* SUSANNAH WOOD, MARY WILSON, RT. WILSON. *Clerk of the Court:* EDMUND HATCH.

NEWBY, FRANCIS. Perquimans County.

January 8, 1752. July Court, 1752. *Brothers:* THOMAS NEWBY, NATHAN NEWBY (all "my lands and houses"), JOHN ROBINSON. *Mother and Executrix:* MARY MOOR. *Witnesses:* ZACH. NIXON, RALPH FLETCHER, ELESABETH NIXON. *Clerk of the Court:* EDMUND HATCH.

NEWBY, GABRIEL.

March 26, 1733. March 1, 1735. *Sons:* JOSEPH (plantation of 300 acres), JESSE (300 acres of land), SAMUEL ("my maner plantation" and also two negroes), FRANCIS. *Grandson:* WILLIAM NEWBY (300 acres of land). *Other legatees:* RICHARD and MARY MOORE. *Wife and Executrix:* MARY. *Witnesses:* WILLIAM HILL, THOMAS MUSE, THOMAS NICHOLSON. Proven before W. SMITH, C. J.

NEWBY, JAMES. Pasquotank County.

November 24, 1739. January Court, 1743. *Son:* JACOB. *Son-in-law:* EDWARD WARD. *Daughters:* SARAH, MAGDALENE and MARY NEWBY. *Wife and Executrix:* HANAH. *Witnesses:* HENRY RAPER, THOMAS OVERMAN, JOSEPH ROBINSON. *Clerk of the Court:* THO. TAYLOR.

ABSTRACT OF WILLS, 1690—1760.

NEWBY, JOSEPH.   Perquimans County.

January 22, 1726. April 21, 1735. *Wife and Executrix:* MARY. No other legatee mentioned. *Witnesses:* NATHAN NEWBY, PETER PEARSON, J. JESSOP. *Clerk of the Court:* JAMES CRAVEN. Coat of arms on seal.

NEWBY, JOSEPH.   Perquimans County.

May 2, 1752. July Court, 1752. *Wife:* ELISABETH. *Daughter:* MARY. *Executors:* SAMUEL NEWBY and JOSEPH WHITE (uncles). *Witnesses:* SAMUEL MOORE, SARAH MOORE, ZACHARIAH MORRIS. *Clerk of the Court:* EDMUND HATCH. Coat of arms on seal.

NEWBY, MARY.   Perquimans County.

October 13, 1739. January Court, 1739. *Son:* JOSEPH MAYO. *Daughter:* ELIZABETH WILLSON. *Grandchildren:* JOHN WILLSON, EDWARD, JEMIMA and ISABELL NEWBY. *Niece:* ELIZABETH WINSLOW. *Executors:* JOHN WILLSON and SAMUEL NEWBY (sons-in-law). *Witnesses:* WILLIAM SITGREAVES, SARAH ELLIT, MIRIAM BOGUE. *Clerk of the Court:* JAMES CRAVEN.

NEWBY, NATHAN.   Perquimans County.

April 1, 1735. October Court, 1735. *Sons:* THOMAS (plantation on Cypress Swamp), FRANCIS ("land whereon I now live"), NATHAN (230 acres of land). *Daughter:* MARY NEWBY. *Wife and Executrix:* MARY. *Executor:* THOMAS NEWBY (brother) and ZACHARIAH NIXON. *Witnesses:* ZACHARIAH NIXON, SENR., FRANCIS TOMES, MARY GIBENS. *Clerk of the Court:* JAMES CRAVEN.

NEWBY, SAMUEL.   Perquimans County.

December 9, 1737. January Court, 1737. *Friends:* JOHN NIXON and ZACHARIAH NIXON. *Cousins and Executors:* THOMAS OVERMAN and JEMES NEWBY. *Witnesses:* ZACHARIAH NIXON, JOSEPH ROBINSON, MARY NIXON. *Clerk of the Court:* JAMES CRAVEN.

NEWBY, WILLIAM.

January 11, 1718–1719. *Wife and Executrix:* ANN. *Witnesses:* SARAH LATON, SARAH PEIRCE, GABRIEL NEWBY. Original missing. Recorded in Book 1712–1722, page 279.

NEWNAM, THOMAS.

September 21, 1723. November 22, 1723. "Now residing at Edenton in North Carolina as Missionary from the Honble the Society for propagating the Gospel in Foreign Parts." *Wife, Executrix and sole legatee:* FRANCES. *Witnesses:* C. GALE, SARAH LLOYD and JOHN FRYARS. Proven before CHRISTOPHER GALE, *Chief Justice.* Coat of arms on seal representing a winged lion.

NEWSUM, JOEL.   Northampton County.

January 10, 1751. February Court, 1752. *Sons:* HOSEA and JOHN ("my plantation to be divided between them"), DAVID, JOEL, WILLIAM and ISAAC (the rest of estate to be divided among them). *Daughter:* MARY NEWSUM. *Executors:* WILLIAM HILYARD (brother), JOHN DUKE. *Witnesses:* ROBT. PEELLE (Quaker), JOHN DICKINSON, ALEXANDER O'QUIN. *Clerk of the Court:* I. EDWARDS.

NEWTON, CHRISTOPHER.   Perquimans County.

May 11, 1759. July Court, 1759. *Wife and Executrix:* SARAH. *Daughter:* CONSTANT. *Witnesses:* THOMAS GILBERT, WALTER NEWTON. *Clerk of the Court:* MILES HARVEY.

NEWTON, THOMAS.   Bladen County.

September 7, 1765. *Son:* JOHN ("my saw mill"). *Daughter:* JANE NEWTON. *Wife and Executrix:* MARY ("my negroes"). *Executor:* CORNELIUS HARNETT. *Witnesses:* WILL'M BARTRAM, JACOB MEZIES. No probate.

NICE, WILLIAM.

April 24, 1757. May Court, 1758. "On Board the Brigantine Hawke of War, THOMAS WRIGHT, Commander." *Sisters:* JANE and KATHERINE NICE in the shire of Murray in Great Britain. *Mother:* JENNET NICE. *Executor:* THOMAS CUNINGHAM. *Witnesses:* JOHN BLYTH, BENJAMIN STONE. *Clerk of the Court:* JA. MORAN.

NICHOLAS, NATHANIEL.   Bertie County.

September 17, 1755. October Court, 1755. This is a nuncupative will proven by THOMAS HUDSON, GEORGE HANDLY and WILLIAM WILLEFORD, and gives to *sons,* JOSAH and WILLIAM NICHOLAS, one plantation each. *Daughter:* ELIZABETH. *Justice:* JOHN BROWN. *Clerk of the Court:* BENJN. WYNNS.

NICHOLSON, JOSEPH.   Albemarle County.

August 6, 1679. January Court, 1697–1698. Plantation on Perquimans River to *brother,* JOHN NICHOLSON. *Brothers:* BENJAMIN, SAMUEL, JOHN, NATHANIEL, CHRISTOPHER. *Executors:* SAML. and JOHN NICHOLSON. *Witnesses:* GABRIEL NUBY, MARY NUBY, THOS. OVERMAN. *Clerk of the Court:* JOHN STEPNEY.

NICHOLSON, NATHANIEL.   Perquimans County.

March 12, 1731–1732. July Court, 1737. *Son:* JONATHAN ("my plantation"). *Daughters:* SARAH and ELIZABETH NICHOLSON. *Wife and Executrix:* SARAH. *Executor:* ZACHARIAH NIXON. *Witnesses:* ALIXANDER STUARD, PETER ALBARDSON. *Clerk of the Court:* JAMES CRAVEN.

NICHOLSON, SAMUEL.

March 22, 1727–1728. No date of probate. *Daughters:* SARAH and ELIZABETH NICHOLSON. *Friend:* SARAH GLOSTER. *Wife and Executrix:* ELIZABETH. *Executor:* JOHN ANDERSON (son-in-law). *Witnesses:* ZACHARIAH NIXON, JOHN KEATON, ELISABETH MONTECUE. *Clerk of the Court:* CHARLES DENMAN.

NICHOLSON, WILLIAM.   Currituck County.

1721. October Court, 1723. *Sons:* JOSIAH ("my manner plantation"). ANTHONY and THEOFILUS NICHOLSON. *Daughters:* SOPHIA, NAOMY and ———— NICHOLSON. *Executor:* JOSIAH NICHOLSON (son). *Witnesses:* DOYLEY LATTER, ANDREW HUDDEY, JOHN CRABB. *Clerk of the Court:* JO. WICKER.

NICKOLLS, JAMES.   Currituck County.

July 13, 1742. October Court, 1743. *Sons:* JAMES ("ye manard plantation"), CALEB (plantation), WILLIS (plantation over the River called Dunkins). *Daughters:* SARAH and FRANKEY NICKOLLS. *Executor:* JOHN ETHERIDGE. *Witnesses:* JAMES BUTT, DARCKES THOMAS, WILLIAM ETHERIDGE. *Clerk of the Court:* JOHN LURRY.

NICKOLSON, CHRISTOFER.   Perquimans County.

May 17, 1723. July 23, 1723. *Son:* THOMAS ("my plantation"). *Daughters:* MARIAM, DABORA, MARY and ANN NICKOLSON. *Wife and Executrix:* MARY. *Executor:* SAMUEL NICKOLSON (brother). *Witnesses:* JEAMES NEWBY, SOLOMON POOL, RICHARD POOL. *Clerk of the Court:* RICHARD LEARY.

NICKOLSON, JOSIAH.   Currituck County.

January 22, 1749–1750. April County Court, 1750. *Sons:* JOHN and JOSIAS ("my land to be divided between them"). To JOHN is also given one negro, and to *son* WILLIAM is given one negro. *Daughter:* CLARE. *Wife and Executrix:* HANNAH. *Witnesses:* BENJAMIN CRABB, PACHANCE EVRAGE, ALEXANDER TRAQUAIR. *Clerk of the Court:* RICH'D MCCLURE.

NICKSON, THOMAS.   Northampton County.

December 1, 1752. February Court, 1753. *Brothers:* JOSEPH and HENRY NICKSON. *Sister:* SARAH JINER. *Executors:* ABRAHAM STEVENSON, JUNR., and WILLIAM ANDREWS. *Witnesses:* WILLIAM TURNER, MARTHA MORE. *Clerk of the Court:* I. EDWARDS.

NICOLS, JOHN.

April 26, 1710. August 12, 1712. *Son:* SAMUEL (land on Sutens Creek). *Daughters:* MARY and HANNAH NICOLS. *Wife and Executrix:* PRESSILLA. *Executor:* SAMUEL NICOLS (father). *Witnesses:* FRANCIS FISHER, ANN DARMAN, HANNAH MODLING. No probate officer.

NIXON, ELIZABETH.   Perquimans County.

March 19, 1747–1748. January Court, 1748. *Son-in-law:* JOHN ANDERSON. *Daughters:* ELIZABETH ANDERSON, SARAH JONES. *Grandsons:* SAMUEL, JOHN and JOSEPH ANDERSON. *Granddaughter:* SARAH ANDERSON. *Friend:* ELIZABETH ALBERTSON, daughter of JOSHUA ALBERTSON. *Executors:* JOHN ANDERSON and JOSEPH ANDERSON. *Witnesses:* THOMAS OVERMAN, JOSHUA ALBERTSON, THOMAS NICHOLSON. *Clerk of the Court:* EDMUND HATCH.

NIXON, JOHN.   Pasquotank Precinct.

February 4, 1687–1688. August 8, 1692. *Wife and Executrix:* EM. *Daughter:* ANN NIXON. *Witnesses:* HENDERSON WALKER, RICHARD PLATER, FRANCIS TOMES, EDWARD MAYO. *Clerk of the Court:* FRANCIS TOMES.

NIXON, RICHARD.   Craven County.

March 5, 1745–1746. June Court, 1746. *Son:* RICHARD (land on Topsail Sound). *Daughters:* GARTRY NIXON (land on southwest), MARY NIXON (land on New Topsail Creek). *Wife and Executrix:* MARY (three negroes). *Executors:* THOMAS GRAVES (brother-in-law), JOHN FONVIELLE. *Witnesses:* JOHN OLIVER, WHEELWRT. PEARSON. *Clerk of the Court:* JNO. RICE. Will provides for investment of proceeds of sale of part of estate in young negroes.

NIXON, ZACHARIAH.   Perquimans County.

September 28, 1739. October Court, 1739. *Sons:* JOHN, PHINEAS, ZACHARIAH, BARNABY (to each is given a plantation, and to all four is given a sawmill and gristmill). *Friend:* MICHAEL MURPHY (land known by the name of Oak Ridge). *Daughter:* REBEKAH TOMS (one negro). To wife is given one-half of negroes. *Executors:* JOHN, PHINEAS and ZACHARIAH NIXON (sons). *Grandchildren:* JOSHUA and MARY MOORE. *Witnesses:* THOMAS OVERMAN, JOHN CHARLES, JOSEPH ROBINSON. OVERMAN and ROBINSON were Quakers. *Clerk of the Court:* JAMES CRAVEN.

NIXON, ZACHARIAH.   Perquimans County.

July 9, 1752. July Court, 1752. *Sons:* FRANCIS, ZACHARIAH (to each is given lands and a lot in Nixon town). *Daughter:* MEHETIBLE NIXON. *Wife and Executrix:* ELIZABETH. *Executor:* JOSEPH WHITE. *Witnesses:* JOHN NIXON, PHINEUS NIXON, MARK NEWBY. *Clerk of the Court:* EDMUND HATCH.

NOBLE, SAMUEL.   Carteret County.

December 26, 1776. January 14, 1776. "As it is customary to bequeath Both The Mortle and Immortal Parts I leave one to the Discression of my Executor and the other to the Marcies of God through my Lord & Savour

Jesus Christ." *Sons:* MARK (land between Miery Branch and White Oak River), WILLIAM (100 acres of land), SAMUEL ("plantation whereon I now live lying between the Black Swamp & Mire branch"). *Daughters:* MARY MAGDILIN BARRY, BETTIE, RACHEL and NANCY NOBLE. *Nephew:* JAMES HOUSTON. *Executors:* MARK, WILLIAM and SAMUEL NOBLE. *Witnesses:* JOHN MUNDINE, BRICE WILLIAMS, LEVI WEST. Proven before RICHARD CASWELL.

NOBLE, WILLIAM. Bath County.

October 22, 1723. June Court, 1724. *Sons:* SAMUEL and WILLIAM (land to be divided between them), JOSEPH (land on White Oak River), JAMES. *Daughter:* HANAH NOBLE. *Wife and Executrix:* ELISABETH. *Witnesses:* ROBERT SMITH, JOHN STARKEY, THOMAS HOLSTON. *Clerk of the Court:* JOHN BAPTISTE ASHE.

NOBLELAND, JOHN. Edgecombe County.

August 12, 1755. November Court, 1755. *Daughters:* MATHEW and REBECCA NOBLELAND, MARY COTTON. *Wife and Executrix:* MARY. *Witnesses:* WM. OGILVIE, NATHANIEL MERRITT, WILLIAM RAINWATER. *Clerk of the Court:* JOS. MONTFORT.

NORCOM, JOHN. Chowan Precinct.

July 26, 1728. September 30, 1728. *Sons:* THOMAS ("plantation I now live on"), STEPNEY, WILLIAM, JOHN, CORNELUS, JEAMES. *Daughters:* SARAH, MARY, ELISABETH. *Wife:* JEAN. *Executor:* THOMAS NORCOM. *Friends:* WILLIAM EGERTON, JOHN CHASTEN, JOHN SIMONS, ABRAHAM WARREN. Proven before RICHARD EVERARD.

NORCOM, JOHN. Chowan County.

February 4, 1745. April Court, 1746. *Daughters:* SARAH and ANN. *Wife and Executrix:* ANN. *Executor:* JOHN HALSEY. *Witnesses:* JOHN PEIRCE, LEVY HAUGHTON, MARY SHELDIN. *Clerk of the Court:* JAMES CRAVEN.

NORCOM, MARY. Chowan County.

May 19, 1718. November 1, 1721. *Sons:* JOHN NORCOM (*Executor*), THOMAS NORCOM. *Daughters:* SARAH, wife of JAMES SMITH; MARY, wife of THOMAS BLICHENDEN. *Granddaughter:* MARY HOPTON. *Grandson:* ABRAHAM WARRIN. *Witnesses:* THOMAS WHITTIS, CORNELIUS LEARY, RICH'D LEARY. *Clerk of the Court:* R. HICKS.

NORCOM, THOMAS. Perquimans Precinct.

May 13, 1707. October 29, 1707. *Sons:* THOMAS and WILLIAM ("my plantation"), JOHN. *Daughters:* ELIZABETH, MARY and SARAH NORCOM.

Grandson: THOMAS NORCOM. *Wife and Executrix:* mentioned, but not named. *Witnesses:* JAMES MING, WALTER TANER. *Clerk of the Court:* J. KNIGHT.

NORCOM, THOMAS.   Perquimans County.

April 23, 1741. April Court, 1744. *Son:* THOMAS ("plantation I now live on left me by the will of my father THOMAS NORCOM"). *Grandson:* RICHARD WHIDBEE (plantation on Sound side joining Lacinse's Creek; also three negroes). *Nephew:* JOHN NORCOM, son of brother, JOHN NORCOM. *Wife and Executrix:* SUSANNA. *Witnesses:* SAMUEL STANDING and JOSEPH ARNOLD. *Clerk of the Court:* EDMUND HATCH.

NORCOM, THOMAS.   Perquimans County.

May 12, 1748. October Court, 1748. *Wife:* MARTHA. *Son:* FREDERICK. *Executor:* JOHN HALSEY. *Witnesses:* GEORGE CHARLTON, MARY HALSEY. *Clerk of the Court:* EDMUND HATCH.

NORFLEET, JAMES.   Perquimans Precinct.

November 28, 1732. January 15, 1732–1733. *Sons:* JOHN ("my plantation, orchards and houses", still, worm and cap, one large silver tankard weighing 33 oz. 16 pwt.; three negroes); THOMAS (three negroes and silver cup, spoon and tobacco box). Cattle divided between sons. *Daughters:* MARY, SARAH, MARGARET and FELISHA NORFLEET. *Wife:* MARY. *Executors:* THOMAS NORFLEET (brother) and WILLIAM HINTON. *Witnesses:* JOHN GORDON, SENR., JOHN GORDON, JUNR., GEORGE GORDON, MARMADUKE NORFLEET. *Clerk of the Court:* CHARLES DENMAN.

NORFLEET, JOHN.   Chowan County.

September 10, 1753. April Court, 1754. *Sons:* ABRAHAM (plantation on Rockahock Creek), JACOB (plantation and houses), JOHN and JAMES *Daughter:* PATIENCE. *Wife and Executrix:* ELISABETH. Gristmill and still ordered to be sold and proceeds divided among children; also island containing 316 acres to be so divided. *Executors:* JOHN and JAMES NORFLEET (sons). All negroes bequeathed to wife. *Witnesses:* DAVID JONES, WILLIAM GWINN, LUKE SUMNER. *Clerk of the Court:* WILL HALSEY.

NORFLEET, MARMADUKE.   Halifax County.

June 29, 1762. November 6, 1762. *Brother:* LEMUEL HOGAN. *Sister:* ELIZABETH NORFLEET (three negroes and silver punch bowl and tankard). *Other legatees:* children of JOHN YOUNG and JOSHUA BEEL. *Executor:* JAMES HOGAN (father-in-law). *Witnesses:* JOHN MORRIS, ELISABETH NORFLEET, THOS. JOYNER, THOMAS KITCHING. Proven before ARTHUR DOBBS, at Newbern.

NORFLEET, MARY.   Perquimans County.

October 12, 1742. January Court, 1742. *Daughters:* MARGARET and FELISHA NORFLEET. *Executor:* JAMES SUMNER. *Witnesses:* JOSEPH RIDDICK, JOHN GORDON, JOSEPH GORDON. *Clerk of the Court:* EDMUND HATCH. Impression of ship on seal.

NORFLEET, THOMAS.   Edgecombe County.

January 23, 1745. August Court, 1746. *Sons:* THOMAS and MARMADUKE (all land of testator to be divided between them; to each is given three negroes and to MARMADUKE is given one silver tankard and one still "and worms"). *Daughters:* SARAH, FARBEY, SUSANAH, MARY, ELISBETH. *Wife and Executrix:* RUTH. *Executor:* MARMADUKE NORFLEET (brother). *Witnesses:* ROBERT HILLIARD, JOHN BLUNT. *Clerk of the Court:* RT. FORSTER.

NORMAN, JOHN.   Onslow County.

March 6, 1753. October 2, 1753. *Sons:* JOHN and WILLIS (to each is given land), PETER (land on Ashes banks). *Daughter:* SARAH NORMAN. *Wife and Executrix:* MARY. *Witnesses:* ELIZABETH CARY, JOB HUNTER, JNO. HUNT. *Clerk of the Court:* JOHN MILTON. Coat of arms on seal.

NORRIS, WILLIAM.   Pasquotank County.

March 24, 1724. *Wife, Executrix and sole legatee:* SUSANAH. *Witnesses:* DAN'LL GUTHRIE, ZACHARIAH FEILD. *Clerk of the Court:* JOHN PARKER.

NORTHEM, JOHN.   Currituck Precinct.

1712. July 14, 1714. *Wife and Executrix:* ELIZABETH. *Sons:* JOHN and PHILIP ("plantation whereon I now live known by the name of Powels Point"). Two negroes bequeathed to each of sons. *Witnesses:* DANIEL MCFARLAND, JOHN WHEDBEE, JOHN BASSFORD. *Clerk of the Court:* JO. WICKER.

NORTON, JOHN.   Currituck County.

September 30, 1744. July 2, 1745. *Sons:* WILLIAM, JOHN, JONATHAN, ASAC. *Daughters:* ABGILL, METABLE, HANAH. *Executors:* WM. and JOHN NORTON (sons). *Witnesses:* JONA. TAGNESS, MARGARET RUSSELL, MARY NORTON. *Clerk of the Court:* RICH'D MCCLURE.

NORTON, WILLIAM.   Bladen County.

December 1, 1746. September Court, 1751. *Sons:* WILLIAM, DANIEL, JACOB, THOMAS. *Daughter:* ELIZBETH. *Executors:* JACOB and THOMAS NORTON. *Witnesses:* WM. LEWIS, JOHN MITCHELL, JOSIAH LEWIS. *Clerk of the Court:* THOS. ROBESON.

NORWOOD, GEORGE.   Northampton County.

April 21, 1749.   August Court, 1749.   *Sons:* SAMUEL (300 acres of land on the River; "one-third part of my still, one-half of my Quince orchard, one-third part of the fruit of my apple orchard, one of the three Pare trees that which stands nearest the river called Norwood's Pare and four of the Catteron Pare trees"), WILLIAM (cattle at Nutbush and one negro). *Grandsons:* GEORGE NORWOOD, son of NATHANIEL (240 acres of land, one horse and one negro girl), NATHANIEL NORWOOD, son of NATHANIEL (310 acres of land at the mouth of Green's Creek, and one negro), JOHN NORWOOD, son of WILLIAM (160 acres of land on Green's Creek, and one negro girl). *Granddaughters:* ELIZABETH, MARY and SARAH, daughters of NATHANIEL NORWOOD. "I give Ten Pounds, Twelve shilling and Six pence Virginia Money to be made in rings with the first letters of my name engraven on them for each grand child I have." *Executors:* WILLIAM, NATHANIEL and SAMUEL NORWOOD (sons). *Witnesses:* JOHN JUSTIS, WILLIAM WOOTEN.   *Clerk of the Court:* I. EDWARDS.

NORWOOD, THOMAS.   Craven County.

December 26, 1757. March 24, 1758. *Son:* WILLIAM (one shilling). *Wife, Executrix and sole legatee:* FRANCES. *Witnesses:* HENRY INCE, SISSELY NORWOOD. Proven before ARTHUR DOBBS.

NORWOOD, WILLIAM.   Craven County.

December 30, 1747. November 14, 1748. *Sister:* MARY LANE. *Niece:* MARY NEVIN. *Brother:* THOMAS NORWOOD. *Nephew:* JOHN NORWOOD. *Executors:* WALTER LANE and BARNABAS RUSSELL. *Witnesses:* THOS. PEARSON, JOSEPH BALCH, W. BETTS, THOMAS PEARSON, JUNR. Proven before E. HALL, *Chief Justice.*

NUSUM, RICHARD.   Bertie County.

February 11, 1753. August Court, 1753. *Wife:* ELIZABETH. *Daughter:* MARY SKINNER. *Grandchildren:* MARY ANDREWS, MARTHA SKINNER. REBECCA, SARAH, LYDIA and ELBE SKINNER (all children of MARY). "*Grandson-in-law*" *and Executor:* WILLIAM ANDREWS. *Witnesses:* ABRAHAM HARRELL, JOHN HARRELL, FRANCIS HARRELL. *Clerk of the Court:* SAM'L ORMES.

OATES, JAMES.   Albemarle Precinct.

July 24, 1703. January Court, 1703–1704. *Son:* JOSEPH OATES. *Wife:* ELIZABETH OATES. JONATHAN EVINS. *Executrix:* ELIZABETH OATES. *Witnesses:* JOSEPH SMITH, JAMES COLES. *Clerk of the Court:* THO. SNODEN.

O'BRIAN, DARBE.   Perquimans Precinct.

February 18, 1723–1724. July 6, 1725. *Legatees:* JOSEPH POTTLE, JOASHAY WILLEBEE, WILLIAM EVANS (*Executor*). *Witnesses:* ANTHO. HATCH, JOSEPH GODFREY, TEMPERANCE PENRICE. Proven before GEO. BURRINGTON.

O'DANIEL, OWEN.   Bertie Precinct.

March 12, 1735–1736. May Court, 1736. *Wife and Executrix:* ELIZABETH. *Executors:* JAMS ROBERTS, LEWIS FRYER and MICHL. RUSSEE. *Witnesses:* WILLIAM KENNADAY, FRA. HOBSON, ROBT. ANDERSON. *Clerk of the Court:* JNO. WYNNS.

ODEON, CHARLES.   Beaufort County.

March 11, 1733. June Court, 1736. *Son:* RICHARD (lands on Town Creek, "at the mouth of the Creek I now live on," and "plantation I now live on"). *Wife and Executrix:* ELISABETH. *Witnesses:* WM. THORNE, WILLIAM CRAWLEY, JNO. WOODARD. *Clerk of the Court:* JOHN COLLISON.

ODOM, JACOB.   Bertie Precinct.

February 16, 1735–1736. November Court, 1736. *Sons:* RICHARD, THOMAS, ABRAHAM (to each is given land). *Daughter:* SARAH ODOM. *Wife and Executrix:* SUSAN. *Witnesses:* JOHN THOMAS and JOHN JENKINS. *Clerk of the Court:* JNO. WYNNS.

ODOM (spelled also ODEOM), JOHN.   Beaufort County.

October, 1740. March Court, 1741. *Son:* JOHN ("my plantation and three negroes"). *Daughters:* MARTHA, ANN, LIDEA and EDY ODOM. *Executors:* JOHN ODOM (son) and LEVI ALDERSON. *Witnesses:* SIMON ALDERSON, CHARLES WHITEHURST, JOHN ALDERSON. *Clerk of the Court:* JNO. FORBES.

ODOM, RICHARD.   Chowan County.

August 12, 1727. January 24, 1728. *Sons:* RICHARD and JOHN, ABRAHAM, JACOB and ARON (to each is given a plantation). *Daughters:* ANN, SARAH, ELIZABETH and JANE ODUM. *Wife:* ANNE. *Executors:* RICHARD and ABRAHAM ODUM (sons). *Witnesses:* EDWARD WARREN, EDWARD VANN, JAMES BRADY and RICHARD TAYLOR. Proven before C. GALE, C. J.

ODYER, DENNIS.   Johnston County.

February 16, 1746. June Court, 1746. *Daughter:* MARY ODYER. *Wife:* ANN. *Executors:* AMBROSS ARIS and JOHN CLARK. *Clerk of the Court:* WILL HODGES; court held at the house of FRANCIS ARINGER on Nuce River.

ABSTRACT OF WILLS, 1690—1760.   273

O'FEYE, DANIELL.   Pasquotank Precinct.

January 18, 1708. *Executor and sole legatee:* JOHN KEMBELL. *Witnesses:* JOHN DANE, JOHN SPARNOR, JOHN ISKET. *Clerk of the Court:* JOHN BISHOP.

OLDFIELD, RICHARD.   Onslow County.

April 19, 1773. September 9, 1773. *Sons:* PITTS ("my house and plantation"), RICHARD, REUBEN, PETER. *Daughters:* NANCE, SARAH and EXSPERANCE OLDFIELD. *Wife:* MARY. *Executors:* PETER STARKEY, EDWARD MORLY. *Witnesses:* WILLIAM CONNAWAY, MARY PITTS, GAIN PITTS. Proven before JO. MARTIN.

OLIVER, FRANCES.   Chowan County.

February 27, 1754. October Court, 1756. *Son-in-law:* JOHN DAVISON of Edenton. *Executor:* JOHN DAVISON. *Other legatees:* Brothers and sister in Virginia, not named. Negroes emancipated. *Witnesses:* ANTHONY CARTEEL, ELIZABETH FLOOD, LEONARD COTTON. *Clerk of the Court:* THOMAS JONES. *Executor* qualified before PETER HENLEY.

OLIVER, JOSEPH.

March 29, 1734. June 11, 1737. *Sons:* THOMAS and JOHN (*Executors*). *Daughter:* SIDNEY OLIVER. *Witnesses:* JOHN MACKEEL, THOMAS MACKEEL and MARTHA MASON. Proven before W. SMITH, C. J.

OLIVER, MOSES.   Chowan Precinct.

January 1, 1728–1729. January 9, 1728. *Executor:* CHARLES RICKETTS. *Legatees:* Children of CHARLES RICKETTS, not named. *Witnesses:* ROBERT JEFFREYS, JOHN GLOVER. Proven before RICHARD EVERARD.

OLIVER, THOMAS.   Hatteras, in Currituck County.

February 4, 1743–1744. April Court, 1745. *Sons:* JOSEPH (plantation called Oyster shell banks), THOMAS (plantation called Peachtree Ridge). *Daughter:* SARAH OLIVER. *Wife and Executrix:* PHEBE. *Executor:* JOB CARR (father-in-law). *Witnesses:* GEORGE HOWARD, ELIZABETH JACKSON, GEORGE SCARBOROUGH. *Clerk of the Court:* RICHD. MCCLURE.

O'NEAL, MICHAEL.   Currituck County.

September 15, 1721. January 10, 1721–1722. *Sons:* CHARLES ("my dwelling plantation"), MICHAEL. *Wife and Executrix:* DEBORAH. *Daughters:* MARY and ELIZABETH O'NEAL and SARAH WALKER. *Friend:* HUMPHREY VINCE. *Witnesses:* ANDREW PEACOCK, WILLIAM BELL, JOHN CRABB. *Clerk of the Court:* JO. WICKER.

18

O'NEAL, MICHAEL.   Currituck Precinct.

March 3, 1722–1723. April 9, 1723. *Sons:* MICHAEL (plantation at Coinjock), THOMAS. *Daughter:* SARAH O'NEAL. *Wife and Executrix:* THOMAZIN. *Witnesses:* THOMAS PARKER, ELIZABETH HANER, RICHD. CHURCH. *Clerk of the Court:* JO. WICKER.

O'QUIN, PATRICK.   Northampton County.

November 23, 1751. February Court, 1752. *Sister:* CHARITY GLASSON. *Executor:* THOMAS DEENS. *Witnesses:* JOHN BROWN, THOMAS COOK, JOHN KNIGHT. *Clerk of the Court:* I. EDWARDS.

ORINDELL, EDWARD.   Chowan County.

November 11, 1732. January 8, 1732. *Sons:* EDWARD ("my plantation"), THOMAS ("land on the Great Swamp"). *Daughters:* RACHEL, MARY and REBECKAH ARENDELL. *Wife and Executrix:* ISEBELL. *Executor:* THOMAS PEIRCE. *Witnesses:* HESHTAN NOE, JOHN BENNET, FRANCIS PETTET. Proven before GEO. BURRINGTON.

ORMOND, WYRIOTT.   Beaufort County.

March 9, 1773. December 1, 1773. *Wife:* ELIZABETH PENELOPE ORMOND (six negroes, one English bay horse and £500 in money). *Daughters:* NANCY and SARAH ORMOND. All profits of estate to be invested in young negroes for benefit of daughters. "My principal desire is that of the education of my daughters * * * and that no expence be thought too great provided etc." *Executors:* ROGER ORMOND (brother) and GEORGE BARROW. Will proven by RICHARD CASWELL, THOMAS RESPESS and THOMAS RESPESS, JR., before JO. MARTIN.

OSBORNE, OBEDIAH.   Onslow County.

August 8, 1758. October Court, 1758. *Wife and Executrix:* ELISEBETH (six negroes and all other estate). *Witnesses:* EDWARD WARD, ENOCH WARD. *Clerk of the Court:* WILL CRAY.

OTTWELL, ISAAC.   Bath County.

October 28, 1732. Town Creek. *Daughters:* ELIZABETH and MARY OTTWELL. *Friends:* EDWARD SALTER and JOHN ODEON. *Witnesses:* PATRICK MAULE, ABRAHAM ADAMS, ROGER JONES, ANN WARREN. *Clerk of the Court:* JNO. COLLISON.

OVERMAN, CHARLES.   Pasquotank County.

August 8, 1755. *Sons:* SAMUEL (plantation), THOMAS, BENJAMIN, ENOCH (two negroes). *Daughters:* ANN MORGAN, MARY ARMOUR, ELIZABETH ARMOUR, HANNAH DESON. *Wife:* ANN. *Executors:* THOMAS NICHOLSON and JOSEPH ROBINSON. *Witnesses:* JOSEPH MORRIS, DAVID JACKSON, MARY TART. *Clerk of the Court:* THOS. TAYLOR.

ABSTRACT OF WILLS, 1690—1760.

OVERMAN, JACOB.

September 12, 1715. *Son:* EPHRAIM. *Daughter:* MARGARET MACKY. *Wife:* DOROTHY. *Executors:* WILLIAM HAIG and THOS. MACKY. *Witnesses:* JAMES BELL, ROBERT WHEATLEY, THOMAS WOODLEY. No probate.

OVERMAN, JAMES.   Pasquotank County.

March 20, 1745–1746. July Court, 1746. *Son:* THOMAS. *Daughter:* HANNAH. *Wife and Executrix:* SUSANNAH. *Witnesses:* THOS. OVERMAN, SAMUEL NEWBY, CHARLES OVERMAN. *Clerk of the Court:* THOS. TAYLOR.

OVERMAN, JOHN.   Pasquotank County.

January 29, 1744–1745. April Court, 1745. *Sons:* JOHN ("my mannor plantation"), WILLIAM. *Daughters:* ELIZABETH and SARAH OVERMAN. *Wife and Executrix:* MARY. *Executor:* THOMAS OVERMAN (brother). *Witnesses:* CHARLES OVERMAN, JAMES OVERMAN, JOHN WHITE. *Clerk of the Court:* THOS. TAYLOR.

OVERMAN, JOSEPH.   Pasquotank County.

September 22, 1739. October Court, 1739. *Brothers:* EPHRAIM, NATHAN and ISAAC OVERMAN. *Friend and Executor:* NATHANIEL MARTIN. *Witnesses:* JOHN NORRIS, THOMAS PALEN and JOHN MARTIN. *Clerk of the Court:* JAMES CRAVEN.

OVERTON, JOHN.   Onslow County.

March 20, 1737–1738. July 4, 1739. *Sons:* JOHN, JAMES, AARON. MOSES, DAVID, JESSE. *Daughters:* SARAH, MARY, NAOMY, ELIZABETH SUSANNAH and ANGEL OVERTON. *Wife and Executrix:* ELIZABETH. *Witnesses:* WM. CRANFORD, JOHN HANSLY. *Clerk of the Court:* WM. CRANFORD. Coat of arms on seal.

OVERTON, ROBERT.   Currituck County.

November 12, 1750. April Court, 1753. *Wife, Executrix and sole legatee:* ALES. *Witnesses:* JAMES BURNHAM, CALEB SIKES, EPHRAIM BRIGHT. *Clerk of the Court:* WILLIAM SHERGOLD.

OWENS, JOHN.   Tyrrell County.

September 16, 1748. March Court, 1750. *Sons:* ZACHARIAH, THOMAS, JOHN (to each is devised a plantation). *Daughter:* SARAH OWENS. Stock mark of daughter: "crop in ye right ear and over keel in ye left." Stock mark of son JOHN: "a slit in the right ear and a crop in the left"; of son THOMAS: "a crop and over keel on right ear"; of son ZACHARIAH: "a crop and underkeel the left ear." *Wife:* ANN. *Executors:* WIFE and son ZACHARIAH. *Witnesses:* NATHANEL SPEENCE WESTE, THOMAS and JAMES FOX. *Clerk of the Court:* EVAN JONES. Coat of arms on seal.

OXENWALL, PETER.   Craven Precinct.

September 9, 1730. September Court, 1730. *Wife, Executrix and sole legatee:* ELIZABETH. *Witnesses:* WILLIAM CARRAWAY, JOHN CARRAWAY, JOHN WARD. *Deputy Clerk of the Court:* CALEB METCALF.

PACE, JOHN, SENIOR.   Bertie Precinct.

March 25, 1726–1727. August Court, 1727. *Sons:* JOHN and WILLIAM (*Executors*), GEORGE. *Daughters:* FRANCIS, ANN, ELIZABETH, MARY MELTON. *Wife:* not named. *Witnesses:* ABRAHAM BURTON, JOHN BOBITT, FRANCIS GARNET. *Clerk of the Court:* RT. FORSTER.

PACE, RICHARD.   Bertie Precinct.

March 13, 1736. February Court, 1738. *Sons:* WILLIAM and THOMAS (plantation to each), RICHARD. *Daughters:* ANN STEWARD, REBECKA BRADFORD, AMY GREEN, FRANCIS GREEN, TABITHA MOORE, MARY JOHNSON, SARAH HOUSE. *Wife:* REBECKA. *Executors:* WILLIAM and THOMAS PACE (sons). *Witnesses:* J. EDWARDS, WILL'M BOONE, BENJAMIN DUKES. *Clerk of the Court:* JOHN WYNNS. Impression of lion rampant on seal.

PACQUINET, MICHAEL.   Beaufort County.

March Court, 1747. Will illegible.

PAGETT, EDWARD.   Chowan Precinct.

February 28, 1727–1728. April 18, 1728. *Brother:* SAMUEL. *Wife and Executrix:* not named. Lands on Bear Creek and "manner plantation" devised to wife. *Witnesses:* WILLIAM ASHLEY, JOHN ROBINSON. Proven before RICHARD EVERARD. Original missing. Recorded in Book 1722–1735, page 138.

PAINE, JOHN.   Craven County.

December 29, 1753. March 2, 1754. *Son and Executor:* THOMAS. *Wife:* ANN. *Witnesses:* CASON SCOTT, ANN SNOW, JOHN SPEIGHT. *Clerk of the Court:* JOHN SNEAD.

PAINE, JOHN.   New Hanover County.

January 9, 1767. March 14, 1767. Wilmington. All estate is devised and bequeathed to *wife*, CATHERINE, and *daughter*, CATHERINE MUSGROVE PAINE. Thirteen pounds proclamation money is ordered paid into the hands of "the church wardens of every County in this province, to be by them distributed among the poor inhabitants of the said several Counties." *Mother:* MARY BREWTON. *Sister:* ELIZABETH, wife of FRANCIS ARTHUR in Georgia. *Executors:* MAURICE MOORE and WILLIAM HILL. *Witnesses:* MARY SNOW, ANN MOUAT, WILLIAM MOUAT. Proven before WM. TRYON.

ABSTRACT OF WILLS, 1690—1760.   277

PAINE, SAMUEL.   Currituck County.
    January 17, 1715. February 17, 1715. *Legatees:* JOHN MCKENNY,
RACHEL MCKENNY (daughter of JOHN), JAMES, JOHN and GEORGE CAROON.
Executors: JAMES and JOHN CAROON. *Witnesses:* THOMAS CROCKER,
KATHERINE JONES, JAMES TOMOOTH. *Deputy Clerk of the Court:* THOS.
BUTT. *Clerk:* JO. WICKER.

PALIN, HENRY, JR.   Pasquotank Precinct.
    January 30, 1700. April 16, 1700. *Sons:* JOHN and THOMAS. *Wife
and Executrix:* ANNE. *Friends:* RICHARD and ELIZABETH HEAT (lands
on Flatty Creek). *Witnesses:* JOHN ROBISON, HUGH CAMPBELL, RICHARD
HEATT. *Clerk of the Court:* THOMAS ABINGTON.

PALIN, JOHN.   Pasquotank County.
    August 16, 1737. October Court, 1737. *Son:* JOHN ("my manner
plantation"). *Nephews:* THOMAS and HENRY PALIN. *Daughter:* MARY
CLEARK ("plantation and land at little flatty creek"). *Other legatees:*
GRISELL BULL (2 negroes), MILLICENT BULL (one negro), SARAH and
CHARLETTA BULL (one negro), ANN GEORGE, JOHN PALIN (1 negro).
To son and daughter is bequeathed ten negroes. *Wife and Executrix:*
SARAH. *Witnesses:* DAVID GEORGE, W. REED, MARY GLAISTER. *Clerk
of the Court:* JAMES CRAVEN. Coat of arms on seal.

PALIN, JOHN.   Pasquotank County.
    February 15, 1755. December Court, 1755. *Legatees:* SARAH PALMER,
daughter of BENJAMIN PALMER; SAMUEL SWANN, son of WILLIAM SWANN;
ANN WINSLOW. *Executors:* CLARK PEOPLES and JOSEPH SCOTT. *Witnesses:* WILLIAM and THOMAS HOSKINS. *Clerk of the Court:* THOS. TAYLOR.

PALIN, THOMAS.   Pasquotank County.
    August 1, 1733. July Court, 1734. *Sons:* HENRY and THOMAS (lands
on Little Flatty Creek). *Daughters:* ANN PALIN, MARY, wife of JOHN
ROSS. *Wife and Executrix:* SUSANNA. *Witnesses:* THOMAS COOK, THOMAS
DAVIS and JOHN PALIN. *Clerk of the Court:* JAMES CRAVEN.

PALIN, THOMAS.   Pasquotank County.
    October 22, 1750. *Sons:* THOMAS and HENRY (land and slaves).
Daughter: ANNE. *Wife:* ELIZABETH. No executor named. *Witnesses:*
JOHN HOPKINS, ANNE HOPKINS, THOS. GRAINGER. No probate.

PALMER, JOSEPH.   Pasquotank County.
    October 4, 1744. October Court, 1744. *Brothers:* ROBERT PALMER,
BENJAMIN PALMER. *Nephew:* MALICHI PALMER. *Cousin:* THOMAS
PALMER. *Sister:* SARAH PINDLETON. *Witnesses:* JNO. MCKEEL, EMANUEL
KNIGHT, THOMAS PALMER. *Executors:* ROBERT and BENJAMIN PALMER.
Clerk of the Court: THO. TAYLOR.

PALMER, ROBERT.   Pasquotank County.

October 5, 1740. October Court, 1740. *Sons:* ROBERT, BENJAMIN, JOSEPH (negroes and land given to each of sons). *Grandsons:* ROBERT and THOMAS PENDLETON, EVAN JONES. *Daughter:* SARAH PENDLETON. *Granddaughter:* NANSE PENDLETON. *Wife and Executrix:* MARY ANN. *Witnesses:* JOHN HASELL, WILLIAM RYALL, JAMES GEORGE. *Clerk of the Court:* JAMES CRAVEN.

PALMER, THOMAS.

January 31, 1720-1721. April Court, 1721. *Son:* THOMAS. *Daughter:* MARY PALMER. *Executor:* ROBERT PALMER (brother). *Witnesses:* ANN IMSON, MARY ———, MATTHEW PRITCHARD. *Clerk of the Court pro tem.:* JNO. PALIN.

PAQUINET, MICHAEL.   Carteret County.

February 20, 1772. March 6, 1772. *Sons:* JAMES ("plantation whereon I now live"), JOHN ("100 acres of land on Cane Creek"), ISAIAH (200 acres of land on Broad Creek). *Daughters:* CHARITY, MARY, MARGARET and REBECKAH PAQUINET. *Wife and Executrix:* MARY. *Witnesses:* JOHN RUSBULL, SEVERN SCOTT, WM. ROBERTSON. Proven before JO. MARTIN.

PARKER, AZRICAM.   Currituck Precinct.

February 18, 1738. *Sons:* JAMES and THOMAS. *Daughter:* SARAH PARKER. *Wife and Executrix:* THOMEZON. *Witnesses:* JOSIAS LITTLE, TIMMOTHY JONES, MICHAEL O'NEAL. *Clerk of the Court:* WILLIAM SHERGOLD.

PARKER, FRANCIS.   Edgecombe County.

April 26, 1746. August Court, 1757. *Sons:* FRANCIS, JOSEPH, SIMON (plantation). *Daughters:* ELIZABETH FOREMAN, CHARITY BRETT, CATHERINE HODGES. *Wife and Executrix:* ELIZABETH. *Witnesses:* GERRARD WALL, JOHN KNIGHT, WALTER MCFARLAN. *Clerk of the Court:* JOS. MONTFORT.

PARKER, JOSEPH.   Chowan County.

November 15, 1749. January Court, 1749. *Daughters:* MARY CANNON, RUTH PARKER, LENINA PARKER. *Sons:* JACOB, TOBE, NATHAN, JOSEPH. *Witnesses:* JEREMIAH CANNON, MARY CANNON. *Clerk of the Court:* WILL MEARNS.

PARKER, MARY.   Edgecombe County.

August 11, 1753. August Court, 1754. *Grandson and sole legatee:* EDMOND GODWIN. No executor named. *Witnesses:* BENJAMIN BRAND, MOSES COLEMAN, CORNELIUS JORDAN. *Clerk of the Court:* BENJAMIN WYNNS.

PARKER, PETER.   Currituck Precinct.

May 2, 1722. July Court, 1722. *Sons:* WILLIAM, WICKER. *Daughters:* SARAH GRIGORY, MARY PARKER, JANE PARKER (land called Beach Ridge), JOANAH PARKER. *Wife and Executrix:* HANAH. *Witnesses:* RICHD. DAUGE, JANE DAUGE, ANN BELL. *Clerk of the Court:* JO. WICKER.

PARKER, PETER.   Currituck County.

April 23, 1750. This is a nuncupative will, proven before STEPHEN WILLIAMS by EDWARD and ELIJAH COX, JOANAH and MIRIAM FEREBEE, and bequeaths all estate to his small children, not named. *Clerk of the Court:* RICHARD MCCLURE.

PARKER, RICHARD.   Chowan County.

September 22, 1749. April Court, 1752. *Sons:* RICHARD, DANIEL, FRANCIS, STEPHEN (about 2,000 acres of land to be divided between the foregoing sons), JONATHAN, JONAS, JACOB, PETER. *Daughters:* ELIZABETH HUNTER, ANN SPRAY, ALICE DAUGHTRY, PATIENCE PARKER. *Grandsons:* RICHARD and WILLIAM PARKER. *Wife and Executrix:* not named. *Witnesses:* JOHN WILLIAMSON, WILLIAM DOUGHTIE, JOHN MOORE. *Clerk of the Court:* JAS. CRAVEN.

PARKER, SIMON.   Edgecombe County.

December 31, 1758. March Court, 1759. *Sons:* FRANCIS, SIMON, WILLIAM, ROBERT (to each is devised a plantation), JAMES. *Daughters:* JUDAH, SARAH, WINNE, CHARITIE and RUTH PARKER. *Wife:* JUDITH. *Executors:* FRANCIS PARKER (brother) and JAMES KNIGHT (brother-in-law). *Witnesses:* CHARLES DANIELL, GIRRARD WALL, MARY CULLENDER. *Clerk of the Court:* JOS. MONTFORT.

PARKER, THOMAS.   Chowan County.

January 23, 1717. October Court, 1717. *Sons:* THOMAS, JOSEPH, JOHN and WILLIAM. *Daughters:* SARAH and FRANCES. *Wife and Executrix:* JEANE. *Witnesses:* JOHN PARKER, HENRY LAM, BENJAMIN EVANS. *Clerk of the Court:* R. HICKS.

PARKER, THOMAS.   Currituck County.

March 16, 1753. March Court, 1755. *Wife:* REBECKAH. *Executors:* EZRICAM PARKER and MICHAEL O'NEIL. *Witnesses:* THOS. TAYLOR, WILLIAM BRABELL, JOHN LURRY. *Clerk of the Court:* WILLIAM SHERGOLD.

PARKER, WILLIAM.   Chowan County.

December 27, 1750. July Court, 1751. *Sons:* JAMES, WILLIAM, THOMAS, BENJAMIN, JOHN. *Daughters:* MARY FRYER and JUDITH DUKE.

Wife and Executrix: ANN. *Witnesses:* WILLIAM WATERS, HENRY GRIFFEN, DEMSEY SUMNER. *Clerk of the Court:* JAMES CRAVEN. Impression of head of Roman soldier on seal.

PARKES, HENRY.   Craven County.

February 27, 1733–1734. September 17, 1734. *Godson:* HENRY GRUM. *Wife:* CATHERINE. No executor. *Witnesses:* JNO. BRYAN, BENJAMIN GRIFEN. *Clerk of the Court:* CALEB METCALFE.

PARLEPOUGH, HENRY.   Craven County.

January 27, 1735–1736. March 17, 1735–1736. *Executor and sole legatee:* JOHN VENDRICK. *Witnesses:* JOHN BRYAN, JOHN JACOB HOAVER, SARAH THOMAS. Proven before RICHARD EVERARD.

PARRISH, JOHN.   Perquimans Precinct.

October 14, 1738. March 24, 1738. *Son:* JOHN (plantation and orchard). *Daughter:* ANNE BARCLIFT (wife of JOHN). *Grandson:* JOHN BARCLIFT. *Wife:* MARGERY. *Executor:* JOHN BARCLIFT, SR. *Witnesses:* JAMES GIBSON, SAMUEL WRIGHT. Proven before W. SMITH, C. J.

PARRISHE, WILLIAM.   Edgecombe Precinct.

January 20, 1735–1736. August Court, 1736. *Daughter:* SARAH PARRISH. *Wife and Executrix:* MARY. *Witnesses:* BUCKLEY KIMBROUGH and ISAAC WINSTON. *Clerk of the Court:* THOS. KEARNEY.

PARROT, JACOB.   Bertie Precinct.

November 3, 1738. November 18, 1738. *Son:* JOHN. *Daughter:* MARY PARROT. *Wife:* MARTHA. *Executors:* WILLIAM FELLTWOOD, EDWARD RASOR. *Witnesses:* LAMB HARDY, LOVICK YOUNG, SARAH MORPHEW. Proven before W. SMITH, C. J.

PARSONS, SAMUEL.   Perquimans County.

May 12, 1745. July Court, 1745. *Sons:* SAMUEL (land on Beaver Cove), BARNABY, JOHN. *Daughters:* SARAH ARNELL, MARY PARSONS. *Wife and Executrix:* SARAH. *Witnesses:* JOHN ANDERSON, LAURENCE ARNEL and JOHN BOYLE. *Clerk of the Court:* EDMUND HATCH.

PARSONS, THOMAS.   Craven County.

February 13, 1747–1748. December Court, 1749. *Sons:* JOHN (one plantation), JEREMIAH, THOMAS (one plantation to each). *Daughters:* SARAH and MARY PARSONS, ELIZABETH MAISON. *Executor:* JOHN MAISON. *Witnesses:* THOS. MASTERS, THOS. COOKE, THOS. WARREN LEE. *Clerk of the Court:* PHIL. SMITH.

PARYER, JOHN.   Craven County.

May 1, 1737. June 20, 1738. *Legatees:* WALPOLIA GILLETH, wife of JOHN GILLETH; JOHN WAXDALE. *Executors:* JOHN SIMON, JOHN WAXDALE, WALPOLIA GILLETH. *Witnesses:* PENELLOPE PARROTT, WILLIAM COOPPER, NATHL. PARROTT. *Clerk of the Court:* JAMES COOR.

PASMORE, JOHN.   Edgecombe County.

May 19, 1754. November Court, 1754. *Sons:* GEORGE, JOHN, ROBERT, JOSEPH. *Daughters:* ELIZABETH SAMMON, SARAH PASMORE. *Wife:* SARAH. *Executors:* GEORGE and JOHN PASMORE (sons). *Witnesses:* JOHN JACKSON, MOSES PENDRY, JAMES SAMON. *Clerk of the Court:* BENJAMIN WYNNS.

PATCHITT, JOHN.   Chowan Precinct.

March 14, 1710–1711. *Wife:* ELIZABETH. *Son:* JOHN ("my plantation"). *Executor:* not named. *Witnesses:* DAVID JONES and WILLIAM TANNER. Original missing. Recorded in Book 1712–1722, page 36.

PATTENSON, HENRY.   New Hanover County.

July 7, 1751. *Wife:* ANNE. *Witnesses:* THOS. NEWTON, JOHN WALKER. *Clerk of the Court:* ISAAC FARIES.

PATTERSON, GEORGE.   Bertie County.

November 19, 1749. December 30, 1749. *Wife and Executrix:* MARY. Other *legatees:* JOHN BURNS, ANN THOMSON, GRISELL BURNS, ANDREW BURNS. *Executors:* JOHN and ANDREW BURNS. *Witnesses:* THOMAS RYAN, ANDREW THOMSON, JAMES FLOOD and DAVID THOMSON. Proven before GAB. JOHNSTON.

PATTERSON, ROBERT.

June 4, 1717. February 15, 1721. *Son:* JOHN. *Daughters:* ELIZABETH and JANET PATTERSON. *Wife and Executrix:* JANET. Other *legatees:* SIMON SIMONS, JOHN PARKE, ANDREW ROSS, ANDREW ROSS, JR., of Nansemond County, Va. *Witnesses:* JAMES LONG, JOSIAH BRIDGERS, WILLM. HAWETT, WILLIAM MOORE, JAMES ALLENN, J. FEHENDEN. Proven before CHAS. EDEN.

PAUL, WILLIAM.   Northampton County.

May 9, 1744. *Wife, Executrix and sole legatee:* MARY. *Witnesses:* R. WILLIAMS, WM. RUSHING, JOHN PAULL. No probate.

PAYNE, PETER.   Chowan County.

March 18, 1754. April Court, 1755. Edenton. *Sons:* WILLIAM (houses and lots in Edenton, silver hilted sword and two negroes), MICHAEL (one negro). *Daughters:* MARY CAROLINA and SARAH EMELIA PAYNE. *Executors:*

JOHN RIEUSSET, JOHN CAMPBELL, THOMAS BARKER. *Witnesses:* JAMES TROTTER, JOHN MCKILDO, MARY MESIGOOD. *Clerk of the Court:* WILL HALSEY. Testator pays his respects to JAMES CAMPBELL of Edenton, in the following language: "she (wife of testator) shall not keep or hold any correspondence with JAMES CAMPBELL of Edenton whom I know to be a man of infamous character, etc."

PEARCE, ROBERT. Edenton.

July 11, 1729. Of the city of Exeter, but now of Edenton. This is a nuncupative will made before C. GALE, G. ALLEYN and ANNE JENOURE and appoints JOHN LOVICK *Executor* and desires that all remainder of estate after payment of debts be forwarded to wife at the house of one JOHN HARRIS in Exon, in Devon County, England.

PEARCY, LAZARUS. Craven County.

April 11, 1760. *Sons:* JOHN, JAMES, EDMON, EPHREM. *Wife and Executrix:* not named. *Witnesses:* EDMUND PEARCE, THOMAS PEARCY, HEZEKIAH PEARCE. No probate.

PEARSON, JOHN. Pasquotank County.

October 8, 1753. June Court, 1755. *Wife and Executrix:* PHEBE. *Witnesses:* MARY JUSTIS, JAMES JUSTIS, JOHN SNOW. *Clerk of the Court:* THOS. TAYLOR.

PEARSON, RACHEL. Perquimans County.

June 25, 1750. January Court, 1750. *Sons:* PETER, JOHN and JONATHAN PEARSON. *Daughters:* RACHEL BOGUE, MARY WINSLOW, BETTY BAGLEY. *Executors:* JOHN WINSLOW and ROBERT BOGUE (sons-in-law). *Witnesses:* JOSHUA HOBART, ARTHUR CROXEN, JOHN MOORE. *Clerk of the Court:* EDMUND HATCH.

PEARSON, THOMAS. Craven County.

December 7, 1748. December Court, 1748. *Sons:* WHEELWRIGHT (land on "News" River), THOMAS (silver watch), HAMMOND. *Daughters:* MARY, ELIZABETH, ANNA and EASTER PEARSON. *Parents:* THOMAS and ELIZABETH PEARSON of Boston. *Executors:* WHEELWRIGHT, THOMAS and MARY PEARSON (children). *Witnesses:* FRS. STRINGER, JOHN SHINE, LEM'LL HARVEY. *Clerk of the Court:* PHIL. SMITH.

PEEKE, JAMES. Bertie County.

November 23, 1728. February Court, 1728. *Son:* WILLIAM. *Executors:* GEORGE WYNN, THOMAS BANKS and RICHARD OLDNER. *Witnesses:* ELIZABETH DAVIS, MARTHA LEE, TRIDDLE KEEFE. *Clerk of the Court:* RT. FORSTER.

ABSTRACT OF WILLS, 1690—1760.   283

PEELLE, JUDITH.   Northampton County.

June 22, 1756. August Court, 1756. *Sons:* JOHN, ROBERT, JOSEPH, JOSIAH, JOSHUA. *Daughters:* SARAH DUKE, MARY GRANBERRY. *Executor:* WILLIAM GRANBERY (son-in-law). *Witnesses:* WILLIAM RUTLAND, ABRAM BRUCE. *Clerk of the Court:* I. EDWARDS.

PEET, WILLIAM.

February 8, 1722–1723. March 12, 1722. "Late of Long Islan in the province of New York." *Sole legatee:* JAMES BULLIN of Chester, in "Penselvany." *Executor:* JAMES NEWBI. *Witnesses:* VALENTINE WALLIS, ANN WALLIS. Proven before WM. REED.

PEGGS, JOHN.   Pasquotank County.

March 20, 1755. June Court, 1755. *Sons:* JOSEPH and JOHN PEGGS (one plantation to each, together with a negro). *Daughters:* MARY and ANN PEGGS. *Executors:* WILLIAM DAVIS, JOHN SMITHIN. *Witnesses:* THOS. HAMLIN, ROBART HOSEA, JONATHAN HOWELL. *Clerk of the Court:* THOS. TAYLOR.

PEGGS, MARGARET.   Pasquotank Precinct.

February 27, 1729. March 14, 1729. *Daughters:* MARY GREGORY, JANE BARECOCK, MIRIAM GREGORY. *Sons:* JOHN PEGGS and PETER BROWN. *Grandsons:* JOHN BROWN, THOMAS BARECOCK. *Granddaughter:* MARY SMITHSON. *Executor:* JOHN PEGGS (son). *Witnesses:* W. MINSON, THOMAS WOODLEY, DANIEL RECKXAKER. Proven before RICHARD EVERARD.

PEIRCE, JOSEPH.   Perquimans County.

1736. October 8, 1736. *Son:* THOMAS ("my plantation whereon I now live"). *Daughters:* MIRIAM (land known as Morises), REBECKAH ("my still"). *Wife and Executrix:* ALIS. *Executor:* THOMAS PEIRCE (brother). *Witnesses:* JOSIAH GILBERT, HANNAH GILBERT, JOSEPH CREECY. Proven before GAB. JOHNSTON.

PENDER, PAUL.   Bertie County.

April 18, 1748. August Court, 1748. *Sons:* JOHN, JOSEPH, SOLOMON, PAUL. *Daughters:* MARY LAURENCE, ELIZABETH LEE, RACHEL ELLIS, CHRISTIAN DAVIS. *Wife:* ELIZABETH. *Executor:* PAUL PENDER (son). *Witnesses:* ALEX. COTTEN, JACOB LASHER. *Clerk of the Court:* JOHN LOVICK.

PENDLETON, HENRY.   Pasquotank County.

March 18, 1727–1728. April 18, 1748. *Daughters:* ELIZABETH WOODLEY, wife of THOMAS; MARY, wife of JOHN BROTHERS; SARAH, wife of JOSEPH REDING; ANNE, wife of THOMAS DAVIS. *Sons:* THOMAS, JOHN.

Grandson: HENRY PENDLETON. *Executor:* THOMAS PENDLETON (son). *Witnesses:* SARAH BULL, MARTHA KELLY, JNO. PALIN. Proven before GAB. JOHNSTON.

PENDLETON, THOMAS.   Pasquotank County.

February 21, 1732. April Court, 1732. *Sons:* THOMAS and JOSEPH ("the manner plantation"), GEORGE, TIMOTHY (plantation called Masons Neck). *Daughters:* ELIZABETH (plantation called Robinsons), ANNE KNIGHT. *Wife:* SARAH. *Executors:* THOMAS and JOSEPH PENDLETON (sons). *Witnesses:* DANIEL ROCKSAKER, WILLIAM DAVIS, J. SWEENY. *Clerk of the Court:* W. MINSON.

PENDLETON, THOMAS.   Pasquotank County.

May 10, 1749. April 18, 1750. *Daughters:* PENELOPE JORDAN, MARY, ELIZABETH. To daughters are given plantations at New Begon Creek, and also an Island in Currituck Sound called Collinton, and also a number of negro slaves. *Wife:* not named. *Executor:* JOSEPH JORDAN. *Witnesses:* DEMSEY CONNER, ROBERT JORDAN, TIMOTHY PENDLETON. Proven before GAB. JOHNSTON.

PENDLETON, THOMAS.   Pasquotank County.

February 21, 1750–1751. July Court, 1751. *Daughters:* MARY, ELIZABETH, TEMINA PENDLETON. *Son:* ROBERT PENDLETON. *Wife and Executrix:* SARAH. *Executor:* BENJAMIN PALMER. *Witnesses:* WILL. GREGORY, JOHN HOSEA, DEMSEY CONNER. *Clerk of the Court:* THOMAS TAYLOR. Coat of arms on seal.

PENRICE, FRANCIS.   Perquimans County.

May 13, 1756. April Court, 1758. *Sons:* FRANCIS, SAMUEL, EDWARD. *Daughters:* MARY LONG, ELIZABETH LONG, ANN SUTTON, HANNAH PENRICE. *Executors:* HANNAH and EDWARD PENRICE (son and daughter). *Witnesses:* JOSHUA SKINNER, WM. AINTON. *Clerk of the Court:* MILES HARVEY.

PENRICE, THOMAS.   Chowan County.

September 5, 1739. October Court, 1739. *Brother, Executor and sole legatee:* FRANCIS PENRICE. *Witnesses:* JOSHA HOBART, LUKE GREGORY, MARY PENRICE. *Clerk of the Court:* JAMES CRAVEN.

PERISH, JOHN.   Perquimans County.

February 12, 1755. April Court, 1759. *Sons:* JOHN, JAMES, JOSEPH, SAMUEL (to each is given land), JOSIAH. *Daughters:* ELINDER, BETTIE and MARY PERISH, JEAN BUNDY. *Executors:* JOHN and JOSIAH PERISH (sons). *Witnesses:* THOMAS HOLLOWELL, PETER PEARSON, CORNELIUS MOORE. *Clerk of the Court:* MILES HARVEY.

ABSTRACT OF WILLS, 1690—1760.

PERISHE, SARAH. Perquimans County.
May 29, 1754. April Court, 1760. *Sons:* SIMON, JAMES. *Daughters:* SARAH, JANE and MORNEN. *Executors:* JAMES PERISHE (son), JOSEPH PERISHE (brother). *Witnesses:* JAS. PIERCE, THOMAS STANTON. *Clerk of the Court:* MILES HARVEY.

PERKINS, HENRY. Currituck County.
July 2, 1715. July 12, 1715. *Wife and Executrix:* ELIZABETH. *Witnesses:* PETER POYNER and JOSEPH POYNER. *Clerk of the Court:* JO. WICKER.

PERRY, JEREMIAH. Chowan Precinct.
October 18, 1694. October Court, 1694. *Wife and Executrix:* JANE PERRY. *Other legatees:* CHRISTIAN and THOS. BLOUNT. *Witnesses:* THO. POLLOCK, ALEX. MCFARLAND, NEAL MCMING, JOHN BUNTIN. *Clerk of the Court:* NATHL. CHEVIN. *Clerk in Secretary's office:* W. GLOVER.

PERRY, PHILIP. Perquimans County.
July 5, 1751. October Court, 1751. *Sons:* JESSE (lands on Little River known by the name of Sandy Hook), PHILIP ("plantation whereon I now live"). *Daughters:* SARAH, MARY, RACHEL, JUDE, ELIZABETH and MIRIAM. *Executor:* JACOB PERRY, son of JACOB PERRY. *Witnesses:* MOSES FEILD, BENJAMIN PERRY, ELIZABETH PERRY. *Clerk of the Court:* EDMUND HATCH.

PERSONS, JOHN. Perquimans County.
December 29, 1753. April Court, 1754. *Daughter:* MIRIAM PERSONS. *Wife and Executrix:* MARY. *Executor:* SAMUEL PERSONS (brother). *Witnesses:* JOHN WHEDBEE, GABRIEL COSAN, JOSEPH PERSHOE. *Clerk of the Court:* WILLIAM SKINNER.

PERSON, PETER. Perquimans Precinct.
March 1, 1751. April Court, 1755. *Sons:* JONATHAN, NATHAN, PETER, JOHN. *Daughters:* RACHEL, MARY and BETTY PERSONS. *Brother:* NATHAN NEWBY. *Wife and Executrix:* not named. *Witnesses:* JESSE NEWBY, WILLIAM BOGUE, WILLIAM HASKIT. *Clerk of the Court:* JAMES CRAVEN.

PETERSON, JACOB. Albemarle County.
January 13, 1697. July Court, 1698. One shilling in silver to REBONAH BOORD, *daughter-in-law*; one shilling each to *daughters* ELIZABETH, CONSTANT. *Daughter:* ANN PETERSON, plantation bought from JNO. DURANT. *Executrix:* MARY PETERSON. *Witnesses:* MARTHA FAGEETT, JAMES FAGEETT, STEPHEN MAINWARING. *Clerk of the Court:* JOHN STEPNEY.

PETERSON, JACOB.   Albemarle County.
1697. This is a nuncupative will leaving everything to *wife*, REBECKAH. Proven before JOHN WHEDBE by EDWARD and MARY GELFF.

PETIT, FRANCIS.   Chowan Precinct.
October 29, 1710. August 12, 1712. *Son:* FRANCIS. *Cousin:* JOHN CHESTNE. *Daughter:* SARAH. *Wife and Executrix:* MARY. *Executor:* THOMAS PEIRCE (brother of wife). *Friend:* JOHN BARROW. *Witnesses:* JONATHAN WILLIAMS, SARAH BARROW, FRANCIS SMITH. No probate officer.

PEYTON, ROBERT.   Bath County.
January 8, 1733. September 10, 1754. *Sons:* THOMAS, ROBERT, WILLIAM (lands up Derhams Creek), AMBROSE. To each of sons is given a plantation. *Daughters:* SARAH PEYTON, DOROTHY PORTER. *Wife and Executrix:* MARY. *Witnesses:* THOMAS GAINS, ELIZABETH BELL, BRYANT KELLY, SOLOMON ROBSON. *Clerk of the Court:* JOHN SNEAD.

PFIFER, JOHN.   Mecklenburg County.
August 14, 1775. January 22, 1777. *Son:* PAUL PFIFER. *Daughters:* MARGARET, ANN ELIZABETH PFIFER. *Wife:* CATHERINE. *Executors:* MARTIN PFIFER (father) and PAUL BARRINGER (father-in-law). *Witnesses:* BENJAMIN PATTON, WILLIAM WALLACE, SAMUEL PATTON. *Clerk of the Court:* SAML. MARTIN. Provision is made for sending son to college and educating daughters.

PHELPS, GODFREY.   Tyrrell County.
February 7, 1750. September Court, 1751. *Sons:* CUDBERD, GODFREY, JOHN (to each is given a plantation; to JOHN "the manner plantation"). *Daughters:* SARAH and ELIZABETH PHELPS. *Wife and Executrix:* ELIZABETH. *Executor:* JOSHUA PHELPS. *Witnesses:* JOHN PAGETT, JOSHUAY PHELPS, JOSEPH SPRUILL. *Clerk of the Court:* EVAN JONES.

PHELPS, HENRY.   Perquimans County.
May 19, 1752. July Court, 1752. *Son:* JONATHAN ("all my lands and plantations * * * the fourth part of my negroes * * * Foxes Journals first and second part &c." *Wife and Executrix:* MARGARET. *Daughter:* ELIZABETH PHELPS. *Executors:* JONATHAN PHELPS (brother) and ZACHARIAH NIXON (father-in-law). *Witnesses:* FRANCIS TOMES, FRANCIS NIXON and SARAH NEWBY. *Clerk of the Court:* EDMUND HATCH.

PHELPS, JONATHAN.   Perquimans Precinct.
March 11, 1688. April 4, 1689. *Son:* JONATHAN. *Wife:* HANNAH. Proven before RICHARD STANRICK, THO. IMPERS, DAVID SHERNOLD. This will is very badly mutilated and so faded as to be illegible.

PHELPS, JONATHAN.   Perquimans County.

December 4, 1732. January Court, 1732. *Sons:* HENRY ("manner plantation"), JONATHAN (300 acres land on Perquimans River). *Daughter:* ELIZABETH PHELPS. Eight negroes and four horses bequeathed to wife and children. *Wife and Executrix:* ELIZABETH. *Executor:* CHARLES DENMAN. *Witnesses:* R. CHEASTEN, ELLEXANDER HOWARD, JAMES ANDERSON. *Clerk of the Court:* CHARLES DENMAN.

PHELPS, SAMUEL.   Perquimans Precinct.

April 21, 1728. July Court, 1728. *Sons:* JONATHAN, JOHN (land in "balehack"), WILLIAM, JAMES. *Wife:* not named. *Executors:* JONATHAN PHELPS (brother), JONATHAN PHELPS (son), ABRAHAM SANDERS and ROBERT WILLSON. *Witnesses:* ABRAHAM SANDERS, RALPH BOSEMAN, CHARLES DENMAN. *Clerk of the Court:* R. EVERARD.

PHELPS, WILLIAM.   Perquimans County.

April 15, 1752. April Court, 1752. *Legatees:* JOHN HARVEY and JAMES LITTESON (cousins), WILLIAM BARKER, SARAH ELIOT, SAMUEL LITTESON. *Executors:* JOHN HARVEY and JAMES LITTESON. *Witnesses:* JOSHUA HOBART, MARGERY MOORE, DERBE MOORE, PENNINAH CHANCEY. *Clerk of the Court:* EDMUND HATCH.

PHENNEY, GEORGE.

June 3, 1736. June 23, 1737. Surveyor Generall of His Majesties Customs Southern District on the Continent of America." *Legatees:* RALPH NODEN, of London; ELIZABETH KIRK, of London. *Nephew:* JOSEPH HARRISON. *Wife and Executrix:* PENELOPE. *Witnesses:* SAMUEL SCOTT, THOMAS ASHLEY, T. BUTLER. Proven before W. SMITH.

PHILLIPS, DANIEL.   Currituck County.

July Court, 1726. *Sons:* JAMES, DANIEL, SAMUEL, BENJAMIN. *Daughters:* MARY DUK, MARGRITT PHILLIPS. *Wife and Executrix:* ABIGALL. *Witnesses:* JOHN MASHELL, WILLIAM SCOTT, ANDR. DUKE. *Clerk of the Court:* J. MARTYN.

PHILLIPS, PAUL.   Craven County.

June 5, 1746. June Court, 1751. *Son:* PAUL. *Grandsons:* PAUL PHILLIPS and PAUL FLOOD. *Daughters:* RACHEL YENSHAW, RUTH SANDERS. *Son-in-law:* WILLIAM FLOOD. *Wife and Executrix:* REBECCA. *Witnesses:* LUKE GRACE, LEONARD LOFTIN, PETER HENDRICKSON. *Clerk of the Court:* CHAS. YOUNG.

PHILLIPS, THOMAS.   Craven County.

June 22, 1743. December 23, 1743. *Wife and Executrix:* ISABELL. *Sons:* JOHN, MASON, THOMAS, JAMES, MARK, WILLIAM. *Daughter:* MARY. *Witnesses:* ROBERT PATERSON, HENRY SUMERLIN. *Clerk of the Court:* N. ROUTLEDGE.

PHILLIPS, THOMAS.   Northampton County.

April 4, 1751. May Court, 1751. *Sons:* THOMAS and MARK (one plantation to each), WILLIAM. *Daughters:* PATTY SIMPSON, MARY PHILLIPS. *Wife and Executrix:* PATTY. *Executor:* WILLIAM PHILLIPS (son). *Witnesses:* SIMON SIMPSON, BEN. EDWARDS, CHRISTOPHER EDWARDS. *Clerk of the Court:* I. EDWARDS.

PHILLIPS, WILLIAM.   Beaufort County.

October 6, 1740. December Court, 1751. *Son:* SAMUEL (land at Swan Point). *Sister:* ANN WILLIAMS. *Wife and Executrix:* ELIZABETH. *Witnesses:* THOMAS MOORE, RICHARD ALLEGOOD, JOHN MCKEEL. *Clerk of the Court:* WILLIAM ORMOND.

PHILPOTT, JOHN.   Albemarle County.

November 19, 1694. JOHN LAWSON, son of NATHL. LAWSON (plantation now living on, ten cows and 6,000 pounds pork to buy a negro), JOHN LAWSON. *Wife:* MARY PHILPOTT. Plantation adjoining home lands to *son-in-law*, WM. WOOLLARD. *Executors:* DANIEL AKEHURST and JOHN LAWSON. *Witnesses:* THO. ROLFE, DANIEL HAWKINS, JOHN CABEGE. (No probate.)

PICKENS, ANDREW.

November 4, 1756. *Sons:* JOHN and ANDREW ("my plantation"). *Daughter:* JEAN PICKENS (saddle horse). *Wife and Executrix:* NANCY. *Witnesses:* ROBERT MCCLENACHAN, JOHN PICKENS. No probate.

PICKERIN, RICHARD.   Bertie County.

January 25, 1739. February Court, 1739. *Legatees:* MARY, JAMES and ROGER SNELL. *Executor:* ROGER SNELL. *Witnesses:* J. HILL. *Clerk of the Court:* RT. FORSTER.

PIERCE, JOHN.   Perquimans County.

September 13, 1682. *Sons:* THOMAS, JOHN and JOSEPH. *Daughter:* REBECKAH. *Other legatees:* THOMAS DAW, WM. BUNDY. *Wife:* not named. *Executors:* WILLIAM BUNDY and JONATHAN PHELPS. *Witnesses:* ROBERT WILSON, FRANCIS TOME and JOHN STANLEY. No probate.

ABSTRACT OF WILLS, 1690—1760.   289

PIERCE, JOHN.   Perquimans County.

October 9, 1726. January 10, 1726. *Sons:* COPELAND, THOMAS. *Daughters:* MARY, ELIZABETH and HANNAH. *Wife and Executrix:* SARAH. *Brothers-in-law:* PETER JONES, JOHN WILLIAMS. *Witnesses:* REBECKAH LONG, RACHEL WEIGHT, THOMAS PIERCE. *Clerk of the Court:* RICHARD LEARY.

PIERCE, JOSEPH.   Perquimans Precinct.

June 6, 1700. *Brother:* THOMAS PIERCE. *Wife and Executrix:* DAMARIS. *Witnesses:* TIMOTHY CLEARE, WM. and THOS. WINSLOW. *Clerk of the Court:* THOS. SNODEN.

PIERCE, THOMAS.   Perquimans Precinct.

February 12, 1731–1732. March 30, 1732. *Sons:* THOMAS, JOSEPH, JOHN. *Daughter:* MARY JONES (1 negro). *Grandchildren:* THOMAS PIERCE, MARY PIERCE. *Wife and Executrix:* MARY. *Executor:* PETER JONES (son-in-law). *Witnesses:* MILES GALE, RICHARD SKINNER, ABRAHAM SANDERS. Proven before GEORGE BURRINGTON.

PIERCE, THOMAS.   Chowan County.

April 6, 1755. October Court, 1756. *Daughters:* MARY NIXON, SARAH MORRIS, JAMIMA NEWBY, KESIAH NEWBY, KERRENHAPPUCH PIERCE. *Grandson:* PIERCE NIXON. *Brother-in-law:* PETER JONES. *Executors:* PHENIASS NIXON, JOHN MORRISS, ROBERT NEWBY, NATHAN NEWBY (sons-in-law), and JOSEPH WHITE. *Witnesses:* JOHN SIMONS, CORNELUS LEARY, MARY CREECY. *Clerk of the Court:* THOMAS JONES.

PIKE, SAMUEL.   Pasquotank Precinct.

December 11, 1716. *Sons:* SAMUEL and BENJAMIN, JOHN. *Daughters:* SUSANNAH PIKE and ANN PIKE. *Wife and Executrix:* JANE PIKE. *Witnesses:* JOHN MARTIN, JOHN MOOR. No probate.

PILKINGTON, SETH.   Beaufort County.

October 7, 1751. March Court, 1754. *Daughters:* SARAH CAUTANCHE (seven negroes), WINIFRED PILKINGTON (ten negroes and "plantation whereon I now live, situated on Lemuel Cherry herring runn"). *Wife's daughter:* ANN LILLINGTON. *Wife's granddaughters:* CATHERINE LOCKHART and MARY EVANS. *Executors:* MICHAEL CAUTANCHE (son-in-law), WINIFRED PILKINGTON (daughter). *Witnesses:* JOHN FRY, WM. STUBBS, MICHAEL CAUTANCHE, JR. *Clerk of the Court:* WALLEY CHAUNCEY.

19

PILSON, GRACE. Craven County.

September 17, 1743. December 23, 1743. *Sister:* MARY FOX, of Perth Amboy, near New York (7 negroes, 3 large looking-glasses). *Kinswomen:* GRACE FOX (4 negroes, 1 silver tankard, 1 looking-glass, 1 gold chain and two gold rings), ELLINOR FOX (2 gold rings, 1 pr. gold earrings). *Brother:* THOMAS FOX (silver watch). *Friend:* RICHARD SCOTT (1 negro man). *Executors:* RICHARD BIDDER and THOMAS PEARSON. *Witnesses:* JAMES COOR, JOSHUA ACKIS, WILLIAM WEBB, JAMES WHITING. Proven before GAB. JOHNSTON. Impression of watchdog on seal.

PILSON, THOMAS. Craven County.

February 17, 1742–1743. September 9, 1743. *Brother:* CHARLES PILSON. *Sister:* ELIZABETH WHEELER. *Wife and Executrix:* GRACE (plantation and 10 negroes). *Witnesses:* JOHN WEST, CHRISTOPHER DAWSON, NICHOLAS PUREFOY. *Clerk of the Court:* N. ROUTLEDGE. *Executor* qualified before J. MONTGOMERY, C. J.

PIMBROUGH, DANIEL.

April 22, 1688. August 2, 1688. *Legatees:* ELIZABETH LILLINGTON, WILLIAM CALLOWAY, son of CALEB CALLOWAY, WILLIAM and ELIZABETH FETTERTON, children of WILLIAM FETTERTON. *Executor:* CALEB CALLOWAY. *Witnesses:* ALEXR. LILLINGTON, JOHN DURANT, ROBERT HERMAN. Proven before DANIEL AKEHURST and EDWARD MAYO.

PINKETT, ELINOR. Beaufort County.

May 17, 1757. March Court, 1758. *Sons:* WILLIAM DANIEL PINKETT, THOMAS and ZACHARIAH PINKETT (one negro to each). *Son-in-law:* WILLIAM MOORE. *Daughter:* HANNAH PINKETT. *Granddaughter:* RACHEL CASON. *Executors:* WILLIAM DANIEL PINKETT and THOMAS PINKETT. *Witnesses:* GEORGE MOYE, JR., WILLIAM PROCTER, MARGARET SMITH. *Clerk of the Court:* WALLEY CHAUNCEY.

PIPKIN, JOHN. Chowan County.

May 21, 1745. July 18, 1745. *Sons:* PHILIP, LEWIS and ISAAC, JOHN and DANIEL (to each is devised a tract of land), JOSEPH (1 negro), JESSE (1 negro). *Wife and Executrix:* MARTHA (1 negro). *Witnesses:* HENRY GOODMAN, JR., TIMOTHY GOODMAN, HENRY GOODMAN, SR. *Clerk of the Court:* EDMUND HATCH.

PIRENT, JAMES. Edgecombe County.

March 7, 1757. May Court, 1757. *Son:* JAMES ("plantation whereon I now live"). *Daughters:* TATION, MARY and SARAH. *Executors:* ARTHUR and JOSHUA BELL. *Witnesses:* JAMES HOGAN, JOSHUA BELL, WILLIAM HOLLOWAY. *Clerk of the Court:* JOS. MONTFORT.

PITMAN, BENJAMIN.   Edgecombe County.

August 3, 1755. May Court, 1756. *Sons:* MOSES, MICAH, SAMSON, JACOB. *Daughters:* PATIENCE FAULK, MARY BOTTOM, ABIGAL PITMAN, LUCY PITMAN, CELA PITMAN, JEMIMA PITMAN. *Wife and Executrix:* ANN. *Witnesses:* JOHN STREATER, JOHN JAMESON, JOHN MURPHREE. *Clerk of the Court:* JOS. MONTFORT.

PITMAN, THOMAS.   Edgecombe County.

April 4, 1754, February Court, 1755. *Sons:* LOT, THOMAS and seven others mentioned, but not named. *Daughters:* two mentioned, but not named. *Brothers:* ROBERT and AMBROSE PITMAN (*Executors*). *Wife:* ANNE. *Witnesses:* JNO. HOPKINS, AMBROSE PITTMAN, JOHN FORT. *Clerk of the Court:* BENJAMIN WYNNS.

PLATER, RICHARD.   Pasquotank Precinct.

September 8, 1705. January Court, 1705. *Legatees:* JOHN HUNT, JOHN MCKEEL, HUGH CAMPBELL, ANTHONY HATCH. Estate in the Kingdom of England devised to mother, DOROTHY PLATER, of Linn, in the County of Norfolk, and MRS. SARAH BEATHER. *Executor:* HUGH CAMPBELL. *Witnesses:* JOSEPH MING, ANTHONY MARCKHAM, JR., JOHN FOURRE. *Clerk of the Court:* J. KNIGHT.

PLATO, THOMAS.   Pasquotank Precinct.

March 12, 1735-1736. *Daughters:* MARTHA, SUSANNAH and MARY PLATO. *Executors:* ANTONY MARCKHAM and JOHN BOYD. *Witnesses:* THOS. WARD, ANTHONY MARCKHAM, JNO. MCKEEL. No probate.

PLOMER, SAMUEL SABANE.

April 12, 1755. May 2, 1755. Surgeon. *Legatees:* PENELOPE and CHARLOTTE BLACKHALL, daughters of DR. ABRAHAM BLACKHALL; SARAH ROWDEN, daughter of SARAH BLACKHALL; CAPT. JOSEPH HERON, SARAH SHARP, ELIZABETH PLOMER SHARP. *Executors:* JOHN CAMPBELL and CHARLES ELLIOT. *Witnesses:* BEN WHEATLEY, JOHN HARVEY, RO. LENOX. Proven before ARTHUR DOBBS. Impression of man's head on seal.

PLOWMAN, JOHN.   Chowan County.

July 1, 1721. August 4, 1721. *Legatees:* JOHN PLOWMAN WHITE (plantation and seven slaves), THOMAS LOVICK, MARY WHITE, JOHN PLOWMAN ASHLEY, GOVERNOR EDEN, JOHN LOVICK, NICHOLAS CRISP, ISAAC HILL (last-named three persons appointed Executors). *Witnesses:* JAMES CASTELLAW, JAS. WINRIGHT, J. CABB. Proven before CHARLES EDEN.

POLLOCK, ESTHER. Chowan County.

May 30, 1712. March Court, 1723. *Executors:* THOMAS LUTEN and THOMAS LUTEN, JR. *Other legatees:* GOVERNOR EDWARD HYDE, MRS. ANN STEWART, HENDERSON LUTEN. Lands on Sasefrick River in Snell County, Maryland, and lands in "this province given me by my late husband, WILLM. WILKISON; lands at Sandy Point." *Witnesses:* ROBERT HICKS, JAMES BEASLEY, JNO. PORTER, JUNR., CONRAD EICHHORN. *Clerk of the Court:* W. BADHAM.

POLLOCK, GEORGE.

October 18, 1736. July 29, 1738. *Brother:* CULLEN POLLOCK (land on Salmon Creek, Chowan River, on the "South Shore," on Moratock River and Canaho Creek; 4,700 acres on north side of Moratock; 710 acres of land on Trent River). *Nephews:* CULLEN and THOMAS POLLOCK (5,000 acres of land at the Haw Fields; 3,300 acres on Tarr River; 2,200 acres on Coor Creek; 220 acres on Coor Creek; 150 acres at Bennys Creek; 500 acres on Wecone Creek; 640 acres on Moratock). *Brother-in-law and Executor:* COL. ROBERT WEST (lands on Trenters and Horn Creeks; island called "the Crow" in Currituck County; sum of money to purchase patents for lands). *Witnesses:* THOMAS ASHLEY, WILLIAM FRYLEY, NEHEMIAH WARRING. Proven before W. SMITH, C. J. The original of this will is missing. Abstract made from recorded copy No. 82 in Book 4, Land Grant Records.

POLLOCK, JAMES. Chowan Precinct.

February 23, 1700. *Legatees:* BULLAH BLOUNT (houses and lands), WILLIAM WARD, THOMAS POLLOCK, EDMOND PEARSE, JOHN WACKER. *Witnesses:* THOMAS BLOUNT, SAM'LL SWANN, THOMAS COOPPER. *Clerk of the Court:* N. CHEVIN.

POLLOCK, THOMAS. Chowan County.

August 8, 1721. August Court, 1753. *Sons:* THOMAS, CULLEN and GEORGE. *Daughter:* MARY, wife of THOMAS BRAY. The following lands are devised: 1,550 acres on Chowan River between MR. KING and THO. DANIEL; lands purchased of THOS. DANIEL, JOHN RASBERRY, JAMES WILKESON, MARTIN FREDERICK RASOR; five tracts of lightwood land on Samon Creek; "land where FIREBENT built ye mill"; 10,000 acres on Mill Creek; 2,560 acres in fork of Raquis called Springfield; 2,500 acres on Moratock River called Canecarora (Coueconora); 640 acres on Bridges Creek at Weekacanaan; 2,800 acres on Cassayah called Rosefield; land on Moratock adjoining BOWMAN; land purchased of RICH'D ROSE; land on Moratock Bay; 900 acres of land on Nuce River fork called New Bern; land bought of MAJOR ROBERT WEST; lands adjoining "land where I now live"; lands adjoining that bought of CARY GOBBEE; land adjoining PARROTS; land where

ABSTRACT OF WILLS, 1690—1760.   293

SAM'LL EDMUNDS lives; land where JOHN GRIFFIN lives near Bavie Swamp; where WILSON lived at Weekacoon Creek; where JOHN MAINARD lived at Pettishore; 2,400 acres of land called Crany Island; 2,200 acres on the south side of Neuse River and west side of Core Creek; 710 acres on Trent River called "ye halfe-way House"; 220 acres on the east side of Core Creek; on the south shore where LEONARD LOFTEN lives; 360 acres on Boag Sound; 215 acres in the fork of Chesters Creek on White Oak River; 150 acres on Neuse River at the head of Bennys Creek; 5,000 acres to the south of Neuse River; 640 acres on Neuse River called Wilkeson's Point; 8,900 acres on the east branch of Salmon Creek; lands lying on South Lancaster. About seventy-five negroes are bequeathed to three sons. The following items may be of interest: "I give * * * one hundred pound to be paid in Boston and 5,000 feet of plank which I have sent for from Boston." "I give * * * lands, mortgages * * * whether in America or Scotland." "* * * what pitch and tarr ye hands in ye woods makes until ye first of aprill next." "* * * I have expended and laid out for a house at Black Rock * * * ten pound more for New England plank." "And whereas also I have been out and expended upon a House for my son CULLEN on the south shore when Mr. WEST the Carpentare is paid for what worke he hath done thereto (to-wit) the covering the house, doeing the Dormant Windoes and making up the Gavell end of the said house and when CULLEN hath what Glass is in the house." "Mr. COKE * * * is to have all the lands that are necessary for him for burning the bricks or what other worke he hath occasion for * * *." *Executors:* THOMAS, CULLEN and GEORGE (sons). *Witnesses:* JOHN BURNNELL, DAVID HENDERSON, WILLIAM HARDY, LAWRENCE SARSOR, JAMES CASTELAW, JAMES CASTELAW, ROBERT WICKS, THOMAS NEWMAN (or NEWNAM), WILLIAM LITTLE, JOSEPH SKITTLETHORP. *Clerk of the Court:* FR. FOSTER. Also SAMUEL ORMES.

POLLOCK, THOMAS.   Bertie County.

April 16, 1732. January 20, 1732. *Sons:* CULLEN, THOMAS, GEORGE. *Wife:* not named. The following lands are devised: plantation called Black Rock; plantation called Great Quarter; plantation called Manuels or Crickits; land on Salmon Creek and Chowan River; 8,900 acres adjoining the aforesaid land; land on Trent River containing 10,000 acres; 2,560 acres in fork of Raquis called Springfield; land at Unaroye Meadows; two tracts nigh Tuskarora Indian Town; 300 acres on Moratuck River; 235 acres on Moratuck River; four tracts on Fishing Creek; land on Briery Branch. *Other legatees:* JACOB PARAT and JOHN HAILES, MRS. ELIZ. DICKSON. About 50 negroes are bequeathed. The following item may be of interest: "I will & order and give by this will to all such persons who are setled on my lands at Trenton Condition of a Certain Writing I give to JACOB MILLER that those already settled thare have leases on ye same terms I promised them." *Witnesses:* GEORGE POLLOCK, FRANCIS RASOR,

JACOB PARAT, ROBERT MINOR, ELIZABETH DICKSON. *Executors:* GEORGE and CULLEN POLLOCK (brothers), ROBERT WEST. Will proven before W. LITTLE, C. J.

POOL, SOLOMON.   Pasquotank County.

July 30, 1739. *Sons:* JOSEPH, SOLOMON, JACOB ("my manner plantation"). *Daughter:* SARAH POOL. To each of children is bequeathed one negro. *Wife and Executrix:* GRACE. *Witnesses:* CHARLES TAYLOR, SOLOMON POOL, JOSEPH ROBINSON. Probate illegible.

POPE, EDWARD.   Pasquotank County.

January 26, 1721–1722. April Court, 1722. *Wife, Executrix and sole legatee:* SARAH. *Witnesses:* W. NORRIS, LUCY JACKSON, EDWARD MAYO. *Clerk of the Court:* EDMD. GALE.

POPE, RICHARD.   Pasquotank Precinct.

June 23, 1701. July 15, 1701. *Son:* EDWARD. *Daughter:* MARY POPE. *Wife and Executrix:* ANN. *Witnesses:* EDWARD MAYO, MATTHEW PRITCHARD, SAMUEL PIKE, GEO. ELLIS, THO. ABINGTON. *Clerk of the Court:* THOS. ABINGTON.

POPE, SAMUEL.   Craven County.

January 5, 1758. February 4, 1758. *Sons:* SAMUEL (land on Core Creek), JOHN and WILLIAM. *Daughters:* ELIZABETH and MARY POPE. *Wife:* SARAH. *Executors:* GEORGE POPE and JOHN TURNER. *Witnesses:* ROBERT TAYLOR, GEORGE POPE, BETTY LANE. *Deputy Clerk of the Court:* PETER CORNEGY.

POPE, WILLIAM.   Edgecombe County.

January 15, 1749. February Court, 1749. *Sons:* JACOB (three negroes), WEST and STEPHEN (one negro each). *Daughters:* REBECCA POPE and JULIAN NEWSOM. *Grandsons:* WILLIAM TAYLOR (two negroes), WILLIAM POPE ("my plantation"). *Executors:* JACOB POPE (son) and JOSEPH NEWSOM (son-in-law). *Witnesses:* HENRY WEST, JOSEPH PEARCE, ARTHUR WALL, JOHN JORDAN. *Clerk of the Court:* BENJAMIN WYNNS. Testator came to this state from Isle of Wight County, in Virginia, and devised to son STEPHEN plantation in said County.

PORSELL, GARRIT.   Albemarle County.

January 31, 1724–1725. August 2, 1725. *Sons:* EDMAN and GARRITT. *Daughters:* MARY, CATHEN, ELIZABETH. *Wife and Executrix:* ELIZABETH. *Witnesses:* WILLIAM WILSON, JOHN SCARBROUGH, WILLIAM WAITE. Proven before RICHARD EVERARD.

PORTER, JOHN, Merchant.   Albemarle County.

January 8, 1712. August 7, 1712. *Wife:* MARY, lands in Chowan Precinct. *Son:* EDMUND, lands in Chowan after death of wife. *Son:* JOHN PORTER, tract of land in Bath County called "Chocowinateh." *Son:* JOSHUA, land called "Quarry's." *Son:* MATTHEW PORTER, 2,000 acres in Bath County, "on other side of river," bought of RICHARD SMITH. *Son-in-law:* JNO. LILLINGTON and *wife* SARAH, mentioned. *Daughter:* ELIZA, three negroes. *Executrix:* MARY PORTER. *Witnesses:* JNO. ALLEN, M. D., JOHN WEBBER. *Notary Public:* JOANE MILLS (WCH.). Original missing. Recorded in Book of Wills No. 2, page 5. This will is proven before JONA THOMAS, Mayor, of Bridgewater, in Sommersett County, England, on the ———— day of February, 1712.

PORTER, JOHN.   "Cape Fair."

October 11, 1727. January 6, 1728. *Son:* JOHN. *Daughter:* SARAH PORTER. *Wife and Executrix:* SARAH PORTER. *Witnesses:* SETH PILKINGTON, JOHN WORTH, J. KNIGHT. Proven before RICHARD EVERARD. Device on seal.

PORTER, JOHN PEYTON.   Beaufort County.

April 29, 1750. March Court, 1755. *Wife:* ELIZABETH (plantation on east side of Durham's Creek called the Garrison containing 644 acres). *Daughters:* MARY PORTER, SARAH PORTER (plantation on east side of Durhams Creek commonly called Hardings, adjoining the plantation called the Garrison). Another tract beginning at SNEADS line "from thence to the Savanna, from thence to the Horsepen Swamp, from thence to the Dismall." Negroes are to be kept on the above described tract "to make Tar, Turpentine in order to raise money, etc." Negroes, cattle and other personal property divided between wife and children. *Executors:* MICHAEL COTANCHE and NATHAN RICHARDSON. *Witnesses:* THOMAS LOUGH, WILLIAM TRIPP, CHARLES LAWTHER. *Clerk of the Court:* WALLEY CHAUNCEY.

PORTER, JOHN.   Hyde County.

November 20, 1750. December Court, 1751. *Sons:* WILLIAM and JOHN ("land whereon I now live including the Houses and plantation"). *Daughter:* PATIENCE PORTER. *Wife:* ELISABETH. *Executors:* THOMAS and JOHN SMITH. *Witnesses:* THOMAS and MARY SMITH, MARY RHODES. *Clerk of the Court:* THOMAS LOVICK.

PORTER, JOHN SWANN.   New Hanover County.

No dates. Rocky Point. House, land, watercourses, etc., devised to JOHN BAPTISTE ASHE, son of SAMUEL ASHE, with remainder to JOHN MOORE, SAM'L SWANN, JR., SAMUEL ASHE (youngest son of SAMUEL) and CINCINNATUS ASHE (son of SAMUEL). Seven slaves are bequeathed to executors for education of two mulatto boys, emancipated by deeds

executed in 1773, which boys were formerly the property of ANN MOSE-
LEY ("now wife of HUGH MUNROE"). To these mulatto boys are be-
queathed slaves. *Executors:* SAMUEL SWANN, JR., and JOHN BAPTISTE
ASHE. No signature, date, witnesses or probate.

PORTER, JOSHUA. Bath County.
January 17, 1733. September 14, 1734. *Son:* JOHN PEYTON PORTER
(land "whereon I now live on Derhams Creek"). *Daughter:* ELIZABETH
(1,000 acres of land on Derhams Creek, together with negro slaves).
Cousin: JOHN FRY. *Other legatees:* ANN LILLINGTON and ELIZABETH FRY
(cousins of testator), WILLIAM TRIPPE, PHILIP CREMER. *Wife:* DOROTHY.
Executors: EDMUND PORTER (brother), PATRICK MAULE and SETH PILK-
INGTON (brothers-in-law), EDWARD MOSELEY and JOHN TRIPPE. *Witnesses:* CHURCHILL READING, JOHN CALDOM, WILLIAM WHITFORD. Proven
before GEORGE BURRINGTON. Original missing. Recorded in Book 1722–
1735, page 329.

PORTER, MARY. Chowan Precinct.
November 12, 1717. January 21, 1717. *Sons:* JOHN (one negro; one-
half dozen Russia leather chairs); EDMUND (one negro; one-half dozen silver spoons, etc.); JOSUA (land at Yawpim adjoining "MR. CLAYTON and
MR. CLARK"; the following personal property: "My negroe woman known
by the name of Edy one Ticken feather bed & bolster and two pillows one
feather bed covered with Canvas and bolster and one Pillowe three pillow
cases Suitable two pair fine sheets, two pair coarse sheets one set of red
watered Curtains and Wallons one Spotted Worsted Rug, Red Rug, Two
pair good blankets 1 flowered Bed coverlid Bedstead that stood in the Hall
Chamber Six Rusia leather chairs one of the large lookeing glasses and my
largest and one midling iron pott the large andirons a large double brass
Skillet and Trevit one brass Candlestick one pair brass Scales and weights,
one pair of Stilliards two Diaper towels a pewter mustard pott the Coarsest
of brass ridles my Dantzick locke Chests a lime sifter a Case of Knives and
forks a Cross cut Sawe a writeing Desk four Pewter Porringers one earthen
Porringer ten Pewter Plates iron pestle Ash Table 1 large Soup Pewter dish
one large small Dito one midle sized Dito 1 large and 1 small Pewter bason
2 earthen bason and 2 pewter Do one set of wedges and six wooden chairs
2 joint stooles to wooden turned chairs 2 Iron tramels 1 brass butter ladle
1 small brass Ketle, 1 pewter chamber pott Milland Salt, 1 Iron chafing
dish the half of my crop now in the ground and one pottle pewter pott and
a pint Pewter pott one Glass Gallon Bottle and one broad Axe"). *Daughters:* ELIZABETH PORTER ("six silver spoons each weighing ten shillings
sterling and one iron pott and pott hooks and twelve soup plates"). SARAH
LILINGTON ("my negro woman called Maria 1 chest of drawers, six painted
Chairs now in her possession one pair of iron fire doggs one small Cedar
table 1 pair of fine sheets two pair Coarse Sheets and two pillow cases Two

Diaper towells my largest quilt one Lignum Vitae Spice Mortar one large Soup Dish one midle sized pewter dish 1 small pewter bason 1 brass Skimer 1 small Iron Kettle the least of my painted trunks two Earthen Bason and Plates 1 English Flasket 1 large glass bottle 1 stone jugg 1 pewter Chamber pott 1 bed pann three of my other which she likes best and the full third part of the Cotten and Wooll that shall belong to me at my decease"). To *daughter* ELIZABETH in addition to above-named legacies is bequeathed the following personal property: "my Indian woman called Judith and her daughter named Sukey 1 chest of drawers one oval table my best Sett of red Curtains and Valent belonging to my lodging rooms three pair fine sheets two pair Coarse Sheets four pillow cases My Green Rugg made of worsted 1 pair of the best rose blankets the least of my quilts my Callico counterpane and Jester Cloath my Bible my Spice box 1 warmeing pann 1 pair Chamber doggs with brass 1 Black trunk and one painted trunk a large brass Keetle and Two Skimers a Brass Shield and Two Iron potts one linked Tramel a brass Flam one Copper Chocolate pott 1 white rugg 1 Gridiron four matted chairs my Silver Salt Marked I p M and Silver peper box with the Same marke one large pewter Soup dish 1 shallow Do two midling pewter dishes 1 large and one Small pewter basons 10 pewter plates Six painted chairs five pewter porringers 1 pr brass candlesticks, Snuffers and snuff dish my Smoothing iron heaters and Frame 1 gallon Stone Jugg 1 Glass Cruit two glass cups one mustard pott two pewter Chamber potts three earthen Bason 1 large Dish Do & Two plates 1 Tin pudding pann 1 Spitt 1 leaden pann and 2 painted brushes a brass Shovel and Tongs a large looking Glass the best of the Bew panns 1 pewter Salt 1 glass decanter 2 tin dish covers 1 brass Ridle a large turned Elbow chair 1 Drippen Pan 1 case of bottles one-half of my Sheep and Cattle one silver tankard." *Granddaughters:* SARAH PORTER, MARY and SARAH LILLINGTON. *Other legatee:* ROBT. HERRICK. *Executors:* JOHN and JOSHUA PORTER (sons). *Witnesses:* J. LOVICK, MARY HARVEY. *Clerk of the Court:* R. HICKS.

PORTER, NICOLESS. Johnston County.

August 24, 1749. September Court, 1749. *Daughters:* JEANE PORTER ("mannor plantation"), ELIZABETH PORTER and ANN PORTER (143 acres of land to each), AGNES PORTER (143 acres of land). *Son:* SAMUELL ("my pole cat land"). *Wife and Executrix:* ELIZABETH. *Executor:* JAMES FARMER. *Witnesses:* NEEDHAM BRYAN, MARY DEES. *Clerk of the Court:* RICHARD CASWELL.

PORTER, SAMUEL. Bladen County.

September 30, 1757. October Court, 1757. *Sons:* JAMES, JOHN, HUGH and SAMUEL. *Executors:* PETER LOARD and WILLIAM McREE. *Witnesses:* MATTHEW BYRNE, NATHL. PLATT, JOHN LOCK. *Clerk of the Court:* J. BURGWYN.

PORTORWIN, PETER.

August 23, 1729. June 10, 1730. *Sons:* JOSEPH and SAMUEL. *Sons-in-law:* JOHN SNOW, FRANCIS DESHUNG. *Witnesses:* JOHN ARTER, THOMAS HUTCHINGS, ANTHONY MARCK. Proven before RICHARD EVERARD.

POTTEL, JOSEPH.   Perquimans County.

February 1, 1747–1748. August 4, 1749. *Daughter and sole legatee:* ELISABETH POTTEL (Bible, gold ring and riding horse, saddle and bridle). *Executor:* PATRICK POOL. *Witnesses:* JOSEPH NEWBY, RALPH FLETCHER, SAMUEL MOORE. Proven before GAB. JOHNSTON.

POWELL, GEORGE.   Bertie Precinct.

March 24, 1735–1736. May Court, 1736. *Sons:* CADE, LEWIS, GEORGE, MOSES (to each is bequeathed a negro). *Executor:* CADER POWELL (son). *Witnesses:* WM. MOOR, CHARLES HORNE, EDMON DOD. *Clerk of the Court:* JNO. WYNNS.

POWELL, JOHN.   Albemarle County.

February 20, 1723–1724. *Wife:* ANN. *Sons:* JOHN and BROOKS POWELL (wife and sons in England and are appointed Executors). *Friends:* WILLIAM DOWNING and JOSHUA TURNER. *Witnesses:* MARY DOWNING, JOHN FREEMAN, JOS. FREEMAN. No probate.

POWELL, THOMAS.   Northampton County.

July 20, 1752. February Court, 1754. *Daughters:* KEZIAH and ANN POWELL. *Wife and Executrix:* ELIZABETH. *Son:* MATTHEW. *Witnesses:* JOHN DEW, HENARY HORTON, BARNEBE JOHNSON. *Clerk of the Court:* I. EDWARDS.

POWELL, WILLIAM.

December, 1748. Will illegible.

POWERS, GEORGE.   Currituck County.

March 27, 1754. June Court, 1755. *Sons:* WILLIAM, GEORGE (plantation between JOSEPH SANDERSON and JOHN WOODHOUSE), CALEB (plantation known as Dicks Field). *Daughters:* LYDDA ETHERIDGE, JEAN ETHERIDGE, ABIGAL POWERS. *Wife and Executrix:* ISABEL. *Witnesses:* JAMES BURNHAM, WILLIAM MARSHAL, RICHARD ETHERIDGE. *Clerk of the Court:* WILLIAM SHERGOLD.

POWERS, ISBELL.   Currituck County.

November 23, 1757. December Court, 1757. *Sons:* WILLIAM, GEORGE and CALEB. *Daughters:* ISBELL, MARY ETHERIDGE, JEANE ETHERIDGE,

ABBEGALL PINER. *Grandson:* JAMES ETHERIDGE. *Witnesses:* WILLIS ETHERIDGE, ELIZABETH MARSHALL, THOS. RICHARDS. *Clerk of the Court:* WM. MEARNS.

POWERS, WILLIAM.   Chowan Precinct.

November 26, 1747. April 14, 1748. *Sister:* AUSTICE (of Cork in Ireland). *Friend and Executor:* BENJAMIN HILL. *Witnesses:* ABRA. BLACKALL, JOSEPH HARRON, ALEXR. MCCULLOCH. Proven before E. HALL, C. J. Testator bequeathes to sister, leases on the following lands in Ireland: Oaten fields, Leckineene Monetane Shanahane, Knockanearkamas, The Bullock Fields, Fort Fields, Currobrodah.

POYNER, JAMES.   Currituck County.

May 7, 1744. March Court, 1755. *Sons:* HUMPHREY and ROBERT. *Wife and Executrix:* SARAH. *Witnesses:* EDWARD COXE, RICHARD ROGERS, SAML. SIMMONS. *Clerk of the Court:* WILLIAM SHERGOLD.

POYNER, JOS.   Currituck County.

August 19, 1712. *Sons:* WILLIAM and JOSEPH. *Wife:* ELIZABETH. *Executors:* HUMPHREY VINCE and *father*, who is not named. *Witnesses:* JOS. WICKER, RUTH WICKER, HENRY SWANN. No probate.

POYNER, PETER.   Currituck County.

July 6, 1710. April 12, 1715. *Sons:* PETER, JOSEPH, ROBERT and WILLIAM (to each is devised land), THOMAS and JAMES. *Daughter:* ELIZABETH. *Granddaughter:* MARY POYNER. *Friend:* SAMUEL BARBER. *Wife and Executrix:* ELIZABETH. *Witnesses:* HUMPHREY VINES (or VINCE), ELIZABETH DAVIS, JOS. WICKER. *Clerk of the Court:* JO. WICKER.

POYNER (or POINER), WILLIAM.   Currituck County.

April 27, 1753. March Court, 1755. *Son:* NATHANIEL ("plantation whereon I now live and plantation in Moyocke"). *Daughter:* ELIZABETH POYNER (plantation on the Beaver Dam). *Executors:* WILLIAM SHERGOLD and CALEB WILLSON. *Witnesses:* SAML. SIMMONS, JONATHAN POYNER, JOHN CHITTOM. *Clerk of the Court:* WILLIAM SHERGOLD.

POYNER, PETER.   Currituck County.

June 22, 1758. December Court, 1758. *Sons:* PETER, JOEL, BENJAMIN (plantation known by the name of Beach Ridge), NATHAN. *Daughters:* SOPHIA BARCO, MARY MERCER, ESTER SALYER, ABIA PINER, KIZIAH POYNER (or PINER), GEMIMA PARKER. *Wife:* SOPHIA. *Executor:* NATHAN (son). *Witnesses:* WILLIAM BRAY, JOSHUA BALL, REUBEN BALL. *Clerk of the Court:* WM. MEARNS.

POYNER, WILLIAM.   Currituck Precinct.

March 14, 1722. July 9, 1723. *Sons:* WILLIAM and SAMUELL (lands on Currotuck Bay). *Daughter:* MARYANN POYNER. *Wife and Executrix:* LIDEE. *Witnesses:* HANNER MEEGS, THOS. SWANN, WM. LUFMAN. *Clerk of the Court:* JO. WICKER.

PRATT, JOB.   Perquimans County.

December 7, 1736. January Court, 1736. *Son:* JOHN. *Wife:* not named. *Executors:* JOSHUA PRATT (brother), JOHN WILKINS. *Friend:* LUKE GREGORY. *Witnesses:* DAN'L HALL, JOSEPH and JEREMIAH PRATT. *Clerk of the Court:* JAMES CRAVEN.

PRATT, JOHN.   Bertie County.

November 4, 1740. August 2, 1742. *Wife, Executrix and sole legatee:* CHRISTIAN (formerly CHRISTIAN CHAMARD). *Witnesses:* HANH. GALE, SARAH CLAYTON, GEORGE PARRIS. Proven before J. MONTGOMERY, C. J.

PRATT, JOHN.   Chowan County.

August 30, 1743. January Court, 1743. *Brother and Executor:* JOSHUA. *Witnesses:* DAVID BUTLER, JOSEPH MING. *Clerk of the Court:* RICHARD MCCLURE.

PRATT, JOSEPH.   Perquimans County.

August 29, 1737. October Court, 1737. *Brothers:* JEREMIAH ("my half of the mill and dwelling house"), JOSHUA. *Executors:* NATHANIEL CARRUTHERS and JOSHUA PRATT (brother). *Witnesses:* NATH'L CARRUTHERS, JOSHUA PRATT and JEREMIAH PRATT. *Clerk of the Court:* JAMES CRAVEN.

PRESCOTT (or PRESCOATE), JOHN.   Beaufort County.

September 21, 1772. March 9, 1773. *Sons:* JOHN, AARON, WILLIAM, BENJAMIN, SIMON. *Daughters:* ANNE MCKINGBUSH, ESBELL WILLIAMS, HANNAH PRESCOTT. No executor named. *Witnesses:* MOSES POOLE, JOHN BREFFILL. Proven before JO. MARTIN.

PRESCOTT, MOSES.   Carteret County.

February 11, 1751. December Court, 1751. *Sons:* WILLIS ("plantation whereon I now live on Bouge Sound"), WILLIAM, MOSES, THOMAS and RUSSELL. *Daughters:* MARY PRESCOTT and SARAH PURDUE. *Wife:* MARY. *Executor:* WILLIAM PRESCOTT (son). *Witnesses:* THO. AUSTIN, MARTHA PRESCOTT, GEORGE MCKEAN. *Clerk of the Court:* GEORGE READ.

PRESCOTT (spelled also PRESTCOAT and PRESCOOT),
WILLIAM. Craven County.
March 17, 1744–1745. September Court, 1745. *Sons:* MOSES, WILLIAM, RICHARD, JOB (land between Troters Creek and Panters Creek). *Daughter:* MARY PRESCOAT. *Granddaughter:* ELIZABETH PRESCOTT. *Wife and Executrix:* MARY. *Witnesses:* JOHN CARROLL, DANIEL CONERLY, AARON WOOD. *Clerk of the Court:* JNO. RICE.

PRESCOTT, WILLIAM. Beaufort County.
October 13, 1755. September Court, 1756. *Son:* THOMAS (two plantations on west side of Durrams Creek). *Wife:* AMEY. *Executors:* JAMES BRINSON and JOHN ROE. *Witnesses:* JOHN ADAMS, ANN ADAMS. *Clerk of the Court:* WALLEY CHAUNCEY.

PRICE, PETER. Beaufort County.
February 3, 1734–1735. March 11, 1734. *Legatees:* MARTHA DICKISON, ELIZABETH, ALIN, JOHN, SARAH, MARTHA, MARY and EZEKIEL DICKISON, JAMES MCKEEL, FRANCIS KNIGHT (*Executrix*). *Witnesses:* BAR. FLEMING, THOS. LEWIS, SARAH LEWIS. *Clerk of the Court:* JOHN COLLISON.

PRICE, RICE. New Hanover County.
September 27, 1756. *Sons:* RICHARD, JAMES, EDMOND (to each is bequeathed negroes). *Wife and Executrix:* TOMZIN. *Executor:* RICHARD PRICE. *Witnesses:* JOHN ROGERS, HENRY HARKER, WM. PEARSE. *Clerk of the Court:* JA. MORAN.

PRICE, THOMAS. Albemarle County.
September 18, 1689. February Court, 1696. *Godson:* ARCHIBALD MCDANIEL. MARY HUMFREYS, JOAN MCDANIEL, JOHN SAWYER. *Witnesses:* MICHAEL CONNER, JOHN SAWYER, GARRETT KEEN. *Clerk of the Court:* WM. GLOVER. (*Executor:* DANIEL PHILLIPS. Appointed by Court.)

PRICE, THOMAS. Edgecombe County.
August 24, 1750. May Court, 1751. *Sons:* WILLIAM, THOMAS and JOHN. *Daughters:* ELIZABETH and RACHEL. *Wife:* not named. *Witnesses:* JOHN HOOKS, WILLIAM RADDAM and JOHN HOOKS, JR. *Clerk of the Court:* BENJAMIN WYNNS.

PRICE, WILLIAM. Perquimans County.
September 21, 1756. January Court, 1757. *Daughters:* RACHEL and ELIZABETH PRICE, MARY and CHRISTIAN PRICE. *Wife and Executrix:* SARAH. *Witnesses:* ISAAC LILLEY, ABRAHAM RIDDICK, ELIZABETH STALLING. *Clerk of the Court:* MILES HARVEY.

PRICKLOVE, ELIZABETH.   Perquimans Precinct.

July 23, 1728. *Daughters:* LEAH SMITH, RACHEL WILLSON, PRISCILA SANDERS, REBECCA CHANCEY, JUDITH. *Grandchildren:* JOHN SMITH, SELVANUS WILLSON, JUDETH and PRESCILLA SANDERS. *Executor:* DANIEL CHANCY. Proven before RICH'D EVERARD by ELIZABETH ELIOT.

PRICKLOWE, SAMUEL.

January 20, 1702–1703. *Sons:* SAMUEL and FRANCIS. *Wife and Executrix:* PENINAH. *Witnesses:* FRANCIS PINVIC, SIMOND TRUMBULL, JOHN ANDERSON. No probate.

PRINGLE, ALEXANDER.   Craven Precinct.

January 29, 1738–1739. March 1, 1739–1740. *Wife, Executrix and sole legatee:* JANE. *Witnesses:* NICHOLAS FOX, ABRAHAM JESSOP, MARGARET WADE. Proven before GAB. JOHNSTON.

PRITCHARD, BENJAMIN.   Pasquotank County.

February 15, 1740. January Court, 1752. *Brother:* JOSEPH PRITCHARD. *Sister:* SARAH PRITCHARD. *Executors:* brother and sister abovementioned. *Witnesses:* WILLIAM DAVIS, JONATHAN REDDING and JOHN BROOKS. *Clerk of the Court:* THOS. TAYLOR.

PRITCHARD, DAVID.

October 2, 1697. January Court, 1697. *Sons:* THOMAS, HENRY, JAMES, SAMUEL, DAVID. *Executors:* GEORGE HARRIS and RICHARD MADREN. *Witnesses:* RICHARD MADREN, GEORGE HARRIS, PHILIP EVANS. *Clerk of the Court:* EDWARD MAYO.

PRITCHARD, DAVID.   Pasquotank Precinct.

October 20, 1707. January 2, 1707. *Devisees:* JAMES, HUGH and SARAH PRITCHARD (land on Nabs Creek). SAMUEL and RICHARD PRITCHARD (the relationship of testator to these parties is not set out). *Wife and Executrix:* mentioned, but not named. *Witnesses:* PAT GORMACKE, RICHARD MADREN, ANNA MADREN. *Clerk of the Court:* JNO. PALEN (or PALIN).

PRITCHARD, HARBERT.   Bertie Precinct.

September 23, 1738. February Court, 1738. *Sons:* JOHN, WILLIAM and JAMES. *Executor:* JONATHAN STANDLEY, JR. *Witness:* ANN WILLIAMS. *Clerk of the Court:* JNO. WYNNS.

PRITCHARD, JAMES.   Pasquotank County.

June 5, 1754. December Court, 1755. *Wife, Executrix and sole legatee:* SUSANAH. *Witnesses:* WM. COALE, THOS. TAYLOR, ELIZABETH TAYLOR. *Clerk of the Court:* THOS. TAYLOR.

PRITCHARD, JEAN. Pasquotank Precinct.

October 25, 1707. January 20, 1707. *Executors:* SAMUEL and JAMES PRITCHARD, PATRICK GORMACKE. No legatees mentioned. *Witnesses:* GEORGE HARRIS, GEORGE HARRIS, JR., ―――― WINBERNE, RICHARD GRAY. *Clerk of the Court:* JNO. PALIN.

PRITCHETT, ABRAHAM. Beaufort County.

January 9, 1749. June Court, 1750. *Sons:* PHILIP, JOSHUA, PETER, ABRAHAM, JAMES (to each is given land and slaves). *Daughters:* SARAH and ELIZABETH. *Wife:* MARGETT. *Executors:* PHILIP and JOSHUA PRITCHETT (sons). *Witnesses:* JOHN WALLIS, WILLIAM BELL, JAMES FLANNAKIN. *Clerk of the Court:* LEVI ALDORSON.

PRITCHETT, JACOB. Beaufort County.

May 4, 1756. September Court, 1756. "On the South Devidings Creek and on the South side of Pamplico River." *Sons:* SIMON and STEPHEN PRITCHETT. *Daughter:* ANNE PRITCHETT. *Other legatees:* JAMES HERINTON (land called Prisces Neck), JOHN HERINTON. *Wife:* REBECKER. *Executors:* NICHOLAS DAW and JOHN WALLIS. *Witnesses:* MARY TINDESLY, ABIGAL DAW, JEANE COLLEBAR. *Clerk of the Court:* WALLEY CHAUNCEY.

PRITCHETT, MARGARET. Beaufort County.

January 12, 1756. March Court, 1756. *Sons:* PETER, JAMES, ABRAHAM, PHILIP, JOSHUAY. *Daughter:* SARAH BOND. *Granddaughters:* ELISABETH, SARAH and MARGET PRITCHETT. *Executor:* PETER PRITCHETT (son). *Witnesses:* THOMAS CAMPAN, MARY TILDESBY. *Clerk of the Court:* WALLEY CHAUNCEY.

PRITLOWE, JOHN. Perquimans Precinct.

September 8, 1720. May 1, 1728. *Daughters:* RACHEL WILLSON, JUDITH SANDERS, ELIZABETH ELIOT. *Grandson:* JOHN SMITH. *Wife and Executrix:* ELIZABETH. *Witnesses:* JOSEPH JESSOP and ROBERT MOORE. Proven before RICHARD EVERARD.

PROUSE, ANNE.

December 14, 1682. *Brother:* CHARLES PROUSE. *Friend:* ELIZABETH WILLIAMS. *Witnesses:* ARNOULD WHITE, WILLIAM MABERY. No probate.

PUGH, FRANCIS. Bertie Precinct.

July 5, 1733. October 4, 1736. *Sons:* JOHN ("plantation whereon I now live"), THOMAS (land "at the Emperors Fields which I bought of CHRISTIAN HITTEBURGH"). Lands at Grindale Creek and lands in Bertie and Edgecombe Precincts divided between two sons; lands in Virginia ordered to be sold. Negroes divided between wife and children. "It is my will that my wife have the management of the ferry where HENRY HORNE lives * * *." Provision for overplus after payment of debts to be laid out in young negroes. *Wife and Executrix:* PHEREBE. *Executors:* COL. ROBERT WEST and CULLEN POLLOCK. *Witnesses:* NEEDHAM BRYAN, HENRY HORNE and WILL'M JONES. *Clerk of the Court:* JOHN WYNNS. Codicil provides for completion of brigantine, and lading and sending same to Great Britain—cargo, tobacco and black walnut. "It is my will & desire that after my sloop Carolina return from New England * * * that my executors purchase a cargo and send the said sloop to the West Indies." *Witnesses:* JOHN CHANCEL, SAM'L SABAN PLOMER, PETER BRITTON. Codicil proven before GAB. JOHNSTON.

PUGH, JOHN.

April 14, 1740. August 5, 1740. *Wife:* HANNAH. *Son:* JOHN. *Brothers and Executors:* THEOPHILUS and DANIEL PUGH (all estate of testator, both in Virginia and North Carolina, bequeathed to these two brothers in trust for son JOHN). *Witnesses:* ABRAHAM BLACKALL, MILES GALE, JAMES CRAVEN. Proven before W. SMITH, C. J.

PURCELL, NEILL.   Craven County.

March 5, 1752. February Court, 1753. *Wife, Executrix and sole legatee:* SARAH. *Witnesses:* FAREBE WILLIAMS, R. MOORE, JNO. SNEAD. *Clerk of the Court:* SOL. REW.

PURDY, GEORGE.

July 10, 1733. August 2, 1733. All estate is left to *wife,* who is not named. *Executors:* RICHARD SANDERSON, EDWARD SALTER. *Witnesses:* GEORGE BURRINGTON, J. POWELL, THOMAS SHERWIN. Proven before WILLIAM LITTLE.

PURKENS, DAVID.   Bath County.

April 26, 1733. March 15, 1734. *Sons:* JAMES, JONATHAN. *Daughters:* ELISABETH WORLEY, MARY PUTTNELL, AFFERECA HARVEY, ANN JONES, REBECKAH and SARAH PURKENS. *Wife and Executrix:* MARY. *Witnesses:* SIMON ALDERSON, JOEL MARTIN, JAMES PIRKINS. *Clerk of the Court:* JNO. COLLISON.

PURSER, ROBERT.   Bath County.

May 10, 1733. September 11, 1733. *Sons:* RICHARD ("plantation I now live on called Ecrepint," on South Dividing Creek), JAMES and BENJAMIN. *Daughter:* MARY PURSER. *Executors:* WILLIAM DAW and JACOB PRITCHETT. *Witnesses:* JOHN LEE, JACOB PRITCHETT, HUMPHRY HAWKINS. *Clerk of the Court:* JNO. COLLISON.

PURYER, ROBERT.   Edgecombe County.

December 25, 1758. June Court, 1759. *Sons:* ROBERT ("my plantation"), WILLIAM. *Daughters:* MARY, MARGARET, ELIZABETH and ANN. *Wife and Executrix:* FRANCES. *Executor:* MOSES HORNE. *Witnesses:* WILLIAM HOBGOOD, RACHEL TANER. *Clerk of the Court:* JOS. MONTFORT.

PUTNELL, WILLIAM.

November 7, 1733. December Court, 1734. Duck Creek. *Sons:* AARON, JOHN. *Wife and Executrix:* MARY. *Brothers:* THOMAS and JOHN WORSELY. *Witnesses:* ROBT. GREAVY, EDD. DOE, JNO. CLIFFORD and ROGER JONES. *Clerk of the Court:* JNO. COLLISON.

QUINN, LOFTIN.   Carteret County.

February 17, 1766. *Sons:* WILLIAM and THOMAS. *Daughter:* MARGRETT QUINN. *Wife and Executrix:* MARY QUINN, formerly MARY CANADY. *Executor:* JAMES FREZER. *Witnesses:* WILLIAM and SARAH COALE, ABIGAIL COALE. Proven before JO. MARTIN.

RAGLAND, FREDERICK.   Northampton County.

August 2, 1757. February Court, 1758. *Brothers and Executors:* GEORGE and WILLIAM. *Witnesses:* JAMES PARHAM, ROGER TAYLOR, EPHRAIM MACGUFFIE. *Clerk of the Court:* I. EDWARDS.

RAGLAND, STEPHEN.   Northampton County.

March 1, 1746. February Court, 1747. *Sons:* STEPHEN, GEORGE, WILLIAM and FREDERICK (plantation to each), EVEN. *Daughter:* AGNESS (one Indian slave). *Wife:* MARY. *Executors:* EVEN and GEORGE RAGLAND (sons). *Witnesses:* ROBERT HICKS, JOHN HAMILTON, JOHN WEBB. *Clerk of the Court:* I. EDWARDS.

RAMAN, WILLIAM.   Albemarle County.

October 12, 1713. *Sons:* THOMAS and EDWARD (plantation to each). *Daughters:* ELIZABETH SCARBOROUGH, SARAH and MARY RAMAN. *Wife and Executrix:* SARAH. *Witnesses:* JNO. HAWKINS, THOMAS PASSINGHAM. No probate.

RAPHELD, WILLIAM.

January 20, 1757. March Court, 1757. *Sons:* BENJAMIN, WILLIAM, THOMAS, ISAAC. *Wife and Executrix:* ANN. *Witnesses:* JOHN ROUTEN, WILLIAM RAPHELD. *Clerk of the Court:* FR. WARD.

20

RASOR, FRANCES.   Bertie County.

April 20, 1747. December 18, 1748. *Son:* EDWARD RASOR. *Daughters:* ELIZABETH HARDY, CHRISTINA BELL. *Daughter-in-law:* ELIZABETH RASOR. *Granddaughter:* FRANCES HARDY. *Executor:* LAMB HARDY (son-in-law). *Witnesses:* WILLIAM HARDY, THOMAS and CHARITY TODD. Proven before E. HALL, C. J.

RASBUARY, JOHN.   Bertie County.

September 11, 1749. February Court, 1749. *Sons:* WILLIAM RASBUARY, THOMAS YAITS, ARTHUR PINNER. *Grandson:* JOHN RASBUARY. *Daughters:* REBECKAH PINNER, BRIDGET YAITS, ELIZABETH WILLIAMS, ANN BEVERLER, MARY UNKERS, CHRISTIAN LOID. *Executors:* BRIDGET RASBUARY (wife), WILLIAM and HOSEA RASBUARY. *Witnesses:* ISAAC HILL, EDWARD WILLIAMS. *Clerk of the Court:* JOHN LOVICK.

RATLIF, DAMARIS.

February 12, 1734. February 24, 1734. *Son:* JOSEPH. *Daughters:* MARY MORE, SARAH WINSLOW. *Sons-in-law:* JOHN MORE, THOMAS WINSLOW. *Granddaughter:* BETTY MORE. *Executors:* ZACHARIAH NIXON (brother), JOHN MORE and THOMAS WINSLOW. *Witnesses:* RICHARD DAVIS, MARY GILBART. Proven before GAB. JOHNSTON.

RATLIFF, RICHARD.   Perquimans Precinct.

June 17, 1724. July 14, 1724. *Sons:* THOMAS and JOSEPH (lands in Virginia and North Carolina). *Daughters:* ELIZABETH, MARY, SARAH, HULDAH. *Wife and Executrix:* DAMARIS. *Executor:* CORNELIUS RATLIFF (brother). *Witnesses:* ZACHARIAH NIXON, FRANCIS CROXTON, MARY NICHOLSON. *Clerk of the Court:* RICHD. LEARY.

RATTLIF, SAMUEL.

February 31, 1733. July 11, 1733. *Son:* ISAAC (plantation on Saman Creek). *Daughters:* ELISABETH and ISBELL. *Other legatees:* PARTHANEY and WILLIAM BALL. *Executors:* NATHANEL HILL and THOMAS ASHLEY. *Witnesses:* WILLIAM BYRD and ANN BALL and WILLIAM ASHLEY. Proven before GEORGE BURRINGTON.

RAWLINGS, BENJAMIN.   Edgecombe Precinct.

December 10, 1738. February Court, 1738. *Legatees:* ROBERT LOCKALEAR, DAVID COLTRAINE, EDMOND KEARNY (son of THOS. and SARAH), JAMES FLOOD, BENJAMIN HILL, JR. (son of BENJAMIN and SARAH), HENRY HILL, SARAH KEARNY, ELIZABETH ALSTON (wife of JOSEPH JOHN), WILLIAM ALSTON, ELIZABETH WILLIAMS (wife of SAMUEL). *Executors:* THOS. KEARNY and DAVID COLTRAINE. *Witnesses:* SAM'L WILLIAMS, R WHITTINGTON, WILLIAM LEE. *Clerk of the Court:* RT. FORSTER.

ABSTRACT OF WILLS, 1690—1760.   307

RAWLINGS, JOHN.   Northampton County.

March 26, 1747. November Court, 1747. *Daughters:* LUCY and SUSANNAH RAWLINGS. *Wife and Executrix:* HANNAH RAWLINGS. *Witnesses:* ART. HARRIS, GEORGE JORDAN, WM. RAWLINGS and GEORGE JORDAN, SENR. *Clerk of the Court:* RT. FORSTER.

RAYFIELD, WILLIAM.   Pasquotank Precinct.

August 4, 1722. March 23, 1731. Of Allegator in the Precinct of Pasquotank. *Sons:* WILLIAM, JAMES (land called the Wild Cat Neck), JOHN. *Wife and Executrix:* ANN. *Executor:* EDWARD LININGTON. *Witnesses:* EDWD. LININGTON, JOHN COMES, SETH PHELPS, RICHARD PUFFENGHALL. Proven before GEORGE BURRINGTON.

RAYFORD, MATTHEW.   Bladen County.

July 21, 1752. April Court, 1758. *Sons:* MATTHEW, ROBERT, WILLIAM and PHILIP. *Daughters:* MARY, ANNE, MOURNING, REBECKAH, GRACE and DRUSILLA. *Wife and Executrix:* MOURNING. *Executor:* ISAAC BUSH. *Witnesses:* MARGARET ARMSTRONG, FRANK ARMSTRONG and THOMAS JONES. *Clerk of the Court of Cumberland County:* JAMES SIMPSON.

RAYMOND, THOMAS.

June 26, 1730. July 31, 1730. "Dover in ye County of Kent, Kingdom of Great Brittain." *Daughter:* ELIZABETH RAYMOND. *Other legatees:* JOB BROOK, ELIZABETH (daughter of JOS. BELL), JAMES WAINWRIGHT (book called Lexicon Technicon), JOHN STARKEY, PETER STARKEY. *Executors:* JOHN STARKEY and THOMAS NELSON. *Witnesses:* RICHD. RUSTULL, PETER STARKEY, JOHN STARKEY. Proven before RICHARD EVERARD.

READ, GEORGE.   Carteret County.

May 26, 1753. September Court, 1753. *Son:* ROBERT (land in Carteret and in Barbadoes). *Daughters:* SARAH and FRANCES READ, MARTHA (wife of ISRAEL CHRISTIAN). *Wife and Executrix:* ANN. *Friends:* THOMAS LOVICK and DAVID SHEPARD. *Witnesses:* GEORGE COGDELL, GRIGG YARBOROUGH, JACOB SHEPARD. Signature of probate officer missing.

READING, CHURCHILL.   Bath County.

September 19, 1734. February 14, 1734. *Nephews:* CHURCHILL CALDOM, JOHN and JACOB BLOUNT. *Brother-in-law:* JOHN CALDOM. *Wife and Executrix:* MARTHA (four negroes). *Executors:* ROBERT WEST, THOMAS WORSLEY and JOHN CALDOM. *Witnesses:* EDW. TRAVIS, HARMAN HILL and EDWARD SALTER. Proven before GAB. JOHNSTON.

READING, JOSEPH.   Pasquotank County.
June 29, 1731. August 3, 1731. *Sons:* SAMUEL, THOMAS, JOHN, JONATHAN and JOSEPH. *Daughters:* MARY, MIRIAM and SARAH READING, ANN PENDLETON. *Wife and Executrix:* SARAH. *Witnesses:* DAVID BOLES, DANIEL RHODES and BENJA. PRITCHARD. Proven before GEO. BURRINGTON.

READING, LIONEL.   Bath County.
July 12, 1708. February 18, 1725. *Sons:* NATHANIEL, CHURCHILL. *Daughters:* SARAH DUPUIS and MARY READING, ANN READING. Negroes bequeathed to sons and daughters. *Wife:* not named. *Executors:* DAVIS DUPUIS and HUMPHREY LEGG. *Witnesses:* JAMES LEIGH, HENRY BROOK, JOHN LAWSON. Proven before RICHD. EVERARD.

READING, THOMAS.   Beaufort County.
January 24, 1749. March Court, 1748–1749. *Niece:* MARGARET CALDOM. *Nephew:* CHURCHILL CALDOM (husband of MARGARET and son of *sister*, ANN CALDOM). *Executors:* ABRAHAM DUNCAN and RICHARD EVANS. *Witnesses:* MARY DUNCAN, MARY POWERS, JOHN MCKENNY. *Clerk of the Court:* JOHN FORBES. Executor qualified before GAB. JOHNSTON.

REAVIS, EDWARD.   Northampton County.
February 21, 1750. February Court, 1752. *Son:* JESSE. *Daughters:* JUDE and MARY REAVIS. *Wife and Executrix:* SARAH. *Executor:* CAPT. JOHN PERSON of Virginia. *Witnesses:* ARTHR. HARRIS, JOHN GILLIAM, ARTHUR JORDAN. *Clerk of the Court:* I. EDWARDS.

RECKSAKER, DANIEL.   Pasquotank Precinct.
February 27, 1732–1733. May 16, 1733. *Legatees:* MARY ANN MITCHELL (daughter), SARAH PINDLETON (Executrix). *Witnesses:* WILLIAM DAVIS, WILLM. AMBLER. Proven before WM. LITTLE, *Chief Justice.*

REDDITT, WILLIAM.   Bertie County.
August 24, 1739. October 29, 1739. *Sons:* JOHN (plantation on the south side of Buckelsberry Swamp), WILLIAM, JOSEPH, JOEL, ISAAC (to each is devised a plantation). *Daughters:* MARGARET, ANN, MARTHA and MARY REDDITT. *Other legatee:* THOMAS YEATES. *Wife and Executrix:* SUSSANNAH. *Executors:* JOHN REDDITT (son) and JOHN OXLEY. *Witnesses:* GEORGE, ROBERT and MARY LAWRENCE. Proven before W. SMITH, C. J.

REDDING, JOHN.   Perquimans County.
January 28, 1754. April Court, 1754. "I give and bequeath to ELIZABETH FULLENTON, my dearly beloved and intended wife, my plan-

tation next to JESSE EASON'S." *Cousin:* JOHN ELLIS. *Executors:* JOHN DAVIS and JOSHUA SMALL (brothers-in-law). *Witnesses:* JESSE EASON, JOSEPH SKETO and JOHN HARRIS. *Clerk of the Court:* WILL. SKINNER.

REDING, JOSEPH. Perquimans County.

October 26, 1751. January Court, 1753. *Sons:* JAMES and JOHN (lands at Ballahack). *Daughters:* MARY, RACHEL and CHARITY. *Executors:* JAMES and JOHN (sons). *Witnesses:* STURGISS EDERINGAME, ABRAHAM BALLARD, JESSE EASON. *Clerk of the Court:* EDMUND HATCH.

REDDING, WILLIAM. Halifax County.

October 26, 1773. February 3, 1774. *Son:* JOSEPH. *Daughters:* PATTY BROWN, MARY, ANN and AMEY REDDING. *Wife and Executrix:* ANN. *Executors:* JAMES BROWN (son-in-law) and WILLIAM WILLIAMS. *Witnesses:* JAMES DAVIS, MARTHA HOOKS. Proven before Jo. MARTIN.

REED, ANDREW. Perquimans Precinct.

February 29, 1723. July Court, 1728. *Grandsons:* WILLIAM and ANDREW WOODLEY, JONATHAN KEETON (to WILLIAM is bequeathed an Indian slave). *Daughter:* ELIZABETH KEETON (Executrix). *Granddaughter:* MARY WOODLEY. *Witnesses:* RICHD. SKINER, RICHD. RATLIF. *Clerk of the Court:* R. EVERARD.

REED, JOSEPH. Anson County.

1750. July Court, 1751. *Son:* WILLIAM. *Wife and other children*, not named. Plantation near the Catawba River. *Executors:* JOHN BRANDON and JOHN NESBET. *Witnesses:* JOSEPH CATE, JOHN RAILY, JOHN ARTLEDGE. *Clerk of the Court:* M. BROWN.

REELL, PETER. Craven County.

November 19, 1739. November 24, 1739. *Sons:* PETER, JOSHUA, JAMES. *Daughters:* ELIZABETH and MARY. *Wife and Executrix:* MARY. *Executors:* SIMON BRIGHT and RICHARD EVANS. *Witnesses:* JOHN BERRY, JOHN JAMES, JOHN HILL. Proven before W. SMITH, C. J.

REESE, OWEN. Pasquotank County.

April 7, 1745. July Court, 1745. *Sons:* JOHN and OWIN. *Daughters:* BETTY, SARAH, MARY and ANN REESE. *Wife and Executrix:* MARY. *Executor:* DANIELL WILLIAMS. *Witnesses:* JOHN BURNHAM, DAVID and WILLIAM CARTRIGHT. *Clerk of the Court:* THOS. TAYLOR.

REGAN, DANIEL.

November 27, 1727. *Son:* DANIEL. *Brother:* THOMAS. *Daughters:* ANN, SARAH, MARY and PRISCILLA REGAN. *Other legatee:* THOMAS GOODSON. *Wife and Executrix:* SARAH. *Witnesses:* WM. BALDWIN, THOMAS REGAN. No probate.

REGGONS, JOSEPH.   Bertie County.

April 2, 1727. August Court, 1727. *Son:* JOSEPH. *Daughters:* MARTHA, MARY, HANNAH, OLIVE REGGONS. *Son-in-law:* JOHN WEEB. *Wife and Executrix:* ELIZABETH. *Witnesses:* WM. BOLDIN, DANIELL REGGONS, THOMAS REGGONS. *Clerk of the Court:* RT. FORSTER.

RELF, JOHN.   Pasquotank County.

September 22, 1742. January Court, 1742. *Sons and Executors:* CORNELIUS and JOHN. *Witnesses:* JOHN and MARY BELL, CORNELIUS JONES. *Clerk of the Court:* THO. TAYLOR.

RELF, MARY.   Pasquotank Precinct.

January 13, 1724–1725. April Court, 1725. *Brother:* WILLIAM RELF. *Brother's grandchildren:* THOMAS and MARY RELF. *Daughters:* SARAH CHANCE, SUSANAH CHANCE. *Son-in-law:* THOMAS PALIN. *Granddaughters:* MARY and ANN PALIN. *Son and Executor:* ROBERT KEEL. *Witnesses:* JAMES SPENCE, ALEXANDER SPENCE, DOROTHY ADAMS. *Clerk of the Court:* JOHN PARK.

RELFE, THOMAS.

April 10, 1704. No probate. *Wife and Executrix:* MARY. *Son:* THOMAS. *Daughter:* DOROTHY RELFE. *Other legatee:* WILLIAM ROADS. *Witnesses:* JOHN BISHOP, ROBERT KEEL, MARY BISHOP.

RENFROW, JOHN.   Edgecombe County.

May 30, 1748. August Court, 1748. *Sons:* ENUCH, JACOB, GEORGE, WILLIAM and JAMES. *Wife:* TOMESON. *Executor:* MATTHEW MCKINNEY. *Witnesses:* JOHN HAYWOOD, NATHANIEL HOLLY, JOHN EVANS. *Clerk of the Court:* BENJN. WYNNS.

RESTON, THOMAS.   New Providence.

March 31, 1723. December 17, 1724. *Wife and Executrix:* ANN. *Witnesses:* WILLIAM JONES, WILLIAM WILLIAMS, WILLIAM WALTERS, JOHN FRENCH. Proven before E. MOSELEY.

REW, SOUTHY.   Craven County.

January, 1754. February Court, 1754. *Sons:* SOLOMON ("plantation whereon I now live on the East side of Owens Creek"), THOMAS (land on Owens' Creek), BEVERLY (land on South River known as Butchers), SOUTHY (two lots in Newbern), SOLOMON. *Daughters:* MARY and EUPHAMA. *Wife:* MARY. Negroes to be divided between wife and children. *Executors:* JOHN STARKEY and SOLOMON REW. *Witnesses:* JOHN SNEAD and CHARLES COGDELL. *Clerk of the Court:* SOL. REW.

REYNAUD, BENJAMIN.   Currituck Precinct.
April 8, 1712.   *Son and Executor:* MOSES.   *Witnesses:* JOSEPH WALTER, ROSMUS HERSLEFF, DANIEL RICE. Original missing. Recorded in Book 1712–1722, page 24.

RHODES, HENRY.   Onslow County.
September 14, 1751. October Court, 1751. *Sons:* HENRY ("my mannor plantation"), THOMAS. *Son-in-law:* DANIEL MASBONE. *Granddaughter:* ELIZABETH MASHBONE. *Wife and Executrix:* MARY. *Witnesses:* THOMAS RHODES, PATIENCE JOHNSON, JOSHUA PAULL. *Clerk of the Court:* THOS. BLACK.

RHODES, HENRY.   Dobbs County.
December 21, 1773. January 25, 1774. *Sons:* JACOB, HENRY, WILLIAM, JAMES. *Daughters:* MARY RINCEY, BABREY RHODES, RACHEL and SARAH RHODES. *Wife:* ELIZABETH. *Executors:* BEEAMAN RHODES, WILLIAM JONES and JOSEPH FEW. *Witnesses:* JOHN FILLYAW, MOSES COX, ROBERT WINSETT. Proven before JO. MARTIN.

RHODES, RICHARD.   Pasquotank Precinct.
March 2, 1693–1694. *Wife and Executrix:* ELISABETH. *Witnesses:* RICHARD MADREN, SARA DAVIS, JOHN SKIPAR. *Clerk of the Court:* EDWARD MAYO.

RHODES, WILLIAM.   Pasquotank County.
January Court, 1734. *Sons:* THOMAS and WILLIAM. *Daughters:* SARAH, DOROTHY, ELIZABETH and MARY RHODES. *Wife and Executrix:* ELIZABETH. *Executor:* WILLIAM RELFE. *Witnesses:* FRANCIS MARTIN, COMFORT CAMMILL, JAMES BIGGERS. *Clerk of the Court:* JOS. SMITH.

RHOADS, WILLIAM.   Tyrrell County.
August 29, 1753. September Court, 1753. *Sons:* WILLIAM ("my manner plantation"), JOHN. *Daughter:* MARGARET COLLINGS. *Wife:* ELIZABETH. *Executors:* WILLIAM and JOHN RHOADS (sons). *Witnesses:* THOMAS BEDFORD, JOHN BROWNING, CHRISTOPHER BUTTERY. *Clerk of the Court:* EVAN JONES.

RICE, BENJAMIN.   Beaufort County.
September 12, 1745. June Court, 1746. *Sons:* ZEBULON, BANJAMIN, JAMES, EVEN, CLANERLY, EPHRIM, HEZEKIAH, GIDEON. *Wife and Executrix:* MARY. *Witnesses:* JAMES HUMES, NATHANIEL DRAPER, THOMAS WILLIA. *Clerk of the Court:* JOHN FORBES.

RICE, EDWARD.   Bertie County.

December 8, 1752. May Court, 1753. *Son:* JOHN. *Daughters:* MARY and BETTY RICE. *Wife and Executrix:* ANN. *Executor:* THOMAS SLATTOR. *Witnesses:* JOHN COKE, SR., JAMES HAIR, WALTER and ELIZABETH JOANES. *Clerk of the Court:* BENJAMIN WYNNS.

RICE, JOHN.   Chowan County.

May 20, 1745. January Court, 1753. *Wife:* SARAH. *Brother and Executor:* EDWARD RICE. *Witnesses:* HARDY HURDELL, BENJAMIN BERREMAN, THOMAS ROWNTREE. *Clerk of the Court:* JAMES CRAVEN.

RICE, LUCY.

February 15, 1720–1721. This is a nuncupative will proven by ROBERT PALMER and THOMAS PALIN before JNO. PALIN and names *daughters,* MARY and CELY.

RICE, MARY.   New Hanover County.

July 9, 1753. February 21, 1754. *Executors:* THOMAS CAMBER and PENNY BUSSY (sister). Proven before MATT. ROWAN. Coat of arms on seal. This will is so torn as to render all other names illegible.

RICE, MORGIN.

October 26, 1684. No date of probate. *Legatee:* SARAH BURNBY, daughter of JOHN BURNBY, who is appointed Executor. *Witnesses:* WILLIAM BURNBY, ANTHONY HATCH. Coat of arms on seal.

RICE, NATHANIEL.   New Hanover County.

December 6, 1752. February 27, 1753. *Son:* JOHN. *Sisters-in-law:* HANNAH and PENNY BURSEY. *Wife's niece:* ELIZABETH DALE. *Wife and Executrix:* MARY. *Niece:* ELIZABETH TWINER of Rumsey, in Hampshire. *Executors:* JAS. HASELL, SAM'L and JOHN SWANN. *Witnesses:* JAMES PORTERFIELD, DAVID LINDSAY, ARC. MACLAINE. *Clerk of the Court:* ISAAC FARIES.

RICHARDS, JOHN.   Pasquotank County.

July 11, 1741. July 14, 1741. *Son-in-law:* LAW. PRIDEES. *Wife and Executrix:* MARY. *Witnesses:* THO. WEEKES, JOHN NELSON, JR., THEOPHILUS MANN. *Clerk of the Court:* THOS. TAYLOR.

RICHARDS, MARY.   Pasquotank County.

October 31, 1743. November 19, 1743. *Daughter:* FRANCES PREDY. *Son-in-law and Executor:* LAWS PREDY. *Witnesses:* J. HULL, ANDREW MOORE, J. HARDY. Proven before J. MONTGOMERY. *Justice of the Peace:* JAS. CRAVEN. Coat of arms on seal.

ABSTRACT OF WILLS, 1690—1760. 313

RICHARDS, RICHARD. Edgecombe County.
October 23, 1758. December Court, 1758. *Sons:* JOHN, JESSE and RICHARD. *Wife and Executrix:* REBECCA. *Executor:* DAVID CRAWLEY. *Witnesses:* WM. KINCHEN, WM. HAYES, JOHN GREEN. *Clerk of the Court:* JOS. MONTFORT.

RICHARDSON, DANIEL. Pasquotank Precinct.
February 28, 1723. March 5, 1723. *Legatees:* GEORGE BURRINGTON (one negro), JOHN LOVICK (one negro), ———— GOFF, MARGARET BERNSBEE, MRS. ANN KNIGHT, wife of LEWIS MCALIXANDER KNIGHT. *Executors:* GEORGE BURRINGTON, JOHN LOVICK and ———— GOFF. *Witnesses:* PATRICK OGLESBEE, WILLIAM JEFFREYS, BARTHOLOMEW SCOTT, THOMAS RAYMOND. Proven before GEORGE BURRINGTON.

RICHARDSON, GEORGE. New Hanover County.
November 15, 1750. *Executor and sole legatee:* JEHU DAVIS, SENR. *Witnesses:* SAML. and THOS. NEALE, ANTHY. WARD. *Clerk of the Court:* JA. MORAN.

RICHARDSON, JOHN. Perquimans County.
November 28, 1743. January Court, 1743. *Son:* JAMES. *Daughter:* ANNE RICHARDSON. *Wife and Executrix:* MARY. *Witnesses:* JAMES GIBSON, JOHN PARRISH. *Clerk of the Court:* EDMUND HATCH.

RICHARDSON, JOHN. Craven County.
September 11, 1773. September 16, 1773. (Newbern.) *Legatees:* WILLIAM EVEN (one negro "now in possession of WILLIAM BROOK SIMPSON Attorney in Newport Rhode Island and one negro man on board my sloop called the Betsey"), PETER GORDON (son of PATRICK GORDON, of Newbern). *Executors:* JOSEPH CRISPIN and RIGDON BRICE. *Witnesses:* JAMES GREEN, JAMES PARRATT, BENJN. GREENAWAY. Proven before JO. MARTIN.

RICHARDSON, STEPHEN. Pasquotank County.
February 7, 1722. July 16, 1723. *Sons:* JOHN ("plantation whereon I live called the Poplars Havin"), STEPHEN (land called the White Oak Neck), RICHARD (land called Blewbootens Neck, the said RICHARD to allow THOMAS BETTYS to live on said land if he, the said BETTYS shall build a house "twenty five foot long and fifteen foot wide and plant ought a orchard of apells trees thirty foot Destent for the Great Stones Sort and Twenty five foot aney other Sort &c."), LEBBEOS and JOSEPH. *Daughter:* ELIZABETH. *Wife and Executrix:* MARY. *Trustees:* JOHN and JAMES TREWBLOOD. *Witnesses:* JAMES GREVES, KATHERINE GREVES and HANNAH EVERTON. *Clerk of the Court:* W. NORRIS.

RICHMOND, HENRY.

September 15, 1714. December 4, 1714. *Wife:* not named. *Cousin and Executor:* CALEB BUNDY. *Witnesses:* CHARLES BULL and MARY STANTON. No probate.

RICKITSON, GORDIUS.   Craven County.

September 25, 1773. March 19, 1774. New Bern. *Sons:* JESSE, BENJAMIN, GORDIUS. *Daughter:* BATHSHABA. *Wife and Executrix:* ABIGAIL. *Witnesses:* JOHN GRANADE, JOHN MERKER, EDW. WHITTY. Proven before JO. MARTIN.

RICKS, BENJAMIN.   Chowan County.

March 31, 1719. November 30, 1721. *Brothers:* JAMES, ROBERT, ABRAHAM and ISAAC RICKS. *Nephew:* ROBERT RICKS, JR. (land on Notaway River). *Sister:* JANE RICKS. *Other legatees:* PATIENCE RICKS (niece) and WILLIAM BROWN, son of BEALE BROWN. *Wife and Executrix:* SARAH. *Witnesses:* BRIDGET ROGERS, MARY ROGERS, JOHN PHIPPS. Proven before C. EDEN, *Governor.*

RICKS, ISAAC.   Edgecombe County.

March 11, 1748. October 28, 1748. *Sons:* ABRAHAM and ROBERT and JOHN (two negroes to each). *Daughters:* MARY POP and MARTHA RICKS. *Wife and Executrix:* SARAH. *Witnesses:* JOHN CROWELL, RICHARD RICHARDS. Proven before E. HALL, *Chief Justice.*

RIDDICK, JOSEPH.   Perquimans County.

September 20, 1759. October Court, 1759. *Sons:* JOSEPH (plantation bought of THOMAS WARD), KADAK (plantation bought of WILLIAM ROUNTREE, MOSES FIELDS and JAMES PRICE; also plantation bought of WILLIAM MOORE and WILLIAM WILLSON lying in Ballahack), ISAAC (lands bought of JOHN BARCLIF and GEORGE SHELL "that lyes over Little River upon deep Creek"). *Daughter:* MARY RIDDICK. *Wife and Executrix:* HANNAH. *Executor:* ROBERT RIDDICK (brother). *Witnesses:* JOSEPH PERRY, BENJAMIN PERRY, JOB RIDDICK. *Clerk of the Court:* MILES HARVEY.

RIDGE, THOMAS.

February 17, 1747–1748. *Sons:* GODFREY and WILLIAM. *Daughters:* ANNE and MARY RIDGE. *Wife and Executrix:* ELIZABETH. *Witnesses:* BENJAMIN BURGESS, ELIZABETH MCGEE, DANIEL MCPETERS. *Clerk of the Court:* JOHN DUNN.

RIGBY, WILLIAM.   New Hanover County.

December 18, 1743. June Court, 1744. Wilmington. Lands on Long Creek, Lockwood's Folly, Black River and lot in Wilmington to be divided between MARGERY RIGBY (mother), JOHN RIGBY (brother) and ALICE MARSDEN. Brigantine "on her return from the West Indies" to be sold and proceeds applied to payment of debts. *Executor:* RUFUS MARSDEN (brother-in-law). *Witnesses:* JAMES SMALLWOOD, THOMAS FINNEY, JOSEPH GARY. *Clerk of the Court:* JAMES SMALLWOOD.

RIGNEY, BENJAMIN. Beaufort County.

December 3, 1750. March 12, 1750. *Daughter:* MARY RIGNEY. *Brother:* JAMES RIGNEY. *Niece:* HANNAH RIGNEY. *Wife and Executrix:* FEBE. *Executors:* WILLIAM WAGGENER and READING BLOUNT. *Clerk of the Court:* WILL. ORMOND.

RIGNEY, JOHN. Beaufort Precinct.

June 14, 1725. April Court, 1726. *Daughter:* ELISABETH. *Executor:* BENJAMIN SLADE (land called the Fork on condition that he "cause my daughter to be teached to read the Bible distinctly and putt her in school"). *Other legatee:* HENRY TRIP. *Witnesses:* JOHN SLADE, WILLIAM SATTERTHWAITE, GI. HOLLIDAY. *Clerk of the Court:* THOMAS JONES. Original missing. Recorded in Book 1722–1735, page 33.

RIORDAME, DENIS. Currituck County.

January 18, 1723–1724. July 14, 1724. *Wife and Executrix:* SARAH. *Daughter:* ANGELICA. *Other legatees:* THOMAS and WM. VINCE. *Witnesses:* JO. WICKER, SAMUEL SIMMONS, ANN IRELAND, DAVID LEGGETT. *Clerk of the Court:* HENRY SWANN.

RISENOUER, MATTHEW. Craven County.

November 18, 1747. September Court, 1747. *Sons:* JOHN and JACOB (Executors). *Daughter:* CATREN SMITH. *Wife:* ELISABETH. *Witnesses:* JACOB TAYLER, GASPER GRANADE, PAUL IVES. *Clerk of the Court:* WILL. HEDGES.

RITEGA, JACOB. Pasquotank Precinct.

March 25, 1735. April Court, 1739. *Daughters:* MARGARET and MIRIAM RITEGA. *Son-in-law:* WILLIAM POWERS. *Wife and Executrix:* PHILLIS. *Witnesses:* WILLIAM LEWIS, THOMAS GASKILLS. *Clerk of the Court:* JOS. SMITH.

RIUSSETT, JOHN.

October 11, 1737. January 17, 1737. Bath Town. "Late of the city of London." *Sons:* JOHN and DAVID RIUSSETT. *Executors:* JOHN MONTGOMERY, THOMAS JONES and PETER RANDON. *Witnesses:* JOHN GARZIA, PETER RANDON. Proven before W. SMITH, C. J.

RIUSSETT, PETER.   Bath County.

January 14, 1734. February 21, 1734. *Nieces:* ANN GALABER, JANE CAILA, .MARY COVEE. *Nephew:* PETTER RANDOWN. *Son:* JOHN BELL. *Brother:* JOHN RIUSSETT. *Executors:* EDWARD SALTER and OLIVER BLACKBURN. *Other legatee:* CHURCH OF BATH. *Witnesses:* OLIVER BLACKBURN, PETER RANDON, MATHIAS COLLIER. Proven before GAB. JOHNSTON.

ROBERTS, ANDREW.   Craven Precinct.

January 22, 1722. June Court, 1723. *Sons:* JOHN and ANDREW. *Daughters:* ANN and ELIZABETH. *Executor:* ADAM MORE. *Witnesses:* WM. WILLSON, NATHANIEL BARAN. *Clerk of the Court:* CALEB METCALFE.

ROBERTS, JAMES.   Craven County.

July 24, 1745. This is a nuncupative will proven before DANL. SHINE by JAMES CONAWAY, and names *Sons:* SAMUEL and JAMES. *Daughter:* MARGRET ROBERTS. *Wife:* ISABLE.

ROBERTS, JAMES.   Craven County.

April 4, 1774. New Bern. *Sons:* RICHARD, JAMES and WILLIAM. *Wife and Executrix:* ELIZABETH. *Witnesses:* ALEX. GARTEN, JOHN MACKAY, JAMES COOR. Proven before JO. MARTIN.

ROBERTS, JOSEPH.   Craven County.

January 15, 1774. This is a nuncupative will proven by JAMES FRAZER and CYNTHIA ROBERTS before JO. MARTIN and names *wife,* ELIZABETH. *Daughters:* SALLY and SABONAH. *Father-in-law:* MICAJAH FRAZIER.

ROBERTSON, HENRY.   Edgecombe County.

June 23, 1749. February Court, 1752. *Sons:* HIGDON, HENRY, PETER, LEWIS (Executor). *Daughter:* DEBORAH ROBERTSON. *Witnesses:* A. J. SMITH, WILLIAM OGILVIE, CHRISTOPHER OGILVIE. *Clerk of the Court:* BENJN. WYNNS.

RORERTSON, JAMES.   Pasquotank County.

January 17, 1753. October Court, 1754. *Sons:* MORDECAI ("my manner plantation"), MALACHI ("my Road plantation"). *Daughter:* SALLEY. *Wife and Executrix:* SARAH. *Executor:* THOMAS TAYLOR. *Witnesses:* SAMUEL OKELY, WILLIAM WOODLY, MARY TAYLOR. *Clerk of the Court:* THOMAS TAYLOR.

ROBINS, JAMES.

November 27, 1725. January 11, 1725. Bath Town. *Brother:* FRANCES ROBINS (one saddle horse). *Wife and Executrix:* MARGARET. *Executor:* THOMAS BOYD. *Witnesses:* CHARLES HOLYDAY, RICHARD FRENCH, WM. SPARRY. Proven before RICHARD EVERARD.

ABSTRACT OF WILLS, 1690—1760. 317

ROBINS, JOSEPH. Rowan County.

November 18, 1754. *Sons:* JOSEPH, WILLIAM and JOHN. *Daughter:* ELENOR. *Wife and Executrix:* ELENOR. *Executor:* JOHN NATION (brother-in-law). *Witnesses:* A. J. SMITH, CH. NATION, RICHARD ROBINS. No probate.

ROBINSON, CHARLES. Anson County.

December 29, 1754. *Sons:* CORNELIUS, TOWNSEND and CHARLES. *Daughters:* SARAH and ELIZABETH. *Wife and Executrix:* SARAH. *Witnesses:* WILLIAM DOWNS, JOHN STON, JAMES DENSON. No probate.

ROBINSON, HUMPHREY. Chowan County.

July 15, 1752. July Court, 1752. *Legatees:* ELIZABETH and SUSANNAH CLELAND (lands in Chowan, houses and lots in Edenton and negroes), JOHN CLELAND, JOHN COOPER. *Executors:* JOHN CLELAND, JOHN WILKINS. No witnesses and no probate.

ROBINSON, JAMES. Albemarle County.

March 12, 1699–1700. All lands and other property to CORNELIUS JONES, Executor. *Witnesses:* THOMAS MILLER, WILLIAM WOOLARD, JOHN POWELL. No probate.

ROBINSON, JOHN. Perquimans County.

October 1, 1757. January Court, 1758. *Sons:* THOMAS and ROWLAND. *Daughter:* SARAH ROBINSON. *Wife:* MARY. *Executor:* JOSEPH ROBINSON (brother) and THOMAS ROBINSON (son). *Witnesses:* JOHN NIXON, JOSHUA MORRIS, SARAH ROBINSON. *Clerk of the Court:* MILES HARVEY.

ROBINSON, JOSEPH. Perquimans County.

June 8, 1717. July 9, 1717. *Son:* JOHN. *Daughter:* SARAH ROBINSON. *Wife and Executrix:* JANE. *Witnesses:* NICHOLAS GUYOR, TIMOTHY CLARE and ELIZABETH WINSLOW. *Clerk of the Court:* RICHARD LEARY.

ROBINSON, THOMAS. Albemarle County.

March 4, 1718–1719. April 2, 1719. Little River in the County of Albemarle. *Sons:* JOSEPH and JOHN (land and negroes). *Daughter:* ANNE ROBINSON. *Executors:* ZACHARIAH NIXON, FRANCIS TOMES and JOHN SYMONS. *Witnesses:* JOSEPH MING, JOSIAH BINGHAM, SAMUEL SHERER. Proven before FRANCIS FOSTER. Also before CHARLES EDEN.

ROBINSON, THOMAS. Chowan County.

April Court, 1755. *Son:* WILLIAM. *Wife and other children:* mentioned, but not named. *Executors:* JOHN HALSEY and JOHN VAIL. *Witnesses:* SAMUEL BENBURY, HANNAH CLAY, SARAH ARINGTON. *Clerk of the Court:* WILL. HALSEY.

RODGERS, JOSEPH.   Bath County.
   January 2, 1704–1705. *Granddaughters:* ELIZABETH DEARAM, LYDIA
COCKERUM. *Grandsons:* JOSEPH COCKERUM and CHARLES HOPTON.
Indian slave freed. *Wife and Executrix:* MARY. *Witnesses:* HENERY
LOCKEY, JOHN PROCTER. *Clerk of the Court:* LEVI TRUEWHITT.

ROE, EDWARD.
   May 3, 1696. July 19, 1696. *Sons:* EDMOND, EBENEZER, VALLENTINE.
Daughter: DEBORAH. *Wife and Executrix:* SARAH. *Witnesses:* DANIEL
FEE, GEORGE ELLES, ELEBETH FEE. *Clerk of the Court:* EDWARD MAYO.
Coat of arms on seal.

ROE, JAMES.   Craven County.
   July 13, 1737. March Court, 1737–1738. *Executor:* FRANCIS STRINGER.
Witnesses: DAN'LL SHINE, JAMES MORE. *Clerk of the Court:* JAMES COOR.

ROE, LUKE.   Craven County.
   December 30, 1774. January 12, 1775. *Brother:* THOMAS ROE.
Nephew: BENJAMIN (son of THOMAS ROE). *Brother-in-law:* JOSHUA
TAYLOR (riding horse and saddle). *Other legatees:* JACOB and other children of JOSHUA TAYLOR. *Executor:* PETER PHYSIOC. *Witnesses:* MATTHEW STEPHENS, NANCE STEPHENS, PETER PHYSIOC. Proven before
JAMES HASELL.

ROE, ROBERT.   Beaufort County.
   December Court, 1756. Formerly of Princess Anne County, now of
Beaufort. *Son:* KITLEY. *Daughters:* BETTY and DOLLY. *Wife and
Executrix:* DOROTHY. *Witnesses:* JAMES DEGGE, JOHN CHAPMAN and
HENRY TRIPPE. *Clerk of the Court:* WALLEY CHAUNCEY.

ROGERS, EMANUEL.   Bertie Precinct.
   November 21, 1727. May Court, 1729. *Wife:* DEBORAH. *Daughters:*
ELIZABETH and MARY. *Executor:* JOHN GRAY. *Witnesses:* RICHD.
HAYNSWORTH, DANIEL CRAWLEY. *Clerk of the Court:* RT. FORSTER.

ROGERS, JOHN.   Bertie Precinct.
   March 4, 1724. July 7, 1726. *Son and Executor:* JOHN. *Witnesses:*
MARY and JOHN RODGERS. Proven before RICHARD EVERARD.

ROGERS, JOSEPH.   Northampton County.
   February 18, 1752. February Court, 1752. *Sons:* JOSEPH, AARON,
ISOM, REUBEN, JOHN, DRURY, MICHAEL. *Daughters:* FAITH ROGERS,
SARAH TARVER, MARY LOWREY. *Executors:* JOHN and JOSEPH ROGERS
(sons). *Witnesses:* NATHN. WILLIAMS, ELY WILLIAMS, NATHAN WILLIAMS. *Clerk of the Court:* I. EDWARDS.

ROGERS, RICHARD. Onslow County.

July 4, 1749. October Court, 1749. *Wife and Executrix:* SARAH. *Witnesses:* JOHN DUDLEY, EZEKIEL HUNTER, JOS. STURGES. *Clerk of the Court:* THOMAS BLACK.

ROGERS, ROBERT. Chowan Precinct.

December 13, 1736. June 11, 1739. *Grandsons:* ROBERT DANIELL and WILLIAM ROGERS. *Son and Executor:* ROBERT. *Daughter:* ELIZABETH (wife of SIMON DANIEL). *Other legatees:* THOMAS and MARY GALLOWAY. *Witnesses:* JOHN WILLIAMS, JANE WILLIAMS, RICHARD TAYLOR. Proven before W. SMITH, C. J.

ROGERS, THOMAS. Bertie County.

August Court, 1749. *Sons:* THOMAS and ROBERT. *Daughter:* MARY. No executor. *Witnesses:* WILLIAM LATTIMORE, JOHN LITLE (or LILLE). No probate officer.

ROGERS, THOMAS. Bertie County.

February 14, 1754. May Court, 1754. *Son:* THOMAS. *Daughters:* MARY and FRANCES ROGERS. *Wife and Executrix:* MARY. *Witnesses:* RICHARD TOMLINSON, RICHARD BRADLEY, ROBERT ROGERS. *Clerk of the Court:* SAML. ORMES.

ROGERS, WILLIAM. Albemarle County.

April 25, 1690. *Legatee:* JONATHAN BATEMAN. No executor. *Witnesses:* JOHN HOLLFAND, JOHN TWIGGER, HANAH EDY. No probate.

ROLFE, THOMAS.

October 15, 1688. February 2, 1690–1691. "Of Yawpim." *Cousin:* JOHN LOVETT. *Wife and Executrix:* ELIZABETH. *Witnesses:* REBECCA WYATE, LAWRENCE CRUISE, HENDERSON WALKER, THOMAS LONGE. *Clerk of the Court:* RICHARD PLATER.

ROOSE, WILLIAM (of Boston, Mariner).

September 26, 1722. This is a nuncupative will proven by RICHARD FARRELL, JANE SPARROW and SAMUEL BERNARD before JOHN SOLLEY, and is so torn that the names of the legatees cannot be ascertained.

ROPER, WILLIAM. Chowan Precinct.

August 18, 1729. February 7, 1729–1730. *Executor and sole legatee:* JACOB BUTLER. *Witnesses:* CORNELIUS LEARY and WILLIAM STACY. Proven before RICHARD EVERARD.

ROSIER, NATHL. Albemarle County.
July 1, 1703. April 5, 1704. *Legatees:* WILLIAM JONES (*Executor*) and HENRY LYSLES. *Witnesses:* HENRY LYSLES, JOHN LEWERTON, ROBERT ONEALE. *Clerk of the Court:* N. CHEVIN.

ROURK, EDMOND. Bladen County.
May 15, 1769. December 16, 1769. "Parish of St. Martins in the County of Bladen." *Son and Executor:* SAMUEL. *Daughter:* MARY ADDISON. *Other legatee:* HENRY McCOY. *Wife:* DOROTHY. *Witnesses:* MARY ADDISON, DAVID MORLEY. Proven before WILLIAM TRYON.

ROWAN, MATTHEW. New Hanover County.
April 18, 1760. July 15, 1760. *Niece:* ROSE ROWAN (daughter of brother ANDREW ROWAN). *Nephew:* MATHEW ROWAN (son of brother ATCHEYSON). *Niece:* ANN ROWAN (daughter of brother WILLIAM). *Other legatees:* RICHARD LYON of Spring Hill in Bladen County, MARGARET ROWAN (niece), MILDRED LYON, daughter of JOHN (ten negroes), MARY LYON (daughter of RICHARD LYON), FREDERICK GREGG of Wilmington (land on the northeast side of Northeast River, opposite to Stag Park in New Hanover County; one gold watch). Eleven negroes and land on White Marsh, in Bladen County, bequeathed to FREDERICK GREGG and RICHARD LYON, in trust for ESTHER ROWAN (wife of ROBERT). ELIZABETH, wife of ARCHIBALD MACLAINE (daughter-in-law). Lands on Northwest River adjoining HENRY SIMMONDS; land on said river adjoining JUDGE LENARD and Nelltown in Bladen County, and land in Craven County opposite Newbern, lying on Trent River, in all about 1,800 acres, devised to Executors to be sold. All remainder of estate is devised and bequeathed to JOHN, the son of JANE STUBBS of Bath, "commonly called and known by the name of JOHN ROWAN." *Executors:* JOHN ROWAN, FREDERICK GREGG, RICHARD LYON. *Witnesses:* SAML. WATTERS, GEO. GIBBS, THOS. CLARK. Proven before ARTHUR DOBBS. *Executors* qualified before CORNELIUS HARNETT, J. P. Coat of arms on seal.

ROW, VALENTINE. Pasquotank County.
March 8, 1739. October Court, 1740. *Sons:* GEORGE and VALENTINE ("my plantation"). *Daughters:* DEBORAH, MARY and SARAH ROW. *Executor:* GEORGE ROW (son). *Witnesses:* RICHARD and THOMAS PRICHARD, JOHN HARRIS. *Clerk of the Court:* JAMES CRAVEN.

ROWELL, ELIZABETH. Northampton County.
January 20, 1745–1746. May Court, 1746. *Son and Executor:* SAMUEL. *Daughter:* MARY ROWELL. *Witnesses:* THOMAS HOLT, JOHN GILL, SAMUEL TARVER. *Clerk of the Court:* RT. FORSTER.

ABSTRACT OF WILLS, 1690—1760. 321

ROWNTREE, FRANCIS.

September 30, 1730. *Wife and Executrix:* not named. *Sons:* FRANCIS, WILLIAM, JESSE, MOSES and JOHN (lands lying in North Carolina and in Nansemond County, Virginia, where testator formerly lived). *Daughters:* REBECCA, SUSANNA, ELIZABETH and CHRISTIAN. *Witnesses:* THOMAS TASLER, THOMAS HOBBS, ISAAC PICKINSON. No probate.

ROUNTREE, FRANCIS.   Johnston County.

July 13, 1748. September Court, 1748. *Sons:* KADOR, FRANCIS, WILLIAM, MOSES. *Wife and Executrix:* MARY. *Executor:* MOSES COLEMAN. *Witnesses:* THEOPHILUS COLEMAN, JOHN BAREFOOT, TARLOW OQUIN. *Deputy Clerk of the Court:* RICHARD CASWELL.

ROUNTREE, HANNAH.   Perquimans County.

September 12, 1758. January Court, 1759. *Sisters:* SARAH HOLLOWELL, LIDY and ANN ROUNTREE. *Brother:* MOSES ROUNTREE. *Mother:* SARAH LELLY. *Brother-in-law:* ELISHA LELLY. *Executor:* NICHOLAS STALLINGS. *Witnesses:* JOE HOLLOWELL, ELIAS STALLINGS, ABNER HOLLOWELL. *Clerk of the Court:* MILES HARVEY.

ROUNTREE, JESSE.   Craven County.

October 17, 1777. November 21, 1777. *Sons:* JESSE, JOHN ("plantation called the Oald Meating House"), WILLIAM. *Daughters:* MARY and ELIZABETH. *Wife:* not named. *Executors:* JOHN ROUNTREE and JAMES FRIZLE. *Witnesses:* THOMAS COLEMAN, MOAB ROUNTREE, EDWD. FITZPATRICK. Proven before RICHARD CASWELL.

ROUNTREE, MOSES.   Perquimans County.

July 21, 1755. October Court, 1755. *Son:* MOSES (plantation and two negroes). *Daughters:* SARAH HOL———, HANAH, LEDY and ANN ROUNTREE. *Wife and Executrix:* SARY. *Executor:* NICHOLAS STALLINGS. *Witnesses:* JOSHUA WHITE, JOHN WHITE, ABRAM HILL. *Clerk of the Court:* MILES HARVEY.

ROUNTREE, THOMAS.   Chowan County.

December 1, 1746. July Court, 1748. *Sons:* CHARLES and THOMAS (to each is devised several tracts of land in Chowan County). *Grandsons:* WILLIAM WALLACE, THOMAS ROUNTREE. *Son-in-law:* ELIAS STALLINGS. *Wife:* ELIZABETH. *Executors:* CHARLES and THOMAS ROUNTREE (sons). *Witnesses:* THOS. WALTON, JOHN FREEMAN. *Clerk of the Court:* WILL. MEARNS.

21

ROWNTREE, THOMAS. Chowan County.

August 6, 1773. January 15, 1774. *Daughters:* ELIZABETH SMALL, SARAH STALLINGS, MARY, RUTH, RACHEL, JUDITH and CHRISTIAN ROWNTREE. *Granddaughter:* SARAH SMALL. *Executor:* AARON HILL. Testator devises lands on Catrin Creek. *Witnesses:* HENRY WALTON, THOMAS SPIVEY. Proven before JO. MARTIN.

RUCKES, THOMAS. Chowan County.

November 9, 1747. April Court, 1748. *Daughters:* MARY, TAMEY and SARAH. *Sons:* DEMSEY, JACOB, JESSE, JOSEPH and THOMAS (the two latter are appointed Executors). *Witnesses:* JACOB ODOM, JAMES BRADY, JACOB RODGERS.

RUSSELL, HABAKKUK. Carteret County.

March 9, 1754. June Court, 1754. *Sons:* DAVID and ABRAHAM. *Daughters:* REBECKAH, SARAH, ABIGAIL and ANN SOPHIA RUSSELL. *Wife:* ANN. *Executors:* GEORGE READ and GEORGE MCKANE. *Witnesses:* LAKKESTER LOVET, HENRY HARTSELL, SAMUEL JORDAN. *Clerk of the Court:* GEORGE READ.

RUSSELL, JOHN. Onslow County.

November 4, 1751. July 3, 1753. *Sons:* JAMES, PETER and MICHAEL. *Daughters:* MARY and ELIZABETH. *Wife:* ELIZABETH. *Executors:* JOHN and PETER STARKEY. *Witnesses:* WILLIAM BARBER, AARON BARBER, WM. FIELDEN. *Clerk of the Court:* WILL CRAY.

RUSSELL, THOMAS. Craven County.

January 4, 1744. March Court, 1744–1745. *Son:* JOHN. *Daughters:* MARY SMITH and JEMIMA CULLING. *Other legatee:* JOHN SMITH, son of WINFREE SMITH. *Wife and Executrix:* ELIZABETH. *Witnesses:* PETER DUKE, JOHN WILLIAMS, WILLIAM MELLAR. *Deputy Clerk of the Court:* N. ROUTLEDGE.

RUSTULL (RUSSELL), RICHARD. Carteret County.

March 15, 1739. June Court, 1747. Core Sound. *Son:* JOHN (land on East side of Newport River). *Daughter:* MARY RUSTULL. *Executors:* RICHARD RUSTULL (father) and HENERY STANTON. *Witnesses:* MARY STANTON, HENRY STANTON, JUNR., ALICE STANTON. *Clerk of the Court:* GEORGE READ.

RYALL, CHARLES. Onslow County.

November 28, 1754. *Sons:* SAMUEL and THOMAS. *Grandson:* CHARLES AUGUSTUS NICKSON. *Executor:* SAMUEL RYALL (son). *Witnesses:* JAMES DENSON, ROBERT NIXON, JOB BROOKES. *Clerk of the Court:* WILL. CRAY.

RYAN, DAVID.   Bertie County.
January 9, 1762. November 13, 1762. *Brothers:* JAMES and GEORGE. *Sisters:* ELIZABETH CAMPBELL and MARY LACKEY. *Executors:* JAMES RYAN, CORNELIUS CAMPBELL, RICHARD LACKEY and JOHN HILL. *Witnesses:* J. PEARSON, JOS. FRITH, WILLIAM SHAW. Proven before ARTHUR DOBBS.

RYAN, THOMAS.   Bertie County.
January 29, 1753. March Court, 1753. *Sons:* DAVID (land "lying in the bottom of Cashy Neck on the thourough-fare commonly known by the name of The Old House"; 1,500 acres of land on Cypress Swamp and four negroes), JAMES (350 acres of land), JAMES (1,120 acres of land and three negroes), GEORGE (plantation in Rocquis formerly known as JAMES CASTELLO'S Islands; plantation at head of Salmon Creek and water mill; two plantations in Chowan and 150 acres of land on Cashy River; three negroes), THOMAS ("The Manor house & Plantation" and also 500 acres of land). *Daughter:* MARY RYAN (two plantations on Chowan River; two plantations on Black Walnut Swamp and two negroes), ELIZABETH CAMPBELL. *Son-in-law:* CORNELIUS CAMPBELL (plantation in Tyrrell County lying on Albemarle Sound and two plantations in Bertie County together with two negroes). *Wife and Executrix:* MARTHA (three negroes). *Executors:* CAPT. JOHN CAMPBELL, CORNELIUS CAMPBELL and THOMAS TURNER. Provision is made for education of children and sale of brig to pay debts. *Witnesses:* EDWD. UNDERHILL, DAVID ALLEN, HUMPHRY NICHOLS. *Witnesses to codicil:* DAVID ALLEN, ELIZABETH ASHBURN, MARY CAPHART. *Clerk of the General Court:* JNO. SNEAD.

RYDING, JONATHAN.   Bertie County.
May Court, 1754. *Son:* JOSEPH ("my mannor plantation"). *Daughters:* MARTHA, ELIZABETH and DOROTHY RIDING. No executor. *Witnesses:* MARK GIBBINS, ELISAH WHITFIELD, EDWARD COLLINS. *Clerk of the Court:* SAMUEL ORMES.

SADLER, RICHARD.   Chowan County.
November 30, 1753. July Court, 1754. *Wife and Executrix:* MARGARET. *Witnesses:* HENRY BONNER, JAMES and DEBORAH THOMPSON. *Clerk of the Court:* WILL. HALSEY.

SADLER, WILLIAM.   Chowan Precinct.
April 13, 1727. April Court, 1727. *Sons:* WILLIAM and RICHARD (plantation divided between them). *Wife and Executrix:* ELIZABETH. *Executor:* MAJR. HENRY BONNER. *Witnesses:* ROBERT JEFFREYS, EDWD. HOWCOTT, WILLIAM THOMPSON. *Clerk of the Court:* RT. FORSTER.

SALISBERY, JAMES.   Pasquotank County.
August 16, 1758. September Court, 1758. *Sons:* JAMES, JOHN, JOSEPH, WILLIAM. *Daughters:* ELIZABETH and FRANCES SALISBERY. *Executors:* JAMES SALISBERY (son) and JOSEPH REED. *Witnesses:* THOMAS ARMOUR, JOSEPH COMMANDER, DAVID SINCLAIR. *Clerk of the Court:* THOS. TAYLOR.

SALTER, EDWARD.   Bath County.
January 6, 1734. February 5, 1734. *Son:* EDWARD. *Daughters:* SARAH, MARY and SUSANNAH. *Sons-in-law:* MILES HARVEY and JOHN HARVEY. *Wife:* ELIZABETH. Following lands devised: 306 acres on south side of Pamlico River called Mount Colvert; land purchased of JOHN SWANN; lands on Bear Creek, Pamlico River and the Beaver Dam of Grays Creek, "whereon JOHN ARRINGTON now dwells." About 25 negroes, one periauger, one brigantine named The Happy Luke, one pair silver spurs, Richard Bloom's History of the Bible and other books "of Divinity, Law and History," large China Punch bowl bequeathed. Brigantine ordered laden with tar and sent to Boston, there to be sold and proceeds invested in young negroes; provision is made for insurance of said vessel with Jacob Windall & Co., in the sum of 1,200 pounds. *Daughter,* SARAH, is left in care of MRS. SARAH PORTER of Cape Fear. Provision is made for education of son "to make him a compleat merchant." *Executors:* EDWARD MOSELEY, JOHN ODEON, JOHN CALDAM, THOMAS BONNER, WILLIAM WILLIS, WILLIAM ADAMS. Proven before GAB. JOHNSTON. Coat of arms on seal. *Witnesses:* WALLEY CHAUNCEY, BENJAMIN RIGNEY, WALTER DIXSON, ROGER JONES.

SANDERS, ABRAHAM.   Perquimans County.
April 6, 1750. October Court, 1751. *Sons:* JOHN (plantation whereon RICHARD WATERS lives), BENJAMIN ("plantation whereon I now live"), ABRAHAM (5s). *Daughters:* JUDE BOIS, ELIZABETH SANDERS. *Wife:* JUDE. *Executors:* RICHARD SANDERS and JOSEPH WHITE. *Witnesses:* JOHN MURDAUGH, JOHN and ELIZABETH WHITE. *Friends:* RICHARD SKINNER and JOHN HARVEY. *Clerk of the Court:* EDMUND HATCH.

SANDERS, ANN.   Perquimans County.
May 12, 1752. July Court, 1752. *Sons:* JOSEPH, BANJAMIN and JOHN SANDERS. *Daughters:* ELIZABETH NEWBY and LYDIA SANDERS. *Granddaughter:* ANN NEWBY. *Executors:* JOHN and JOSEPH SANDERS (sons). *Witnesses:* THOS. NEWBY, JOSHUA ELLIOT, THOMAS ELLIOT. *Clerk of the Court:* EDMUND HATCH.

SANDERS, BENJAMIN.   Perquimans County.
September 30, 1744. October Court, 1744. *Sons:* BENJAMIN ("dwelling plantation"), JOSEPH and JOHN. *Daughters:* BETTY and LIDA. *Wife*

and Executrix: ANN. *Executor:* SAMUEL NUBE (son-in-law). *Witnesses:* JOSHUA ELIOT, ANN ELLIOT. *Clerk of the Court:* EDMUND HATCH.

SANDERS, JOHN.   Onslow County.

January 6, 1732–1733. April 3, 1733. New River. *Brother:* ROBERT SANDERS. *Other legatees:* STEPHEN, RICHARD and EASTER WILLIAMS (children of JOHN WILLIAMS), EDWARD and STEPHEN HOWARD (sons of STEPHEN HOWARD), THOMAS FARNELL. *Sister:* ANN WILLIAMS. *Executor:* ROBERT SANDERS (brother). *Witnesses:* JOB BROOKES, STEPHEN HOWARD, JAMES FOYLE. *Clerk of the Court:* WILLIAM CRANFORD.

SANDERS, JOHN.   Chowan County.

August 18, 1751. October Court, 1751. *Sons:* FRANCIS ("plantation I now live on"), JOHN (plantation on Cypress Swamp where THOMAS RUTTER lives), ROBERT, JESSE, THOMAS. To each of above-named sons is bequeathed negroes. *Daughters:* MILLE, FERIBE and ELIZABETH SANDERS. *Wife and Executrix:* MARY. *Witnesses:* JOHN LOE (or LOCE), JR., JOHN LOE (or LOCE), SR., JACOB RUTH. *Clerk of the Court:* JAMES CRAVEN.

SANDERS, MARY.   Bertie County.

June 1, 1734. August Court, 1734. *Son:* ISAAC. *Daughters:* MARY and CHRISTINA ELIZABETH SANDERS. *Grandson:* ISAAC SNODEN. *Godson:* JOHN WILLSON. *Executors:* GEORGE WYNNS and ROBERT EVANS. *Witnesses:* JOSEPH THOMPSON and BENJN. WYNNS. *Clerk of the Court:* BENJAMIN WYNNS.

SANDERS, WILLIAM.   Edgecombe County.

June 5, 1756. February Court, 1757. *Sons:* HENRY (land on Panther Branch), WILLIAM ("the Mannor plantation"). Land called Simmonses Neck to be sold. *Wife and daughters:* not named. *Executors:* JOSEPH SHAW, JR., JOHN BRADFORD, TRISTRIM LOWTHER and SOLOMON WILLIAMS. *Witnesses:* WM. IRBY, JOHN GRICE, WM. HORNSBY. *Clerk of the Court:* JOSEPH MONTFORT.

SANDERSON, BAZIL.

January 22, 1721–1722. April 2, 1722. "Island of Antegua." *Legatees:* WILLIAM HILL, of Antegua, ELIZABETH SANDERSON (wife of BARTHOLEMY SANDERSON), JOHN LOVICK (saddle and bridle and gold studs), HENRY CLAYTON, WILLIAM LITTLE, WILLIAM BADHAM, MARY BADHAM (wife of WILLIAM), SARAH HAZARD (wife of ROBERT). *Sisters:* KATHERINE DYE and FRANCES PEATE (both of London). *Executors:* BART. SANDERSON, KATHERINE DYE, JOHN LOVICK and HENRY CLAYTON. Proven before Court at Edenton by WILLIAM LITTLE. *Clerk of the Court:* W. BADHAM.

SANDERSON, BENJAMIN.   Craven County.

October 1, 1757. January 3, 1758. *Sons:* JOSEPH, BENJAMIN (*Executor*). *Daughter:* DINA FOSCUE, HANNAH BARBER. *Granddaughter:* SARAH FOSCUE (one negro). *Executor:* BENJAMIN BROCKETT. *Witnesses:* WILLIAM GARDNER, SIMON FOSCUE, JOHN GRANADE. Proven before ARTHUR DOBBS.

SANDERSON, JOSEPH.   Currituck County.

January 13, 1743. October Court, 1746. *Wife:* JULIA. *Sons:* RICHARD ("the manner plantation," also the plantation on Sandy Banks known as Pawmers, and other tracts of land, location not given), SAMUEL and JOSHUA (plantation and land to each), THOMAS and WILLIAM (plantation to each), BENJAMIN (1 negro and land on North River), JOSEPH (land on Sandy Banks). *Executor:* JOHN LURRY. *Witnesses:* JOHN WOODHOUSE, WILLIAM BAGLY, SAMUEL JARVES. *Clerk of the Court:* RICHARD McCLURE.

SANDERSON, JOSEPH.   Currituck County.

April 26, 1758. December Court, 1758. *Sons:* JOSEPH ("plantation whereon I now live"), RICHARD (plantation known as the Deep Branch), CALEB (70 acres land). *Daughters:* JULIAN, ANN, LIDA and SUSANNAH SANDERSON. *Wife:* CESIAH. *Executor:* JOSEPH SANDERSON (son). *Witnesses:* JOHN WOODHOUSE, GEORGE POWERS, SAMUELL SALLYER. *Clerk of the Court:* WM. MEARNS.

SANDERSON, JOSEPH.   Craven County.

February 12, 1774. March 19, 1774. *Sons:* JESSE, THOMAS, JOSEPH, BENJAMIN, SHADRACH, JOHN, JAMES, ISAAC (land at Miskeeto Point). Negroes bequeathed to each of sons. *Daughters:* PRUDENCE FOSTER, LIDDY LEE. *Executors:* JESSE SANDERSON (son), THOS. LEE (son-in-law), EDWARD WHITLEY. *Witnesses:* THOS. FOY, JOHN MEEKET, WILLIAM GRIFFITH. Proven before JO. MARTIN.

SANDERSON, JULIAN.   Currituck County.

July 31, 1749. April 17, 1752. *Granddaughters:* ELIZABETH CHURCH and ANN WHITE. *Executor:* HENRY WHITE (son-in-law). *Witnesses:* SAMUEL JONES, MARGITT BARRIT, EASTHER WHITE. *Clerk of the Court:* WILLIAM SHERGOLD.

SANDERSON, RICHARD.   Perquimans County.

August 17, 1733. October 15, 1733. *Son:* RICHARD ("ye Island of Ocreecock," three negroes and one Indian slave; "the mannor plantation"; "all my lots in Ronoak Town"; "two thirds of ye Sea Flower Brigantine"; one-half of sloop Swallow). *Son-in-law:* TULLY WILLIAMS (five negro slaves; 140 acres of land in Perquimans bordering on son RICHARD and JOHN WILLOUGHBY; one-third of Sea Flower Brigantine and one-half of sloop Swallow). *Nephews:* JOSEPH and RICHARD SANDERSON. *Brother-in-law:* HENRY WOODHOUSE (one Mustee fellow). *Sister:* SUSANNA ERWIN. *Daughter:* ELIZABETH POLLOCK. *Cousin:* ELIZABETH DICKSON. *Nephew:* HEZEKIAH WOODHOUSE (land "on ye Sandy Bank by the name of Point Lookout"). *Daughter:* GRACE (wife of TULLY WILLIAMS). *Executors:* RICHARD SANDERSON (son) and TULLY WILLIAMS (son-in-law). *Witnesses:* CLEMT. HALL, THOMAS SNOWDEN, THOMAS TRUMBAL. *Clerk of the Court:* CHARLES DENMAN.

SANDERSON, RUTH.

(Wife of COL. RICHARD SANDERSON of Little River). September 4, 1727. January 29, 1727. *Relatives:* THOS. HARVEY, MILES GALE of Boston (two negroes each), PENELEAP LETTELL, wife of WILLIAM LITTLE (one negro), ELIZABETH CLAYTEN (one negro). *Executors:* THOS. HARVEY and MILES GALE. *Witnesses:* JOSHUA WHEREY, ELIZABETH HARVEY. Proven before RICHARD EVERARD.

SARSON, LAURENCE. Bertie Precinct.

May 6, 1726. "Formerly of the County of Suffolk in Great Brittain but now of Bertie precinct," etc. *Devisees and legatees:* WILLIAM WATERS (land on Salmon Creek), JAMES WATERS, brother of WILLIAM (land on the "east end of the Great Pocoson"), KATHERINE ARNOLD, SARAH WATERS. *Executor:* THOMAS LOVICK. *Witnesses:* JAMES CASTLETON, HERCULES COYTE. Coat of arms on seal. Attached to this will is a lease from testator to one HUGH HYMAN, dated January 24, 1723, of a plantation called Bucklesbury on the condition that the said HYMAN "clear on the plantation six thousand corn hills att five foot distant * * * and to raise and plant out at twelve foot distance three hundred peach trees." Lease witnessed by JOHN DUKINGFIELD, JOHN SHORT. No probate to will. Coat of arms on seal.

SAWYER, CHARLES. Pasquotank County.

October 21, 1750. January Court, 1750. *Sons:* JOHN (plantation on North River), JESSE (land on North River), CHARLES ("land I now live on," riding horse and cattle); WILLIS (land adjoining Butterworth, JOHN SAWYER, etc.). *Daughters:* DOROTHY and MIRIAM. To each of above-named children is bequeathed a negro. *Wife:* not named. *Executor:* WILLIS SAWYER. *Witnesses:* BENNETT MORGAN, LODWICK WILLIAMS, S. S. PLOMER. *Clerk of the Court:* THOS. TAYLOR.

SAWYER, DANIEL. Pasquotank County.

May 15, 1749. April Court, 1752. *Sons:* CORNELIUS, ISAAC and EZEKIEL (land divided among them). *Daughters:* TAYMER, BETTY and SARAH

SAWYER. *Wife:* MARY. *Executors:* CORNELIUS and ISAAC (sons). *Witnesses:* GRIFFITH GRAY, JOHN SAWYER, JOAB DAUGE. *Clerk of the Court:* THO. TAYLOR.

SAWYER, HENRY. Pasquotank County.

June 24, 1728. August 3, 1729. *Sons:* CHARLES, BENJAMIN, DANIEL. *Daughters:* TAMER, CAEN and ELIZABETH WILLIAMS, CHARITY GRAY and SUSANNER WILLIAMS. *Executors:* DANIELL and BENJAMIN SAWYER (sons). *Witnesses:* CORNELIUS ROSE, JOHN KELLY, WILLIAM ———. Proven before RICHARD EVERARD.

SAWYER, JEREMIAH. Pasquotank County.

October 10, 1755. June Court, 1756. *Sons:* ROBERT and CHARLES (land divided between them). *Son-in-law:* THOS. HAYSTENS. *Daughter:* BRIDGET JOLLEY. *Grandson:* WILLIS HAYSTENS. *Executor:* CHARLES SAWYER (son) *Witnesses:* JOS. JONES, WILLIAM HIXSON. *Clerk of the Court:* THO. TAYLOR.

SAWYER, JOHN. Albemarle County.

December 22, 1713. *Sons:* JOHN, THOMAS, ROBERT, SOLOMON (a plantation to each). *Grandson:* CHARLES GRANDY. *Wife and Executrix:* JEAN. *Witnesses:* THOMAS and ROBERT SAWYER, TIMOTHY READING. No probate.

SAWYER, JOHN. Pasquotank County.

June 2, 1743. January Court, 1743. *Sons:* JOHN, TULLE (plantation called Gumberry), STEPHEN, WILLIAM (land in Currituck known as Peters Ridge). To each son is given negroes and a horse. *Daughters:* GRACE and SARAH. *Wife and Executrix:* ABIGAL. *Witnesses:* WILLES SAWYER, SARAH SAWYER. *Clerk of the Court:* THOS. TAYLOR.

SAWYER, JOSHUA. Pasquotank County.

May 19, 1753. July Court, 1753. *Sons:* JOSHUA and DAVID (plantation divided between them), WILLIAM, NATHAN, JESSE. *Daughters:* MARY and SARAH SAWYER. *Executor:* JOSHUA SAWYER (son). *Witnesses:* ROBERT MURDEN, JOSHUA JENNINGS, JACOB MITCHELL. *Clerk of the Court:* THOS. TAYLOR.

SAWYER, ROBART. Pasquotank County.

April Court, 1735. *Sons:* JEREMIAH (land adjoining JOHN SPENCE), JOSEPH and ZACHARIAH ("plantation whereon I now live"), DENIS (land on Sawyers Creek), JOHN SCARBOROUGH (land called the light place). *Daughter:* ESTER SAWYER (land between DENIS SAWYER and the light place). *Granddaughter:* SUSANNAH SAWYER (land called the Great Island). *Wife and Executrix:* FRANCES. *Witnesses:* CHARLES and DANIEL SAWYER, SAMUELL SIMMONS. *Clerk of the Court:* JOSU SMITH.

SAWYER, SOLOMON.   Pasquotank County.

August 15, 1742. October Court, 1742. *Sons:* JOHN ("my manner plantation"), SOLOMON (plantation known by the name of Dogwood Ridge). *Daughters:* CHARITY, ELISABETH, MARY, PETTYATH and CHRISTIAN SAWYER. *Witnesses:* BARTLETT MORGAN, THOMAS HASTINS. *Clerk of the Court:* THOS. TAYLOR.

SAWYER, THOMAS.

October 22, 1750. January Court, 1750. *Daughters:* DOLLY SMITHSON, JEMIMA, MARY and MIRIAM SAWYER. *Son-in-law and Executor:* JOHN SMITHSON. *Wife and Executrix:* ELISABETH. *Witnesses:* HENRY NICKELES, WILLIAM HARRIS, HEZ. CARTWRIGHT. *Clerk of the Court:* THOS. TAYLOR.

SAWYER, THOMAS.   Pasquotank County.

May 19, 1756. June Court, 1756. *Sons:* ALEXANDER, JOSEPH, THOMAS, SAMUEL ("my plantation"). *Daughters:* JANE HUMPHRIES, TAMER WILLIAMS, CATTREN and REBECKAH SAWYER. *Grandsons:* SAMUEL HASTINGS, MAIKD MORGAN. *Granddaughter:* ANNE SAWYER. *Daughter-in-law:* SARAH SAWYER. *Executors:* SAMUEL and REBECKAH SAWYER (son and daughter). *Witnesses:* BENJAMIN SAWYER, GRIFFITH GRAY, BENTT. MORGAN. *Clerk of the Court:* THOS. TAYLOR.

SAWYER, WILLIS.   Pasquotank County.

April 3, 1753. April Court, 1753. *Wife and Executrix:* HANOR (plantation on Pasquotank River). *Daughter:* BETTY SAWYER. *Brother:* CHARLES SAWYER. *Father:* CHARLES SAWYER. *Witnesses:* WILLIAM SYMONS, BETY SYMONS, ANN SAWYER. *Clerk of the Court:* THOS. TAYLOR. Executrix qualified before JARVIS JONES.

SCANER, ISAAC.   Albemarle County.

August 6, 1693. October 2, 1693. *Friends:* WILLIAM JACKSON and ELIZABETH NIXON. *Neighbors:* WILLIAM SIMSON, ROBERT LEWIS, JOHN GODFREY, ANN BOYSE. No executor appointed. *Witnesses:* WILLIAM TANNER, WILLIAM JACKSON, THOMAS SYMONS. *Clerk of the Court:* EDWARD MAYO.

SCARFE, JOHN.   Pasquotank County.

February 15, 1751. April Court, 1751. *Sons:* JAMES, JOHN, EDWARD, JONATHAN, ISRAEL. *Daughters:* ANNE RICHARDSON, MARY JONES. *Wife:* MARY. *Witnesses:* WILLIAM ABERCROMBIE, JAMES GREVES, WILLIAM RODES. Codicil to this will of even date and witnessed by same parties appoints *wife* and *son* JAMES as Executors, and makes bequests to *grandson,* JOHN SCARFE. *Clerk of the Court:* THOS. TAYLOR.

SCARBROUGH, CHARLES.   Pasquotank County.

January 20, 1750–1751. *Son:* BENJAMIN (land on Poplar Swamp). *Daughter:* LYDA SCARBROUGH. *Wife and Executrix:* JOICE. *Witnesses:* JAMES FORBES, JOHN SCARBROUGH, ELIZABETH TORKSEY. No probate.

SCARBROUGH, JOHN.   Pasquotank County.

December 27, 1754. June Court, 1756. *Daughters:* SARAH BURGES (three negroes), TAMAR SCARBROUGH ("my plantation"). *Executor:* WILLIAM BURGES. *Witnesses:* PAUL SHARP, BENJAMIN WILLSON, THOMAS CLUF and BENJAMIN TORKSEY. *Clerk of the Court:* THOMAS TAYLOR.

SCARBROUGH, MACRORA.   Perquimans County.

January 31, 1752. February 18, 1752. *Sons:* BENJAMIN, MACRORA and WILLIAM. To BENJAMIN is given plantation "whereon I now dwell called Springfield," with four negroes, six silver spoons, silver-headed cane, silver shoe buckles, knee buckles, 14 silver vest buttons, black walnut desk and also half of land at Yawpim, called Point Pleasant. To MACRORA is devised land at Oak Ridge and four negroes, a silver can, silver watch and black walnut desk. To WILLIAM is given land bought of MR. HARVEY and ROBERT WILSON. *Daughter:* ELIZABETH SCARBROUGH. *Wife and Executrix:* ELIZABETH. *Trustees:* JOHN SCARBROUGH (brother), EDMUND HATCH (brother-in-law) and WILLIAM BURGIS. *Witnesses:* WALTER KIPPIN, JOSHUA HOBART, CORNELIUS MULLIN, ROBERT AVERY, MARTHAANN KIPPIN. Proven before GAB. JOHNSTON. Coat of arms on seal.

SCHWANNER, MATHIAS TOBIAS.   Tyrrell County.

September 21, 1743. March Court, 1744. *Sons:* JOHN, SAMUEL, WILLIAM and MATHIAS (land on the "Right hand of the road as thou goest upward the said County on the westward side of Tuk Creek, and four negro slaves"). *Grandson:* WILLIAM BRYAN (son of DARBY BRYAN). *Daughters:* SARAH BRYAN, MARY SCHWANNER. *Wife and Executrix:* JANE. *Witnesses:* WILLIAM BARRETT, ROBERT LANIER, ROBERT LANIER DANIEL. *Clerk of the Court:* THOMAS LEE.

SCOLLAY, ELIZABETH.   Bertie County.

December 1, 1766. January 12, 1767. *Sons:* THOMAS POLLOCK (three negroes and one teapot, milk pot, tankard, two salts, three table, one soup and all teaspoons). CULLEN POLLOCK ("all my books and a mourning ring"). *Other legatees:* children of TULLY WILLIAMS, children of RICHARD SAUNDERSON; DR. ROBERT LENNOX and *wife,* FANNY; JOHN SCOLLAY, of Boston (one negro man); PEGGY CATHCART, daughter of DOCTOR WILLIAM CATHCART (negro girl); SARAH BLOUNT, daughter of JOSEPH (one negro girl); SOPHIA RASOR, daughter of EDWARD RASOR (one negro girl); FANNAY CATHCART, daughter of WILLIAM (one negro girl); THOMAS BLOUNT, son of

ABSTRACT OF WILLS, 1690—1760.   331

JOSEPH BLOUNT. *Former husband:* THOMAS POLLOCK. *Executors:* THOMAS POLLOCK, ROBERT LENOX, RICHARD SAUNDERSON and JOSEPH BLOUNT. *Witnesses:* HARDY HARDISON, FREDERICK HARDISON. Proven before WILLIAM TRYON.

SCOLLAY, SAMUEL.

February 18, 1752. *Friends:* THOMAS GILFORD, of Busty in Zetland; MAGNIS HENDERSON, of Guards in Zetland; GEORGE TRIEL, of Broh in Orkney, in the Island of Sandy (fifty pounds to each), "MRS. MARGARET STEWART, alias TRIEL, late Lady of Eleoness in Orkney, in the Island of Sandy" (twenty pounds); MRS. MARY TULINTON, alias DAVIS, relict of ROBERT DAVIS, shipbuilder in Leath, Scotland; HUGH BLACKBURN, of Norfolk; DR. WILLIAM CATHCART, ROBERT TODD, of Norfolk. *Brother:* JERMAN ROBERT SCOLLAY, of Lerwick in Zetland. *Sons-in-law:* THOMAS and CULLEN POLLOCK (land on "the Plank Bridge" in Pasquotank County). To TULLY WILLIAMS is bequeathed his father's sword and cattle at Kettyhauk. *Wife and Executrix:* not named. *Executors:* THOMAS and CULLEN POLLOCK. *Witnesses:* ANN ANDERSON, ED. RASOR, JOHN NICHOLLS. Proven before GAB. JOHNSTON.

SCOTT, JOHN.   Pasquotank County.

September 13, 1738. January 8, 1738. *Daughters:* ELIPHEL and HANNAH SCOTT. *Wife and Executrix:* SARAH. *Witnesses:* DAVID GEORGE, JOSEPH JORDAN. *Clerk of the Court:* JOS. SMITH.

SCOTT, JOHN.   Craven County.

October 4, 1764. September 27, 1773. Newbern. *Wife and Executrix:* MARTHA. *Executor:* JAMES REED. *Witnesses:* HANNAH LANGSONE, FRANK ROMBOUGH, JAMES DAVIS. *President of the Island of Antigua:* THOS. JARVIS. Will proven before JO. MARTIN and also before THOS. JARVIS.

SCOTT, JOSEPH.

October 26, 1685. *Son and Executor:* JOSHUA. *Clerk of the Court:* EDWARD MAYO. Remainder of will illegible.

SCOTT, JOSHUA.   Albemarle County.

January 8, 1685–1686. *Daughters:* GRACE and SARAH SCOTT (lands, orchards, etc.). *Wife and Executrix:* MARY. *Witnesses:* JOHN KINSAY, RICHARD EVENS, JOHN WOLFENDEN. No probate.

SCOTT, MARY.   Perquimans County.

March 17, 1691–1692. October 3, 1692. *Daughters:* HEPTHENIA WALKING, JULYANAH TAYLOR. *Granddaughter:* JOHENAH TAYLOR. No executor. *Witnesses:* ANTHONY DAWSON ―――― BUTLER. *Clerk of the Court:* JOHN STEPNEY.

SCOTT, MATTHEW.   Pitt County.

August 26, 1771. December 6, 1771. *Brothers:* WILLIAM and JAMES SCOTT, fullers and clothiers in Pennsylvania. *Father:* JOHN SCOTT (plantation and storehouse in Woodstock). Testator desires all bonds, notes, lot and houses near one CLARK'S, lot and house in Woodstock town, Bay Boat, periauger and seine to be delivered to one SAMUEL PURVIANCE, in Baltimore, in payment of account due him, said PURVIANCE, by testator and CALHON trading as partners. *Executors:* JAMES SCOTT (brother) and MRS. ELIZABETH SPEIR. *Witnesses:* SUSANNA EVANS, RICHD. EVANS. Proven before JO. MARTIN.

SCOTT, RICHARD.   New Hanover County.

March 6, 1756. April 16, 1762. *Wife and Executrix:* MARY (stock marked and branded as set out in will and also dwelling plantation). *Son-in-law:* OSWELL SILL. *Other legatees:* WILLIAM, son of RICHARD EARLE; ELIZABETH, daughter of JOHN SIMPSON. *Witnesses:* ELIZABETH MORRIS, ALICE HUDSON, JOHN EARLE. Proven before ARTHUR DOBBS.

SCOTT, STEPHEN.

March 12, 1711. September 11, 1716. *Sons:* EDWARD ("plantation I now live on on Newbegun Creek"), STEPHEN and HENRY (plantation to each), JOHN and JOSHUA. *Daughters:* SARAH and ELIZABETH SCOTT. *Wife and Executrix:* ELIZABETH. *Witnesses:* MATTHEW PRITCHARD, JOHN SHEARLY, BENJAMIN PRITCHARD. Proven before CHARLES EDEN.

SCOTT, STEPHEN, SR.   Pasquotank County.

November 21, 1752. January Court, 1753. *Sons:* JOSEPH (land on Beaver Dam Swamp, one-half of "plantation whereon I now live, together with one negro man"), SAMUEL (half of the "plantation whereon I now live," land known by the name of the Rigg, land known as Newbegun Creek meeting-house land, seven negroes and one "New England mare & colt" and one silver watch). *Daughter:* MARY CONNER, wife of JOHN CONNER (three negroes and one riding horse). *Grandchildren:* JOSEPH and MARY SCOTT (6 negroes), MARY, JOHN and CADO CONNER (5 negroes), STEPHEN and WILLIAM SCOTT (2 negroes). *Executors:* JOSEPH and SAMUEL SCOTT (sons). *Witnesses:* ROBERT JORDAN, KATHARNA WHITE, THOMAS NICHOLSON. *Clerk of the Court:* THOMAS TAYLOR. Device on seal.

SEAGRAVE, ADAM.   Currituck Precinct.

October 7, 1723. January 14, 1723–1724. *Legatees:* JOHN SMITH (Executor), SAMSON WOODHOUSE. *Witnesses:* HENRY WOODHOUSE, THOMAS LARRY, JOHN STONE. *Clerk of the Court:* JOS. WICKER.

ABSTRACT OF WILLS, 1690—1760.

SEARS, WILLIAM.   Albemarle County.

August 29, 1679. *Wife and Executrix:* ANN. *Brother:* THOMAS SEARS ("now in Bermudas"). *Friend:* RICHARD ROADES. *Witnesses:* RALPH COATES, DANIEL FRISSELL. No probate. Impression of ship on seal.

SEAY, JAMES.   Bertie County.

May 18, 1772. January 6, 1774. *Sons:* ISAAC, JOHN, JAMES (plantation to each). *Daughters:* ONEY SEAY, MARY BROWN. *Executors:* ISAAC SEAY, ARTHUR BROWN, JOEL BROWN (son-in-law). *Witnesses:* EZEKIEL TOMLINSON, JOSEPH HORNE, ANN WILLIAMS. Proven before JO. MARTIN.

SETTON, NATHANIEL.   Perquimans Precinct.

February 23, 1724-1725. March 30, 1725. *Legatees:* JOHN WARD, RUTH GLOSTER, JOSEPH SETTON, ELISABETH WHEDBEE, PATHANNA SETTON, JAMES ANDERSON, THOMAS SETTON, GEORGE SETTON and RICHARD WHEDBEE. *Executors:* RICHARD WHEDBEE and THOMAS SETTON. *Witnesses:* RICHARD DAVES, RICHARD SKINNER, REBECKA SETTON. *Clerk General Court:* SAMUEL SWANN.

SHACKLEFORD, JAMES.   Carteret County.

July 10, 1759. September Court, 1759. *Sons:* JAMES (600 acres "of my Quarter of the Banks"), JOSEPH (plantation formerly belonging to Jo. WICKER), PELEG. Negroes divided among children. *Wife and Executrix:* KEZIAH. *Witnesses:* ANANIAS CAVENAGH, THOMAS ADDISON, ANDREW HENDERSON, ROBERT FINNEY. *Clerk of the Court:* WM. ROBERTSON.

SHACKLEFORD, JOHN.   Carteret County.

March 25, 1734. September Court, 1734. *Son:* JAMES ("land on Bancks lying to the Eastward of Old Topsail Inlet, called by the name of Shackelfords Banks"; island named Carrot Island and one negro). *Daughters:* MARY, ELIZABETH and ANN SHACKELFORD (one gold ring to each), SARAH MOSS (wife of JOSEPH). *Grandsons:* JOHN and WILLIAM ROBERTS. *Wife and Executrix:* ANN. *Executor:* JOHN SHACKELFORD (son, to whom is devised all remainder of estate after legacies mentioned). *Witnesses:* SAMUEL CHADWICK, EPHRAIM CHADWICK. *Clerk of the Court:* JAS. WINRIGHT.

SHARP, JACOB.   Bertie County.

October 30, 1748. January 27, 1748. *Son:* STARKEY ("all my lands and Manner plantation"). *Wife and Executrix:* ELISABETH. *Nephew:* SAMUEL TANNER. *Friends:* WILLIAM HOOKER, WM. WITHERIN, JOHN BAKER, of Littletown, PETER EVANS (*Executor*). *Witnesses:* WILLIAM WILLINGTON, ISAAC LASSITER, MARY LASSITER. Proven before GAB. JOHNSTON.

SHARWOOD, DAVID.   Perquimans Precinct.

November 16, 1722. April 9, 1723. *Sons:* JONATHAN and DAVID (a plantation to each). *Wife and Executrix:* JANE. *Executor:* SAMUELL PHELPS. *Witnesses:* GABRIELL NEWBY, SAMUEL PHELPS, JAMES CITESON (or CYTISON). *Clerk of the Court:* RICHD. LEARY.

SHAVER, JOHN.   Bath County.

October 25, 1730. December Court, 1730. *Friends and Executors:* JOHN THOMAS, THOMAS BLAKE, THOMAS FLIBUS and NICHOLAS ROUTLEDGE. *Witnesses:* JACOB HOOVER, R. ATKINS. *Clerk of the Court:* C. METCALFE.

SHEARD, DAVID.   Perquimans County.

August 10, 1740. December 3, 1740. *Son:* THOMAS ("my plantasion and all my lands"). *Daughters:* ELIZABETH and MARY SHEARD. *Executors:* WILLIAM and JOHN JONES. *Witnesses:* JOHN ANDERSON, JEREMIAH BARNES, ROBERT HALL. Proven before W. SMITH, C. J.

SHEARER, ROBERT.   Bertie Precinct.

October 7, 1727. *Sons:* ROBERT and ARTHUR (land on Little Swamp), JOHN (land called the "Poynt Land"), WILLIAM. *Daughters:* PRUDENCE and SUSANNAH. *Wife and Executrix:* ELIZABETH. *Overseers:* JOHN DEW and ARTHUR WILLIAMS. *Witnesses:* HENRY GAY, JOSEPH BOON. No probate.

SHELLEY, JOHN PHILIP.   Edgecombe County.

June 28, 1749. August Court, 1749. *Sons:* PHILIP (land on Swift Creek and four negroes), DANIEL (land on Swift Creek at the mouth of Tumbling Run, and two negroes). *Daughter:* JUDETH SHELLEY (two negroes). *Executor:* THOMAS MANN. *Witnesses:* WILLIAM SMITHES, JEREMIAH MALPASS, MARGARET TERRY. *Clerk of the Court:* BENJAMIN WYNNS. Impression of head on seal.

SHEPARD, DAVID.   Carteret County.

May 30, 1774. January 13, 1775. *Sons:* SOLOMON (land on west side of Black Creek bought of LANKISTHUR LOVETT, land on Boague Sound known as Smith's Hammock, land on the head of Broad Creek and three negro men), ELIJAH ("plantation whereon I now live," land on south side of Newport River called Snow Neck, land on Boague Sound known as Bartrom's Point, and four negroes). To two above-named sons is devised land on south side of Newport River known as Read's Neck. To heirs of son JACOB is devised land on Boague Sound called Whitehall, land on Newport River known as Mount Pleasant, and another tract on north side of Newport River, together with one negro man. *Grandsons:*

DAVID (son of SOLOMON SHEPARD, plantation on Boague Sound at the mouth of Goose Creek, known as Townley's Point, and one negro), JOHN (son of JACOB SHEPARD), SOLOMON and ABSOLOM SHEPARD (to SOLOMON is given a plantation on Boague Sound and three negroes), DAVID WARD, DAVID SANDERS (one negro), DAVID TAYLOR. *Daughters:* SARAH WALLIS (five negroes), REBECKAH SANDERS (one negro), ABIGAIL WARD (six negroes), ELISABETH TAYLOR (negroes). *Wife:* not named. *Executors:* SOLOMON and ELIJAH SHEPARD (sons), COL. WILLIAM THOMSON. *Witnesses:* CORNELIUS CANADY, ELISABETH CANADY, GIDEON CANADAY. Proven before JAS. HASELL.

SHEPARD, THOMAS.   Currituck County.

March 20, 1721–1722. July 10, 1722. *Daughters:* ELIZABETH and GWINEFOLD SHEPARD. *Son:* SAMSON ("my plantation"). *Wife and Executrix:* RUTH. *Witnesses:* JO. WICKER, HUMPH. VINCE. *Clerk of the Court:* JO. WICKER.

SHERARD, JOHN.   Northampton County.

October 21, 1751. August Court, 1753. *Sons:* JOSEPH, WILLIAM, ROBERT (plantation devised to each), Thomas. *Daughter:* CHARITY SHERARD. *Wife:* not named. Two negroes bequeathed. *Witnesses:* JOHN DAWSON, WILLIAM BRIDGERS, AGNES LASSITER, JOHN BRIDGERS. *Clerk of the Court:* I. EDWARDS.

SHERWOOD, THOMAS.   Albemarle County.

December 22, 1693. April 17, 1694. *Wife and Executrix:* ELIZABETH ("one-half the plantation I now live on, including the mantion house"). *Daughter:* SARAH. *Executor:* GEORGE MUSCHAMP. *Witnesses:* WILLIAM RAWLINSON, ELIZABETH RAWLINSON, BARBARA MIDLETON. *Clerk of the Court:* EDWARD MAYO.

SHETTS, JACOB.   Craven County.

September 25, 1751. *Daughters:* ZILLPMAN JOHN, CEVEL SHETTS, CATRRON FELD. *Wife:* CEVEL. *Executors:* LEWIS BRYAN and JOHN CORNOT. *Witnesses:* HARDY BUSH, SAML. FEILD, CATHRINE BUSH. No probate.

SHINE, DANIEL.   Craven County.

May 5, 1757. August Court, 1757. *Sons:* JOHN (1 shilling), THOMAS (1 negro), WILLIAM (2 negroes), JAMES ("all the rest of my estate, negroes, lands, horses, cattle, hogs, etc."). *Daughter:* ELIZABETH VAUGHAN. *Executors:* JAMES SHINE and JOHN OLIVER. *Witnesses:* FARLD GREEN, JOHN WILLIAMSON, CHARLES SHENEWOLF. *Deputy Clerk of the Court:* PETER CONWAY. Impression of stag on seal.

SHIRLEY, JAMES.
December 9, 1737. February 18, 1737. Cape Fear. *Son:* DESMINIERE. *Daughters:* SUSANNAH and ANN SHIRLEY. *Wife and Executrix:* ANN. *Witnesses:* DUN. CAMPBELL, ARMAND DEROSSETT, M. D., DR. ROGER ROLFE. Proven before GAB. JOHNSTON at Newton.

SHIRORD, ALEXANDER. Bertie Precinct.
July 10, 1731. *Sons:* ALEXANDER ("my plantation in Virginia"), AARON, JOHN ("plantation where I now live"). *Daughters:* MARTHA, CATREN and ELIZABETH. *Wife and Executrix:* MARY. *Witnesses:* ALXR. DOWNING, WILLIAM HOMES, WILLIAM WORRELL. No probate.

SHORTER, WILLIAM. Northampton County.
December 7, 1752. May Court, 1753. *Son:* BENJAMIN ("my plantation"). *Other legatee:* DORCAS HUGGINS. *Wife and Executrix:* ELIZABETH. *Witnesses:* THOS. PACE, JOHN MOORE. *Clerk of the Court:* I. EDWARDS.

SHROCK, PETER. Bertie County.
July 11, 1750. July 10, 1751. *Brothers:* MYCHEL, GEORGE and JOHN CAPHEART. *Father and Executor:* GEORGE CAPHEART. *Witnesses:* EDY CETER, JNO. CRICKET, JR. Proven before GAB. JOHNSTON, at Eden House.

SHUBRIDGE, WILLIAM. Onslow County.
January 30, 1744–1745. April Court, 1746. *Grandchildren:* WILLIAM and ELISABETH AHAIR, SHUBRIDGE and WILLIAM RAMSEY. *Executors:* JOHN AHAIR and SAMUELL RAMSEY (sons-in-law), JOHN STARKEY. *Witnesses:* JOHN GILLETT, WILLIAM RAMSEY, DENIS OMAR. *Clerk of the Court:* GEO. CLOPTON.

SHUTE, GYLES. Bath County.
February 11, 1729–1730. June Court, 1730. *Sons:* PHILIP, SAMUEL ("plantation I now live on lying on the Mouth of Towne Creek"), JOSEPH. *Daughter:* PENELOPE SHUTE (gold ring). *Wife and Executrix:* CHARITY. *Witnesses:* ISAAC OTTIWELL, JOHN MATTOCKE, JOHN LAWSON. *Clerk of the Court:* JNO. MATTOCKE. Device of some description on seal.

SHUTE, REBECCA.
May 28, 1732. August 12, 1732. Port Royall, in the Island of Jamaica. *Daughter:* REBECCA SHUTE (plantation in Cape Fear with negroes, etc.). *Mother:* MARY EARLE. *Friend:* JNO. EARLE. *Executors:* MARY and JOHN EARLE. *Witnesses:* GEORGE CAVANISS, JOHN PHIPPS, JACOB PHIPPS, JOSIAH EASON. *Clerk of the Court at Port Royall:* LOUIS GALDY. *Justice of the Peace, North Carolina:* W. BADHAM. Coat of arms on seal.

ABSTRACT OF WILLS, 1690—1760.   337

SIGLEY, JOHN.   Beaufort County.

May 10, 1750. December Court, 1754. *Son:* AARON. *Daughters:* ANN and JEAN SIGLEY. *Wife and Executrix:* MARGRET SIGLEY. *Witnesses:* COLEMAN ROE, HENRY LOCKEY. *Clerk of the Court:* WALLEY CHAUNCEY.

SILVERTHORN, GILFORD.   Hyde Precinct.

April 5, 1737–1738. March 7, 1737. *Sons:* JOHN, SABASTIN (*Executor*). *Daughter:* MARY. *Wife and Executrix:* MARY. *Witnesses:* ROGER MASON, NICKLES BOOTY, JOHN MASON. *Clerk of the Court:* J. MARDNER.

SILVERTHORN, SABASTIN.   Hyde County.

December 22, 1751. March Court, 1752. *Son:* JOHN ("my manner plantation"). *Daughters:* LYDIA, MARY, AGNES and SARY SILVERTHORN. *Wife and Executrix:* MARY. *Executor:* BENJAMIN MASON. *Witnesses:* ROGER MASON, JR., JONATHAN BELL and MARK REW. *Clerk of the Court:* FRANCIS EGLETON.

SILVESTER, RICHARD.   Beaufort County.

January 11, 1728. June 10, 1729. *Son:* RICHARD WILLIAM SILVESTER (land at Bridge Town in Norfolk County, Virginia; also two tracts of land on Machapungo River). *Other legatee:* WILLIAM WORMINTUN ("two bitts of Ground in Virga att ye Bridge Town"). *Wife:* not named. *Grandsons:* EBENEZER and HENRY SLADE. *Witnesses:* JOHN SMITH, JILES WILLIAMS, JAMES ARTREE. No executor named. *Clerk of the Court:* JNO. MATTOCKE.

SIMMONS, BULLOCK.   Currituck County.

April 14, 1746. October Court, 1746. *Sons:* SOLOMON and WILLIS. *Daughter:* MARY SIMMONS. *Wife and Executrix:* ELISABETH. *Witnesses:* THOMAS LEGITT, WILLIS SIMMONS, ROBERT SIMMONS. *Clerk of the Court:* RICHARD MCCLURE.

SIMMONS, EDWARD.   Edgecombe Precinct.

October 5, 1735. November Court, 1735. *Daughters:* ELIZABETH and JANE HOLLEY, TOMAZIN, HANNAH. *Grandchildren:* JOHN and MARY JACKSON. *Wife and Executrix:* MARY. *Witnesses:* ANDREW JOHNSON, FRANCIS JOHNSON, BEN. RAWLINS. *Clerk of the Court:* RT. FORSTER.

SIMMONS, FRANCIS.   Currituck County.

October 25, 1757. December 20, 1757. *Son:* SAMUEL. *Brother and Executor:* JOHN SIMMONS. *Witnesses:* SAMUEL HOLSTEAD, JOHN BRABBELL, WILLIAM CHITTUM. *Clerk of the Court:* WM. MEARNS.

SIMMONS, HENRY.   Currituck County.

March 4, 1753. March Court, 1755. *Sons:* HILARY, SOLOMON, ASA, THOMAS. *Daughters:* RHODA and ABIAH. *Wife and Executrix:* DEBORAH. *Witnesses:* JAMES PHILLIPS, JOHN SIMMONS, SOLOMON SIMMONS. *Clerk of the Court:* WILLIAM SHERGOLD.

SIMMONDS, HENRY.   Bladen County.

January 9, 1758. January Court, 1758. *Brothers:* WILLIAM SIMMONDS, BENINJR MOORE. *Sisters:* ANN MOORE, JUDITH DAVIS. *Other legatee:* EDMUND FOGARTY. *Executors:* BENINJR MOORE, WILLIAM SIMMONDS, THOS. HALL. *Witnesses:* MARY SMITH, JOHN GRANGE, SAM'L WATTERS. *Clerk of the Court:* J. BURGWIN. Impression on seal of two fighting cocks under a crown.

SIMMONS, HENRY.   Onslow County.

August 7, 1770. April 18, 1774. *Sons:* EDWARD, JAMES, HENRY, JOSEPH, ELIJAH, SAMUEL and BENJAMIN (to these sons is devised lands on Holstons Creek, Browns Harrows, etc.). *Wife and Executrix:* MARTHA. *Witnesses:* THOS. DULANEY, MARY WARD, THOS. DULANEY. Proven before JO. MARTIN.

SIMMONS, JACOB.   New Hanover Precinct.

February 24, 1735–1736. June 16, 1736. Shallotte. *Sons:* JOHN (land on Little River and the Sound), JACOB (250 acres of land in the fork of Shallotte). *Daughter:* MARY SIMMONS. *Wife and Executrix:* MARY. *Trustee for minor son:* JONATHAN SWAIN, of Lockwoods Folly. *Witnesses:* PHEEBE MILLER, THOMAS HOPCRAFT, JEHOSHAPHAT HALLANDS. Proven before GAB. JOHNSTON.

SIMMONS, JAMES.   Currituck County.

August 15, 1753. March Court, 1755. *Son:* ISLES. *Brother:* SAMUEL SIMMONS. *Executor:* WILLIAM FERREBEE. *Witnesses:* SAMUEL SIMMONS, PETER SPRALLIN, GEORGE FISHER. *Clerk of the Court:* WM. SHERGOLD.

SIMMONS, MARY.   Perquimans County.

September 19, 1722. July 14, 1724. *Son:* THOMAS PEIRCE. *Daughter:* REBECKAH TOMES. *Grandchildren:* SARAH, JOSEPH, THOMAS, JOSEPH PEIRCE, MARY JONES, SARAH PETTELL, MARY and ISAIAH SMITH. *Executor:* THOMAS PEIRCE (land on Sound side). *Witnesses:* BENJAMIN SANDERS, CHARLES DENMAN. *Clerk of the Court:* RICHD. LEARY. *Executor* qualified before C. GALE, C. J.

SIMMONS, MATTHEW.   Albemarle County.

February 16, 1691–1692. *Daughters:* ANN and MARGARET SIMMONS. Remainder of will illegible.

SIMMONS, NICHOLAS.
   Will illegible.

SIMMONS, THOMAS.   Currituck County.
   February 22, 1755. September Court, 1755. *Sons:* THOMAS, SAMUEL
and SAMPSON ("my plantation to be divided between them"), EDOM, CALEB
and ASALEL. *Daughters:* MARY SIMMONS and ELIZABETH MUNCREEF and
SARAH MERCER. *Wife and Executrix:* SARAH. *Witnesses:* BENJAMIN
PRESCOOT, BENJAMIN COWEL, ELISABETH COWEL. *Clerk of the Court:*
WILLIAM SHERGOLD.

SIMONS, ANDREW.   Beaufort County.
   January 6, 1746-1747. April 7, 1752. *Sons:* WILLIAM, THOMAS, JOHN
JOSHUA ("This Beaverdam plantation whereon I now live"), GEORGE and
LEVI (100 acres of "Beaverdam land" to each). *Wife and Executrix:* MARY.
Executor: JOHN ODEON. *Witnesses:* ROBT. CUTLER, JOHN CARROL, ED-
WARD POYNER. Proven before GAB. JOHNSTON, at Bath Town. Impres-
sion of winged dragon on seal.

SIMONS, ARGILL.   Chowan Precinct.
   April 13, 1714. December 17, 1714. *Son:* JOHN. *Daughter:* MAR-
GREAT. *Cousin and Executor:* FRANCES FOSTER. *Witnesses:* THOMAS
HORTON, SARAH GRAY, P. SMITH. Proven before CHARLES EDEN. Device
on seal.

SIMONS, JOHN.   Chowan Precinct.
   June 2, 1731. June 25, 1732. *Sons:* JOHN, ARGILL. *Executors:* FRAN-
CIS BEASLEY, EDWARD STANDING. *Witnesses:* JAMES BEASLEY, FRANCIS
HARRISON. Proven before GEO. BURRINGTON.

SIMONS, JOHN.   Craven County.
   July 14, 1741. September 24, 1742. *Sons:* JOHN, DANIEL, MANUELL,
BENJAMIN, BUSETT (to each is devised a plantation). *Daughters:* KATH-
ERINE BANTER, MARY and ELIZABETH SIMONS. *Brother:* ABRAHAM BU-
SETT. *Wife:* MARGERETT (two negroes). No executor named. *Wit-
nesses:* MARTIN FRANCK, JOHN GOURLAY, CIVILL FRANCK. *Clerk of the
Court:* N. ROUTLEDGE.

SIMONS, JOHN.   Craven County.
   December 22, 1760. *Son:* WILLIAM. *Wife and Executrix:* MARY.
Executor: THOMAS SIMONS (brother). Land on Bay River and Trent sold
for debts. *Witnesses:* WILLIAM FULSHER, ANTHONY MOORE, ROBERT
BURNEY. No probate.

SIMPSON, ALEXANDER.

November 29, 1737. June 9, 1738. "Late of the Parish of Kennoway in the shire of Fife in that part of Great Britain called Scotland." *Executor and sole legatee:* JOHN CALDOM. *Witnesses:* R. EVERARD, HARMAN HILL, THOMAS HARVEY, WALLEY CHAUNCEY. Proven before GAB. JOHNSTON. Coat of arms on seal.

SIMPSON, WALTER. New Hanover County.

November 9, 1758. February Court, 1759. *Executor and sole legatee:* JOHN GARNES. *Witnesses:* BENJN. MORISON, ALEXANDER ADAMSON and ROBERT MCNAIR. *Clerk of the Court:* JA. MORAN.

SIMS, ROBERT. Bertie Precinct.

February Court, 1729. *Sons:* ROBERT ("my dwelling plantation"), THOMAS (land lying upon Oachoneche Neck), JAMES (land on Conaconara Swamp). *Brother and Executor:* JOHN SIMS. *Other devisee:* JOHN FYBASH. *Witnesses:* WILLIAM BOON, ELIAS FORD, NATHANIEL COOPER. *Deputy Clerk of the Court:* THOS. CREW.

SIMSON, JOHN. Knott's Island, in Currituck County.

March 19, 1744–1745. March Court, 1754. *Sons:* JAMES ("plantation I live on"), SOLOMON ("plantation THOMAS EVANS now lives on"), JOSHUA. *Wife:* SARAH. *Daughter:* MARY EVANS. *Executor:* THOMAS EVANS (son-in-law). *Witnesses:* HENRY WHITE, HILRA WHITE. *Clerk of the Court:* JOHN SNOAD.

SIMSON, WILLIAM. Albemarle County.

January 15, 1693–1694. April 17, 1694. *Sons:* WILLIAM and JOHN (negro to each). *Wife:* DORITY. *Executors:* JOHN THOMLIN and JOHN RAPER. *Witnesses:* ROBERT LOWRY and CHARLES TAYLOR. *Clerk of the Court:* EDWARD MAYO.

SINCLAIR, SAMUEL. Hyde County.

January 3, 1755. January 7, 1755. *Daughters:* ANN, CATHERINE, FRANCES and LUCIE. *Grandchildren:* WILLIAM and ANN THOMAS. *Wife and Executrix:* ELISABETH. *Executors:* JOHN STARKIE and STEPHEN LEE. Sawmill and land to be sold for debts. *Witnesses:* SAMUEL SWANN, THOMAS LOVICK, WILL MONAT. Proven before ARTHUR DOBBS.

SINGLETON, JOHN. Northampton County.

October 29, 1754. May Court, 1755. *Wife and Executrix:* MARTHA. *Other legatee:* ANNE MORRIS, daughter of wife (500 acres of land and one negro). *Executor:* GEORGE ROBERTSON. *Witnesses:* ARTHUR DICKESON, MATT HUBBARD, ARTHUR DICKESON, JR. *Clerk of the Court:* I. EDWARDS.

SINGLETON, SAMUEL.   Dobbs County.
   December 4, 1762. *Son:* SPYERS ("my plantation"). *Daughter:* MARTHA CASWELL. *Executors:* HANNAH (wife), RICHARD CASWELL, BENJAMIN CASWELL (son-in-law). *Witnesses:* ARTHUR YOUNG, FRANCIS WILLIAMS. Proven before ARTHUR DOBBS.

SITGREAVES, WILLIAM.   Carteret County.
   July 26, 1744. March Court, 1747. Port Beaufort. *Sons:* WILLIAM and THOMAS. *Executors:* STEPHEN FORD, MARY LINGARD (aunt, residing in Philadelphia). *Witnesses:* MICHEL PAQUINET, MARY PAQUINET, MICHEL PAQUINET. *Clerk of the Court:* GEORGE READ.

SITTERSON, JAMES.   Perquimans County.
   January 13, 1748. January Court, 1750. *Wife:* HANNAH SITTERSON. *Sons:* JAMES and SAMUEL. *Daughter:* MARY BARKER. *Executors:* Wife, HANNAH, and *son,* JAMES. *Witnesses:* JOHN HARVEY, JOHN NICKOLS, THOMAS NICKOLS. *Clerk of Court:* EDMUND HATCH.

SKINNER, JOHN.   Perquimans County.
   July 26, 1769. December 12, 1771. *Wife and Executrix:* SARAH. *Son:* STEVEN (silver shoe buckles, knee buckles and stock buckle, and all remainder of estate real and personal. Provision is made for his schooling in Carolina and other parts). *Executors:* EVAN, JOSHUA and WILLIAM SKINNER (brothers). *Witnesses:* DUKE BOGUE, WILLIAM JACKSON, JOSHUA SKINNER, JR. Proven before JO. MARTIN.

SKINNER, RICHARD, JR.   Perquimans County.
   January 10, 1746. January Court, 1746. *Wife and Executrix:* SARAH. *Executor:* JOHN HARVEY. *Witnesses:* SAMUEL STANDIN, ABRAM SANDERS, JOSHUA SKINNER. *Clerk of the Court:* EDMUND HATCH.

SKINNER, RICHARD.   Perquimans County.
   May 18, 1752. July Court, 1752. *Sons:* SAMUEL ("my plantation"), EAVENS ("plantation where JOHN SIMPSON now lives in Chowan"), JOSHUA (plantation on the Sound Side "formerly called Fendall's," being land purchased of CHRISTIAN REED), WILLIAM ("my backe plantation"), JOHN (plantation lying on the Sound side called "Petifers," being land purchased of CHRISTIAN REED). *Wife:* SARAH ("land where THOMAS MUNDS now lives in Chowan County"). Negroes divided among sons. *Friends:* JOSEPH WHITE, JOHN and BENJAMIN HARVEY. *Executrix:* SARAH SKINNER (wife). *Witnesses:* JOS. WHITE, PETER JONES and JOHN HARVEY. *Clerk of the Court:* EDMUND HATCH.

SLADE, GEORGE.   Chowan Precinct.

June 3, 1710. *Wife and Executrix:* MARY. *Other legatee:* JAMES PATCHETT. *Witnesses:* DANIEL LEIGH, RICHARD LAWRENCE, WILL NEWLAND. Original missing. Recorded in Book 1712–1722, page 32.

SLADE, HEZEKIAH.   Hyde County.

January 10, 1752. March Court, 1752. *Son:* JEREMIAH. *Daughters:* DINAH and REBECCA. *Wife and Executrix:* SARAH. *Executor:* BENJAMIN JEWEL. *Witnesses:* THOS. SMITH, BENJAMIN SLADE, JAMES HAMILTON. *Clerk of the Court:* FRANCIS EGLETON.

SLADE, JOHN.   Hyde County.

September 6, 1743. December Court, 1743. *Sons:* JOHN ("the plantation whereon I now live"), BENJAMIN (land bought of JOHN SMITH COOPER), HEZEKIAH and WILLIAM HODGES SLADE (land bought of FRANCIS BANKS). *Daughters:* MARY (wife of BENJAMIN JEWEL), SARAH and KEZIA SLADE. Stock marks of children are as follows: WM., "under square ye left ear"; BENJN., "crop & an under bit and one slit in the Right ear"; SARAH, "under square the right ear". *Wife and Executrix:* ABIGAIL. *Witnesses:* RICHARD LEATH, WILLIAM WILKINSON, URIAH COLLINS. *Clerk of the Court:* WILLIAM BARROW.

SLADE, SAMUEL.   Beaufort County.

March 17, 1746. December Court, 1746. *Daughters:* ELIZABETH (wife of WILLIAM DUNBARR), HANNAH (wife of WILLIAM FOSQUE), JANE (wife of JAMES BLOUNT), SUSANNAH ("my manner plantation"). *Grandchildren:* SAMUEL BLOUNT, MARY BLOUNT (1 slave to each), MARY DUNBARR (1 negro), SAMUELL DUNBARR (plantation on south side of Pamtico River "att the head of Blount's Creek and on a Branch known by the name of good neighborhood branch"). *Executors:* BENJAMIN RIGNEY and JACOB NEVELL. *Witnesses:* THOS. JAMES, PHILIP SHUTE, MARY DUNBAR. *Clerk of the Court:* JOHN FORBES.

SLAUGHTER, MICHAEL.   Chowan County.

February 2, 1741. February 6, 1741. Edenton. *Daughters:* ANAH, ABIGAIL, ELIZABETH, NANCY, REBECKAH and DEBORAH SLAUGHTER. *Wife and Executrix:* ELIZABETH. *Witnesses:* JOHN PARK, ROBERT and ABIGAL FRENCH. Proven before GAB. JOHNSTON.

SLOBOCK, JACOB.   Carteret County.

October 13, 1755. March Court, 1756. *Son:* NATHAN. *Executor and brother-in-law:* JAMES SMITH. *Witnesses:* PHILEMON HUNTT, AMOS SMALL, SARAH SMALL. *Clerk of the Court:* JOHN SMITH.

SLOCKUM, ANTHONY.   Albemarle County.
November 26, 1688. *Son:* JOHN ("plantation I now live upon").
Grandsons: JOHN SLOCKUM, SAMUEL SLOCKUM (200 acres of land), JOSEPH
(200 acres of land), THOMAS and JOSEPH GILBERT. *Granddaughter:*
SARAH GILBERT. *Executor:* JOHN SLOCKUM (son). *Witnesses:* JOHN
WIMPELE, WILLIAM DOBSON, NICHOLAS CRISP. No probate.

SLOCOMB, JOHN.   Craven Precinct.
March 28, 1722. September 19, 1722. *Sons:* JOHN ("my dwelling
plantation"), JOSEPH (land known as JOSIAS SLOCUM'S), JESEWAY and
JOSIAS (land on Mill Branch and one Mustee boy). *Daughter:* ELISABETH
SLOCOM (land on Mill Branch and one mustee boy). Proven before
RICHARD GRAVES by CAPT. WILLIAM HANDCOCK. *Clerk of the Court:* C.
METCALFE. No signature of testator or witnesses.

SLOCUMB, JOHN.   Craven County.
December 17, 1759. *Cousins:* JOSEPH and JOHN CHARLES SLOCUMB.
Mother: MARY SLOCUMB. *Wife:* MARY. *Executors:* JOHN DONELSON,
JACOB TAYLOR. *Witnesses:* GRIGG YARBOROUGH, HUGH HOWY. No
probate.

SLOCOM, SAMUEL.   Bath County.
May 8, 1712. April 25, 1713. *Brothers:* WILLIAM and SOLOMON
SMITH, and JOHN SLOCOM. *Sister:* ISEBLE SMITH. *Other legatee:* MARGET
DAVIS. *Witnesses:* WM. BRICE, LOUIS THOMAS, ANN BRICE. Proven
before WM. BRICE. *Clerk of the Court:* J. PALIN.

SMALL, BENJAMIN.   Carteret County.
January 11, 1751. March Court, 1752. *Sons:* BENJAMIN (plantation
bought of DAVID BALY), JONAS (land adjoining BENJAMIN), AMOS (100
acres of land adjoining THOMAS JESSOP), JOHN KNITE SMALL ("my
manna plantation"). *Daughter:* SARAH JESSOP. *Wife and Executrix:*
MIRIAM. *Witnesses:* HENRY STANTON, PATIENCE BULL. *Clerk of the
Court:* GEORGE READ.

SMALL, BENJAMIN.   Carteret County.
June Court, 1756. *Sons:* BENJAMIN and JONAS SMALL. *Wife:* not
named. *Executor:* JOHN LOVET (father-in-law). *Witnesses:* LEWIS
WELCH, JOHN KNIGHTS SMALL. *Clerk of the Court:* JNO. SMITH.

SMELAGE, EDWARD.   Onslow County.
December 9, 1744. New River. *Daughter:* SARAH SMELAGE. *Wife
and Executrix:* ANNE. *Witnesses:* WILLIAM MARCHMENT, DAVID BUM-
PUS, THOMAS BUMPUS. No probate.

SMEWIN, HENMAN.   Albemarle County.
July 17, 1673. November 3, 1673. *Friend and Executor:* THOMAS EAST-
CHURCH, who is appointed guardian for JOHN, MARGARET and ELIZABETH
WHITE, children of HENRY WHITE, dec'd. *Witnesses:* GEORGE WALKER,
THO. HASSOLD. *Clerk of the Court:* THOMAS HARRIS.

SMITH, ANDREW.
March 22, 1756. April 14, 1760. Cape Fear. *Wife and Executrix:* ANN.
Witnesses: ISAAC WALDRON, JACOB WALDRON, RACHEL WALDRON. Proven
before ARTHUR DOBBS.

SMITH, EDWARD.   Pasquotank Precinct.
July 10, 1690. July Court, 1690. *Witnesses:* THO. DAVIS, DAVID
PRICHARD, ANN BARTLETT. *Clerk of the Court:* PAUL LATHUM. Will illegible.

SMITH, EDWARD.
August 20, 1727. June 10, 1735. *Executor and sole legatee:* ROGER
MOORE. *Witnesses:* JNO. MOORE, JUSTINA MOORE, RICHARD JAMES
PARKER. *Clerk of the Court:* HUGH CAMPBELL.

SMITH, GEORGE.   Bertie County.
March 1, 1735. April 16, 1736. *Sons:* RICHARD and GEORGE ("the
manner plantation"), JOHN and LEWIS (land at Cottanoe). *Daughter:*
MARY (plantation in Tyrrell). *Wife and Executrix:* ELIZABETH (two negroes). *Witnesses:* EDWARD COLLINS, THOMAS GAINS, CHARLES ARRINGTON. Proven before W. SMITH, C. J.

SMITH, GEORGE.   Northampton County.
January 21, 1745–1746. February Court, 1746. *Sons:* WILLIAM, JEREMIAH ("my plantation"). *Daughters:* MARTHA JONES, ELIZABETH BALDWIN, MARY BARRETT, SUSANNAH, SARAH, RACHEL and CAROLINE PENELLOPE SMITH, ELIZABETH SMITH. *Executors:* JEREMIAH SMITH and THOMAS
BARRETT. *Witnesses:* JAMES SMITH, JAMES JONES. *Clerk of the Court:*
RT. FORSTER.

SMITH, HENRY.   Craven County.
August 4, 1748. November 2, 1748. *Sons:* DAVID ("plantation I now
live on" and all cattle in his mark "which is a crop in the right ear and slit
in ye left Ear"), HENRY (land on Nuse River), JOHN (one negro boy "and
one gray mare that has been much bit with wolves"), SAMUEL (one negro).
Daughters: SARAH (cattle), NANNEY (one negro boy), ELIZABETH (one

mustee boy), OLIF (one negro) and REBECKAH SMITH (one negro). *Executor:* DAVID SMITH (son). *Witnesses:* HENRY GARRALD, CHARLES SMITH, JOHN HARDEE. Proven before E. HALL, C. J.

SMITH, JAMES.   Perquimans County.

December 8, 1735. April Court, 1736. *Sons:* JAMES ("plantation I now live on"), SOLOMON (land called Forte Point), JOHN (land called Beaver Dam Neck). *Daughters:* ELIZABETH SMITH ("1 mulatter boy"), MARY SMITH. *Wife and Executrix:* ANN. *Executor:* MACKRORA SCARBOROUGH. *Witnesses:* FRANCIS PENRICE, SAMUELL BOUNDS, JOHN HARMAN. *Clerk of the Court:* JAMES CRAVEN.

SMITH, JAMES.   Craven County.

March 27, 1745. April 8, 1745. *Son and Executor:* JAMES. *Daughters:* MARY and MARTHA SMITH. *Wife and Executrix:* MARTHA. *Executor:* WILLIAM BRICE. *Witnesses:* THOMAS SMITH, BENJAMIN SANDERSON, JNO. SNOAD. Proven before GAB. JOHNSTON.

SMITH, JAMES.   Beaufort County.

September 3, 1744. March Court, 1749. *Wife and Executrix:* ANN ("my manner plantation"). *Executor:* JAMES DODLEY. *Witnesses:* JAMES SINGLETON, MARY DUDLEY, JOHN SMITH. *Clerk of the Court:* JOHN ALDORSON.

SMITH, JEREMIAH.

June 10, 1720. July 12, 1720. *Wife:* MARGARET. *Executor:* THOMAS SIMMONS. *Witnesses:* THO. TAYLOR, ESTER TAYLOR, THO. TAYLOR, JR. *Clerk of the Court:* JO. WICKER.

SMITH, JOHN.   Bertie Precinct.

December 12, 1728. August Court, 1729. *Son:* JOHN ("my manour plantation"). *Daughters:* MARY and JANE SMITH. *Wife and Executrix:* JUDITH. *Executors:* JAMES BOONE and THOMAS MACKELENDING. *Witnesses:* GEORGE WHITE, WILLIAM JONES and CHARITY WHITE. No probate.

SMITH, JOHN.   Chowan Precinct.

January 30, 1731–1732. *Wife and Executrix:* ELIZABETH. *Witnesses:* JOHN CHAMPEN, HUMPHREY WEBB, RICHARD BOND. No probate.

SMITH, JOHN.   Hyde County.

December 17, 1748. March 7, 1748. *Sons:* WILLIAM (lands on Matchapungo River and Slades Creek), THOMAS, JAMES, BENJAMIN, JOHN (plantation to each), SAMUEL (lands known as Mouse harbor). *Daughters:* MAR-

THA and ELIZABETH. *Wife and Executrix:* MARY. *Witnesses:* JONATHAN JASPER, CATHERINE JASPER, URIAH COLLINS. *Clerk of the Court:* THOS. LOACK.

SMITH, JOHN.   Craven County.

August 15, 1768. October 9, 1770. Newbern. *Son:* JOHN TRINK SMITH ("all my estate"). *Mother:* MARTHA SMITH. *Mother-in-law:* HANNAH FRINK and her daughter HANNAH FRINK (twenty pounds to each). *Wife:* DEBORAH. *Daughter-in-law:* SARAH OUTERBRIDGE (two negroes). *Son-in-law:* RAMSEY WHITE OUTERBRIDGE (two negroes). *Sister:* HANNAH FRINK. *Uncle and Aunt:* JOHN and PRUDENCE HARDY, in Blossom Street, Norton Falgate, London. *Other legatee:* RICHARD SALTER, of Newgate in London. *Executors:* JAMES REED, RICHARD BLACKLEDGE, JACOB SHEPPARD and JAMES COOR. *Witnesses:* JOSEPH CRISPIN, MARY HAWK, FRANCIS CHILD. Proven before WM. TRYON.

SMITH, JOHN.   Hyde County.

March 20, 1772. *Sons:* JOSHUA, THOMAS and STEPHEN SMITH (land and negroes), JOHN (one negro). *Grandson:* JOHN SMITH. *Executors:* STEPHEN, JOSHUA and THOMAS SMITH (sons). *Witnesses:* SAMUEL DAVIS, THOMAS MACKWILLAMS, ABIGAL SLAID. No probate.

SMITH, JOSEPH.   Perquimans County.

October 2, 1724. July 17, 1732. *Sons:* JOHN, JOSEPH (land in Ballyhack). *Daughter:* ELISABETH SMITH. *Wife and Executrix:* LEAH. *Executor:* SAMUEL PHELPS. *Witnesses:* ROBERT WILSON, LUKE NOBLIN, THOMAS ELLIOT. *Clerk of the Court:* CHARLES DENMAN.

SMITH, LEVI.   Currituck Precinct.

August 29, 1709. January 10, 1715–1716. *Son:* JEREMIAH. *Wife and Executrix:* SARAH ("all my estate"). *Witnesses:* THO. TAYLOR, EDWD. TAYLOR, JOS. WICKER. *Clerk of the Court:* JOS. WICKER.

SMITH, NICHOLAS.   Beaufort County.

April 14, 1751. June Court, 1751. *Son and Executor:* SIMON. *Wife and Executrix:* MARY. *Witnesses:* ANDREW and RICHARD BROWN, THOMAS WILLIAMS. *Clerk of the Court:* WILLIAM ORMOND.

SMITH, RICHARD.   Pasquotank County.

January 10, 1750–1751. April Court, 1751. *Wife and Executrix:* MARY ANN SMITH. *Executor:* HENRY PENDLETON. *Witnesses:* HENRY PENDLETON, GEORGE PENDLETON, ANN MEADS. *Clerk of the Court:* THO. TAYLOR.

SMITH, RICHARD.   Northampton County.

July 26, 1751. February Court, 1756. *Legatees:* DRURY and MARY ALDRIDG and RICHARD SMITH (grandson). *Executors:* HENRY ARTHUR SMITH (son), ROBERT STURT. *Witnesses:* JOHN PETERSON, ROBERT STUART, WM. COCKE. *Clerk of the Court:* I. EDWARDS.

SMITH, RICHARD.   Edgecombe County.

December 17, 1756. May Court, 1757. *Sons:* RICHARD, STEPHEN, WILLIAM (to each is devised 73 acres of land), BENJAMIN ("my plantation"). *Wife and Executrix:* SARAH. *Witnesses:* JOHN DOYLE, CHARLES DODSON. *Clerk of the Court:* JOS. MONTFORT.

SMITH, ROBERT.   Perquimans Precinct.

February 13, 1692–1693. May 1, 1693. *Son:* JOSEPH. *Daughter:* ELIZABETH. *Son-in-law:* SAMUEL WOOD. *Executors:* WILLIAM and JOHN GODFREY. *Witnesses:* THOMAS STEELE, ELIZABETH GODFREY, SAMUEL WOOD. *Clerk of the Court:* EDWARD MAYO.

SMITH, ROBERT.   Bertie County.

January 26, 1726. May Court, 1726. *Son:* ROBERT (one plantation). *Daughters:* ELIZABETH and MARY SMITH. *Wife and Executrix:* MARY. *Executor:* BARRABY MELTON. *Witnesses:* WILLIAM LOW, JOHN LOW, JOHN WERHAM. *Clerk of the Court:* RT. FORSTER.

SMITH, SARAH.   Currituck Precinct.

February 22, 1721–1722. *Son and Executor:* THOMAS TAYLOR. *Witnesses:* CORNELIUS JONES, ANN PEACOCK, AND. PEACOCK. *Clerk of the Court:* JOHN MARTYN.

SMITH, THOMAS.   Albemarle County.

November 4, 1706. *Legatees:* MARGRITT CUTTLER and JAMES WARD (*Executor*). *Witnesses:* JNO. ALLCOCK, STEPHEN SWAINE, PATRICKE CAVYELTON. No probate.

SMITH, THOMAS.   Beaufort County.

December 12, 1752. March Court, 1753. *Son:* JAMES. *Daughter:* MARY SMITH. *Wife and Executrix:* MARY. *Witnesses:* GEORGE GERRARD, THOMAS HENLY, SAMLL. TAYLOR. *Clerk of the Court:* WILLIAM ORMOND.

SMITH, THOMAS.   Edgecombe County.

March 10, 1757. May Court, 1757. *Wife and Executrix:* not named. *Executor:* BANJAMIN HAILE. *Witnesses:* JOHN and SUSANA JONES. *Clerk of the Court:* JOSEPH MONTFORT.

SMITH, WILLIAM.

December 28, 1716. October 24, 1724. Little River. *Wife and Executrix:* ELISABETH. *Witnesses:* RO. BUCKNER, JOHN FOURRE. *Clerk of the Court:* JOHN CORNICK. Will proven before GEORGE BURRINGTON.

SMITH, WILLIAM. Pasquotank Precinct.

March 14, 1719–1720. May 11, 1734. *Son:* JOHN ("my land and plantation"). *Daughter:* LYDIA SMITH. *Wife and Executrix:* ELIZABETH SMITH. *Executors:* JOHN SMITH (brother), WM. RELFE. *Witnesses:* W. NORRIS, WM. RELFE, RICHARD RELFE. Proven before NATH. RICE.

SMITH, WILLIAM. Tyrrell County.

February 12, 1741–1742. March 16, 1742. *Sons:* THOMAS, SAMUEL and JOHN (1 shilling to each). *Wife and Executrix:* ELIZABETH. *Witnesses:* WINEFORD COMBS, MARY MACKEY, ANN MACKE. Proven before W. SMITH, C. J. *Clerk of the Court:* W. DOWNING.

SMITH, WILLIAM. Chowan County.

March 30, 1743. July Court, 1743. *Legatees:* ROBERT HALTON (box of china at ABRAHAM BLACKALL'S), BENJAMIN HILL, DAVID COLETRANE, JAMES CRAVEN, JOSEPH ANDERSON, JOSEPH HARREN, DR. WILLIAM CATHCART and DR. ABRAHAM BLACKALL, THOMAS JONES, GABRIEL JOHNSTON, JAMES TROTTER. *Executors:* GABRIEL JOHNSTON and ROBERT HALTON. *Witnesses:* T. BARKER, WILLIAM HERRITAGE, ALEXR. MCCULLOCH. *Clerk of the Court:* RICHD. MCCLURE.

SMITH, WILLIAM. Craven County.

September 4, 1749. March 20, 1749. *Sons:* JAMES ("my plantation"), RICHARD. *Daughters:* MARY and ELIZABETH (one mulatto slave to each), SARY ANN SMITH. *Wife and Executrix:* SARAH. *Witnesses:* LEVI TREWHITT, ANDREW BASS, ISABELLA KEITH. *Clerk of the Court:* PHIL. SMITH.

SMITH, WILLIAM. Chowan County.

April 26, 1755. July Court, 1755. "Late of the Shire of Perth in North Britain, but now of Chowan Precinct in Carolina." *Brothers:* JOHN and JAMES SMITH. *Sister:* ISABEL SMITH, relict of THOMAS EMERS. *Executor:* WILLIAM MEARNS. *Witnesses:* THOMAS BARKER, ROBERT LENOX. *Clerk of the Court:* THOMAS JONES.

SMITHSON, THOMAS. Pasquotank County.

November 2, 1743. January Court, 1743. *Sons:* JOSHUA ("plantation whereon I now live to him and his ears, and so from eair to eair so long as there is a SMITHSON to be found"), JOSEPH and JOHN (land to each). *Daughters:* MERIAM and DORKIS SMITHSON (1 negro to each), MARY MURDEN, TAMER NORRIS. *Wife and Executrix:* ANN. *Witnesses:* EDMOND JACKSON, RICHARD PRICHARD. *Clerk of the Court:* THO. TAYLOR.

SMITHWICK, ANN.   Bath Precinct.

November 5, 1711. *Executors and legatees:* Brothers and sisters, not named. *Witnesses:* CHARLES HOPTON, ——— GATLING. No probate.

SMITHWICK, EDWARD.   Chowan County.

January 21, 1715. October 16, 1716. *Sons:* EDWARD, SAMUEL and JOHN. *Daughter:* SARAH (land on Morattock River). *Executors:* WILLIAM CHARLTON and LUKE MIZELL. *Witnesses:* ROBERT ANDERSON, STEPHEN ALDERSS. *Clerk of the Court:* R. HICKS.

SMITHWICK, JOHN.

August 28, 1696. January Court, 1696. Archdaill. *Wife and Executrix:* HANNA. *Daughter:* SARY SMITHWICK. *Witnesses:* THOMAS HARLOE, CHARLES SMITH. *Clerk of the Court:* CHARLES DENMAN.

SNEDEKER, GARRET.   New Hanover County.

July 7, 1770. August 24, 1770. *Wife:* MARGARET. *Brothers:* TUNIS and THEODORANS SNEDEKER. *Nephew:* THEODORANS WARING, son of JAMES WARING (land on the Widow Moore's Creek). No executor appointed. *Witnesses:* DANIEL AUSTIN, ANNE AUSTIN, FRANCIS TOMLINSON. Proven before WM. TRYON.

SNELL, ROGER.

June, 1708. November 26, 1708. *Son:* ROGER. *Wife and Executrix:* ELIZABETH. *Daughter:* KATHERINE. *Witnesses:* WILL FRILIE, WILLIAM BOULER, NICHOLAS TYLOR. Proven before STEPHEN CARY, *Governor*.

SNELL, ROGER.   Duplin County.

October 27, 1758. April 11, 1759. *Sons:* JAMES (land and two negroes), ROGER ("my plantation and three negroes"). *Daughters:* PURTHANY SNELL, MARY KING, REBECCA HERRING (negroes to each). *Sons-in-law:* ABRAHAM HERRING and MICHAEL KING. *Wife:* ANN. *Executors:* MICHAEL KING and GEORGE BELL. *Witnesses:* JOHN KING, JOHN CANADY, JESSE BELL. *Clerk of the Court:* JOHN DICKSON.

SNELLIN, ISRAEL.   Albemarle County.

August 31, 1700. September 6, 1700. *Daughter:* RACHELL SNELLIN (plantation after decease of *wife*, HANNAH SNELLIN). *Daughter:* ESTER

SNELLIN. *Executors:* HANNAH SNELLIN, ISAAC WILLSON. *Witnesses:* SAMUEL NICHOLSON, JOSEPH PEINE, FRANCIS TOMES, JR. *Secretary of State:* SAML. SWANN.

SNOAD, HENRY. Beaufort County.

May 20, 1752. December 12, 1752. *Sons:* JOHN PEYTON SNOAD ("plantation whereon I now live, plantation I bought of JOHN LANE, my silver watch, silver-hilted sword, silver shoe and knee buckles, six silver spoons, silver can, gold sleeve buttons, mahogany desk, gilt framed looking-glass and large china bowl"), BENJAMIN SNOAD (plantation in the Cow-pen Neck, plantation at the mouth of White Oak River on Queens Creek, "my silver-hilted sword that was my father's, six large silver spoons, black walnut looking-glass and all my china"). *Daughter:* ANN SNOAD (plantation at the mouth of Blount's Creek, six silver spoons, silver tea tongs and silver pepper box). *Sister:* MARY LANE (money "to purchase head stones for her son, JOHN SNOAD LANE, who lies buried in my orchard"). *Friends and Executors:* WALLEY CHAUNCEY (1 horse, bridle and saddle and one case pistols and gun. To wife of WALLEY, AUNT CHAUNCEY, is bequeathed 40s for ring), JAMES BONNER (gun and sword), JOHN HARDEE. *Apprentice:* WILLIAM OGLESBY. *Witnesses:* SAMUEL BOUTWELL, ANNE WILLOUGHBY, GRIFFITH HOWELL. *Clerk of the Court:* WILL. ORMOND.

SNOAD, JOHN. Beaufort County.

June 21, 1743. September 1, 1743. *Sons:* HENRY ("my plantation," land on Little Beaver Dam, Maule's Neck; land on Herring Run, on the north side of Pamlico River; land on Grindell Creek), WILLIAM (lands on Pamlico River and in the fork of May's Beaver Dam), JOHN (land on Grindell Creek). To each of sons is bequeathed negroes. *Daughters:* MARY, ANNE and ELIZABETH SNOAD (negroes to each). To sons HENRY and WILLIAM is bequeathed two periaugers. *Son-in-law:* JOHN FRY. *Wife:* ELIZABETH (6 negroes). *Executors:* WILLIAM MARTIN and WALLEY CHAUNCEY (brothers-in-law), HENRY SNOAD (son). *Witnesses:* HENRY, ELIZABETH and ZACHR. LUCAS. Proven before J. MONTGOMERY.

SNOAD, WILLIAM. Beaufort County.

March 15, 1746. April 8, 1747. *Wife:* PATIENCE (lands on White Oak and Queens Creeks). *Other legatees:* MARY LANE, ANNE BONNER, ELIZABETH SNOAD (sisters). *Executors:* THOMAS BONNER, SIMON JONES, EDWARD SALTER and JAMES BONNER. *Witnesses:* JOEL MARTIN, ANN MARTIN, SARAH MARTIN, ANN SALTER, MARY BRICKLE. Proven before E. HALL, C. J.

ABSTRACT OF WILLS, 1690—1760. 351

SNODEN, SAMUEL. Pasquotank County.

December 5, 1750. July Court, 1753. *Wife and Executrix:* SARAH. *Other legatee:* GRACE, daughter of GEORGE SNODEN. *Executor:* ROBERT BAILEY. *Witnesses:* JAMES GREGORIE, ROBERT BAILEY, DEBORAH SUTTON. *Clerk of the Court:* THO. TAYLOR.

SNODEN, THOMAS. Perquimans County.

February 24, 1727–1728. October Court, 1736. *Sons:* JOHN (land in Bertie and stock in his mark, "the said mark being upon Record"), JOSEPH (land in Bertie), WILLIAM, GEORGE and SAMUEL (land in Perquimans divided among them), SOLOMON and LAMUELL. *Executors:* SAMUEL SWANN and JNO. SNODEN. *Witnesses:* RICHARD ROBINS, ABRAHAM JENETT, THOS. TRUMBLE. *Clerk of the Court:* JAMES CRAVEN.

SNOUCK, DANIEL. Perquimans Precinct.

June 1, 1712. *Friends:* THOMAS LILY, JOHN, SARAH, MARGARET and ELIZABETH LILY (children of THOMAS). *Wife and Executrix:* MARGRETT. *Executor:* WILLIAM KITSHING. *Witnesses:* WILLIAM CARMAN, TIMOTHY TAYLOR, FRANCIS JOHNES. *Clerk of the Court:* RICHARD LEARY.

SNOWDEN, JOSEPH. Perquimans County.

November 20, 1740. January Court, 1740. *Brothers:* JOHN, GEORGE and WILLIAM SNOWDEN. *Niece:* THOMSON SNOWDEN. *Executors:* JOHN and WILLIAM SNOWDEN (brothers). *Witnesses:* BENJAMIN BAPTISS, AARON MOSES, WILLIAM LAYDEN. *Clerk of the Court:* EDMUND HATCH.

SNOWDON, ELIZABETH. Perquimans County.

May 31, 1744. January Court, 1744. *Sons:* WILLIAM, FRANCIS, GEORGE and ISACK LAYDEN. *Granddaughter:* ELIZABETH LAYDEN. *Grandsons:* ROBERT and JOSEPH WARREN. *Executors:* GEORGE and FRANCIS LAYDEN (sons). *Witnesses:* SAMLL. SWANN, SARAH SWANN, MARY SWANN. *Clerk of the Court:* EDMUND HATCH.

SOANE, JOHN. Bertie County.

March 16, 1732–1733. August Court, 1733. *Sons:* HALLEDAY and WILLIAM. *Daughters:* ELIZABETH and ANNA. *Wife and Executrix:* HANNAH. *Witnesses:* LEWIS BRYAN, ELIZABETH DUNCAN. *Clerk of the Court:* RT. FORSTER.

SOLLEY, JOHN. Pasquotank County.

June, 1751. April Court, 1752. *Sons:* THOMAS (land on Neuse River bounding on Beards Creek), JOSEPH ("my plantation whereon I now live").

To each son is given two negroes. *Daughters:* MARY CLEVES, ANN WIAT. *Executor:* JOSEPH (son). *Witnesses:* TABITHA EMERSON, THOMAS EMERSON, JOHN GRAY. *Clerk of the Court:* THO. TAYLOR.

SOMERSET, SEYMORE.   Northampton County.

December 20, 1751. February Court, 1752. *Sons:* JOHN ("my plantation"), SEYMORE. *Daughters:* EASTER SOMERSETT, ELIZABETH EARP (*Executrix*). *Witnesses:* EDWARD EARP, MANUAL EARP, WM. WINBORNE. *Clerk of the Court:* I. EDWARDS.

SOTHELL, SETH.   Albemarle County.

January 20, 1689–1690. February Court, 1693–1694. *Executrix:* ANNA SOTHELL. THOMAS HARTLEY (plantation for five years, Signory on Flatty Creek and Pasquotank River until death). *Father-in-law:* EDWARD FOSTER (plantation at Cuscopincum and 30 head of cattle). WILLIAM DUNKINFIELD, WILLIAM WILKESON and HENDERSON WALKER (five pounds each for gold ring), EDWARD WADE (plantation on Little River until death). ANNA BLUNT, *wife* (all estate and personal property not otherwise willed). *Witnesses:* WM. WILKESON, HENDERSON WALKER, JOHN LOWES, WILL. WOLLARD, SARAH WOLLARD. *Clerk of the Court:* EDWARD MAYO.

SOUTHERLAND, JOHN.   Donwoody County, Virginia.

March 27, 1771. April 5, 1771. *Son:* FENDALL. *Daughters:* ELIZABETH, SARAH and MARY ANN. *Wife:* ANN (lot in Peters Burg). *Executor:* FENDALL SOUTHERLAND (brother). *Witnesses:* WILLIAM ROBERTSON, JOSEPH BELL, WM. ROBERTS. Proven before WILLIAM TRYON.

SOWELL, CHARLES.   Bertie Precinct.

November 25, 1738. February Court, 1738. *Sons:* RICHARD (land on Bear Swamp), THOMAS (plantation "where ADAM HARRELL now dwells"), LEWIS (land on horse swamp), CHARLES ("my manner plantation"). *Daughters:* ELIZABETH, HANNAH, MARY and SARAH SOWELL. *Wife and Executrix:* MARTHA. *Executor:* BENJAMIN WYNNS. *Witnesses:* EBANAZAR SLASON, THOMAS SOWELL, RICHARD HOLMES, ELIZA HARRELL, JNO. WYNNS. *Clerk of the Court:* JNO. WYNNS.

SOWELL, JOHN.   Bertie County.

March 28, 1750. February Court, 1755. *Sons:* JOHN (land), JAMES (one negro), FRANCIS. *Daughters:* MARY, ELIZABETH, FERIBY, ANN. *Wife and Executrix:* ANN. *Executor:* JAMES JONES. *Witnesses:* ADHAM HARRILL, JOHN FREEMAN, PAUL BUNCH. *Clerk of the Court:* SAML. ORMES.

Abstract of Wills, 1690—1760.   353

SOWELL, RICHARD.   Bertie County.

July 5, 1751. August Court, 1751. *Sons:* RICHARD, AARON ("my maner plantation"). *Wife:* MARTHA. *Executors:* JOHN and OBEDIAH SOWELL. *Witnesses:* ELEAZR. QUINBY (?), AARON OLIVER, WILLIAM BENNET. *Clerk of the Court:* SAML. ORMES.

SOWERBY, HENRY.   Northampton County.

June 22, 1747. August Court, 1747. *Son:* JOHN ("my plantation" and one negro). *Wife and Executrix:* SARAH. *Witnesses:* CHAS. STEVENS, BENJAMIN DEBERRY, ELIZA STEVENS. *Clerk of the Court:* RT. FORSTER.

SPARKMAN, JOHN.   Chowan County.

April 19, 1728. October Court, 1728. *Grandsons:* JOHN and STEPHEN SPARKMAN (land on the "Liking Root Branch"). *Sons:* JOHN, RICHARD, THOMAS, WILLIAM. *Daughters:* SARAH and MARY SPARKMAN. *Executor:* JOHN GREEN. *Witnesses:* JOHN WIGGINS, JOHN HORNE, JOHN GREEN. *Clerk of the Court:* RT. FORSTER.

SPARKMAN, JOHN.   Chowan County.

April 25, 1738. July 14, 1739. *Sons:* THOMAS, JOHN. *Wife:* SARAH. *Executors:* ROBERT and WILLIAM REDDICK. *Witnesses:* THOMAS PILAND, THOMAS HARRELL, THOMAS HARRELL. Proven before W. SMITH.

SPARNON, JOSEPH.   Pasquotank County.

May 15, 1718. *Legatees:* WILLIAM BRETTNO, WILLIAM and ANN BRETTNO (children of WILLIAM), JOHN BLISH, ABRAHAM THOMAS. *Executor:* not named. *Witnesses:* JOSEPH COOPER, THOMAS SHEPARD, ELIZABETH COOPER, JOHN BELL. No probate.

SPARROW, THOMAS.

May 20, 1717. May 27, 1717. *Sons:* SOLOMON ("my maner plantation"), JOHN and KINSEY (plantations above the "maner" plantation), SOLOMON (cattle). *Wife:* not named. *Brother and Executor:* THOMAS HARDING. *Witnesses:* JAMES LEIGH, ELIEZER LILLINGTON, JOHN LILLINGTON. Proven before CHAS. EDEN.

SPEIGHT, FRANCIS.   Chowan County.

October 16, 1749. January Court, 1749. *Sons:* MOSES (plantation at Contenteny and four negroes), JOHN and JOSEPH (land on wolfpit valley). *Brother:* WILLIAM SPEIGHT. *Wife and Executrix:* KATHERN. *Witnesses:* JOHN SANDERS, FRANCIS SANDERS, DANIEL CARCH. *Clerk of the Court:* WILL. MEARNS.

23

SPEIR, ELIZABETH. Pitt County.

October 9, 1773. March 23, 1774. *Nephews:* JOSEPH WARREN (two negroes), WILLIAM SMYDICK, MARKE MESELL (three negroes). *Other legatees:* MARY SMYDICK, JOHN SMYDICK, EDMOND SMYDICK, FAMALER SMYDICK, MARY MEESEL, ELIZABETH WARREN, JOSEPH WARREN, JAMES and MATHEW SCOTT, WILLIAM MEESEL. *Executors:* MARK MEESEL and JOSEPH WARREN, JR. *Witnesses:* GEO. EVANS, JOHN HARDEE, MAJOR HARRIS. Proven before JO. MARTIN.

SPEIR, JAMES. Bertie County.

December 12, 1731. February Court, 1731. *Son:* JAMES (plantation on Ahoskie). *Wife and Executrix:* ANN ("my manner plantation" and two negroes). *Daughters:* MORNING SPEIR, SARAH EVERITT. *Daughters-in-law:* SARAH and PATIENCE STALLINGS. *Witnesses:* ROBERT GREAVES, CULMER SESSOMS, JNO. SUTTON. *Clerk of the Court:* RT. FORSTER.

SPEIR, JOHN.

January 8, 1761. June Court, 1767. *Wife:* ELIZABETH (negro boy and other chattels). *Daughters:* CLEARE HARDEE ("all my lands in North Carolina"), PATIENCE JEFFREYS, APSELE HOLLAND. *Executors:* JOHN and WILLIAM SPEIR (brothers) and ALEXANDER STEWART. *Witnesses:* WM. SPEIR, ALEXR. STEWART, JOHN SPEIR, JUNR. *Clerk of the Court:* AMB COX BAYLEY.

SPELLER, HENRY. Bertie Precinct.

April 5, 1727. *Son:* THOMAS ("plantation I now dwell on lying on the North side of Moratock River"). *Daughter:* ANN SPELLER (land on Smithwick Creek below Scewocca). *Wife:* PATIENCE. *Executor:* THOMAS PARRIS, of Edenton (brother). *Witnesses:* WILLIAM LITTLE, THO. BETTERLEY, W. BADHAM, ANN ISMAY. No probate. Impression of lion rampant on seal.

SPELLER, PATIENCE. Bertie Precinct.

February 3, 1738–1739. February Court, 1738. *Sons:* JAMES SWAIN and THOMAS SPELLER (one mulatto boy to each), RICHARD SWAIN. *Daughters:* PATIENCE RAY, ANNE WARD (negroes to each). *Grandchildren:* SARAH, JOHN and ELIZABETH SMITHWICK, WILLIAM SWAIN. *Executors:* JAMES SWAIN and THOMAS SPELLER (sons). *Witnesses:* CHARLTON MIZELL, PHILIP WARD. *Clerk of the Court:* JOHN WYNNS.

SPENCE, ALEXANDER. Pasquotank Precinct.

August 2, 1734. April Court, 1735. *Sons:* JAMES (240 acres of land on the Eastern Shore in Maryland), ALEXANDER, JOSEPH (land on Pasquotank River), ROBERT (land adjoining RICHARD FERRIL, ABEL ROSS, JOHN TRUE-

BLOOD), TRUMAN (appointed *Executor*). *Daughters:* JANE and CATHERINE
SAWYER. *Witnesses:* JEREMIAH MURDEN, THOMAS SAWYER, EVIN LURRY.
Clerk of the Court: JOS. SMITH.

SPENCE, JAMES.   Pasquotank Precinct.

March 20, 1739–1740. October Court, 1740. *Sons:* ALEXANDER, DAVID,
JAMES. *Daughters:* BRIDGET SPENCE and BETTY MARDRUM. *Wife and
Executrix:* SARAH. *Witnesses:* JOHN JONES, BERD BANGER, ELIZABETH
PERISHE. *Clerk of the Court:* JAMES CRAVEN.

SPENCE, JAMES.   Pasquotank County.

November 19, 1753. April Court, 1755. *Sons:* ALEXANDER, JOHN and
JAMES. *Daughters:* SARAH COOK, LETTESHA, AREY and DOROTHY SPENCE.
Wife and Executrix: ELIZABETH SPENCE. *Witnesses:* SAMUEL SMITH, SAML.
EDNYE, DAVID DAVIS. *Clerk of the Court:* THOS. TAYLOR.

SPENCE, JOHN.   Pasquotank County.

March 14, 1735–1736. April 13, 1736. *Sons:* DAVID and ALEXANDER
(lands divided between them). *Daughters:* DOROTHY DAVIS, ELIZABETH
SPENCE. *Granddaughter:* REACHELL SAWYER. *Executors:* CHARLES SAW-
YER and JOHN DAVIS. *Witnesses:* GEO. ROWE, ALEXANDER LEFLEAR,
ELIZABETH LEFLEARE. *Clerk of the Court:* JOS. SMITH. Device on seal:
Letters S. S., three circles and square.

SPIGHT, MARY.   Bertie County.

February 25, 1740–1741. May 7, 1743. *Sons:* MOSES, ISAAC (*Executor*).
Daughter: RACHEL and RUTH JORDAN, ZILPAH BLANCHARD. *Granddaugh-
ters:* MARY and ELIZABETH SPIGHT. *Cousins:* JACOB HINTON, RUBEN
HINTON, WILLIAM, BETTIE and MARY HINTON, JOSEPH PEREY (*Executor*).
Witnesses: GUY HILL, MOSS ROWNTREE, THOMAS ROWNTREE. Proven
before GAB. JOHNSTON, at Edenton.

SPIGHT, THOMAS.   Perquimans Precinct.

April 9, 1737. April 27, 1737. *Sons:* ISAAC ("plantation whereon I
now dwell"), MOSES. *Daughters:* RACHEL and RUTH JORDEN and ZILPAH
BLANCHARD. *Wife and Executrix:* MARY. *Witnesses:* RICHARD PEARCE,
GEFERY HUBBARD, THOS. ROWNTREE. Proven before W. SMITH, C. J.

SPIGHT, THOMAS.   Craven County.

October 3, 1756. November Court, 1756. This is a nuncupative will
proven before JOHN CLITHERALL by JOHN SPEIGHT, PHRUSAN SPEIGHT and
ANN PAYN. *Wife:* ELIZABETH (one negro). *Sister:* PRUSANE SPIGHT.
Other legatees: JOHN and SIMON SPIGHT. *Clerk of the Court:* WM. POWELL.

SPIVEY, THOMAS.   Chowan Precinct.

December 23, 1729. February 5, 1729–1730. *Sons:* JACOB (plantation) and BENJAMIN, WILLIAM and THOMAS (12 pence and a Bible). *Son-in-law:* WILLIAM HILL (90 acres land). *Daughter:* MARY HILL. *Grandchildren:* JACOB SPIVEY, SARAH, MARY and SUSANAH HILL. *Other legatee:* MARKE CHAPEL. *Executor:* JACOB SPIVEY (son). *Witnesses:* WILLIAM WESTTON, ROBART BLANCHARD, THOMAS MANSFIELD. Proven before RICHARD EVERARD.

SPRATTEN, HENRY.   Currituck County.

January 10, 1750. April Court, 1751. *Wife and Executrix:* MARY. *Daughter:* ESTHER SPRATTON. *Brother:* PETER SPRATTON. *Brother-in-law:* THOMAS TATUM. *Witnesses:* ROBERT FLETCHER, WILLIAM WHITE. *Clerk of the Court:* RICHD. MCCLURE.

SPRING, ARON.   Beaufort County.

April 18, 1755. June Court, 1756. *Sons:* ROBERT ("my plantation"), JAMES and ABRAHAM (440 acres of land divided between them). *Daughters:* DINAH (wife of WILLIAM JESSOP), ELIZABETH SPRING. *Wife:* MARTHA. Negroes bequeathed to children. *Executor:* JOHN BARROW (brother-in-law). *Witnesses:* THOMAS BARROW, LITTLETON EBORN, JUN. *Clerk of the Court:* WALLEY CHAUNCY.

SPROT, THOMAS.   Anson County.

January 15, 1757. *Daughters:* MARY and ANN BARNET, JEAN NEEL, SUSANNAH POLK, MARTHA SPROT (land on Sugar Creek). *Sons:* THOMAS (land on Twelve Mill (Mile) Creek), JOHN CLARK. *Executors:* ANDREW SPROT and THOMAS POLK. *Witnesses:* WILLIAM BARNET, JAMES SPROT, JAS. CAMPBELL. No probate.

STACEY, CHARLES.   Chowan Precinct.

January 2, 1724–1725. July 19, 1725. *Wife and Executrix:* MARY. *Witnesses:* DAVID BUTLER, JAMES WARD, GEORGE DEAR. Proven before C. GALE, C. J.

STAFFORD, JOHN.   Bath County.

May 15, 1733. March Court, 1735. *Sons:* WILLIAM (plantation on South side of Broad Creek), JOHN ("my plantation I now dwell on"), JOSHUA (180 acres land), EDWARD (land on Creek Swamp), THOMAS (land on Broad Creek). *Daughter:* DINAH STAFFORD. *Executor:* JOHN STAFFORD (son). *Witnesses:* MARY, DARKIS and THOMAS BATTERS. *Clerk of the Court:* JOHN COLLISON.

STAFFORD, WILLIAM.   Currituck Precinct.

February 17, 1727–1728. April 9, 1728. *Sons:* JOHN and EDWARD (1 shilling to each), WILLIAM ("my plantation"), SAMUEL (300 acres of land). *Daughters:* ANN, FRANCES and MARY STAFFORD. *Wife and Executrix:* JEAN. *Executor:* PHILIP NORTHAN. *Witnesses:* MARY JOHNS, GEORGE POWERS. *Clerk of the Court:* J. MARTYN.

STAFFORD, WILLIAM.   Currituck County.

August 28, 1742. October Court, 1742. *Sons:* JAMES ("plantation whereon I now live"), WILLIAM. *Wife and Executrix:* FRANCES. *Executor:* RICHARD HODGES. *Witnesses:* SOLOMON BRIGHT, WILLIAM BOWIN. *Clerk of the Court:* JOHN LURRY.

STAFFORD, WILLIAM.   Pasquotank County.

November 12, 1750. *Sons:* JOHN and STEPHEN (land to each). *Daughters:* SUSANNAH and MARY. *Wife and Executrix:* ELENDER. *Other legatee:* RACHEL REW. *Executor:* WILLIAM WAYMAN. *Witnesses:* JAMES DUFFY, JOB NICKOLES, HEZ. CARTWRIGHT. No probate.

STAFFORD, WILLIAM.   New Hanover County.

August 31, 1765. October Court, 1765. *Sons:* RICHARD, WILLIAM and JOHN (plantation divided between them and one negro each), SAMUEL (plantation in Pitt County lying on SAML. TISON'S branch, and one negro), SETH (plantation). *Daughters:* MARY MAY, ANN FORBES, PRUDENCE STONE and ELIZABETH STAFFORD. *Wife:* ELIZABETH. *Executors:* WILLIAM and JOHN STAFFORD (sons). *Witnesses:* JOHN ALEXR. WILLEY, CHAS. HOLLINGSWORTH. *Clerk of the Court:* JNO. BURGWIN.

STALLINGS, LOTT.   Chowan County.

November 5, 1749. January 31, 1749. *Son:* SAMUEL (land in Belleyhack known by the name of Elbo). *Son-in-law:* ISAAC HILL (land adjoining THOS. NEWBY). *Daughter:* ANN STALLINGS. *Granddaughter:* SARAH HILL. *Executor:* SAMUEL STALLINGS (son). *Witnesses:* JAMES COPELAND, BENJ. BERRYMAN, GILBERT SCOTT. Proven before GAB. JOHNSTON at Eden House.

STAMP, RICHARD.   Pasquotank Precinct.

October 20, 1721. April 17, 1722. *Sons:* THOMAS ("my plantation"), RICHARD (225 acres of land). *Daughters:* MARY, ANN, ELIZABETH and TAMER. To each of above-named children is bequeathed one negro. *Wife and Executrix:* MARY ANN. *Witnesses:* DANIEL RICHARDSON, JOSEPH OLIVER, MARGARETT BOURNSBY, MARY CALLIHAN. *Clerk of the Court:* EDMUND GALE. Impression of church spire on seal.

STAMP, THOMAS.   Pasquotank Precinct.
    October 9, 1729. *Brothers:* BENJAMIN PALMER and RICHARD STAMP
(*Executor*). *Mother:* MARY ANN PALMER. *Witnesses:* JOHN MCKEELL,
JOHN CLARKE, WILLIAM ASKINES. *Clerk of the Court:* WM. MINSON.

STANDING, EDWARD.   Chowan Precinct.
    July 9, 1718. January 17, 1721. *Sons:* WILLIAM (land on Cossia),
SAMUEL, EDWARD. *Daughter:* SARAH STANDING. *Wife and Executrix:*
SARAH ("my manner plantation"). *Witnesses:* JNO. HARLOE, ROBERT
STASEY, THOMAS HEARTH (or HEATH). *Clerk of the Court:* W. BADHAM.

STANDIN, SAMUEL.   Perquimans County.
    March 28, 1752. April Court, 1752. *Sons:* SAMUEL and WILLIAM
(plantation to each), EDWARD (250 acres of land and one negro man).
Daughters: MARY and PENELOPE STANDIN. *Wife:* not named. *Execu-
tors:* JOHN HARVEY, WILLIAM WYATT and JOSHUA SKINNER. *Witnesses:*
JOHN NICKOLS, THOS. NICKOLS, ELISABETH SUTTON. *Clerk of the Court:*
EDMUND HATCH. Device on seal: man mounted on lion.

STANDIN, WILLIAM.   Perquimans County.
    November 4, 1759. April Court, 1760. *Son:* JOHN (plantation and
two negroes). *Daughter:* SARAH (two negroes). *Wife and Executrix:*
MARY. *Executor:* WILLIAM WYATT. *Witnesses:* JOHN CREECY, THOMAS
STRATTON, ABRAHAM JENNETT. *Clerk of the Court:* MILES HARVEY.
Provision is made for schooling of son JOHN, "to read, rite and cifer as
far as the rule of three."

STANDLEY, JONATHAN.   Bertie County.
    March 5, 1773. April 3, 1773. *Sons:* DAVID (plantation on Rocquis
and one negro), EDMOND (Pine woods land and one negro). *Daughters:*
ELISABETH ROADES, JEMIMA KITTRELL, ESTHER SPIVEY, SUSANNAH
BAKER, MARY STALLINS, MARTHA STANDLEY. *Wife:* ANN (land at Lum-
ber Bridge, three negroes, one "smoaking chair," etc.). *Executors:*
DAVID STANDLEY (son) and THOMAS ROADES (son-in-law). *Witnesses:*
CADER CHERRY, SOLLOMON CHERRY, MARTHA CHERRY. Proven before
JO. MARTIN.

STANFIELD, JOHN.   Orange County.
    August 4, 1755. September Court, 1755. *Sons:* JOHN (land on Haw
River), THOMAS (land known as the Meeting-house tract), SAMUEL ("plantation whereon I now live"). To THOMAS and SAMUEL is also devised
land near the Rich Hills. *Wife:* HANNAH. *Executors:* JOHN JONES and

ABSTRACT OF WILLS, 1690—1760.   359

JOSEPH MADDOX. Codicil provides for education of three sons. *Witnesses:* THOMAS LINDLEY, HUGH LAUGHLIN, THOMAS LOWE. *Clerk of the Court:* JAS. WATSON.

STANFORD, LEVIN.   Beaufort County.

December 16, 1772. May 15, 1773. *Daughter:* SARAH SHUFORD. *Executor:* JAMES BRINSON. *Witnesses:* MOSES POOLE, JOHN and NANCY COVINGTON. Proven before Jo. MARTIN.

STANSELL, JOHN.   Tyrrell County.

August 22, 1750. March Court, 1750. *Sons:* JOHN and GODFREY. *Daughters:* ELIZABETH BARBRE, REBECKAH STANSELL, MARY BENTELY. *Wife and Executrix:* SARAH. *Witnesses:* EDMUND SMITHWICK, REBECKAH STANSELL, SAMUEL SMITHWICK. *Clerk of the Court:* EVAN JONES.

STANTON, HENRY.   Carteret County.

May 1, 1751. September Court, 1751. *Sons:* HENRY (land called the Swimming Point), JOSEPH (land on Queens Creek), BENJAMIN, JOHN (land called Bare Banks). *Wife and Executrix:* LIDDY. *Daughters:* HANNAH SPOONER, MARY ALBURTSON, SARAH STANTON. *Witnesses:* ELIAS ALLERTSON, THOMAS WHITE, ISAAC WHITE. *Clerk of the Court:* GEORGE READ.

STANTON, MARY.

February 2, 1720–1721. April Court, 1721. *Sons:* JOHN and ROBERT ARMOUR, ELIJA STANTON. *Daughters:* MARY BROTHERS, ANN KELLY. *Other legatees:* MARY STANTON and REBECCA BROTHERS. *Executor:* ELIJA STANTON (son). *Witnesses:* SAMUEL GUTHRIE, TERRENCE SWEENY, MARY ARMOUR. *Clerk pro tem.:* JNO. PALIN. Fleur-de-lis on seal.

STANTON, THOMAS.   Pasquotank Precinct.

August 25, 1720. October 18, 1720. *Wife and Executrix:* MARY. *Witnesses:* JOHN BUNDY, RICHD. SAMS, ANN MEIDS. *Clerk of the Court:* W. NORRIS.

STASEY, THOMAS.   Chowan Precinct.

April 19, 1697. July 5, 1697. *Sons:* JOHN, THOMAS and CHARLES. *Wife and Executrix:* REBECKAH. *Witnesses:* KATHERINE WATTS, FRANC SEGRAVE, LUSEAH SEGRAVE. *Clerk of the Court:* N. CHEVIN.

STEELL, ALEXANDER.   Onslow County.

September 18, 1751. January Court, 1751. *Sons:* PETER and JAMES (plantation on Trent River). *Daughters:* ELIZABETH, SARAH, MARGARET,

ANN and RACHELL. *Wife and Executrix:* MARY. *Executors:* PETER STEELL (son) and JOHN STARKEY. *Witnesses:* SUSANNA BARBARA, MITCHELL BARBARA, RICHARD BARBER. *Clerk of the Court:* THO. BLACK.

STEELE, AMBROSE.   Beaufort County.

December 25, 1724. April Court, 1725. *Son:* AMBROSE (land in town of Freehold, in the County of Monmouth, in East Jersey). *Wife:* REBECKAH. Land at Neuse leased of CULLEN POLLOCK ordered sold. *Executors:* WILLIAM LITTLE, CORNELIUS FOWLER and EDWARD SALTER. *Witnesses:* WILLIAM LITTLE, DEBORAH PILSON, J. STONOR and THO. UNDAY. Codicil witnessed by J. STONOR, DEBORAH PILSON and WILLIAM BEVAN. *Clerk of the Court:* JNO. SWANN. *Justice:* THOS. BOYD.

STEELY, THOMAS.   Chowan County.

May 28, 1719. June 4, 1719. *Brother:* THOMAS HAWKINS. *Sister:* JANE ADDERLY. *Witnesses:* JAMES SMITH, JAMES and ELIZABETH HAWKINS. No probate.

STEPHENS, EDWARD.   Johnston County.

October 19, 1751. December Court, 1751. *Sons:* EPHRAIM, EDMUND, JACOB (plantation to each). *Daughters:* SARAH, PATIENCE, MORNIN. *Executors:* WILLIAM STEPHENS (brother) and EPHRAIM STEPHENS (son). *Witnesses:* ARTHUR FORT, BENNET BLACKMAN, RACHEL STEPHENS. *Clerk of the Court:* CHAS. YOUNG.

STEPHENSON, GEORGE.   Edgecombe County.

June 25, 1753. August Court, 1754. *Nephews:* JOSEPH STEPHENSON (son of brother, WILLIAM), JESSE and WILLIAM STEPHENSON (sons of brother, CHARLES). *Executor:* WILLIAM STEPHENSON. *Witnesses:* HENRY HORN, ELIZABETH HORN, SION HORNE. *Clerk of the Court:* BENJAMIN WYNNS.

STEPNEY, JOHN.   Perquimans County.

November 11, 1750. January Court, 1750. *Sons:* JOHN (three plantations, one lying on Indian Creek, and one negro), SAMUEL ("plantation whereon I now live" and plantation on Indian Creek, together with one negro). *Daughters:* SARAH, MARY, MARCEY, ELIZABETH and RACHEL. *Wife and Executrix:* SARAH. *Executors:* JOHN STEPNEY (son) and ZACHARIAH NIXON. *Witnesses:* THOMAS CALLAWAY, WILLIAM WYATT, LEVY HAUGHTON. *Clerk of the Court:* EDMUND HATCH.

STEPNEY, JOHN.   Perquimans County.

February 2, 1754. April Court, 1754. *Sons:* WILLIAM, JOHN. *Daughter:* MARY STEPNEY. *Wife and Executrix:* ELIZABETH. *Executor:* WILLIAM WYATT. *Witnesses:* JOSHUA HARMAN, BREATHARD TRUELOVE. *Clerk of the Court:* WILLIAM SKINNER.

STEVENS, JAMES.   Bath County.

   September 5, 1739. November 15, 1739. *Wife and Executrix:* JENET. *Witnesses:* RICHARD CHEEK, JOHN QUIN, JAMES CHEEK. Proven before GAB. JOHNSTON.

STEVENS, JEREMIAH.   Currituck County.

   August 24, 1757. September Court, 1757. *Daughters:* EASTER and ELIZABETH STEVENS. *Executor:* SAMUEL JARVIS. *Witnesses:* JOHN LURRY, WILLIAM FEREBE, JOHN BARNES. *Clerk of the Court:* WM. MEARNS.

STEVENS, THOMAS.   Craven County.

   June 11, 1751. June Court, 1751. *Sons:* JOHN ("my plantation"), THOMAS. *Daughters:* SARAH, MARY and FRANCES STEVENS. *Wife:* MARY. *Executors:* THOMAS STEVENS (sons), BENJAMIN BROCKIT. *Witnesses:* JOHN GRANADE, JOHN KINSEY, SARAH BROCKETT. *Clerk of the Court:* CHAS. YOUNG.

STEVENS, THOMASEN.   Currituck County.

   April 20, 1748. October 5, 1748. *Sons:* MICHAEL ONEAL, JOHN STEVENS. *Daughter:* MARY STEVENS. *Executors:* THOMAS PARKER and JOHN STEVENS. *Witnesses:* THO. TAYLOR, GILBIRD PORTWOOD, JAMES MERCER. *Clerk of the Court:* RICHD. MCCLURE.

STEVENS, WILLIAM.   Chowan Precinct.

   October 24, 1697. January Court, 1697. *Legatees:* ROBERT WEST, THOMAS GILLAM (*Executor*). *Witnesses:* HENDERSON WALKER, JOHN HOULDBROOK, ANN WALKER. *Clerk of the Court:* N. CHEVIN.

STEVENS, WILLIAM.   Beaufort County.

   February 22, 1750. March 13, 1750. *Son:* JAMES ("my plantation"). *Wife and Executrix:* PENNELOPE. *Witnesses:* RICHARD NEWMAN, EZEKIEL DICKINSON, SALATHIEL MIXON. *Clerk of the Court:* WILLIAM ORMOND. Will almost illegible.

STEVENSON, CHARLES.   Northampton County.

   July 4, 1748. November Court, 1751. *Sons:* BENJAMIN, GEORGE, WILLIAM and JESSE (land divided among them). *Daughters:* MARTHA, SUSANNA and OLIVE. *Wife:* ELIZABETH. *Executor:* WILLIAM STEVENSON (son). *Witnesses:* JOHN DAWSON, ABRM. HOOD, EDWARD STREATER. *Clerk of the Court:* I. EDWARDS.

STEVENSON, WILLIAM.   Perquimans County.

   July 18, 1738. July Court, 1739. *Grandsons:* WILLIAM ("1 Church Bybel and silverware marked W. S."), JOHN, JOSEPH and THOMAS STEVENson ("all the residue of my estate"). *Son and Executor:* JOHN. *Witnesses:* WILLIAM AMBLER, JOSEPH BUNCOMBE, JAMES TURNBULL. *Clerk of the Court:* JAMES CRAVEN.

STEWARD, WILLIAM.   Perquimans Precinct.

August 11, 1709. *Wife and Executrix:* ELIZABETH. *Sons:* WILLIAM and JOSEPH. *Daughters:* MARY and PATIENCE. *Witnesses:* ——— FRENCH and ELIZ. FRENCH. No probate. The signature of JOHN LAWSON appears on the back of this will.

STEWARD, WILLIAM.   Perquimans Precinct.

April 11, 1711. *Sons:* WILLIAM and JOSEPH. *Daughters:* PATIENCE, ELIZABETH and MARY. *Wife and Executrix:* ELIZABETH. *Witnesses:*——— FRENCH and ——— FRENCH. *Clerk of the Court:* EDWD. BENWICKE.

STEWART, JOHN.   Craven County.

October 13, 1741. June 22, 1742. *Legatees:* JACOB TOMSON, JOHN, son of RICHARD BYRD; ELIZABETH, daughter of SAMUEL PRESENT. *Executors:* DENIS ODYER (father-in-law), RICHARD BYRD. *Witnesses:* JNO. HERRING, RICHARD BYRD. *Registrar:* EDWARD GRIFFITH.

STEWART, JOHN.   Bertie County.

August 5, 1773. December 13, 1774. *Wife and Executrix:* JENNET. *Executors:* ANDREW BUNN and GEORGE LOCKHART. *Witnesses:* GEORGE MATTHEWS, THOMAS CLARKSON, MATTHEW CRAWFORD. Proven before Jo. MARTIN.

STEWART, LEVI.   Currituck County.

July 15, 1752. January Court, 1753. *Sons:* JOHN ("plantation I now live on"), LEVI (one negro). *Wife and Executrix:* ANN (one negro). *Witnesses:* JOSEPH STEWART, JOHN BENNET, WILLIS MILLER. *Clerk of the Court:* WILLIAM SHERGOLD. Impression of head on seal.

STIBALL, RICHARD.   Chowan County.

September 18, 1695. April Court, 1695. *Daughters:* MARY, PASHENCE. *Executors:* WILLIAM PREVES, WILLIAM CHALTON. *Witnesses:* WILLIAM PREVES, WILLIAM CHALTEN, ARTHUR CARLETON. *Clerk of the Court:* N. CHEVIN.

STIRING, GEORGE.   Carteret County.

March 29, 1745. June Court, 1745. *Sons:* GEORGE, JOHN and HENRY. *Wife and Executrix:* MARY. *Daughters:* ELIZABETH and JOYCE STIRING. *Witnesses:* WILLIAM SALTER, HENRY SMITH. *Clerk of the Court:* GEORGE READ.

STOAKLEY, JOSEPH.   Pasquotank County.

December 12, 1729. January 3, 1729–1730. *Sons:* ISAAC, JOSEPH. *Daughter:* MARY STOAKLEY. *Other legatees:* ISACK DELLEMAR, WILLIAM CARTRIGHT. *Wife and Executrix:* ANN. *Witnesses:* THOMAS MERREDAY, JOHN RICKS, WM. MINSON. Proven before RICHARD EVERARD. To children is bequeathed six negroes and one gold ring each.

STOCKLEY, THOMAS.   New Hanover County.

September 5, 1757. February Court, 1758. *Brothers:* CAPEWELL STOCKLEY (*Executor*), PETER STOCKLEY. *Sister:* ANN STOCKLEY. *Sons:* JOHN and THOMAS. *Witnesses:* JOHN WILKINSON, JONATHAN STURGES, JACOB STOCKLEY. *Clerk of the Court:* JA. MORAN.

STONE, JOHN.   Perquimans County.

October 14, 1744. January Court, 1744. *Sons:* JOHN, WILLIAM and MOSES. *Wife and Executrix:* MARY (land on Veases Creek). *Executor:* RALPH FLETCHER. *Witnesses:* JOHN PERRY, JOHN MUNDLEN, ROGER KENYON. *Clerk of the Court:* EDMUND HATCH.

STONE, RICHARD.   Currituck County.

August 19, 1749. October Court, 1749. *Daughters:* ALES and AMAY STONE, MARY PARKER. *Son-in-law:* JOHN PARKER. *Wife and Executrix:* SINNA. *Executor:* PETER DAUGE. *Witnesses:* JOHN WHITEHURST, PETER DAUGE. *Clerk of the Court:* RICHARD MCCLURE.

STRICKLAND, JOSEPH.   Northampton County.

September 25, 1755. November Court, 1755. *Son:* AXEM ("my plantation"). *Daughters:* RACHEL STRICKLAND (land on Great Branch), ABEGILL STRICKLAND, OLLIEF STRICKLAND. *Wife and Executrix:* ELISABETH. *Executor:* JOSEPH SIKES. *Witnesses:* WILLIAM MOORE, JOHN POWELL. *Clerk of the Court:* I. EDWARDS.

STRICKLAND, WILLIAM.   Bertie County.

May Court, 1728. *Sons:* WILLIAM, JOHN (100 acres of land at Roanoak), JOSEPH (100 acres of land at Roanoak), MATTHEW, SAMUEL ("my dwelling plantation"). No wife or executor named. *Witnesses:* NATHANIEL COOPER and ELIAS FORD. *Clerk of the Court:* RT. FORSTER.

STRINGER, FRANCIS.   Craven County.

January 8, 1749. March 30, 1753. *Mother:* MARY STRINGER (plantation on Contentne bought of HENRY SUMMERLIN and two negroes). *Brothers-in-law:* JOHN SHINE (land on Stoney Town Creek, in Chowan County bought of DERHAM HANDCOCK), DANIEL SHINE (land on Falling Creek).

Brother: WILLIAM STRINGER (lots in Newbern). *Daughter:* ELIZABETH STRINGER (eight slaves). *Other legatees:* ANNE GOFFEE, JOHN STRINGER, son of GEORGE STRINGER of Core Creek; WILLIAM BOND, GEORGE STRINGER, son of brother RALPH; and THOMAS STRINGER (land commonly called Dover). Provision is made for fund for poor of parish. *Wife:* HANNAH (eight negroes). *Executors:* DANL. SHINE, JAMES GREEN and THOMAS GRAVES. *Witnesses:* ABNER NEALE, JNO. KANNADY, JOHN JONES, JOS ATHERLY. Codicil witnessed by JNO. OLIVE and JNO. CANNADY bequeaths slaves to wife. Proven before MATT. ROWAN.

STRINGER, MARY. Chowan County.

April 27, 1744. May 10, 1748. *Sons:* JOHN and FRANCIS SANDERS (*Executors*). *Daughters:* MARY DAWSON, MARTHA SUMNER. *Granddaughters:* FRUSAN MORRIS, ELIZABETH COTTING and MARY GARDNER. *Witnesses:* EDWARD HARE, HENRY CLAYTON, EDWARD HARE, JR. Proven before GAB. JOHNSTON.

STRINGFIELD, RICHARD. Northampton County.

July 19, 1747. November Court, 1747. *Sons:* JAMES, RICHARD, JOSEPH (*Executor*). *Witnesses:* THOMAS SHORN, SAMUEL WARREN. *Clerk of the Court:* RT. FORSTER.

STROWDE, JOHN. Currituck County.

January 28, 1693. January 25, 1703–1704. *Daughters:* MARY and ELIZABETH ("all my estate"). *Executor:* JOHN BENNETT. *Witnesses:* WILLIAM STAFFORD, MARY BENNETT, RICHARD EVERINGTON. *Clerk of the Court:* EDWD. TAYLER.

STUART, JOHN. Chowan Precinct.

January 5, 1702–1703. January Court, 1706–1707. *Wife and Executrix:* not named. *Daughter:* MARY. *Witnesses:* WM. WILKINS, ALEXR. GILLAGIN. *Clerk of the Court:* N. CHEVIN.

STUART, JOHN. New Hanover Precinct.

June 27, 1736. July 9, 1736. *Legatees:* SARAH SMITH, HENRIETTA STUART (sister, of Inverness in North Britain). *Executors:* THOMAS WARDROPER (Surveyor General of the Province) and JAMES MURRAY, of Brunswick. *Witnesses:* JAMES FERGUS, WM. ELLISON. Proven before W. SMITH, C. J.

STUBBS, RICHARD. Tyrrell County.

February 25, 1754, March Court, 1754. *Brothers:* EVERITT ("my manner plantation"), WILLIAM, THOMAS, JOHN. *Sister:* MARY. *Other legatee:* ANN JONES. *Executors:* THOMAS and EVERETT STUBBS. *Witnesses:* DAVID AIRS, ESTHER WALKER, MARY STUBBS. *Clerk of the Court:* EVAN JONES.

STUBBS, THOMAS.   Beaufort County.

January 17, 1738. August 7, 1737. (Letters issued May 23, 1739.) *Sons:* WILLIAM ("my maner plantation lying near Moratock Bridge"), THOMAS (plantation on Flat Swamp "on Pantico Road"), EVERET ("land on Pantico Road"), JOHN (land on Coneke Creek called Briles Neck), RICHARD (land called Saverges). *Daughters:* HANAH and MARY. *Wife and Executrix:* MARY. *Witnesses:* JAMES DWIGHT, NATHANIEL EVERET. *Clerk of the Court:* ANDERSON SAGG.

STUBBS, WILLIAM.

December 8, 1756. June Court, 1757. Bath Town. *Son:* WILLIAM. *Daughter:* MARGARET. *Wife and Executrix:* JANE. *Witnesses:* JOHN ALDORSON, SAMUEL THOMSON, PETER CAILA. *Clerk of the Court:* WALLEY CHAUNCEY.

SUGG, GEORGE.   Beaufort County.

October 29, 1758. November Court, 1758. *Sons:* NIMROD (land on Tison Creek), JOEL, GEORGE and ALLEN SUGG. *Daughters:* LUCEY TISON, FANNY and SARAH SUGG. *Executors:* AQUILA SUGG, ABRAHAM TISON, JOEL and ALLEN SUGG. *Witnesses:* THOS. TILDESLEY, FRIEDRICH SERGNT, JOHN ANDERS. Proven at Enfield Court. I. EDWARDS, *Clerk of the Court.*

SUMNER, JAMES.   Perquimans County.

March 26, 1750. May 14, 1750. *Sons:* LUKE (two plantations), JAMES (three plantations), SETH (land on Sutton's Creek), DAVID (plantation "where DAVID KELLEY now lives"), ROBERT, WILLIAM and JOSIAH (200 pounds current money of Virginia to each). To each of sons is bequeathed negro slaves, and to JOSIAH is devised houses and lots in Suffolk, Virginia. *Daughters:* MARY and PENELOPE (200 pounds in money and two negroes to each). *Wife and Executrix:* MARY. *Witnesses:* THOMAS HURDLE, DEMSEY SUMNER. Good impression of castle on seal.

SUMNER, JOHN.   Chowan County.

April 18, 1754. January Court, 1755. *Sons:* SAMUEL ("plantation whereon I now live"), WILLIAM (land bought of JOSEPH and GRIGORY STALLINGS and JOHN KNIGHT, and three negroes), JACOB (land on west side of Orapeak Swamp known as Kilmaney, six negroes), JOSEPH (land at Tar River bought of ABRAHAM ODUM, and five negroes), MOSES (land bought of WILLIAM WEBB in Bertie County, and four negroes). *Daugh-*

ter: ELISABETH BATTLE (four negroes). *Wife and Executrix:* ELISABETH (nine negroes). *Witnesses:* JOSEPH JONES, JOHN BENTON, SR., JASEN CAMPBELL, ROSANNA RIDDICK, JETHRO BENTON. *Clerk of the Court:* WILL HALSEY. Impression of coronet on seal.

SUMNER, RICHARD.   Bertie County.

April 12, 1729. May Court, 1729. *Son and Executor:* JAMES ("my manner plantation"). *Wife:* MARY. *Daughter:* CHARITY SUMNER. *Executor:* JAMES BRYANT (father-in-law). *Witnesses:* JAMES WOOD, EDWARD GREEN, JOHN SUTTON. *Clerk of the Court:* RT. FORSTER.

SUTTON, GEORGE.

March 11, 1699. No probate. *Son:* RICHARD. *Daughters:* ELIZABETH (plantation at the Richland), DEBORAH (plantation at the hickory land). *Wife:* not named, and no executrix appointed.

SUTTON, JOSEPH.   Perquimans County.

January 20, 1694–1695. April Court, 1696. *Sons:* JOSEPH, CHRISTOPHER, GEORGE and NATHANIEL. *Wife and Executrix:* DELIVERANCE. *Witnesses:* JENKIN WILLIAMS, FRANCIS FOSTER, WILLIAM BARROW. *Clerk of the Court:* W. GLOVER.

SUTTON, JOSEPH.   Perquimans County.

January 11, 1723–1724. March 10, 1723. *Sons:* GEORGE and JOSEPH ("plantation I now live on"). To JOSEPH is also given two negroes, and to GEORGE two negroes. *Daughters:* PASHENCE and ELIZABETH (six silver spoons, one silver cup and silver tankard). *Grandson:* THOMAS SUTTON. *Executors:* RICHARD WHIDBEE (brother) and GEORGE SUTTON (son). *Witnesses:* RICHARD RATLIFF, WILLIAM WOOD, WILLIAM BARBER. Proven before GEO. BURRINGTON.

SUTTON, JOSEPH.   Perquimans County.

January 15, 1723–1724. March 26, 1724. *Son:* CHRISTOPHER (land and negroes). *Daughters:* SARAH and ELIZABETH (land called Edghill Leavels), MARY (land on Sutton's Creek), HANNAH (land on Sipros (Cypress) Swamp). *Brothers:* GEORGE and NATHANIEL SUTTON. *Wife and Executrix:* REBECKAH. *Executors:* PETER JONES and RICHARD WHIDBY. *Witnesses:* FRANCIS CRAXTON, RICHARD RATTLIFF, WILLIAM JONES. Proven before GAB. JOHNSTON.

SUTTON, MARY.   Perquimans County.

November 14, 1738. January Court, 1738. *Mother:* REBECKA DENMAN. *Sisters:* SARAH THOMAS and ELIZABETH MOULIN. *Brother and*

ABSTRACT OF WILLS, 1690—1760. 367

Executor: CHRISTOPHER SUTTON (plantation on Sutton's Creek). *Cousin and Executor:* JOSEPH SUTTON. *Witnesses:* BENJAMIN BAPTIST, ANN BARBER. *Clerk of the Court:* JAMES CRAVEN.

SUTTON, NATHANIEL.

December 20, 1682. March 12, 1682. *Sons:* GEORGE ("plantation whereon I now live"), JOSEPH (plantation where EDWARD POULTER lives), NATHANIEL (150 acres of land). *Daughter:* REBECKAH. *Cousin:* JOHN GODBY. *Wife:* not named. *Witnesses:* EDWARD POULTER, JOHN KINSE. *Clerk of the Court:* THOS. SNODEN.

SUTTON, THOMAS.   Bertie County.

February 3, 1750–1751. March 2, 1750. *Sons:* THOMAS, WILLIAM, GEORGE, JOSHUA, JASPER (land divided among these sons). *Daughters:* PARTHENIA, MARY, ELIZABETH, JUDITH. *Wife:* ELIZABETH. *Executors:* JOHN HARDISON and EDWARD RASOR. *Witnesses:* PETER WINANTS, ARTHUR WILLIAMS, ELIZABETH RASOR. Proven before GAB. JOHNSTON at Eden House. Eight negroes are divided among children.

SWAIN, JEREMIAH.   Tyrrell County.

June 28, 1746. September Court, 1746. Scuppernong. *Wife and Executrix:* MARY. *Son:* JOHN ("my plantation"). *Brother:* JAMES SWAIN (100 acres of land). *Witnesses:* JOHN SWAIN, WILLIAM TARKINGTON, MARY WEST. *Clerk of the Court* in 1746: JAMES CONNOR; in 1747: JOSIAH HART.

SWAIN, JOHN.   Tyrrell County.

April 6, 1749. December Court, 1749. *Sons:* JAMES: (land on Riders Creek), JOHN (plantation on the Sound Side), WILLIAM and STEPHEN ("the manor plantation"). *Daughters:* ELIZABETH MARY HOOKER, ROSANNA and MARTHA SWAIN. *Grandson:* JOHN SWAIN (son of JEREMIAH). *Wife and Executrix:* MARY. *Witnesses:* JOSEPH SPRUILL, JOANNE CHESTON, MARGARET GENKKENS. *Clerk of the Court:* EVAN JONES.

SWAIN, WILLIAM.   Tyrrell County.

December 15, 1752. March Court, 1753. *Brothers:* JOHN and JAMES SWAIN. *Wife and Executrix:* MAREY. *Witnesses:* JOSEPH SPRUILL, WILLIAM RHOADS, MARTHA SWAIN. *Clerk of the Court:* EVAN JONES.

SWAINE, STEPHEN.   Chowan County.

January 24, 1712–1713. *Sons:* JOHN, JAMES, RICHARD (plantation devised to each). *Daughters:* ELIZABETH SPRUILL, MARY and PATIENCE SWAINE. *Wife and Executrix:* PATIENCE. Proven before J. PALIN, *Clerk of the Court,* by the deposition of THOS. SNODEN.

SWANN, SAMUEL.   Perquimans County.

January 8, 1753. April Court, 1753. *Daughters:* MARY, wife of RICH-ARD CLATEN (lands on sound side, and lands lying to westward of aforesaid), SARAH, ANN, ELIZABETH, MARTHA, JANE and MARGARET. *Other legatees:* JESSE HENDLEY ("one-half my Allegator land"), JOHN VAIL (brother). *Executors:* JOHN and JEREMIAH VAIL (brothers). *Witnesses:* JOHN SMITH, SUSANNAH VAIL (?), WILLIAM WOLLARDS. *Clerk of the Court:* EDMUND HATCH. SWANN seal used.

SWANN, SAMUEL.   Perquimans Precinct.

September 12, 1707. April 20, 1708. *Sons:* WILLIAM (bible and seal ring), SAMPSON, HENRY and THOMAS (land between Muddy Creek and Marshy Gutt; lightwood on Grassy Point land, one pitch kettle "to Boyle Tarr"; "all the goods I have sent for from London—shagathee, shalloon and silk to make them a suit"); SAMUEL and JOHN. *Daughters:* ELIZABETH and SARAH SWANN. *Brother:* RICHARD BLAND, of Virginia. *Wife and Executrix:* ELIZABETH ("my plantation whereon I now live during her life and then to son, SAMUEL"). *Witnesses:* ELIZABETH THICKPEN, ANN MOSELEY, JOHN LILLINGTON, FRANCIS FOSTER, EDWD. MOSELEY. *Clerk of the Court:* J. KNIGHT. Impression of what seems to be a coronet on seal. Letters testamentary with a copy of will is annexed to this will, signed by W. GLOVER and sealed with the seal of the proprietors—A cross surrounded by coat of arms of the eight lords proprietors.

SWANN, THOMAS.   Pasquotank County.

May 7, 1733. August 9, 1733. *Sons:* SAMUEL (one plantation), WILLIAM (plantation bought of ROBERT WALLIS). "But in case either of my said sons shall sell, alien, mortgage or any other way convey either of ye sd plantations hereby given out of ye name of SWANN then it shall and may be lawful for ye other of my sd sons to reenter and take possession of the same." *Daughters:* REBECCA and ELIZABETH SWANN (land at Moyock, in Currituck). To each of sons is bequeathed a horse, bridle and saddle. All estate, consisting of negroes, lands, cattle, etc., is given to wife for education of children. *Wife and Executrix:* ELIZABETH. *Executor:* EDWARD MOSELEY. *Witnesses:* BANJA. PRITCHARD, MARY EDWARDS, SAML. WISE. Proven before GEORGE BURRINGTON. Coat of arms on seal illegible.

SWIFT, EPHERAM.   White Oak, in Onslow County.

November 4, 1744. *Sons:* EPHERAM, EBENEZER. *Wife:* PHEBY. *Executor:* JOHN STARKEY. *Witnesses:* THOS. CUMMINS, EMEL JONES, FRANCIS REAVIS. No probate. Portion of this will is missing.

SWINSON, RICHARD.   Chowan County.

April 24, 1716. July Court, 1716. *Sons:* RICHARD ("my plantation"), JOHN (200 acres of land), WILLIAM (land on Creek). *Son-in-law:* RICHARD

ABSTRACT OF WILLS, 1690—1760.   369

KANADY (land "from pecoson to the Little Bridges"). *Wife and Executrix:* ELIZABETH. *Witnesses:* MARY SWINSON, GI. HALLIDAY. *Clerk of the Court:* R. HICKS.

SYERS, GERRARD.

March 29, 1755. "Late of Perth Amboy but now of Cape Fear." *Wife and Executrix:* JANE. *Other legatees:* PHILIP KEARNY, of Perth Amboy; ANDREW GOUTEY (sea books and instruments). *Executors:* CORNELIUS HARNETT and DANIEL DUNBIBIN. *Witnesses:* SAML. DUNBIBIN, JOHN EDE, JNO. LYELL. Proven before ARTHUR DOBBS. Impression of anchor and ropes on seal.

SYMONS, BENJAMIN.   Pasquotank County.

October 24, 1748. *Son:* ABRAHAM (plantation and one negro). *Daughters:* ANN, MARY and HANNAH SYMONS. *Wife and Executrix:* ELIZABETH. *Executor:* WILLIAM SYMONS (uncle). *Witnesses:* JOSEPH BAILEY, JOHN DAVIS, HANNAH SYMONS. No probate.

SYMONS, JEREMIAH.   Pasquotank County.

March 30, 1713. December 12, 1713. *Sons:* JEREMIAH, WILLIAM and SAMUELL (plantation divided between them). *Daughters:* TAMER, wife of SAMUEL RUNDEY; DEBORAH, wife of WM. CHANCEY; SARAH, wife of THOS. ROBINSON; MARY SYMONS (to these are bequeathed negroes), ANN OVERMAN and ELIZABETH SYMONS. *Executors:* JEREMIAH SYMONS, SAMUELL BUNDEY and CHARLES OVERMAN. *Witnesses:* W. NORRIS, JOHN SYMONS, HENRY WHITE. No probate.

SYMONS, JEREMIAH.   Pasquotank County.

November 1, 1740. January Court, 1740. Little River in the County of Pasquotank. *Sons:* BENJAMIN, JEREMIAH ("my manor plantation"). *Daughters:* SARAH READING, ANN SPENCE, HANNAH SYMONS. *Wife and Executrix:* RACHEL. *Witnesses:* WILLIAM SYMONS, JEHOSAPHAT SYMONS, JAMES OVERMAN. *Clerk of the Court:* THO. TAYLOR.

SYMONS, JOHN.   Pasquotank County.

November 13, 1741. January Court, 1741. *Sons:* THOMAS and PETER (plantation divided between them). All estate is bequeathed to aforementioned sons. No executor or other legatees named. *Witnesses:* WILLIAM SYMONS, AARON MORRIS, JONATHAN WHITE. *Clerk of the Court:* THOS. TAYLOR.

24

SYMONS, JOHN. Pasquotank Precinct.

September 11, 1748. January 19, 1748. *Wife and Executrix:* ELIZABETH (two negroes). *Executor:* JOSEPH ROBERTSON. *Witnesses:* MARY SYMONS, JOSEPH SYMONS, JONATHAN LANGWITHTHA. Proven before GAB. JOHNSTON.

SYMONS, RACHEL (relict of JEREMIAH). Pasquotank Co.

October 12, 1748. April 11, 1749. *Daughters:* SARAH READING, ANN SPENCE and HANNAH SYMONS. *Son:* BENJAMIN. *Grandson:* ABRAHAM SYMONS. *Granddaughter:* ANN REDDING. *Executor:* BENJAMIN SYMONS (son). *Witnesses:* TERENCE SWEENY, ROBERT LOWRY, JEHOSHAPHAT SYMONS, RACHEL SYMONS. Proven before E. HALL, C. J.

SYMONS, THOMAS. Pasquotank Precinct.

January 20, 1702–1703. February 16, 1706. *Sons:* JOHN and PETER (plantation to each). *Wife and Executrix:* REBECCA. *Witnesses:* JEAMS WHITE, JOHN MOVIS, JOHN WHITE, ZACHARIAH NIXON. *Clerk of the Court:* THO. ABINGTON.

SYMONS, THOMAS. Pasquotank County.

February 30, 1757. March Court, 1758. *Sons:* JOHN, ABRAHAM, THOMAS (to each is devised land). *Daughters:* MIRIAM and ANN. *Wife and Executrix:* ANN. *Witnesses:* JEHOSHAPHAT SYMONS, NATHAN OVERMAN, JOHN SANDERS. *Clerk of the Court:* THO. TAYLOR. Coat of arms on seal.

SYMS, WILLIAM. Edgecombe County.

October 24, 1755. *Daughter:* SARAH WHOOPER (plantation lying on Kehukey). *Son:* WILLIAM. *Executor:* JOHN WHITAKER. *Witnesses:* THOS. TAYLOR, MARY TREE, XTR. HAYNES. No probate.

TARKINGTON, JOHN.

November 14, 1715. August 2, 1716. "Scoppernun." *Son:* WILLIAM (lands). *Daughters:* MARY and REBECCA TARKINGTON. *Wife and Executrix:* MARTHA. *Executor:* EDWARD PHELPS "of Scoppernun" (Scuppernong). *Witnesses:* JOHN WINGET, MARY LASON, J. WATKINS. *Clerk of the Court:* R. HICKS.

TARKINGTON, WILLIAM. Tyrrell County.

February 21, 1747. September Court, 1748. *Sons:* JOHN (land on Sheep Neck Branch), JOSHUA, BENJAMIN and JOSEPH, WILLIAM and ZEBULON (to each is given land). *Daughters:* ANN, SARAH and JOANNA. *Wife and Executrix:* mentioned, but not named. *Witnesses:* MATTHEW CASWELL, EDWARD PHELPS, ELIZABETH CASWELL. *Clerk of the Court:* EVAN JONES.

ABSTRACT OF WILLS, 1690—1760.

TART, JOSEPH.   Hyde County.

June 19, 1748. September 6, 1748. *Sons:* NATHAN and JOSEPH. *Daughters:* MARY MCCEALE and TABITHA TART. *Wife and Executrix:* SARAH (plantations in Hyde and Beaufort). *Executors:* RICHARD NEWMAN and RICHARD LEIRMONT. *Witnesses:* WILLIAM MORE, JACOB CONER, RD. LEIRMONT. *Clerk of the Court:* THOMAS LOACK.

TATUM, NATHANIEL.   Edgecombe County.

November 9, 1750. February Court, 1750. *Sons:* EDWARD, NATHANIEL, PETER and JOSE. *Daughter:* REBECKER TATUM. All lands divided among children. One negro bequeathed to children. *Wife and Executrix:* ELIZABETH. *Witnesses:* JAMES CANE, ELLENER WEVER, REBECCA CANE. *Clerk of the Court:* BENJN. WYNNS.

TAYLOR, ABRAHAM.   Johnston County.

April 2, 1751. December Court, 1751. *Sons:* ROBERT, JACOB, JOSEPH and ABRAHAM. *Daughters:* PRUDENCE TAYLOR, ANNE CALTON, RACHEL BEEZLEY. *Grandchildren:* DINAH and ABRAHAM TAYLOR. *Wife:* EDE. *Executor:* JOSEPH TAYLOR (son). *Witnesses:* HENRY ROBERTS, SARAH PRIVAT, J. ATKINSON. *Clerk of the Court:* CHAS. YOUNG.

TAYLOR, ANDREW.   Northampton County.

March 1, 1759. April Court, 1759. *Sons:* CALEB (plantation and two negroes), DEMSY (one negro). *Daughters:* GRACE and JUDITH. *Wife and Executrix:* ANNE. *Witnesses:* I. EDWARDS, JOHN HAYES, SAMUEL HAYES. *Clerk of the Court:* I. EDWARDS.

TAYLOR, ANN.

February 4, 1764. March 16, 1764. This is a nuncupative will proven by SAMUEL SWANN before ARTHUR DOBBS, and bequeaths negroes to grandchildren of SAML. SWANN, and an annuity to one MRS. SAUNDERS.

TAYLOR, EBENEZER.

April 21, 1711. *Cousins:* SAMUEL and ELINOR CROSS. *Wife:* AGNES (house and plantation). *Brothers:* SAMUEL TAYLOR, BENJAMIN TAYLOR. Library bequeathed to son of BENJAMIN who entered the ministry. Land on Forsters Creek ordered sold. *Son-in-law:* GOWEN LONDON. *Brother:* EDWARD WALKER (*Executor*). *Executor:* SAMUEL CROSS. *Witnesses:* EBENEZER TAYLOR, GIDEON JOHNSON, SAMUEL and JOSEPH WRAGG. No probate. Original missing. Recorded in Book 1712–1722, page 273.

TAYLOR, EDWARD.

December 3, 1710. *Daughters:* SARAH, DORCAS, ANNE. *Wife:* SARAH. *Executrix:* SARAH TAYLOR. *Witnesses:* TIMOTHY EIVES, RACHEL EIVES, AZRIKAM PARKER, JR. *Clerk of the Court:* ROBT. BUCKNER.

TAYLOR, JANE (widow of NATHANIEL). Carteret Precinct.

April 17, 1754. This is a nuncupative will, proven before ENOCH WARD by FRANCIS DAVIS. All estate of testatrix is bequeathed to one ISHMAEL TAYLOR, who was formerly a slave of her husband. Deposition approved by NATHANIEL RICE.

TAYLOR, JOHN.   Chowan County.

March 19, 1715–1716. September Court, 1716. *Son:* JOHN. *Wife and Executrix:* MARTHA. *Executors:* HENRY and WILLIAM CONER. *Witnesses:* JERE. VAIL, ROBERD STECEY. *Clerk of the Court:* R. HICKS.

TAYLOR, JOHN.   Craven County.

March 24, 1772. March 28, 1772. *Sons:* ABSOLAM, JOHN. *Grandson:* JOHN TAYLOR. *Daughters:* VIOLATER GARDE, TAMER TAYLOR, COURTNEY TAYLOR. *Granddaughter:* ALSE GARDE. *Executor:* BAZELL SMITH. *Witnesses:* JACOB SIKES, ANN SIKES, ELIZABETH THOMPSON. Proven before JO. MARTIN.

TAYLOR, LEMUELL.   Perquimans Precinct.

November 3, 1719. July Court, 1720. *Son:* LEMUELL (plantation and one negro). *Wife and Executrix:* JEAN. *Witnesses:* DANELL HALL, JAMES CHESON, JO. OATES. *Clerk of the Court:* WM. HABEL.

TAYLOR, LUKE.   Chowan County.

December 18, 1773. February 8, 1774. *Sons:* JOHN and THOMAS (plantation divided between them). *Wife:* DEBORAH. *Executors:* JOSEPH CREECY, JOHN WILKINS and JOHN TAYLOR. Proven before JO. MARTIN.

TAYLOR, NATHANIEL.

April 3, 1734. May 13, 1734. *Wife and Executrix:* JANE (silver plate and remainder of estate). *Witnesses:* JAMES BELL, FRANCIS DAVIS, HENRY BLURTON. Proven before NATHL. RICE.

TAYLOR, RALPH.   New Hanover County.

November 18, 1757. February Court, 1758. Wilmington. *Wife and Executrix:* MARY. *Executors:* BENJAMIN MORRISON and WILLIAM LORD. *Witnesses:* ARMAND DeROSSET, DANIEL DUNBIBIN and ARTHUR MABSON. *Clerk of the Court:* JA. MORAN. Provision made for payment of debts due merchants in Liverpool.

TAYLOR, ROBERT.   Albemarle Precinct.

September 7, 1700. *Wife:* ANN TAYLOR (all real and personal estate). *Executrix:* ANN TAYLOR. *Witnesses:* THO. ROLFE, THO. LEWISS, ROBT. LOVE. No probate.

TAYLOR, ROBERT.   Edgecombe County.

September Court, 1758. *Sons:* ROBERT and EDWARD (1 shilling to each), JOSEPH, WILLIAM, HENRY, RICHARD, THOMAS, BILLINGTON, NIM-. ROD and HUDSON. *Daughters:* JUDITH and RACHEL TAYLOR, ANN HUSE. *Wife and Executrix:* ANN. *Witnesses:* WILLIAM HUDSON, JAMES VAULX, WM. HUDSON, JR. *Clerk of the Court:* JOS. MONTFORT.

TAYLOR, SAMUEL.   Northampton County.

1746. *Sons:* ROBERT ("my plantation" and two negroes), ETHD. (land and two negroes), HARRY (lands). *Daughters:* ELIZABETH and MARTHA TAYLOR (negro and increase). *Wife:* CELA. *Executor:* ETHD. TAYLOR (son). Bequests made to *son*, SAMUEL TAYLOR, "in case he returns to Meherrin to enjoy same." No signature, witnesses or probate.

TAYLOR, THOMAS, SR.   Currituck Precinct.

August 20, 1734. July Court, 1736. *Sons:* EDWARD (negroes) and THOMAS. *Daughters:* SARAH (wife of JEREMIAH STEPHENS), BRIDGET (wife of SAMUEL JARVES), BETHIA TAYLOR. *Grandsons:* BENJAMIN TAYLOR and EZEKIEL PHILLIPS. *Wife and Executrix:* EASTHER. *Witnesses:* STEPHEN WILLIAMS, SOLO. JARVES, J. MARTYN. *Clerk of the Court:* JOS. SMITH.

TAYLOR, WILLIAM.   Pasquotank County.

December 30, 1772. January 23, 1773. *Brother:* JAMES TAYLOR. *Wife and Executrix:* MARY (four negroes). *Executors:* JOHN RICHARDSON (brother-in-law) and CALEB NASH. *Witnesses:* W. NORRIS, JOHN CRAWFORD, JER. SEDLEY. Proven before JO. MARTIN.

TERNELL, JACOB.

December 18, 1711. July 1, 1713. Little River. *Cousins:* ANN HILL, ROUGER HILL ("my land in Kakcomak). *Executor:* RICHARD HILL (brother). *Witnesses:* JOHN MACKIE, JOHN SMITH, EDWD. ———. Proven before JOHN NELSON.

TERRILL, WILLIAM.   Albemarle County.

June 3, 1682. Little River. *Sons:* WILLIAM, "in Weymouth, New England" (plantation on Little River, commonly called the Quarter), GIDEON, "of Weymouth afsd" (land on Little River and Deep Creek). *Daughter:* MARY (wife of WILLIAM MANSON). *Other legatees:* MARY, daughter of NATHANIEL BAXTER; JOHN, son of RICHARD TULE. *Executors:* GEORGE DURRANT of "Bertey Point," JOHN HUNT of Little River. *Witnesses:* SAM WOODROW, WILLIAM HUGHES, NATHANIEL BAXTER. No probate. Impression of swan on seal.

TESTER, ROBERT.
January 8, 1695. January 13, 1696. This is a nuncupative will, proven before JOHN STEPNEY by THOMAS and KATHERINE CLARK, and names *legatees:* JOHN HOPKINS and ROBERT TESTER.

THOMAS, BARNABEE.
October 5, 1735. December 11, 1735. *Son:* ELISHA (plantation and two negroes). *Wife:* SARAH ("ye use of all my negroes, she using them as a Christen ought to do"). *Brother and Executor:* PHILIP. *Witnesses:* WILLIAM THOMAS, JNO. DAWSON, JACOB CARR. Proven before GAB. JOHNSTON.

THOMAS, FRANCIS. Chowan County.
September 16, 1738. January 15, 1739. *Sons:* STEPHEN, JOHN and WILLIAM, FRANCIS ("plantation I live on, called the forck of the Duckinstool"). *Daughter:* ELIZABETH THOMAS. *Wife and Executrix:* MARY. *Witnesses:* JOHN JORDAN, EDMOND CONELL, JAMES WILLIAMS. Proven before W. SMITH, C. J.

THOMAS, FRANCIS. Bladen County.
June 8, 1756. October Court, 1756. *Son:* GEORGE. *Wife and Executrix:* JOAN. *Witnesses:* THOS. HALL, LUCY HALL, THOMAS SMITH. *Clerk of the Court:* J. BURGWIN.

THOMAS, JOHN. Northampton County.
March 18, 1745. May Court, 1746. *Son:* JOSEPH (plantation and negro). *Wife and Executrix:* ANN. *Witnesses:* I. EDWARDS, JOHN GOODALL, MATTHEW LOWRY. *Clerk of the Court:* RT. FORSTER.

THOMAS, JOSEPH. Bertie Precinct.
December 10, 1735. February Court, 1735. *Sons:* JOSEPH, MIKEL, LUKE and JAMES (lands divided among them). *Daughter:* CHARITY THOMAS. To sons is also given negroes. *Wife:* ELISABETH. *Executor:* JOHN SPIVEY. *Witnesses:* FRANS. HOBSON, WM. SIMONS. *Clerk of the Court:* JNO. WYNNS.

THOMAS, JOSEPH. Bertie County.
April 26, 1752. April Court, 1758. *Sons:* MICHAEL (640 acres of land "now in the possession of GRIFFIN SUMMERELL," together with stock of cattle and hogs and two negroes), JOSIAH (land "on which NATHANIEL KEEL lives," together with cattle, etc., and one negro boy), JOSEPH ("my plantation," stock and one negro). *Daughters:* MARY (land adjoining JOHN SPIVEY, and one negro), ELISABETH THOMAS (land "Whereon

Abstract of Wills, 1690—1760.

Judith Thomas now lives"). *Wife and Executrix:* Ann. *Executors:* Thomas Whitmill and Arthur Williams. *Witnesses:* Josiah Collins, Nathaniel Keel, Joseph Keel, Richard Sparkman. *Clerk of the Court:* Benjamin Wynns.

Thomas, Joseph.   Edgecombe County.

October 24, 1757. June Court, 1758. *Daughters:* Mary, Priscilla and Charity Thomas (to each is devised lands on Pigg Basket Creek, and one negro), Morning ("my plantation"). *Wife and Executrix:* Mourning (or Morning). *Executor:* John Thomas (brother). *Witnesses:* Micajah Thomas, William Defnall, Mourning Thomas. *Clerk of the Court:* Jos. Montfort.

Thomas, Josiah.   New Hanover County.

January 30, 1751. May Court, 1752. *Brothers:* Hannaniah and Azriah Thomas. *Cousin:* James Williams (lot "on the Town Sandhills"). *Daughter:* Ann Thomas (lot in Wilmington, ten acres "of ye aforesaid Sand Hills, and plantation whereon I now live"). *Wife and Executrix:* Hannah (land on Long Creek). *Witnesses:* Mary Ann Dubose, Elizabeth Carter. *Clerk of the Court:* Isaac Faries.

Thomas, Louis.   Craven County.

October 30, 1730. March 16, 1730–1731. *Wife and Executrix:* Ann Martha. *Daughter:* Elizabeth Thomas. *Son-in-law:* John Michel Shilfer. *Witnesses:* Joshua Platt, John Page. *Clerk of the Court:* C. Metcalfe.

Thomas, Luke.   Edgecombe County.

June 20, 1751. August Court, 1751. *Brother and Executor:* Jacob Thomas ("my plantation," together with one negro). *Sister:* Mary Thomas (one negro). *Other legatee:* Ezekiah Keel. *Witnesses:* Edwd. Brown, John Tanner, Elizabeth Keel. *Clerk of the Court:* Benjamin Wynns.

Thomas, Morgan.

1709. *Legatees:* James Martin and John Anderson. *Witnesses:* James Luton, Edward Harper. No executor or probate.

Thomas, Thomas.   Bladen County.

March 6, 1758. April Court, 1758. *Sons:* Samuel, Joseph, Cornelius, Thomas (land in Craven on Flat Swamp), John and Amos (land on Dunn's Creek). *Daughters:* Phebe, Martha and Elizabeth Thomas, Priscilla Dunn. *Wife and Executrix:* Prudence. *Witnesses:* Josiah Evans, Jonathan Evans. *Clerk of the Court:* J. Burgwin.

THOMSON, DAVID.   Duplin County.

March 6, 1773. October 26, 1773. *Sons:* WILLIAM (two negroes, and land lying between Buck Hall and the spring branch), DAVID (two negroes, and land on Cow Marsh), JAMES (two negroes, and land on Buck Hall), STEPHEN ("my plantation," three negroes, and "my large Book called Burket on the New Testament"). *Daughters:* AMELIA and MARTHA THOMSON (three negroes to each). *Sons-in-law:* ROGER SNELL and JESSE DARDEN (one negro to each). *Executors:* ANDREDO THOMSON (brother) and ROGER SNELL. *Witnesses:* HENRY HOLLINGSWORTH, JOHN THOMSON and THOMAS THOMSON. Proven before Jo. MARTIN.

THOMPSON, JOHN.   Craven County.

1738. September 27, 1738. *Son:* WILLIAM (half of all estate). *Brother:* ALEXANDER THOMPSON. *Wife:* AGNES. *Executors:* WILLIAM THOMPSON (brother) and FRANCIS STRINGER (surgeon). *Witnesses:* JOSEPH SLOCUMB, JOHN THOMPSON, JR., WILLIAM BOND. *Clerk of the Court:* JAMES COOR. Crest on seal.

THOMPSON, JOHN.   Chowan County.

August 8, 1755. *Son:* ROBERT. *Wife:* MARY (three negroes and plantation). *Other legatees:* WILLIAM THOMPSON (son of JAMES THOMPSON) and MARY TULLINGTON (daughter of MATTHIAS TULLINGTON). *Executors:* MATTHIAS TULLINGTON, JOHN LEWIS and HENRY BONNER. *Witnesses:* MICAJAH BUNCH, THOMAS LUTEN, WILLIAM JONES. No probate. Impression of head on seal.

THOMS, JOSEPH.   Perquimans Precinct.

February 9, 1728. March Court, 1727-1728. *Brothers:* JAMES and JOHN. *Other legatees:* JOSEPH, MARY, SARAH and DAMMERES RATLEFF. *Executor:* RICHARD DAVIS. *Witnesses:* THOMAS RATLIFF, HANNAH NICKLESON. Proven before RICHARD EVERARD.

THORAGOOD, FRANCIS.   Bath County.

June, 1714. April Court, 1716. *Sons:* FRANCIS, ADAM and EARLEY. *Daughters:* SARAH and ANN THORAGOOD. *Wife and Executrix:* ANN. *Witnesses:* JOSEPH FULFORD and ROBERT TURNER. *Clerk of the Court:* JNO. DRINKWATER.

THORNTON, JOHN.   Granville County.

November 10, 1754. September 2, 1755. *Wife and Executrix:* SARAH (three negroes). *Son:* FRANCIS (lands in Granville). *Daughter:* MARY THORNTON (lands in Virginia and Northampton County). *Executor:* ROBERT JONES, JR. *Witnesses:* WILLIAM PERSON, MARY JORDAN, WILLIAM LANKFORD. *Clerk of the Court:* DANIEL WELDON.

ABSTRACT OF WILLS, 1690—1760. 377

THURSTON, JOHN.   Albemarle County.
April 10, 1692. *Son and Executor:* JOHN. *Witnesses:* FRANCIS TOMES, THOMAS HOLMSON (?), SAMUEL NICKELLSON. No probate.

TIBBIT, JOHN.   Carteret County.
April 9, 1755. June Court, 1755. This is a nuncupative will proven by EPHRAIM BULL and names: *Wife and Executrix:* SARAH (land and negro). *Son:* GEORGE TIBBIT and *daughters,* MARY HOPKINS, AVES SOLE, ANNE BALA and ALSEY HILL.

TIGNER, JAMES.   Craven County.
November 25, 1749. March 20, 1749. *Sons:* THOMAS, WILLIAM and TOULSON (lands divided among them). *Daughter:* MARY ANN TIGNER. *Wife and Executrix:* SUSANNAH. *Witnesses:* ABNER NEALE, EDMUN CULLEN, DANIEL SMITH. *Clerk of the Court:* PHIL. SMITH.

TIMMERMAN, JOHN GASPER.   Craven Precinct.
May 21, 1722. September Court, 1722. *Legatees:* SEVILLA TIMMERMAN (wife) and MARY MAGDALEN TIMMERMAN (daughter). *Witnesses:* JACOB MILLER, JOHN LEILKER MILLER, JACOB SHEETS. *Clerk of the Court:* CALEB METCALFE.

TISON, SAMUEL.   Bath County.
May 1, 1736. September 16, 1736. Buford Parish. *Son:* MAGER. *Daughter:* SARAH TISON ("all cattle marked with smooth crop on ye right ear and half flower deluse on ye under side of ye left ear"). *Wife and Executrix:* MARGERA. *Executors:* CORNELIUS and THOMAS TISON. *Witnesses:* JNO. HARDEE, EDMD. TISON, JNO. KING. Provision is made for land on Horn Creek or Little Contentnea to be patented for son MAGER, and to daughter SARAH is devised land on Swift Creek. *Clerk of the Court:* JNO. COLLISON.

TISSON, MATHIAS.   Bath County.
April 5, 1710. *Sons:* JOHN, EDWARD, EDMOND, THOMAS, SAMUEL (land on Slaids Creek), MATHYAS. *Daughter:* SUSANNA. *Wife and Executrix:* MARY. *Witnesses:* BENJAMIN SANDERSON, BENJAMIN SLADE, CHARLES SMITH. No probate.

TOMES, FRANCIS.   Perquimans County.
September 5, 1729. No probate. *Daughters:* MARY NEWBY (plantation bought of JAMES THICKPEN, also a tract of land on Usess Creek bought of WILLIAM MORE), ELIZABETH PHELPS ("land I had in exchange from STEPHEN GIBBONS for my land called ye Image," also plantation adjoining RACHELL BARROW called Clagisters), PRISCILLA JONES, MARGARET TOMES

(land on Bull Branch), PLEASANT WINSLOW (land on Usess Creek). *Son:* FRANCIS (land "whereon I now live"). Negroes bequeathed to children. *Wife and Executrix:* REBECKAH. *Friends:* JOSEPH and THOMAS JESSOP and WILLIAM MORE and THOMAS WINSLOW. *Executor:* NATHAN NEWBY (son-in-law). *Witnesses:* J. JESSOP, RICHARD CHESTEN, RALPH FLETCHER, R. EVERARD. Letters granted October 6, 1729.

TOMES, JOSHUA.   Perquimans Precinct.

March 4, 1731–1732. April Court, 1732. *Son:* FOSTER (land and negroes). *Daughters:* SARAH TOMES (one negro), HANNAH MAUDLIN and MERIAM SUTTON. *Son-in-law:* CHRISTOPHER SUTTON. *Grandsons:* JOSHUA and WILLIAM SHERRO. *Wife and Executrix:* REBECKAH (plantation and three negroes). *Executors:* FOSTER TOMES (son), JOSEPH SUTTON and CHARLES DENMAN. *Witnesses:* CHARLES DENMAN, MARGARET and JOHN CHARLES. *Clerk of the Court:* CHARLES DENMAN.

TOMLIN, JOHN.   Perquimans Precinct.

July 7, 1715. *Son:* WILLIAM (plantation, live stock, etc.). *Brother and Executor:* WILLIAM TOMLIN. *Witnesses:* ALBERT ALBERTSON, SR., ALBERT ALBERTSON, JR., and THOMAS STAFFORD. No probate.

TOMLINSON, JOHN.   Albemarle County.

October 14, 1697. March Court, 1697–1698. *Children:* WILLIAM and MARY, JOHN and ELIZABETH. Land called "Cabin Neck" to be divided between *sons*, WILLIAM and JOHN. *Executrix:* ELIZABETH TOMLINSON. *Witnesses:* JACOB OVERMAN, DOROTHY OVERMAN. *Clerk of the Court:* WM. GLOVER.

TOMS, MARY.   Perquimans Precinct.

March 30, 1713. January Court, 1717–1718. *Legatees:* WILLIAM PLATER, VESTY LEWIS, ELISABETH PRITLOW, RACHELL LORENCE, ELIZABETH, daughter of *brother*, WILLIAM NICKOLLSON. *Executors:* JOSEPH and MARY GLOSTER. *Witnesses:* RALPH FLETCHER, JEAN FLETCHER, EDWARD THOMAS, JAMES BALES, ELIZABETH IEEDLETT (?), JAMES THECKPU. *Clerk of the Court:* RICHARD LEARY.

TOMSON, JACOB.   Johnston County.

May 25, 1750. June Court, 1750. *Sons:* THOMAS and JACOB THOMSON. *Executors:* THOMAS LUES and RICHARD BYRD. *Wife:* MARY. *Witnesses:* MIKEL RASHER, ROBERT BYRD. *Clerk of the Court:* RICHARD CASWELL. Courthouse on Walnut Creek.

TOMSON, WILLIAM (son of JOHN TOMSON).

June 11, 1736. July 27, 1736. "County of Medlesex, London March." *Legatees:* JOHN TOMSON ("fine house and two acres of land called ye

Charey Gardens in Barken being eight miles from London"). *Wife and Executrix:* SUSANNAH. *Witnesses:* JOSEPH THORNE, JOHN STINSON, ANTHONY WHITE, JUDATH STRATCH (?). Proven before GABRIEL JOHNSTON. Impression of head on seal.

TOOKE, JAMES.   Pasquotank Precinct.

February 6, 1719–1720. April Court, 1720. *Legatees:* JOHANNAH SCOTT (sister), JAMES TOOKE SCOTT (plantations known as Proctors and Floyds), THOMAS SCOTT, MARY SCOTT, ELIZABETH and SARAH SCOTT, MARY RICKS, JOHN SYMONS, JOHN TAWNYHILL, JOHN SCOTT, JOHN, SARAH and WILLIAM EVERIGIN, THOMAS and JOSEPH COMMANDER, JAMES COMMANDER. *Executors:* THOMAS COMMANDER and WILLIAM EVERIGIN. *Witnesses:* EVAN JONES, DAVID PRINCE, ANNE PALMER, DANIEL MACKEEL. *Clerk of the Court:* W. NORRIS.

TOOPS, JOSEPH.

July 26, 1755. *Brother:* JOHN TOOPS ("in Jermaney"). *Executors:* GEORGE SMITH and CHARLES HUNTER. *Witnesses:* JONATHAN HUNT, JAMES MACAY, ZEBULON STOUT. No probate.

TORKSEY, ELIZABETH.   Pasquotank County.

January 25, 1758. March Court, 1758. *Son:* JOHN TORKSEY. *Executor:* ABEL GALLUP. *Witnesses:* JUDITH WHITE and FRANCES BROCKSAT. *Clerk of the Court:* THOMAS TAYLOR.

TORKSEY, JOHN.   Pasquotank County.

November 10, 1745. April Court, 1747. *Sons:* THOMAS (one negro), BENJAMIN ("my plantation"). *Daughters:* ELIZABETH and SUSANA (four negroes). *Executors:* THOMAS and BENJAMIN (sons). *Witnesses:* WM. BURGES, JOHN RIGHT (WRIGHT) and ABASANA PERKINS. *Clerk of the Court:* THOS. TAYLOR.

TORKSEY, PHILLIP.   Albemarle County, Pasquotank Precinct.

January 16, 1720–1721. July 20, 1727. *Sons:* PHILLUP and JOHN TORKSEY, ROBERT MORGIN and HENRY HAMAN. *Executors:* ROBERT MORGAN and *wife*, not named. *Witnesses:* ROBERT and SARAH HARRISON, MARY GILBART, WILLIAM GRIFFIN. *Clerk of the Court:* THO. WEEKES. Executors qualified before WM. WILLSON.

TORKSEY, PHILIP.   Pasquotank County.

February 25, 1755. June Court, 1755. *Brothers:* EZEKIEL and JOHN TORKSEY. *Cousin:* MARGARET NEEDHAM (one negro). *Wife and Executrix:* ELISABETH. *Witnesses:* WM. BURGES, ABEL GALLEP, BENJAMIN TORKSEY. *Clerk of the Court:* THOS. TAYLOR.

TORVERSON, JAMES.   Albemarle County.

August 5, 1675. *Executor and sole legatee:* THOMAS JARVIS. *Witnesses:* PAUL LATHUM, THOMAS DEWBERY. Proven before SETH SOTHELL.

TOTEWINE, WILLIAM.   Craven County.

April 5, 1776. February 7, 1777. *Sons:* WILLIAM (plantation on Flat Swamp), SIMON (silver shoe buckles and "Rifeld Gun"), WINDER (horse, saddle and bridle), COLBORN. *Executor:* WILLIAM TOTEWINE (son). *Witnesses:* JOSIAH HOLT, RACHEL BANKS. Proven before RICHARD CASWELL.

TOWNSEN, JOHN.   Perquimans County.

August 10, 1737. October Court, 1739. *Brother and Executor:* WILLIAM TOWNSEN. *Daughter of brother:* ANN TOWNSEN. *Witnesses:* ZACH. CHANCEY, PRISCILLA SANDERS, REBECCA CHANCEY. *Clerk of the Court:* JAMES CRAVEN.

TRANTER, JOHN.   Bath County.

December 15, 1723. *Wife and Executrix:* ANNE. *Other legatees:* HENRY and ROBERT WHITHURST, SAMUEL, WILLIAM and ELINOR WHITHURST. *Witnesses:* THOMAS MOUNT, J. BAPTA. ASHE. No probate.

TRAVIS, EDWARD.   Beaufort County.

December 30, 1739. December Court, 1740. Parish of St. Thomas. *Sons:* JOHN, WILLIAM, THOMAS (land "where I now dwell in the fork of Goose Creek"). *Daughter:* MARY TRAVIS. To *son,* THOMAS is bequeathed negroes. *Executors:* SIMON ALDERSON and JOHN BOYDE. *Witnesses:* JNO. BOYDE, BENJAMIN HAWKINS, ROBERT CURTIS. *Clerk of the Court:* ROG. JONES.

TREMAIN, JONATHAN.   Onslow County.

July 3, 1739. January 4, 1742. *Friends:* ROGER MOORE and WILLIAM DRY. *Executors:* JOHN and PETER STARKEY. *Witnesses:* JANTT. NOBLE, CHAR. HAY and JOSEPH NOBLE. *Clerk of the Court:* WM. CRANFORD.

TROTTER, WILLIAM.   Perquimans Precinct.

March 28, 1729. December 16, 1729. *Daughter:* DOROTHY TROTTER ("my plantation"). *Wife and Executrix:* MARY. *Sisters:* ELISABETH NEWBY and ELISABETH TROTTER. *Witnesses:* FRANCIS NEWBY, MOSES and MARGARET ELLIOT. Proven before RICHD. EVERARD. Nuncupative codicil dated December 10, 1729, and proven before EZEKIEL MAUDLIN by WILLIAM GREEN, JESSE NEWBY and WILLIAM MORRIS, devises lands in York County, Virginia, to daughter.

TROWELL, JOSEPH.   Perquimans County.

January 29, 1735. April Court, 1736. *Wife and Executrix:* TABITHA. *Son:* JOSEPH. *Witnesses:* SAM. TAYLOR, JAMES BEASLY. *Clerk of the Court:* JAMES CRAVEN.

ABSTRACT OF WILLS, 1690—1760.

TRUEBLOOD, AGNES.   Pasquotank Precinct.

September 15, 1692. October 3, 1692. *Sons:* JOHN and AMOS. *Daughters:* MARY and ELIZABETH TRUBLOOD. Negroes bequeathed to above-named. No witnesses. No executor. *Clerk of the Court:* PAUL LATHUM.

TRUEBLOOD, JOHN.   Pasquotank County.

October 28, 1734. January 14, 1734. *Sons:* JOHN ("my manner plantation," also plantation on Arrannuse Creek known by the name of Cretches Old Field, and one negro), FISKER (land known by the name of Ieve Neck), DANIEL (one negro). *Daughters:* MIRIAM and ELIZABETH TRUBLOOD (negroes given to each). *Wife and Executrix:* SARAH (negroes). *Executors:* ABEL ROSS (brother) and JARVIS JONES. *Witnesses:* JOHN SAULS, WILLOUGHBY RICE and DUGLESS ROOD. *Clerk of the Court:* JAMES SMITH.

TRUITT, JOSEPH.   Craven County.

March 29, 1755. August Court, 1756. *Sons:* LEVI ("my plantation and riding horse"), JOHN. *Wife and Executrix:* PERSILLAR. *Witnesses:* LUKE RUSSELL, JEMINEA RUSSELL, JAMES SMITH. *Clerk of the Court:* WM. POWELL.

TRUMBULL, THOMAS.

October 22, 1733. November 8, 1733. *Son:* WILLIAM (plantation and one negro). *Daughter:* SARAH TRUMBULL. Two other children mentioned, but not named, to each of whom is bequeathed a negro. "My desire is that each one of my children shall have a maire branded by my executors and their brand recorded." *Wife and Executrix:* ELIZABETH. *Executors:* SAMUEL BARTLETT and JEAMES TURNULL. *Witnesses:* RICHARD SANDERSON, THOMAS CLARK, JOHN SNODEN. Proven before GEO. BURRINGTON.

TUCKER, NATHANIEL.'   Onslow County.

January 7, 1750. April 2, 1751. *Brother:* HENRY TUCKER. *Executor:* JOHN STARKEY. *Witnesses:* J. ROBERTS, JNO. HOLMES, ANN FRAZER. *Clerk of the Court:* THOS. BLACK.

TULLEY, JANE.   Pasquotank Precinct.

August 1, 1729. October 11, 1732. *Grandson and Executor:* DAVID BOLES. *Other legatees:* MARY and DANIEL RODES, JR. *Witnesses:* JONATHAN HIBBS, WILLM. LEE and DANIEL RODS. *Clerk of the Court:* W. MINSON (or H. MINSON).

TULY (or TULLE), THOMAS.   Hyde County.

December 3, 1740. June Court, 1741. *Sons:* THOMAS, JOHN, NATHANIEL and ANTHONY TULY. *Daughters:* MARY LEITH, SARY TULY, ELIZA-

BETH EASTER, RACHEL JUEL. *Wife and Executrix:* not named. *Witnesses:* EDW. HADLEY, FOSTER JONES (or JAMES), EZEKIEL RICHARDS. *Clerk of the Court:* W. BARROW.

TURBAVELL, RICHARD.   Bertie Precinct.

December 4, 1725. May Court, 1726. *Sons:* JOHN (land on "ye reedy run"), FRANCIS (land on Moratock River), WILLIAM ("plantation where he lives"), WALTER ("plantation where I now live"). *Daughter:* ELIZABETH TURBAVELL. *Grandchildren:* DANIEL and MARY COLSON. *Executor:* WILLIAM TURBAVELL (son). *Witnesses:* JOHN HOG, RICHARD CAERTON (?), JOHN HATCHER. *Clerk of the Court:* RT. FORSTER.

TURNBULL, JAMES.   Tyrrell County.

September 26, 1753. June Court, 1754. *Legatees:* YREOT ORMOND, THOMAS BARKER, MARY PANTRY (niece), ROBERT and JAMES PANTRY (land at Scuppernong called the Brak Oake, and the Rich Levills), MARY TURNBULL BUTCHER, BELL BUTCHER (lands called Bell's gift, Gards Island and land in Edenton), HENRY JORDAN, ELIZABETH HANMORE, DANIEL HANMORE. Periauger and canoes ordered sold for debts. *Executors:* MARY BUTCHER and WILLIAM GARDNER. *Witnesses:* ANN DENEM, JOHN MATHEWS, CHARLES DENEM, JAMES TATTERTON. *Clerk of the Court:* EVAN JONES.

TURNER, HENRY.   Henrico County, Va.

January 17, 1712–1713. *Son:* ABELL (plantation on Falling Creek in Henrico County). *Daughters:* JOAN, ELIZABETH, ANN, HANNAH, JANE, MARY. *Wife and Executrix:* PATIENCE. *Witnesses:* JAMES FLEMMING, ARTHUR DOUGALL, WILLIAM FISHER. *Clerk of the Court:* EDWD. BONWICKE (or RENWICKE).

TURNER, HENRY.   Edgecombe County.

January 20, 1748–1749. February Court, 1748. *Sons:* JOSEPH and THOMAS TURNER (land on the "Cattale Marsh"), SOLOMON (land on Deep Creek). *Daughters:* SARAH, MARY and OLLIF (negro to each). *Wife and Executrix:* MARY (three negroes). To sons is also bequeathed negroes. *Executor:* MATTHEW JOYNER. *Witnesses:* MATTHEW JOYNER, JAMES HARRIS, MARMADUKE NORFLEET. *Clerk of the Court:* BENJN. WYNNS.

TURNER, JOHN.

October 30, 1715. *Cousins:* EDWARD and WILLIAM TURNER. *Brother:* WILLIAM TURNER. *Executor:* JOHN SYMONS. *Witnesses:* HENRY ARNOLD and MARY WHITE. No probate.

ABSTRACT OF WILLS, 1690—1760.

TURNER, JOHN.   Perquimans Precinct.

March 3, 1717–1718. April 8, 1718. *Brother:* WILLIAM BASTABELL. *Other legatees:* THOMAS PEIRCE (*Executor*) and MARY PIERCE. *Witnesses:* WM. WOOD, CATTRON DAVIS, THOMAS PEIRCE. *Clerk of the Court:* RICHARD LEARY. Impression of head on seal with letters "o a v."

TURNER, RICHARD.   Perquimans Precinct.

April 14, 1719. *Daughters:* ELIZABETH NEWBY and HANNAH BASTABLE. *Son-in-law:* WILLIAM BASTABLE. *Grandson:* SAMUEL NEWBY. *Wife and Executrix:* BRIDGET. *Witnesses:* ROBERT WILSON, SAMUEL PHELPS, JAMES LITTLESON. *Clerk of the Court:* RICHD. LEARY.

TURNER, ROBART.   Perquimans County.

April 15, 1742. July Court, 1743. *Son:* JOSEPH. *Daughter:* MARY TURNER. *Wife and Executrix:* ANN. *Witnesses:* PETER ALBORDSON, THOMAS JESSOP. *Clerk of the Court:* EDMUND HATCH.

TURNER, ROBERT.   Beaufort County.

March 6, 1745. March Court, 1745. *Sons:* ROBERT (in England), JOHN (land on South Dividing Creek, lot No. 27 in Bath Town, large Bible, sermon books, law books, silver watch, mourning ring). *Daughters:* ANN WILLIAMS, SARAH GRAVES (land on Nevil's Creek), MARY BENSON (land on Nevil's Creek). *Sons-in-law:* JOHN BENSON (lot No. 38 in Bath Town), THOMAS WILLIAMS (lot No. 39 in Bath Town), THOMAS GRAVES. *Grandson:* ROBERT WILLIAMS ("my plantation"). *Executors:* JOHN TURNER, THOMAS WILLIAMS, THOMAS GRAVES, JOHN BENSON. *Witnesses:* HENRY WEST, JACOB NEVILL, SAMLL. TAYLOR, WILLM. LANE. *Clerk of the Court:* JOHN FORBES.

TURNER, WILLIAM.   Albemarle County.

April 28, 1696. July 27, 1698. Little River. *Sons:* WILLIAM and JOSHUA (plantation to each). *Daughter:* SARAH TURNER. *Wife and Executrix:* KATHERINE. *Witnesses:* RICHARD PLATER, HUGH CAMPBELL, HENRY PALIN, THOMAS SIMMONS. *Clerk to Council:* W. GLOVER.

TURNER, WILLIAM.   Albemarle County.

October 28, 1696. Little River. *Sons:* WILLIAM (orchard on Little Creek), JOHN (plantation bought of PATRICK BALEY). *Daughter:* SARAH TURNER. *Executors:* MATTHEW KELLY and JAMES DAVIS. *Witnesses:* RICHARD PLATOR, HUGH CAMBELL, HENRY PALIN, THOMAS SIMONS. This is a copy made by J. KNIGHT. No probate.

TURNER, WILLIAM.

May 23, 1709. October 17, 1709. *Sons:* WILLIAM and EDWARD. *Brother:* JOHN. *Wife and Executrix:* not named. *Witnesses:* THOS. TWEDIE, ZACHARIAS NIXON, ELIZABETH NIXON. *Clerk of the Court:* THOS. ABINGTON.

TURNER, WILLIAM.   Pasquotank County.

December 23, 1749. April Court, 1750. *Son:* JAMES. *Wife and Executrix:* ELIZABETH (estate divided between son and wife). *Executor:* EZEKIEL TURNER (brother). *Witnesses:* JOSEPH MORRIS, WILLIAM TURNER, PATRICK POOL. *Clerk of the Court:* THOS. TAYLOR.

TURNER, WILLIAM.   Pasquotank County.

April 6, 1753. July Court, 1753. *Sons:* EZEKIEL (land on Gumbridge Branch, on CHARLES OVERMAN's line), JOSEPH (land on Gumbridge Branch), WILLIAM ("two lotts lying next to Nixonton), JOHN ("my plantation"). *Grandson:* JAMES TURNER (two lots next to son WILLIAM's). *Wife and Executrix:* KESIAH. *Witnesses:* ISAAC PARKER, SAML. OVERMAN and RT. WILSON. Codicil dated April 13, 1753, and witnessed by RT. WILSON, ISAAC SWEENIE and JAMES GREGORIE, gives negro man to son WILLIAM. *Clerk of the Court:* THOMAS TAYLOR.

TWEOX, JAMES.

May 5, 1711. *Son:* ROBERT ("all cattle in his possession," "land he now lives on, running from ye south side of his new dwelling house to a place called Selpshis (?) Swamp"). JOHN LAWSON (one horse, and land beginning at Mahomets Swamp running to WM. HARDY's line), MARY LAWSON, JUNR., SAML. HARDY (son of WM. HARDY). *Wife:* ANN TWEOX. "Plantation I now live on" to MARY LAWSON (widow of NATHL. LAWSON). ROBERT TWEOX, JOHN LAWSON and MARY LAWSON to have privilege of grinding at mill, and daughter of MARY LAWSON, provided she marry and "seat in this Neck." *Witnesses:* GEORGE GLADSTENIES, JOSEPH CANINGS, JOHN SNELL (?). *Clerk of the Court:* ROBERT BUCKNER.

TWIDDY, THOMAS.   Pasquotank Precinct.

April 12, 1705. August 19, 1706. *Wife, Executrix and sole legatee:* ELENER. *Witnesses:* THOMAS STAFFORD, RICHARD POOL, JOHN RAPER. *Clerk of the Court:* THO. ABINGTON.

TWIGG, WILLIAM.   Chowan County.

June 20, 1741. July Court, 1741. *Legatees:* ELIZABETH HALE (30 pounds "bill money of this province"), MARY MARSH ("that came in with me into North Carolina," one silver tankard, two silver salts, one silver punch ladle, two silver spoons). *Daughter:* MARY ANN TWIGG, of

London. *Executor:* MILES GALE. *Witnesses:* BENJAMIN TALBOT, KATHERINE DELOGG and PRISTER PERRY. *Clerk of the Court:* JAMES CRAVEN. Coat of arms on seal.

TYLER, MOSES.   Bladen County.

June 25, 1762. August 9, 1762. *Sons:* NEEDHAM ("my plantation"), OWEN ("my cattle"), MOSES (one negro). *Daughters:* PENELEBY, ELISABETH, CHRISTIAN and LUCRETIA TYLER. *Wife and Executrix:* SARAH. *Executor:* JOS. HOWARD. *Witnesses:* ROBERT STEWART, ITHAMAR SINGLETARY, JOHN FLOYD. Proven before ARTHUR DOBBS.

TYLER, THOMAS.   Bath County.

June 5, 1722. July Court, 1722. *Executor and sole legatee:* JOHN JORDAN. *Witnesses:* THOMAS MCKENNY and DAVID BLAIR. *Clerk of the Court:* RT. FORSTER.

TYNER, NICHOLAS.   Northampton County.

December 12, 1752. November Court, 1753. *Grandson:* JAMES TYNER (lands on Gaulberry). *Other children:* NICHOLAS and JOHN TYNER (the children of JAMES TYNER, decd.), WILLIAM TYNER, SARAH WOODARD, ELIZABETH JOHNSON and ANN CORBETT. *Executor:* WILLIAM TYNER (son). *Wife:* ELIZABETH. All estate divided among children abovenamed. *Witnesses:* J. DEW, WILLIAM CORBETT. *Clerk of the Court:* I. EDWARDS.

UNDAY, THOMAS.   Bath County.

October 13, 1722. July Court, 1725. *Wife and Executrix:* MARTHA (houses and lot in Bath town). *Witnesses:* ROBERT FORRESTER, JAMES ROBINS, RALPH SEYMOUR. *Clerk of the Court:* JOHN SWANN.

UPTON, EDWARD.   Pasquotank County.

July 7, 1753. January Court, 1755. *Sons:* EDWARD and JOSHUA (lands adjoining MATTHEW WINN). *Daughters:* SARAH FIRBISH, SABELLA, ELIZABETH, SUSANNA and ANN UPTON. *Wife and Executrix:* ELIZABETH. *Witnesses:* EDWARD and MARY SCOTT, ABRAHAM MILLER. *Clerk of the Court:* THOS. TAYLOR.

UPTON, JOHN.   Pasquotank Precinct.

June 30, 1715. *Sons:* JOHN (plantation known as Buckingham), WILLIAM, JOSEPH and THOMAS (plantation on Pasquotank River), EDWARD (plantation known as Abington). *Daughters:* MARY and RUTH. *Wife and Executrix:* not named. *Witnesses:* GRIFFITH GRAY, METHUSALEM VAUGHAN. *Clerk of the Court:* W. NORRIS.

UPTON, THOMAS.   Pasquotank County.

May 19, 1750. July Court, 1750. *Sons:* WILLIS ("my maner plantation"), THOMAS and WILLIAM (land known as Johnskintown). *Daughters:* ELIZABETH, MERAM and CHARETON UPTON. *Wife and Executrix:* CHRISTIAN. *Witnesses:* JOHN UPTON, ISAAC SAWYER, JOSEPH TEMPLE. *Clerk of the Court:* THO. TAYLOR.

URQUHART, WILLIAM.   Chowan County.

September 5, 1738. September 26, 1738. (Edenton). *Legatees:* JAMES MITCHELL of Edenton, ROBERT ANDERSON of New York (*Executor*). *Witnesses:* ROBERT INNES, JAMES WALLACE, JA. BALLENTINE. Proven before W. SMITH, C. J.

VALLENTINE, RICHARD.

June 4, 1731. December 7, 1731. Northwest branch of Cape Fear River. *Devisees:* JOHN BENNITT, of Pennsylvania (estate on Cape Fear River), JAMES BENNITT, son of JOHN (one-half of estate in Pennsylvania), RUTH BENNITT, daughter of JAMES (one-half of estate in Pennsylvania), ANN BENNITT (wife of JAMES). *Executors:* JOHN CLAYTON, of Cape Faire River, THOMAS LINDLEY, of Philadelphia. *Witnesses:* EDWD. WINGATE, JEFF. POLLARD. Proven before R. MOORE, DA. EVANS and JNO. CLAYTON, *Justices.*

VANLUVEN, CHRISTOPHER.   Bertie County.

September 23, 1732. November 1, 1732. *Sons:* JOHN and HENRY. *Wife and Executrix:* ELISABETH. *Witnesses:* MARTIN FREDERICK RASOR, THOMAS ASHBURN. Proven before GEORGE BURRINGTON.

VAN PELT, JOHN.

November 22, 1734. June 17, 1748. City of New York, Mariner. *Sons:* JOHN (land in Bertie known as JOHN SWANN'S plantation), DANIEL, (land in Bertie known as Chinckapin Neck and JOHN WILSON'S plantation). *Daughters:* MARY and ELSLIE (five lots in Bath Town). *Wife:* MARY. *Executor:* JOHN VAN PELT (son). *Witnesses:* ANDREW MOOR, JOHN PRATT, HENRY DEMEYER. Proven before GAB. JOHNSTON.

VANN, EDWARD.   Chowan County.

February 14, 1738. June 4, 1752. *Son:* EDWARD (land on Swamp). *Daughters:* ANN VANN, SARAH, ELIZABETH. *Executor:* EDWARD VANN (son). *Wife:* not named. *Witnesses:* JOHN VANN, WILLIAM VANN, JOHN LEWIS. Proven before GAB. JOHNSTON.

VANN, JOSEPH.   Chowan County.

April 27, 1752. April Court, 1753. *Sons:* GEORGE, JACOB ("my manner plantation"). *Daughters:* ANN LANGSTON, DARKES, MARY, ELIZABETH and

JUDEY. *Executors:* GEORGE and ELIZABETH VANN (children). *Witnesses:* JACOB ODOM, THOMAS LANGSTONE, SARY LANGSTONE. *Clerk of the Court:* JAMES CRAVEN.

VANN, WILLIAM.   Chowan Precinct.

April 16, 1735. August 11, 1740. *Son:* EDWARD (lands between THOMAS NORICE and STEPHEN SHEPARD; land on the Lands Ridge between JOSEPH BRADDY and JAMES BRADDY). *Daughters:* SARRAH HOGH, ANN VANN. *Grandson:* WILLIAM VANN, son of EDWARD. *Wife and Executrix:* SARRAH. *Witnesses:* JAMES and JOHN BRADY, HENRY GOODMAN. Proven before W. SMITH, C. J.

VARNUM, JACOB.   Chowan County.

September 25, 1715. March 29, 1716. Boston in New England. Chowan in North Carolina. "Mariner." *Wife:* not named. *Other legatee:* WILLIAM GARDINER ("one sad coloured Broad Cloth Coat and breeches and Vest, ye Vest and breeches being in Boston"). *Executor:* ANTHONY ALEXANDER. *Witnesses:* JOHN BLISH, JOHN MIXON, JOHN NEWMAN, GRIFF JONES. *Clerk of the Court:* R. HICKS. Impression of head on seal.

VAUGHAN, JOHN.   Northampton County.

August Court, 1750. *Sons:* WILLIAM and JOHN. *Daughters:* LUCEY, MOLLIE and FANNY. *Wife and Executrix:* CASSIAH. *Witnesses:* SAMUEL TARVER (*Executor*), WILLIAM BAKER, JOHN MANDER. *Clerk of the Court:* I. EDWARDS.

VAUGHAN, VINSON.   Northampton County.

June 29, 1749. August Court, 1749. *Sons:* VINSON (350 acres of land and three negroes), JOSHUA (one negro), NOEL HUTCHENS (one negro). *Daughters:* MARGARET BREATHAN, SARAH VAUGHAN, NAOMY VAUGHAN (one negro to each). *Executors:* JOHN BRETHEN and FRANSES VAUGHAN. *Witnesses:* RICHARD BROWN, JOHN BREEDING, JOHN BROWN. *Clerk of the Court:* I. EDWARDS.

VEALE, WILLIAM.   New Hanover County.

June 11, 1760. November 22, 1760. Wilmington. *Son:* WILLIAM. *Wife and Executrix:* ABIGAIL. *Executor:* DANIEL DUNBIBIN. *Witnesses:* JOHN CAMPBELL, THOMAS MUTTED (?), JOHN FORSTER. Proven before ARTHUR DOBBS.

VINCE, HUMPHREY.   Currituck County.

April 4, 1738. January Court, 1739. *Cousins:* JAMES and SARAH POYNER, PETER, son of JAMES (plantation and negroes), WILLIAM and VINCE WHITE. *Other legatees:* JOSIAS NICKOLS, SARAH SIMMONS, THOMAS MEGGS,

LAZARUS and JOHN FLOWER, ANDREW PEACOCK, LUKE WHITE (cousin). *Executor:* JAMES POYNER. *Witnesses:* THOS. TAYLOR, JOSHUA DEEL, MARY TAYLOR. *Clerk of the Court:* WM. SHERGOLD.

VINCE, THOMAS.   Currituck County.

August 31, 1721. October 10, 1721. *Sons:* THOMAS and WILLIAM. *Daughters:* HANNAH VINCE, MARGRETT WHITE, SARAH POYNER. *Grandchildren:* MARGRETT WHITE, WILLIS POYNER. *Executor:* HUMPHREY VINCE (brother). *Witnesses:* JO. WICKER, WILLIAM PARKER. *Clerk of the Court:* JO. WICKER.

VINES, SAMUEL.   Beaufort County.

March 15, 1740. *Sons:* JOHN (plantation on Goose Creek), SAMUEL and WILLIAM (plantation "wherein I now dwell" called the Point). *Daughters:* FRANSES, ELIZABETH, MARY, REBECCA and ESTER. *Wife and Executrix:* MARY. *Witnesses:* JOHN LAWSON, MARTHA ELLIOTT, ROGER JONES. *Clerk of the Court:* ROGER JONES.

VINSENT, STEPHEN.

September 26, 1696. April 13, 1698. *Wife and Executrix:* MARY. *Witnesses:* JOHN BILLETT, ALSE BILLETT, ———? *Clerk of the Court:* EDWARD MAYO.

WADE, JOHN.   Pasquotank County.

Will not dated. October Court, 1750. *Daughters:* MARY and MAGDALENE WADE. *Executors:* ROBERT LOWRY, WILLIAM DAVIS and JOHN SKINNER. *Witnesses:* JOSIAH CARTRIGHT, ROBERT PALMER, THOMAS WILCOCKS. *Clerk of the Court:* THOMAS TAYLOR.

WADE, JOSEPH.   Orange County.

January 3, 1757. March Court, 1757. *Sons:* JOHN (one dollar), JAMES (three negroes, land on Eno River). *Daughters:* MARY STRAWTHER, SUSANNAH HART, ELIZABETH TALLY, LUCY POWELL (two negroes), SARAH FOUNTIN (one negro). *Wife:* SARAH. *Grandson:* JOSEPH STRAWTHER. *Executors:* JAMES WADE (son) and JOSEPH POWELL (son-in-law). *Witnesses:* WILLIAM BURFORD, SAMUEL BURTON. *Clerk of the Court:* JOSEPH WATSON.

WADE, MARY.   Pasquotank County.

December, 1736. January Court, 1736. *Sister and Executrix:* MAGDALEN WADE. *Witnesses:* JOSHUA MARKHAM, SARAH LOWRY. *Clerk of the Court:* JAMES CRAVEN.

WAHAB, JAMES.   Currituck County.

October 15, 1772. March 25, 1774. Hatteras Banks. *Daughters:* SARAH and BARBARA (negroes to each). *Sons:* JOBE (land at Armiskeat and at Wissockin Creek), JAMES, WILLIAM (land at Hatteras Banks). *Executors:* JAMES and JOB WAHAB (sons). *Witnesses:* JOSEPH WILLIAMS, GEORGE PRICE, ANDREW DONALDSON. Proven before Jo. MARTIN.

WAIDE, ALICE. Chowan County.

April 25, 1700–1701. *Grandsons:* THOMAS and JOHN HAWKINS, THOMAS and JAMES LONG. *Granddaughters:* MARY and ELIZABETH LONG. *Daughter:* ELIZABETH LONG. *Executor:* JOHN HAWKINS. *Witnesses:* GEORGE SLAID, VINES CROPLEY, GEORGE SWAINE. *Clerk of the Court:* N. CHEVIN.

WAIN, THOMAS. Beaufort County.

November 16, 1747. *Son and Executor:* JOHN. *Daughter:* SARAH WHARTON. *Granddaughter:* MAHETABEL WHATNOUGH. *Witnesses:* JOHN FOURER. JOHN HARRISON, WILLIAM DOWS. No probate.

WAINS, THOMAS. Craven County.

Will illegible.

WALBUTTEN, ROBERT. Bertie Precinct.

March 25, 1733. July 31, 1733. *Wife and Executrix:* SARAH. *Sons:* JOHN and SMITHWICK (lands). *Daughter:* SARAH. *Witnesses:* ROBERT ROGERS, HUGH HIGHMAN, JOSEPH WIGHT. Proven before GEORGE BURRINGTON.

WALDRON, JACOB.

May 13, 1763. October Court, 1765. *Sons and Executors:* ISAAC and JACOB. *Brother:* CORNELIUS WALDRON. *Executor:* RICHARD QUINCE. *Witnesses:* RICHARD QUINCE, REVELL MUNROE, PARKER QUINCE. *Clerk of the Court for Wilmington District:* J. BURGWIN.

WALKER, HENDERSON.

October 27, 1701. July 4, 1704. *Wife and Executrix:* ANN. *Other legatees:* MAJ. SWANN ("my sword"), JOHN, GEORGE and SARAH LILLINGTON, ELIZABETH WALKER. *Witnesses:* PR. GODFREY, ROBERT HARMAN, GEORGE CHAMBERY. *Clerk of the Court:* N. CHEVIN.

WALKER, JOHN. Albemarle County.

January 12, 1709. *Wife and Executrix:* ELISABETH. *Sons:* JAMES, THOMAS (land called Barsees Neck). *Daughter:* SARAH. *Executors:* THOMAS and ROBERT WEST. *Witnesses:* ELIZABETH POWELL, ZACHARIAH GARKIN, WILL MITCHELL. Original missing. Recorded in Book 1712–1722, page 37.

WALKER, THOMAS.   Craven County.

February 19, 1753. March 19, 1753. *Son:* JOHN. *Daughters:* SARAH and MARY. *Executors:* BENJAMIN CUMMINGS, THOMAS TIGNER. *Witnesses:* ABNER NEALE, CHRISR. NEALE, JOHN CUMMINGS. Proven before JAS. HASELL, C. J.

WALL, JOSEPH.   Beaufort County.

December 29, 1755. September Court, 1756. *Sons:* JAMES, JOSEPH and HOWEL ("lands on Bear Creek and ye horse pen"), ROBERT. *Daughters:* MARY BALLARD, ANN and ELIZABETH WALL. *Wife and Executrix:* DEBORAH. *Witnesses:* SAMUEL PHILLIPS, JAMES WALL, JOSEPH WALL. *Clerk of the Court:* WALLEY CHAUNCEY.

WALL, JOSHUA.   Currituck County.

November 10, 1744. April Court, 1745. *Sons:* JOSHUA, THOMAS and JOSEPH. No executor. *Witnesses:* THOMAS ROBB, MARY ROOUSALL (RUSSELL), PATTRICK GOODIN. *Clerk of the Court:* RICHARD MCCLURE.

WALL, JOSHUA.   Currituck County.

January 16, 1749. April Court, 1752. Hatteras Banks. *Brother:* THOMAS. *Wife and Executrix:* MARY. *Witnesses:* JOSEPH WILLIAMS and JOSHUA CAMPBELL. *Clerk of the Court:* WILLIAM SHERGOLD.

WALL, RICHARD.   Northampton County.

February 29, 1752. August Court, 1755. *Sons:* SAMPSON (1 negro), RICHARD, ARTHUR, SAMUEL. *Daughters:* JUDITH DELOATCH, SARAH BOYKIN, PRECILA BENSON, JANE LEWIS. *Wife:* LUCY. *Witnesses:* CHAS. CAMPBELL, JAMES LEWIS. *Clerk of the Court:* I. EDWARDS.

WALL, SARAH.   Edgecombe County.

November 2, 1754. June Court, 1756. *Sons:* HENRY, ARTHUR and JOHN WALL. *Grandson:* WILLIAM FRENCH. *Daughter:* FAITH. *Executor:* JOHN WALL (son). *Witnesses:* HENRY, ELIZABETH and SIHON HORN. *Clerk of the Court:* JOS. MONTFORT.

WALLACE, THOMAS.   Currituck County.

January 26, 1746–1747. April 27, 1747. *Wife and Executrix:* SARAH ("my perriauger"). *Daughter:* BARBARA WALLACE. *Witnesses:* CHRIS. BUTLER, ELIZABETH MATTHEWS. Proven before GAB. JOHNSTON.

WALLACE, THOMAS.   Chowan County.

October 28, 1750. January Court, 1750. *Sons:* WILLIAM, JONATHAN, JOHN. *Daughters:* JUDITH and SUSANAH (lands in Bertie County), ELIZABETH WALLACE (land on "the old Soune Neck"), MARY WALLACE

ABSTRACT OF WILLS, 1690—1760.

(land on the east side of the "old Toune Road to Warreck"). *Wife and Executrix:* ELISABETH. *Witnesses:* THOMAS and TIMOTHY WALTON. *Clerk of the Court:* WILL MEARNS.

WALLACE, WILLIAM.   Martin County.

September 19, 1774. February 13, 1775. *Son:* WILLIAM (plantation and six negroes). *Daughters:* KEZIAH, DINAH, QUOTINA, AGNESS, ALBA (one negro to each). *Wife and Executrix:* MARTHA. *Witnesses:* JAMES RAWLINS, WILLIAM LEWELLING, DAVID TAYLOR, WILLIAM BOWERS. Proven before Jo. MARTIN.

WALLER, THOMAS.   Albemarle County.

June 30, 1687. July 10, 1687. *Son:* GEORGE. *Daughters:* ANNE and ELIZABETH. *Wife and Executrix:* not named. *Witnesses:* JOHN HALLAN, WILLIAM BILLINGS, JOHN HARRIS, JOHN DURANT. Proven before SETH SOTHELL.

WALLIS, ANDREW.   Craven County.

March 18, 1742-1743. *Sons:* JAMES, ANDREW. *Wife and Executrix:* MARY. *Witnesses:* WILLIAM WICKLIFFE, JOS. WILSON, ROBERT JARMAN. No probate.

WALLIS, JOHN.   Onslow County.

November 21, 1748. April Court, 1751. *Son and Executor:* RICHARD. *Wife:* ELIZABETH. *Witnesses:* ARTHUR ROYALL, JOHN ROYALL, JOB BROOKES. *Clerk of the Court:* THOMAS BLACK.

WALLIS, STEPHEN.   Craven County.

April 28, 1757. August Court, 1757. *Sons:* BENJAMIN (lands), ROBERT and STEPHEN (*Executors*). *Wife:* SUSANA. *Witnesses:* BERRY NELSON, SARAH NELSON, JOHN CUMMINGS. *Clerk of the Court:* PETER CONWAY.

WALLIS, WILLIAM.   Beaufort County.

December 29, 1748. March Court, 1749. *Sons:* WILLIAM and JOHN (land and negroes). *Daughters:* LIDIA BOND, ABIGAL DAW (negroes to each). *Wife and Executrix:* MARY WALLIS. *Executor:* NICHOLAS DAW. *Witnesses:* PHIL. PRITCHETT, JOHN BENSTED, JEAN BRANNOCK. *Clerk of the Court:* JOHN ALDORSON.

WALSTON, LONDON.   Bath County.

May 26, 1728. April Court, 1728. *Devisees:* THOMAS BATTERS (*Executor*), MARY BATTERS, daughter of THOMAS (land on "Papleco River" adjoining Blunts Town). *Witnesses:* JAMES BACKALDER, THOMAS RIGNE, MARY CORDING. *Clerk of the Court:* THOMAS JONES.

WALTERS, MARY.   New Hanover County.

April, 1756. May 25, 1756. *Brothers:* JOHN and JOSEPH WALTERS. *Sisters:* ELIZABETH WALTERS and MARY GRAINGER. *Son:* WILLIAM WALTERS. *Other legatees:* BARBARA MURRAY, ISABEL MACNEIL, KATHERINE MACLAINE (daughter of ARCHIBALD MACLAINE). *Executor:* JAMES MURRAY (lands on Black River). *Witnesses:* B. MURRAY, ANN BRITTON, WALTER ———. Codicil dated April 21, 1756, bequeaths estate to sister, MARY GRAINGER, in event of death of son. *Witnesses to codicil:* JOSEPH and ELIZABETH WALTERS. Proven before ARTHUR DOBBS. *Clerk of the Court:* ISAAC FARIES.

WALTON, THOMAS.   Chowan County.

November 12, 1750. July 5, 1751. *Son and Executor:* WILLIAM. *Daughters:* ELIZABETH TROTMAN, SUSANAH WALTON, JUDETH ROUNTREE, ANN HUNTER, SARAH PERY (1 negro). *Grandson:* THOMAS WALTON (plantation). *Witnesses:* WILLIAM WALTON, HARDY HUNTER, TIMOTHY WALTON. Proven before GAB. JOHNSTON at Eden House.

WAMAN, WILLIAM.   Pasquotank County.

March 18, 1721. July 18, 1721. *Sons:* WILLIAM, ROBERT and JOHN. The following lands are devised: land on Nobesbruke Creek, lands between DAVID PRICHARD and BENJAMIN LONEWELL, lands between the mouth of Pasquotank River and Flatty Creek. *Daughter:* ELENDER WAMAN. *Wife and Executrix:* HANNAH. *Witnesses:* JNO. MCKEELE, JNO. FOURRE, THOMAS REES. *Clerk of the Court:* EDMUND GALE.

WAR, WILLIAM.   Northampton County.

December 16, 1754. May Court, 1756. *Sons:* HENRY, THOMAS (200 acres of land on the Horse Hole). *Daughter:* ANN WAR. *Wife:* ANN. *Executor:* WILLIAM WINBORNE. *Witnesses:* THOMAS FLANNER, PHILIP WINBORNE. *Clerk of the Court:* I. EDWARDS.

WARD, ENOCH.   Carteret County.

February 13, 1750. March Court, 1750. *Sons:* RICHARD and ENOCK. *Daughters:* ANN, MARY, ELIZABETH, SARAH, ABIGALL and SUSANAH (lands on Banks). *Son-in-law:* JOSEPH SUTTON (husband of daughter ANN). *Other devisee:* JAMES SHACKELLFORD. *Wife:* MARY. *Executors:* RICHARD WARD and EDWARD SIMPSON. *Witnesses:* ANANIAS CAVENAGH, JOSHUA and JOHN SIMPSON. *Clerk of the Court:* GEO. READ. Five negroes bequeathed.

WARD, JOHN.   Chowan County.

May 9, 1747. December 16, 1748. *Sons:* THOMAS, JAMES and JOSEPH (land bought of GEORGE TURNIDGE), WILLIAM, JOBE, AMOS (plantation known by the name of the Indian Creek), BENJAMIN. *Daughters:* ELIZABETH TOMSON, CATTERINE EVINS. *Wife and Executrix:* CATTERENE WARD. *Witnesses:* THOMAS ROWNTREE, CHARLES COPELAND, JOHN COPELAND. Proven before GAB. JOHNSTON.

WARD, JOHN.   Tyrrell County.

March 5, 1748–1749. September Court, 1750. *Sons:* MICHAEL, JOHN (1 negro and "all cattle running on Little Cantanknee"), DAVID. *Daughters:* ELIZABETH NOBLE (100 acres of land), DORCAS OVERSTREET (land lying on Little Cantanknee). *Executors:* MICHAEL and JOHN (sons). *Witnesses:* GRIFFITH HOWELL, JOHN BUTLER, ELIZABETH BUTLER. *Clerk of the Court:* EVAN JONES.

WARD, THOMAS.   Chowan County.

October 16, 1750. July Court, 1751. *Wife and Executrix:* CHRISTIAN. *Son:* MICHAEL ("the Shop Plantation"). *Witnesses:* WILLIAM WRIGHT, HARDY and JOSEPH HURDLE. *Clerk of the Court:* JAMES CRAVEN.

WARMING, ABRAHAM.   Albemarle County.

No date or probate. *Legatees:* JOHN WHEATLEY, WILLIAM WINSEY. *Witnesses:* JOHN LEWIS, ELINOR LUTON, THOMAS LUTEN, JOHN CHANDLER.

WARRIN, ABRAHAM.   Perquimans County.

October 26, 1739. July Court, 1740. *Son:* HENRY (plantation "I now live on"). *Other children:* mentioned, but not named. *Other legatees:* JOHN and JEAMES CHESSON, CHRISTOPHER DENMAN. *Creditors:* SARAH and SUSANNAH SUTTEN. *Wife and Executrix:* SARAH. *Executor:* RICHARD SKINNER. *Witnesses:* JOHN CREESE, MARY CREESE, JOHN STEPNEY. *Clerk of the Court:* JAMES CRAVEN.

WARREN, HENRY.   Matchepungo Creek, in Bath County.

February 15, 1716. April 2, 1717. *Son:* ABRAHAM (lands). *Daughters:* MARY, ELIZABETH and ANN (cattle to each). *Wife and Executrix:* ELIZABETH. *Executor:* JOHN PORTER, of Bath. *Witnesses:* JOHN MARTIN, WILLIAM HARRIS, GI. HALLIDAY. Codicil of even date and witnessed by same persons bequeaths negro to son, ABRAHAM. *Clerk of the Court:* JNO. DRINKWATER.

WARREN, ROBERT.   Edgecombe County.

Not dated. June Court, 1759. *Daughters:* MARY WARREN (one negro), SARAH, JANE and MILSSON WARREN. *Wife and Executrix:* MARGRET. *Executor:* GEORGE DAWKINS. *Witnesses:* BENJAMIN MERRYMAN, WILLIAM LANE. *Clerk of the Court:* JOSEPH MONTFORT.

WARREN, SARAH.   Perquimans Precinct.

October 1, 1730. *Sons-in-law:* ABRAHAM JONES, JOHN ARNOLD *(Executor). Other legatee:* ANN CRAWTHERS, daughter of NATHAN CRAWTHERS. *Witnesses:* JOHN FALCONER, ABRAHAM WARREN, SARAH WARREN. No probate.

WARREN, WILLIAM.

October 3, 1723. November 26, 1723. *Friend and Executor:* JOSEPH REDING. *Witnesses:* ALEXR. CRUIKSHANK, DUGLIS ROD. Proven before WILLIAM REED.

WATERS, WILLIAM.   Onslow Precinct.

January 18, 1751. July Court, 1754. *Son:* JOSIAS. *Daughter:* MARY. *Wife and Executrix:* MARTHA. *Witnesses:* LEWIS JENKINS, JOHN AVIRETT. *Clerk of the Court:* WM. RAY.

WATKINS, THOMAS.   Perquimans County.

January 3, 1754. January Court, 1754. *Legatees:* JOHN and RICHARD WHEDBEE, JOHN MORRIS and SAMUELL NEWBY. *Executor:* JOHN WHIDBEE. *Witnesses:* WILLIAM FOSTER, POTSEFULL PIERCE, MARY WHEDBEE. *Clerk of the Court:* EDMUND HATCH.

WATKINS, WILLIAM.   Pitt County.

November 9, 1771. October 14, 1773. *Sons:* JOHN and WILLIAM. *Sons-in-law:* FRANCIS BUCK, JAMES CASON, WILLIAM ORMOND, JAMES JONES. *Daughters:* SARAH BUCK, ELIZABETH, ANN and RACHEL. *Wife and Executrix:* CHRISTIAN. *Witnesses:* CATHERINE CROFTON, JOHN SALTER, RANDEL MCDANIEL. Proven before JO. MARTIN.

WATSON, JOHN.   New Hanover County.

January 3, 1743–1744. March Court, 1743. "Of ye Sound." *Sons:* JOHN, JOSEPH and JONATHAN. *Daughter:* SARAH. *Wife and Executrix:* SARAH. *Witnesses:* ARCHD. NICKELLS, JOSEPH JONES, FRANCIS BEALE. *Clerk of the Court:* JAMES SMALLWOOD.

WATSON, JOHN.   New Hanover County.

December 15, 1773. March 3, 1774. *Son:* JOHN. *Daughters:* ELIZABETH WATSON, MARY, wife of SAMUEL MARSHALL, SARAH, wife of NIXON CHESTER. *Wife and Executrix:* ANN. *Witnesses:* JNO. ROBESON, JOHN GAILLARD, WILLM. NICHOLS. Proven before JO. MARTIN.

WAXDALE, JOHN.   Bath County.

November 12, 1733. December Court, 1734. Trent River. *Son:* JOHN. *Wife and Executrix:* WALPOLIA. *Witnesses:* DAVID DUPUIS, WILLIAM DUPUIS, JOHN SIMONS, JOHN PARKER, JAMES CLEMENT. *Clerk of the Court:* CALEB METCALFE.

ABSTRACT OF WILLS, 1690—1760.

WAXDALE, JOHN. Craven County.

March 5, 1738–1739. December 18, 1739. *Daughters:* LOVICE, MARGARET, KATHERINE, MARIAM, ANNACIVILLA. *Executors:* ABRAHAM BUSSETT, PHILIP MILLER. *Witnesses:* HUGH STANALAND, NATHANIEL PARROTT. *Clerk of the Court:* JAMES COOR.

WAYMAN, WILLIAM. Pasquotank County.

March 9, 1737. July Court, 1740. *Legatees:* MARY, HANER, THAMER, THOMAS and ROBERT LOWRY. *Executor:* ROBERT LOWRY. *Witnesses:* ROBERT and MARY LOWRY. *Clerk of the Court:* JAMES CRAVEN.

WEAVER, JOHN. Chowan County.

September 18, 1750. October Court, 1750. *Legatees:* JOHN POLSON (*Executor*) and CALEB POLSON, son of JOHN. *Witnesses:* MARY STUART, GEORGE POLSON, DEMSEY SUMNER. *Clerk of the Court:* WILLIAM MEARNS.

WEAVER, WILLIAM. Bertie Precinct.

February Court, 1735. *Sons:* WILLIAM, JOHN (land at Pea Hill), HENRY (land on Fountains Creek), EDWARD, THOMAS (one "Clankibone pot"). *Brother:* STEPHEN WEAVER. *Wife and Executrix:* not named. *Witnesses:* JOHN COOK and JOHN ARNOL. *Clerk of the Court:* JOHN WYNNS.

WEBB, ANTHONY. Bertie County.

August 27, 1748. November Court, 1750. *Sons:* SAMUEL, WILLIAM (plantation on Deep Creek "whereon I now live" and two negroes). *Daughters:* PERSILLO, KEZIER, ANNE. *Wife:* MARTHA. *Executor:* WILLIAM. *Witnesses:* WILLIAM and JOHN BARTON, ISAAC PIERCE. *Clerk of the Court:* SAMUEL ORMES.

WEBB, HENRY. Orange County.

January 10, 1756. March Court, 1759. *Sons:* WENTWORTH and JOHN (negro to each). *Wife and Executrix:* ELIZABETH. *Witnesses:* GEORGE LAWS, ELIAS DOWNES. *Clerk of the Court:* JAMES WATSON.

WEBB, JOHN. Northampton County.

February 11, 1749. February Court, 1749. *Sons:* JOLLEY, JAMES and JESSE. *Daughter:* JUDITH WEBB (estate divided among children above named). *Wife and Executrix:* ELIZABETH. *Witnesses:* ROBERT HICKS, WILLIAM RAGLAND. *Clerk of the Court:* I. EDWARDS.

WEBB, SAMUEL. Bertie County.

May 24, 1754. May Court, 1754. *Sons:* BENJAMIN and SAMUEL (lands on Horse Creek). *Daughters:* PENELOPE, ANN and ELIZABETH WEBB (negro to each). *Wife and Executrix:* MARGET. *Witnesses:* MOSES SUMNER, TAMER WILLIFORD, EASTER WILLEFORD. *Clerk of the Court:* SAMUEL ORMES.

WEBSTER, ELISABETH.   Carteret County.

March 4, 1754. June Court, 1754. *Sons:* JOHN WEBSTER, JOSEPH, JAMES and SAMUEL NOBLE, BENJAMIN WEBSTER. *Daughters:* HANNAH ROBERTS and RACHEL HOURTON. *Executor:* SAMUEL NOBLE (son). *Witnesses:* MOSES HOUSTON, RACHEL PEARSON, HANNAH SIMMONS. *Clerk of the Court:* GEO. READ.

WEBSTER, JOHN.   Carteret County.

July 8, 1745. February 27, 1746. *Sons:* JOHN, JOSEPH, BENJAMIN. *Daughters:* ELIZABETH and MARY. *Executors:* PETER PEERY and NICHOLAS HUNTER. *Witnesses:* MOSES HOUSTON, JAMES NOBLE, RICHARD WILLIAMSON. Proven before GAB. JOHNSTON.

WEBSTER, JOHN.   Hyde County.

December 25, 1773. April 6, 1774. *Sons:* RICHARD, SAMUEL, JAMES and HENRY. *Daughter:* MARY. *Wife and Executrix:* LYDIA. *Executors:* SAMUEL SMITH and WILLM. PORTER. *Witnesses:* JOHN MARKDORY (?), RICHARD CAPPS. Proven before JO. MARTIN.

WEBSTER, WILLIAM.   Hyde County.

October 16, 1745. February 3, 1745. *Son:* WILLIAM (plantation and two negroes). *Wife and Executrix:* ANN. *Grandchildren:* JOHN THOROGOOD WEBSTER and ANN WEBSTER, children of JAMES WEBSTER, deceased (one negro girl to each). *Witnesses:* JOHN WEIGHT, LODWICK MARTIN, THOMAS LOACK. *Clerk of the Court:* THOMAS LOACK.

WEEKES, BENJAMIN.   Carteret County.

November 9, 1744. June Court, 1745. *Sons:* ISAAC, JARBUS, THEFFLUS, ARCHELAS, BENGUMEN. *Daughters:* LIDDA WITTON, MARY WILLIMS, CHRISTIAN WEAKS, THANKFULL HICKS, ELIZABETH WEEKS. *Wife and Executrix:* MARY. *Witnesses:* JEHOSHAPHAT HOLLANDS, FRANCIS BURNS, THOMAS PERSON. *Clerk of the Court:* GEORGE READ.

WELCH, JOHN.   Chowan County.

April 23, 1730. *Sons:* EDWARD and JOHN (plantation to each, JOHN'S lying on Cockfighting Branch), JAMES (land on Cockfighting Branch). *Daughter:* SARAH (150 acres of land). *Wife and Executrix:* ELIZABETH. *Witnesses:* JOHN and JAMES PARKER, BENJAMIN EVANS. No probate.

WELCH, NATHANIEL. Pasquotank County.
February 13, 1734–1735. April Court, 1735. *Legatees:* TERENCE SWEENY, THOMAS GASKILL, ELIZABETH GASKILL, JOSEPH PENDLETON, DANIEL DUNN, JOHN CORP. *Executor:* TERENCE SWEENY. *Witnesses:* JOHN SMEDLEY, THOMAS PENDLETON. *Clerk of the Court:* JOS. SMITH.

WELLS, WILLIAM.
January 31, 1742–1743. *Sons:* WILLIAM and NATHANIELL, JOHN and JOSEPH (lands), HENRY. *Daughters:* SARAH EVANS, ELIZABETH ———. *Executor:* JOHN STARKEY. *Witnesses:* JOHN DUDLEY, JOHN MCGRAH, EPH. SWIFT. No probate. County not given.

WENHAM, ROBERT.
May 16, 1735. August 9, 1735. *Sons:* ROBERT (*Executor*), WILLIAM. *Witnesses:* FRANCIS BROWN, JOHN GREEN, JOHN GOURDON. Proven before W. SMITH, C. J.

WEST, ARTHUR. Bertie County.
April 12, 1727. May Court, 1730. *Devisees and legatees:* ROBERT, son of HENRY WEST (land on Fishing Creek), NATHANIEL HICKMAN (land on Fishing Creek). *Brother:* JOSEPH WEST. *Sister:* MARY WEST. *Wife and Executrix:* MARY. *Witnesses:* ARTHUR WHITCHED, WILLIAM WEST, EDWARD TOWERSON. *Clerk of the Court:* RT. FORSTER.

WEST, CHARLES. Pasquotank County.
August 8, 1747. October Court, 1748. *Sons:* LEMUEL (four negroes), JONATHAN (three negroes and cattle), HEZEKIAH (two negroes). *Daughters:* WINEFRUIT WEST (two negroes), DINAH WEST. *Grandson:* BENJAMIN WEST, son of CHARLES, dec'd (plantation known as Cowpen Neck and Rollinseas). *Wife and Executrix:* DINAH. *Executors:* LEMUEL WEST (son) and THOMAS MACKEEL (son-in-law). *Witnesses:* JOHN GUTHRAY, ANN DANIEL, JOHN MCKEEL. *Clerk of the Court:* THOS. TAYLOR.

WEST, HENRY. Beaufort County.
August 14, 1752. December Court, 1752. *Sisters:* MARY SOJORNER, SARAH PEYTON, CEILA TYNES. *Nephew:* JOHN PEYTON. *Niece:* HOLLAND APPLEWHITE. *Executors:* JOHN GILES, MICHAEL COUTANCHE, WILLIAM PEYTON and THOMAS PIERCE. *Witnesses:* THOMAS and JOHN JASPER, JOHN PORTER. *Clerk of the Court:* WILL ORMOND. Original missing. Abstract made from recorded copy.

WEST, JOHN. Chowan Precinct.
July 16, 1713. *Wife and Executrix:* ELIZABETH. *Witnesses:* LAWRENCE SARSON, ELIZABETH ROSE. Original missing. Recorded in Book 1712–1722, page 27.

WEST, JONATHAN. Pasquotank County.

August 28, 1751. July Court, 1751. *Legatees:* LAMUEL and HEZEKIAH WEST, THOMAS MCKEEL, WILLIAM WOODLEY, DINAH and BENJAMIN WEST. Negroes are divided among above-named. *Executors:* THOMAS WOODLY and THOMAS MACKEEL. *Witnesses:* JONATHAN HOWELL, ISAAC COX, ANTHONY WHITE. *Clerk of the Court:* THOMAS TAYLOR.

WEST, PETER. Bertie County.

July 31, 1749. ʻMay Court, 1751. *Daughters:* SARAH WEST, ELIZABETH COTTON (four negroes). *Son:* PETER (lands and negroes). *Grandson:* WILLIAM WEST. *Executor:* CHARLES HORNE. *Witnesses:* HENRY WINBORNE, BRYAN HARE, WUSTRUM (?) ROGERS. *Clerk of the Court:* SAMUEL ORMES.

WEST, ROBERT. Chowan Precinct.

March 28, 1689. June 4, 1689. *Sons:* ROBERT, THOMAS, JOHN and RICHARD (lands and negroes). *Wife and Executrix:* MARTHA. *Witnesses:* JAMES DAMERELL, JAMES HARLA. Proven before SETH SOTHELL.

WEST, THOMAS. Bertie County.

November 6, 1756. April Court, 1757. *Wife and Executrix:* ELIZABETH. *Daughter:* ELIZABETH WEST. *Son:* WILLIAM. (7 negroes divided among foregoing). *Executor:* ROBERT WEST (brother). *Witnesses:* JOHN CORBERT, WM. FLEETWOOD, JOSEPH WHITE. *Clerk of the Court:* BENJN. WYNNS.

WEST, WILLIAM. Bertie Precinct.

July 28, 1735. *Legatees and Executors:* ROBERT WEST, JR., and THOMAS WEST, his brother (all estate devised and bequeathed to these two). *Witnesses:* WILLIAM LATTIMER, ROBERT WEST. No probate officer.

WEST, WILLIAM. Beaufort County.

December 4, 1744. December 10, 1745. *Daughters:* SARAH PEYTON (negro), CAHIA TYNES, MARY SOJOURNER. *Grandson:* JACOB SOJOURNER. *Wife and Executrix:* SUSANNA. *Executor:* HENRY WEST (son). *Witnesses:* RICHRD. JONES, MARY SMITH, JEREMIAH SMITH. *Clerk of the Court:* JOHN FORBES.

WEST, WILLIAM. Edgecombe County.

November 26, 1749. February Court, 1749. *Son and Executor:* WILLIAM (lands on Rocky Swamp, together with water mill). *Brother:* HENRY WEST. *Nephew:* WILLIAM WEST (son of HENRY). *Daughter:* MARY WILLIAMS. *Witnesses:* WALLIS JONES, JOHN LONG, JOEL JONES. *Clerk of the Court:* BENJAMIN WYNNS.

Abstract of Wills, 1690—1760.

West, William. — Craven County.
February Court, 1750. *Sons:* JOHN, DANIEL, WILLIAM, SAMEWILL (SAMUEL). *Daughters:* MARY LANE, ELIZABETH and LYDIA WEST. *Wife and Executrix:* REBECKOR. *Executors:* JOHN LANE and DANIEL DAUGHITY. *Witnesses:* JONATHAN MCKFARSON, DANIEL DAUGHITY, ELIZABETH DAUGHITY. *Clerk of the Court:* PETER CONWAY.

Weston, William. — Bertie County.
November 12, 1747. February Court, 1748. *Sons:* EPHRAIM, JOHN and WILLIAM (lands "upon the Loosing Swamp" and other tracts described in will), MALICHI and THOMAS WESTON ("plantation whereon I live"). *Daughter:* RACHEL WESTON. *Wife:* CATHERINE. *Executors:* JOHN and WILLIAM (sons). *Witnesses:* JOSEPH WATFORD, MOSES GREEN. *Clerk of the Court:* JOHN WESTON.

Whaltone, Thomas. — Chowan County.
May 8, 1719. June 8, 1719. *Wife:* ANNE, of King and Queen County in Virginia. All estate is left to wife and seven children, not named. *Executor:* JOHN PLOWMAN. *Witnesses:* AB. COKBURNE, JOHN WHITE, MARY WHITE. Proven before Governor CHARLES EDEN. Impression of what appears to be cherub with wings on seal.

Wharrey, Anthony. — Perquimans Precinct.
September 17, 1716. July 8, 1718. *Son:* JOSHUA. *Wife and Executrix:* SARAH. *Executor:* THOMAS HARVEY. *Witnesses:* FRANCIS SMITH. SAMUELL WYATT, ANN RAY. *Clerk of the Court:* RICHARD LEARY.

Whary, Joshua. — Perquimans Precinct.
January 28, 1729. August 18, 1730. *Brother:* ANTHONY WHARY. *Sisters:* ELIZABETH, RACHEL, SARAH and MARY WHARY. *Executor:* ROBERT BEVINES. *Witnesses:* JOHN ARNAL, ELIZABETH ARNAL, JOHN STEPNEY. Proven before GAB. JOHNSTON.

Wheatley, John. — Chowan County.
December, 1706. January 1, 1706–1707. *Daughters:* ELIZABETH, ANN and MARTHA. *Wife and Executrix:* ANNE (land on Indian Towne Creek). *Executor:* SAMUEL PASCKEL. *Witnesses:* THOMAS LUTON, HENRY BONER, NATHL. CHEVIN. *Clerk of the Court:* NATHL. CHEVIN.

Wheatley, Samuel. — Tyrrell County.
January 21, 1739–1740. June Court, 1740. *Wife and children:* mentioned, but not named. *Executors:* SAMUEL WHEATLEY and WILLIAM KENNEDY. *Witnesses:* WM. KENNEDY, SARY PELL, MARY WENTHAM. *Clerk of the Court:* THOMAS LEARY.

WHEDBEE, RICHARD.   Perquimans County.

January, 1746. July Court, 1746. *Sons:* JOHN (plantation and one negro), RICHARD (land known as Broken Beeches and one negro), GEORGE (three negroes), BENJAMIN and JOSEPH (two negroes to each). *Daughters:* ELIZABETH PRATT, DEBORAH WILKENS, SARAH HASKENS (two negroes to each). *Wife and Executrix:* HANNAH (two negroes). *Executors:* CHRISTIAN and JOSEPH REED (brothers-in-law). *Witnesses:* SAMUEL SNOWDEN, ELIZABETH REED, CATHERINE DAVIS. *Clerk of the Court:* EDMUND HATCH.

WHEEDBEE, ANN.   Pasquotank County.

September 24, 1750. January Court, 1750. *Sons:* WILLIAM BOYD and THOMAS BOYD. *Other legatees:* ELIZABETH BAILEY, WINIFORT BOYD, ANN BAILEY. *Executors:* ANTHONY MARCKHAM and WILLIAM BOYD. *Witnesses:* JOHN WILKINS, JOSEPH COMMANDER. *Clerk of the Court:* THOS. TAYLOR.

WHELLER, HENRY.   Bertie Precinct.

June 24, 1726. November Court, 1727. *Sons:* EMPRER, HENRY, JOHN. *Daughter.* SARAH. *Wife and Executrix:* ANNE. *Witnesses:* ROBERT SIMES, ANDREW IRELAND. *Clerk of the Court:* ROBERT FORSTER.

WHIDBE, GEORGE.   Pasquotank Precinct.

March 22, 1718. July 29, 1718. *Sons:* RICHARD, GEORGE (land on Alegator River), JOHN. *Cousin:* RICHARD WHIDBE. *Daughter:* RUTH WHIDBE. *Executors:* GEORGE and RICHARD WHIDBE (sons). *Witnesses:* JOHN MIXON, AUTHO. ALLEXANDER, REBECKAH BALEY. *Clerk of the Court:* R. HICKS.

WHIDBE, GEORGE.   Albemarle County.

April 21, 1722. *Daughters:* ANN and ELIZABETH (land on Cow Ridge). *Brother:* RICHARD WHIDBEE. *Other legatees:* JOHN GARDENER (son of JANE GARDENER) and JOHN WHIDBEE (son of JOHN WHIDBEE). *Wife and Executrix:* WINEFORD. *Witnesses:* JOSEPH WINSHIP, WILLIAM HUDSON, WILLIAM WILLSON. Proven before WM. REED, *"Presidente of North Carolina."*

WHIDBEE, GEORGE.   Pasquotank County.

June 16, 1749. August 11, 1749. *Brothers:* JOHN and RICHARD WHIDBEE. *Nephews:* GEORGE (son of RICHARD), JOHN and THOMAS WHIDBEE (sons of JOHN). To above-named is bequeathed negroes. *Wife and Executrix:* ANN. *Witnesses:* ANTHONY MARKHAM, JNO. MCKEEL. Proven before GAB. JOHNSTON at Eden House. Coat of arms on seal.

WHIDBE, RICHARD.   Tyrrell County.
   March 29, 1736. June Court, 1740. *Cousin and Executor:* GEORGE
PHILPS. *Other legatee:* CUDBATH PHILPS. *Witnesses:* JOHN WOODLAND,
THOMAS and JANE BEST. *Clerk of the Court:* THOMAS LEARY.

WHITE, ABRAHAM.   Pasquotank County.
   January 7, 1746. January Court, 1746. *Brother:* JOHN WHITE.
Nephew: JAMES WHITE, son of JOHN (plantation). *Wife and Executrix:*
SARAH. *Executor:* JAMES WHITE (brother). *Witnesses:* AARON MORRIS,
THOMAS SYMONS, JOSEPH ROBINSON. *Clerk of the Court:* THOMAS TAY-
LOR. Device on seal.

WHITE, ARNOLD.
   March 22, 1690. *Daughter:* ELIZABETH. *Son and Executor:* ARNOLD.
Brother: HENRY WHITE. *Witnesses:* STEPHEN MUNDEN, WILLIAM MAN,
JEAMS DAVIS. *Clerk of the Court:* HENDERSON WALKER.

WHITE, ARNOLD.   Perquimans County.
   April 24, 1751. July Court, 1752. *Sons:* SAMUEL and ARNOLD (plantation divided between them). *Wife and Executrix:* ELIZABETH. *Witnesses:* PETER PARKER, JACOB OVERMAN, MARY PARKER. *Clerk of the
Court:* EDMUND HATCH.

WHITE, GEORGE.   Craven County.
   October 7, 1741. September 22, 1744. *Sons:* GEORGE and LUKE.
Daughters: SARAH and PERSILLA. *Wife:* FRANCESS. *Witnesses:* ROBERT
CLARK, JOHN WHITE, EDWD. VANN. Proven before GAB. JOHNSTON.

WHITE, GEORGE.   Chowan County.
   April, 1747. Will illegible.

WHITE, HENRY.
   November 14, 1669–1670. May 16, 1670. *Wife:* ELENER. *Son:* ARNULL.
No executor appointed. *Witnesses:* GEORGE RICHARDS, HENRY MAN-
NERLY. *Clerk of the Court:* THOS. HARRIS. *Justice:* PETER CARTERET.

WHITE, HENRY.   Albemarle County.
   September 19, 1706. *Sons:* HENRY, ARNOLD, ISACK, ROBERT and JOHN.
(Negroes and "maner" plantation devised and bequeathed to sons.) *Daugh-
ters:* CONTENT, MARY and NAOMY. *Wife and Executrix:* not named. *Wit-
nesses:* ZACHARIAH NIXON, JOHN SYMONS, JOHN MARTIN, JEREMYAH
SYMONS, JOHN RAPER. No probate.

26

WHITE, HENRY.   Pasquotank County.

March 25, 1739. April Court, 1739. *Sons:* THOMAS and ISAAC (all estate left to these two sons). *Executors:* HENRY STANTON and WILLIAM BURDEN (or BENDER). *Witnesses:* WILLIAM SYMONS, JOHANA WHITE, BENJAMIN NEWBY. *Clerk of the Court:* JOSEPH SMITH. *Clerk of Carteret County:* JOHN SIMPSON.

WHITE, HENRY.   Currituck County.

December 22, 1751. September 10, 1754. *Sons:* HILARY (two negroes), HENRY, JOSEPH (land at Navis Creek), CALEB (plantation called Dunkeleys), JOSHUA, CHURCH. To four sons is given land over Indian Creek, and also plantation at Black Water. *Daughter:* MARY. *Executors:* HILARY and HENRY WHITE (sons). *Witnesses:* JOS. CAMPBELL, CHARLES WILLIAMS, WILLIAM DUDING (?). *Clerk of the Court:* JOHN SNOAD.

WHITE, JOHN.   Albemarle County.

April 4, 1690–1691. *Legatees:* WILLIAM and ELIZABETH EDLETON, JAMES RIGG (*Executor*). *Wife and Executrix:* MARGRET. *Witnesses:* JOHN STEPNEY, STEPHEN HANREFFE (?), THOMAS LEFFER (?). Signature of probate officer illegible.

WHITE, JOHN.   Hyde County.

April 7, 1724. April Court, 1726. *Wife and Executrix:* SARAH. *Witnesses:* ROBERT PEYTON, PATRICK MAULE. *Clerk of the Court:* THOMAS JONES. Executrix qualified before SAMUEL SLADE. Coat of arms on seal.

WHITE, JOHN.   Perquimans Precinct.

February 16, 1730–1731. March 10, 1730. *Son:* JOHN. *Daughters:* RACHEL WHITE (land bought of FRANCIS NUBE (NEWBY), SARAH, ELIZABETH and HULDE. *Sister:* MARY. *Wife and Executrix:* SARAH. *Witnesses:* JOHN LILLE, JAMES ———, WILLIAM WHITE. Proven before GEORGE BURRINGTON.

WHITE, JOHN.   Carteret County.

April 11, 1744. February 26, 1745. *Brother:* ROBERT WHITE, of the County of Norfolk, in Great Britain. *Executors:* JOHN STARKEY and SAMUELL WILSON. *Witnesses:* RALPH CAVES, SARAH STARKEY, JACOB BIDDLE. Proven before GAB. JOHNSTON.

WHITE, JOHN.   Pasquotank County.

May 19, 1754. July Court, 1754. *Son:* SAMUEL. *Sister:* ELIZABETH WHITE. *Wife:* ANN. *Other legatee:* JOHN MAN. *Executor:* JAMES DAVIS. *Witnesses:* TIMOTHY MEEDS, JAMES DAVIS, WILLIAM BUNDY. *Clerk of the Court:* THOMAS TAYLOR.

ABSTRACT OF WILLS, 1690—1760. 403

WHITE, LUKE. Currituck County.

June 8, 1757. March Court, 1758. *Sons:* VINSON (land called Absalom Poiner's), JOSHUA (plantation and one negro). *Daughters:* CHRISTIAN WHITE, KEZIAH ELLES, wife of MICHAEL ELLES, MARY, wife of JOHN TOMSON. *Wife and Executrix:* MARGARET. *Witnesses:* WILLIAM BRAY, JOSEPH POYNER, JOHN WHEATLEY. *Clerk of the Court:* WM. MEARNS.

WHITE, MEDIA. Bertie County.

August 27, 1744. January 17, 1749. Chowan. *Wife and Executrix:* ELIZABETH. *Witnesses:* ABIGAIL WHITE, JOSEPH BUTTERTON, SARAH BUTTERTON. Proven before GAB. JOHNSTON. Impression of winged dragon on seal.

WHITE, NEHEMIAH. Pasquotank County.

September 5, 1751. July Court, 1751. *Sons:* BENJAMIN and JOSHUA (land to each). *Daughters:* SARAH, MARY and MARTHA WHITE. *Wife and Executrix:* MARTHA. *Executor:* JOSEPH PRITCHARD (brother-in-law). *Witnesses:* JOSEPH COMMANDER, ROBERT WHITE, JOSEPH ROBINSON. *Clerk of the Court:* THOMAS TAYLOR.

WHITE, ROBERT. Albemarle County.

April 19, 1698. Probate illegible. *Sons:* VINCENT and ROBERT. *Daughter:* MARY. *Friend:* THOMAS JONES. *Executor:* VINCENT WHITE (son). *Witnesses:* EPHREAM COSTE, JOHN FOURRE, FRANCIS DeLaMARE.

WHITE, ROBERT. Pasquotank Precinct.

January 1, 1732. April 16, 1733. *Sons:* JONATHAN and ZEFENIAH ("the manah plantation adjoining ROBERT LOWRY"), JOSEPH ("back land" and two negroes). To each of sons is bequeathed negroes. *Daughters:* ANN and ELIZABETH WHITE. *Wife and Executrix:* REBECKAH. *Witnesses:* AARON MORRIS, ROBART DAVIS, HENRY WHITE. Proven before GEO. BURRINGTON.

WHITE, ROGER. Albemarle County.

September 10, 1686. *Wife and Executrix:* JOAN. *Other legatees:* WILLIAM MORRISON, RICHARD WILLIAMSON and GEORGE LONODAY (?). *Witnesses:* WM. CHAPMAN, GEORGE LONODAY (?), RICHARD WILLIAMSON, THOMAS WALLEN. No probate.

WHITE, SARAH. Hyde County.

January 6, 1726. April Court, 1727. *Legatees:* BENJAMIN MORDICKE (plantation on Machepungo River), ELIZABETH MONTGOMERY, JOHN SNOAD, JR., ARDLEY THOROWGOOD, SARAH BELL (*Executrix*). *Witnesses:* GI. HALIDAY, WILLIAM WEBSTER. *Clerk of the Court:* THOMAS JONES.

WHITE, THOMAS.   Albemarle County.

March 11, 1695. No probate. *Wife and Executrix:* DIANA. *Other legatee:* WILLIAM COLLINS. *Witnesses:* DEBORA WILLOBY, WILLIAM COLLINS, THOMAS HASSOLD.

WHITE, THOMAS.   Chowan County.

April 26, 1752. January Court, 1754. *Wife and Executrix:* SARAH. *Son:* not named. *Children of wife:* JOB and JOHN CHARLTON, MARY CRECY, SUSANAH LEARY. *Executors:* JOB and JOHN CHARLTON, LEVI CRECY. *Witnesses:* J. BENBURY, M. POTTER, JOSH. PRATT. *Clerk of the Court:* WILL HALSEY. Impression on seal: man mounted on horse or lion.

WHITE, THOMAS.   Carteret County.

November 28, 1757. December 8, 1757. *Sons:* HENRY (plantation), THOMAS (one negro). *Executors:* HENRY STANTON and ISAAC WHITE (brother). *Witnesses:* EPHRAIM BULL, JAMES BROWN, KATHERINE WHITE. *Clerk of the Court:* WILLIAM ROBERTSON.

WHITE, WILLIAM.   Chowan County.

December 14, 1723. April 14, 1724. *Wife and Executrix:* MARY. *Daughter:* MARY. *Witnesses:* JEREMIAH PRATT, THOMAS MERCER. Proven before C. GALE, C. J.

WHITE, WILLIAM.   Currituck County.

March 10, 1753. March Court, 1755. *Sons:* HENRY, WILLOUGHBY (lands to each), LUKE, JAMEY (negro to each). *Daughters:* CORTNA, LOVE and MERIAM WHITE (negroes). *Wife and Executrix:* MARGARET. *Witnesses:* GEORGE POWERS, SAM. SIMMONS, THOMAS MILLER. *Clerk of the Court:* WILLIAM SHERGOLD.

WHITE, WILLIAM.   Cumberland County.

May 5, 1774. July 13, 1774. *Granddaughter:* CATRINE KNOWLAN. *Nephews:* JAMES and GERALD WHITE. *Brother:* JAMES WHITE. *Executors:* WM. MCREE, JAMES WHITE, JOSEPH KEMP. *Witnesses:* GRIFFITH JONES, MARY WHITE, MARY WHITE. Proven before Jo. MARTIN.

WHITEHEAD, ALICE.   Craven County.

March 12, 1741-1742. June 21, 1743. *Brother:* EDWARD WHITEHEAD of London. *Nephews:* JAMES and ROBERT WHITEHEAD (sons of brother, EDWD.). *Niece:* ELIZABETH WHITEHEAD (daughter of brother, EDWARD). *Other legatees:* TABITHA SMITH, MILDRED TRAVERS, THOMAS (son of JOHN FEARN), MARY (wife of JOHN FEARN), ANN BENDIS, SARAH BENDIS, MARY (wife of JAMES COOR, youngest daughter of THOMAS SMITH of New River), NICHOLAS ROUTLEDGE of New Bern, MADAM HANNIS (wife of JOSEPH HAN-

NIS), SUSANNAH (wife of WILLIAM HERRITAGE), WILLIAM BRICE, JOSEPH HANNIS, JR. (*Executor*), MANUEL and PETER ("two Portugee servants"). Codicil revokes legacy of two Portugese slaves and gives them their freedom. All legacies are in money or clothing. *Witnesses:* THOMAS HILDERSLEY SKERRETT, CATHERINE ROUTLEDGE, HENRY HERTWELL, RALPH YEOMAN. Device on seal. *Clerk of the Court:* N. ROUTLEDGE.

WHITEHOUSE, SAMUEL.   Carteret County.

October 28, 1756. December Court, 1756. *Sons:* ROBERT (plantation at the Straights lying to the eastward of Old Topsail Inlet and one negro). *Son-in-law:* WILLIAM WILKINS TAYLOR (plantation "on which I now live" on Bouge and Newport Sounds). *Daughters:* ESTHER and ANNE WHITEHOUSE. *Wife and Executrix:* ABIGAIL. *Executor:* VALINTINE WALLIS. *Witnesses:* FRANCES SHEPARD, JOHN OGELSBEE, GEO. MACKANE. *Clerk of the Court:* JOHN SMITH.

WHITEHURST, THOMAS.

"Lieutenant in the Royal Navy." March 22, 1765. June 23, 1766. Unto WILLIAM GRENFELL LOBB, youngest son of JACOB LOBB, commander of "His Majesty's sloop the Viper," is bequeathed money in hands of GEORGE MARSH of Savage Gardens, Tower Hill, London. Unto *sister*, ANN WHITEHURST is devised lands known as Styles Copp within six miles of the town of Stafford, England; sister also named as *Executrix*. *Witnesses:* J. EUSTACE, THOMAS COBHAM, THOMAS MCGUIRE. Proven before WM. TRYON. Impression of head on seal.

WHITLEY, SAMUEL.   Tyrrell County.

January 21, 1739–1740. March 4, 1739. Lands and property bequeathed to wife and children, who are not named. *Son-in-law:* WILLIAM ARCHDECON. *Executors:* SAMLL. WHITLEY and WILLIAM KENNEDY. *Clerk of the Court:* THOMAS LEARY.

The original of this will missing. Abstract made from recorded copy No. 117, in Grant Book No. 4.

WHITLEY, WILLIAM.   Northampton County.

August 15, 1751. April Court, 1759. *Sons:* JACOB, JAMES, WILLIAM, ARTHUR, JOSEPH. *Daughters:* ELIZABETH, JULIAN and SUSANNA. *Wife and Executrix:* JULIAN. *Witnesses:* JAMES GAY, ELISHA DARDEN, CHARLES BARNES. *Clerk of the Court:* I. EDWARDS.

WHITMELL, THOMAS.   Bertie County.

November 23, 1735. December 13, 1735. *Sons:* THOMAS, LEWIS, WILLIAM. *Daughters:* SARAH and MARTH. WHITMELL and ELIZABETH POLLOCK. *Wife:* ELIZABETH. The following lands devised: plantation (home) on Kesia River; land on Buck Swamp. Horses and other live stock, together with eight or ten negroes bequeathed to above-named. *Executors:* THOS. WHITMELL (son) and JOHN GRAY. *Witnesses:* SIMON GALE, GARRAD VAN UPSTALL, MARY CANNADY. Proven before GAB. JOHNSTON.

The original of this will missing. Abstract made from recorded copy No. 22, in Grant Book No. 4.

WHITNEY, JOSHUA.

December 26, 1735. January 21, 1735. *Sons:* DAVID, JEREMIAH, SAMUEL (one negro and one-fourth share of sloop Ketring to each), JOSEPH, FRANCIS. *Daughters:* KETRING (negro), RUTH. About 12 silver spoons and one silver tankard bequeathed to sons and daughters. *Wife:* MARTHA. *Executors:* DAVID and JEREMIAH WHITNEY (sons). *Witnesses:* JOHN and JEREMIAH BENTLEY, JAMES BLAIR. Proven before W. SMITH.

WIAT, JOHN. Perquimans County.

April 9, 1738. June 15, 1739. *Son:* WILLIAM (lands and negroes). *Daughters:* SARAH STANDING (lands on Mings Creek and Bridge Creek), ELIZABETH OATES. *Brother:* JOSHEWAY LONG (land known as Normond's Folly). *Wife and Executrix:* RACHEL. *Executors:* WILLIAM WIAT and THOMAS PEIRCE. *Witnesses:* THOMAS CALLOWAY, WM. HOSKING, WILLIAM LONG. Proven before W. SMITH.

WIAT, THOMAS. Perquimans Precinct.

April 28, 1735. July 23, 1735. *Brothers:* THOMAS LONG, SAMUELL WIAT, WILLIAM LONG, JOSHUA LONG (*Executor*). *Witnesses:* JOHN STEPNEY, WILLIAM HOSKINS (or HORKINS). No probate officer.

WICKER, RICHARD. Currituck County.

January 30, 1699–1700. *Wife:* MARTHA. *Granddaughters:* ANNA and ELIZABETH (daughters of GEORGE BOOTH). *Other legatee:* ROBERT LINNEY. *Witnesses:* ANN THOMAS, PEETER PARKER, NATHANIEL TOMS. *Clerk of the Court:* WILL SWANN.

WICKLIFFE, WILLIAM. Craven County.

September 30, 1753. December 15, 1754. *Son:* WILLIAM. *Daughters:* ELIZABETH, ALICE and KATHERINE WICKLIFFE. *Executors:* JOHN FRANKS (son-in-law), WILLIAM WICKLIFFE (son), JOHN STARKEY. *Witnesses:* JERE. VAIL, DANIEL DUPEE, SOUTHY REW. Proven before ARTHUR DOBBS.

WICKSTEAD, PALL. New Hanover County.

August 4, 1738. August 12, 1738. This is a nuncupative will proven before MATT. ROWAN, J. P., by MARY BRYAN and FRANCIS BOYLAN, and bequeaths books to said ROWAN's children, and remainder of estate to said BOYLAN.

WILCOCKS, JOHN. Craven County.

May 9, 1761. No probate. *Sons:* BENJAMIN (land bought of LEMUEL HATCH), THOMAS and STEPHEN. *Grandson:* JOHN WILCOCKS. Saw and grist mill mentioned. *Wife:* JANE. *Daughter:* ANN. *Executor:* LEMUEL HATCH. *Witnesses:* ELENER WILCOCKS, GERSHOM WOOD, EDMUND HATCH.

WILKINS, CHARLES. Chowan Precinct.

January 23, 1733–1734. February 15, 1734. *Sons:* JOHN ("my plantation," bounded by Mattacomack Swamp and Queen Anne's Creek, and the road from Hoskins Bridge to Yawpim), WILLIAM (plantation called Britains and Fordyces, and also lands called the Wett Ground). *Daughters:* SARAH (wife of LUKE GREGORY), ANN, MARY and ELISABETH. *Brother-in-law:* NICHOLAS CRISP. *Wife:* not named. *Executors:* JOHN and WILLIAM (sons). *Witnesses:* SAMUEL and SARAH WARNER, EDWARD STANDIN. Proven before GAB. JOHNSTON.

WILKINS, JOHN. Chowan County.

January 18, 1774. March 17, 1774. *Sons:* CHARLES ("thick neck" plantations in Perquimans and Chowan, together with three negroes), JOHN (plantation near Hoskins' Mill and plantation known as McClenny's, together with three negroes). *Daughters:* KATHERINE BAINS, DEBORAH TAYLOR, ELIZABETH WILKINS. *Wife and Executrix:* JUDITH (three negroes). *Executors:* ANDREW KNOX and THOMAS OLDHAM. *Witnesses:* CHARLES COPELAND, WILLIAM COPELAND, REBECCA BARBER. Proven before JO. MARTIN.

WILKISON, PHILIP. Bladen County.

February 24, 1757. July Court, 1758. *Sons:* THOMAS (land on Wilkeson's Creek), RICHARD, JOHN, WILLIAM. *Daughters:* ELIZABETH, MARY and MARGARET WILLIAMS. *Wife and Executrix:* MARTHA (negroes). *Witnesses:* BENJAMIN SLUYTER, THOMAS PLATT, ALEXANDER MCCONKEY. *Clerk of the Court:* J. BURGWIN.

WILKISON, WILLIAM.

July 4, 1704. May 9, 1706. *Wife and Executrix:* ESTHER. *Other legatees:* WM. GLOVER, THOMAS LUTTEN, THOMAS BLUNT, JNO. BLUNT (1 ring to each). *Witnesses:* JAMES BENBERY, DANLL. LEIGH, SILAS SMITH, JAMES BEASLEY, JOHN SHAW, RACHELL BACKER. *Clerk of General Court:* J. KNIGHT.

WILLCOX, JEREMIAH. Pasquotank County.

April 22, 1754. July Court, 1754. *Son:* STEPHEN (lands on sound side). *Daughters:* SARAH and RUTH. *Wife and Executrix:* ELIZABETH.

Other legatee: ELIZABETH WAKEFIELD. *Executor:* ZACHARIAH KEETON. *Witnesses:* NATHAN OVERMAN, JOB NICHOLS. *Clerk of the Court:* THO. TAYLOR.

WILLIAMS, ANTHONY.   Chowan County.

December 3, 1717. April Court, 1718. *Sons:* LEWIS, WILLIAM, JOHN, ANTHONY (land on Beach Swamp). *Daughters:* SARAH, MARY and ELLINORE WILLIAMS. *Wife and Executrix:* MARTHA (land at Catawatsky). *Other devisee:* JAMES CORLEE (land on Holly Swamp). *Father-in-law:* JOHN EARLY. *Witnesses:* WILLIAM CRANFORD, PETER WEST, PRECILLA WEST. *Clerk of the Court:* R. HICKS.

WILLIAMS, ANTHONY.   Duplin County.

July 3, 1751. April Court, 1752. *Sons:* STEPHEN (plantation and negroes), BENJAMIN (land "I now live on called the Beaverdam Neck"). To son BENJAMIN is also given two negroes, and son STEPHEN is requested to build for him a "sufficient dwelling of ye Bigness of twenty and sixteen foot." *Daughters:* MARY (wife of MOSES POWELL), PENELLIPY WILLIAMS (one negro), PHERIBE WILLIAMS (one negro), EASTER WILLIAMS, SIVELITY WILLIAMS. *Cousin:* ANTHONY BEVELY. *Other devisee:* EDWARD CARTER. *Wife:* MARY. *Executors:* JOB BROOKES, WILLIAM HAIRS. *Witnesses:* SAMUELL JONES, GEORGE SMITH, JOHN WILLIAMS. *Clerk of the Court:* JOHN DICKSON.

WILLIAMS, ARTHUR.   Bertie County.

August 8, 1735. February Court, 1739. *Sons:* ARTHUR (water mill and lands on Creek), ROBERT (lands on Potecasi Creek above ye Wildcat Swamp, land on Mahering River at Walnut Field, lands called the Goose Pond), JOHN ("plantation I now live on" and land called the Reedy Branch), MOAB (lands on River and land on Pottecasi called the Roundabout). To JOHN and MOAB is bequeathed small water mill. All negroes divided among sons. *Executors:* ROBERT and WILLIAM (sons). *Witnesses:* ABRAHAM BURTON, NICHOLAS BOONE, NICHOLAS BOONE, JUNR. *Clerk of the Court:* JOHN WYNNS.

WILLIAMS, EDWARD.   Chowan County.

February 9, 1713–1714. July Court, 1714. "Prodigall and disobedient" *son:* JOHN. *Wife and Executrix:* MARY. *Witnesses:* JOHN BRYAN, LAWRENCE MAGUE. *Clerk of the Court:* EDWD. BENWICKE (or RENWICKE).

WILLIAMS, EDWARD.   Pasquotank County.

October Court, 1739. *Sons:* LEMAND, JOSIAH, LODWICK and JOSEPH (lands and negroes). *Daughter:* SARAH. *Wife and Executrix:* ELISEBETH. *Witnesses:* DANIEL SAWYER, B. MORGAN. *Clerk of the Court:* JAMES CRAVEN.

WILLIAMS, ELISHA.   Edgecombe County.

August 13, 1751. February Court, 1755. *Brothers:* SOLOMON WILLIAMS, GEORGE WILLIAMS, DANIEL WILLIAMS, JOSHUA WILLIAMS, JOHN WILLIAMS. *Nephew:* RICHARD WILLIAMS (son of JOHN). *Sisters:* MARY CAR, ELIZABETH DAUGHTRY. *Executor:* JOSHUA WILLIAMS. *Witnesses:* JAMES SMITH, DREW SMITH, GEORGE BELL. *Clerk of the Court:* BENJAMIN WYNNS.

WILLIAMS, ELIZA.   Perquimans County.

November 8, 1745. December 3, 1745. *Sons:* JOHN and ANTHONY HATCH. *Daughter:* PENELOPE WILLIAMS (1 negro). Ten silver spoons bequeathed to son and daughter. *Other legatees:* BENJAMIN BAPTIST and BRYAN FOSSETT. *Executors:* McRORA SCARBROUGH and EDMUND HATCH (brother). *Witnesses:* SAMUEL SNOWDEN, SARAH SNOWDEN, FRANCIS LAYDEN. Proven before E. HALL.

WILLIAMS, GEORGE.   Northampton County.

January 6, 1749–1750. May Court, 1750. *Sons:* ROBERT (one negro), GEORGE (land bought of MATTHEW KINCHEN, and one negro), SAMUEL (one negro), JACOB (one negro), WILLIAM (one negro). Lands lying on Hopkins Howell's spring branch, and Kerby's Creek. *Daughters:* SARAH, ANN and MELDRED. *Wife:* SARAH (seven negroes). *Other legatees:* ETHEL TAYLOR and JAMES TURNER, JR. *Executors:* ROBERT WILLIAMS (son). *Witnesses:* JNO. SIMPSON, ETHD. TAYLOR, NICHOLAS MONGER, WILLIAM MONGER. *Clerk of the Court:* I. EDWARDS.

WILLIAMS, GEORGE.   Edgecombe County.

July 19, 1758. June Court, 1759. *Sons:* GEORGE ("my plantation"), SAMUEL (land on Deer Creek bought of WILLIAM WHITEHEAD). *Daughter:* CLOE. *Deceased Sister:* LUCRETIA WILLIAMS. *Wife and Executrix:* PRISCILLA. *Witnesses:* GEORGE CRUDUP, MOSES BAKER, JOHN NORWOOD. *Clerk of the Court:* JOS. MONTFORT.

WILLIAMS, JAMES.   Bertie Precinct.

August 21, 1736. February Court, 1737. *Son:* EZEKIEL. *Daughters:* FERIBE and JERUSHA WILLIAMS (two negroes). *Wife and Executrix:* ELIZABETH. *Executor:* THEOPHILUS WILLIAMS (brother). *Witnesses:* ROBERT HINES, WILLIAM STANDLEY, GEORGE PRICE. *Clerk of the Court:* JNO. WYNNS.

WILLIAMS, JAMES.   Carteret County.

October 31, 1770. November 19, 1770. *Sons:* BRICE (land in Duplin County on Stewart's Creek, and four negroes), BENJAMIN and JAMES ("plantation I now live on" divided between them, and five negroes bequeathed to each). *Wife and Executrix:* SARAH (½ dozen cushion chairs, ½ dozen chairs, silver spoons and other household furniture, together with three negroes). *Daughters:* CHRISTIAN NIXON, SARAH HATCH (negroes), CASSANDRA (three negroes), MARY (three negroes), CLARISSICA (three negroes). *Executor:* LEMUEL HATCH. *Witnesses:* STEPHEN BALL, STEPHEN YEATS, CHARLES MACKLAND. Proven before WM. TRYON.

WILLIAMS, JESSE.   Onslow County.

September 27, 1773. *Sons:* LOT (one negro and land on N. W. Branch of New River "above DR. CARRUTHERS' bridge at a place called Gerald's neck"), JESY (plantation and one negro), HILL (one negro and land on N. W. branch of New River adjoining MATTHEW GREGORY). *Daughters:* SARAH, ESTHER and HANNAH WILLIAMS (negro to each). *Wife:* ANNE (three negroes). *Executors:* OBED and UZ WILLIAMS (brothers). *Witnesses:* MOSES COX, MATTHEW GREGORY, BENJAMIN WILLIAMS. Proven before JO. MARTIN.

WILLIAMS, JOANNA.   Bertie County.

January 12, 1747–1748. July Court, 1756. *Sons and Executors:* RICHARD and THOMAS WILLIAMS. *Daughter:* ELIZA SMITH. *Grandchildren:* SIMON WILLIAMS, ARTHUR BROWN (negro boy to each), MARY SMITH, PENELOPE WILLIAMS, MARY HARRELL (negro to each). *Witnesses:* JOHN HARRELL, EASTHR CHITTAM. *Clerk of the Court:* BENJAMIN WYNNS.

WILLIAMS, JOHN.   Albemarle County.

January 29, 1727–1728. *Daughter:* MARY. *Brother:* NATHANIEL WILLIAMS (plantation). *Wife and Executrix:* SARAH. *Witnesses:* THOMAS and MARY PEIRCE, CHARLES CENMAN. *Clerk of the Court:* CHARLES DENMAN.

WILLIAMS, JOHN.

January 26, 1721. May 18, 1722. *Brothers:* THEOPHILUS, JAMES, ISAAC and ARTER WILLIAMS (lands at Runaroy). *Cousins:* JOHN WILLIAMS, ANTHONY HERRING. No executor named. *Witnesses:* JOHN and ANN WILLIAMS, MARY MONDS. Proven before THOS. POLLOCK, SENR.

WILLIAMS, JOHN.   Edgecombe County.

August Court, 1737. *Wife and Executrix:* ANN. *Sons:* JOHN and JOSHUA. *Daughter:* MARY. *Witnesses:* HENRY TANTON, THOMAS CARTA. *Clerk of the Court:* THOMAS KEARNY.

WILLIAMS, JOHN.   Bertie County.

March 13, 1745. January Court, 1758. *Sons:* ISAAC (one negro), ARTHUR ("my maner plantation"), THEOPHILUS (one negro). *Daughters:*

ANN HERRING, SARAH CASTELAW. *Grandson:* JOHN WILLIAMS. *Wife and Executrix:* ANN. *Witnesses:* WILLIAM BYRD, JOHN MOORE, THOMAS CASTELLAW. *Clerk of the Court:* BENJAMIN WYNNS.

WILLIAMS, JOSEPH.
1682. Will illegible.

WILLIAMS, JOSEPH.   Perquimans County.

June 28, 1772. *Sons:* JAMES and JOSEPH (plantation between Garrgut and the Mill Swamp "whereon I now live"), WILLIAM, NATHANIEL. *Daughters:* ELIZABETH, MARY and ANN WILLIAMS. *Wife and Executrix:* FRANCES. *Witnesses:* WILLIAM SKINNER, ROBERT HAINES, NICHOLAS BRAINER. *Clerk of the Court:* MILES HARVEY.

WILLIAMS, LEWIS.   Chowan County.

October 1, 1716. April 16, 1717. *Son:* ANTHONY. *Grandsons:* LEWIS WILLIAMS (land on Poplar Swamp), JOHN JONES, CHARLES SAWELL, JOSHUA PATCHETT. *Daughter:* PRISCILLA WEST (land on Katherine's Creek). *Wife and Executrix:* MARY (land at Catawatsky). *Witnesses:* WILLIAM CRANFORD, GRISSIE LITTLESON. *Clerk of the Court:* R. HICKS.

WILLIAMS, LODWICK.   Albemarle County.

November 7, 1684. December 1, 1684. *Son:* EDWARD. *Wife and Executrix:* HANNAH. *Witnesses:* THOMAS FRENCH, JOHN JONES. Proven before JOHN ARCHDALE.

WILLIAMS, LOTT.   Onslow County.

June 16, 1757. October Court, 1757. *Son:* BENJAMIN. *Daughter:* ANN. Negroes bequeathed to each. *Executors:* JESSE and OBED. WILLIAMS. *Witnesses:* BENJAMIN WILLIAMS, MOSES COX, JUNR., UZ WILLIAMS. *Clerk of the Court:* WILL CRAY.

WILLIAMS, MOAB.   Northampton County.

May 19, 1751. May Court, 1752. Lands on Potecasi Creek called the Roundabout, and also lands purchased of ROBERT EDWARDS. *Son:* DENTON (water mill and still). *Wife and Executrix:* SARAH WILLIAMS. *Father of wife:* JAMES DENTON (*Executor*). *Witnesses:* JOHN BROWN, ANNE WILLIAMS, JOHN THORN. *Clerk of the Court:* I. EDWARDS.

WILLIAMS, NATHAN.   Northampton County.

April 8, 1751. July Court, 1758. *Sons:* ELEY and NATHAN (lands on Plumtree and Cyprus Branch), THOMAS. *Daughters:* MARTHA WILLIAMS and four others, not named. *Wife and Executrix:* REBECCA (four negroes). *Witnesses:* CHAPLIN WILLIAMS, JOHN FORDHAM. *Clerk of the Court:* I. EDWARDS.

WILLIAMS, ROWLAND.   Northampton County.

March 8, 1754. May Court, 1754. *Son:* JOHN ("all my lands in North
Carolina"). *Daughters:* CASIAH BALL, MARTHA and LEWSY WILLIAMS.
Wife and Executrix: PHELIS. *Witnesses:* WILLIAM ARMISTEAD, JAMES
WALLACE, FRA. JONES. *Clerk of the Court:* I. EDWARDS.

WILLIAMS, SAMUEL.   Bertie Precinct.

April 16, 1736. November Court, 1736. *Legatees:* ELIZABETH and
SAMUEL WILLIAMS (children of GEORGE). *Brother and Executor:* GEORGE.
Witnesses: JNO. SIMPSON, EDWARD HERRIN, WALTER PITTS. *Clerk of the
Court:* JNO. WYNNS.

WILLIAMS, SAMUEL.   Edgecombe County.

November 18, 1748. February Court, 1748. *Sons:* SAMPSON and WIL-
LIAM (land "adjoining to the Taylor's in the Island as I leased of MRS.
JOHNSTON"), JACOB and GEORGE ("the manner plantation" and land on
Beaverdam Swamp), SAMUEL. *Daughter:* CREESE WILLIAMS. To sons
and daughter are bequeathed five negroes. *Wife and Executrix:* JANE.
Witnesses: JOHN POPE, JOHN CRUDUP, MOURNING CRUDUP. *Clerk of the
Court:* BENJAMIN WYNNS.

WILLIAMS, SAMUEL.   Edgecombe County.

October 21, 1753. February Court, 1754. *Sons:* WILLIAM, SOLOMON,
SAMUEL (land on Mush Island bought of ROBERT LANG), JOSEPH JOHN
WILLIAMS (about 800 acres of land bought of JOHN BURT and JOHN EGER-
TON, and adjoining YANCEY's line and the Reedy Branch). To two last
named sons are devised 11 negroes. *Grandson:* SAMUEL WILLIAMS. *Wife:*
ELIZABETH. *Executors:* PHILIP ALSTON and BENJAMIN WYNNS. *Wit-
nesses:* THOMAS and EDMUND KEARNY, JAMES ALSTON. *Clerk of the Court:*
BENJAMIN WYNNS. Coat of arms on seal.

WILLIAMS, THOMAS.   Currituck County.

December 12, 1732. Probate not dated. *Sons:* SAMUEL (land called
the New Desire), JOSEPH (land on the Sand Banks). *Wife:* MARY. *Daughter:* MARY. Negroes bequeathed to sons and daughter. Wife appointed
Executrix. *Witnesses:* MARGRET NORTON and CHARLY NORTON. *Clerk of
the Court:* THOMAS LOWTHER.

WILLIAMS, THOMAS.   Beaufort County.

December 13, 1748. December Court, 1753. "Southwark Parish in the
County of Surry." Will probated in Beaufort County, N. C. *Wife and
Executrix:* ELIZABETH. *Wife's children:* MARY WILLIAMS, WILLIAM FLAKE,
ARTHUR, ELIZABETH and ROBERT FLAKE. *Witnesses:* CHAS. BINNS, WIL-
LIAM CLARK, JAMES CLARK, JOHN WILLIAMS, ROBERT FLAKE. *Clerk of the
Court:* not given.

ABSTRACT OF WILLS, 1690—1760.

WILLIAMS, THOMAS.   Beaufort County.

February 17, 1757. March Court, 1758. *Sons:* THOMAS (land on the East side of the mouth of Bath Town Creek, bought of WM. BAKER, and lot in Bath Town No. 39), CHARLES and JOHN (land in the fork of Cuckolds Creek), ROBERT. *Daughters:* TEMPERANCE, ANN, MARY, SARAH and HANAH WILLIAMS, ELIZABETH PRITCHARD. Land in the fork of Nevils Creek devised to *son*, CHARLES. Estate in England and Wales ordered divided among wife and children. *Wife and Executrix:* ANN. *Executors:* WYRIOTT ORMOND, JAMES ELLISON, COLEMAN ROE and THOMAS WILLIAMS. *Witnesses:* WILLIAM DOWD, JACOB NEVIL, JR., MOSES NEVIL. *Clerk of the Court:* WALLEY CHAUNCY.

WILLIAMS, WILLIAM.   Currituck Precinct.

February 2, 1724–1725. No probate. *Sons:* THOMAS (plantation up Tulls Creek together with one negro), STEPHEN (land at the mouth of Tulls Creek), TULLE (land bought of WILLIAM SWANN together with one negro). To three sons is devised land up Tulls Creek called Long Leet. *Daughters:* JANE BRENT, ABIGAIL PHILLIPS (one negro to each). *Granddaughter:* MARY BRENT. *Grandson:* JONATHAN BRENT. To sons TULLE and STEPHEN is devised land called "Gibeses Island." *Wife and Executrix:* MARY. *Witnesses:* WILLIAM DAVIS, CHARLES BRENT, ROBERT ERVIN.

WILLIAMS, WILLIAM.   Albemarle County.

December 9, 1711. April 15, 1712. *Wife and Executrix:* MARY. *Sons:* SAMUEL, JOHN (lands on Blak Water called Littel Town), STEVEN (lands). *Witnesses:* TREDELL KEEFE, LUIS WILLIAMS, ROBERT LANIER. *Clerk of the Court:* EDWARD BONWICKE.

WILLIAMS, WILLIAM.   Edenton, Chowan County.

May 7, 1730. December 20, 1732. *Sons:* WILLIAM and THOMAS. *Daughters:* SARAH and ELIZABETH. *Wife and Executrix:* FRANCES. *Witnesses:* JAMES BREMEN, JOHN RICHARDS, JOHN MATTHEWS. Proven before GEO. BURRINGTON.

WILLIAMS, WILLIAM.

February 7, 1760. *Son:* JESSE. *Daughters:* ZELPHA and LUCY WILLIAMS. *Executor:* ISAAC BARRENTON. *Witnesses:* DAVID LEWIS, WILLIAM WEST, BENJAMIN WILLIAMS. No probate.

WILLIAMSON, CHARLES.   Onslow County.

June 18, 1746. June 18, 1746. This is a nuncupative will proven before GABRIEL JOHNSTON by DANIEL RAYNER, JOHN SHEPHERD and SAMUEL RAYNER, and bequeaths all estate to *wife*, HANNAH.

WILLIAMSON, JOHN. Onslow County.

March 13, 1733–1734. October 2, 1734. New River. *Sons:* CHARLES (land on southwest fork of New River), ZACHARY and JOHN (plantation on New River). *Daughter:* MARGARET. *Wife and Executrix:* ROSE. *Witnesses:* ALLEXANDER FRAZER, PETER STARKEY, JOSEPH WATTS. *Clerk of the Court:* WM. CRANFORD.

WILLIAMSON, RICHARD. Carteret Precinct.

January 15, 1723. *Sons:* WILLIAM, JOHN (land on White Oak River). *Daughters:* MARY, JANE and ANNE WILLIAMSON. *Wife and Executrix:* JANE. *Executors:* ENOCH WARD, JOHN STARKEY, JOHN ROBERTS, SARAH and NATHANIEL PIGOTT. No probate.

WILLIS, WILLIAM. Beaufort County.

Will so torn as to be illegible.

WILLOUGHBY, THOMAS. Pasquotank County.

June 6, 1753. July Court, 1753. *Half-brother:* THOMAS EVINS. *Wife and Executrix:* ANN. *Witnesses:* SOLOMON POOL, JOHN BAYLEY, PATRICK POOL. *Clerk of the Court:* THOS. TAYLOR.

WILSON, CHARLES.

County and all dates missing. *Witnesses:* COLEMAN ROE, EDETH ODEON. Will illegible.

WILLSON, ELIZABETH. Perquimans County.

Only a portion of this will is found, and mentions *sons,* JAMES, ISAAC and ROBERT. All dates missing.

WILLSON, ELIZABETH.

December 18, 1753. Will so torn as to be illegible.

WILLSON, ISAAC. Perquimans County.

June 13, 1714. July 13, 1714. *Sons:* BENJAMIN, ROBERT and ISAAC. *Daughter:* ANN. *Wife and Executrix:* ANN. *Witnesses:* JA. CAVANA, THOMAS WILKISON. *Clerk of the Court:* HENRY CLAYTON.

WILLSON, MARGARET.

April 14, 1706. *Daughters:* ELENOR and MARY. *Witnesses:* JOHN DUNN, MATTHEW BRAYE, HANNAH WHITLOCK. Proven before PHIL. TORKSEY.

WILLSON, ISAAC. Perquimans Precinct.

October 3, 1724. December 29, 1724. *Brothers:* ROBERT and BENJAMIN WILLSON. *Nephews:* JOSEPH WILLSON, ISAAC WILLSON (plantation on Perquimans River "where CAPT. PETTIVER now lives"). *Niece:* RACHEL WILLSON. *Other legatees:* JOSEPH and THOMAS ELLIOTT. *Mother:* ANN PETTIVER. *Uncle and Executor:* RALPH BOZMAN. *Witnesses:* RUTH MINGE, ROBERT MORE, ELIZABETH FLOWER. Proven before EDWARD MOSELEY.

WILLSON, ROBERT.   Perquimans Precinct.

April 28, 1693. January 11, 1696. *Grandchildren:* ROBERT and ANN WILLSON, SARAH and ESTER BELMAN. *Son:* ISAAC. *Daughter:* SARAH BELMAN. *Wife and Executrix:* ANN. Plantation devised to son, location of land not given. *Witnesses:* JOHN COPELAND, RICHD. RATCLYFE, ELIZABETH RATCLYFE. Proven before JOHN ARCHDALE, DANIEL AKEHURST, FRANCIS TOMES and SAMUEL SWANN, Justices of Court, sitting at house of SAMUEL SWANN.

WILLSON, SAMUEL.   Onslow County.

October 13, 1758. April Court, 1759. *Wife and Executrix:* SARAH. *Nephew:* SAML. WILSON, son of brother ROBART, decd., "in Penselvany." *Witnesses:* EZEKIEL HUNTER, LEBBEUS HUNTER, REBKAH HUNTER. *Clerk of the Court:* WILLM. CRAY.

WILLSON, SARAH.   Pasquotank County.

January 2, 1751–1752. April Court, 1754. *Sons:* WILLIAM, BENJAMIN (one negro), THOMAS (one negro). *Daughters:* REBECKAH FURBUSH, ELIZABETH BARTLET. *Executors:* BENJAMIN and THOMAS (sons). *Witnesses:* WILLIAM BARNARD, SAMUEL LOWMAN. *Clerk of the Court:* THOMAS TAYLOR.

WILLSON, WILLIAM.   Tyrrell County.

June 19, 1740. June Court, 1741. *Sons:* PATTESON (land called Aoses), WILLIAM and THOMAS (land bought of CORNELIOUS FITCHPATRICK), BENJAMIN (land bought of BENJAMIN ALEXANDER). *Daughters:* REBECKA, SARAH and ROSAMAN (land called Pope land), MARY SCARBOROUGH, ELIZABETH BARCLIFTE. *Wife and Executrix:* SARAH (use of all negroes). *Witnesses:* BENJAMIN BIDGOOD, WILLIAM RAPYULD, BENJAMIN ALEXANDER. *Clerk of the Court:* W. DOWNING.

WILLSON, WILLIAM.   Northampton County.

January 1, 1745. No probate. *Sons:* JOHN, ISAAC (land on south side of Tarr River), ELISHA MOORE WILSON. *Daughters:* CHARITY, ANNE, KATHERINE, ELINOR and MARY WILLSON. Negroes bequeathed to above-named. *Wife:* JUDITH. *Executor:* JOHN EDWARDS. *Witnesses:* ABRM. HOOD, JOHN GOODALL, MICHAEL TURNER.

WILSON, CALEB.   Currituck County.

1754. September Court, 1754. *Sons:* JAMES (land inherited from father, land bought of THOMAS BURGES, land bought of brother, JOSIAH WILSON, eight negroes and one silver tankard and gold ring), TATUM and WILLIAM (three negroes to each). *Nephew:* DANIEL SWEENEY. To son WILLIAM are bequeathed seven negroes and one gold ring. *Daughter:* LOVE WILSON (lands bought of THOMAS LOWTHER and "the Muncreefs," and five negroes). To TATUM is devised land bought of FRANCIS ETHERIDGE, BENJAMIN CROWELL, JOHN HUGHES and JOSEPH COOPER and seven negroes. Seven negroes over and above what had been already bequeathed are bequeathed to four children. *Wife and Executrix:* SARAH. *Executors:* JOSIAH WILSON (brother) and DANIEL SWEENEY. *Witnesses:* DREW HOLSTEAD, THOS. BURGES, MALACHI WILSON, JOS. NORBURY, WM. BLUNT. *Clerk of the Court:* JNO. SNOAD.

WILSON, ISAAC.   Perquimans County.

October 30, 1749. April Court, 1751. *Sons:* ROBERT, JAMES. *Daughters:* RACHEL and MIRIAM WILLSON. *Wife and Executrix:* ELIZABETH. *Witnesses:* JACOB PERRY, SENR., JACOB PERRY, ISRAEL PERRY. *Clerk of the Court:* EDMUND HATCH.

WILSON, JOSEPH.   Perquimans County.

April 24, 1752. July Court, 1752. *Daughters:* ELIZABETH (land on Wilson's Creek), MARY (land adjoining MATTHEW PRITCHARD). *Son:* REUBEN ("maner plantation"). *Wife and Executrix:* MARY. *Executor:* ROBERT NEWBY. *Witnesses:* JACOB WILSON, WILLIAM TOWNSEND, RACHEL WINSLOW. *Clerk of the Court:* EDMUND HATCH.

WILSON, PATTISON.   Pasquotank County.

March 15, 1746. July 12, 1746. *Son:* WILLIAM. *Daughter:* MARY. *Wife and Executrix:* ELIZABETH. *Executor:* WILLIAM WILSON (brother). *Witnesses:* JOHN SCARBROUGH, JOHN BELL, JOHN SQUIERS. *Clerk of the Court:* THOS. TAYLOR.

WILSON, ROBERT.   Albemarle County.

February 26, 1693. December Court, 1697. *Son:* ISAIAH WILSON. *Grandchildren:* ROBERT and ANN WILSON, SARAH and HESTER BOLMAN. *Son:* ISAACK WILSON. *Executrix:* ANN WILSON. *Witnesses:* JOHN COPELAND, RICHD. RATCLIFF, ELIZ. RATCLIFF. *Clerk of the Court:* W. GLOVER.

WILSON, ROBERT.   Pasquotank County.

April 22, 1757. June Court, 1758. Nixonton. *Grandsons:* RUBEN WILSON (lands between Reedy Branch and Ferry Causey), OBED. WINSLOW (land at Grassie Point), CALEB WINSLOW (land known by the name of the

Glade). *Sons:* ISAAC and SILVANUS. *Daughter:* RACHEL TOWNSEND. *Granddaughters:* ELISABETH and MARY WILSON (lands on Reedy Branch, etc.). Negroes bequeathed to granddaughters. *Executor:* BARNABY NIXON, JACOB WINSLOW. *Witnesses:* WILLIAM, GEORGE and ELISABETH WOOD. *Clerk of the Court:* THO. TAYLOR.

WILTON, WILLIAM.   Craven County.

January 7, 1773. New Bern. *Wife:* JANE. *Executors:* TIMOTHY CLEAR, JOHN GREEN, WILLIAM RUMSEY. *Witnesses:* JOSEPH DOWSE, JOHN MACE, JAMES BIGGLESTON. Proven before Jo. MARTIN.

WIMBERLEY, JOHN.   Bertie County.

September 2, 1742. November Court, 1749. *Sons:* EZEKIEL, BENJAMIN, JOHN, LEVY, MOSES (land and negroes bequeathed to sons). *Wife:* ELIZABETH. *Executors:* THOMAS WIMBERLEY (brother), JOHN SMITH (brother-in-law). *Clerk of the Court:* JOHN LOVICK.

WIMBERLY, THOMAS.   Bertie Precinct.

October 22, 1731. February Court, 1732. *Sons:* GEORGE (land on Swift Creek and Tar River), JOSEPH (land between Tar River and Swift Creek). *Daughter:* SARAH WIMBERLEY. *Wife:* SUSANA. *Executors:* GEORGE and JOSEPH WIMBERLEY (sons). Negroes bequeathed to wife. *Witnesses:* JOHN DUFFIELD, SAMUEL WILLIAMS, ELINOR BRASWELL. *Clerk of the Court:* RT. FORSTER.

WIMBERLY, THOMAS.   Bertie County.

January 27, 1751. February Court, 1752. *Sons:* ABRAHAM and six others mentioned, but not named. *Daughter:* JUDITH. *Wife and Executrix:* MARY. *Witnesses:* NEEDHAM BRYAN, WILLIAM LEVENER (?). *Clerk of the Court:* SAMUEL ORMES.

WINDLEY, ROBERT.   Albemarle County.

July 31, 1688. Probate illegible. *Son and Executor:* WILLIAM. *Daughter:* LIDIA. *Other legatees:* JOHN PERRY, GEORGE PERRY, JOHN and ELIZABETH EATON. *Witnesses:* EDWARD and ELIZABETH SMITHWICK.

WINFELD, RICHARD.

April 3, 1733. September 12, 1733. *Daughter:* ABIGALL, SUSANA, ELISABETH, MARY, ANNE, PRUDENCE. *Sons:* ROBERT and JOHN. *Wife and Executrix:* MARY. *Witnesses:* ROBERT SPRING, WILLIAM GRAY, JONAS WINFIELD. *Clerk of the Court:* JNO. COLLISON. *Justices of the Court at Bath Town:* ROBERT TURNER, BENJAMIN PEYTON, HENRY CROPTON.

WINGATE, SAMUEL.
January 9, 1770. January 19, 1770. "Formerly of Cape Fear but Now resident in the Island of Grenada." *Wife and Executrix:* ALICE. Schooner "Charming Peggy" ordered sent to CORNELIUS HARNET in Cape Feare to be sold for benefit of wife. *Executor:* JOHN KNIGHT. *Witnesses:* JOHN O'DONNELL, JOHN MACKEAND, ELIAS HOWELL. Will proven before ULYSSES FITZMAURICE, "Lieutenant-Governor and Commander-in-Chief in and over the Southern Carribee Islands." Proven in North Carolina before WILLIAM TRYON. Executrix qualified before FREDERICK GREGG. Impression of head on seal.

WINHAM, ROBERT.   Craven County.
January 19, 1754. November Court, 1753. *Wife and Executrix:* MARY (land on Broad Creek). *Son:* WILLIAM. *Executor:* JOHN LENFIELD. *Witnesses:* ROBERT BIERNEY, WILLIAM WILLIAMS, KAZIA WILLIAMS. *Clerk of the Court:* PETER CONWAY.

WINN, JOHN.   Pasquotank County.
December 18, 1739. January Court, 1739. *Son:* EZEKIAH. *Daughter:* ELISABETH WINN. *Nephew:* DANIEL TEMPLE. *Sister:* BEETY WINN. *Wife and Executrix:* DINAH. *Executors:* ABEL ROSS and WILLOUGHBY PRICE. *Witnesses:* WILL CRETCH, DANIEL TEMPLE, BETEY WINN. *Clerk of the Court:* JAMES CRAVEN.

WINRIGHT, JAMES.   Carteret County.
August 13, 1744. March Court, 1744. Lands on Newport River between MR. LOVICK and DAVID SHEPARD ordered sold. Land on Newport River called Newfoundland devised to wife, ANN, together with all negroes owned by testator. Lots in Beaufort Town bought of JOHN PINDAR devised to wife. *Sister:* ELIZABETH WHITE of Boston. *Other legatees:* ELIZABETH and SUSANNAH MABSON, ANN (wife of JAMES BLOUNT), THOMAS FLYBUS. Rents and profits of land and houses in Beaufort Town to be applied "for the encouragement of a sober Discreet Quallified Man to teach a School at Least Reading Writing Vulgar and Decimal Arithmetick in the aforesaid town of Beaufort, which said man shall be chosen and appointed by the Chairman of the Cartret County Court, etc." *Other legatees:* THOMAS LOVICK, ROBERT READ, GEORGE READ, ARTHUR MABSON, WILLIAM WHITE (boat and sails), JAMES MALIN. Lands on Suttons Creek ordered sold. *Executors:* THOMAS LOVICK and GEORGE READ. *Witnesses:* DAVID SHEPARD, DAVID SHEPARD "younger," WILLIAM DENNIS. *Clerk of the Court:* GEORGE READ.

ABSTRACT OF WILLS, 1690—1760.   419

WINSHIP, JOSEPH.   Currituck County.

April 2, 1733. January Court, 1746. *Wife and Executrix:* APPELONE. *Witnesses:* JOHN COX, JOHN WILLIAMS, NICHOLAS LUND, SAM. WILLIAMS. *Clerk of the Court:* RICHD. McCLURE.

WINSLOW, JOHN.   Perquimans County.

January 25, 1753. *Daughters:* ELIZABETH, HANNAH and EASTER. *Sons:* BENJAMIN and ISRAEL (lands divided between them), JOHN and JOSEPH. *Wife and Executrix:* EASTER. *Witnesses:* NICHOLAS STALLINGS, JOSHUA and THOMAS WHITE. *Clerk of the Court:* MILES HARVEY.

WINSLOW, JOHN.   Perquimans County.

April 17, 1754. July Court, 1754. *Sons:* JOSIAH (one negro), THOMAS and SAMUEL (lands divided between them). *Daughter:* MIRIAM. *Wife and Executrix:* MARY. *Witnesses:* WILLIAM WEEKES, THOMAS WEEKES, JR., BENJAMIN ROBERTS. *Clerk of the Court:* RICHARD CLAYTON.

WINSLOW, JOSEPH.   Perquimans County.

September 26, 1750. January Court, 1750. *Son:* JOSEPH (land on Core Neck). *Daughters:* LYDIA WINSLOW (lands near head of Little River), MARY WINSLOW, MIRIAM WINSLOW (land called Grassy Ridge). Negroes bequeathed to son. *Wife and Executrix:* PLEASANT. *Executors:* WILLIAM WHITE and FRANCIS TOMS. *Witnesses:* JOSHUA HOBART, TRUMAN MOORE, JOHN ROBERTSON. *Clerk of the Court:* EDMUND HATCH.

WINSLOW, THOMAS.   Perquimans County.

January 9, 1744. January Court, 1745. *Sons:* THOMAS and TIMOTHY (negro to each), JOHN (1 negro), JOB (plantation in Pasquotank County near Newbegun Creek). *Daughters:* ELIZABETH and MIRIAM (negroes to each). *Executors:* THOMAS and JOBE WINSLOW (sons). *Witnesses:* THOMAS HOLLOWELL, JOSIAH BOGUE, TRUMAN MOORE. *Clerk of the Court:* EDMUND HATCH.

WINSLOW, THOMAS.   Perquimans County.

January 21, 1746-1747. April Court, 1747. *Sons:* JESSE, THOMAS ("my manah plantation"). Negroes are bequeathed to above-named sons. *Daughter:* ELIZABETH WINSLOW. *Wife and Executrix:* SARAH. *Executors:* FRANCIS TOMES and ZACHARIAH NIXON. *Witnesses:* ABRAHAM ELLIOT and MARY WINSLOW. *Clerk of the Court:* EDMUND HATCH.

WINSLOW, TIMOTHY.   Perquimans County.

April 26, 1752. July Court, 1752. *Sons:* JACOB, TIMOTHY, OBED (land to each), CALEB (land on Little River). *Daughter:* MARY WINSLOW.

To sons and daughter are bequeathed negroes. *Wife and Executrix:* RACHEL. *Executor:* JOHN WINSLOW (brother). *Witnesses:* ESTHER WINSLOW, SARAH ELLIOT, THOMAS NEWBY. *Clerk of the Court:* EDMUND HATCH.

WINTER, JOSEPH.   Bath County.

December 1, 1735. December 12, 1735. *Executrix and sole legatee:* MARGRETT PENDERGEST. *Witnesses:* RICHD. RIGBY, ROBERT CONLAHANE, MARGRETT RIGBY. *Clerk of the Court:* JNO. COLLISON.

WINWRIGHT, ANN.   Carteret County.

March 7, 1751. June Court, 1751. Newport River. *Legatees:* SARAH and BETSEY (daughters of THOS. LOVICK), SARAH (wife of THOMAS LOVICK), PENELOPE LOVICK, SARAH BENNERS (mulatto boy), GEORGE PHENIS LOVICK, JOHN BENNERS. *Executors:* SARAH and PENELOPE LOVICK. *Witnesses:* JOHN BENNERS, DAVID EVANS. *Clerk of the Court:* GEORGE READ.

WOOD, EDWARD.   Chowan Precinct.

August 9, 1691. *Wife:* ALICE (land at Yaupim). *Executor:* FRANCIS HARDLEY. *Witnesses:* SAML. PRICKLOVE, JOHN SLOCOMB, ROBERT MELLYNE. No probate.

WOOD, EDWARD.   Onslow Precinct.

April 5, 1728. January 2, 1738. *Sons:* WILLIAM (lands on Harrys Creek), EDWARD (lands known as Broad Neck). To son WILLIAM is bequeathed cattle branded with his brand "as by record may appear." *Daughters:* SARAH and BETHIA. *Mother:* MARY. *Wife and Executrix:* ANN. *Other legatee:* DANLL. RAINER. *Witnesses:* JNO. MURFREY, JOHN MOORE, ELINOR MURFREY. *Clerk of the Court:* WILLIAM CRANFORD.

WOOD, JAMES, SR.   Northampton County.

June 25, 1751. March 18, 1752. Northwest Parish. *Sons:* JAMES (lands on Cuttowhisky Marsh and pasture lands on Cuttowhisky Swamp, together with five negro slaves), JOSEPH (land on Cuttowhisky, together with six negroes), JONAS ("plantation whereon I now live" on Cuttowhisky Marsh, together with six negroes and a still), MOSES (one shilling). Plantation at Coniritratt given to three sons. *Daughters:* ELIZABETH, SUSANNAH and MARY WOOD, MARY OUTLAW, SARAH DUFFIELD, ANN and CHARITY WOOD, ROSANNAH BOND, WINNY WOOD (negroes given to above-named daughters). *Sister:* SARAH KILLINGSWORTH. *Executors:* JOSEPH and JONAS WOOD (sons). *Witnesses:* BARNABA BAGGOTT, JOHN PARKER, WM. FRYER. Proven before GAB. JOHNSTON at Eden House.

ABSTRACT OF WILLS, 1690—1760. 421

WOOD, JOHN. Johnston County.
August 4, 1748. June Court, 1750. *Daughters:* ALICE, MARY and ESTHER. *Son:* JOHN (land, cattle, etc.). *Wife:* JANE. *Executors:* JOHN WOOD (son) and JOHN SMITH. *Witnesses:* ROBERT and ANN BUTLER, WILLIAM BUTLER. *Clerk of the Court:* R. CASWELL. Courthouse on Walnut Creek.

WOOD, MOSES. Bertie County.
March 8, 1757. April Court, 1757. *Brother:* JAMES WOOD, Executor. *Sister:* SARAH BAKER. *Witnesses:* THOMAS BAKER, JONATHAN WOOD, JOSEPH FARMER, THOS. CREW. *Clerk of the Court:* BENJAMIN WYNNS.

WOOD, THOMAS. Hyde County.
July 19, 1740. December Court, 1740. *Sons:* SCARBROUGH (plantation), RICHARD, ABRAHAM and ISAAC. *Daughters:* RACHEL and SARAH WOOD. *Wife and Executrix:* NAOMI. *Witnesses:* URIAH COLLINS, LEMUEL WHYN, MARTHA WHYN. *Clerk of the Court:* W. BARROW.

WOOD, WILLIAM. Pasquotank County.
November 4, 1732. April 15, 1733. *Friend and Executor:* ROBERT CARTRITT. *Witnesses:* ALEXANDER SPENCE, JER. SYMONS. Proven before GEO. BURRINGTON.

WOODHOUSE, HENRY. Currituck County.
November 27, 1750. April Court, 1751. *Son:* HEZEKIAH (land and negroes). *Wife:* CESIAH (six negroes). *Daughter:* MARY WEST (three negroes). *Daughter-in-law:* MARY JARVES. *Friend:* ABRAHAM LEACHFIELD. *Witnesses:* JOHN WOODHOUSE, THOMAS LURRY, PETER BAWM. *Clerk of the Court:* RICHARD MCCLURE.

WOODHOUSE, HORATIO. Onslow County.
January 28, 1755. July Court, 1755. *Wife and Executrix:* CATHERINE. *Son:* JOHN (three negroes). *Daughter:* ALISS HAINES (wife of ERASMUS HAINES of Va.). *Executors:* HENRY RODES and WILLIAM CRAY. *Witnesses:* HENRY MOORE, CASSON MOORE, WM. WILLIAMS. *Clerk of the Court:* WILL CRAY.

WOODNOT, HENRY. Chowan Precinct.
December 29, 1718. June 29, 1719. *Legatees:* ROBERT BELL (one negro), ISABELL FERGUSON (daughter of ANNE FERGUSON "and now the wife of ROBERT BELL"). Above-named legatees appointed Executors. *Witnesses:* ARTHUR DUGALL, THOMAS ROGERS, JAMES CASTELLAW. Proven before CHARLES EDEN.

WOODROW, ALEXANDER.

June 12, 1754. September 6, 1759. Wilmington. *Mother:* JEAN WOODROW, of the City of Edenburgh. *Executor:* BENJAMIN MORRISON. *Witnesses:* ALEX. MCALESTER, JOHN CAMPBELL, ALEXR. MCGILLIVRAY. *Clerk of the Court:* A. MACLAINE.

WOODS, THOMAS. Northampton County.

October 20, 1751. November Court, 1751. *Son:* JESSE. *Daughter:* ANN WOODS. *Wife:* MARY. *Witnesses:* CHARLES COUNSELL, ANDREW TAYLOR, MICHAEL COUNCILL. *Clerk of the Court:* I. EDWARDS.

WOOLARD, RICHARD.

January 22, 1706-1707. April 8, 1707. *Sons:* JOHN and RICHARD. *Daughters:* HANNAH BOROS, ANN WOOLARD. *Wife and Executrix:* JANE. *Witnesses:* JAMES WARD, WM. BREATHET, JNO. ALLCOCK. *Clerk of the Court:* THOS. SNODEN.

WOLFENDEN, JOHN. Perquimans County.

September 4, 1691. No probate. *Executor:* RICHARD EVANS. *Witnesses:* JOHN LILLY, STEPHEN MANWARING.

WOODARD, JOHN. Bath County.

November 21, 1734. St. Thomas Parish. *Sons:* HENRY (land "adjoining the school house"), JOHN ("manner plantation"). *Daughter:* MARY WOODARD (plantation on Pamplyco River). *Brother:* JOEL WOODARD. *Other legatee:* ELIZABETH CORTNEY. *Executors:* WILLIAM MARTIN and HENRY LUCAS. *Witnesses:* ROBERT SHEARD, HENRY ODOM, ELIZABETH CORTNEY. *Overseers:* EDWARD SALTER and JOHN ODOM. No probate.

WOODLEY, THOMAS. Pasquotank County.

March 20, 1752. January Court, 1753. *Grandchildren:* WILLIAM, THOMAS, MARY, ELIZABETH and PEGGY TAYLOR. *Daughters:* MARY SPEIGHT, ELIZABETH TAYLOR. *Son:* WILLIAM (lands and negroes). *Executors:* THOMAS TAYLOR, WILLIAM GREGORY, WILLIAM WOODLEY (son). *Witnesses:* JONATHAN REDING, JAMES PRICHARD, THOMAS TWEEDY. *Clerk of the Court:* THOS. TAYLOR.

WOODWARD, SAMUELL. Chowan County.

March 13, 1752. April Court, 1752. *Sons:* SAMUEL (250 acres of land). EDWARD, RICHARD (negroes to each). *Daughter:* ELIZABETH WHITE (negroes). *Wife:* SARAH. To sons is bequeathed tar—118 barrels. *Executors:* SAMUEL WOODWARD, LUKE WHITE. *Witnesses:* CHARLES ROBERTS, RICHARD WOODWARD. *Clerk of the Court:* JAMES CRAVEN.

WOOLWARD, WILLIAM.   Albemarle County.
November 12, 1684. February 2, 1691–1692. *Wife:* SARAH. *Granddaughter:* MARGRETT HOLLBROCK. *Executor:* EDWARD WADE. *Witnesses:* GEORGE GUNNETTE, HENRY GOODMAN, HENRY BONNER, WILLIAM CHARELTON, NICHOLAS DAW. *Clerk of the Court:* RICHARD PLATER.

WOMBWELL, BENJAMIN.   Beaufort County.
November 5, 1750. March Court, 1750. *Sons:* NATHAN, WILLIAM, BENJAMIN and JORDAN (land on Tison's Creek). Land in "Miana Government in South Hampton" devised to Executors. *Wife and Executrix:* ANNE. *Executor:* BENJAMIN BROWN. *Witnesses:* JOS. BARROW, JOHN EVANS. *Clerk of the Court:* WILLIAM ORMOND.

WORDEN, JAMES.   Chowan County.
April 23, 1755. July Court, 1755. *Sons:* JOHN (saddle, clothes and silver buckles), JAMES and WILLIAM ("such money as will buy him a small Bible and pair of silver shoe buckles" to each). *Executor:* JOHN HALSEY. *Witnesses:* STEPHEN and ELENER CREECH. *Clerk of the Court:* THOMAS JONES. Coat of arms on seal.

WORKMAN, ARTHUR.
August 1, 1695. April 19, 1697. "Late of Jamaica but now of Ronoch." *Legatees:* CAPT. JOHN HUNT (one silver tankard, value of twelve pounds), MRS. ELIZABETH HUNT (gold mourning ring), ANTHONY HATCH, son of MRS. ELIZABETH HUNT (plantation on Little River), JOHN ROBINSON, CHARLES SADLER of Jamaica, THOMAS SHERWOOD of Jamaica, MARY and MILLESAINT WORKMMAN (sisters, all estate in Kingdom of Ireland), SARAH and HENRY FRANKLIN, MARY CLERKE (*Executrix*), widow of JOHN CLERKE. *Witnesses:* JOHN HUNTT, JOHN ROBISON, RICHARD PLATER, JOHN LEGG. *Clerk of the Court:* EDWARD MAYO.

WORLEY, JOHN.   Tyrrell County.
February 8, 1740–1741. March 3, 1740. *Son:* JOSHUA ("my maner plantation"). *Daughters:* ELIZABETH LURRY (three negroes), PENELOPE WEIGHT (cattle, "crop in ye right Eare and over Caele in left"). *Grandson:* JOHN NORCOMB (or NORKOM). *Executors:* JOSHUA WORLEY, THOMAS LURREY and WILLIAM WEIGHT. *Witnesses:* EBENEZER SLAD, JOHN and JANE ROGERS. Proven before W. SMITH, C. J.

WORLEY, LOVICK.   Tyrrell County.
January 24, 1754. March Court, 1754. *Daughter:* ANN GRAY WORLEY. *Wife and Executrix:* ANN WORLEY. *Brother:* JOHN WORLEY. *Brother-in-law:* WILLIAM GRAY. *Sisters-in-law:* LUCRETIA, AMELIA and

LOUISA GRAY. *Executors:* JAMES BLOUNT (uncle), THOMAS WHITMELL. *Witnesses:* DAVID JERNIGAN, THOMAS KINSY, DAVID CANADAY. *Clerk of the Court:* EVAN JONES.

WORSLEY, JOHN.   Beaufort County.

1750. Probate not dated. *Sons:* ABRAHAM and STEPHEN. *Daughter:* DORCAS. *Wife and Executrix:* not named. *Witnesses:* JNO. BARROW, SAMUEL BARROW, LYDIA ODEON. *Clerk of the Court:* PHTT. PRITCHETT.

WORSLEY, JOHN.

October 17, 1760. *Half-brothers:* LEWIS BRYAN, ISAAC, THOMAS, WILLIAM, HARDY and NATHAN BRYAN. *Half-sister:* MARY BRYAN. *Mother:* SARAH BRYAN (Executrix). To above-named are bequeathed negroes, lands and horses. *Witnesses:* JOHN STEVENS, FREDERICK ISLER, FREDERICK BECTON. No probate.

WORSLEY, THOMAS.   Bath County.

January 18, 1737. March Court, 1737. *Sons:* THOMAS (lands on Swift Creek), JOSEPH (lands on Swift Creek), JOHN (lands on Bear Creek). Negroes divided between sons. *Cousin:* RICHARD CLEMENS. *Wife:* SARAH. *Executors:* JOHN HODGSON, THOMAS and JOSEPH BLOUNT. *Witnesses:* R. EVERARD, PHILIP WILLIAMS, JOHN CALDOM. *Clerk of the Court:* ROGER JONES. Impression of lion rampant on seal.

WORTH, JOHN.   Bladen County.

August 1, 1743. September Court, 1743. *Father:* JOHN WORTH, of New Jersey. *Sister:* ELIZABETH. *Cousin and Executor:* JOSEPH CLARK of New Hanover County. *Witnesses:* THOMAS WAMAN, E. VERNON, JOHN WILLIAMSON. *Clerk of the Court:* JOHN CLAYTON. Executor qualified before SAMUEL BAKER. Impression of dog on seal.

WOTSFORD, JOSEPH.   Bertie County.

July 27, 1737. November Court, 1739. *Sons:* JOHN ("my mannor plantation"), JOSEPH. *Daughters:* MARY WOTSFORD, ELIZABETH VALLENTINE. *Other legatee:* MARTHA MAYNOR. *Wife and Executrix:* ELINOR. *Trustee:* WM. WESSON (brother). *Witnesses:* JNO. WYNNS, BENJAMIN HARGROVE, EDWARD TIDMON. *Clerk of the Court:* JOHN WYNNS.

WRIGHT, AUGUSTINE.   Pasquotank County.

May 27, 1741–1742. April Court, 1742. *Brothers:* WILLIAM and CHARLES. *Mother and Executrix:* ELIZABETH. *Witnesses:* JOHN MARTIN, JOHN BROWN. *Clerk of the Court:* THOMAS TAYLOR.

WRIGHT, JOHN.   New Hanover County.
   May 30, 1747. *Son:* SAMUEL. *Daughter:* SARAH WRIGHT. *Wife and Executrix:* ANN. *Witnesses:* JOHN LYON, WILLIAM VERNON, JOHN MERRICK. No probate.

WRIGHT, SAMUEL.   Perquimans Precinct.
   September 9, 1717. July 29, 1718. *Sons:* THOMAS (land on Little River), SAMUEL. *Wife and Executrix:* not named. *Witnesses:* THOMAS STAFFORD, GEORGE GORDEN. *Clerk of the Court:* R. HICKS.

WRIGHT, SAMUEL.   Perquimans County.
   March 6, 1754. April Court, 1754. *Sons:* THOMAS and SAMUEL. *Daughters:* MARY and HANNAH WRIGHT. *Wife and Executrix:* ELIZABETH. *Executor:* NATHANIEL WELCH. *Witnesses:* HANNER ELLET, JEMIME DOWDY, ISAAC SITTERSON. *Clerk of the Court:* RICHARD CLAYTON.

WYNNS, WILLIAM.   Bertie County.
   December 3, 1757. April Court, 1758. *Wife and Executrix:* ELIZABETH. *Daughter:* PENELOPE. *Son:* "unnamed." *Executors:* BENJAMIN WYNNS (brother), JOHN HARRELL. *Witnesses:* THOMAS BONNIFANT, GEO. WYNNS, WILLIAM BARTON. *Clerk of the Court:* BENJAMIN WYNNS. Coat of arms on seal.

WYNNS, GEORGE.   Bertie County.
   February 2, 1750–1751. May Court, 1751. *Sons:* JOHN (two negroes), JOSEPH (one negro), BENJAMIN (three negroes), WILLIAM (three negroes), GEORGE (lands and five negroes, copper brandy still). *Daughter:* MARY SESSUMS, wife of CULMEN SESSUMS (one negro); SARAH, wife of PETER EVANS (one negro). *Wife:* ROSE. *Executors:* BENJAMIN and WILLIAM (sons). *Witnesses:* JNO. BAKER, THOS. LEE, JNO. HARRELL, JAS. BOON. *Clerk of the Court:* SAMUEL ORMES.

WYNNS, JOHN.   Bertie County.
   February 10, 1750. May Court, 1753. "Winnson." *Sons:* JAMES BOON ("the mannour plantation" and two negroes), WATKIN WILLIAM (Ferry plantation, and land called Blind Islands), JOHN AUGUSTUS (land called Bridge Neck, 400 acres of "lightwood land" and two negroes). *Daughters:* MARY ANNE (lands bought of PEEKE and HALLUM, and two negroes), SARAH AMELIA (plantation called Morrises and Cuba, and two negro slaves), WYNNEY CAROLINE (land called Sharpe's Neck, and two negroes). *Wife and Executrix:* SARAH. *Executors:* BENJAMIN and WILLIAM WYNNS (brothers), JAMES BOONE and WATKIN WILLIAM WYNNS (sons). *Witnesses:* JOS. WYNNS, STEPHN. HOOKER, WILLIAM HOOKER, JUNR., EPHRAIM HUNTER, BENJAMIN BASKER. *Clerk of the Court:* BENJAMIN WYNNS.

YEATS, JAMES.   Carteret County.

November 8, 1750. March Court, 1750. *Wife and Executrix:* MARY. *Executor:* GEO. READ. *Witnesses:* MARY STEM, SAMUEL O'STEEN, GEO. MCKEAN. *Clerk of the Court:* GEORGE READ.

YEATES, WILLIAM.   Bertie County.

December 3, 1751. May Court, 1752. *Daughters:* MARY YEATES, SUSANNAH PIPKIN, MARTHA LANGSTON (one negro), JUDITH YEATES (one negro), AMY YEATES (one negro). *Sons:* WILLIAM, ROBERT (land n Bertie on Pottecasi Creek), RICHARD (land in Bertie on Blew Water Branch and Raccoon Marsh adjoining BRYAN HARE; also one negro man), CHARLES (land in Bertie on Cuttewhiski Swamp), DANIEL ("my plantation"). *Wife and Executrix:* MARY. *Witnesses:* JNO. BRICKELL, ISAAC CARTER, BRYAN HARE. *Clerk of the Court:* SAMUEL ORMES.

YOUNG, GEORGE.

March 12, 1696. 1698. *Son:* FOSTER. *Daughters:* ANN and MARY. *Friend:* WM. LEDFORD. *Wife and Executrix:* PROTHESIA. *Witnesses:* WILLIAM LEDFORD, SENIOR, WILLIAM LUDFORD, JUNIOR, HUMPHREY LEGG. *Clerk of the Court:* N. CHEVIN.

SUPPLEMENT.

Records of the following wills were found after the foregoing pages had been printed:

ANSWELL (ANSELL or ANCELL), JAMES.   Currituck County.

September 12, 1738. April Court, 1740. *Son and Executor:* JOHN. *Daughter:* SARAH ROBERTS. *Grandson:* JAMES ROBERTS. "* * * My will and desire is that the negro wench called ESTOR which I gave to my son JOHN ANSELL by Deed be Sett att liberty During the term of sixty years and in case my Son JOHN should not allow her my Desire then all that I have given to him I give to my Daughter SARAH ROBERTS except five pounds * * *." *Witnesses:* HENRY WHITE, HILARY WHITE, LEADY WHITE. *Clerk of the Court:* WM. SHERGOLD. Original missing. Recorded in Book No. 4, Will No. 110, Record of Grants.

CHRISTIAN, CHRISTOPHER.   Montgomery County.

November 29, 1781. March Court, 1783. *Sons:* JOHN and JAMES. *Daughters:* PATTY and LUCY. *Friend:* PATTY COLLY. *Executors:* JOHN MACK, NICHOLAS CHRISTIAN and WILLIAM MACK. *Witnesses:* CHRISTOPHER CHRISTIAN, DRURY COLLIER, THOMAS BULLOCK. *Clerk of the Court:* GEO. DAVIDSON.

JORDAN, JOSEPH.   Pasquotank County.

May 4, 1742. February Court, 1752. *Wife:* MARY. *Daughter:* MARY HENLEY. *Sons:* JOSEPH (" my Plantation whereon I now live, containing Two hundred Acres of Land more or Less"); ROBERT (" Two Plantations on the River Side Called by the names of Overmans and Hacket, running as far as to the head of a Branch to the plantation called the Old plantation across from this Line where I live on by that line Called Lufmans line"), MICAJAH (" my Plantation called the Old Plantation withall the Woodland belonging to it Except that part I gave to my son Robert"). *Witnesses:* SAMUEL HUGHE, DEMPSEY CONNER, JOSEPH ROBINSON. *Clerk of the Court:* THOMAS TAYLOR.

MARSH, EDWARD.   Guilford County.

May 18, 1778. September Court, 1779. *Son:* DARIUS MARSH (plantation whereon I now live). *Wife:* KATHERINE. *Other legatees:* KATHERINE and BRYANT (children). *Executors:* KATHERINE MARSH, ROBERT HARGROVE, JACOB SHEPPARD. *Witnesses:* ROBT. HARGROVE, AMORY SPINKS, JA. SHEPPARD. Will proven in Randolph County. *Clerk of the Court:* A. TATOM.

ROE, JOHN.   Richmond County.

November 15, 1780. March Court, 1783. *Sons:* EDWARD ROE (one shilling and no more), JOHN EDWARD ROE and SAMUEL ROE. *Daughters:* SARAH RICHARDSON PHILLIPS, JEAN ROE, RACHEL ROE. *Grandson:* SAMUEL SALSBURY CHEARS. *Other legatee:* MARTHA USSERY. *Wife:* SUSANNAH. *Executors:* SUSANNAH ROE and JOSEPH CHAPLAIN. *Witnesses:* JOSEPH HINES, JAMES DOWNING, WM. LEAGO. *Clerk of the Court:* WM. LOVE.

INDEX TO ABSTRACT OF WILLS.

[Names of testators are printed in capitals.]

	PAGE.
Abbott, John	261
Abel, Richard	62
ABERCROMBIE, HANNAH	1
Abercrombie, William	329
Abett, Thos.	136
ABINGTON, JOSEPH	1
Abington, Mary	1
Abington plantation	385
Abington, Sarah	317
ABINGTON, THOMAS	1
Abington, Thos.	.27, 51, 54, 56, 65, 129, 132 (2), 201 (2), 230 (2), 231 (2), 277, 294 (2), 370, 384 (2).
Abington, William	1
Absalom Poiner's land	403
Accomack Entry, land called.	213
Ackis, Joshua	290
Acock, James	47
ADAMS, ABRAHAM	1
ADAMS, ABRAHAM	1
ADAMS, ABRAHAM	1
Adams, Abram	1
Adams, Abraham	2 (2)
Adams, Abraham	274
Adams, Anne	1
Adams, Ann	213, 301
Adams, Bathia	1
ADAMS, CHARLES	2
Adams Creek, land on	120, 242, 261
Adams, Dorothy	310
Adams, Elizabeth	1, 2
Adams, Emanuel	2
Adams, Frances	2
Adams, Hanah	48
Adams, James	1 (2), 2 (2), 50, 105, 187, 213, 238, 256
ADAMS, JOHN	2
ADAMS, JOHN	2
Adams, John	2 (2), 301
Adams, Joseph	1
Adams, Leath	71
ADAMS, MARGARET	2
Adams, Margaret	2
Adams, Martha	2
Adams, Mary	2 (2), 49, 187
Adams, Mathias	116
ADAMS (ADDOMES) MATTHEW	2
Adams, Matthew (son of Matthew)	2

	PAGE.
Adams, Matt	49
Adams, Obia	1
ADAMS, PETER	2
Adams, Rachel	2, 181
Adams, Richard	1
ADAMS, ROGER	2
Adams, Sarah	1, 2, 213
Adams, Thomas	2
Adams, Will	51
Adams, William	1, 71, 324
Adams, Wiloby	1
Adamson, Alexander	340
Adderly, Jane	360
Addison, Mary	320 (2)
ADDISON, RICHARD	2
Addison, Sarah	2
Addison, Thomas	333
Addison, William	165
Ahair, Elizabeth	336
Ahair, John	336
Ahair, William	336
Aharskey Swamp, land on	174
AHIER, JOHN	3
Ahier, Elizabeth (wife of John)	3
Ahier, Elizabeth (daughter John)	3
Ahier, William	3
Ahoskie Marsh, land on	15, 84
Ahoskie, plantation on	354
Ainslee, Thomas	45
Ainton, Wm.	284
Airs, David	365
Akehurst, Daniel	51, 73, 79, 105, 157, 245, 288, 290, 415
Akehurst, Samuel	129
Albardson, Peter	265
Albemarle Sound, land on	87, 248
Albemarle Sound, manor fronting on	35
Albemarle Sound, plantations on	323
Albertson, Aaron	3 (2)
ALBERTSON, ALBERT, Sr.	3
Albertson, Albert	3 (2)
Albertson, Albert, Jr.	3, 378
Albertson, Albert, Sr.	378
Albertson, Benjamin	3
Albertson, Chalkley	3
Albertson, Easaw	3
Albertson, Elias	359
Albertson, Elizabeth	3 (2), 267

Index.

	PAGE.
Albertson, Francis	3
Albertson, Hannah	3
Albertson, Isaac	3
Albertson, Jemima	3
Albertson, John	3
Albertson, Joshua	3
Albertson, Joshua	3, 7, 267
Albertson, Mary (daughter of Joshua)	3
Albertson, Mary (wife of Joshua)	3
Albertson, Mary	3
Albertson, Mary (granddaughter of Mary)	3
Albertson, Mary	256, 359
Albertson, Nathaniel	3
Albertson, Nathaniel	3 (2)
Albertson, Penelopy	3
Albertson, Peter	3 (2)
Albertson, Ruth	3
Albertson, William	3 (2), 7
Albordson, Peter	383
Alburt, Nathaniel	70
Alden of the Hill plantation,	257, 258
Aldershire, John	2
Alderson, Ann	225
Alderson, Elizabeth	3
Alderson, James	225
Alderson, John	3, 167, 240, 272
Alderson, Leven	3
Alderson, Levi	219, 272, 303
Alderson, Mary	240
Alderson, Sarah	3, 156
Alderson, Simon	3
Alderson, Simon	42 (2), 64, 71, 187, 272, 304, 380
Alderss, Stephen	349
Aldorson, John	345, 365, 391
Aldridg, Drury	347
Aldridg, Mary	347
Aldridge, Dorothy	4
Aldridge, John	4
Alegator, land at	26
Alegator River, land on	400
Alexander, Anne	4
Alexander, Anthony	4
Alexander, Anthony (son of Anthony)	4
Alexander, Anthony	387
Alexander, Benjamin	4, 225, 415
Alexander, Casiah	4
Alexander, Christian	4
Alexander, Elizabeth	185
Alexander, George, Sr.	230
Alexander, Giddeon	4

	PAGE.
Alexander, Isaac	4
Alexander, Jane	4
Alexander, John	4
Alexander, Joseph	4
Alexander, Josias	4
Alexander, Joshua	4, 127
Alexander, Samuel	4
Alexander, Naomi	4
Alexander, Nathan	123
Alexander, Priscilla	4
Alexander, Rachel	4
Alexander, Samuel	140
Alexander, Sarah	4
Alexander, Seth	4
Alexander, Susannah	127
Alford, Ann	4
Alford, Jabez	4
Alford, Jabus	154
Alford, Jebaz	208
Alford, John	4
Alford, Joseph	4
Alford, Sarah	4, 189
Alford, Tabitha	4, 189
Allaire, Louis	130
Allaire, Margaret	130
Allbird, John	182
Allcock, Jno.	347, 422
Allday, Thomas	4
Allen, Andrew	4
Allen, Cathrine	5
Allen, David	323 (2)
Allen, Ealce	5
Allen, Eleazar	5
Allen, Eleazar	5 (2), 61, 258
Allen, Elizabeth	5 (2)
Allen, George	5
Allen, Go.	49
Allen, Hugh	5
Allen, James	5
Allen, Jemima	27
Allen, John	5
Allen, John	5
Allen, Jno. (M. D.)	295
Allen, Josia	5
Allen, Margaret	5
Allen, Mary	5
Allen, Priscilla	4 (2)
Allen, Richard	5
Allen, Rode	180
Allen, Sarah	5
Allen, Sarah	5 (2), 253
Allen, Shadrack	53
Allen, Thomas	235
Allen, Timothy	30
Allen, William	5, 263
Allenn, James	281

INDEX.

	PAGE.
Alleyn, George	197
Alleyn, G.	282
Allexander, Autho.	400
Allin, Ann	250
Alligator land	368
Alligator, lands in	156, 217
Alligood, Hillery	6
Alligood, John	6
ALLIGOOD, RICHARD	6
Alligood, Richard	288
Alligood, William	6
Almes, Jane	56
Alsop and Carroll	254
Alston, Elizabeth	6, 306
Alston, James	6 (2)
ALSTON, JOHN	6
Alston, John (grandchild of John)	6
Alston, John	237
Alston, Joseph John	6, 306
Alston, Mary	237
Alston, Patty	6
Alston, Phillip	6
Alston, Solomon	6, 237
Alston, William	6 (2), 306
Amason, Benjamin	50
Amason, James	50
Amason, Jesse	50
Amason, William	50
AMBLER, WILLIAM	6
Ambler, William	362
Ambler, Willm.	308
AMBROS, DAVID	7
Ambros, David (son of David)	7
Ambros, Israel	7
Ambros, Jesse	7
Ambros, Mary	7
Ambros, Morning	7
Ambros, Susannah (daughter of David)	7
Ambros, Susannah (wife of David)	7
Ambros, William	7
Ambrose, William	256
Ames, James	71
Ancrum, John	105, 106
Anderson, Ann	8, 68, 147, 331
ANDERSON, CAROLUS	7
Anderson, Carolus	7
Anderson, Eave	7
Anderson, Elmar	54
ANDERSON, ELISABETH	7
ANDERSON, ELIZABETH	7
Anderson, Elizabeth (granddaughter of Elizabeth)	7

	PAGE.
Anderson, Elizabeth	8, 267
ANDERSON, GEORGE	7
Anderson, George (son of William)	7
ANDERSON, JAMES	7
Anderson, James (son of James)	7
Anderson, James	7, 8, 287, 333
Anderson, James, Junr.	228
Anderson, James, Senr.	228
Anderson, Jane	255
ANDERSON, JOHN	8
Anderson, John	3, 7 (3), 20, 229, 230, 255, 260, 266, 267 (2), 280, 302, 334, 348, 375.
Anderson, John (grandson of Elizabeth Nixon)	267
ANDERSON, JOSEPH	8
ANDERSON, JOSEPH	8
Anderson, Joseph	13, 32, 38, 65, 68 (2), 83, 130, 142, 251, 267 (2)
Anderson, Katherine	22
Anderson, Leah	227
Anderson, Mararet	8
Anderson, Mary	7 (2), 8
Anderson, Moses	96
Anderson, Rob't	272, 349, 386
Anderson, Samuel	7, 8, 148, 160, 267
Anderson, Sarah	7 (3), 22, 267
Anderson Swamp, land on	108
Anderson, William	7 (2)
Anders, John	365
Andress, Elizabeth	157
Andrew, Walter	205
Andrews, Agnes	8
Andrews, Edmund	8, 58
Andrews, Elisabeth	8
Andrews, Etheldred	8
Andrews, Henry	152
Andrews, James	8 (2)
Andrews, Janet	8
ANDREWS, JOHN	8
Andrews, John (son of John)	8
Andrews, Levi	8
Andrews, Mary	152, 205, 242, 271
Andrews, Rebecca	152
Andrews, Ruben	205
Andrews, Sarah	8
Andrews, Stephen	92
ANDREWS, THOMAS	8
Andrews, Thomas	8
ANDREWS, WARREN	8
Andrews, William	25, 54, 152 (2), 266, 271

INDEX.

	PAGE.
Anelyn, Ann	8
Anelyn, Henry	8
Anelyn, John	8
ANELYN, PETER	8
Anelyn, Peter (son of Peter)	8
Angely, John	225
Ansell, Caleb	9
Ansell, James	9
ANSELL, JOHN	9
Ansell, John (son of John)	9
Ansell, John (son of John). 9	(2)
ANSELL, JOHN OF NETSILAND.	9
Ansell, John	190, 427
Ansell, Letessha	9
Ansell, Mary	9
Ansell, William	9
ANSWELL (ANSELL or AN-CELL), JAMES	427
Answell (Ansell or Ancell) John	427
Ansley, Ann	9
Ansley, Easter	9
Ansley, Elizabeth	9
Ansley, John	9, 192
Ansley, Joseph	9
Ansley, Mary	9
Ansley, Rachel	9
Ansley, Sarah (daughter of Solomon)	9
Ansley, Sarah (wife of Solomon)	9
ANSLEY, SOLOMON	9
Aoses land	415
Apperson, William	178
Apple Tree, land on	71
Applewhite, Holland	397
Arbuthnot, John	218
Archbald, Nathan	215
Archbell, Nathan	113
Archdale, John	105, 411, 415
Archdecon, William	405
Archebald, Nathan	167
Archir, Michl.	148
ARDERNE, JOHN	9
Arendell (Orindell), Mary.	274
Arendell (Orindell), Rachel.	274
Arendell (Orindell), Rebeckah	274
ARENTON, CHRISTOPHER	9
Arenton, Leah	9
Arenton, Mary (daughter of William)	9
Arenton, Mary (wife of William)	9
Arenton, Rebeckah	9
Arenton, Sarah	9

	PAGE.
ARENTON, WILLIAM	9
Arenton, William	9
Argy, John	130
Aringer, Francis	272
Arington, Thomas	223
Arinton, Mary	255
Aris, Ambross	272
Arkill, Wm.	31, 44
Arlin, John	68
Arlin, Mary	68
Arlord, James	244
Arlow, Bridget	9
ARLOW, JAMES	9
Arlow, John	9
Armiskeat, land at	388
Armistead, William	412
Armor, John	10 (2), 262
Armor, Robert	10
Armor, Theophilus	10
Armor, Thomas	10
ARMOR, WILLIAM	10
Armore, Thomas	115
Armour, Ann	10
Armour, Elizabeth	274
ARMOUR, JOHN	10
Armour, John (son of John)	10
Armour, John	359
Armour, Mary	10, 274, 359
Armour, Thomas	324
Armour, Robert	359
Armstrong, Asiah	10
Armstrong, Frank	307
Armstrong, Isabel	57
ARMSTRONG, JEAMS	9
ARMSTRONG, JOHN	10
Armstrong, Margaret	307
Arnal, Alice	177
Arnal, Edward	177
Arnal, Elizabeth	399
Arnal, John	129, 399
Arnal, Martha	129
Arnech, Moses	161
Arnel, Laurence	280
Arnell, John	18
Arnell, Sarah	280
Arnell, William	10
ARNOLD, EDWARD	10
Arnold, Edward (son of Edward)	10
Arnold, Elizabeth	10 (2)
Arnold, Jane	115
ARNOLD, JOHN	10
ARNOLD, JOHN	10
Arnold, John	11, 394
Arnold, John (son of John).	10
Arnold, John (son of John).	10

Index. 433

	PAGE.
Arnold, Joseph	10
Arnold, Joseph	10, 156, 269
Arnold, Henry	382
Arnold, Katherine	327
Arnold, Lawrence	11
Arnold, Lawrence	10 (2)
Arnold, Mary	10 (2)
Arnold, Peter	249
Arnold, Pleasant	10
Arnold, Sarah	17
Arnold, Tho.	9
Arnold, Thomas, Jr.	137
Arnold, William.7 (2), 10 (2),	22
Arnol, John	395
Arranton, Sarah	157
Arranuse Creek, land on	381
Arrington, Briggs	11
Arrington, Charles	344
Arrington, John	324
Arrington, William	11
Arrington, William (son of William)	11
Arter, John	298
Arter, Matthew	53
Arthand, Go.	229
Arthur, Ann	11
Arthur, Bridget	11
Arthur, Elizabeth	276
Arthur, Francis	276
Arthur, James	11, 48
Arthur, John	11
Arthur, John	11
Arthur, John (son of John)	11
Arthur, Mary	11
Arthur, Matthew	11
Arthur, Sarah	48, 132
Arthur, William	11, 174
Artledge, John	309
Artree, James	337
Artry, Mary	30
Ash Branch, land on	110
Ashburn, Elizabeth	323
Ashburn, Sarah	96
Ashburn, Thomas	169, 386
Ashe's Banks, land on	270
Ashe, Cincinnatus	295
Ashe, John	11
Ashe, Capt. John	13
Ashe, John Baptista	11
Ashe, John Bapta...128, 216 (2), 224, 231, 250, 268, 295, 296, 380	
Ashe, Mary	11
Ashe, Sam	82
Ashe, Samuel	11, 295
Ashe, Samuel (son of Samuel)	295

	PAGE.
Asheton, Thomas	23 (2)
Ashford, Jonathan	29
Ashlee, Solomon	104
Ashley, Dinah	183
Ashley, Francis	12
Ashley, John	12
Ashley, John (son of John)	12
Ashley, John	20
Ashley, John Plowman	291
Ashley, Joseph	20, 150, 166
Ashley, Jurden	12
Ashley, Mary	12
Ashley, Nell	183
Ashley, Sarah	12, 20
Ashley, William..12, 183, 194, 276, 306	
Ashly, Thomas...8, 103, 163, 287, 292, 306	
Ashly, Thomas, Jr.	163, 169
Ashton, John	147
Ashwood plantation	11
Askines, William	358
Askins, Anne	112
Askue, John	12
Askue, Nicholas	12
Askue, William	12
Aspell, Jean	204
Aspill, Martin	77
Asskew, John	39
Atherly, Jos.	364
Atkins, James	31, 119
Atkins, Lewis	250
Atkins, R.	334
Atkinson, Amos	218
Atkinson, J.	371
Atkinson, Jane	218
Atkinson, Richard	188
Atkison, James	27
Atkison, Winnifred	198
Atkison, William	198
Aurendell, Edwd.	117
Austin, Ann	349
Austin, Daniel	349
Austin, Dnl.	118
Austin, Tho.	300
Avent, Thomas	12
Avent, Uslea	12
Avent, William	12
Avera, Alexander	168
Avera, Elizabeth	168
Averet, Ann	173
Averett, John	135
Averitt, Arthur	13
Averitt, Benjamin Nathaniel	13
Averitt, Ephaly	13
Averitt, John	13, 394

28

INDEX.

	PAGE.
Averitt, Nancy	13
AVERITT, NATHANIEL	13
Avery, Jane	13
Avery, James	13 (2)
AVERY, JOHN	13
Avery, Robert	330
Aweedy, Thomas	126
Aydlett, Phillip	42
Backalder, James	391
Backcus, John	118
Backer, Rachell	407
Bacon, John	169
Bacon, Richd.	169
Bacon, Dr. Solomon	41
Badham, Martha	13
Badham, Mary	109, 325
Badham, W.	16, 109 (2), 292, 325, 336, 354, 358
BADHAM, WILLIAM	13
Badham, William	86, 130, 325 (2)
Baeley, Wm.	108
Baget, Nicholas	45
Baggitt, Abraham	13
Baggitt, Barnabey	13
Baggitt, Benjamin	13
Baggitt, Hardy	13
Baggitt, John	13
Baggitt, Joseph	13 (2)
Baggitt, Martha	13
Baggitt, Mary	13
BAGGITT, NICHOLAS	13
Baggitt, Nicholas (son of Nicholas)	13
Baggitt, Sarah	13
Baggitt, Thomas	13 (2)
Baggott, Barnaba	420
Bagley, Amblox	216
Bagley, Betty	282
Bagley, Hanna	13
Bagley, Rebeca	249
Bagley, Samuel	112
Bagley, Susana	14
Bagley, Susannah	13
BAGLEY, THOMAS	13
Bagley, Thomas (son of Thomas)	13
Bagley, Thomas	37, 74
Bagley, William	13, 326
Bailey, Ann	14, 400
Bailey, Barbarie	126
Bailey, Benjamin	14
BAILEY, DAVID	14
Bailey, David	14
Bailey, Elizabeth	400

	PAGE.
Bailey, James	262
BAILEY, JOHN	14
Bailey, John	14
BAILEY, JOSEPH	14
Bailey, Joseph	14 (2), 369
Bailey, Margaret	14
Bailey, Patrick	14 (2)
Bailey, Robert	14 (2), 351 (2)
Bailey, Simon	14 (2)
Bailey, Tamor	14
Bailey, Tnamor	14 (2)
Bains, Katherine	407
Baird, Jeane	14 (2)
BAIRD, RICHARD	14
Baird, Robert	241 (2)
Baire Swamp, land on	22
Baire Swamp, plantation on	23
Baker, Benett	15
Baker, Benjamin	171
Baker, Benjamin, Jr.	171
Baker, Mrs. Betsey	32
Baker, Blake	15, 68, 203
Baker, David	15
Baker, Elizabeth	95
BAKER, HENRY	15
Baker, Henry (son of Henry)	15
Baker, Henry, Jr.	107, 197
Baker, Honer	59
Baker, James	15, 33
Baker, John	15, 68 (2), 166, 333, 425
Baker, Lawrence	15
Baker, Mary	15
BAKER, MOSES	15
Baker, Moses	69, 409
Baker, Robert	226
Baker, Ruth (wife of Henry)	15
Baker, Ruth (daughter of Henry)	15
Baker, Ruth	68
Baker, Ruth (daughter of Ruth)	68
Baker, Samuel	214, 424
Baker, Sarah	15, 68, 421
Baker, Susannah	358
Baker, Thomas	59, 421
Baker, William	15 (2), 95, 387
Baker, Wm.	233, 413
Baker, Zadock	15, 68
Balch, Benjamin	15
Balch, Joseph (son of Benjamin)	15
BALCH, JOSEPH	15
Balch, Joseph	2 (2), 271
Balch, Mary	15

Index. 435

	PAGE.
Balch, Phoebe	15
Balch, Susannah	15
Bald Ridge plantation	87
Baldwin, Elizabeth	344
Baldwin, Wm.	309
Balehack, land in	287
Bales, James	378
Baley, Ann	69
Baley, David	147
Baley, Deborah	69
Baleyhack, plantation in	251
BALEY, JOHN	15
Baley, Joseph	69
Baley, Mary	15 (2), 69
Baley, Patrick	147, 383
Baley, Rebeckah	400
Ball, Ann	16, 306
Ball, Casiah	412
Ball, Elizabeth	16
Ball, James	41
Ball, Jacob	245
Ball, James	15
BALL, JOHN	15
Ball, Joshua	299
Ball, Magdalene	15 (2)
Ball, Nathan	15
Ball, Parthaney	306
Ball, Rachel	15
Ball, Reuben	299
Ball, Sarah	15
Ball, Stephen	15, 410
BALL, THOMAS	16
Ball, William	16, 306
Ball, Wm.	80
Ballahack, lands at	309 (2)
Ballahack, land in	314
Ballance, John	114
Ballance, Richard	79
Ballance, Samll.	48
BALLARD, ABRAHAM	16
Ballard, Abraham	309
Ballard, Ann	16
Ballard, Anne	16
Ballard, Apsilla	16
Ballard, Bathsheba	16
Ballard, Elias	16
Ballard, Elisher	16
Ballard, Elizabeth	16 (2)
Ballard, Esther	16
Ballard, Jethro	16
Ballard, Keadah	16
Ballard, Jemima	93
BALLARD, JOHN	16
Ballard, John	16
BALLARD, JOSEPH	16

	PAGE.
Ballard, Joseph (son of Joseph)	16 (2)
Ballard, Lewis	108
Ballard, Martha	16
Ballard, Mary	16, 390 (2)
Ballard, Peter	247
Ballard, Sarah	16
Ballard, Susanne	16
Ballard, William	124
Ballards plantation	54
Balleau, Andrew	123
Ballentine, Alexander	16
Ballentine, Dinah	16
BALLENTINE, GEORGE	16
Ballentine, Henry	77
Ballentine, Ja.	386
Ballyhack, land in	254, 346
Baly, David	343
Bampfield, William	6
Banbow Creek, land on	92
Banger, Berd	355
BANGS, ABIAH	16
Bangs, Abiah	16 (2), 63
Banckes, John	220
Banckey, John	206
Bangs, Betty	16 (2)
BANGS, JONATHAN	16
Bangs, Jonathan	16
Banks, Anne	17
Banks, Francis	342
Banks, John	220
Banks, Jonathan	17 (2)
Banks, Rachel	380
Banks, Thomas	282
BANKS, WILLIAM	17
Banks, Wynn & Askew, land joining	15
Banter, Katherine	339
Baper, Edw'd.	72
Baptism, ministers bequest to	30
Baptiss, Benjamin	351
BAPTIST, BENJAMIN	17
Baptist, Benjamin	7, 367, 409
Baptist, Edmund	17 (2)
Baptist, Mary Clark	17 (2)
Baptiste, Benjamin	73, 122
Baran, Nathaniel	316
Barbara, Mitchell	360
Barbara, Susanna	360
Barber, Aaron	322
Barber, Ann	367
Barber, Charles	103
Barber, Charley	54
Barber, Elisabeth	198
Barber, George	77
Barber, Hannah	326

	PAGE.
Barber, Jacob	54
BARBER, JOHN	17
Barber, John	4, 42
Barber, Joshua	54
Barber, Lem'll.	54
Barber, Margaret	142
Barber, Moses	198
Barber, Rebecca	407
Barber, Richard	360
Barber, Samuel	299
Barber, William	322, 366
Barbour, Charles	9
Barbre, Elizabeth	359
Barclif, Charles	137
Barclif, John	314
Barcliff, Elizabeth	176
Barclift, Ann	17
Barclift, Anne	280
Barclift, Asa	17
Barclift, Benjamin	17
Barclift, Blake	17
Barclift, Demson	17
Barclift, Elizabeth	17 (2), 169 (2)
Barclift, James	17
Barclift, John of Wearneck.	7
BARCLIFT, JOHN	17
Barclift, John (cousin of William)	18
Barclift, John (son of William)	18
Barclift, John	17 (3), 18, 73, 132, 158, 280
Barclift, John (grandson of John Parish)	280
Barclift, John, Sr.	280
Barclift, Joseph	17, 18, 243
BARCLIFT, JOSHUA	17
Barclift, Joshua	18
Barclift, Mary	17 (2)
Barclift, Miriam	17
Barclift, Noah	17
Barclift, Samuel	17, 18, 260
Barclift, Sarah	18 (2), 245
BARCLIFT, THOMAS	17
Barclift, Thomas (son of Thomas)	17
Barclift, Thomas	18
Barclift, Thos.	169
BARCLIFT, WILLIAM	18
BARCLIFT, WILLIAM	18
Barclift, William (son of Joshua)	18
Barclift, William (son of William)	18

	PAGE.
Barclift, William	17 (2), 160, 176
Barclifte, Elizabeth	415
Barco, Sophia	299
Barcock, Ann	18
Barcock, Daniell	18
Barcock, Jane (daughter of William)	18
Barcock, Jane (wife of William)	18
Barcock, John	18
Barcock, Joseph	18
Barcock, Luke	18
Barcock, Peter	18
Barcock, Thomas	18
BARCOCK, WILLIAM	18
Barcock, William (son of William)	18
Barcroft, William	198
Bard, Hannah	14
Bard, Mary	193
Bard, Richard	193
Bardin, John	47
Bare, Banks	359
Barecock, Jane	283
BARECOCK, THOMAS	18
Barecock, Thomas (son of Thomas)	18
Barecock, Thomas	283
Barecock, William	18 (2)
Bare Creek, land on	12
Barefield, Elizabeth	18
Barefield, Henry	18
Barefield, Isham	18
Barefield, James	18, 19
BAREFIELD, JOHN	18
Barefield, Judith	18
Barefield, Luke	18, 96
Barefield, Mary	18, 19, 228
BAREFIELD, RICHARD	18
Barefield, Richard (son of Richard)	18 (2)
Barefield, Richard (grandson of Richard)	18
Barefield, Rose	18
Barefield, Solomon	18
Barefield, Thomas	18
Barefield, William	18
Barefoot, John	321
Bare Swamp, land at	34
Barfield, Eeth	19
Barfield, Elizabeth	228
Barfield, Henry	19
Barfield, James	18
Barfield, Jane	218
Barfield, Jesse	19 (2)

INDEX. 437

	PAGE.
Barfield, John	61
BARFIELD, RICHARD	19
Barfield, Richd.	83, 218
Barfield, Solomon	19 (3)
Barfield, Thomas	228 (2)
Barfield, William	219
Barkcake, William	186
Barker, Mary	113, 341
Barker, T.	348
Barker, Thomas	8 (2) 123, 147 (2), 153, 282, 348, 382
Barker, William	287
Barkett, Mary	174 (2)
Barkock, Thomas	131
Barlow, Thomas	14
BARLOW, ROBERT	19
Barley, David	10
Barnard, William	415
Barnes, Charles	405
Barnes, Demsey	19
Barnes, Elizabeth	19
Barnes, Hezekiah	19
Barnes, Jacob	19
Barnes, James	19, 21
Barnes, Jeremiah	334
Barnes, Jesse	151
Barnes, Jethro	19
Barnes, Jno.	84
Barnes, John	361
BARNES, JOSEPH	19
BARNES, JOSEPH	19
Barnes, Mycah	19
Barnes, Nathan	170, 237
Barnes, William	21
Barnet, Ann	356
Barnet, Mary	356
Barnet, Samuel	78
Barnet, William	213, 356
BARNETT, EDWARD	19
Barnett, J. J.	57
Barnett, Sarah	19
Barnett, William	330
Barnham, Gabriel	199
Barns, Ann	19 (2)
Barns, Edward	41
Barns, James	251
BARNSFELD, ANN	19
Barnsfeld, William	230
Baron, Henry	111 (2)
BAROS, MOSES	19
Barrah, George	109
Barrah, Thomas	109 (2)
Barrah, Zaceria	109
Barran, Jas.	174
Barran, Thomas	87, 174
Barran, Wm., Jr.	153

	PAGE.
Barren Branch and Wickacorn Creek, land on	170
Barrenton, Isaac	413
Barrett, Mary	344
Barrett, Thomas	344
Barringer, Paul	286
Barrit, Margitt	326
Barrow, Ann	20 (2), 21
Barrow, Benjamin	19
Barrows Creek, land on	219
BARROW, EDMUND	19
Barrow, Elizabeth	19, 20
Barrow, Eliza	21 (2)
Barrow, Frederick	20
Barrow, George	20, 21, 29, 109, 274
Barrow, H.	241
Barrow, Hedrick	21
Barrow Hole, land at	35
BARROW, JAMES	20
Barrow, James	19, 20 (3), 21, 216
Barrow, Jeams	21
Barrow, Jean	21, 30
Barrow, Johanah	20
BARROW, JOHN	20
BARROW, JOHN	20
BARROW, JOHN	20
BARROW, JOHN, SR.	20
Barrow, John (son of John)	20
Barrow, John (uncle of John)	20
Barrow, John (son of Joseph)	21
Barrow, John (brother of Joseph)	21
Barrow, John (son of William)	21
Barrow, John (brother of William)	21
Barrow, John	19, 20 (3), 21 (2), 29 (2), 60, 61, 101, 164, 196, 198, 215, 216, 231, 286, 356, 424
BARROW, JOSEPH	20
Barrow, Joseph, Jr.	20
BARROW, JOSEPH	21
BARROW, JOSEPH, JR.	21
Barrow, Joseph (son of Joseph)	21
Barrow, Joseph	20 (4), 21, 56, 136, 165, 198, 216 (2)
Barrow, Jos.	423
Barrow, Joseph, Jr.	20, 196, 198
Barrow, Margaret	20 (2)
Barrow, Mary (daughter of Edmund)	19

438 INDEX.

	PAGE.
Barrow, Mary (wife of Edmund)	19
Barrow, Mary	20, 21, 216
Barrow, Moses	20, 21
Barrow, Mr.	46
Barrow, Orpah	20 (2)
Barrow, Rachell	20 (2), 377
Barrow, Rebeca	20
Barrow, Rebecca	20
BARROW, REBEKAH	21
Barrow, Rebekah	21
Barrow, Richard	21, 216 (2)
Barrow, Samuel	21, 216, 424
Barrow, Sarah (wife of James)	20 (2)
Barrow, Sarah (daughter of James)	20
Barrow, Sarah (cousin of James)	20
Barrow, Sarah	20 (2), 21 (4), 55, 145, 165, 259, 286
Barrow, Thomas	20, 21, 346
BARROW, WILLIAM	21
BARROW, WILLIAM	21
BARROW, WILLIAM	21
Barrow, William (son of Joseph)	20 (2)
Barrow, William (son of William)	21 (4)
Barrow, William (grandson of Joseph)	20
Barrow, William	13, 21 (2), 29 (4), 109, 156, 216, 342, 366
Barrow, Wm.	77, 145, 216
Barrow, W.	382, 421
Barrow, Zachariah	20, 21, 109
Barry, Daniel	163
Barry, David	21
Barry, Mary Magdilin	266
Barry, Marion	21
Barry, James	235
Barry, Sarah	62
BARRY, WILLIAM	21
Barsus Neck	389
Bartlet, Elizabeth	415
Bartlet, Thomas	138
Bartlett, Ann	344
Bartlett, Elizabeth	22
Bartlett, Pashe	30
Bartlett, Samuel	381
Bartlett, Thomas	22
BARTLETT, WILLIAM	22
Bartlett, William (son of William)	22 (2)
Barton, Hannah	22
Barton, Hanna	22

	PAGE.
Barton, Joel	19
Barton, John	114, 395
BARTON, VALLENTIN	22
Barton, William	395, 425
BARTRAM, ELIZABETH	22
Bartram, Elizabeth	218
Bartram, William	73, 92, 106, 168
Bartram, Wm.	22, 265
Bartre, Joel	78
Bartrom's Point	334
Baset, James	30
Basker, Benjamin	425
Basley, Sarah	219
Bass, Andrew	76, 348
Bass, Aron	22
Bass, Benjamin	22 (2)
Bass, Dinah	22 (2)
BASS, EDWARD	22
Bass, Edward (son of Edward)	22
Bass, Edward	22, 23 (2)
Bass, Elijah	22
Bass, James	22
BASS, JOHN	22
Bass, John (son of John)	22, 23
Bass, Joseph	22
Bass, Kiziah	22
Bass, Lovewell	22
Bass, Lovey	22
Bass, Mary	22
Bass, Mary (daughter of John)	22
Bass, Mary (wife of John)	23
Bass, Moses	22
Bass, Paceunce	22
Bass, Reuben	22
Bass, Sampson	22
Bass, William	22 (2)
Bassett, Abraham	395
Bassett, Richard	50
Bassford, John	270
Bastabell, William	383
Bastable, Hannah (wife of William)	23
Bastable, Hannah (daughter of William)	23
Bastable, Hannah	383
BASTABLE, WILLIAM	23
Bastable, William	383
Basteba plantation	191
Batchelors Creek, land on	153
BATCHELOR, EDWARD	23
BATCHELOR, EDWARD	23
Batchelor, Edward (son of Edward)	23

	PAGE.
Batchelor, Elizabeth	23
Batchelor, Francis (wife of Edward)	23 (2)
Batchelor, Francis (daughter of Edward)	23
Batchelor, John	23, 96
Batcher, Joseph	49
Bate, Ann	23
Bate, Augustine	23, 198
Bate, H.	57
BATE, HENRY LAWRENCE	23
Bate, Humphrey	23
Bate, Martha	23
Bateman, Elisebeth	171
Bateman, Eliza	24
Bateman, Elizabeth	24, 62
Bateman, Isabell	24
BATEMAN, JOHN	23
Bateman, John	24
BATEMAN, JONATHAN	24
Bateman, Jonathan (son of Jonathan)	24 (2)
Bateman, Jonathan	23 (2), 62, 175, 319
Bateman, Josher (or Joseph)	24
Bateman, Margaret	24 (2)
Bateman, Mary	24 (2), 169 (2)
Bateman, Samuell	24
Bateman, Thomas (brother of John)	23 (4)
Bateman, Thomas (nephew of John)	23
Bateman, Thomas	4, 7, 24, 62
BATEMAN, WILLIAM	24
Bateman, William (son of William)	24
Bateman, William	10, 23 (2)
Bateman, Wm.	144
Bates, James	200
Bath, Richd.	110, 121
Bath Town Creek, land on	413
Battle, Elisabeth	366
Battle, Jesse	24
BATTLE, JOHN	24
Battle, John	52, 195
Battle, Prissilla	24
Battle, Sarah (wife of John)	24 (2)
Battle, Sarah (daughter of John)	24
Battle, William (brother of John)	24
Battle, William (son of John)	24
Batters, Darkers	24

	PAGE.
Batters, Darkis	356
Batters, Diana	24
Batters, Mary	24, 356, 391
BATTERS, THOMAS	24
Batters, Thomas	356, 391
Bauer, Mathew	6
Bawne, Peter	421
Baxter, Mary	373
Baxter, Nathaniel	373 (2)
BAYER, DAVID	24
Bayes, Ann	24
BAYES, EDWARD	24
Bayes, Eliz.	24
Bayes, John	24
Bayes, Mary	24 (2)
Bayes plantation	38
Bayley, Ambcox	2
Bayley, Amb. Cox	354
Bayley, John	414
Bayley, Martha	39
Bayley, Patrick	168
Bayley, Thomas	168
Baynard, Phillip	231
Bay River, land on	63
Bay River and Trent, land on	339
Bays, William	122
Beach Reag plantation	56
Beach Ridge plantation	279, 299
Beach Swamp, land on	408
Beahan, Eliz.	187
Beale, Francis	394
Beally, David	86
Beally, Patrick	86
Beally, John	86
Beally, Thomas	117
Beally (or Bayley)	183
Bear Creek, plantation on	175
Bear Creek, lands on	276, 324, 424
Bear Creek and Horse Pen, land on	390
Bear River, land on	176
Bear Swamp, land at	35 (2)
Bear Swamp, land on	352
Beard, Daniel	218
Beard, Neil	218
Beards Creek, plantation on	173
Bearcock, John	142
BEASLEY, FRANCES	24
Beasley, Francis	25, 339
Beasley, Jeams (brother of Francis)	24
Beasley, Jeames (son of Francis)	24
Beasley, James	89 (2), 117 (4), 215, 339, 380, 407

440 INDEX.

	PAGE.
BEASLEY, JAMES	25
Beasley, James (son of John)	117
Beasley, James, Jr.	25
Beasley, Johanna	218
Beasley, John..25, 28, 36, 117 (2)	
Beasley, Mary..........24, 25, 89	
Beasley, Robert..........24, 117	
BEASLEY, SAMUEL	25
Beasley, Sarah	218
Beasley, Thomas	25
Beather, Mrs. Sarah	291
Beaufort, legacy for church at	214
Beaufort, legacy for school in	418
Beaver Cove, land in	152
Beaver Cove, land on	280
Beaver Dam of Grays Creek, land on	324
Beaver Dam, land at	22
Beaverdam, land in fork of..	205
Beaverdam, land on.......71,	240
Beaver Dam, plantation on..	299
Beaver Dam Neck.......345,	408
Beaverdam plantation	339
Beaver Dam Swamp, land on 33,	412
Beaver Dam Swamp, plantation on	332
Beaver Ponds, land on	260
Beay, Eliza	54
Beck, Moses	113
Becton, Ann	25
Becton, Edmond	25
Becton, Frederick.....25 (2),	424
Becton, George	25
BECTON, JOHN	25
Becton, Mary	25
Becton, Michael	25
Becton, Sarah	25
Bedarrin, Hannah	168
Bedford, Thomas...112, 263,	311
Beech Island land	35
Beech Run, land on	67
Beels, Ann	25
Beels, Barbray	25
Beels, Elizabeth	25
BEELS, JACOB	25
BEELS, JAMES	25
Beel, John	25
Beel, Joshua, children of	269
Beels, John..............25 (2)	
Beels, Mary	25
Beels, Tabitha	25
Beesley, Ann	117
Bee Tree Neck, land on	18
Beetree Neck, land at	87
	PAGE.
Beety, Martha	227
Beezley, Eliza	25
Beezley, Elizabeth	25
Beezley, John............25 (2)	
Beezley, Rachel	371
BEEZLEY, THOMAS	25
Beezley, Thomas (son of Thomas)	25
BEFRET, BENJAMIN	25
Befret, Benjamin (son of Benjamin)	25
Beitelle, Francis	151
Belcher, Bourleay	249
Belcher, Robert	234
Belknap, Elisha	239
Bell, Ann.................8,	279
Bell, Anne...............27, (2)	
Bell, Archibald	74
Bell, Arthur..26 (3), 27 (2), 129,	290
Bell, Benjamin	26
Bell, Caleb	114
Bell, Christiana	306
BELL, CORNELIUS	26
Bell, Cornelius (son of Cornelius) 26 (2)	
Bell, David	26
Bell, E.	250
BELL, ELIZABETH	26
Bell, Elizabeth...27, 108, 286,	307
Bell, Ester	129
BELL, GEORGE	26
Bell, George (son of George) 26 (2)	
Bell, George...26 (3), 27, 40, 74, 95, 127, 183, 211, 349,	409
Bell's Gift	382
Bell, Henry	26
Bell, Isabell Ferguson	421
Bell, James...26, 31 (2), 275,	372
Bell, Jane	27
Bell, Jesse	349
BELL, JOHN	26
Bell, John (son of John)	26
Bell, John.18 (2), 26 (2), 27, 74, 130, 142, 310, 316, 353,	416
Bell, John Lathy	26
Bell, Jonathan..........145,	337
BELL, JOSEPH	26
Bell, Joseph.......26, 27 (2),	352
Bell, Jos.	307
Bell, Joshua......27 (2), 290 (2)	
Bell, Margrett	27
Bell, Margret	26
Bell, Marmaduke	114
Bell, Mary (wife of John)..	26

INDEX. 441

	PAGE.
Bell, Mary (daughter of John)	26
Bell, Mary	26 (2), 27, 114, 252, 310
Bell, Nathaniel	26
Bell, Rilind	95
Bell, Robert	8, 74, 127, 421
BELL, ROSS	27
Bell, Ross (son of Ross)	27
Bell, Sarah	26 (2), 114 (2), 403
Bell, Th.	137
Bell, Thos.	26
BELL, THOMAS	27
BELL, THOMAS	27
Bell, Thomas	26 (2), 27
Bell, Penelope	8, 74
BELL, WILLIAM	27
BELL, WILLIAM	27
Bell, William (son of William)	27
Bell, William	5, 26 (2), 27, 129, 272, 303
BELLMAN, JOHN	27
Bellman, Mary	27 (2)
Bellman, William	239
Belman, Esther	415
BELMAN, JOHN	27
Belman, John (son of John)	27
Belman, John	256
Belman, Robert	27
Belman, Sarah	27 (2), 415 (2)
Belt, John	87
Bembridge, John	251
Benberry, James	28, 407
Benbow, Charles	28, 65 (2)
Benbow, Evans	28
BENBOW, GERSHON	28
Benbow, Gershon	59, 189
Benbow, Mary	65
Benbow, Powel	28 (2)
Benbow, Richard	28
Benbow, Susannah	28
Benbow, Will	158
Benbury, Bridgett	28
Benbury, Edmund	28
Benbury, J	28, 158, 404
Benbury, John (brother of William)	28
Benbury, John (son of William)	28
Benbury, John	28, 38, 145, 172
Benbury, Joseph	28
Benbury, Miles	28
Benbury, Samuel	28, 317
Benbury, Sarah	28
BENBURY, WILLIAM	28

	PAGE.
Benbury, William (son of William)	28
Benbury, Wm.	28, 35
Bender, Daniel	28
Bender, John	28
BENDER, MARTIN	28
Bender, Mary	28
Bender, Salome	28
Bendis, Ann	404
Bendis, Sarah	404
Beniman, Joseph	232
Benners, John	222, 420
Benners, Sarah	420
Bennet, Alice	28
Bennet, Anne	28
Bennet, Arthur	105
Bennet, Benjamin	28, 29
Bennet, Betsse	29
Bennet, Darkes	29
Bennet, Elizabeth	28
BENNET, JOHN	28
Bennet, John	28 (2), 57, 168, 274, 362, 364, 386
Bennet, Jno.	104
BENNET, JOSEPH	28
Bennet, Joseph (son of John)	28
Bennet, Joseph (son of Joseph)	28
Bennet, Joseph (brother of John)	28
Bennet, Josiah	28
Bennet, Mary	28, 29, 364
Bennet, Moses	29
BENNET, NEHEMIAH	28
Bennet, Nehemiah	57
Bennet, Rebecker	29
Bennet, Samuel	28
BENNET, SOLOMON	29
Bennet, Solomon	28, 57
Bennet, Susan	28
Bennet, William	28, 84, 353
Bennett, James	386
Bennett, Jane	46
Bennett, Ruth	386
Bennett, Will	61
Benning, James	99
Bennington, Cornelius	90
Bennitt, Ann	386
Bennys Creek, land on	292, 293
Benson, Edy	215
Benson, John	383 (2)
Benson, Mary	383 (2)
Benson, Precila	390
Benson, Sarah	140
Bensted, John	391
Benston, Mathias	123

442 INDEX.

	PAGE.
Benthall, Joseph	205 (2)
Bentley, Ann	29 (2)
Bentley, Hanah	29
Bentley, Isaac	29
Bentley, James	29 (2), 118
Bentley, Jeremiah	29
Bentley, Jeremiah	406
BENTLEY, JOHN	29
BENTLEY, JOHN	29
BENTLEY, JOHN	29
BENTLEY, JOHN	29
Bentley, John (son of John)	29
BENTLEY, JOHN OF MORATOCK RIVER	29
Bentley, John (son of John of Moratock River)	29
Bentley, John (grandson of John of Moratock River)	29
Bentley, John	25 (2), 406
Bentley, Joseph	29
Bentley, Lidia	29
Bentley, Mary	29, 359
BENTLEY, RICHARD	30
Bentley, Richard	29 (2)
Bentley, Sarah	29 (2), 118
Bentley, Thomas	25
Bentley, William	25, 29 (2), 201, 245
Benton, Elijah	30, 62, 181 (2)
Benton, Epophroditus	30
Benton, Francis	84
Benton, Jethro	30 (2), 366
BENTON, JOHN	30
Benton, John (son of John)	30 (2)
Benton, John, Sr.	366
Benton, Lazarus	135
Benton, Martha	84
Benton, Moses	30
Benton, Samuel	181
Benton, Susannah	177
Benwick (Renwicke), Edwd.	408
Benwicke, Edwd.	362
Bergeron, Elias	30 (2)
Bergeron, John	21, 30
BERGERON, JUDITH	30
Bermuda, "an island in the sound"	248
Bernard, Samuel	319
Bernsbee, Margaret	313
Berreman, Benjamin	312
Berry, Comfort	30 (2)
BERRY, CORNEALUS	30
Berry, Cornealus	30
Berry, Hepzibah	74
Berry, John	30, 309

	PAGE.
Berry, Littleton	30
Berry, Sarah	207
Berryman, Benj.	357
Best, Jane	401
Best, Mary	60
Best, Thomas	4, 401
Beteithelly (Bathelly), Fran.	244
Bets, Doser	183
Bets, John	190
Betsworth, Sarah	63
Betsworth, Wm.	176
Bett, John, Sr.	34
Betterley, Thomas	49
Betterley, Tho.	354
Bettes, Francis	36
Bettesworth, John	103
Betts, James	49
Betts, W.	144, 271
Bettys, Thomas	313
Bevan, William	360
BEVANS, MARY	30
BEVANS, RICHARD	30
Bevely, Anthony	408
Bever Dam, land on	32
Beverdams, land called the.	216
Beverler, Ann	306
Beverley, Henry	30
BEVERLEY, JOHN, SR.	30
Beverley, John (son of John, Sr.)	30
Beverley, Margarett	30
Beverley, Rachel	30
Beverley, Robert	30
Beverley, Sarah	30
Beverley, William	30
Bevin, William	214
Bevines, Robert	399
Bevins, Ann	30
Bevins, Elizabeth	30
Bevins, John	30, 31
BEVINS, MARY	30
Bevins, Mary (daughter of Mary)	30
Bevins, Robert	30, 31
Bexley, Rebeckah	31
BEXLEY, WILLIAM	31
BIARD, RICHARD	14
Bidder, Richard	290
Biddle, Ann	31 (2)
Biddle Isaac (son of Isaac)	31
Biddle, Isaac (son of Jacob)	31 (4)
BIDDLE, JACOB	31
Biddle, Jacob (son of Jacob)	31
Biddle, Jacob	56 (2), 402
Biddle, William	31

INDEX. 443

	PAGE.
Bidgood, Benjamin..136, 236,	415
Bidgood, Sarah	17
Bierney, Robert	418
Bigford, Magdaline	215
Biggers, James	311
Biggleston, J.	22
Biggleston, James	417
Biggs, John............141	(2)
Biggs, Mary	141
Biggs, Sarah	114
Biggs, W.	49
Billet, Allice	31
Billet, Daniel	31
BILLET, JOHN	31
Billet, Sarah	31
Billett, Alse	388
Billett, Jean	88
Billett, John	94
Billett, John	388
Billings, William	391
Bingham, Josiah	317
Binns, Chas.	412
Bird, Ann	59
Bird, Nathaniel	66
Bird, Sarah	59
Bird, Wm.	170
Birnie, Illin.............31	(2)
BIRNIE, WILLIAM	31
Birote, Benjamin	31
BIROTE, PETER	31
Bishop, Elizabeth	32
BISHOP, GEORGE	31
Bishop, George...........32,	203
Bishop, Hannah	148
Bishop, John........78, 273,	310
Bishop, Mary	310
Bishop, Stoakley	31
BLACK, ISAAC	32
Black, Jane	32
Black, John	32
BLACK, MICHAEL	32
Black, Samuel	117
Black, Tho.	43
Black, Thomas.....311, 319,	391
Black, Thos., 85, 103, 147, 189, 249, 254, 360,	381
Black Creek, land on	334
Black River, land on	392
Black Rock plantation	293
Black Swamp and Mire Branch, land between	266
Black Walnut, land at head of	81
Black Walnut Swamp, land on	214

	PAGE.
Black Walnut Swamp, plantation on...............80,	323
Black Water, plantation at..	402
Blackall, Abner	43
Blackall, Abra	299
BLACKALL, ABRAHAM	32
Blackall, Dr. Abraham, 222, 291,	348
Blackall, Abraham......304,	348
Blackall, Abram	38
Blackall, Charlot	32
Blackall, Dr.	32
BLACKALL, SARAH	32
Blackall, Sharlot	32
Blackhall, Charlotte	291
Blackhall, Penelope..32 (2),	291
Blackhall, Sarah 32 (2),	291
Blackburn, Benjamin	125
Blackburn, Hugh	331
Blackburn, Oliver.........2,	316
Blackledge, Ann 32	(2)
Blackledge, Benjamin	32
Blackledge, Benjamin, Sr...	32
BLACKLEDGE, RICHARD, SR...	32
Blackledge, Richard (son of Richard, Sr.)..........32	(2)
Blackledge, Richard	346
Blackledge, Thomas	32
Blackledge, William	32
Blackman, Allison........33	(2)
Blackman, Arthur.......33,	124
Blackman, Bennet...33 (2), 197,	360
Blackman, Bennett	186
Blackman, Elizabeth	33
BLACKMAN, JOHN	33
Blackman, John (son of John)	33
Blackman, Joseph	33
BLACKMAN, NICHOLAS	33
Blackman, Sarah	33
Blackman, Steaven	33
Blackmoor, Zacharia	226
Black River, lands on	314
Blackshire, Alexander	120
Blainye, Geo.	9
Blair, David	385
Blair, James	406
BLAKE, DAVID	33
Blake, David (son of David)	33
Blake, David	69
Blake Elizabeth	33
Blake, Mary	107
Blake, Mathew	33
Blake, Sarah	33
Blake, Thomas 33,	334

INDEX.

	PAGE.
Blakeney, John	226
Blak Water, land on	413
Blanchard, Aaron	15, 33, 116
Blanchard, Absalom	33
BLANCHARD, BENJAMIN	33
Blanchard, Benjamin (son of Benjamin)	33
Blanchard, Catherine	33 (2)
BLANCHARD, EPHRAIM	33
Blanchard, Ephraim (son of Ephraim)	33 (2)
Blanchard, Isabel	33 (2)
Blanchard, Micajah	33
Blanchard, Robart	356
Blanchard, Robert	33
Blanchard, Zilpah	355 (2)
Blanchet, Elizabeth	242
Blanck, Sara	137
Bland, Judith	177
Bland, Richard	368
Bland, William	250
Blaning, Elizabeth	33 (2)
BLANING, HUGH	33
Blank, Sarah	137
Blanning, Hugh (Capt.)	101
Blanshard, Christopher	98
Blanshard, Demsey	116
Blanshard, Huldah	116
Blanshard, Robert	116
Bleighton, George	206
Blewbootens Neck plantation	313
Blew Water plantation	106
Blew Water Branch and Raccoon Marsh, land on	426
Blichenden, Abraham	34 (2)
Blichenden, John	34
Blichenden, Mary	34 (2), 268
Blichenden, Sarah	34
Blichenden, Thomas	34, 128, 268
Blichenden, William	34 (2)
BLIN, DANIEL	34
Blin, Daniel	187, 240
Blin, Morning	34
Blind Islands	425
BLISH, JOHN	34
Blish, John, 186, 190 (2), 353, 387	
Blitchenden, Abraham	39
Bliz, Dan'l.	50
Blount, ——	17
BLOUNT, ——	35
Blount, Anne	35 (5), 418
BLOUNT, BENJAMIN	34
Blount, Benjamin (son of Benjamin)	34 (2)
Blount, Benjamin	34 (2), 117, 211

	PAGE.
Blount, Bullah	292
Blounts Creek, land on	342
Blounts Creek, mill on	243
Blounts Creek, plantation on,	98, 350
Blount, Charles	34, 35, 36
Blount, Christian	285
BLOUNT, EDMUND	34
Blount, Edmund (son of Edmund)	34
Blount, Edmund	34
BLOUNT, ELIZABETH	34
Blount, Elizabeth (wife of John)	35 (2)
Blount, Elizabeth (wife of James)	35 (2)
Blount, Elizabeth	34 (4), 35, 36, 163
Blount, Esther	34
Blount, Frederick	36
Blount, Henry	114
Blount, Isaac	34
Blount, J.	32
Blount, Jacob	32, 34 (2), 101, 211, 307
BLOUNT, JAMES	35
BLOUNT, JAMES	35
Blount, James (son of James)	35 (2)
Blount, James (grandson of James)	35
Blount, James (son of John)	35
Blount, James	34 (2), 35, 36 (3), 251, 342, 418, 424
Blount, Jane	342
Blount, Jesse	219
BLOUNT, JOHN	35
BLOUNT, JOHN	36
Blount, John (son of John)	35
Blount, John	34, 35 (3), 36, 153, 307
Blount, Joseph	8, 34, 35 (2), 36, 68, 243, 330, 331 (2), 424
Blount, Mary	34, 35, 36 (2), 342
Blount, Martha	36
Blount, Rachele	34
Blount, Rachel	35 (2)
Blount, Reading	32, 116, 243, 315
Blount, Samuel	342
Blount, Sarah	34, 35, 36, 86, 330
Blount, Capt. Thos.	211
Blount, Thomas, of Cape Fear	219
Blount, Thomas, of Chowan	219
Blount, Thomas (son of John)	35

INDEX. 445

	PAGE.
BLOUNT, THOMAS	36
Blount, Thomas....2, 34, 79, 211 (2), 292, 330,	424
Blount, Thos.....35 (2), 72, 130, 206,	285
Blount, Thomas, Jr.	2
Blount, Wilson	36
Blount, Zilplia	211
Blount, Zilpha	212
Blounts and Nevils creeks, land on	243
Blue Water, land at	83
Blunt, John	270
Blunt, Jno.	404
Blunt, Thomas	407
Blunt, Miller	8
Blunt, William	159
Blunt, Wm.	416
Blurton, Henry	372
Blyth, Ander	229
Bly, Elizabeth	68
Blye, Elizabeth (daughter of Wm.)	36
Blye, Elizabeth (wife of Wm.)	36 (2)
Blye, Sarah	36
Blye, Thomas	36
BLYE, WILLIAM	36
Blye, William (son of Wm.)	36 (2)
Bly, Harral	96
Bly, James	68
Bly, William	68
Blyth, John	265
Boag Sound, land on	293
Boague Sound, plantation on	335
Bobbit, Amey	36
Bobbit, Frances	36
BOBBIT, JOHN	36
Bobbit, Mary	36
Bobbit, Thomas	36
Bobbit, William	36 (2)
Bobbitt, John	276
Boddie, Elizabeth	184 (2)
Boddie, John	184
Boddie, Mary	51
Boddie, Wm.	51
Boge, ——	14
Boge, or (Bogue), Deborah,	36 (2)
Boge, Ellender	37
Boge, Jean	37
Boge (or Bogue), Jesse	36
Boge (or Bogue), Jobe	36
Boge (or Bogue), Joseph	36
BOGE (OR BOGUE), JOSIAH	36

	PAGE.
Boge, Josiah	37
Boge, Lidy	36
Boge, Margaret	14
Boge, Mary	36
Boge, Miriam	36
Boge, Myriam	37
Boge, Rachel	37
BOGE, WILLIAM	37
Boge, William (son of Wm.),	37 (2)
Boge, William........14 (2),	70
Bogue and Newport sounds, plantation on	405
Bogue, Duke	341
Bogue, Jak	37
Bogue, Josias	14
Bogue, Josiah	419
Bogue, Miriam	264
Bogue, Rachel	282
Bogue, Robert 255,	282
Bogue, Sarah	37
BOGUE, WILLIAM	37
Bogue, William (son of Wm.)	37
Bogue, William 208, 218,	285
Boid, Ann	68
Boide, John	69
Bois, Jude	324
Boldin, William 144,	310
Boles, David 163, 308,	381
Bollen, Rachel	184
Bolman, Hester	416
Bolman, Sarah	416
Bolton, Humphry	157
Bond, Anna	37
Bond, Elisabeth	37
Bond, Elisebeth	37
Bond, Elizebeth	38
Bond, Francis	37
Bond, Hance	37
Bond, Henry	37
Bond, James 5, 37 (3),	38
Bond, Jane	38
BOND, JOHN	37
Bond, John (son of John)	.37 (2)
Bond, John (son of William)	38
Bond, John 37, 42,	218
BOND, LEWIS	37
Bond, Lewis	37
Bond, Lidia	391
Bond, Luke	38
Bond, Margaret	38
Bond, Martha	37
Bond, Mary 37 (2), 38 (2)	
Bond, Rebecca	38
BOND, RICHARD	37

	PAGE.
Bond, Richard (son of Richard)	37
Bond, Richard (brother-in-law of Lewis)	37
Bond, Richard (son of Lewis)	37
Bond, Richard..5, 37, 38 (2),	345
BOND, ROBERT	37
Bond, Robert....37, 141 (2),	158
Bond, Rosannah	420
BOND, SAMUEL	38
Bond, Samuell 38	(2)
Bond, Sarah (wife of Robert)	37
Bond, Sarah (daughter of Richard)	37
Bond, Sarah (sister of Vinyard)	38
Bond, Sarah (wife of Vinyard) 38	(2)
Bond, Sarah (daughter of Vinyard)	38
Bond, Sarah 37 (2), 94,	303
Bond, Susana	38
Bond, Sweeting	38
BOND, VINYARD	38
Bond, Vinyd	2
BOND, WILLIAM	38
Bond, William (son of William)	38
Bond, William ..37 (2), 364,	376
Bondfield, Chas.	95
Boner, Henry.......193, 399	(2)
Boner, Robert	251
Boni, Jacob, Sr.	204
Boni, Jacob, Jr.	204
Bonnefaut, Thomas	425
Bonner, Anne	350
Bonner, Deborah	38
Bonner, Elizabeth	38
Bonner, Elisebath........39	(2)
BONNER, HENRY	38
Bonner, Henry (son of Henry) 38	(2)
Bonner, Henry (son of Thos.)	39
Bonner, Henry.....2, 38, 39, 118, 130, 170, 192, 215, 240, 323 (2), 376, 423.	
Bonner, James 2, 350	(2)
Bonner, Jas.	79
BONNER, JOHN	38
Bonner, John	80
BONNER, MARY	39
Bonner, Mary 38, 39,	195

	PAGE.
Bonner, Moses	39
BONNER, THOMAS	39
Bonner, Thomas (son of Thomas)	39
BONNER, THOMAS	39
Bonner, Thomas (son of Thos.)	39
Bonner, Thos., Jr.	79
Bonner, Thomas..21, 38 (2), 198, 324,	350
Bonner, William	39
Bonwicke (Renwicke), Edwd.	382
Bonwicke, Edward	413
Booge, William	219
Boon, ——	39
Boon, Ann	39
Boon, James	39
Boon, Jas.	425
BOON, JOSEPH	39
Boon, Joseh (son of Joseph)	39
Boon, Joseph (son of Nicholas)	39
Boon, Joseph	334
Boon, Martha	39
Boon, Mary (daughter of Nicholas)	39
Boon, Mary (wife of Nicholas) 39	(2)
Boon, Mary	39
BOON, NICHOLAS	39
Boon, Nicholas (son of Nicholas)	39
Boon, Nicholis	125
Boon, Ratlif	39
Boon, Thomas..........39	(2)
Boon, Thomas, Jr.	39
Boone, Elizabeth.........39	(2)
BOONE, JAMES	39
Boone, James	345
Boone, Nicholas 7, 188,	408
Boone, Nicholas, Jr.	408
Boone, Willm.	276
Boone, William...7, 39 (2), 47, 125,	340
Boord, Rebonah	285
Booseman, Ralph	99
Booth, Anna	406
Booth, Elizabeth	406
BOOTH, GEORGE	39
Booth, George	406
Booth, George (son of George)	39
Booth, John	39
BOOTH, JAMES	40
BOOTH, JOHN	40

Index. 447

	PAGE.
Booth, Martha	26
Booth, Mary	39 (2)
Booth, Rachel	26, 40
Booty, Nickles	337
BOOZMAN, RALPH	40
Boras, Hannah	422
Borden, Benjamin	40 (2)
Borden, Hannah	40
Borden, Katherine	40
Borden, Susannah	40
Borden, Thomas	40
BORDEN, WILLIAM	40
Borden, William (son of Wm.)	40
Borden, William (nephew of William)	40
Boseman, Ralph	287
Boswell, Ezibell	40
BOSWELL, GEORGE	40
Boswell, George (son of George)	40
Boswell, George	40
Boswell, Hannah	255 (2)
Boswell, Ichabod	40
Boswell, Isac	40
Boswell, John	7 (2), 40 (3), 85, 255
Boswell, Joseph	255
Boswell, Mary	40
Boswell, Thomas	40
Boswell, William	40
Bosworth, Ephraim	41
BOSWORTH, JOSEPH	41
Bosworth, Joseph (son of Joseph)	41
Bosworth, Mary	41 (2)
Bosworth, Robert	41
BOTNETT, JOHN	41
Bottom, Mary	291
Bould, Joseph	41
BOUDE, JOHN	41
Boude, John (cousin of John)	41
Boude, Katherine	41 (2)
Boude, Thomas	41
Bouge Sound, plantation on.	300
BOULD, GEORGE	41
Bould, Mary	41 (2)
Bouler, William	349
Boulton, Abraham (Dr.)	86
Bound, Abigall (wife of Richd.)	41 (2)
Bound, Abigall (daughter of Richard)	41
Bound, Edward	41
Bound, Elizabeth	41
Bound, Horner	41
BOUND, RICHARD	41
Bound, Samuel	41
Bounds, Samuell	345
BOUREN, EDMUND	41
Bouren, Jane	41
Bouren, Joseph	41
Bouren, Sarah (wife of Edmund)	41
Bouren, Sarah (daughter of Edmund)	41
Bouren, Susannah	41
Bourn, Joseph	114
Bournsby, Margaret	357
Boutwell, Lionel	43
Boutwell, Samuel	350
Bowds, John	71
Bowers, William	391
Bowen, Arthur	110
Bowin, John	167
Bowin, William	357
Bowman, ——	292
Bownd, John	86
Bownd, Margaret	86
Bownin, Frances	167
Bowsers plantation	108
Boxly, Thomas	41
Boyce, Ann	17
Boyce, Ann	42 (2)
Boyce, Benjamin	41
Boyce, Elizabeth	42
BOYCE, ISAAC	41
Boyce, Isaac	42 (2)
Boyce, Jean	42
Boyce, Job	41, 42
BOYCE, JOHN	42
Boyce, John (son of John)	42
Boyce, Joseph	41
Boyce, Jude	41
Boyce, Mary	42
Boyce, Moses	42
Boyce, Rachel	42
Boyce, Susannah	42 (2)
Boyce, William	17
BOYCE, WILLIAM	42
BOYCE, WILLIAM	42
Boyd, Ann	42
Boyd, Anne	42, 237
Boyd, Elizabeth	69
BOYD, JOHN	42
Boyd, John (son of Thomas)	42
BOYD, JOHN	42
Boyd, John	42, 84, 88, 140, 291, 380 (2)

448   INDEX.

	PAGE.
Boyd, Katherine	42
Boyd, Lydia	42 (2)
Boyd, Lydiar	42
Boyd, Marion	42
Boyd, Robert	244
BOYD, THOMAS	42
Boyd, Thos.	27, 123, 201, 360
Boyd, Thomas	42 (2), 69, 262, 316, 400
BOYD, WINEFRED	42
Boyd, Winefred	69
Boyd, Winifort	400
Boyd, Winefruit	42
Boyd, William	42 (2), 69, 109, 118, 400 (2)
Boykin, Benj.	166
Boykin, Benjamin	43
BOYKIN, EDWARD	43
Boykin, Edward (son of Edward)	43
Boykin, Hardy	43
Boykin, Henry	43
Boykin, Judith	43 (2)
Boykin, Meldred	43 (2)
Boykin, Sarah	390
Boykin, Solomon	43 (2)
BOYKIN, THOMAS	43
Boykin, Thomas (son of Thos.)	43 (2)
Boykin, Thomas	43, 259
Boyle, John	280
Boyintone, Benjamin	43
BOYINTONE, JOSEPH	43
Boylan, Francis	406
Boyse, Ann	329
Boyte, James	82
Bozman, Ralph	415
Brabbell, John	337
Brabell, William	279
Brabham, John	189
Brace, George	154
Brack, Eliazar	43
Brack, Elizabeth	43
Brack, Gean	43
BRACK, GEORGE	43
Brack, George (son of George)	43 (2)
Brack, Richard	43
Brack, William	43
Braddish, ——	139
Braddy, Grace	43 (2)
BRADDY, JAMES	43
Braddy, James (son of James)	43 (2)
Braddy, James	387
Braddy, John	43
Braddy, Joseph	43, 387
Bradey, Ellis	73
BRADEY, JOHN	43
Bradford, John	44, 207, 325
Bradford, Mary	44
BRADFORD, NATHANIEL	44
Bradford, Nathaniel (son of Nathaniel)	44
Bradford, Patience	44
Bradford, Rebecka	276
Bradford, Sarah	44
Bradley, Abel	44
Bradley, Dority	44 (2)
Bradley, Elizabeth	44
Bradley, Haner	44
Bradley, John	44
Bradley, Mary	44
Bradley, Rachel	212
BRADLEY, RICHARD	44
Bradley, Richard	44, 259, 319
Bradley, Richd.	208
Bradley, Robert	42
Bradley, William	44 (2)
Bradshaw, Joseph	261
Brady, Abigail	43
Brady, Elisebeth	78
Brady, James	272, 322, 387
Brady, John	15, 44, 387
BRADY, JOSEPH	44
Brady, Joseph	44, 234
Brady, Tamer	44 (2)
Braezar, James	7
Braham, Patrick	34
Brainer, Nicholas	411
Brak Oake, land at Scuppernong	382
Branch, Anne	44 (3)
Branch, Elizabeth	44, 174 (2)
BRANCH, FRANCIS	44
Branch, Francis	44
Branch, Isaac	44
Branch, Issachar	44
Branch, Margaret	44 (2)
Branch, Solomon	44
Branch, Thomas	44
BRANCH, WILLIAM	44
Branch, William (son of William)	44
Branch, William	44
Brand, Andrew	44
Brand, Benjamin	278
BRAND, ISABELLA CAMERON	44
Brandon, John	309
Brannock, Jean	391
Brantley, John	88

INDEX.

	PAGE.
Brantley, William	115
Branton, Thomas	25
BRASKE, LAWRENCE	45
Brassell, John	202
Brassiers, Richard	146
Braswell, Ann	123
Braswell, Benjamin	133
Braswell, Elinor	417
Braswell, James	133
Braswell, Jean	45
Braswell, Jobe	45
Braswell, Mary	45
Braswell, Richard	45, 53
BRASWELL, ROBERT	45
Braswell, Robert (son of Robert)	45
Braswell, Sarah	45
Braswell, Valentine	45
Braswell, William	123
Britton, Peter	304
Brawler, Isaac	151
Bray, Christopher	45
Bray, Daniel	45
Bray, Dinah	45
Bray, George	45 (3), 56
Bray, Henere	45
BRAY, HENRY	45
Bray, Henry	56
Bray, Jacob	45
Bray, Jeremiah	45
Bray, John	45
Bray, Joseph	67
Bray, Mary	292
Bray, Sarah	176
Bray, Thomas	292
BRAY, WILLIAM	45
Bray, William	45, 56, 122 (2), 135, 299, 403
Braye, Matthew	414
Brayen, Derby	75
Breathan, Margaret	387
Breathet, Wm	422
Breeding, John	387
Breffill, John	300
Brefot, Jones	88
Bremen, James	413
Brenn, Jesse	206
Brent, Ann	45 (3)
Brent, Charles	45, 413
BRENT, JAMES	45
Brent, James (son of James)	45
BRENT, THOMAS	45
Brent, James (son of Thos.)	45
Brent, Jane	413
Brent, Jonathan	413
Brent, Joshua	10

	PAGE.
Brent, Keziah	45
Brent, Mary	413
Brent, Richard	45
Brethen, John	387
Brett, Charity	278
Brettno, Ann	353
Brettno, William	353
Brettno, William (son of William)	353
Breuitt, Samuel	23
Brewer, Catherine	46
BREWER, GEORGE	46
Brewer, George (son of Geo.)	46
Brewer, Hannah	46
BREWER, JANE	46
Brewer, John	46
Brewer, Mary	46
Brewer, Matthew	46
Brewer, Rawle	46
Brewton, Mary	276
Brian, Eliz	262
BRIANT, SAMUEL	46
Brice, Ann	46, 343
Brices Creek, mill at	253
Brice, Eliza	46
Brice, Francis	46, 213
Brice plantation	15
Brice, Rigdon	216, 313
BRICE, WILLIAM	46
Brice, William (son of William)	46
Brice, William	217, 345, 405
Brice, Wm	169, 343
Brickell, Ann	46
BRICKELL, JAMES	46
Brickell, James (son of James)	46 (2)
Brickell, John	137
Brickell, Jno	426
Brickell, Mary	46
Brick House plantation	86, 220
Brickle, Mary	350
Bridge Creek, land on	406
Bridge Neck land	425
Bridg Nack plantation	56
Bridgen, Edward	46
Bridgen, John (Rev.)	46
BRIDGEN, SAMUEL	46
Bridgen, Sarah	46
Bridgen, William	46
Bridgens Hall plantation	46
Bridgens Pastime plantation	46
Bridgers, Benjamin	47 (2)
Bridgers, Elizabeth	47
Bridgers, John	47, 84, 335

29

INDEX.

Bridgers, Joseph....47 (2), 84 (2), 87, 166
Bridgers, Josiah 281
Bridgers, Mary 47
Bridgers, Samuel 47 (2)
Bridgers, Sarah (wife of Wm.) 47
Bridgers, Sarah (daughter of Wm.) 47
BRIDGERS, WILLIAM 47
BRIDGERS, WILLIAM 47
BRIDGERS, WILLIAM 47
Bridgers, William (son of William) 47
Bridgers, William...84 (3), 335
Bridgers, W................ 76
Bridger, Elizabeth 210
Bridger, Mary Johnson..... 188
Bridges, Bracewell 166
Bridgess, Joseph 47
Bridgess, Mary 47
Bridgess, Patience 47
BRIDGESS, SAMUEL 47
Bridgetown, land at........ 337
Briery Branch, land on..... 293
Briery Branch, land on waters of 48
Briery Branch, plantation on 79
Briery Swamp, land on..... 71
Briffet, Samll.............. 134
Briffets Island plantation... 66
Briggs, Christian 47
Briggs, Elizabeth 47
Briggs, James 47
Briggs, John 47
Briggs, Moses 47
Briggs, Rachel 47
BRIGGS, RICHARD 47
Briggs, Richard (son of Rich'd) 47
Briggs, Solomon 47
Briggs, Tilpah 47
Bright, Adam 47
Bright, Ann 47, 48 (2), 132
Bright, Bridges 47
Bright, Caleb 47
Bright, Casiah 48
Bright, Cortney 47
Bright, Edee 48
Bright, Elizabeth (wife of Rich'd) 48
Bright, Elizabeth (daughter of Richard) 48
Bright, Elizabeth 47, 48
Bright, Elenar 48

Bright, Ephram 48, 275
Bright, Graves 48, 140
Bright, Hance 48
Bright, Hanson 48
BRIGHT, HENRY 47
BRIGHT, HENRY 47
Bright, Henry (son of Henry) 47 (2)
Bright, Isaac 142
Bright, Isack 67 (2)
BRIGHT, JAMES 48
Bright, James (son of Simon) 48
Bright, James (brother of Simon) 48
Bright, James 48, 66
Bright, John 47
Bright, Mary (wife of Simon) 48
Bright, Mary (daughter of Simon) 48
Bright, Mary (daughter of William) 48
Bright, Mary (granddaughter of William).......... 48
Bright, Mary 48, 67
Bright, Mary Ann.......... 47
Bright, Nancy 48
BRIGHT, RICHARD 48
BRIGHT, RICHARD 48
Bright, Richard (son of Rich'd) 48
Bright, S.................. 66
Bright, Sally 48
Bright, Samuel 47
Bright, Samll 48
Bright, Sarah (daughter of William) 48
Bright, Sarah (granddaughter of William).......... 48
Bright, Silas 47
BRIGHT, SIMON 48
Bright, Simon (son of Simon) 48
Bright, Simon...66 (2), 140, 149, 233, 309
Bright, Sollomon 48
BRIGHT, SOLOMON 48
Bright, Solomon (son of Solomon) 48
Bright, Solomon 357
Bright, Stockwell 48
Bright, Susanah 48
Bright, Susy 47
BRIGHT, WILLIAM 48

INDEX. 451

	PAGE.
Bright, William	.48 (2), 141, 142
Bright, Wm	149
Brights Branch, land on	67
Briles Neck	365
Brill, Acton	49
Brill, Francis	49
Brill, Rigdon	49
BRILL, WILLIAM	49
Brill, William (son of William)	49
Brin, Francis	49
Brinkley, Ann	169
Brinkley, James	63
Brinkley, Michael	69
Brinley, Francis	15
Brinn, Richard	158
Brins plantation	38
Britains and Fordyces plantation	407
Britt, Elizabeth	49
Britt, Mary	49
Britt, "Old Madum"	262
BRITT, WILLIAM	49
Britton, Francis	178
Britton, Henery	178
Britton, Ann	392
Britton, Moses	178
Broad Creek, land at	37
Broad Creek, land on	21, 108, 180, 278, 334, 418
Broad Creek, plantation on,	42, 96, 356
Broader, James	179
Broad Neck Branch, land on	110
Broad Neck lands	420
Broad Neck plantation	23
Broadwell, Hester	83
BROCHETT, BENJAMIN	49
Brochett, Sarah	49
Brockett, Benjamin	326
Brockett, Sarah	361
Brockit, Benjamin	361
Brock, John	11, 113, 215
Brocksat, Frances	379
BRODERICK, THOMAS	49
Brodie, Jane	140 (2)
Brodrick, Andrew	49
Brodrick, Dan'l	49
Brogden, James	36
Brogden, John	4
Brogden, Peter	4
Broken Beeches	409
BROMLEY, GEORGE	49
Brook, Henry	308
Brook, Jno.	250

	PAGE.
Brook, Job	307
Brooke, Samuel	121
Brookes, Job	322, 325, 391, 408
Brooks, Elizabeth	49
Brooks, Frances	49
Brooks, Henry	4
Brooks, Job	200
BROOKS, JOHN	49
Brooks, John (son of John)	49
Brooks, John	152, 302
Brooks, Mary (wife of John),	49 (2)
Brooks, Mary (daughter of John)	49
Brooks, Sarah	174
Brooks, Sibbe	174
Broomfield, courthouse in	50
Brosyer, Elizabeth	226
Brothers, Benjamin	50
Brothers, Darcus	69
Brothers, Doroty	50
Brothers, Elizabeth	.50 (2), 162
Brothers, Hanah	50
BROTHERS, JOHN	50
Brothers, John (son of John)	50
Brothers, John	50, 245, 283
Brothers, Joseph	50 (2)
Brothers, Mary	.50 (3), 283, 359
Brothers, Rebekah	50, 359
Brothers, Richard	..10, 50 (2), 83
Brothers, Samuell	50 (2)
Brothers, Sarah (wife of Wm.)	50
Brothers, Sarah (daughter of William)	50
BROTHERS, WILLIAM	50
Brothers, William (son of Wm.)	50
Brothers, William (brother of John)	50
Brothers, William (son of John)	50
Brothers, William	10
Brothers, Thomas	50 (2), 69
Broughton, Edward	97
Browns Creek, land on	261
Brown, Agnis	51 (2)
Brown, Andrew	346
Brown, Ann	50, 52, 126
Brown, Anne	50
Brown, Anny	50
Brown, Arthur	333, 410
Brown, Beale	314
Brown, Benjamin	50, 423
Brown, Catharine	50
Brown, Charity	170

	PAGE.
Brown, Christian	51
Brown, David	67
Brown, Dorothy	50
Brown, Dan'l.	50, 51
Brown, Edith	51
Brown, Edward	54
Brown, Edwd.	375
Brown, Elizabeth	50, 51 (2), 52 (2), 228
Brown, Fortune	51
BROWN, FRANCES	50
Brown, Francis (son of Francis)	50
Brown, Francis	171, 397
Brown, George	148, 227
Brown, Hanrenittia	51
Brown, Hardy	51
Brown, Henry	161
Brown, Howell	51
Brown, Isabella	51
Brown, Jacob	52
Brown, James	46
BROWN, JAMES	50
BROWN, JAMES	50
BROWN, JAMES	50
Brown, James (son of James)	50
Brown, James	51 (2), 92, 217, 309, 404
Brown, Dr. James	182
Brown, Jane	50, 144, 170
Brown, Jean	51
Brown, Joel	333
BROWN, JOHN	51
BROWN, JOHN	51
Brown, John	50, 51 (2), 52 (2), 67, 79, 90, 91, 95 (2), 98, 101, 126, 137, 159, 182, 251, 265, 274, 283, 387, 411, 424.
Brown, John, Sr.	90
BROWN, JONAS	51
Brown, Jonas (son of Wm.)	51
Brown, Jos.	147
Brown, M.	309
Brown, Margaret	51
Brown, Margarett (wife of Richard)	51 (2)
Brown, Margarett (daughter of Richard)	51
Brown Marsh, lands on	61 (2)
Brown Marsh plantation	147
Brown, Martha	52 (2)
Brown, Mary	50 (3), 52 (2), 112, 126, 228, 333
Brown, Molly	50
Brown, Nathan	51 (2)

	PAGE.
Brown, Olive	51
Brown, Patience	51
Brown, Patty	309
Brown, Peeter	51
Brown, Peter	56, 124, 283
BROWN, PHILLIP	51
Brown, Phillip	134
Brown, Priscilla	51, 228
Brown, Rachel	50
BROWN, RICHARD	51
Brown, Richard (son of Richd.)	51
Brown, Richard	346, 387
Brown, Sally	50
Brown, Sarah	22 (2), 50, 51, 52 (2), 56, 124, 228
Brown, Stephen	51
Brown, Temsin	51 (2)
BROWN, THOMAS	51
BROWN, THOMAS	51
Brown, Thomas (son of Thos.)	51
Brown, Thomas	22 (2), 52, 248
Brown, Tomsin	134
BROWN, WILLIAM	52
BROWN, WILLIAM	52
Brown, William	50 (2), 51, 314
Brown, Wm.	51
Browne, Anne	52
Browne, Elizabeth	12
Browne, Howell	50, 154 (2)
Browne, Jesse	52
Browne, Jesse	164
BROWNE, JOHN	52
Browne, John	12, 45, 52
Browne, Josiah	52
Browne, Margaret	45 (2)
Browne, Mary	51 (2)
BROWNE, WALTER	52
Browne, William	236
Browney, Sarah	116
Browning, Darkess	52
Browning, Elizabeth	52
Browning, Jane	132
BROWNING, JOHN	52
Browning, John (son of John)	52 (2)
Browning, John	132, 133 (2), 311
Browning, Margett	52 (2)
Browning, Sarah	132
Brownrigg, Richd.	162
Browns Harrows, land on	338
Bruce, Abram	283
Brucle (or Breecle), Mary	83
Brun, Ann	75
Bruton, Charles	226

INDEX.

	PAGE.
BRYAN, ANNE	52
Bryan, Anne (wife of William)	53 (2)
Bryan, Anne (daughter of William)	53
Bryan, Ann	53 (5), 187
Bryan, Darbey	160
Bryan, Darby	115, 330
Bryan, David	53 (2)
Bryan, E.	229
BRYAN, EDWARD	53
Bryan, Edward (son of Edwd.)	53
Bryan, Edward	53 (2), 81, 141, 164, 219, 232, 262
Bryan, Elice	232 (2)
Bryan, Elizabeth	53, 178
BRYAN, HARDY	53
Bryan, Hardy (son of Hardy)	53
Bryan, Hardy	53 (2), 424
Bryan, Isaac	53, 424
Bryan, Jess	53
Bryan, Jesse	52 (2), 63
Bryan, John	52 (2), 53 (2), 134 (2), 207 (2), 229, 230, 232, 250, 261, 280 (2), 408.
Bryan, Joseph	53
Bryan, Lewis	53 (3), 335, 351, 424
Bryan, Martha	53
Bryan, Mary	53, 406, 424
Bryan, Millborough	62
Bryan, Nathan	53, 424
Bryan, Needham	57, 131, 168, 192, 254, 297, 303, 417
Bryan, Penelipy	53
Bryan, Rachel	53 (2)
Bryan, Sarah	53 (3), 330, 424
BRYAN, SIMON	53
Bryan, Simon	79 (2)
Bryan, Susan	57
BRYAN, THOMAS	53
Bryan, Thomas	53 (2), 84, 424
BRYAN, WILLIAM	53
Bryan, William	53
Bryan, William (son of Wm.)	53 (2)
Bryan, William	52 (2), 53, 168, 330, 424
Bryant, Arthur	54
Bryant, Drewseller	207
Bryant, Elener	239
Bryant, Elias	250
Bryant, Elizabeth	14, 54
BRYANT, JAMES	53

	PAGE.
Bryant, James	45, 53 (2), 102, 246, 366
Bryant, Jas.	47
BRYANT, JOHN	54
Bryant, Joseph	54
Bryant, Needham	250
Bryant, Paccence	45
Bryant, Patience	54
Bryant, Simon	14
Bryant, Thomas	23, 53, 84
Bryant, Thos.	45
BRYANT, WILLIAM	54
Bryant, William (son of William)	54
Bryant, William	47 (3), 53, 54
Bryly, John	198
Buchar, Mary	250
Buck, Anne	54
Buck Creek, land on	191
Buck, Francis	394
Buck Hall, land on	376
Buck Hall and Spring Branch, land between	376
Buck Horn, land on	71
Buckhorse Swamp, land on	98
BUCK, JOHN	54
Buck, John	224
Buck, Sarah	394
Buckelsberry Swamp, plantation on	308
Buck Swamp, land on	406
Buckingham (plantation)	385
Buckingham, Stephen	167
Buckler, John	16
BUCKLY, ELLENDER	54
Buckly, Elizabeth	54
Buckly, Henry	54
Buckly, Jorge	54
Buckly, Rowland	100
Bucklesbury plantation	327
Buckner, Robert	54, 120, 163, 384
Buckner, Ro.	348
Buckner, Robt.	371
Buford, John	178 (2)
Buford, William	178 (2)
Bugnion, Elizabeth	54
Bugnion, Margaret	54
Bugnion, Mr.	257
BUGNION, RALPH	54
Buie, Wm.	76
Bula, Anne	377
Bull Branch, land on	378
Bull, Chas.	83, 135, 223
Bull, Charles	314
Bull, Charletta	277

454 Index.

	PAGE.
Bull, Ephraim	377, 404
Bull, Grisell	277
Bull, Grizell	81
Bull, John	57
Bull, Millicent	277
Bull, Patience	343
Bull, Sarah	83, 112, 135, 277, 284
Bullin, James	283
Bullock, Joseph	40
Bullock, Mary	40
Bullock, Sarah	40
Bullock, Thomas	40, 427
Bull Yard plantation	114
Bulock, James	115
Bumpas, Cornelius	54 (2)
Bumpas, David	54 (2), 343
BUMPAS, JOB	54
Bumpas, John	54
Bumpas, Tabas	54
Bumpus, Thomas	343
Bun, Ann	55
Bun, Benjamin	54
Bun, David	54
Bun, Eleaner	55
BUN, JOHN	54
Bun, John (son of John)	54
Bun, William	55
Bunch, Micajah	376
Bunch, Paul	60, 352
Buncombe, Joseph	362
Buncomb, Mary	83
Bunday, Elizabeth	20
Bunday, Jean	183
Bunday, John	245
Bunday, Josiah	20
Bunday, Samuel	183
Bundey, Samuel	369
Bundy, Abraham	55 (3)
BUNDY, ANNE	55
Bundy, Anne	55 (2), 211
BUNDY, BENJAMIN	55
Bundy, Benjamin	55 (2), 72 (2)
BUNDY, CALEB	55
BUNDY, CALEB	55
Bundy, Caleb	55, 84, 314
BUNDY, DAVID	55
Bundy, Eliza	72
Bundy, Gideon	55 (3)
Bundy, Hannah	55 (2), 72
Bundy, Jane	84
Bundy, Jean	284
Bundy, Jeremiah	55
Bundy, John	55, (3), 72, 359
Bundy, Josah	259
Bundy, Josiah	40, 55 (3), 251

	PAGE.
Bundy, Liday	55
Bundy, Lydia	55
Bundy, Mary	55 (2)
Bundy, Miriam	55
Bundy, Moses	55
BUNDY, SAMUEL	55
Bundy, Samuel	55 (3)
Bundy, Saml	92
Bundy, Samuel (brother of Caleb)	55
Bundy, Samuel (son of Caleb)	55
BUNDY, WILLIAM	55
Bundy, William	55 (4), 402
Bundy, Wm	40, 288 (2)
Bunker, Simon	162
Bunn, Andrew	362
Bunn, William	237 (2)
Buntin, John	285
Bunting, John	77
Burden (Bender), William	402
Burdet, Jonathan	91
Burford, William	388
Burges, Elizabeth	45, 56 (2)
Burges, George	57
Burges, J	144
Burges, Mary	151 (2)
Burges, Sarah	330
Burges, Stephen	45
Burges, Thomas	45, 129, 416
Burges, Thos	416
Burges, William	45, 56, 330 (2)
Burges, Wm	141, 379 (2)
Burgess, Benjamin	314
Burgess, Elizabeth	56
BURGESS, STEPHEN	56
Burgess, Stephen (son of Stephen)	56
BURGESS, STEPHEN	56
Burgess, Stephen (son of Stephen)	56
Burgess, Thomas	56 (2), 416
Burgwin, C	65
Burgwin, J	101, 255, 297, 338, 374, 375, 389, 407
Burgwin, Jno	214, 357
Burk, Ann	256
Burke, Edward	249
Burke, William	39
Burket, Esbel	120
Burket, Thomas	158
BURKETT, JOHN	56
Burkett, John (son of John)	56
Burkett, Joseph	56 (2)
Burleigh, James	56

INDEX. 455

	PAGE.
BURLEIGH, ROBERT	56
Burleigh, Robert (son of Robt.)	56
Burleigh, Sarah	56
Burn, Andr	219
Burn, John	81, 195, 219
Burnap, Nathnell	103
BURNASS, JOHN	56
Burnby, Elizabeth (wife of John)	56
Burnby, Elizabeth (granddaughter of John)	56
Burnby, Hannah	57 (2)
BURNBY, JOHN	56
Burnby, John (son of John)	56
Burnby, John (father of Thomas)	57
Burnby, John (brother of Thomas)	57
Burnby, John	312
Burnby, Marguerett	56
Burnby, Sarah	312
BURNBY, THOMAS	57
Burnby, William	57, 312
BURNET, GEORGE	57
Burnet, James	250
Burnet, Susanna	57
Burnett, Archibald	91
Burney, Elizabeth	71
Burney, John	71
Burney, Robert	339
Burnham, Benjamin	67
BURNHAM, ELIZABETH	57
BURNHAM, ESEBEL	57
Burnham, Gabr.	67
Burnham, Gabrell	167
Burnham, James	28, 47, 275, 298
Burnham, John	309
Burnham, Sarah	167
Burnham, Susias Abiar	57
Burnnell, John	293
Burns, Andrew	281 (2)
Burns, Francis	396
Burns, Grisell	281
Burns, John	281 (2)
Burns, Mary	147
Burnside, John	138
Burrington, Geo.	33, 87, 114, 115, 150, 159, 163, 174, 178, 179, 180, 183, 186, 215 (2), 218, 255, 272, 274, 289, 296, 304, 306, 307, 308, 313 (3), 339, 348, 366, 368, 381, 386, 389, 402, 403, 413, 421.
Burroes, Hannah	41
Bursey, Hannah	312

	PAGE.
Bursey, Penny	312
BURT, MARY	57
Burt, Wm.	57
Burtenshall, Margaret	57 (2)
BURTENSHALL, RICHARD	57
Burtenshall, Richard (grandson of Richard)	57
Burton, Abraham	89, 99, 242, 276, 408
Burton, Elizabeth	168
Burton, Samuel	388
Burwell, Lewis	210
Burwell, Martha	210
Busbe, Thomas	117
BUSBEY, CATHERINE	57
Busbey, Thomas	236
Busby, Thomas	74
Busett, Abraham	256, 339
Bush, Catherine	335
Bush, David	7, 129
Bush, Elizabeth	58
Bush, Hardy	335
Bush, Issac	307
Bush, James	87, 241
Bush, John	58
Bush, Martha	58
Bush, William (son of Wm.)	58
BUSH, WILLIAM, SR.	58
Bussly, Rowland	100
Bussy, Penny	312
Butcher, Bell	382
Butcher, Mary	382
Butcher, Mary Turnbull	382
Butchers plantation	310
Butler,	331
Butler, Andrew	58
Butler, Anhoretta	88
Butler, Ann	421
Butler, Chris	158, 390
Butler, Christopher	21, 58 (3), 88
BUTLER, DAVID	58
Butler, David	58, 142, 172, 173, 243, 300, 356
Butler, Elizabeth	58 (2), 393
BUTLER, JACOB	58
Butler, Jacob	21, 319
Butler, James	58 (3)
Butler, Jethro	229
BUTLER, JOHN	58
Butler, John (son of John),	58 (3)
Butler, John (son of James)	58
Butler, John	76, 151, 393

INDEX.

	PAGE.
Butler, Mary....58 (3), 172,	243
Butler, Robt.	121
Butler, Robert 125,	421
Butler, Sarah	58
Butler, Simon	58
Butler, T.	287
Butler, Thomas	19
Butler, William......58, 218,	421
Butt, James	266
Butt, Thos.	277
Butterre, Sarah	23
Butterton, Joseph 207,	403
Butterton, Sarah	403
Butterworth, land adjoining.	327
Buttery, Christopher	311
Buttlor, Rachel	199
Butts Grove Island	87
Buxton, Ann (daughter of Samuel)	58
Buxton, Ann (wife of Samuel)	58
Buxton, Edwd.	170
Buxton, George	58
Buxton, Jacob	58
Buxton, Lewis	58
Buxton, Petronelia	58
BUXTON, SAMUEL	58
Buxton, Samuel (son of Samuel)	58
Buxton, William	58
Byard, Jane	218
Byard, Thomas	6
Byfield, Samuel	243
Bynum, Faith	207
Bynum, Mary	125
Byrd, Anne	59
Byrd, Edman	59
Byrd, Edward	59
Byrd, Elizabeth	59
Byrd, Jeane	219
BYRD, JOHN	59
Byrd, John (son of John)..	59
Byrd, John	362
Byrd, Rebecca...........59	(2)
Byrd, Richard...59, 362 (3),	378
Byrd, Robert	378
BYRD, THOMAS	59
Byrd, Thomas (son of Thomas)	59
Byrd, William 59, 306,	411
Byrde, Anna	39
Byrde, Edmon	39
Byrde, Pachence	39
Byrne, Lawrence	255
Byrne, Matthew	297
BYROM, THOS.	59

	PAGE.
Cabage, John	177
Cabb, J.	291
Cabbidge, John	253
Cabbage Inlet, land opposite to	257
Cabbin Necke	36
Cabbin Neck plantation..212	(2)
Cabbing Ridge plantation...	134
Cabege, John 248,	288
Cabey, John	73
Cabin Neck	378
Caerton, Richard	382
Caila, Jane	316
Caila, Peter	365
Cailag (or Cailaugh), Peter	1
Cain, Abijah	59
Cain, Christian	49
Cain, Elizabeth	59
CAIN, HARDY	59
Cain, Hardy	59
Cain, Isabell	59
Cain, James 59	(2)
CAIN, JOHN	59
Cain, Jonathan 59 (2),	245
Cain, Patience	59
Cain, Plurity	59
Cain, Rachell 59	(2)
Cain, Rebekah...........27,	251
Cain, Sary	59
Cain, Unis	59
CAIN, WILLIAM	59
Cain, William (son of William)	59
Cain, William	27
Cain, Zipporah	59
Calden, Capn. John	160
Caldone, Ann	308
Caldone, Churchill......307,	308
Caldone, John..244, 296, 307 (2), 324, 340,	424
Caldone, Margaret	308
Caldwell, Joshua 59	(2)
CALDWELL, ROBERT	59
Calef, James	128
Caleps, Jas.	90
Caley, Nathaniel	72
Calheart, Dr. William	142
Calhon,	332
Calihan, John	260
CALLAWAY, CALEB	60
Callaway, Caleb 60,	215
Callaway, Elizabeth	60
Callaway, Elizabeth (wife of Joshua)	60
Callaway, Elizabeth (daughter of Caleb)	60

	PAGE.
Callaway, John	60 (2)
CALLAWAY, JOSHUA	60
Callaway, Joshua	60
Callaway, Thomas	60, 360
Callaway, Thos.	146
Callaway, Tho.	249
Callebar, Jeane	303
Calleton, Elizabeth (wife of George)	123 (2)
Calleton, George	123
Callihan, Mary	357
Callihern, Dennis	240
Callio, Elizabeth	60
Callio, Jane	60
CALLIO, JOSEPH	60
Calloway, Caleb	188
Calloway, Caleb	290 (2)
Calloway, Job	69
Calloway, Joshua	221
Calloway, Thomas	92, 111, 406
Calloway, William	290
Calloway, Zebulon	152
Callums Creek, land on	164
Calvart, Mary	121
Cambal, William	108
Cambel, Rachel	249
Cambell, Hugh	383
Camber, Thomas	312
CAMBRELL, ALEXANDER	60
Cambrell, Anne	60
Cambrell, Sarah	60
Cambridge, Elizabeth	60
CAMBRIDGE, FRANCIS	60
CAMBRILL, ANNE	60
Camerlen, Ann	60
Camerlen, Belason	60
CAMERLEN, DANIEL	60
Camerlen, Phillip Alexander	60
Camerlen, Rachel	60
Cammill, Comfort	311
Cammill, John	260
Campan, Thomas	303
Campbell, Ann	61 (2)
Campbell, Chas.	43, 123, 390
Campbell, Cornelius	323 (3)
Campbell, Dun	336
Campbell, Elizabeth	323 (2)
Campbell, Fergd	323 (2)
Campbell, Henry	203
CAMPBELL, HUGH	61
Campbell, Hugh	123, 182, 229, 248, 277, 291 (2), 344, 383
CAMPBELL, JAMES	61
Campbell, James	27, 282

	PAGE.
Campbell, Jas.	32, 356
Campbell, Jas., Jr.	74
Campbell, Jasen	366
CAMPBELL, JOHN	61
Campbell, John	31, 118, 133, 162, 197, 229 (2), 235, 282, 291, 387, 422.
Campbell, John (of Lazy Hill)	197
Campbell, Capt. John	323
Campbell, Josa	100
Campbell, Jos.	85, 402
Campbell, Joshua	390
Campbell, Magdalen	61, 229, 248
Campbell, Mary (wife of John)	61
Campbell, Mary (daughter of John)	61
Campbell, Mary	164
Campbell, Rachel	61
Campbell, Robert	61
Campbell, Samuel	61
Campbell, Thomas	101
CAMPBELL, WILLIAM	61
Campbell, William (son of William)	61
Campbell, William	61 (2)
Campbell, Wm.	159
Campen, Edmond	104
Campen, Edward	95
Campen, Robert	104, 213
Canada, Patrick	189
Canaday, David	424
Canaday, Gideon	335
Canady, Brigett	191
Canady, Cornelius	335
Canady, Elizabeth	61, 335
Canady, Jeudath	22
Canady, John	61 (2), 349
Canady, John	349
Canady, Katherine	61
Canady, Kezia	61
CANADY, RICHARD	61
Canady, Richd.	189
CANADY, SAMUEL	61
Canady, Samuel (son of Samuel)	61
Canady, William	61
Canaho Creek, land on	292
Cane, James	371
Cane, Rebecca	371
Cane, William	59
Cane Creek, land on	278
Canings, Joseph	384
CANLEPI, MICHAEL	62

INDEX.

	PAGE.
Cannady, Jno.	364
Cannady, Mary	406
Cannady, Richard	79
Cannesby in Cathness, legacy for church bell	179
CANNINGS, JOSEPH	62
Cannings, Rebekah	62
Cannon, David	62
Cannon, Dennis	62
CANNON, EDWARD	62
Cannon, Edward (son of Edward)	62
Cannon, Henry	32, 62
Cannon, Jaen	62
Cannon, Jeremiah	278
Cannon, John	62
Cannon, Margaret	62
Cannon, Mary	62, 278 (2)
Cannon, Olif	62
Cannon, Ruth	62
Cannon, Sarah	62
Cannon, William	62
Canterbury, Archbishop of	103
Cape, Joseph	34
Cape Fair, house and lott in	179
Cape Fear, land on North East of	205
Cape Fear, plantation in	336
Cape Fear River, estate on	386
Cape Fear River, land on	188
Cape Fear River, lands on	257
Caphart, Mary	323
Capheart, George	336 (2)
Capheart, John	336
Capheart, Mychel	336
Cappell Point plantation	176
CAPPS, DENNIS	62
Capps, Dennis (son of Dennis)	62
Capps, Edward	62
Capps, Elizabeth	62
Capps, Enoch	62
Capps, Henry	62
Capps, Moses	62 (2)
Capps, Phillip	62
Capps, Richard	396
Capps, William	62
Caps, Moses	213
Car, Jonathan	62
Car, Margaret	62
Car, Mary	409
CAR, PATRICK	62
Car, Tamar	62
Car, Thomas	62
Carch, Daniel	353
Cardin, Jesse	47

	PAGE.
Carell, John	239
Carey, Elizabeth	13
Carissur, Joseph	19
Carkeet, Mary	150
CARLETON, ARTHUR	62
Carleton, Arthur	88, 362
Carlton, John	215
Carlyle, John	179
Carman, Ann	62
Carman, Elizabeth	62
CARMAN, WILLIAM	62
Carman, William	351
Carnal, Thomas	242
Carney, Elizabeth	196
Carnick, John	73, 82
Caron, George	185
Caron, Patrick	102
Caron, William	107
Caroon, George	277
Caroon, James	277 (2)
Caroon, John	277 (2)
Carp, Elinor	50
Carp, John	146 (2)
Carr, Archbald	63
Carr, Hannah	63
Carr, Jacob	374
Carr, James	141
Carr, Jane	63
Carr, Job	273
Carr, Will	238
CARR, WILLIAM	63
Carraway, Ann	52, 63
Carraway, Enoch	63
Carraway, Fanny	63
Carraway, Francis	63
Carraway, Gideon	52, 63 (2)
CARRAWAY, JAMES	63
Carraway, James	52, 53
Carraway, John	276
Carraway, Joseph	63 (2)
Carraway, Nancy	63
Carraway, Thomas	63
Carraway, William	276
Carraway, William, Jr.	53
Carrell, John	188
Carril, Elizabeth	101
Carrill, Molley	100
Carrol, John	186, 339
Carroll, John	301
Carrot Island	333
Carruthers, Nath'l	34, 165, 300
Caruthers, Content	63
Caruthers, Dr.	410
Caruthers, Elizabeth	16, 63
Caruthers, J.	152
Caruthers, Jacob	62, 63 (2)

INDEX. 459

	PAGE.
Caruthers, James	63 (3)
Caruthers, Jane	261
CARUTHERS, JOHN	63
CARUTHERS, JOHN	63
Caruthers, John (son of John)	63 (2)
Caruthers, John	16 (3), 38, 63 (2)
Caruthers, Jno., Jr	261
Caruthers, Joseph	63 (2)
Caruthers, Joseph	149
Caruthers, Mary	16
CARUTHERS, NATHANIEL	63
Caruthers, Nathaniel	63, 220, 300
CARUTHERS, ROBERT	63
Caruthers, Robert	63
Caruthers, Unice	63
Caruthers, William, Sr.	13
Caruthers, W., Jr.	48
Caruthers, William	16 (2), 63, 261
Carswell, Matthew	9
Carta, Thomas	410
Carteel, Anthony	273
CARTER, ANN	64
Carter, Benjamin	131
Carter, Cattren	200
Carter, Edward	408
Carter, Elizabeth	375
CARTER, HENRY	64
Carter, Henry (son of Henry)	64
Carter, Isaac	205 (2), 426
Carter, James	200, 208
Carter, John	64 (2)
Carter, Margret	64
Carter, Solomon	64, 241
Carter, Walter	64
Carter, William	57
Carteret, Peter	401
Cartlidge, E.	244
Cartlidge, Edmo.	76
Cartreet, Benjamin	175
Cartriet, Jno.	45
Cartright, Ann	132
Cartright, Caleb	65
Cartright, David	65
Cartright, Elizabeth (daughter of John)	65
Cartright, Hannah	65
Cartright, John	65
Cartright, Joseph	65
Cartright, Robert	65
Cartright, Sarah	65
Cartright, Tamer	65
Cartright, Thomas	65
CARTRIGHT, WILLIAM	65

	PAGE.
Cartritt, Robert	421
Cartus, Ann	113
Cartwright, Benjamin	64
Cartwright, Catherine	64
Cartwright, Catren	64
Cartwright, Claudius	64
Cartwright, David	309
Cartwright, Eliza	64
Cartwright, Elizabeth	64 (2), 110
Cartwright, Ezekiel	64
CARTWRIGHT, GRACE	64
Cartwright, Grace	64, 65
Cartwright, Hezekiah	64 (2)
Cartwright, Hez	329, 357
Cartwright, Job, Sr	64
Cartwright, Job	64 (2)
CARTWRIGHT, JOHN	64
Cartwright, John	64, 65, 158
Cartwright, Joseph	64 (2)
Cartwright, Jos	64
Cartwright, Josiah	64, 388
Cartwright, Martha (wife of Robert)	64
Cartwright, Martha (daughter of Robert)	64
Cartwright, Mary	64, 181
CARTWRIGHT, ROBERT	64
Cartwright, Robert	64, 65
CARTWRIGHT, THOMAS	64
Cartwright, Thos	64 (2)
Cartwright, Thomas (son of Thomas)	64 (2)
Cartwright, Thomas	65, 163
CARTWRIGHT, WILLIAM	65
Cartwright, William	64, 303
Carver, Ann	65
Carver, Arcadia	65
Carver, Elizabeth	65
Carver, Elizabeth (wife of James)	65
Carver, Elizabeth (daughter of James)	65
CARVER, JAMES	65
CARVER, JAMES	65
Carver, James (son of James)	65
Carver, James	65
Carver, Job	65
Carver, Mary	65
CARVER, SAMUEL	65
Carver, Samuel (son of Samuel)	65
Carver, Samuel	65 (3)
Carver, Sarah	65

460 INDEX.

	PAGE.
Carvers Creek Meeting, legacy to	176, 191
Cary, Elizabeth	270
Cary, James, Jr	20
Cary, Richard	76
Cary, Stephen	349
Cary, Thomas	2, 176
Cary, Thos	36
Cary, William	106
Casan, Gabriel	285
Cashai River, land on	160
Cashia Neck, land in	164
Cashia River, land on	199
Cashie River, land on	142
Cashie Swamp, land on	200
Cashoak, plantations at	219
Cashy River, land on	323
Casle, Rhoda	190
Cason, Hester	104
Cason, James	394
Cason, Rachel	290
Cass, John	138
Casshi River, land on	77
Castelaw, James	293 (2)
Castellaw, Bathiah	66
Castellaw, Katherine	66
Castellaw, James	66, 115, 225, 291, 421
Castellaw, John	66
Castellaw, Sarah	66 (2), 411
Castellaw, Thomas	66, 211
CASTELLAW, WILLIAM	66
Castello, James	323
Casten, Demsey	37
Caster, Hennery	25
Castleton, James	327
Caswell, Benjamin	66, 341
Caswell, Dallam	66 (4)
Caswell, Eleanor	66
Caswell, Elisha	66
Caswell, Elizabeth (wife of Matthew)	66
Caswell, Elizabeth (daughter of Matthew)	66
Caswell, Elizabeth	370
Caswell, Joanna	66
Caswell, John	66 (4)
Caswell, Martha	341
Caswell, Martin	66 232
Caswell, Mary	66
CASWELL, MATTHEW	66
Caswell, Matthew (son of Matthew)	66 (2)
Caswell, Matthew	370
Caswell, N	66

	PAGE.
CASWELL, RICHARD	66
Caswell, Richard	23, 48 (3), 82, 125, 163 (4), 207, 216, 248, 268, 274, 297, 321 (2), 341, 378, 380.
Caswell, Richard, Jr	66
Caswell, Mrs. Richard	66
Caswell, R	32, 48 (2), 117, 151, 152, 157, 162, 232, 421
Caswell, Richard William	66
Caswell, Samuel	66 (2)
Caswell, Samuel (brother of Matthew)	66
Caswell, Samuel (son of Matthew)	66
Caswell, Sarah	66, 163
Caswell, Shine	66
Caswell, Susannah	66 (2)
Caswell, Tabitha	66
Caswell, William	66
Caswell, Wm.	125
Caswell, Winston	66 (4)
Catabee River, plantation on	228
Catawaske Marsh, plantation on	52
Catawatsky, land at	408, 411
Catawba River, plantation near	309
Cate, Joseph	309
Cates, Peter	255
Cathcart, Fannay	330
Cathcart, Johnston	187
Cathcart, Margaret	248
Cathcart, Peggy	330
Cathcart, Will	23, 195
Cathcart, Dr. William	147 (2), 330, 331, 348
Cathcart, William	187, 188, 249, 330
Cathey, John	218
Cathright, Lydia	13
Catrin Creek, land on	322
Cattale Marsh, land on	382
Cautanche, Michael	116, 289
Cautanche, Michael, Jr	289
Cautanche, Sarah	289
Cavana, Ja	414
Cavaniss, George	336
Cavena, Aquilla	67
Cavena, Arther	67
CAVENA, CHARLES	67
Cavena, Charles (son of Charles)	67
Cavena, David	67
Cavena, Henry	67

INDEX. 461

	PAGE
Cavena, Mary	67
Cavena, Needham	67
Cavena, Nicolas	67
Cavenaugh, Ananias, 149, 333, 392	
Caves, Ralph	402
Cavyelton, Patricke	347
CAWDREY, THOMAS	67
Cawen, Enoch	160
Cedar Point plantation	212
Cedy Branch, land on	69
Cenaday, Patrick	218
Cenman, Charles	410
Certis, Mary	232
Ceter, Edy	336
Chabanas, Isaac	199
Chadwick, E.	261
Chadwick, Ephraim	41, 333
Chadwick, Gayer	67
Chadwick, Isaiah	67
Chadwick, Josiah	67
Chadwick, Mary (wife of Samuel)	67
Chadwick, Mary (daughter of Samuel)	67
Chadwick, Rebeckah	67
CHADWICK, SAMUEL	67
Chadwick, Samuel	333
Chadwick, Sarah	67
Chadwick, Tamor	67
Chadwick, Thomas	67 (2)
Chalkhill, Dorcas	67
CHALKHILL, JOHN	67
Chalkhill, Lydia	67
Chalkhill, Mary	67
Chalten, William	362
Chalton, William	362
Chambars, Edward	185
Chamberlain, Jeremiah	67
CHAMBERLAIN, JOHN	67
Chamberlain, John (son of John)	67 (2)
Chamberlain, Katherine	117
Chamberlain, William	67
Chamberlayne, Edwd.	205
Chamberlin, Aby	1
Chamberlin, Amy	67
Chamberlin, Ann	67
Chamberlin, Bettie	67
Chamberlin, Cathrein	1 (2)
Chamberlin, Courtney	1
Chamberlin, Jeremiah	1
Chamberlin, Lucy	1, 67
Chamberlin, Martha	67
Chamberlin, Robert	67
CHAMBERS, EDMOND	67

	PAGE
Chambers, Elizabeth	235
Chambery, George	389
CHAMPEN, JOHN	68
Champen, John	345
Champen, Sarah	68 (2)
Champion, Benj.	95
CHAMPION, EDWARD	67
Champion, Edward (son of Edward)	68
Champion, Edward	68
Champion, Elizabeth	68
Champion, Jane	192
Champion, Joseph	67
Champion, Mary (wife of Edward)	68
Champion, Mary (daughter of Edward)	68
CHAMPION, ORLANDO	68
Champion, Orlando	131
Champion, Thomas	67
Chance, Sarah	310
Chance, Susanah	310
Chancel, John	304
Chancey, Daniel	68, 302
Chancey, Deborah	68, 369
CHANCEY, EDMUND	68
Chancey, Edmund (son of Stephen)	68
Chancey, Edmund (son of Jacob)	68
Chancey, Edmund (son of Zachariah)	68
Chancey, Edmund	243 (2)
Chancey, Hannah	68
Chancey, Jacob	68
Chancey, Jeremiah	68, 69
Chancey, Mary	68
Chancey, Penniah	287
Chancey, Rachel	68
Chancey, Rebecca	302, 380
Chancey, Stephen	68
CHANCEY, WILLIAM	68
Chancey, William (father of William)	68
CHANCEY, WILLIAM	69
Chancey, William (grandson of William)	69
Chancey, Wm.	369
Chancey, Zach	34, 380
Chancey, Zachariah	68 (2)
Chancy, Mary	68
Chandler, John	393
Chaney, Zachariah	87 (2)
Channel, Rafe	26
Chapel, Marke	356

	PAGE.		PAGE.
Chaplain, Joseph	427	Charlton, Jasper	181
Chapman, Benjamin	127	Charlton, Job...70, 158, 404 (2)	
CHAPMAN, CHAS	69	CHARLTON, JOHN	70
Chapman, Charles (son of Chas.)	69	Charlton, John (son of John)	70
Chapman, Charles	69	Charlton, John..........404 (2)	
Chapman, Edward	237	Charlton, Sarah	70
Chapman, Frances	69	Charlton, William........70, 349	
Chapman, Henry 69 (2)		Chase, Amy	40
Chapman, James	31	Chason, James	132
CHAPMAN, JOHN	69	Chasten, John	268
Chapman, John 19, 318		Chastlon, Sarah	172
CHAPMAN, MARY	69	Chatwin, Joseph	222
Chapman, Robert	103	Chauncey, Aunt (wife of Walley)	350
Chapman, Samuel	69	Chauncey, Walley....38, 71,	
Chapman, Sarah	69	75, 79, 88, 115 (2), 119, 164,	
Chapman, William 46, 69		167, 218, 289, 290, 295, 301, 303	
Chapman, Wm..............	403	(2), 318, 324, 337, 340, 349, 350	
Chapmen, Alexander	105	(2), 356, 365, 390, 413.	
Chappel, Eliza	69	Chears, Samuel Salsbury....	427
Chappel, Judah	69	Cheasten, Anne	70
Chappel, Michaiah	69	CHEASTEN, RICHARD	70
Chappel, Moses	69	Cheasten, Richard (son of Richard) 70 (2)	
CHAPPEL, RICHARD	69	Cheasten, Richard...93, 122, 206	
Chappel, Richard (son of Richard)	69	Cheasten, R........175 (2), 287	
Chappel, Sarah	69	Cheat Neck Branch, land on	150
Charelton, William	423	Cheat Neck Island..........	150
Charey Gardens in Borken..	379	Cheat Neck, land on........	150
Charles, Abigail	7	Cheek, Ann	71
CHARLES, DANIELL	69	Cheek, James............71, 361	
Charles, Elizabeth........70 (2)		Cheek, Jane (wife of Richard)	71
CHARLES, HANNAH	70		
Charles, Hannaugh	70	Cheek, Jane (daughter of Richard)	71
Charles, Jane	70		
Charles, Jann	70	Cheek, John	71
CHARLES, JEANE	70	Cheeks Mill Creek, land on..	218
Charles, Jeane	69	Cheek, Randolph	71
CHARLES, JOHN	70	CHEEK, RICHARD	71
Charles, John....69, 70 (3), 267, 378		Cheek, Richard, Jr.........	71
Charles, Josuay	70	Cheek, Richard.........198, 361	
Charles, Lidey	70	Cheek, Robt.............71 (2)	
Charles, Margaret	378	Cheek, William	71
CHARLES, SAMUEL	70	Cheek, Wm.................	71
Charles, Samuel (son of Saml)	70	Chenifen Ridge plantation..	206
Charles, Samuell 69, 70 (2)		Cherry, Abigail	71
Charles, Sarah	70	Cherry, Cader	358
CHARLES, WILLIAM	70	Cherry, Cado	71
Charles, William	210	Cherry, Charles	71
Charlescraft, Anthony	31	Cherry, Courtney	71
Charlescraft, Jacob	31	Cherry, George	71
Charlton, Abigail	181	Cherry, Elizabeth 58, 71	
Charlton, George	269	Cherry, James	58
		Cherry, John.............71 (2)	

INDEX. 463

	PAGE.
Cherry, Martha	58 (2), 358
Cherry, Mary	71
Cherry, Patience	71
CHERRY, SAMUEL	71
Cherry, Samuel (son of Saml.)	71 (2)
Cherry, Solomon	71, 358
Cherry, William	71
Cherry, Willis	71
Cheryholme, John	103
Cheson, James	372
Chesher, Mary	71
Chesher, Sarah	71
CHESSON, ANNE	71
Chesson, Ann	71
CHESSON, JAMES	71
Chesson, James (son of James)	71
Chesson, James	71, 221 (2), 393
Chesson, John	71 (2), 393
Chesson, Joshua	71
Chesten, Richard	378
Chesters Creek, land on	293
Chester, Elizabeth (wife of John)	71
Chester, Elizabeth (daughter of John)	71
Chester, Elizabeth	71, 181 (2)
CHESTER, JOHN	71
CHESTER, JOHN	71
Chester, John (son of John)	71
Chester, John	52, 181
Chester, Martha	72
Chester, Mary	71
Chester, Nixon	394
CHESTER, SAMUEL	72
Chester, Sarah	394
Chester, Sary	71
Chestne, John	286
Cheston, Joanne	367
CHEVIN, NATHANIEL	72
Chevin, Na	90, 119
Chevin, Nathaniel	88, 186
Chevin, Nathl	24, 163, 214 (2), 246, 285, 399 (2)
Chevin, N	4, 90, 98, 119, 143, 225, 262, 292, 320, 359, 361, 362, 364, 389 (2), 426.
Chevin, Thos.	24
Chew, Alice	137
CHEW, HENRY, SR.	72
Chew, Henry (son of Henry, Sr.)	72
Chew, Henry	150
Chew, Joseph	72 (2)

	PAGE.
Chickconacomock plantation	147
Child, Francis	66, 346
Chinagam, Thomas	100
Chinckapin Neck	386
Chincquapine Ridge plantation	210
Chinkapin Swamp, land on	13
Chinkopin Creek, land on	95
Chinpin plantation	127
Chittam, Easthr	410
Chittom, John	299
Chittum, William	337
Chitty, Edward	47
Chivers, Edward	102
Chocowinateh plantation	295
Chocowinity Bay, land on	167
Chorley, Jane	102
Chorley, John	102 (2)
Chowan River, land on	81, 292, 293
Chowan River, plantations on	323
CHRISTIAN, CHRISTOPHER	427
Christian, Christopher	427
Christian, Israel	307
Christian, James	427
Christian, John	427
Christian, Lucy	427
Christian, Martha	307
Christian, Nicholas	427
Christian, Patty	427
Church, Ann	72
Church of Bath, legacy to	316
Church, Elizabeth	136, 326
CHURCH, JOSEPH	72
Church, Julian	72
Church, Richard	72 (2)
Church, Richd	274
Church Wardens, legacy to	276
Churchwell, James	153
Churton, Wm	147
Cidden, Benjamin	115
Cirby (or Cobey), John	157
Cishooke, land in	195
Cissai River, land on	143
Citeson (Cytison), James	334
Clagisters plantation	377
Clanton, William	234
CLAPHAM, JOSEPH	72
Clapham, Josias	72 (2)
Clapham, Samuell	72
Clappor, John	105
Clarck, Thomas	89
CLARE, HANNAH	72
Clare, Timothy	190, 317
Clark,	332

464 INDEX.

	PAGE.
Clark, Mr.	296
Clark, Aaron	73
Clark, Ann	73
Clark, Elisabeth	65 (2), 73
CLARK, GEORGE	72
Clark, Henrey	15 (2)
CLARK, JAMES, SR.	73
Clark, James	412
Clark, Jean	73
CLARK, JOHN	73
Clark, John (son of John)	73
Clark, John	198, 231, 272
Clark, Joseph	59, 148, 262, 424
Clark, Katherine	374
Clark, Levi	73
Clark, Moses	73
CLARK, ROBERT	73
Clark, Robert (son of Robert)	73
Clark, Robert	401
Clark, Thomas	73, 374, 381
Clark, Thos.	320
Clark, William	73, 412
Clarke, Bridgit	73
Clarke, Cathern	14
Clarke, Catring	14
Clarke, Elizabeth	73
Clarke, Grace	73
CLARKE, JOHN	73
Clarke, John	73, 112, 144, 358
Clarke, Julius Cæsar	246
Clarke, Lewis	73
Clarke, Mary	73 (2)
Clarke, Matthew	73
CLARKE, THOMAS	73
Clarke, Thomas (son of Thomas)	73 (2)
Clarke, Thomas	112, 113
Clarke, William	73
Clarkson, Thomas	362
Clasco (or Glasco), Susannah	100
Clash, Eleanor	259
Claten, Mary	368
Claten, Richard	368
Clay, Hannah	317
Clayton, Mr.	296
CLAYTON, ELIZABETH	73
Clayton, Elizabeth	74, 155, 327
Clayton, H.	109
CLAYTON, HENRY	74
Clayton, Henry	76, 325 (2), 364, 414
Clayton, John	92, 243, 252, 386 (2), 424

	PAGE.
Clayton, Mary	73
Clayton, Richard	20, 74, 145, 243, 419, 425
Clayton, Sarah	74, 130, 300
Clayton, Zebulan	105
Clayton, Zeb	106, 243
Cleare, Hannah (wife of Timothy)	74
Cleare, Hannah (daughter of Timothy)	74
CLEARE, TIMOTHY	74
Cleare, Timothy	38, 218, 219, 289, 417
Clearey, Mary	64
Cleark, Mary	277
Cleaves, Benjamin	227
Cleland, Elizabeth	317
Cleland, John	317 (2)
Cleland, Susannah	317
Clemens, Richard	111, 424
Clement, James	394
CLEMENT, JOHN	74
Clements, Benjamin	74
Clements, Elizabeth	74
CLEMENTS, GEORGE	74
Clements, George (son of George)	74
Clements, Susanna	74
Clemet, John	127
Clerke, John	423
Clerke, Mary	423
Cleves, Mary	352
Clewes, Ann	96
Clifford, John	215 (2), 305
Clifford, Mary	74
CLIFFORD, THOMAS	74
Clitherall, John	355
CLOASE, GEORGE	74
Clopton, Geo.	97, 170, 226, 261, 336
Clows, Anne	97
Clubfords Creek, land on	191
Clur plantation	257
Cluf, Thomas	330
Clybun, Jean	73
Coak, Ann	82
Coakson, Samuel	52
Coale, Abigail	305
Coale, Sarah	305
Coale, William	1, 305
Coale, Wm.	163, 302
Coar, James	41
Coar, Mary	41
Coart, John	66
Coates, Ralph	136, 333

INDEX. 465

	PAGE.
Cob, Edward	28
Cobb, Elizabeth	56
Cobb, Jesse	66
Cobb, Jno	42
Cobham, Thomas	105, 405
Cochran, John	258
Cock, Anthony	248
Cock, Samuel	26, 248
Cock, Samuel, Jr	223
Cockbern, Sarah	143
Cockburn, Richd	222
Cocke, Wm	347
Cockfighting Branch, land on	396
Cockran, Margaret	164
Cockrum, Joseph	318
Cockrum, Lydia	318
Cocks, John	223
Cocks, Robert	161, 202
Cocks, W.	179
Codgan, Cha.	139
Coe, Lydia	95
Coen, Beley	75
COEN, BENJAMIN	75
Coen, Bridget	75
Coen, Caleb	94
Coethred, William	143
Coffield, Ann	210
Coffield, William	210
COFFINE, MARY	75
Cofft. Susanna	57
Cogan, Mary	144
Cogdell, Charles	104, 310
Cogdell, Charles, Jr	126
Cogdell, George	307
Cogdell, Rd	64
Cogdell, Richard	23
Cogwell, Bettie	75
COGWELL, HENRY	75
Cogwell, Mary	75
Cogwell, Sarah	75
Cohary Swamp, land on	125
Cohernan, George	139
Cohookey Creek, land on	191
Coinjock, plantation at	274
Cokburn, Ab.	399
Coke, Mr.	293
Coke, John, Sr	312
Coke, Rebecca	253
Coker, Agnes	75
COKER, CALEB	75
Coker, James	75 (2)
Coker, Margreat	75
Coker, Margret	75
Coker, Mary	75 (2)
COKER, RICHARD	75

	PAGE.
Coker, Richard	75
Coker, Sarah	75
Coker, Thomas	75
Colaxe, Docr. Petter	113
Cole, John	156
Cole, John (son of John)	156
Cole, Spencer	178
Cole, William	227
Coleman, Elisabeth	76
Coleman, James	76
Coleman, Jane	75
Coleman, Jervis	211, 212
Coleman, John	76
Coleman, Mary	75
Coleman, Mary	76
Coleman, Moses	75, 278, 321
Coleman, Richd	108
COLEMAN, ROBERT	75
Coleman, Robert	75
Coleman, Samuel	75, 76
Coleman, Sarah	75
Coleman, Susannah	75
Coleman, Theophilus	321
Coleman, Thomas	76, 321
COLEMAN, WILLIAM	75
COLEMAN, WILLIAM	76
Coleman, William (son of William)	76
Coles, James (father of James)	76
Coles, Elizabeth	76
COLES, JAMES	76
Coles, James	21, 271
Coles, Mary	76
Coleson, Abraham	76
Coleson, Joseph	76
Coleson, Mary	35
COLESON, WILLIAM	76
Coleston, Kathn	31
Coletrane, David	348
Colla, Smith	74
Collehan, Cornelius	116
Colles, Cotton	88
Collet, Joseph	102, 103 (2)
Colley, Elizabeth	76
Colley, James	76
Colley, John	76
Colley, Katherine	76
COLLEY, MAGDALEN	76
COLLEY, MATTHEW	76
Colley, Mathhew	76
Colley, Rebecca	76 (2)
COLLEY, ROBERT	76
COLLIER, CORNELIUS	77
Collier, Drury	427

30

466   INDEX.

	PAGE.
Collier, Mathias	316
Collings, Elisibeth	78
Collings, James	263
Collings, Margaret	311
Collings, Mary	85
COLLINGS, WILLIAM	78
Collings, William	177
Collins, Absolum	77
Collins, Alie	77
Collins, Allie	77
Collins, Ann	77
Collins, Annarito	249
Collins, Baily	227
COLLINS, CHARLES	77
Collins, David	77, 91
Collins, Demsey	77
Collins, Edward	76, 323, 344
Collins, Edwd	33, 76
Collins, Elizabeth	13, 77
Collins, Hannah	77
Collins, Henry	78
COLLINS, JAMES	77
Collins, James	112, 262
Collins, Jesse	77
COLLINS, JOHN	77
COLLINS, JOHN	77
Collins, John (son of John)	77
Collins, John (grandson of John)	77
Collins, John	59, 129
Collins, Joseph (son of John)	77
Collins, Joseph	77, 249
Collins, Josiah	375
COLLINS, LUIEE	77
Collins, Luiee	77
Collins, Luce	262
Collins, Mary	77 (2)
Collins, Mikell	77
COLLINS, RICHARD	77
Collins, Samuel	77 (2)
Collins, Thomas	77 (2)
COLLINS, URIAH	78
Collins, Uriah	13 (2), 107, 125, 126, 342, 346, 421
Collins, William (son of John)	77
Collins, William	77 (3), 403, 404
Collinton Island	284
COLLIS, THOMAS	78
Collison, John	1 (2), 19, 24, 48, 64, 71, 107, 109, 155, 187, 213, 238 (2), 243, 244, 272, 274, 301, 304 (2), 305, 356, 377, 417, 420.
Collson, Jacob	78

	PAGE.
COLLSON, JOHN	78
Collson, John (son of John)	78 (2)
Collson, Joseph	78
Collson, Martha	78
Collson, Mary	78
Collson, Sandows	78
Collson, Susannah	78 (2)
Collson, Thomas	78
Collson, William	137
Colly, Patty	427
Colpeper, John	155
Colson, Daniel	382
Colson, James	6
Colson, John	204
Colson, Mary	382
Colston, Jacob	78
COLSTON, MARY	78
Colston, William	78
Coltraine, David	306 (2)
Coltrane, David	101
Colvell, Maturin	22
Colvell, Malunn	148
Comber Creek and Morattock River, land between	213
Combs, James	78, 149
Combs, John	78
Combs, Mary	78, 106
Combs, Robert	78 (2)
Combs, Samuell	78
Combs, Wineford	348
COMBS, WINNIFITT	78
Comes, John	307
Comminfort, Andrew	79
Cominfort, Hendrick	79
COMMINFORT, HENDRICK	79
Comminfort, Margaret	79
COMINFORT, RICHARD	79
Cominfort, William	79
Commander, Benjamin	79
Commander, Elisabeth	79
Commander, James	379
Commander, John	79
Commander, Joseph (son of Thomas)	79 (2)
Commander, Joseph (brother of Thomas)	79
Commander, Joseph	69, 79, 84, 324, 379, 400, 403
COMMANDER, JOSEPH MATTHEW	79
Commander, Mary	69, 79 (2)
Commander, Samuel	79
Commander, Sarah	79 (2)
COMMANDER, THOMAS	79

Index. 467

	PAGE.
COMMANDER, THOMAS	79
Commander, Thomas (son of Thomas)	79 (2)
Commander, Thomas	79, 176, 379 (2)
Commander, William Chancey	69
Conaby, plantation at	212
Conaconara Swamp, land on,	340
Conahoe plantation	187
Conaway, James	151, 316
Conaway, John	257
Conecarora plantation	292
Conehoe Pocoson, land on	252
Conell, Edmond	374
Coner, Henry	372
Coner, Jacob	371
Coner, James	88
Coner, William	372
Conerly, Daniel	301
Conet, Elmer	19
Conetoe, plantation on	242
Congleton, Abraham	79
Congleton, David	79
Congleton, Elizabeth	79
Congleton, Henry	79
Congleton, James	79 (2)
Congleton, John	79
Congleton, Sarah	79 (2)
CONGLETON, WILLIAM	79
Congleton, William (son of William)	79 (2)
Coniritratt, plantation at	420
Connaway, William	273
CONNER, ANDREW	80
Conner, Andrew	155
Conner, Annlatitia	80
Conner, Cado	332
Conner, Cador	80
Conner, Cathern	182
CONNER, DEMSEY	80
Conner, Demsey	284 (2)
Conner, Elisebeth	80
Conner, James	43, 367
Conner, Jas	116
CONNER, JOHN	80
Conner, John (son of John)	80
Conner, John	223, 332 (2)
Conner, Mary	80 (2), 332 (2)
Conner, Michael	301
Conner, Ruth	80
Conner, Sarah	80
Connerly, Cullen	80
CONNERLY, JOHN	80
Connerley, Jno	162

	PAGE.
Connerly, Kesiah	80
Connerly, Patience	80
Connerly, William	80
Connor, Demsey	199
Conohoe, plantation and mill at	125
Contanche, Michael	219
Conteneney Creek, land on	212
Contentne, plantation on	363
Contentney, plantation at	353
Contentney, land on	241
Contentny, land on	149
Conway, Ann	259
CONWAY, MARY	80
Conway, Peter	49, 102, 132, 192, 207, 335, 391, 399, 418
Conway, William	80
Cook, Anna (wife of John)	80
Cook, Anna (daughter of John)	80
Cook, Arnol	395
Cook, Benjamin	80
Cook, Daniel	81
Cook, David	80
Cook, Elizabeth	80, 81 (3)
Cook, Elimeleach	81
Cook, Ephraim	81
Cook, Frances	81
Cook, Henery	81
Cook, Isaac	80 (2)
Cook, James	81
Cook, Jesse	81
COOK, JOHN	80
COOK, JOHN	81
Cook, John	81 (4), 129, 395 (2)
Cook, Lazarus	81
Cook, Leml.	162
Cook, Mary (wife of Samuel)	81
Cook, Mary (daughter of Samuel)	81
Cook, Mary	52, 81
Cook, Mercurius	81
Cook, Neomy	81
COOK, SAMUEL	81
Cook, Samuel	80, 160
Cook, Sarah	80, 355
COOK, THOMAS	81
Cook, Thomas	81, 94, 242 (3), 264, 274, 277
COOK, WILLIAM	81
Cook, William (son of William)	81
Cook, William	81, 249
Cooke, E.	48
Cooke, John	48, 258
Cooke, Thos.	224, 242, 280

468   INDEX.

	PAGE.
Cooker, Elizabeth	123
Cookoo, Mary	1
Cooneriskatt Swamp, land on	174
Cooper, Edward	78, 143 (2)
Cooper, Elizabeth	143, 353
Cooper, Frances	249
Cooper, James	81
Cooper, John	317
Cooper, John Smith	342
COOPER, JOSEPH	81
Cooper, Joseph (son of Joseph)	81
Cooper, Joseph	353, 416
Cooper, Marget	82
Cooper, Mary	81, 131
Cooper, Nathaniel	39 (2), 143, 233 (2), 340, 363
Cooper, Samuel	216
Cooper, Samuel	225
Cooper, Sarah	81
Cooper, Sarah Ann	81
Coopper, Thomas	292
Coopper, William	281
Coor Creek, land on	292
Coor, James	17, 37, 127, 137, 281, 290, 316, 318, 346, 376, 395, 404.
Coor, Mary	404
Coothen, John	52
Copeland, Anne	82
Copeland, Charles	81, 82, 393, 407
Copeland, Christian (daughter of William)	81
Copeland, Christian (wife of William)	82
Copeland, Diana	81
COPELAND, JAMES	81
Copeland, James (son of James)	81
Copeland, James	81, 93, 357
Copeland, Jesse	82
Copeland, John	81, 393, 415, 416
Copeland, Judath	82
Copeland, Mary	81
Copeland, Peter	68
Copeland, Sarah	68, 81, 82
COPELAND, WILLIAM	81
Copeland, William (son of William)	81
COPELAND, WILLIAM	82
Copeland, William (son of William)	82
Copeland, William	68, 407
Coper (Cooper)	189
Coper (Cooper), George	161

	PAGE.
Copland, Thomas	88
Corbert, John	398
Corbett, Ann	385
CORBETT, THOMAS	82
Corbett, William	385
Corbill, Alidea	44
Corbin, Francis	82, 86
CORBIN, JEAN	82
Cording, Mary	391
Cording, Wm.	14
Cording, William	174
Core, Arthur	82 (2)
Core Creek, land on	40, 128, 293, 294
Core, Elizabeth	82
Core, Grace	82
Core, John	47
Core, Margett	82
Core Neck, land on	419
Core Point, plantations on	38
CORE, THOMAS	82
Core, Thomas (son of Thomas)	82
Corey, Thomas	231
COREY, JOHN	82
Corey, John (son of John)	82
Corey, Joseph	82
Corey, Luca	82
Corey, Thomas	82 (2)
Corlee, James	408
Corlew, John, Jr.	192
Cornegy, Peter	294
Cornick, John	96, 164, 348
Cornish, Elias	62
Cornish, Eliash	213
Cornot, John	335
Cornwell, Capt. James	105
Corp, Elinor	82
Corp, Elizabeth	83
Corp, Elner	82
CORP, JOHN	82
CORP, JOHN	83
Corp, John	56, 397
Corp, Richard	83
Corp, William	82
Corprew, George Durant	83
Corprew, John	83
Corprew, Joshua	83
Corprew, Sarah	83 (2)
CORPREW, THOMAS	83
Corree, David	83
Corree, Jacob	83
CORREE, JAMES	83
Corree, James (son of James)	83
Corree, Janet	83

	PAGE.
Corree, John	83, 95
Corree, Margret	83
Corree, Mary	83
Correll, James	59
Corry, Jo.	126
Corry, Mary	126
Corry, Rebecca	199
Corry, Thomas	126
Corsaks Swamp, land on	16
Cortney, Elizabeth	422 (2)
Cortney, Peter	210
Cory, Mary	201
Cosan, Elizabeth	255
Cossia, land on	358
COSTE, EPHRAIM	83
Coste, Ephream	403
Coster, John	21
Cotanche, Michael	295
Cotohney, land on	4
Cotrell, William	60
Cottanoe, land at	344
Cotten, Alexander	126
Cotten, Alexr	239
Cotten, Alex	283
Cotten, Ann	126, 195
Cotten, Anne (wife of Jno.)	83
Cotten, Anne (daughter of John)	83
Cotten, Arther	78
Cotten, Benjamin	83
Cotten, Charles	84 (2), 166
Cotten, Christian	78
Cotten, Henry	78
COTTEN, JAMES	78
Cotten, James (son of James)	78
Cotten, Jemima	126
COTTEN, JOHN	83
Cotten, John (son of John),	83 (2)
Cotten, John	78
Cotten, Lydia	83
Cotten, Mary	84
Cotten, Patience	84
Cotten, Robert	84
COTTEN, SAMUELL	83
Cotten, Samuell (son of Samuell)	83
Cotten, Samuell	78
Cotten, Samll	251
COTTEN, SARAH	84
Cotten, Sarah	78, 83, 84
Cotten, Solomon	78
Cotten, Susannah	126
Cotten, Theophilus	78

	PAGE.
Cotten, William	83, 84
Cotting, Elizabeth	364
Cotton, Alexander	18, 84
Cotton, Anne	371
Cotton, Arthur	84
Cotton, Elizabeth	398
Cotton, Humfre	84
Cotton, James	84
COTTON, JOHN	84
COTTON, JOHN	84
Cotton, John (son of John)	84
Cotton, Joseph	84, 226
Cotton, Leonard	273
Cotton, Martha	84
Cotton, Mary	268
Cotton, Priscilla	84
Cotton, Samuel	84
Cotton, Susannah	84
Cotton, Thomas	84
Cotton, William	84
Cough, John Roner	95
Coulahane, Robert	420
Coulson, Elizabeth	84
COULSON, WILLIAM	84
Council, Michael	422
Counsell, Charles	422
Coupland, Sarah	169
Coupper, Elizabeth	24
Coupper, James	167
Coupper, Samuell	24
Courtney, Hannah	84
Courtney, Jonathan	84, 85
Courtney, John	84
COURTNEY, ROBERT	84
Courtney, Robert (son of Robert)	84, 85
Courtney, Rowlan	84
Coutanche, Michael	50
Covee, Mary	316
Covell, Thankfull	16
Covington, John	359
Covington, Nancy	359
Cow Island plantation	209
Cow Marsh, land on	376
Cow Ridge, land on	400
Cowan, John	248
Coward, Benjamin	4
Coward, Bevard	85
Coward, Elizabeth	85
COWARD, JOHN	85
Coward, John (son of John)	85
Coward, William	4, 85
Cowel, Benjamin	339
Cowel, Elisabeth	339
COWELL, BENJAMIN	85

	PAGE.
Cowell, Benjamin (son of Benjamin)	85
Cowell, Butlar	85
Cowell, Dorcas	85
Cowell, Edmond	85
Cowell, Elizabeth (wife of Benjamin)	85
Cowell, Elizabeth (daughter of Benjamin)	85
Cowell, John	85
Cowell, Rebecca	85
Cowell, Solomon	85 (2)
Cowell, Thomas	85
Cowell, William	85
Cowen, Daniel	85
COWEN, GARRETT	85
Cowles, Ann	19
Cowman, Thomas	83
Cowpen Neck, plantation in	350
Cowpen Neck and Rollinseas plantation	397
Cox, Abraham	31
Cox, Absalom	85 (2)
Cox, Ann (wife of Thomas)	86
Cox, Ann (daughter of Thomas)	86
Cox, Ann	48, 70
Cox, Anne	85
COX, CHARLES	85
Cox, Charles	240
Cox, Christian	85
Cox, Daniel	172
Cox, Daniel, Jr	172
Cox, Dinah	86
COX, EDWARD	85
Cox, Edward	28, 86, 226, 279
Cox, Elijah	279
Cox, Eliza	85 (2)
Cox, Francesina	85
Cox, Isaac	398
Cox, Jemima	134
COX, JOHN	85
Cox, John	70, 144, 419
Cox, Marmaduke	86
Cox, Martha	85
Cox, Mary	86, 160
Cox, Moses	311, 410
Cox, Moses, Jr	411
Cox, Pernigan	2
Cox, Robert	70 (2)
Cox, Sarah	30
Cox, Solomon	86
Cox, THOMAS	86
Cox, Thomas	85 (2)
Cox, William	30

	PAGE.
Coxe, Edward	299
Coxe, Elizabeth	85
COXE, ROBERT	85
Coxe, Robert (son of Robert)	85
Coxe, Sarah	85
Coyte, Hercules	327
Crabb, Benjamin	266
Crabb, John	266, 273
Crabtree Creek, land on	191
Craddock, Elizabeth	86
Craddock, Quith	57
CRADDOCK, RICHARD	86
Cradock, Charles	2, 171 (2)
Craduck, Elizabeth	45 (2)
Crafford (Crawford), Arthur	93
Crafford, Wm.	174
Craford, Ann	43
Craford, Margaret	155
Craford, Capt. William	155
Craford (Crawford), William	93
Craford, William	201
Crafton, Henry	19
Crage, Richard	9
Craghill, land adjoining	203
Craghill, Thomas	3, 145
Craghill, Thos.	161
CRAIG, RICHARD	86
Crambie, Jno.	59
Cranford, James	86
Cranford, John	86
Cranford, Katherine	86
Cranford, William	58
Cranford, Wm.	85
CRANFORD, WILLIAM	86
Cranford, William	171, 408, 411, 420
Cranford, Wm.	140, 156, 173, 175, 260, 275 (2), 325, 380, 414.
Crank, Ann	115, 237
Crank, Elizabeth	237 (2)
Crank, Mary	237
Crank, Thomas	10
Crank, William Markham	237
Crany Island	293
CRAVEN, JAMES	86
Craven, James	1, 7, 8, 10 (2), 11, 17, 27 (2), 30, 37, 42, 43, 47, 50, 55, 58, 68, 69, 70, 79, 82, 94, 117, 118, 120, 123, 128, 131, 135, 141, 158, 165, 169, 171 (2), 176, 177 (2), 178, 180, 181, 182, 184, 194, 195, 202, 206, 208, 215, 216,

INDEX. 471

	PAGE.
228, 247, 248, 251, 256, 259, 263, 264 (4), 265, 267, 268, 275, 277 (2), 278, 279, 280, 284, 285, 300 (2), 309, 312 (2), 320, 325, 345, 348, 351, 355, 362, 367, 380 (2), 385, 387, 388, 393 (2), 395, 408, 418, 422.	
Craven, John (Dr.)	86
Craven, Penelope (formerly Hodgson)	86
Crawford, Arthur	93
Crawford, Henery	93
Crawford, John	373
Crawford, Mary	86
Crawford, Matthew	362
CRAWFORD, WILLIAM	86
Crawford, Wm.	86
Crawford (Cranford), Wm.	25
Crawley, Daniel	318
Crawley, David	234, 313
Crawley, William	272
Crawthers, Ann	394
Crawthers, Nathan	394
Crawman, William	236
Craxton, Arthur	206
Craxton, Francis	366
Cray, Will..13, 19, 247, 249, 274, 322 (2), 411, 421	
Cray, William....31, 64, 118, 189, 415, 421	
Cray, Willm	96, 140, 183
Cray, Wm	141, 240
Creacy, Paciana	206
Crecy, Levi	404
Crecy, Mary	404
Cree, Wm.	148
Creech, Elener	423
CREECH, HENRY	87
Creech, Henry (son of Henry)	87
Creech, Henry	25
Creech, Joyce	87
Creech, Richard	87
Creech, Stephen	423
Creech, Tamer	87
Creech, Thomas	87
Creech, William	87
Creecy, John	117, 358
Creecy, Joseph	221, 283, 372
Creecy, Mary	9, 289
Creecy, Sarah	150
Creek Swamp, land on	356
Creekmore, William	16
Creese, John	393
Creese, Mary	393
Creessie, Eliazor	253

	PAGE.
Cremen, Martin	199
Cremer, Philip	296
Cressey, Levi	161
Cressy, Elizabeth	87
Cressy, John	87 (2)
Cressy, Joseph	87
CRESSY, LEVI	87
Cretch, Will	418
Cretches Old Field plantation	381
Crew, Mary	155
Crew, Thomas	122
Crew, Thos	169, 340, 421
Cricket, Charles	87
CRICKET, JOHN	87
Cricket, John (son of John)	87 (2)
Cricket, Jno., Jr.	336
Cricket, Mary	87
Cricket, Thomas	87
Crickman, Mary	176
Crisp, Elizabeth	87
Crisp, John	87
CRISP, NICHOLAS	87
Crisp, Nicholas	291, 343, 407
Crisp, Richard	87
Crispin, Joseph	313, 346
Crocker, Mary	245
CROCKER, PETER	87
Crocker, Sarah	87 (2)
Crocker, Thomas	277
Crockitt, John	228
Crofort Branch, land on	143
Crofton, Ambros	87
Crofton, Catherine	394
Croftons Cut, plantation in	88
Crofton, Elizabeth	88 (2)
CROFTON, HENRY	87
Crofton, Martha	88
Crofton, Mary	88
Crofton, Theophilus	87
Crofton, Thomas	87
Crofton, William	87
CROKER, ANTONY	88
Croker, Arter	88 (2)
Croker, Jacob	88 (2)
Croker, Thomas	88
CROMEN, MARTIN	88
Cromen, Thomas	88
Cromwell, Thomas	117
Cromwell, Thom. Sreton	241
Croney, Anne	88
CRONEY, DINNIS	88
Croney, Elender	88
Croney, Mary	88
Croney, William	88 (2)

INDEX.

	PAGE.
Croom, Joshua	66
Crompton, Henry	7
Cropely, Peter	119
Cropley, Ann	88
CROPLEY, JOHN	88
CROPLEY, VINES	89
Cropley, Vins	88, 389
Croply, William	25, 89
Cropton, Henery	238
Cropton, Henry	417
CROSLAND, ELIZABETH	88
CROSLEN, JOHN	88
Crossllan, John	135
Crossman, Margaret	196
CROSSOT, JOSEPH	89
Cross, Elinor	371
Cross, Samuel	371 (2)
Crounes Creek, land in the fork of	174
Crow Island	292
Crowell, Benjamin	416
Crowell, Edward	159
Crowell, John	218, 233, 314
Croxen, Arthur	282
Croxton, Francis	306
Crudup, George	51, 409
Crudup, John	412
Crudup, Mourning	412
Cruickshank, Alexr	141
Cruickshank, Ann	141
Cruikshank, Alexander	138, 394
Cruikshank, John	138
Cruikshank, Patrick	138
CRUISE, LAWRENCE	89
Cruise, Lawrence	319
Cruise, Mary	89
Crump, Cassandra	89 (2)
Crump, Charles	89 (2)
Crump, Katy	89
CRUMP, JOSEPH	89
Crump, Joseph (son of Joseph)	89
Crump, Josias	89
Crump, Patty	89
Crump, Richard	89
Crumpton, Anne	89
Crumpton, Elizabeth	89
CRUMPTON, HENERY	89
Crumpton, Henery (son of Henery)	89
Crumpton, Jane	89
Crumpton, John	153
Crumpton, Susannah	89
Crumpton, William	89

	PAGE.
Cuckolds Creek	413
Culbertson, Isaiah	161
Cullen, Edmun	377
Cullen, Martha	89
Cullender, Mary	279
Cullens, Nathan	116
Cullers, John	191
Cullers, Mary	191
Culling, Jemima	322
Cully, John	105
Culpeper, John	136
Cumbo, Cannon	233
Cumboes plantation	108
Cuming, John	165, 238
Cummin, James	98
Cummings, Benjamin	120, 242, 262, 390
Cummings, John	120, 239, 390, 391
Cummins, Thos	368
Cuningham, Thomas	265
CUNNINGHAM, MORRIS	89
Cunningham, Thomas, Jr.	105
Cunnyngham, Alex	44
Curlee, James	106
Curlin, Keziah	167
Curling, Sarah	146
CURRIR, JOHN	89
Currir, Sarah	89
Currotuck Bay, land on	300
Curry, William	73
Curtis, Phebe	85
Curtis, Richard	84
Curtis, Robert	380
Curtis, Silvanus	162
Cuscopincum, plantation at	352
Cushake Creek, plantation on	158
Cuthris, Amos	151
Cutler, Rob't.	339
Cuttewhiski Swamp, land on	426
Cuttler, Margrett	347
Cuttowhisky Marsh and Swamp, land on	420
Cypress Creek, land on	187
Cypress Swamp, land in	50
Cypress Swamp, land on	43, 107, 323
Cypress Swamp, plantation on	264, 325
Dale, Elizabeth	312
Dale, Mary	106 (2)
Dailie, John	87
Dallison, Mr.	253
Dalrymple, Sir John	89

INDEX.

	PAGE.
DALRYMPLE, JOHN	89
Dalrymple, Martha	89
DeGrafinred, Mary	68
DAMERELL, JAMES	90
Damerell, James	189, 398
Damerell, Lucy	90
Damerell, Rachel	90
Damevall, James	4
Damevall, Mary	4, 59
Damorell, James	208 (2)
Damorell, Mary	208
Damorell, Rachel	208
Dancy, James	195
Dane, John	273
Daniel, Aaron	90
Daniel, Aron	90
Daniel, Abraham	90
Daniel, Ann	397
Daniel, Arthur	106
Daniel, Elizabeth	90
DANIEL, ELISABETH	90
Daniel, Elisabeth (wife of Thomas)	90
Daniel, Elisabeth (daughter of Thomas)	90
Daniel, Elisabeth (daughter of Elisabeth)	90
Daniel, Elizabeth	114, 319
Daniel, Ephraim	90
Daniel, Ezekiel	90
Daniel Halls plantation	221
Daniel, Isaac	90
DANIEL, JOHN	90
Daniel, John (son of John)	90 (2)
Daniel, John	53, 90 (3)
Daniel, Joseph	90 (2)
Daniel, Josiah	90 (2)
Daniel, Mary	90 (2)
Daniel, Pricilah	90
Daniel, Prisilia	90
Daniel, Robert	90
Daniel, Robert Lanier	90, 207, 330
Daniel, Ruth	90 (2)
Daniel, Sarah (wife of John)	90
Daniel, Sarah (daughter of John)	90
Daniel, Sarah	98 (3)
Daniel, Simon	319
DANIEL, THOMAS	90
Daniel, Thomas (son of Thomas)	90
Daniel, Thos	292 (2)
Daniel, William	90 (2)

	PAGE.
Daniell, Charles	279
Daniell, Frances	90
DANIELL, OWEN	90
Daniell, Robert	207, 319
Daniell, Thomas	4, 90 (3)
DANIELL, WILLIAM	90
Dann, Elizabeth	91
Dann, Jane	112
Dann, Jeane	91
DANN, JOHN, SR	91
Dann, John	91
Dann, Lina	91
Dansbe, Clearemon	91
DANSBE, DANIEL	91
Dansbe, Elizabeth (wife of Daniel)	91
Dansbe, Elizabeth (daughter of Daniel)	91
Dansbe, Isome	91
Dansbe, Mary	91
Danse, William	199
Darby, William	111
Darden, Alse	91
Darden, America	91
Darden, Elisha	405
Darden, Henarey	91
Darden, Jacob	213
Darden, Jesse	376
DARDEN, JOSEPH	91
Darden, Joseph (son of Joseph)	91
Darden, Joseph	71, 200, 213
Darden, Rebec	91
Darden, Samuel	213 (2)
Darden, West	91
Dardon, Jacob	145
Dargan, Cornelius	12
Darman, Ann	266
DARNALL, ANN	91
Darnall, William	91
Darling, Elizabeth	91
Darling, Richard	91
Darling, Thomas	91
Dart, Elizabeth	160
Dart, Simon	160
Dauge, Jane	279
Dauge, Joab	328
Dauge, Peter	91, 135, 363 (2)
Dauge, Richard	91, 279
Dauge, Susannah	91
Daughity. Daniel	399 (2)
Daughity, Elizabeth	399
Daughtrey, Alexandria	91
Daughtrey, Bryan	91
Daughtrey, John	91

	PAGE.
Daughtrey, John (grandson of Thomas)	91
Daughtrey, Joshaway	45
Daughtrey, Joshua	91
Daughtrey, Mary	91
Daughtrey, Pleasants	91
Daughtrey, Samuel	91
DAUGHTREY, THOMAS	91
Daughtrey, Thomas (son of Thomas)	91
Daughtry, Alice	279
Daughtry, Elizabeth	409
Daughtry, Jesse	91
Dauson, Christopher	188
Davenport, Ann	91
DAVENPORT, JACOB	91
Davenport, James	91
Davenport, John, Sr.	91
Davenport, John	91, 248
Davenport, Rachel	91
Davenport, William	91
Daves, David	160
Daves, Joseph	224
Daves, Samuell	38
Davey, Jane	92
Davey, Joseph	92
Davey, Margarett	92
Davey, Rachell	92
Davey, Samuell	92
DAVEY, WALTER	92
David, David	92
DAVID, PHILLIP	92
David, Phillip	160
Davidson, Geo.	427
Davie, Andrew	188
DAVIES, FRANCIS	92
Davies, Judith	92
Davise's plantation	110
Davis, ————	21
Davis, Aaron	181
Davis, Abigarl	95
Davis, Abigill	93
Davis, Alee	93
Davis, Ann	95, 283
Davis, Anne	224
DAVIS, ARTHUR	92
Davis, Arthur (son of Arthur)	92 (2)
Davis, Beniemen	95
Davis, Callip	95
Davis, Catherine	24, 400
Davis, Cattron	383
Davis, Charity	94
Davis, Christian	283
Davis, Cornelius	92

	PAGE.
DAVIS, DAVID	92
Davis, David	108, 355
Davis, Davis	93
Davis, Dorothy	94, 354
Davis, Edward	108
Davis, Elizabeth (sister of Richard Eagle)	106
Davis, Elizabeth (cousin of Richard Eagle)	106
Davis, Elizabeth (wife of Thomas)	94
Davis, Elizabeth (daughter of Thomas)	94
Davis, Elisebeth	107
Davis, Elisibeth	78, 92, 93 (3), 94 (4), 286, 299
Davis, Francis	372 (2)
Davis, George	28
Davis, Henry	93
DAVIS, HUGH	92
DAVIS, ISAAC	92
DAVIS, JAMES	93
Davis, James (son of James)	93
Davis, James	76, 94 (2), 201, 309, 331, 383, 402 (2)
Davis, Jeams	401
Davis, Jean	106
Davis, Jehu, Sr.	313
Davis, Jehu	139
DAVIS, JOHN	93
DAVIS, JOHN	93
DAVIS, JOHN	93
DAVIS, JOHN	93
Davis, John (son of John)	93 (2)
Davis, John	10, 12, 47 (2), 86, 93 (2), 94, 123, 139 (2), 214, 224, 238, 309, 355, 369.
Davis, John, Jr.	54
Davis, Joseph	93 (3), 95 (2)
Davis, Joshua	93
Davis, Judith	338
Davis, Lewis	92 (2)
Davis, Margaret	18
Davis, Marget	343
Davis, Martha	39
Davis, Mary	69, 93, 94 (2), 95
Davis (Tulinton), Mrs. Mary	331
Davis, Moses	94
Davis, Naithane	30
Davis, Nathan	95 (2)
Davis, Nathaniel	93
DAVIS, PETER	93
Davis, Phillip	94
Davis, Rachel	92 (2)
DAVIS, RICHARD	93
Davis, Richard	94, 306, 333, 376

	PAGE.
Davis, Robart	403
DAVIS, ROBERT	94
Davis, Robert	69 (2), 93, 331
Davis, Rubin	94
Davis, Ruth	94, 182
Davis, Sam	76
DAVIS, SAMUELL	94
Davis, Samuel	78, 86, 93 (3), 132, 138, 140, 163, 181, 346
Davis, Sara	311
Davis, Sarah	69, 93, 94 (3)
Davis, Sary	93
DAVIS, SOLOMON	94
Davis, Solomon	95, 248
DAVIS, THOMAS	94
DAVIS, THOMAS	94
DAVIS, THOMAS	94
DAVIS, THOMAS	94
Davis, Thomas (son of Thos.)	94
Davis, Thos.	48, 94 (2), 107, 167, 174, 196, 225 (2), 250, 253, 277, 283.
Davis, Thos.	160, 344
Davis, Thomasin	94
Davis, Thomeson	94
Davis, Wicker	95
DAVIS, WILLIAM	95
Davis, Wiliam (son of Wm.)	95
Davis, William	10, 21, 93 (3), 94 (2), 95, 170, 181, 200, 239 (2), 245, 283, 284, 302, 308, 388, 413.
Davis, Winnifred	245
Davison, Eleshea Christiana.	95
DAVISON, JOHN	95
DAVISON, JOHN	95
Davison, John (son of Jno.)	95
Davison, John (grandson of Jno.)	95
Davison, John	154, 273 (2)
Davison, Mary (wife of Jno.)	95
Davison, Mary (granddaughter of Jno.)	95
Davison, Robert	95
Davy, Thomas	8
Daw, Abigal	303, 391
Daw, Nicholas	99, 172, 303, 391, 423
Daw, Thomas	288
Daw, William	304
Dawe, Diana	95
Dawe, Dinah	95
Dawe, John	95
Dawe, Nicholas	95

	PAGE.
DAWE, WILLIAM	95
Dawe, William (son of William)	95
Dawe, William	95
Dawes, John	226
Dawkins, George	393
Dawley, John	97
Daws, Abraham	64
Daws, Elyjah	95
DAWS, WILLIAM	95
Daws, William (son of William)	95
Dawson, Anthony	82, 138, 331
Dawson, Capt. Anthony	208
Dawson, Charity	6
Dawson, Chrisr.	140
Dawson, Christopher	290
Dawson, Coll. J	174
Dawson, Demey	95
Dawson, Elizabeth	52
Dawson, F.	37
Dawson, George	239
Dawson, Henry	11, 203
DAWSON, JOHN	95
Dawson, John (son of John)	95
Dawson, John	11, 47, 52, 83, 84 (2), 184, 251, 335, 361, 374
Dawson, Martha	95
Dawson, Mary	95, 364
Dawson, Patience	95
Dawson, Rabackah	111
Dawson, Sollomon	95
Dayes, Thomas	196
Dayton, John	41
Day, John	136
Deadmans Swamp, land on..	63
Deal, Isabel	53
Deal, Sarah	72
Deane, Christian	96
Deane, Elizabeth	96
DEANE, GEORGE, SR.	96
Deane, Geo.	96
Dear, George	356
Dearam, Elizabeth	318
DeBerry, Benj'n	111, 353
Deberry, Jno.	111
DeBruhl, Mary	205
Deed, Catherine	41
Deedan, Rebecker	108
Deel, Joshua	388
Deens, Daniel	91
Deens, Thomas	274
Deep Branch, land on	77
Deep Branch plantation	326
Deep Creek, plantation on	395
Deep Creek, land at	10

INDEX.

	PAGE.
Deep Creek, land on.	314, 373, 382
Deep Creek, land on, in New Corotuck	182
Deep, John	149
Deep River, land on	187
Deep Run, land on	150, 197
Deep Run Swamp (land on)	197
Deer Creek, land on	409
Dees, Mary	297
Defuall, William	375
Degge, James	318
Dehorty, Jas.	59
Dehorty, Rebekah	59
Deiptt, Ann	96
Deiptt, Penon	96
Deiptt, Petter	96
DEIPTT, JOHN	96
Deiptt, John (son of John)	96
Delabastie, A.	229
Delamare, Francis	96, 196, 262
De La Mare, Francis	127, 237, 403
DELAMARE, STEPHEN	96
Delemare, Stephen	65, 244
DELAMAR, FRANCIS	96
Delamar, Francis (son of Francis)	96
Delamar, Francis	232
Delamar, Susannah	96
Delamar, Thomas	96
Deleney, William	122
Dellemar, Isack	363
Deloatch, Francis	165
Deloatch, Judith	390
Delogg, Katherine	385
DELOHOIDE, WILLIAM	96
Demeyer, Henry	386
Denby, Elizabeth	44
Denem, Ann	382
Denem, Charles	382
DENEHAM, ELIZABETH	96
Deneham, Elezabeth	96
Deneham, John	96
Denillard, Jacob	189
Denman, Charles	13, 23, 56, 70, 106, 149, 156, 201, 204, 210, 228 (2), 243, 247, 266, 269, 287 (3), 327, 338, 346, 349, 378 (3), 410.
Denman, Christopher	204, 251, 293
Denman, Rebecca	196
Denman, Rebecka	366
Denman, Sarah	149, 204
Denning, Stephen	14, 31, 109 (3), 124, 133, 155 (2), 188, 190, 195, 227, 241, 418.

	PAGE.
Denson, Elizabeth	96
DENSON, JAMES	96
Denson, James	317, 322
Denton, Christian	126
Denton, James	411
Deon, John	239
Dept, Ann	97
Dept, Elizabeth	97
Dept, Jane	97
Dept, John	97, 149
DEPT, PENELOPE	97
Dept, Peter	97
Derby, Judith	97
DERBY, WILLIAM	97
Derhams Creek, land on	109, 296
Derhams Creek, land up	286
DERHAM, ELIZABETH	97
Derham, Elizabeth (legatee of Elizabeth)	97
Derham, John	97
Derham, Joseph	97
Derham, Katherine	97
Dering, Emelius	81
De Rosset, ——	139
DeRossett, Armand	46, 372
DeRossett, Armand, M. D.,	123, 336
DeRosset, Armond John	97
DeRosset, Elizabeth Cathrine	6, 46
DeRosset, Lewis Henry	82, 97
DeRosset, Lewis	99
DeRosset, Magdalene Mary	97
DeRosset, Mary	97
DEROSSET, MOSES JOHN	97
DeRosset, Moses Jno.	31, 61, 102, 257 (2)
DeRossett, Mrs., Sr.	6
Derring, Rebekah	120
Deshung, Francis	298
DeSon, Hannah	274
DeSon, Henry	14, 59, 62, 145, 168, 190, 229
DEVIS, JOHN	97
Dew, Abram	54
Dew, Abraham	133
Dew, Charles	120
Dew, Constant	98
Dew, J.	385
Dew, John, Senor	47
DEW, JOHN	97
Dew, John (son of John)	97
Dew, John	47, 53 (2), 71, 120, 298, 334
Dew, Joseph	97, 98, 120
Dew, Morven	98

INDEX.

	PAGE.
Dew, Patience	98
Dew, Spenser	98
Dew, Susannah	98
Dew, William	98
Dewbery, Thomas	380
Dewise, Edward	254
Dexter, Foye	261
DEXTER, HOPE	97
Dexter, Hope	97
Dexter, Phillip	97
Dias, Ann	98
DIAS, HENRY	98
Dias, Henry (son of Henry)	98
Dias, John	98
Dias, Rebecca	98
Dias, Richard	98
Dias, Thomas	98
Dick, John	115
Dickenson, Daniel	98 (2)
Dickenson, Isaac	98
DICKENSON, JOHN	98
Dickenson, John (son of John)	98 (2)
Dickenson, Rebecca	98
Dickeson, Arthur	340
Dickeson, Arthur, Jr.	340
Dickins, Eady	44
Dickins, John	44
Dickins, Suffrah	44
Dickinson, Charity	98 (2)
Dickinson, Daniel	98
Dickinson, David	98 (3)
Dickinson, Ezekiel	361
Dickinson, Isaac	98 (2)
Dickinson, John	98 (2), 102, 265
DICKINSON, MARY	98
Dickinson, Mary	98 (2)
DICKINSON, REBEKAH	98
Dickison, Alin	301
Dickison, Elizabeth	301
Dickison, Ezekiel	301
Dickison, John	301
Dickison, Martha	301 (2)
Dickison, Mary	301
Dickison, Sarah	301
Dicks, Ann	30
DICKS, JOHN	98
Dicks, Joshua	106
Dicks, Phelis	98
Dicks Field plantation	298
Dickson, David	207
Dickson, Mrs. Eliz.	293
Dickson, Elizabeth	294, 327
Dickson, James	98
Dickson, Jennet	98
DICKSON, JOHN	98
Dickson, John	26, 63 (2), 85, 167, 180, 194, 216, 222, 235, 349, 408.
Dicson, David	184
Dillday, Edward	86
Dillday, Hanner	86
DISCORAH, THOMAS	99
Dix, John	119
Dixon, Biatha	99
Dixon, Choosewell	99
Dixon, Christiana	99
Dixon, Frances	99
Dixon, James	99
DIXON, JOHN	99
Dixon, Nicholas	51
DIXON, ROBERT	99
Dixon, Robert	223
Dixon, Robert (son of Robert)	99
Dixon, Robert	223
Dixon, Sarah	95
Dixon, Thomas	99
Dixon, Tobias	99
Dixson, Robert	145
Dixson, Walter	145, 324
Dobbins, John	171
DOBBS, ARTHUR	99
Dobbs, Arthur	2, 6 (2), 32, 38, 53, 61, 64, 74, 86, 136, 173, 179, 197, 203, 209, 229, 238, 239, 242, 245, 257, 262, 269, 271, 291. 320, 323, 326, 332, 340, 341, 344, 369, 371, 385, 387, 392, 406.
Dobbs, Conway Richard	99 (2)
Dobbs, Edward Brice	99
Dobbs, Justina	99
Dobbs, Richard (Rev. Dr.)	99
Dobson, Kateren	100
DOBSON, WILLIAM	100
Dobson, William	35, 343
Docton, Sarah	177
Dod, Edmon	298
Dodd, Edwd.	250
Dodley, James	345
Dodson, Charles	347
Doe, Edd	305
Doe, Ralph	185
Dogwood Ridge plantation	329
DOLEER, GYLES	100
Donaho, Daniel	11
Donaldson, Andrew	389
Donelson, John	343
Donnavan, Sarah	44

	PAGE.
Donnavon, James	44
DONOHO, JOHN	100
Dooles, Bitha	100
Dooles, Catteren	100
Dooles, John	100
Dooles, Joseph	100 (3)
Dooles, Patience	100
Dooles, Sarah	100
DOOLES, THOMAS	100
Dormon, Richard	138
Dothery, Percila	236
Dothry, Mandue	236
Dougall, Arthur	382
Douge, James	100
Douge, Joab	100
Douge, John	100
Douge, Mary	100
Douge, Peter	114
DOUGE, TULL	100
Dough, Josiah	44
Doughtery, Sarah	45
Doughtie, William	279
DOUGHTY, JOHN	100
Doughty, Marian	100
Douglas, Ann	101
Douglas, Elizabeth (wife of James)	101
Douglas, Elizabeth (granddaughter of James)	101
DOUGLAS, JAMES	101
Douglas, James (son of James)	101
Douglas, Kesia	101
Douglas, Thomas	8
DOUGLASS, DAVID	100
Douglass, Eliza	30
Douglass, Elizabeth	101
Douglass, James	30
Douglass, James	195
Douglass, John	100, 101
Douglass, Margarett	139
Douglass, Susanah	100
Douglass, William	100, 101
Dover,	364
Doway, Catherine	101
Doway, Elizabeth	101
Doway, James	101
DOWAY, ROBERT	101
Doway, Robert (son of Robert)	101
Dowd, William	413
Dowdy, Elizabeth	114
Dowdy, Hellena	114
Dowdy, Jemime	425
Dowe, Dianah	114
Dowers, Hannah	144

	PAGE.
Dowie, Robert	34
DOWNER, WILLIAM	101
Downes, Elias	395
Downing, Ann	20, 21, 101
Downing, Alexr.	336
Downing, Elizabeth	101
Downing, Henry	101
Downing, James	427
Downing, Mary	101, 298
Downing, W.	27, 210, 348, 415
DOWNING, WILLIAM	101
DOWNING, WILLIAM	101
Downing, William (son of William)	101
Downing, William	12, 21, 84, 212, 298
Downs, William	317
Dows, William	389
Dowse, Joseph	80, 417
Doyle, John	347
Drake, Aron	53
Drake, Francis	191
Drake, James	102
Drake, Jesse	52
DRAKE, JOHN	102
Drake, Sarah	102
Draper, Mary	193
Draper, Nathel.	206
Draper, Nathaniel	206, 311
Draper, Richard	61
Dreace, Mary	197
Dreding, Charity	102
DREDING, JOHN	102
DRINKWATER, JOHN	102
Drinkwater, John	94, 97, 393
Drinkwater, Jno.	96, 174, 175, 181, 215, 239 (2), 376
Driny, Thomas	140
Droughan, Walter	128
Dry, Mrs. Mary Jane	5, 6
Dry, Miss Rebecca	6 (2)
Dry, William	6 (3), 113, 380
Dry, Wm	67, 106
Duan, Matthew	183
DuBois, Ann Jean	102
DuBois, Isaac	102
DuBois, James	102
DuBois, Jean	102 (2)
DUBOIS, JOHN	102
DuBois, John (son of John)	102 (2)
DuBois, John	97
DuBois, Magdalene Margaret	102
DuBois, Margaret	102

INDEX. 479

	PAGE.
DuBois, Peter	102 (2)
DuBois, Walter	102 (2)
Dubose, Mary Ann	375
Duckenfield, Ann	103
Duckenfield, Jane	103
Duckenfield, John	103 (3)
Duckenfield, Judith	103
Duckenfield, Katherine	103
Duckenfield, Margaret	102, 103
Duckenfield, Mary	103
DUCKENFIELD, NATHANIL.	102
Duckenfield, Nathaniel	103 (2)
Duckenfield, Sir Robert	103
Duckenfield, Samuel	103 (2)
Duckenfield, Sarah	103
Duckenfield, Susannah	103
DUCKENFIELD, WILLIAM	103
Duckenfield, William	9 (2), 105
Duckson (or Dickson), John	19
Dudley, Abraham	104
Dudley, Ambrose	85
Dudley, Anne	103
Dudley, Bettie	31
Dudley, Bishop	31
DUDLEY, CHRISTOPHER	103
Dudley, Christopher (son of Christopher)	103
Dudley, Christopher (son of Thomas)	103
Dudley, Christopher	104
Dudley, David	103
DUDLEY, EDWARD	103
Dudley, Edward	103
Dudley, Elijah	104
Dudley, Elizabeth (wife of Thomas)	104
Dudley, Elizabeth (daughter of Thomas)	104
Dudley, Elizabeth (daughter of Wm. Hardin)	150
Dudley, Elizabeth (granddaughter of Wm. Hardin)	150
Dudley, Elizabeth	89, 103, 183
Dudley, Esther	32, 111
Dudley, George	103 (2)
Dudley, Hannah	103
Dudley, Jacob	104
Dudley, Jemima	173
Dudley, Jane	150
DUDLEY, JOHN	103
Dudley, John (son of John)	103
Dudley, John	103, 319, 397
Dudley, Malakie	104
Dudley, Mary	103 (2), 104, 134, 215, 345

	PAGE.
Dudley, Sarah	103
Dudley, Stephen	104
DUDLEY, THOMAS	104
DUDLEY, THOMAS	104
Dudley, Thomas (son of Thos.)	104 (2)
Dudley, Thomas	89, 103 (2)
Dudley, Thomas, Jr.	150
Dudley, William	103 (2), 104, 190, 402
Duffield, John	417
Duffield, Sarah	420
Duffy, James	357
Dugall, Arthur	230, 421
Dugen, John	175
Duggan, Jesse	104
DUGGAN, THOMAS	104
Duggan, Thomas (son of Thomas)	104
Duggan, Mary	104
Dugles, Anne	35
Duglis, Mary	73
Duk, Mary	287
Duke, Andr.	287
Duke, John	265
Duke, Judith	279
Duke, Mary	184
Duke, Peter	242, 322
Duke, Sarah	283
Dukes, Benjamin	276
Dukes, Robert	110
Dukingfield, John	327
Dulaney, Thos.	338 (2)
DUNBAR, DUN	104
Dunbar, Elisabeth	104
Dunbar, Ester	104
Dunbar, Hannah	104
Dunbar, Jane	197
Dunbar, Mary	104, 342
Dunbar, Richard	36
Dunbar, Robt.	198
Dunbar, Samll.	88
Dunbar, Samuell	104
Dunbar, Sarah	104
Dunbar, Sarah Barr	104
Dunbarr, Elizabeth	342
Dunbarr, Mary	342
Dunbarr, Samuel	124, 342
Dunbarr, William	342
Dunbarr, Wm.	124, 219
Dunbibin, Daniel	56, 151, 244, 369, 372, 387
Dunbibin, Jonas	248
Dunbibin, Saml.	369
DUNCAN, ABRAHAM	104

INDEX.

	PAGE.
Duncan, Abraham (nephew of Abraham)	104
Duncan, Abraham	46, 50, 92, 308
DUNCAN, ALEXANDER	105
Duncan, Alexander	45, 74, 139, 257
Duncan, David	78
Duncan, Elizabeth	351
Duncan, George	104
Duncan, Honnora	227
Duncan, James	104
Duncan, John	104 (2), 123, 219
Duncan, Mary	46, 104, 308
Duncan, Robert	104, 105
Duncan, William	104
Dunkeley's plantation	402
Dunkenfield, Wm.	208
Dunkinfield, William	352
Dunkin, Daniel	116
Dunkins plantation	266
Dunn, Daniel	397
Dunn, John	180, 202, 204, 314, 414
Dunn, Priscilla	375
Dunns Creek, land on	375
Dunston, Barnaby Stely	13
Dunston, Ellen	13
Dunston, John	13 (3)
Dunston, Martha	13
Dunston, Mary	13
Dunston, Richard William	13
Dupartall, Ann	217
Dupee, Daniel	105, 185, 406
DUPEE, ELIAS	105
Dupuis, Davis	308, 394
Dupuis, Sarah	308
Dupuis, William	394
Dupuise, David	75
Durant, Aaron Moses	106
Durant, Abraham Jetnett	106
DURANT, ANN	105
Durant, Ann (wife of George)	105
Durant, Ann (daughter of George)	105
Durant, Ann	87, 155
Durant, Anne	105
Durant, Elizabeth	87, 105, 132
DURANT, GEORGE	105
DURANT, GEORGE	105
Durant, George (son of George)	105
Durant, George (nephew of Geo.)	105

	PAGE.
Durant, George	87, 105, 137, 156 (2), 157, 160 (2)
Durant, Hagar	87
Durant, Henry	105
Durant, John (brother of George)	105
Durant, John (son of George)	105
Durant, Jno.	285, 290, 391
Durant, Mary	73, 87, 105, 137
Durant, Matytya	105
Durant, Pertyenia	105
Durant, Sarah	87, 105 (2)
DURANT, THOMAS	106
Durant, Thomas	105 (2), 155
Durham, Milly	213
Durhams Creek, land on	95
Durrance, Elizabeth Durant	106
Durrance, Francis	106
DURRANCE, SAMUEL	106
Durrance, Samuel	27, 116 (2), 148, 150, 165, 199, 247
Durrance, Wellcom	106
Durrance, William	106
Durrams Creek, plantations on	301
Durrant, George, of Bertey Point	373
Dutten, William	238
Dwight, Elizabeth	106
Dwight, James	365
DWIGHT, MATHEW	106
Dyckes, George	133
Dye, Katherine	325 (2)
Dyson, Clement	25
Eadey, Elizabeth	106
EADEY, HENRY	106
Eadey, John	106
EAGAN, JAMES	106
Eagle, Joseph	106
Eagle, Margaret Henrietta	106
EAGLE, RICHARD	106
Eagle, Susannah	106
Eagles, Richd. (father of Richard Eagle)	106
Eagles, Jams.	244
Eagleson, John	106
Eardan, John	82
Earle, John	332
Earle, Jno.	336 (2)
Earle, Mary	336 (2)
Earle, Richard	332
Earle, William	332
Earls, Cormelial	108
Earley, John	228

INDEX. 481

	PAGE.
Early, Ann	107
EARLY, ELIONÒR	106
Early, Eliza	39
Early, J.	256
Early, James	39
EARLY, JOHN	107
Early, John (son of John),	107 (2)
Early, John	39, 408
Early, Mary	58
Earp, Edward	352
Earp, Elizabeth	352
Earp, Manual	352
Eason, Anne	107
Eason, Benjamin	84, 85
Eason, George (son of William)	107
Eason, George (brother of William)	107
Eason, George	107
Eason, Jane	107
Eason, Jesse	47, 138, 309 (3)
Eason, Josiah	336
Eason, Mary (wife of William)	107
Eason, Mary (daughter of William)	107
Eason, Moses	138
Eason, Rachel	107
Eason, Susanna	107
Eason, Thomas	94, 107 (2), 194 (2)
EASON, WILLIAM	107
EASON, WILLIAM	107
Eason, William (son of William)	107
Eason, William (son of William)	107
Eason, William	42, 94
East Branch of Long Creek, land on	82
Eastchurch, Thomas	344
EASTER, ABRAHAM	107
Easter, Abraham	107 (2), 126
Easter, Ann	107
Easter, Dinah	107
Easter, Elizabeth	107, 381
Easter, James	107
EASTER, JOHN	107
EASTER, JOHN	107
Easter, John	107 (2), 108
Easter, Lida	107
Easter, Lydia	107
Easter, Mary	107 (2)
EASTER, MARY	107
Easter, Sarah	107, 108

	PAGE.
Easter, Thomas	107 (4), 108, 241
Easter, William	107 (2)
Eastern Shore, land on	354
Eastis, Silvester	136
Eaton, Charles Rust	108
Eaton, Elizabeth	417
EATON, JAMES	108
Eaton, John	417
Eaton, Mary	108 (2)
Eaton, Martha	108
Eaton, Robert	179
Eaton, Thomas	108
EATON, WILLIAM	108
Eaton, William (son of William)	108
Eborn, Elizabeth	108 (2), 109 (3)
EBORN, HENRY	108
Eborn, Henry (son of Henry)	108
Eborn, Henry	108, 109
Eborn, James	109 (3)
EBORN, LITTLETON	109
Eborn, Littleton	108, 109 (2), 196
Eborn, Littleton Jun.	356
Eborn, Martha	109
Eborn, Mary	108
EBORN, NATHANIEL	109
Eborn, Nathaniel	108, 109
Eborn, Rebecca	109
Eborn, William	109 (3)
Eborne, Aaron	109 (3)
Eborne, Elizabeth	109
Eborne, Henry	21, 108 (2), 109
Eborne, Littleton	109
Eborne, Martha	21
Eborne, Nathaniel	20, 21
EBORNE, REBEKAH	109
Eborne, Rebekah	21
Eborne, William	109
EBURN (or EBORNE), ELIZABETH	108
Eburn, Henry	108 (2)
Eburn, Littleton	108 (2)
Eburn, Nathaniel	108
Ecleston, Thomas	38
Ecrepint plantation	304
Ede, John	369
EDEN, CHARLES	109
Eden, Charles	20, 73, 212, 222, 291, 317, 332, 339, 399, 421
Eden, Chas.	25, 102, 103, 158, 204, 281, 353
Eden, C.	151, 190, 314
Eden, Gov. Charles	160 (2)

31

INDEX.

	PAGE.
Eden, Governor	291
Eden, Henry	111
Edens, Phillip	83
Edenton, land in and near	44
Ederingame, Sturgiss	309
Edghill, Leavels	366
Edleton, Elizabeth	402
Edleton, William	402
Edmonds, David	109
Edmonds, Elizabeth (daughter of Richard)	109
Edmonds, Elizabeth (wife of Richard)	109
Edmonds, Henry	109
Edmonds, Marey	109
Edmonds, Rebekah	109
EDMONDS (EDDMONDS), RICHARD	109
EDMONDS, SAMUEL	109
Edmonds, Sarah	109
Edmonds, Susannah	109
Edmonds, Thomas	109
Edmondson, John	110
EDMONDSON, JOSEPH	110
Edmondson, Priselow (wife of Joseph)	110
Edmondson, Priselow (daughter of Joseph)	110
Edmondson, Thomas	110
Edmunds, John	195
Edmunds, Saml	293
Edmunds, Samuel	49
Ednye, Ahinoam	110
Ednye, Ann	110 (2)
Ednye, Nuton Rensher	110
Ednye (Edney), Robert	110
Ednye, Samuel	110
Ednye, Saml	355
Edny, Samuel	201
Education, bequest for	28
Education, legacy for	418
Edwards, Ann	110 (2)
Edwards, Ben	288
Edwards, Britain	110
EDWARDS, CATHERINE	110
Edwards, Charity	111
Edwards, Christopher	288
Edwards, Edward	110, 175, 223
Edwards, Elisabeth	51
Edwards, Elizabeth	58, 110
EDWARDS, HENRY	110
Edwards, Henry (son of Henry)	110
EDWARDS, ISAAC	110

	PAGE.
Edwards, Isaac	58
Edwards, I..7, 11, 12, 19, 20, 22, 43 (2), 46, 47, 51, 58 (2), 60, 69, 81, 82, 83, 89, 90, 91, 98 (3), 101, 109, 111, 112, 113, 116, 120, 123, 131, 136, 150, 154 (2), 159, 165 (2), 166, 184 (3), 188, 192 (2), 195, 198, 199, 202, 224 (2), 236, 237, 252, 265, 266, 271, 274, 283, 288, 298, 305 (2), 308, 318, 335, 336, 340, 347, 352, 361, 363, 365, 371 (2), 374, 385, 387 (2), 390, 392, 395, 405, 409, 411 (2), 412, 422.	
Edwards, J. (I.)	110
Edwards, J	110, 150, 276
Edwards, Jane	108
Edwards, Jesse	110
Edwards, John, Sr	110
EDWARDS, JOHN	111
Edwards, John (son of John)	111
Edwards, John (grandchild of Isaac)	110
Edwards, John (of Roanoke)	136
Edwards, John	110 (2), 211, 212, 261, 415
Edwards, Josiah	110
Edwards, Mary	18, 111, 368
Edwards, Nathan	110
Edwards, Col. Nathaniel	108
Edwards, Robert	110 (2), 411
Edwards, Samuel	51, 110
Edwards, Thomas	110, 111
Edwards, William	110
Edy, Diana	111
Edy, Hanah	319
Edy, Henry	111
EDY, JOHN	111
Eelbech, Montfort	249
Egarton, William	71
Egerton, Ann	111
EGERTON (EGGERTON), JAMES	111
Egerton, James (son of James)	111
Egerton, John	91
Egerton, Mary	111
Egerton, Sarah	111
Egerton, William	71, 111, 268
Egerton, Wm.	75
Eggerton, James	157
Egleton, Francis	15, 78, 211, 241, 337, 342
Egleton, Frans	19, 93, 107, 125, 214, 236, 241
Eichhorn, Conrad	292

	PAGE.
Eivens, Ann	115
Eivens, Elizabeth	115
Eivens, Jonathan	115
Eivens, Rabakah	115
Eivens, Richard (son of Richard)	115
Eives, Rachel	371
Eives, Timothy	371
Elbeck, Mary	233
Elbeck, Montfort	233 (2)
Elbo plantation	357
Elder, David	121
Eldridge, Martha	111
Eldridge, Mary	111
Eldridge, Samuel	111
ELDRIDGE, WILLIAM	111
Eless, John	192
Elfisk, William	93
Eliot, Elizabeth	253, 302, 303
Eliot, Joshua	325
ELIOT, MICHEL	112
Eliot, Sarah	287
Elison, Paul	9
Eliss, John	141
Elks, Amanuel	111
ELKS, JOHN	111
Elks, John (son of John)	111
Elks, Marmaduke	110
Elks, Mary	111
ELKS, RICHARD	111
Elks, Thomas	111
Ellebar, Elizabeth	102
Ellegood, Margreat	111
ELLEGOOD, MATTHIAS	111
Elles, George	318
Elles, Gorg	56
Elles, Keziah	403
Elles, Michael	403
Ellet, Hanner	425
Ellice, Even	214
Ellice, Phillis	214
Elliot, Abraham	112, 419
Elliot, Ann	325
Elliot, Benjamin	112
Elliot, Caleb	112
Elliot, Charles	291
Elliot, Elizabeth	254, 255
Elliot, Isaac	112
Elliot, Joseph	112
Elliot, Joshua	112, 324
Elliot, Margaret	112
Elliot, Margaret	112, 380
Elliot, Mary	255
Elliot, Moses	112, 380
Elliot, Sarah	420

	PAGE.
Elliot, Solomon	112
ELLIOT, THOMAS	112
Elliot, Thomas (son of Thomas)	112
Elliot, Thomas	324, 346
Elliot, Ursely	112
Elliot, William	112
Elliott, Abraham	255
Elliott, Benjamin	112
ELIOTT, CHARLES	112
ELLIOTT, GEORGE	112
Elliott, Joseph	112, 415
Elliott, Judah	112
Elliott, Martha	388
Elliott, Mary	255
ELLIOTT, MOSES	112
Elliott, Moses (son of Moses)	112
Elliott, Moses	208
Elliott, Rob't	68
Elliott, Thomas	122
Elliott, Thomas	415
Ellis, Ann	112
Ellis, Benjamin	230
Ellis, Elizabeth	253
Ellis, Evan	176, 180
ELLIS, GEORGE	112
Ellis, George	1, 163
Ellis, Geo.	294
Ellis, Hannah	112
Ellis, Jno. (son of Robert)	112
Ellis, John (grandson of Robert)	112
Ellis, John	309
ELLIS, MARY	112
Ellis, Michal	88 (2)
Ellis, Rachel	283
ELLIS, ROBERT	112
Ellis, Robert (grandson of Robert)	112
Ellis, William	8
Ellison, Andrew	113
Ellison, James	225, 413
Ellison, Jas.	80
ELLISON, WILLIAM	113
Ellison, Wm.	364
Ellit, Sarah	264
Ellitt, Daniel	148
Elmsley, Elizabeth	80
Elson, Zack	27
Elton, Robert	66
ELTON, ZACHARIAH	113
Elwin, Fountain	139
Emers, Isabel Smith	348
Emers, Thomas	348

INDEX.

	PAGE.
Emerson, Tabitha	352
Emerson, Thomas	352
Emewhitt, Levi	77
Emly, Wm.	125
Enecks, Ann	191
Enecks, Isaac	191
Enecks, Jane	191
Enecks, William	191
ENGEL, PETER	113
ENGLISH, JOSEPH	113
English, Joseph	250
Ennet, Edmond	113
ENNET, EDMUND	113
Ennet, Ellinor	113
Ennet, John	113
Ennet, Joseph	110
Ennett, Johnathan	13
Eno Old Fields, land at	253
Eno River, land on	124, 388
Episcopal Church at Dover, Delaware, bequest to	229
Erkman, Kniga	38
Erkman, Mary	38
Erwin, Susanna	327
Ervin, Robert	413
Esleck, Isaac	124
Esler, Fredrick	25
ESPY, JAMES	113
Espy, James	179, 229
Espy, Margaret	113
Espy, Sarah	113
Espy, Usher	113
Estor (negro wench)	427
Etheridg, Agness	73
Etheridg, Rachel	73
Etheridge, Abner	114
Etheridge, Absalom	114
Etheridge, Adam	114 (2)
Etheridge, Amos	114
Etheridge, Andrew	225
Etheridge, Andrew, Jr.	225
Etheridge, Ann	44, 113, 114
Etheridge, Barby	114
Etheridge, Caleb	114
Etheridge, Callib	114
Etheridge, Christon	114
Etheridge, Dorothy	114
Etheridge, Elener	48
Etheridge, Elliner	114
Etheridge, Ellizabeth	114
Etheridge, Francis	416
ETHERIDGE, HENRY	113
Etheridge, Henry (son of Henry)	113
Etheridge, James	114, 299
Etheridge, Jean	298
Etheridge, Jeane	298
ETHERIDGE, JOHN	114
Etheridge, John (son of John)	114
Etheridge, John	48, 113, 266
Etheridge, Josias	114
Etheridge, Lettisha	114
ETHERIDGE, LUKE	114
Etheridge, Lydda	298
ETHERIDGE, MARMADUKE	114
Etheridge, Mary	114, 298
Etheridge, Prissella	114
Etheridge, Redah	114
Etheridge, Richard	113, 114, 298
Etheridge, Rich.	48
Etheridge, Sampson	114 (2)
Etheridge, Sam'l.	67
Etheridge, Samuel	113
Etheridge, Sarah	114 (3)
ETHERIDGE, SOLOMON	114
Etheridge, Solomon (son of Solomon)	114
Etheridge, Solomon	114
Etheridge, Susey	114
Etheridge, Tedy	113
Etheridge, Thos.	111
Etheridge, William	113, 114, 266
Etheridge, Willis	114, 159, 167, 299
Etherigs, Mary	29
Ethrigs, Timothy	29
Etoms, Francis	20
Eubank, Elizabeth	114
EUBANK, GEORGE	114
Eubank, Geo.	110
Eubank, Isabella	114
Eubank, James	114
Euere, Ann	161
Eustace, J.	102, 405
Evans, Alce	116
Evans, Ann	115, 141, 170, 252
Evans, Bartholomew	115, 176
EVANS, BARWELL	115
Evans, Barwell (nephew of Barwell)	115
Evans, Benjamin	11 (4), 279, 396
Evans, Catherine	116
EVANS, CHARLES	115
Evans, Charles (son of Benjamin)	115
Evans, Charles (son of Charles)	115 (3)

INDEX.

	PAGE.
Evans, Charles, Jr.	115
Evans, Charles	115
Evans, C.	36
Evans, Da.	386
Evans, David	420
Evans, Elener	116
Evans, Elisabeth	116
Evans, Elizabeth	115 (2), 116, 176
Evans, Ellener	116
Evans, George	116
Evans, Geo.	354
EVANS, HUNT	115
Evans, Isaac	56
Evans, Jacob	115
Evans, Jacob (brother of Barwell)	115
Evans, Jacob (nephew of Barwell)	115
Evans, Jane (wife of John)	115
Evans, Jane (daughter of John)	115
EVANS, JOHN	115
Evans, John (son of John)	115
Evans, John	33, 115 (2), 116, 240, 310, 423
Evans, John Hunt	176
Evans, Jonathan	92, 176, 375
Evans, Josiah	375
EVANS, MARY	115
Evans, Mary	115, 116 (2), 289, 340
Evans, Mary (wife of Thomas)	116
Evans, Mary (daughter of Thomas)	116
Evans, Peter	246, 333, 425
Evans, Phillip	302
Evans, Rachel	115
EVANS, RICHARD	116
EVANS (EIVENS), RICHARD.	115
Evans, Richard (son of Richard)	116
Evans, Richard	98, 308, 309, 422
Evans, Richd.	332
EVANS, ROBERT	116
Evans, Robert (son of Robert)	116
Evans, Robert	170 (2), 325
Evans, Rob't	106
Evans, Sarah	115, 116, 397, 425
Evans, Stephen	252
Evans, Susanna	332

	PAGE.
Evans, Susannah (wife of Barwell)	115
Evans, Susannah (daughter of Barwell)	115
EVANS, THOMAS	116
EVANS, THOMAS	116
Evans, Thomas (son of Thomas)	116
Evans, Thomas	33, 115, 147, 340 (2)
Evans, William	115, 272
Evatt, Mary	116
Evatt, Sarah	116
EVATT, WILLIAM	116
Even, William	313
Evens, Even	148
Evens, Jonathan	191
Evens, Richard	331
Evens, Sarah	76, 128
Evens, William	210
Everard, Richard	16, 35, 64, 65, 77, 105, 108, 118, 126, 149, 156 (2), 193, 205, 222, 223, 224, 244, 256, 268, 273, 276, 280, 283, 294, 295, 298, 303, 307, 316, 318, 319, 327, 328, 356, 363, 376.
Everard, Rich'd	49, 56, 60 (2), 62 (2), 69, 71 (2), 74, 77, 85, 99, 112, 119, 127, 135, 209, 235, 248, 302, 308, 380.
Everarde, R.	124, 126, 161 (2), 287, 309, 340, 378, 424
Everay, Patiens	117
Everenden, Thomas	154
Everet, John	242
Everet, Nathaniel	113, 365
Everett, Elisabeth	116
EVERETT, JOHN	116
Everett, John	116
Everett, Joshua	116
Everett, Mary	116
Everett, Nathaniel	116, 199
Everett, Thomas	116
Everigin, John	132, 146, 158, 379
Everigin, Joseph	141
Everigin, Sarah	379
Everigin, William	175, 379 (2)
Everigin, Wm., Sr.	158
Everigin, Wm., Jr.	158
Everigin, W.	176
Everington, Richard	364
EVERITT, NATHANIEL	116
Everitt, Nathaniel	116
Everitt, Nathaniel (of Mereland)	116

	PAGE.
Everitt, Nathaniel (of New River)	116
Everitt, Nathaniel (of the parish of St. Andrews)	116
Everitt Nathaniel (of St. Andrews)	117
Everitt, Sarah	354
Everitt, Thomas	117
Everton, Daniel	1
Everton, Frances	199
Everton, Hannah	1, 117, 313
Everton, James	1, 117
EVERTON, JEREMIAH	117
Everton, Jeremiah	67, 199
Everton, John	61
Everton, Rachel	117
Everton, Sarah	199
Everton, Solomon	117, 199
Everton, William	1
Eves, Mary	147
Eves, Ralph	147
Evines, Thomas	164, 414
Evins, Bartholomew	237
Evins, Catterine	393
Evins, Jonathan	271
Evins, Joshua	237
Evins, Timer	237
Evitt, Charles	11
Evrage, Pachance	266
Evregan, John	142
Ewell, Elisabeth Cotten	83
Ewell, Roderick Cotten	83
Ewell, Sally Cotten	83
EYRES, RICHARD	117
FAGAN, ENOCH	117
Fagan, Mary	117
Fagan, Ruina	117
Fageett, James	285
Fageett, Martha	285
Fagon, Bedford	26
Faircloth, Edward	78
Fairless, Nicholas	106, 228
Falaw, William	11
Falconer, Ann	117
Falconer, George	117
FALCONER, JOHN	117
Falconar, Jno.	3, 153, 394
Falconer, Sarah	117 (2)
FALCONER, THOMAS	117
Falconer, Thomas	76, 117
Falk, Elizabeth	117
Falk, James	71
Falk, John	117
Falk, Jonathan	117

	PAGE.
FALK, RICHARD	117
Falk, Richard (son of Richard)	117
Falk, Richard	117
Falk, William	117
Fallaw, James	81
Falle, David	228
Falling Creek, land on	125, 205, 363, 382
Fallow, William	16
Fanings, Joseph	120
Fanning, Wm.	195
Fareclof, Sarah	159
Faries, Isaac	5, 31, 32, 54, 100, 195, 222, 238, 253, 254, 258, 281, 312, 375, 392.
Farlee, Christiana	118
FARLEE, JAMES	118
Farlee, James (son of James)	118
Farlee, James	118
Farlee, Rachel	118
Farlee, Samuel	118
Farlee, Sarah	118
Farmer, James	297
Farmer, Joseph	421
Farmer, Sarah	256
Farmer, Wm.	32
Farnell, Thomas	325
Farquharson, Charles	97
Farquharson, Cosmas	254
Farr, Hannah	118
Farr, James	118
FARR, RICHARD	118
Farr, Richard (son of Richard)	118
Farr, Titus Green	118
Farr, William	118
Farrell, Richard	319
Farren, Thomas	96
Farrow, Barbary	118
FARROW, FRANCIS	118
Farvy, John	72 (2)
Faulk, Patience	291
Faulks Point	155
Feare, Ann	118
FEARE, OBADIAH	118
Fearn, John	404
Fearn, Mary	404
Fearn, Thomas	404
Fee, Daniel	318
Fee, Elebeth	318
Fehenden, J.	281
Feld, Cathron	335
Fellow, Rob't	202

Index. 487

	PAGE.
Felltwood, William	280
Felte, Sarah	154
Felthen, Ann	119
FELTHEN, JAMES	119
Felts, Elisabeth	119
FELTS, HUMPHREY	119
Felts, John	119
Fendall, Elizabeth	119, 215
FENDALL, JOHN	119
Fendall, John	215
Fendall's plantation	341
FENDALL, ROBERT	119
Fendall, Robert (brother of John)	119
Fendall, Robert	155
Fendal's plantation	87
Fener, John	246
Feneson, James	227
Fennell, John	9
Fennison, James	68
Feps, Josiah	119
Feps, Mary	119
Feps, Molle	119
Feps, Nathaniel	119
Feps, Sarah	119
FEPS, WILLIAM	119
Feps, William (son of William)	119
Ferebee, George	120
Ferebee, Joanah	279
Ferebee, Joseph	120
Ferebee, Miriam	279
Ferebee, William	120
Ferebe, William	361
Fergus, James	364
Fergus, John	106
FERGUSON, ADAM	119
Ferguson, Adam	119
Ferguson, Alickander	171
Ferguson, Anne	421
Ferguson, Elizabeth	110, 119, 120, 214
Ferguson, Jane	119
Ferguson, Joan Martin	239
FERGUSON, MARK	119
Ferguson, Mark	119, 239
Ferguson, Sarah	119
Ferguson, Slocumb	119, 238
Feriel, Erasmus	120
Feriel, John	120
FERIEL, RICHARD	120
Ferny Ridge plantation	191
Ferrebee, William	338
Ferrill, Ann	121
Ferrill, Elizabeth	77

	PAGE.
Ferril, Ann	120
Ferril, Caleb	120
Ferril, Joseph	120
Ferril, Mary	120
Ferril, Richard	354
Ferril, Samuel	120
Ferril, Sarah	120
Ferril, Tamer	120
FERRIL, WILLIAM	120
Ferry plantation	425
Fetterton, Elizabeth	290
Fetterton, William	290
Fetterton, William (son of William)	290
Few, Joseph	311
Fewox, Ann	120
FEWOX, JAMES	120
Fewox, John	23
Fewox, Mary	169
Fewox, Robert	2, 23, 120
Fibath, Phelis	125
Ficher, Moses	180
Field, Ambrose	153
Field, Ann	118
Field, James	119, 169
Field, John	118
Field, Moses	285
FIELD, RICHARD	118
Field, Richard (son of Richd.)	118
Field, Samuel	118
Field, Saml	335
Field, Sarah	177
Field, Smith	119
Field, Zachariah	55, 270
Fielden, Wm	322
Fields, Ann	118
Fields, Deborah	114
Fields, Jacob	42
FIELDS, JAMES	118
Fields, Moses	118, 314
Fields, Rubin	118
Fields, Zebiah	118
FIGURES, BARTHOLOMEW	120
Figures, Bartholomew (son of Bartholomew)	120 (3)
Figures, Bartholomew	224
Figures, John	120 (3), 224
Figures, Joseph	120
Figures, Richard	120
Figures, William	120, 224
Fillbert, Nicholas	214
Filliaw, Ann	120
Filliaw, James	120
Filliaw, Jane	120

INDEX

	PAGE.
FILLIAW, JOHN	120
Filliaw, John (son of John)	120
Filliaw, Joseph	120
Filliaw, Mary	120
Filliaw, Prisillar	120
Fillingham, Benjamin	120
Fillingham, Jarvis	120
FILLINGHAM, JOHN	120
Fillingham, John (son of John)	120 (2)
Fillingham, Margaret	120
Fillingham, Robert	120 (2)
Fillingham, Samuel	120
Fillyaw, John	203, 311
Finch, Dorothy	122
Finch, Porter	122
Finney, Isaac	115
Finney, John	230
Finney, Robert	333
Finney, Thomas	315
Finsinger, Phillip	86
Firebent, ———	292
Firbish, Sarah	385
Fish, John (son of William)	121
Fish, John (grandson of William)	121
Fish, Mary (wife of William)	121
Fish, Mary (daughter of William)	121
FISH, WILLIAM	121
Fish, William (son of William)	121
Fish, Wm. (grandson of William)	121
Fisher, Francis	266
Fisher, George	32, 121, 161, 338
FISHER, JAMES	121
Fisher, John	46
FISHER, RANDOLPH	121
Fisher, Thomas	121
Fisher, Thos.	161
Fisher, William	382
Fishing Creek, plantation on,	47, 251
Fishing Creek, land on	293, 397
Fishing Creek, surveys on	84
Fitchjarrel, Richard	70
Fitchpatrick, Cornelius	415
Fitzgarald, Ann	121
FITZGARALD, JOHN	121
Fitzgarald, John (son of John)	121
Fitzgarald, Thomas	121
Fitzgerald, James	4
FitzMaurice, Ulysses	418

	PAGE.
FITZPATRICK, BRYAN	121
Fitzpatrick, Bryant	121
FITZPATRICK, CORNELIUS	121
Fitzpatrick, Cornelius (son of Cornelius)	121
Fitzpatrick, Cornelius	121 (2)
Fitzpatrick, Dinis	121
Fitzpatrick, Edwd.	321
Fitzpatrick, Elender	121
Fitzpatrick, Elizabeth (daughter of Cornelius)	121
Fitzpatrick, Elizabeth (wife of Cornelius)	121
Fitzpatrick, Isack	225
Fitzpatrick, John	121
Fitzpatrick, Mary	121
Fitzpatrick, Sarah	121
Fitzpatrick, Vinney	121
Fitzrandolph, Benj.	227
Fitzrandolph, Benjamin	191, 235
Flagg Run, land on	173
Flake, Arthur	412
Flake, Elizabeth	412
Flake, Robert	21, 412
Flake, William	412
Flanakin, Katherine	122
Flanakin, James	121, 122
Flanakin, Leah	121
FLANAKIN, RICHARD	121
Flanakin, Richard (son of Richard)	121
Flanakin, Thomas	121
Flanakin, William	121
Flannakin, James	303
Flanner, Thomas	392
Flat Branch, land east of	79
Flat Swamp, plantation on	365
Flat Swamp, land on	375, 380
Flatty Creek, lands on	277
Flatty Creek, land on	392
Flatty Creek and Pasquotank River, Signory on	352
Fleetwood, Wm.	398
Flemen, Elizabeth	34
Fleming, Bart.	244
Fleming, Bar.	301
Fleming, Elizabeth	122 (2)
FLEMING, GEORGE	122
Fleming, James	122
Fleming, Martha	122
Fleming, Mary	122
FLEMING, ROSANNA	122
Flemming, George	208
Flemming, James	382
Flemming, Maria	208
FLETCHER, CURTIS	122

INDEX. 489

	PAGE.
Fletcher, Doratha	122
Fletcher, Elizabeth	122
FLETCHER, FRANCIS	122
Fletcher, George	122
Fletcher, James	122
Fletcher, Jane	122 (2)
Fletcher, Joshua	122
Fletcher, Josua	122
Fletcher, Jean	378
Fletcher, Margaret	122
Fletcher, Mary	122
Fletcher, Miriam	122
FLETCHER, RALPH	122
FLETCHER, RALPH	122
Fletcher, Ralph (son of Ralph)	122 (2)
Fletcher, Ralph	93, 253, 263, 298, 363, 378 (2)
Fletcher, Robert	356
Fletcher, Ruth	122
FLETCHER, THOMAS	122
Fletcher, Thomas	122
Flibus, Thomas	334
Flood, Elizabeth	123 (2), 273
FLOOD, JAMES	123
FLOOD, JAMES	123
Flood, James	281, 306
Flood, Paul	287
Flood, Wm.	261
Flood, William	191, 287
Floaryday, William	165
FLORELL, WILLIAM	123
Flower, Elizabeth	415
Flower, John	388
Flower, Lazarus	388
Flowrey, Lazerus	160
Floyd, Elizabeth	26
Floyd, Francis	26
Floyd, Griffin	71
Floyd, Jessee	123
FLOYD, JOHN	123
Floyd, John (son of John)	123
Floyd, John	385
Floyd, Morrise	123
Floyd, Peter	71
Floyd, Stephen	123
Floyd, Thomas	123 (2)
Floyd, Thos.	26
Floyd, William	123 (2)
Floyds plantation	379
Flybus, Thomas	418
FLYN, COLLUMB	123
Flyn, Collumb (son of Collumb)	123
Flyn, Columb	91
Flynn, Thomas	23

	PAGE.
Fogarty, Edmund	338
Foger, Edmund	139
Fogg, Grace	123
Fogg, Johnwats	123
FOGG, MOSES	123
Fokes, William	212
Folley plantation	193
Fontaine, Fran.	174
Fonveille, Brice	153
Fonvielle, Elizabeth	124
Fonvielle, Easter	124
Fonvielle, Francis	124 (2)
Fonvielle, Frederick	124
Fonvielle, Isaac	123
Fonvielle, Jeremiah	124
FONVIELLE, JOHN	123
Fonvielle, John (son of John)	123, 124
Fonvielle, John	96, 153 (2), 267
Fonvielle, Mary	124
Fonvielle, Richard	140
Fonveille, Sarah	140
Fonvielle, Stephen	124
Fonveille, William Brice	124 (2), 140
Fonville, Anna	66 (2)
Fonville, Francis	157
Fonville, John	62
Fontaine, Fran.	105
Foraster, Ann	124
Foraster, Benjamin	124
FORASTER, JAMES	124
Foraster, James (son of James)	124
Foraster, Thomas	124
Foraster, William	124
Forbes, Alexr.	176
Forbes, Ann	357
Forbes, Elizabeth	45, 142
Forbes, James	124, 142, 330
Forbes, Jas.	45
FORBES, JOHN	124
Forbes, John	30, 46, 71, 77, 95, 96, 104, 176, 187, 219, 272, 308, 311, 342, 383, 398.
Forbes, Martha	124
Forbes, Wm.	139, 253, 258
Forbus, Alice	159
Forbus, Baley	18
Forbus, James	18, 159
Forbus, Martha	18
Forbus, Rebekah	18
Forbus, Rebecca	18
Forck of the Duckinstool plantation	374
Ford, Alexander	197

	PAGE.
Ford, Alexr.	87
Ford, Elias	340, 363
Ford, Hanna	22
Ford, John	39
Ford, Stephen	341
Fordham, Benjamin	17
Fordham, John	411
Fordise, George	22
Fordyse, George	88, 159
Forehand, Anthony	81
FOREHAND, CORNELIUS	124
Forehand, Cornelius (son of Cornelius)	124
Forehand, Elizabeth (daughter of Cornelius)	124
Forehand, Elizabeth (wife of Cornelius)	124
Forehand, James	124
Forehand, John	124
Forehand, Mary	124
Forehand, Richard	124
Forehand, Sarah	117
Forehand, Thomas	124
Foreman, Alexander	124, 240
Foreman, Caleb	124
Foreman, Elizabeth	278
FOREMAN, JOHN	124
FOREMAN, JOHN TIDINGS	124
Foreman, John Fydings	124
Foreman, John	199
Foreman, John (son of Sanders)	124
Foreman, Joseph	124
Foreman, Joshua	124 (2)
Foreman, Lazarus	124
Foreman, Margarett	124 (2), 199
Foreman, Sanders	124
Foreman, William	124
Foreman, Wm.	90
Fork Bridge, land beginning at	193
Fork, William	92
Forke Neck plantation	98
Forrester, Robert	385
Forsha, Robt.	244
Forshaw, Henry	48
Forster, ——— (wife of Capt. John)	105
Forster, Capt. John	105
Forster, John	241, 387
Forster, Margaret	94
Forster, Robert	5, 7, 15, 222, 244, 400
Forster, Rob't.	237

	PAGE.
Forster, Rt.	21, 23, 32, 47 (2), 71, 72, 74, 84, 88, 91, 93, 98, 99, 102, 136, 144, 154, 165, 166, 170, 178, 186, 200 (2), 211, 242, 243, 259, 270, 276, 282, 288, 293, 306, 307, 310, 317, 318, 320, 323, 337, 344, 347, 351, 352, 353 (2), 354, 363, 364, 366, 374, 382, 385, 397, 417.
Forsters Creek, land on	371
Fort, Alice	125
Fort, Anna	21
Fort, Arther	125
Fort, Arthur	125 (2), 203, 360
Fort, Author	125
Fort, Benjamin	125
Fort Branch, plantations on.	251
Fort, Catherine	125
Fort, Dunly	125
Fort, Druly	125 (2)
Fort, Elias	125 (4)
Fort, Elisabeth (wife of George)	125
Fort, Elizabeth	21
Fort, Elizebeth (daughter of George)	125
FORT, GEORGE	125
Fort, George (son of George)	125
Fort, Jerusha	125
Fort, Jerushah	125
FORT, JOHN	125
FORT, JOHN	125
Fort, John (son of John)	125 (2)
Fort, John	125, 202, 291
Fort, John, Jr.	125
Fort, Mary	125
Fort, Moses	125 (2)
FORT, RICHARD	125
Fort, Samuell	125
Fort, Thomas	125 (2)
Fort, William	125
Forte Point	345
Fortescue, Luke	227
FORTSEN, MARY	125
Fortsen, Theophilus	125
Fortt, Ealcer	7
Fortt, Elias	7
Foscue, Abigail	125
Foscue, Bell	125, 126
Foscue, Dina	326
FOSCUE, JOHN	125
Foscue, John (son of John).	125
Foscue, John	125, 126
Foscue, Luke	125, 126
Foscue, Lydia	125
Foscue, Mary	125

Index. 491

	PAGE.
Foscue, Moses	125
Foscue, Moses	125
Foscue, Sarah	326
FOSCUE, SIMON	125
Foscue Simon (son of Simon)	125
Foscue, Simon	125, 326
Foscue, William	125 (2)
Fossett, Bryan	409
Foster, Diana	126
Foster, Elizabeth	126 (3)
Foster, Frances	339
Foster, Francis	126, 366, 368
FOSTER, HANNAH	126
Foster, Hannah	126
FOSTER, JAMES	126
FOSTER, JOHN	126
Foster, John	221
Foster, Jno.	105
Foster, Lydie	126
Foster, Martha	34
Foster, Parker	126
Foster, Prudence	326
Foster, Richard	122
FOSTER, ROBERT	126
Foster, Robert	2
Foster, R.	186
Foster, Thomas	32, 126
FOSTER, WILLIAM	126
Foster, William	394
Fosque, Hannah	342
Fosque, William	342
Foulks (or Foleks) Point	155
Fountaine, John	67
Fountain, Richard	22
Fountains Creek, land on	395
Fountin, Sarah	388
Fourer, John	389
Fourre, Elizabeth	126
Fourre, Isaac	126
FOURRE, JOHN	126
Fourre, John	127, 291, 348, 403
Fourre, Jno.	146, 392
Fourre, Maher	126
Fourre, Nathaniel	126
Fourree, Catherine	127
Fourree, Margueritt	127
Fourree, Mary	127
Fourree, Nicole	127
FOURREE, PETER	127
Fowler, Cornelius	360
Fox, Ann	127
Fox, Ellinor	290
Fox, Elizabeth	157
Fox, Grace	290
FOX, JAMES	127

	PAGE.
Fox, James	275
Fox, Judith	203
Fox, Mary	290
Fox, Nicholas	302
Fox, Sarah	156
Fox, Thomas	127, 275, 290
Fox, Thos.	41, 149
Foxhall, Thomas	154
Foy, Thos.	326
Foyle, James	136, 325
Francis, James	117
Franck, Barbara	127
Franck, Catherine	127
Franck, Civill	339
Franck, Edward	127
Franck, John	127
FRANCK, JOHN MARTIN	127
Franck, Martin	123, 207, 339
Franck, Sevil (wife of John Martin)	127
Franck, Sevil (daughter of John Martin)	127
Franck, Susannah	127
Frank, Edward	53
Frank, Martin	46, 53
Frankland, Miss Hariat	6
Frankland, Miss Mary	6
Frankland, Mrs. Sarah	5 (2)
Frankland, Thomas	5
Franklin, Henry	423
Franklin, John	84
Franklin, Sarah	423
Franks Creek, land on	221
Franks, John	406
Franks, Mary Ann	12
FRASER, DUNCAN	127
Frazer, Alexander	414
Frazer, Ann	381
Frazer, James	316
Fraziar, Micajah	173
Frazier, Ann	54
FRAZIER, DAVID	127
Frazier, Elizabeth	127
Frazier, James	214, 245
Frazier, Mary (wife of Samuel)	127
Frazier, Mary (daughter of Samuel)	127
Frazier, Mary	117
Frazier, Micajah	69, 316
FRAZIER, SAMUEL	127
Frazier, Samuel	127
Frazier, Sarah	214
Frederick, John	25
Freehold, land in	360
Freeman, Aron	128

	PAGE.
Freeman, James	127
FREEMAN, JOHN	128
FREEMAN, JOHN	127
Freeman, John (son of John)	127 (2), 128
Freeman, John	95, 97, 128, 298, 329, 352
Freeman, John, Jr.	128
Freeman, Jos.	298
Freeman, Mary	127, 128 (2)
Freeman, Mathew	127
Freeman, Richard	128
Freeman, Robert	72
Freeman, Samuel	128
Freeman, Sarah	117
Freeman, Thomas	117, 128
FREEMAN, WILLIAM	128
Freeman, William (son of William)	128
Freeman, William	127
Free School, legacy for	179
French, ———	362 (3)
French, Abigal	342
French, Elizabeth	122, 128
French, Eliz.	76, 362
French, Mrs. Elizabeth	221
French, George	74
French, John	310
FRENCH, RICHARD	128
French, Richard	155, 206, 219, 221, 316
French, Rich.	76
French, Robert	342
French, Thomas	140, 411
French, William	390
Freshwater, Elizabeth	128
Freshwater, Frances Armstead	128
FRESHWATER, JOHN	128
Freshwater, John (son of John)	128
Freshwater, Phaddus	128
Freshwater, Sarah	152
Freshwater, William Armsted	128
Frezer, James	305
Frilie, Will	349
Frink, Hannah	346 (2)
Frink, Hannah (daughter of Hannah)	346
Frissell, Daniel	333
Frith, Jas.	323
Frizle, James	321
Frog Hall plantation	71
Frohock, William	226
Frost, Elenor	128

	PAGE.
Frost, Elizabeth	88
Frost, James	128
Frost, Joan	128
FROST, WILLIAM	128
Frost, William (son of William)	128
Frowing, Mary	204
Frume, Jane	127
Fry, Elizabeth	296
Fry, Elizabeth (mother of Thomas)	128
Fry, Elizabeth (wife of Thomas)	128
Fry, John	289, 296, 350
FRY, THOMAS	128
Fryard, John	174
Fryars, John	264
Fryer, Jeames	130
Fryer, Lewis	272
Fryer, Mary	279
Fryer, Thomas	130
Fryer, William	130
Fryer, Wm.	420
Fryley, William	292
Fryly, Grace	128
FRYLY, WILLIAM	128
Fuggin, Sary	117
Fulford, Joseph	89, 376
Fulford, Prudence	238
Fulgham, Anthony	121
Fulker, John	113
Fullard, Thomas	260
Fullenton, Elizabeth	308
Fullerton, Mary	129, 197
Fullerton, Matthias	129
FULLERTON, ROBERT	129
Fullerton, Robert	197
Fullerton, Susanna	129
Fulsher, William	339
Furbish, Abigail	129
Furbish, Alice	129
Furbish, Isaac	129
FURBISH, THOMAS	129
Furbish, Thomas (son of Thomas)	129
Furbish, William	129
Furbush, James	68
Furbush, Rebeckah	415
Fussell, Ann	129
Fussell, Benjamin	167
Fussell, Jacob	167
Fussel, Aaron	129
Fussel, Sarah	129
FUSSEL, THOMAS	129
Futrell, Elizabeth	98 (3)
Fyam, William	22
Fybash, John	340

INDEX.

	PAGE.
GAD, JAMES	129
Gad, Joseph	110
Gad, Sarah	129
Gadd, Wm.	230
Gaddy, William	233
Gaddy, Wm.	234
Gailors Hammock plantation	241
Gailes Branch, land on	177
Gailliard, John	394
Gainer, Arther	129
Gainer, Benjamin	129
Gainer, Eliza	129
Gainer, Hester	129 (2)
Gainer, James	129
Gainer, Joseph	129 (4)
Gainer, Lydda	129
GAINER, MARY	129
Gainer, Mary	129
Gainer, Martha	129 (3)
Gainer, Sary	129
GAINER, SAMUEL	129
Gainer, Samuel (son of Samuel)	129 (2)
Gainer, Thomas	129 (2)
GAINER, WILLIAM	129
Gainer, William (son of William)	129 (2)
Gainer, William	129 (4)
Gains, Ann	252
Gains, Thomas	286, 344
Gainwell, George	226
Galaber, Ann	316
Galdy, Louis	336
GALE, CHRISTOPHER	129
Gale, Christopher	35, 74 (2), 82, 218, 222 (2), 264
Gale, C	21 (2), 38, 55, 73, 76, 87, 164, 167, 192, 209, 212, 264, 272, 282, 338, 356, 404.
GALE, EDMOND	130
Gale, Edmond (son of Edmond)	130
Gale, Edmond (nephew of Christopher)	130
Gale, Edmond (brother of Christopher)	130
Gale, Edmond	222
Gale, Edmund	81, 160 (2), 218, 357, 392
Gale, Edmd.	223, 294
Gale, Edward	18
Gale, Edwd.	25, 55
Gale, Hanh.	300
Gale, Mary	130

	PAGE.
Gale, Miles	83, 130, 155, 156, 176, 289, 309, 327 (2), 385
Gale, Roger	130 (2)
Gale, Sarah Catherine	130
Gale, Simon	406
Galland, John	27, 89, 189
Gallop, Abel	379
GALLEY, JOHN	130
Galley, Jno.	166
Galloway, Mary	319
Galloway, Thomas	319
Galluay, Mary	130
GALLUAY, THOMAS	130
Gallup, Abel	379
GAMBELL, ADAM	130
Gambell, James	130
Gambell, John	130
Gambling, Joshua	193
GAMMIDGE, FRANCIS	130
Ganey, Thomas	226
Garde, Alse	372
Garde, Violater	372
Gardiner, Jane	400
Gardiner, John	400
Gardiner, Elizabeth	29
Gardiner, Euridice	84
Gardiner, William	387
Gardner, Ann	130 (2)
Gardner, Annah (daughter of Martin)	131
Gardner, Annah (wife of Martin)	131
Gardner, Dunsila	130
Gardner, Elisabeth	130
Gardner, Elizabeth	29
Gardner, Isaac	29, 131 (2)
Gardner, Joan	131
Gardner, James	29, 131
Gardner, James Smeathwick	130
GARDNER, JOHN	130
Gardner, John	131
Gardner, Martain	135
GARDNER, MARTIN	131
Gardner, Mary	29, 49, 364
Gardner, Samuel	131 (2)
Gardner, Thomas	131 (2)
GARDNER, WILLIAM	131
Gardner, William (son of William)	131 (2)
Gardner, William	29, 130, 131, 143, 326, 382
Gardner, William, Jr.	130
Gard's Island	382
GARFORT, GREGORY	131
Garkin, Zachariah	389
Garner, Arthur	58 (2)

	PAGE.		PAGE.
Garner, Elizabeth	131	GASKILL, WILLIAM	132
Garner, Elizabeth Cherry	58	Gaskill, William (son of William)	132
Garner, Estor	131	Gaskins, Ann (wife of Fisher)	132
Garner, Hanner	131		
Garner, James	58	Gaskins, Ann (daughter of Fisher)	132
GARNER, JOHN	131		
Garner, John (son of John)	131	Gaskins, Benjamin	132
Garner, John (grandson of John)	131	GASKINS, CATRIN	132
Garner, Mary	131 (2)	GASKINS, FISHER	132
GARNER, RALFE	131	Gaskins, Harmon	48
Garner, Sarah	58 (3)	Gaskins, Joseph	132
Garnes, John	340	Gaskins, Thomas	132 (2)
Garnet, Francis	276	GASKINS, WILLIAM	132
Garnet, Mary	132	Gaskins, William (son of William)	132
GARNET, WILLIAM	132		
Garnett, John	148	Gaston, Alex.	240
Garnett, Ralph	100	Gaston, Mary	31
Garnett, Mary	100, 148	Gate, John	23
Garrad, Eliz.	139	GATHIN, EDWARD	132
Garrald, Henry	345	Gathin, Elizabeth	132 (2)
Garrell, John	116	Gathin, John	132 (2)
Garret, Daniel	247	Gatling, ———	349
Garret, Esbell	71	Gattellen, John	151
GARRET, JOHN	131	Gaulberry, land on	385
Garret, John (son of John)	131	Gay, Henry	19, 334
Garret, Jonathan	131	Gay, James	405
Garret, Mary	186	Gearsham, Spear	2
Garret, Ralph	185	Geekie, James	248
Garret, Sarah	131	Gelff, Edward	286
Garret, William	15	Gelff, Mary	286
Garrett, Daniel	71	Genkkens, Margaret	367
Garrett, Easter	157	George, Ann	277
Garrett, Everard	82	GEORGE, DAVID	132
Garrett, Humphrey	131 (2)	George, David (son of David)	132
Garrett, Jane	131		
Garrett, Joshua Haughton	157	George, David	135, 277, 331
Garrett, Lettes	131	George, Elizabeth	132
Garrett, Mary	131	GEORGE, HENRY	132
Garrett, Prudence	131, 168	George, James	132, 278
Garrett, Sarah	131	George, John	210
GARRETT, THOMAS	131	George, Margaret	132
Garrett, Thomas (son of Thomas)	131	GERFORT, GREGORY	133
		Gerkin, Zacharial	34
Garrett, William	71, 199	Geralds Neck. land at	410
Garrgut and Mill Swamp, land between	411	Gerrard, Forbis	243
Garten, Alex.	316	Gerrard, George	347
Gary, Joseph	315	Gerrard, William	243
Garzia, John	315	GEWIN, CHRISTOPHER	133
Gaskill, Ann	183	Gewin, Christopher (son of Christopher)	133
Gaskill, Elizabeth	397		
Gaskill, Fane	132	Gibbs, George	148
Gaskill, Jane	132	Gibbs, Geo.	320
Gaskill, Jean	132	Gibbs, Henry, Jur.	195
Gaskill, Thomas	132, 315, 397	Gibbs, John	94, 106
		Gibbins, Henry	149

INDEX. 495

	PAGE.
Gibbins, Mark	32, 323
Gibble, Anna	4
GIBBLE, DEDERICK	133
Gibble, Dederick (son of Dederick)	133
Gibble, Frederick	4, 133
Gibble, Hannah	133
Gibble, Susannah	133
Gibbons, Stephen	377
Gibens, Mary	264
Gibeses Island, land on	413
GIBLE, DEDERICK	133
Gible, Dederik (son of Dederick)	133
Gible, Frederick	133
Gible, Mary (daughter of Dederick)	133
Gible, Mary (wife of Dederick)	133
Gibson, Elizabeth	105
Gibson, James	10 (2), 17 (3), 98, 122, 136, 169, 172, 260, 280, 313.
Gibson, Margaret	199
Gibson, Mary	18, 133 (2)
GIBSON, THOMAS	133
Gibson, Walter	133 (2), 199
Gibson, William	31
Giddings, Abraham	133
Giddings, Agnis	133
Giddings, Benjamin	133
Giddings, Elizabeth	133
Giddings, Darkis	133
Giddings, Frances	133
Giddings, Hugh	140
Giddings, Isaac	133
Giddings, Jacob	133 (2)
Giddings, John	133
Giddings, Lidea	133
GIDDINGS, THOMAS	133
Giddings, Thomas	133
Giddings, William	133
GIDDINGS, WILLIAM	133
Giddins, Margret	30
Giddins, William	13
Giddinses Point plantation	180
Gidgood, Benjamin	4
Gidon, Benjamin	82
Gidon, Johannah	82
Gilbart, Mary	306, 379
Gilberd, John	134
GILBERD, THOMAS	134
Gilberd, Thomas (son of Thomas)	134
Gilberd, William	134
Gilbert, Dinah	134

	PAGE.
Gilbert, Elizabeth	134
GILBERT, FRANCIS	134
Gilbert, Francis (son of Francis)	134
Gilbert, Francis	1
Gilbert, Frs.	38
Gilbert, Henry	134
Gilbert, Hannah	283
Gilbert, Jeremiah	134
Gilbert, Joseph	343
Gilbert, Josiah	56, 283
Gilbert, Mary	207
Gilbert, Sarah	207, 343
Gilbert, Thomas	250, 265, 343
Gilbert, Thos.	260
Gilbirt, Dinah	134
Gilbirt, Jeremiah	134
Gilbirt, Joel	134
Gilbirt, Joseph	134
GILBIRT, JOSIAH	134
Gilbirt, Thomas	134
Gilbirt, Sarah	134
Gilbord, Thomas	150
Giles, John	397
Giles, Mathias	190
Gilford, Isaac	122
Gilford, Joseph	134
GILFORD, JOHN	134
Gilford, Thomas	331
Gill, John	320
Gillagin, Alexr.	364
Gillam, Thomas	361
Gillespye, Lydia	64
Gillet, Betty	134
Gillet, Sarah	134
Gilleth, Walpolia	281 (2)
Gillett, Anderson	134 (2)
GILLETT, JOHN	134
GILLETT, JOHN	134
Gillett, John (son of John)	134
Gillett, John	177, 281, 336
Gillett, Moses	134 (3)
Gillett, Paterson	134
Gillett, Patterson	67, 134
Gilliam, John	308
Gillim, William	234
Gillitt, Elizabeth	104
Gillitt, John	104
Gillitt, Sarah (daughter of Thos. Dudley)	104
Gillitt, Sarah (granddaughter of Thomas Dudley)	104
Gillyam, Sarah	134
GILLYAM, THOMAS	134
Girkin, Hannah	27
Given, Allis	169

INDEX.

Gladstain, Geo..........120 (2)	Glyon, James 57
GLADSTAINE, GEORGE 134	Glyon, Mary 57
Gladstemis, George 384	Gobbee, Cary 292
Glair, Peter 67	Godard, Sarah 207
Glaister, Joseph....146 (2), 175, 201	Godbe, Cary 189
	Godbe, Henry 136
GLAISTER, MARY 135	Godby, Ann 136
Glaister, Mary..........146, 277	GODBY, CARY 136
Glascoe, Daniel 250	Godby, Elizabeth 136
Glascoine, Elizabeth 154	Godby, John 367
Glasco, Caleb 100	Godby, Mary 136
Glasco, Jan. 135	Godby, Rachel 136
GLASCO, ROBERT 135	Godby, Sarah 136
Glasgoe, Ruth 142	Godby, William 136
Glasgow, Abiah 135	Godfree, Elisabeth 142
Glasgow, Caleb 135	Godfrey, Ann 136
Glasgow, Elizabeth 135	Godfrey, Ellinor (wife of Thomas) 136
Glasgow, J. 48	
Glasgow, James 66	Godfrey, Ellinor (daughter of Thomas) 136
Glasgow, Lowdenner 135	
Glasgow, Sarah 135	Godfrey, Elizabeth 347
Glasgow, Susannah 135	Godfrey, Fillamer 136
GLASGOW, WILLIAM 135	GODFREY, FRANCIS 136
Glasson, Charity 274	Godfrey, Francis 136
Glaster (or Glauster), Ruth 135	Godfrey, James 136
Glaster (or Glauster), Sarah 135	Godfrey, Joane 136
Glauster, James 139	Godfrey, John......136, 329, 347
GLAUSTER, JOSEPH 135	Godfrey, Joseph........136, 272
Glauster, Mary 135	Godfrey, Lawrence 11
GLIN, RICHARD 135	Godfrey, Mathew 261
Glishan, Jean 135	Godfrey, Mathew 136
GLISHAN, JOHN 135	GODFREY, MATTEW 136
Gloster, Joseph 378	Godfrey, Peter 42
Gloster, Mary 378	Godfrey, P. 42
Gloster, Ruth 333	Godfrey, Pr. 389
Gloster, Sarah 266	Godfrey, Sarah..........136 (2)
Glover, Benjamin 135	GODFREY, THOMAS 136
Glover, Elizabeth 205	Godfrey, Thomas (son of Thomas) 136
Glover, George 135	
Glovers Hammock plantation 214	Godfrey, Thomas 22
	Godfrey, William...136 (2), 347
Glover, John.......135, 136, 273	Godly, Amy 136
Glover, Joseph 135	GODLY, JOHN 136
Glover, Mary 136	Godly, John (son of John).. 136
GLOVER (GLOVEYER), WILLIAM 135	Godly, Katherine 136
	Godly, Mary 136
Glover, William (son of William) 135	Godly, Nathan 136
	Godly, Thomas 136
Glover, William.....22, 136, 182	Godwin, Barnsby 137
Glover, Wm........301, 378, 407	Godwin, Bridget 60
Glover, W...1, 24, 29 (2), 30, 79, 81, 91, 105, 127, 130, 138, 155, 177, 182, 183, 189, 215, 261, 285, 366, 368, 383, 416.	Godwin, Courtney 137
	Godwin, Edmond 278
	Godwin, Joseph 60
	Godwin, Josias 137
Glyn, Elizabeth 135	Godwin, Julian 137
Glyon, Ego 57	Godwin, Kearney 137

INDEX. 497

	PAGE.
Godwin, Martha (wife of William)	137
Godwin, Martha (daughter of William)	137
Godwin, Mary (daughter of Nathan)	136
Godwin, Mary (wife of Nathan)	136
Godwin, Nathan	162
GODWIN, NATHAN	136
Godwin, Capt. Thomas	210
Godwin, Silvia	137
GODWIN, WILLIAM	137
Godwin, Willis	137
Goff, ———	313 (2)
Goffee, Anne	364
GOFFE, ARTHUR	137
Goldsmith, Daniel	229
Goldsmith, John Clark	105
GOMM, JOHN	137
Gomm, John	212
Gomm, Mary	137
GONSOLVO, LAURENCE	137
GONSOLVO, LAWRENCE	137
Gonsolvo, Lawrence	188
GONSOLVO, THOMAS	137
Good, Christian	234
Good, John	37
Good Neighborhood Branch, land on	342
GOODALL, GILBERT	137
Goodall, Gilbert	22
Goodall, John	374, 415
Gooden, John	154
Goodin, Pattrick	390
Goodin, Samuel	122
Goodin, Thomas	164
Gooding, Davenport	70, 116
Gooding, Jos.	47
Gooding, Thomas	107
Goodman, Henry, Sr.	290
Goodman, Henry	43, 141, 387, 423
Goodman, Henry, Jr.	290
Goodman, John	151
Goodman, Timothy	290
Goodson, Sarah	309
Goodson, Thomas	309
Goodwin, Wm.	261
Goold, Fr.	113
Goold, M.	61
Goold, The	206, 251
Goolde, Fre.	165
Gooldsberry, William	11
Goos Creek, land on	104
Goose Creek, land on	261, 380

	PAGE.
Goose Creek, plantation on	388
Goose Pond	408
Gorams Neck plantation	142
Gorden, Anne	17, 138
Gorden, Elizabeth	138
GORDEN, GEORGE	138
Gorden, George	138, 425
Gorden, Hanner	138
Gorden, John	93
GORDEN, NATHANIEL	138
Gorden, Nathaniel	138
Gorden, Sarah	93
Gorden, Tamer	138 (2)
Gorden, William	93 (2), 138
Gordin, George	126
Gording, George	182
Gordon, David	163
Gordon, George	138 (2), 269
Gordon, Jacob	138
GORDON, JOHN	138
Gordon, John (son of John),	138 (2)
Gordon, John, Sr.	269
Gordon, John, Jr.	269
Gordon, John	270
Gordon, Joseph	270
Gordon, Mary	80, 138 (2), 177
Gordon, Nathanell	138
GORDON, PATRICK	138
Gordon, Patrick	313
Gordon, Peter	313
Goreham, Elinor	137
GOREHAM, JOHN	137
Goreham, John (nephew of John)	137
Goremge, Charles	210
Gormack, Elizabeth	138
Gormack, Joane	138
GORMACK, PATRICK	138
Gormacke, Pat	302
Gormacke, Patrick	303
Gorman, John	26
Gorman, Michl.	23
GOSBE, JOHN	138
Gosbe, John (son of John)	138
Goshaen, land at Mattehapungo, known as	35
Goshan, land at Matchepungo, known as	35
Gough, Robert	138
Gough, Sarah (wife of Thomas)	138
Gough, Sarah (daughter of Thomas)	138
GOUGH, THOMAS	138

32

	PAGE.
Gould, George	147
Goulds plantation	108
Gourdon, John	178, 397
Gourlay, John	339
Gourley, Elizabeth	139
Gourley, George	139
Gourley, Grisle	139
GOURLEY, JOHN	139
Gourley, Mary	139
Goutey, Andrew	369
Gowel, John	2
Grace, Luke	287
Gracey, Robert	98
Gradless, Timothy	78
Grady, An	19
Grainger, Ann	139
Grainger, Col. Caleb	102
GRAINGER, CALEB	139
Grainger, Caleb (son of Caleb)	139
Grainger, Caleb..54, 61, 102, 105, 139, 179	
Grainger, Cornelius	102
Grainger, Cornelius Harnett	139
Grainger, Elizabeth	139
Grainger, Josa	100
GRAINGER, JOSHUA	139
Grainger, Joshua (son of Joshua)	139
Grainger, Mary (wife of Caleb)	139
Grainger, Mary (daughter of Caleb)	139
Grainger, Mary....105, 139, 392 (2)	
Grainger, Thos.	277
Grainger, William	139
Graham, George	174
Grahams Place, plantation	230
Grahms, George	121
Granade, Gasper	315
Granade, John...28, 49, 174, 204, 205, 314, 326, 361	
Granbary, Frances	139
Granbary, John	139
GRANBARY, SAMUEL	139
Granbary, William	139
Granberry, Mary	283
Granberry, William	283
Grandin, Daniell	185, 207
Grandy, Charles	328
Grandy, Sarah	142
Grandy, Thomas	111
Grange, Hugh	139

	PAGE.
Grange, James (son of John)	139
Grange, James (brother of John)	139
Grange, James	141
GRANGE, JOHN	139
Grange, John (son of John)	139
Grange, John	338
GRANT, ALEXANDER	139
Grant, Alexander (son of Alexander)	139
Grant, Alexander	140
Grant, Experience	172
Grant, John	139, 140
Grant, Mary	139
Grant, Reuben	172
Grant, Solomon	139
Grant, Stephen	212
GRANT, WILLIAM	140
Granville Court House	108
Grassie Point, land at	416
Grassy Point land	368
Grassy Ridge land	419
Grave, George	188
Gravenor, Hester	117
Graves, Ann	140
Graves, Francis	140
Graves, Hannah	140
Graves, Mary	140
GRAVES, RICHARD	140
GRAVES, RICHARD	140
Graves, Richard (nephew of Richard)	140
Graves, Richard...149, 214, 343	
Graves, Sarah	147, 383
Graves, Thomas (son of Richard)	140
Graves, Thomas (brother of Richard)	140
Graves, Thomas....153, 267, 364, 383 (2)	
Gray, Abraham	77
GRAY, ALEN	140
Gray, Amelia	141, 423
GRAY, ANN	140
Gray, Ann (wife of John)	141
Gray, Ann (daughter of John)	141
Gray, Ann (daughter of Richard)	141
Gray, Ann (wife of Richard)	141
Gray, Ann	112, 242
Gray, Barbara	141

INDEX. 499

	PAGE.
Gray, Charity	328
Gray, Cornelius	77
Gray, Elinor	140
Gray, Elizabeth..46, 77, 140,	154
Gray, Geo.	95
Gray, Godfrey	137
GRAY, GRIFEN	140
Gray, Grifen (son of Grifen)	140
Gray, Griffith..176, 328, 329,	385
Gray, Hannah	140
Gray, Hannar	140
Gray, Henry	137
Gray, Hugh	140
GRAY, JAMES	140
Gray, James (son of James)	140
Gray, James	140
Gray, Maj. Joseph	202
Gray, Jenot	140
GRAY, JOHN (Surveyor)	141
Gray, John (son of John)	141
Gray, John, Sr.	142
Gray, John, Jr.	88
Gray, John.......73, 78, 88, 94, 115, 140, 191, 235, 244, 318, 352, 406.	
Gray, Louisa.........141,	424
Gray, Lucretia........141,	423
Gray, Mary (wife of Alen)	140
Gray, Mary (daughter of Alen)	140
Gray, Mary............141,	176
Gray, Peter, Jr.	205
Gray, Priscilla	142
Gray, Rebeckah	77
GRAY, RICHARD	141
Gray, Richard (son of Richard)	141
Gray, Richard......112, 140,	303
Gray, Sarah............140,	339
Gray, Thomas	140
Gray, William..46, 115, 140, 141, 244 (2), 417,	423
Gray, Wm.........113, 120,	234
Gready, Katherine	94
Gready, Mary	94
Great Branch, land on...13,	363
Great Bridge, land on road to	167
Great Bridges, land at	241
Great Flatty Creek, plantation at mouth of	132
Great Island	328
Great Neck, land on	227
Great Pocoson, land on	327

	PAGE.
Great Quonkee, mill on	233
Great Quarter plantation	293
Great Swamp, land in	114
Great Swamp, land on	274
Greaves, James	65
Greaves, Robert	354
Green, A.	147
Green, Amy	276
Green, Ann	21
Green, Anthony	212
Green, Catherine	141
Green, Edward	366
Green, Elizabeth	175
Green, Elee (or Else), (wife of Richard)	141
Green, Else (daughter of Richard)	141
Green, Farnifold	188
Green, Farld	335
Green, Fernifold	140
Green, Francis	276
Green, Furnifold......207,	232
Green, Henry	280
GREEN, JACOB	141
Green, Jacob	141
Green, James..140, 141, 149, 313,	364
GREEN, JOHN	141
Green, John (son of John)	141
Green, John, Sr.	242
Green, John.....2, 141, 313, 353 (2), 397,	417
Green, Leonard	141
Green, Lucy	2
Green, Mary...........141,	147
Green, Moses	399
Green, Peter	76
Green Pond Neck plantation	84
GREEN, RICHARD	141
Green, Robert 36,	141
Green, Dr. Samuell	257
Green, Samuell	139
Green, Sam'll	56
Green, Sarah	141
GREEN, SUSANNAH	141
Green, Thomas 141	(3)
Green, Thos.	36
Green, Timothy	133
Green, William.....141 (2),	380
Greenaway, Benjn	313
Greenhall, plantation in	38
Greens Creek, land on	271
Grefen, Martin (son of Martin)	143

	PAGE.
Gregg, Frederick	320 (3), 418
Gregg, Fredk.	49
Gregorie, James	351, 384
Gregory, Affiah	142
Gregory, Anne	142, 143
Gregory, Barbra	142
Gregory, Caleb	18, 142
Gregory, Charity	142
Gregory, Charles	198
Gregory, Cornelius	142
Gregory, Dempsey	142
Gregory, Demsey	141
Gregory, Elizabeth (wife of Samuel)	142
Gregory, Elizabeth (daughter of Samuel)	142
Gregory, Frederick	142
Gregory, Griffith	142
Gregory, Isaac	141, 142
Gregory, Jacob	142 (2)
Gregory, James	142 (4), 151
Gregory, Jas.	200
Gregory, Job	142 (2)
Gregory, John	142 (2), 225
Gregory, Joseph	142
GREGORY, JUDATH	141
Gregory, Judith	143
Gregory, Luke	142, 171, 284, 300, 407
Gregory, Lovey	141, 143
Gregory, Nathan	142
GREGORY, MARGARET	142
Gregory, Margaret	18 (2)
Gregory, Mark	142
Gregory, Mary	141, 142, 143, 160, 283
Gregory, Matthew	410 (2)
Gregory, Miriam	283
Gregory, Priscilla	18
GREGORY, RICHARD	142
Gregory, Richard	142 (2)
Gregory, Richard	130
Gregory, Robert	142 (2), 305
Gregory, Sampson	142
GREGORY, SAMUEL	142
Gregory, Samuell (son of Samuel)	142
Gregory, Sarah	142, 279, 407
GREGORY, THOMAS	142
Gregory, Thomas	142
Gregory, Thos.	130
GREGORY, WILLIAM	142
GREGORY, WILLIAM	142
Gregory, William	142 (2), 422
Gregory, Will	32, 132, 384

	PAGE.
Gregory, W.	257
Greves, James	313, 329
Greves, Katherine	313
Grey, Peter, Jr.	226
Grey, Peter, Sr.	205, 226
Grey, Peter	69
Grice, Elizabeth (wife of Francis)	143
Grice, Elizabeth (daughter of Francis)	143
Grice, Faith	143
GRICE, FRANCIS	143
Grice, Jacob	143
Grice, James	143
Grice, John	143, 325
Grice, Robert	143 (2)
Grice, Thomas	143
Grice, William	143
Grifen, Benjamin	280
Grifen, Edward	143
Grifen, Elizabeth (wife of Martin)	143
Grifen, Elizabeth (daughter of Martin)	143
Grifen, John	143
GRIFEN, MARTIN	143
Grifen, Martin (son of Martin)	143
GRIFEN, RICHARD	143
Grifen, Sarah	143
Grifen, William	143
Griffen, Andrew	143
Griffen, Ann (daughter of Epenetus)	143
Griffen, Ann (wife of Epenetus)	143
Griffen, Edward	130
Griffen, Elisabeth	143
Griffen, Elizabeth	129
GRIFFEN, EPENETUS	143
Griffen, Epenetus (son of Epenetus)	143
Griffen, Henry	280
Griffen, James	24
Griffen, John	143
Griffen, Matthew	143
Griffeth, Arther	144
Griffeth, Edmond	144
Griffeth, Jemima	144
GRIFFETH, JOHN	144
Griffeth, John	144
Griffeth, Mary	144
Griffin, Ann	143
Griffin, Betty	182
Griffin, Charles	1

INDEX. 501

	PAGE.
GRIFFIN, EDWARD	143
Griffin, Edward (son of Edward)	143
Griffin, Elisabeth	160
Griffin, Elizabeth	148
Griffin, Elizabeth Hammond	182
Griffin, Grace	143
GRIFFIN, JAMES	143
Griffin, James (son of James)	143
Griffin, James	165, 182
Griffin, John	143 (2), 293
Griffin, Joseph	143
Griffin, Lydia	144
Griffin, Mary	33, 143, 144
Griffin, Sarah	116, 143 (2)
GRIFFIN, WILLIAM	144
GRIFFIN (GRIFFON), WILLIAM	144
Griffin, William (son of William)	144
Griffin, William	143 (2), 379
Griffing, George	158
Griffith, Edward	362
Griffith, William	326
Griggs, Elizabeth	144
GRIGGS, SAMUEL	144
GRILLS, RICHARD	144
Grills, Sarah	144
GRIMES, ABSOLOM	144
Grimes, Lidea	144
Grindale Creek, land on	303
Grindell Creek, land on	350
Grisard, Thos.	133
Grising, James	33
Grist, Frances	144
Grist, John	144
Grist, Mary	144
GRIST, RICHARD	144
Grist, Richard	144
Grist, William	144
Groenendeyk, Cornelius	127
Groome, Moses	29
Grosvenor, Elizabeth	144
Grosvenor, Ester	144
Grosvenor, Sarah	144
Grosvenor, Susannah	144
Grosvenor, William	144
Grosvenor, Wm.	62
Grove, Richd.	133
Groveley plantation	12
Grum, Henry	280
Guerad, Paul	139
Guie, James	23
GUILLIAMS, GEORGE	145

	PAGE.
Guilliams, George (son of George)	145 (2)
Guilliams, Isaac	145
Guilliams, Samuel	145 (3)
Gulliver, Wm.	230
Gumberry plantation	328
Gumbridge Branch, land on	384
Gumbs, Abraham	145 (2)
Gumbs, Elisha	145 (2)
Gumbs, Leah	145
GUMBS, MATTHEW	145
Gumbs, Rachel	145
Gumbs, Ruth	145
Gumbs, Sarah	145
Gum Pole Swamp, land on	50
Gum Swamp, land on	70
Gum Swamp and Bull Branch, land on	70
Gunnette, George	423
GUNTER, JOHN	145
Gurganus, Joseph	236
GUTAN, JOSEPH	145
Gutan, Rebecca	145
Guthray, John	397
Guthrie, Daniel	118, 161
Guthrie, Dan'l.	154, 270
GUTHRIE, JOHN	145
Guthrie, Samuel	359
Guy, Briggit	145
Guy Hall Swamp, plantation on	77
Guy, James	145
Guy, James (son of James)	145
Guy, John	145
Guy, Mary	145
Guy, William	145
Guyor, Nicholas	317
Gwinn, William	269
Habel, Wm.	372
HACKLEFIELD, JOHN	145
Hackman, Thomas	195 (2)
Hackney, Jenings	109
Hackney, Samuel	109
Hadley, Edward	19
Hadley, Edwd.	24, 26, 64, 107, 382
Hadley, Keziah	13
Hadley, Keziah	145
Hagin, Marten	242
Haghton (or Raghton), Tho.	133
Haig, Ann	146
HAIG, MARY	146
Haig, Mary (daughter of William)	146

INDEX.

	PAGE.
Haig, Mary (wife of William)	146
Haig, Sarah	146 (3)
HAIG, WILLIAM	146
HAIG, WILLIAM	146
Haig, William (son of William)	146 (3)
Haig, William (son of Mary)	146
Haig, William	146, 275
Haile, Benja	238
Haile, Benjamin	347
Haile, Hanna	111
Hailes, John	293
Haines, Aliss	421
Haines, Erasmus	421
Haines, Robert	411
Hair, James	312
Hairs, William	408
HAKONY, JOHN	146
Hakony, John (son of John)	146
Halcey, John	111
Halfe-Way House plantation	293
Hale, Elizabeth	384
Hale, John	164
Hale, William	123
Hale's plantation	38
Haliday, Gilbert	215 (2)
Haliday, Gi	403
HALL, AN	146
Hall, Ann	54, 146, 247
Hall, Benjamin	147
Hall, Clement	83
Hall, Clemt	327
Hall, Danell	372
Hall, Danl	300
Hall, Dolly	248
Hall, Ebenezer	14
Hall, Edward	147 (2), 157 (2)
Hall, Elinor	147
Hall, Elizabeth	33, 93, 147, 178
Hall, Enoch	7
Hall, Enoch	14, 30, 142
Hall, E	2, 53, 133, 175 (2), 227, 271, 299, 306, 314, 345, 350, 370, 409.
Hall, Hannah	262
Hall, Henry	157
HALL, HEZEKIAH	146
Hall, Jane	147
Hall, J	158
HALL, JOHN	146
Hall, John	35
HALL, JOSEPH	147
Hall, Joseph	147
Hall, Lucy	374
Hall, Mary	146, 157
HALL, NATHANIEL	147
Hall, Natt	167
Hall, Priscilla	134
Hall, Rachel	157
Hall, Robert	68, 334
Hall, Samuel	146, 185
Hall, Sarah	146
Hall, Thos	34, 95, 178, 262, 338, 374
HALL, WILLIAM	147
Hall, William	33, 111, 147
Hall, Will	247
Hall, Wm	89
Hallan, John	391
Hallands, Jehoshaphat	338, 396
Halle, Edward	207
Halliday, Gi	369, 393
Halliman, Saml	166
Hallis, Ann	34
Halloman, Christofer	59
Hallowell, Thomas	40
Hallsey, Daniell	90, 168
Hallsey, John	118
Hallsey, Wm	118
Halsbrook, Joseph	77
HALSEY, DANIEL	147
Halsey, John	8, 117, 157, 171, 268, 269, 317, 423
Halsey, J	36, 63, 68
Halsey, Mary	147, 269
Halsey, Will	9, 28, 32, 36, 38, 44, 47, 130, 145, 171, 192, 269, 282, 317, 323, 366, 404.
Halsted, Drew	416
Halton, Elizabeth	147
Halton, Jno	205 (2)
Halton, Mary (sister of Robt.)	147
Halton, Mary (wife of Robert)	147
HALTON, ROBERT	147
Halton, Robert, Jr	147
Halton, Robert	92, 348 (2)
Halton, Robt	96, 113
Haltons Lodge	147
Haman, Henry	379
Haman, Jane	147
Haman, Joseph	147
Haman, Luke	4
Haman, Sarah (wife of Thomas)	147

INDEX. 503

	PAGE.
Haman, Sarah (daughter of Thomas)	147
HAMAN, THOMAS	147
Hambleton, Elizabeth	238
HAMBLETON, JANE	148
HAMBLETON, JOSEPH	147
Hambleton, Rachell	147
Hamblin, Elizabeth	148
Hamblin, John	148
Hamblin, Martha (daughter of Thomas)	148
Hamblin, Martha (wife of Thomas)	148
HAMBLIN, THOMAS	148
Hamer, John	76
Hamilton, Andrew	148
Hamilton, Catherine	148
Hamilton, Douglas	249
Hamilton, Esabel	148
Hamilton, Esther	148
Hamilton, James	148 (2), 342
HAMILTON, JOHN	148
HAMILTON, JOHN	148
HAMILTON, JOHN	148
Hamilton, John (son of Jno.)	148
Hamilton, John	305
Hamilton, Mary	125, 148
Hamilton, Stewart	148
Hamilton, William	148
Hamlin, Thos	283
Hamlin, Thomas	237
Hammond Creek, land on	61
Hammond, Martha	153
Hammontree, Rubin	16
Hampton, Leey	158
Han, William	10
Hanah, John	11
Hanbox (or Hancox), Jacob	174
Hanbury, Juda	129
Hanby, Amee	246
Hanby, Demsie	148
Hanby, Hannah	148
HANBY, JOHN	148
Hanby, John (grandson of John)	148
Hanby, Mary	148
Hanby, Salvanias	148
Hanby, Selvanus	148
Hanby, William	246
Hancock, Ann	149
Hancock, Benjamin	149 (3)
Hancock, Eliz	164
HANCOCK, HECTOR	149

	PAGE.
Hancock, Henry	149
Hancock, John	149, 258
Hancock, Joseph	149
Hancock, Ledlay	149
Hancock, Mary	149
Hancock, Nathaniel	149 (3)
Hancock, Stephen	215
Hancock, Will	158
Hancock, William	149
Hand, Ann	149
Hand, Elizabeth	149
Hand, Jane	53
Hand, Jean	149
Hand, Mary	149
HAND, PETER	149
Hand, Peter	96, 113, 205
Handcock, Derham	363
Handcock, Elenor	149
HANDCOCK, ELISEBETH	149
Handcock, Elizabeth	149
Handcock, John	149
Handcock, Mary	149
HANDCOCK, WILLIAM	149
Handcock, William (son of William)	149 (2)
Handcock, William (grandson of William)	149
Handcock, William	260
Handcock, Capt. William	343
Handcock, Wm	219
Handley, George	265
HANDWORKER, DANIEL	149
Handworker, Katherine	149
Haner, Elizabeth	274
Hanford, P	195
Hanmore, Daniel	382
Hanmore, Elizabeth	382
Hannis, Catherine	149
HANNIS, JOSEPH	149
Hannis, Joseph (son of Joseph)	149
Hannis, Joseph, Sr.	62
Hannis, Joseph	62, 217, 404
Hannis, Joseph, Jr.	405
Hannis, Katherine	217
Hannis, Madam	404
Hanreffe, Stephen	402
Hansley, John	275
Haraery, Sol	176
HARBERT, EDWARD	149
Harbert, Edward (son of Edward)	149 (2)
Harbert, John	149
Harbertt, Mary	41
Hardee, Cleare	354

504 INDEX.

	PAGE.
Hardee, John..209, 345, 350,	354
Hardee, Jno.	377
Hardesty, Anna	150
Hardesty, Dorotha	150
Hardesty, Joseph	150
Hardesty, Lucy	150
Hardesty, Mary	150
Hardesty, Robert	150
Hardesty, Samuel	150
HARDESTY, THOMAS	150
Hardesty, Thomas (son of Thomas)	150
Hardie, Geo.	151
Hardie, George	217
Hardin, Jane	150
Hardin, Mr.	49
HARDIN, WILLIAM	150
Harding, Ann	150
Harding, James	150
HARDING, JOSIAH	150
Harding, Josiah (son of Josiah)	150
HARDING, MARY	150
Harding, Mary	150
Harding, Rebecca	142
HARDING, RICHARD	150
Harding, Thomas...128, 150,	353
Hardings plantation	295
Hardison, Charles 150,	222
Hardison, Frederick	331
Hardison, Hardy	331
Hardison, Jaspar (son of Jasper)	150
HARDISON, JASPER	150
Hardison, Jasper	132
Hardison, Capt. John	104
Hardison, John.....132, 150 (2),	367
Hardison, Joseph 132,	150
Hardison, Josuah	150
Hardison, Mary	150
Hardison, Richard......132,	150
Hardison, Thomas......132,	150
Hardley, Francis	420
Hardy, Elizabeth...150, 242,	306
Hardy, Frances	306
Hardy, Jacob	150
HARDY, JOHN	150
Hardy, John....59, 158, 189, 214, 260,	346
Hardy, Jos..............203,	252
Hardy, J.	312
Hardy, Lamb......163, 280,	306
Hardy, Mary	150
Hardy, Prudence	346

	PAGE.
Hardy, Rebecca.........151,	214
HARDY, RICHARD	151
Hardy, Rd.	67
Hardy, Robert	164
Hardy, Samuel	120
Hardy, Saml.	384
Hardy, Sarah	151
Hardy, Thomas	150
Hardy, William..53 (2), 150, 151, 293,	306
Hardy, Wm........120, 384	(2)
Hare, Bryan...151 (3), 398,	426
HARE, EDWARD	151
HARE, EDWARD	151
Hare, Edward (son of Edward) 151	(2)
Hare, Edward	364
Hare, Edward, Jr.	364
Hare, Edward Bryan	151
Hare, John.........151 (3),	194
Hare, Lucretia	151
Hare, Mary 151	(2)
Hare, Moses............240,	243
Hare, Mourning	131
Hare, Penelope	251
Hare, Thomas..........151	(3)
Hare, William	243
Hareck, Sarah	243
Hareck, Richard	243
Haren, Richard	55
Harendeen, Matthew	56
Harenton, Charles	78
Hargrove, Benjamin	424
Hargrove, Robert	427
Hargrove, Robt.	427
Harison, Elizabeth	151
HARISON, JOHN	151
Harison, John (son of John)	151
Harison, Mary	151
Harison, Thomas	151
Harison, William	151
Harkel, Elisabeth	151
HARKEL, GEORGE	151
Harkel, George (son of George)	151
Harkel, Joseph	151
Harkel, Margaret	151
Harkel, Mary	151
Harkel, Miriam	151
Harker, Ebenezer	152
HARKER, ELIZABETH	152
Harker, Henry	301
Harker, James 152	(2)
Harker, Sarah	152

INDEX. 505

Harker, Zachariah 152 (2)
Harla, James 398
Harlee, John 70
Harloe, Jno................. 358
Harloe, Thomas 349
Harlors Creek, land on..... 40
Harlow, Eliza 163
Harlow, Wm................ 132
Harlston, Mrs. Mary........ 5
HARMAN, CALEB 152
Harman, Caleb (son of
  Caleb) 152
Harman, Caleb 152 (2)
Harman, Elizabeth...60, 152 (2)
Harman, James 152
Harman, John 92, 152, 345
Harman, Joshua....... 152, 360
Harman, Mary.......92, 152 (2)
Harman, Orpah 152
HARMAN, ROBERT 152
Harman, Robert.....92, 152,
  215, 220, 389
Harman, Stephen 152
Harman, Thomas........152 (2)
Harnett, Cornelius....49, 56, 61
  (2), 105, 139, 168, 241, 248, 257,
  265, 320, 369, 418.
Harnett, Elizabeth 123
Harold, William 7
Harper, Edward 375
Harper, George 252
Harper, John............67, 134
Harper, Nicholas 151
Harper, Robert 17
Harrell, Abbagill 152
Harrell, Abbe (or Able)..152 (2)
Harrell, Abell 133
HARRELL, ABRAHAM 152
Harrell, Abraham 271
Harrell, Adam 352
Harrell, Ann 152, 153
Harrell, Benjamin 152
Harrell, Christopher 133, 152
Harrell, David 153 (2)
HARRELL, EDWARD 152
Harrell, Elisha 152
Harrell, Eliza 352
Harrell, Esias 153
Harrell, Esias (deceased).. 153
Harrell, Ezekiel 153
Harrell, Francis 271
Harrell, George 152 (2)
Harrell, Grace 152
Harrell, Henry 152 (2)
Harrell, Israel Hardy...152 (2)

Harrell, Jesse (brother of
  John) 152
Harrell, Jesse (son of John) 152
Harrell, Jesse 152, 153 (2)
HARRELL, JOHN 152
HARRELL, JOHN 153
Harrell, John..152 (3), 166,
  271, 410, 425
Harrell, Jno.............213, 425
Harrell, Joshewa 152
HARRELL, JOSIAH 153
Harrell, Josiah (son of
  Josiah) 153
Harrell, Josiah..........153 (2)
Harrell, William 153
Harrell, Zachariah 152
Harrell, Lot 133, 152
Harrell, Mary (wife of
  John) 152
Harrell, Mary (daughter of
  John) 152
Harrell, Mary 133, 410
Harrell, Sarah 153
Harrell, Solomon 153
Harrell, Susannah 152
Harrell, Thomas....152, 353 (2)
Harrell, Thos...........141 (2)
Harren, Joseph 348
Harren, Robert 159
Harres, John 23
Harrill, Abram 95
Harrill, Adham 352
Harrill, Thomas 95
HARRINGTON, HUMPHREY ... 153
Harrington, Ann 153
Harrington, Charles 241
Harrington, Elizabeth 153
Harris, Art................. 307
Harris, Arthr.............. 308
Harris, Cheary 153
Harris, David 42
Harris, Elender............ 153
Harris, Eli 153
Harris, George, Sr......... 138
Harris, George, Jr......138, 303
Harris, George..65, 302 (2), 303
Harris, Jacob 58
HARRIS, JAMES 153
Harris, James (son of
  James) 153
Harris, James 382
HARRIS, JOHN 153
Harris, John..167, 282, 309,
  320, 391
Harris, J.................. 146

	PAGE.
Harris, Liddy	135
Harris, Major	354
Harris, Morning	136
Harris, Samuel	136
Harris, Sarah	216
HARRIS, THOMAS	153
Harris, Thomas (son of Thomas)	153
Harris, Thomas....125, 136, 146, 182, 251,	344
Harris, Thos.	401
Harris, William........329,	393
Harris, Wm.............108,	109
Harrison, Chas.	257
HARRISON, DANIEL	153
Harrison, Edmond	154
Harrison, Edward, Jr.	180
Harrison, Edward	88
Harrison, Elizabeth..153, 154,	167
Harrison, Frances	190
Harrison, Francis	339
HARRISON, JOHN	154
Harrison, John	389
Harrison, Joseph...153, 154,	287
Harrison, Joshuay	154
Harrison, Lidy	22
HARRISON, ROBERT	154
Harrison, Robert (son of Robert) 154	(2)
Harrison, Robert........158,	379
Harrison, Sarah (wife of Robert)	154
Harrison, Sarah (daughter of Robert)	154
Harrison, Sarah........158,	379
Harrison, Thomas	154
HARRISON, VINES	154
Harrison, William........154,	244
Harrison, Wm.	92
Harriss, Job 47	(2)
Harriss, John	235
Harriss, Thomas	26
Harold, Elizabeth	127
Harron, Joseph 86,	299
Harrow plantation	163
Harrys Creek, land on	420
Harrys, Thomas	60
Hart, Benjamin.........154	(2)
Hart, David............154	(2)
Hart, Henry...........154,	166
Hart, Jesse.............154	(2)
HART, JOHN	154
Hart, John.............154	(2)
Hart, Josee	154
Hart, Josiah........61, 178,	367

	PAGE.
Hart, Luce	154
Hart, Lusee	154
HART, MARY	154
Hart, Mary	154
Hart, Richard...........53,	149
Hart, Sarah............154	(2)
Hart, Susannah	388
HART, THOMAS	154
Hart, Thomas	2
HARTLEY, FRANCIS	154
Hartley, Francis	217
Hartley, Rd.	254
Hartley, Susannah	154
Hartley, Thomas	352
Hartlock, Elizabeth	44
Hartsell, Henry	322
Hartshorn, Elizabeth	158
Hartshorn, Joyce	158
Hartshorn, Thomas	158
Harvey, Col.	87
Harvey, Mr.	330
Harvey, Afereca	304
Harvey, Arthur	155
Harvey, Benjamin..155, 156,	341
Harvey, Bridget	155
HARVEY, DOROTY	155
Harvey, Elizabeth...... 156,	327
Harvey, Eliz.	46
Harvey, Francis	155
Harvey, James	155
HARVEY, JOHN	155
Harvey, John (grandson of John)	155
Harvey, John (brother of Thomas)	156
Harvey, John (nephew of Thomas)	156
Harvey, John (decd.)	155
Harvey, John..20, 155 (2), 196, 198, 202, 251, 287 (2), 291, 324 (2), 341 (4), 358.	
Harvey, John Mark......155	(2)
Harvey, Joshua	155
Harvey, Josias	155
Harvey, Lamll.	231
Harvey, Lemll.	282
Harvey, Mary......155 (2),	297
Harvey, Miles.....7, 17 (2), 116, 134, 138 (2), 152, 155, 156, 157, 161, 206, 221, 243, 253, 254, 259, 260, 265, 284 (2), 285, 301, 314, 317, 321 (2), 324, 358, 411, 419.	
Harvey, M.	122
Harvey, Peter	155
Harvey, Rebecca	155
HARVEY, RICHARD	155

INDEX.

	PAGE.
Harvey, Richard (son of Richard)	155
Harvey, Richard (brother of Richard)	155
Harvey, Richard.21, 155 (2),	202
Harvey, Richd.	231
Harvey, Robert	155
Harvey, Samuel	155
Harvey, Sam'l	44, 155
Harvey, Sarah	155, 206
HARVEY, THOMAS	155
HARVEY, THOMAS	155
HARVEY, THOMAS	156
Harvey, Thomas (nephew of Thomas)	155, 156
Harvey, Thomas (son of Thomas)	155 (2)
Harvey, Thomas.....46 (2), 154, 340,	399
Harvey, Thos...155, 261, 327	(2)
Harvy, Miles	112
Harwell, Elizabeth	100
HARWOOD, EDWARD	156
Hase, William	131
Hasell, James, Jr.	258
Hasell, James........99, 257,	318
Hasell, Jas.....191, 259, 312, 335,	390
Hasell, John	278
Hasell, Mary	6
Hasell, Susann	5, 6 (2)
Hasell, Mrs. Susannah	257
Haskens, Sarah	400
Hasket, Joshua	36, 255
Hasket, William	260
Hasking, Wm.	406
HASKINS, HANNIBAL	156
"Haskins land"	48
Haskins, mill at	218
Haskins, William.....70, 83,	157
Haskit, Abraham	112
Haskit, Anne	70
Haskit, Anthony	70
Haskit, Tabitha	70
Haskit, William	259, 285
Haslen, Thos.	64
Hassale, Thomas	24
Hassell, Benjamin	156
Hassell, Caswell	66
Hassell, Esther	156
Hassell, Isaac	156
Hassell, James	5 (2)
HASSELL, JOHN	156
Hassell, John (son of John)	156
Hassell, Joseph	156
Hassell, Rachell	156

	PAGE.
Hassold, Thomas	404
Hassold, Tho.	344
Hastel, John	134
Hastine, Dr. Thomas	23
Hastings, Samuel	329
Hastins, Thomas	329
HATCH, ANTHONY	156
HATCH, ANTHONY	157
Hatch, Anthony (son of Anthony)	156
Hatch, Anthony.....86, 157, 291, 312, 409,	423
Hatch, Antho.	272
Hatch, Arthur	59
Hatch, Durant	157
Hatch, Edmund....3 (2), 7, 8, 9, 10, 17 (2), 18 (3), 21, 24, 34, 36, 37, 40, 42, 55, 56, 63 (2), 70, 94, 111, 113, 118, 122, 123, 124, 136, 138, 146, 148, 150, 156 (2), 157 (3), 158, 160, 161, 169 (2), 172 (2), 173, 185, 194, 196 (2), 198, 202, 216, 220, 243, 245, 249, 253, 254 (2), 255 (2), 259, 260, 263 (2), 264, 267 (2), 269 (2), 270, 280, 282, 285, 286, 287, 290, 309, 313, 324 (2), 325, 330, 341 (3), 351 (2), 358, 360, 363, 368, 383, 394, 400, 401, 407, 409, 416 (2), 419 (3), 420.	
Hatch, Edmd.	157 (2)
Hatch, Elisabeth (wife of Anthony)	156
Hatch, Elisabeth (daughter of Anthony)	156
Hatch, Elizabeth	157 (2)
Hatch, John	157 (3), 409
Hatch, Joy	157
Hatch, Lamb	156
HATCH, LEMUEL	157
Hatch, Lemuel (son of Lemuel)	157 (2)
Hatch, Lemuel	407 (2), 410
Hatch, Mary (wife of Lemuel)	157
Hatch, Mary (daughter of Lemuel)	157
Hatch, Mary	124
Hatch, Samell	49
Hatch, Sarah	410
Hatcher, John	382
Hath (Heath), Robert	160
Hatteras Banks, land at	389
HATTON, JOHN	157
HAUGHTON, CHARLES	157

508 INDEX.

Haughton, Charles (son of Charles) 157
Haughton, Charles 157
Haughton, David 158
Haughton, Easter 158
Haughton, Elizabeth.....157 (2)
HAUGHTON, GEORGE 157
HAUGHTON, JAMES 157
Haughton, James 158
Haughton, Jeremiah.....157 (2), 215
Haughton, Job. 158
Haughton, John 157
Haughton, Jonathan 158
Haughton, Joshua 158
Haughton, Judith 157
Haughton land 34
Haughton, Levy 268, 360
Haughton, Mary (wife of William) 158
Haughton, Mary (granddaughter of William)..... 158
Haughton, Mary 158
Haughton, Rachel 158
HAUGHTON, RICHARD 158
Haughton, Richard (son of Richard) 158
Haughton, Sarah 158
Haughton, Thomas 157
Haughton, Tho. 188
HAUGHTON, WILLIAM 158
Haughton, William 158
HAUSINGTON, BENIDICTUS ... 158
Hausington, Cattern 158
Hausington, Dinah (wife of Benedictus) 158
Hausington, Dinah (daughter of Benedictus) 158
Hausington, Elisebeth 158
Hausington, Mary 158
Hausington, Sarah 158
Haward, James 60
Hawes, Elizabeth 90
Haw Fields, land at........ 292
Hawett, Willm............. 281
Hawk, Mary 346
Hawkins, Anne 158
Hawkins, Benjamin 380
Hawkins, Daniel.....69 (2), 288
Hawkins, Elizabeth (wife of Thomas) 159
Hawkins, Elizabeth (daughter of Thomas).......... 159
Hawkins, Elizabeth 360
Hawkins, Eliz. 35
Hawkins, Humphrey 304

Hawkins, James....158, 220, 360
HAWKINS, JOHN 158
HAWKINS, JOHN 158
HAWKINS, JOHN 158
Hawkins, John (son of John) 177
Hawkins, John....12, 23, 35, 73, 155, 177, 189, 248, 253, 389 (2)
Hawkins, Jno. 305
Hawkins, Joshua 158
Hawkins, Mary (wife of John) 158
Hawkins, Mary (daughter of John) 158
Hawkins, Mary.....23, 158, 159
Hawkinses Neck, plantation, 119
HAWKINS, SARAH 158
Hawkins, Sarah....159, 195, 253
Hawkins, Solomon 198
HAWKINS, THOMAS 159
Hawkins, Thomas (son of Thomas) 159
Hawkins, Thomas..177, 195, 360, 389
Hawks, John............80, 127
Hawks, Mary 2
Hawley, Ann 159
Hawley, Benjamin......159 (2)
Hawley, Christopher 159
Hawley, Elizabeth 159
Hawley, Joseph 159
Hawley, Mary 159
HAWLEY, MIKELL 159
Hawley, William 159
Hawren, John 131
Haw River, land on........ 358
Hay, Char................. 380
Hayes, John...........203, 371
Hayes, Samuel 371
Hayes, Wm. 313
Hayles, Lewis 173
Hayman, Anne 159
Hayman, Charles 159
Hayman, Elinor 159
HAYMAN, HENRY 159
HAYMAN, HENRY 159
Hayman, Henry (son of Henry) 159
Hayman, Henry 223
Hayman, James 159
Hayman, Mary......... 159 (3)
Hayman, Thomas 159
Hayman, William 159
Haynes, Andrew 108
Haynes, Anne 108
Haynes, Eaton 108

	PAGE.
Haynes, Francis Bythell....	95
Haynes, Xtr.	370
Haynsworth, Richd.	318
Hays, Mary	120
Haystens, Thos..............	328
Haystens, Willis	328
Haywood, John	246
Haywood, Deborah......159	(2)
Haywood, Egbert........159	(3)
Haywood, Harwood	159
HAYWOOD, JOHN	159
HAYWOOD, JOHN	159
Haywood, John (son of John)	159
Haywood, John	310
Haywood, Mary.........159	(2)
Haywood, Sherwood	159
Haywood, William......159	(2)
Hazard, Robert	325
Hazard, Roger..........167,	192
Hazard, Sarah.........167,	325
Hazell, Samuel	262
Head, Richard	129
Headly, Elizabeth	127
Hearendeen, Thomas	193
Hearison, Elisabeth	159
HEARESON, JOHN	159
Heareson, John (son of John)	159
Heareson, Thomas	159
Heareson, William......159	(2)
Hearring, Jonathan	111
Hearth (Heath)	358
Heath, Elizabeth	160
Heath, Holland	45
HEATH (HATH), NEHEMIAH.	160
Heat, Elizabeth	277
Heat, Richard	277
Heatt, Richard	277
Hecklefield, Elizabeth	1
HECKLEFIELD, JOHN	160
Hecklefield, John (son of John)	160
Hecklefield, John	1
Hedges, Ann	160
HEDGES, THOMAS	160
Hedges, William.........160	(2)
Hedges, Will..3, 53, 54, 176,	315
Heldersham	13
Hellier, Ann	65
Hellier, Richard 65,	113
Henagan, John (Swenny)...	103
Henbe, Elizabeth	7
Henbe, James 3,	8
Henbe, Sarah	7

	PAGE.
Henbe, Silvanus	8
Henby, Clarkey	160
Henby, James	160
Henby, John 160	(2)
HENBY, JOSEPH	160
Henby, Mary	160
Henby, Silvanus	160
Henderson, Andrew	333
HENDERSON, DAVID	160
Henderson, David........84,	293
Henderson, George	160
Henderson, George 160	(2)
HENDERSON, HENMAN	161
Henderson, James 109,	147
Henderson, Jennett	160
Henderson, Joseph	174
Henderson, Magnis	331
Henderson, Mary	161
Henderson, Thos.........61,	175
Hendersons Creek, land on..	104
Hendley, Jesse	368
Hendrick, Abraham	55
Hendrick, Daniel	11
Hendrick, Elisha	161
HENDRICK, FRANCIS	161
HENDRICK, FRANCIS	161
Hendrick, George	161
HENDRICK, JEREMIAH	161
Hendrick, Jeremiah	138
Hendrick, Mary	161
Hendrick, Sarah	161
Hendrick, Thomas	161
Hendricks, Frances	161
Hendricks, Jeremiah	161
Hendricks, Mary (wife of Solomon)	161
Hendricks, Mary (daughter of Solomon)	161
Hendricks, Sarah 161	(2)
HENDRICKS, SOLOMON	161
Hendrickson, Peter	287
Hendrikson, Eilzth..........	31
Hendrikson, Peter	31
Hendrixon, Abraham....202, 251,	259
Heninton, John	198
Henley, Elizabeth	161
Henley, Isabell	161
Henley, Jesse	161
Henley, John	135
HENLEY, JOHN	161
HENLEY, JOHN	161
Henley, John (son of John) 161	(3)
Henley, John 162	(3)

INDEX.

Henley, Joseph 161
Henley, Mary 161 (2)
Henley, Miriam 161
HENLEY, PETER 162
Henley, Peter 273
Henley, Samuell 136
Henly, Benjamin 161
Henly, Edward 161
Henly, Elizabeth (wife of John) 161
Henly, Elizabeth (daughter of John) 161
Henly, Esayah 4
HENLY, JOHN 161
Henly, John (son of John).. 161
Henly, Thomas 347
Henly, William 161
Henman, Thomas 134
Henman, Thos.............. 110
Hennard, John 107
Hennunteh, land at and near 87
Henry, Francis......67, 100 (2)
Henry, Lewis 102
Hepburn, Chas. 168
Herbert, John 215
Herinton, James 303
Herinton, John 303
Heritage, William 86
Herman, Robert 290
Hern, Elizebeth 162
Hern, Ellinder 162
HERN, JAMES 162
Hern, James (son of James) 162
Hern, John 162
Hern, Mary 162
Hern, Mason 162
Hern, Mason (wife of James) 162
Hern, Rachel 162
Hern, Sarah 162
Hern, William 162
Heron, Benjn. 102
Heron, Joseph 197
Heron, Capt. Joseph........ 291
Heron, Rachel 43
Herrenden, Hannah 162
HERRENDEN, HEZEKIAH 162
Herrenden, Hezekiah 252
Herricks Creek, land on..... 174
Herrick, Rob't. 297
Herrin Creek, land on...... 182
Herrin, Edward 412
Herring, Abraham 349
Herring, Ann 411
Herring, Anthony....80, 98, 410

Herring, Anthony........162 (3)
Herring, Barthena 162
Herring, Jno. 362
Herring, Joseph 162
Herring, Michael 162
Herring, Rebecca 349
Herring, Richard 260
Herring Run, land on....... 350
HERRING, SAMUELL 162
Herring, Samuel 101
Herring, Stephen.........80, 162
Herritage, Elizabeth 163
Herritage, Heneage......163 (3)
Herritage, John......66, 163 (2)
Herritage, Susannah....163, 405
HERRITAGE, WILLIAM 163
Herritage, William..247 (2), 348, 405
Herritage, Wm. 2
Herritage, William Martin.. 163
Hersleff, Rosmus 311
Hertwell, Henry 405
Heteier, Richard 106
Hewit, Bartholomew 157
HEWITT, BARTHOLOMEW 163
Hewitt, Bartholomew 59
Hewitt, Barzilla 186
Hibbs, John 163
HIBBS, JONATHAN 163
Hibbs, Jonathan (son of Jonathan) 163
Hibbs, Jonathan.........65, 381
Hickman, Nathaniel 397
Hickney, Richard 14
Hickory Land, plantation at. 366
Hicks, Abigail 164
HICKS, AFRICA 163
HICKS, DAVID 163
Hicks, David.............163 (2)
Hicks, Elizabeth 163
Hicks, Hannah..........163, 164
HICKS, JOHN 163
Hicks, Lucretia 163
Hicks, Robert......292, 305, 395
Hicks, Robt. 163
Hicks, R....15, 26, 35 (2), 46, 51, 52 (2), 58, 59, 62, 68, 89, 95, 125, 128, 138, 143, 147, 171 (2), 189, 203, 211, 230, 246, 268, 279, 297, 349, 369, 370, 372, 387, 400, 408, 411, 425.
Hicks, Thankfull 396
HICKS, THOMAS 164
Hicks, Thomas..........163, 242
Hickson, Jo. Rd............ 16
Hickson, Robert 134

INDEX.

	PAGE.
Higgines, Mich.	123
Higgins, Ann (wife of Michall)	164
Higgins, Ann (daughter of Michall)	164
Higgins, Ann	100
Higgins, Hannah	164
Higgins, Mary	164
Higgins, Michael	164 (2), 185
HIGGINS, MICHALL	164
Higgins, Sarah	164
Higgins, William	164
Highe, Elizabeth	245
Highman, Hugh	389
Highman, William	4
Highman, Thomas	4
Higman, Sarah	203
Hill, Aaron (son of William)	165
Hill, Aaron (grandson of William)	165
Hill, Aaron	322
Hill, Abraham	207
Hill, Abram	321
Hill, Adam	130
Hill, Alsey	377
Hill, Ann (wife of William)	165
Hill, Ann (daughter of William)	165
Hill, Ann	165, 171, 373
HILL, BENJAMIN	164
Hill, Benjamin	13, 147, 182 (2), 299, 306
Hill, Benjamin, Jr.	306
Hill, Benjamin	348
Hill, Christian	207
Hill, Daniel	165 (2)
Hill, Elizabeth	37, 144, 165, 253 (2)
Hill, Francis	165, 217
HILL, GEORGE	164
Hill, George (son of George)	164
Hill, George	79, 164
Hill, Green	154
Hill, Guy	355
HILL, HARMAN	164
Hill, Harman (son of Harman)	164
Hill, Harman	164, 165, 307, 340
Hill, Henry	164, 196, 306
HILL, ISAAC	164
Hill, Isaac	50, 291, 306, 357
Hill, Isack	164
Hill, Jacob	37, 255
Hill, James	164
HILL, JOHN	165
HILL, JOHN	165

	PAGE.
Hill, John (son of John)	165
Hill, John	161, 164 (3), 209, 219, 309, 323
Hill, Capt. John	234
Hill, Jno.	178, 204
Hill, Joshua	165
Hill, J.	288
Hill, Lewis	165
Hill, Martha	164
Hill, Mary	164, 356 (2)
Hill, Michael	164
Hill, Mikell	143
HILL, MOSES	165
Hill, Moses	77
Hill, Nathaniel	164, 165 (2), 306
Hill, Peter	165
Hill, Priscilla	164
Hill, Rachel	164 (2), 165
Hill, Rachel	165
HILL, RICHARD	165
Hill, Richard	373
HILL, ROBERT	165
Hill, Robert (son of Robert)	165
Hill, Robert	165
Hill, Rouger	373
Hill, Sarah	164, 165, 207, 306, 356, 357
Hill, Susannah	356
Hill, Thomas	198, 249
Hill, Thos.	118
HILL, WILLIAM	165
HILL, WILLIAM	165
Hill, William (son of William)	165 (2)
Hill, William	37, 143, 164, 263, 276, 325, 356
Hill, Will	33
Hill, Wm.	15
Hille, Hannah	14
Hillard, Tho.	201
Hilliard, Ann (wife of William)	166
Hilliard, Ann (daughter of William)	166
Hilliard, Charity	166
Hilliard, Elias	166, 184
Hilliard, Isaac	166, 184
Hilliard, Jacob	166, 184
Hilliard, James	166 (2), 184 (2)
Hilliard, Jeames	166
Hilliard, Jeremiah (son of Jeremiah)	166
Hilliard, Jeremiah	166, 184
HILLIARD, JOHN	165
Hilliard, John (son of John)	165

INDEX.

	PAGE.
Hilliard, John (son of Elizabeth Jeffreys)	184 (2)
Hilliard, John (grandson of Elizabeth Jeffreys)	184
Hilliard, Mary	165, 166
HILLIARD, ROBERT	166
Hilliard, Robert (son of Jeremiah)	166
Hilliard, Robert	84, 165, 184, 270
Hilliard, Samsone	166
Hilliard, Sarah	165, 184
Hilliard, Thomas	175
HILLIARD, WILLIAM	166
Hilliard, William (son of William)	166 (2)
Hilliard, William (son of Elizabeth Jeffreys)	184 (2)
Hilliard, William (grandson of Elizabeth Jeffreys)	184
Hilliard, William	166 (2)
Hillyard, Robert	232
HILORY, SAMEL.	166
Hilton, John	225
Hilyard, William	265
Hines, Charles	98
Hines, James	27
Hines, Joseph	427
Hines, Robert	409
Hinton, Bettie	355
Hinton, Elizebeth	166
Hinton, Hardy	166 (2)
Hinton, Jacob	355
Hinton, James	166, 209
HINTON, JOHN	166
Hinton, John (son of John)	166
Hinton, John	166
Hinton, Jonas	166
Hinton, Mallacie	166
Hinton, Martha	252
Hinton, Mary	166, 355
HINTON, MICAJAH	166
Hinton, Micajah	62
Hinton, Noah	153
Hinton, Ruben	355
Hinton, William (brother of John)	166
Hinton, William (son of John)	166
Hinton, William	166, 269, 355
Hires (?), Daniel	90
Hires (?), James	90
Hitteburgh, Christian	303
Hix, Daniel	202
Hix, Thomas	202
Hix, Wm.	71

	PAGE.
Hixon, Elinor	207
Hixon, Walter	207
Hixson, William	328
Hoaver, John Jacob	280
Hobard, Joshua	146
Hobart, Josha	284
Hobart, Joshua	40, 282, 287, 330, 419
Hobbs, Elizabeth	16
Hobbs, John	237
Hobbs, Thomas	321
Hobbs, Thos.	52, 199
Hobbs, Tho.	116
Hobby, Frances	166
HOBBY, JACOB	166
Hobby, Jemime	166
Hobby, Mathew	166
Hobby, Rhoda	166
Hobby, Sarah	166
Hobby, Thomas	111
Hobgood, Mary	148
Hobgood, William	305
Hobs, Frances	166
HOBS, JOHN	166
Hobson, Fra.	272
Hobson, Frans.	374
Hockings, Ann	167
Hockings, Benjamin	71
Hockings, Lattess	167
Hockings (Hawkins), John.	167
Hockings, Mary	167
Hockings, Rachell	71
HOCUT, EDWARD	167
Hocut, Edward (son of Edward)	167
Hocut, Martha	167
Hocut, Nathaniel	167
Hocut, William	167
Hodesin, Aaron	85
Hodges, Catherine	278
Hodges, Elisebeth	167
Hodges, Frances	167 (2)
Hodges, Francis	1, 63, 92, 149
Hodges, Henry	167
HODGES, JAMES	167
HODGES, JAMES	167
Hodges, James (son of James)	167
Hodges, John	167 (2)
Hodges, Joseph	167
Hodges, Josiah	167
Hodges, Lamb	167
Hodges, Mariam	167
Hodges, Mary	167
Hodges, Miriam	167
Hodges, Molly	167

INDEX. 513

	PAGE.
Hodges, Portlock	167
Hodges, Rebeckah	71
HODGES, RICHARD	167
HODGES, RICHARD	167
Hodges, Richard	357
Hodges, Robert	158
Hodges, Sarah (wife of Richard)	167
Hodges, Sarah (daughter of Richard)	167
Hodges, Sarah Catherine	167
Hodges, Uphan	167
Hodges, Will	272
Hodges, Willis	167
HODGSON, JOHN	168
Hodgson, John	1, 424
Hodgson, Margaret	168
Hodgson, Mary	168
Hodgson, Penelope (wife of James Craven)	86
Hodgson, Thomas Craven	86
Hoens, Margaret	189
Hog, Elizabeth	168, 188
Hog, John	382
HOG, RICHARD	168
Hogan, James	269, 290
Hogan, Lemuel	269
Hogben, William	245
Hogbin, Elizabeth	168
Hogbin, Margett	168
Hogbin, Sarah	168
HOGBIN, WILLIAM	168
Hogg, James	70 (2), 188
Hogg, John	168
Hogg, Robert	168
Hogges, Elias	168 (2)
Hogges, John	168
Hogges, Richard	168 (2)
HOGGES, ROBERT	168
Hogh, Sarrah	387
Hogpen Neck plantation	166
Hokins, Joyce	57
HOLBROOK, FARMANESS	168
HOLBROOK (or HOLEBROUGH), JOSEPH	168
Holbrook, Margrett	134
Holebrough, John	168
Holederley, Elizabeth	179
Holderley, Fortune	179 (2)
Holederley, Henry	179
Holeman, Jonathan	126
Holladay, Elizabeth	168
Holladay, Samuell	168
HOLLADAY, THOMAS	168
Holladay, Thomas	168
Holladay, William	168

	PAGE.
HOLLADAY, WILLIAM	168
Holland, Annie	169
Holland, Apsele	354
HOLLAND, DANIEL	169
Holland, Demcy	251
Holland House plantation	196
Holland, John	169
Holland, Joseph	131
Holland, Otho	1, 114
Holland, Mary	82
Hollbrook, Dorothy	169
Hollands, Jehoshaphat	338, 396
HOLLBROOK, JOHN	169
Hollbrook, John (son of John)	169
Hollbrook, Margrett	423
Holley, Elizabeth	337
Holley, Jane	337
HOLLERY, SAMUEL and SAMUELL WOODARD	169
Hollfand, John	319
Holliday, Gilbert	211
Holliday, Gi.	315
Holliman, Absalom	212
Hollingsworth, Chas.	357
Hollingsworth, Henry	376
Hollingsworth, Isaac	110
Hollingsworth, John	110
Hollingsworth, Samuel	110
Hollingsworth, Valentine	110
Hollis, Ann	169
Hollis, Armit	169
HOLLIS, JAMES	169
Holloman, Christefer	190
Holloman, Chrisfor	59
Holloman, Margerrit	59
Holloway, John	109, 169
HOLLOWAY, THOMAS	169
Holloway, Thomas	82
Holloway, Upherasha	169
Holloway, William	188, 290
Hollowell, Abner	169, 321
HOLLOWELL, EDMUND	169
Hollowell, Elizabeth	169
Hollowell, Joe	321
Hollowell, Joel	169
Hollowell, John	169 (6)
Hollowell, Jos.	240
Hollowell, Levy	169 (2)
HOLLOWELL, LUKE	169
HOLLOWELL, RUBIN	169
Hollowell, Sarah	321
Hollowell (?), Sarah	321
Hollowell, Thomas, Sr.	169
Hollowell, Thomas	36, 169, 284, 419

33

514   INDEX.

	PAGE.
Hollowell, William	169
HOLLY, JOHN	170
Holly, Nathaniel	310
Holly, Richard	170
Holly, Sarah	170
Holly Shelter Creek, land on	256
Holly Shelter Creek and the Bald White Sand Hills, land between	257
Holly Swamp, land on	408
Hollyman, Christopher	246
Hollyman, Samuel	246
Holmes, Abigil	170
Holmes, Ann	256
Holmes, Archibald	156
Holmes, Barnabas	170
HOLMES, EBENEZER	170
Holmes, Ebenezer (son of Ebenezer)	170
Holmes, Edward	170
Holmes, Gabriel	170
Holmes, Hannah	170
Holmes, Hardy	170 (2)
HOLMES, JOHN	170
Holmes, John (son of John)	170
Holmes, John	97, 170
Holmes, Jno.	381
Holmes, Lydel	170
Holmes, Richard	352
Holmes, Rose	170
Holmes, Seth	170
Holmes, Tamar	170
Holmes, Thomas	205, 377
Holmes, William	125
Holstead, Samuel	337
Holston's Creek, land on	338
Holston, Thomas	268
Holt, Josiah	380
Holt, Martha	113
Holt, Thomas	320
Holyday, Charles	316
HOMES, EDWARD	170
HOMES, EDWARD	170
Homes, Elizabeth	170, 209
Homes, John	170
Homes, Liddea	170
Homes, Solomon	203
Homes, Thomas	170, 209, 226
Homes, William	336
Honor, John Jacob	175
Hood, Abrm	361, 415
Hood, Edward	73
Hood, Robert	125
Hook, Elisebath	170
HOOK, JOHN	170
Hook, John (son of John)	170

	PAGE.
Hook, Mary	170
Hook, Robert	170
Hook, Ruth	170
Hook, Sarah	170
Hook, Thomas	170
Hook, William	170
Hooker, Benjamin	170
Hooker, Elisabeth (wife of Godphrey)	170
Hooker, Elisabeth (daughter of Godphrey)	170
Hooker, Elizabeth Mary	367
Hooker, Godfree	170
HOOKER, GODPHREY	170
Hooker, James	171
Hooker, John	171
Hooker, Nathan	171
Hooker, Sarah	171
Hooker, Stephen	171, 425
HOOKER, WILLIAM	170
HOOKER, WILLIAM	171
Hooker, William (son of William)	170, 171
Hooker, William	171, 333
Hooker, William, Jr.	425
Hooks, Charles	171
Hooks, John	13, 16, 171 (2), 301
Hooks, John, Jr.	301
Hooks, Martha	309
Hooks, William	140
Hooks, Thomas	171
HOOKS, WILLIAM	171
Hooks, William (son of William)	171
Hooks, William (grandson of William)	171
Hooper, Martha	119
Hoopper, Thomas	220
Hoover, Jacob	334
Hopcraft, Thomas	338
Hopkins, Anne	277
Hopkins Howells Spring Branch, land on	409
HOPKINS, JAMES	171
Hopkins, James	112
HOPKINS, JOHN	171
HOPKINS, JOHN	171
Hopkins, John	171, 277, 374
Hopkins, Jno.	291
Hopkins, Mary	171, 377
Hopkins, Samuel	225
Hopkins, Sarah	171
Hopkins, William	112, 171
Hopper, David	54 (2)
Hopson, Francis	197

INDEX.

Hopton, Charles..........318, 349
Hopton, Mary 268
Horn, Charles 171, 251
Horn Creek, land on....292, 377
Horn, Elizabeth........360, 390
Horn, Henry...171, 194, 360, 390
Horn, Josiah 194
Horn, Margaret 171
Horn, Michaell 171
Horn, Moses 171
Horn, Richard 204
Horn, Sarah 212
Horn, Sihon 390
Horn, Sikon 194
Horn, Thomas 171
HORN, WILLIAM 171
Horn, William (son of William) 171
Horne, Charles..13, 236, 298, 398
Horne, Henry......229, 304 (2)
Horne, John 353
Horne, Joseph 333
Horne, Moses...........100, 305
Horne, Sion 360
Horns Quarter plantation... 192
Hornsby, William 200
Hornsby, Wm...........171, 325
Horny, Jos................. 181
Horse Creek, land on....... 395
Horse Hole, land on........ 392
Horse Meadow or Pasture plantation 222
Horse Pasture Swamp, land on 91
Horse Swamp 174
Horse Swamp, land on...... 352
Horse Swamp, plantation on 107
HORTH, THOMAS 171
Horton, Henary 298
Horton, John 98
Horton, Parmenas 262
Horton, Susanah 98
Horton, Thomas 339
Hosea, Abraham....128, 172, 245
HOSEA, ABRAM 172
Hosea, Abram (nephew of Abram) 172
Hosea, Ann 172
Hosea, Elizabeth 137
Hosea, John........172, 245, 284
HOSEA, JOSEPH 172
Hosea, Joseph (son of Joseph) 172
Hosea, Joseph 172
Hosea, Mary............172 (2)

HOSEA, ROBERT 172
Hosea, Robert..172, 200, 245, 283
Hosea, Thomas 172
Hosea, William..........172 (2)
Hoskie Swamp, land on..... 101
Hoskins, John 215
Hoskins, Mathew Mary..... 172
Hoskins Mill, plantation near 407
Hoskins, Sarah 145
Hoskins, Thomas 145
HOSKINS, THOMAS 172
Hoskins, Thomas........172, 277
HOSKINS, WILLIAM 172
Hoskins, William.....2, 145 (2), 172, 215, 220, 277
Hoskins (Horkins), William 406
HOSMER, HANNAH 172
Hossten, Frances 105
Hostler, Alexr............. 248
Hott, Richard 46
Houghton, David 173
Houghton, Elizabeth 172
Houghton, James 173
Houghton, Jonathan 172
Houghton, Joshua 172
Houghton, Mary (wife of William) 172
Houghton, Mary (daughter of William) 172
Houghton, Mary........172, 173
Houghton, Sarah 172
HOUGHTON, THOMAS 172
Houghton, Tho.............. 131
HOUGHTON, WILLIAM 172
Houghton, William......172, 173
Houghton, Wm.............. 62
Houldbrook, John 361
Houren, John..107, 109, 114, 120
Hourton, Rachel 396
House, Ann 173
House, Balis 173 (2)
House, Edith 173 (2)
HOUSE, GEORGE 173
House, George (grandson of George) 173
House, George......152 (2), 173
House, James 173
House, John 173
House, Robert 152
House, Sarah 173, 276
HOUSE, THOMAS 173
House, Thomas 173
House, William 173
Houston, Ann 103

	PAGE.
Houston, Elizibeth	173
Houston, James	173, 268
Houston, Margrett	173
Houston, Mary	173
HOUSTON, MOSES	173
Houston, Moses	104, 134, 173, 177, 235, 396 (2)
Houston, Rachel	173
HOUSTON, THOMAS	173
Houston, Thomas (son of Thomas)	173
HOUSTON, WILLIAM	173
Houston, William (son of William)	173
Houston, William	104, 173, 235
Houston, Wm.	180, 212
Hover, Henry	173
Hover, John	173
HOVER, JOHN JACOB	173
Hover, Jacob	173
Hover, Margareth	173
Hover, Mary Magdalena	173
Hover, Samuel	173
HOWARD, CHARLES	174
Howard, Charles (son of Charles)	174
Howard, Charles	119, 240
Howard, Edward	174, 260 (2), 325
Howard, Eleanor	216
Howard, Elizabeth	193
Howard, Ellexander	287
Howard, George	273
HOWARD, JAMES	174
Howard, James (son of James)	174 (2)
Howard, James	96, 251
Howard, John	56, 96, 174, 203
Howard, Jos.	385
Howard, Mary	61, 174
Howard, Robert	3, 61, 216
Howard, Samuell	174
Howard, Sarah (wife of James)	174
Howard, Sarah (daughter of James)	174
Howard, Sarah	225
Howard, Solomon	174, 194
Howard, Stephen (son of Stephen)	325
Howard, Stephen	3, 325 (2)
Howard, Stephen, Jr.	3
Howard, William	193
Howcott, Edward (brother of John)	174

	PAGE.
Howcott, Edward (son of John)	174 (2)
Howcott, Edward	11, 38, 92, 174
Howcott, Edwd	323
Howcott, Elizabeth	38
Howcott, Frances	197
HOWCOTT, JOHN	174
Howcott, John (son of John)	174
Howcott, Mary (wife of John)	174
Howcott, Mary (daughter of John)	174
Howcott, Mary	38
Howcott, Nathaniel	174
Howcott, Richard	174
Howcott, William	38
Howe, Arthur	95
Howe, Job	253
Howel, Caleb	244
Howel, Nathaniel	166
Howell, Elias	418
Howell, Griffeth	164, 350, 393
Howell, Jonathan	231, 283, 398
HOWELL, JOSEPH	174
Howell, Joseph (son of Joseph)	174 (2)
Howell, Marget	174
Howell, Martha	174
Howell, Mary	174
Howell, Murphrey	174
Howell, Thomas	174 (2)
Howells, Joseph	249
Howes, Arthur	46
Howes, Job, Sr.	46
Howes, Job, Jr.	46
Howison, Rachel	67
Hows, Job	12
HOWSON, WILLIAM	174
Howey, Hugh	343
Hoyle, Elizabeth	261
Hoyle, James	85, 232, 261
Hubard, Abegell	9
Hubard, James	194
Hubbard, Gefery	355
Hubbard, Matt	340
HUBBARD, RANE	175
Hubbard, Sarah	202
Hubbs, Mary	169
Hubbs, Thos.	169
Huchleroy, Elisabeth	176
Huckins, Ann	175
HUCKINS, DANIEL	175
Huckins, Solomon	175
Huckins, Vallinty	175

INDEX.   517

	PAGE.
HUDDE, CHRISTOPHER	175
Hudde, Prusily	175
Huddey, Andrew	266
Hudler, John	256
Hudson, Abell	227
Hudson, Alice	332
Hudson, Elesebeth	175
HUDSON, JOSEPH	175
Hudson, Joseph (son of Joseph)	175
Hudson, Joseph	16, 150
Hudson, Lewis	175
Hudson, Mary	175
Hudson, Susanah	175
Hudson, Thomas	265
Hudson, Thos.	213
Hudson, William	373, 400
Hudson, Wm., Jr.	373
Hudson, Zekill	232
Huey & Crymble	99
HUGGENS, ANN	175
Huggens, Benjamin	175
Huggens, Charles	175
Huggens, Jacob	175
Huggens, Lucreasea	175
Huggens, Matthew	175 (2)
Huggens, Nehemiah	175
Hugger, Edm'd.	156
Huggins, Abraham	175
Huggins, Benjamin	175
Huggins, Charles	175
Huggins, Dorcas	336
HUGGINS, EDMOND	175
Huggins, Jacob	175
HUGGINS, JAMES	175
HUGGINS, JOHN	175
Huggins, John (son of John)	175
Huggins, John	175
Huggins, Lucresea	175
Huggins, Mary	175, 176
Huggins, Mathew	175 (2)
Huggins, Nehemiah	175
Huggins, Philip	175
Hughe, Samuel	199
Hughes, John	101, 212, 416
Hughes plantation	108
Hughes, William	126, 373
Hughes, William, Jr.	145
Hughes, Willis	218
Huise, Mary	47 (2)
Hull, Catherine	176
Hull, Daniel	245
HULL, JOHN	176
Hull, John	2

	PAGE.
Hull, J.	312
Hull, Mary	176
Hull, Peter	115
Humes, Abigail	176
Humes, Elisabeth	176
HUMES, JAMES	176
Humes, James	207, 311
Humes, Mary	176
Humes, Rennis	176
Humfreys, Mary	301
HUMPHREY, JOSEPH	176
Humphrey, Joseph (nephew of Joseph)	176
Humphries, Ann	258
Humphries, Christopher	176, 195
Humphries, Dinah	195
Humphries, Jane	329
HUMPHRIES, JOHN	176
Humphries, John (son of John)	176
Humphries, John (another son of John)	176
Humphries, Joseph	195
HUMPHRIES, RICHARD	176
Humphries, William	176 (2)
Hunt, Andrew	177
Hunt, Elisabeth	72 (2), 130, 176
Hunt, Mrs. Elizabeth	423
Hunt, Capt. John	130 (2), 423
Hunt, John (Capt.)	78
HUNT, JOHN	176
Hunt, John	4, 13, 176, 291
Hunt, John, of Little River	373
Hunt, Jno.	270
Hunt, Jonathan	379
Hunt, Lawrence	209
HUNT, THOMAS	177
Hunter, Agness	177
Hunter, Alce	177
Hunter, Allise	178
HUNTER, ANN	177
Hunter, Ann (wife of William)	178
Hunter, Ann (daughter of William)	178
Hunter, Ann	392
Hunter, Catrin	177
Hunter, Charles	379
Hunter, Daniel	177
Hunter, Easter	178
Hunter, Elisha	177 (2), 178
Hunter, Elizebath	177, 279
Hunter, Ephraim	178, 425
Hunter, Esekel	249

518　Index.

	PAGE.
Hunter, Ezekiel	319, 415
Hunter, Ezekil	134
Hunter, Ezekill	104, 177 (2)
Hunter, E. ———	177
Hunter, Hardy	178, 392
Hunter, Henry	4, 23, 177
HUNTER, ISAAC	177
Hunter, Isaac (son of Isaac)	177
Hunter, Isaac	83, 178
Hunter, Jacob	177
Hunter, James	178
Hunter, Jesse	177
Hunter, Joab	177
Hunter, Job	178, 223, 270
HUNTER, JOHN	177
Hunter, John	178 (2)
Hunter, Judith	178
Hunter, Lebbeus	177, 415
Hunter, Mary	177, 178, 248
Hunter, Moses	4, 177
HUNTER, NICHOLAS	177
Hunter, Nicholas	173, 178, 396
Hunter, Reachell	177
Hunter, Rebecca	177
Hunter, Rebeckah	173
Hunter, Rebkah	415
HUNTER, ROBERT	177
Hunter, Robert	178
Hunter, Ruth	177
Hunter, Sarah	23, 177 (2), 178
Hunter, Stephen	177
Hunter, Timothy	178
HUNTER, WILLIAM	178
HUNTER, WILLIAM	178
Hunter, William (son of William)	178 (2)
Hunter, William	177, 232
Hunter, Wm.	177 (2)
Hunter, Zillah	177
Hunts plantation	121
Hunts Point plantation	214
Huntt, John	231, 245, 423
Huntt, Philemon	342
Hurdell, Hardy	312
HURDLE, BENJAMIN	178
Hurdle, Elizabeth	178
Hurdle, Hardy	393
Hurdle, Joseph	393
Hurdle, Moring	178
Hurdle, Thomas	365
Hurdle, William	178
Hurley, Ann	170, 175 (2)
Hurley, Jacob	175 (2)
Hurley, James	261

	PAGE.
Hurley, Richard	115
Hurst, Elizabeth	217
Hurst, Judath	251
Hurst, William	261
Husbands, Jane	178, 262
Husbands, John	178
HUSBANDS, RICHARD	178
Husbands, Richard (son of Richard)	178
Huse, Ann	373
Hutchenson, Mary	183
Hutchings, Amea	142
Hutchings, Anthony	76
Hutchings, Thomas	142, 298
Hutchins, Antho.	213
Hutchins, Anthony	167, 202, 213
Hutchins, Noel	387
Hutson, Francis	119, 178
Hutson, Hardy Holladay	168
Hutson, John Holladay	168
Hutson, Joseph	57
Hutson, Mary	168
Hutson, Neptuania	206
Hutson, Thomas Holladay	168
HUTSON, WILLIAM	178
Hutssoon, Thomas	25
Huyandine, Thomas	54
Hyde, Governor Edward	292
Hydlebyrd, Catherine	228
Hyland, Lawrence	242
Hyman, Hugh	327
Hyman, John	29
Hyman, Thomas	4, 250
HYRNE, HENRY	178
Hyrnes, Henry	6
Ieedlett (?), Elizabeth	378
Ieve Neck	381
Ilands, Sarah	180
Impers, Tho.	286
Imson, Ann	278
Inbason, Robert	199
Ince, Henry	271
Indian Creek, land on	360
Indian Creek, land over	482
Indian Creek plantation	392
Indian Grave Branch, land on	245
Indian Towne Creek, land on	399
Indian Town plantation	214
Ingram, Abraham	179
INGRAM, ABSALOM (OR ABRAHAM)	179
Ingram, David	179 (2)

	PAGE.
Ingram, Isaac	179
Ingram, James	179
Ingrim, Jean	74
Ingrim, Nework	74
INNES, JAMES	179
Innes, James	2, 12, 208
Innes, John	208
Innes, Robert	386
Irby, Ann	179
Irby, Elizabeth	179 (2)
IRBY, HENRY	179
Irby, Henry	179
Irby, William	179
Irby, Wm.	325
Ireland, Andrew	400
Ireland, Ann	315
Ireland, lands in	299
Irving, Andrew	42
IRVING, ROBERT	179
Irwing, Andrew	166
Isaac (a molato boy)	4
Isenmanger, Joseph	259
Isham, Charles	180
ISHAM, JAMES	180
Isham, James (son of James)	180
Isham, Jane	180
Isham, Margaret	180
Isket, John	273
Island Lands plantation	29
Island of Carolina, land in.	234
Islands, Elizabeth	180
Islands, George	180
ISLANDS (ILANDS), RICHARD	180
Islands, Richard (son of Richard)	180
Islands, Robert	180
ISLER, CHRISTIAN'	180
Isler, Christian	127
Isler, Elizabeth (wife of Christian)	180
Isler, Elizabeth (daughter of Christian)	180
Isler, Elizabeth	75
Isler, Frederick	127 (2), 180, 424
Isler, John	180 (2)
Isler, Mary	75
Isler, Susannah	180
Isler, William	180 (2)
Ismay, Ann	354
ISMAY, JOHN	180
Ismay, Nancy	180
Ismay, Sarah	180
Ives, Courtney	174
Ives, Elisabeth	180
Ives, Esther	180
Ives, Job	180 (2)
IVES, JOHN	180
Ives, Jonas	180
Ives, Mary	180
Ives, Paul	315
IVES, THOMAS	180
Ivy, Ludford	4
Jackit Swamp	191
Jacks Creek, land on	21
Jackson, Aaron	182
Jackson, Absalom	181
Jackson, Ace	182
Jackson, Ann (wife of Daniel)	181
Jackson, Ann (daughter of Daniel)	181
Jackson, Ann	181 (2)
Jackson, Anne	71
Jackson, Benjamin	164
Jackson, Christopher	204
JACKSON, DANIEL	180
Jackson, Daniel (son of Daniel)	180
Jackson, Daniel	181, 182 (2)
Jackson, Daniell	181, 182
Jackson, Darkes	182
JACKSON, DAVID	181
Jackson, David	180, 182 (2), 274
Jackson, Demce	182
Jackson, Edmond	349
Jackson, Edward	182
Jackson, Elisabeth	181
Jackson, Elizabeth	181 (3), 182 (3), 273
Jackson, Hanah	181
Jackson, Hester	182 (2)
JACKSON, ISAAC	181
Jackson, James	182
Jackson, Joab	180, 182
JACKSON, JOHN	181
Jackson, John	181 (2), 182, 281, 337
Jackson, Joshua	181 (2)
Jackson, Lamuel	182
Jackson, Lucy	181, 294
Jackson, Margaret (wife of William, Jr.)	182
Jackson, Margaret (daughter of William, Jr.)	182
Jackson, Margret	181
Jackson, Mary (wife of Samuel)	181

	PAGE.
Jackson, Mary (daughter of Samuel)	181
Jackson, Mary	17, 181, 337
Jackson, Mathias	181
Jackson, Moses	182
Jackson, Parthenia	182
JACKSON, ROBERT	181
Jackson, Ruth	181
JACKSON, SAMUEL	181
JACKSON, SAMUEL	181
Jackson, Samuel	180, 181 (2), 182
Jackson, Saml.	182
Jackson, Simon	182
Jackson, Stephen	207
JACKSON, THOMAS	182
Jackson, Thomas (son of Thomas)	182
Jackson, Thomas	13, 181 (2)
JACKSON, WILLIAM, SR.	182
JACKSON, WILLIAM, JR.	182
JACKSON, WILLIAM	182
Jackson, William	9, 180, 182 (2), 329 (2), 341
Jackson, Will, Jr.	182
Jackson, Wm., Sr.	182
Jackson, Zachariah	182 (3)
JACKSON, ZACHARIAS	182
Jackson, Zacharias	181, 182
Jacob, Jane	182
JACOB, ISAAC	182
Jacob, Sarah	183
Jacob, Susanah	182
Jacobbs Wells plantation	25
Jacobs, Pasley	173
Jacocks, Charles	195
Jacocks, Jonathan	34
Jacocks, Mary	35
JACOCKS, THOMAS	183
Jacocks, Thos.	219
Jacocs, Mary	35
James, Andrew	208
James, Ann	183
JAMES, EDWARD	183
James, Edward (son of Edward)	183
James, Edward	34
James, Elinor	87
James, Elizabeth	183
James, Francis	208
James, Gilbert	183
James, Jane	183
James, John	309
James, Joshua	97
James, Milly	183
James, Peter	75

	PAGE.
James, Rebecca	183
James Robinson's plantation	190
James, Samuel	183
James, Thomas	120, 183 (2), 231
James, Thos.	56, 160, 342
JAMES, WILLIAM	183
JAMES, WILLIAM	183
James, William (son of William)	183 (2)
James, William	10, 237
James, Willis	120
Jameson, John	291
Jameson, William	64 (2)
Jaques, Elisha	178
Jarman, Elijah	262
Jarman, John	183 (3), 240
Jarman, Larrance	183
Jarman, Little	236 (2)
Jarman, Mary (daughter of Thomas)	183
Jarman, Mary (grandchild of Thomas)	183
Jarman, Moses	183
Jarman, Robert	391
JARMAN, THOMAS	183
Jarman, Thomas (son of Thomas)	183
Jarman, William (son of Thomas)	183 (2)
Jarman, William (grandson of Thomas)	183
Jarnagand, David	237
Jarnagand, Thos.	237
Jarratt, Abraham	183
Jarratt, Catherine	183
Jarratt, Esther	183
Jarratt, Isaac	183
Jarratt, Jacob	183
JARRATT, JOHN	183
Jarratt, John (son of John)	183
Jarratt, Sarah	183
Jarratt, Susannah	183
Jarrell, Thomas	202
Jarrot Hays Place plantation	230
Jarves, Bridget	373
Jarves, Elizabeth	184
Jarves, Mary	421
Jarves, Samuel	326, 373
Jarves, Solo.	373
Jarvis, Dorcas	155
JARVIS, FOSTER	183
Jarvis, Foster (son of Foster)	184
Jarvis, Frances	239
Jarvis, Francis	184

INDEX.

Jarvis, Hester, Sr.	72
Jarvis, Jonathan	183
Jarvis, Martain	183, 184
Jarvis, Samuell	183
Jarvis, Samuel	131, 184, 361
Jarvis, Thomas	155, 380
Jarvis, Thos.	331 (2)
Jarvis, William	183
Jasper, Ann (wife of Samuel)	184
Jasper, Ann (daughter of Samuel)	184
Jasper, Ann	108, 184, 211
Jasper, Catherine	346
Jasper, Elizabeth	184
Jasper, Israel	184
Jasper, John	397
Jasper, Jonathan	184 (2), 211 (2), 346
Jasper, Lyddela	184
Jasper, Mary	184
JASPER, RICHARD	184
JASPER, SAMUEL	184
Jasper, Samuel (son of Samuel)	184
Jasper, Samuel	241
Jasper, Samuell	184
Jasper, Thomas	397
Jasper, William Richard	211
Jasper, William	184 (2)
Jeames, John	161
JEFFREYS, CHRISTOPHER	184
JEFFREYS, ELIZABETH	184
JEFFREYS, ELIZABETH	184
Jeffreys, Osborne.	7, 166. 184 (4)
Jeffreys, Patience	354
Jeffreys, Robert	60 (2), 118, 273, 323
Jeffreys, William	313
Jenett, Abraham	351
Jenkin, Thos.	140, 202
JENKINS, CHARLES	184
Jenkins, Charles (son of Charles)	184
Jenkins, Charles (son of William)	185
Jenkins, Charles	185, 194
Jenkins, Elizabeth	11, 185
Jenkins, George	6
Jenkins, Henry	184, 185
Jenkins, Isabella	203
Jenkins, James	226
Jenkins, John	146, 217, 272
Jenkins, Lewis	203, 247, 394
Jenkins, Marget	141
Jenkins, Martha	6
Jenkins, Shurard	185
Jenkins, Thomas	86, 141, 226
Jenkins, Thos.	202
Jenkins, William	184, 185 (2)
Jenkins, Winbourne	185
Jenkisson, Elizabeth	89
Jenkisson, Robert	89
Jennet, Abraham	127
Jennet, An	146
Jennet, Mary	146
Jennett, Abraham	358
JENNETT, ABRAHAM	185
Jennett, Abraham (son of Abraham)	185
Jennett, Abraham (son of John)	185
Jennett, Abraham (grandson of John)	185
Jennett, Ann (Jabez's daughter)	185
Jennett, Ann (wife of John)	185
Jennett, Ann (daughter of John)	185
Jennett, Ann	185
Jennett, Dorothy	185
Jennett, Elizabeth	185 (2)
Jennett, Isakiah	185
Jennett, Jabez	185 (2)
Jennett, Jean	185
Jennett, Jeremiah	185
JENNETT, JOHN	185
JENNETT, JOHN	185
Jennett, John (son of John)	185
Jennett, John (son of John)	185
Jennett, John	188
Jennett, Mary	185
Jennett, William	185 (2)
Jennings, Elliner	185
Jennings, Isaac	185
JENNINGS, JOHN	185
Jennings, John	185, 193, 201
Jennings, Joshua	328
Jennings, Luse	185
JENNINGS, MARY	185
Jennings, Mary	186
JENNINGS, THOMAS	185
Jennings, Thomas (son of Thomas)	185
JENNINGS, WILLIAM	185
JENNINGS, WILLIAM	186
Jennings, William	244
Jenoure, Ann	186
Jenoure, Anne	282
JENOURE, JOSEPH	186
Jerkins, Sarah	194

	PAGE.
Jernagan, David	186
Jernagan, George	186
Jernagan, James	186
JERNAGAN, JOHN	186
Jernagan, Temperance	186
Jernagan, Thomas	186
Jernigan, David	424
Jernigan, Henry	197
Jernigan, John	186
Jernigan, Phebe	33
Jernigin, Dempsie	186
Jernigin, Henry	186
JERNIGIN, HENRY	186
Jernigin, Henry (son of Henry)	186
Jernigin, Jacob	186 (2)
Jernigin, Jesse	186
Jernigin, Phebe	186
Jerrett, Jno.	146
Jervis, Foster	13 (2), 19
Jessop, Abraham	302
Jessop, Dinah	356
Jessop, Elizabeth	186
Jessop, Jane	74
Jessop, Jonathan	186
JESSOP, JOSEPH	186
Jessop, Joseph	14, 38, 70, 77 (2), 219, 245, 303, 378
Jessop, Jos.	38
Jessop, J.	74, 186, 255, 264, 378
Jessop, Margaret	186
Jessop, Maryann	239
Jessop, Mary	186
Jessop, Sarah	343
Jessop, Timothy	186
Jessop, Thomas	7, 74 (2), 186 (4), 239, 244, 343, 378, 383
Jessop, William	356
JEVINS, ELIZABETH	186
Jevins, Elizabeth	187
JEVINS, JOHN	187
Jewel, Benjamin	187, 343 (3)
Jewel, Frances	187
Jewel, James	187
Jewel, John	187 (2)
Jewel, Mary	342
Jewel, Samuel	187
JEWEL, THOMAS	187
Jewel, Anne	187
Jewell, Benjamin	211
JEWELL, JOHN	187
Jewell, Martha	187
Jewell, Mary	211
Jilks, Ann	188
Jiner, Sarah	266

	PAGE.
Joanes, Elizabeth	312
Joanes, Walter	312
John (a mulatto child)	127
John Simsons Branch, land binding on	31
John, Zillpman	335
Johnes, Francis	351
Johns, John	261
Johns, Mary	357
Johnson, Andrew	337
Johnson, Anne	188
Johnson, Barnebe	298
Johnson, Benjamin	189
Johnson, Catherine	188
Johnson, Charles	108, 109
Johnson, Elizabeth	58, 188, 385
Johnson, Ezekel	189
Johnson, Francis	46, 337
Johnson, Gideon	371
Johnson, Henry	218
JOHNSON, JAMES	188
Johnson, James	188 (2)
JOHNSON, JOHN	188
JOHNSON, JOHN	188
JOHNSON, JOHN	188
JOHNSON, JOHN	188
Johnson, John	159
Johnson, John Stephen	189
JOHNSON, LEWIS	188
Johnson, Martha	188
Johnson, Mathias	17
Johnson, Mary	128, 188, 189, 276
Johnson, Patience	311
Johnson, Richard	118, 188
Johnson, Sarah	108, 188 (2), 189
JOHNSON, SUSANAH	189
Johnson, Thomas	189 (2)
JOHNSON, WILLIAM	189
JOHNSON, WILLIAM	189
Johnson, William (son of William)	189
Johnson, William	188 (3), 217
Johnson, Wm.	188
Johnston, Ann	188, 189
Johnston, Benjamin	189
Johnston, Esther	198
Johnston, Frances	187
JOHNSTON, GABRIEL	187
Johnston, Gabriel	2 (2), 11, 46, 81, 147 (2), 206, 225, 239, 261, 348 (2), 379, 413.
Johnston, Gab.	1, 8, 12, 14, 23, 26, 29, 39, 40 (3), 61, 65, 68, 69, 74 (2), 77 (2), 80, 92, 103 (2), 107, 113 (3), 123 (3), 130, 131, 132,

INDEX. 523

134, 139 (2), 147, 148, 160, 168, 176, 178, 179, 181, 182, 193, 195, 200 (2), 218, 229 (2), 230, 242, 246, 247, 251 (3), 252, 255, 260, 262, 281, 283, 284 (2), 290, 298, 302, 304, 306, 307, 308, 316, 324, 330, 331, 333, 336 (2), 338, 339, 340, 342, 345, 355, 357, 361, 364, 366, 367, 370, 374, 386 (2), 390, 392, 393, 396, 399, 400, 401, 402, 403, 406, 407, 420.
Johnston, Hannah 188
Johnston, Henry 187
Johnston, Isobell 188
Johnston, Joan 188
Johnston, John.....187, 188, 189
Johnston, Lillah 168
Johnston, Mrs. 412
Johnston on New River, Courthouse at 103
Johnston, Penelope......187, 188
Johnston, Robert 168
Johnston & Robinson....... 219
JOHNSTON, SAMUEL 188
Johnston, Samuel (son of Samuel) 188
Johnston, Samuel.......139, 187
JOHNSTON, THOMAS 189
Johnston, Thomas (son of Thomas) 189 (2)
Johnstoun, Richard 18
Johnstun, Aaron 22
Jolley, Bridget 328
Jones, ——— 140
Jones, Abigall 191
Jones, Abraham.190 (2), 195, 394
Jones, Absalom 188
Jones, Absalum 190
Jones, Albridgton 191
Jones, Amey 198
Jones, An. 198
Jones, Ann....108, 165, 186, 189, 190 (2), 191, 193, 194 (3), 195 (2), 197 (2), 214, 304, 365.
Jones, Anne 108
JONES, ARTHUR 189
Jones, Arthur 190
Jones, Barsheba 44
Jones, Benjamin 193
Jones, Bette Day........... 191
Jones, Bridget 190
Jones, Bridgett 81
Jones, Britton 198
Jones, Catharine 191
Jones, Catherine 191
JONES, CHARLES 189

JONES, CHARLES 190
Jones, Charles (son of Charles) 190
Jones, Charles....4 (2), 191 (2), 197 (2)
Jones, Christopher 190
JONES, CORNELIUS 190
JONES, CORNELIUS 190
Jones, Cornelius (son of Cornelius) 190 (3)
Jones, Cornelius.....92, 154, 190, 195, 310, 317, 347
Jones, Creacy 193
JONES, DANIELL 190
JONES, DAVID, SR........... 190
JONES, DAVID 190
Jones, David...190, 193 (2), 197, 269, 281
Jones, Demsey 194
Jones, Dinah 195
Jones, Dorothy 193
Jones, Dreury 198
Jones, Edah 198
Jones, Edmond 194
JONES, EDWARD 191
JONES, EDWARD 191
Jones, Elesebeth.........195 (2)
Jones, Elezebeth (wife of David, Sr.)............... 190
Jones, Elezebeth 192
Jones, Elisabeth (granddaughter of John)........ 193
Jones, Elisabeth (daughter of John) 193
Jones, Elisabeth 190
Jones, Elisebeth 77
Jones, Eliza 156
Jones, Elizabeth (wife of Cornelius) 190
Jones, Elizabeth (daughter of Cornelius) 190
Jones, Elizabeth..59, 80, 91, 154, 178, 190, 192, 193 (2), 194 (2), 195, 196 (2), 197, 198.
Jones, Elizebeth (daughter of David, Sr.)............ 190
Jones, Elizebeth 122
Jones, Ellener 32
Jones, Emel................ 368
Jones, Eml................. 134
Jones, Ephraim 197
Jones, Etheldred 194
JONES, EVAN 191
JONES, EVAN 191

	PAGE.
Jones, Evan (son of Evan),	191 (2)
Jones, Evan..9, 19, 29, 34, 61, 66, 78, 90, 101, 104, 116, 117, 129, 130, 131, 132, 137, 143, 156, 165, 168, 185 (2), 193, 212, 213, 220, 234, 275, 278, 286, 311, 359, 365, 367 (2), 370, 379, 382, 393, 424.	
Jones, Even	128
Jones, Evin	193
Jones, Florance	194
Jones (or James), Foster	382
Jones, Fraley	193
Jones, Fra	412
Jones, Frances	253
JONES, FRANCIS	191
Jones, Francis	152, 191, 196
Jones, Francis, Jr.	209
JONES, FREDERICK	192
JONES, FREDERICK	192
Jones, Frederick (son of Frederick)	192 (2)
Jones, Frederick	178 (2), 194, 195, 197, 212
Jones, Frederick, of the Oak	6
Jones, Fryly	128
Jones, George	196
Jones, Gray	192
Jones, Griff	387
Jones, Griffin	80
Jones, Griffith..78, 189, 235,	404
Jones, Hannah	195, 196
Jones, Harding	192 (2), 204
Jones, Henrietta	22
JONES, HENRY	192
JONES, HENRY	192
JONES, HENRY	192
Jones, Henry, of Greenhall.	235
Jones, Henry (son of Henry)	192
Jones, Henry	195, 197 (3), 198, 246
Jones, Henry Restove	192
Jones, Holland	196
Jones, Howel	149
JONES, ISAAC	193
Jones, Isaac (son of Isaac)	193
Jones, Isaac	124, 176, 191, 260
JONES, ISAM	193
Jones, Isam	198
Jones, Izayah	196
Jones, Jacob	180
JONES, JAMES	193
Jones, James (son of James)	193

	PAGE.
Jones, James...10, 101, 141, 191 (3), 192, 194 (5), 195 (2), 197, 198 (2), 238, 261, 344, 352, 394	
Jones, Jas	191
Jones, Jane	192, 196
Jones, Jarnas	193
Jones, Jarvis	81, 329, 381
Jones, Jemima	191
Jones, Jeruas	256
Jones, Jesse	206
Jones, Joel	398
JONES, JOHN	193
JONES, JOHN	193
JONES, JOHN	193
JONES, JOHN	193
JONES, JOHN	194
JONES, JOHN	194
JONES, JOHN	194
JONES, JOHN	194
JONES, JOHN	194
JONES, JOHN	194
JONES, JOHN	194
JONES, JOHN, SR.	195
Jones, John (son of John),	193 (2), 194 (4), 197
Jones, John..8, 10, 28, 30, 90, 190, 191, 192, 193 (2), 194 (2), 195 (2), 196, 197 (2), 244, 246, 259, 260 (2), 334, 347, 355, 358, 364, 411 (2).	
Jones, John, Jr.	16
Jones, Cap. John	32 (2)
Jones, Jno	22
Jones, Jon	98
JONES, JONATHAN	195
Jones, Jonathan (son of Jonathan)	195
Jones, Jonth	31
JONES, JOSEPH	195
Jones, Joseph (son of Joseph)	195
Jones, Joseph	30, 92, 143, 194, 195, 196, 366, 394
Jones, Jos	328
Jones, Joshua	253
Jones, Josiah	104
Jones, Josias	176, 194
Jones, Judith (daughter of John)	194
Jones, Judith (wife of John)	194
Jones, Katheran	190
Jones, Katherine	277
Jones, Katy	192
Jones, Lancelot	190
Jones, Lewis	129, 189, 194

INDEX. 525

Jones, Lovick 191
Jones, Lucy 191
Jones, Lydia 191, 229
Jones, Malachy 196
Jones, Margaret 196
Jones, Marget 198
Jones, Margret 196
Jones, Marmaduke 61, 97
Jones, Martha..145, 192, 195
  (3), 344
JONES, MARY 195
Jones, Mary (cousin of
  Ephraim) 214
Jones, Mary (sister of
  Ephraim) 214
Jones, Mary (wife of
  Morris) 195
Jones, Mary (daughter of
  Morris) 195
Jones, Mary (daughter of
  Peter) 196
Jones, Mary (wife of Peter) 196
Jones, Mary..44, 72. 77, 101, 108,
  128, 129, 135, 190, 191, 192 (2),
  193 (3), 194, 195 (2), 196 (3),
  214, 225, 235, 289, 329, 338.
Jones, Mary Ann........... 194
Jones, Matthew 191, 193
Jones, Moris 190
JONES, MORRIS 195
Jones, Morris (son of
  David, Sr.) 190
Jones, Morris (brother of
  David, Sr.).............. 190
Jones, Morris.............. 190
Jones, Nann 87
Jones, Nathaniel 191 (2)
Jones, Neomy 195
Jones, Nehemiah 193
Jones, Patte 194
JONES, PETER 195
JONES, PETER 196
JONES, PETER, SR........... 196
Jones, Peter (son of Peter),
  195, 196
Jones, Peter....121, 150, 198
  (2), 203, 251, 289 (3), 341, 366
Jones, Phillip 47, 192
Jones' plantation 38
Jones, Prior 192
Jones, Priscilla.....191, 194, 377
Jones, Rebecca..........108, 196
Jones, Rebeckah....192 (2), 198
Jones, Richard.......80, 190, 398

Jones, Ridley 191
Jones, Robert........16, 108, 195
Jones, Robert, Jr........... 376
JONES, ROGER 196
Jones, Roger (son of
  .Roger) 196
Jones, Roger..3, 90 (2), 98, 191
  (3), 238, 262, 274, 305, 324, 388
  (2), 424.
Jones, Rog..............122, 380
Jones, Ruth............195, 197
JONES, SARAH 196
Jones, Sarah (wife of
  Peter) 195
Jones, Sarah (daughter of
  Peter) 195
Jones, Sarah (wife of Wil-
  liam) 198
Jones, Sarah (daughter of
  William) 198
Jones, Sarah..4, 18, 159, 190 (2),
  191, 192, 194, 195, 198 (3), 223,
  267.
Jones, Samuel......114, 194, 326
Jones, Samuel (son of
  Samuell) 196
JONES, SAMUELL 196
Jones, Samuell 408
Jones, Sam'll, Jr........... 173
Jones, Silva 198
Jones, Simon..........198, 350
Jones, Siphres 189
Jones, Solomon.....190, 194, 195
Jones, Susan 195
Jones, Susana 347
Jones, Susanna 191
Jones, Taylor 190
JONES, THOMAS 196
Jones, Thomas (son of
  Frederick) 192 (2)
Jones. Thomas (brother of
  Frederick) 192 (2)
Jones, Thomas, of Petty
  Shore 164
Jones, Thomas..4, 12, 13 (2), 76,
  90, 92, 117, 128, 135, 143, 151,
  165, 188, 190 (3), 193, 194 (2),
  195, 196 (3), 197, 221, 238, 240,
  244, 273, 289, 307, 315 (2), 348
  (2), 391, 402, 403 (2), 423.
Jones, Tho..............134, 181
Jones, Thos.............162, 193
Jones, Timmothy 278
Jones, Tingnall 191

	PAGE.
Jones, Vini	77
Jones, Wallis....59, 193, 194 (2), 198 (2), 398	
Jones, Walter	25, 149
JONES, WILLIAM	197
JONES, WILLIAM	197
JONES, WILLIAM	197
JONES, WILLIAM	197
JONES, WILLIAM	198
JONES, WILLIAM	198
JONES, WILLIAM	198
JONES, WILLIAM	198
Jones, William (son of Henry)	197 (2)
Jones, William (son of John)	197 (2)
Jones, William (grandson of William)	197
Jones, William (son of William)	198 (3), 214
Jones, William...18, 20, 72, 163, 168, 190, 192 (2), 193, 194 (2), 196 (3), 198, 214 (2), 310, 311, 320, 334, 345, 366, 376.	
Jones, Willm	90, 143, 304
Jones, Wm	208 (2)
JONES, WILLIAM HARDING	197
Jones, William Harding	192 (2)
Jones, Winnifred	198
Jones, Zackaryath	196
Jones, Zechariah	196
Jones, Zephaniah	196, 221
Johnskintown	386
Jons, Rebecca	250
Jons, Thomas	250
Jonson, John	75
Jordan, Abraham	83, 199
JORDAN, ARTHUR	198
JORDAN, ARTHUR	199
Jordan, Arther (son of Arthur)	198, 199
Jordan, Arthur	308
Jordan, Benjamin	198 (2)
Jordan, Charles	115
Jordan, Cornelius	75, 278
JORDAN, DEBORAH	199
Jordan, Elin	75
Jordan, Elizabeth	80, 198
Jordan, Ester	199
Jordan, Fortune	198
Jordan, George, Sr.	307
Jordan, George	198, 307
Jordan, Henry	198, 382
Jordan, James	198

	PAGE.
JORDAN, JOSEPH	199
Jordan, Joseph..80, 98, 146, 162, 223, 284, 331	
Jordan, Jos.	80
JORDAN, JOHN	199
Jordan, John (son of John)	199
Jordan, John...49, 133, 181 (2), 198, 199, 294, 374, 385	
Jordan, Luarresia	199
Jordan, Matthias	80
Jordan, Mary..146, 199 (2), 376	
Jordan, Penelope	80, 284
Jordan, Rachel	355
Jordan, Rebecca	199 (2)
Jordan, Robert	284, 332
Jordan, Ruth	355
Jordan, Samuel	109, 199, 322
Jordan, Sarah (daughter of Arthur)	199
Jordan, Sarah (wife of Arthur)	199
Jordan, Sarah	198, 199
JORDAN, SOLOMON	199
Jordan, Thomas	190, 198, 214
Jordan, Thos.	184
JORDAN, WILLIAM	199
Jorden, Rachel	355
Jorden, Ruth	355
Jossey, Sarah	84
Joy, Margare	41
Joy, Margery	199
JOY, WILLIAM	199
Joy, Wm.	41
Joyner, Isabell	259
Joyner, Mathew	153
Joyner, Matthew	382 (2)
Joyner, Nehemiah	73
Joyner, Thos.	269
Judkins, Mary	218
Juel, Rachel	382
Jumping Run plantation	140
Justes, Elies	52
Justis, James	282
Justis, John	271
Justis, Mary	282
Justuce, E. (?)	97
Kakcomak, land in	373
KALBIN, JOHN	199
Kanady, Richard	369
Kannady, Jno.	364
KASEWELL, FRANCIS	200
Kasewell, Martha	200
Kasewell, Mary	200
Kasewell, Sarah	200

INDEX. 527

	PAGE.
Katherins Creek, land on....	411
Kearney, Edmond	306
Kearney, Philip	369
Kearney, Sarah......6, 306	(2)
Kearny, Thomas	410
Kearney, Thos.......78, 170, 246, 260, 280, 306	(2)
Kearsey, James	200
Kearsey, John	200
Kearsey, Peter	200
Kearsey, Susanna	200
KEARSEY (CEARSEY) THOMAS	200
Kearsey, Thomas (son of Thomas) 200	(2)
Kearsey, Thomas, Jr.	200
Kearsey, William (son of Thomas)	200
Kearsey, William (grandson of Thomas)	200
Keaton, John	266
Keatten, John	70
Kechen, William	111
Keefe, Elizabeth	200
Keefe, Ellinor	200
KEEFE, FREDERICK	200
Keefe, Frederick (son of Frederick)	200
Keefe, John	200
Keefe, Margrett	200
Keefe, Mary	238
Keefe, Tredell	413
Keefe, Triddle	282
Keel, Ann	189
Keel, Charles..........145,	200
Keel, Elizabeth	375
Keel, Ezekiah	375
KEEL, JOHN	200
Keel, Joseph	375
KEEL, LEMUEL	200
Keel, Mary	189
Keel, Nathaniel.....200, 374,	375
Keel, Priscilla	189
Keel, Robert............115,	310
KEEL, TAMAR	200
Keel, Tamer	200
KEELAND, JOHN	200
Keele, Hardy	77
Keele, Nathaniel	106
Keell, Rob't	226
Keels, Robert	72
Keen, Garrett..........131,	301
Keen, John	77
Keen, Martha	141
Keep, John	238
Keeter, James..........57,	160
Keeton, Elisabeth	201

	PAGE.
Keeton, Elizabeth.......200,	309
KEETON, HENRY	200
Keeton, Jonathan	309
Keeton, Joseph	200
Keeton, Merriam	200
Keeton, Patrick.........201	(2)
Keeton, Sarah	201
KEETON, ZACHARIAH, SR.	201
Keeton, Zachariah (son of Zachariah) 201	(2)
Keeton, Zachariah.......185,	408
Kehukey, plantation on	370
Kehukey Swamp, plantation on	21
Keile, Mary	201
Keile, Robert	201
Keile, Sarah	201
KEILE, THOMAS	201
Keile, Thomas (son of Thomas)	201
Keith, Isabella	348
Keith, James	149
Kelley, Asa	201
Kelley, David	365
Kelley, James	5
KELLEY, JOHN	201
Kelley, Joseph	166
Kelley, Martha	201
Kelley, Mary	145
Kelley, Matthew	89
KELLEY, SARAH	201
Kelley, Sarah (daughter of Sarah)	201
Kelly, Ann	359
Kelly, Bryant	286
Kelly, Elisabeth (wife of John)	201
Kelly, Elizabeth (daughter of John)	201
Kelly, Elizabeth.....14, 146,	201
Kelly, James	201
Kelly, John............201,	328
Kelly, Magdalen	201
Kelly, Martha	284
Kelly, Mary...........201	(2)
KELLY, MATHEW	201
Kelly, Matthew	383
Kelly, Nanna	201
Kelly, Nicholas	201
Kelly, Patrick	201
Kelly, Rebecca	201
KELLY, SMITH	201
Kelly, William	116
Kelly, William, Jr.	146
Kembell, John	273
Kemp, Allen	201

	PAGE.
Kemp, Elizabeth	202
KEMP, GEORGE	201
Kemp, George (son of George)	201
Kemp, Joseph	202, 404
Kemp, John	202 (2)
Kemp, Mary	201
Kemp, Sarah	201, 202
Kemp, Steven	202
Kemp, Thomas	202
KEMP, WILLIAM	202
Kemp, William (son of William)	202 (2)
Kenady, Patrick	188
Kendall plantation	253
Kendricks Creek, land at mouth of	36
Kendricks Creek, land on. 27, 119,	212
Kenedy, Francis	88
Kenedy, Grace	88
Kenedy, James	219
Kenedy, John	202
Kenedy, Patrick	219
Kenedy, Sarah	202
KENEDY, WALTER	202
Kenedy, William	88 (2)
Kenedy, Wm., Jr.	88
Keniday, James	218
Kennaday, William	272
Kennan, Thomas	25
Kennan, William	235
Kennedy, John	202
Kennedy, Mary	202
Kennedy, Thomas	219
Kennedy, William	399 (2), 405
Kenney, John	148
Kenny, Lazarus	179
Kennekinn, Ann	140
KENT, JOHN	202
Kent, Mary	202
Kengues Mill Creek, land on.	1
Kenyon, Joab	202
KENYON, JOHN	202
Kenyon, Mary	202
Kenyon, Roger	24, 363
Kenyons Savannah, land on.	104
Kesia River, plantation on.	406
Kesiah River, land on	138
Kesler, Joanna	42
Kessler, Phillip	31
Keton, Elizabeth	202
KETON, JOHN, SR.	202
Keton, John (son of John, Sr.)	202
Keton, Joseph	202

	PAGE.
Keton, Lewis	202
Ker, Gilbert	4
Kerbys Creek, land on	409
Kerney, Thomas	233
Kerr, Joseph	4
Kershaw, Susannah	38
KIBBLE, ABRAHAM	202
Kibble, Edith	202
Kibble, James	202
Kibble, Luse	202
Kight, John	124
Kilbe, John	133
KILBEE, CHRISTOPHER	202
Kilbee, Elizabeth	202
Kilbee, Epaphroditus	202
Kilbee, Frances	202
Kilbee, Katherine	202
Kilbee, Sarah	202
Kilbee, Xpher	202
Killam Swamp, land on	236
KILLINGSWORTH, FRANCIS	203
Killingsworth, Mary	203
Killingsworth, Nicholas	198
Killingsworth, Nols	203
Killingsworth, Rebeckah	203
KILLINGSWORTH, RICHARD	203
Killingsworth, Richard (cousin of Richard)	203
Killingsworth, Sarah	420
Kilmaney	365
Kimbrough, Buckley	260, 280
KINCE, CHRISTIAN	203
Kince, Edward	203
Kince, Elizabeth	203
Kince, John	203 (2)
Kince, Joseph	203
Kince, Samuel	203
Kince, William	203
Kinchen, Elizabeth	203
Kinchen, John	203 (2)
Kinchen, Lemuel	233
Kinchen, Martha	203
Kinchen, Mary	203
Kinchen, Matthew	409
Kinchen, Temperance	203
KINCHEN, WILLIAM	203
Kinchen, William (son of William)	203
Kinchen, William	233
Kinchen, William, Jr.	233
Kinchen, Wm.	313
Kinchen, W.	233
Kindrecks Creek, Courthouse on	117
King, Ann (wife of Henry).	203

INDEX. 529

	PAGE.
King, Ann (daughter of Henry)	203
King, Catherine	204
King, Catren	203
King, Cattren	203
King, Charles	203 (2)
King, Chas.	171
King, Elisabeth	203
KING, HENRY	203
KING, HENRY	203
King, Henry (son of Henry)	203
King, Henry	203, 204
King, Higason	104
King, Isbel (wife of Michael)	204
King, Isbel (daughter of Michael)	204
King, Jacob	203
King, Joell	139
KING, JOHN	203
King, John (son of John)	203
King, John	25, 158, 204, 261, 349
King, Jno.	377
King, Mary	203, 204, 349
KING, MICHAEL	204
King, Michael (son of Michael)	204
King, Michael	203 (2), 349
King, Mikel	74
King, Nicholas	203
King, Penelope	204
King, Priscilla	203
King, Prudence	203
King, Solomon	151
King, William	104, 203
King, Mr.	292
KINGSTAN, JAMES	204
Kinsay, John	331
KINSE, JOHN	204
Kinse, John	367
Kinse, Presillah	204
Kinsey, Absalom	204
Kinsey, Christian	204
Kinsey, Easter	204
Kinsey, Elizabeth	204
KINSEY, JOHN	204
Kinsey, John (son of John)	204
Kinsey, John	361
Kinsey, Joseph	204
Kinsey, Mary	204
Kinsey, Samuel	204
Kinsy, Thomas	424
Kinyards, plantation at	211

	PAGE.
Kinzey, Henry	184
Kittrell, Jemima	358
Kippin, Marthaann	330
Kippin, Walter	330
Kipps, Dorothy	124
Kirby, Charles	204
Kirby, Easter (wife of Thomas)	204
Kirby, Easter (daughter of Thomas)	204
Kirby, Edward	204
Kirby, Mabel	204
KIRBY, THOMAS	204
Kirby, Thomas (son of Thomas)	204
Kirk, Elizabeth	287
Kirks plantation	50
Kisable Creek, land on	113
KISABLE, MICHAEL	204
Kitching, Thomas	269
KITCHING, WILLIAM	204
Kitshing, William	351
Knight, Ann	205
Knight, Anne	284
Knight, Mrs. Ann	313
Knight, Catherine	205
Knight, Francis	301
Knight, Emmanuel	205, 231, 277
Knight, Hester	177
Knight, James	279
Knight, John	205 (2), 274, 278, 365, 418
Knight, J.	70, 269, 291, 295, 368, 383, 407
Knight, Lewis	42, 205
KNIGHT, LEWIS ALLEXANDER.	205
Knight, Lewis McAlexander.	313
Knight, Martha	24, 205
Knight, Nemiah	205
Knight, Thomas	149
KNIGHT, TOBIAS	205
Knight, Tobias	1
KNIGHT, WILLIAM	205
Knight, William (son of William)	205
Knight, William	24, 205
Knights, Edward	83
Knights, William	83
Knott, Agnee Marvell	203
Knott, Nathaniel	13
Knotts Island, land on	150
Knox, Andr.	221
Knox, Andrew	157, 407
KNOX, JOHN	205
Knox, Margret	205

34

	PAGE.
Knox, Mary	205
Knox, Thomas	205
Knowis, John	62
Knowlan, Catrine	404
Knowls, Robert	2
Koen, Caleb	75
Koen, Daniel	94, 167
Koone, Mikel	183
Kornegey, Abraham	205
Kornegey, Daniel	205
Kornegey, David	205
Kornegey, Elijah	205
KORNEGEY, GEORGE	205
Kornegey, George (son of George)	205 (2)
Kornegey, Jacob	205
Kornegey, John	205
Kornegey, John Jacob	205
Kornegey, Joseph	205
Kornegey, William	205
Kowen, Elizabeth	85
Kubys Creek, land on	7
Laban plantation	147
Lacey, Margreat	126
Lacinse's Creek, plantation adjoining	269
Laciter, George	122
Laciter, Robert	122
Lackey, Mary	323
Lackey, Richard	323
Lacy, Christopher	209
Lacy, Joseph	206
Lacy, Thomas	206
LACY, WILLIAM	206
Lacy, William (son of William)	206
Lacye, Barbary (daughter of William, Sr.)	205
Lacye, Barbary (daughter of William, Jr.)	205
Lacye, Mary (daughter of William, Jr.)	205
Lacye, Mary (daughter-in-law of William, Sr.)	205
Lacye, Mary (granddaughter of William, Sr.)	205
LACYE, WILLIAM, SR.	205
Lacye, William (son of William, Sr.)	205
Lacye, William, Jr.	205 (2)
Ladman, James	14
Laffitte, Sarah	206
LAFFITTE, TIMOTHY	206

	PAGE.
LAKARO (LAKERS), BENJAMIN	206
Lakaro, Juliana	206
Laker, Juliana	92
LAKER, JULIANA	206
Lakers, Mrs. Juliana	42
Lakers, Julian	42
LAMBERSON, HENRY	206
Lamberson, John	207
Lamberson, Mary	206
Lambert, Uriah	176
Lamberthson, Th.	133
Lambirtson, Richard	210
Laman, John	154
Lamon, John	154
Lambrosher, Joseph	185
Lamb, Elizabeth	206
Lamb, Mary	206
Lamb, Miriam (wife of William)	206
Lamb, Miriam	206
LAMB, WILLIAM	206
Lamb, William	113
Lands Ridge, land on	387
Landwell, Elizabeth	69
Lane, Abraham	207
Lane, Barnabas	207
Lane, Barnaby	233
Lane, Betty	294
LANE, CHRISTIAN	207
Lane, Elizabeth	207 (2)
LANE, EPHRAIM	207
Lane, George (brother of Walter)	207
Lane, George (son of Walter)	207
Lane, George	207, 261
Lane, Henry	279
Lane, James	240
Lane, John	123, 207, 233, 261, 350, 399
Lane, John Snoad	350
LANE, JOSEPH	207
Lane, Joseph	44, 233 (2)
Lane, Mary	97, 207 (2), 271, 350 (2), 399
Lane, Rachel	207
Lane, Samuel	207
Lane, Sarah	207 (2)
LANE, THOMAS	207
Lane, Tobe	19
LANE, WALTER	207
Lane, Walter (grandson of Walter)	207

INDEX. 531

	PAGE.
Lane, Walter	271
Lane, William	19, 207 (2), 393
Lane, Willm	383
Lane, Wm	31 (2), 217
Lang, John	86
Lang, Joshua	20
Langathen, Jonathan	122
Langsone, Hannah	331
Langston, Ann	386
Langston, Christian	208
Langston, Martha	426
Langstone, Sary	387
Langstone, Thomas	387
Langworthy, Jonathan	227
Langwiththa, Jonathan	370
Lanier, Annanazah Cristanah	207
Lanier, Clemt	89
Lanier, Elizabeth	207
Lanier, Grase	207
Lanier, Jean	207
Lanier, John	207 (3)
LANIER, ROBERT	207
Lanier, Robert	330, 413
Lanier, Samariah	207
Lanier, Sarah (wife of Robert)	207
Lanier, Sarah (daughter of Robert)	207
Lanier, William	144, 207 (2)
Lankford, William	376
LANKTON, THOMAS	208
Lapierre, John	207
Laporte, John	13
Larance, John	244
Larkins, James	208
LARKINS, JOHN	208
Larkins, John (son of John)	208
Larkins, Tabitha	208
Larkins, William	208
Larness, William	14
Larry, Thomas	332
Lasater, Lidday	129
LASEY, FRANCIS	208
Lasey, Jemima	208
Lasey, John	208
Lasey, Mary Ann	208
Lasey, William	122
Lasher, Jacob	283
Lashly, Lidda	208
LASHLY, PATRICK	208
Lasiter, Ann	171
Lasiter, Jacob	95
Lasittor, Ann	131

	PAGE.
Lason, Mary	370
Lassiter, Agnes	335
Lassiter, Isaac	333
Lassiter, Mary	333
Laster, Sarah	250
Laten, Benjamin	105
Laten, Thomas	259
Latham, Paul	42, 84
Lathan, Deliverance	216
Lathum, Ann	185
Lathum, Elizabeth (wife of Paul)	208
Lathum, Elizabeth (daughter of Paul)	208
Lathum, George	208
LATHUM, PAUL	208
Lathum, Paul	100 (2), 136, 168, 344, 380, 381
Laton, Sarah	264
Latten, Richd	136
Latter, Doyley	62, 266
Lattimer, Elizabeth	29, 208
LATTIMER, WILLIAM	208
Lattimer, Will	29, 128
Lattimer, William	398
LATTIMORE, ELIZABETH	208
Lattimore, William	319
Laughlin, Hugh	359
Laughlin, Patrick	130
Laurence, Mary	283
Laurence, William	210
Laurency, Ann D	110
Lavender, John	53
Lawhon, John	62
Lawler, Danby	209
Lawler, David	209
LAWLER, PATRICK	209
Lawler, Pashent	209
Lawrence, Ann	209
Lawrence, Elisabeth	8 (2)
LAWRENCE, GEORGE	209
Lawrence, George (son of George)	209
Lawrence, George	209, 308
Lawrence, Jane	209
Lawrence, John	209 (2)
Lawrence, Joshua	209
Lawrence, Ju.	125
Lawrence, Margaret	209
Lawrence, Mary	308
Lawrence, Rachell	209
Lawrence, Richard	342
Lawrence, Robert	209, 308
Lawrence, Sarah	209 (2)
Lawrence, Thomas	209 (2)

Index

	PAGE
LAWRENCE, WILLIAM	209
Lawrence, Wm	209
Laws, George	260, 395
Lawson, Durram	209
Lawson (Smith), Isabella,	209 (2)
LAWSON, JOHN (Gent.)	209
Lawson, John..112, 288 (2), 308, 336, 362, 384 (2), 388	
Lawson, John (son of Nathl. Lawson)	288
Lawson, Jno	120
Lawson, Margaret	209
Lawson, Mary..120, 134, 384 (2)	
Lawson, Mary, daughter of.	384
Lawson, Mary (widow of Nathaniel)	120
Lawson, Mary, Jr	384
Lawson, Mary Pallis	209
Lawson, Nathaniel	120
Lawson, Nathl	288, 384
Lawsons plantation	246
LAWSON, SAMUEL	209
Lawter, Ann	209
Lawter, Darby	209
LAWTER, DAVID	209
Lawter, Mary	209
Lawther, Charles	295
Laydain, Francis	115
Laydan, George	351
Layden, Elizabeth	210, 351
LAYDEN, FRANCIS	210
Layden, Francis (son of Francis)	210
Layden, Francis..7, 24, 260, 351 (2), 409	
Layden, George	210, 351
Layden, Isaac	210
Layden, Isack	351
Layden, Mary	210
Layden, William	210, 351 (2)
Layson, Evens Rhoda	108
Layson, Rhoda	108
Layson, Salathyel	108
Layton, Daniell	70
Lazy, Abigail	210
LAZY (LACY), JOHN	210
Lazy (Lacy), Sarah	210
Lea, Godfrey	41
Leachfield, Abraham	421
Leagett, Agness	78
Leagett, John	78
Leago, Wm	427
Leagwit, James	208
Leake, Andrew	187

	PAGE
Lear, Elizabeth	210
LEAR, JOHN	210
Lear, John (grandson of John)	210
Learge, Christian	210
LEARGE, JACOB	210
Learge, Jacob	210
Learge, Mary	210
LEARY, CORNELIUS	210
Leary, Cornelius	117, 210 (2), 220 (2), 268, 289, 319
Leary, Elizabeth	29
Leary, James	210
Leary, James	210
Leary, John	59, 210 (3)
Leary, Mary	210 (2)
Leary, Rebecca	210
Leary, Rebekah	210
LEARY, RICHARD	210
Leary, Richard (son of Richard)	210
Leary, Richard...3, 20 (2), 117, 204, 220 (2), 266, 289, 317, 351, 378, 383, 399.	
Leary, Rich'd...10, 37, 41, 75, 107, 119, 128, 159, 210, 219, 221 (3), 247, 268, 306, 334, 338, 383.	
Leary, Sarah (wife of Richard)	210
Leary, Sarah (daughter of Richard)	210
Leary, Sarah	210, 221
Leary, Sary	210
Leary, Susanah	404
Leary, Thomas	210, 220, 399, 401, 405
Leary, Thos	34
Leath, Agnes	211
Leath, Casia	211
Leath, Catherine	211
Leath, Charles	210, 211
Leath, Dorcas	184, 211
Leath, Frances	211
Leath, Hannah	184, 211, 241
LEATH, JOHN, SR	210
LEATH, JOHN	211
Leath, John (son of John, Sr.)	211 (2)
Leath, John	164, 184, 211
Leath, Keatren	133
Leath, Kezia	184
Leath, Keziah	211
Leath, Lydia	211
Leath, Mary	211 (2)
Leath, Peter	210

INDEX. 533

	PAGE.
Leath, Rachel	211
LEATH, RICHARD	211
Leath, Richard	342
Leath, Samson	211
Leath, Samuel	210
Leath, Sarah	211
Leath, Thomas	210
Leavet, Elizabeth	249
Leay, James	110
Lecky, Adam	177
Ledford, William, Sr.	426
Ledford, Wm.	426
Lee, Arthur	212
Lee, Edward	211, 212
Lee, Elisabeth	212
Lee, Elizabeth	96, 212, 283
Lee, Elizabeth (wife of George)	211
Lee, Elizabeth (daughter of George)	211
Lee, Ferrebee	212
Lee, Ferreby	212
Lee, Frances	212
LEE, GEORGE	211
Lee, George (son of George)	211
Lee, George	17
LEE, JAMES	211
Lee, James (son of James)	211
Lee, James, Jr.	96
Lee, Jane	212
Lee, John	211, 304
Lee, Liddy	326
Lee, Lucreacy	253
Lee, Martha	212, 282
LEE, MARY	211
Lee, Mary	211, 212 (2), 213
Lee, Prissilla	213
Lee, Rachel	212
LEE, RICHARD	212
Lee, Richard (son of Richard)	212
Lee, Robert	211
Lee, Samll.	48
Lee, Sarah	41, 121, 211 (2), 212
Lee, Solomon	212
LEE, STEPHEN	212
Lee, Stephen (son of Stephen)	212
Lee, Stephen	13, 56, 64 (2), 101 (2), 118, 261, 340
Lee, Stephens	212
Lee, Steven	213
LEE, STEVENS	212
Lee, Stevens (son of Stevens)	212

	PAGE.
Lee, Stevens	61 (2), 101, 128, 213
LEE, THOMAS	212
LEE, THOMAS	212
LEE, THOMAS	213
LEE, THOMAS	213
Lee, Thomas (son of Thomas)	213
Lee, Thomas	38, 39, 101, 128, 212, 330
Lee, Thos.	26, 207, 236, 247, 326, 425
Lee, Thos. Warren	280
Lee, Timothy	212
Lee, William (son of William)	212
Lee, William	211 (2), 212 (2), 213, 238, 306
Lee, Willm.	381
Leech, Joseph	23 (3), 192
Leeming, Mary	86
Lees, Capt. Thomas	220
Leeth, George	213
LEETH, JOHN	213
Leeth, Joseph	213
Leffer, Thomas	402
Leflear, Alexander	355
Lefleare, Elizabeth	355
Leftin, Leonard	220
Legard, Wm.	103
Legett, Absalom	45, 114
Legitt, Alexander	213
Legitt, Elisabeth (wife of Thomas)	213
Legitt, Elisabeth (daughter of Thomas)	213
Legitt, James	213
LEGITT, THOMAS	213
Legitt, Thomas	337
Legg, Humphrey	96 (2), 308, 426
Legg, John	423
Legget, Anderson	128
Leggett, David	315
Leggett, Humphrey	156
Leggett, John	78
Leggitt, Mary	58
LEIGH, ANN	213
Leigh, Ann	213
Leigh, Daniel	342
Leigh, Danll.	407
Leigh, Elizabeth	96, 97
LEIGH, JAMES	213
Leigh, James (son of James)	213 (2)
Leigh, James	97 (2), 168, 209, 308, 353

Index.

	PAGE.
Leigh, John	96, 97, 213 (2)
Leigh, Lyonall	213
Leigh, Peter	213
Leigh, Sarah	213
Leirmont, Margaret	214
LEIRMONT, RICHARD	213
Leirmont, Richard	371
Leirmont, Rd.	371
Leirmont, Willielma	214
Leith, Mary	381
Lelly, Elisha	321
Lelly, Sarah	321
Lemuel Cherry herring runn, plantation on	289
Lenard, Judge	320
Lendion, John	20
Lenerton, Levi Markham	83
Lenfield, John	418
Lenning, Peter	86
Lennon, Ann	214
Lennon, Denis	214
Lennon, Ephraim	214
LENNON, JOHN	214
Lennon, John (son of John)	214
Lennox, Fanny	330
Lennox, Dr. Robert	330
Lenox, Ro.	291
Lenox, Rob.	87
Lenox, Robert	331, 348
LEONARD, LOFTIN	219
Leonard, Theophilus	93
Lepper, Anne	214
LEPPER, THOMAS	214
Lepper, Tho.	188
Lerry, Elizabeth	29
Leson, Mary	19
Lesshons, John	25
Lester, John	231
Letel Flate Creek, plantation in	132
Lettel River, plantation on	126
Lettell, Peneleap	327
Levener, William	417
Lewelling, William	391
Lewerton, Elizabeth	214
Lewerton, Elizabeth (wife of William)	214
Lewerton, Elizabeth (daughter of William)	214
LEWERTON, EPHRAIM	214
Lewerton, John (son of John)	214
Lewerton, John	214 (2), 320
Lewerton, Mary	214
LEWERTON, WILLIAM	214

	PAGE.
Lewerton, William (son of William)	214
Lewess, Jacob	213
Lewess, Jno.	213
Lewinton, John	61
Lewis, Abiggail	54
Lewis, Ann	230
Lewis, Anthony	189
LEWIS, DAVID	214
Lewis, David	139, 413
Lewis, Deborah	38
Lewis, Eff	151
Lewis, Elizabeth	120, 215
LEWIS, EVAN	215
Lewis, Eve	163
Lewis, Henry	101
Lewis, Jacob	232
Lewis, James	390
Lewis, Jane	390
Lewis, John	2, 39, 43, 100, 111, 129, 151 (5), 165, 194, 198, 376, 386, 393.
Lewis, John, Jr.	39
Lewis, Joshua	202
Lewis, Josiah	270
Lewis, Luke	151
Lewis, Margarett	170
Lewis, Martha	64, 163
Lewis, Mary	214, 215
Lewis, Mathew	43 (2)
Lewis, Matthew	85
Lewis, Mills	151
Lewis, Mourning	43
Lewis, Phillip	151
Lewis, Prudence	133
Lewis, Richard	38
Lewis, Right	98
Lewis, Robert	329
Lewis, Sarah	38, 301
Lewis, Solomon	215
Lewis, Thomas	183
Lewis, Thos.	301
Lewis, Vesty	378
LEWIS, WILLIAM	215
Lewis, William (son of William)	215 (2)
Lewis, William	2, 11, 64, 171, 315
Lewis, Wm.	44, 270
Lewiss, John	16
Lewiss, Tho.	372
Lickblat, Sarah	180
Liddle, Catherine	227
Liking Root Branch, land on	353
LILE, GEORGE	215
Lile, George (son of George)	215

INDEX. 535

	PAGE.
Lile, John	215
Liles, George	38
Liley, John	14
Lille, John	402
Lilley, Isaac	301
Lilley, John	204, 216
Lilley, Joseph	216
Lilley, Sarah	77, 216
LILLEY, THOMAS	216
Lilley, Thomas (son of Thos.)	216 (2)
Lilley, Thos.	77
Lilley, Timothy	216
Lilley, William	204, 216
LILLINGTON, ALEXANDER	215
Lillington, Alexander	30, 115, 119, 216, 257
Lillington, Alexr.	290
LILLINGTON, ANN	215
Lillington, Ann	215, 216, 289, 296
LILLINGTON, ELIEZER	215
Lillington, Eliezer	353
Lillington, Eliezr.	224
LILLINGTON, ELIZABETH	216
Lillington, Elizabeth	119, 215 (2), 216, 290
Lillington, George	215, 389
LILLINGTON, JOHN	216
Lillington, John	215, 295, 353, 368, 389
Lillington, Mary	215, 216, 297
Lillington, Sarah	90, 215, 216, 295, 296, 297, 389
Lilliput plantation	6
Lilly, Isaac	216
LILLY, JOHN	216
Lilly, John	422
Lilly, Joseph	216
Lilly, Joshua	216
Lilly, Kazeiah	216
Lilly, Thomas, Jr.	204
Lily, Elizabeth	351
Lily, John	82, 351
Lily, Margaret	351
Lily, Sarah	82, 351
Lily, Thomas	351
Lindley, Thomas	359, 386
Lindsay, David	312
LINDSAY, JAMES	216
Lindsay, James	98
Lindsay, Peter	216
Lindsay, Robert	97, 216 (2), 230
Lindsay, William	216
Lingard, Mary	341
Linington, Ann Hutchinson	217
Linington, Christian	217

	PAGE.
LININGTON, EDWARD	217
Linington, Edward (son of Edward)	217
Linington, Edward	225, 307
Linington, Edwd.	118, 307
Linington, Elizabeth	217
LININGTON, GEORGE	217
Linington, George	217
Linington, G.	225
Linington, Hannah	217
Linn, James	228
Linn, William	238
Linney, Robert	406
Linsey, Ann	217
Linsey, Benjamin	217
LINSEY, DANIEL	217
LINSEY, DAVID	217
Linsey, David	185, 217
Linsey, Mary	217
LINSEY, ROBERT	217
Linsey, Sarah	217
Linton, John	52
Linton, Margaret	217
Linton, Moses	48, 114, 228
LINTON, WILLIAM	217
Lipscomb, William Mansfield	209
Lisle, Henry	226
Lisle, Jane	226
Lisle, William	226
Lisler, Henry	68
Lisles, Dorothy	197
Lisles, Henry, Sr.	197
Lisles, Henry, Jr.	197
Lisles, Jane	197 (2)
Lisles, William	197
Lister, Edward	154
Litte (Lille), John	319
Littel Town lands	413
Litteson, James	287 (2)
Litteson (or Sitteson), Samuel	206
Litteson, Samuel	287
Little, Abraham	218
Little, Alexander	218
Little Alligator, land on	172
Little, Andrew	95
Little, Archibald	218
Little Beaver Dam, land on	350
Littlebridge, Joseph	64
Little Bridges, land at	369
Little Cantanknee, land on	393
Little Contentnea, land on	377
Little Creek, land at	25
Little Creek, orchard on	383
Little Creek, plantation on	242
Little Flatty Creek, land on	277

	PAGE.
Little Flatty Creek, plantation at	277
Little, For., plantation	65
LITTLE, GEORGE	217
Little, George	218
Little, Isaac	218 (3)
Little, Jacob	165, 218 (2)
Little, James	218 (2)
LITTLE, JOHN	218
Little, John (son of John)	218
Little, John	218 (2)
Little, Joseph	218
Little, Josiah	120
Little, Josias	278
Little, Margaret	218
Little, Mary	217
Little, Morning	218
Little, Penelope	130, 156, 217
Little, Penelope (wife of William)	218
Little, Penelope (daughter of William)	218
Little River, land at head of	40
Little River, land on	373, 419 (2), 425
Little River, land up	55
Little River, plantation at	215
Little River, plantation on,	352, 423
Little River and the Sound, land on	338
Little Roquis, land on	173
Little Swamp, land on	334
Little Swamp, plantation on	252
Little, Thomas	21
Little, Thomas (grandson of John)	218
Little, Thomas (of Rowan County)	218
Little Town, land at	15
LITTLE, WILLIAM	218
LITTLE, WILLIAM	218
Little, William (son of William)	218 (2)
Little, William	74 (2), 156 (2), 217, 218, 222 (3), 293, 304, 325 (2), 327, 354, 360 (2).
Little, Wm	116, 186, 199, 308
Little, W	52, 294
Littleson, Grissie	411
Littleson, James	383
Littleton, Hannah	40
Littleton, James, Jr.	40
Littman, Mary	143
Littman, Samuell	143
Livingstone, William	165

	PAGE.
Lloyd, Sarah	264
Lloyd, Thos.	90
Loach, Thos.	14
Loack, Elis	124
Loack, Elizabeth	107
Loack, R.	126
Loack, Thomas	20
Loack, Thomas	21, 124, 371, 396 (2)
Loack, Thos.	107, 108 (2), 124, 211 (2), 227 (2), 235, 240, 346.
Loadinar, James	14
LOADMAN, JAMES	218
Loads (Rhodes), Thos.	110
Loard, Peter	297
Lobb, Jacob	405
Lobb, William Grenfell	405
LOCK, BENJAMIN	218
Lock, Benjamin	218
Lock, David	218
Lock, Elizabeth	218
Lock, Hannah	191
Lock, John (son of Benjamin)	218
Lock, John (brother of Benjamin)	218
Lock, John	297
Lock, Joseph	218
Lock, Leonard	218
Lock, Mary	218
Lock, Miriam	218
Lock, Susannah	218
LOCK, THOMAS	218
Lock, Thomas	106
Lockalear, Robert	306
Lockey, Frazer	219
Lockey, Henry	38, 219, 318, 337
Lockey, James	219
LOCKEY, JOSEPH	219
Lockey, Joseph (son of Joseph)	219
Lockey, Sarah (wife of Joseph)	219
Lockey, Sarah (daughter of Joseph)	219
Lockhart, Catherine	289
Lockhart, Elizabeth	219
Lockhart, George	219, 362
Lockhart, Geo.	90
LOCKHART, JAMES	219
Lockhart, James (son of James)	219
Lockhart, James	225
Lockhart, Jas.	53
Lockhart, Lillington	53, 219 (2)

INDEX. 537

	PAGE.
Lockwoods Folly, lands on..	314
LODMAN, JAMES	219
Loe (Loce), John, Sr.	325
Loe (Loce), John, Jr.	325
Loer Broad Creek, plantation on	48
Loften, Leonard	293
Loftin, Benoniea	219
Loftin, Cornelius	219 (2)
Loftin, Jane	219
Loftin, Joyce	219
LOFTIN, LEONARD	219
Loftin, Leonard (son of Leonard)	219 (2)
Loftin, Leonard	287
Loftin, Leonard of Handcock's Creek	239
Loftin, Percelly	219
Loftin, Sarah	238, 239
Log House plantation	66
LOGAN, ALEXANDER	219
Logan, Geo.	253
Loid, Christian	306
Lombroser, Marjory	129
Lombrosker, Joseph	201
London, Gowen	371
Long, Andrew	220 (2)
Long, Ann	221
Long Branch and Creek Swamp, land on	3
Long Creek, lands on	314, 375
LONG, DANIEL	219
Long, Elisabeth	152
Long, Elizabeth	210, 219, 220 (2), 284
Long, Elizabeth (wife of James)	220
Long, Elizabeth (daughter of James)	220
Long, Elizabeth	389
Long, Ester	220
LONG, GILES	220
Long, Giles	220 (3)
Long, Gilles	220
Long Glade plantation	180
Long, Ichabod	221
LONG, JAMES	220
LONG, JAMES	220
LONG, JAMES	220
Long, James (son of James),	220 (3)
Long, James	91, 221 (3), 281, 389
Long, Jemima	220
Long, John	119, 159, 210, 220 (2), 221, 398

	PAGE.
Long, Josheway	406
LONG, JOSHUA	220
LONG, JOSHUA	220
Long, Joshua (son of Joshua)	220
Long, Joshua (son of Thomas)	221
Long, Joshua (brother of Thomas)	221
Long, Joshua	119, 220, 221 (2), 406
Long, Joshuway	220
Long, Keziah	220
Long Leet land	413
Long, Lemuel	221
Long Marsh, land on	72
Long, Mary	220, 284, 389
Long, Reuben	221 (2)
Long, Rebeckah	221, 289
Long, Reuben	221 (2)
Long Ridge, land on	110
LONG, SARAH	220
Long, Sarah	221 (2)
Long, Simeon	221 (2)
Long, Stephen	220
LONG, THOMAS	221
LONG, THOMAS	221
Long, Thomas	60 (2), 119, 152, 220 (3), 221 (4), 389, 406
Long, Thomas (brother of Joshua)	220
Long, Thomas (son of Joshua)	220
Long, Thomas (son of Thomas)	221 (2)
Long, Thos.	221
LONG, WILLIAM	221
LONG, WILLIAM	221
Long, William (son of William)	221
Long, William (nephew of William)	221
Long, William	119, 121, 220, 221, 406 (2)
Longe, Thomas	319
Longlad, Ann	92
Longlarther, Anne	105
Longlather, Ann	219
Longleather, Anne	221
LONGLEATHER, DANIEL	221
Longleather, Elizabeth	221
Lonoday, George	403 (2)
Looking Glass Swamp, plantation on	136
Loosing Swamp, land at	194
Loosing Swamp, land on	399

	PAGE.
Lord, Amelia	222
Lord, Mary	222
Lord, Margaret (wife of William)	222
Lord, Margaret (daughter of William)	222
Lord, Peter	222
Lord, Thomas	222
LORD, WILLIAM	222
Lord, William..105, 222, 253, 372	
Lorence, Rachell	378
Lots, Mary	113
Lough, Thomas	295
Lourre, Pierre	236
Lousin Swamp, plantation on	194
LOVE, AMOS	222
Love, Amos (son of Amos), 222 (2)	
Love, Ann	244
Love, Catherine	222
Love, Charles	222
LOVE, DANIEL	222
Love, Elishe	222
Love, Elizabeth	222
Love, James	222
Love, John	130
Love, Margaret	222
Love, Mary (wife of Amos)	222
Love, Mary (daughter of Amos)	222
Love, Robt.	372
Love, Sarah	222
Love, Thomas	222
Love, Winnefred	222
Love, Wm.	427
Lovel, Mary	192
Lovel, Mary Ann	181
Lovet, John	343
Lovet, Lakkester	327
Lovett, John	319
Lovett, Lankisthur	334
Lovett, Rd.	2
Lovewell, Benjamin.....209, 392	
Lovewell, Christiana	209
Lovick, Anna	163
Lovick, Betsey	420
Lovick, George	163
Lovick, George Phenis	420
Lovick, George Phenney	222
LOVICK, JOHN	222
Lovick, John (nephew of John)	222
Lovick, John....34, 35, 36, 66, 74 (2), 109, 156, 180, 218, 247, 253,	

	PAGE.
282, 283, 291, 306, 313 (2), 325 (2), 417.	
Lovick, J.	297
Lovick, Mr.	418
Lovick, Penelope....218, 222, 420	
Lovick, Sarah....35, 222, 420 (2)	
LOVICK, THOMAS	222
Lovick, Thomas (grandson of Thomas)	223
Lovick, Thomas.....191, 222, 291, 295, 307, 327, 340, 418 (2)	
Lovick, Thos.	420
Low, Ann	223
Low, Ann Letitia	223
Low, Barnabe	223
Low, EMANUEL	223
Low, Emanuel	158
Low, George.......223 (2), 255	
Low, Hannah	223
Low, JOHN	223
Low, John	263, 347
Low, John (son of John)	223
Low, Lidie	223
Low (?), Robinson	223
Low, Thomas	223 (2)
Low, William	347
Lowden, Ann	223
LOWDEN, JOHN	223
Lowden, Robert	223
Lowden, Sarah	223
LOWE, ANN	223
Lowe, Ann	223
Lowe, Anna Latitia	223
Lowe, George	223
Lowe, John.........99, 210, 223	
Lowe, Thomas	359
Lowe, Thos.	112
LOWE, WILLIAM	223
Lowe, William (son of William)	223
Lowe, William	99
Lowell, Abigaill	223
LOWELL, EDMUND	223
Lowes, John	352
Lowie, Richard	246
Lowman, Samuel.......106, 415	
Lowrey, Mary	318
Lowry, Benjamin	224
Lowry, Betey	224
Lowry, Elisabeth	224
Lowry, Elizebeth	224
LOWRY, GEORGE	224
Lowry, Hannah	224
Lowry, James	94
Lowry, John........224 (3)	
LOWRY, JOSEPH	224

INDEX. 539

	PAGE.
Lowry, Joseph	93, 224
Lowry, Lidea	224
Lowry, Mary	69, 224 (2), 395
Lowry, Matthew	129, 374
Lowry, Noah	224
Lowry, Richard	119, 241
LOWRY, ROBERT	224
Lowry, Robert (son of Robert)	224
Lowry, Robert	69, 79, 163, 340, 370, 388, 395 (3), 403
Lowry, Robert, Jr.	147
Lowry, Sarah	224, 388
Lowry, Thomas	93, 224
Lowry, William	224 (3)
Lowther, George	224
Lowther, John	224
Lowther, Margaret	224
Lowther, Nancy	224
Lowther, Nelly	224
Lowther, Thomas	48, 412, 416
Lowther, Thos.	114 (2), 196
LOWTHER, TRISTRIM	224
Lowther, Tristrim	325
Lowther, William	224 (2)
Loyd, David	148 (2)
Loyd, Joseph	202 (2)
LOYD, ROBERT	224
Loyd, Roderick	222
Loyd, Sarah Catherine	224
Loyd, Tho.	49
Loyd, William	202 (2)
Loyde, Elizabeth	224
Loyde, John (son of John)	224
LOYDE (LIDE), JOHN	224
Loyde, Robert	224
Loyde, Sarah	224
Loyde, Thomas	224
Loyed, Mary	141
Luarton, Anne	224
LUARTON, JOHN	224
Lucas, Charity	124
Lucas, Elizabeth	350
Lucas, Henry	350, 422
Lucas, John	94, 95
LUCAS, MARY	225
Lucas, Zachr.	350
Ludford, Ann	225 (2)
Ludford, Anne	118
Ludford, Christian	36, 118, 225 (2)
Ludford, Hanah	225
Ludford, Johana	225
LUDFORD, JOHN	225
Ludford, John	225 (2)
Ludford, Martha	118, 225
Ludford, Mary	72, 118, 225
Ludford, Sarah	118, 225 (3)
Ludford, Thomas	118, 225 (2)
Ludford, Tomson	118, 225
LUDFORD, WILLIAM	225
LUDFORD, WILLIAM	225
Ludford, William (son of William)	225 (3)
Ludford, William (grandson of William)	225
Ludford, William	118
Ludford, William, Jr.	426
Ludlow Castle plantation	46
LUERTON, JOHN	225
Luerton, John	151
Lues, Thomas	378
Lufman, Daniel	225 (2)
LUFMAN, WILLIAM	225
LUFMAN, WILLIAM	225
Lufman, William (son of William)	225 (3)
Lufman, Wm.	300
Lufty (Lutty), Mary (daughter-in-law of William)	226
Lufty (Lutty), Mary (granddaughter of William)	226
LUFTY (LUTTY), WILLIAM	226
Lufty (Lutty), William (son of William)	226 (2)
Luis, Benjamin	226
Luis, Elizabeth	226
Luis, Hudson	226
Luis, John	226
LUIS, RICHARD	226
Luis, William	226
Luker, Ruth	155
LUMBROSIER, JOHN	226
Lumbrosier, Joseph	226
Lumber Bridge, land at	358
Lumley, George	18, 25, 78
Lund, Nicholas	419
Lundy, Sarah	76, 78
Lunr, Nicholas	242
Lurrey, Thomas	423
Lurry, Elizabeth	423
Lurry, Evin	355
Lurry, John	92, 114, 120, 153, 266, 279, 326, 357, 361
Lurry, Miriam	226
Lurry, Thomas	226, 421
LURRY, WILLIAM	226
Luten, Constant	11, 194
Luten, Const.	44
Luten, Hanah	197
Luten, Henderson	292
Luten, John	192

	PAGE.
Luten, Rachel	198
Luten, Samuel	192
Luten, Thomas..11, 197 (2), 246, 292, 376,	393
Luten, Thomas, Jr.	292
Luten, Thos.	24, 98
Luten, William	2, 8
Luten, Wm.	44 (2)
Luton, Adam	226
Luton, Elinor	393
Luton, Elizabeth	226
Luton, James	375
Luton, Mary	226
Luton, Thomas	89, 399
Luton, Thos.	24
Luton, Wm.	172
Lutten, Thomas	407
Lyal, Mathew	93
Lyell, Jno.	369
Lyles, Jefery	15 (2)
Lyles, Wm.	197
Lyncey (or Lynch), Mich.	130
Lynch, Elizabeth (wife of John)	226
Lynch, Elizabeth (daughter of John)	226
LYNCH, JOHN	226
Lynch, Nelly	226
Lyon, Ann	226
Lyon, Elizabeth	226
Lyon, George	226
LYON, JAMES	226
Lyon, James	113
Lyon, John	226, 320, 425
Lyon, Mary	226, 320
Lyon, Mildred	320
Lyon, Richard	97 (2), 320 (3)
Lyon, Richard of Spring Hill	320
Lyon, Zillah	226 (2)
Lysle, Henry	9
Lysle, Jeane	197
Lysles, Henry	320 (2)
Mabery, William	303
MABSON, ARTHUR	227
Mabson, Arthur (son of Arthur)	227
Mabson, Arthur	10, 372, 418
Mabson, Elizabeth	418
Mabson, Mary	227
Mabson, Susanna	227
Mabson, Susannah	417
Mabry, Elizabeth	57
MCADAM, JAMES	227
McAdam, Sarah	227
McAdams, Joseph	227

	PAGE.
MCADAMS, SARAH	227
McAlester, Alexr	232
McAlester, Alex.	422
McAlexander, Sarah	235
McAlexander, Susannah	63
McAlister, Alezr	133
McAlpin, Hannah (wife of William)	227
McAlpin, Hannah (daughter of William)	227
MCALPIN, WILLIAM	227
Macay, James	379
McBride, Fr.	176
Macbride, John	201
Macbride, Sarah	201
McBrie, Robert	128
McBurney, John	177
McCan, James	49
McCanne, Hough	26
McCanne, Nat	204
McCanne, Wm.	204
MCCARTY, BAILEY	227
MCCARTY, DENNIS	227
McCarty, Dennis	227
McCarty, Elinor	227
McCarty, Mary	227
McCeale, Mary	371
MCCLALLAND, ANDREW	227
McClalland, Andrew (grandson of Andrew)	227
McClalland, Andrew (son-inlaw of Andrew)	227
McClalland, James	227
McClalland, Jane	227
McClalland, Thomas	227
McClammy, Luke	228 (2)
McClammy, Mark	228
McClammy, Peter	228 (2)
MCCLAMMY, THOMAS	228
McClammy, Woney	228 (2)
McClee, Robert	27
McClenachan, Robert	288
McClenacken, Robt.	228
MCCLENDEN, DEBORAH	228
Macclelean, Alexander	106
MACCLENDON, DENNIS	228
MacClendon, Dennis (son of Dennis)	228
MacClendon, Elizabeth	228
MacClendon, Francis	228
MacClendon, John	228
MacClendon, Margaret	228
MacClendon, Mary	228
MacClendon, Thomas	228
McClennys plantation	407

INDEX. 541

McClure, Richard...31, 100, 123, 167, 226, 279, 300, 326, 337, 363, 390, 421.
McClure, Richd....47, 57, 62, 85, 114 (3), 135, 141, 150, 153, 160, 172, 180, 184, 190, 213, 217, 266, 270, 273, 348, 356, 361, 419.
McConkey, Alexander....176, 255, 407
McConkey, Patrick 65
McCorkel, Archibald 228
McCorkel, James 228
McCorkel, Margaret 228
McCORKEL, ROBERT 228
McCorkel, Robert (son of Robert) 228
McCorkhill, Margaret 67
MacCoulaskie, Duncan 235
MacCoulaskie, Neill 235
McCoy, Christian 228
McCOY, DANIELL 228
McCoy, Henry 320
McCoy, John 228
McCoy, Lidia 228
McCoy, William 228
MACCRARY, ROBERT 228
McCulloch, Alexr........348, 299
McCulloch, Benjamin 164
McCulloch, Dorothy Berisford 228
McCulloch, Elizabeth Margaret 228
McCulloch, Henrietta Mary.. 228
MCCULLOCH, HENRY 228
McCulloch, Mary 228
McCulloch, Patt............ 124
McCulloch, Penelope Martha 228
McCulloch, Sarah 162, 164
McCwean, James 76
McDaniel, Archibald 301
McDaniel, Charles 14
MACDANIEL, JAMES 229
MacDaniel, James (son of James) 229
MacDaniel, John 229
MacDaniel, Levinah 229
MacDaniel, Margaret 229
MacDaniel, Risdon 229
McDaniel, James 54
McDaniel, Joan 301
McDaniel, Randel 394
McDaniel, Sarah (daughter of Daniel) 229
McDaniell, Ann 229
MacDaniell, Ellener 229
MACDANIELL, OWEN 229
MCDANIELL, DANIEL 229
McDaniell, Daniel (son of Daniel) 229
McDaniell, James 229
McDaniell, Nicholas 229
McDaniell, Sarah (wife of Daniel) 229
Macdesley, John 252
Macdonel, Sarah 51
MacDonald, Archibald 234
McDonald, Dun............. 45
McDonald, James 245
McDoule (McDowell), Peter, 231
McDowell, Christian 229
MCDOWELL, JAMES 229
McDowell, James 229
MCDOWELL, JOHN 229
McDule, Peter 199
Mace, Ann 229
Mace, Anne 230
Mace, Benjamin 230
Mace, Elizabeth 229
MACE, FRANCIS 229
Mace, Francis (son of Francis) 229
Mace, Hanna 230
Mace, John 229, 417
Mace, Jonas 230
Mace, Sarah 229
MACE, WILLIAM 230
Mace, William (son of William) 230
Mace, William (nephew of William) 230
McFarlan, Daniell.......119 (2)
McFarlan, Walter 278
McFarland, Alex............ 285
McFarland, Daniel 270
McFarlane, Daniel 214
McFarling, Jeanet 106
MacFee, Duncan 234
McFeters, Daniel 97
McGee, Andrew 230
McGee, Ann ....,...... 252
McGee, Elizabeth 314
McGee, Jean 230
MCGEE, JOHN 230
McGee, John (son of John).. 230
McGee, Martha..........230 (2)
McGee, Samuel 230
McGee, Susanah 230
McGee, William 230
McGibbins, John 153
McGillivray, Alexr. 422

542 INDEX.

McGrah, John............56, 397
McGregor, Africa 230
McGregor, Gregor 230
McGREGOR, HUGH 230
McGregor, John 230
McGregor, Patrick 230
McGregore, Hem............ 130
MacGuffie, Ephraim 305
McGuire, Thomas 405
Machapongo, plantation in.. 96
Machapungo River, land on.. 337
McHarlin, John 51 (2)
Machecomock Creek, plantation on.................... 13
McHenry, George Augustus.. 58
McHenry, Phereby.......58 (2)
McHenry, Sarah Ann....... 58
McHenry, Susanna 58
McHenry, Wineford 58
Machenry, Margaret 107
Machepungo River, plantation on.................... 403
Mack, John 427
Mack, William 427
McKane, George 322
MacKane, John 230
MACKANE, GEORGE 230
Mackane, Geo............... 405
MacKane, Margaret 230
MacKane, Mary (wife of George) 230
MacKane, Mary (daughter of George) 230
MacKane, Sophia 230
MACKARTY, TIMOTHY 230
MacKarty, Mary 230
McKay, John 127
Mackay, Hugh 101
Mackay, John 316
Mackay, William 27
Mackbride, James 75
Mackcone, John 131, 170
Mackdaniel, Ann 230
Mackdaniel, Ele 193
Mackdaniel, Elexander 230
Mackdaniel, Daniel (son of Daniel) 230
Mackdaniel, Dority 193
Mackdaniel, William 195
Mackdaniell, Archbell 230
MACKDANIELL, DANIEL 230
Mackdaniell, James 230
Mackdaniell, Mary 230
Mackdaniell, Sarah (wife of Daniel) 230

Mackdaniell, Sarah (daughter of Daniel) 230
Macke, Ann 348
McKean, George 163, 300
McKean, Geo................ 426
Makeand, John 418
McKee, William 222
McKee, Wm. 180
McKeel, Anthony 231
McKEEL, BENJAMIN 231
McKeel, Benjamin........231 (2)
McKeel, Daniel 231
McKeel, Elizabeth.......231, 232
McKeel, Grace..........232 (2)
McKeel, James 301
McKEEL, JOHN 231
McKeel, John (son of John). 231
McKeel, John....42, 82, 140 (2), 145, 202, 231 (4), 232, 288, 291, 397.
McKeel, Jno.........277, 291, 400
McKeel, Joseph 231
McKeel, Margaret 231
McKeel, Mary.......145, 231 (2)
McKeel, Milla 232
McKeel, Miriam 232
McKeel, Nathaniel 231
McKEEL, REBECCA 231
McKeel, Sarah 231
McKeel, Thamar 231
McKEEL, THOMAS 231
McKEEL, THOMAS 231
McKEEL, THOMAS 232
McKeel, Thomas (son of Thomas) 231 (2)
McKeel, Thomas....231 (3), 398
McKeel, Thos................ 231
McKeel, Wineyfruit (Winifred) 232
Mackeel, Daniel.........201, 379
Mackeel, John..........201, 273
Mackeel. Thomas...273, 397, 398
MacKeele. Francis 183
McKeele, Jno. 392
McKeell, John 358
McKEELL, JOHN 231
McKeell, John (son of John) 231
McKeell, Margrett 231
McKeell, Sophia 231
McKeell, Thomas 231
McKeell, Thomas, Jr........ 231
McKeell, Thos............... 245
Mackeell, Ann 231
MACKEELL, ANTHONY 231
Mackeell, Anthony (son of Anthony) 231

INDEX. 543

	PAGE.
Mackeell, John	231, 262 (2)
Mackeell, Joseph	231
Mackeell, Rabackey	231
Mackeell, Sarah	231
Mackeel, Thomas	231
McKeels, Thomas	83
McKeithan, Donald	232
McKEITHAN, DUGALD	232
McKeithan, James	232 (2)
McKeithan, John	232
McKeithan, Mary	232 (2)
McKeithan, Sarah	232
McKeithen, A.	74
McKeithen, Mary	92
Mackelending, Thomas	345
Mackelroy, Adam	232
Mackelroy, David	232
Mackelroy, Elizabeth (daughter of James)	232
Mackelroy, Elizabeth (wife of James)	232
MACKELROY, JAMES	232
Mackelroy, James	232 (2)
Mackelroy, John	232
Mackelroy, Sarah	232
Mackelroy, Thomas	232
Mackelway, James	206
McKenny, John	277, 308
McKenny, Rachel	277
McKenny, Thomas	385
Macker, John	121
Mackey, Isaac	206
Mackey, Jane	227
Mackey, Mary	348
Mackey, William	213
Mackey, Capt. William	26, 27
Mackey, Wm.	26, 212
Mackfarrell, Jacob	232
MACKFARRELL, JOHN	232
Mackfarson, Jonathan	399
Mackgregory, Gregory	163 (2)
Mackgregory, Patrick	163 (2)
MACKGUE, LAWRENCE	232
Mackie, John	373
Mackie, Susanah	226
Mackie, William	226
McKildo, John	8, 123, 282
McKildo, Jno.	171
Mackilwean, Elizabeth	232
Mackilwean, Elinor	232
MACKILWEAN, FRANCIS	232
Mackilwean, Francis (son of Francis)	232
Mackilwean, Fras.	216
Mackilwean, Gatsey	232
Mackilwean, Hanah	232

	PAGE.
Mackilwean, John	233
Mackilwean, Jos.	185
Mackilwean, Mary (daughter of Francis)	232
Mackilwean, Mary (wife of Francis)	232
Mackilwean, Nancy	232
Mackilwean, Penelopy	232
Mackilwean, Richard Francis	66
McKingbush, Anne	300
MACKINNE, BARNABEE, JR.	233
MacKinne, William	233 (2)
Mackinne, Barnaby	233 (2)
MACKINNE, JOHN	233
Mackinne, Martha	233
Mackinne, Mary (wife of John)	233
Mackinne, Mary (daughter of John)	233
Mackinne, Mary	233 (3)
Mackinne, Patience	233 (2)
MACKINNE, RICHARD	233
Mackinne, Robert	233 (2)
McKinne, Martha	234
McKinne, Mary (daughter of Mary)	234
McKinne, Patience	234
McKinney, Barnaby	234
McKinney, John	234
MCKINNEY, MARY	233
McKinney, Matthew	310
McKinnie, Barnaby	233
McKinzie, Ann	234
McKinzie, Janet	141, 234
MCKINZIE, JOHN	234
McKinzie, John (son of John)	234
McKinzie, Kenneth	234
McKinzie, William	234
McKithan, Dugald	141
Mackkey, Mary	214
Mackland, Charles	410
Macknary, Gilbert	13
Macknight, ——	82
Macknights plantation	257
Macknicol, Elizabeth	108
MacKoone, Thomas	131
Mackwilliams, Thomas	31, 346
Macky, Daniel	235
Macky, John	163
Macky, Margeret	235, 275
Macky, Thos.	275
MACKY, WILLIAM	235
Maclaine, A.	97, 241, 422

544 INDEX.

	PAGE.
Maclaine, Archibald	102, 320, 392
MacLaine, Arc.	312
MacLaine, Elizabeth	320
Maclaine, Katherine	392
McLauchlin, Nancy	232
MACLEARAN, ARCHIBALD	234
MacLearan, Archibald (son of Archibald)	234
MacLearan, Duncan	234
MacLearan, Florence	234
MacLearan, John	234
MACKLEMORE, ABRAHAM	234
Macklemore, Abraham	234
Macklemore, Atkin	234
Macklemore, Charles	234
Macklemore, Ephraim	234
Macklemore, Fortain	234
MACKLEMORE, JAMES	234
Macklemore, James (son of James)	234
Macklemore, John	234
Macklemore, Mary	234
Macklemore, Margory	234
Macklemore, William	234 (2)
Macklemore, Young	234
Maclendon, Elinore	58
Mackley, Anne	234
Mackley, Marey	234
Mackly, Barbery	234
MACKLY, HENRY	234
McLin, Thomas	238
MACMIEL, JOHN	235
McMing, Neal	285
McNair, Robert	340
McNallin, Hannah	19
McNary, Elisabeth	235
MCNARY, GILBERT	235
McNary, Gilbert	145
McNary, Jane	235
McNary, Mary	235
McNary, William	235
MacNaughten, Charles	235
MacNaughten, Isbell	235
MacNaughten, Mary	235
MACNAUGHTEN, RANALD	235
McNaughten, Niell	235
McNeary, Gilbert	64
MacNeil, Isabel	392
McNeill, Catherine	133
McNeill, Hect.	232
McNeill, Huton	133
McNeill, Neill	133
Macnoral, William	109
McPeters, Daniel	314
Macquin, John	118

	PAGE.
Macrae, Robert	41
McRee, James	235
McRee, John	235
McRee, Robert	235
McRee, Samuel	235
McRee, Susannah	235
MCREE, WILLIAM	235
McRee, William (son of William)	235 (2)
McRee, William	63, 297
McRee (McKee), Wm.	214
McRee, Wm.	404
McWilliams, Jno.	243
MADDOX, JOHN	235
Maddox, Joseph	359
Maddox, Miriam	235
Maddren, Richard	138, 302
Maddux, Sarah	173
Madling, Hannah	266
Madlin, Joseph	101
Madren, Anna	302
Madren, Ann	67, 138, 235
Madren, Elizabeth	235
Madren, Jacob	181, 236
Madren, Joseph	236
Madren, Reuben	235
MADREN, RICHARD	235
Madren, Richard	193, 302 (2), 311
Madren, Ruth	235
Madren, Sarah	236
Madren, Thomas	235
Magett, Jane	237
Magett, Niclas	237
Magnier, Phillip	44
Magnier, Phillip, Jr.	44
Magnier, Samuel	44
Mague, Lawrence	408
Mahains, Sarah	238
Maherin, land at	192
Maheron River, land on	117
Mahomets Swamp, land on.	384
Maidenhare Creek, land on.	37
Maikdsunace, Arthur	33
Mainard, John	293
Mainner, John	200
Mainner, Sarah	200
Mainner, William	200 (2)
Mainner, William (son of William)	200
Mainwaring, Stephen	285
Maio, Edward	159
Maison, Elizabeth	280
Maison, John	280
Major, Ann	153

INDEX.

	PAGE.
Major Harves Quarter, land on	221
Makee, Catherine	236
MAKEE, DANIELL	236
Makee, Daniell (son of Daniell)	236
Makee, Elinor (daughter of Daniell)	236
Makee, Elinor (wife of Daniell)	236
Makee, John	236
Makefarson, Joseph	47
Makefashion, Andrew	24
Makefashion, Danniell	24
Makefashion, William	114
Malin, James	418
Mallard Creek and Goose Creek, land between	102
Mallard, Francis	146
Mallden, Thos.	213
Mallington, Richard	65
Malpass, Jeremiah	334
Mals, George	113
Maltimer, Hannah	203
Malto, Elizabeth	207
Man, Absalom	236
Man, Bridgett	236
Man (?), Dorrity	236
Man, Edward	236 (2)
Man, Elizabeth	236
Man, Frederick	236
Man, Jesse	236
MAN, JOHN	236
MAN, JOHN	236
Man, John (son of John)	236
Man, John	146, 236, 402
Man, Joseph	236 (2)
Man, Lizebeth (wife of John)	236
Man, Lizebeth (daughter of John)	236
Man, Mary	236
Man, Theophalos	236
Man, Theophalus	236
MAN, THOMAS	236
Man, Thomas (son of Thomas)	236
Man, Thomas	236
Man, William	225, 236, 401
Mandar, John	192
Manden, Mary	237
MANDEN, THOMAS	236
Manden, Thomas	5
Mander, John	387
Mandovel, Diney	236
Mandovel, Elizabeth (wife of John)	236

	PAGE.
Mandovel, Elizabeth (daughter of John)	236
MANDOVEL, JOHN	236
Mandovel, John (son of John)	236
Mandovel, Rebeckah	236
Mandovel, Samuel	236
Mandovel, Stephen	236
Manear, John	95
Maner, Henry	237 (2)
Maner, Jacob	183, 237
MANER, JOHN	237
Maner, William	237
MANEY, JAMES	237
Maney, James (son of James)	237
Mann, Bridget	170
Mann, Theophilus	312
Mann, Thomas	334
Mannerly, Henry	401
Manning, John	124
Mansfield, Hannah	200
Mansfield, Thomas	356
Manson, Mary	373
Manson, William	373
Manuel (Portugee servant)	405
Manuels or Creekits plantation	293
Manwaring, Stephen	422
Many, James	16
Marchant, Kedar	44
Marchel, James	127
Marchment, William	113, 343
Marck, Anthony	298
MARCKHAM, ANTHONY	237
Marckham, Anthony (son of Anthony)	237
Marckham, Anthony	291 (2), 400
Marckham, Anthony, Jr.	291
Marckham, Charles	237
Marckham, Joshua	237
Marckham, Joy	237
Marckham, Levy	237 (2)
Marckham, Lewy	141
Marckham, Mary	237
Marckham, Tamar	237
Marckhum, Anthony	127
Marcum, Charles	72
Marcum, Levi	72
MarkDory, John	396
Mardner, J.	337
Mardrum, Betty	355
Mareman, Andrew	202
Margaret Jordans Fork plantation	214

	PAGE.
Margin, Jacob	70
Marke, John	122
Markham, Antho.	237
Markham, Anthony..42, 83, 202, 231, 232, 237 (2),	400
Markham, Charles..148, 231,	237
Markham, Elizabeth 83,	237
MARKHAM, JOSHUA	237
Markham, Joshua	388
Markham, Josua	237
Markham, Joy	262
MARKHAM, LEVI	237
Markham, Levi	231
Markham, Louis	115
Markham, Mary	237
Markham, Thomas	148
Markland, Chas.	157
Marks, John	15
Marlington, Richard	65
Marr, Alif	237
MARR, JOSEPH	237
Marr, Joseph	178
MARSDEN, ALICE	238
Marsden, Alice (daughter of Alice)	238
Marsden, Alice	315
Marsden, Elizabeth	238
Marsden, Peggy	238
Marsden, Richard	238
Marsden, Rufus......46, 123,	315
MARSDEN, THOMAS	238
Marsden, William	238
Marsh Branch, land on	121
Marsh, Bryant	427
Marsh, Darius	427
MARSH, EDWARD	427
Marsh, George	405
Marsh, Katherine (wife of Edward)	427
Marsh, Katherine (child of Edward)	427
Marsh, Katherine	427
Marsh, Mary	384
Marshal, William	298
Marshall, Absolem	238
Marshall, Amy 238,	262
Marshall, Elizabeth 238,	299
Marshall, Humphrey	238
MARSHALL, JOHN	238
Marshall, John (son of John).	238 (2)
Marshall, John	262
Marshall, Jno.	238
Marshall, Margaret 238	(2)
Marshall, Mary	394
Marshall, Priscilla	238

	PAGE.
Marshall, Samuel	394
Marshall, Thos.	238
MARSHALL, WILLIAM	238
Marshel, James	180
Marston, Ann 238	(2)
MARSTON, ELIZABETH	238
Marston, Mary	238
Marston, Mourning......238	(2)
Martain, John	209
Marten, Else (daughter of John)	239
Marten, John	8
Marten, Mary	239
Martin, Agnes	8
Martin, Ann....225, 239 (2), 240,	350
Martin, Annah	176
Martin (Scott), Anne	240
Martin (Scott), Annes	240
Martin, Charles Ardison	225
Martin, Edne	240
Martin, Elias	110
MARTIN, ELIZABETH	238
Martin, Elizabeth...239 (2),	240 (2)
Martin, Else (wife of John).	239
Martin, Frances	225
Martin, Francis	311
MARTIN, GEORGE	239
Martin (Scott), Henry	240
Martin, James 39,	375
Martin (Scott), James	240
MARTIN, JOEL	239
Martin, Joel.....47, 225, 240 (2), 304,	350
Martin, Jo...2, 8, 17, 22, 50, 52, 58, 63, 80, 82, 84, 95, 99, 111, 120, 124, 127 (2), 138, 140 (2), 152, 153, 172 (2), 173, 178, 185, 198, 205, 207, 212, 214, 222, 228, 230, 232, 233, 235, 241, 242 (2), 243, 245, 249, 250, 262, 273, 274, 278, 300, 305, 309, 311, 313, 314, 316 (2), 322, 326, 331, 332, 333, 338, 341, 354, 358, 359, 362, 372 (2), 373, 376, 389, 391, 394 (2), 396, 404, 407, 410,	417.
MARTIN, JOHN	239
Martin, John (son of John).	239
Martin, John......8, 62, 196, 239 (2), 240 (3), 275, 289, 393, 401,	424.
Martin, Jos.	64
Martin, Joseph.........239,	240
Martin, Joshua.........239	(2)

INDEX.

	PAGE.
Martin, Lodowick	214
Martin, Lodwick	396
Martin, Lucrece	47
Martin, Lucy	8
Martin (Scott), Lurane	240
Martin, Mary	155, 225, 240 (2)
Martin (Scott), Mary	240
Martin, Miriam	239
Martin, Moses	239
MARTIN, NATHANIEL	239
Martin, Nathaniel	135 (2), 239, 275
Martin, Richard	182, 239 (2), 240
Martin, Robert	239
Martin, Roger	144
Martin, Saml	286
Martin, Sarah	3, 135, 225, 239, 350
Martin, Stephin	156
Martin, Susannah	225
MARTIN, THOMAS	239
Martin, Thomas	113, 239
Martin (Scott), Thomas	240
Martin, Thos.	21
MARTIN, WILLIAM	239
MARTIN, WILLIAM	240
MARTIN, WILLIAM	240
MARTIN, WILLIAM	240
Martin, William (son of William)	240 (2)
Martin (Scott), William (son of William)	240
Martin, William	2, 239, 350, 422
Martindale, John	168
Martyn, J.	39, 45, 185, 186, 225 (2), 287, 347, 357, 373
Martyn, John	183, 185, 217, 240
Maryland, Caleb	72
Masbone, Daniel	311
Mashbone, Elizabeth	311
Mashborne, Daniel	240
Mashborne, Edward	240
MASHBORNE, JETHRO	240
Mashborne, Mary	240
Mashborne, Sarah	240
Mashborne, Susanna	240
Maschamp, G.	155
Maschamp, George	154
Mashell, John	287
Mash Swamp, land on	195
Maskil, Daniel	240
Maskil, Dorothy	240
MASKIL, WILLIAM	240
Mason, Agnes	241

	PAGE.
Mason, Ann	240, 241
Mason, Benjn.	195
Mason, Benja.	190
Mason, Benjamin	241 (4), 337
Mason, Caleb	254
Mason, Catharina	241
Mason, Charity	241
Mason, Christopher	241
Mason, David	241
Mason, Dorcas	241
Mason, Elisebeth	190
Mason, Elizebeth	241
MASON, JOHN, SR.	241
MASON, JOHN	240
MASON, JOHN	240
MASON, JOHN	241
Mason, John (son of John)	241
Mason, John	33 (2), 56, 108, 241 (2), 337
Mason, John, Jr.	241
Mason, Joseph	241
Mason, Joshua	241
Mason, Moses	241 (2)
Mason, Margaret	241
Mason, Martha	273
MASON, MARY	241
Mason, Mary (wife of John)	241
Mason, Mary (daughter of John)	241
Mason, Mary	31, 56, 175, 241
Masons Neck plantation	284
Mason, Rachel	227
MASON, ROGER	241
MASON, ROGER	241
Mason, Roger (son of Roger)	241
Mason, Roger (son of Roger)	241
Mason, Roger, Jr. (grandson of Roger)	241
Mason, Roger	214, 240, 241, 337
Mason, Roger, Jr.	184, 211, 241, 337
Mason, Sarah	56, 241
Mason, Susannah	241
Mason, Thomas	240, 241 (4)
Mason, Thomas, Jr.	241
Massapungo Swamp, plantation on	196
Massenburg, Major Nicholas	20
Massey, Elizabeth	242
MASSEY, HEZEKIAH	242
Massey, Hezekiah (son of Hezekiah)	242

INDEX.

Massey, John 242 (3)
Massey, Lucy 242
Massey, Richard 242
Massey, Sarah 242
Massey, William 242
Massy, Francis 36
Massy, John 36
Massy, Richard 36
Masters, Arcala 242
MASTERS, JOHN 242
Masters, John 242
MASTERS, JOSEPH 242
Masters, Joseph (son of
  Joseph) 242
Masters, Joseph 242 (2)
Masters, Julyann 242
Masters, Samuel.....242 (2), 262
Masters, Samll.............. 238
Masters, Sarah 242
MASTERS, THOMAS 242
Masters, Thomas 242 (2)
Masters, Thos............... 280
Mastres, Josiah 136
Mastres, Thos............... 136
Matchapungo Creek, land on,
                    109, 239
Matchapungo Swamp, land
  at 244
Matchapungo River, land on. 345
Matchapungo Creek, land on. 108
Matchepungo River, land on. 94
MATHAM, RALPH 242
Matham, Ralph 33
MATHERS, EDWARD 242
Mathers, Mathers Lurenia.. 242
Mathers, Mary 242
Mathers, Priscilla 242
Mathers, Sarah...........31, 242.
Mathews, Ann 217
MATHEWS, CHARITY 242
Mathews, James 242
Mathews, John 382
Mathews, Jno............... 49
Mathews, Precilla 243
MATHEWS, THOMAS 243
Matlock, Jno................ 62
Mattchacomak Creek, plantation on 44
Matthews, Elizabeth 390
Matthews, George 362
Matthews, John 108, 413
Matthews, Jno............... 180
Matthews, Nathaniel 68
Matthews Point plantation.. 27
Matthias, Elizabeth 243

MATTHIAS, JOHN 243
Matthias, William 243
Mattock, John 215
Mattocke, Ann 243
Mattocke, Elizabeth 243
MATTOCKE, JOHN 243
Mattocke, John..26, 181, 213,
                    231, 336
Mattocke, Jno............336, 337
Mattocke, Mary 243
Maudlin, Edward 204
MAUDLIN, EZEKIEL 243
Maudlin, Ezekiel........204, 380
Maudlin, Hannah.......243, 378
Maudlin, James 243
Maudlin, Jeremiah.......243 (2)
Maudlin, Joshua 243
Maudlin, Sarah 243
MAUDLIN, THOMAS 243
Maule, Anne 243
Maule, Barbara 244
Maule, Elizabeth (wife of
  John) 243
Maule, Elizabeth (daughter
  of John) 243
Maule, Elizabeth 243
Maule, Jemima 243
MAULE, JOHN 243
Maule, John 244
Maule, Mary 244
Maule, Moses 243
Maule, Pat 216
MAULE, PATRICK 243
Maule, Patrick......128, 244,
                274, 296, 402
Maule, Penelope (wife of
  William) 244
Maule, Penelope (daughter
  of William) 244
Maule, Penelope 243
Maule, Sarah 244
MAULE, WILLIAM 244
Maule, William 117, 164
Maules Neck, land on....... 350
MAULTSBY, JOHN 244
MAULTSBY, JOHN 244
Maultsby, John (son of
  John) 244
Maultsby, John (nephew of
  John) 244
Maultsby, John 31
Maultsby, Mary (mother of
  John) 244
Maultsby, Mary (sister of
  John) 244

INDEX. 549

	PAGE.
Maultsby, Mary	244
Maultsby, William	65, 244 (2)
Maultsbys Point plantation	253
Maverts plantation	65
Maxwell, Wm.	101
May, Mary	357
May, Richard	28
Mayberry, Benjamin	162
Mayfield, Ann	244
MAYFIELD, PETER	244
Maynor, Martha	424
Mayo, Ann	38, 244
MAYO, EDWARD	244
MAYO, EDWARD	245
Mayo, Edward (son of Edward)	244
Mayo, Edward	17 (2), 42, 67, 70, 86, 89, 96, 105, 122, 131, 157, 187 (2), 200, 236, 248 (2), 253, 267, 290, 294 (2), 302, 311, 318, 329, 331, 335, 340, 347, 352, 388, 423.
Mayo, Elizabeth	244
Mayo, John	213
Mayo, Joseph	244, 264
Mayo, Lenine	114
Mayo, Mary	74, 162, 186, 187, 215
Mayo, Mary (wife of Edward)	244, 245
Mayo, Mary (daughter of Edward)	244, 245
Mayo, Sarah	244
Mayo, Thomas	114
Mays Beaver Dam, land in fork of	350
Mead, James	173
Meades, Thomas	245
Meades, Timothy	205
Meadow Branch, lands on,	43 (2), 71
Meadowes, plantation in	154
Meads, Ann	10, 245, 346
Meads, Elizabeth	200
Meads, John	245
Meads, Susannah	200
Meads, Thomas	200 (2)
MEADS, TIMOTHY	245
Mearns, William	8, 195, 348, 395
Mearns, Will	8, 32, 33, 39, 43, 58, 83, 104, 118, 129, 143, 147, 178, 278, 321, 353, 391.
Mearns, Wm.	142, 299 (2), 326, 337, 361, 403
Meavis, Benjamin	245

	PAGE.
Meavis, John	245
Meavis, Leah	245
Meavis, Pigo	245
MEAVIS (MEVOIS), MARK	245
Meavis, Nathan	245
Medford, Daniel	245
Medford, Elizabeth (daughter of Henry)	245
Medford, Elizabeth (wife of Henry)	245
Medford, Ferrebee	245
MEDFORD, HENRY	245
Medford, Henry (son of Henry)	245
Medford, James	245
Medford, John	245 (2)
Medford, Mary	245
Medleton, Elisabeth	109
Medlin, Richard	229
Meed, John	245
Meed, Mary	245
Meed, Milloson	245
Meed, Thomas	245
MEED, TIMOTHY.	245
Meeds, John	189
Meeds, Elizabeth	245
MEEDS, SUSANNAH	245
Meeds, Sussanah	245
MEEDS, THOMAS	245
Meeds, Timothy	245 (3), 402
Meegs, Hanner	300
Meeket, John	326
Meers, Grace	4
Meesel, Mark	354
Meesel, Mary	354
Meesel, William	354
Meetinghouse tract	358
Meggs, Thomas	387
Meglohon, Alce	246
MEGLOHON, JAMES	246
Meglohon, James (son of James)	246
Meglohon, Margerit	246
Meherin Creek, land on	126
Meherin Cypress Swamp, land on	144
Meherrin Neck, land in	218
Meherring Landing, land at.	15
Meids, Ann	359
Meline, Ellliner	189
Mellar, William	322
Mellyne, Robert	236, 420
Melhen, Robert	86
Melhen, Richd.	86
Melton, Ancel	246
Melton, Barraby	347

INDEX.

	PAGE.
Melton, Berabe	109
Melton, Isesum	246
Melton, James	246
Melton, Jonathan, court held at house of	240
Melton, Nathan	246 (2)
Melton, Nathaniel	246
MELTON, ROBERT	246
Meltune, Saml	215
Menzies, James	2
Mercer, Jacob	30
Mercer, James	361
Mercer, Mary	299
Mercer, Sarah	339
Mercer, Thomas	30, 404
Merchant, Abiah	155
Merchant, Christopher	155 (2)
Merker, John	314
Merrick, Geo	51
Merrick, John	425
Merriday, Elizabeth (daughter of Thomas)	246
Merriday, Elizabeth (wife of Thomas)	246
Merriday, Mary	246
Merriday, Sarah	246
MERRIDAY, THOMAS	246
Merriday, Thomas	363
Merriday, Thos	158
Merringer, Francis	2
Merrit, Benjamin	246
Merrit, Efrum	246
Merrit, Mary	246
Merrit, Mary (wife of Nathaniel)	246
MERRIT, NATHANIEL	246
Merrit, Nathaniel (son of Nathaniel)	246
Merrit, Sarah	246
Merrit, Thomas	159
Merritt, Ann	246
Merritt, Betty	246
MERRITT, CHARLES	246
Merritt, Charles (son of Charles)	246
Merritt, Hardy	246
MERRITT, JOHN	246
Merritt, John (son of John)	246
Merritt, John	246
Merritt, Mary	246
Merritt, Nathaniel	246, 268
Merritt, Sarah	246
Merritt, Thomas	246
Merritt, Thos	246
Merritt, William	246

	PAGE.
Merryman, Benjamin	207, 393
Mesell. Marke	354
Mesigood, Mary	282
MESLER, CEARSMEAR	246
Mesler, Phillis	246
Messex, Aron	247
Messex, Dorothy	247
Messex, Ester	247
Messex, Grace (wife of Joseph)	247
Messex, Grace (daughter of Joseph)	247
MESSEX, JOSEPH	247
Messex, Joseph (son of Joseph)	247
Messex, Joshua	247
Messex, Leven	247
Messex, Sarah	247
Metcalfe, Ann	219
Metcalfe, Caleb	46, 132, 141, 149 (2), 161, 165, 175, 210, 217, 219 (2); 280, 316, 377, 394.
Metcalfe, C	96, 113, 132, 140, 204, 214, 247, 334, 343, 375
METCALF, CALEB	247
Metcalf, Caleb	276
Mets, Anne Curtisse	247
METS, GEORGE	247
Mets, George (son of George)	247
Mets, Susannah	247
Mewboorn, Eleannar	247
Mewboorn, George	247
Mewboorn, John	247
Mewboorn, Joshua	247
Mewboorn, Mary	247
Mewboorn, Moses	247
Mewboorn, Nicholas	247
MewBoorn, Nicholess	247
MEWBOORN, THOMAS	247
Mewboorn, Thomas (son of Thomas)	247
Mewboorn, Thomas	247
Mezies, Jacob	265
Miana Government, land in	423
Michaels Bridge, land at	150
Michalle, William	155
Michener, Jereh	38
Middle Creek, land on	238
Middle Swamp, land on	87
Middle Swamp, land on W. side of	37
Middleton, Ann	247
Middleton, Edward	248
Middleton, Elizabeth	247

INDEX. 551

	PAGE.
MIDDLETON, HENRY	247
Middleton, Henry (son of Henry)	247
Middleton, Isaac	247
Middleton, Jane	248
Middleton, James	247 (2), 248
MIDDLETON, JOHN	247
MIDDLETON, JOHN	247
MIDDLETON, JOHN	248
Middleton, John (son of John)	247
Middleton, John	20, 247
Middleton, Martha	247
Middleton, Mary	247 (2), 248
Middleton, Mildred	248
Middleton, Sabra	247
Middleton, Samuel	247
Middleton, Sarah (wife of John)	247
Middleton, Sarah (daughter of John)	247
Middleton, Sarah	223, 248, 249
Middleton, Sussanna	247
Middleton, William	210
Midleton, Barbara	335
Midyett, Ann	248
Midyett, Cateran	248
Midyett, Dina	248
Midyett, John	248 (2)
Midyett, Joseph	248 (2)
MIDYETT, MATTHEW	248
Midyett, Matthew	248
Midyett, Samuel	248
Midyett, Thomas	248
Miery Branch, land on	67
Miery Branch and White Oak River, land between.	268
Mihand, Ann	235
Mile Branch, land on	196
Milhons, Saml.	65
Mill Branch, land on	343
Mill Creek, land on.	115, 120, 292
Mill, Elizabeth	238
Mill, John	105
Mill Swamp, land on	221
Mill Swamp, plantation on	111
MILLARD, CHARLES	248
Millchell, George	177
Millchell, Kisiah	177
Miller, Abraham	385
Miller, Andrew	249 (2)
Miller, Anna	248
Miller, Benjamin	64
Miller, Daniel	248
Miller, Eleanor	248
Miller, Evan	79

	PAGE.
Miller, Fletcher	204
Miller, Jacob	32, 210, 293, 377
Miller, James	248
Miller, Jane	35, 93
Miller, John (brother of William)	248
Miller, John (father of William)	248
Miller, John	151
Miller, John Leilker	377
Miller, Martin	234
Miller, Mary	34
Miller, Pheebe	338
Miller, Nathaniel	248
Miller, Philip	395
Miller, Ralph	94, 95
Miller, Richard	248
MILLER, THOMAS	248
MILLER, THOMAS	248
Miller, Thomas	30, 144, 189, 248, 317, 404
MILLER, WILLIAM	248
Miller, William	248
Miller, Willis	57, 362
Millerton, R. W.	57
Mills, Joane (WCH)	295
Mills, John	126, 155
Milner, Arthur	248
MILNER, JAMES	248
Milton, Ann	249
Milton, Barrabee	224
Milton, Berebe	99
Milton, John	13, 118, 189, 270
MILTON, JONATHAN	249
Milton, Jonathan (son of Jonathan)	249
Milton, Jonathan	19
Milton, Purify	249
Milton, Robert	118
Ming, James	269
MING, JOSEPH	249
Ming, Joseph (son of Joseph)	249 (2)
Ming, Joseph	58, 142, 291, 300, 317
Ming, Martha	58, 171
Ming, Mary	249
Ming, Nathaniel	58
Ming, Rachel	249
Ming, Sarah	171 (2)
Ming, Thomas	171, 249 (2)
Ming, Thos.	157
Minge, James	41, 190
Minge, Ruth	415
Mings Creek, land on	406
Minor, Robert	294

552 INDEX.

Minse's Creek, land on...... 221
Minsey, John 237
Minshon, Richard 15
Minson, H...96, 115, 129, 140,
141, 167, 211, 223
Minson, W......56, 126, 205,
283, 284, 381
Minson, Wm........112, 130,
231, 358, 363
Minton, Joseph 57
Miskeeto Point, land at..... 326
Mistres, Thomas 217
Mitchel, Capt. George...... 173
Mitchell, Abra...........119, 175
MITCHELL, ABRAHAM 249
Mitchell, Abraham......119, 247
MITCHELL, ABRAM 249
Mitchell, Abm. 56
Mitchell, Alexr. 247
Mitchell, Amey 188
Mitchell, Ann...........154, 249
Mitchell, Anthony.......249 (2)
Mitchell, Benjamin 249
Mitchell, Cathrine 249
Mitchell, Elizabeth 132
Mitchell, George........249 (2)
Mitchell, Jacob 328
MITCHELL, JAMES 249
Mitchell, James (son of
James) 249
Mitchell, James..........43, 386
Mitchell, John.......73, 106,
156, 249 (3), 270
Mitchell, Mary 249
Mitchell, Mary Ann........ 308
Mitchell, Peter 194
MITCHELL, RANDALL 249
Mitchell, Rebecca 249
Mitchell, Rebeckah 249
Mitchell, Sarah 247
Mitchell, Susannah 132
Mitchell, William...21, 132,
154, 159, 249
Mitchell, Will............15, 389
Mitchell, Wm...........170, 198
Mitchener, John 172
Mitem, Moning 196
Mitiams Creek, land on.... 97
Mixon, George..........108, 109
Mixon, John.......156, 387, 400
Mixon, Salathiel 361
Mix, Wm. 207
Mizell, Charlton........106, 354
Mizell, Luke........29, 208, 349
Mizell, Sarah 29
Mizell, Susannah 106

Mizell, William 25
Mobley, Edward (son of
John) 250 (2)
Mobley, Edward (brother of
John) 250
MOBLEY, JOHN 250
Mobley, John (son of John). 250
Mobley, Mordeca 250
Mobley, Samuel 250
Mobley, Rachell 250
Mobson, Alice 238
Mobson, Arthur 238
Modlin, Edmond 75
Modling, Hannah 202
Modling, John 202
Mockason plantation 4
Mohoon, Ann 250
Mohoon, Edee 250
Mohoon, James 250
Mohoon, Jesse 250
Mohoon, John 250
MOHOON, JOSIAH 250
Mohoon, Josiah (son of
Josiah) 250
Molbron, Sarah 190
Molines, Elenor 105
Molseed, W. 136
Moltan, John 165
Monat, Ann 276
Monat, William 276
Monders, Thomas 52 (2)
Mondlin, Edward.........70 (2)
Mondlin, Hannah 70
Mondlin, John 70 (3)
Mondlin, Mary...........70, 410
Monereif, George 250
MONEREIF, JOHN 250
Monereif, John (son of
John) 250
Monereif, Mary (wife of
John) 250
Monereif, Mary (daughter
of John) 250
Monereif, Thomas 250
Monereif, William 250
Money, Thomas 19
Monger, Nicholas 409
Monger, William 409
Monk, Nehemiah 244
Monley, David 141
Mons, Ann 250
MONS, THOMAS 250
Monson, Patience 91
Montecue, Elisabeth 266
Montfort, Elizabeth 248

INDEX. 553

Montfort, Joseph....44, 162, 249 (2), 325, 347, 393
Montfort, Jos...21, 26, 51, 59 (2), 67, 100, 110, 115, 159 (2), 166, 191, 194, 198, 203, 207, 212, 233, 238, 249, 252, 262, 278, 279, 290, 291, 305, 313, 347, 373, 375, 390, 409.
Montfort, Mary 248
MONTGOMERY, ANN 250
Montgomery, Ann 251
Montgomery, Elizabeth..244, 250, 403
MONTGOMERY, GEORGE 250
Montgomery, George 250
Montgomery, James 250
MONTGOMERY, JOHN 251
Montgomery, John..101, 113, 239, 315
Montgomery, Josias 250
Montgomery, J.....4, 40, 92 (2), 117, 145, 198, 204, 219, 290, 300, 312, 350.
Monticue, Elizabeth 251
MONTICUE, THOMAS 251
Moor, Andrew 160, 386
Moor, Ann 252
Moor, Arthur 39
Moor, Benja................ 227
Moor, Charity 111
Moor, Cornelius 251
Moor, Edward 208
Moor, Gideon 254
MOOR, JOHN 251
MOOR, JOHN 252
Moor, John......36, 37, 185, 289
Moor, Joseph 251 (2)
Moor, Martha 111
Moor, Mary.........36, 252, 263
Moor, Matthew 111
Moor, Mela 111
MOOR, THOMAS 254
Moor, Thomas 160
Moor, Truman 36
Moor, William 134
Moor, Wm.................. 298
Moore, ——— (sister of Sarah Allen)............. 5
Moore, Aaron 254
Moore, Abigail 253
Moore, Adam....60, 113, 247 (2)
Moore, Allethea 254
Moore, Andrew.........160, 312
Moore, Ann.....97, 168, 204, 251 (2), 252 (2), 253, 338

Moore, Anne 253
Moore, Ammey 11
Moore, Anthony 339
Moore, Beninjr..........388 (2)
Moore, Benjamin 252
Moore, Betey 252
Moore, Casson 140, 421
Moore, Celia 252
Moore, Charles 218, 251
Moore, Christian 251
Moore, Cornelius....252, 254, 284
MOORE, DAVID 251
Moore, Derbe 287
Moore, Edward.........144, 202
Moore, Elizabeth (daughter of William) 255
Moore, Elizabeth (wife of William) 255
Moore, Elizabeth....173, 252 (2), 254, 258
MOORE, EPAPHRODITUS 251
Moore, Ezekiel 252
Moore, Fillder 17
Moore, George..6, 67, 90, 253 (2)
Moore, Grace 251
Moore, Hanna 254
Moore, Hardy 66
Moore, Henry 421
Moore, Hodges 252
Moore, Isham 252
MOORE, JAMES 251
Moore, James...97, 105, 173, 252, 254, 255
Moore, Jane 254
Moore, Jesse 254
Moore, Jessee 252
MOORE, JOHN 251
MOORE, JOHN 252
MOORE, JOHN 252
Moore, John (son of John), 252 (2)
Moore, John (uncle of John) 252
Moore, John (son of Richard) 253
Moore, John (brother of Richard) 253
Moore, John..12, 17 (2), 87, 251, 252, 253, 254 (2), 255 (2), 279, 282, 295, 336, 411, 420.
Moore, Jno................. 344
Moore, Jonathan 254
MOORE, JOSEPH 252
Moore, Joseph (son of Joseph) 252
MOORE, JOSHUA 252

INDEX.

	PAGE.
Moore, Joshua	254, 255 (2), 267
Moore, Justina	344
Moore, Leah	254
Moore, Levi	148
Moore, Margery	287
Moore, Mark	252
Moore, Martha	253, 254
MOORE, MARY	252
Moore, Mary (daughter of Roger)	253
Moore, Mary (wife of Roger)	253
Moore, Mary (wife of Samuell)	254
Moore, Mary (niece of Samuell)	254
Moore, Mary	49, 192, 251 (3), 253 (2), 254 (3), 263, 267
Moore, Col. Maurice	212, 258
Moore, Maurice	105, 139, 216, 277
Moore, ——— (wife of Maurice)	105
Moore, Melia	252
Moore, Miriam	252, 253
Moóre, Morice	251
Moore, M.	74
Moore, Nathaniel	252
Moore, Obadiah	254
Moore, Rachel	251, 253
MOORE, RICHARD	253
Moore, Richard	12, 33, 252 (2), 263
MOORE, ROBERT	253
Moore, Robert	11, 15, 119, 219, 221, 303
MOORE, ROGER	253
Moore, Roger	12, 61, 89, 90, 168, 344, 380
Moore, Rogr.	258
Moore, R.	304, 386
MOORE, SAMUEL	253
MOORE, SAMUEL	254
MOORE, SAMUEL	254
Moore, Samuel (son of Samuel)	253, 254
Moore, Samuel	252, 254 (2), 264, 298
MOORE, SAMUELL	254
Moore, Samuell	93, 252, 253 (2), 255
Moore, Sam'll	150, 202
Moore, Sarah (wife of Samuel)	254
Moore, Sarah (daughter of Samuel)	254

	PAGE.
Moore, Sarah	251, 252 (2), 253, 254, 264
Moore, Surity	113
Moore, Susan	113
Moore, Susanah	251
Moore, Susannah	17
Moore, Tabitha	252, 276
Moore, Thomas	251, 254 (2), 288
MOORE, TITUS	254
MOORE, TRUEMAN	254
Moore, Truman	252, 255 (2), 419
MOORE, WILLIAM	255
Moore, William (son of William)	255
Moore, William	14, 17, 203, 252, 253 (2), 254, 281, 290, 314, 363
MOORHEAD, JAMES	255
Moorhead, James	255
Moorhead, Jane	255
Moorhead, Sarah (wife of James)	255
Moorhead, Sarah (daughter of James)	255
Moorhead, William	255
Moran, James	56
Moran, Ja.	10, 46, 67, 72, 241, 244, 265, 301, 313, 340, 363, 372.
Moran, Jas.	45
Moratock Bay, land on	292
Moratock Bridge, plantation near	365
Moratock, plantation at	220
Moratock River, land on,	101, 292, 354, 382
Moratoke River, land on	87, 192
Morattock River, land on	24, 349
Moratuck River, land on	293
Mordicke, Benjamin	403
More, Adam	316
More, Betty	306
More, Edward	110
More, Ester	39
More, James	318
More, John	37, 211, 306 (2)
More, Martha	255, 266
More, Mary	306
More, Richard, Jr.	211
More, Robert	415
More, Samuell	252
More, Thomas	256
MORE, WILLIAM	255
More, William	18, 113, 252, 371, 377, 378

INDEX. 555

More, Willm. 80
Morean, John 165
Morey, Edward 64
Morgan, ——— (wife of
  Robert) 379
Morgan, Aaron 256
Morgan, Allis 256
Morgan, Ann.......255, 256, 274
Morgan, B................94, 408
Morgan, Bartlett 329
Morgan, Bennet.........256 (2)
Morgan, Bennett.75 (2), 134, 327
Morgan, Bentt. 329
Morgan, Charles 255
Morgan, Daniel 82
Morgan, David 82
Morgan, Elizabeth (wife of
  Robert) 256
Morgan, Elizabeth (daughter
  of Robert) 256
Morgan, Elizabeth 255
Morgan, Goer 256
Morgan, Hannah 255
Morgan, Jacob 255
MORGAN, JAMES 255
Morgan, James..230 (2), 255 (2)
MORGAN, JANE 255
Morgan, Jane 32
MORGAN, JOHN 255
Morgan, John (son of John) 255
Morgan, Joseph.141, 255, 256 (3)
Morgan, Juda 256
Morgan, Maikd 329
Morgan, Mary 255
Morgan, Miriam 255
Morgan, Morgan 32
Morgan, Morgan, Jr........ 32
Morgan, Moses 256
MORGAN, NATHAN 256
Morgan, Rebekah 255
Morgan, Richard 256
MORGAN, ROBERT 256
Morgan, Robert (son of
  Robert) 256
Morgan, Robert 379
Morgan, Rob't............. 167
Morgan, Sukee 256
Morgan, William (son of
  Nathan) 256
Morgan, William (brother
  of Nathan) 256
Morgan, William 255
Morgans Swamp, land on... 255
Morgin, Hannah..........40 (2)
Morgin, Henry 30
Morgin, Jane 239

Morgin, John 239
Morgin, Robert 379
Moring, Jane 218
MORIS, JOHN 256
Moris, John (son of John).. 256
Moris, John 370
Moris, Thomas 172
Morison, Benjamin 10
Morison, Benjn......92, 244, 340
Morley, David 320
Morly, Edward 273
Morphew, Sarah 280
Morrel, Elizabeth 256
MORRELL, HUMPHREY 256
Morrey, Elizabeth 28
Morris, Aaron..256, 369, 401, 403
Morris, Anne 340
Morris, Bethshaba 107
Morris, Charles 256
Morris, Elizabeth...181, 256, 332
Morris, Frusan 364
Morris, Hannah 256
Morris, Isac 256
Morris, James..........256, 257
Morris, Jane 256
MORRIS, JOHN 256
Morris, John (son of John). 256
Morris, John....19, 170, 256,
                         269, 394
Morris, Jonathan 66
Morris, Joseph..256 (2), 274, 384
Morris, Joshua 317
Morris, Mary....3, 135, 256 (2)
Morris, Matthew 256
Morris, Rebekah........107, 256
Morris, Richard 153
Morris, Sarah..........256, 289
Morris, Solomon........256, 257
Morris, Susaner 43
MORRIS, THOMAS 256
Morris, Thomas (son of
  Thomas) 256
Morris, Thomas (grandson
  of Thomas) 256
Morris, Thomas..........21, 177
Morris, Tho. 181
Morris, William (son of
  Thomas) 256, 257
Morris, William (brother of
  Thomas) 257
Morris, William....119, 154,
                         256, 380
Morris, Zachariah......256, 264
Morrises and Cuba planta-
  tion 425
MORRISON, BENJAMIN 257

	PAGE.
Morrison, Benjamin	372, 422
Morrison, William	230, 403
Morriss, Benjamin	256
Morriss, Jacob	256
Morriss, James Early	256
MORRISS, JOHN	256
Morriss, John (son of John)	256
Morriss, John	289
Morriss, Nathan	256
Morriss, Richard	256
Morriss, William	256
Morse, Francis	180
Mortimer, Hannah	257
MORTIMER, JOHN	257
Mortimer, Mary	257
Mortimer, Rebecca	257
Mortimore, Thos.	43
Morton, Margret	19
MOSLER, CEARSMER	259
Mosler, Philis	259
Moseley, Ales	98
Moseley, Ann.	257, 258, 296, 368
Moseley, Aner	257
MOSELEY, EDWARD	257
Moseley, Edward (son of Edward)	257
Moseley, Edward.	12, 42 (2), 71, 87, 92, 98, 118, 156 (2), 192 (2), 212, 258 (2), 296, 324, 368, 415.
Moseley, Edwd.	52, 180, 255, 368
Moseley, E.	51, 57, 74 (2), 103 (2), 111, 130, 150, 174, 250, 310.
Moseley, James	257 (2), 258
Moseley, Joel	192
Moseley, John	257, 258 (2)
Moseley, Sampson	257 (2), 258
Moseley, Thomas	257 (2), 258
Moseley, William	188, 258
Moseleys Creek, land on	32
Moses, Aaron	351
Moses Creek, land on	8
Moss, GRACE	259
Moss, Joseph	259, 333
Moss, Sarah	333
Mott, Hannah	46
Mott, John	46
Mott, Stephen	229
Moulin, Elizabeth	366
Mounce, Mary	2
MOUND, NOAH	259
Mount Calvert plantation	324
Mount Galland plantation	244
Mount Gallard, islands near.	187
Mount Garriot plantation	182

	PAGE.
Mount Misery plantation	253
Mount Misseary plantation	204
Mount Pleasant	334
Mount Thomas	380
Mountain Creek, land on	76
MOUNTEAGUE, ELIZABETH	259
Mounticue, Elizabeth	259
MOUNTICUE, THOMAS	259
Mountery, Roger	77
Mouse Harbor	345
Moy, Annie	259
Moy, Ashe	130
Moy, Elisabeth	130
Moy, Jane	259
MOY, JOHN	259
Moy, John (son of John)	259
Moye, Elizabeth	259
Moye, George, Jr.	290
MOYE, THOMAS	259
Moyock, land at	368
Moyocke, plantation in	299
Mozark Creek, land on	29
Mozor, Denel	259
Mr. Allen's Creek, land on	253
Muddy Creek and Marshy Gutt, land between	368
Mulford, Ephm.	199
Mulkey, David	260
Mulkey, Eve	260
Mulkey, Jane	260
Mulkey, Jonathan	260
Mulkey, Judith	260
MULKEY, PHILIP	260
Mulkey, Philip (son of Philip)	260
Mulkey, Sarah	260
Mulkey, Scarborough	260
Mullen, Abraham	8, 260 (2)
Mullen, Elender	8
Mullen, Elizabeth	260
Mullen, Hannah	260
Mullen, Isaac	260
MULLEN, ISAAC	260
MULLEN, JACOB	260
Mullen, Jacob (son of Jacob)	260
Mullen, Jacob	172, 260
Mullen, Jane	8
Mullen, Joseph	260
Mullen, Rebecca	260
Mullen, Thomas	260
Mullin, Cornelius	330
Mullington, Richd.	226
Mumford, Edward	260
Mumford, Elizabeth	260
MUMFORD, JOSEPH	260

INDEX. 557

	PAGE.
Mumford, Joseph (son of Joseph)	260
Muncreef, Elizabeth	339
Munday, Elizabeth	260
Munday, Emmay	260
MUNDAY, WILLIAM	260
Munday, William (son of William)	260
Munden, Peter	56
Munden, Stephen	401
Mundine, John	268
Mundlen, John	363
Munds, Thomas	341
Mundy, Benjamin	37
Munroe, Hugh	296
Munroe, Revell	389 (2)
Muns, Anne	260
MUNS, THOMAS	260
Muns, Thomas	60, 100
Murdaugh, John	324
Murden, Elizabeth	64
MURDEN, JEREMIAH	260
Murden, Jeremiah	64, 65, 355
Murden, Jerrom	64
Murden, John	64 (2), 167
Murden, Mary	64, 65, 175, 260, 349
Murden, Colo. Robert	167
Murden, Robert	1, 260, 328
Murfey, Joseph	183
Murfey, Mary	183
Murfree, William	185
Murfree, Wm.	82
Murfrey, Elinor	420
Murfrey, Jno.	420
Murphey, Ann	261
Murphey, Martha	261
Murphey, Mary	261
MURPHEY, WILLIAM	261
Murphree, John	67, 291
Murphy, Benjamin	261
Murphy, Bridgett	261
MURPHY, EDMOND	261
Murphy, Edmund (son of Edmond)	261
Murphy, Elizabeth	261
Murphy, Esther	261
MURPHY, JEREMIAH	261
Murphy, Jeremiah	261
Murphy, John	164, 261
Murphy, Josua	261
Murphy, Michael	161, 267
Murphy, Sarah	261
MURPHY, THOMAS	261
Murphy, Thomas (son of Thomas)	261

	PAGE.
Murphy, Thomas	261 (2)
MURRAY, ANDREW	261
Murray, Andrew	119, 170, 223
Murray, Andr.	56, 86, 247
Murray, B.	392
Murray, Barbara	392
Murray, Elizabeth	260
Murray, Ja.	26, 113
Murray, James	2, 6, 113, 260, 364, 392
Murray, John	44
Murray, Robina Cameron	44
Murray, Robert	44
Muschamp, G.	236
Muschamp, George	335
Muse, Thomas	263
Mushrow, John	198
Mutted, Thomas	387
Myhan, James	100
Myhand, James	54
Myhand, John	235
Myhand, Mary	235
Myhand, Sarah	54
Nahale, James	236
Nairne, John	5
Nairn, John	244
Nairns, John	72
Nanson, Richard	195
Naris Creek, land on	402
Narron, Mary	75
Nash, Abner	249
Nash, Caleb	373
Nash, Frances	180
Nation, Ch.	317
Nation, John	317
Nayler, Margaret	261
Nayler, Mary	261
NAYLER, WILLIAM	261
Neal, Christopher	15
Neal, Elizabeth	68
NEALE, ABNER	261
Neale, Abner (son of Abner)	261
Neale, Abner	364, 377, 390
Neale, Barre	261
NEALE, CHARLES	262
Neale, Charles (son of Charles)	262
Neale, Chrisr.	390
Neale, Christopher	17, 32, 140, 261, 262
Neale, Dorcas	262
Neale, Elizabeth (wife of Abner)	261
Neale, Elizabeth (daughter of Abner)	261

558 INDEX.

Neale, Elizabeth 262
Neale, Hannah 261
NEALE, HENRY 262
Neale, Henry (son of Henry) 262
Neale, Jane 262
Neale, Mrs. Mary 32
Neale, Mary............262 (2)
Neale, Mathew 261
Neale, Patience 261
Neale, Philip 261
Neale, Richard..........261, 262
Neale, Saml. 313
Neale, Samuel...........59, 262
Neale, Thomas 262
Neale, Thos. 313
Neale, William 59
Neales Creek, land on....... 232
Needham, Ann 262
Needham, Christopher 262
Needham, Gedeon 262
Needham, John..........262 (2)
Needham, Margaret 379
NEEDHAM, THOMAS 262
Needham, Thomas (son of Thomas) 262
Neel, Jean 356
Neeltown, land adjoining.... 320
Nekelles, Sarah 175
"Negro, Betty" 208
Nelson, Ann...............48, 97
Nelson, Archd. 138
Nelson, Berry 391
Nelson, John....26 (2), 214, 259, 373
Nelson, John, Jr............ 312
Nelson, Jno. 146
Nelson, Rachel 160
Nelson, Sarah 391
Nelson, Thomas.........259, 307
Nelson, Thos. 63
Nesbet, John 309
Nessfeild, Ann 262
NESSFEILD, JOHN 262
Nett, Richard 132
Neuse, land at............. 360
Neuse, lands in............. 156
Neuse River, land on...217, 257, 293 (2)
Neuse River and Beards Creek, land on........... 351
Nevel, James 26
Nevell, Jacob 342
NEVIL, BENJAMIN 262
Nevil, Benjamin (son of Benjamin) 262

Nevil, Elizabeth (wife of Benjamin) 262
Nevil, Elizabeth (daughter of Benjamin) 262
Nevil, Jacob, Jr............. 413
Nevil, Jesse 262
Nevil, John 243
Nevil, Moses 413
Nevile, William 242
NEVILL, FRANCIS 262
Nevill, Jacob 383
Neville, Benj'n............. 238
Nevils Creek, land on...383, 413
Nevin, Mary 271
New Abbey plantation...... 223
New Begon Creek, plantations on 284
Newbegun Creek meeting house 332
Newbegun Creek, plantation on 332
Newbegun Creek, plantation near 419
New Begun Creek, plantation at 200
New Bern plantation....... 292
Newbern, land opposite to... 320
Newbern Town, marsh opposite to 41
Newby, Ann............264, 324
New, Jno................44, 144
NEWBY, BENJAMIN 263
Newby, Benjamin (son of Benjamin) 263
Newby, Benjamin 402
NEWBY, EDWARD 263
Newby, Edward 264
Newby, Elisabeth........264, 380
Newby, Elizabeth.3, 253, 324, 383
NEWBY, FRANCIS 263
NEWBY, FRANCIS 263
Newby, Francis (son of Francis) 263
Newby, Francis.....122, 148, 254 (2), 263 (2), 264, 380
NEWBY, GABRIEL 263
Newby, Gabriel.....146, 263, 264, 334
Newby, Hannah.........259, 263
Newby, Isabell 264
Newby, Jacob 263
NEWBY, JAMES 263
Newby, James.......94, 224, 230, 263, 283
Newby, Jamima 289
Newby, Jeames 266

INDEX. 559

	PAGE.
Newby, Jemes	264
Newby, Jemima	264
Newby, Jesse...263 (2), 285, 380	
Newby, Jessee	263
NEWBY, JOSEPH	264
NEWBY, JOSEPH	264
Newby, Joseph..40, 263 (2), 298	
Newby, Kesiah	289
Newby, Magdalene	263
Newby, Margaret	263
Newby, Mark......263 (2), 267	
NEWBY, MARY	264
Newby, Mary (wife of Nathan)	264
Newby, Mary (daughter of Nathan)	264
Newby, Mary...263 (2), 264 (2), 377	
Newby, Naomy	259
NEWBY, NATHAN	264
Newby, Nathan........148, 196, 252, 254, 263 (2), 264, 285, 289, 378.	
Newby, Robert..196, 263 (2), 289, 416	
Newby, Robt.	255
Newby, Samivel	135
NEWBY, SAMUEL	264
Newby Samuel..40, 230, 251, 259 (2), 263, 264 (2), 275, 383	
Newby, Samuell	394
Newby, Sarah......263 (3), 286	
New. Susanah	263
Newby, Thomas....252, 263, 264 (2), 420	
Newby, Thos. 324, 357	
NEWBY, WILLIAM	264
Newby, William..206, 230, 263(3)	
New Corotuck, plantation at.	182
New Desire land	412
Newfoundland	418
New Germany	53
New Hyrnham plantation	178
Newland, Will	342
Newman, John	387
Newman, Richard....77, 361, 371	
Newman (Newnam), Thomas	293
Newnam, Frances	264
NEWNAM, THOMAS	264
New Market, land at	59
Newport River, land on..72, 322, 334, 418	
Newport Sound, land in	239
New River, Court House on.	31
New River, land at mouth of	116

	PAGE.
New River, land on	124
New River, land on southwest fork	414
New River, plantation on	414
Newsom, Joseph	294
Newsom, Julian	294
Newsom, Rebeccah	98
Newsom, Rebeckah	98
News River, land on	282
Newsum, David	265
Newsum, Hosea	265
Newsum, Isaac	265
NEWSUM, JOEL	265
Newsum, Joel (son of Joel)	265
Newsum, John	265
Newsum, Mary	265
Newsum, William	265
NEWTON, CHRISTOPHER	265
Newton, Constant	265
Newton, Jane	265
Newton, John	265
Newton, Mary	265
Newton, Sarah	265
NEWTON, THOMAS	265
Newton, Thomas	56
Newton, Thos............95, 281	
Newton, Walter	265
New Topsail Creek, land on.	267
Niblack, William 8 (2)	
Nice, Jane	265
Nice, Jennet	265
Nice, Katherine	265
NICE, WILLIAM	265
Nicholas, Elizabeth	265
Nicholas, Geo.	222
Nicholas, Jos.	41
Nicholas, Josah	265
NICHOLAS, NATHANIEL	265
Nicholas, William	265
Nicholls, John..116, 168, 213, 331	
Nichols, Humphry	323
Nichols, Job	408
Nichols, Susanah	257
Nichols, William	165
Nichols, Willm.	394
Nicholson, Anthony	266
Nicholson, Benjamin	265
Nicholson, Christopher..145, 259 (2), 265	
Nicholson, Elizabeth (wife of Samuel)	266
Nicholson, Elizabeth (daughter of Samuel)	266
Nicholson, Elizabeth	265
Nicholson, George	198

Nicholson, John 265 (3)
Nicholson, Jonathan 265
NICHOLSON, JOSEPH 265
Nicholson, Joseph...138, 259 (2)
Nicholson, Josiah 266 (2)
Nicholson, Mary 306
Nicholson, Naomy 266
NICHOLSON, NATHANIEL 265
Nicholson, Nathaniel 265
Nicholsoh, Saml............. 265
NICHOLSON, SAMUEL 266
Nicholson, Samuel.......265, 350
Nicholson, Samuell 138
Nicholson, Sarah....265 (2), 266
Nicholson, Sophia 266
Nicholson, Theofilus 266
Nicholson, Thomas....40 (2), 55
 (2), 145, 165, 172 (2), 196, 227
 (2), 259 (2), 263, 267, 274, 332
Nicholson, Thos............. 254
NICHOLSON, WILLIAM 266
Nicholson, William 79
Nicholson, —— (daughter
 of William) 266
Nickeles, Henry 329
Nickells, Archd............. 394
Nickellson, Samuel 377
Nicker, Joseph 28
Nickleson, Hannah 376
Nickless, Nathaniel 190
Nickole, William 176
Nickoles, Job 357
Nickolls, Caleb 266
Nickolls, Frankey 266
NICKOLLS, JAMES 266
Nickolls, James (son of
 James) 266
Nickolls, Sarah 266
Nickolls, Willis 266
Nickollson, Elizabeth 378
Nickollson, William 378
Nickols, John...18, 156, 341,
 358, 387
Nickols, Thos............... 358
Nickolson, Ann 266
NICKOLSON, CHRISTOFER 266
Nickolson, Clare 266
Nickolson, Dabora 266
Nickolson, Hannah 266
Nickolson, John 266
NICKOLSON, JOSIAH 266
Nickolson, Josias 266
Nickolson, Mariam 266
Nickolson, Mary (wife of
 Christofer) 266

Nickolson, Mary (daughter
 of Christofer) 266
Nickolson, Mary 204
Nickolson, Nathaniel 3
Nickolson, Samuel.......204, 266
Nickolson, Thomas 266
Nickolson, William 266
Nickson, Charles Augustus.. 322
Nickson, Henry 266
Nickson, Joseph 266
NICKSON, THOMAS 266
Nickson, Zachariah 202
Nicols, Hannah 266
NICOLS, JOHN 266
Nicols, Mary 266
Nicols, Pressilla 266
Nicols, Samuel (father of
 John) 266
Nicols, Samuel (son of John) 266
Night, William 126
Nights, Ann 245
Nisbett, Eleanor 229
Nisbrale, Cristifer 70
Niscon, Em................. 17
Nixon, Ann 267
Nixon, Barnaby 267, 417
Nixon, Christian 410
Nixon, Elisabeth 263
NIXON, ELIZABETH 267
Nixon, Elizabeth...252, 267,
 329, 384
Nixon, Ellender 228
Nixon, Em.................. 267
Nixon, Francis..251, 259, 267, 286
Nixon, Gartry 267
NIXON, JOHN 267
Nixon, John.....55, 251, 259,
 264, 267 (3), 317
Nixon, Mary (wife of
 Richard) 267
Nixon, Mary (daughter of
 Richard) 267
Nixon, Mary............264, 289
Nixon, Mehetable 259
Nixon, Mehetible 267
Nixon, Pheniass 289
Nixon, Phineas 55, 267 (2)
Nixon, Phineus 3, 267
Nixon, Pierce 289
NIXON, RICHARD 267
Nixon, Richard (son of
 Richard) 267
Nixon, Richard............. 232
Nixon, Robert..........254, 322
Nixon, Thomas 111

INDEX. 561

	PAGE.
Nixon, Zach.....93, 252, 254,	263
Nixon, Zachariah	267
Nixon, Zachariah	267
Nixon, Zachariah (son of Zachariah) 267	(2)
Nixon, Zachariah...6, 8, 20, 148, 251 (2), 252 (2), 254, 255, 259 (2), 264 (3), 265, 266, 267, 286, 306 (2), 317, 360, 370, 384, 401, 419.	
Nixon, Zachariah, Sr........	264
Nixon, Zachariah, Jr.......	259
Nixon, Richard	217
Nixon, Toune, lots at......	224
Nobesbruke Creek, land on.	392
Noble, Bettie	268
Noble, Betty	173
Noble, Elisabeth	268
Noble, Elizabeth	393
Noble, Hanah	268
Noble, James..173, 268, 396	(2)
Noble, Jantt.............	380
Noble, Joseph..173, 268, 380,	396
Noble, Mark........173 268	(2)
Noble, Nancy	268
Noble, Rachel	268
Noble, Racll (Rachel)......	140
Noble, Samll.	140
Noble, Samuel	267
Noble, Samuel...15, 173, 268 (3),	396
Noble, William	268
Noble, William (son of William)	268
Noble, William 268	(2)
Nobleland, John	268
Nobleland, Mary	268
Nobleland, Mathew	268
Nobleland, Rebecca	268
Noblin, Luke	346
Nobs Creek, land on........	302
Noden, Ralph	287
Noe, Heshton	274
Nolson, Ann	77
Norbury, Jos.	416
Norcam, Mary	137
Norcam, Thomas	137
Norcom, Ann (wife of John)	268
Norcom, Ann (daughter of John)	268
Norcom, Cornelius	268
Norcom, Elisabeth	268
Norcom, Elizabeth	268
Norcom, Frederick	269
Norcom, Jeames	268
Norcom, Jean	268

	PAGE.
Norcom, John	268
Norcom, John	268
Norcom, John (son of John)	268
Norcom, John (brother of Thomas)	269
Norcom, John (nephew of Thomas)	269
Norcom, John 268	(2)
Norcom, Martha	269
Norcom, Mary	268
Norcom, Mary 268	(2)
Norcom, Sarah 268	(3)
Norcom, Stepney	268
Norcom, Susanna	269
Norcom, Thomas	268
Norcom, Thomas	269
Norcom, Thomas	269
Norcom, Thomas (father of Thomas)	269
Norcom, Thomas (son of Thomas) 268,	269
Norcom, Thomas (grandson of Thomas)	269
Norcom, Thomas........268	(3)
Norcom, William 268	(2)
Norcomb (Norkom), John...	423
Norcomb, Mary	137
Norcomb, Thomas	156
Norfleet, Abraham	269
Norfleet, Elisabeth.......269	(2)
Norfleet, Elisbeth	270
Norfleet, Elizabeth	269
Norfleet, Farbey	270
Norfleet, Felisha........269,	270
Norfleet, Jacob	269
Norfleet, James	269
Norfleet, James 269	(2)
Norfleet, John	269
Norfleet, John (son of John)	269
Norfleet, John......178, 269	(2)
Norfleet, Margaret......269,	270
Norfleet, Marmaduke	269
Norfleet, Marmaduke (brother of Thomas).....	270
Norfleet, Marmaduke (son of Thomas) 270	(2)
Norfleet, Marmaduke....138, 173, 269,	382
Norfleet, Mary.............	270
Norfleet, Mary (wife of James)	269
Norfleet, Mary (daughter of James)	269
Norfleet, Mary	270
Norfleet, Patience	269

36

	PAGE.
Norfleet, Phillisia	16
Norfleet, Ruth	270
Norfleet, Sarah	16, 269, 270
Norfleet, Susanah	270
NORFLEET, THOMAS	270
Norfleet, Thomas (brother of James)	269
Norfleet, Thomas (son of James)	269
Norfleet, Thomas (son of Thomas)	270
Norice, Thomas	387
Norman, Henry	155, 185
NORMAN, JOHN	270
Norman, John (son of John)	270
Norman, John	175 (2)
Norman, Joseph	137
Norman, Mary	270
Norman, Peter	270
Norman, Samuel	137
Norman, Sarah	270
Norman, Willis	270
Norment, Elizabeth	157
Norment, Stokes	157
Normonds, Folly	406
Norris, John	163, 275
Norris, Samuel	163
Norris, Susanah	270
Norris, Tamer	349
Norris, W.	31, 133, 146, 161, 201, 223 (3), 244, 294, 313, 348, 359, 369, 373, 379, 385.
Norris, Will	64
NORRIS, WILLIAM	270
Norris, William	163
Norsem, Thos.	137
North Dividing and Jacks Creeks, land on	244
North East of New River, land on	54 (3)
North East River, land on	92
North River, islands in	159
North River, land on	326
North River plantation and land on	327
North River Swamp, land on	142
Northwest Branch of Cape Fear River, land on	11
North West Branch of Cape Fear, land on	82
N. W. Branch of New River, land on	410
North West plantation, up the	51
North West plantation, up.	179

	PAGE.
North West River, land on,	65, 218, 320
No. West River, land up	139
Northan, Philip	357
Northan, Solomon	242
Northan, William	242
Northcoat, John	22
Northcoate, John	105
Northem, Elizabeth	270
NORTHEM, JOHN	270
Northem, John (son of John)	270
Northem, Philip	270
Northern, Phillip	29, 57
Northerns plantation	114
Northuntee Mach, land on	67
Norton, Abgill	270
Norton, Asac	270
Norton, Charly	412
Norton, Daniel	270
Norton, Elizbeth	270
Norton, Hanah	270
Norton, Jacob	270 (2)
NORTON, JOHN	270
Norton, John (son of John)	270
Norton, John	185, 186, 217, 270
Norton, Jonathan	270
Norton, Margaret	186
Norton, Margret	412
Norton, Mary	270
Norton, Metable	270
Norton, Thomas	270 (2)
NORTON, WILLIAM	270
Norton, William (son of William)	270
Norton, William	242, 270
Norton, Wm.	270
Norwood, Anne	158
Norwood, Elizabeth	97, 271
Norwood, Frances	271
NORWOOD, GEORGE	271
Norwood, George (grandson of George)	271
Norwood, John	110, 271 (2), 409
Norwood, Mary	271
Norwood, Nathaniel (grandson of George)	271
Norwood, Nathaniel	271 (4)
Norwood, Samuel	271 (2)
Norwood, Sarah	271
Norwood, Sissely	271
Norwood, Theo.	189
NORWOOD, THOMAS	271
Norwood, Thomas	271
NORWOOD, WILLIAM	271
Norwood, William	271 (4)

INDEX. 563

	PAGE.
Notaway River, land on	314
Nouell, Frances	144
Nowell, James	233
Nube, Francis	402
Nube, Samuel	325
Nuby, Gabriel	265
Nuby, John	76
Nuby, Mary	265
Nuce River, land on	124, 234
Nugent, Edward	110
Nuse River, land on.	123, 147, 344
Nusum, Elizabeth	271
NUSUM, RICHARD	271
Nuss, Anne	214
Nuss, Katherine	214
Nutt, John	241
Oachoneche Neck, land on	340
Oak Ridge, land at	330
Oak Ridge plantation	267
Oar, James	27
Oates, Elizabeth	271 (3), 406
OATES, JAMES	271
Oates, James	121, 143, 202
Oates, Jo	372
Oates, Joseph	71, 271
Oaverman, Elizabeth	70
Oald Meeting House plantation	321
O'BRIAN, DARBE	272
O'Bryan, William	96
Ocreecock Island	326
O'Daniel, Elizabeth	272
Odaniel, Jacob	249
O'DANIEL, OWEN	272
Oden, Chas	145
Oden, John	145, 219
ODEON, CHARLES	272
Odeon, Edith	414
Odeon, Elisabeth	272
Odeon, John	3, 274, 324, 339
Odeon, Lydia	424
Odeon, Richard	272
Odier, Dennis	75
Odom, Abraham	272 (3)
Odom, Ann	272
Odom, Anne	272
Odom, Aron	272
Odom, Edy	272
Odom, Henry	422
Odom, Lidea	272
ODOM, JACOB	272
Odom, Jacob	130, 272, 322, 387
Odom, John (son of John)	272 (2)

	PAGE.
Odom, John	272, 422
Odom (Odeom), John	272
Odom, Martha	272
Odom, Mary	254
ODOM, RICHARD	272
Odom, Richard (son of Richard)	272 (2)
Odom, Richard	272
Odom, Sarah	272
Odom, Susan	272
Odom, Thomas	272
O'Donnell, John	418
Odum, Abraham	365
Odum, Ann	272
Odum, Elizabeth	272
Odum, Jane	272
Odum, Sarah	272
Odyer, Ann	272
ODYER, DENNIS	272
Odyer, Denis	362
Odyer, Mary	272
O'FEYE, DANIELL	273
Offill, William	112
Ogden, Jonathan	40 (2)
Ogden, Jonathan, Sr.	40
Ogden, Richard	40
Ogelsbee, John	405
Ogilby, Patr.	137
Ogilby, Patrick	144
Ogilvie, Christopher	316
Ogilvie, William	316
Ogilvie, Wm.	268
Oglesbee, Patrick	313
Oglesby, William	350
Ohone, Alise	137
Okaneechy, land at	218
Okely, Samuel	316
Old, Edward, Jr.	111
Old, Rebekah	111
Oldfield, Exsperance	273
Oldfield, Mary	273
Oldfield, Nance	273
Oldfield, Peter	273
Oldfield, Pitts	273
Oldfield, Reuben	273
OLDFIELD, RICHARD	273
Oldfield, Richard (son of Richard)	273
Oldfield, Richard	212
Oldfield, Sarah	273
Oldner, Thos.	16, 145, 282, 407
Old Box Neak	38
Old Field plantation	231
Old Ford plantation	232
Old Soune Neck, land on	390

INDEX.

Old Towne Creek, land on..11, 46
Old Town Creek, plantation
  on eastern branch........ 187
Old Town plantation........ 139
Old Town Swamp, land on.. 1
Old Town Road to Warreck,
  land on 391
Olive, Jno.................. 364
Oliver, Aaron 16, 353
Oliver, Alexander 86
Oliver, Andrew 118
Oliver, Elizabeth 86
Oliver, Ellicksander 166
OLIVER, FRANCES 273
Oliver, Francis 32
Oliver, John...208, 229, 267,
                  273, 335
OLIVER, JOSEPH 273
Oliver, Joseph 273, 357
Oliver, Mary 86
OLIVER, MOSES 273
Oliver, Phebe 273
Oliver, Robert 238
Oliver, Sarah 273
Oliver, Sidney 273
OLIVER, THOMAS 273
Oliver, Thomas (son of
  Thomas) 273
Oliver, Thomas 273
Olover, Andrew 171
Olover, Joseph 248
Omar, Denis 336
O'Neal, Charles 273
O'Neal, Deborah 273
O'Neal, Elizabeth 273
O'Neal, Mary 273
Oneal, Mary 27
O'NEAL, MICHAEL 273
O'NEAL, MICHAEL 274
O'Neal, Michael (son of
  Michael) 273, 274
O'Neal, Michael 278
Oneal, Michael 361
O'Neal, Sarah 274
O'Neal, Thomas 274
Oneal, Thomasin 27
O'Neal, Thomazin 274
Oneale, Robert 320
O'Neel, Michael 184
O'Neil, Charles 148 (2)
O'Neil, Michael 279
Optan, John 235
O'Quin, Alexander 265
Oquin, Elizabeth 195
O'QUIN, PATRICK 274

Oquin, Tarlow 321
Orapeak Swamp, land on... 365
Orched Creek, land on...... 47
Orey, Peter 14
Orindell, Anne 229
ORINDELL, EDWARD 274
Orindell, Edward (son of
  Edward) 274
Orindell, Isebell 274
Orindell, Thomas 274
Orme, Robert 212
Ormes, Sam'l.....50, 57, 83, 101,
  147, 152, 162, 170, 176, 194, 203,
  208, 219, 252 (2), 271, 319, 352,
  353.
Ormes, Samuel....4, 29, 164, 178,
  187, 205, 207, 213, 293, 323, 395,
  398, 417, 425, 426.
Ormond, Mr................ 46
Ormond, Elizabeth Penelope. 274
Ormond, Henry 80
Ormond, Nancy 274
Ormond, Roger......80, 145, 274
Ormond, Sarah 274
Ormond, William....52, 105,
  288, 346, 347, 361, 394, 423
Ormond, Will.......6, 21, 34, 80,
  90, 128, 136, 144, 162, 315, 350,
  397.
Ormond, W................ 105
Ormond, Wy............128, 145
Ormond, Wyriot 86
ORMOND, WYRIOTT 274
Ormond, Wyriott..46, 80 (2), 413
Ormond, Yreat 382
Orraneechey Neck, land in.. 36
Orreroy Swamp, land on.... 54
Orton plantation 253
Osborn, Alexr.............. 76
Osborn, Sary 177
Osborne, Elisebeth 274
OSBORNE, OBEDIAH 274
Osburn, Thomas 225
Oserow Meadow, land in.... 84
O'Sheal, David 130
O'Steen, Sam'll. 207
O'Steen, Samuel 426
Ottiwell, Isaac 336
Ottwell, Elizabeth 274
OTTWELL, ISAAC 274
Ottwell, Mary 274
Otway, Geo..............174 (2)
Oughtree, Sarah 190
Outerbridge, Ramsey White. 346
Outerbridge, Sarah 346

INDEX. 565

	PAGE.
Outlaw, Mary	420
Overenton, William	47
Overman, Ann......79, 274,	369
Overman, Benjamin	274
OVERMAN, CHARLES	274
Overman, Charles.....40, 56, 255, 275 (2), 369,	384
Overman, Dorothy......275,	378
Overman, Elizabeth	275
Overman, Enoch	274
Overman, Ephraim......275	(2)
Overman, Hannah	275
Overman, Isaac	275
OVERMAN, JACOB	275
Overman, Jacob..55, 76, 201,	378, 401
OVERMAN, JAMES	275
Overman, James....161, 275,	369
OVERMAN, JOHN	275
Overman, John (son of John)	275
Overman, John.......259,	263
OVERMAN, JOSEPH	275
Overman, Mary	275
Overman, Miriam.......14,	259
Overman, Nathan..185, 275,	370, 408
Overman, Rachel	255
Overman, Saml	384
OVERMAN, SAMUEL	274
Overman, Sarah	275
Overman, Susannah.....143,	275
Overman, Thomas....40, 56, 161, 225, 263, 264, 267 (3), 274, 275 (2).	
Overman, Thos.........265,	275
Overman, William	275
Overstreet, Dorcas	393
Overton, Aaron	275
Overton, Ales	275
Overton, Angel	275
Overton, David	275
Overton, Elizabeth	275
Overton, Elizabeth Susannah	275
Overton, James........190,	275
Overton, Jesse	275
OVERTON, JOHN	275
Overton, John (son of John)	275
Overton, Mary	275
Overton, Moses	275
Overton, Naomy	275
OVERTON, ROBERT	275
Overton, Sarah	275
Owen, Geo	100
Owen, Thomas.........95,	106

	PAGE.
Owen, Thos	90
Owen, Wm	243
Owens, Ann	275
Owens Creek, land on	310
OWENS, JOHN	275
Owens, John (son of John),	275 (2)
Owens, Sarah	275
Owens, Thomas.........275	(2)
Owens, Zachariah......275	(3)
Owin, Thomas 25, 175	(2)
Oxenwall, Elizabeth	276
OXENWALL, PETER	276
Oxley, John	308
Oyster Creek, W. side of Pamlico River, land on...	94
Oyster Shell Banks plantation	273
Oyster Shell Creek, land on.	227
Pace, Ann	276
Pace, Elizabeth.....203, 223,	276
Pace, Francis	276
Pace, George	276
PACE, JOHN, SR	276
Pace, John (son of John)...	276
Pace, Mary Melton	276
Pace, Rebecca ...,........	276
PACE, RICHARD	276
Pace, Richard (son of Richard)	276
Pace, Richard, Jr	59
Pace, Thomas..252, 276 (2),	336
Pace, William......224, 276	(3)
PACQUINET, MICHAEL	276
Padeth, Samuel	193
Padge, John	170
Padggett, Edward	153
Page, James	228
Page, Jesse	57
Page, John	375
Paget, Eliza	35
Paget, Elizabeth	35
PAGETT, EDWARD	276
Pagett, John..........137,	286
Pagetts plantation	86
Pagett, Saml	34
Pagett, Samuell	118
Pagett, Samuel	276
Pain, Mary	117
Paine, Ann	276
Paine, Catherine	276
Paine, Catherine Musgrove.	276
PAINE, JOHN	276
PAINE, JOHN	276

	PAGE.
Paine, Jos.	108
PAINE, SAMUEL	277
Paine, Thomas	276
Paire, Thomas	81
Palen, Thomas	275
Palin, Ann	163, 277, 310
Palin, Anne	277 (2)
Palin, Ann Reading	135
Palin, Elizabeth	277
Palin, Henry	67, 135, 277 (3), 383
Palin, Henry, Sr.	73
PALIN, HENRY, JR.	277
Palin, Henry, Jr.	157
PALIN, JOHN	277
PALIN, JOHN	277
Palin, John (son of John),	135, 277
Palin, John	1, 19, 59, 72, 135, 163, 183, 193, 223, 234, 263, 277 (3), 284.
Palin, Jno.	10, 135, 197, 245, 278, 302, 303, 312, 359
Palin, Jo.	45, 96
Palin, Jon	167
Palin, J.	55, 83, 85, 112, 138, 220, 221, 343, 367
Palin, Mary	310
Palin, Mary Clark	135 (2)
Palin, Mary Glaister	135
Palin, Sarah	135 (2), 277
Palin, Susanna	277
PALIN, THOMAS	277
PALIN, THOMAS	277
Palin, Thomas (son of Thomas)	135, 277 (2)
Palin, Thomas	1, 17, 112, 135 (2), 277 (2), 310, 312
Palmer, Anne	379
Palmer, Benjamin	277 (3), 278, 284, 358
Palmer, Elizabeth	234
Palmer, Isaac	18
Palmer, J.	17
Palmer, Joanna	206
PALMER, JOSEPH	277
Palmer, Joseph	278
Palmer, Malichi	277
Palmer, Mary	278
Palmer, Mary Ann	278, 358
Palmer, Martha	206
PALMER, ROBERT	278
Palmer, Robert (son of Robert)	278

	PAGE.
Palmer, Robert	19, 277 (2), 278, 312, 388
Palmer, Samuell	206
Palmer, Sarah	277
PALMER, THOMAS	278
Palmer, Thomas (son of Thomas)	278
Palmer, Thomas	183, 277 (2)
Pamlico River, land on	1, 324, 350
Pamplico River, land on	80, 104, 164
Pamplico River, land on S. side of	37
Pamplyco River, plantation on	422
Pamtico River, land on	342
Pane, Benj'n.	209
Pantego plantation	108
Panther Branch, land on	325
Pantico Road, land on	365
Pantry, James	382
Pantry, Mary	382
Pantry, Robert	382
Papleco River, land on	391
Paquinet, Charity	278
Paquinet, Isaiah	278
Paquinet, James	278
Paquinet, John	278
Paquinet, Margaret	278
Paquinet, Mary	341
Paquinet, Mary (wife of Michael)	278
Paquinet, Mary (daughter of Michael)	278
PAQUINET, MICHAEL	278
Paquinet, Michel	341 (2)
Paquinet, Rebekah	278
Paradice plantation	53
Parat, Jacob	293, 294
Pargiter, William	131 (2)
Parham, James	305
Parise, Joseph	176
Parish, Angelina	233
Parishe, Joshua	36
Parishes Creek, land on	206
Park, John	310, 342
Parker, Amos	118
Parker, Ann	280
Parker, Azriam	72
PARKER, AZRICAM	278
Parker, Azrikam, Jr.	371
Parker, Benjamin	173, 192, 279
Parker, Charitie	279
Parker, Charity	30 (2)
Parker, Daniel	279

INDEX. 567

	PAGE.
Parker, Elizabeth	240, 278
Parker, Ezricam	279
Parker, Frances	279
PARKER, FRANCIS	278
Parker, Francis (son of Francis)	278
Parker, Francis (brother of Simon)	279
Parker, Francis (son of Simon)	279
Parker, Francis	279
Parker, Gemima	299
Parker, Hanah	279
Parker, Isaac	98 (2), 384
Parker, Jacob	278, 279
Parker, James	30, 180, 278, 279 (2), 396
Parker, Jane	72, 279
Parker, Jeane	279
Parker, Jemima	85
Parker, Joanah	279
Parker, John	177, 193, 218, 263, 270, 279 (3), 281, 363, 394, 396, 420.
Parker, Jonas	279
Parker, Jonathan	279
PARKER, JOSEPH	278
Parker, Joseph	46, 177, 278 (2), 279
Parker, Judah	279
Parker, Judith	279
Parker, Lenina	278
PARKER, MARY	278
Parker, Mary	30 (2), 84, 118, 123, 279, 363, 401
Parker, Nathan	278
Parker, Patience	279
PARKER, PETER	279
PARKER, PETER	279
Parker, Peter	279, 401, 406
Parker, Rebeckah	279
PARKER, RICHARD	279
Parker, Richard (son of Richard)	279
Parker, Richard (grandson of Richard)	279
Parker, Richard James	344
Parker, Robert	279
Parker, Ruth	278, 279
Parker, Samuel	90
Parker, Sarah	192, 278, 279 (2)
PARKER, SIMON	279
Parker, Simon (son of Simon)	279
Parker, Simon	278

	PAGE.
Parker, Stephen	279
Parker, Susannah	98
PARKER, THOMAS	279
Parker, Thomas (son of Thomas)	279
Parker, Thomas	72, 226, 274, 278, 279 (2), 361
Parker, Thomezon	278
Parker, Tobe	278
Parker, Wicker	279
PARKER, WILLIAM	279
Parker, William (son of William)	279
Parker, William	30 (2), 279 (4), 388
Parker, Winne	279
Parker, Zilphea	177
Parkes, Catherine	280
PARKES, HENRY	280
Parkington, Bernard	2
Parkinson, James	222
PARLEPOUGH, HENRY	280
Parly, J.	246
Parnera, Mr.	49
Parris, George	300
Parris, Thomas	354
PARRISH, JOHN	280
Parrish, John (son of John)	280
Parrish, John	313
Parrish, Margery	280
Parrish, Sarah	135, 280
Parrishe, Mary	280
PARRISHE, WILLIAM	280
Parrot, Elizabeth	189
PARROT, JACOB	280
Parrot, Jacob	189
Parrot, John	280
Parrot, Martha	280
Parrot, Mary	280
Parrot, Susanah	189
Parrots	292
Parrott, Mr. Francis	208
Parrott, Francis	155
Parrott, James	313
Parrott, Jane	147
Parrott, Nathaniel	395
Parrott, Nathl.	281
Parrott, Penellope	281
Parse, Edmon	77
Parson, Jeremiah	280
Parsons, Barnaby	280
Parsons, Jeremiah	241
Parsons, John	280 (2)
Parsons, Mary	280 (2)
PARSONS, SAMUEL	280

	PAGE.
Parsons, Samuel (son of Samuel)	280
Parsons, Samuel	10
Parsons, Sarah	255, 280 (2)
PARSONS, THOMAS	280
Parsons, Thomas (son of Thomas)	280
Partis, William	26
Parton, James	222
Partree, Thomas	240
PARYER, JOHN	281
Pasly, Johana	219
Pasckel, Samuel	399
Pasmore, George	281 (2)
PASMORE, JOHN	281
Pasmore, John (son of John)	281
Pasmore, John	281
Pasmore, Joseph	281
Pasmore, Robert	281
Pasmore, Sarah (wife of John)	281
Pasmore, Sarah (daughter of John)	281
Pasquotank River, land on	26, 354, 392
Pasquotank River, plantation on	329, 385
Pasquotank River Bridge, plantation and islands on N. E. side of	167
Passingham, Thomas	305
Patchet, Mary	145
Patchett, James	342
Patchett, Joshua	411
Patchitt, Elizabeth	281
PATCHITT, JOHN	281
Patchitt, John (son of John)	281
Paterson, Ja	113
Paterson, Robert	288
Pattecasi Creek, land on the Beaverdam	89
Patten, John	243
Pattenson, Anne	281
PATTENSON, HENRY	281
Patter, James	32
Patter, Mary	113
Patterson, Elizabeth	281
PATTERSON, GEORGE	281
Patterson, Janet (wife of Robert)	281
Patterson, Janet (daughter of Robert)	281
Patterson, John	281
Patterson, Mary	281
PATTERSON, ROBERT	281

	PAGE.
Patton, Benjamin	286
Patton, Samuel	286
Pattycasey, plantation at	154
Paul, Mary	281
PAUL, WILLIAM	281
Paul, William	195
Paull, Catrine	175 (2)
Paull, John	281
Paull, Joshua	254, 311
Paupoy Ridge plantation	241
Pawmers plantation	326
Paylen, John	81
Payn, Ann	355
Payne, Mary Carolina	281
Payne, Michael	281
PAYNE, PETER	281
Payne, Peter	8, 31, 63, 101, 249
Payne, Sarah Emelia	281
Payne, Simon	254
Payne, William	281
Payton, Benjamin	83
Pea Hill, land at	395
Peachtree Ridge plantation	273
Peacock, And	130, 347
Peacock, Andrew	273, 388
Peacock, Ann	347
Peacock, Elizabeth	111
Peacock, Patty	111
Peacock, Samuell	89
Pearce, Edmund	116, 164, 282
Pearce, Hezekiah	282
Pearce, Johanna	223 (2)
Pearce, Joseph	294
Pearce, Joshua	116, 164
Pearce, Richard	355
PEARCE, ROBERT	282
Pearcy, Edmon	282
Pearcy, Ephrem	282
Pearcy, James	282
Pearcy, John	282
PEARCY, LAZARUS	282
Pearcy, Thomas	282
Pearry, Adam	250
Pears, Edmund	165
Pears, John	256
Pears, Joseph	256
Pearse, Edmond	292
Pearse, Lazarus	53
Pearse, Martha	8
Pearse, Wm	301
Pearson, Anna	282
Pearson, Easter	282
Pearson, Elizabeth (mother of Thomas)	282

Pearson, Elizabeth (daughter of Thomas).......... 282
Pearson, Hammond 282
Pearson, J.................. 323
PEARSON, JOHN 282
Pearson, John 282
Pearson, Jonathan 282
Pearson, Mary 282 (2)
Pearson, Peter......264, 282, 284
Pearson, Phebe 282
PEARSON, RACHEL 282
Pearson, Rachel 396
PEARSON, THOMAS 282
Pearson, Thomas (father of Thomas) 282
Pearson, Thomas (son of Thomas) 282 (2)
Pearson, Thomas 105, 290
Pearson, Thomas, Jr........ 271
Pearson, Thos.............. 271
Pearson, Wheelwright....282 (2)
Pearson, Wheelwrt.......... 267
Peate, Frances 325
Pecoson Point, land on...... 32
Peek, Mary 30
Peek, Samuel 134
PEEKE, JAMES 282
Peeke, Sarah (printed Puke) 238
Peeke, Thomas Parrot (printed Puke) 238
Peeke, William 282
Peeke, Wm.................. 238
Peeke and Hallem.......... 425
Peelle, Charity 98
Peelle, John 283
Peelle, Joshua 283
Peelle, Joseph 283
Peelle, Josiah 283
PEELLE, JUDITH 283
Peelle, Robert........91, 98, 283
Peelle, Robt................ 265
Peery, Peter 396
PEET, WILLIAM 283
Peeterick, John 252
Peggott, John 134
Peggs, Ann 283
PEGGS, JOHN 283
Peggs, John 283 (3)
PEGGS, JOSEPH 283
PEGGS, MARGARET 283
Peggs, Mary 283
Peggy (a mulatto child).... 127
Pegs, Joseph 132
Peine, Joseph 350
Peirce, Alis 283

Peirce, James 77, 260
Peirce, John 268
PEIRCE, JOSEPH 283
Peirce, Joseph 338 (2)
Peirce, Mary 410
Peirce, Miriam 283
Peirce, Rebekah 283
Peirce, Sarah........36, 264, 338
Peirce, Thomas.........150, 154, 221, 274, 283 (2), 338 (3), 406, 410.
Peirce, Thomas, Jr......... 150
Pell, Deborah 27
Pell, Sary 399
Pelwood, Mary 85
Pender, Elizabeth 283
Pender, John 283
Pender, Joseph 283
PENDER, PAUL 283
Pender, Paul (son of Paul), 283 (2)
Pender, Solomon 283
Pendergest, Margrett 420
Pendleton, Ann..........128, 308
Pendleton, Elizabeth.....284 (3)
Pendleton, George.......284, 346
Pendleton, Mary 284
Pendleton, Hen............. 200
PENDLETON, HENRY 283
Pendleton, Henry...145 (2), 284, 346 (2)
Pendleton, John 283
Pendleton, Joseph..128, 135, 245, 284 (2), 397
Pendleton, Mary........145, 284
Pendleton, Nanse 278
Pendleton, Robert.......278, 284
Pendleton, Sarah....278, 284 (2)
Pendleton, Temina 284
PENDLETON, THOMAS 284
PENDLETON, THOMAS 284
PENDLETON, THOMAS 284
Pendleton, Thomas (son of Thomas) 284
Pendleton, Thomas..146, 278, 283, 284 (2), 397
Pendleton, Thos............ 230
Pendleton, Timothy 284 (2)
Penket, William Daniell.... 90
Penney, Richard 167
Penny, Elizabeth 239 (2)
Penny, John 239
Penrice, Edward 284 (2)
PENRICE, FRANCIS 284

	PAGE.
Penrice, Francis (son of Francis)	284
Penrice, Francis	284, 345
Penrice, Hannah	284 (2)
Penrice, Mary	158, 284
Penrice, Samuel	284
Penrice, Sarah	158
Penrice, Temperance	272
PENRICE, THOMAS	284
Penrice, Thomas	156
Penrie, Francis	215
Penrim, Francis	115
Peoples, Clark	277
Perce, Mary	220
Perce, Thomas	220
Perce, Thos.	221
Perdue, James	98
Perey, Joseph	355
Pergifer, William	133
Perish, Bettie	284
Perish, Elinder	284
Perish, James	284
PERISH, JOHN	284
Perish, John (son of John)	284
Perish, John	284
Perish, Joseph	284
Perish, Josiah	284 (2)
Perish, Mary	284
Perish, Samuel	284
Perishe, Elizabeth	355
Perishe, James	285 (2)
Perishe, Jane	285
Perishe, John	254
Perishe, Joseph	285
Perishe, Mornen	285
PERISHE, SARAH	285
Perishe, Sarah (daughter of Sarah)	285
Perishe, Simon	285
Perisho, Joshua	3
Perkins, John	25
Perkins, Abasana	379
Perkins, Daniel	43
Perkins, David	89
Perkins, Elizabeth	285
PERKINS, HENRY	285
Perkins, Mary	98
Permenter, James	212
Perquimans River, land on,	6, 24, 38 (2), 155, 287
Perquimans River, plantation on	265, 415
Perrey, Elizabeth	248
Perries, Jesse	177
Perries, Phillip	177

	PAGE.
Perries, Mary	177
Perry, Benjamin	285, 314
Perry, Elizabeth	177, 285 (2)
Perry, George	417
Perry, Israel	416
Perry, Jacob	285, 416
Perry, Jacob, Sr.	416
Perry, Jacob (son of Jacob)	285
Perry, Jane	285
PERRY, JEREMIAH	285
Perry, Jesse	285
Perry, John	81, 194, 363, 417
Perry, Joseph	314
Perry, Jude	285
Perry, Judeth	51
Perry, Judith	177
Perry, Lewis	251
Perry, Mary	285
Perry, Miriam	285
PERRY, PHILIP	285
Perry, Philip (son of Philip)	285
Perry, Prister	385
Perry, Rachel	285
Perry, Sarah	70, 285
Perry, Thomas	51
Persey, William	207
Persher, Joseph	260
Pershoe, Joseph	285
Person, Capt. John	308
Person, John	285
Person, Jonathan	285
Person, Nathan	285
PERSON, PETER	285
Person, Peter (son of Peter)	285
Person, William	376
Person, Wm.	108
Persons, Betty	285
PERSONS, JOHN	285
Persons, Mary	285 (2)
Persons, Miriam	285
Persons, Rachel	285
Persons, Samuel	285
Persons, Thomas	396
Pery, Sarah	392
Pesket (Prescott), Thomas	212
Peter (Portugee servant)	405
Peters, Ann	165
Peters Ridge plantation	328
Peterson, Ann	285
Peterson, Constant	285
Peterson, Elizabeth	285
PETERSON, JACOB	285
PETERSON, JACOB	286
Peterson, John	347
Peterson, Mary	285

INDEX. 571

	PAGE.
Peterson, Rebeckah	286
Petifers plantation	341
PETIT, FRANCIS	286
Petit, Francis (son of Francis)	286
Petit, Mary	286
Petit, Sarah	286
Pettell, Sarah	338
Pettishore, land at	293
Pettit, Francis	274
Pettiver, Ann	415
Pettiver, Capt.	415
Peugh, Margaret	109
Peugh, Robert	109
Peyton, Ambrose	286
Peyton, Benj.	238
Peyton, Benja.	213
Peyton, Benjamin	417
Peyton, Benjn.	24
Peyton, John	397
Peyton, Mary	286
PEYTON, ROBERT	286
Peyton, Robert (son of Robert)	286
Peyton, Robert..19 (2), 213 (2), 402	
Peyton, Rob't.	24
Peyton, Sarah	286, 397, 398
Peyton, Thomas	286
Peyton, William	286, 397
Peyton, Will'm	38
Pfifer, Ann Elizabeth	286
Pfifer, Catherine	286
PFIFER, JOHN	286
Pfifer, Margaret	286
Pfifer, Martin	286
Pfifer, Paul	286
Phelps, Cudberd	286
Phelps, Edward...46, 66, 91, 134, 370 (2)	
Phelps, Edwd.	66
Phelps, Elizabeth (wife of Godfrey)	286
Phelps, Elizabeth (daughter of Godfrey)	286
Phelps, Elizabeth (wife of Jonathan)	287
Phelps, Elizabeth (daughter of Jonathan)	287
Phelps, Elizabeth..6, 23, 134, 218, 219, 286, 377	
PHELPS, GODFREY	286
Phelps, Godfrey (son of Godfrey)	286
Phelps, Hannah	286
PHELPS, HENRY	286
Phelps, Henry...7, 251, 259, 287 (2)	
Phelps, John...209, 286 (2), 287	
PHELPS, JONATHAN	286
PHELPS, JONATHAN	287
Phelps, Jonathan (brother of Henry)	286
Phelps, Jonathan (son of Henry)	286
Phelps, Jonathan (son of Jonathan)	286, 287
Phelps, Jonathan (brother of Samuel)	287
Phelps, Jonathan (son of Samuel)	287 (2)
Phelps, Jonathan..7, 113, 253, 288	
Phelps, Jonathan, Sr.	113
Phelps, Joshua	286
Phelps, Joshuay	286
Phelps, Margaret	286
Phelps, Mary	23
Phelps Point, Court House at,	18, 37
PHELPS, SAMUEL	287
Phelps, Samuel..23, 99, 334, 346, 383	
Phelps, Sarah	286
Phelps, Seth	307
Phelps, Walters	209
PHELPS, WILLIAM	287
Phelps, William	287
Phelps, Willm.	79
PHENNEY, GEORGE	287
Phenney, Penelope	287
Phetts, Elizabeth	41
Philer, Vendal	210
Philips, Elizabeth	110
Philips, Jonathan	70
Philips, Samuel	110
Phillips, Abigail	413
Phillips, Abigall	287
Phillips, Benjamin	287
Phillips, Celia	165
PHILLIPS, DANIEL	287
Phillips, Daniel (son of Daniel)	287
Phillips, Daniel	301
Phillips, Daniell	92
Phillips, Danll.	196
Phillips, Elizabeth	288
Phillips, Ezekiel	373
Phillips, Hannah	125
Phillips, Isabell	288
Phillips, James	287, 288, 338

Index.

Phillips, John 125, 259, 288
Phillips, Mason 288
Phillips, Margritt 287
Phillips, Mark 288 (2)
Phillips, Mary 288 (2)
Phillips, Patty 288
PHILLIPS, PAUL 287
Phillips, Paul (son of Paul) 287
Phillips, Paul (grandson of
  Paul) 287
Phillips, Paul 261
Phillips, Rebecca 287
Phillips, Robt.............. 88
Phillips, Samuel....287, 288, 390
Phillips, Sara 35
Phillips, Sarah Richardson.. 427
PHILLIPS, THOMAS 288
PHILLIPS, THOMAS 288
Phillips, Thomas 259
Phillips, Thomas (son of
  Thomas) 288 (2)
PHILLIPS, WILLIAM 288
Phillips, William...112, 124,
  171, 191, 288 (3)
Phillis (a free negro woman) 127
PHILPOTT, JOHN 288
Philpott, John..105, 122, 189, 208
Philpott, Mary 288
Philps, Cudbath 401
Philps, George 401
Philps Point, Court house on 34
Phipps, Jacob 336
Phipps, John............314, 336
Phitt, John 55
Physioc, John 206 (2)
Physioc, Peter 318 (2)
PICKENS, ANDREW 288
Pickens, Andrew (son of
  Andrew) 288
Pickens, Jean 288
Pickens, John 288 (2)
Pickens, Nancy 288
Pickeren, Richard 143
PICKERIN, RICHARD 288
Pickering, Richard 151
Pickinson, Isaac 321
Pierce, Ann 121
Pierce, Arthur 121
Pierce, Copeland 289
Pierce, Damaris 289
Pierce, Elizabeth 289
Pierce, Hannah 289
Pierce, Isaac 395
Pierce, James 158
PIERCE, JOHN 288

PIERCE, JOHN 289
Pierce, John (son of John).. 288
Pierce, John 289
PIERCE, JOSEPH 289
Pierce, Joseph..........288, 289
Pierce, Jos. 285
Pierce, Kerrenhappuch 289
Pierce, Mary (wife of
  Thomas) 289
Pierce, Mary (grandchild of
  Thomas) 289
Pierce, Mary 289, 383
Pierce, Patsefull 394
Pierce, Rebekah 288
Pierce, Richard 121
Pierce, Sarah 289
PIERCE, THOMAS 289
PIERCE, THOMAS 289
Pierce, Thomas (son of
  Thomas) 289
Pierce, Thomas (grandson of
  Thomas) 289
Pierce, Thomas........9, 20 (2),
  117, 286, 288, 289 (3), 383 (2),
  397.
Pierson, Samuel 31
Piert, John 155
Pigg Basket Creek, land on. 375
Pigott, Nathaniel 414
Pigott, Sarah 414
Pike, Ann 289
Pike, Benjamin..........55, 289
Pike, James 64
Pike, Jane 55, 289
Pike, John 289
Pike, Jonathan 113
PIKE, SAMUEL 289
Pike, Samuel (son of
  Samuel).................. 289
Pike, Samuel 189, 294
Pike, Samuell 56
Pike, Susannah 289
Piland, Edward 209
Piland, Thomas 209, 353
Pilcher, Edward 228
Pilkington, James 128
PILKINGTON, SETH 289
Pilkington, Seth........295, 296
Pilkington, Winifred 289 (2)
Pilkinton, Seth 64, 187
Pill, Edward 77
Pilson, Charles 290
Pilson, Deborah 360 (2)
PILSON, GRACE 290
Pilson, Grace 290

INDEX. 573

	PAGE.
PILSON, THOMAS	290
PIMBROUGH, DANIEL	290
Pinbrow, Daniell	70
Pindleton, Joseph	186
Pindleton. Sarah	277, 308
Pindor, John	86, 418
Pindor, William	4
Pindry, Moses	281
Piner, Abbegall	299
Piner, Abia	299
Piners, land called	37
Piney Point plantation	14
PINKETT, ELINOR	290
Pinkett, Hannah	290
Pinkett, Thomas	290 (2)
Pinkett, William Daniel	290 (2)
Pinkett, Zachariah	290
Pinner, Arthur	306
Pinner, Rebeckah	306
Pinnil, Richard	94
Pinvic, Francis	302
Pipken, John	151
Pipkin, Daniel	290
Pipkin, Isaac	151 (3), 290
Pipkin, Jesse	290
Pipkin, Jethro	125
PIPKIN, JOHN	290
Pipkin, John (son of John)	290
Pipkin, John	125 (2)
Pipkin, Joseph	290
Pipkin, Lewis	290
Pipkin, Martha	290
Pipkin, Phillip	290
Pipkin, Susannah	426
PIRENT, JAMES	290
Pirent, James (son of James)	290
Pirent, Mary	290
Pirent, Sarah	290
Pirent, Tation	290
Pirkens, John	114
Pirkins, James	304
Pirkins, Samuell	91
Pitman, Abigail	291
Pitman, Ambrose	291
Pitman, Ann	291
Pitman, Anne	291
PITMAN, BENJAMIN	291
Pitman, Cela	291
Pitman, Elizabeth	7
Pitman, Jacob	291
Pitman, Jemima	291
Pitman, John	11
Pitman, Lot	291
Pitman, Lucy	291
Pitman, Micah	291

	PAGE.
Pitman, Moses	291
Pitman, Robert	291
Pitman, Samson	291
Pitman, Samuel	159
Pitman, Sidney	259
PITMAN, THOMAS	291
Pitman, Thomas (son of Thomas)	291
Pitt, John	164
Pittman, Abigal	67
Pittman, Ambrose	291
Pittman, Ambrus	125
Pittman, Joseph	261
Pittman, Mary	261
Pittman, Thomas	238
Pitts, Gain	273
Pitts, Hannah	103
Pitts, Mary	132
Pitts, Mary	273
Pitts, Robert	132
Pitts, Walter	412
Plains plantation	156
Plank Bridge, land on	331

PLANTATIONS.

Abington	385
Alden of the Hill	257, 258
Ashwood	11
Bald Ridge	87
Ballards	54
Basteba	191
Bayes	38
Beach Reag	56
Beach Ridge	299
Beaverdam	339
Black Rock	293
Blewbootens Neck	313
Blew Water	106
Bowsers	108
Brick House	86, 220
Bridg Nack	56
Bridgens Hall	46
Bridgens Pastime	46
Briffits Island	66
Brins	38
Britains and Fordyces	407
Broadneck	23
Brown Marsh	147
Buckingham	385
Bucklesbury	327
Bull Yard	114
Butchers	310
Cappell Point	176
Cabin Neck	36, 212 (2)
Cabbing Ridge	134
Cedar Point	212

574 INDEX.

Entry	Page
Chenifin Ridge	206
Chickconacomock	147
Chincquapine Ridge	210
Chinpin	127
Chocowinateh	295
Clagisters	377
Clur	257
Conahoe	187
Coneconara	292
Coopers	257
Cow Island	209
Cowpen Neck and Rollinseas,	397
Cretches Old Field	381
Cumboes	108
Daniel Halls	221
Davise's	110
Deep Branch	326
Dicks Field	298
Dogwood Ridge	329
Dunkeleys	402
Dunkins	266
Ecrepint	304
Elbo	357
Faulks Point	155 (2)
Fendalls	341
Fendals	87
Ferny Ridge	191
Ferry	425
Floyds	379
Folley, The	14, 193
Forck of the Duckinstool	374
Fork, The	315
Forke Neck	48
Frog Hall	71
Gailors Hammocks	241
Garrison, The	295
Giddinses Point	180
Glovers Hammock	214
Gorams Neck	142
Goulds	108
Graham's Place	230
Great Quarter	293
Green Pond Neck	84
Groveley	12
Gumberry	328
Hales	38
Half-way House	293
Haltons Lodge	147
Hammock, The	228
Hardings	295
Harrow	163
Hawkinses Neck	119
Heldersham	13
Hill, The	66
Hogpen Neck	166
Holland House	196
Horns Quarter	192
Horse Meadow or Pasture	222
Hughes	108
Hunts	121
Hunts Point	214
Image, The	377
Indian Creek	393
Indian Town	214
Island Lands	29
Jacobs Wells	25
James Robinsons	190
Jarrot Hays Place	230
Jones, ——	38
Jumping Run	140
Kendall	253
Kirks	50
Kinyards	211
Laban	147
Lawsons	246
Light Place, The	328
Lilliput	6
Little For.	65
Log House	66
Long Glade	180
Ludlow Castle	46
McClenny's	407
Macknights	257
Manuels or Crickits	293
Masons Neck	284
Matthews Point	27
Maultsbys Point	253
Maverts	65
Meadowes	154
Middle plantation	36
Mockason	4
Morrises and Cuba	425
Mount Calvert	324
Mount Galland	244
Mount Garriot	182
Mount Messeary	204
Mount Misery	253
New Abbey	223
New Bern	292
New Germany	53
New Hyonham	178
Northerns	114
Oak Ridge	267
Oald Meeting House	321
Old Box Neak	38
Old Field	231
Old Ford	232
Old House, The	323
Old Town	139
Orton	253
Oyster Shell Banks	273
Pagetts	86

INDEX. 575

	PAGE.
Pantego	108
Paradice	53
Paupoy Ridge	241
Pawmers	326
Peachtree Ridge	273
Peters Ridge	328
Petiphers	341
Piney Point	14
Plains	156
Point, The	388
Point Pleasant	179, 330
Poplars Haven	313
Possum Quarter	187
Powels Point	270
Prisces Neck	303
Proctors	379
Quarys	295
Quarter, The	155 (2)
Red Banks	66
Red House	66
Renocooset	138
Rick Neck	111
Rigg, The	332
Robinsons	284
Rosefield	292
Roses	150
Salmon Creek	9
Sandy Hook	285
Sandy Run	65
Scotts Hall	244
Shop, The	393
Simmonses Neck	325
Snow Hills	25
Springfield	163, 292, 293, 330
Stamping Place	116
Stancells	174
Stults Hall	137
Stumpy Island or New River banks	11
Thick Neck	407
Thurrefare Ridge	196
Tower Hill	99
Town Point	223
Townleys Point	335
Tubbago's Folly	136
Tuckers Ridg	45
Turkey Point	11
Tuttellfields	4
Vinyard	74
Volls Island	236
Wallins	84
Walnut Hill	66
Whale House	114
Whitemarsh	257
White Oak Neck	313

	PAGE.
Whites Old field	232
Wild Cat Neck	307
Wilkesons Point	293
Windlys	87
Wolf Pit Ridge	86
Wolf Point Ridge	45
Youngs	108
Plater, Dorothy	291
Plater, Martha	261
PLATER, RICHARD	291
Plater, Richard	4, 11, 267, 319, 383, 423 (2)
Plater, Richd	182
Plater, William	378
Plato, Martha	291
Plato, Mary	291
Plato, Susannah	291
PLATO, THOMAS	291
Plator, Richard	383
Platt, Jashua	247 (2), 375
Platt, Nathl	297
Platt, Thomas	79, 407
Platts, Lucy	86
Plomer, Sam'l. Saban	304
PLOMER, SAMUEL SABANE	291
Plomer, Dr. Samuel Sabine.	8
Plomer, S. S.	327
Plommer, Dr. Samuel Laban	32
PLOWMAN, JOHN	291
Plowman, John	399
Plowman, John	222, 399
Plowman, Magnes	35
Plumtree, land at	260
Plumtree and Cyprus Branch, land on	411
Pohagon, Mary	200
Poheagin, Mary	200
Point Lookout	327
Point Pleasant plantation	179, 330
Pointer, John	231
Pole Cat land	297
Polk, Susannah	356
Polk, Thomas	356
Pollard, Jeff.	386
Pollock, Cullen (brother of George)	292
Pollock, Cullen (nephew of George)	291
Pollock, Cullen	26, 101 (2), 160, 165, 212, 250, 292, 293 (3), 294, 304, 330, 331 (2), 360.
Polloćk, Collin	52
Pollock, Col.	170

	PAGE.
Pollock, Elizabeth......327,	405
POLLOCK, ESTHER	292
Pollock, Frances	250
POLLOCK, GEORGE	292
Pollock, George.....292, 293 (3),	294
POLLOCK, JAMES	292
POLLOCK, THOMAS	292
POLLOCK, THOMAS	293
Pollock, Thomas (son of Thomas) 292,	293
Pollock, Thomas..4, 90, 111, 130 (2), 142, 151, 156 (2), 176, 208, 212, 291, 292, 293, 330, 331	(4)
Pollock, Thos....35 (2), 121,	199
Pollock, Thos., Sr...........	410
Pollock, Tho.	285
Pollocke, Thomas	8
Polson, Caleb	395
Polson, George	395
Polson, John	395
Pongo Creek, plantation on.	124
Pool, Grace	294
Pool, Jacob	294
Pool, John	172
Pool, Joseph........183, 294	(2)
Pool, Miriam	181
Pool, Patrick....14, 298, 384,	414
Pool, Richard..........266,	384
Pool, Sarah	294
POOL, SOLOMON	294
Pool, Solomon (son of Solomon)	294
Pool, Solomon..224, 266, 294,	414
Poole, Moses............300,	359
Pop, Mary	314
POPE, ANNJELEANY	234
Pope, Ann	294
Pope, Barnaby	234
POPE, EDWARD	294
Pope, Edward	294
Pope, Elizabeth	294
Pope, George...........294	(2)
Pope, Henry	207
Pope, Jacob............294	(2)
Pope, John..51, 233, 261, 294,	412
Pope, Joseph	159
Pope land	415
Pope, Patience	51
Pope, Mary............294	(2)
Pope, Rebecca	294
POPE, RICHARD	294
POPE, SAMUEL	294
Pope, Samuel (son of Samuel)	294
Pope, Sarah...........294	(2)

	PAGE.
Pope, Stephen	294
Pope, Thos.	54
Pope, West	294
POPE, WILLIAM	294
Pope, William..........294	(2)
Pope, Winifred	207
Poplar Swamp, land on..330,	411
Poplar Swamp, plantation on	194
Poplars Havin plantation...	313
Poptewell, Dorothy	185
Porgen, William	136
Porsell, Cathen	294
Porsell, Edman	294
Porsell, Elizabeth (wife of Garrit)	294
Porsell, Elizabeth (daughter of Garrit)	294
PORSELL, GARRIT	294
Porsell, Garritt (son of Garrit)	294
Porsell, Mary	294
Porter, Agnes	297
Porter, Ann	297
Porter, Dorothy.........286,	296
Porter, Edmund....295, 296	(2)
Porter, Elisabeth	295
Porter, Eliza	295
Porter, Elizabeth (wife of Nicoless)	297
Porter, Elizabeth (daughter of Nicoless)	297
Porter, Elizabeth....295, 296 (2),	297
Porter, Hugh	297
Porter, James	297
Porter, Jeane	297
PORTER, JOHN	295
PORTER, JOHN (Merchant)..	295
Porter, John (son of John), 295	(2)
Porter, John...11, 156, 188, 216, 239, 253, 295, 296, 297 (2), 393,	397.
Porter, John, Sr............	205
Porter, John, Jr............	205
PORTER, JOHN PEYTON......	295
Porter, John Peyton	296
PORTER, JOHN SWANN......	295
Porter, Mrs. John..........	258
Porter, Jno., Jr............	292
PORTER, JOSHUA	296
Porter, Joshua.....157, 295,	297
Porter, Josua	296
PORTER, JOHN	295
PORTER, MARY	296
Porter, Mary...........295	(3)

INDEX. 577

	PAGE.
Porter, Matthew	295
PORTER, NICOLESS	297
Porter, Patience	295
PORTER, SAMUEL	297
Porter, Samuel	297
Porter, Samuell	297
Porter, Sarah (daughter of John)	295
Porter, Sarah (wife of John)	295
Porter, Sarah	295, 297
Porter, Mrs. Sarah	324
Porter, William	295
Porter, Willm.	396
Porterfield, James	312
Portorwin. Joseph	298
PORTORWIN, PETER	298
Portorwin, Samuel	298
Portwood, Gilbird	361
Possum Quarter plantation	187
Potecasi Creek, land on	408, 411
Pottecasi Creek, land on	426
Pottel, Elizabeth	298
POTTEL, JOSEPH	298
Potter, James	38
Potter, Mary	113
Potter, M.	404
Pottle, Elizabeth	184
Pottle, Joseph	184 (2), 272
Potts, Dorothy	103
Poulter, Edward	367 (2)
Powel, William	171
Powels Point plantation	270
Powell, Ann	298 (2)
Powell, Brooks	298
Powell, C.	97
Powell, Cade	298
Powell, Cader	298
Powell, David	206
Powell, Elizabeth	298, 389
Powell, Fielder	41
POWELL, GEORGE	298
Powell, George	41, 298
POWELL, JOHN	298
Powell, John (son of John)	298
Powell, John	41, 103, 135, 206, 317, 363
Powell, J.	304
Powell, Joseph	388
Powell, Keziah	298
Powell, Lewis	298
Powell, Lucy	388
Powell, Mary	43, 408
Powell, Matthew	298
Powell, Moses	298, 408
Powell, Robert	173

	PAGE.
Powell, Sarah	189
POWELL, THOMAS	298
POWELL, WILLIAM	298
Powell, William	135
Powell, Wm.	229, 355, 381
Power, William	179
Power, Wm.	182
Powers, Abigall	298
Powers, Austice	299
Powers, Caleb	298 (2)
POWERS, GEORGE	298
Powers, George (son of George)	298
Powers, George	167, 179, 298, 326, 357, 404
Powers, Isabel	298
POWERS, ISBELL	298
Powers, Isbell (daughter of Isbell)	298
Powers, Joseph	199
Powers, Mary	91, 308
POWERS, WILLIAM	299
Powers, William	226, 298 (2), 315
Poyner, Benjamin	299
Poyner, Edward	181, 339
Poyner, Elizabeth (wife of Peter)	299
Poyner, Elizabeth (daughter of Peter)	299
Poyner, Elizabeth	299 (2)
Poyner, Humphrey	299
POYNER, JAMES	299
Poyner, James	299, 387, 388
Poyner, Joel	299
Poyner, Jonathan	299
Poyner, Joseph (son of Joseph)	299
Poyner, Joseph	285, 299, 403
POYNER, JOS.	299
Poyner (Pinar), Kiziah	299
Poyner, Lider	300
Poyner, Mary	299
Poyner, Maryann	300
Poyner, Nathan	299 (2)
Poyner, Nathaniel	299
POYNER, PETER	299
POYNER, PETER	299
Poyner, Peter (son of Peter)	299 (2)
Poyner, Peter	285, 387
Poyner, Robert	299 (2)
Poyner, Samuell	300
Poyner, Sarah	299, 387, 388
Poyner, Sophia	299
Poyner, Thomas	41, 299

37

	PAGE.
POYNER, WILLIAM	300
Poyner, William (son of William)	300
Poyner, William	299 (2)
Poyner (Poiner), William	299
Poyner, Willis	388
"Poynet" land	334
Prather, Josiah	37
Pratt (Chamard), Christian	300
Pratt, Elizabeth	400
Pratt, Jeremiah	71, 300 (3), 404
PRATT, JOB	300
Pratt, Job	71
PRATT, JOHN	300
PRATT, JOHN	300
Pratt, John	300, 386
PRATT, JOSEPH	300
Pratt, Joseph	300
Pratt, Josh	404
Pratt, Joshua	300 (5)
Pratt, Sarah	40
Predy, Frances	312
Predy, Laws	312
Presbyterian church at Dover, Del., bequest to	229
Prescoat, Mary	301
Prescoot, Benjamin	339
Prescott, Aaron	300
Prescott, Amey	301
Prescott, Benjamin	300
Prescott, Elizabeth	301
Prescott, Hannah	300
Prescott, Job	301
PRESCOTT (PRESCOATE), JOHN	300
Prescott, John (son of John)	300
Prescott, Martha	300
Prescott, Mary (wife of Moses)	300
Prescott, Mary (daughter of Moses)	300
Prescott, Mary	301
PRESCOTT, MOSES	300
Prescott, Moses (son of Moses)	300
Prescott, Moses	301
Prescott, Richard	301
Prescott, Russell	300
Prescott, Simon	300
Prescott, Thomas	300, 301
PRESCOTT, WILLIAM	301
Prescott, William (son of William)	301
PRESCOTT (PRESTCOAT, PRESCOOT), WILLIAM	301
Prescott, William	230, 300 (3)
Prescott, Willis	300

	PAGE.
Present, Elizabeth	362
Present, Samuel	362
Preves, William	362 (2)
Previt, Mary	145
Price, Christian	301
Price, Edmond	301
Price, Elizabeth	301 (2)
Price, George	222, 389, 409
Price, James	118, 301, 314
Price, John	301
Price, Mary	301
PRICE, PETER	301
Price, Rachel	301 (2)
PRICE, RICE	301
Price, Richard	301 (2)
Price, Sarah	301
PRICE, THOMAS	301
PRICE, THOMAS	301
Price, Thomas (son of Thomas)	301
Price, Tomzin	301
PRICE, WILLIAM	301
Price, William	231, 301
Price, Willoughby	418
Prichard, Benjamin	201
Prichard, David	41, 344, 392
Prichard, James	422
Prichard, Richard	320, 349
Prichard, Thomas	320
Prickett, Patience	166
PRICKLOVE, ELIZABETH	302
Pricklove, Judith	302
Pricklove, Saml	420
Pricklovell, Samuel	126
Pricklowe, Francis	302
Pricklowe, Peninah	302
PRICKLOWE, SAMUEL	302
Pricklowe, Samuel (son of Samuel)	302
Pridees, Law	312
Prince, David	379
Pringell, Mary	49
PRINGLE, ALEXANDER	302
Pringle, Jane	302
Pringle, Joseph	102
Prior, William	103
Prisces Neck plantation	303
Priscod, Isabell	130
Priscod, Moses	130
Prise (Price), Thomas	189
Prishet, David	122
Prisket, Ann	197
Prisket, John	197
Pritchard, Banja	368
Pritchard, Benja.	239, 308

INDEX. 579

	PAGE.
PRITCHARD, BENJAMIN	302
Pritchard, Benjamin	31, 332
PRITCHARD, DAVID	302
PRITCHARD, DAVID	302
Pritchard, David (son of David)	302
Pritchard, Elizabeth	413
PRITCHARD, HARBERT	302
Pritchard, Henry	302
Pritchard, Hugh	302
Pritchard, Jacob	52
PRITCHARD, JAMES	302
Pritchard, James	302 (3), 303
PRITCHARD, JEAN	303
Pritchard, Joana	54
Pritchard, John	302
Pritchard, Joseph	239, 302, 403
Pritchard, Margaret	123
Pritchard, Matthew	172, 278, 294, 332, 416
Pritchard, Richard	302
Pritchard, Samuel	302 (2), 303
Pritchard, Sarah	302 (2)
Pritchard, Susannah	125, 302
Pritchard, Thomas	186, 236, 302
Pritchard, William	302
Pritchet, Joshua	104
PRITCHETT, ABRAHAM	303
Pritchett, Abraham (son of Abraham)	303
Pritchett, Abraham	303
Pritchett, Abrm	37, 122
Pritchett, Anne	303
Pritchett, David	100
Pritchett, Elisabeth	303 (2)
PRITCHETT, JACOB	303
Pritchett, Jacob	304 (2)
Pritchett, James	303 (2)
Pritchett, Joshua	37, 303 (2)
Pritchett, Joshuay	303
PRITCHETT, MARGARET	303
Pritchett, Marget	303
Pritchett, Margett	303
Pritchett, Peter	303 (3)
Pritchett, Phil	391
Pritchett, Philip	303 (3)
Pritchett, Phillip	37
Pritchett, Phtt	424
Pritchett, Rebeckar	303
Pritchett, Sarah	303 (2)
Pritchett, Simon	303
Pritchett, Stephen	303
Pritlow, Elisabeth	378
Pritlowe, Elizabeth	303
PRITLOWE, JOHN	303

	PAGE.
Privat, Sarah	371
Privet, Jacob	89
Privett, Jacob	7, 194
Privett, John	97
Privit, Jacob	11
Privit, William	89, 137
Prockter, John	182
Procter, John	164, 318
Procter, William	290
Proctor, John	96
Proctors plantation	379
Prothro, James	110
Prothro, Jeremiah	110
PROUSE, ANNE	303
Prouse, Charles	303
Prows, Charles	117
Pryor, Phillip	208
Puffields, John	61
Puffenghall, Richard	307
Pugh, Daniel	304
PUGH, FRANCIS	303
Pugh, Hannah	304
Pugh, James	234 (2)
PUGH, JOHN	304
Pugh, John (son of John), 304 (2)
Pugh, John	303
Pugh, Mrs. Margaret	222
Pugh, Pherebe	304
Pugh, Theophilus	304
Pugh, Thomas	303
Pullen, Henry	148
PURCELL, NEILL	304
Purcell, Sarah	304
Purdue, Sarah	300
PURDY, GEORGE	304
Purefoy, Nicholas	174, 290
PURKENS, DAVID	304
Purkens, James	304
Purkens, Jonathan	304
Purkens, Mary	304
Purkens, Rebeckah	304
Purkens, Sarah	304
Purrer, Robert	100
Pursell, Garrett	154
Pursell, John	98
Purser, Benjamin	304
Purser, James	304
Purser, Mary	304
Purser, Patience	213
Purser, Richard	304
PURSER, ROBERT	304
Pursey, Garrett	158
Purviance, Samuel	332 (2)
Purviance, Wm.	257

Purves, Alexander 105
Purvis, John 16
Puryear, Robert 100
Puryer, Ann 305
Puryer, Elizabeth 305
Puryer, Frances 305
Puryer, Margaret 305
Puryer, Mary 305
PURYER, ROBERT 305
Puryer, Robert (son of Robert) 305
Puryer, William 305
Putnell, Aaron 305
Putnell, John 305
PUTNELL, WILLIAM 305
Puttnell, Mary 304, 305
Putt, Lucy 10
Pyrent, Mary 27

Quakers, land devised to.... 65
Quarlay, John 18
Quarter Swamp, plantation on 22
Quarrys plantation 295
Queen Annes Creek, court held at 26
Queen Anne Creek, plantation on 137
Queens Creek, land on...249, 359
Quidle, Patrick 184
Quin, John 361
Quinby, Eleazr. 353
Quince, Parker 389
Quince, Richard..51, 222, 389 (2)
Quince, Richard (Capt.).... 101
Quince, Richd. 253
QUINN, LOFTIN 305
Quinn, Margaret 305
Quinn (formerly Canady), Mary 305
Quinn, Thomas 305
Quinn, William 305
Quinn, Wm. 198

Rabey, Adam 168
Rabey, Jethro 165
Rabey, Judith 30
Raccoon Creek, land on..... 232
Raddam, William 301
Ragland, Agness 305
Ragland, Even..........305 (2)
RAGLAND, FREDERICK 305
Ragland, Frederick 305
Ragland, George.........305 (3)
Ragland, Mary 305
RAGLAND, STEPHEN 305

Ragland, Stephen (son of Stephen) 305
Ragland, William...305 (2), 395
Ragsdale, W. 148
Raily, John 309
Rainbow Banks, land on.... 92
Rainer, Danll. 420
Rainer, Lee 119
Rainwater, John 129
Rainwater, Mary 129
Rainwater, William 268
Ralier, Lydia 63
Raman, Edward 305
Raman, Mary (wife of William) 305
Raman, Mary 305
Raman, Sarah (daughter of William) 305
Raman, Thomas 305
RAMAN, WILLIAM 305
Ramsey, David..........136, 242
Ramsey, Robt. 119
Ramsey, Samuel 336
Ramsey, Shubridge 336
Ramsey, William........173, 336
Randon, Peter......315 (2), 316
Randown, Petter 316
Raner, Richard 259
Raner, Ruth 246
Rankhorn, Abraham 181
Ransher, Samuell 191
Raper, Henry 263
Raper, John....168, 340, 384, 401
Raper, Josiah 259
Rapheld, Ann 305
Rapheld, Benjamin 305
Rapheld, Isaac 305
Rapheld, Thomas 305
RAPHELD, WILLIAM 305
Rapheld, William 305 (2)
Raphell, William 225
Rapyuld, William 415
Rasbarry, William 190
Rasberry, John 292
Rasbuary, Bridget 306
Rasbuary, Hosea 306
RASBUARY, JOHN 306
Rasbuary, John 306
Rasbuary, William......306 (2)
Rasbuery, Wm. 246
Rasher, Mikel 378
Rason, Edward 87
Rasor, Ed. 331
Rasor, Edward....280, 306, 330, 367
Rasor, Edward Frederick.. 189

INDEX. 581

	PAGE.
Rasor, Elizabeth	306, 367
RASOR, FRANCES	306
Rasor, Frances	189
Rasor, Francis	293
Rasor, Fred.	119
Rasor, Mart Fred.	163
Rasor, Martin Frederick,	292, 386
Rasor, Sophia	330
Ratcliff, Eliz.	416
Ratcliff, Richd.	416
Ratclyfe, Elizabeth	415
Ratclyfe, Richd.	415
Ratleff, Dammeres	376
Ratleff, Joseph	376
Ratleff, Mary	376
Ratleff, Sarah	376
RATLIF, DAMARIS	306
Ratlif, Joseph	196, 251, 255, 259 (2), 306
Ratlif, Richd.	309
Ratlif, Sarah	306
Ratliff, Cornelius	306
Ratliff, Damaris	306
Ratliff, Elizabeth	306
Ratliff, Huldah	306
Ratliff, Isaac	80
Ratliff, Joseph	122, 160, 251, 252, 306
Ratliff, Mary	306
RATLIFF, RICHARD	306
Ratliff, Richard	204, 306, 366, 376
Rattlesnake Branch, land on,	174
Ratlif, Elisabeth	306
Rattlif, Isaac	306
Rattlif, Isbell	306
RATTLIF, SAMUEL	306
Rattliff, Mary	122
Rattliff, Richard	366
Rattliff, Thomas	122
Rawley, John	174
RAWLINGS, BENJAMIN	306
Rawlings, Hannah	307
RAWLINGS, JOHN	307
Rawlings, Joseph	127
Rawlings, Lucy	307
Rawlings, Susannah	307
Rawlings, Wm.	307
Rawlins, Ben.	337
Rawlins, James	391
Rawlinson, Elizabeth	335
Rawlinson, William	335
Ray, Ann	399
Ray, Chrissmass	101
Ray, Elisabeth	117

	PAGE.
Ray, John	160 (2), 193 (2), 225
Ray, Patience	354
Ray, Wm.	394
Rayfield, Ann	307
Rayfield, James	307
Rayfield, John	307
RAYFIELD, WILLIAM	307
Rayfield, William (son of William)	307
Rayford, Anne	307
Rayford, Drusilla	307
Rayford, Grace	307
Rayford, Mary	307
RAYFORD, MATTHEW	307
Rayford, Matthew (son of Matthew)	307
Rayford, Mourning (wife of Matthew)	307
Rayford, Mourning (daughter of Matthew)	307
Rayford, Philip	307
Rayford, Rebeckah	307
Rayford, Robert	307
Rayford, William	307
Raymond, Elizabeth	307
RAYMOND, THOMAS	307
Raymond, Thomas	313
Rayner, Daniel	413
Rayner, Samuel	413
Read, Ann	72, 307
Read, Frances	307
Read, Geo.	15, 26, 40, 67, 104, 133, 149, 163, 177, 227, 392, 396, 426.
READ, GEORGE	307
Read, George	72, 183, 249, 300, 322 (3), 341, 343, 359, 362, 396, 418 (3), 420, 426.
Read, John	7
Read, Robert	307, 418
Read, Sarah	307
Reading, Ann	308
READING, CHURCHILL	307
Reading, Churchill	296, 308
Reading, John	308, 309
Reading, Jonathan	308
READING, JOSEPH	308
Reading, Joseph (son of Joseph)	308
READING, LIONEL	308
Reading, Martha	308
Reading, Mary	308 (2)
Reading, Miriam	308
Reading, Nathaniel	308
Reading, Samuel	308

582   INDEX.

	PAGE.
Reading, Sarah (wife of Joseph)	308
Reading, Sarah (daughter of Joseph)	308
Reading, Sarah	369, 370
READING, THOMAS	308
Reading, Thomas	308
Reading, Timothy	328
Reads Neck	334
Reason, Matthew	113
REAVIS, EDWARD	308
Reavis, Francis	368
Reavis, Jesse	308
Reavis, Jude	308
Reavis, Mary	308
Reavis, Sarah	308
RECKSAKER, DANIEL	308
Reckxaker, Daniel	283
Recton, Ruth	55
Red Banks plantation	66
Red House plantation	66
Redbud, survey on	77
Reddick, John	216
Reddick, Margaret	216
Reddick, Robert	353
Reddick, Thomas	169
Reddick, William	353
Redding, Amey	309
Redding, Ann (wife of William)	309
Redding, Ann (daughter of William)	309
Redding, Ann	370
REDDING, JOHN	308
Redding, Jonathan	302
Redding, Joseph	309
Redding, Mary	309
REDDING, WILLIAM	309
Redditt, Ann	308
Redditt, Isaac	308
Redditt, Joel	308
Redditt, John	308 (2)
Redditt, Joseph	308
Redditt, Margaret	308
Redditt, Martha	308
Redditt, Mary	308
Redditt, Susannah	308
REDDITT, WILLIAM	308
Redditt, William (son of William)	308
Redford, Robt.	54
Reding, Charity	309
Reding, James	309 (2)
Reding, Joseph	283, 309 (2)
Reding, Jonathan	422
REDING, JOSEPH	309

	PAGE.
Reding, Joseph	394
Reding, Mary	309
Reding, Rachel	309
Reding, Samuel	96
Reding, Sarah	283
REED, ANDREW	309
Reed, Christian	73, 341 (2)
Reed, Elizabeth	7, 400
Reed, Hannah	169
Reed, James	53, 169, 331, 346
Reed, John	77, 218
REED, JOSEPH	309
Reed, Joseph	324, 400
Reed, Margtt.	77
Reed, Martha	218
Reed, William	51, 193, 196, 309, 394
Reed, Wm.	118, 158, 167, 283, 400
Reed, W.	277
Reef, Sarah	107
Reedy Branch	417
Reedy Branch land	408
Reedy Branch and Ferry Causey	416
Reedy Run, land on	382
Reell, Elizabeth	309
Reell, James	309
Reell, Joshua	309
Reell, Mary (wife of Peter)	309
Reell, Mary (daughter of Peter)	309
REELL, PETER	309
Reell, Peter (son of Peter)	309
Rees, Mary	65
Rees, Owen	65
Rees, Thomas	392
Reese, Ann	309
Reese, Betty	309
Reese, Daniel	133
Reese, John	309
Reese, Mary (wife of Owen)	309
Reese, Mary (daughter of Owen)	309
REESE, OWEN	309
Reese, Owen (son of Owen)	309
Reese, Sarah	309
Reffer, Thomas	189
Regan, Ann	309
REGAN, DANIEL	309
Regan, Daniel (son of Daniel)	309
Regan, Mary	309
Regan, Priscilla	309
Regan, Sarah	309
Regan, Thomas	309 (2)

INDEX. 583

	PAGE.
Reggons, Daniell	310
Reggons, Elizabeth	310
Reggons, Hannah	310
REGGONS, JOSEPH	310
Reggons, Joseph (son of Joseph)	310
Reggons, Martha	310
Reggons, Mary	310
Reggons, Olive	310
Reggons, Thomas	310
Reigs, Abraham	10
Reigs, John	10
Relf, Cornelius	310
RELF, JOHN	310
Relf, John (son of John)	310
Relf, John	185
RELF, MARY	310
Relf, Mary	310
Relf, Thomas	224, 310
Relf, William	310
Relfe, Dorothy	310
Relfe, Mary	310
Relfe, Richard	348
RELFE, THOMAS	310
Relfe, Thomas	310
Relfe, William	311
Relfe, Wm	348 (2)
Rembough, John	83
Remm, John Peter	261
Remm, Melchor	127, 180
Renneroy Marshes, land in	153
Renfrow, Enuch	310
Renfrow, George	310
Renfrow, Jacob	310
Renfrow, James	310
RENFROW, JOHN	310
Renfrow, Tomeson	310
Renfrow, William	310
Renick, Mary	218
Renocooset plantation	138
Rese, Oen	65
Respess, Thomas	274
Respess, Thomas, Jr	274
Reston, Ann	310
RESTON, THOMAS	310
Retton, Ruth	55
Rew, Beverly	310
Rew, Euphama	310
Rew, Mark	337
Rew, Mary (wife of Southy)	310
Rew, Mary (daughter of Southy)	310
Rew, Rachel	357
Rew, Sol	15, 25, 43, 48, 63, 105, 126, 149, 164, 240, 304, 310

	PAGE.
Rew, Solomon	310 (3)
REW, SOUTHEY	310
Rew, Southy	241, 310, 406
Rew, Thomas	214, 310
REYNAUD, BENJAMIN	311
Reynaud, Moses	311
Reynolds, John	43
Reynolds, Joyce	171
Reynolds, Wm.	171
Rheam, Jeremiah	43 (2)
Rhoads, Elizabeth	311
Rhoads, James	213
Rhoads, John	311 (2)
RHOADS, WILLIAM	311
Rhoads, William (son of William)	311 (2)
Rhoads, William	367
Rhodes, Barbrey	311
Rhodes, Beeaman	311
Rhodes, Daniel	308
Rhodes, Dorothy	311
Rhodes, Elisabeth	311
Rhodes, Elizabeth (wife of William)	311
Rhodes, Elizabeth (daughter of William)	311
Rhodes, Elizabeth	311
RHODES, HENRY	311
RHODES, HENRY	311
Rhodes, Henry (son of Henry)	311 (2)
Rhodes, Henry	141
Rhodes, Jacob	311
Rhodes, James	311
Rhodes, John	152
Rhodes, Jno.	152
Rhodes, Mary	295, 311 (2)
Rhodes, Rachel	311
RHODES, RICHARD	311
Rhodes, Sarah	311 (2)
Rhodes, Thomas	311 (3)
RHODES, WILLIAM	311
Rhodes, William (son of William)	311
Rhodes, William	311
Rhoudes, James	117
Ribinson, Joseph	198
Rice, Ann	312
Rice, Benja.	96
Rice, Banjamin (son of Benjamin)	311
RICE, BENJAMIN	311
Rice, Betty	312
Rice, Cely	312
Rice, Clanerly	311
Rice, Daniel	311

584 INDEX.

	PAGE.
RICE, EDWARD	312
Rice, Edward	247, 312
Rice, Ephrim	311
Rice, Even	311
Rice, Gideon	311
Rice, Hezekiah	311
Rice, James	311
Rice, John	120, 125, 149, 208, 267, 312 (3)
Rice, Jno	41, 151, 168, 301
RICE, LUCY	312
RICE, MARY	312
Rice, Mary	96, 311, 312 (2)
RICE, MORGIN	312
RICE, NATHANIEL	312
Rice, Nathaniel	5, 12, 148, 372
Rice, Nath	239, 348
Rice, Nathl.	372
Rice, Rice	32
Rice, Mary	312
Rice, Sarah	63, 91, 164, 312
Rice (Secretary)	94
Rice, Simon	122
Rice, William	253
Rice, Willoughby	381
Rice, Zebulon	311
Rich Hills, land near	358
Rich Levills	382
Rich Neck, land on head of.	43
Rich Neck plantation	111
Rich Theck'tt in Virginia, land at	197
Rich, Wm.	55
Richard, Andre	249
Richards, Ezekiel	382
Richards, George	401
Richards, Jesse	313
RICHARDS, JOHN	312
Richards, John	43, 313, 413
Richards, Jno.	140
RICHARDS, MARY	312
Richards, Mary	68, 312
Richards, Rebecca	313
RICHARDS, RICHARD	313
Richards, Richard	313, 314
Richards, Thomas	107
Richards, Thos.	299
Richards, William	68 (2)
Richardson, Ann	194, 313
Richardson, Anne	329
Richardson, Benjamin	194
RICHARDSON, DANIEL	313
Richardson, Daniel	72 (2), 109, 357
Richardson, Elizabeth	313
RICHARDSON, GEORGE	313

	PAGE.
Richardson, James	313
RICHARDSON, JOHN	313
RICHARDSON, JOHN	313
Richardson, John	65, 313, 373
Richardson, Joseph	313
Richardson, Lebbeos	313
Richardson, Mary	313 (2)
Richardson, Nathan	295
Richardson, Nathl.	2
Richardson, Richard	313
RICHARDSON, STEPHEN	313
Richardson, Stephen (son of Stephen)	313
Richardson, William	111
Richey, Thomas	227
Richland	49
Richland plantation	49
Richland, plantation at	366
Rickets, Charles	232
Rickets, John	232
Rickets, William	232
Ricketts, Charles	273
Ricketts, Charles, children of	273
Rickitson, Abigail	314
Rickitson, Bathshaba	314
Rickitson, Benjamin	314
RICKITSON, GORDIUS	314
Rickitson, Gordius	314
Rickitson, Jesse	314
Ricks, Abraham	314 (2)
RICKS, BENJAMIN	314
RICKS, ISAAC	314
Ricks, Isaac	5, 237, 261, 314
Ricks, James	314
Ricks, Jane	314
Ricks, John	314, 363
Ricks, Martha	314
Ricks, Mary	379
Ricks, Patience	314
Ricks, Robert	314 (2)
Ricks, Robert, Jr.	314
Ricks, Sarah	314 (2)
RICHMOND, HENRY	314
Riddick, Abraham	301
Riddick, Hannah	177, 314
Riddick, Isaac	314
Riddick, Job	314
RIDDICK, JOSEPH	314
Riddick, Joseph (son of Joseph)	314
Riddick, Joseph	178, 270
Riddick, Kadak	314
Riddick, Mary	314
Riddick, Robert	314
Riddick, Rosanna	366
Riddick, Samuel	234

INDEX. 585

Riders Creek, land on...... 367
Ridge, Anne 314
Ridge, Elizabeth 314
Ridge, Godfrey 314
Ridge, Mary 314
RIDGE, THOMAS 314
Ridge, William 314
Ridges, land up the........ 216
Riding, Dorothy 323
Riding, Elizabeth 323
Riding, John 143
Riding, Jonathan 88
Riding, Martha 323
Riding, Mary 214
Riding, Thomas 143
Rieusett, John............34, 282
Rigbe, Elizbeth 242
Rigby, John 315
Rigby, Margery 315
Rigby, Margrett 420
Rigby, Richd. 420
RIGBY, WILLIAM 314
Rigg, James 402
Riggins, Elizabeth 129
Riggsby, William 149
Right, John 82
Right (Wright), John...... 379
Riging, Daniel 144
Rigne, Thomas 391
RIGNEY, BENJAMIN 315
Rigney, Benjamin.......324, 342
Rigney, Elisabeth 315
Rigney, Febe 315
Rigney, Hannah 315
Rigney, James............50, 315
RIGNEY, JOHN 315
Rigney, Mary 315
Rincey, Mary 311
Riordame, Angelica 315
RIORDAME, DENIS 315
Riordame, Sarah 315
Risenouer, Elizabeth 315
Risenouer, John 315
RISENOUER, MATTHEW 315
Risenouer, Jacob 315
Risnover, Mathew 204
Rissonover, Mathias 247
Rit, Comfort 126
Rit, Jeremiah 126
Rit, Samuel 126
RITEGA, JACOB 315
Ritega, Margaret 315
Ritega, Miriam 315
Ritega, Phillis 315
Riussett, David 315
RIUSETT, JOHN 315

Riussett, John (son of John) 315
Riussett, John 316
RIUSSETT, PETER 316
River Island, land in....... 27
Rivet, George 50
Roads, Elisabeth 358
Roades, Richard 333
Roades, Thomas 358
Roads, William.........246, 310
Roanoak, land at.......... 363
Roanoak River, land on..... 164
Roanoke River, islands in... 187
Roanoke River, land on..192, 197
Roanoke, land up.......... 63
Roanoque River and Uraha Swamp, land between..... 110
Robb, Thomas 390
Robens, John 237
Roberson, John 194
Roberson, Thomas 234
ROBERTS, ANDREW 316
Roberts, Andrew (son of Andrew) 316
Roberts, Ann 316
Roberts, Benjamin 419
Roberts, Charles........145, 422
Roberts, Cynthia 316
Roberts, Elizabeth......316 (3)
Roberts, Hannah 396
Roberts, Henry 371
Roberts, Houston 173
Roberts, Isable 316
ROBERTS, JAMES 316
ROBERTS, JAMES 316
Roberts, James (son of James) 316
Roberts, James (son of James) 316
Roberts, James 9, 427
Roberts, James 272
Roberts, John..142, 238, 316, 333, 414
ROBERTS, JOSEPH 316
Roberts, J. 381
Roberts, Margaret.......238, 316
Roberts, Richard........137, 316
Roberts, Sabonah 316
Roberts, Sally 316
Roberts, Samuel 316
Roberts, Sarah...9, 176, 204, 427
Roberts, Thos. 86
Roberts, William....205, 316, 333
Roberts, Wm. 352
Robertson, Deborah 316
Robertson, Elizabeth 101

Index.

Robertson, George 340
ROBERTSON, HENRY 316
Robertson, Henry (son of Henry) 316
Robertson, Higdon 316
ROBERTSON, JAMES 316
Robertson, James 52
Robertson, John 135, 419
Robertson, Joseph 370
Robertson, Lewis 316
Robertson, Malachi 316
Robertson, Mordecai 316
Robertson, Peter 316
Robertson, Salley 316
Robertson, Sarah 316
Robertson, William..150, 223 (2). 352, 404
Robertson, Wm......72. 229, 230, 278, 333
Robeson, Ann...........207, 241
Robeson, John......241 (2), 262
Robeson, Jno. 394
Robeson, Mary 22
Robeson, Thomas........22, 234
ROBESON, THOS. 244
Robeson, Thos....34, 59, 65, 141, 176, 189, 191, 218, 226 (2), 227, 232, 235, 270.
Robetson, Abell 146
Robins, Edward 117
Robins, Elenor..........317 (2)
Robins, Frances 316
ROBINS, JAMES 316
Robins, James 385
Robins, John 317
ROBINS, JOSEPH 317
Robins, Joseph (son of Joseph) 317
Robins, Margaret 316
Robins, Richard........317, 351
Robins, William 317
Robinson, Ann 207
Robinson, Anne 317
ROBINSON, CHARLES 317
Robinson, Charles........76, 317
Robinson, Cornelius 317
Robinson, Elizabeth 317
ROBINSON, HUMPHREY 317
Robinson, Humphrey 176
Robinson, Humphry 31, 87
ROBINSON, JAMES 317
Robinson, James 122
Robinson, Jane 317
Robinson, Jemime 252
ROBINSON, JOHN 317

Robinson, John..........74, 207, 253, 254, 263 (2), 276, 317 (2), 423.
ROBINSON, JOSEPH 317
Robinson, Joseph......17, 40, 55, 181, 199, 256, 259, 263, 264, 267 (2), 274, 294, 317 (2), 401, 403
Robinson, Jos. 255
Robinson, Mary....252, 253, 317
Robinson, Rowland 317
Robinson, Samuel 176
Robinson, Sarah (wife of Charles) 317
Robinson, Sarah (daughter of Charles) 317
Robinson, Sarah....253, 317 (3), 369
ROBINSON, THOMAS 317
ROBINSON, THOMAS 317
Robinson, Thomas.......317 (2)
Robinson, Thos. 369
Robinson, Townsend 317
Robinson, William 317
Robison, Casten 24
Robison, Cotton 24
Robison, Capt. John........ 138
Robison, John...83, 135, 277, 423
Robson, Haner 197
Robson, Solomon....197, 198, 286
Robson, Wm. 198
Roche, Mary 78
Roche, P. 228
Roche, Thomas 78
Rockahock Creek, land on... 13
Rockahock Creek, plantation on 269
Rockahock Neck, land in.... 155
Rockey Point, land opposite to 257
Rockey Point, plantation at. 257
Rockfish Creek, land near... 11
Rodners, plantation at fork of 29
Rockquis Swamp, plantation on 252
Rocksaker, Daniel 284
Rocky Point, land at........ 253
Rocky Swamp, land on...... 398
Rocquis, plantation in...... 323
Rocquis, plantation on...... 358
Rod, Duglis, ... 394
Rodes, Daniel, Jr. 381
Rodes, Henry 421
Rodes, Mary 381
Rodes, William 329
Rodgers, Frances 143

Index. 587

Rodgers, Jacob 322
Rodgers, John 143, 318
RODGERS, JOSEPH 318
Rodgers, Mary 318 (2)
Rodgers, Thomas 143 (2)
Rods, Daniel 381
Roe, Benjamin 318
Roe, Betty 318
Roe, Coleman 337, 413, 414
Roe, Deborah 318
Roe, Dolly 318
Roe, Dorothy 318
Roe, Ebenezer 318
Roe, Edmond 318
ROE, EDWARD 318
Roe, Edward 427
ROE, JAMES 318
Roe, Jean 427
ROE, JOHN 427
Roe, John 301
Roe, John Edward 427
Roe, John Vallentine 100
Roe, Kikley 318
ROE, LUKE 318
Roe, Rachel 427
ROE, ROBERT 318
Roe, Samuel 427
Roe, Sarah 318
Roe, Susannah 427 (2)
Roe, Thomas 318 (2)
Roe, Valentine 318
Roes Bay, land on 241
Roes, land up 241
Rogers, Aaron 318
Rogers, Briget 314
Rogers, Deborah 318
Rogers, Drury 318
Rogers, Elizabeth 318
ROGERS, EMANUEL 318
Rogers, Faith 318
Rogers, Frances 319
Rogers, Francis 158
Rogers, Isom 318
Rogers, Jacob 44
Rogers, Jane 423
ROGERS, JOHN 318
Rogers, John (son of John), 318
Rogers, John 301, 318 (2), 423
Rogers, Jordan 85
ROGERS, JOSEPH 318
Rogers, Joseph (son of
 Joseph) 318
Rogers, Joseph 43, 318
Rogers, Mary (wife of
 Thomas) 319

Rogers, Mary (daughter of
 Thomas) 319
Rogers, Mary 57, 314, 318, 319
Rogers, Michael 318
Rogers, Peleg 106
Rogers, Reuben 318
Rogers, Reuben 199
ROGERS, RICHARD 319
Rogers, Richard 299
ROGERS, ROBERT 319
Rogers, Robert (son of
 Robert) 319
Rogers, Robert..208, 319 (2), 389
Rogers, Sarah 319
ROGERS, THOMAS 319
ROGERS, THOMAS 319
Rogers, Thomas (son of
 Thomas) 319 (2)
Rogers, Thomas 421
Rogers, Thos 158
ROGERS, WILLIAM 319
Rogers, Williams 319
Rogers, Wustrum 398
Rogerson, Casiah 204
Rogerson, Daniel ...204, 216 (3)
Rogerson, Danll. 205
Rogerson, Hanna 216
Rogerson, Josiah 169, 204, 216
Rogerson, Margret 204
Rogeson, Daniel 178
Rognes Swamp, land on 78
Rokquis Creek, planta-
 tions on 143
Rolf, Jno 167, 193
Rolfe, Ann 40
Rolfe, Elizabeth 193, 319
Rolfe, John 193
Rolfe, Dr. Roger 336
Rolfe, Roger 40 (2), 46, 123
ROLFE, THOMAS 319
Rolfe, Tho 100, 201 (2),
                    244, 288, 372
Rolfe, Thos 185, 189
Rolfe, Wm 41, 185
Rolfe, W 161
Rollins, Comft 238
Rollison, William 118
Rolton, Dorothy 153
Rombough, Frank 331
Roneoake River, land on.... 57
Ronoak Town, lots in 326
Ronoke River, land on 234
Rood, Dugless 381
Rooke, Mary 117
Rooke, Richard 117, 183

Index.

	PAGE.
Rooks, Joseph	151
Rooks, Mary	91
Roos, William	191
ROOSE, WILLIAM	319
Root, John	95
Roots, Hannah	244 (2)
Roots, Mary	244
Roots, Roger	244
Roots, Sarah	244
Roousall (Russell), Mary	390
Roper, John	176
ROPER, WILLIAM	319
Roper, William	123
Rose, Cornelius	328
Rose, Elizabeth	397
Rose, John	180
Rose, Richd	292
Rose, Sarah	75
Rosefield plantation	292
Roses plantation	150
Rosewell, Benjamin	103
Roshall, Peter	172
ROSIER, NATHL.	319
Ross, Mr.	253
Ross, Abel	193, 256, 354, 381, 418
Ross, Andrew	60, 199, 210, 281
Ross, Andrew, Jr.	281
Ross, David	61, 248
Ross, James	11, 83
Ross, John	277
Ross, Mary	277
Ross, Tamar	256
Ross, William	222
Ross, Wm.	253
Rosy, Elizabeth	125
Roundabout land	408, 411
Roulings, Elizabeth	180
Rountree, Ann	321 (2)
Rountree, Charles	321 (2)
Rountree, Chas.	33
Rountree, Elizabeth	321 (2)
ROUNTREE, FRANCIS	321
Rountree, Francis (son of Francis)	321
ROUNTREE, HANNAH	321
Rountree, Hanah	321
ROUNTREE, JESSE	321
Rountree, Jesse (son of Jesse)	321
Rountree, Jethro	77
Rountree, John	321 (2)
Rountree, Judith	392
Rountree, Kadar	321
Rountree, Ledy	321 (2)
Rountree, Mary	321 (2)

	PAGE.
Rountree, Moab	321
ROUNTREE, MOSES	321
Rountree, Moses	118, 321 (3)
Rountree, Sary	321
ROUNTREE, THOMAS	321
Rountree, Thomas (son of Thomas)	321 (2)
Rountree, Thomas (grandson of Thomas)	321
Rountree, Thomas	33, 169
Rountree, Thos.	33, 166, 209
Rountree, Thos., Sr.	33
Rountree, William	314, 321 (2)
Rourk, Dorothy	320
ROURK, EDMOND	320
Rourk, Samuel	320
Rousham, John	63, 117
Routen, John	305
Routledge, Ao	151
Routledge, Catherine	405
Routledge, Nicholas	123, 334, 404
Routledge, Nichs	31
Routledge N,	62, 76, 97, 149, 217, 256, 288, 290, 322, 339, 405.
Routlidge, W.	16
Row, Deborah	320
Row, George	320 (2)
Row, Mary	320
Row, Sarah	320
Row, VALENTINE	320
Row, Valentine (son of Valentine)	320
Rowan, ———, Capt.	96
Rowan, Andrew	320
Rowan, Ann	320
Rowan, Atcheyson	320
Rowan, Elizabeth (Mrs.)	96
Rowan, Esther	320
Rowan, John	320
Rowan (Stubbs), John	320
Rowan, Margaret	320
Rowan, Mathew	320
Rowan, Matthew	34, 320
Rowan, Matt	12, 49, 92, 97, 142, 187, 226, 258, 312, 364, 406
Rowan, Robert	320
Rowan, Rose	320
Rowan, William	320
Rowden, Isaac	11
Rowden, Sarah	32, 180, 224, 291
Rowden, Will	224
Rowe, Geo.	355
ROWELL, ELIZABETH	320
Rowell, Mary	320
Rowell, Samuel	320

INDEX. 589

	PAGE.
Rowntree, Christian.....321,	322
Rowntree, Elizabeth	321
ROWNTREE, FRANCIS	321
Rowntree, Francis (son of Francis)	321
Rowntree, Jesse	321
Rowntree, John	321
Rowntree, Judith	322
Rowntree, Mary	322
Rowntree, Moses	321
Rowntree, Moss	355
Rowntree, Rachel	322
Rowntree, Rebecca	321
Rowntree, Ruth	322
Rowntree, Susannah	321
ROWNTREE, THOMAS	322
Rowntree, Thomas..127, 128, 312, 355,	393
Rowntree, Thos.	355
Rowntree, William	321
Rowsom, John	42
Rowsum, Elizabeth	117
Rowsum, William	98
Royal, Cornilus	19
Royal, Elizabeth (granddaughter of Ann Barnsfeld)	19
Royal, Elizabeth (daughter of Ann Barnsfeld).......	19
Royal, Wm.	96
Royall, Arthur	391
Royall, John	391
Rozier, David	91
Rozier, Reuben	91
Ruckes, Demsey	322
Ruckes, Jacob	322
Ruckes, Jesse	322
Ruckes, Joseph	322
Ruckes, Mary	322
Ruckes, Sarah	322
Ruckes, Tamey	322
RUCKES, THOMAS	322
Ruckes, Thomas	322
Rue, Comfort	126
Ruffin, Etheldred	154
Ruffin, Robert	154
Ruffin, Robt	251
Ruffin, Samuel	174
Rumney Marsh, plantation at	244
Rumsey, William	417
Runaroy, land at...........	410
Runaroy Marshes, land on..	72
Rundey, Samuel	369
Rundey, Tamer	369
Runnills, Christopher	76

	PAGE.
Rurner, Robert	213
Rus, Elias	152
Rusbull, John	278
Rusel, Jane	234
Rushing, Wm.	281
Rush Marsh and Goose Creek, land on...........	104
Russ, John	199
Russ, Mary	148
Russ, Thomas	148
Russee, Michl.	272
Russell, Abigail	322
Russell, Abraham	322
Russell, Ann	322
Russell, Ann Sophia........	322
Russell, Barnabas	271
Russell, Benja.	19
Russell, Benjamin	13
Russell, David	322
Russell, Elizabeth (daughter of Thomas)	322
Russell, Elizabeth.......322	(2)
RUSSELL, HABAKKUK	322
Russell, James	322
Russell, Jemima	381
RUSSELL, JOHN	322
Russell, John.............11,	322
Russell, Luke	381
Russell, Lydia	13
Russell, Margaret	270
Russell, Mary	322
Russell, Michael	322
Russell, Peter	322
Russell, Rebeckah	322
Russell, Sarah	322
RUSSELL, THOMAS	322
Rustull, John	322
Rustull, Mary	322
Rustull (Russell), Richard.	322
Rustull, Richard (father of Richard)	322
Rustull, Richd.	307
Ruth, Jacob	325
Rutherford, Frances	105
Rutherford, Francis	82
Rutherford, John.44, 82 (2),	105
Rutherford, Hon. John.....	112
Rutherford, John, Jr.......	82
Rutherford, William Gordon	82
Rutherford, James	257
Rutland, Martha	91
Rutland, William	283
Rutter, Mehittobel	12
Rutter, Mich.	12
Rutter, Thomas	325
RYALL, CHARLES	322

	PAGE.
Ryall, Samuel	322 (2)
Ryall, Thomas	322
Ryall, William	278
RYAN, DAVID	323
Ryan, David	323
Ryan, George	323 (2)
Ryan, James	323 (4)
Ryan, Martha	323
Ryan, Mary	323
RYAN, THOMAS	323
Ryan, Thomas (son of Thomas)	323
Ryan, Thomas	169, 281
Ryan, Thos.	80
RYDING, JONATHAN	323
Ryding, Joseph	323
Sadler, Charles	423
Sadler, Elizabeth	323
Sadler, Margaret	323
SADLER, RICHARD	323
Sadler, Richard	323
SADLER, WILLIAM	323
Sadler, William (son of William)	323
Sadler, William	68
Sagg, Anderson	210, 225, 365
Saint, Daniel	152, 254 (3)
St. Ely, Peter	103
St. Paul's Parish, legacy to poor of	83
Salem, land at	148
Salisbery, Elizabeth	324
Salisbery, Frances	324
SALISBERY, JAMES	324
Salisbery, James (son of James)	324 (2)
Salisbery, John	324
Salisbery, Joseph	324
Salisbery, William	324
Sall, Stephen	34
Sallyer, Samuell	326
Salmon Creek, land on	80, 214, 292, 293 (2), 327
Salmon Creek plantation	9
Salmon Creek, plantation on	187
Saltar, William	148
Salter, Ann	350
Salter, Elizabeth	324
SALTER, EDWARD	324
Salter, Edward (son of Edward)	324
Salter, Edward	88, 218, 274, 304, 307, 316, 350, 360, 422
Salter, Hannah	156
Salter, John	394

	PAGE.
Salter, Mary	324
Salter, Richard	348
Salter, Sarah	324 (2)
Salter, Susannah	324
Salter, William	51, 362
Salyer, Ester	299
Salyer, Samuel	184
Saman Creek, plantation on	306
Samin, Matthew	49
Saml. Tisons Branch, land on	357
Sammon, Elizabeth	281
Samon Creek, land on	292
Samon, James	281
Sampson, Mr.	258
Sampson, John	99
Sams, Richd.	359
Sand Banks, land on	412
Sanderlin, Diana	4
Sanderlin, Sarah	18
SANDERS, ABRAHAM	324
Sanders, Abraham (son of Abraham)	324
Sanders, Abraham	41, 253, 289
Sanders, Abram	28, 341
SANDERS, ANN	324
Sanders, Ann	170, 325
SANDERS, BENJAMIN	324
Sanders, Benjamin (son of Benjamin)	324
Sanders, Benjamin	23, 51, 263, 324 (2), 338
Sanders, Betty	324
Sanders, Christina Elizabeth	325
Sanders, David	335
Sanders, Elizabeth	41, 324, 325
Sanders, Euridice	154
Sanders, Feribe	325
Sanders, Francis	325, 353, 364
Sanders, Graham	55
Sanders, Henry	325
Sanders, Isaac	325
Sanders, Jesse	325
SANDERS, JOHN	325
SANDERS, JOHN	325
Sanders, John (son of John)	325
Sanders, John	154, 324 (4), 353, 364, 370
Sanders, Joseph	324 (3)
Sanders, Jude	324
Sanders, Judith	302, 303
Sanders, Lida	324
Sanders, Lydia	324
SANDERS, MARY	325
Sanders, Mary	154, 325 (2)

INDEX.

	PAGE.
Sanders, Mille	325
Sanders, Morgan Smith	205
Sanders, Prescilla	302
Sanders, Priscilla	302, 380
Sanders, Rebeckah	335
Sanders, Richard	324
Sanders, Robart	262
Sanders, Robert	287, 325 (3)
Sanders, Rose	154
Sanders, Ruth	287
Sanders, Sarah	23, 154
Sanders, Thomas	154, 325
SANDERS, WILLIAM	325
Sanders, William (son of William)	325
Sanderson, Ann	326
Sanderson, Bart	325
Sanderson, Bartholemy	325
SANDERSON, BAZIL	325
SANERSON, BENJAMIN	326
Sanderson, Benjamin (son of Benjamin)	326
Sanderson, Benjamin	183, 326 (2), 345, 377
Sanderson, Caleb	326
Sanderson, Cesiah	326
Sanderson, Eliza	17
Sanderson, Elizabeth	50, 325
Sanderson, Isaac	326
Sanderson, James	326
Sanderson, Jesse	326 (2)
Sanderson, John	326
SANDERSON, JOSEPH	326
SANDERSON, JOSEPH	326
SANDERSON, JOSEPH	326
Sanderson, Joseph	50, 183, 298, 326, 327
Sanderson, Joseph (son of Joseph)	326 (4)
Sanderson, Joshua	326
Sanderson, Julia	326
SANDERSON, JULIAN	326
Sanderson, Julian	326
Sanderson, Lida	326
SANDERSON, RICHARD	326
Sanderson, Richard (son of Richard)	326, 327 (2)
Sanderson, Richard (nephew of Richard)	327
Sanderson, Richard	73, 304, 326 (2), 331, 381
Sanderson, Richard, children of	330
Sanderson, Col. Richard of Little River	327
Sanderson, Richd.	72

	PAGE.
SANDERSON, RUTH	327
Sanderson, Samuel	326
Sanderson, Sara	126
Sanderson, Sarah	66
Sanderson, Shadrach	326
Sanderson, Susannah	326
Sanderson, Thomas	326 (2)
Sanderson, William	326
Sandy Banks, land on	326
Sandy Creek, plantation on	88
Sandy Hook plantation	285
Sandy Point, lands at	292
Sandy Run plantation	65
Sandy Run and Bear Swamp, land betwixt	81
Sandwell, Benjamin	101
Sandwell, Mary	101
Sarsan, Laurance	8
SARSON, LAURENCE	327
Sarson, Lawrence	397
Sarson, Lawrence	293
Sarton, Laurence	151, 189
Satchwell, John	145
Satten, Deborah	69
Satten, Joseph	69
Satterthwaite, William	315
Saul, Stephen	183
Sauls, John	381
Saunders, Mrs.	371
Savage, Hill	153
Savage, William	26
Saverges, ——	365
Savig, Mary	255
Sawell, Charles	411
Sawkill, John	110
Sawtell, Zechariah	126 (2)
Sawyer, Abigal	328
Sawyer, Alexander	329
Sawyer, Ann	329
Sawyer, Anne	329
Sawyer, Benjamin	193, 328 (2), 329
Sawyer, Betty	327, 329
Sawyer, Bridget	142
Sawyer, Caen	328
Sawyer, Caleb	163, 244
Sawyer, Catherine	355
Sawyer, Cattren	329
Sawyer, Charity	329
SAWYER, CHARLES	327
Sawyer, Charles (son of Charles)	327
Sawyer, Charles (brother of Willis)	329
Sawyer, Charles (father of Willis)	329

INDEX.

Sawyer, Charles.75, 328 (4), 355
Sawyer, Christian 329
Sawyer, Cornelius......327, 328
Sawyer, Daniell 328
SAWYER, DANIEL 327
Sawyer, Daniel.....328 (2), 408
Sawyer, Denis 328
Sawyer, Dennis 262
Sawyer, Dorothy 327
Sawyer, Easter 142
Sawyer, Elisabeth......329 (2)
Sawyer, Ester 328
Sawyer, Ezekiel 327
Sawyer, Frances 328
Sawyer, Grace 328
Sawyer, Hanor 329
SAWYER, HENRY 328
Sawyer, Henry 193
Sawyer, Isaac......327, 328, 386
Sawyer, Jane 355
Sawyer, Jean 328
Sawyer, Jemima 329
SAWYER, JEREMIAH 328
Sawyer, Jeremiah 328
Sawyer, Jesse..........327, 328
SAWYER, JOHN 328
SAWYER, JOHN 328
Sawyer, John (son of John),
328 (2)
Sawyer, John...94, 301 (2),
327 (2), 328, 329
Sawyer, Colo. John......... 111
Sawyer, John Scarborough.. 328
Sawyer, Joseph.........328, 329
SAWYER, JOSHUA 328
Sawyer, Joshua (son of
Joshua) 328
Sawyer, Joshua 328
Sawyer, Judah 142
Sawyer, Mary..328 (2), 329 (2)
Sawyer, Miriam........327, 329
Sawyer, Nathan 328
Sawyer, Peter 134
Sawyer, Pettyath 329
Sawyer, Reachell 355
Sawyer, Rebeckah.......329 (2)
SAWYER, ROBART 328
Sawyer, Robert.....328 (3),
329 (2)
Sawyer, Sarah.327, 328 (3), 329
SAWYER, SOLOMON 329
Sawyer, Solomon........328, 329
Sawyer, Stephen 328
Sawyer, Susannah 328
Sawyer, Tamer 328
Sawyer, Taymer 327

SAWYER, THOMAS 329
SAWYER, THOMAS 329
Sawyer, Thomas (son of
Thomas) 329
Sawyer, Thomas....328 (2), 355
Sawyer, Thos. 31
Sawyer, Tulle 328
Sawyer, William........328 (2)
Sawyer, Willes 328
SAWYER, WILLIS 329
Sawyer, Willis..........327 (2)
Sawyer, Zachariah 328
Sawyer's Creek, land on and
below 195
Sawyer's Creek, land on.... 328
Saxpahaw Old Fields, land
near 253
Sayes, Mathew..........250, 260
Sayrs, Mary 28
SCANER, ISAAC 329
Scarborough, Benj. 24
Scarborough, Benjamin..206,
330 (2)
SCARBROUGH, CHARLES 330
Scarborough, Elizab 196
Scarbrough, Elizabeth (wife
of Macrora) 330
Scarbrough, Elizabeth
(daughter of Macrora).... 330
Scarborough, Elizabeth 305
Scarborough, George 273
Scarbrough, Joice 330
SCARBROUGH, JOHN 330
Scarborough, John...88, 248,
294, 330 (2), 416
Scarbrough, Lyda 330
Scarborough, Mac. ..34, 159,
196, 201
Scarborough, Col. McArora.. 157
Scarborough, Mackeora..206 (2)
Scarborough, McKrona 167
Scarborough, Mackrora 345
SCARBOROUGH, MACROBA 330
Scarbrough, Macrora (son
of Macrora) 330
Scarborough, McRora 409
Scarborough, Mary 415
Scarbrough, Tamar 330
Scarbrough, William 330
Scarf, James 117
Scarf, John 117
Scarfe, Edward 329
Scarfe, Israel 329
Scarfe, James 329 (2)

INDEX. 593

	PAGE.
SCARFE, JOHN	329
Scarfe John (son of John)	329
Scarfe, John	329
Scarfe, Jonathan	329
Scarfe, Mary	329
Scittison, Ann	23
Scittison, James	23
Scittison, Mary	23
Sciwocco, land below	340
Schaw, Neil	241
Schaw, Robert	105
Schonnewolf, Johann Barnhart	133
Schwanner, Jane	330
Schwanner, John	330
Schwanner, Mary	330
Schwanner, Mathias	330
SCWANNER, MATHIAS TOBIAS	330
Schwanner, Samuel	330
Schwanner, William	330
Scoggan, William	108
Scollay, Elise	142
SCOLLAY, ELIZABETH	330
Scollay, Jerman Robert	331
Scollay, John	330
Scollay, Sam	7, 101, 157
SCOLLAY, SAMUEL	331
Scollay, Samuel	237
Scot, Ann	151 (2)
Scot, Gilbert	169, 204
Scott, Andrew	160
Scott, Andrew (son of Andrew)	160
Scott, Bartholm	74
Scott, Bartholomew	313
Scott, Cason	276
Scott, Edward	163, 332, 385
Scott, Eliphel	331
Scott, Elisabeth	135
Scott, Elizabeth (wife of Stephen)	332
Scott, Elizabeth (daughter of Stephen)	332
Scott, Elizabeth	379
Scott, George	160
Scott, Gilbert	216, 357
Scott, Grace	331
Scott, Hannah	331
Scott, Henry	332
Scott, Hugh	160 (2)
Scott, Johannah	379
SCOTT, JOHN	331
SCOTT, JOHN	331
Scott, John	84 (2), 186, 223, 245, 332 (2), 379

	PAGE.
Scott, James	332 (2), 354
Scott, James Tooke	379
SCOTT, JOSEPH	331
Scott, Joseph	245, 277, 332 (3)
Scott, Jos.	80
SCOTT, JOSHUA	331
Scott, Joshua	135, 223, 331, 332
Scott, Martha	84, 331
SCOTT, MARY	331
Scott, Mary	331, 332 (2), 379, 385
Scott, Mathew	354
SCOTT, MATTHEW	332
SCOTT, RICHARD	332
Scott, Richard	175, 290
Scott, Samuel	132, 141, 287, 332 (2)
Scott, Sarah	331 (2), 332, 379
Scott, Severn	278
SCOTT, STEPHEN	332
SCOTT, STEPHEN, SR.	332
Scott, Stephen (son of Stephen)	332
Scott, Stephen (grandson of Stephen, Sr.)	332
Scott, Stephen	129, 132, 135, 186, 201, 223
Scott, Thomas	140, 379
Scott, William	49, 287, 332 (2)
Scotts Hall plantation	244
Scoules, Joseph	46
Scrimsher, Sarah	122
Scuppernong River, land on,	66, 156
SEAGRAVE, ADAM	332
Seals, John	104
Sears, Ann	333
Sears, Thomas	333
SEARS, WILLIAM	333
Seavern, James, Jr.	259
Seay, Isaac	333 (2)
SEAY, JAMES	333
Seay, James	333
Seay, John	333
Seay, Oney	333
Sechewraa, Mary	96
Sedley, Jer.	373
Segrave, Franc.	359
Segrave, Luseah	359
Selby, Samuel	190
Selby, William	190
Sellars, James	246
Sellers, Auther	89
Sellwood, Jno.	224
Selpshis Swamp, land on	384

38

	PAGE.
Sergut, Frederich	365
Sessoms, Culmer	354
Sessums, Culmen	425
Sessums, Cullineur	39
Sessums, Mary	425
Setton, George	333
Setton, Joseph	333
SETTON, NATHANIEL	333
Setton, Pathanna	333
Setton, Rebecka	333
Setton, Thomas	333 (2)
Seward, Mary	6
Seymour, Ralph	385
Shackelford, Ann (wife of John)	333
Shackelford, Ann (daughter of John)	333
Shackelford, Banks	333
Shackelford, Elizabeth	333
Shackelford, James (son of John)	333
Shackelford, James	392
SHACKELFORD, JOHN	333
Shackelford, John	333
Shackelford, Mary	333
SHACKLEFORD, JAMES	333
Shackleford, James (son of James)	333
Shackleford, Joseph	333
Shackleford, Keziah	333
Shackleford, Peleg	333
Shaford (Shackleford), James	95
Shallotte, land in fork of	338
Sharar, Robert	204
Sharbo, William	13
Sharman, Lucy	74
Sharman, Rob't	74
Sharp, Charles	147
Sharp, Elisabeth	333
Sharp, Elizabeth Plomer	291
SHARP, JACOB	333
Sharp, Robert	159
Sharp, Paul	330
Sharp, Sarah	291
Sharp, Starkey	333
Sharpe, David	70
Sharpes Neck land	425
Sharples, Robert	2
SHARWOOD, DAVID	334
Sharwood, David (son of David)	334
Sharwood, Jane	334
Sharwood, Jonathan	334

	PAGE.
Shauwaukee, land at and near	87
SHAVER, JOHN	334
Shaw, Anguish	235
Shaw, Angus	232
Shaw, Dusher	234
Shaw, John	407
Shaw, Joseph, Jr.	325
Shaw, Richard	61
Shaw, Robert	106
Shaw, William	323
Shawdaily, Mary	45
SHEARD, DAVID	334
Sheard, Elizabeth	334
Sheard, Mary	334
Sheard, Robert	422
Sheard, Thomas	334
Shearer, Arthur	334
Shearer, Elizabeth	334
Shearer, John	334
Shearer, Prudence	334
SHEARER, ROBERT	334
Shearer, Robert (son of Robert)	334
Shearer, Susannah	334
Shearer, William	334
Shearlock, Francis	217
Shearly, John	332
Shearwood, David	115
Shearwood, Jonathan	23
Shearwood, Mary	99
Shearwood, Sarah	99
Sheep Neck Branch, land on,	370
Sheering, Mathew	242
Sheets, Jacob	377
Sheldin, Mary	268
Shell, George	314
Shelley, Daniel	334
SHELLEY, JOHN PHILLIP	334
Shelley, Judith	334
Shelley, Philip	334
Shelton, Bural	51
Shenewolf, Charles	335
Shepard, Absalom	335
SHEPARD, DAVID	334
Shepard, David	214, 307, 335, 418 (2)
Shepard, David-Younger	418
Shepard, Elijah	334, 335
Shepard, Elizabeth	335
Shepard, Frances	405
Shepard, Gwinefold	335
Shepard, Jacob	307
Shepard, John	214 (2), 335
Shepard, Jacob	335

INDEX. 595

Shepard, Jacob, heirs of..... 334
Shepard, Richard 214
Shepard, Ruth 335
Shepard, Samson 335
Shepard, Sarah 183
Shepard, Solomon...214, 334, 335 (2)
Shepard, Stephen 387
SHEPARD, THOMAS 335
Shepard, Thomas 353
Shepard, William 214
Shepherd, David 89
Shepherd, John 413
Shepherd, Sarah 244
Sheppard, Ja............... 427
Sheppard, Jacob 346, 427
Sheslow, Daniel 261
Sherard, Charity 335
SHERARD, JOHN 335
Sherard, Joseph 335
Sherard, Thomas 335
Sherard, William........120, 335
Sherer, Samuel 317
Shergold, William..9 (2), 10, 28, 30, 44, 45, 48, 85, 135, 275, 278, 279, 298, 299 (3), 326, 338, 339, 362, 390, 404.
Shergold, Wm....48, 85, 179, 338, 388, 427
Sherlock, ——— 185
Sherlock, Dennis 217, 219
Sherlock, Francis 217
Sherlock, Mary 217
Sherlow, Daniel 176
Shernold, David 286
Sherrard, James 242
Sherrard, Robert 335
Sherrard, Sussanah 242
Sherro, Joshua 378
Sherro, William 378
Sherrod, David 69
Sherrod, Roben 8
Sherwin, Thomas 304
Sherwood, Elizabeth 335
Sherwood, Mary 21
Sherwood, Sarah 335
SHERWOOD, THOMAS 335
Sherwood, Thomas......196, 423
Shetts, Cevel (wife of Jacob) 335
Shetts, Cevel (daughter of Jacob) 335
SHETTS, JACOB 335
Shilfer, John Michel........ 375

Shilo, Dorithy 57
SHINE, DANIEL 335
Shine, Daniel..........363, 364
Shine, Danl.............316, 318
Shine, James 335 (2)
Shine, John.........282, 335, 363
Shine, Jno................. 232
Shine, Thomas 335
Shine, William 335
Shines, Mrs................ 66
Shipherd, Cyprian 189
Shippard, Henry 9
Shippard, Martin 9
Shippen, Edward 177
Shipurd, David 146
Shirley, Ann (wife of James) 336
Shirley, Ann (daughter of James) 336
Shirley, Desminiere 336
Shirley, Ann 40
SHIRLEY, JAMES 336
Shirley, Susannah 336
Shirord, Aaron 336
SHIRORD, ALEXANDER 336
Shirord, Alexander (son of Alexander) 336
Shirord, Catren 336
Shirord, John 336
Shirord, Martha 336
Shirord, Mary 336
Shockley Creek, plantation on 230
Shorly, Daniel 85
Shorn, Thomas 364
Short, John 327
Shorter, Benjamin 336
Shorter, Elizabeth 336
SHORTER, WILLIAM 336
SHROCK, PETER 336
SHUBRIDGE, WILLIAM 336
Shuford, Sarah 359
Shurley, John 86
Shute, Charity..102 (4), 196, 336
SHUTE, GYLES 336
Shute, Gyles....94, 102 (4), 212
Shute, Joseph 336
Shute, Mary 1
Shute, Penelope 336
Shute, Philip 336, 342
Shute, Phillip 1, 102
SHUTE, REBECCA 336
Shute, Rebecca (daughter of Rebecca) 336
Shute, Samuel 336

	PAGE.
Sibbly, Wm.	191
Sidbury, Comfort	32
Sidbury, James	31
Sidbury, Moses	32
Sidbury, Woodman Stoakley	31
Sigley, Aaron	337
Sigley, Ann	337
Sigley, Jean	337
SIGLEY, JOHN	337
Sigley, Margret	337
Sikes, Ann	372
Sikes, Benjamin	242
Sikes, Caleb	275
Sikes, Jacob	372
Sikes, Joseph	236, 363
Silk, Edward	42
Sill, Oswell	332
Silverthorn, Agnes	337
Silverthorn, Gild	64
SILVERTHORN, GILFORD	337
Silverthorn, John	337 (2)
Silverthorn, Lydia	337
Silverthorn, Mary (wife of Gilford)	337
Silverthorn, Mary (daughter of Gilford)	337
Silverthorn, Mary (wife of Sabastin)	337
Silverthorn, Mary (daughter of Sabastin)	337
Silverthorn, Mary	126
SILVERTHORN, SABASTIN	337
Silverthorn, Sabastin	337
Silverthorn, Sabbastin	107
Silverthorn, Sary	337
SILVESTER, RICHARD	337
Silvester, Richard William	337
Silvester, Richd. Wm.	48
Silvester, William	13, 19 (2)
Simens, Elisabeth	136
Simes, Robert	400
Simes, William	256
Simmond, Henry	191
SIMMONDS, HENRY	338
Simmonds, Henry	320
Simmonds, William	338 (2)
Simmons, Abiah	338
Simmons, Ann	338
Simmons, Asa	338
Simmons, Asalel	339
Simmons, Bassett	229
Simmons, Benjamin	28, 214, 338
SIMMONS, BULLOCK	337
Simmons, Caleb	339
Simmons, Daniel	214
Simmons, Deborah	338

	PAGE.
Simmons, Edom	339
SIMMONS, EDWARD	337
Simmons, Edward	338
Simmons, Elijah	338
Simmons, Elisabeth	337
Simmons, Emmanuel	134
Simmons, Emanuell	245 (2)
SIMMONS, FRANCIS	337
Simmons, Hannah	39, 337, 396
SIMMONS, HENRY	338
SIMMONS, HENRY	338
Simmons, Henry	82, 100, 338
Simmons, Henry, Jr.	45
Simmons, Hilary	338
Simmons, Isles	338
SIMMONS, JACOB	338
Simmons, Jacob (son of Jacob)	338
SIMMONS, JAMES	338
Simmons, James	214, 338
Simmons, Jamima	44
Simmons, John	28, 45, 134, 214 (2), 337, 338 (2)
Simmons, Joseph	338
Simmons, Margaret	338
Simmons, Martha	338
SIMMONS, MARY	338
Simmons, Mary (wife of Jacob)	338
Simmons, Mary (daughter of Jacob)	338
Simmons, Mary	337 (2), 339
SIMMONS, MATTHEW	338
SIMMONS, NICHOLAS	339
Simmons, Rhoda	338
Simmons, Robert	62, 213, 337
Simmons, Sam	404
Simmons, Saml	299 (2)
Simmons, Sampson	339
Simmons, Samuel	315, 337, 338 (3), 339
Simmons, Samuell	328
Simmons, Sarah	62, 339, 387
Simmons, Solomon	337, 338 (2)
SIMMONS, THOMAS	339
Simmons, Thomas (son of Thomas)	339
Simmons, Thomas	338, 345, 383
Simmons, Tomazin	337
Simmons, Willis	62, 337 (2)
Simmonses Neck plantation.	325
Simon, John	281
SIMONS, ANDREW	339
Simons, Argell	81
SIMMONS, ARGILL	339
Simons, Argill	339

INDEX. 597

	PAGE.
Simons, Benjamin	339
Simons, Busett	339
Simons, Daniel	339
Simons, Elizabeth	339
Simons, George	339
Simons, Jacob	58
Simons, Jeremiah	168
SIMONS, JOHN	339
SIMONS, JOHN	339
SIMONS, JOHN	339
Simons, John (son of John),	339 (2)
Simons, John....72, 215, 268, 289, 339 (2),	394
Simons, Joshua	339
Simons, Levi	339
Simons, Manuell	339
Simons, Margerett	339
Simons, Margreat	339
Simons, Mary	339 (3)
Simons, Simon	281
Simons, Thomas..20, 168, 339,	383
Simons William	339 (2)
Simons, Wm	374
SIMPSON, ALEXANDER	340
Simpson, Canon	225
Simpson, Edward	392
Simpson, Elizabeth	332
Simpson, James	307
Simpson, Jane	103
Simpson, John...40, 43, 103, 154, 165, 189, 259, 262, 332, 341, 392, 402.	
Simpson, Jno	409, 412
Simpson, John, Jr	105
Simpson, Joshua	392
Simpson, Patty	288
Simpson, Simon	288
SIMPSON, WALTER	340
Simpson, William	103
Simpson, William Brook	313
Sims, James	340
Sims, John	340
SIMS, ROBERT	340
Sims, Robert (son of Robert)	340
Sims, Thomas	340
Simson, Abram	31
Simson, Dorethy	340
Simson, James	340
SIMSON, JOHN	340
Simson, John	201, 340
Simson, John, Jr	181
Simson, Joshua	340
Simson, Mary	54

	PAGE.
Simson, Sarah	340
Simson, Solomon	340
SIMSON, WILLIAM	340
Simson, William (son of William)	340
Simson, William	175, 329
Simson, Wm	54, 182
Simson, Wm., Jr	181
Sinclair, Ann	340
Sinclair, Catherine	340
Sinclair, David	324
Sinclair, Elisabeth	340
Sinclair, Frances	340
Sinclair, Lucie	340
SINCLAIR, SAMUEL	340
Sinclar, David	148
Sinclare, Elizabeth	215
Singletary, Deborah	199
Singletary, Ithamar..199 (2),	385
Singletary, John	199 (2)
Singleton, Hannah	341
Singleton, James	167, 345
SINGLETON, JOHN	340
Singleton, Martha	340
SINGLETON, SAMUEL	341
Singleton, Spyers	32, 66, 341
Sipros Swamp, land on	366
Sirgener, William	166
Sisemore, Elizabeth	170
Sisemore, Samuel	170
Site, John	139
Siterson, James	99
Sitgreaves, John	127
Sitgreaves, Thomas	341
Sitgreaves, Thos	127
SITGREAVES, WILLIAM	341
Sitgreaves, William (son of William)	341
Sitgreaves, William	264
Sitten (or Litten), Isaac	3
Sitterson, Hannah...156, 341 (2)	
Sitterson, Isaac	425
SITTERSON, JAMES	341
Sitterson, James (son of James)	341 (2)
Sitterson, James	156
Sitterson, Samuel	341
Sittersun, James	27
Sivells, Charity	114
Sivilenant, Darbey	26
Skebell, Richard	135
Skeehawkee, land at	234
Skerrett, Thomas Hildersby.	405
Sketo, Joseph	309
Skiles, Mary	148

INDEX.

	PAGE.
Skiner, Charles	237
Skiner, James	150
Skiner, Richd.	309
Skiner, Susane	237
Skiner, Susannah	205
Skinner, Charles	19
Skinner, Eavens	341
Skinner, Elbe	271
Skinner, Evan	196, 341
Skinner, James	20, 150
SKINNER, JOHN	341
Skinner, John	152, 341, 388
Skinner, Jonathan	251
Skinner, Joshua	251, 284, 341 (3), 358
Skinner, Joshua, Jr.	341
Skinner, Lydia	271
Skinner, Martha	271
Skinner, Mary	271 (2)
Skinner, Rebecca	271
SKINNER, RICHARD	341
Skinner, Richard	7, 55, 122, 253, 289, 324, 333, 393
Skinner, Richard, Sr.	150 (2)
SKINNER, RICHARD, JR.	341
Skinner, Richard, Jr.	128, 150
Skinner, Richd.	254
Skinner, Samuel	341
Skinner, Sarah (child of James)	150
Skinner, Sarah	122, 150, 196, 271, 341 (4)
Skinner, Steven	341
Skinner, Will	221 (2), 309
Skinner, William	16, 151, 285, 341 (2), 360, 411
Skinner, Willm.	196
Skinner, Wm.	153
Skinner, Zachariah	150
Skipar, John	311
Skipwith, Henry	249 (2)
Skittlesharp, Joseph	143
Skittlesharp, Mary	143
Skittlethorp, Joseph	293
Slabbach, Elizabeth	173
Slabbach, Mary	173
Slad, Ebenezer	423
Slade, Abigail	342
Slade, Agnes	13
Slade, Ann	164
Slade, Benjamin	133, 315, 342 (3), 377
Slade, Dinah	342
Slade, Ebenezer	101, 337
Slade, Elizabeth	211
SLADE, GEORGE	342

	PAGE.
Slade, Hannah Hodges	211
Slade, Henry	101, 174, 337
SLADE, HEZEKIAH	342
Slade, Hezekiah	211, 342
Slade, Jeremiah	227, 342
Slade, Jer.	93
SLADE, JOHN	342
Slade, John (son of John)	342
Slade, John	88, 102, 133, 219, 315
Slade, Joseph	164
Slade, Kezia	342
Slade, Mary	342
Slade, Rebecca	342
SLADE, SAMUEL	342
Slade, Samuel	102, 402
Slade, Samuel, Jr.	102
Slade, Sarah	342 (3)
Slade, Susannah	342
Slade, William	125
Slade, William Hodges	342 (2)
Slades Creek, land on	345
Slaid, Abigal	346
Slaid, George	389
Slaids Creek, land on	377
Slason, Ebanazor	357
Slater, Margaret	217
Slater, Margarett	137
Slater, Richard	155
Slater, Thomas	217
Slatter, John	178
Slatter, Keziah	178
Slatter, Littleton	178
Slatter, Oen	104, 178
Slattor, Thomas	312
Slaughter, Abigail	32, 342
Slaughter, Anah	342
Slaughter, Deborah	342
Slaughter, Elizabeth	342 (2)
SLAUGHTER, MICHAEL	342
Slaughter, Nancy	342
Slaughter, Rebeckah	342
Slider, George	210
SLOBOCK, JACOB	342
Slobock, Nathan	342
SLOCKUM, ANTHONY	343
Slockum, John (son of Anthony)	343
Slockum, John (grandson of Anthony)	343
Slockum, John	343
Slockum, Joseph	343
Slockum, Samuel	343
Slocom, Elisabeth	343
Slocom, John	343
SLOCOM, SAMUEL	343

INDEX. 599

	PAGE.
Slocomb, Jeseway	343
SLOCOMB, JOHN	343
Slocomb, John (son of John)	343
Slocomb, John	420
Slocomb, Joseph	343
Slocomb, Josias	343
Slocum, Ann	35 (2)
Slocum, Josias	343
SLOCUMB, JOHN	343
Slocumb, John	149
Slocumb, John Charles	343
Slocumb, Joseph	343, 376
Slocumb, Mary (mother of John)	343
Slocumb, Mary (wife of John)	343
Slocumb, Samuel	4
Slocumbs Creek, land on	119
Sluyter, Benjamin	407
Small, Amos	342, 343
SMALL, BENJAMIN	343
SMALL, BENJAMIN	343
Small, Benjamin (son of Benjamin)	343 (2)
Small, Elizabeth	322
Small, John Knights	343
Small, John Knite	343
Small, Jonas	343 (2)
Small, Joshua	138, 309
Small, Miriam	343
Small, Sarah	322
Small, Thomas	82
Smallwood, Charlotte	92
Smallwood, James	32 (2), 92 (2), 100 (2), 101, 160, 257, 315 (3).
Smart, Samuel	213
Smear, Elizabeth	187, 188
Smedley, John	397
Smelage, Anne	343
SMELAGE, EDWARD	343
Smelage, Sarah	343
SMEWIN, HENMAN	344
Smith, ——— ———	67
Smith, Ambrose Joshua	248
Smith, A. J.	316, 317
SMITH, ANDREW	344
Smith, Ann	109, 173, 344, 345 (2)
Smith, Bazell	173, 372
Smith, Benet	131
Smith, Beneta	49
Smith, Benjamin	345, 347
Smith, Caroline Penelope	344
Smith, Catren	315
Smith, Charles, Jr.	184

	PAGE.
Smith, Charles	184, 345, 349, 377
Smith Creek, land on	253
Smith Creek, plantation on	102
Smith, Daniel	377
Smith, David	171, 344, 345
Smith, Deborah	346
Smith, Dinah	19, 214
Smith, Dorcas	13
Smith, Drew	21, 409
Smith, Ed	215
SMITH, EDWARD	344
SMITH, EDWARD	344
Smith, Edward	12 (2), 73, 177
Smith, Elisabeth	346
Smith, Elisabeth	348
Smith, Eliza	410
Smith, Elizabeth	13, 113, 173, 208, 227, 237, 344 (3), 345 (2), 346, 347 (2), 348 (3).
Smith, Frances	166
Smith, Francis	20 (3), 286, 399
SMITH, GEORGE	344
SMITH, GEORGE	344
Smith, George (son of George)	344
Smith, George	33, 73, 192, 379, 408
Smith, Gilbert	75
Smith, Hannah	209 (3)
SMITH, HENRY	344
Smith, Henry (son of Henry)	344
Smith, Henry	185, 239, 362
Smith, Henry Arthur	347
Smith (Lawson), Isabella,	209 (2)
Smith, Isaiah	338
Smith, Iseble	343
SMITH, JAMES	345
SMITH, JAMES	345
SMITH, JAMES	345
Smith, James (son of James)	345 (2)
Smith, James	38, 166, 172, 196, 208 (2), 260, 268, 342, 344, 345, 347, 348 (2), 360, 381 (2), 409
Smith, Jas	56
Smith, Jane	345
Smith, Jarves	38
Smith, Jean	181
SMITH, JEREMIAH	345
Smith, Jeremiah	344 (2), 346, 398
SMITH, JOHN	345
SMITH, JOHN	345

SMITH, JOHN 345
SMITH, JOHN 346
SMITH, JOHN 346
Smith, John (son of John),
        345 (2), 346
Smith, John (grandson of
 John) 346
Smith, John (nephew of
 James McDowell) 229
Smith, John (brother-in-law
 of James McDowell)..... 229
Smith, John..4, 13 (3), 14, 21, 38,
 58, 61, 95 (2), 148, 172 (2), 191,
 222, 235, 295, 302, 303, 322, 332,
 337, 342, 344 (2), 345 (4), 346,
 348 (4), 368, 373, 405, 417, 421
Smith, Jno...........36, 225, 343
Smith, John, Sr............. 235
Smith, John, Jr............. 235
Smith, John Trink.......... 346
Smith, Jos..50, 75, 146, 181, 186,
 311, 315, 331, 355 (2), 373, 397
Smith, Josa 88
SMITH, JOSEPH 346
Smith, Joseph (son of
 Joseph) 346
Smith, Joseph...38, 140, 271,
        347, 402
Smith, Josu................ 130
Smith, Josu................ 328
Smith, Joshua..........346 (2)
Smith, Judith..........248, 345
Smith, Leah............302, 346
SMITH, LEVI 346
Smith, Lewis 344
Smith, Lovey 172
Smith, Lydia 348
Smith, Margaret........290, 345
Smith, Martha (wife of
 James) 345
Smith, Martha (daughter of
 James) 345
Smith, Martha....13, 19, 345, 346
Smith, Mary (wife of
 Robert) 347
Smith, Mary (daughter of
 Robert) 347
Smith, Mary (wife of
 Thomas) 347
Smith, Mary (daughter of
 Thomas) 347
Smith, Mary....34, 123, 164, 173,
 184, 196, 208, 295, 322, 338 (2),
 344, 345 (3), 346 (2), 348, 398,
 410.

Smith, Mary Ann........245, 346
Smith, Menes 217
Smith, Mich................ 64
Smith, Nanney 344
Smith, Nathan 49, 217
Smith, Nathaniel 227
SMITH, NICHOLAS 346
Smith, Nicholas 181
Smith, Olif 345
Smith, Patrick 73, 99
Smith, Phil.....2, 28, 63, 77, 113
 (2), 120, 144, 153, 180, 191, 204,
 241, 261, 280, 282, 348, 377.
Smith, Priscilla 57
Smith, P................... 339
Smith, Rachel 344
Smith, Rebeckah 345
SMITH, RICHARD 346
SMITH, RICHARD 347
SMITH, RICHARD 347
Smith, Richard (son of
 Richard) 347
Smith, Richard...4, 209, 295,
        344, 347, 348
Smith, Richd............... 33
SMITH, ROBERT 347
SMITH, ROBERT 347
Smith, Robert (son of
 Robert) 347
Smith, Robert.......24, 133, 268
Smith, Rob't............... 204
Smith, Samuel..13, 110, 344,
        345, 348, 355, 396
Smith, Samuel 107
Smith, Mrs. Sarah.......... 5
SMITH, SARAH 347
Smith, Sarah..235, 253, 268,
 342, 344 (2), 346, 347, 348, 364
Smith, Sary Ann........... 348
Smith, Silas 407
Smith, Simon 346
Smith, Solomon....217, 343, 345
Smith, Stephen..223, 346 (2), 347
Smith, Susana 38
Smith, Susanah 77
Smith, Susannah 344
Smith, Tabitha 404
SMITH, THOMAS 347
SMITH, THOMAS 347
SMITH, THOMAS 347
Smith, Thomas.....7, 13, 52, 60,
 105, 109, 214, 227 (2), 253, 295
 (2), 345 (2), 346 (2), 348, 374,
 404.

INDEX.   601

Smith, Thos.....93 (2), 217, 342
Smith, W.....7, 8, 12, 13, 15, 16,
  20, 38, 41, 44, 69, 73, 76, 79, 86,
  93, 97, 101, 115, 128, 130, 142,
  154, 160 (2), 165, 169, 186, 197,
  205, 206, 219, 227, 228, 239, 263,
  273, 280 (2), 287, 292, 308, 309
  (2), 315, 319, 334, 344, 348, 353,
  355, 364, 373, 386, 387, 397, 406
  (2), 423.
Smith, Walter 227
SMITH, WILLIAM 348
SMITH, WILLIAM 348
SMITH, WILLIAM 348
SMITH, WILLIAM 348
SMITH, WILLIAM 348
SMITH, WILLIAM 348
Smith, William...13, 33, 71,
  74, 77, 227, 343, 345, 347
Smith, Winfree 322
Smithes, John 208
Smithes, William 334
Smithin, John 283
Smiths Creek, land on...... 248
Smiths Creek and No. Et.
  River, land on............ 139
Smiths Hammock 334
Smithson, Ann 349
Smithson, Dolly 329
Smithson, Dorkis 349
Smithson, Jno. 236
Smithson, John..........329, 348
Smithson, Joseph 348
Smithson, Joshua 348
Smithson, Mary 283
Smithson, Meriam 349
SMITHSON, THOMAS 348
Smiths Point and Blunts
  Creek, land at............ 244
SMITHWICK, ANN 349
Smithwick, Cloanah 131
Smithwick Creek, land on... 354
Smithwick, Edmund 25, 359
SMITHWICK, EDWARD 349
Smithwick, Edward 417
Smithwick, Edward (son of
  Edward) 349
Smithwick, Elizabeth....354, 417
Smithwick, Hanna 349
Smithwick, Jno............. 73
SMITHWICK, JOHN 349
Smithwick, John.....25 (2),
  143, 349, 354
Smithwick, Jon. 25
Smithwick, Luke 25

Smithwick, Samuel......349, 359
Smithwick, Sarah.......349, 354
Smithwick, Sary 349
Smithwicke, Edward 220
Smydick, Edmond 354
Smydick, Famaler 354
Smydick, John 354
Smydick, Mary 354
Smydick, William 354
Snead, Henry 240
Snead, Jno...15, 80, 123, 191,
  204, 304, 323
Snead, John....41, 175, 225,
  240, 276, 286, 310
SNEDEKER, GARRET 349
Snedeker, Margaret 349
Snedeker, Theodoraus 349
Snedeker, Tunis 349
Snell, Ann 349
Snell, Elizabeth 349
Snell, James 288, 349
Snell, John 120, 384
Snell, Katherine 349
Snell, Mary 288
Snell, Purthany 349
SNELL, ROGER 349
SNELL, ROGER 349
Snell, Roger (son of Roger).
  349 (2)
Snell, Roger....169, 204, 288
  (2), 376 (2)
Snellin, Ester 349
Snellin, Hannah 349, 350
SNELLIN, ISRAEL 349
Snellin, Rachell 349
Snelling, Israel 209
Snelling, Rachel 209
Snoad, Ann 350
Snoad, Anne 350
Snoad, Benjamin 350
Snoad, Elizabeth (wife of
  John) 350
Snoad, Elizabeth (daughter
  of John) 350
Snoad, Elizabeth 350
SNOAD, HENRY 350
Snoad, Henry 350 (3)
SNOAD, JOHN 350
Snoad, John (son of John).. 350
Snoad, Jno..............345, 416
Snoad, John.............340, 402
Snoad, John, Jr............. 403
Snoad, John Peyton......... 350
Snoad, Mary 350
Snoad, Patience 350

INDEX.

	PAGE.
Snoad, William	350
Snoad, William	350 (2)
Snoden, Ann	169
Snoden, George	351 (2)
Snoden, Grace	351
Snoden, Isaac	325
Snoden, Jno.	351
Snoden, John	351, 381
Snoden, Joseph	351
Snoden, Samuell	351
SNODEN, SAMUEL	351
Snoden, Samuel	351
Snoden, Sarah	351
Snoden, Solomon	351
Snoden, William	351
SNODEN, THOMAS	351
Snoden, Thomas	226
Snoden, Tho.	131, 205, 271
Snoden, Thos.	42, 60, 75, 133, 289, 367 (2), 422
SNOUCK, DANIEL	351
Snouck, Margrett	351
Snow, Ann	276
Snow, John	282, 298
Snow Hills plantation	25
Snow Neck	334
Snow, Mary	276
Snowden, George	351
Snowden, John	351 (2)
SNOWDEN, JOSEPH	351
Snowden, Samell	197
Snowden, Samuel	81, 400, 409
Snowden, Sarah	409
Snowden, Solomon	157
Snowden, Thomas	105, 327
Snowden, Thomson	351
Snowden, William	351 (2)
SNOWDON, ELIZABETH	351
Snowdon, Sarah	14 (2)
Soames, Benj.	103
Soane, Anna	351
Soane, Elizabeth	351
Soane, Halliday	351
Soane, Hannah	351
SOANE, JOHN	351
Soane, William	351
Sojorner, Mary	397, 398
Sojournor, Jacob	398
Sole, Aves	377
Sole, Petter	113
SOLLEY, JOHN	351
Solley, John	124, 193, 319
Solley, Joseph	351, 352
Solley, Thomas	351
Solomon, ——	51

	PAGE.
Solomon, Shepard	335
Somerset, John	352
SOMERSET, SEYMORE	352
Somerset, Seymore (son of Seymore)	352
Somersett, Easter	352
Somertown and Buckland, land at	76
Soper, Ben.	161
Sorey, Peter	100
Sorey, Sarah	100
Sothell, Anna	352
Sothell, Anna Blunt	352
SOTHELL, SETH	352
Sothell, Seth	35, 45, 57, 73, 89, 93, 97, 111, 140, 155, 158, 176, 217, 244, 245, 260, 380, 391, 398
Sound Neck, place known as,	33
Sound Side and Flatty Creek, land on	141
South Dividing Creek, land on	102, 104, 383
South, John	231
South Lancaster, land on	293
South Shore, land on	292, 293
Southerland, Ann	352
Southerland, Elizabeth	352
Southerland, Fendall	352 (2)
SOUTHERLAND, JOHN	352
Southerland, Mary Ann	352
Southerland, Sarah	352
Southwest, land on	267
So. West River, land on	253
Sowell, Aaron	353
Sowell, Ann (wife of John),	352
Sowell, Ann (daughter of John)	352
SOWELL, CHARLES	352
Sowell, Charles (son of Charles)	352
Sowell, Elizabeth	352 (2)
Sowell, Feriby	352
Sowell, Francis	352
Sowell, Hannah	352
Sowell, James	352
SOWELL, JOHN	352
Sowell, John (son of John)	352
Sowell, John	353
Sowell, Lewis	352
Sowell, Martha	352, 353
Sowell, Mary	352 (2)
Sowell, Obediah	353
SOWELL, RICHARD	353
Sowell, Richard (son of Richard)	353

INDEX. 603

	PAGE.
Sowell, Richard	352
Sowell, Sarah	352
Sowell, Thomas	352 (2)
SOWERBY, HENRY	353
Sowerby, John	353
Sowerby, Sarah	353
Spaight, Elizabeth	192
Spaight, Richd	136
Span, Moses	208
Span, Richard	179
SPARKMAN, JOHN	353
SPARKMAN, JOHN	353
Sparkman, John (son of John)	353 (2)
Sparkman, John (grandson of John)	353
Sparkman, John	141
Sparkman, Mary	353
Sparkman, Richard	353, 375
Sparkman, Sarah	353 (2)
Sparkman, Stephen	353
Sparkman, Thomas	353 (2)
SPARNON, JOSEPH	353
Sparnor, John	273
Sparrow, Jane	319
Sparrow, John	353
Sparrow, Kinsey	353
SPARROW, THOMAS	353
Sparry, Wm	134, 316
Spearman, Edward	167
Spears, John	84
SPEIGHT, FRANCIS	353
Speight, Francis	151, 174
Speight, Henry	151
Speight, Isaac	94
Speight, John	276, 353, 355
Speight, Joseph	151, 353
Speight, Kathern	353
Speight, Mary	422
Speight, Moses	353
Speight, Phrusan	355
Speight, Tho.	107
Speight, William	139, 353
Speir, Ann	354
SPEIR, ELIZABETH	354
Speir, Elizabeth	75 (2), 332, 354
SPEIR, JAMES	354
Speir, James (son of James)	354
Speir, James	75
SPEIR, JOHN	354
Speir, John	75, 354
Speir, John, Junr.	354
Speir, Jos.	174, 203
Speir, Morning	354
Speir, Penelope	242

	PAGE.
Speir, Penelopy	242
Speir, William	354
Speir, Wm	75 (2), 209, 235
Speirs, Thomas	176
Spell, Thomas	194
Speller, Ann	354
SPELLER, HENRY	354
Speller, Henry	230
SPELLER, PATIENCE	354
Speller, Patience	230, 354
Speller, Thomas	354 (3)
SPENCE, ALEXANDER	354
Spence, Alexander (son of Alexander)	354
Spence, Alexander	310, 355 (3), 421
Spence, Ann	369, 370
Spence, Arey	355
Spence, Bridget	355
Spence, David	355 (2)
Spence, Dorothy	355
Spence, Elizabeth	355 (2)
SPENCE, JAMES	355
SPENCE, JAMES	355
Spence, James (son of James)	355 (2)
Spence, James	310, 354
SPENCE, JOHN	355
Spence, John	328, 355
Spence, Joseph	110, 354
Spence, Lettesha	355
Spence, Lyman	148
Spence, Mary	260
Spence, Robert	354
Spence, Samuel	111
Spence, Sarah	355
Spence, Truman	355
Spencer, Thomas	111
Spenser, Edward	190, 195
Spier, Dorothy	170
Spier, Elizabeth	197
Spier, William Lewse	197
Spiers, Elizabeth	197
Spight, Elizabeth	355 (2)
Spight, Isaac	355 (2)
Spight, John	355
SPIGHT, MARY	355
Spight, Mary	355 (2)
Spight, Moses	355 (2)
Spight, Prusane	355
Spight, Simon	355
SPIGHT, THOMAS	355
SPIGHT, THOMAS	355
Spinks, Amory	427
Spinks, Ann	174

	PAGE.
Spire, George	216
Spivey, Benjamin	356
Spivey, Champen	68
Spivey, Esther	358
Spivey, Jacob (son of Thomas)	356 (2)
Spivey, Jacob (grandson of Thomas)	356
Spivey, John	274 (2)
Spivey, Jonathan	153
Spivey, Martha	68
Spivey, Nathaniel	68 (2)
SPIVEY, THOMAS	356
Spivey, Thomas	322, 356
Spivey, William	356
Spooner, Hannah	359
Spooner, John	172
Spooner, Stanton	172 (2)
Sprallin, Peter	338
SPRATTEN, HENRY	356
Spratten, Mary	356
Spratton, Esther	356
Spratton, Peter	356
Spray, Ann	279
Sprick, William	88
Spring, Aaron	219
Spring, Abraham	356
SPRING, ARON	356
Spring, Elizabeth	356
Spring, James	356
Spring, Martha	37, 356
Spring, Robert	30, 119, 356, 417
Springfield plantation	163, 292, 293, 330
Sprot, Andrew	356
Sprot, James	356
Sprot, John Clark	356
Sprot, Martha	356
SPROT, THOMAS	356
Sprot, Thomas	356
Spruell, Elisabeth	195
Spruill, Elizabeth	367
Spruill, Godfrey	225
Spruill, Jos.	185
Spruill, Joseph	286, 367 (2)
Spruill, Saml.	185
Spruill, Capt. Samuell	225
Spruill, Samuel	2, 9, 66
Spruill, Samuel, Jr.	9
Squiers, Amos	232
Squiers, John	416
Squires, Jonas	77
Squiers, Sarah	45
STACEY, CHARLES	356
Stacey, Mary	356

	PAGE.
Stack, John	73, 101
Stacy, William	319
Stafford, Amey	136
Stafford, Ann	357
Stafford, Dinah	356
Stafford, Edward	28, 356, 357
Stafford, Elender	357
Stafford, Elizabeth (wife of William)	357
Stafford, Elizabeth (daughter of William)	357
Stafford, Frances	357
Stafford, Francis	92, 357
Stafford, Hannah	65
Stafford, James	357
Stafford, Jean	357
STAFFORD, JOHN	356
Stafford, John (son of John)	356
Stafford, John	174, 356, 357 (4)
Stafford, Joshua	356
Stafford, Mary	357 (2)
Stafford, Richard	357
Stafford, Samuel	357 (2)
Stafford, Seth	357
Stafford, Stephen	357
Stafford, Susannah	357
Stafford, Thomas	3, 356, 378, 384, 425
STAFFORD, WILLIAM	357
STAFFORD, WILLIAM	357
STAFFORD, WILLIAM	357
STAFFORD, WILLIAM	357
Stafford, William (son of William)	357 (3)
Stafford, William	356, 364
Stag Park, land opposite to	320
Stallings, Ann	357
Stallings, Elias	41 (2), 118, 321 (2)
Stalling, Elizabeth	301
Stallings, Gregory	365
Stallings, Hannah	10
Stallings, Henry	42
Stallings, Jacob	256
Stallings, Joseph	365
STALLINGS, LOTT	357
Stallings, Mary	256
Stallings, Nicholas	41, 42, 118, 169, 216, 321 (2), 419
Stallings, Patience	354
Stallings, Richard	5
Stallings, Samuel	357 (2)
Stallings, Sarah	322, 354
Stallins, Mary	358

	PAGE.
Stamp, Ann	357
Stamp, Elizabeth	357
Stamp, Mary	357
Stamp, Mary Ann	357
STAMP, RICHARD	357
Stamp, Richard (son of Richard)	357
Stamp, Richard	42, 358
Stamp, Tamer	357
STAMP, THOMAS	358
Stamp, Thomas	357
Stamping Place plantation	116
Stanaland, Hugh	395
Stanard, William	270
Stancell, Katherine	151
Stancell, John	128
Stancells plantation	174
Standin, Edward	358, 407
Standin, Edwd.	119
Standin, John	358
Standin, Mary	358 (2)
Standin, Penelope	358
STANDIN, SAMUEL	358
Standin, Samuel (son of Samuel)	358
Standin, Samuel	341
Standin, Sarah	358
STANDIN, WILLIAM	358
Standin, William	358
STANDING, EDWARD	358
Standing, Edward (son of Edward)	358
Standing, Edward	339
Standing, Samuel	269, 358
Standing, Sarah (wife of Edward)	358
Standing, Sarah (daughter of Edward)	358
Standing, Sarah	406
Standing, William	358
Standley, Ann	358
Standley, David	358 (2)
Standley, Edmond	358
STANDLEY, JONATHAN	358
Standley, Jonathan	77, 146
Standley, Jonathan, Jr.	302
Standley, Martha	358
Standley, William	409
Standley, Margrett	146
Standly, Rachel	251
Stanfield, Hannah	358
Stanfield, John (son of John)	358
STANFIELD, JOHN	358
Stanfield, Samuel	358 (2)

	PAGE.
Stanfield, Thomas	358 (2)
STANFORD, LEVIN	359
Stanford, Levin	99
Stanley, John	288
Stanley, Richd.	142
Stanly, Edward	57
Stanly, William	57
Stanrick, Richard	286
Stansell, Godfrey	359
STANSELL, JOHN	359
Stansell, John (son of John)	359
Stansell, Rebeckah	359 (2)
Stansell, Sarah	359
Stansill, Catherine	143
Stansill, John	143
Stansill, Mary (daughter of Mary)	143
Stansill, Mary	143
Stansill, William	143
Stanton, Alice	40, 322
Stanton, Benjamin	359
Stanton, Elezbeth	126
Stanton, Elija	359 (2)
Stanton, Elijah	126, 138
Stanton, Elizah	138
Stanton, Henery	322
STANTON, HENRY	359
Stanton, Henry (son of Henry)	359
Stanton, Henry	40, 343, 402, 404
Stanton, Henry, Jr.	322
Stanton, James	123
Stanton, John	359
Stanton, Joseph	359
Stanton, Liddy	359
STANTON, MARY	359
Stanton, Mary	314, 322, 359 (2)
Stanton, Sarah	359
STANTON, THOMAS	359
Stanton, Thomas	55, 285
Star, Sarah	33
Starkey, Edward	212
Starkey, John	2, 15, 31, 56 (2), 85, 97, 103 (3), 104, 119, 136, 139, 147, 156 (2), 175, 176, 179, 189, 223, 227, 247, 249, 268, 307 (3), 310, 322, 336, 360, 368, 380, 381, 397, 402, 406, 414.
Starkey, Peter	176, 212, 273, 307 (2), 322, 380, 414
Starkey, Sarah	176, 402
Starkie, John	340
Stasey, Charles	359
Stasey, John	359

Stasey, Rebeckah 359
Stasey, Robert 358
STASEY, THOMAS 359
Stasey, Thomas (son of
  Thomas) 359
Stecey, Roberd 372
Steds and Reasonovers
  Runs, land between....... 157
Steel, Alexander 204
STEELE, AMBROSE 360
Steele, Ambrose (son of
  Ambrose) 360
Steele, Rebeckah 360
Steele, Thomas 347
STEELL, ALEXANDER 359
Steell, Ann 360
Steell, Elizabeth 359
Steell, James 359
Steell, John 70
Steell, Margaret 359
Steell, Mary 360
Steell, Peter............359, 360
Steell, Rachel 360
Steell, Sarah 359
Steell, Thomas 70
STEELY, THOMAS 360
Steers, Thomas 257
Stell, Steven 86
Stem, Mary 426
Stephen, Edmund 360
STEPHENS, EDWARD 360
Stephens, Ephraim......360 (2)
Stephens, Hen. 103
Stephens, Jacob 360
Stephens, Jeremiah 373
Stephens, Mary 108
Stephens, Matthew 318
Stephens, Mornin 360
Stephens, Nance 318
Stephens, Patience 360
Stephens, Rachel........203, 360
Stephens, Sarah........360, 373
Stephens, Willm.........111, 360
Stephenson, Charles 360
STEPHENSON, GEORGE 360
Stephenson, Jesse 360
Stephenson, Joseph 360
Stephenson, William (son of
  Charles) 360
Stephenson, William (broth-
  er of George)............ 360
Stephenson, William 360
Stepney, Elizabeth.......360 (2)
STEPNEY, JOHN 360
STEPNEY, JOHN 360

Stepney, John (son of John),
                       360 (3)
Stepney, John.......3, 60, 63, 70,
  82, 115, 137 (2), 138 (2), 170,
  188, 206, 209, 210, 219, 221, 265,
  285, 331, 374, 393, 399, 402, 406
Stepney, Marcey 360
Stepney, Marie 70
Stepney, Mary..........360 (2)
Stepney, Rachel 360
Stepney, Samuel 360
Stepney, Sarah (wife of
  John) 360
Stepney, Sarah (daughter of
  John) 360
Stepney, William 360
Stepny, John 218
Stevens, Ann 238
Stevens, Chas. 353
Stevens, Easter 361
Stevens, Eliza 353
Stevens, Elizabeth 361
Stevens, Frances 361
STEVENS, JAMES 361
Stevens, James 361
Stevens, Jenet 361
STEVENS, JEREMIAH 361
Stevens, John..105, 156, 210,
                  243, 361, 424
Stevens, Mary (wife of
  Thomas) 361
Stevens, Mary (daughter of
  Thomas) 361
Stevens, Mary 361
Stevens, Parthenia 156
Stevens, Penelcpe 361
Stevens, Richard 103
Stevens, Samuel 131
Stevens, Sarah 361
STEVENS, THOMAS 361
Stevens, Thomas (son of
  Thomas) 361 (2)
STEVENS, THOMASEN 361
STEVENS, WILLIAM 361
STEVENS, WILLIAM 361
Stevens, William 137
Stevens, Wm. 208
Stevenson, Abraham, Jr..... 266
Stevenson, Benjamin 361
STEVENSON, CHARLES 361
Stevenson, Charles 84
Stevenson, Elizabeth 361
Stevenson, George 361
Stevenson, Jesse 361
Stevenson, John.....6, 7, 73,
                       361, 362

INDEX. 607

	PAGE.
Stevenson, Joseph	361
Stevenson, Martha	361
Stevenson, Olive	361
Stevenson, Susanna	361
Stevenson, Thomas	17, 361
STEVENSON, WILLIAM	361
Stevenson, William (grandson of William)	361
Stevenson, William	6, 242, 361 (2)
Steward, Ann	276
Steward, Elizabeth (wife of William)	362
Steward, Elizabeth (daughter of William)	362
Steward, Elizabeth	206, 362
Steward, Joseph	221, 362 (2)
Steward, Mary	362 (2)
Steward, Patience	362 (2)
STEWARD, WILLIAM	362
STEWARD, WILLIAM	362
Steward, William (son of William)	362 (2)
Steward, William	221
Stewart, Alexander	27, 354
Stewart, Alexr.	120, 354
Stewart, Anna	215
Stewart, Mrs. Ann	292
Stewart, Ann	362
Stewart, Charles	31
Stewarts Creek, land on	409
Stewart, Jennet	362
STEWART, JOHN	362
STEWART, JOHN	362
Stewart, John	362
Stewart, Joseph	362
STEWART, LEVI	362
Stewart, Levi (son of Levi)	362
Stewart, Levi	153
Stewart (Triel), Mrs. Margaret	331
Stewart, Mary	134, 215
Stewart, Robert	37, 385
Stewart, Sarah	192
Stewart, William	137
Steyne, John	70
Stiball, Mary	362
Stiball, Pashence	362
STIBALL, RICHARD	362
Stibett (Stiver), Richard	88
Still, Robert	242
Stillwell, Samuel	249
Stinson, John	379
Stiring, Elizabeth	362
STIRING, GEORGE	362

	PAGE.
Stiring, George (son of George)	362
Stiring, Henry	362
Stiring, John	362
Stiring, Joyce	362
Stiring, Mary	362
Stiver, Ann	88
Stiver, Constant	88
Stiver, Haner	88
Stiver, Johaner	88
Stiver, Rich.	88 (2)
Stivers, John	137
Stoakley, Ann	363
Stoakley, Isaac	363
STOAKLEY, JOSEPH	363
Stoakley, Joseph (son of Joseph)	363
Stoakley, Mary	363
Stockley, Ann	96, 363
Stockley, Capewell	363
Stockley, Isaac	96
Stockley, Jacob	363
Stockley, John	363
Stockley, Joseph	52, 65, 96, 139
Stockley, Peter	363
STOCKLEY, THOMAS	363
Stockley, Thomas (son of Thomas)	363
Stockum, Eliza	260
Stockum, John	260
Stoddart, James, and his wife	42
Stokes, William	115
Ston, John	317
Stone, Ales	363
Stone, Amay	363
Stone, Ann	5, 174
Stone Bay, land on	124
Stone, Benjamin	265
Stone Creek, land on	124
Stone, James	135
STONE, JOHN	363
Stone, John (son of John)	363
Stone, John	5, 246, 332
Stone, Lemuel	172
Stone, Mary	363
Stone, Moses	363
Stone, Pegee	246
Stone, Prudence	357
STONE, RICHARD	363
Stone, Linna	363
Stone, William	363
Stones Creek, plantation on branch of	254
Stoney Town Creek, land on	363
Stonor, J.	360 (2)

	PAGE.
Stoping Creek, land on	68
Stout, Charles	97
Stout, Zebulon	379
Strachan, George	160
Strahorns Neck, land on	190
Straights, plantation at	405
Strange, Thos.	83
Stratch, Judath	379
Stratton, Mary	246
Stratton, Thomas	358
Strawther, Joseph	388
Strawther, Mary	388
Streater, Edward	361
Streater, John	291
Strickland, Abegill	363
Strickland, Axem	363
Strickland, Elisabeth	363
Strickland, Elizabeth	43
Strickland, John	39, 261, 363
STRICKLAND, JOSEPH	363
Strickland, Joseph	363
Strickland, Matthew	363
Strickland, Ollief	363
Strickland, Pattience	43
Strickland, Rachel	363
Strickland, Samuel	363
STRICKLAND, WILLIAM	363
Strickland, William (son of William)	363
Stringer, Elizabeth	364
STRINGER, FRANCIS	363
Stringer, Francis	41, 149, 227, 318, 376
Stringer, Francis (Dr.)	76
Stringer, Frs.	282
Stringer, George (son of Ralph)	364
Stringer, George (of Cove Creek)	364
Stringer, Hannah	364
Stringer, John	232, 364
STRINGER, MARY	364
Stringer, Mary	363
Stringer, Ralph	364
Stringer, Thomas	364
Stringer, William	364
Stringfield, James	364
Stringfield, Joseph	364
STRINGFIELD, RICHARD	364
Stringfield, Richard (son of Richard)	364
Stripes, Mary	62
Strowde, Elizabeth	364
STROWDE, JOHN	364
Strowde, Mary	364
Stuard, Alexander	265
Stuart, Eliz.	42
Stuart, Henrietta	364
STUART, JOHN	364
STUART, JOHN	364
Stuart, Mary	364, 395
Stuart, Robert	347
Stubble, Elizabeth	158
Stubble, John	158
Stubble, Mary	158
Stubbs, Everet	365
Stubbs, Everett	365
Stubbs, Everitt	364
Stubbs, Hanah	365
Stubbs, Jane	320, 365
Stubbs, John	141, 364, 365
Stubbs (Rowan), John	320
Stubbs, Margaret	365
Stubbs, Mary (wife of Thomas)	365
Stubbs, Mary (daughter of Thomas)	365
Stubbs, Mary	364, 365
STUBBS, RICHARD	364
Stubbs, Richard	365
STUBBS, THOMAS	365
Stubbs, Thomas (son of Thomas)	365
Stubbs, Thomas	364, 365
STUBBS, WILLIAM	365
Stubbs, William (son of William)	365
Stubbs, William	364, 365
Stubbs, Wm.	289
Stutts Hall plantation	137
Stumpy Island on New River Banks	11
Sturges, Jonathan	363
Sturges, Jos.	85, 189, 319
Sturges, Joseph	96, 256
Sturgon, Colleton	217
Sturgon, John	217
Sturgon, Mary	217
Sturt, Robert	347
Styles, Copp	405
Sugar Creek, land on	356
Sugg, Allen	365 (2)
Sugg, Aquila	249, 259, 365
Sugg, Fanny	365
SUGG, GEORGE	365
Sugg, George (son of George)	365
Sugg, George	115, 136, 162
Sugg, Joel	365 (2)
Sugg, Nimrod	365
Sugg, Sarah	365
Sugnion, Ralph	101

	PAGE.
Sumerlin, Henry	288, 363
Summerell, Griffin	374
Summersetts Creek, land on.	186
Sumner, Ann	171
Sumner, Charity	366
Sumner, David	365
Sumner, Demsey	280, 365, 395
Sumner, Diomee	45
Sumner, Elisabeth	366
Sumner, Francis	256
Sumner, Jacob	365
SUMNER, JAMES	365
Sumner, James (son of James)	365
Sumner, James	270, 366
SUMNER, JOHN	365
Sumner, John	10, 16 (2), 60, 117, 194
Sumner, Joseph	365 (3)
Sumner, Luke	269, 365
Sumner, Martha	171, 364
Sumner, Mary (wife of James)	365
Sumner, Mary (daughter of James)	365
Sumner, Mary	366
Sumner, Moses	177, 365, 396
Sumner, Penelope	365
SUMNER, RICHARD	366
Sumner, Richard	102
Sumner, Robert	365
Sumner, Samuel	177, 365
Sumner, Seth	365
Sumner, Thomas	171
Sumner, William	365 (2)
Suten's Creek, land on	37, 266
Suton, Joseph	3
Suttain, Anne	228
Sutten, James	210
Sutten, Joseph	138
Sutten, Sarah	393
Sutten, Susannah	393
Sutton, Ann	110, 284, 392
Sutton, Christopher	8, 366 (2), 367, 378
Suttons Creek, land on	260, 365, 366, 367, 418
Sutton, Deborah	68, 351, 366
Sutton, Deliverance	366
Sutton, Elinor	12
Sutton, Elesabeth	68, 358
Sutton, Elizabeth (wife of Thomas)	367
Sutton, Elizabeth (daughter of Thomas)	367

	PAGE.
Sutton, Elizabeth	195, 366 (3)
SUTTON, GEORGE	366
Sutton, George	195, 366 (5), 367 (2)
Sutton, Hannah	366
Sutton, Jasper	367
Sutton, Jno.	354
Sutton, Jo.	160
Sutton, John	22, 30, 102, 143, 195 (2), 366
SUTTON, JOSEPH	366
SUTTON, JOSEPH	366
SUTTON, JOSEPH	366
Sutton, Joseph (son of Joseph)	366 (3)
Sutton, Joseph	7, 68, 220, 228, 252, 367 (2), 378, 392
Sutton, Joseph, Jr.	164 (2)
Sutton, Joshua	367
Sutton, Judah	150
Sutton, Judith	367
SUTTON, MARY	366
Sutton, Mary	366, 367
Sutton, Merlam	378
SUTTON, NATHANIEL	367
Sutton, Nathaniel	366 (2), 367
Sutton, Nathaniel, Sr.	164
Sutton, Nathaniel, Jr.	164
Sutton, Parthenia	367
Sutton, Pashence	366
Sutton, Rebeckah	366, 367
Sutton, Richard	156, 366
Sutton, Samuel	17
Sutton, Sarah	106, 196, 366
SUTTON, THOMAS	367
Sutton, Thomas (son of Thomas)	367
Sutton, Thomas	195, 366
Sutton, Thos.	106, 195
Sutton, William	367
Swain, James	354 (2), 367 (3)
SWAIN, JEREMIAH	367
Swain, Jeremiah	367
SWAIN, JOHN	367
Swain, John (son of John)	367
Swain, John (grandson of John)	367
Swain, John	20, 367 (3)
Swain, Jonathan	338
Swain, Joshua	220
Swain, Marey	367
Swain, Margaret	368
Swain, Martha	367 (3)
Swain, Mary	367
Swain, Richard	354

INDEX.

	PAGE.
Swain, Rosanna	367
Swain, Stephen	367
SWAIN, WILLIAM	367
Swain, William	354, 367
Swaine, George	389
Swaine, James	367
Swaine, John	367
Swaine, Mary	367
Swaine, Patience (wife of Stephen)	367
Swaine, Patience (daughter of Stephen)	367
Swaine, Richard	367
SWAINE, STEPHEN	367
Swaine, Stephen	347
Swan, Jane	250
Swan, John	72
Swan Point, land at	288
Swan Quarter, land on	107
Swanquarter Bay, land at	241
Swan, Samuel	250 (3)
Swann, Ann	368
Swann, Mrs. Ann	5
Swann, Eliza	52, 74
Swann, Elizabeth (daughter of Samuel)	368
Swann, Elizabeth (wife of Samuel)	368
Swann, Elizabeth (daughter of Thomas)	368
Swann, Elizabeth (wife of Thomas)	368
Swann, Elizabeth	368
Swann, Henry	299, 315, 368
Swann, Jane	192, 368
Swann, Jno.	145, 360
Swann, John	11, 12, 90, 238, 257, 312, 324, 368, 385, 386
Swann, Maj.	389
Swann, Martha	368
Swann, Mary	351
Swann, Rebecca	368
Swann, Saml. (grandchildren of)	371
SWANN, SAMUEL	368
SWANN, SAMUEL	368
Swann, Samuel (son of Samuel)	368 (2)
Swann, Sam'l	292, 312, 350
Swann, Samll.	178, 351
Swann, Samuel	11, 12, 23, 106, 184, 207, 257, 277, 333, 340, 351, 368, 371
Swann, Saml., Jr.	295, 296
Swann, Samuell	415 (2)
Swann, Sampson	368

	PAGE.
Swann, Sarah	128, 351, 368 (2)
SWANN, THOMAS	368
Swann, Thomas	368
Swann, Thos.	300
Swann, William	277, 368 (2), 413
Swann, Will.	79, 406
Swann, Wm.	49, 68
Swanson, Swan	168, 215
Sweeney, Daniel	416 (2)
Sweeney, Jer.	205
Sweeny, J.	156, 183, 284
Sweeny, Mary	205
Sweeny, Terence	237, 359, 370, 397 (2)
Sweney, T.	79
Swennie, Isaac	384
Swenny (or Sweney), John.	170
Sweny, Isaac	245
Swift Creek, land on	166, 199, 334, 377, 424
Swift Creek and Tar River, land on	417
Swift, Ebenezer	368
Swift, Eph.	397
SWIFT, EPHERAM	368
Swift, Epheram (son of Epheram)	368
Swift, Pheby	368
Swifts Creek, land on	104, 136
Swimming Point	359
Swinney, Isam	186
Swinson, Elizabeth	369
Swinson, John	368
Swinson, Mary	369
SWINSON, RICHARD	368
Swinson, Richard (son of Richard)	368
Swinson, William	106, 211, 368
Swope, George	217
SYERS, GERRARD	369
Syers, Jane	369
Symons, Abraham	369, 370 (2)
Symons, Ann (wife of Thomas)	370
Symons, Ann (daughter of Thomas)	370
Symons, Ann	22, 369
SYMONS, BENJAMIN	369
Symons, Benjamin	369, 370
Symons, Bety	329
Symons, Elizabeth	369 (2), 370
Symons, Hannah	369 (3), 370
Symons, Jaramiah	84
Symons, Jehosaphat	369, 370 (2)
SYMONS, JEREMIAH	369

INDEX. 611

	PAGE.
SYMONS, JEREMIAH	369
Symons, Jeremiah (son of Jeremiah)	369 (2)
Symons, Jeremiah	79, 369, 370, 401
Symons, Jer.	69, 421
Symons, Joe	69
SYMONS, JOHN	369
SYMONS, JOHN	370
Symons, John	55, 69, 93, 158, 317, 369, 370 (2), 379, 382, 401
Symons, Joseph	370
Symons, Mary	229, 369 (2), 370
Symons, Miriam	370
Symons, Peter	230, 369, 370
SYMONS, RACHEL	370
Symons, Rachel	369, 370
Symons, Rebecca	370
Symons, Samuell	369
SYMONS, THOMAS	370
SYMONS, THOMAS	370
Symons, Thomas (son of Thomas)	370
Symons, Thomas	79, 84, 89, 189, 329, 369, 401
Symons, Thos.	100
Symons, William	93, 224, 329, 369 (4), 402
SYMS, WILLIAM	370
Syms, William (son of William)	370
Syon (or Lyon), Mary	22
Tabbs Creek, land on	108
Tadlock, Edward	64
Tadlock, Thomas	236
Tagness, Jona	270
Tailer, Charles	227
Tainless, Nichs	51
Talbot, Benjamin	16, 31 (2), 385
Talbot, Benjn.	206
Taler, Johnathan	85
Talksey, Susannah	158
Tally, Elizabeth	388
Talor, John	9, 157
Taner, Rachel	305
Taner, Walter	269
Tanner, John	59, 375
Tanner, Samuel	333
Tant, William	225, 281, 329
Taneyhill, John	191
Tanton, Henry	410
Tapley, Hosea	165
Tarkill Branch, land on	47
Tarkington, Ann	370

	PAGE.
Tarkington, Benjamin	370
Tarkington, Joanna	370
TARKINGTON, JOHN	370
Tarkington, John	370
Tarkington, Joseph	370
Tarkington, Joshua	370
Tarkington, Martha	370
Tarkington, Mary	370
Tarkington, Rebecca	370
Tarkington, Sarah	370
Tarkington, William	367, 370 (3)
Tarkington, Zebulon	370
Tar River, land at	365
Tar River, land on	104, 235
Tar River and Town Creek, land on	115
Tar River, plantation over	238
Tart, James	251
TART, JOSEPH	371
Tart, Joseph (son of Joseph)	371
Tart, Jos.	240
Tart, Mary	93, 274
Tart, Nathan	371
Tart, Sarah	371
Tart, Tabitha	371
Tarver, Samuel	320, 387
Tate, James	241
Tate, William	62
Tater, Beth	19
Tater, Cattren	19
Tatom, A.	427
Tatterton, James	382
Tatum, Ann	73
Tatum, Edward	371
Tatum, Elizabeth	371
Tatum, Jose	371
TATUM, NATHANIEL	371
Tatum, Nathaniel (son of Nathaniel)	371
Tatum, Peter	371
Tatum, Rebecker	371
Tatum, Thomas	73, 356
Tawnyhill, John	379
Tayler, George	4
Tayler, Jacob	77, 315
TAYLOR, ABRAHAM	371
Taylor, Abraham (son of Abraham)	371
Taylor, Abraham (grandson of Abraham)	371
Taylor, Absolam	372
Taylor, Agnes	371
TAYLOR, ANDREW	371
Taylor, Andrew	422
TAYLOR, ANN	371

612 INDEX.

	PAGE.
Taylor, Ann........372 (2),	373
Taylor, Anne............371	(2)
Taylor, Benjamin........371,	373
Taylor, Bethia.............	373
Taylor, Billington.........	373
Taylor, Caleb..............	371
Taylor, Cela...............	373
Taylor, Charles..........294,	340
Taylor, Courtney...........	372
Taylor, C. E...............	84
Taylor, David...........335,	391
Taylor, Deborah........372,	407
Taylor, Demsy.............	371
Taylor, Dinah.............	371
Taylor, Dorcas.............	371
Taylor, Easther............	373
TAYLOR, EBENEZER..........	371
Taylor, Ebenezer...........	371
Taylor, Ede................	371
TAYLOR, EDWARD............	371
Taylor, Edward.....49, 373	(2)
Taylor, Edwd........24, 346,	364
Taylor Elisabeth...........	335
Taylor, Elizabeth...302, 373, 422	(2)
Taylor, Ester..............	345
Taylor, Ethd........373 (2),	409
Taylor, Ethel..............	409
Taylor, George.............	137
Taylor, Grace..............	371
Taylor, Harry..............	373
Taylor, Henry..............	373
Taylor, Hudson.............	373
Taylor, Ishmael............	372
Taylor, Jacob.......318, 343,	371
Taylor, James..........165,	373
TAYLOR, JANE...............	372
Taylor, Jane...............	372
Taylor, Jean...............	372
TAYLOR, JOHN...............	372
TAYLOR, JOHN...............	372
Taylor, John (son of John),	372 (2)
Taylor, John (grandson of John)....................	372
Taylor, John.......259, 372	(2)
Taylor, Johenah............	331
Taylor, Jonathan..23, 72 (2), 144,	220
Taylor, Joseph......371 (2),	373
Taylor, Joshua.............	318
Taylor, Joshua (children of),	318
Taylor, Judith..........371,	373
Taylor, Julian.............	138
Taylor, Julyanah...........	331

	PAGE.
TAYLOR, LEMUELL..........	372
Taylor, Lemuell (son of Lemuell)................	372
TAYLOR, LUKE.............	372
Taylor, Martha..........372,	373
Taylor, Mary...316, 372, 373, 388,	422
TAYLOR, NATHANIEL........	372
Taylor, Nathaniel..........	372
Taylor, Nimrod............	373
Taylor, Peggy..............	422
Taylor, Prudence..........	371
Taylor, Rachel.............	373
TAYLOR, RALPH............	372
Taylor, Richard..86, 272, 319,	373
TAYLOR, ROBERT............	372
TAYLOR, ROBERT...........	373
Taylor, Robert (son of Robert)..................	373
Taylor, Robert..91, 294, 371,	373
Taylor, Roger.............	305
Taylor, Sam................	380
Taylor, Samll..........347,	383
TAYLOR, SAMUEL...........	373
Taylor, Samuel (son of Samuel).................	373
Taylor, Samuel............	371
Taylor, Sarah..........371	(3)
Taylor, Tamer.............	372
TAYLOR, THOMAS, SR........	373
Taylor, Thomas (son of Thomas, Sr.).............	373
Taylor, Thomas....1 (2), 67, 72, 79, 162, 167, 181, 284, 316 (2), 321, 330, 332, 347, 372, 373, 379, 384, 388, 398, 401, 402, 403, 415, 422 (2), 424.	
Taylor, Tho....148, 224, 227, 231, 239, 245, 255, 263, 277, 310, 328 (2), 345, 346 (2), 349, 352, 361, 369, 370, 386, 408, 417.	
Taylor, Tho., Jr............	345
Taylor, Thos.....3, 25, 27, 42, 55, 64, 68, 80 (2), 81, 82, 83, 93 (2), 94, 106, 110, 111, 122, 124, 128, 132 (2), 134, 141, 142 (2), 143, 144, 145, 163, 183, 200, 201 (2), 223, 224 (2), 226, 231 (2), 232, 236, 237 (2), 239, 245, 246, 262, 274, 275 (2), 277, 279, 282, 283, 302 (3), 309, 312, 324, 327, 328, 329 (5), 355, 369, 370, 379 (2), 384, 385, 388, 397, 400, 414, 416, 422.	
Taylor, Timothy...........	351

Index. 613

	PAGE.
Taylor, William	373
Taylor, William..33, 200, 220, 294, 373,	422
Taylor, William Wilkins	405
Teachy, Daniel	204
Teachy, Marget	204
Teare River, plantation on falls of	166
Teel, William	230
Teer, Richard	207
Telar, Matthew	53
Temple, Daniel	418 (2)
Temple, Joseph	386
Tenell, Robert	251
Tennett, William	243
Ternell, Jacob	373
Terrill, Gideon	373
Terrill, William	373
Terrill, William (son of William)	373
Terry, Margaret	334
Tester, Robert	374
Tester, Robert	374
Tetherton, Willm	221
Tetterton, William	53
Tewe, Elezin	60
Thach, John	81, 168
Thearsse, Richd	54
Theckpu, James	378
Thems, Thomas	218
The Folly plantation	14
The Fork plantation	315
The Garrison plantation	295
The Glade	417
The Hammock plantation	228
The Hill	66
The Image plantation	377
The Light Place plantation	328
The Old House plantation	323
The Point plantation	388
The Quarter plantation..155,	373
The Rigg plantation	332
The Shop plantation	393
Thick Neck plantation	407
Thickpen, Elizabeth	368
Thickpen, James	377
Thigpen, John	71
Thomas, Abner	261
Thomas, Abraham	353
Thomas, Amos	375
Thomas, Ann Martha	375
Thomas, Azriah	375
Thomas, Barnabee	374
Thomas, Charity	374, 375
Thomas, Cornelius	375

	PAGE.
Thomas, Dorkes	266
Thomas, Edward	88, 378
Thomas, Elisha	374
Thomas, Elizabeth	374 (2)
Thomas, Elizabeth..374, 375	(2)
Thomas, Francis	374
Thomas, Francis	374
Thomas, Francis (son of Francis)	374
Thomas, Francis	153
Thomas, George	374
Thomas, Hannah	375
Thomas, Hannaniah	375
Thomas, Jacob	375
Thomas, James	374
Thomas, Joan	374
Thomas, John	374
Thomas, John....36, 84, 261, 272, 334, 374, 375	(2)
Thomas, Jona	295
Thomas, Joseph	374
Thomas, Joseph	374
Thomas, Joseph (son of Joseph)	374 (2)
Thomas, Joseph	375
Thomas, Joseph 249, 374,	375
Thomas, Josiah	375
Thomas, Josiah	374
Thomas, Judith	375
Thomas, Louis	375
Thomas, Louis	60, 343
Thomas, Luke	375
Thomas, Luke	374
Thomas, Martha	375
Thomas, Mary..374 (2), 375	(2)
Thomas, Micajah	375
Thomas, Michael	374
Thomas, Mikel	374
Thomas, Morgan	375
Thomas, Morning	375
Thomas, Mourning (or Morning)	375
Thomas, Mourning	375
Thomas, Moses	149
Thomas, Phebe	375
Thomas, Philip	374
Thomas, Priscilla	375
Thomas, Prudence	375
Thomas, Sarah..261, 280, 366,	374
Thomas, Stephen	374
Thomas, Thomas	375
Thomas, Thomas (son of Thomas)	375
Thomas, Thomas	84
Thomas, William....340, 374	(2)

614 INDEX.

	PAGE.
Thomas, William, Sr.	204
Thomas, Wm., Jr.	204
Thomas, Winifred	261 (2)
Thomases Creek, land on	176
Thomlin, John	340
Thomlinson, John	262
Thomlinson, John, of Clubfoots Creek	239
Thompson, Agnes	376
Thompson, Alex.	144
Thompson, Alexander	376
Thompson, Ann	28
Thompson, Archbold	54
Thompson, Deborah	323
Thompson, Debroh	39
Thompson, Elizabeth	372
Thompson, George	28
Thompson, James	323, 376
THOMPSON, JOHN	376
THOMPSON, JOHN	376
Thompson, John	129
Thompson, John, Jr.	376
Thompson, Joseph	325
Thompson, Mary	376
Thompson, Robert	376
Thompson, William	323, 376 (3)
Thompson, Wm.	149
Thoms, James	376
Thoms, John	376
THOMS, JOSEPH	376
Thomson, Amelia	376
Thomson, Andredo	376
Thomson, Andrew	281
Thomson, Ann	281
THOMSON, DAVID	376
Thomson, David (son of David)	376
Thomson, David	281
Thomson, Jacob	378
Thomson, James	97, 170, 376
Thomson, Martha	107, 376
Thomson, Samuel	365, 375
Thomson, Stephen	376
Thomson, Thomas	376
Thomson, Thomson	378
Thomson, William	335, 376
Thoragood, Adam	376
Thoragood, Ann	376
Thoragood, Earley	376
THORAGOOD, FRANCIS	376
Thoragood, Francis (son of Francis)	376
Thoragood, Sarah	376
Thorla, Edmond	249
Thorla, Edmund	223

	PAGE.
Thorla, Rebecca	223
Thormain, John	213
Thorn, John	411
Thorne, Joseph	379
Thorne, Wm.	272
Thornton, Francis	376
THORNTON, JOHN	376
Thornton, John	135
Thornton, Martha	43
Thornton, Mary	376
Thornton, Sarah	376
Thorowgood, Ardley	403
Thorp, Paul	165
Thrower, Thomas	198
Thurman, Mary	213
Thurrefare Ridge plantation,	196
Thurston, Deborah	206
Thurston, Hannah	75
THURSTON, JOHN	377
Thurston, John (son of John)	377
Thurston, John	75
Tibbit, George	377
TIBBIT, JOHN	377
Tibbit, Sarah	377
Ticehore, Fecey	133
Tidman, Edward	51
Tidmon, Edward	424
TIGNER, JAMES	377
Tigner, Mary Ann	377
Tigner, Susannah	377
Tigner, Thomas	377, 390
Tigner, Toulson	377
Tigner, William	377
Tildesby, Mary	303
Tildesley, Thos.	365
Tilten, John	140
TIMMERMAN, JOHN GASPER.	377
Timmerman, Mary Magdalen,	377
Timmerman, Sevilla	377
Tindesly, Mary	303
Tison, Aaron	211 (3), 235
Tison, Abraham	365
Tison, Cornelius	377
Tison Creek, land on	365
Tison, Edmd.	377
Tison, John	115
Tison, Lucey	365
Tison, Mager	377
Tison, Margera	377
Tison, Mason	241
TISON, SAMUEL	377
Tison, Sarah	377
Tison, Thomas	165 (2), 241, 377
Tisons Creek, land on	422

Index.

	PAGE.
Tisson, Edmond	377
Tisson, Edward	377
Tisson, John	377
Tisson, Mary	377
TISSON, MATHIAS	377
Tisson, Mathyas	377
Tisson, Samuel	377
Tisson, Susanna	377
Tisson, Thomas	377
Todd, Charity	306
Todd, Robert	331
Todd, Thomas	306
Todvine, Frederick	207
Toler, James	240
Toler, Mary	1
Toler, Mathias	1
Toler, Matthias	240
Tomas, Francis	69
Tomblin, William	260
Tomblin, Wm.	138, 172
Tome, Francis	288
Tomes, Foster	378 (2)
TOMES, FRANCIS	377
Tomes, Francis (son of Francis)	378
Tomes, Francis	70 (2), 133, 138, 148, 160, 264, 267 (2), 286, 317, 377, 415, 419.
Tomes, Francis, Jr.	131, 350
TOMES, JOSHUA	378
Tomes, Margaret	133, 377
Tomes, Margarett	131
Tomes, Sarah	378
Tomes, Rebeckah	338, 378 (2)
TOMLIN, JOHN	378
Tomlin, William (brother of John)	378
Tomlin, William (son of John)	378
Tomlinson, Abenezar	208
Tomlinson, Elizabeth (wife of John)	378
Tomlinson, Elizabeth (daughter of John)	378
Tomlinson, Ezekiel	333
Tomlinson, Francis	349
TOMLINSON, JOHN	378
Tomlinson, John (son of John)	378 (2)
Tomlinson, Mary	378
Tomlinson, Richard	29, 208 (3), 319
Tomlinson, William	378 (2)
Tomooth, James	277
Tompson, James	39
Toms, Foster	158

	PAGE.
Toms, Francis	122, 419
TOMS, MARY	378
Toms, Nathaniel	406
Toms, Rebekah	267
Tomson, Elizabeth	393
Tomson, Hezekiah	166
TOMSON, JACOB	378
Tomson, Jacob	362
Tomson, John	378 (2), 403
Tomson, Mary	129, 378, 403
Tomson, Susannah	379
TOMSON, WILLIAM (son of John)	378
Toner, Kathern	129
Tonie, Mary	70
Tooke, Abraham	155
Tooke, Dorotey	155
TOOKE, JAMES	379
Tooke, James	155
Tooke (Toole), James	176
Tooke, Joane	155
Tooke, John	155
Tooke, Thomas	155
Tooke, Thomas (son of Thomas)	155
Tooke, William	155
Tookes, James	231
Tool, Edward	153
Tool, Jonathan	153
Tool, Mary	153
Toole, Edward	152, 153
Toole, Jonathan	153
Toomer, Henry	61, 257
Toomer, Joshua	32
Toops, John	379
TOOPS, JOSEPH	379
Topsail Sound, land on	267
Torksey, Benjamin	330, 379 (3)
TORKSEY, ELIZABETH	379
Torksey, Elizabeth	330, 379 (2)
Torksey, Ezekiel	379
TORKSEY, JOHN	379
Torksey, John	379 (3)
Torksey, Phil	414
TORKSEY, PHILIP	379
TORKSEY, PHILIP	379
Torksey, Phillup	379
Torksey, Robert	262
Torksey, Susana	379
Torksey, Thomas	379 (2)
TORVENSON, JAMES	380
Totewine, Colborn	380
Totewine, Simon	380
Totewine, Winder	380
TOTEWINE, WILLIAM	380

Index

	PAGE.
Totewine, William (son of William)	380 (2)
Touchstone, Christopher	12
Touchstone, Rose	12
Tower Hill plantation	99
Tower, Kath	112
Towerson, Edward	397
Towler, Mathias	33
Town Creek, land on	154, 272
Town Creek, plantations on.	38
Town Point plantation	223
Town Sandhills, lot on	375
Towne Creek, plantation on.	336
Townleys Point plantation..	335
Townsen, Ann	380
TOWNSEN, JOHN	380
Townsen, William	113, 380
Townsend, Rachel	417
Townsend, William	416
Toxey, John	201
Trams, Wm	129
Tranter, Anne	380
TRANTER, JOHN	380
Tranter, John	216
Tranters Creek, land at	244
Traquair, Alexander	266
Traver, Samuel	387
Travers, Mildred	404
TRAVIS, EDWARD	380
Travis, Edw	307
Travis, John	380
Travis, Mary	380
Travis, Thomas	380 (2)
Travis, William	380
Tree, Mary	370
TREMAIN, JONATHAN	380
Trent River, land on	127, 157, 187, 245, 292, 293
Trent River, plantation on,	261, 359
Trent River, plantations on..	38
Trent and New Rivers, land on	187
Trenters Creek, land on	292
Trenton, lands at	293
Trents Creek, land on	232
Trevethan, Wm	69
Trewblood, John	313
Trewblood, James	313
Trewett, Joseph	96
Trewhitt, Levi	348
Triel, George	331
Trip, Henry,	315
Tripp, William	295
Trippe, Henry	318

	PAGE.
Trippe, John	296
Trippe, John, Jr	104
Trippe, William	296
Trippe, Will'm	38
Trombell, Elizabeth	73
Trombell, Sarah	73
Trombell, Simon	73
Trombell, Thomas	73
Troters Creek and Panters Creek, land between	301
Trotman, Dancy	198
Trotman, Elizabeth	392
Trott, Mary	103
Trott, Mrs. Sarah	253
Trotter, Dorothy	380
Trotter, Elisabeth	380
Trotter, James	32, 229, 282, 348
Trotter, Mary	380
TROTTER, WILLIAM	380
TROWELL, JOSEPH	380
Trowell, Joseph (son of Joseph)	380
Trowell, Tabitha	380
Trublood, Elizabeth	381 (2)
Trublood, Mary	381
Trublood, Miriam	381
TRUEBLOOD, AGNES	381
Trueblood, Amos	381
Trueblood, Daniel	381
Trueblood, Elizabeth	64 (2)
Trueblood, Fisker	381
TRUEBLOOD, JOHN	381
Trueblood, John (son of John)	381
Trueblood, John	64, 354, 381
Trueblood, Joshua	64
Trueblood, Josiah	64
Trueblood, Lydda	3
Trueblood, Miriam	64
Trueblood, Sarah	381
Truelove, Breathard	360
Truewhit, Levi	4
Truewhitt, Levi	318
Truitt, John	381
TRUITT, JOSEPH	381
Truitt, Levi	381
Truitt, Persellar	381
Trumbal, Thomas	327
Trumball, William	17, 172
Trumbell, Simon	73
Trumble, Thos	351
Trumbull, Elizabet	381
Trumbull, Mary	158
Trumbull, Sarah	381
Trumbull, Simond	302

INDEX.

	PAGE.
TRUMBULL, THOMAS	381
Trumbull, William	243, 352
Truwitt, Joseph	97
Tryon, William	320, 331, 352, 418
Tryon, Wm	49, 61, 64, 69, 97, 99, 102, 105, 106, 147, 168, 169, 173, 199, 257, 276, 346, 349, 405, 410.
Tubbagus Folly	136
Tuder, H.	237
Tudor, Henry	5, 256
Tuckahoe, lands on	188
Tucker, Agnes	162
Tucker, Goodwin	238
Tucker, Henry	381
Tucker, James	261
TUCKER, NATHANIEL	381
Tucker, Robert	114
Tuckers Ridge plantation	45
Tuk Creek, land on	330
Tuke, James	79
Tuke, John	79
Tule, Jacob	108, 241
Tule, Jean	241
Tule, John	241 (2), 373
Tule, Nathaniel	145
Tule, Richard	373
Tulle, Benjamin	54
Tulle, Thomas	26
Tullington, Mary	376
Tullington, Matthias	376 (2)
Tulley, Benjamin	122
TULLEY, JANE	381
Tulley, Thomas	122
Tulls Creek, land and plantation on	413
Tully, Mary	1
Tuly, Anthony	381
Tuly, John	381
Tuly, Nathaniel	381
Tuly, Sary	381
TULY (TULLE), THOMAS	381
Tuly, Thomas (son of Thomas)	381
Tumbling Run, land on	334
Turkey Point	11
Turkey Swamp, plantation on	58
Turbavell, Elizabeth	382
Turbavell, Francis	382
Turbavell, John	382
TURBAVELL, RICHARD	382
Turbavell, Walter	382
Turbavell, William	382 (2)
TURNBULL, JAMES	382
Turnbull, James	34, 250 (2), 362

	PAGE.
Turnbull, Jeames	381
Turnbull, Mary	250
Turnbull, Rachel	169
Turnbull, Thomas	257
Turnedge, Elizabeth	82
Turnedge, George	82
Turner, Abell	382
Turner, Ann	382, 383
Turner, Benjamin	232
Turner, Bridget	383
Turner, David	15
Turner, Edward	382, 384
Turner, Elizabeth	382, 384
Turner, Ezekiel	384 (2)
Turner, Hannah	382
TURNER, HENRY	382
TURNER, HENRY	382
Turner, Henerrey	166
Turner, Henry	169
Turner, J.	35
Turner, James	54, 93, 384 (2)
Turner, James, Jr.	409
Turner, Jane	382
Turner, Joan	382
TURNER, JOHN	382
TURNER, JOHN	383
Turner, John	20, 37, 93 (3), 124, 148, 294, 383, 384 (2)
Turner, Jno.	94, 113, 187, 196
Turner, Jno., Jr.	127
Turner, Joseph	382, 383, 384
Turner, Joshua	57, 62, 66, 298, 383
Turner, Katherine	383
Turner, Kesiah	384
Turner, Mary (wife of Henry)	382
Turner, Mary (daughter of Henry)	382
Turner, Mary	57, 62, 382, 383
Turner, Michael	415
Turner, Ollif	382
Turner, Pasco	234
Turner, Patience	254, 382
Turner, Rebecca	15
TURNER, RICHARD	383
TURNER, ROBART	383
TURNER, ROBERT	383
Turner, Robert (son of Robert)	383
Turner, Robert	42 (2), 64, 221, 238, 262, 376, 417
Turner, Robt.	187, 250
Turner, Sarah	318, 382, 383 (2)
Turner, Solomon	382
Turner, Thomas	323, 382

Index

	PAGE
Turner, Walter	231
TURNER, WILLIAM	383
TURNER, WILLIAM	383
TURNER, WILLIAM	384
TURNER, WILLIAM	384
TURNER, WILLIAM	384
Turner, William (cousin of John)	382
Turner, William (brother of John)	382
Turner, William (son of William)	383 (2), 384 (4)
Turner, William	254, 266, 384
Turner, Wm.	237
Turnidge, George	392
Tuskarora Indian Town, land nigh	293
Tuttellfields plantation	4
Tuttsnia, plantation at	29
Twedie, Thos.	384
Twedy, Thos.	22
Tweedy, Thomas	422
Twelve Mile Creek, land on	355
Tweox, Ann	384
TWEOX, JAMES	384
Tweox, Lawson	384
Tweox, Robert	384 (2)
Twiddy, Elener	384
TWIDDY, THOMAS	384
Twiddy, Thomas	65
Twigg, Mary Ann	384
TWIGG, WILLIAM	384
Twigger, John	24, 319
Twiner, Elizabeth	312
Tye, Antony	224
Tyler, Billah	36
Tyler, Christian	385
Tyler, Elisabeth	385
Tyler, John	134
Tyler, Kellem	36
Tyler, Lucretia	385
TYLER, MOSES	385
Tyler, Moses	385
Tyler, Needham	385
Tyler, Owen	385
Tyler, Peneleby	385
Tyler, Sarah	385
TYLER, THOMAS	385
Tyler, Thomas	199
Tylor, Nicholas	349
Tyner, Elizabeth	385
Tyner, James	385
Tyner, James (dec'd.)	385
Tyner, John	385
TYNER, NICHOLAS	385
Tyner, Nicholas	385

	PAGE
Tyner, William	385 (2)
Tynes, Colia	398
Tynes, Ceila	397
Tysar, William	169
Tyson, Mary	162
Ulan, John	176
Umpheris, Mary	142
Umpheris, Sarah	142
Unaroye Meadows, land at	293
Unday, Martha	385
Unday, Tho.	360
UNDAY, THOMAS	385
Underhill, Edwd.	323
Underwood, Daniel	94
Underwood, Elizabeth	7, 213
Underwood, Hannah	73
Underwood, John	7
Unkers, Mary	306
Upton, Ann	385
Upton, Chareton	386
Upton, Christian	386
UPTON, EDWARD	385
Upton, Edward (son of Edward)	385
Upton, Edward	385
Upton, Elizabeth (daughter of Edward)	385
Upton, Elizabeth (wife of Edward)	385
Upton, Elizabeth	18, 386
UPTON, JOHN	385
Upton, John (son of John)	385
Upton, John	386
Upton, Joseph	385
Upton, Joshua	385
Upton, Levinah	47
Upton, Mary	385
Upton, Meram	386
Upton, Ruth	385
Upton, Sabella	385
Upton, Susanna	385
UPTON, THOMAS	386
Upton, Thomas (son of Thomas)	386
Upton, Thomas	385
Upton, William	385, 386
Upton, Willis	386
Uraha Swamp, land on	110
URQUHART, WILLIAM	386
Usess Creek, land on	377, 378
Ussery, Martha	427
Vail, J.	2
Vail, Jere	372, 406

INDEX.

	PAGE.
Vail, Jer.	1
Vail, Jeremiah..87, 164, 257,	368
Vail, John.........317, 368	(2)
Vail, Mary 192,	258
Vail, Moseley....27, 122, 172,	220
Vail, Susannah	368
Vaile, Jeremiah	126
Vallentine, Elizabeth	424
VALLENTINE, RICHARD	386
Valls Island plantation	236
Vandermulen, Jane	79
Vandermulen, Thomas	79
Vandermuler, Jane	79
Vandermuler, Thomas	79
Van Golder, Tunis	124
Vanluan, Christopher	203
Vanluvan, Christopher	119
VANLUVEN, CHRISTOPHER	386
Vanluven, Elizabeth	386
Vanluven, Henry	386
Vanluven, John	386
Van Pelt, Daniel	386
Vanpelt, Danl	50
Van Pelt, Elslie	386
VAN PELT, JOHN	386
Van Pelt, John (son of John) 386	(2)
Van Pelt, Mary (wife of John)	386
Van Pelt, Mary (daughter of John)	386
Van Upstall, Garrad	406
Vann, Ann 386,	387
Vann, Anne	86
Vann, Darkes	386
VANN, EDWARD	386
Vann, Edward (son of Edward) 386	(2)
Vann, Edward...15, 85, 272,	387
Vann, Edwd.	401
Vann, Elizabeth.....386 (2),	387
Vann, George 386,	387
Vann, Henry	85
Vann, Jacob	386
Vann, John	386
VANN, JOSEPH	386
Vann, Joseph	86
Vann, Judey	387
Vann, Mary	386
Vann, Sarah	386
Vann, Sarrah	387
VANN, WILLIAM	387
Vann, William (son of Edward)	387
Vann, William	386

	PAGE.
Vansselt, Anthony	4
Vansselt, Jacob	4
Vansselt, John	4
VARNUM, JACOB	387
Vaughan	72
Vaughan, Cassiah	387
Vaughan, Elizabeth	335
Vaughan, Fanny	387
Vaughan, Franses	387
VAUGHAN, JOHN	387
Vaughan, John (son of John)	387
Vaughan, Joshua	387
Vaughan, Lucey	387
Vaughan, Methusalem....159,	385
Vaughan, Mollie	387
Vaughan, Naomy	387
Vaughan, Sarah	387
VAUGHAN, VINSON	387
Vaughan, Vinson (son of Vinson)	387
Vaughan, William 195,	387
Vaughan, Will	154
Vaughan, Wm.	190
Vaulx, James	373
Veale, Abigail	387
VEALE, WILLIAM	387
Veale, William (son of William)	387
Veases Creek, land on	363
Vendrick, John	280
Verlin, John	68
Vernon, E.	424
Vernon, Ephraim	239
Vernon, John	21
Vernon, William	425
Vialon, Gaspar	217
Vince, Hannah	388
Vince, Humph	335
VINCE, HUMPHREY	387
Vince, Humphrey...130, 299,	388
Vince, Humphry........179,	273
Vince, Margaret	79
Vince, Mary	79
Vince, Sarah	79
VINCE, THOMAS	388
Vince, Thomas (son of Thomas)	388
Vince, Thomas 79,	315
Vince, William..........315,	388
Vines, Elizabeth	388
Vines, Ester	388
Vines, Franses	388
Vines (Vince), Humphrey	299
Vines, John	388

	PAGE.
Vines, Mary (wife of Samuel)	388
Vines, Mary (daughter of Samuel)	388
Vines, Rebecca	388
VINES, SAMUEL	388
Vines, Samuel (son of Samuel)	388
Vines, William	388
Vins, Ann	82
Vins, John	88
Vins, Jonathan	82
Vins, Rebekah	82
Vins, Richard	82
Vins, Richard, Sr. 82	(2)
Vinsent, Mary	388
VINSENT, STEPHEN	388
Vinyard plantation	74
Vipon, Henry	80
Viriana, land in	39
Waccamaw Swamp, land on,	214
Wacker, John	292
Waddal, James	27
Waddell, Hu.	262
Wade, Edward 352,	423
Wade, James 388	(2)
WADE, JOHN	388
Wade, John	388
WADE, JOSEPH	388
Wade, Magdalen 388	(2)
Wade, Margaret	302
WADE, MARY	388
Wade, Mary	388
Wade, Sarah	388
Waggener, William	315
Wahab, Barbara	388
WAHAB, JAMES	388
Wahab, James 389	(2)
Wahab, Job	389
Wahab, Jobe	388
Wahab, Sarah	388
Wahab, William	389
WAIDE, ALICE	389
Wain, John	389
WAIN, THOMAS	389
WAINS, THOMAS	389
Wainwright, James	307
Waite, Ebenr.	200
Waite, William	294
Wakefield, Elizabeth	408
Waker (or Walker), Jos. . . .	111
Walbutten, John	389
WALBUTTEN, ROBERT	389
Walbutten, Sarah 389	(2)

	PAGE.
Walbutten, Smithwick	389
Waldron, Cornelius	389
Waldron, Isaac 344,	389
WALDRON, JACOB	389
Waldron, Jacob........344,	389
Waldron, Rachel	344
Waldron, William	41
Walker, Abigail	247
Walker, Ann....81, 119, 215, 361,	389
Walker, Benj.	247
Walker, Charity	198
Walker, Edward	371
Walker, Elisabeth	389
Walker, Elizabeth	389
Walker, Elizebeth	116
Walker, Esther	365
Walker, George	344
WALKER, HENDERSON	389
Walker, Henderson..81, 117, 119, 151, 155 (2), 159, 215 (2), 250, 260, 267, 319, 352 (2), 361,	401
Walker, Henry 72,	235
Walker, James	389
WALKER, JOHN	389
Walker, John..105, 106, 116, 281,	390
Walker, Judeth	72
Walker, Mary 106,	390
Walker, Sarah..27, 273, 389,	390
WALKER, THOMAS	390
Walker, Thomas	389
Walker, Thos.	92
Walking, Hepthenia	331
Wall, Ann	390
Wall, Arthur........294, 390	(2)
Wall, Deborah	390
Wall, Elizabeth.........144,	390
Wall, Faith	390
Wall, Francis	75
Wall, Gerrard	278
Wall, Girrard	279
Wall, Henry	390
Wall, Howel	390
Wall, James.............390	(2)
Wall, John..............390	(2)
WALL, JOSEPH	390
Wall, Joseph (son of Joseph)	390
Wall, Joseph 390	(2)
WALL, JOSHUA	390
WALL, JOSHUA	390
Wall, Joshua (son of Joshua)	390
Wall, Lucy	390

INDEX.

	PAGE.
Wall, Mary	390
WALL, RICHARD	390
Wall, Richard (son of Richard)	390
Wall, Richard	43
Wall, Robert	390
Wall, Sampson	390
Wall, Samuel	390
WALL, SARAH	390
Wall, Sarah	125
Wall, Thomas	390 (2)
Wallace, Agness	391
Wallace, Alba	391
Wallace, Barbara	390
Wallace, Dinah	391
Wallace, Elisabeth	391
Wallace, Elizabeth	230, 390
Wallace, Elizth	249
Wallace, James	249, 386, 412
Wallace, John	390
Wallace, Jonathan	390
Wallace, Judith	390
Wallace, Keziah	391
Wallace, Martha	391
Wallace, Mary	390
Wallace, Quotina	391
Wallace, Sarah	390
Wallace, Susanah	390
WALLACE, THOMAS	390
WALLACE, THOMAS	390
WALLACE, WILLIAM	391
Wallace, William (son of William)	391
Wallace, William	286, 321, 390
Wallard, Sarah	88
Wallases Creek, land on	98
Wallbutton, Jemimah	130
Wallbutton, John	130
Wallen, Thomas	403
Waller, Anne	391
Waller, Elizabeth	391
Waller, George	391
WALLER, THOMAS	391
Wallins plantation	84
Wallis, Adam	120, 238
WALLIS, ANDREW	391
Wallis, Andrew	391
Wallis, Ann	283
Wallis, Benjamin	391
Wallis, David	14
Wallis, Elizabeth	391
Wallis, James	391
Wallis, Jane	140
Wallis, Jean	238
WALLIS, JOHN	391

	PAGE.
Wallis, John	193, 303 (2), 391
Wallis, Mary	112, 140, 391 (2)
Wallis, Richard	391
Wallis, Robert	94, 100, 120, 193, 238, 244, 368, 391
Wallis, Sarah	140, 335
WALLIS, STEPHEN	391
Wallis, Stephen (son of Stephen)	391
Wallis, Stephen	239
Wallis, Susana	391
Wallis, Valentine	283, 405
Wallis, Vallentine	140
WALLIS, WILLIAM	391
Wallis, William (son of William)	391
Wallis, William	112, 140 (2), 200, 237, 249
Wallis, Wm.	42
Walls, Richard	43
Wallson, Peter	218
Walnut Creek, courthouse on	378, 421
Walnut Field, land at	408
Walnut Hill plantation	66
Walpole, Charles	179
Walroy Swamp, land on	33
Walson, Mary	106
Walston, Charity	251
Walston, Dorothy	197 (2)
WALSTON, LONDON	391
Walston, Rachel	251
Walston, William	197
Walter, Joseph	311
Walters, Elizabeth	392 (2)
Walters, George	178
Walters, Henry	178
Walters, John	90, 392
Walters, Joseph	12, 90 (2), 178, 392 (2)
WALTERS, MARY	392
Walters, Samuel	90
Walters, William	189, 310, 392
Walters, Wm.	89, 90, 260
Walton, Hannah	4
Walton, Henry	322
Walton, Rachel	177
Walton, Susannah	392
WALTON, THOMAS	392
Walton, Thomas	4, 391, 392
Walton, Thos.	321
Walton, Timothy	391, 392
Walton, William	392 (2)
Waman, Elender	392
Waman, Hannah	392

	PAGE.
Waman, John	392
Waman, Robert	392
Waman, Thomas	424
WAMAN, WILLIAM	392
Waman, William (son of William)	392
War, Ann (wife of William),	392
War, Ann (daughter of William)	392
War, Henry	392
War, Thomas	392
WAR, WILLIAM	392
Ward, Abigail	335
Ward, Abigall	392
Ward, Amos	392
Ward, Ann	354
Ward, Anthony	139, 238
Ward, Anthy	313
Ward, Archy	49
Ward, Benjamin	393
Ward, Catterene	393
Ward, Christian	393
Ward, David	335, 393
Ward, Edward	263, 274
Ward, Elizabeth	13, 392
WARD, ENOCH	392
Ward, Enoch	189, 274, 372, 414
Ward, Enock	392
Ward, Fr.	106 (2), 117, 127, 143, 305
Ward, Francis	106, 201
Ward, James	62, 76, 347, 356, 392, 422
Ward, Jobe	392
WARD, JOHN	392
WARD, JOHN	393
Ward, John (son of John)	393
Ward, John	29, 78, 130, 250, 276, 333, 393
Ward, Jno	25
Ward, Joseph	392
Ward, Margret	68
Ward, Mary (wife of Enoch)	392
Ward, Mary (daughter of Enoch)	392
Ward, Mary	90, 338
Ward, Michael	393 (3)
Ward, Micheall	127
Ward, Mikel	30
Ward, Phillip	354
Ward, Rebecca	130
Ward, Rebekah	29
Ward, Richard	40, 392 (2)
Ward, Sarah	392

	PAGE.
Ward, Susanah	392
WARD, THOMAS	393
Ward, Thomas	249 (2), 314, 392
Ward, Thos	291
Ward, William	292, 392
Wardell, Elliner	125
Warden, John	259
Wardnar, Sarah	70
Wardroper, Thomas	364
Wardsworth, Edward	255
Waring, James	349
Waring, Theodoraus	349
Warley, Anne	34
WARMING, ABRAHAM	393
Warner, Frances	38
Warner, Samuel	407
Warner, Samll	35
Warner, Sarah	112, 407
Warnsley, Andrew	76
Warren, Abraham	268, 393 (2), 394
Warren, Ann	274, 393
Warren, Bray	151
Warren, Ed	43
Warren, Edward	15, 151 (3), 272
Warren, Elizabeth (wife of Henry)	393
Warren, Elizabeth (daughter of Henry)	393
Warren, Elizabeth	354
WARREN, HENRY	393
Warren, Jane	393
Warren, John	113
Warren, Joseph	151, 351, 354 (2)
Warren, Joseph, Jr	354
Warren, Margret	393
Warren, Mary	393 (2)
Warren, Milsson	393
Warren, Rachel	7
WARREN, ROBERT	393
Warren, Robert	159, 351
Warren, Samuel	39, 131, 364
WARREN, SARAH	394
Warren, Sarah	393, 394
WARREN, WILLIAM	394
Warren, William	65, 151
Warren, Wm	41
Warrenton, George, Sr.	111
Warrenton, George, Jr.	111
WARRIN, ABRAHAM	393
Warrin, Abraham	268
Warrin, Henry	393
Warrin, Joseph Hilson	143
Warrin, Sarah	146, 393

INDEX. 623

	PAGE.
Warring, Nehemiah	292
Warsley, Martha	35
Warsley, Thomas	145
Washington, Jas.	111
Wastands, Margret	61
Waters, James	327
Waters, Josias	394
Waters, Martha	394
Waters, Mary	394
Waters, Richard	324
Waters, Sarah	327
Waters, Thomas	243
WATERS, WILLIAM	394
Waters, William	250, 280, 327 (2)
Watford, John	233
Watford, Joseph	399
Watkins, Ann	394
Watkins, Christian	394
Watkins, Elizabeth	394
Watkins, Jane	213
Watkins, J.	370
Watkins, John	151, 159, 394
Watkins, Mary	213
Watkins, Rachel	394
WATKINS, THOMAS	394
WATKINS, WILLIAM	394
Watkins, William (son of William)	394
Wats, Elizabeth	256
Watson, Ann	394
Watson, Elizabeth	394
Watson, James	112, 157 (2), 246, 395
Watson, Jas.	141, 171, 359
WATSON, JOHN	394
WATSON, JOHN	394
Watson, John (son of John),	394 (2)
Watson, John	86
Watson, Jonathan	394
Watson, Jos.	124
Watson, Joseph	388, 394
Watson, Robert	217
Watson, Sarah (wife of John)	394
Watson, Sarah (daughter of John)	394
Watson, Thomas	146, 186
Watters, Saml.	320, 338
Watts, Doreas	57
Watts, Joseph	176, 414
Watts, Katherine	359
Waxdale, Annacivilla	395
WAXDALE, JOHN	394

	PAGE.
WAXDALE, JOHN	395
Waxdale, John (son of John)	394
Waxdale, John	281 (2)
Waxdale, Katherine	395
Waxdale, Lovice	395
Waxdale, Margaret	395
Waxdale, Mariam	395
Waxdale, Walpolia	394
Waxfield, John	204
Waye, Jane	180
Wayman, Haner	395
Wayman, Mary	395
Wayman, Thamer	395
Wayman, Thomas	395
WAYMAN, WILLIAM	395
Wayman, William	357
Wayne, Gabriel	92
Weakes, Iland	179
Weakes, John	202
Weaks, Christian	396
Weathersbee, Thomas	245
Weaver, Edward	395
Weaver, Elizabeth	129
Weaver, Gilbert	129
Weaver, Henry	395
WEAVER, JOHN	395
Weaver, John	30, 395
Weaver, Stephen	395
Weaver, Thomas	395
WEAVER, WILLIAM	395
Weaver, William (son of William)	395
Weaver, William	129
Webb, Ann	395
Webb, Anne	395
Webb, Apsilla	10
WEBB, ANTHONY	395
Webb, Antho.	59
Webb, Benjamin	395
Webb, Eliza	259
Webb, Elizabeth	395 (3)
WEBB, HENRY	395
Webb, Humphrey	11, 345
Webb, Isham	117
Webb, James	395
Webb, Jesse	395
WEBB, JOHN	395
Webb, John	305, 395
Webb, Jolley	395
Webb, Judith	395
Webb, Kezier	395
Webb, Marget	396
Webb, Margret	196
Webb, Martha	395
Webb, Penelope	395

INDEX.

	PAGE.
Webb, Persillo	395
WEBB, SAMUEL	395
Webb, Samuel (son of Margret)	196
Webb, Samuel (son of Samuel)	395
Webb, Samuel	196, 395
Webb, Wentworth	395
Webb, William	223, 290, 365, 395 (2)
Webb, Zachariah, Sr.	122
Webb, Zachariah, Jr.	122
Webber, John	295
Webster, Ann	396 (2)
Webster, Amelia	213
Webster, Benjamin	396 (2)
WEBSTER, ELISABETH	396
Webster, Elizabeth	396
Webster, Henry	396
Webster, James	396
Webster, James (dec'd.)	396
WEBSTER, JOHN	396
WEBSTER, JOHN	396
Webster, John (son of John)	396
Webster, John	396
Webster, John Thorogood	396
Webster, Joseph	396
Webster, Lydia	396
Webster, Mary	396 (2)
Webster, Richard	396
Webster, Samuel	396
WEBSTER, WILLIAM	396
Webster, William (son of William)	396
Webster, William	155, 214, 403
Wecone Creek, land on	292
Weeb, John	310
Weekacanaan, land at	292
Weekacoon Creek, land at	293
Weekes, Anne	211
Weekes, Archelas	396
WEEKES, BENJAMIN	396
Weekes, Benjamin	396
Weekes, Isaac	396
Weekes, Jarbus	396
Weekes, Mary	396
Weekes, Thefflus	396
Weekes, Tho	45, 161, 199, 312, 379
Weekes, Thomas	147, 159, 182, 243
Weekes, Thomas, Jr.	419
Weekes, Thos.	72, 211, 223
Weekes, Thos., Jr.	161
Weekes, William	419

	PAGE.
Weeks, Anne	85
Weeks, Elizabeth	396
Weeks, Joseph	41
Weeks, Thomas	14
Weeks, Zack	151
Weight, Alexr.	230
Weight, John	396
Weight, Penelope	423
Weight, Rachel	289
Weight, William	423
Welborn, Thomas	230 (2)
Welch, Elizabeth	396
Welch, Edward	396
Welch, James	396
WELCH, JOHN	396
Welch, John (son of John)	396
Welch, Lewis	150, 343
WELCH, NATHANIEL	397
Welch, Nathaniel	425
Welch, Robert	150
Welch, Sarah	396
Welches Creek, land on	35
Welches Creek up Moratock, land on	35
Weldon, Dan	147
Weldon, Daniel	7, 94, 108 (2), 208, 226, 376
Weldon, Danl.	88
Weldon, Elizabeth	108
Weldon, Frances	246
Weldon, Samuel	194
Wells, Elizabeth	25
Wells, Francis	158
Wells, Henry	397
Wells, John	103, 397
Wells, Joseph	397
Wells, Nathaniell	397
WELLS, WILLIAM	397
Wells, William (son of William)	397
Wellson, Sarah	90
Welsh, Elizabeth	170
Wendley, Elizabeth	109
Wendley, Israel	109
WENHAM, ROBERT	397
Wenham, Robert (son of Robert)	397
Wenham, Robert	96
Wenham, William	397
Wentford, Eliner	16
Wentham, Mary	399
Werham, John	347
Werrill, John	47
Wesbrook, Thomas	202
Wesson, William	15
Wesson, Wm.	424

INDEX. 625

	PAGE.
WEST, ARTHUR	397
West, Benj'n.	27
West, Benjamin	42, 59 (2), 397, 398
WEST, CHARLES	397
West, Charles	42, 141
West, Charles (dec'd.)	397
West, Christian	151
West, Daniel	399
West, Dinah (wife of Charles)	397
West, Dinah (daughter of Charles)	397
West, Dinah	398
West, Eliza	242
West, Elizabeth (wife of Thomas)	398
West, Elizabeth (daughter of Thomas)	398
West, Elizabeth	57, 397, 399
WEST, HENRY	397
West, Henry	294, 383, 397, 398 (2)
West, Hezekiah	397, 398
WEST, JOHN	397
West, John	48, 73, 130, 290, 398, 399 (2)
WEST, JONATHAN	398
West, Jonathan	397
West, Joseph	397
West, Samuel	398
West, Samuel	397 (3)
West, Levi	268
West, Lydia	399
West, Martha	35, 155, 398
West, Mary (wife of Arthur)	397
West, Mary (sister of Arthur)	397
West, Mary	13, 155, 367, 421
West, Miriam	173
West, Mr. ———	293
WEST, PETER	398
West, Peter	408
West, Peter (son of Peter)	398
West, Peter	151
West, Precilla	408
West, Priscilla	411
West, Rebeckor	399
West, Richard	398
WEST, ROBERT	398
West, Robert	8, 49, 81 (2), 130, 151, 164, 165, 212, 294, 307, 361, 389, 397, 398 (3).
West, Col. Robert	155, 169, 204, 292, 304

	PAGE.
West, Robert (son of Coll. Robert)	204
West, Maj. Robert	199, 230, 292
West, Robert, Jr.	212, 398
West, Colo. Robt.	160
West, Rob't.	203
West, Samewill	399
West, Sarah	398
West, Sarney	155
West, Susanna	398
WEST, THOMAS	398
West, Thomas	49, 130, 389, 398 (2)
WEST, WILLIAM	398
WEST, WILLIAM	398
WEST, WILLIAM	398
WEST, WILLIAM	399
West, William (son of Henry)	398
West, William (son of William)	398
West, William	158, 397, 398 (2), 399, 413
West, Wm.	139
West, Winefruit	397
West, Wynne	151
Westbeere, Charles	81
West, Nathaniel Spence	275
Westerman, Wm.	136
Weston, Catherine	33, 399
Weston, Ephraim	252, 399
Weston, John	399 (3)
Weston, Malichi	399
Weston, Rachel	399
Weston, Samuel	162
Weston, Samuel, Jr.	162
Weston, Thomas	399
WESTON, WILLIAM	399
Westtton, William	33, 356, 399 (2)
Wett Ground	407
Wever, Ellener	371
Whale House plantation	114
Whale, Rachel	190
Whaley, Wm.	240
Whaltone, Ann	399
WHALTONE, THOMAS	399
WHARREY, ANTHONY	399
Wharrey, Joshua	399
Wharrey, Sarah	399
Wharton, Sarah	39, 389
Whary, Anthony	399
Whary, Elizabeth	399
WHARY, JOSHUA	399
Whary, Mary	399
Whary, Rachel	399

	PAGE.
Whary, Sarah	399
Whatnough, Mahetabel	389
Wheatley, Anne (wife of John)	399
Wheatley, Ann (daughter of John)	399
Wheatley, Ben	10, 243, 291
Wheatley, Elizabeth	399
WHEATLEY, JOHN	399
Wheatley, John	393, 403
Wheatley, Jon	98
Wheatley, Mary	225
Wheatley, Robert	275
WHEATLEY, SAMUEL	399
Wheatley, Samuel	92, 399
Wheatley, Martha	399
Whedbe, John	286
Whedbee, Benjamin	400
Whedbee, Christian	400
Whedbee, Elisabeth	333
Whedbee, George	400
Whedbee, Hannah	400
Whedbee, John	270, 285, 394, 400
Whedbee, Joseph	400
Whedbee, Mary	394
WHEDBEE, RICHARD	400
Whedbee, Richard	333 (2), 394, 400
WHEEDBEE, ANN	400
Wheedbee, Richard	228
Wheedbey, Ann	69
Wheeler, Elizabeth	290
WHEELER, HENRY	400
Wheler, Elisebath	39
Wheller, Anne	400
Wheller, Emprer	400
Wheller, Henry	400
Wheller, John	400
Wheller, Sarah	400
Wherey, Joshua	327
Wherry, Anthony	60, 156 (2)
Wherry, Elizabeth	156
Wherry, Joshua	156
Whidbe, Ann	400
Whidbe, Elizabeth	400
WHIDBE, GEORGE	400
WHIDBE, GEORGE	400
Whidbe, George (son of George)	400
Whidbe, George	400
Whidbe, John	400
WHIDBE, RICHARD	401
Whidbe, Richard	137, 400 (3)
Whidbe, Ruth	400
Whidbe, Sarah	137

	PAGE.
Whidbe, Wineford	400
Whidbee, Ann	400
Whidbee, Elizabeth	121
WHIDBEE, GEORGE	400
Whidbee, George (nephew of George)	400
Whidbee, Geo.	121
Whidbee, George	121
Whidbee, John (son of John)	400
Whidbee, John (brother of George)	400 (2)
Whidbee, John (nephew of George)	400
Whidbee, John	394, 400
Whidbee, Richard (brother of George)	400
Whidbee, Richard	105, 121 (2), 269, 366, 400
Whidbee, Thomas	400
Whidby, Richard	156, 366
Whipple, Thomas	18
Whitaker, Geo.	27
Whitaker, John	370
Whitched, Arthur	397
White, ——	41
White, Abigail	403
WHITE, ABRAHAM	401
White, Abraham	69
White, Ann	200, 262, 326, 402, 403
White, Anthony	379, 398
White, Arnall	245
White, Arnold	401
WHITE, ARNOLD	401
WHITE, ARNOLD	401
White, Arnold (son of Arnold)	401 (2)
White, Arnold	89
White, Arnold, Jr.	93
White, Arnold, Sr.	93
White, Arnould	303
White, Arnull	401
White, Benjamin	403
White, Caleb	9, 402
White, Catren	131
White, Charity	345
White, Christian	403
White, Church	402
White, Content	401
White, Cortna	404
White, Damaris	93
White, Diana	24, 30, 403
White, Easther	326
White, Elener	401

INDEX. 627

White, Elisabeth 70
White, Elizabeth....... 324, 344, 401 (2), 402 (2), 403 (2), 418, 422.
White, Esther 190
White, Euphemia 97
White, Francess 401
White, Fenn. 76
WHITE, GEORGE 401
WHITE, GEORGE 401
White, George (son of George) 401
White, George......... 127, 345
White, Gerald 404
White, Hall 334
White, Hardy 245
WHITE, HENRY 401
WHITE, HENRY 401
WHITE, HENRY 402
WHITE, HENRY 402
White, Henry.....9 (2), 76, 150, 201 (2), 326, 340, 369, 401, 403, 404 (2), 427.
White, Henry (decd.)...... 344
White, Hilary....9, 402 (2), 427
White, Hillary 184
White, Hilra 340
White, Hulde 402
White, Isaac........ 359, 402, 404
White, Isack 401
White, James (brother of Abraham) 401
White, James (nephew of Abraham) 401
White, James.... 88, 101, 404 (3)
White, Jamey 404
White, Jeams 370
White, Joan 403
White, Johana 402
WHITE, JOHN 402
WHITE, JOHN 402
WHITE, JOHN 402
WHITE, JOHN 402
WHITE, JOHN 402
White, John (son of John).. 402
White, John.....51, 93, 152 (2), 179, 195, 275, 321, 324, 344, 370, 399, 401 (2).
White, John Plowman...... 291
White, Jonathan 369, 403
White, Jos.................. 341
White, Joseph.... 21, 76 (2), 113 (2), 134, 152 (2), 196, 198, 213, 253, 254, 264, 267, 289, 324, 341, 398, 402, 403.

White, Joseph, Jr........... 254
White, Joshua..9, 18, 94, 227 (2), 321, 402, 403 (2), 419
White, Judith 379
White, Katharna 332
White, Katherine 404
White, Leady.............9, 427
White, Ledy 72
White, Love 404
WHITE, LUKE 403
White, Luke...388, 401, 404, 422
White, Margaret....344, 403, 404
White, Margret 402
White, Margrett 388 (2)
White, Marsh, land on...226, 320
Whitemarsh plantation 257
White, Martha (wife of Nehemiah) 403
White, Martha (daughter of Nehemiah) 403
White, Mary (wife of William) 404
White, Mary (daughter of William) 404
White, Mary....75, 146, 213, 291, 382, 399, 401, 402 (2), 403 (2), 404 (2).
White, Mathew 120
WHITE, MEDIA 403
White, Meriam 404
White, Naomy 401
WHITE, NEHEMIAH 403
White, Nehemiah.........18, 227
White Oak Neck plantation.. 313
White Oak River, land on. 28, 104, 118, 268, 293, 414
White Oak and Queens creeks, land on......... 350
White, Patrick 122
White, Persilla 401
White, Rachel 402
White, Rackes 23
White, Rebeckah 403
WHITE, ROBERT 403
WHITE, ROBERT 403
White, Robert (son of Robert) 403
White, Robert...66, 93, 401, 402, 403
WHITE, ROGER 403
White, Samuel 401, 402
WHITE, SARAH 403
White, Sarah...74, 401 (2), 402 (3), 403, 404, 422
WHITE, THOMAS 403

	PAGE.
WHITE, THOMAS	404
WHITE, THOMAS	404
White, Thomas (son of Thomas)	404
White, Thomas.....158, 262, 359, 402,	419
White, Thos.	158
White, Vince	387
White, Vincent 403	(2)
White, Vinson	403
WHITE, WILLIAM	404
WHITE, WILLIAM	404
WHITE, WILLIAM	404
White, William....100, 150, 186, 190, 254 (2), 356, 387, 402, 418, 419.	
White, W.	179
White, Will	30
White, Willoughby	404
White, Wm.	53
White, Zefeniah	403
Whiteard, Sarah	242
WHITEHEAD, ALICE	404
Whitehead, Edward	404
Whitehead, Elizabeth	404
Whitehead, James	404
Whitehead, Robert	404
Whitehead, William	409
Whitehouse, Abigail	405
Whitehouse, Anne	405
Whitehouse, Esther	405
Whitehouse, Robert	405
WHITEHOUSE, SAMUEL	405
Whitehurst, Ann	405
Whitehurst, Charles	272
WHITEHURST, THOMAS	405
Whitehurst, John.........58,	363
Whites Old Field plantation.	232
Whitfield, Ann	189
Whitfield, Elisah	323
Whitfield, William......141,	194
Whitfield, Wm.	125
Whitford, William..181 (2),	296
Whitford, Wm.	53
Whithurst, Elinor	380
Whithurst, Henry	380
Whithurst, Richd.	161
Whithurst, Robert	380
Whithurst, Samuel.......67,	380
Whithurst, William	380
Whiting, Elizabeth	240
Whiting, James.....180, 240,	290
Whitington, Elizabeth	46
Whitley, Ann	60
Whitley, Arther	405

	PAGE.
Whitley, Edward	326
Whitley, Elisabeth	60
Whitley, Elizabeth	405
Whitley, Jacob	405
Whitley, James	405
Whitley, Joseph	405
Whitley, Julian 405	(2)
Whitley, Julion	19
Whitley, Saml.	405
WHITLEY, SAMUEL	405
Whitley, Susanna	405
WHITLEY, WILLIAM	405
Whitley, William........60,	405
Whitlock, Hannah	414
Whitmell, Elizabeth.....115,	405
Whitmell, Lewis	405
Whitmell, Martha	405
Whitmell, Martha	115
Whitmell, Sarah	405
WHITMELL, THOMAS	405
Whitmell, Thomas (son of Thomas)	405
Whitmell, Thomas........23, 76, 83, 115 (2), 141, 142, 187, 223, 424.	
Whitmell, Thos...66, 72, 178,	406
Whitmell, William	405
Whitmill, Mary	252
Whitmill, Thomas	375
Whitmill, Tho.	144
Whitney, David 406	(2)
Whitney, Francis	406
Whitney, Jeremiah......406	(2)
Whitney, Joseph	406
WHITNEY, JOSHUA	406
Whitney, Ketring	406
Whitney, Martha	406
Whitney, Ruth	406
Whitney, Samuel	406
Whittey, Mary	129
Whittington, R.	306
Whittis, Thomas	268
Whittmeal, Thomas	78
Whittock River, land on....	173
Whitty, Edw.	314
Whooper, Sarah	370
Whorten, Edward	65
Whyn, Lemuel	421
Whyn, Martha	421
Wiat, Ann	352
Wiat, James	141
WIAT, JOHN	406
Wiat, John........119, 156,	221
Wiat, Rachel	406
Wiat, Samuell	406

INDEX.

	PAGE.
WIAT, THOMAS	406
Wiat, William	406 (2)
Wiatt, Elizabeth	60
Wiatt, John	60 (2), 220
Wiatt, Rachel	60
Wiatt, Samuel	119
Wickacone Creek, plantation on	236
Wickacorn Creek and Barren Branch, land on	170
Wicker, James	28
Wicker, Jno.	54
Wicker, Jo.	33, 41, 217, 240, 266, 270, 273, 274, 277, 279, 285, 300, 315, 333, 335 (2), 345, 388 (4).
Wicker, Jos.	72, 79, 91, 183, 250, 299 (3), 332, 346 (2)
Wicker, Martha	406
WICKER, RICHARD	406
Wicker, Ruth	299
Wickliffe, Alice	406
Wickliffe, Elizabeth	406
Wickliffe, Katherine	406
WICKLIFFE, WILLIAM	406
Wickliffe, William (son of William)	406 (2)
Wickliffe, William	391
Wickliffe, Wm.	164, 256
Wicks, Robert	293
WICKSTEAD, PALL	406
Widow Moores Creek, land on	349
Wier, Robert	61
Wier, Thomas	218
Wiggins, Elizabeth	202
Wiggins, George	149
Wiggins, John	353
Wiggins, Margret	163
Wiggins, Thos.	191
Wiggons, Mary	73
Wiggons, Wm.	73
Wight, Alex.	229
Wight, Joseph	389
Wigmore, Mary	97
Wigons, Olive	168
Wilcocks, Ann	407
Wilcocks, Benjamin	407
Wilcocks, Elener	407
Wilcocks, Jane	407
WILCOCKS, JOHN	407
Wilcocks, John	407
Wilcocks, Stephen	407
Wilcocks, Thomas	388, 407
Wild Cat Neck plantation	307
Wilkes, Thos.	55

	PAGE.
Wilkeson, James	292
Wilkeson, Wm.	352
Wilkesons Creek, land on	407
Wilkesons Point plantation	293
Wilkings, James	41
Wilkins, Ann	407
Wilkins, Charles	407
WILKINS, CHARLES	407
Wilkins, Deborah	63, 400
Wilkins, Elizabeth	228
Wilkins, Elisabeth	407
Wilkins, Elizabeth	147, 407
Wilkins, James	41, 228
WILKINS, JOHN	407
Wilkins, John (son of ·John)	407
Wilkins, John	15, 63, 111, 222, 300, 317, 372, 400, 407 (2)
Wilkins, Joseph	249
Wilkins, Judith	30, 407
Wilkins, Mary	147, 407
Wilkins, Sarah	249
Wilkins, Susannah	147
Wilkins, Thomas	15
Wilkins, William	157, 407 (2)
Wilkins, Wm.	364
Wilkinson, John	363
Wilkinson, William	342
Wilkinson, Col. Wm.	155
Wilkinson, Wm.	72
Wilkinson, Wm. and his wife	42
Wilkison, Esther	407
Wilkison, Elizabeth	407
Wilkison, John	407
Wilkison, Martha	407
WILKISON, PHILIP	407
Wilkison, Richard	407
Wilkison, Thomas	407, 414
Wilkison, William	121, 352, 407
WILKISON, WILLIAM	407
Wilkison, William	93
Wilkison, Col. William	215
Wilkison, Willm.	292
Wilkison, Wm.	39
Wilkjon, William	22 (2), 88 (2)
Wilkjon, Wm.	134
Willard, Catherine (sister of Eleazar Allen)	5
Willard, Catherine (niece of Eleazar Allen)	5
Willard, Daniel	5
Willard, Josiah	5
Willard, William	5
Willborn, Thomas	116
Willcocks, Elizabeth	201
Willcocks, James	174
Willcocks, John	177, 184, 202

INDEX.

Willcox, Elizabeth 407
WILLCOX, JEREMIAH 407
Willcox, Ruth 407
Willcox, Sarah 407
Willcox, Stephen 407
Willebee, Joshay 272
Willeford, Easter 396
Willeford, William 256, 265
Willey, John Alexr. 357
Willia, Thomas 311
Williams, Alice 235
Williams, Ann..... 136, 194, 288, 302, 325, 333, 383, 409, 410 (3), 411 (4), 413.
WILLIAMS, ANTHONY 408
WILLIAMS, ANTHONY 408
Williams, Anthony (son of Anthony) 408
Williams, Anthony 411
Williams, Arter 410
WILLIAMS, ARTHUR 408
Williams, Arthur (son of Arthur) 408
Williams, Arthur..71, 83 (2), 89, 91, 200, 230, 237, 334, 367, 375, 410.
Williams, Benjamin 178 (2), 408, 409, 410, 411 (2), 413
Williams, Boneta 173
Williams, Brice..... 173, 268, 409
Williams, Cassandra 410
Williams, Chaplin 411
Williams, Charles...104, 402, 413
Williams, Clarissica 410
Williams, Cloe 409
Williams, Creese 412
Williams, Daniel 409
Williams, Daniell 309
Williams, David 235
Williams, Denton 411
Williams, Easter 408
Williams, Easter 325
WILLIAMS, EDWARD 408
WILLIAMS, EDWARD 408
Williams, Edward..107, 203, 306, 411
Williams, Ellinore 408
Williams, Elisebeth 408
WILLIAMS, ELISHA 409
WILLIAMS, ELIZA 409
Williams, Elizabeth..... 6, 7, 91, 178, 252, 303, 306 (2), 328, 409, 411, 412 (2), 413.
Williams, Eley 411
Williams, Ely 318
Williams, Esbell 300

Williams, Esther 410
Williams, Ezekiel 409
Williams, Farebe 304
Williams, Feribe 409
Williams, Frances 411, 413
Williams, Francis 341
WILLIAMS, GEORGE 409
WILLIAMS, GEORGE 409
Williams, George (son of George) 409
Williams, George...161, 236, 409 (2), 412 (3)
Williams, George, Sr. 236
Williams, George, Jr. 236
Williams, Giles 48
Williams, Gilstrap 137
Williams, Grace 327
Williams, Hanah 413
Williams, Hannah..170, 410, 411
Williams, Hester 57
Williams, Hill 410
Williams, Isac 81
Williams, Iseac..... 168, 410 (2)
Williams, Jacob........ 409, 412
WILLIAMS, JAMES 409
WILLIAMS, JAMES 409
Williams, James (son of James) 409
Williams, James....374, 375, 410, 411
Williams, James Conner.... 242
Williams, Jas. 42
Williams, Jane 319, 412
Williams, Jenkin 366
Williams, Jenkins 29
Williams, Jerusha 409
WILLIAMS, JESSE 410
Williams, Jesse 411, 413
Wiliams, Jesy 410
Williams, Jiles 337
WILLIAMS, JOANNA 410
WILLIAM, JOHN 410
WILLIAM, JOHN 410
WILLIAM, JOHN 410
WILLIAM, JOHN 410
Williams, John....20, 29 (2), 86, 107, 110, 138, 198, 250, 289, 319, 322, 325, 408 (4), 409, 410 (3), 411, 412 (2), 413 (2), 419.
Williams, Jno. 77
Williams, Jonathan 286
WILLIAMS, JOSEPH 411
WILLIAMS, JOSEPH 411
Williams, Joseph (son of Joseph) 411

Williams, Joseph..... 22, 26, 202, 389, 390, 408 (2), 412
Williams, Joseph John...... 242
Williams, Joshua..... 60, 409 (2), 410
Williams, Kazia 418
Williams, Lemand 408
WILLIAMS, LEWIS 411
Williams, Lewis 408, 411
Williams, Lewsy 412
WILLIAMS, LODWICK 411
Williams, Lodwick...... 327, 408
WILLIAMS, LOTT 411
Williams, Lot 410
Williams, Lucretia 409
Williams, Lucy 413
Williams, Luis 413
Williams, Margaret 407
Williams, Martha.... 58, 408, 411, 412
Williams, Mary (wife of Thomas) 412
Williams, Mary (daughter of Thomas) 412
Williams, Mary.... 104, 136, 396, 398, 407, 408 (3), 410 (3), 411 (2), 412, 413 (3).
Williams, Mathew 168
Williams, Mildred 409
WILLIAMS, MOAB 411
Williams, Moab 408
WILLIAM, NATHAN 411
Williams, Nathan (son of Nathan) 411
Williams, Nathan 11, 318
Williams, Nathaniel... 11, 36, 178, 410, 411
Williams, Nathn 318
Williams, Obed 410, 411
Williams, Penelippy 408
Williams, Penelope...... 409, 410
Williams, Phelis 412
Williams, Pheribe 408
Williams, Phillip 424
Williams, Philo........... 24, 71
Williams, Priscilla 409
Williams, Rebecca 411
Williams, Richard... 62, 137, 152, 325, 409, 410
Williams, Robert.... 383, 408 (2), 409 (2), 413
Williams, Roger 29 (2)
WILLIAMS, ROWLAND 412
Williams, R................ 281
Williams, Sam............. 419

Williams, Saml............. 306
Williams, Samll............ 259
Williams, Sampson 412
WILLIAMS, SAMUEL 412
WILLIAMS, SAMUEL 412
Williams, Samuel (son of George) 412
Williams, Samuel... 121, 306, 409 (2), 412 (2), 413, 417
Williams, Samuell 121
Williams, Sarah (wife of George) 409
Williams, Sarah (daughter of George) 409
Williams, Sarah.... 153, 212, 408 (2), 410 (3), 411, 413
Williams, Simon 410
Williams, Sivelity 408
Williams, Solomon...... 325, 409
Williams, Stephen.. 153, 279, 325, 373, 408, 413
Williams, Steven 413
Williams, Susannah 59
Williams, Susanner 328
Williams, Tamer 329
Williams, Temperance 413
Williams, Theophilus...... 33, 57 (2), 110, 135, 186, 254, 409, 410 (2).
WILLIAMS, THOMAS 412
WILLIAMS, THOMAS 412
WILLIAMS, THOMAS 413
Williams, Thomas (son of Thomas) 413
Williams, Thomas.... 80, 104, 152 (2), 153, 167, 221, 346, 383 (2), 410, 411, 413 (3).
Williams, Thos..... 10, 45, 48, 114, 152
Williams, Timothy 36
Williams, Tulle.. 17, 157, 243, 248, 413
Williams, Tully.. 326, 327 (2), 331
Williams, Tully, children of.. 330
Williams, Uz........... 410, 411
Williams, Will.............. 12
WILLIAMS, WILLIAM 413
WILLIAMS, WILLIAM 413
WILLIAMS, WILLIAM 413
WILLIAMS, WILLIAM 413
Williams, William(son of William) 413
Williams, William.. 41, 48, 74, 108, 153, 189, 196, 242, 309, 310, 408 (2), 409, 411, 412, 418.

INDEX.

Williams, Willm....... 49, 87, 180
Williams, Wm... 153, 195, 252, 421
Williams, Zelha 413
Williamson, Allis 116
Williamson, Ann 414
WILLIAMSON, CHARLES 413
Williamson, Charles..... 247, 414
Williamson, Elizabeth 109
Williamson, Francis 87
Williamson, Hannah 413
Williamson, James 87
Williamson, Jane (wife of Richard) 414
Williamson, Jane (daughter of Richard) 414
WILLIAMSON, JOHN 414
Williamson, John (son of John) 414
Williamson, John ..279, 335, 414, 424
Williamson, Jos. 174
Williamson, Margaret 414
Williamson, Mary 414
WILLIAMSON, RICHARD 414
Williamson, Richard..... 240, 247, 396, 403 (2)
Williamson, Rose 414
Williamson, Thomas 150
Williamson, William 414
Williamson, Zachary 414
Willie, Rev. William........ 249
Williford, Tamer 396
Williford, Wm.............. 246
Willington, William 333
Willis, Elizabeth 112
Willis, James 32
Willis, Joseph 32
Willis, Mary 90
WILLIS, WILLIAM 414
Willis, William...... 144, 207, 324
Willis, Wm............. 71 (2), 90
Williss, George 65
Williss, Wm. 90
Willoby, Debora 404
Willoughby, Ann 414
Willoughby, Anne 350
Willoughby, Harris 115
Willoughby, John 327
WILLOUGHBY, THOMAS 414
Wills, Priscilla 84
Wills, Richard 84
Willson, Ann (daughter of Isaac) 414
Willson, Ann (wife of Issac), 414
Willson, Ann 415 (2)

Willson, Anne 415
Willson, Benjamin.. 330, 414 (2), 415 (3)
Willson, Caleb 299
Willson, Charity 415
Willson, Elenor 414
Willson, Elinor 415
WILLSON, ELIZABETH 414
WILLSON, ELIZABETH 414
Willson, Elizabeth....... 107, 264
WILLSON, ISAAC 414
WILLSON, ISAAC 414
Willson, Isaac (son of Isaac) 414
Willson, Isaac..119, 350, 414, 415
Willson, James 414
Willson, John..... 39, 45, 90, 186, 264 (2), 325, 415
Willson, Joseph.......... 85, 414
Willson, Judith 415
Willson, Katherine 415
WILLSON, MARGARET 414
Willson, Mary.......... 414, 415
Willson, Miriam 416
Willson, Patteson 415
Willson, Rachel..... 302, 303, 415
Willson, Rebecka 415
WILLSON, ROBERT 415
Willson, Robert (grandson of Robert) 415
Willson, Robert... 23, 27, 414 (3)
Willson, Rosaman 415
WILLSON, SAMUEL 415
WILLSON, SARAH 415
Willson, Sarah.. 90, 106, 415 (3)
Willson, Selvanus 302
Willson, Thomas 415 (3)
WILLSON, WILLIAM 415
WILLSON, WILLIAM 415
Willson, William (son of William) 415
Willson, William (Mairener), 34
Willson, William..... 26, 34, 107 (2), 314, 400, 415
Willson, Wm.... 36, 147, 248, 316, 379
Wilson, ——— 293
Wilson, Ann......... 36, 416 (2)
WILSON, CALEB 416
Wilson, Caleb 167
WILSON, CHARLES 414
Wilson, Elisabeth 417
Wilson, Elisha 251
Wilson, Elisha Moore....... 415
Wilson, Elizabeth....... 416 (3)

INDEX.

	PAGE.
Wilson, Ellis	112
WILSON, ISAAC	416
Wilson, Isaac	417
Wilson, Isaack	416
Wilson, Isaiah	416
Wilson, Jacob	206, 416
Wilson, James	75, 416 (2)
Wilson, John	4, 28, 112, 217, 220, 254, 386
WILSON, JOSEPH	416
Wilson, Josiah	416 (2)
Wilson, Jos.	391
Wilson, Judith	191
Wilson, Love	416
Wilson, Malachi	85, 416
Wilson, Mary	263, 416 (3), 417
Wilson, Nathl.	85
WILSON, PATTISON	416
Wilson, R.	99, 112
Wilson, Rachel	416
Wilson, Reuben	416
Wilson, Robart (dec'd.)	415
WILSON, ROBERT	416
WILSON, ROBERT	416
Wilson, Robert	226, 288, 330, 346, 383, 416 (2)
Wilson, Rt.	263, 384 (2)
Wilson, Ruben	416
Wilson, Sam'l.	415
Wilson, Samuell	402
Wilson, Sarah	416
Wilson, Scasbrook	6
Wilson, Silvanus	417
Wilson, Solo.	58 (2)
Wilson, Tatum	416
Wilson, Th.	137
Wilson, William (son of Pattison)	416
Wilson, William (brother of Pattison)	416
Wilson, William	255, 294, 416
Wilson, Wm.	225
Wilsons Creek, land on	416
Wilton, Jane	417
WILTON, WILLIAM	417
Wimberley, Abraham	417
Wimberley, Benjamin	417
Wimberley, Elizabeth	417
Wimberley, Ezekiel	417
Wimberley, George	417 (2)
WIMBERLEY, JOHN	417
Wimberley, John	417
Wimberley, Joseph	85, 417 (2)
Wimberley, Judith	417
Wimberley, Levy	417

	PAGE.
Wimberley, Mary	417
Wimberley, Moses	417
Wimberley, Sarah	417
Wimberley, Susanna	417
WIMBERLEY, THOMAS	417
WIMBERLEY, THOMAS	417
Wimberley, Thomas	417
Wimpele, John	343
Winants, Peter	367
Winberne, ———	303
Winberry, John	137
Winbery, Elliner	201
Winborn, Ann	177
Winborn, Sarah	185
Winborne, Henry	398
Winborne, Phillip	392
Winborne, Thomas	185
Winborne, William	110, 392
Winborne, Wm.	150, 352
Windall, Jacob, & Co.	324
Windley, Lidia	417
WINDLEY, ROBERT	417
Windley, William	417
Windly, Sarah	107
Windlys plantation	87
Winfeld, Abigall	417
Winfeld, Anne	417
Winfeld, Elizabeth	417
Winfeld, John	417
Winfeld, Mary (daughter of Richard)	417
Winfeld, Mary (wife of Richard)	417
Winfeld, Prudence	417
WINFELD, RICHARD	417
Winfeld, Robert	417
Winfeld, Susana	417
Winfield, Elezebeth	242
Winfield, Jonas	417
Wingate, Alice	418
Wingate, Edwd	386
Wingate, Elizabeth	203
Wingate, John	100 (2), 135, 260
WINGATE, SAMUEL	418
Winget, John	370
Winham, Mary	418
WINHAM, ROBERT	418
Winham, William	418
Winly, John	107
Winn, Beety	418
Winn, Betey	418
Winn, Dinah	418
Winn, Elizabeth	418
Winn, Ezekiah	418
WINN, JOHN	418

	PAGE.
Winn, Matthew	385
Winns, Rose	58
Winright, Ann	418
WINRIGHT, JAMES	418
Winright, James 137,	291
Winright, Jas 41, 146,	333
Winsett, Robert	311
Winsey, William	393
Winshaff, Joseph	118
Winship, Appelone	419
WINSHIP, JOSEPH	419
Winship, Joseph	400
Winsloe, Timothy	62
Winslow, Ann	277
Winslow, Benjamin	419
Winslow, Caleb 416,	419
Winslow, Easter (wife of John)	419
Winslow, Easter (daughter of John)	419
Winslow, Elizabeth 264, 317, 419	(3)
Winslow, Esther	420
Winslow, Hannah	419
Winslow, Hester	72
Winslow, Israel	419
Winslow, Jacob 417,	419
Winslow, Jesse 74,	419
Winslow, Job 245,	419
Winslow, Jobe	419
WINSLOW, JOHN	419
WINSLOW, JOHN	419
Winslow, John 282, 419 (2),	420
WINSLOW, JOSEPH	419
Winslow, Joseph (son of Joseph)	419
Winslow, Joseph 254, 255,	419
Winslow, Josiah	419
Winslow, Lydia	419
Winslow, Mary 282, 419	(4)
Winslow, Miriam 419	(3)
Winslow, Obed 416,	419
Winslow, Pleasant 378,	419
Winslow, Rachel 416,	420
Winslow, Samuel	419
Winslow, Sarah 306,	419
WINSLOW, THOMAS	419
WINSLOW, THOMAS	419
Winslow, Thomas (son of Thomas)	419
Winslow, Thomas 74 (2), 252, 306 (2), 378, 419	(3)
Winslow, Thos.	289
WINSLOW, TIMOTHY	419

	PAGE.
Winslow, Timothy (son of Timothy)	419
Winslow, Timothy 74,	419
Winslow, Wm.	289
Winslowe, Elizabeth	74
Winslowe, Leah	186
Winslowe, Thomas	186
Winston, Isaac	280
WINTER, JOSEPH	420
WINWRIGHT, ANN	420
Wise, Mary	127
Wise, Saml.	368
Wissockin Creek, land at	389
Wite, Samuel	126
Wite, Samuel (son of old Samuel)	126
Witherin, Wm.	333
Witherington, Rocksolanah	63
Witherinton, John	63
Witton, Lidda	396
Wmson (Williamson), J.	144
Wodley, Thomas	78
Wolf, N.	120
Wolfpit Ridge plantation	86
Wolf Point Ridge	45
WOLFENDEN, JOHN	422
Wolfenden, John 111,	331
Wolfpit Valley, land on	353
Wollard, Richard	135
Wollard, Sarah	352
Wollard, Will	352
Wollards, William	368
Wombwell, Anne	423
WOMBWELL, BENJAMIN	423
Wombwell, Benjamin (son of Benjamin)	423
Wombwell, Jordan	423
Wombwell, Nathan	423
Wombwell, William	423
Wood, Aaron 247,	301
Wood, Abraham	421
Wood, Alice 420,	421
Wood, Ann 420	(2)
Wood, Benjamin	203
Wood, Bethia	420
Wood, Charity	420
WOOD, EDWARD	420
WOOD, EDWARD	420
Wood, Edward (son of Edward)	420
Wood, Edward	127
Wood, Elisabeth	417
Wood, Elizabeth	420
Wood, Esther	421
Wood, Francis	203

INDEX. 635

	PAGE.
Wood, George	8, 417
Wood, Gershom	407
Wood, Hannah	4
Wood, Hugh	124
Wood, Isaac	421
WOOD, JAMES, SR.	420
Wood, James	366, 420, 421
Wood, Jane	421
WOOD, JOHN	421
Wood, John (son of John)	421
Wood, John	421
Wood, Jonas	420 (2)
Wood, Jonathan	421
Wood, Joseph	420 (2)
Wood, Mary	420 (2), 421
WOOD, MOSES	421
Wood, Moses	420
Wood, Naomi	421
Wood, Rachel	421
Wood, Richard	14, 78, 93, 421
Wood, Rosannah	62
Wood, Samuel	347 (2)
Wood, Sarah	420, 421
Wood, Scarbrough	421
Wood, Susannah	263, 420
WOOD, THOMAS	421
WOOD, WILLIAM	421
Wood, William	366, 417, 420
Wood, Wm.	45, 383
Wood, Winny	420
Woodard, Henry	240, 422
Woodard, Joel	422
WOODARD, JOHN	422
Woodard, John	422
Woodard, Jno.	272
Woodard, Mary	239, 422
WOODARD, SAMUELL, AND SAMUEL HOLLERY	169
Woodard, Samuel	155, 166
Woodard, Sarah	62, 385
Woodas, Henry	1
Woodhous, Horatius	254
Woodhouse, Catherine	421
Woodhouse, Cesiah	421
WOODHOUSE, HENRY	421
Woodhouse, Henry	217, 327, 332
Woodhouse, Hezekiah	327, 421
WOODHOUSE, HORATIO	421
Woodhouse, John	27, 85, 180, 183, 262, 298, 326 (2), 421 (2).
Woodhouse, Samson	332
Woodland, John	121, 122, 401
Woodley, Andrew	309

	PAGE.
Woodley, Elizabeth	283
Woodley, Mary	50, 309
WOODLEY, THOMAS	422
Woodley, Thomas	50, 55 (2), 275, 283 (2)
Woodley, William	309, 398, 422 (2)
Woodly, Thomas	398
Woodly, William	316
Woodly, Wineyfruit (Winnifred)	232
WOODNOT, HENRY	421
WOODROW, ALEXANDER	422
Woodrow, Jean	422
Woodrow, Sam	373
Woods, Ann	422
Woods, Elizabeth	32
Woods, Jesse	422
Woods, Mary	422
WOODS, THOMAS	422
Woodstock Town, courthouse at	19
Woodstock Town, courthouse in	78
Woodstock, plantation and storehouse in	332
Woodward, Edward	422
Woodward, Richard	422 (2)
WOODWARD, SAMUELL	422
Woodward, Samuel (son of Samuel)	422
Woodward, Samuel	2, 422
Woolard, Ann	422
Woolard, Jane	422
Woolard, John	422
WOOLARD, RICHARD	422
Woolard, Richard (son of Richard)	422
Woolard, William	317
Woollard, Wm.	288
Woolward, Sarah	423
WOOLWARD, WILLIAM	423
Wooten, William	271
Word, Margaret	183
WORDEN, JAMES	423
Worden, James	423
Worden, John	423
Worden, William	423
WORKMAN, ARTHUR	423
Workman, Mary	423
Workman, Millesaint	423
Worldly, Dorcas	13
Worley, Ann	423
Worley, Ann Gray	423

INDEX.

	PAGE.
Worley, Elisabeth	304
Worley, Hester	35
WORLEY, LOVICK	423
WORLEY, JOHN	423
Worley, John	423
Worley, Joshua	423 (2)
Wormintun, William	337
Worrell, Richard	81
Worrell, William	336
Worseley, John	305, 424
Worseley, Thomas	305, 307
Worsley, Abraham	424
Worsley, Dorcas	424
WORSLEY, JOHN	424
WORSLEY, JOHN	424
Worsley, Joseph	424
Worsley, Mary	127
Worsley, Sarah	424
Worsley, Stephen	424
WORSLEY, THOMAS	424
Worsley, Thomas	424
Worth, Elizabeth	424
WORTH, JOHN	424
Worth, John (father of John)	424
Worth, John	295
Wortham, Hutson	206
Wortham, Juliana	206
Wotsford, John	424
WOTSFORD, JOSEPH	424
Wotsford, Joseph	424
Wotsford, Elinor	424
Wotsford, Mary	424
Wragg, Joseph	123, 371
Wragg, Samuel	371
Wren, Ann	78
Wren, Peter	106
Wrenford, Edmund	80 (2)
Wrenford, Susannah	80
Wright, Ann	51, 425
WRIGHT, AUGUSTINE	424
Wright, Charles	25, 424
Wright, Elizabeth	17, 424, 425
Wright, Hannah	425
Wright, Henry	51
Wright, James	154, 234
WRIGHT, JOHN	425
Wright, John	155
Wright, Joseph	170
Wright, Mary	25, 425
Wright, Rebecca	170
WRIGHT, SAMUEL	425
WRIGHT, SAMUEL	425
Wright Samuel (son of Samuel)	425 (2)

	PAGE.
Wright, Samuel	280, 425
Wright, Sarah	425
Wright, Thomas	265, 425
Wright, William	45, 393, 424
Wright, Wm.	126
Writ, Jeremiah	126
Writ, Thos.	126
Wyate, Rebecca	319
Wyatt, Joshua	221
Wyatt, Mary	221
Wyatt, Samuell	399
Wyatt, Thomas	119
Wyatt, William	18, 60, 358 (2), 360 (2)
Wyatt, Wm.	196
Wyne, Jacobina	248
Wynn, John	52
Wynn, Ruth	101
Wynn, William	101
Wynne, George	282
Wynne, Jeremiah	156
Wynne, Mary	156
Wynne, Peter	156
Wynne, Richd.	148
Wynne, Thos.	156
Wynnes, James	171
Wynns, Benjamin	13, 26, 27, 73, 87, 104, 129 (2), 131, 152 (2), 153 (2), 166, 171, 174, 182 (2), 188, 197, 198, 209, 213, 248, 251, 254, 259, 278, 281, 291, 294, 301, 312, 334, 352, 360, 375 (2), 382, 398, 409, 410, 411, 412, 421, 425 (6).
Wynns, Benj.	78, 81, 91, 325 (2)
Wynns, Benj., Jr.	151
Wynns, Benjn.	25, 39, 53, 54, 75 (2), 87, 95 (2), 121, 133, 137, 166, 193, 200, 207, 208, 233, 234, 250, 256, 265, 316, 371, 398.
Wynns, Elizabeth	425
WYNNS, GEORGE	425
Wynns, George (son of George)	425
Wynns, George	325
Wynns, George Augustus	39
Wynns, Geo.	425
Wynns, James Boone	425 (2)
WYNNS, JOHN	425
Wynns, John	5, 30, 33, 36, 39, 50, 78, 89, 146, 186, 195, 236, 237, 238 (2), 239, 276, 304, 354, 395, 408, 424, 425.
Wynns, John Augustus	425

INDEX. 637

	PAGE.
Wynns, Jno.....24, 45, 51, 57, 85, 107, 126, 144, 169, 232, 234, 272 (2), 298, 302, 352 (2), 374, 409, 412, 424, 425 (2).	
Wynns, Mary	39
Wynns, Mary Anne	425
Wynns, Penelope	425
Wynns, Rose	425
Wynns, Sarah	425
Wynns, Sarah Amelia	425
Wynns, Watkin William..425 (2)	
WYNNS, WILLIAM	425
Wynns, William.....182, 425 (2),	427
Wynns, Wm..............39,	171
Wynns, Wynnry Caroline...	425
Yaits, Bridget	306
Yaits, Thomas	306
Yarborough, Grigg.......307,	343
Yarborough, Richard	12
Yarbrough, Elizabeth	223
Yarrett, Daniel	116
Yates, Wm.	193
Yaupim, land at.........296,	420
Yawpim, plantation at	217
Yawpim, plantation on	60
Yawpim River, plantation at	215
Yawpin River, plantation upon	111
Yenshaw, Rachel	287
Yeates, Amy	426
Yeates, Charles	426
Yeates, Daniel	426
Yeates, Judith	426
Yeates, Mary 426 (2)	
Yeates, Richard	426
Yeates, Robert	426
Yeates, Thomas	308

	PAGE.
YEATES, WILLIAM	426
Yeates, William (son of William)	426
YEATS, JAMES	426
Yeats, John	209
Yeats, Mary	426
Yeats, Stephen	410
Yelverton, Elizabeth	35
Yelverton, James	35
Yelverton, John (grandson of James Blount)	35
Yelverton, John 35 (2)	
Yeoman, Joseph	152
Yeoman, Ralph	405
Yetts, Thomas	16
Yopim, plantation on	63
Yopim River, land on	220
Young, Ann	426
Young, Arthur..........199,	341
Young, Charles	360
Young, Chas......47, 80, 203, 287, 361,	371
Young, Foster	426
YOUNG, GEORGE	426
Young, Gerard	116
Young, John (children of)..	269
Young, Joseph	138
Young, Lovick	280
Young, Peter	81
Young, Prothesia	426
Young, Mary	426
Young, Matthew	197
Young, Rachel	67
Youngman, Eb.	161
Young's plantation	108
Youpim Ridge, land on	41
Zacee, Thomas	94

APPENDIX.

INDEX TO WILLS.

BOOK 1 "A."

	PAGE.		PAGE.
Alford, Jabez	33	Hicks, Africa	37
Arderne, Jno.	47	Lakor, Benj.	9
Blount, Thos.	7	Lacy, Wm., Sr.	22
Boyce, William	26	Oates, James	20
Buck, John	44	Pricklove, Saml.	27
Collins, Richard	13	Pope, Richard	15
Daniel, Owen	5	Steward, Wm.	46
Fendall, Robt.	39	Stiball, Richd.	17
Fisher, James	25	Taylor, Edw.	42
Garfort, Gregory	23	Taylor, Robt.	13
Gormack, Patrick	35	Tweox, James	40

BOOK 1.

	PAGE.		PAGE.
Arnold, Lawrence	50	Lillington, Alexander	78
Blount, James	120	Lankton, Thos.	86
Bentley, Jno.	61	Muns, Thos.	42
Bateman, Jonathan	68	Mesler, Ceasmore	82
Bayes, Edward	89	Nicholson, Jos.	95
Bartlett, Wm.	97	Neal, Chas.	126
Boyce, Wm.	169	Perry, Jeremiah	65
Barber, Jno.	170	Price, Thomas	87
Calley, Matthew	123	Pollock, Jas.	173
Croslen, Jno.	43	Palin, Henry, Junior	128
Crosland, Elizabeth	42	Phillpott, Jno.	104
Comander, Joseph Mathew	75	Peterson, Jacob	98
Craig, Richard	88	Roe, Edmund	84
Cooke, Jno.	80	Robison, Jas.	127
Dann, Jno., Sr.	82	Smith, Robt.	38
Deane, Geo., Senr.	121	Sothell, Seth.	40
Foure, Peter	75	Sutton, Joseph	66
Fendall, John	81	Stasi, Thomas	91
Gambell, Adam	55	Stevens, Wm.	92
Gough, Thomas	64	Smithwike, Jno.	93
Garner, Ralfe	84	Sutton, Geo.	122
Gonsolvo, Lawrence	95	Snellin, Israel	175
Harrison, Jno.	43	Tester, Robt.	63
Johnson, Jno.	44	Tomlinson, Jno.	94
Jones, Chas.	60	Turner, Wm., Sen.	102
Johnson, Jas.	62	Wilson, Robt.	72
Jackson, Wm.	90	White, Robt.	96
Kelley, Sarah	127	Workman, Arthur	119
Lawrence, Wm.	47	Wade, Alice	172
Loadman, James	59		

APPENDIX.

LIST OF WILLS IN GRANT BOOK No. 76.

Name.	Page.	Date.	Counties.
Allen, Andrew	278	1762	Dobbs and Craven.
Adair, James (deed of gift)	256	1759	Dobbs and Craven.
Adair, James (deed of gift)	259	1763	Dobbs and Craven.

LIST OF WILLS RECORDED IN GRANT BOOK 4.
Date, 1724–1743.

Name.	Number of Will.	County.
Alderson, Simon	131	Beaufort.
Andrews, Thomas	135	Bertie.
Abington, Joseph	10	Currituck.
Allin, John	35	
Answell, James	110	
Bond, Robert	71	Bath.
Brown, Richard	41	Bertie.
Brown, Walter	54	Bertie.
Boade, John	87	Bertie.
Battle, John	127	Bertie.
Ballard, John	59	Chowan.
Baker, Henry	81	Chowan.
Boyd, John	86	Chowan.
Badham, William	136	Chowan.
Bonner, Henry	162	Chowan.
Bright, Richard	111	Currituck.
Bryant, John	4	Edgecombe.
Burgess, Stephen	44	Pasquotank.
Bundy, Samuel	122	Pasquotank.
Boyd, John	168	Pasquotank.
Belman, John	133	Perquimans.
Boswell, George	156	Perquimans.
Blunt, Benjamin	114	Tyrrell.
Booth, George	2	
Beezley, Thomas	17	
Beasley, Samuel	27	
Bate, Henry Lawrence	113	
Branch, Francis	123	
Bright, Henry	134	
Baigeron, Judith	150	
Carter, Henry	33	Bath.
Crompton, Henry	56	Bertie.
Collins, John	138	Bertie.
Charlton, John	50	Chowan.
Crawford, W.	140	Chowan.
Craven, James	201	Chowan.
Cox, Thomas	143	Currituck.
Convey, Dennis	13	Pasquotank.

APPENDIX. 641

Name.	Number of Will.	County.
Cox, John	141	Onslow.
Chappel, Richard	11	
Chancey, W., Jr.	30	
Delamar, Francis	161	Bath.
Dias, Henry	76	Beaufort.
Dwight, Matthew	70	Chowan.
Davis, Isaac	146	Currituck.
Donohoe, Job	149	New Hanover.
Davis, Solomon	100	Pasquotank.
Davis, Richard	67	Perquimans.
Downing, William	92	
Etheridge, Henry	147	Currituck.
Everton, Jeremiah	164	Pasquotank.
Ferrel, Richard	124	Albemarle.
Forster, Robert	128	Bertie.
Green, Susannah	18	
Griffin, William	36	
Gale, Edmund	69	
Goffe, Arthur	74	
Gregory, Thomas	106	
Harrison, Vines	78	Albemarle.
Henderson, George	64	Bertie.
Hollbrook, John	126	Bertie.
Horth, Thomas	28	Chowan.
Houston, Thomas	14	Onslow.
Hall, Ann	163	Perquimans.
Haig, William	3	
Irving, Robert	65	Currituck.
Jessop, Joseph	46	Albemarle.
Jones, William	31	Bertie.
Jones, John	42	Bertie.
Jeffries, Eliza	151	Northampton.
Jeffries, Eliza	142	
Jones, Jonathan	108	Pasquotank.
Jackson, William	48	Perquimans.
Jewel, Thomas	57	
King, Michael	160	Bertie.
Ketchings, William	32	Perquimans.
Lovick, John	39	
Lilley, Thomas	52	
Leary, Richard	85	
Ludford, John	90	
Lillington, Elizabeth	154	
Man, Thomas	7	
Moys, John	9	
McKeels, Rebecca	15	

Name.	Number of Will.	County.
Moore, James	24	
Mauden, Thomas	45	
Martin, William	55	
Mackinne, Barnaby, Jr.	58	
Middleton, Henry	89	
Morris, John	103	
Macrary, Robert	115	
Mackgue, Lawrence	118	
Mason, John, Sr.	155	
Martin, John	157	
Mereday, Thomas	158	
Nicholson, Nathaniel	66	
Newby, Mary	99	
Newby, Benjamin	102	
Odeon, John	165	Beaufort.
Odeon, Charles	49	
Overman, Joseph	107	
Parish, John, Sr.	91	Albemarle.
Pugh, Francis	34	Bertie.
Purrei, Joseph	43	
Power, George	53	Bertie.
Prichards, Harbert	95	Bertie.
Pukerin, Richard	109	Bertie.
Peyton, Robart	121	Bertie.
Pratt, John	167	
Parke, Henry	21	Craven.
Parish, William	139	Edgecombe.
Plato, Thomas	26	Pasquotank.
Pools, Solomon	98	Pasquotank.
Pendleton, Henry	105	Pasquotank.
Palmer, Robert	125	Pasquotank.
Pratts, Job	62	Perquimans.
Phenny, George	68	
Pollock, George	82	
Parrot, Jacob	84	
Pugh, John	112	
Redditt, William	116	Bertie.
Rogers, Robert	88	Chowan.
Roe, James	72	Craven.
Ritegas, Jacob	12	Pasquotank.
Spellers, Patience	79	Bertie.
Snoad, John	145	Beaufort.
Smith, George	63	Bertie.
Smith, James	51	Perquimans.
Sowell, Charles	80	Bertie.
Stafford, William	169	Currituck.
Simmons, Edward	16	Edgecombe.
Spence, Alexander	5	Pasquotank.
Spence, James	129	Pasquotank.
Spence, John	60	
Symons, Jeremiah	132	Pasquotank.

Appendix.

Name.	Number of Will.	County.
Snowden, Thomas	61	Perquimans.
Sharred, David	153	Perquimans.
Shackelford, John	19	
Shavers, John	20	
Stubs, Thomas	83	
Silberton, Gilford	77	
Simpson, Alexander	75	
Stevenson, William	93	
Scot, John	96	
Snowden, Joseph	132	
Symons, John	159	
Tayler, Thomas	47	
Thomas, Barnaba	23	
Townsens, John	101	Perquimans.
Trublood, John	6	Pasquotank.
Thomas, Joseph	37	
Vann, William	119	Chowan.
Williams, Thomas	22	Bertie.
Williams, John	94	
Williams, Edward	103	Pasquotank.
Wills, William	152	Onslow.
Winn, John	104	Pasquotank.
Wiat, John	97	Perquimans.
Weaver, William	38	Bertie.
Wade, Mary	137	Pasquotank.
Warrens, Abraham	120	Perquimans.
Whetley, Samuel	117	Tyrrell.
Whedbee, Richard	130	Tyrrell.
Whitmell, Thomas	22	Bertie.
Whitehead, Alice	144	Craven.
Whitney, Joshua	25	
Worth, John	148	Bladen.

INDEX TO WILL BOOK, No. 2, 1712-1722.

Name.	Will Book.	Page.
Avelin, Peter	1712-1722	2
Askue, John	1712-1722	31
Adams, James (inventory)	1712-1722	78
Alderson, Simon	1712-1722	80
Armor, William	1712-1722	276
Albertson, Mary	1712-1722	315
Bannfield, Walter	1712-1722	1
Borsene, John	1712-1722	3
Bodeet, Jacob	1712-1722	10
Brent, Thomas	1712-1722	25
Brett, William	1712-1722	34
Benbury, William	1712-1722	39
Bowrem, Edmund	1712-1722	42

644 APPENDIX.

Name.	Will Book.	Page.
Burnby, John	1712–1722	46
Bennet, John	1712–1722	49
Bell, George (jury before him)	1712–1722	58
Bell, John	1712–1722	316
Bonesly, John	1712–1722	61
Bounsell, Walter	1712–1722	62
Burke, Richard	1712–1722	73
Britt, William	1712–1722	73
Berry, Ed.	1712–1722	75
Berry, John	1712–1722	86
Berey, John (inventory)	1712–1722	184
Beard, James	1712–1722	76
Burchenhead, George (inventory)	1712–1722	76
Bray, William	1712–1722	81
Barrass, John	1712–1722	85
Browne, Daniele	1712–1722	86
Brown, William	1712–1722	152
Browne, James	1712–1722	284
Browne, John	1712–1722	300
Brown, Thomas	1712–1722	158
Baley, John	1712–1722	108
Blount, James	1712–1722	113
Blount, James (inventory)	1712–1722	255
Barrow, William	1712–1722	115
Barrow, John	1712–1722	146
Barrow, James	1712–1722	151
Barrow, James (inventory)	1712–1722	248
Barrow, John	1712–1722	174
Beasley, Francis	1712–1722	172
Beesly, Francis (inventory)	1712–1722	206
Beesly, Walter (inventory)	1712–1722	290
Beaseley, James	1712–1722	239
Beaseley, James (inventory)	1712–1722	278
Britnoe William (inventory)	1712–1722	184
Britnoe, William (inventory)	1712–1722	289
Barnes, Henry (inventory)	1712–1722	189
Blysh, John (inventory)	1712–1722	192
Busby, John (inventory)	1712–1722	207
Billet, John	1712–1722	223
Brice, William	1712–1722	227
Boyd, Winefred	1712–1722	242
Bonner, Katherine	1712–1722	252
Batchelor, Richd. (account)	1712–1722	256
Berkley, John, Eliz. Berkely and Sarah Catchmayd (letter).	1712–1722	281
Broem, William (inventory)	1712–1722	289
Branch, William	1712–1722	294
Bounds, Richard	1712–1722	298
Barcocks, Thomas	1712–1722	303
Boge, William	1712–1722	318
Barnsfield, Anne	1712–1722	319
Bundy, Caleb	1712–1722	328
Bundy, Caleb	1722–1722	322
Ball, Thomas	1712–1722	333
Beels, James	1712–1722	336
Barry, William	1712–1722	338

Appendix.

Name.	Will Book.	Page.
Coles, James	1712-1722	22
Creech, Henry	1712-1722	28
Comminfort, Hendrick	1712-1722	44
Cominfort, Richard	1712-1722	244
Coulson, William	1712-1722	53
Coffins, Mary (inventory)	1712-1722	70
Clarke, John	1712-1722	137
Cheven, Nathaniel	1712-1722	218
Clarke, John (inventory)	1712-1722	258
Clarke, John (inventory—concluded)	1712-1722	289
Clarke, Thomas	1712-1722	149
Clarke, Francis (inventory)	1712-1722	256
Cogwell, Henry	1712-1722	150
Cogwell, Henry (inventory)	1712-1722	272
Clarke, Thomas (inventory)	1712-1722	262
Corp, John	1712-1722	178
Corp, Elinor	1712-1722	221
Coleman, Thomas (inventory)	1712-1722	183
Coleman, Robert	1712-1722	346
Collis, Thomas	1712-1722	217
Collis, Thomas (inventory)	1712-1722	260
Callio, Joseph	1712-1722	217
Carpenter, Francis (inventory)	1712-1722	254
Conty, Ephram (inventory)	1712-1722	261
Coste, Ephraim	1712-1722	332
Cropley, Vines (inventory)	1712-1722	181
Cambridge, Francis	1712-1722	36
Cowan, Garret	1712-1722	303
Denoise, Alexander (inventory)	1712-1722	58
Dawson, Francis	1712-1722	81
Derham, Elizabeth	1712-1722	125
Daves, William	1712-1722	151
Davis, James	1712-1722	179
Davis, Samuell (inventory)	1712-1722	204
Dann, John (inventory)	1712-1722	253
Drake, Arnold (inventory)	1712-1722	256
Danis, James	1712-1722	179
Duckenfeild, William	1712-1722	312
Ellis, George	1712-1722	295
Edwards, Humphrey	1712-1722	25
Edmunds, Samuell	1712-1722	310
Eivens, Richard	1712-1722	327
Eden, Charles, Governor	1712-1722	299
Fordice, George (inventory)	1712-1722	52
Fordice, George (will)	1712-1772	9
Fewox, James (inventory)	1712-1722	62
Fitzpatrick, Bryan	1712-1722	64
Fitzpatrick, Cornelass	1712-1722	307
Fulver, John (jury on him)	1712-1722	75
Falk, Richard	1712-1722	27
Fort, George	1712-1722	154
Frost, William	1712-1722	156
French, Richard	1712-1722	104

Appendix.

Name.	Will Book.	Page.
Gregory, Thomas (children's estate)	1712–1722	73
Gregory, Richard	1712–1722	235
Goodlett, Alexander	1712–1722	4
Goodlatt, Alexander (inventory)	1712–1722	60
Green, Farnifold	1712–1722	10
Green, Farnifold (order)	1712–1722	77
Giles, Mathias	1712–1722	14
George, Henry	1712–1722	34
Gladstains, George	1712–1722	44
Goodale, Gilbert	1712–1722	46
Graylin, Thomas (inventory)	1712–1722	58
Goodpatt, Thorough (inventory)	1712–1722	74
Goodgrave, Ann (order)	1712–1722	77
Gibson, Elinor	1712–1722	85
Gergamus, N.	1712–1722	90
Goreham, John	1712–1722	158
Griffen, Martin	1712–1722	165
Griffen, Martin (inventory)	1712–1722	186
Glover, Joseph (inventory)	1712–1722	199
Gardiner, James (inventory)	1712–1722	211 and 256
Grill, Richard	1712–1722	221
Grill, Richard (inventory)	1712–1722	250
Goble, Dederith	1712–1722	236
Godson, Benj. (inventory)	1712–1722	247
Gale, Christopher	1712–1722	291
Glanville, William	1712–1722	293
Garrett, Cowan	1712–1722	303
Glaister, Joseph	1712–1722	142
Grosvenor, William	1712–1722	322
Holebrough, Joseph	1712–1722	16
Harrington, Humphrey	1712–1722	19
Hodgson, John	1712–1722	24
Harrison, John	1712–1722	32
Hill, Isack	1712–1722	33
Harris, John	1712–1722	48
Hancock, John (inventory)	1712–1722	59
Hawkins, John	1712–1722	227
Hawkins, John	1712–1722	111
Hawkins, Sarah	1712–1722	340
Hooker, William	1712–1722	144
Houghton, George	1712–1722	171
Houghton, George (inventory)	1712–1722	249
Hudson, Edwd. (inventory)	1712–1722	185
Hall, Peter (inventory)	1712–1722	273
Haig, William (inventory)	1712–1722	200
Haig, Mary	1712–1722	169
Horner, Elinor	1712–1722	220
Horner, Elinor (inventory)	1712–1722	257
Halsey, Danll.	1712–1722	222
Hardy, John	1712–1722	233
Hewitt, Bartholomew	1712–1722	242
Hopkins, John	1712–1722	301
Heicklefeild, John	1712–1722	305
Haman, Thomas	1712–1722	320
Harvy, Dorothy	1712–1722	332

Appendix.

Name.	Will Book.	Page.
Hodges, James	1712–1722	343
Haig, William	1712–1722	167
Harman, Robert	1712–1722	269
Jones, Thomas (inventory)	1712–1722	74
Jones, Thomas (will)	1712–1722	29
Jones, Fran., admr. to Arthur Jones	1712–1722	9
Jones, Daniel	1712–1722	13
Jones, John	1712–1722	21
Jones, John (inventory)	1712–1722	187
Jones, Cornelius	1712–1722	93
Jones, Edwd.	1712–1722	245
Jones, Edwd. (inventory)	1712–1722	253
Jones, David (inventory)	1712–1722	255
Jones, Arthur (inventory)	1712–1722	278
James, Edward	1712–1722	321
Jordine, Solomon	1712–1722	296
Jennings, Ann (inventory)	1712–1722	251
Jennings, Ann (will)	1712–1722	224
Jennings, John (inventory)	1712–1722	253
Jennings, John (will)	1712–1722	223
Jordan, John	1712–1722	219
Johnson, Susannah	1712–1722	166
Johnson, Lewis	1712–1722	53
Jackson, Isaac	1712–1722	128
King, Henry	1712–1722	100
Knight, Simon (admr. to John Porter)	1712–1722	108
Knight, Tobias	1712–1722	147
Knight, Tobias (inventory)	1712–1722	263
Kerby, Thomas	1712–1722	173
Kent, John	1712–1722	219
Kent, John (inventory)	1712–1722	254
Kasewell, Fran	1712–1722	41
Lewerton, Ephraim	1712–1722	30
Lewerton, John (inventory)	1712–1722	68
Lawson, John	1712–1722	39
Lawson, John	1712–1722	98
Long, James	1712–1722	51
Long, William	1712–1722	54
Long, Sarah	1712–1722	160
Long, Sarah (inventory)	1712–1722	194
Lee, Thomas	1712–1722	161
Lee, William (inventory)	1712–1722	191
Lepper, Thomas	1712–1722	163
Lepper, Thomas (inventory)	1712–1722	248
Lowden, John	1712–1722	171
Lowden. John (inventory)	1712–1722	185
Luis, Richard	1712–1722	176
Lewis, Thomas, Sen.	1712–1722	237
Lewis, Thomas (inventory)	1712–1722	260
Lockey, Henry (admstr.)	1712–1722	84
Ligo, John	1712–1722	117
Ligo, John (inventory)	1712–1722	118
Loftin, Leonard	1712–1722	317

648 APPENDIX.

Name.	Will Book.	Page.
Lowe, William	1712–1722	336
Lee, Thomas	1712–1722	343
Martin, Joel	1712–1722	131
Martin, James	1712–1722	244
Monereif, John	1712–1722	43
Mitchel, Archibald (inventory)	1712–1722	72
Mackarty, Timothy	1712–1722	157
Malbe, George	1712–1722	164
Moore, Richard (inventory)	1712–1722	189
Mathews, Edmund (inventory)	1712–1722	250
Meads, John (inventory)	1712–1722	255
Markham, Anthony (inventory)	1712–1722	265
Machley, Henry	1712–1722	323
Nicholson, Benjamin	1712–1722	15
Norcom, Mary	1712–1722	313
Newby, Edward	1712–1722	270
Newby, William	1712–1722	279
Nortly, David (James Nortly, admr.)	1712–1722	84
Oglebey, George (inventory)	1712–1722	254
Odeon, Elinor (inventory)	1712–1722	252
Porter, Mary	1712–1722	139
Porter, John	1712–1722	5
Porter, John	1712–1722	45
Patnel, John	1712–1722	24
Patchitt, John	1712–1722	36
Pettit, Mary	1712–1722	79
Parry, Adam (inventory)	1712–1722	204
Peirce, John (inventory)	1712–1722	204
Pearce, Joseph (inventory)	1712–1722	256
Prescot, Aron	1712–1722	279
Plowman, John	1712–1722	301
Palmer, Thomas	1712–1722	325
Pike, Samuel	1712–1722	150
Pruet, William (inventory)	1712–1722	189
Pope, Edward	1712–1722	337
Phelps, Edwd. (inventory)	1712–1722	196
Parker, Peter	1712–1722	229
Paterson, Robert	1712–1722	330
Robinson, Susanna	1712–1722	13
Robinson, John	1712–1722	238
Rountree, William (inventory)	1712–1722	247
Rice, Danll.	1712–1722	251
Relf, Thos.	1712–1722	270
Rice, Lucy	1712–1722	315
Reverly, John	1712–1722	41
Reynaud, Benjamin	1712–1722	24
Russel, Sarah (admrx. to Wm. Russel)	1712–1722	135
Robinson, Thomas	1712–1722	169
Robinson, Thomas (inventory)	1712–1722	208
Ross, William	1712–1722	342
Ricks, Benjamin	1712–1722	344

Appendix.

Name.	Will Book.	Page.
Scot, Stephen	1712-1722	106
Slade, Joseph (Ed. Traverse, admr.)	1712-1722	136
Slade, George	1712-1722	32
Sparrow, Thomas	1712-1722	120
Slocum, Samll.	1712-1722	8
Standing, Richd.	1712-1722	13
Standing, Edward	1712-1722	311
Sadler, William	1712-1722	35
Smith, Alexander	1712-1722	54
Smith, Mary	1712-1722	225
Smith, Mary (inventory)	1712-1722	249
Swain, Stephen	1712-1722	57
Swain, Stephen (inventory)	1712-1722	65
Stansel, John (inventory)	1712-1722	69
Sparnon, Joseph	1712-1722	155
Sparnon, Joseph (inventory)	1712-1722	202
Steely, Thomas	1712-1722	177
Steely, Thomas	1712-1722	199
Steely, Thomas (inventory)	1712-1722	272
Simon, Rebecca (inventory)	1712-1722	197
Simons, George	1712-1722	238
Snell, John (inventory)	1712-1722	211
Sayer, Thomas	1712-1722	233
Smithwick, Edwd. (inventory)	1712-1722	249
Sanderson, Richd. (inventory)	1712-1722	264
Sanderson, Basil	1712-1722	339
Spruill, Godfrey	1712-1722	271
Spruill, Godfrey (inventory)	1712-1722	280
Stone, Willm.	1712-1722	277
Stanton, Thos.	1712-1722	308
Stanton, Mary	1712-1722	309
Stanton, Thomas	1712-1722	324
Stamp, Richard	1712-1722	334
Toms, Francis (inventory)	1712-1722	78
Toms, Francis (will)	1712-1722	55
Toms, Mary	1712-1722	156
Tayler, John	1712-1722	98
Tayler, Lemuell (inventory)	1712-1722	260
Tayler, Ebenezer	1712-1722	273
Tayler, Peter	1712-1722	275
Tyler, Thomas	1712-1722	346
Thorowgood, Fran.	1712-1722	129
Thomas, Morgan	1712-1722	3
Tanner, Walter	1712-1722	18
Turner, Henry	1712-1722	26
Turner, Richard	1712-1722	175
Tomlins, John (inventory)	1712-1722	183
Tomlin, John (will)	1712-1722	212
Tooke, James	1712-1722	228
Thorp, Richd.	1712-1722	239
Tucker, Robert	1712-1722	243
Upton, John	1712-1722	241
Upton, John	1712-1722	326

650 APPENDIX.

Name.	Will Book.	Page.
Vendemulen, Thomas	1712–1722	234
Williams, Edward	1712–1722	103
Williams, William	1712–1722	38
Williams, William (inventory)	1712–1722	72
Williams, Pilgrim (inventory)	1712–1722	247
Williams, John	1712–1722	306
Welsch, John	1712–1722	40
Walker, John (inventory)	1712–1722	60
Warren, Henry	1712–1722	123
Wallace, Robert (inventory)	1712–1722	63
Wallis, William (inventory)	1712–1722	290
Waltone, Thomas	1712–1722	145
Woodnott, Henry	1712–1722	176
Woodnott, Henry (inventory)	1712–1722	289
Watkins, John (inventory)	1712–1722	189
Weyley, Thos. (inventory)	1712–1722	193
Wilson, Samll.	1712–1722	240
Wilson, Samll. (inventory)	1712–1722	261
Wire, John (inventory)	1712–1722	250
Waman, William	1712–1722	306
Warren, Abraham	1712–1722	19
West, John	1712–1722	27
Wharton, David	1712–1722	1

INDEX TO WILL BOOK, No. 3, 1722-1735.

Ames, John (inventory)	1722–1735	88
Allen, James (will)	1722–1735	286
Allen, George	1722–1735	387
Adams, Abraham	1722–1735	289
Adams, John	1722–1735	317
Adams, Abraham	1722–1735	362
Anderson, Elizabeth	1722–1735	327
Baker, Moses	1722–1735	21
Baker, Moses (inventory)	1722–1735	162
Blount, John	1722–1735	43
Blount, Elizabeth	1722–1735	307
Bell, William	1722–1735	48
Bell, William (inventory)	1722–1735	75
Bell, Ross	1722–1735	149
Bell, Thos.	1722–1735	276
Blewlet, Abraham (inventory)	1722–1735	62
Bends, Samuel	1722–1735	15
Barns, Jeremiah (inventory)	1722–1735	91
Boyd, Thomas	1722–1735	95
Boyd, Thomas (inventory, etc.)	1722–1735	112
Brent, Thomas	1722–1735	103
Bagley, Thomas	1722–1735	118
Bagley, Thomas (inventory)	1722–1735	185
Bastable, William	1722–1735	123
Bastable, William (inventory)	1722–1735	172
Bundy, Benjamin	1722–1735	129

APPENDIX. 651

Name.	Will Book.	Page.
Bray, William, Senr.	1722–1735	130
Bromley, George	1722–1722	131
Bunch, Paul	1722–1722	138
Burket, John	1722–1735	172
Burket, John (inventory)	1722–1735	182
Ballard, Joseph, Senr.	1722–1735	198
Burgess, Stephen	1722–1735	200
Bailey, William (inventory)	1722–1735	228
Blanchard, John (inventory)	1722–1735	229
Barecock, William	1722–1735	237
Baros, Moses	1722–1735	269
Browning, John	1722–1735	280
Barclifts, William	1722–1735	285
Bryan, James	1722–1735	297
Bass, John	1722–1735	305
Church, Joseph	1722–1735	5
Clerk, George	1722–1735	8
Clerk, Thomas (inventory)	1722–1735	68
Clayton, Henry	1722–1735	40
Cambril, Alexander	1722–1735	50
Cape, John (inventory)	1722–1735	62
Clear, Timothy (inventory)	1722–1735	71
Clare, Hannah	1722–1735	118
Clare, Hannah (inventory)	1722–1735	177
Chesson, Ann	1722–1735	127
Chesson, Ann (inventory)	1722–1735	164
Chesson, James (inventory)	1722–1735	165
Cheston, James	1722–1735	105
Crisp, Nicholas	1722–1735	93
Cameril, Alexander and Ann (inventory)	1722–1735	108
Carman, William	1722–1735	137
Cotton, Jno.	1722–1735	141
Cockshell, Andrew (inventory)	1722–1735	158
Coward, William	1722–1735	166
Charles, Samuel (inventory)	1722–1735	167
Charles, Samuel (will)	1722–1735	186
Crossot, Joseph	1722–1735	191
Collens, James	1722–1735	192
Collens, Lucy	1722–1735	192
Cannings, Joseph	1722–1735	197
Copeland, William	1722–1735	14
Cartwright, Grace (inventory)	1722–1735	170
Chapman, Mary	1722–1735	207
Clapham, Joseph	1722–1735	315
Cartwright, William	1722–1735	260
Cartright, William, Senr.	1722–1735	354
Colson, Mary	1722–1735	298
Cane, William	1722–1735	302
Cromen, Martin	1722–1735	320
Chester, John	1722–1735	328
Creasy, Levi	1722–1735	330
Cook, Thomas	1722–1735	344
Deiptt, John	1722–1735	4
Davis, Hugh	1722–1735	36

Name.	Will Book.	Page.
Davis, Peter	1722–1735	104
Davis, William (inventory)	1722–1735	188
Davis, Jno. (inventory)	1722–1735	223
Discorah, Thomas	1722–1735	38
Discorah, Thomas (inventory)	1722–1735	188
Dauge, Richard (inventory)	1722–1735	82
Dunston, John	1722–1735	107
Dixon, Robert	1722–1735	125
Delamare, Stephen	1722–1735	254
Durant, Thomas	1722–1735	302
Darden, Joseph	1722–1735	326
Engel, Peter	1722–1735	22
Evans, Jeffry	1722–1735	60
Evans, Jonathan (inventory)	1722–1735	83
Evans, Hunt (inventory)	1722–1735	226
Evans, Thomas	1722–1735	258
Edy, John	1722–1735	107
Ellis, Francis (inventory)	1722–1735	166
Elleot, George	1722–1735	132
Elliott, Aaron (inventory)	1722–1735	169
Elliott, Thomas	1722–1735	203
Everendon, Thomas (inventory)	1722–1735	176
Eaton, James	1722–1735	209
Eubank, George	1722–1735	233
Easters, John	1722–1735	272
Early, Elenor	1722–1735	296
Eborn, Henry	1722–1735	310
Farrow, Francis	1722–1735	11
Felts, Humphrey	1722–1735	38
Flint, Richard (inventory)	1722–1735	87
Fry, Thomas (inventory)	1722–1735	92
Fry, Thomas (will)	1722–1723	101
Frost, William (inventory)	1722–1735	93
Farlee, James	1722–1735	97
Forster, James	1722–1735	107
Foster. Hannah	1722–1735	131
Foster, James (inventory)	1722–1735	169
Feltham, James	1722–1735	132
Fraser, David	1722–1735	228
Fourre, John	1722–1735	242
Freeman, John	1722–1735	243
Gunter, John	1722–1735	36
Guilbert, Francis	1722–1735	38
Guilbert, Francis (inventory)	1722–1735	85
Guilbert, Francis (inventory)	1722–1735	91
Guilbert, Joseph (inventory)	1722–1735	122
Gatlin, Edward	1722–1735	54
Gavins, Charles (inventory)	1722–1735	74
Garmack, James (inventory)	1722–1735	88
Griffith, John	1722–1735	135
Guthrie, Samuel (inventory)	1722–1735	169
Galley, John	1722–1735	203
Grey, Richard	1722–1735	209

APPENDIX.   653

Name.	Will Book.	Page.
Gray, Ann	1722-1735	239
Godley, John	1722-1735	255
Glesson, John	1722-1735	286
Hicks, Thomas	1722-1735	30
Hicks, Thomas (inventory)	1722-1735	77
Hicks, David	1722-1735	263
Hicks, Robert	1722-1735	297
Heclefield, John (inventory)	1722-1735	69
Hassell, Jane (inventory)	1722-1735	73
Hatch, Anthony	1722-1735	57
Hatch, Anthony (inventory)	1722-1735	189
Hill, George	1722-1735	26
Hill, Richard	1722-1735	181
Hill, John	1722-1735	238
Hardin, Thomas (inventory)	1722-1735	121
Hayman, Henry	1722-1735	122
Harrison, Daniel	1722-1735	143
Harrison, Danl. (inventory)	1722-1735	168
Henley, John	1722-1735	146
Hackley, Henry (inventory)	1722-1735	171
Henderson, Henman (inventory)	1722-1735	171
Hopton, Charles (inventory)	1722-1735	173
Hambleton, John	1722-1735	174
Handworker, Daniel	1722-1735	213
Harvey, Thomas	1722-1735	216
Harvey, Richard	1722-1735	278
Hollowell, Edmund	1722-1735	208
Hinton, John	1722-1735	240
Husbands, Richard	1722-1735	263
Hunter, William	1722-1735	265
Hawkins, Thomas	1722-1735	268
Hardison, Jasper	1722-1735	279
Howcott, John	1722-1735	283
Hall, Hezekiah	1722-1735	292
Hamilton, Jane	1722-1735	293
Hooks, John	1722-1735	296
House, Thomas	1722-1735	299
Hoskins, Thomas	1722-1735	304
Irby, Henry	1722-1735	290
Ismay, John	1722-1735	312
Jesper, Richard	1722-1735	28
Jasper, Richard, Senr. (inventory)	1722-1735	65
Jasper, Richard, Jun. (inventory)	1722-1735	93
Jones, Samuel	1722-1735	37
Jones, David (inventory)	1722-1735	66
Jones, John, Senr.	1722-1735	98
Jones, Frederick	1722-1735	115
Jones, John	1722-1735	193
Jones, Wm. Harding	1722-1735	251
Jones, William	1722-1735	306
Jones, William	1722-1735	308
Joy, William	1722-1735	39
Johnson, William	1722-1735	140

APPENDIX.

Name.	Will Book.	Page.
James, Guilbert (inventory)	1722–1735	171
James, William	1722–1735	313
Jordan, William	1722–1735	257
Jenoure, Joseph	1722–1735	265
Jarnagan, John	1722–1735	269
Kemp, George	1722–1735	29
Keede, Freddle	1722–1735	102
Knight, Lewis Alexander	1722–1735	246
Kearseys, Thomas	1722–1735	273
Kelly, Smith	1722–1735	294
Lillington, Ann	1722–1735	47
Lumley, George (inventory)	1722–1735	73
Lee, Thomas (inventory)	1722–1735	73
Lee, Anne	1722–1735	270
Leigh, James	1722–1735	217
Loaden, Richard (inventory)	1722–1735	86
Lenton, William	1722–1735	97
Luffman, William	1722–1735	134
Luffman, William	1722–1735	147
Lloyd, Robert	1722–1735	150
Low, Emanuel	1722–1735	156
Leyden, Francis (inventory)	1722–1735	168
Leyden, Francis (inventory)	1722–1735	173
Leyden, Francis (will)	1722–1735	183
Long, Thomas	1722–1735	136
Lawley, Patrick	1722–1735	180
Lewis, William	1722–1735	252
Ludford, William	1722–1735	275
Mayo, Edward	1722–1735	17
Maule, William	1722–1735	34
Mouk, Joseph (inventory)	1722–1735	67
Marden, Richard (inventory)	1722–1735	80
Ming, James (inventory)	1722–1735	81
Moor, John (inventory)	1722–1735	89
Moor, John (inventory)	1722–1735	91
Moore, William (will)	1722–1735	253
Moye, Thomas	1722–1735	103
Miller, Thomas	1722–1735	104
Miller, Thomas (inventory)	1722–1735	167
Mackintosh, Margery	1722–1735	107
Massey, Hezekiah, Senr.	1722–1735	128
Metts, George, Sen.	1722–1735	133
McBride, Truman (inventory)	1722–1735	158
McReel, Thomas (inventory)	1722–1735	196
Matthews, Thomas	1722–1735	233
Maudlin, Ezekiel	1722–1735	248
McClendon, Deborah	1722–1735	257
Marstons, Elizabeth	1722–1735	274
Mattocks, John	1722–1735	282
Martin, George	1722–1735	288
McDaniel, Daniel	1722–1735	295
Norris, William	1722–1735	6
Newby, John (inventory)	1722–1735	74

APPENDIX. 655

Name.	Will Book.	Page.
Nolam, James (inventory)	1722–1735	76
Navell, Francis (inventory)	1722–1735	88
Navell, Francis (will)	1722–1735	106
Nicholson, Samuel	1722–1735	119
Norcomb, Jno.	1722–1735	139
Norfleet, James	1722–1735	281
Obrian, Darby	1722–1735	31
Obrian, Darby (inventory)	1722–1735	89
O'Neal, Michael	1722–1735	52
Ogilby, Patrick	1722–1735	108
Ogleby, Patrick (inventory)	1722–1735	109
O'Neal, Michael (will)	1722–1735	153
Oliver, Moses	1722–1735	169
Oadam, Richard (inventory)	1722–1735	225
Orandle, Edward	1722–1735	271
Ottiwell, Isaac	1722–1735	285
Powell, John	1722–1735	23
Poyner, Joseph	1722–1735	46
Poyner, William (inventory)	1722–1735	223
Philips, Daniel	1722–1735	55
Phillips, Thomas (inventory)	1722–1735	227
Palmer, Thomas (inventory)	1722–1735	58
Palmer, Nathaniel (inventory)	1722–1735	159
Pavy, Weebly	1722–1735	87
Peirce, John	1722–1735	100
Pearse, Thomas	1722–1735	234
Pearce, Robert	1722–1735	212
Pace, John, Senr.	1722–1735	126
Pagett, Edward	1722–1735	137
Phelps, Samuel	1722–1735	145
Phelps, Humphrey (inventory)	1722–1735	175
Phelps, Jonathan	1722–1735	266
Pollock, Hester	1722–1735	152
Pollock, Thomas	1722–1735	309
Parris, Thomas	1722–1735	155
Parris, Thomas (inventory)	1722–1735	219
Pricklove, John and Elizabeth (inventory)	1722–1735	160
Pendleton, Thomas	1722–1735	245
Purdy, George	1722–1735	276
Purser, Robert	1722–1735	287
Putnell, William	1722–1735	291
Porter, Joshua	1722–1735	329
Pirkins, David	1722–1735	309
Richardson, Daniel	1722–1735	2
Rigney, John	1722–1735	32
Rigney, John (inventory)	1722–1735	86
Robins, James	1722–1735	33
Reading, Lionel	1722–1735	41
Reading, Lionel (inventory)	1722–1735	86
Rogers, John	1722–1735	52
Roggers, John (inventory)	1722–1735	228
Reston, Thomas	1722–1735	55
Rice, Lucy (inventory)	1722–1735	58
Ratliff, Samuel	1722–1735	318

APPENDIX.

Name.	Will Book.	Page.
Ratliff, Richard (inventory)	1722–1735	62
Reggons, Joseph	1722–1735	127
Rednapp, Joseph (inventory)	1722–1735	159
Reed, Andrew	1722–1735	151
Reed, William (inventory)	1722–1735	178
Raymond, Thomas	1722–1735	199
Roper, William	1722–1735	213
Reyfeeld, William	1722–1735	231
Racksaker, Daniel	1722–1735	279
Roundtree, Francis	1722–1735	316
Smith, William	1722–1735	7
Smith, Sarah	1722–1735	33
Smith, Robert	1722–1735	53
Smith, Sarah (inventory)	1722–1735	63
Smith, James (inventory)	1722–1735	167
Smith, John	1722–1735	294
Smith, Joseph	1722–1735	314
Smith, William	1722–1735	299
Sutton, George (inventory)	1722–1735	64
Sutton, Nathaniel	1722–1735	35
Sutton, Joseph (inventory)	1722–1735	78
Sutton, Joseph (will)	1722–1735	19
Slade, Abigal (inventory)	1722–1735	60
Seizmoor, Samuel (inventory)	1722–1735	61
Stamp, Richard (inventory)	1722–1735	66
Stamp, Thomas (inventory)	1722–1735	226
Sathaucks, Capt. (inventory)	1722–1735	67
Slocomb, John (inventory)	1722–1735	71
Snider, Ralph (inventory)	1722–1735	72
Sullivant, Darby (inventory)	1722–1735	73
Simmons, Mary (inventory)	1722–1735	79
Simmons, Mary (will)	1722–1735	12
Sigley, William (inventory)	1722–1735	84
Steel, Ambrose (inventory)	1722–1735	88
Skinner, Richard, Senr. (inventory)	1722–1735	91
Steward, William (inventory)	1722–1735	115
Sanderson, Richard	1722–1735	321
Sanderson, Ruth	1722–1735	120
Sanders, John (inventory)	1722–1735	172
Sanders, Mary	1722–1735	287
Silvester, Richard, Senr.	1722–1735	194
Spivey, Thomas, Senr.	1722–1735	195
Stoakley, Joseph	1722–1735	210
Swann, Henry (inventory)	1722–1735	220
Swann, Thomas	1722–1735	319
Sadler, William	1722–1735	227
Stringer, John	1722–1735	229
Saraon, Lawrence	1722–1735	232
Speir, James	1722–1735	236
Symons, John	1722–1735	250
Shute, Rebecca	1722–1735	261
Sherrard, Alexander	1722–1735	298
Scot, William (inventory)	1722–1735	169
Sherrar, Samuel	1722–1735	165
Speller, Henry	1722–1735	124

APPENDIX. 657

Name.	Will Book.	Page.
Strickland, William	1722–1735	145
Stafford, William	1722–1735	148
Smithson, John (inventory)	1722–1735	166
Soan, John	1722–1735	325
Stephenson, Elizabeth	1722–1735	331
Taylor, Nathaniel	1722–1735	300
Taylor, Lemuel	1722–1735	29
Taylor, Jane	1722–1735	301
Turbervil, Richard	1722–1735	51
Thorowgood, Thomas (inventory)	1722–1735	68
Tannahill, John (inventory)	1722–1735	90
Torksey, Philip	1722–1735	106
Torksey, Philip (inventory)	1722–1735	168
Thomas, Joseph	1722–1735	121
Toms, Joseph (inventory)	1722–1735	166
Toms, Francis	1722–1735	201
Toms, Francis (inventory)	1722–1735	222
Toms, Joshua	1722–1735	247
Trotter, William	1722–1735	204
Tinnins, Mary	1722–1735	228
Tully, Jane	1722–1735	259
Unday, Thomas	1722–1735	47
Vanluven, Christopher	1722–1735	256
White, William	1722–1735	10
White, John	1722–1735	53
White, Sarah	1722–1735	99
White, Arnold (inventory)	1722–1735	225
White, Robert	1722–1735	324
White, Arnold, Senr.	1722–1735	205
Widbey, George	1722–1735	24
Wilson, Isaac	1722–1735	35
Wilson, Isaac (inventory)	1722–1735	224
Williams, William	1722–1735	48
Williams, Johanna (inventory)	1722–1735	90
Williams, John	1722–1735	119
Williams, William	1722–1735	264
Williams, Thomas	1722–1735	284
Warren, William	1722–1735	61
Wheeler, Henry	1722–1735	124
Walston, London	1722–1735	134
Wherry, Joshua	1722–1735	207
Wimberly, Thomas	1722–1735	244
Walburton, Robert	1722–1735	274
Wingfield, Richard	1722–1735	301
Wood, William	1722–1735	325
Young, Joseph	1722–1735	175
Zearge, Jacob	1722–1735	261

INDEX TO WILL BOOK, No. 4, 1738-1752.

Name.	Will Book.	Page.
Adams, Roger	1738–1752	146
Boyintone, Joseph	1738–1752	74
Blin, Daniel	1738–1752	340
Barrow, William	1738–1752	344
Barrow, John	1738–1752	258
Bell, Joseph	1738–1752	350
Ball, James	1738–1752	280
Barr, Danelun	1738–1752	37
Bumpas, Job	1738–1752	56
Brewer, Jane	1738–1752	120
Bond, John	1738–1752	147
Busbey, Catirina	1738–1752	184
Busbey, Thomas	1738–1752	236
Booth, James	1738–1752	217
Brown, James	1738–1752	269
Bryan, William		27
Collins, Charles	1738–1752	79
Cawdry, Thomas	1738–1752	106
Carver, James	1738–1752	93
Carver, James, Senr.	1738–1752	233
Clifford, Thomas	1738–1752	125
Carter, Edmond	1738–1752	142
Clayton, Elizabeth	1738–1752	176
Campbell, Hugh	1738–1752	187
Campbell, John	1738–1752	316
Coleman, William	1738–1752	270
Chadwick, Samuel	1738–1752	308
Daw, William	1738–1752	35
Dudley, Edward	1738–1752	347
Dudley, Thomas	1738–1752	95
Daniel, Thomas	1738–1752	102
Daves, Dughter	1738–1752	164
Delahnide, William	1738–1752	204
Delahnide, William	1738–1752	227
Downer, William	1738–1752	294
Doughty, John	1738–1752	298
Edwards, John	1738–1752	15
Espy, James	1738–1752	140
Ennet, Edmond	1738–1752	156
Eagon, James	1738–1752	160
Ellison, William	1738–1752	178
Flyn, Collumb	1738–1752	72
Fryly, William	1738–1752	194
Freemain, John	1738–1752	250
Fort, John	1738–1752	254
Flavell, William	1738–1752	190
Foort, Richard	1738–1752	104
Flood, James	1738–1752	162
Frank, Martin John	1738–1752	371
Fillian, John	1738–1752	42

APPENDIX. 659

Name.	Will Book.	Page.
Green, John	1738–1752	100
Gourley, John	1738–1752	101
Grange, John	1738–1752	131
Grant, Alexander	1738–1752	245
Griggs, Samuel	1738–1752	273
Gillitt, John	1738–1752	329
Hedges, Thomas	1738–1752	31
Higgins, Ann	1738–1752	41
Huggins, Edmond	1738–1752	181
Heneley, John	1738–1752	45
Hollis, James	1738–1752	114
Hutson, William	1738–1752	137
Hendrick, Francis	1738–1752	167
Hambleton, Joseph	1738–1752	183
Hodgson, John	1738–1752	186
Howcott, Edward	1738–1752	267
Harvis, John	1738–1752	322
Hunter, Nicholas	1738–1752	324
Hannis, Joseph	1738–1752	337
Hicks, John	1738–1752	292
Ingram, Abram	1738–1752	334
Keel, John	1738–1752	76
King, John	1738–1752	312
Lamberson, Henry	1738–1752	18
Laker, Juliana	1738–1752	82
Lord, William	1738–1752	85
Lawkins, John	1738–1752	212
Luton, Adam	1738–1752	248
Love, Daniel	1738–1752	92
Lockey, Joseph	1738–1752	361
Lyon James	1738–1752	367
Logan, Alexander	1738–1752	139
Lock, Thomas	1738–1752	122
Leath, Richard	1738–1752	296
Moseley, Edward	1738–1752	1
Mackferrell, John	1738–1752	17
Murphey, Edmond	1738–1752	34
Mitchel, Abram	1738–1752	53
Mason, John	1738–1752	57
Maskill, William	1738–1752	80
McDowell, John	1738–1752	200
Millard, Charles	1738–1752	218
Metcalfe, Caleb	1738–1752	219
Maule, Patrick	1738–1752	238
McCalpin, William	1738–1752	299
Murphy, Thomas	1738–1752	327
Marr, Joseph	1738–1752	336
Marsden, Thomas	1738–1752	226
Neal, Henry	1738–1752	196
Newby, Samuel	1738–1752	215
Norwood, William	1738–1752	51

Name.	Will Book.	Page.
Norman, John	1738–1752	87
Nixon, Zachariah	1738–1752	133
Nixson, Richard	1738–1752	357
Overton, John	1738–1752	77
Ohier, John	1738–1752	21
Owan, Daniel	1738–1752	23
Odyer, Dennis	1738–1752	252
Parker, Azricom	1738–1752	241
Purcell, Neal	1738–1752	14
Pollock, Thomas	1738–1752	66
Powell, William	1738–1752	59
Pringle, Alexander	1738–1752	170
Pearson, Thomas	1738–1752	277
Parsons, Thomas	1738–1752	304
Porter, Nicholas	1738–1752	314
Pritchett, Abraham	1738–1752	352
Paquinet, Michael	1738–1752	49
Russell, Thomas	1738–1752	19
Roberts, James	1738–1752	26
Risonover, Matthew	1738–1752	29
Rawlings, Banjamin	1738–1752	63
Rontree, Francis	1738–1752	116
Reading, Thomas	1738–1752	118
Rustull, Richard, Jr.	1738–1752	259
Rogers, Richard	1738–1752	263
Smith, James	1738–1752	24
Smith, John, Senr.	1738–1752	153
Smith, Edward	1738–1752	170
Smith, William	1738–1752	256
Smith, Henry	1538–1752	288
Smith, James	1738–1752	320
Sterring, George, Senr.	1738–1752	47
Sitgraves, William	1738–1752	55
Sanders, John	1738–1752	112
Stevens, James	1738–1752	128
Stafford, John	1738–1752	166
Sherley, James	1738–1752	172
Stuart, John	1738–1752	179
Sutton, Mary	1738–1752	221
Simmonds, Jacob	1738–1752	223
Swift, Ephraim	1738–1752	301
Stover, Jacob John	1738–1752	331
Tomson, William	1738–1752	188
Thompson, John	1738–1752	230
Tignar, James	1738–1752	286
Valentine, Richard	1738–1752	108
Vince, Humphrey	1738–1752	205
Waxdale, John	1738–1752	174
West, William	1738–1752	20
Wallis, Andrew	1738–1752	33

APPENDIX. 661

Name.	Will Book.	Page.
Wallis, William	1738–1752	264
Winn, Sam.	1738–1752	110
White, Henry	1738–1752	129
White, John	1738–1752	342
Wickstead, Pall	1738–1752	193
William, James	1738–1752	225
Wood, John	1738–1752	275
Walker, Thomas	1738–1752	284
Wain, Thomas	1738–1752	303
Wright, John	1738–1752	342

INDEX TO WILL BOOK, No. 5, 1749-1753.

Name	Will Book	Page
Allen, Eleazar	1749–1753	11
Albertson, Joshua	1749–1753	229
Brown, Thomas	1749–1753	1
Benbow, Gershon	1749–1753	15
Bishop, George	1749–1753	24
Burnap, John	1749–1753	31
Bryan, Edward	1749–1753	36
Bryan, Simon	1749–1753	207
Brickell, James	1749–1753	61
Befret, Benjamin	1749–1753	79
Boulds, George	1749–1753	119
Bevin, Richard	1749–1753	125
Cranford, William	1749–1753	58
Cheek, Richard	1749–1753	144
Coker, Calep	1749–1753	205
Dexter, Hope	1749–1753	27
Dudley, Christopher	1749–1753	29
Davis, Thomas	1749–1753	166
Davis, Benja. and David Davis (power of attorney to John Sampson).	1749–1753	174
Dupee, Elias	1749–1753	190
Edmondson, Joseph	1749–1753	111
Fort, John	1749–1753	76
Frazier, John	1749–1753	133
Godfrey, Matthew	1749–1753	50
Giddins, Thomas	1749–1753	67
Grainger, Joshus	1749–1753	86
Godwin, William	1749–1753	199
Hall, Joseph	1749–1753	7
Huggins, John	1749–1753	98
Harket, George	1749–1753	103
Humes, James	1749–1753	129
Hunter, Robert	1749–1752	184
Hill, Benjamin	1749–1753	187
Hollowell, Rubin	1749–1753	223
Handcock, William	1749–1753	69

Name.	Will Book.	Page.
Holms, Ebenezer	1749–1753	138
Isler, Christian	1749–1753	148
Jennings, Thomas	1749–1753	92
John, Arthur	1749–1753	13
Jarrott, John	1749–1753	154
Jasper, Sam	1749–1753	163
Jackson, Thomas	1749–1753	217
Kingston, James	1749–1753	3
Kenyon, John	1749–1753	227
Lowell, Edmond	1749–1753	96
Lattemare, Elizabeth	1749–1753	204
Morris, Thomas	1749–1753	23
Mackay, William	1749–1753	25
Middleton, John	1749–1753	33
Mabson, Arthur	1749–1753	40
Murray, Andrew	1749–1753	74
McNary, Gilbert	1749–1753	81
Mason, Roger, Jr.	1749–1753	90
McClalland, Andrew	1749–1753	100
Martin, William	1749–1753	114
Mitchel, Abraham	1749–1753	141
Mewboorn, Thomas	1749–1753	196
Mobley, John	1749–1753	202
Mackinne, John	1749–1753	214
Norton, William	1749–1753	136
Nusum, Richard	1749–1753	182
Prescott, William	1749–1753	151
Pain, John	1749–1753	167
Rigby, William	1749–1753	21
Reel, Peter	1749–1753	47
Rice, Benjamin	1749–1753	52
Rice, Mary	1749–1753	192
Rice, Edward	1749–1753	212
Smelage, Edward	1749–1753	19
Slade, Samuel	1749–1753	45
Slade, John	1749–1753	55
Subridge, William	1749–1753	65
Simson, John	1749–1753	169
Tarkington, William	1749–1753	4
Tart, Joseph	1749–1753	8
Turner, Robert	1749–1753	105
Thomas, Josiah	1749–1753	127
White, George	1749–1753	20
White, Henry	1749–1753	171
Waine, Thomas	1749–1753	44
Watson, John		54
Weekes, Bingman	1749–1753	62

APPENDIX. 663

Name.	Will Book.	Page.
Wood, Edward	1749–1753	72
Webster, John	1749–1753	84
Webster, William	1749–1753	93
Winright, James	1749–1753	158
West, Henry	1749–1753	194
Watkins, Thomas	1749–1753	225
Wynns, John	1749–1753	208

INDEX TO WILL BOOK, No. 6, 1750-1758.

Name	Will Book	Page
Adams, William	1750–1758	30
Allday, Thomas	1750–1758	161
Brown, Francis	1750–1758	3
Bell, Elizabeth	1750–1758	6
Beavens, Mary	1750–1758	71
Bennet, Nehemiah	1750–1758	87
Blin, Daniel	1750–1758	117
Bright, William	1750–1758	119
Burnat, George	1750–1758	143
Brent, James	1750–1758	146
Bentley, John	1750–1758	165
Black, Isaac	1750–1758	176
Bradford, Nathl.	1750–1758	203
Belchar, George	1750–1758	232
Biddle, Jacob	1750–1758	261
Baily, John	1750–1758	267
Carr, William	1750–1758	66
Collins, John	1750–1758	52
Cherry, Samuel	1750–1758	94
Caswell, Matthew	1750–1758	133
Cavenah, Charles	1750–1758	208
Cain, John	1750–1758	218
Congilton, William	1750–1758	242
Crofton, Harry	1750–1758	254
Coker, Richard	1750–1758	258
Douglas, James	1750–1758	61
Dickinson, Rebeckah	1750–1758	184
Dickinson, Mary	1750–1758	191
Doolos, Thomas	1750–1758	216
Durrane, Saml.	1750–1758	222
Evans, Richard	1750–1758	106
Evans, Berwell	1750–1758	238
Eborn, Nathaniel	1750–1758	108
Freeman, John	1750–1758	112
Foster, John	1750–1758	114
Fipes, William	1750–1758	101
Gray, John	1750–1758	1
Gibble, Dederick	1750–1758	63

Name.	Will Book.	Page.
Gainer, Samuel	1750-1758	81
Gomm, John	1750-1758	97
Giddings, William	1750-1758	269
Homes, Edward	1750-1758	9
Hall, John	1750-1758	46
Harbrett, Edward	1750-1758	78
Higgins, Michael	1750-1758	84
Holladay, William	1750-1758	124
Hassell, John	1750-1758	129
Harrington, Hezekiah	1750-1758	147
Harrell, Edward	1750-1758	170
Ives, Thomas	1750-1758	89
Jones, John	1750-1758	14
Jones, James	1750-1758	126
Jones, Thomas	1750-1758	173
Johnson, John	1750-1758	189
Johnston, Gabriel	1750-1758	153
King, Henry	1750-1758	17
Knight, William	1750-1758	40
Kemp, William	1750-1758	136
Lattimer, William	1750-1758	10
Lee, Thomas	1750-1758	39
Lockhart, James	1750-1758	149
McDowal, James	1750-1758	44
McRee, William	1750-1758	64
Moore, John	1750-1758	159
Moore, John	1750-1758	167
Moore, Thomas	1750-1758	179
Moore, John	1750-1758	192
Moore, Joseph	1750-1758	211
Mountague, Elizabeth	1750-1758	224
Meltons, Jonathan	1750-1758	264
Owense, John	1750-1758	5
Pollock, Cullen	1750-1758	23
Pilkington, Seth	1750-1758	103
Parker, Mary	1750-1758	122
Parker, Francis	1750-1758	196
Powel, Thomas	1750-1758	183
Pirent, James	1750-1758	201
Prescott, William	1750-1758	236
Russell, Habbakkuk	1750-1758	68
Redding, John	1750-1758	74
Rogers, Thomas, Senr	1750-1758	169
Rogers, Thomas	1750-1758	141
Ryding, Jonathan	1750-1758	145
Roe, Robert	1750-1758	248
Stansell, John	1750-1758	11
Sutton, Thomas	1750-1758	12

APPENDIX. 665

Name.	Will Book.	Page.
Smith, Richard	1750-1758	35
Smith, Richard	1750-1758	199
Smith, Thomas	1750-1758	205
Shrocks, Peter	1750-1758	29
Sowell, Richard	1750-1758	37
Scollay, Saml.	1750-1758	42
Stevenson, George	1750-1758	131
Sinclare, Samuel	1750-1758	150
Sigley, John	1750-1758	178
Shorter, William	1750-1758	186
Sherrard, John	1750-1758	188
Sanders, William	1750-1758	207
Stubbs, William	1750-1758	234
Spring, Aaron	1750-1758	250
Tyner, Nicholas	1750-1758	195
Vaughan, Vincent	1750-1758	229
Webb, Anthony	1750-1758	7
Webb, Samuel	1750-1758	158
Wynns, George	1750-1758	18
West, Peter	1750-1758	22
Wood, James	1750-1758	48
Wimberly, Thomas	1750-1758	56
Walters, William	1750-1758	72
Wright, Samuel	1750-1758	75
Worley, Lovick	1750-1758	79
Winslow, John	1750-1758	91
Williams, Thomas	1750-1758	99
Yeates, William	1750-1758	58

INDEX TO WILL BOOK, No. 7, 1755-1758.

Averett, Nathaniel	1755-1758	28
Allen, Elizabeth	1755-1758	136
Andrews, John	1755-1758	137
Adams, Charles	1755-1758	176
Barfield, Richard	1755-1758	10
Bridgess, Samuel	1755-1758	46
Bright, Solomon	1755-1758	63
Benbury, William	1755-1758	73
Barclif, Joshua	1755-1758	105
Brandon, William	1755-1758	133
Bently, John	1755-1758	182
Bently, Richard	1755-1758	208
Bonner, Thomas	1755-1758	252
Baker, John	1755-1758	265
Craven, James	1755-1758	12
Chapman, Charles	1755-1758	23
Carruthers, John	1755-1758	62
Cowell, Benjamin	1755-1758	67

Appendix.

Name.	Will Book.	Page.
Daniel, John	1755–1758	41
Denson, James	1755–1758	55
Duckenfield, Nathaniel	1755–1758	144
Davis, William	1755–1758	186
Davison, John	1755–1758	261
Everett, John	1755–1758	86
Eliot, Moses	1755–1758	121
Eliot, Michael	1755–1758	194
Evans, Aberwall	1755–1758	204
Evans, Robert	1755–1758	213
Foraster, James	1755–1758	56
Falconer, Thomas	1755–1758	108
Fox, James	1755–1758	180
Gray, Allen	1755–1758	17
Gardner, John	1755–1758	48
Gardner, William	1755–1758	102
Gordon, Nathaniel	1755–1758	118
Gordon, John	1755–1758	227
Gillett, John	1755–1758	176
Griffen, Epenetus	1755–1758	178
Howard, Charles	1755–1758	33
Haughton, Charles	1755–1758	89
Hendrick, Jeremiah	1755–1758	123
Hunter, John	1755–1758	131
Harrell, John, Jr.	1755–1758	164
Hockings, John	1755–1758	173
Hooker, William	1755–1758	241
Hinton, Micajah	1755–1758	254
Hillard, William	1755–1758	52
Jordan, Arthur	1755–1758	51
Jones, Morris	1755–1758	82
Jones, John	1755–1758	112
Jones, David, Sr.	1755–1758	139
Johnson, John	1755–1758	141
Little, John	1755–1758	127
Lee, Richard	1755–1758	157
Laurence, George	1755–1758	160
Moore, Samuel	1755–1758	116
Moore, John	1755–1758	35
Moore, Titus	1755–1758	245
McCulloh, Henry	1755–1758	24
Mullen, Jacob	1755–1758	222
Mason, Roger	1755–1758	39
Nickson, Thomas	1755–1758	22
Nobland, John	1755–1758	155
Nicholas, Nathaniel	1755–1758	159
Norwood, Thomas	1755–1758	206
Oliver, Francis	1755–1758	71

APPENDIX.

Name.	Will Book.	Page.
Parker, Thomas	1755–1758	20
Pierce, Thomas	1755–1758	75
Payne, Peter	1755–1758	95
Plomer, Samuel S.	1755–1758	99
Peeble, Judith	1755–1758	120
Pitman, Benjamin	1755–1758	154
Price, William	1755–1758	188
Pritchett, Margaret	1755–1758	200
Powers, Isobell	1755–1758	233
Pope, Samuel	1755–1758	238
Ryall, Charles	1755–1758	8
Rountree, Moses	1755–1758	37
Read, George	1755–1758	57
Robinson, Charles	1755–1758	129
Robinson, Thomas	1755–1758	88
Robinson, John	1755–1758	217
Robins, Joseph	1755–1758	134
Syers, Gerard	1755–1758	1
Sumner, John	1755–1758	2
Stevenson, John	1755–1758	26
Seville, Stephen	1755–1758	32
Smith, Richard	1755–1758	43
Smith, William	1755–1758	92
Singleton, John	1755–1758	49
Speight, Thomas	1755–1758	126
Small, Benja	1755–1758	184
Shine, Danll.	1755–1758	191
Spring, Aaron	1755–1758	202
Simmons, Francis	1755–1758	321
Syms, William	1755–1758	152
Trewett, Joseph	1755–1758	60
Thompson, John	1755–1758	100
Toops, Joseph	1755–1758	135
Woodhouse, Horatio	1755–1758	19
War, William	1755–1758	44
Wall, Richard	1755–1758	45
Worden, James	1755–1758	94
Whitehouse, Saml.	1755–1758	142
Williams, Joanah	1755–1758	163
Wallis, Stephen	1755–1758	190
Wade, Joseph	1755–1758	193
West, Thomas	1755–1758	256
Wood, Moses	1755–1758	258

INDEX TO WILL BOOK, No. 8, 1753-1768.

Arenton, Christopher	1753–1768	99
Anderson, George	1753–1768	155
Albertson, Isaac	1753–1768	179
Allen, Sarah	1753–1768	193
Alton, Andrew	1753–1768	270

APPENDIX.

Name.	Will Book.	Page.
Bradley, John	1753–1768	1
Barrow, Joseph	1753–1768	32
Barrow, William	1753–1768	221
Bell, William	1753–1768	107
Bond, Lewis	1753–1768	103
Bond, Vinyard	1753–1768	263
Ballard, Abraham	1753–1768	96
Blackall, Sarah	1753–1768	92
Brockett, Benja	1753–1768	145
Bray, Henry	1753–1768	176
Brown, John	1753–1768	206
Barclift, John	1753–1768	242
Crocker, Peter	1753–1768	34
Clark, Robert	1753–1768	45
Chancey, Edmund	1753–1768	55
Carruthers, Robert	1753–1768	135
Connor, John	1753–1768	120
Connor, Demsey	1753–1768	83
Corps, John	1753–1768	81
Cooper, Joseph	1753–1768	82
Cloase, George	1753–1768	149
Campbell, James	1753–1768	186
Crutchfield, Edmund (depo.)	1753–1768	278
Davis, John	1753–1768	18
Davis, Thomas	1753–1768	161
Danbe, Daniel	1753–1768	40
Duggan, Thomas	1753–1768	110
Dalrymple, John	1753–1768	300
Dobbs, Arthur, Governor	1753–1768	290
Duncan, Alexander	1753–1768	302
Eaton, William	1753–1768	156
Eavans, Charles	1753–1768	225
Freshworter, John John	1753–1768	88
Grigory, Margaret	1753–1768	13
Grigory, William	1753–1768	20
Gregory, Richard	1753–1768	166
Griffin, Edward	1753–1768	113
Galluay, Thomas	1753–1768	94
Gardner, Martin	1753–1768	211
Galland, Mary	1753–1768	288
Hosea, Joseph	1753–1768	47
Hunter, Isaac	1753–1768	100
Hopkins, John	1753–1768	93
Hopkins, James	1753–1768	251
Hodges, James	1753–1768	179
Harrell, John	1753–1768	180
Houston, William	1753–1768	184
Horn, William	1753–1768	202
Hobby, Jacob	1753–1768	218
Haywood, John	1753–1768	223

APPENDIX. 669

Name.	Will Book.	Page.
Isham, James	1753-1768	24
Innes, James	1753-1768	191
Jordan, Joseph	1753-1768	26
Jones, Peter	1753-1768	42
Jones, Isham	1753-1768	50
Jones, William	1753-1768	208
Johnston, Saml.	1753-1768	133
Jasman, Thomas	1753-1768	148
Kelley, John	1753-1768	177
Kinchen, William, Jun.	1753-1768	197
Kince, Christian	1753-1768	215
Lelly, John	1753-1768	7
Long, Thomas	1753-1768	48
Long, Joshua	1753-1768	117
Long, William	1753-1768	233
Lawson, Saml.	1753-1768	137
Lashly, Patrick	1753-1768	154
Lynch, John, Sen.	1753-1768	162
Low, John	1753-1768	173
Moore, Trueman	1753-1768	37
Moore, Roger	1753-1768	62
MacKane, George	1753-1768	140
Messex, Joseph	1753-1768	140
Mckeel, Thomas, Senr.	1753-1768	78
Mackeel, Benjamin	1753-1768	80
Meed, Timothy	1753-1768	87
Morison, Benjamin	1753-1768	150
Morris, John	1753-1768	213
Meares, Mark	1753-1768	228
Maudlin, Thomas	1753-1768	230
Melton, Robert	1753-1768	254
Neville, Benjamin	1753-1768	189
Newton, Christopher	1753-1768	236
Norfleet, Marmaduke	1753-1768	267
Nessfield, John	1753-1768	280
Overton, Robert	1753-1768	86
Peyton, Robert	1753-1768	104
Poyner, Peter	1753-1768	168
Parker, Simon	1753-1768	200
Puryer, Robert	1753-1768	204
Perisho, John	1753-1768	261
Paine, John Captaine	1753-1768	298
Reding, Joseph	1753-1768	22
Ridge, Thomas	1753-1768	35
Rew, Southy	1753-1768	52
Robertson, James	1753-1768	121
Rhoads, William	1753-1768	75
Rowan, Matthew	1753-1768	151
Richards, Richard	1753-1768	219

APPENDIX.

Name.	Will Book.	Page.
Riddick, Joseph	1753-1768	239
Ryan, David	1753-1768	272
Swann, Samuel	1753-1768	2
Sawyer, Willie	1753-1768	5
Sawyer, Joshua	1753-1768	84
Scarfe, John	1753-1768	10
Stepney, John	1753-1768	30
Swain, William	1753-1768	115
Stubbs, Richard	1753-1768	73
Snowden, Saml.	1753-1768	90
Sanderson, Joseph	1753-1768	164
Salisbury, James	1753-1768	175
Smith, Andrew	1753-1768	185
Scott, Richard	1753-1768	257
Singleton, Samuel	1753-1768	268
Scolley, Elizabeth	1753-1768	295
Turner, William	1753-1768	15
Turnbull, James	1753-1768	123
Taylor, Robert	1753-1768	217
Taylor, Ann	1753-1768	279
Tyler, Moses	1753-1768	259
Veal, William	1753-1768	274
Willoughby, Thomas	1753-1768	9
Webster, Elisabeth	1753-1768	61
Wickliffe, William	1753-1768	127
White, Thomas	1753-1768	118
White, John	1753-1768	77
Williams, Samuel	1753-1768	109
Williams, Thomas	1753-1768	142
Williams, George	1753-1768	190
Woodrow, Alexander	1753-1768	188
Warren, Robert	1753-1768	226
Webb, Henry	1753-1768	250
Watters, Sarah	1753-1768	275
Wilson, Caleb	1753-1768	68